This is a comprehensive study of minor landowners – the gentry – in one county in fifteenth-century England. In common with other recent local studies of the later middle ages, it builds upon the seminal work of K. B. McFarlane, looking at the political and social world in the localities from which the nobles drew their power.

The book aims to present a fully-rounded picture of the experiences of the gentry, relating their private to their public lives, their permanent concerns to the changing needs of local and national politics. Its approach is thus both thematic, exploring the main elements, often private in nature, which moulded their public actions, such as marriage, estate management and sense of family, and chronological, presenting a detailed narrative of politics and account of political structures and relationships.

The work takes a conscious stand for a return to a more 'constitutional' form of political history than the orthodoxy of the moment for the period, which takes patronage and personalities to be the prime movers in politics. This is evident in its concern with issues of stability and disorder (much influenced by recent work on law and society) and with the structure of the polity, with the inter-relationship of local and national politics, and with the ideas of the political classes. The book is intended as a contribution to the history of England as a whole in the fifteenth century and to the study of the long-term development of the English landed classes and the English constitution.

LOCALITY AND POLITY

LOCALITY AND POLITY

A STUDY OF WARWICKSHIRE LANDED SOCIETY, 1401–1499

CHRISTINE CARPENTER

Lecturer in History, University of Cambridge, and Fellow of New Hall

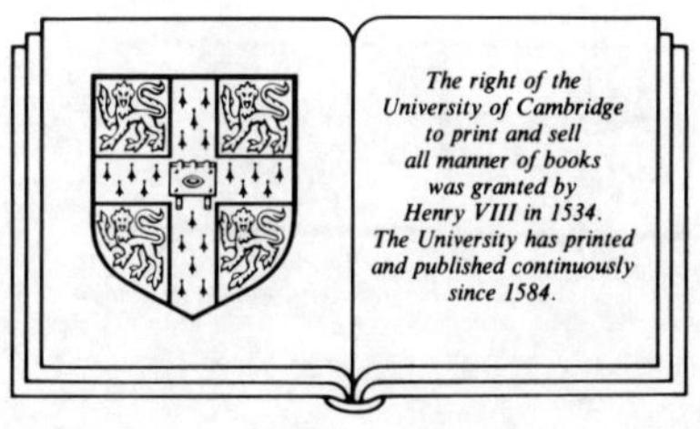

CAMBRIDGE UNIVERSITY PRESS

Cambridge
New York Port Chester
Melbourne Sydney

Published by the Press Syndicate of the University of Cambridge
The Pitt Building, Trumpington Street, Cambridge CB2 1RP
40 West 20th Street, New York, NY 10011–4211, USA
10 Stamford Road, Oakleigh, Melbourne 3166, Australia

First published 1992

Printed in Great Britain at the University Press, Cambridge

British Library cataloguing in publication data

Carpenter, Christine
Locality and polity: a study of Warwickshire landed society, 1401–1499.
1. Warwickshire. Social life, history
I. Title
942.48

Library of Congress cataloguing in publication data

Carpenter, Christine.
Locality and polity: a study of Warwickshire landed society, 1401–1499 / Christine Carpenter.
p. c.
Includes bibliographical references and index.
ISBN 0-521-37016-7 (hardback)
1. Warwickshire (England) – Gentry – History. 2. Landowners – England – Warwickshire – History. 3. Land tenure – England – Warwickshire – History. I. Title. II. Series.
HT657.C37 1991
333.3'09424'8 – dc20 90-43062 CIP

ISBN 0 521 37016 7 hardback

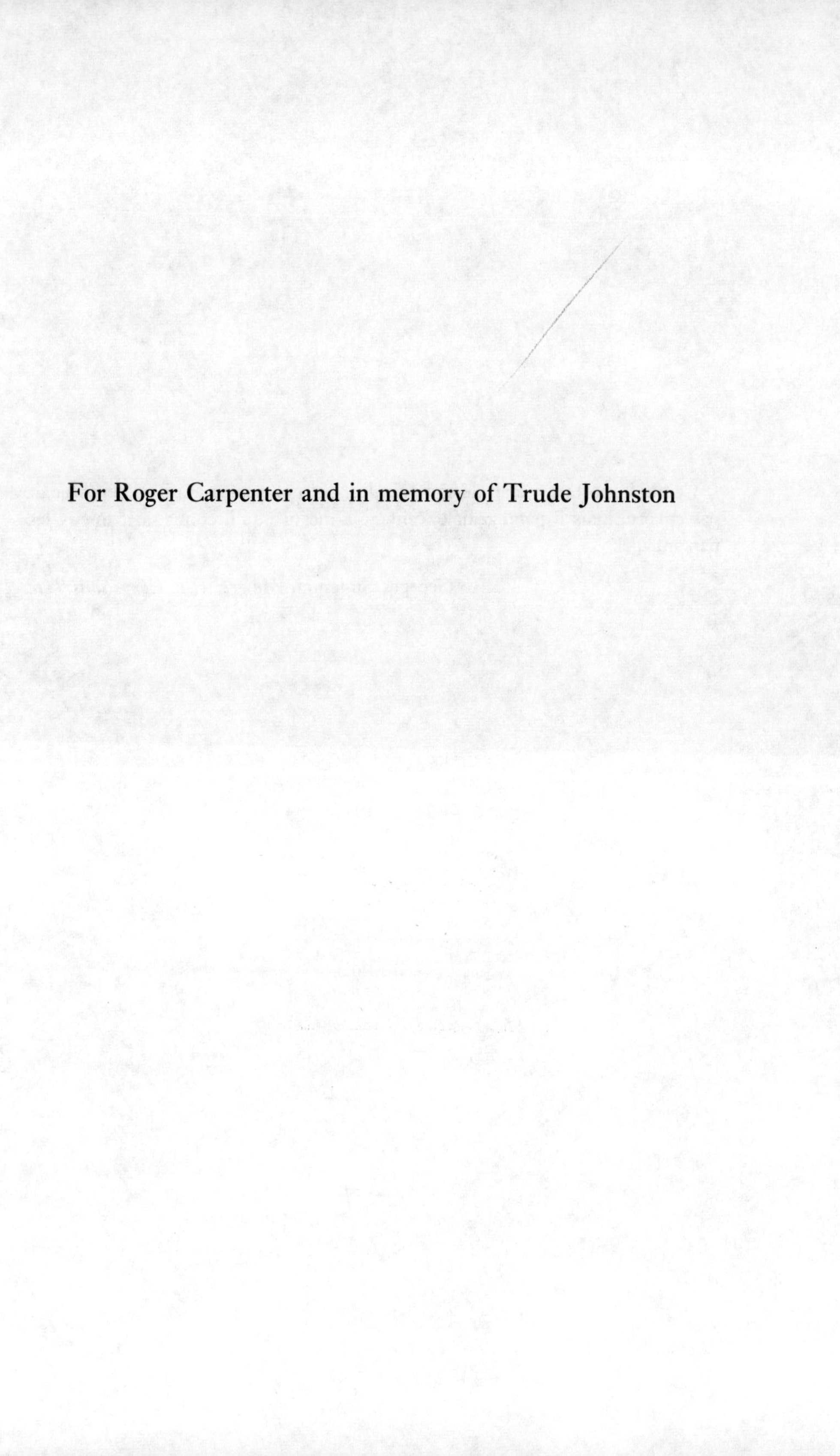

For Roger Carpenter and in memory of Trude Johnston

Ce qui importait, c'était de comprendre. Or, non seulement il ne comprenait pas encore, mais il pataugeait davantage à mesure qu'il connaissait mieux les personnages.

Georges Simenon, *Maigret et le Corps sans Tête*

CONTENTS

FIGURES

TABLES

PREFACE

One cannot spend nearly twenty years, albeit with intermissions, on a piece of work without incurring a considerable number of debts. As the last stage on a long journey it is a pleasure to acknowledge the most important of these. First and foremost I must thank Dr Gerald Harriss, the supervisor of the PhD thesis on which this book is based, not only for his unfailing help and support while I was his research student, but also for his continued encouragement and friendship afterwards. I am also especially grateful to Professor Sir Geoffrey Elton, who not only began to teach me what history was about when I was an undergraduate, but offered assistance and advice both during and after my time as a research student, and to Professor Sir James Holt, Professor Wallace MacCaffrey, Mr Ralph Bennett, Dr John Morrill and Dr Gillian Sutherland, to all of whom I owe a very great deal. The same is true of my colleagues at New Hall – especially Dr Zara Steiner – both for being prepared to offer a secure job to a semi-retired mother of young children and for subsequent friendship and stimulus. Others to whom I am indebted are Professors John Baker, Christopher Brooke, Barrie Dobson, Roderick Floud (if I failed to take his generous advice on how to do proper statistical tests, it was merely the result of my own mathematical ineptness), Hassell Smith, the late Professor Christopher Cheney, Drs Caroline Barron, George Bernard, Jeremy Boulton, Brendan Bradshaw, Christopher Dyer, Steven Ellis, Steven Gunn, Michael Hicks, Michael K. Jones, Edward Miller, Ruth Morse, Dorothy Owen, Simon Payling, Sandra Raban, Carole Rawcliffe, Miri Rubin, Richard Tuck, Roger Virgoe and Susan Wright. Above all I must thank the two people who were for many years my late-medieval colleagues at Cambridge, Dr Edward Powell and Dr Rosemary Horrox. Rosemary will know how much factual information she passed to me at my request; neither will know quite how much they have enlarged my understanding of our shared period. Unfortunately, their books and Dr Harriss' study of Cardinal Beaufort – all three works of enormous importance for the period – came out too late for me to read before this study was virtually complete. As is evident from some of the footnotes, however, I enjoyed lengthy discussions with Dr Horrox and Dr Powell about their work. (It will also be evident that, the last stages of the work having taken rather a long time, I missed other very recent works, including those by J. C. K. Cornwall and Professors Bean and Lander.) Professor Holt and Drs Dyer, Harriss, Horrox, Morrill and Powell, and Professor Holt's then co-editors of the Cambridge medieval series, in which this book was originally to appear, Professors Brooke and David Luscombe, were kind enough to offer comments on parts of the manuscript. Needless to say, any remaining faults are my own, but the help I received saved me from worse ones. In this context I am particularly indebted to my research students, Dr Benjamin Thompson and Dr John Watts, for reading the entire manuscript and taking seriously my instructions not to be kind. To both of them and to my former research student, Mr Julian Turner, I owe more than I can say. I remain convinced that I learned considerably more from them than they from me. Similarly, I must thank those other Cambridge students who have helped me to a greater understanding of medieval history, including, during the last two years, the members of my Special Subject class on the fifteenth-century gentry. I used many libraries and record offices and would like to thank the people who helped me in all of them. Special thanks are owed to the long-suffering staff of the Cambridge University Library, notably those in the Reading Room and the old and new Anderson Room; the staff at the Public Record Office, especially Mr David Lee, Miss Margaret Condon, Dr David Crook and Dr John Post; Dr Robert Bearman of the Shakespeare Birthplace Trust archives; and Mr Alan Cameron, erstwhile keeper of manuscripts at Nottingham University Library. The Marquess of Bath and Sir Robert Throckmorton kindly allowed me to consult their manuscripts at Longleat and Coughton Court, and I am grateful to their librarians, Miss Austin and Miss Thompson, for their assistance and also to Mrs Clare McLaren Q.C. for subsequent permission to use the Throckmorton papers in this work. The British Academy and the Twenty-Seven Foundation helped with my research expenses. I owe my thanks to everyone at the Cambridge University Press who has been concerned in the production of this book, including the editors of the series, past and present, and especially Mr William Davies, for their encouragement and not least their patience as they awaited its arrival. Finally there remains my family. My children, Jamie and Alison, have lived their entire lives under the shadow of the Warwickshire gentry, and I thank them for their forebearance, as also for their help with the final stages. The dedicatees, my husband and my mother, are the ones, who, with practical help and moral support, made it all possible.

ABBREVIATIONS

Bod. Lib.	Bodleian Library, Oxford
Br. Lib.	British Library
Cal. Close Rolls	*Calendar of the Close Rolls Preserved in the Public Record Office, 1399–1509*, 18 vols., London, H.M.S.O., 1927–63.
Cal. Fine Rolls	*Calendar of the Fine Rolls Preserved in the Public Record Office, 1399–1509*, 11 vols., London, H.M.S.O., 1931–62.
Cal. Pat. Rolls	*Calendar of the Patent Rolls Preserved in the Public Record Office, 1399–1509*, 17 vols., London, H.M.S.O., 1903–16.
Cat. Anc. Deeds	*A Descriptive Catalogue of Ancient Deeds in the Public Record Office*, 6 vols., London, H.M.S.O., 1890–1915.
Colls. Hist. Staffs.	*Collections for a History of Staffordshire*, ed. by the William Salt Archaeological Society, 1, 1880– .
Dep. Keep.'s Rep.	*Reports of the Deputy Keeper of the Public Records* – No. 41, London, 1880, 'Calendar of Norman Rolls', Hen. V, pp. 671–810. – No. 44, London, 1883, 'Calendar of French Rolls', Hen. V., pp. 543–638. – No. 48, London, 1887, 'Calendar of French Rolls', Hen. VI, pp. 217–450.
Derbys. R. O.	Derbyshire Record Office.
D.N.B.	Stephen, L. and Lee, S. eds., 1885–1900, *Dictionary of National Biography*, 63 vols., London.
Dugdale	Dugdale, Sir William, 1730, *The Antiquities of Warwickshire*, 2 vols. in one, London, rpt. Manchester, s.d.

Dugdale (1765 edn)	Dugdale, Sir William, 1765, *The Antiquities of Warwickshire*, Coventry.
E.E.T.S.	Early English Text Society
Feud. Aids	*Inquisitions and Assessments Relating to Feudal Aids ... Preserved in the Public Record Office, 1284–1431*, 6 vols., London, H.M.S.O., 1899–1920.
G.E.C.	Gibbs, V., Doubleday, H. A. etc. eds., 1910–40, *The Complete Peerage*, 13 vols., London.
Gloucs. R. O.	Gloucestershire Record Office
H.M.C.	Royal Commission on Historical Manuscripts
I.P.M.	Inquisition *post mortem*
I.P.M.	*Calendarium Inquisitionum Post Mortem Escaetarum*, III, Ric. II–Hen. IV, Record Commissioners, London, 1821. *Calendarium Inquisitionum Post Mortem Escaetarum*, IV, Hen. V–Ric. III, Record Commissioners, London, 1828.
I.P.M. Hen. VII	*Calendar of Inquisitions Post Mortem ... Preserved in the Public Record Office, Hen. VII*, 3 vols., London, H.M.S.O., 1898–1955.
Leics. R. O.	Leicestershire Record Office
List of Escheators	Wood, A. C., 1971, *Typescript List of Escheators for England and Wales* in the P.R.O., issued as List and Index Society, 72.
Lists and Indexes, 9	Hughes, A., ed., 1898, *A List of Sheriffs for England and Wales*, P.R.O. Lists and Indexes, main series, 9, London, H.M.S.O., rpt. N. York, 1963.
Northants. R. O.	Northamptonshire Record Office
Nott. Univ. Lib.	Nottingham University Library
N.R.A.	National Register of Archives
Oxon. L. R. O.	Oxford Local Record Office
Paston Letters	*Paston Letters and Papers of the Fifteenth Century*, ed. N. Davis, 2 vols., Oxford, 1971–6.
P.R.O.	Public Record Office
Procs. Priv. Counc.	*Proceedings and Ordinances of the Privy Council of England*, ed. N. H. Nicolas, 7 vols., Record Commissioners, London, 1834–7.
Return: 1878	*Return: Members of Parliament*, 1878, 2 vols., London, House of Commons.

Rot. Parl.	*Rotuli Parliamentorum, 1377–1503*, 4 vols., London, 1783.
S.B.T.	Shakespeare Birthplace Trust Records Office
S.C.R.O.	Staffordshire Record Office
Test. Ebor.	*Testamenta Eboracensia*, ed. J. Raine II, III, IV Surtees Soc., 30 (1855), 45 (1864), 53 (1869).
Test. Vetust.	*Testamenta Vetusta*, ed. N. H. Nicolas, 2 vols. in one, London, 1826.
V.C.H.	*V.C.H. Warwicks.*, 1904–69, *The Victoria History of the County of Warwick*, 8 vols. with index, London.
W.C.R.O.	Warwick County Record Office
Wedgwood: Biographies	Wedgwood, J. C., 1936, *History of Parliament: Biographies of the Members of the Commons House 1439–1509*, London.
Wedgwood: Register	Wedgwood, J. C., 1938, *History of Parliament: Register of the Ministers and of the Members of both Houses 1439–1509*, London.
W.F.F.	*Warwickshire Feet of Fines*, III, ed. L. Drucker, Dugdale Soc. Publications, 18, 1943.
Wm. Salt Lib.	William Salt Library
Worcs. R. O.	Hereford and Worcester Record Office

NOTE ON TEXT

To avoid confusion Humphrey Stafford, earl of Stafford and later duke of Buckingham, is referred to throughout as 'Buckingham' and similarly James Boteller, son and eventual heir of the earl of Ormond, created earl of Wiltshire during his father's lifetime, is referred to as 'Wiltshire'.

1

INTRODUCTION

This is a study of the life of the rulers of late-medieval England. England in the middle ages, and well beyond, was ruled by the landowning classes, because wealth and, more importantly, political power, were founded in land.[1] Although the focus is local, this close analysis of a relatively small number of families is offered as a contribution to the study of the ruling aristocracy as a whole, itself an indispensable prerequisite for the analysis of the political life of the time. The emphasis will be on the public lives of these families, on the way in which their actions affected local and national politics, but many aspects of their more private lives – marriage, land settlements, estate management and religious beliefs – must be seen as inseparable from their public concerns. As politics had an inevitable bearing on the conduct of private matters, so private concerns could not fail to influence political viewpoints and, indeed, must to a large extent have determined political responses. Equally, landowners, like all people at all times, required an atmosphere of peace and security in which to carry on those parts of their lives as divorced from the public domain as relations with spouses and young children. As with any other group of politically active people, the political attitudes of these families were made up of a confused amalgam of personal experiences and prejudices, political ideas and public and private loyalties. This study is aimed at reconstructing the totality of experiences that went into the making of fifteenth-century political man.

To do so it has to cross some of the traditional historiographical boundaries. The starting point was originally the politics of late-medieval England, specifically the causes and effects of the political upheavals of the fifteenth century. The technique of the local study was borrowed from the Tudor and Stuart historians who had already put it to such effective use.[2] If this was an innovative approach at the time, interest even then in late-medieval local

1 This point is pursued below, pp. 283–5.

2 Carpenter, M. C. 1976. Many of the works on later local history are cited below, ch. 17, nn. 57–8. The work on the seventeenth century is summarised in Morrill 1976a: Intro.

history was far from new.[3] The work of K. B. McFarlane had already drawn attention to the importance of the nobility, whose power rested in the localities, individual local conflicts had been discussed in several notable articles, and the problem of 'bastard feudalism' and local order, by its very nature, called for a local approach.[4] But it also demanded that attention be given to the role of the king's law, since it was the effectiveness of the king's government in the shires that was often at issue in discussions of bastard feudalism,[5] and for landowners the key area of government was the law that defended their property.[6] As it happened, the development of this project coincided with the coming together of legal and social history in a marriage that has proved fruitful for both disciplines. The study of law in society has particular relevance for the fifteenth century. First, it enables us to bring more precise analytical tools to bear on the question of how the law operated in a world in which there was frequent resort to extra-legal processes of all kinds, from informal arbritration to violence. Secondly, it focuses attention on the problem, highly germane to fifteenth-century politics, of what makes a society stable or unstable.[7] Here, both law and history have profited from the insights offered by sociology and anthropology.[8] Curiously, the new approach to legal history, which seems so peculiarly apt for the study of the landed society of late-medieval England, has so far failed to impinge substantially on the work of political historians of the period. More surprisingly still, it has yet to inform many of the local studies that have burgeoned in recent years.[9]

It was then a logical step from asking questions about the interplay of law

3 Local studies that appeared about the same time or not long after include Bennett 1975, 1983; Astill 1977; Tyldesley 1978; Saul 1978, 1981; Wright 1978, 1983; Pollard 1979; Rowney 1981; Cherry 1981a; Payling, 1987b.

4 McFarlane 1973; Harriss 1981; Griffiths 1968; Jeffs 1961b; Lewis 1958; Virgoe, 1972–3, 1973; Storey 1966: chs. 5, 7–8, 10–11, 13; Rosenthal 1970; Bellamy 1964, 1973; Stones 1957. More recent contributions include Virgoe 1980; McClane 1984; Waugh 1977; Kaeuper 1979; Smith, A. 1984; Payling 1986.

5 The literature is surveyed in Harriss 1981: pp. xviii–xxv, starting from McFarlane's classic exposition, 'Bastard feudalism', 1981a; also sections on retaining and disorder in the local studies cited above, n. 3.

6 For a general survey showing how the law was essentially a law of property and how it developed, Milsom 1981.

7 E.g. Gatrell, Lenman and Parker eds. 1980; Sharpe 1982, 1984; Hay 1984; Knafla 1983; Cockburn ed. 1977; Weisser 1979; Stone 1983; Stone and Sharpe 1985; Ives 1981b, 1983a,b; Hanawalt 1979; Given 1977; Wormald 1980; Maddicott 1978b; Clanchy 1974, 1983; Powell 1979, 1983a, 1984b; Post 1976; Green 1972; also works cited in p. 283, n. 4. The more ambitious medieval studies by social historians, notably those by Given and Hanawalt, have tended to suffer from the existence of so many unresolved critical problems with the sources: on some of these and on the critical literature, app. 4 below.

8 E.g. Banton ed. 1966; Deutsch 1973; Gluckman 1955; Boissevain 1974; Roberts 1983.

9 A notable exception in local history is Wright 1983, and, in more general studies, Powell's seminal articles on arbitration (1983a, 1984b); on arbitration, also Rawcliffe 1984; Rowney 1982; Hicks 1983; Rosenthal 1970.

and society to analysing the attitude to the law of the members of that society[10] and thence to broader questions touching the beliefs – the *mentalités*, to use the fashionable term – of these landowning families. And since it was clear that any investigation of the attitudes of landowners must start with their dealings with their most prized possession, their land, it became apparent that a thorough examination of the gentry's management of their estates was essential. 'Management' has been taken to include family settlements and inheritance practices, economic exploitation of the estate, consumption patterns and gifts to the church. The political, social and economic concerns of these families all in their own way constituted a significant part of the family interest and the study of each particular area can be a means of shedding light on the others. Often these concerns would conflict, and the ways in which such conflicts were resolved may tell us much about a landowning family's priorities.[11]

It is the search for attitudes and beliefs among the landowners who dominated the medieval polity that seems to be the most urgent task for historians of late-medieval English politics. Since Stubbsian constitutionalism was finally – indeed, quite recently – laid to rest, the emphasis in this field has been on the politics of personalities.[12] The move to abandon the imposition of anachronistic concepts on past societies in favour of closer study of the individual figures who comprise society has been by no means confined to late-medieval English politics,[13] but it undoubtedly owes its particular force in this field to the work of K. B. McFarlane. He it was who first urged historians to look less at kings and governments and more at the nobility on whose power their rule ultimately rested, pointing out as he did so that it was 'An excessive addiction to constitutional issues' that had made medieval English history 'much too royalist'. It was McFarlane who said of the nobility, 'it seemed to me that it was time that an attempt were made to find out something about these

10 A preliminary exploration is Carpenter 1983; also an early but passable effort, Carpenter 1980b.

11 A first summary of the work on this is Carpenter 1986b.

12 A reflection of how recent the abandonment of Stubbs has been is the introduction to Fryde 1979. In 1953, when Stubbs had been dead over half a century, McFarlane said: 'he . . . stamped English medieval historiography so deeply with his image that we have hardly escaped the imprint yet' (1973: p. 1); arguably (below, p. 6), the imprint is still there, more explicitly in American historiography (McKenna 1979: pp. 485–6), but also in some writing on political theory (Genet 1981: pp. 23–4). For the classic statement of Stubbsian attitudes to the fifteenth century, Fortescue, *Governance*, Intro. by Plummer. It is no accident that this is to be found in an edition of a work by Fortescue (below, p. 6). For a survey of the literature to the 1970s, see Guth 1977.

13 The historiography of the seventeenth century in particular has followed a similar course to that of the later middle ages (a fact exemplified by G. L. Harriss' examination of the use of medieval arguments in seventeenth-century debates (Harriss 1978). Although historians of the two periods have not followed an identical path in their flight from the Whig Interpretation, they seem now to have reached about the same point, but those of the seventeenth century are responding with greater intellectual ambition (see particularly Morrill 1976b; ch. 1 and preface to 2nd edn (1980); Hirst 1981; and Sharpe 1986: pp. 322–3).

men.'[14] There can be no doubt that his injunction has been taken to heart; the last fifteen years have seen an enormous number of studies of the noblemen and gentry who, together with the crown, constituted political society in late-medieval England. Many of these studies are now coming into print.[15]

In many ways the effect of this work has been liberating, freeing the period of the aridity that arose from over-emphasis on institutions and focusing research where it belongs, on the interplay of the small number of people in whose hands political power lay: the king and his magnates or, at the local level, the leading gentry and their noble lords. And yet it is becoming increasingly evident that this avenue is ending in a cul-de-sac, and that the more we learn factually about these people the less we seem to understand about them. The 'new history' of the period has two particular characteristics. One is a strong concentration on the politics of patronage, seen by many as the key to governmental success or failure.[16] Frequently this has entailed limiting politics almost exclusively to the personal relations of king and nobility, and it is this limitation that has contributed to the other principal feature of recent work, the separation of high from low politics. Studies of individual noblemen have been most successful in their analysis of great political events, less so in describing the roots of noble power, while explorations of local societies have tended to be thematic and, even in examining the interconnections of local and national politics, have rarely attempted to delineate the place of the locality within the body politic. Accounts of particular local conflicts, including those whose importance lies in their effect on national politics, have lacked a framework within which their true importance for the body politic might be judged.[17]

Put more generally, there has been too much concentration on the personal politics of kings and noblemen and too little examination of enforcement – the whole debate has tended to suffer from what could be called 'Glendower's

[14] McFarlane 1973: pp. 2, 3; also Cooper 1983b: p. 78.

[15] E.g. Jack 1961; Pollard 1968, 1983; Kent 1973; Rawcliffe 1974, 1978; Woodger 1974; Hicks 1974, 1978, 1980; Crawford 1975; Archer 1984a; Walker 1986; Sinclair 1987a; Weiss 1976; Thomson 1979. Amongst studies of noble affinities are the pioneering Dunham 1955; Pollard 1975–6; Cherry 1979; Carpenter 1980a. For gentry studies, see the work cited above, n. 3. For the nobility, the revolution began in the fourteenth century, with Maddicott 1970 and Phillips 1972. On its significance, see Davies, R. R. 1972–3.

[16] E.g. Fryde 1979: pp. 13–14; Phillips 1972; pp. 284–5; Kaeuper 1988: p. 293; Rosenthal 1976: pp. 52–3; Ross 1976: pp. 19–20; Ross ed. 1979: 'Intro.', pp. 9–10; Lander 1969: pp. 179–80, 188–9, 1980, pp. 86–7; Griffiths 1974: p. 69; Griffiths ed. 1981: 'Intro.', pp. 12–13; Cherry 1981b: pp. 123–4; Tuck 1985a, pp. 94, 132–3, 146, 292; 1971. More generally, this interpretation informs such works as Tuck 1973 (see esp. p. 72) and Griffiths 1981. For a contrary view, see Harriss 1981: p. xxiv, and Harriss 1985c: p. 47. Also Richmond 1983: pp. 57–60, whose remarks on patronage were anticipated by McFarlane 1973a: pp. 287–97, and 1981d.

[17] Recent work that has looked at the problem of centre and locality is Given-Wilson 1986 and 1987b.

disease'[18] – and consequently too little investigation of the roots and uses of power.[19] This makes it difficult to produce much more than a surface narrative of political events, and, when acute dislocation at the centre of power renders even this limited ambition problematic, as in the 1310s and 1450s, the narrative itself breaks down. We still await an account of the 1450s that looks more coherent than the seemingly unconnected series of battles and beheadings depicted in Parts II and III of *Henry VI*, two of Shakespeare's least coherent works.[20] Another result has been an over-emphasis on the importance of the state of the royal finances. No one, least of all anyone working on Henry VI's reign, would deny that gross royal indebtedness could be a serious problem. However, the placing of patronage and, therefore, the king's capacity to offer rewards at the centre of analysis, and reluctance to examine the real basis of royal power, have tended towards too-ready acceptance of the dictum that sound royal finances equal a stable monarchy.[21] The obvious facts that both Edward II and Richard II were very rich at the ends of their reigns should make us at least hesitate before using this equation unthinkingly.[22]

It might almost be said that the constitutionalism of the Whigs which McFarlane demolished so effectively has produced amongst political historians of this period an aversion for political or constitutional ideas of any sort.[23] Yet all societies have a constitution, even if, as at this period, it consists only of the largely unspoken assumptions of the politically aware about what may or may not be done. Similarly, all active politicians must have some sense of why they do what they do. Indeed, the political history of the fourteenth and fifteenth centuries now being written implies a constitution, one where all leverage comes from the centre, in the shape of the king's power to grant money and offices to his nobility, while they in turn raise the gentry's support in the same

18 GLEND: I can call spirits from the vasty deep.
HOTSPUR: Why, so can I, or so can any man, But will they come when you do call for them?
(Shakespeare, *Henry IV Part I*, III, i). Cf. for France, Lewis 1981. Ironically, a similar comment was made at the height of the 'constitutionalist' phase: local government was neglected in favour of 'the flashy episodes of national life' (Maitland, 1911: pp. 468–9).

19 One notable exception is Davies, R. R. 1978.

20 Interesting comments on how this style of history can lead to the collapse of any kind of narrative framework are to be found in Butterfield's discussion of the 'Namierisation' of eighteenth-century politics (1957: Book III, esp. pp. 297–8).

21 E.g. Ross 1974: ch. 16; Wolffe 1970; Chrimes 1972a: chs. 6 and 11 (with reservations). Above all, this theme is a *leitmotiv* in the work of Lander: e.g. 1969: pp. 103–14, 166–8, 192–4, 1976a: pp. 35, 39–40, 48, 54–5, 1980: pp. 4–5 and ch. 3.

22 Fryde 1979: ch. 7; Buck 1983; Saul 1984: pp. 31–3; Barron 1968. It was as much as anything the way they made themselves rich that caused their downfall.

23 McKenna 1979. A notable exception has been Harriss 1975; also, more recently, Harriss 1985a,c,e; Powell 1985. The important pioneering work of Chrimes 1936 has not been followed up. Note also Kaeuper 1988.

way. It is in fact remarkably like the constitution assumed by Fortescue, complete with his conviction that money lay at the root of the problem. And Fortescue's trustworthiness as a guide to fifteenth-century political life should not go unquestioned.[24] Reluctance to admit the inseparable concepts of political ideas and constitutional history has allowed this particular interpretation of the late-medieval constitution to slip furtively into the position of orthodoxy. Yet, its assumption that kings had to buy the loyalty and co-operation of their nobility is at odds with the essence of McFarlane's interpretation. It may well be the influence of Fortescue that accounts for a lingering sense in some recent work that, contrary to one of McFarlane's most important insights, the nobility were at heart hostile to effective kingship.[25]

But the origins of the problem lie deeper than this. To paraphrase McFarlane, in the search for the individual baron we are in danger of losing our sense of the class as a whole.[26] Although it is clearly undesirable to generalise about a group before we know something of the people of whom it consisted, it is equally unsatisfactory to leave the analysis at the level of isolated case studies. If all politics is seen in terms of individual protagonists, each driven by his own inner daemon, we can come to no other conclusion than that politics were exclusively personal and, regardless of what ideological front might be put up to justify political action, each was out for what he could get.[27] This premiss leads inescapably to the conclusion that politics were wholly dominated by patronage, which can then justify the opinion that everybody was out for what he could get, and so on in a never-broken circle.[28] That is another reason why the

24 Fortescue, *Governance*, passim. For a brief comment on his interpretation, see Carpenter 1983: p. 234.

25 This can lead to internally contradictory statements: e.g. Ross 1976, essentially a school-of-McFarlane interpretation, seems to approve of the tougher Tudor policies towards the nobility (pp. 152–57, and, on the early Tudors, cf. McFarlane 1973: pp. 2–3); Lander has a shrewd understanding of the importance of the nobility to the king, including in the localities, but is very dismissive of their conduct and aspirations: e.g. 1969: pp. 30, 67–8, 81–2, 161–73, 175–84, 187–90, 1976a: pp. 13–16, 30–6, 55–6, 1980: pp. 3, 34–5, 48, 190–3, 221, 335, 362–8. Also e. g. Ross 1974: pp. 331–41; Griffiths 1981: pp. 569–97. Cf. in particular, McFarlane 1973: pp. 120–1.

26 McFarlane 1981f: p. 232.

27 This point was made to me by Julian Turner, late of Magdalene College, Cambridge. I cannot over-emphasise my debt to Mr Turner in dealing with the problems of the historiography of the late-medieval polity. See also Davies, R. R. (1972–3: p. 201): 'Medieval historians . . . have come to suspect that behind every constitutional bush lurks a mean-minded baron or a profit-seeking king.' Cf. McFarlane 1973: p. 119.

28 Lander is particularly hostile to the idea that politics went any further than a '"pork-barrel" morality' and the pursuit of personal ambitions; see, e.g., 1969: pp. 30, 81, 166, 167, 169, 179, 182, 189–91, 1976a: pp. 16, 21–8, 55–6, 1980: pp. 265, 285, 360, 1986: p. 37 ('Fundamentally based as it was on property and personalities, political life was even more of a jungle than it is today, when it is at least to some extent tempered by principles'). Also e.g. Ross 1981: p. lii; Storey 1966: pp. 15–16; Griffiths 1981: pp. 597, 735–6; Tuck 1985a: p. 293; Starkey 1987a: p. 24

Victorian idea of The Bad Baron (so accurately and hilariously pilloried by Sellar and Yeatman in their section on Warwick the Kingmaker) still persists.[29] As with Fortescue's constitution, the answer to the question why the members of the political community behaved as they did has been assumed rather than thought out. The answer may indeed be that they all acted out of pure egotism (although they would probably be unique in history were this the case, and the *Somnium Vigilantis*, in condemning the Yorkists precisely for this moral failing, clearly felt it was preaching to a converted audience), but the proposition needs to be examined.[30] When magnates and gentry reacted to a particular type of rule in a particular way, it is worth asking whether anything beyond personal pique or ambition governed their responses. Did they realise that their individual interests might often be best served by pursuing collective aspirations? If so, how may aspirations be investigated and defined?[31] In a stimulating series of articles, Michael Hicks has been posing some thoughtful questions about the personal morality of great landowners in this period.[32] The aim of the present study is to investigate the *political* morality and ideologies of landowners as a group in the later middle ages.

The genius of McFarlane was to see not only that the nineteenth-century constitution was wholly alien to late-medieval England, but also that the only way we should ever begin to understand the nature of the constitution of this time was by thinking ourselves imaginatively into the minds of the people who were its constituent parts, and so learn how they saw their relationships with each other and with their king. Long before *mentalités* were commonplace in English historiography, McFarlane was asking questions about the collective beliefs of the English ruling classes in the late middle ages. Particular case-histories were to be merely a prelude to a deeper comprehension of the body politic. This was to be achieved by generalising from the information acquired by sensitive explorations of the careers of late-medieval politicians. Even in the fragmentary form in which we have it, it is clear that McFarlane's work on the

('the sordid, confused machinations of fifteenth-century power politicians'); Wood 1986: p. 165; Kaeuper 1988: p. 287. Cf. Rosenthal and Richmond eds. 1987: 'Intro.', pp. ix–x.

29 Sellar and Yeatman 1975: pp. 54–5.

30 Kekewich 1982. A fifteenth-century poem says explicitly that service to a lord solely for profit is of no use to the lord (Kail ed., *Political Poems*, p. 73 v. 4).

31 See McFarlane on the complexities of motivation (1973: pp. 280–1), and Gillingham 1981: p. 6, which makes a serious attempt to grapple with the problems the nobility themselves were grappling with in the fifteenth century. The problem is well summed up by Holmes, when he writes of the need for 'an effort of the imagination, exercised . . . without nostalgia, sentimentality, or contempt', while pointing out the unchanging nature of many features of humanity: 'They were, so far as we know, neither more nor less intelligent, grasping, or pious than people are today' (Holmes 1962: pp. 4–5). Also Reynolds 1984: p. 1, and p. 4 on the dangers of assuming that political thought is 'the prerogative of . . . philosophers . . . or theologians'.

32 Hicks 1985a, 1986b,c, 1987.

nobility was to be a major contribution to a reassessment of the constitution of this time.[33]

The difficulties in uncovering the unspoken assumptions of any age are obvious enough; for the fifteenth century, whose protagonists have left us almost no explicit explanations of their behaviour, they verge on the insuperable. The single substantial source, the Paston letters, has proved awkward to use, because of problems in judging whether this family was representative or wholly unrepresentative of landowning mores.[34] In any case, people do not necessarily expatiate on their political ideas in personal or business correspondence, let alone on ideas they take for granted.[35] We have no choice but to rely on deductions of motive drawn from the analysis of actions, and it is here above all that McFarlane has shown the way in his work on the nobility.[36] As J. C. Holt has demonstrated, political ideas both grow out of and inform daily political experience.[37] If the present study reconstructs the experience of a particular landowning society, it is with the aim of making some progress towards achieving McFarlane's goal; to move by way of the study of the individuals who comprised that society, first in isolation then in relation to each other, to an understanding of the fundamental beliefs and attitudes that informed their political actions and their view of the constitution. Put another way, we may find out whether there *was* a political morality in this period, or whether political life was indeed as Hobbesian as J. R. Lander would have us believe.[38] For these individuals, what, if any, was the meaning of the words that described their foremost preoccupations; words like 'family', 'lineage', 'gentility', 'friendship', 'allegiance', 'neighbourhood', 'locality', 'power', 'stability', 'public', 'private', 'law', 'justice', 'crime', 'good government', or their

[33] McFarlane 1973: pp. x, xviii, xxxii, 297; in particular two key statements: his objection to constitutional studies because they were not 'concerned . . to prove *the realities of political power*' (my italics) (p. xviii) and his comment on the studies which undermined Stubbs: 'they have discredited it without putting anything coherent in its place. This failure to substitute anything for it *as a whole* has produced utter confusion' (McFarlane's italics) (p. 280). Although these words were written in 1938, they serve as a fitting epitaph on the present state of affairs.

[34] E.g. Du Boulay 1970, which generally takes the former view, Thomson 1983: p. 65, which is agnostic, and Richmond 1981: *passim*, and summing-up, pp. xv–xvi, which seems to lean to the latter view.

[35] Hence the comment on the Plumptons in Taylor 1975: pp. 86–7.

[36] See in particular, 1973a: p. 281: 'Men have to be judged from their actions alone . . . But it is a mistake to suppose therefore that motives were less complex and characters more consistent. To do so is to submit to the tyranny of one's materials.' This early and rather neglected essay is an extraordinarily powerful and imaginative statement of the whole problem and its points remain highly relevant.

[37] Holt 1961a,b, 1965.

[38] Richmond's pioneering work, which aims to present one member of the gentry in the round (1981), is at its most successful when it places Hopton in the context of his friends and neighbours (ch. 4).

medieval equivalents? The meaning of such words, which one may hope to deduce from their actions, would lie at the heart of their political beliefs.

Placing the local society within the national political and constitutional framework is an unavoidable part of the inquiry. Central government and the provinces were inseparable parts of the body politic, and the local society's view of itself inevitably moulded and was moulded by the role it played within the larger political world. Here the key issue was the fluctuating relationship between government and localities which remained at the core of national politics until modern technology finally sealed the victory of centripetal over centrifugal forces. As Wallace MacCaffrey has written of England in the sixteenth and seventeenth centuries, '[It] was a hybrid political society in which a centralized monarchy existed side by side with a kind of confederation of local political interests . . . all held together in a certain rough unity by the powerful hand of the monarchy, yet stubbornly retaining in wide areas independence of aims and of action.'[39] For the fifteenth century there are important questions to be asked about the nature of the 'rough confederation of political interests' and the extent of the 'rough unity'. How much control over the localities, unfettered by the crown, did the nobility have? If they were largely free of governmental control, how much lawlessness did this cause? What determined the precise relationship of king, nobility and gentry in this period, and did this change during the century? In this context particular attention will be given to the resurgence of monarchical power at the end of the century, its possible causes and the significance this may have had for the Tudors in the sixteenth century.

Most important of all is the question of how and with what consequences government came to break down in the middle of the century. A political crisis on this scale and the deposition of the king were more surprising occurrences than has sometimes been supposed. How Henry VI came to lose his unchallengeable authority will be examined through the experience of one part of his realm. Still more pressing is the question of how this landed society coped with the enormous uncertainty engendered by monarchical failure and consequent disorder from 1440 to 1471 and even beyond. All societies are in some respects inherently unstable but most have 'fail-safe devices' which prevent the forces for instability overwhelming the methods of conflict resolution.[40] It remains to be seen whether these existed in fifteenth-century England and, if so, whether their role in neutralising conflict in such an extreme situation itself became the agent of fundamental change. Behind the discussion of the whole problem of law and order in a landowning society lies a growing body of work, the product of the new school of legal historians, that recognises the need to see the private processes of late-medieval litigation and conflict resolution not as aberrations from the norm of royal law-enforcement but as adjuncts to it.[41] In the light of

39 MacCaffrey 1975: p. 204.

40 Gluckman 1955; Boissevain 1974; Lewis ed. 1968.

41 In particular the work of Clanchy and Powell (cited n. 7, above).

this work it has been necessary to recast questions about late-medieval law, in particular to ask what landowners expected from it and where they thought the dividing line between normal private influence and unacceptable interference should lie.[42]

Although this is a study of the political society of one county, it must not be forgotten that the county represented only one aspect of the identity of an area. It may be argued, indeed, that most counties had very little existence as political and social units until the later sixteenth century.[43] On this hypothesis, the only justification for using the county as the basis for study is simply one of convenience; that the royal records were organised on a county basis. If there was a variety of local identities in all parts of England, it will be evident that Warwickshire was a peculiarly fragmented county, in which other localisms, owing their existence to geography, tenure and magnate affinities, could exert a stronger influence. The tension between administrative, political and tenurial boundaries will be a major theme throughout. So will the difficulties this caused for the nobility who, to offer the right sort of protection to their clients, needed to control the whole county. The tension poses even more problems for the historian of Warwickshire, who should ideally be able to trace the course of events throughout the midlands and even beyond. Since this is clearly an impossibility, and since little work has been done on the neighbouring counties in this period, some of the conclusions on the significance of particular political events must remain provisional until more is known about Warwickshire's neighbours in the fifteenth century.

This, however, is a relatively minor obstacle to the successful completion of a late-medieval local study. The real problems lie with the sources. The detailed use of sources will be discussed in the text as particular issues arise, but there are some general points which should be made first. The backbone of the work consists of the records of the king's government, particularly of the law-courts, and of gentry families, particularly deeds, wills and estate accounts. The famous correspondences[44] and a certain amount of literary evidence have also been used, but with a full awareness of the dangers of drawing conclusions from these records alone. The use of private records to investigate status, land acquisition and dispersal, economic resources, estate management and religious bequests is relatively straightforward, and is facilitated by the existence of a corpus of work which shows what can be done with these sources in dealing with most of these issues. The problems begin when it comes to reconstructing political and social relationships and the course of local politics. Of themselves the sources will give few answers to the essential questions. This is not a reason for abandoning the questions but for evolving a method of inquiry which will make the sources speak effectively. If one confines one's conclusions to what

42 Carpenter 1983.

43 Morrill 1984: pp. 157–8; below, p. 33, n. 50, and *passim*, esp. ch. 9.

44 *Paston Letters*; *The Plumpton Correspondence*; *The Stonor Letters and Papers*.

can readily be demonstrated, one automatically biases the interpretation towards the more fully documented areas, notably in perpetuating the mistake of seeing everything from the governmental point of view. Speculation founded on observable fact, often buttressed by the insights offered by the correspondences, can legitimately be used to breathe life into the dry bones of the data. For example, we know about the mechanics of the appointment of local officials; we do not know how the names were actually chosen. However, there is evidence – such as comments in the Stonor and Paston letters, and the Bedford riot, which resulted from the failure to make the commission of the peace reflect the realities of local power – which lends weight to the reasonable supposition that some cognisance was normally taken of local power structures and of what the locals had to say.[45]

Even while being prepared to speculate about what the evidence means, the historian has to be careful to remain firmly anchored in it. This means piecing together a large number of often very small fragments of information, using methods not far removed from those of the classic fictional detective. However, unlike Lord Peter Wimsey, at the end of the inquiry the historian has no idea of how complete his material is. Telling pieces of evidence tend to be few and far between; they have to be mined for, and a large amount of spoil will usually contain only the occasional nugget. This is especially true of the royal records, which are peculiarly unhelpful for the local historian of the later middle ages. Up to about 1300 they are almost manageable and have the great advantage that many aspects of the crown's dealings with the shires were brought together in the work of a single body, the eyre, whose records can be very informative. In the early years of Henry VIII governmental records, notably the State Papers, become much more explicit about governmental intentions, and letter evidence, both public and private, begins to proliferate. Between lies a period of voluminous records, most of them singularly uninformative about local affairs, when the crown communicated with the shires through a large number of diverse channels, some of which, conciliar supervision in particular, have left little documentation.[46]

A choice has to be made between saturation coverage of a small period or less dense concentration on a longer time-span from which more can be learned about long-term change. In this case the second option has been chosen. The fifteenth century encompassed such extremes of effective and ineffective government that it seemed that the advantages of being able to study a single area through a period of change and upheaval outweighed the disadvantages of possible superficiality. It is in any case an obvious period to take for Warwickshire, as it runs from the accession of Richard Beauchamp to the earldom of Warwick in 1401 to the execution of the last medieval earl,

[45] Below, p. 349.

[46] *Rolls of the Justices in Eyre*; *Civil Pleas of the Wiltshire Eyre*; *The 1235 Surrey Eyre*; Elton 1969: ch. 2.

Clarence's son, in 1499. Evidence from beyond this *terminus* has been examined, especially the wills of the gentry who died in the sixteenth century, but these dates give the essential parameters of the study.

The impossibility of reading everything compounds the most insuperable problem facing a historian of late-medieval local politics and that is to reconstruct *in toto* the political structure of a region. To describe a local conflict is relatively easy, but to place it in its local context and discover its links with other conflicts and sources of tension, and then go on to elucidate the developments in local and national politics that caused, shaped and were shaped by it is an altogether more demanding proposition. Uncovering and evaluating political linkages is a dangerous, perhaps foolhardy, occupation, in which guilt may be attributed, wholly erroneously, by association. And there is always the nagging suspicion that an unread group of manuscripts may contain the information that invalidates one's conclusions. Nevertheless, the attempt is worth making even at the risk of being wrong. As a general principle the evidence has been pushed as far as it will reasonably go, on the grounds that it is better to be wrong asking the right questions than not to ask the questions at all. Ultimately, the use of the evidence comes down to the unsatisfactory justification of 'feel'; after living long enough with the records and the families they record, one begins to sense what the evidence can and cannot do. For that reason the thesis which was the first fruit of the work is a less reliable guide to county affairs than this book into which it eventually metamorphosed. To those who query whether the unreliability of some of the detailed analysis in the thesis might not indicate the infirmity of all attempts at a narrative of this sort, it can only be said that the re-evaluation of parts of the thesis is offered in the belief that time has brought a closer approximation to the truth.[47]

Any portrait of a society that considers both structure and change over time must falter in the face of the need to divide, for analytical purposes, what should be an indivisible whole. The present study is divided into two halves. The first concentrates on long-term structures and aims essentially to depict the nature and concerns of the gentry. It concludes with a summarising chapter on family and lineage. A major theme in this section is the question of who the gentry were; in particular, it draws comparisons between the nobility at one end of the social hierarchy and the admissibility of the very minor gentry to a study of political society at the other. To avoid pre-empting the second question – of whether the minor gentry are part of the landed elite – the analysis of social structures is based on a complete tenurial survey of the county. The second, chronological part deals with political and social relationships among Warwickshire landowners, including the nobility, and with the course of local politics. A short chapter on the local officers links the two. The first half lays the

[47] One encouraging feature has been the number of times that deductions about allegiances have been confirmed by subsequent evidence.

foundations for the second, in showing what determined the political actions of the gentry, while the second shows the political life within which many of the decisions described in the first half were taken. One important area scarcely touched on is the political influence of the church in the localities; in the end it was decided that this was too complex a problem to deal with adequately, although it is self-evidently one that demands serious attention. However, the fact that Warwickshire, unlike say Worcestershire or parts of Kent, was not dominated by ecclesiastical estates except near Coventry makes this less serious an omission than it might have been.[48]

This is a history of the fifteenth-century body politic and those who comprised it, written from the perspective of Warwickshire, and its view may consequently be skewed at times. It tackles a number of important questions about late-medieval politics and society in England, which is the principal justification for its length, and many of the answers may be felt to be unsatisfactory; some are openly provisional. It will have served its purpose if it makes a contribution to the difficult problem of how to do late-medieval local history – whether, indeed, properly speaking it can be done at all – and above all to changing the agenda for the study of politics in late-medieval England.

[48] Dobson has tackled this problem in parts of his work on Durham Priory: 1973: chs. 1, 5–6, and Benjamin Thompson is working on it in his study of the church and the local landowners in fourteenth-century Norfolk. For ecclesiastical estates in Warwickshire, see below, pp. 32–3.

Part I

STRUCTURAL

2

GEOGRAPHY, ECONOMY AND REGIONAL IDENTITY

Warwickshire lies in a region that has been called 'the centre of England', and the centre of England does indeed lie in this county, at Meriden just south of Coventry. As befits its position, the county is one of the principal crossroads of England, where two great Roman roads, Watling Street and the Fosse Way, and one minor one, Ryknield Street, converge, along with a later road from Worcester to Birmingham that Higden, not quite accurately, also called Ryknield Street and described as one of the 'Four great Royal Roads of England'. Coventry itself lay at a nodal point of the medieval road network. The county accordingly possessed enormous strategic importance, not only because of its command of central communications but also because it links north midlands to south, and east midlands to the Welsh borderland.[1] That the midlands should become a major battleground four times during 'The Wars of the Roses', at Blore Heath, Northampton, Edgcote and Bosworth (five times if we include Tewkesbury, just over the south-west Warwickshire border), was perhaps inevitable. But, as Goodman has shown, it was also vital to control the area because of its importance as a recruiting ground; in practice whoever got there first tended to win not only the recruiting contest but the battle that followed.

Goodman's work also reveals the indispensability of the towns in raising forces and as providers of war loans.[2] Coventry can be shown to have played a part in offering both men and money to kings and their adversaries, and towns such as Coventry, which had accumulated substantial wealth since the fixing of subsidies in 1334, could really only be effectively exploited by rulers needing both kinds of support if they could command their direct contribution of

[1] Skipp 1979; Pevsner and Wedgwood 1966: p. 15; Skipp 1979: pp. 17–18; Cronne 1951: p. 7; Pelham 1950: p. 138; Hilton 1967: p. 10 and reproduction of Gough Map, plate 4, between pp. 150 and 151 (I owe the point about Coventry's position in the road network and the supporting reference to the Gough Map to Dr Dyer).

[2] Goodman 1981b: Part 1 *passim* and pp. 143–4, 219–20.

both.[3] Coventry, Warwick, Birmingham and Stratford were the county's most successful boroughs. Others, such as Henley in Arden and Alcester in the west and Kineton in the south, had done less well.[4] Even Warwick, despite Richard Beauchamp's attempts at resuscitation, was stagnating by the fifteenth century, doubtless suffering from the proximity of the more thriving Stratford to the south and Coventry to the north, as well as from the over-attentive control of the earls of Warwick in their *caput honoris*.[5] The great urban success story of the century in Warwickshire and England was Coventry, whose wool and cloth penetrated into most parts of England and into overseas markets; in 1451 the city gave its prosperity outward form with the act of incorporation. Coventry's trade clearly benefited from its excellent communications, giving it ready access to all parts of England, and the same is true of Birmingham, which had grown rapidly during the period of assarting and colonisation in the late twelfth and thirteenth centuries, and was to continue to develop during the later middle ages. Both Coventry and Birmingham, natural stopping-places on the drove-roads from Wales and Chester to London, were thriving cattle-markets, but Birmingham was already beginning to make its later reputation as a centre of metal-work. Raw materials and wood for charcoal all lay to hand in its immediate environs, and it has been suggested that, at least after 1400, metal working was as important to the town's economy as the older cloth and leather trades.[6] Both towns were desirable places to control for economic reasons, but the Birmingham region in particular, as we shall see shortly, had considerable strategic importance as well.

Otherwise Warwickshire's economy was predominantly agrarian. There were numbers of other markets, most of them established in the great phase of market growth in the late twelfth and thirteenth centuries, but these, although most were reasonably successful, did no more than fulfil their main purpose of acting as local exchange centres.[7] A few of the gentry families of this period had perhaps emerged from the wool trade[8] but outside Coventry this was a county dominated by landowners. The point is illustrated by the enthusiasm

3 *Coventry Leet Book*, pp. 282–3, 313–5, 344–6, 354–8, 364–6, 381–2, 408–13, 426–8, 474–81 etc.; Gill 1938: pp. 33–6; Rowlands 1987: p. 62; Goodman 1981b: pp. 219–20.

4 Harley 1964: pp. 124–8; Hilton 1967: ch. 7. (I owe particular thanks to Dr Dyer for saving me from a number of errors on Warwickshire towns and markets).

5 Cronne 1951: pp. 18–19; *V.C.H.*, VIII, pp. 480–1; Hilton 1967: p. 174; 1975: pp. 83–4.

6 Gill 1930: pp. 44–9; *V.C.H.*, VIII, pp. 3, 155–8; Pelham 1951: p. 260 (diagram based on Gough Map); 1938; 1945–6; 1950; Holt 1985: pp. 3–11, 18–19; Coss 1974a; Skipp 1979: pp. 207–9; Leland 1907–10: II, pp. 96–7; Hilton 1967: p. 175, 1975: pp. 86–7; Bonser 1970: map on pp. 186–7. An indication of Birmingham's wealth can be gained from the value of £40 placed on it in 1478 by the Inquisition *Post Mortem* (C.140/65/17), since these notoriously undervalued. For discussion of the possible decay of Coventry (Phythian-Adams 1979, pp. 35–39), see below, p. 00. For the colonisation of the Arden, see below, pp. 20–2.

7 *V.C.H.*, II, pp. 146–7; Barker 1984–7; Watkins 1983–4; Rowlands 1987: p. 43; Britnell 1981.

8 Pelham 1939–40.

with which the towns courted the local nobility and gentry, enrolling them in their gilds and fraternities and entertaining them.[9] This was true even of Coventry. Moreover, Coventry proper was surrounded by a number of manors under the jurisdiction of the leet, such as Exhall, Caludon, Wyken and Whitley, all of them incorporated into the city in 1451. These acted as avenues of 'gentrification' for merchants like the Bristowes and also as a base from which landowners could bring influence to bear on the city. Two particular occasions stand out when Coventry was dragged by the landowners of the leet into the politics of the county: the Betley affair in the 1440s and the enclosure disputes which began in the 1470s.[10]

Warwickshire was not only under-urbanised compared with some other parts of England, it was also under-populated. Despite being among the richer English counties, in the Poll Tax returns for 1377 it lies only equal eighteenth in the league table of population density, measured in persons to the square mile, above another twenty counties but below all the midland counties except for Berkshire, Staffordshire and Derbyshire, and both the last two, unlike Warwickshire, had substantial areas of upland.[11] Some parts of the county were almost entirely empty of settlement, notably the heathland around Sutton Coldfield in the north and, in the east, Dunsmore Heath, a notorious haunt of criminals, which rather unfortunately lay on the main Coventry to London road.[12]

Warwickshire's geography and economy have always lain in two distinct segments, the Feldon and the Arden. As Leland noted in the 1530s

> I lernyd . . . that the moste parte of the shire of Warwike, that lyeth as Avon river descendithe on the right hand or rype of it, is in Arden . . . and the grownd in Arden is muche enclosyd, plentifull of gres, but no great plenty of corne. The othar part of Warwyk-shire that lyethe on the lefte hond or ripe of Avon river, muche to the southe, is for the moste parte champion, somewhat barren of wood, but very plentifull of corne.

The difference was remarked on again by Camden some years later and was still evident to some extent in the agricultural regions described by Wedge in the eighteenth century.[13] Roughly speaking, the Avon forms the boundary

9 *Register of the Gild of Stratford-upon-Avon*; S.B.T., Stratford Corporation Records; *Register of the Guild of Knowle; Register of the Guild of Coventry*; cf. Horrox 1981; see also below, pp. 338–9.

10 *V.C.H.*, VIII, pp. 40–1; below, pp. 402–10, 540–2. On urban gentry, see Horrox 1988.

11 Russell 1948: p. 313; Donkin 1976: pp. 78–9.

12 Skipp 1979: p. 44; Wedge 1794: pp. 38–9; Agricola 1762: p. 18; Millward and Robinson 1971: pp. 25–6; Tate 1943–4: p. 59. In 1430 a suspected receiver of felons was said to live at Harbury, a village some four to five miles south-west of Dunsmore Heath (*Colls. Hist. Staffs.*, 17, p. 129). Note also the extent of heathland on Wolvey Heath, about six miles north of Dunsmore, implied in the agreement of 1414/5 between Giles Astley and the abbot of Combe over grazing rights there (*Dugdale*, p. 67; and below, pp. 383–5 for more on this dispute).

13 Hilton 1967: pp. 14–15; Leland 1907–10: II, p. 47; Camden 1610: pp. 561, 565; Wedge 1794: pp. 7–8; Hooke 1982.

between the two, although there is another area of Feldon towards the north-east border with Leicestershire.[14] The distinctiveness of the geography and economy of each region can be deduced from the fact that the major towns, the exchange points, lay more or less along the line where they met. The Feldon, the open countryside, was settled first, the earliest settlements being probably those along the light and easily worked Avon terraces and amongst the heavier but fertile alluvial soils of the Avon basin, after which there was movement south into the heavy Lower Lias clays of southern Warwickshire. Domesday Book makes evident the preponderance of Feldon over Arden in 1086 in terms of settlement, population and wealth, even allowing for the under-recording of detached Arden hamlets dependent on manors in the Feldon.

Although parts of the Tame-Blythe basin in the Arden were colonised early from Tamworth, and there was some early penetration into the south-west Arden from Stratford, the area as a whole was less inviting. Partly this was because much of it was on rather higher ground (the Birmingham plateau, divided into two segments – the south Staffordshire plateau and the east Warwickshire plateau – by the Tame-Blythe basin), but principally because it required clearing. It was heavily wooded, and the southern end of the south Staffordshire plateau, known as the Arden plateau, the bulk of which was covered by the four large parishes of Kings Norton and Yardley in Worcestershire and Tanworth and Solihull in Warwickshire, seems to have had almost no pre-Conquest settlement at all. It has been suggested that the real barrier to colonisation was the oak forests that flourished on the Keuper Marl soils which cover much of the region, and that, where possible, the earlier settlers would 'leap over' these areas, making the first clearances on the lighter soils, where the woodland was less intractable.

The soils of the Arden are variable in quality, although by no means generally infertile, but they tend to be heavy. In some of the river valleys, such as those of the Rea and the Blythe and the area between the Alne and the Avon in the south-west Arden, there were drainage problems and, in places, a tendency to flood. Parts of the Arden, notably the acid heathland near Sutton Coldfield and Balsall, and the coal measures in the east Birmingham plateau, are distinctly unfertile. Moreover, clearance may sometimes have led to degeneration and reversion to heath, which may be how the Arden heathland originated.[15] All these disadvantages meant that the main colonisation of the

[14] Nicklin 1932; Hilton 1967: pp. 14–15; Kinvig 1950: pp. 120–2.

[15] For geography and settlement of the Arden, see Millward and Robinson 1971: pp. 25–9; Kinvig 1962: pp. 266–70, 1950: pp. 121–9; Roberts 1965: pp. 56–62, 136–43, 1977: pp. 76–7; Skipp 1979: pp. 100–2, 1981: pp. 162, 165–6, 177–9, 181–2; Hooke 1985: p. 249; Watts 1978–9: pp. 17, 29; Bond 1973: pp. 3–6; Wedge 1794: pp. 38–9; Kinvig 1954: pp. 274–94; and see works cited below, n. 16. For problems in using Domesday evidence, see Sawyer 1976: pp. 1–7; Harvey 1976; and, specifically for Warwickshire, Ford 1976: pp. 149–57, which also discusses early settlement along the Avon.

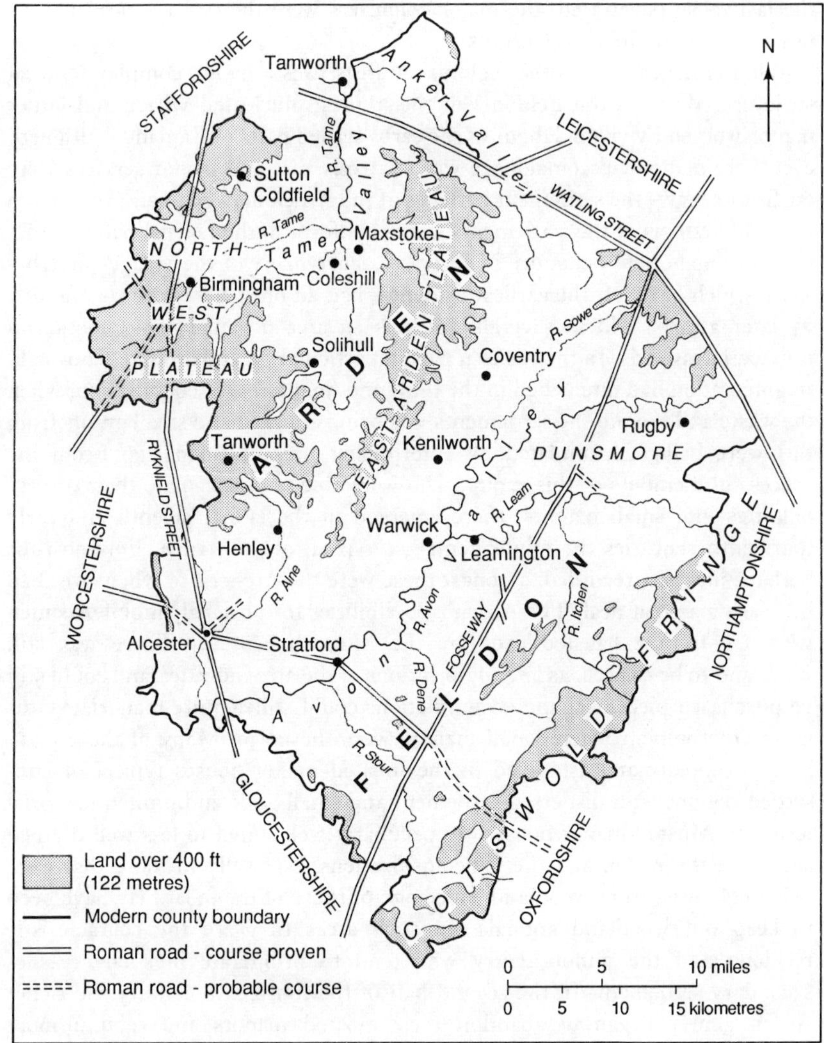

Figure 1 Warwickshire: main geographical features (from Thorpe 1962: p. 39)

Arden took place between about 1000 and 1300, when many of the agriculturally secondary parts of England first came under the plough. Much of the Arden, particularly in the west, was colonised with the encouragement of the earls of Warwick. The earls' 'super-parishes' can be observed breaking up, under the pressure of comital grants of the twelfth and thirteenth centuries, into separate hamlets and new sub-manors. In the area near Coventry, perhaps the last to be penetrated, the major colonisers were the ecclesiastical institutions, especially the newer orders.[16]

What emerged, as in other colonising areas, was a highly complex tenurial structure. Whereas the Feldon had the 'typical' nucleated village and larger manor worked by villein labour of the early-settled parts of England – although even here manor-vill coincidence was relatively rare and labour services were far from heavy – the settlement patterns of the Arden defy generalisation. Even the field systems of the settlements fail to conform to the normal pattern, that is, either open field or tenure in severalty, since many of the villages, notably those which have left the earliest evidence, had an open-field core surrounded by later assarts held in severalty. It was an area of small sub-manors and isolated farmsteads. In the western part in particular, in and around Tanworth, fragmentation had intensified in the third and final phase of colonisation, when the wasteland around the settlements was being attacked and small grants from this were being accumulated by enterprising peasant colonisers. From the successful members of this group, who were able to amalgamate their diverse holdings into small manors, there emerged in the late thirteenth and early fourteenth centuries the minor gentry so typical of the Arden. Foremost, or perhaps just best recorded, amongst these were the Archers, of whom we shall be hearing a great deal. The Arden's possibilities for upwardly mobile yeomen were far from exhausted even by the fifteenth century. There was still woodland to be cleared, as later descriptions of the area indicate; land could still be purchased piecemeal and accumulations could still acquire manorial status in an environment where small manors were the norm. Many of these petty lords, originally at least, lived in the moated manor-houses typical of late-settled regions with dispersed settlement and small-scale and limited manorial lordship. Moated manor houses are peculiarly well suited to less well drained areas like the Arden and the Lincolnshire fens, especially to those that were being colonised from woodland, since one purpose of the moat may have been to keep out woodland animals. In such areas they are the characteristic residences of the minor gentry who tend to proliferate in such areas of secondary settlement. In the second half of the fourteenth century the richer Arden gentry began to abandon their moated manors and rebuild more imposingly on higher ground, as the Archers were doing on one of their estates in about 1500, an indication that some at least were beginning to think of themselves as rather more than 'parish gentry' of purely local interests.[17]

[16] The colonisation of the Arden is discussed in Kinvig 1954: pp. 292–4; Harley 1964: pp. 122–4; Skipp 1960: pp. 6–17, 1979: pp. 100–2, 141, 1970b: pp. 21–35, 1981; Skipp and Hastings 1963: pp. 9–20; Roberts 1965: chs. 2 and 3, 1968; Hilton 1967: pp. 36–7, 1975c: pp. 122–3; *V.C.H.*, II, pp. 78–9, 82, 86; Rowlands 1987: p. 50.

[17] For settlement patterns and tenurial structure in the Arden, see Hilton 1975c, 1985b; Hilton ed., *Stoneleigh Leger Book*, pp. xlv–xlvii; Harley 1958–9; Skipp 1979: pp. 101–2, 1970b: pp. 24–33, 36–42; and other works by Skipp cited in n. 16; Roberts 1962, 1961–2, 1965: chs. 2–7,

Contrasts of agriculture are equally evident between the two regions. The Feldon, with its nucleated villages, open fields and unfree peasants, was a major grain-producing area until the later fourteenth century. Then, like other older parts of England, it began to suffer the delayed effects of the Black Death. The grain market collapsed, the peasantry either resisted the demands of lordship or voted with their feet and villages began to be seriously depopulated. The problem was particularly acute on the wetter Lower Lias soils of the south of the county which required more labour. There followed in many settlements what Dyer has described as a long-drawn-out 'wasting process', beginning in many cases in about the mid fourteenth century and sometimes taking a century or more to complete. The lords responded, if not always with noticeable alacrity, by converting to pasture, either enclosing an already empty village or ejecting the last remaining tenants. At the end of the fifteenth century John Rous lamented the destruction of sixty villages, the bulk of them in Warwickshire; on the most recent published reckoning the process of desertion was completed on twelve villages between about 1350 and 1450 and on another seventy-three in the next 250 years, many of these at the end of the middle ages. They were nearly all in the Feldon and although some, like Fulbrook, were imparked, most were converted to sheep. The thriving trade in wool and cloth and Coventry's proximity made sheep-farming, and in some areas cattle-grazing, obviously attractive. Although the bottom dropped out of the wool market in the middle of the century, this could be all to the good as far as gentry and yeomen pastoral farmers were concerned as it made leased pastures, abandoned by the greater lords, more readily available. We shall see at a later stage how some made the most of such opportunities.[18]

The Arden, with its more variable and sometimes rather ungrateful soils, its small estates and its lack of villein labour, had never been an area given over primarily to grain. Skipp has estimated that even at the late-thirteenth-century peak of arable farming the Arden contained two acres of grass for every acre of tilth. Although Dyer's estimates for the mid fourteenth century, based on the Feet of Fines, rate the arable acreage much higher (the exclusion of, for

1968: pp. 103–12, 1973: pp. 227–30, 1976–7; Emery 1962; Perry 1980; Rowlands 1987: pp. 21–2. For a short general discussion of the effects of colonisation on settlement patterns, see Miller and Hatcher 1978: pp. 85–7; for the tenurial structure of the midlands, see Kosminsky 1956: pp. 68–151. A good idea of the tenurial complexity of the Arden can be gained from a rental of Codbarrow: S.C.12/22/86. The distinctive Arden political and social structure is discussed further below, pp. 70, 77, 296–7, 318.

18 The agrarian economy of the Feldon is treated in Dyer 1965–7, 1967–8, 1968, 1980b: ch. 11, 1981, 1982; Beresford 1945–6, 1971; Bond 1969, 1982; Rous, *Historia Regum Angliae*, pp. 122–3; Thorpe 1962; Hilton 1975d; Tate 1943–4: pp. 58–62; Alcock 1977; *Domesday of Enclosures*, II, pp. 389–453. For the abandonment of pasture by the great lords, see Dyer 1981: p. 16, and, for warnings against naive use of the commissions which are the main evidence for depopulation and enclosure, see Kerridge 1955. For more details on leasing and agriculture in general, see below, ch. 5 and for rebuilding of moated manor houses, see below, pp. 199, 202.

example, unenclosed pasture from Feet of Fines would exaggerate the percentage of arable), both writers are agreed that 'the balance [was] shifting still further in favour of grass' in the later middle ages.[19] The Arden's mixed economy was much better insulated than the Feldon against sudden collapses in grain or wool trades and the area seems to have prospered on a variety of enterprises, agricultural and non-agricultural, in this period. Apart from some wheat-growing in more fertile parts like the Tame valley, the principal grain crop was oats. The availability of marl in plentiful supply and the relative ease with which engrossment and enclosure could be done meant that soil improvement could be easily carried out. There was plenty of rough pasture on the heathland and during this period there was enclosure of pasture, both private and common, some of it converted from arable. As early as 1221 it was said 'Such is the law in Arden that where there is a great pasture, he whose land it is may well make buildings and raise hedges and ditches within that pasture, provided that it is not in their exit or entry or to their hurt'.[20] Stock-farming is already evident in the early fourteenth century, both sheep and cattle. Cattle-raising was indeed a peculiarly apt occupation in an area lying between Birmingham and Coventry. Smaller livestock were also exploited in rabbit-warrens and in the fish-ponds which could be easily created in the less well drained parts of the region, particularly in the water-courses feeding the moats around the moated manor houses.

The greater lords had parks in the Arden, notably in the south-west where there were more noble lands and fewer small-scale gentry: the dukes of Norfolk at Claverdon for example and the earls of Warwick at Wedgenock. Wood was an obvious natural resource to exploit, especially in the western Arden with its proximity to the salt pits of Droitwich in Worcestershire, which in Leland's day were consuming an estimated 6,000 loads of wood a year. The Arden was also an area of rural craftsmen: smiths near Birmingham, as we would expect, tanners as an offshoot from cattle-raising, coopers, weavers and tilers. The contrast between the Feldon and the Arden in terms of urbanisation may well owe something to the more diversified nature of the Arden economy which was likely to stimulate specialisation and exchange. Although the county's wealth still lay predominantly in the Feldon in 1334, comparison of the subsidy assessments of 1327 and 1524 indicates growing prosperity in the Arden during this period of generalised agricultural slump, a conclusion supported by the rate

[19] Skip 1970b: p. 87. For the Arden economy, see Dyer 1980a, 1981, *passim* (I must thank Dr Dyer for pointing out to me the inbuilt bias in his Feet of Fines figures); Skipp 1970b: chs. 18 and 19, 1970a; Harley 1964: pp. 124–5; Agricola 1762: p. 18; Roberts 1965: chs. 8 and 9; Smith, L. W. D. 1980; *Court Rolls of the Manor of Bromsgrove*, pp. 4–5; Leland 1907–10: II, p. 94; Rowlands 1987: p. 62; Glasscock 1976: p. 139; and for more detail, including conditions for animal husbandry, see below, pp. 180–3. An equivalent degree of prosperity has been observed in the similar 'wood-pasture' region of Norfolk and Suffolk in the following century (MacCulloch 1986: p. 29).

[20] Harley 1964: pp. 125, 129 n. 33.

of church building in the area. By 1524 the size of the local population may have been restored to the high level of 1300, and both Skipp and Dyer note the region's ability to adapt to changing economic and demographic conditions, which enabled it to sustain the next great period of population growth. The relative buoyancy of the Arden economy was probably the most important single reason for the survival of its minor gentry whom we shall meet shortly.[21]

It will become increasingly apparent that regionalism was a key factor in the history of Warwickshire at this time, but it was not a regionalism that divided only the north from the south. The county was in fact a wholly artificial creation, consisting of a number of areas, each of them facing outwards to the neighbouring county.[22] In descriptions of the midlands Warwickshire has been variously incorporated with Worcestershire into the west midlands and with a number of other counties into the south midlands. The agriculture of the Avon valley in both Warwickshire and Worcestershire was in fact largely undifferentiable. The Birmingham plateau, which is generally agreed to be a single geographical unit, is shared among Warwickshire, Worcestershire and Staffordshire.[23] The heathland north of Birmingham ran into Staffordshire. Eastern Warwickshire, as landscape studies of its neighbours show, had more in common geographically and agriculturally with the western parts of Leicestershire and Northamptonshire than with the rest of the county. The pastoral areas of southern and south-western Warwickshire lay within a broader sheep-rearing tract of country running across the Cotswolds in Gloucestershire, Oxfordshire and Warwickshire; Warwickshire pastures were for example incorporated into the Westminster Abbey sheep runs in this area. The western Arden was part of a belt of wood-pasture country, much of it in the royal forest of Feckenham, in Worcestershire and west Warwickshire. It has been noted that new families in this area would tend to be offshoots of other Arden families, and later parts of this study will emphasise the extent to which the Warwickshire/Worcestershire woodland was a distinct region.[24]

Although one would not expect a county to constitute a geographical and economic unit, Warwickshire is more fragmented than most. In some sense this

21 Cf. the area in the seventeenth century (Hughes 1987: p. 4–5).

22 This is nicely reflected in the local building materials (Pevsner and Wedgwood 1966; p. 15); also Hughes 1987: pp. 40–1.

23 Hilton 1967: *passim*; Beckinsale and Beckinsale 1980: p. vii; For the Birmingham plateau: British Association, 1950: *passim*; and map in Skipp 1979: p. 20.

24 The artificiality of boundaries in relation to geography, soil etc. is clearly shown in the following maps: Skipp 1979: p. 20; Pelham 1950: p. 137; Kinvig 1962: p. 267; Millward and Robinson 1971: p. 25; Beckinsale and Beckinsale 1980: pp. 2, 12–13. For particular instances described here, see Kinvig 1962: pp. 275–6 for the north-west; Hoskins 1950a, Steane 1974: p. 161, Dyer 1981: pp. 19–21 and works cited above, n. 18 for east Warwickshire; Bond 1973: pp. 1–7 and Millward and Robinson 1971: pp. 26–8 for the Avon Valley; Dyer 1981: pp. 16–17, and Hilton 1967: p. 82, for the south-west pastoral region; Hilton 1967: pp. 14–15, 242, Ford 1976: pp. 146–9 and Skipp 1970b: pp. 84–5, and 1981: pp. 181–2, for the Warwickshire/Worcestershire Arden.

Figure 2 Warwickshire: Hundreds and settlements (from Gover, Mawer and Stenton eds., 1936; and Pevsner and Wedgwood 1966). Modern county boundaries: detached portions of counties not shown.

applies to all the midland counties and is due to the artificiality of their original shiring. In the case of Warwickshire, however, regionalism was particularly acute. The formation of the county had not only cut across geographical boundaries, but across the territories of existing peoples and kingdoms and had also left a number of anomalies in the 'detached' parts of counties lying outside the boundaries. For Warwickshire, the diocesan divisions, corresponding with the old kingdoms – Lichfield for the Mercians, Worcester for the subkingdom of the Hwicce – fitted far better with the geographical ones, but this meant that the geographical disunity was matched by an ecclesiastical one which only emphasised the divide between Arden and Feldon.[25]

The separation of north and south was further accentuated by two of the oldest surviving lay tenurial units in the region, the earldom of Chester and the Honor of Tutbury. The connection with the former had existed since the late eleventh century when the town of Coventry had been granted to Earl Hugh. The earls remained heavily involved in the town's affairs until their interests were acquired by the crown which showed itself equally watchful of its rights. The road from London to the north-west was diverted via Coventry and Lichfield; another, known significantly as the 'Earlsway', ran from Chester to the earl's properties in the east midlands, as far as Leicester, and from it came a connecting link to Coventry. Throughout the fifteenth century the crown as earl of Chester took an active interest in the affairs of the town, whether the earldom was held by the king himself or, as under Edward IV, by his son and heir.[26] This interest, given added weight by the crown's tenure of the Duchy of Lancaster property of Kenilworth nearby, where much of the crown ordnance was stored, reached its peak in the late 1450s when Henry VI's capital was transferred to Coventry.[27] That Coventry's link with Chester was more than a matter of overlordship can be seen from the presence among Coventry's Trinity Gild of men from Cheshire and Lancashire. Coventry men in turn traded to Chester and even to Ireland beyond. One of Warwickshire's leading gentry in the early fifteenth century, Thomas Crewe, had come from Cheshire. This was not an obvious path for a Cheshire landowner to take and there must be a serious case for arguing that the ancient Coventry–Cheshire connection had played a part in bringing him to Warwickshire.[28]

The Honor of Tutbury was now normally part of the Duchy of Lancaster

[25] Finberg 1976: pp. 21, 147; Skipp 1979: pp. 105–8, 110, 119–20, 1981: p. 182; Kinvig 1950: pp. 114–15, 1962: p. 274; Rowlands 1987: pp. 5, 7; Hooke 1985: *passim*, esp. map, p. 7. For the detached portions, see Kinvig 1954: pp. 270–1, where they are listed. See also the comments in Everitt 1985a: pp. 14–20.

[26] Sanders 1960: pp. 32–3; *V.C.H.*, VIII, pp. 2–3; Coss 1974a; Davis 1976; Palliser 1976: pp. 79–81; *V.C.H.*, VIII, p. 34; *Coventry Leet Book, passim*; Pelham 1950: p. 138; Goodman 1981b: pp. 14–15.

[27] Goodman 1981b: pp. 160, 268; below, pp. 475–83.

[28] Bennett 1983: pp. 14, 106, 121, 123, 130, 188–9; Gill 1930: pp. 48–9.

and therefore of the crown lands. It straddled the Staffordshire/Derbyshire border, the bulk of it lying in western Derbyshire, but so many prominent north Warwickshire landowners had lands in one or both of these counties and were linked to the Duchy through the Tutbury connection that the affairs of the north midlands were often closely tied in with those of Warwickshire. Duchy property within Warwickshire itself had come from the crown, to which Earl Edmund owed his grant of Kenilworth. The direct influence of the Duchy within the county owed much to the crown's connections with Coventry, since the actual amount of land owned by the Duchy in Warwickshire was rather small, but the proximity of Kenilworth to Coventry made both Duchy castle and royal town important midlands bases for the crown after 1399. Moreover, the Warwickshire properties were all in the north of the county, so that the combined weight of the Honors of Tutbury and Leicester, the one primarily a north-midland unit, the other centred on Leicestershire, which borders on the northern parts of Warwickshire, was another factor in separating north from south.[29]

In at least one case we can demonstrate the effect of Tutbury Honor in moving the interests of a Warwickshire family into the north midlands. At the time of the Domesday survey the Shirleys were tenants of the Ferrers, the first lords of the Honor, for their residence of Lower Ettington in southern Warwickshire and for other lands elsewhere, including some nearer the centre of the Honor, in Derbyshire. It was these lands to the north that were eventually to form the main focus of the family's estate and by the fifteenth century the Ettington property had become in every sense peripheral.[30] The affairs of Tutbury were a thread running through Warwickshire politics throughout the century. If the crown chose to be an active duke of Lancaster, Tutbury and Leicester together gave the king a substantial springboard from which the administration of northern and north-eastern Warwickshire could be directed. If a north midland magnate held the Honor or its major offices, north Warwickshire could be drawn into the politics of the north midlands. In this context it is worth remembering that the Warwickshire shrievalty was a joint one, shared with Leicestershire, and that, through the Leicestershire-based incumbents of the office, considerable influence could be exercised from that county.[31]

Regionalism was to some extent reinforced by poor communications. Although the county was reasonably well served by roads from north to south,

[29] Sanders 1960: pp. 148–9; *V.C.H. Staffs.*, IV, pp. 48–9; *V.C.H. Leics.*, II, p. 97; *V.C.H. Derbys.*, I, pp. 336–46; *V.C.H.*, I, p. 327, VI, pp. 135–7; Wright 1983: ch. 6; Somerville 1953: pp. 2, 111 n. 2; Fox 1939; *Dugdale* (1765 edn), pp. 165–72; Wylie 1884–98: IV, pp. 287–302; Wylie and Waugh 1914–29: I, pp. 190, 315, 427, III, pp. 41, 86, 270; Griffiths 1981: pp. 57, 237, 253, 613–4, 777–85; for lands of Warwickshire gentry in the north midlands and in other counties in general, Carpenter, M. C. 1976: App. IIC and for connections with these, below, ch. 9.

[30] *Dugdale*, pp 619–22; *V.C.H.*, V, p. 78; below, pp. 149, 234.

[31] *P.R.O. Lists and Indexes*, 9, pp. 145–6; for Leicestershire involvement in Warwickshire politics, see especially below, pp. 325–7.

those running south from Birmingham to Warwick, Coventry and Stratford had to pass through some of the muddier parts of the Arden; it was indeed easier to move north from Birmingham over the lighter soils of Staffordshire.[32] Furthermore, in terms of distance and access to towns and markets, Warwick was by no means an obvious place for inhabitants of the north and north-east of the county to visit. This is an important consideration when we come to examine the significance of the county as a force in local political life, for Warwick was the site for meetings of the county court and, normally speaking, for quarter sessions, and both these administrative assemblies have been identified as focuses of local solidarity based on the shire.[33] A direct demonstration of the effects of poor communications in the fifteenth century is not usually possible but in the better documented seventeenth 'the appalling state of the roads' in parts of Sussex may have helped contribute to the separation of the gentry of east and west Sussex. It is at least something that we should bear in mind when we come to examine local networks and local identities. More immediately pertinent is Ann Hughes' demonstration of the north's reluctance to come south to sessions at Warwick in the seventeenth century and the lack of connections between north and south Warwickshire at that time, which may well have owed something to poor communications.[34] It is hard to believe that things had been much better 200 years earlier. We shall find that separation of north and south is a phenomenon that grows in importance in the later fifteenth century. Within the different parts of the county, localism was reinforced by the sometimes quite complex networks of tracks and pathways. This was especially true of the areas in the west of the county bordering on Worcestershire where the Droitwich saltways ran, reinforcing the separate identity of this cross-county region.[35]

The routes that the major roads had to take, to make use of river crossings and to avoid ground that was too high or too low to be passable with ease, gave crucial significance to certain key points, several of which were outside the county. Not surprisingly these tended to be castles, since castle builders will have had at least as much strategic sense as historians and geographers. Dudley Castle in Staffordshire commanded the road from Birmingham to north-west Staffordshire and Shropshire, two counties with which Warwickshire landowners were extensively connected. Tamworth, part in Warwickshire, part in Staffordshire, was situated near a crossroads where roads to Birmingham,

[32] Map in Skipp 1979: p. 125; *V.C.H.*, VII, p. 26.

[33] Maddicott 1978a, 1981; Bennett 1973, 1983: ch. 2; Saul 1981: ch. 4 and p. 168; Wright 1983: p. 109 (but note her reservations, p. 146). Note also Everitt's comments on the importance of the later growth of the county town in creating a sense of county solidarity, 1985a: pp. 21–39, and similarly Fletcher 1986: pp. 98–9.

[34] Pelham 1950: pp. 138–9; Kinvig 1950: p. 116; Fletcher 1975: pp. 5–7, 44–53; Hughes 1982: pp. 43–55.

[35] Hilton 1967: pp. 11–12; Pelham 1950: p. 139.

Lichfield and Tutbury met Watling Street, which linked Chester to London. Worcester lay on the main road from Tewkesbury to Birmingham, a road which connected two important areas of Beauchamp property and ran past Weoley Castle in north-east Worcestershire. Worcester Castle could also block the way up the rivers Teme and Severn.

Within the county the importance of Warwick, the earls' *caput honoris*, commanding the Avon where Arden and Feldon met, is self-evident, but some attention should be given to Maxstoke, which will be seen to play a large part in the politics of the county. This north Warwickshire castle was close to Coleshill, where the four minor roads linking the four compass points in north Warwickshire met. Coleshill itself was in consequence one of the two most considerable unfortified communications centres in the county. The other was Birmingham, the nearest passable point beyond the Clent and Lickey Hills which stand between the north-west of England and Warwickshire. Birmingham was also the point at which the Arden roads met as they 'picked their way from sandy patch to sandy patch across the Keuper Marl country'. Most of these roads converged on the ford across the River Rea at Deritend to the east of Birmingham; to the south was Solihull, at the crossing-point of the Coventry–Birmingham and Coventry–Worcester roads.[36] Birmingham was indeed *the* crossroads between north and south midlands in this part of England. It is clear that, given a struggle for control of the administrative unit of Warwickshire, the problems of uniting north and south were going to make some of these places strategically very sensitive. Points of communication in the less well drained parts of the western and north-western Arden would assume particular significance in any kind of direct confrontation. Moreover, landowners in the north of the county and over the Staffordshire border might find themselves, so to speak, facing the other way, their lands acting as vantage points in a fight for dominance beyond the borders of Warwickshire.

The distribution of great estates in the fifteenth century accentuated the tendencies already described.[37] There was first of all a clear-cut division between the areas north and south of the Avon, in that the early settled south, except for the southern tongue of Kineton Hundred, was largely denuded of directly held lands of the lay nobility, most of their property here having been subinfeudated or granted to the church at an early stage. North of the Avon there was much more noble land, including the great majority of the Warwick estates in Warwickshire. The Coventry region, however, which had been colonised late by the church, was dominated by ecclesiastical lords and by the

36 Maps in Skipp 1979: pp. 20, 125, and see also p. 144; Leland 1907–10: II, p. 106 (Coleshill 'a praty thrwgh-faire'); Kinvig 1962: p. 274; Pearson 1894: p. 31; map in *Dugdale*, between pp. 868 and 869; Gill 1930: p. 91; Pelham 1950: pp. 137–9. On Coleshill as a focal point for north Warwickshire, see Watkins 1983–4.

37 For all refs. to noble estates, *V.C.H.*, III–VIII, *passim* and *Dugdale, passim*. There is further discussion of these below, ch. 9. See fig. 8 below, p. 301.

presence of the king at Coventry and Kenilworth.[38] Then, the territorial geography of the great lay estates mirrored the natural and agrarian environment in taking the county's centres of gravity to its peripheries. Hilton noted the absence of resident nobility in the thirteenth century and the pattern holds equally good for the fifteenth.[39] In the case of every magnate with lands in Warwickshire, the king as duke of Lancaster included, their Warwickshire properties were part of an estate whose focal point lay elsewhere. This was even true of the earls of Warwick; although Warwick was their *caput honoris*, the Beauchamps had originally come from Elmley in Worcestershire. At the time of Richard Beauchamp's accession in 1401 the estate lay along a Warwickshire–Worcestershire axis, roughly divided between the two but situated predominantly to the west of Warwick, with a small but significant body of lands on the north-west Warwickshire/south-west Staffordshire border and some outlying properties in midland counties to the south and east, as well as some further afield. Richard Beauchamp's marriage to the Berkeley heiress in about 1397 had shifted the focus of his lands towards the south-west, as the Berkeley estates were situated in the southern parts of Gloucestershire. The death of Elizabeth in 1422, leaving three co-heiresses, refocused the estate yet again. First, it meant that the house of Warwick would retain the Berkeley lands only as long as Beauchamp himself survived, holding them in courtesy. Secondly, Beauchamp married again the following year, his bride being the Despenser heiress. The Despenser lands dovetailed with those of the Beauchamps – they had indeed already been partially amalgamated once, under Thomas Lord Despenser, during Thomas Beauchamp's disgrace in the last years of Richard II – and provided a third centre to the estate. This was the old Despenser/Clare capital of Tewkesbury, which turned the Warwick–Elmley–Worcester axis into a triangle with Tewkesbury as its third point.[40] Thus, the weight of the Beauchamp lands produced another formidable division in Warwickshire, this one separating west from east down the middle of the county; east of a line running roughly from Tamworth through Warwick to Brailes in the far south, the earls' interests were negligible, although the need to protect estates in Northamptonshire and in other south midland counties would discourage them from neglecting eastern Warwickshire. The addition of the Berkeley lands on a temporary basis and of the Despenser lands more permanently created a continuous area of interest west of Warwick, from south Staffordshire in the north to south-west Gloucestershire in the south.

The two lesser families to be as fully committed to Warwickshire as the Beauchamps of Warwick also straddled the borders. William Beauchamp of

38 Above, pp. 20–2.

39 Hilton 1967: p. 40.

40 *Beauchamp Cartulary*, esp. Intro.; Dugdale 1675–6: I, pp. 396–7; *Calendar of Inquisitions Post Mortem 1–6 Henry IV*, pp. 171–3; Carpenter 1986a: pp. 26–7; Sinclair 1987a: ch. 1. For a full listing of the Warwick estates, see Hicks 1980: App. II.

Bergavenny, Richard Beauchamp's uncle, and Bergavenny's long-lived widow, Joan, had an estate roughly divided between Worcestershire and west Warwickshire.[41] The estates of the Ferrers of Chartley were focused on north Warwickshire and south Staffordshire.[42] Then there were the Botellers of Sudeley whose lands lay in a band stretching across the county from Sudeley Castle in Gloucestershire, through Henley in Arden and Beaudesert Castle in west Warwickshire and up to Griff in north-east Warwickshire.[43] It will be apparent that the Sudeley connection was potentially one of the more powerful links between north and south. The other noble family of the first rank with major Warwickshire interests was the Staffords, earls of Stafford and later dukes of Buckingham. It was the expansion of the Stafford estate that was to do most to change the political geography of Warwickshire.[44] Initially the Stafford lands in Warwickshire consisted of some sizeable but scattered manors in the south-west and east of the county, seemingly of little interest beyond the revenues they brought to a family whose most important English holdings were in Staffordshire, Kent and south-west Gloucestershire; but the ambitions of Humphrey Stafford, later duke of Buckingham, were to change all that. In 1438 he bought Maxstoke Castle, one of the crucial strategic points in north Warwickshire, from Lord Clinton, a minor north Warwickshire magnate, along with the adjacent manor also owned by the Clintons. By this single act he changed the face of Warwickshire politics; where the county had traditionally been subject to the influence of the earls of Warwick wielded from their base in the west midlands, an alternative source of local authority from the north midlands was now available.

We have seen that the county's diocesan structure tended to pull it apart at the middle, and the territorial power of the major ecclesiastical institutions in the region worked in the same way. To the north lay Lichfield, the true centre of the combined diocese of Coventry and Lichfield and the focal point of the diocesan estates. Several north Warwickshire families, particularly those with Staffordshire lands, served the bishops. Because there must be some territorial limits to a local study, it has proved barely possible to investigate the bishops' role in local politics, but the potential power of this other north Warwickshire–north midlands unit should not be underestimated, especially in periods when the lay powers were weak. The bishops' influence also ran far into the south of the county, to Bishops Itchington and Bishops Tachbrook.[45] The lands of the Worcester see had a similar effect, in this case in emphasising the unity of the west Warwickshire–Worcestershire region. If the overwhelming local territorial

41 Dugdale 1675–6: I, pp. 239–40.

42 *I.P.M.* 14 Hen.VI/33.

43 Dugdale 1675–6: I, pp. 596–7.

44 The estate is listed in full in Rawcliffe 1978, App. A; *Dugdale* (1765 edn), pp. 704, 743.

45 See the bishops' estate accounts e.g. Wm. Salt Lib. Wm. Salt Orig. Coll. 335/1; Heath 1974: pp. 7–8, 23–41; below, pp. 567–8. And cf. Saul 1986: p. 38 on the influence of ecclesiastical lordship in parts of fourteenth-century Sussex.

dominance of the earls of Warwick meant that the bishops were able to make less of an impact politically than their colleagues at Lichfield, the leases and estate offices that they and the other great ecclesiastical institutions of Worcestershire, such as Evesham and Bordesley and Worcester Priory, had to offer made them focal points for the gentry of the west midlands.[46] The fact that nearly all these religious houses had lands on either side of the Warwickshire/Worcestershire boundary reinforced local solidarity across the county boundary.[47] Similarly, on the Warwickshire/Northamptonshire borders there were desirable lands, paticularly for stock-farmers, to be leased from such institutions as the abbey of Combe and Coventry and Nuneaton Priories, which helped draw together east Warwickshire and Northamptonshire.[48]

A similar regionalism, compounded of economic and tenurial localism and indifferent communications, has been observed by Ann Hughes in seventeenth-century Warwickshire.[49] It would seem that in this county fragmentation was the norm; it was the region formed by a segment of the shire and the adjacent segment of its neighbour or neighbours that had the sharpest identity. For better or for worse, this has to be a study of 'greater Warwickshire'; the county itself plus those parts of neighbouring counties with histories inseparable from those of Warwickshire. It will be seen that connections with some counties were stronger than with others and that the relative importance of individual neighbouring counties varied with time, but there is no escaping the fact that their history was often integral to the affairs of Warwickshire. This was not the case in all parts of England: Cheshire seems to have been a much more cohesive unit, the Paston letters indicate that Norfolk and Suffolk together made an entity that had some reality beyond the purely administrative. Nevertheless, if Warwickshire was an extreme case, it is well to remember that no county was likely to contain within itself all possible identities: geographical, economic, agricultural, ecclesiastical, tenurial, social, political. If seventeenth-century historians are now questioning the concept of the 'county community', surely it behoves the historian of late-medieval England, a period when the shires were far less subject to the governmental intrusions that could nourish a sense of county identity, to approach the term rather more critically than has tended to be the case.[50]

Some vital questions need to be asked. For example, in the fifteenth century,

[46] Dyer 1980b: pp. 67–74, 210–11; Hilton 1967: pp. 25–40. A family that did particularly well from ecclesiastical leases and grants in this area are the Throgmortons of south-west Warwickshire and south-east Worcestershire (*V.C.H.*, III, pp. 80–2; Coughton Court, Throckmorton MS Exhib. Box No. 9, Box 35 (Studley lease); *Cal. Pat. Rolls 1413–16*, p. 340, *1494–1509*, p. 64).

[47] Dyer 1980b: *passim*; Bond 1973: esp. map, p. 4; Rahtz and Hirst 1976: pp. 16–19.

[48] See particularly the leases of the Catesbys and Spensers (discussed at greater length below, ch. 5); also *V.C.H.*, VI, p. 183.

[49] Hughes 1982.

[50] Pollard 1979; Bennett 1983: *passim*, 1973; *Paston Letters*, *passim*; MacCulloch 1986: *passim*; Hassell Smith 1974: pp. 108–9; Holmes 1980; Fletcher 1983: pp. 151–2; and above, n. 33. Also Saul 1986: pp. 58–60. For further discussion of this subject, below. pp. 340–4.

when the nobility's power in comparison with the gentry's was so much greater than it was to be 200 years later, how far did the magnates' management of their authority in and around their estates dictate the shape of local politics? Were there any areas, whether officially demarcated or not, where geography, economy, the estates of greater and lesser landowners, power structures and networks of association combined to create a recognisable community, or was there a variety of overlapping regionalisms? And how did all these possible regional identities relate to the administrative unit itself; for, after all, both hundred and shire had important functions, and, as we shall see, without control of the shire in some sense, no magnate could hope to harness potential support from the segments of the county where his estates lay. Somehow he had to marry region to county. In Warwickshire the nobility were likely to have a particularly hard time in achieving this objective. How they attempted to do it will be one of the main themes of this work. But it could not be done without sensitivity to the susceptibilities of their lesser partners in local politics, the gentry. The regionalism of the gentry did not automatically dovetail with that of the nobility, although we have already seen that the great landowners, as lessors or as feudal lords, could exert some influence on the structure of gentry estates. If we wish to understand how the nobility handled their relations with the gentry, we must first try to acquire some fraction of that familiarity with the world of the gentry that would have been the automatic heritage of any child of the nobility; the obvious starting point for such an exploration is to find out who the gentry were.

3

WHO WERE THE GENTRY?

I

The purpose of this chapter is to discover the composition of the political classes in the localities: those who mattered, whose interests, however indirectly expressed, had to be taken into account by local nobility and ultimately by the king. There are immediate problems of definition in deciding which landowners were not members of the nobility, and indeed in the use of the word 'nobility' itself. As far as the first is concerned, the development of the concept of parliamentary peerage during the fourteenth and fifteenth centuries provides firmer dividing lines than existed before.[1] Even so, there were men like Ralph Boteller, later Lord Sudeley, and the Ferrers of Chartley, who came of a lineage that could be claimed to qualify them for the peerage, or had married into one, who were not reckoned to be peers unless specially created. For the purposes of this study they have nevertheless been counted as nobility, since family history, lands, lifestyles and connections clearly put them with the peerage.[2] Whether there were in fact real differences in these respects between nobility and gentry is an important question, and one to which an answer will be attempted at the end of the first section of this study.[3] Whether 'nobility' should be used as a synonym for the peerage is another matter. McFarlane, following contemporary practice, quite rightly referred to the entire ruling class as the 'noblesse', although in effect his book on the nobility was almost exclusively about the peerage.[4] The terms used in this study, although mildly anachronistic, are designed primarily to avoid confusion. 'Nobility' or 'magnates' will be reserved for the peerage or men of equivalent standing, even when they were not legally

1 Powell and Wallis 1968: pp. 284–5; McFarlane 1973: pp. 122–5.
2 Powell and Wallis 1968: pp. 470–1, 509–10; McFarlane 1973: pp. 123–4; *G.E.C.*, *passim*.
3 Below, pp. 254–7.
4 McFarlane 1973: pp. 6–7, and note his later views, pp. 122–5.

peers, while the word 'aristocracy' will be used for landed society as a whole, nobility and gentry.[5]

It has been variously estimated that lesser, non-noble landowners held anything from slightly under 60 per cent to about 75 per cent of the land in any one county in the later middle ages. Potentially they were therefore the most powerful element in the shires.[6] It is thus essential, as a basis for all subsequent discussion of local society and politics, to establish who they were, how and why they were marked out and how the local hierarchy of landowners was structured. The core of this chapter is an analysis of the Warwickshire gentry taken at three points in the century, 1410, 1436 and 1500. These three cross-sections of society are designed to reveal both its structure and the dynamics of change. The obvious starting-point is 1436, a year which chooses itself because of the survival of the oath-lists of 1434 and the detailed income-tax returns of 1436.[7] Unfortunately, Warwickshire, unlike Derbyshire, is blessed with detailed returns for this year alone, so the earlier and later analyses lack any discussion of income, beyond a generalised assessment based on numbers of manors owned, and this in itself is not entirely reliable, since manorial histories are confused at times about both the identification and the histories of manors.[8] For the first cross-section, the date of 1410 has been chosen as the furthest back the present study can reach if there is to be a reasonable expectation of picking up most of the notable local figures. The third and final cross-section is taken at 1500. Although this leaves a much bigger gap between the last two points of analysis, this can be bridged to some extent by looking backwards from 1500, to 1450 and 1470, to see whether any changes observed at the end of the century were already discernible earlier on.

The basis of this survey consists of a complete tenurial analysis, using the *V.C.H.* and Dugdale's *History and Antiquities of Warwickshire*, and a biographical register which includes not only all Warwickshire landowners of the fifteenth century but also men who by their designation or by the company they kept may be deemed of any local significance (see app. 1).[9] These data establish the 'pool' from which the local elite can be selected and the pool itself has to be as all-inclusive as possible to avoid *a priori* definitions of who the Warwickshire gentry were and how local hierarchies were defined. In short, the

5 In this sense the word only comes into common currency in the seventeenth century (*O.E.D.*, *sub verb.*).

6 Dyer 1981: p. 3 (based on material in Carpenter, M. C. 1976, which would now require some slight revision, but not enough to affect his figures substantially); Saul 1981: p. 5; Bennett 1983: p. 81; Payling 1987b: pp. 1–18.

7 *Cal. Pat. Rolls 1429–36*, pp. 384–5; E.179/192/59, 200/68, 238/90, 240/266; E.163/7/31 Part 1; Gray 1934; Carpenter, M. C. 1976: App. III.

8 Wright 1983; p. 3. Some detailed returns from 1524–7 survive for Warwickshire, but they are not very informative (E.179/192/120, 122, 128).

9 Most of this material, up to *c.* 1472, is in Carpenter, M. C. 1976: Apps. I and II, although some parts have been slightly revised in the light of later research.

object of the exercise is to let the society speak for itself, to use its own definitions of gentility and to try to understand the meaning of the words that were employed. Nevertheless, unavoidably, certain decisions have to be made at an early stage which will to some extent predetermine the later discussion.

First, there is the problem of who should be counted as a Warwickshire landowner, a particularly pressing one in a county with such artificial boundaries. Here, there are real dangers, for unless we give consideration to the claims of all those with some sort of stake in Warwickshire affairs to be included as possible members of the county society we bias the analysis from the start. It is quite easy to show the existence of a 'county community' once one has excluded all landowners with major interests elsewhere.[10] Here, the only criterion of inclusion is that such figures should have had at least some fragment of manorial lordship in Warwickshire and taken some part in the affairs of the county. Accordingly, among those included are families such as the Staffordshire Astons, whose Warwickshire interests were peripheral but who nevertheless consorted with figures who are more properly termed Warwickshire gentry. Also included are those such as the more distant Culpeppers of Kent, as long as they can be shown to have been actively concerned about their quite substantial Warwickshire properties. By no means all families of this type were non-resident: some, such as the Chetwynds, seem to have spent equal time in their Warwickshire and Staffordshire residences, many of the others, such as the Cokayns and Willoughbys and, initially, the Culpeppers, had secondary residences in the county. On the other hand, some families, like the Botellers of Middleton, the Hortons of Kingsbury, and the Langleys of Atherstone, are excluded, despite their Warwickshire properties, on the grounds that there is no evidence that they would have seen themselves as part of Warwickshire society or been seen as such by other Warwickshire landowners.[11] Although all families who are defined as Warwickshire gentry on these terms are given equal weight in the cross-sectional analyses, in the political sections the more peripheral figures have to be treated as such. That certain parts of the county had stronger concentrations of landowners with equal or greater interests in other parts of England is in itself an important fact, and even those families excluded from the lists of landowners which form the basis of this analysis may have played a significant role. The neglect of their Warwickshire lordships could create power vacuums in certain areas, giving perhaps an additional and sometimes unexpected influence in local politics and society to other land-

[10] Saul 1981: pp. 31–5; Wright 1983; p. 4.

[11] See, for the Chetwynds, Chetwynd-Stapylton 1892, for the Cokayns, *Dugdale*, p. 1120, for the Willoughbys, below, pp. 00, for the Culpeppers, their presence on the 1434 list. The Langleys had been an important Warwickshire family in earlier centuries, but had little to do with the county by the early fifteenth century (*Langley Cartulary; V.C.H.*, VIII, p. 84).

owners.[12] Only by refusing to confine the discussion to purely local figures can we establish the degree of localism.

Problems of this kind occur mostly in defining the upper end of the social and economic hierarchy of gentry society. There are also the difficulties of demarcating its lower end, the people hovering perilously close to the level of the richer peasantry. Again, it is wise to avoid *a priori* decisions on which, if any, of these should be included amongst the gentry.[13] The discussion of terminology which follows will show that increasingly in the later middle ages titles, hitherto confined to the upper levels of society, were used to signify rank lower down, but they are not necessarily the best guide. Whatever the terms of nomenclature might indicate about the attributes of gentility, we have to ask ourselves whether those at the bottom of the gentle hierarchy can be accounted a significant part of political society, and the answer to this difficult question can come only from a series of different approaches, of which this discussion is merely the first stage. The meaning of 'gentility' in its political, governmental and tenurial context, the role in local affairs taken by these men, their connections with more elevated personages, must all be taken into account. Is it possible to say that in these respects they had more in common with the upper echelons of the local gentry than with the peasants just beneath them? Are we indeed justified in lumping all lesser landowners with a claim to gentility into a single status group and labelling it 'the gentry'?

Finally, there are decisions about how to count the families included in the cross-sections. The nature and composition of the family will be treated in later chapters. The guiding principle used for the moment is that brothers and sons of the head are counted as separate entities only if they can be shown to have had independent means of support.[14] Tenure of a landed estate, by marriage or family settlement, is one form of qualification, as is possession of a competence from service to the king, the nobility or the law. In the case of professionals of this kind, evidence of marriage is a good indication that they were wealthy enough to count as a distinct unit. All these choices have been made with one end in view, to determine the size and composition of the group that saw itself as pre-eminent in Warwickshire affairs, and conceived it had a right to a say in these. The peripheral families, whether socially or geographically marginal, and the independent junior lines, especially if the wealth of this second group was

[12] Below, ch. 9; Payling 1987b: ch. 2 on the Stanhopes.

[13] Cf. the remarks on this in Pugh 1972: p. 96. On inclusion of minor figures, compare Wright 1983: p. 6, and Astill 1977: p. 4, both of which exclude them at an early stage.

[14] Below, chs. 6 and 7 on the nature of the family. Younger sons are not always readily identifiable unless the settlement documents survive, so the evidence is biased towards identifying independent holdings amongst the more prominent families. On the other hand, these families were better placed to set up younger sons and heirs. A useful source for all families are the registers of the gilds (above, p. 19 n. 9 for refs.), since the acquisition of independence was often marked by joining a gild.

meagre, could have a profound effect on the behaviour and aspirations of the rest, in intensifying or reducing competition for an accepted place in local society.

II

Difficulties in exploring the late-medieval landowning hierarchy are compounded by problems of terminology. Status in late-medieval England is now recognised to be a very complex issue. The problems for the historian begin in the early thirteenth century. For the previous century or more, as far as we know, landed position, title, rank, service and economic position had generally matched. The titles used to designate the two principal ranks in the landed classes, baron and knight, were defined by tenure but also denoted service. Lesser landowners were known collectively as knights, they served the king militarily – perhaps in declining numbers by now, but at least their lands were defined as tenures owing scutage – and increasingly as minor local officers in the fast-growing common law.[15] By 1224, when the first distraint of knighthood was levied, tenure, title, rank, wealth and service were already out of phase.[16] Indeed, it could be argued that they had begun to get out of phase as soon as the title of knight began to be used less to designate a particular rank in the 'feudal' hierarchy, the main obligations of which were reckoned to be military, than as an honorific title for the landed class as a whole, including the nobility. From this point on, confusion between titles that described a particular form of tenure and of service, usually to the crown, and those that were broadly social was set to become rampant.

It was further confounded by the fact that titles conferred for service could themselves be understood to honour the recipient. The expansion of lay documentation from this time, especially that of the lesser landowners, makes possible some understanding of how they saw themselves. Paradoxically, even while fewer of these men were troubling to be knighted, those that did so were now at pains to identify themselves as knights on their own and their neighbours' documents because knighthood was becoming something to be valued.[17] Why knights should have chosen to emphasise their title at this point is on the face of it far from clear. The number of men ready and willing to serve

[15] Mortimer 1985; Williams, A. 1985; Keefe 1983: chs. 1 and 2; Stenton 1961; Du Boulay 1966: ch. 3; Miller 1951: ch. 6; King 1973: ch. 2; Carpenter, D. A. 1980: p. 722; Wagner 1972: p. 114; Nichols 1863: pp. 200–1. The historiography of the early knight and the 'feudal settlement' is undergoing rapid revision, but probably not so far as to diminish substantially the force of this generalisation, at least as far as the developed 'feudal' structure is concerned. See, in addition to the works cited above, Holt 1982–5; Chibnall 1986: Part I.

[16] Powicke 1962: p. 72.

[17] Keen 1984: chs. 3 and 4; Hilton 1967: p. 52; Astill 1977: p. 268; Clanchy 1979: ch. 6; Juriça 1976: p. 11. But cf. Carpenter, D. A. 1980: p. 738. On another aspect of self-awareness among lesser thirteenth-century landowners, see Coss 1983.

the king as *strenui milites* was declining and was to continue to do so. This was partly on the grounds of the growing costs of the equipment, partly because lesser landowners had acquired so many other private and public responsibilities. The accumulation of local chores was in itself an added incentive for both the *strenui* and their non-military fellows to avoid knighthood.[18] The distraints made periodically over the rest of the thirteenth century, first at the twenty librate level and finally settling at forty librates, were an attempt to remedy the consequent lack of both fighting men and officers.[19]

If distraints were necessary, it must be assumed that for those who chose to become knights the rank had an additional attraction, and the fact that they chose increasingly to advertise their title would suggest that for them it was coming to be bound up with status. This was a more indefinable quality expressed in the literal translation of the word, that is, one's 'standing' in the locality. Apparently, knighthood was thought to give an edge over fellow landowners that compensated for the burdens it brought. It seems indeed that from the early thirteenth century on there were two views of title: generally speaking the government continued to see it as something related to service and tenure, while for local societies there was a growing tendency to equate it with status. However, for the king, who was merely trying to find ways of ensuring the continuation of knightly services, status was of no interest at all. He saw little reason to mark knights out. To him there was no hierarchy of lesser landowners: all of them were supposed to be knights, ready to serve him in a military or administrative capacity, and it was to be some time before the governmental records bothered to identify regularly those who actually had been knighted. Since this was a period when social aspirations were increasingly expressed in distinctive and ever more precise titles, confusion between government and landowners over the implications of title was likely to be reflected in confusion in its use.[20]

It was the government's attempts to come to terms with the new realities that account for some of the changes, as also for much of the further muddle, in the terminology of rank in the thirteenth and fourteenth centuries. First, it had to accept that there were men who were not knights but might be worthy in tenurial terms of local office; this it had done by the end of the thirteenth century.[21] However, recognising reality in this respect immediately created

[18] Saul 1981: pp. 46–7; Treharne 1946–8: pp. 5–10; Powicke 1962: ch. 4; Denholm-Young 1965: pp. 19–20, 1969a: pp. 88–9; Carpenter, D. A. 1980: pp. 737–8; Painter 1943: ch. 2; Naughton 1976: pp. 11–12 (but the bias of her sample towards local office-holders – e.g. pp. 15–16 – may exaggerate the decline of fighting knights); Given-Wilson 1987a: pp. 17–18; Waugh 1983: esp. pp. 941–71.

[19] Powicke 1962: pp. 63–81, 103–17; Waugh 1983: pp. 937–44; Carpenter, D. A. 1980: pp. 739–40.

[20] Saul 1981: ch. 1; McFarlane 1973: pp. 122–5; Brown, A. L. 1981: pp. 115–16; Carpenter, D. A. 1980: p. 738.

[21] Saul 1981: p. 38; Denholm-Young 1965: pp. 147–59, 1969b: pp. 22–3, 1969a: p. 89; Nichols 1863: p. 201; Carpenter, D. A. 1980: pp. 722, 738–9.

another problem, for it meant that there were numbers of men with enough land to hold office, their position enhanced by their role in the crown's administration, but without any special mark of distinction in a world where distinctions were beginning to matter. Secondly, the king was obliged to initiate searches for potential fighting knights, those who by tenure, ancestry and income might be asked to perform military service. It was these enquiries that produced the early-fourteenth-century rolls of arms that have been so profitably exploited by social historians.[22] Prestwich has shown that the enquiries of 1322 and 1324 were undoubtedly intended as a preliminary to the compulsory creation of a body of fighting men.[23]

Despite the government's efforts, in the late thirteenth and fourteenth centuries there was a mass of contradictions where war service, the original core of knighthood, and title were concerned. There was no guarantee that the men who could best afford the burden of being knighted and the ever-growing expenses of war would be willing or even competent to serve, despite the continuance of knightly traditions in some families and the encouragement of the mass knighting ceremonies which provided a cheap method of receiving the accolade. Conversely, some knights, presumably those who had won the accolade in war, were exceedingly minor local figures, their title scarcely congruous with the new socially loaded meaning of knighthood, whose descendants were to be esquires or even mere gentlemen.[24] At the same time, although knights seem to have accepted the obligation to fight in Edward III's wars, knighthood was rapidly losing its meaning in relation to arms, and already in the fourteenth century some non-knights were serving as mounted soldiers, part of an undifferentiated body of *homines ad arma*.[25] Nevertheless, that their service was still reckoned inferior to a knight's can be seen very clearly in the differentiation between annuities of retained knights and esquires, of which there is a telling instance in fourteenth-century Leicestershire: John Talbot was retained by John of Gaunt at 10 marks a year, the fee to be quadrupled were he knighted.[26]

Compounding the more general confusion over title was the fact that, despite their growing awareness of the importance of status, local landowners continued to see it largely as a function of service in both its older military and newer official forms. But increasingly the newer kind was the commoner, for by the

[22] Saul 1981: *passim*, esp. chs. 1 and 2; Denholm-Young 1965: *passim*, 1969a: *passim*; Wagner 1956: ch. 6; Prestwich 1972: pp. 80–81.

[23] Prestwich 1984: p. 155.

[24] Astill 1977: p. 270; Saul 1981: pp. 40–4; Powicke 1962: pp. 69–70, 115–16; Denholm-Young 1965: pp. 25–9, 1969b: pp. 87, 91–2; Maddicott 1970: p. 57; Carpenter, D. A. 1980: p. 737. An example of a 'poor' knight of the late thirteenth century is Henry Hyband/Hubaud (Hilton 1967: p. 59), for details of whose lowly fifteenth-century descendant, see app. 2. Cf. Payling 1987b: pp. 120–3; Waugh 1983: pp. 958–60.

[25] Astill 1977: p. 274; Carpenter, D. A. 1980: pp. 737–8; Saul 1981: p. 17; Prestwich 1984: p. 149.

[26] Astill 1977: pp. 223–4.

fourteenth century the weight of official business bearing on local men had increased massively.[27] It remained however for the crown to recognise its importance by accepting that a title might be appropriate for its non-knightly local officers. In the localities the belief that they should be dignified in some way was given an added edge by circumstances that encouraged the merging of the governmental concept of title as an indication of service into the landowners' developing concept of title as an indication of status. This was that service was inseparable from land. In a sense this had almost always been the case, since, once the post-Conquest settlement was complete, a knight was defined by the form of his tenure.[28] Similarly, local office-holding and tenure had always been inseparable; the knights and the non-knightly landowners who began to succeed them as officers were chosen because they had enough land 'to answer king and people', that is, to make good out of their own pockets any financial short-fall or compensation for wrongs done in the locality.[29] But it is arguable that in the later middle ages the landed wealth that was intrinsic to royal service was assuming a new importance in relation to local status. Partly this was a question of life-style, of having the means to maintain a standard of living consonant with one's degree.[30] This in itself was nothing new, but the ever-deepening penetration of the royal government into local affairs began to give the possession of estates an added dimension.

During the thirteenth century local societies had been drawn more immediately into contact with the king through their responsibility to the eyre and as a result of the growth of national taxation.[31] The greater local landowners might already in consequence have begun to see their leadership of local society as something that was in itself a form of service to the crown and might need to be indicated by a mark of special distinction. This may be one reason why those who were knights began to record that fact on private deeds. When the king began to incorporate manorial franchises, such as frankpledge and some of the functions of the court leet, into his all-embracing peace-keeping system in the late thirteenth and early fourteenth centuries, it must have seemed that all landowners who held any of these privileges were becoming in some sense the king's officers.[32] The belief that all manorial lords were therefore possessors of a special status would have been given added force by the fact that during the

[27] Cam 1930: *passim*; Willard, Morris and Dunham eds. 1950: *passim*; below, p. 44.

[28] Works cited in n. 15, above.

[29] Jewell 1972: pp. 33–4, 192.

[30] McFarlane 1973: pp. 92–101; Stone 1967: p. 74; and below, ch. 6, for more on consumption patterns.

[31] Cam 1930: pp. 29–30; Harriss 1975: chs. 1 and 2; Maddicott 1975, 1984.

[32] Waugh 1983: pp. 985–6, for the suggestion that by the end of the thirteenth century knighthood was coming to imply 'community leadership' rather than military leadership (but see also the comments in n. 80 below). Morris 1910: pp. 155–6; Harding 1960; Putnam 1929; *Proceedings before the Justices of the Peace*, Intro., *passim*; Cam 1930: pp. 124–8, 1950: pp. 169–71; Crowley 1975; Post 1983; Sharpe 1984: pp. 25–6; McIntosh 1984: pp. 78, 84–5; Kent 1986, pp. 15–20.

course of the middle ages this jurisdiction had come to define manorial lordship.[33] The process by which royal lordship subsumed manorial jurisdiction was a gradual one, not to be completed for centuries to come,[34] and its implications for minor landowners were to emerge only later, but it had the effect of making owners of manors seem partners with the crown at the lowest level of administration. They were marked out both as landowners and as carriers of royal power, on however small a scale. The need for a means of distinguishing the greater non-knightly landowners, most of them owners of several manors, especially those now serving the crown in the major local offices, became therefore all the more pressing.[35]

This process, as far as the fourteenth century is concerned, has been definitively catalogued by Saul. A variety of designations was employed, most, like *scutifer, domicellus, serviens* and *armiger*, being drawn from military usage. Since there was still a strong military element to the great households at this time, some of these terms, such as *domicellus* and *serviens*, were also in use in domestic and administrative service, as was 'yeoman', which surfaced later in the century. A third category indicated status by tenure: 'franklin', *firmarius*. A complicating factor, evident from this list, was that England was by now a country where three different languages were at various times in use amongst the governing classes. So what seem different terms – *armiger* and *esquier*, for example – are essentially translations. As Saul points out, the choice of term used in a particular document, especially in the early fourteenth century, seems to have been largely a matter of the administrative practice of the governmental institution that issued it, and a significant determinant would have been the language in use in the department concerned.

However, without wanting to push the argument too far, it is worth noting that *esquier* and *armiger*, the titles that were eventually to be fixed on to describe the highest ranks below the knights, are in French and Latin, the languages of the governing class; that they appear early in the century; and that they have strong connotations not just of service but of the military service that had originally distinguished the landowning elite from the rest. On the other hand, the terms eventually used for the most minor landowners – 'husbandman', 'franklin', *firmarius*, 'yeoman' – mostly appear in this particular guise towards the end of the century; they are nearly all English, the universal language by this time of lesser landowners; and, in all but the last case, they denote not

33 Holdsworth 1922: 1, pp. 180–1 (I owe this reference to Dr. Edward Miller); and see works cited in n. 32, above. *Select Pleas in Manorial and other Seignorial Courts*, p. lxiii, quotes a judge as saying in 1456, 'Chescun manoir de common droit ad un court baron incident al manoir'; also p. xli.

34 Williams, P. 1981: chs. 5–7; Zell 1977; Sharpe 1984: chs. 2 and 4.; on its serious implications for local conflict and the role of the J.P.s in this, see below, p. 264.

35 Astill 1977: p. 278 on fourteenth-century esquires and lordship over lands and men; on thirteenth-century developments in status and terminology, cf. France (Duby 1971: pp. 470–2).

service but tenure.[36] The implication is that what was taking shape in the first part of the fourteenth century, when *esquier* and *armiger* were coming into use, was a means of distinguishing the greater local landowners who had failed to become knights, but saw themselves still as partaking of the knightly culture, perhaps even to the point of learning French,[37] and were rendering some form of service to the crown.

By the later fourteenth century at this level some clarification had been achieved. If there was still some confusion about the exact nature of an esquire or an *armiger*, whether official or military, at least there was a fairly general measure of agreement that they were superior to the lesser men who were as yet unlikely to hold office. And by this time an *armiger* was so called no longer from bearing his lord's arms (literally, at first), but from being entitled to his own.[38] Undoubtedly this development was due largely to the mounting weight of responsibility being carried by local landowners as the royal administration continued to grow and, under Edward III, was increasingly devolved to the localities.[39] Even the king was now coming to realise that official service to the crown, if still a second best to military service, had an importance of its own and was no longer merely an aspect of knightly duties.

But there were other forces producing both greater definition and greater uniformity. The king's law demanded precision, and its impact was considerably intensified by the effects of the Black Death. It is clear that the Pestilence shook landed society; suddenly the old certainties about peasant obedience and subordination were gone.[40] Indeed the existence of an aggressive, newly prosperous peasantry was enough in itself to encourage the drawing of more precise hierarchical lines to show the peasants that they were still firmly at the bottom. The process was speeded up, however, by the fact that it was the government alone that had the power to put the lower classes in their place. Some of the many legislative measures that ensued, notably the Sumptuary

[36] Saul 1981: pp. 6–29. My debt to his magnificent collation of evidence is obvious throughout this chapter. For language, see Clanchy 1979: chs. 6 and 7; Wilson 1943; Rothwell 1975–6; Legge 1979. Also Holt 1982: pp. 119–26 and the *O.E.D.* for further discussion of these terms. For 'franklin', see Saul 1983: pp. 12–13. For discussion of the meaning of 'yeoman', notably Holt 1982; *Rymes of Robyn Hood*, p. 35–6; Campbell, M. 1960: pp. 8–10; Camden 1610: p. 177. For 'husbandman', see *O.E.D.* The word could clearly have gentlemanly connotations, even in the fifteenth century: e.g. Thomas atte Wode 'gentleman' 1436, 'husbandman' 1443 (K.B.27/699 Coram Rege rot.42d., /728 Coram Rege rot.5). For noble households, e.g. Painter 1943: p. 29; McFarlane 1973: pp. 110–13.

[37] Clanchy 1979: pp. 151–4.

[38] Saul 1981: pp. 16–23; Denholm-Young 1969b: p. 23.

[39] Putnam 1929; *Proceedings before the J.P.s*, Intro., esp. pp. xliii–viii; Harriss 1975: pp. 401–10; Willard, Morris and Dunham eds. 1950: *passim*; Saul 1981: pp. 256–7.

[40] This is a vast subject in itself, but see e.g. the Commons' complaints (e.g. *Rot. Parl.*, II, pp. 233–4, III, pp. 268–9; Dobson ed., *Peasants' Revolt*, pp. 72–8); Langland, *Piers Plowman*, Prologue ll.22–4, 40–5, Passus V, ll.13–36, VI, ll.115–98, 302–330; Harriss 1975: pp. 333–4, 340–6, 507; Coleman 1981: pp. 126–56.

Laws, required the drawing up of a generally recognised hierarchy of titles covering the whole spectrum of society. The Poll Taxes, another response to the redistribution of wealth that followed the Black Death, demanded a similar conspectus of society, in this case the equation of rank and wealth.[41] Furthermore, the legislation greatly accelerated the move towards making the social control of the peasantry the responsibility of the king's law. This was particularly true of the labour laws, which effectively gave the king's courts the job of enforcing the lord's labour services. That could only give an added impetus to the belief that the jurisdictional authority of manorial lords placed all of them, even the least, in some sense in the king's service and that they should therefore have the title that was now recognised as due to the king's local officers.[42]

Even so, at this point, despite the precision of the titles listed in the statutes, the exact dividing line at the bottom end of the landowning scale between the well-born and the rest was yet to be drawn. It seems that yeomen, franklins, serjeants and *firmarii* were still sitting uneasily on that boundary.[43] Yet it was now the lowest group of landowners that was beginning to demand recognition. This was both because many of them were lords of manors and because the presence of uppity peasants beneath them, living in a style to which the peasantry was not supposed to aspire, was a strong incentive to the landowning class as a whole to make a firm separation of the *gentil* from the rest. The Statute of Additions of 1413, in itself a direct response to the demands for precision occasioned by the growth of the law, was to be the catalyst that finally produced the extrapolation from *gentil* for all well-born people to 'gentlemen' for the lowest of the well born.[44] The title itself is very telling, in signifying not only freedom but also the ability to sustain a certain way of life, and this included subsisting without manual labour.[45] These qualities, despite the growth of freedom after the Black Death, would automatically signal separation from the peasantry. However, both 'franklin', which had originally meant

41 Field 1965; Bennett 1983: pp. 105–6; Bolton 1980: p. 47; *Statutes of the Realm*, I, pp. 380–1; *Rot. Parl.*, III, pp. 57–8, V, pp. 504–6; Harte 1976; Munro 1983. Regularisation of status was also required by other legislation of the period, not bearing on the peasantry, e.g. Statute of Livery, 1390 (*Statutes of the Realm*, II, pp. 74–5); this emphasises that the need for definition was partly simply a function of the growth of law. On consumption and hierarchy, see below, p. 199 n. 9.

42 Harriss 1975: ch. 17; Dobson ed., *Peasants' Revolt*, pp. 63–8. On the close relationship of jurisdiction and administrative regulation in the English peace-keeping system, see Maitland 1911: pp. 477–8.

43 Saul 1981: p. 25, 1983: pp. 13–14.

44 *Statutes of the Realm*, II, p. 171; Sitwell 1902; Powell 1979: pp. 188–9.

45 Agnes Paston regrets that her two youngest sons had not enough to 'leve theron wythouȝt they shuld hold the plowe be the tayle' (*Paston Letters*, I, p. 44); an apprentice was not to do any 'vile and bestial service' because 'he was a gentleman' and 'allied to many worshipful persons' (Myers ed., *English Historical Documents*, IV, p. 1124); requiring a gentleman to show his title is seen as 'enthralling' him (*Paston Letters*, I p. 135).

freeman, and 'yeoman' could still on occasion be used in the fifteenth century interchangeably with 'gentleman'; it was to be some time before the term gained universal acceptance as the title of the lowest rank of gentry.[46] These reservations notwithstanding, the statute represents the last stage along the road to precision of social terminology, the end of a long-drawn-out process in which the growth of royal government and the demand for definition which the king's law brought had played a considerable part;[47] from soon after 1413 we have the classic three-fold division of knight, esquire and gentleman.

But the government for its part seems to have continued to think for the most part in terms that had begun to be out of date nearly two centuries before. For the king, rank remained primarily an attribute of military service. Even as late as the Poll Tax returns 'esquire' could still be used for landless men who held this rank in a military sense.[48] The insistence that all landed families of any local standing were by definition fighting knights could give rise to administrative nonsense, as when a Warwickshire return made in 1419 of men who carried arms from their ancestors and could be asked to serve in person in defence of the realm listed such figures as Thomas Hugford, son of a professional administrator of obscure origins, and William Shukburgh, whose family lay at the very bottom of the class of esquires. The commissioners added with perplexity and perhaps despair that certain other knights and esquires had given various excuses before them, which they had been unable to determine.[49] It also meant that, whereas knights had proclaimed their title in their own documents since the thirteenth century, few non-military governmental records bothered to do so until the fifteenth.[50] Esquires, apart from the king's own, are rarely designated in non-legal royal documents until the 1440s, gentlemen until the 1460s, and commissions listed on the Patent Rolls scarcely designate either

[46] Above, n. 44; Wagner 1972: p. 118; Saul 1981: pp. 26–7; Campbell 1960: pp. 11–13; Dyer 1980b: chs. 15 and 16, 1983: p. 210; Bennett 1983: pp. 105–7. For the use of 'franklin' and 'yeoman' for gentlemen, see C.67/41 m.10; C.P.40/802 rot.202, and below, p. 75. Bennett suggests the term may have had this more specific meaning earlier than has been supposed (1984), but his example is not convincing and there is a clear difference in the way the word 'gentil' is used in the fifteenth century and its earlier uses (Compare e.g. *Statutes of the Realm*, I, p. 380 with *Statutes of the Realm*, II, p. 399).

[47] Note the contrasting reluctance to define terms in Scotland, where the king's law was a much less all-pervasive force (Wormald 1986b).

[48] *Rot. Parl.*, III, p. 58; Saul 1981: p. 17; also Astill 1977: pp. 267–9. Cf. earlier purely military esquires (Denholm-Young 1965: pp. 21–2).

[49] Bod. Lib. Dugdale MS 7, p. 272; S.B.T. D.R.503 fo. 60v.; *Dugdale*, p. 278; E. 28/97/32B (ref. from Morgan 1986: p. 32 n. 44); and app. 1 for Shukburgh. A list discussed by Goodman seems to belong to the same inquiry and produced the same sort of response, showing that those qualified by tenure were on the whole neither able nor willing to fight (Goodman 1981b, cited in Morgan 1986: p. 32 n. 45).

[50] Above, n.17; Astill 1977: pp. 268–9; Wood-Legh 1931: pp. 382–3. Knights were not designated as such on the J. P. commissions until the later years of Henry V, presumably because their status was thought to be irrelevant to this particular non-military job.

rank until some time after these dates.[51] That even the crown had nevertheless tacitly recognised the disparity between income and military status is evident from the fact that from the 1340s distraint had ceased to be a means of getting the wealthier gentry to fight and had become a purely fiscal measure. The discussion of knightly incomes will show that fixing the level of distraint at £40 was in any case to take the process out of the realm of economic reality.[52]

The reality understood by local society was that, while the king might on occasion continue to need knights for France and Scotland, the real value to him of all these lesser landowners was as local officials. Furthermore, their awareness of their ever-growing importance to the crown, both as conduits of authority – through royal office and their own lordship over their peasant tenants – and as taxpayers, could only reinforce the belief that title acknowledged status as well as service. If the royal government was reluctant to recognise these facts, provincial society was beginning to understand them very well. It was also realising with ever greater clarity that local office, although burdensome and, if possible, to be avoided, might be regarded as a significant attribute to status. It brought, perhaps most importantly, considerable authority over the officer's own and others' peasant tenants, as these became decreasingly amenable to manorial authority and increasingly subject to the king's law.[53] There was the additional inducement that, despite continuing problems with the shrieval farm, officers suffered fewer financial disabilities than in the days when kings had relied heavily on their local officers for their income.[54] They were accordingly now generally spared the embarrassment of pillaging their neighbours on the king's behalf. Moreover, the localities' near-independent role in the administration of the king's law meant that the key executive offices of J. P. and sheriff conferred enormous political power. Even if some of the gentry had no ambitions to wield it, those who were clients of the local nobility were likely to be encouraged to do so by their lords.[55]

If office could be perceived to be an attribute of local status, legislation reinforced this view by relating it to both land and title. The major local offices carried qualifications of property and rank, the J. P. being the last to be brought into line in 1439.[56] Leaving aside the financial imperatives lying behind these qualifications, the fact that all administrative power had to be backed up with

[51] Note the fact that the term 'gentleman' is not found among the king's household servants in 1445, but is there in 1478 (Myers, *Household of Edward IV*, esp. pp. 63, 64, 69–75, 91, 106, 114–5).

[52] Saul 1981: pp. 41–2. On the costs of knighthood, see above, n.18.

[53] Works cited above, n. 32; Putnam 1908: *passim*; below, p. 264.

[54] Morris 1910; Harriss 1975; Cam 1930; Chrimes 1966 (all *passim*); Jeffs 1961a: chs. 3 and 4. Cf. Naughton 1976: p. 37.

[55] On the consequences of devolved power for local politics, see below, Part II; on the attractions or otherwise of office, see below, pp. 274–5.

[56] Qualifications for office are usefully summarised in Saul 1981: p. 110 and in Jewell 1972: pp. 33–4.

the readily available force that came in the first instance from the officer's tenants meant that considerable landed power was desirable, if not essential, for the major local officers.[57] Furthermore, the localities' sense of their own importance can hardly have failed to have increased as their administrative responsibilities and financial importance to the crown grew in the course of the fourteenth century. In the middle and upper echelons, leadership of local society, expressed in lands and office, would have required local recognition by some sort of title. Among the minor landowners, minor office and the possession of manorial lordship were beginning to nurture similar aspirations. All this was bound to encourage the equation of office, wealth, rank, tenurial position and status within the local societies. Accordingly, by the 1420s esquires were beginning to be designated on private deeds with reasonable frequency, by the 1430s regularly so. Gentlemen follow a decade or so later.[58] The nobility, as we shall see, were almost as reluctant as the crown to recognise status of this sort; it remained at this stage very much a home-grown phenomenon.

But curiously, judging by the literature with which these landowners were likely to be familiar, their perception of the structures of society drew as heavily as the king's on the outdated archetypes. Langland's division of society is the traditional threefold one of those who fight, those who work and those who pray. Chaucer's squire is an apprentice knight. His pilgrims include a man of law and a knight, who is clearly a near-professional fighting-man, but only a single country gentleman, the franklin; although evidently prosperous and locally eminent, he is not accorded the title of esquire, which would by now have been the due of a man of this standing. That title is employed only in its now outdated military usage. Chaucer's yeoman is, as Holt has shown, a household serving-man. If these writers were perhaps a little recherché for most landowners, there is plenty of more 'popular' chivalric literature, but it contains few role models for the provincial owners of estates, clients of the nobility and officers of the crown and the courts who made up the bulk of gentle society. Malory's depiction of a noble retinue, in Arthur's round table, is a heavily militarised vision of what was a normal part of local political society. Even to the end of the middle ages the crusade remained part of every knight's aspirations.[59] In Caxton's translation of *The Order of Chivalry*, 'gentylesse' is still equated with 'chyualrye'. The reality of the life of the gentry was barely recognised in literature except when they were berated in

[57] For amplification of this point, see below, pp. 283–4.

[58] Morgan 1986: p. 33 n. 54 for the first instance of 'gentleman' in a monumental inscription, significantly from 1445.

[59] *Piers Plowman*, Passus VI, ll.24–36; Duby 1978: *passim*; Chaucer, *Complete Works*, pp. 17–25; Mann 1973: *passim*; Saul 1983; Holt 1982: pp. 120–2; Hilton 1975: pp. 25–6; Malory, *Works, passim*; Mathew 1948; Ferguson 1960: pp. 4–10, 134–5; Keen 1983.

The Order of Chivalry and *The Boke of Noblesse* for failing to conform to the literary conventions.[60]

And yet chivalric fictions were the common property of the whole of landed society in this period. Landowners as a body, whether knighted or not, had continued to see themselves as the repository of the knightly virtues throughout the period in which knighthood itself was in decline.[61] Military prowess, even if no longer universally indicated by knightly rank, remained the spiritual *raison d'être* of the landed class for many centuries to come and these were qualities that were still associated in the landowning psyche with the knightly caste. The gentry's mostly vicarious involvement in the king's wars by paying for them was transformed in their reading into an active pursuit of military glory.[62] If they themselves remained content to see the world in terms that were so at odds with their actual experience, is it to be wondered at that the king was slow to respond to changes in the nature of local society?

Perhaps the literary sources do all the same give us some sense of contemporary awareness of the disparity between ideal and reality in the debate about 'nature' and 'nurture'; whether gentility was the product of birth or of breeding.[63] Undoubtedly it was to a considerable degree a reflection of a world in which, in some respects if not in others, social mobility was on the increase, and the manuals of etiquette produced at this time must surely be seen as further evidence of this, being guide books to polite society for the *nouveaux riches*.[64] But at a deeper level the controversy may have acquired a sharper edge from the contradictions that have been discussed here. Status seems still to have been primarily a function of service, but crown and locality seem to have been at odds over the exact nature of this service, even while the local landowners in their idealised world clung as obstinately as their rulers to a wholly outmoded view of the whole issue. The hierarchy of status did not necessarily reflect the hierarchy of wealth and territorial power. Qualification for office was financial, that for knighthood a compound of wealth and ancient family tradition. Locally speaking, a parvenu esquire might be more important than an absentee knight of ancient lineage. These problems will now be brought into sharper focus in the detailed examination of the hierarchy of Warwickshire landed society that follows.

60 *Order of Chivalry*, pp. 97–101; *Boke of Noblesse*, pp. 76–8.

61 Powicke 1962: pp. 71, 178–81; Saul 1981: pp. 36–59; Bennett 1983: pp. 81–2, 231–3, 1986: pp. 9–10; Pierce 1986; Wright 1983: p. 8; Ferguson 1960; Keen 1984: chs. 9–13. Thomas Ralegh, who was not knighted and is not known to have given military service, bequeathed a full suit of armour (Canterbury Dioc., Reg. Arundel, 1, fo. 219).

62 Ferguson 1960: pp. 128–41.

63 See, e.g., the Wife of Bath's remarks or the *Promptorium Parvulorum* (*c.* 1440), both quoted in Smythe-Palmer n.d.: pp. 30–1; Keen 1984: pp. 157–61 (showing that this was a European-wide phenomenon); Cooper 1983a: pp. 46–9; Morgan 1986: p. 20.

64 E.g. *Manners and Meals in Olden Time*. For fuller comments and references on social mobility in the fifteenth century, see below, ch. 4.

III

The first cross-section to be taken will be that for 1436, the year for which information is most complete; we can then work backwards and forwards from that date. Significantly, in the case of Warwickshire, neither the commissioners for the income-tax of that year nor those for the oaths of 1434 took much interest in indicating the ranks below that of esquire. Practices varied in other counties but the point holds generally true throughout the returns.[65] In Warwickshire, unlike some other counties, esquires were designated in the oath lists – twenty-one in this case – but we shall see that this was a very inadequate count, and in the tax-returns a mere nine were picked out. The two lists are mutually inconsistent in other ways. The nature and purpose of the 1434 list will be discussed later in relation to crown listings of landowners throughout the period, but some of the discrepancies between the two lists need to be considered here, as they are indicative of a general lack of system and hence incompleteness in both of them.

First, there is disagreement about the localising of figures with widespread lands, so that Sir John Culpepper sits near the top of the Warwickshire list of 1434 but does not appear in the Warwickshire tax return of two years later, presumably being assessed on a lost list for Kent, Northamptonshire or Rutland where he also had lands. Some people seem simply to have been passed over by the tax commissioners; perhaps the commissioners in different counties each assumed that a landowner with widespread lands was being assessed elsewhere. Of these, Sir Edward Doddingselles is found in a miscellaneous additional list which includes other men omitted from the original returns for Warwickshire and elsewhere and was possibly the outcome of attempts to remedy earlier mistakes. Richard Brasebrugge, whose father had died the year before, between the compilation of the two lists, may have escaped altogether. Alternatively, he may appear on another additional record, now lost.[66] Conversely, Thomas Ferrers, Thomas Harewell and William Lisle, whose inclusion on the 1434 list would seem inevitable, feature on the tax return alone. Here, we seem to encounter the normal medieval governmental problem: trying to do too much too quickly with inadequate administrative resources. The failure of the exchequer to make use of the convenient list of local landowners returned to the chancery only two years before made its task no easier. There was, however, more prolonged pursuit of accuracy for the tax return, where the king's immediate interests were more obviously at stake.

[65] *Cal. Pat. Rolls 1429–36*, pp. 370–413; Gray 1934: pp. 631–9. Gray's lists are incomplete: also documents in n.7, above.

[66] C.139/73/3. Below, n. 73 for the question of taxing of minors. Culpepper's absence in 1436 may also be explained by death (below, app. 1). His Warwickshire lands were subsequently held by his widow and her second husband John Braunspath (*W.F.F.*, 2596; *V.C.H.*, IV, p. 132), but there is no tax return either for Braunspath or for a Culpepper heir in Warwickshire.

The two lists must, in short, be regarded as merely a starting point in compiling a register of the Warwickshire gentry in 1436 and must in any case be supplemented with the returns for other counties: the possible movement of John Culpepper alone should be warning against assuming the lists for each county to be comprehensive. As soon as we extend our search into other records, it becomes apparent not only that the recording of the non-knightly ranks in the returns of 1434 and 1436 is grossly inadequate but also that confusion existed between different types of record on whether and by what criteria these ranks should be recorded. Something has already been said about the chronology of designation of status in governmental and private documentation. Judicial records of all sorts, including pardons, are the only source for title which regularly cover all levels of landowning society until about mid-century, since they were obliged by the statute of 1413 to record additions,[67] although bishops' registers seem to give surprisingly full and varied information even earlier.[68] But as long as the law courts almost alone thought fit to make such distinctions, did they have much meaning in themselves? And, at this early stage, were they based on the status to which the litigants and defendants themselves admitted or on some private system worked out by the clerks? King's Bench seems fairly consistently to have underestimated status,[69] and it is from these records principally that we are able to trace the early stages in the matching of the profession of lawyer and the status of gentleman.[70] If that is certainly an important statement about status and one which was later to be generally accepted, it is conceivable that at this point it was not one that was acknowledged outside the legal profession itself.[71] We should probably take deeds as the most reliable indication of the status which the participants claimed and their neighbours conceded, but will always have to allow for over-

[67] The same point is made in Wright 1983: pp. 3–4. In the early years of the statute status was not universally recorded even in the Pardon Rolls, perhaps because the entries referred to judicial records from before the statute, where status would not normally be recorded (C.67/36,37). However, status was being recorded surprisingly early, if haphazardly, in the rolls of the Common Pleas (e.g. C.P.40/579 rot. 53d., /599 roti.341,435d.).

[68] See the excerpts in *Dugdale* used for recording presentations to livings; also the surprisingly full recording of status in the tax returns for Hampshire and one or two other counties for 1431 (*Feudal Aids*, II, espec. pp. 359–75).

[69] E.g. Thomas Sydenhale, 'gentleman' in K.B.27/725 Coram Rege rot.62d. (but also in one or two deeds), or Richard Hubaud, 'gentleman' in K.B.27/745 Coram Rege rot.40. For more information on variation in status, Carpenter, M. C. 1976: App. I and notes.

[70] Ives 1955: pp. 52, 153; Storey 1982: pp. 95–6. But note the opinion of a fourteenth-century judge that a man could not be a gentleman because he was a lawyer (Denholm-Young 1969b: p. 130), but could be admitted to the status on account of being the son of a knight. So convinced were the compilers of the Pardon Rolls in the period following the Statute of Additions that 'lawyer' and 'gentleman' were the same thing that they quite often designated all lawyers and crown administrators 'gentleman of London' (e.g. C.67/38 m.7).

[71] Below, n.115.

optimism,[72] while the failure of most deeds to record gentlemen until about the 1440s must raise doubts about how seriously the title was taken before then as an indication of status. It is in fact insufficient merely to count the numbers in each group; inconsistencies and the bias of the records need to be taken into account. The process by which it became normal practice to record titles at the lower levels of local society is in any case of considerable importance to the whole issue.

The reliability of the returns of income is unfortunately less amenable to confirmation. These figures were supposed to represent clear income after deduction of costs. They were therefore presumably equivalent to the sums recorded on valors.[73] They certainly inspire more confidence than the sums recorded on the I.P.M.s, which were so variable, mostly so low and so often supplied by the interested parties that here they have been ignored entirely.[74] Some comparisons can be made between incomes drawn from estate accounts and those recorded by the commissioners. The nearest in time, based on a Mountford account of 1433–4, is encouraging in that it implies a clear income – recorded revenue minus immediate expenses – of about £260, to set beside a tax assessment of £258, although this was merely the revenue paid to the receiver and omits sums paid direct to the lord.[75] However, valor evidence is probably a more reliable indicator, in that we are more likely to be comparing

72 Compare the seventeenth-century yeomen who style themselves gentlemen in their wills (Fletcher 1975: p. 22).

73 *Rot. Parl.*, IV, pp. 486–7. On valors, e.g. Jack ed., *Valor of Edmund Grey, Earl of Kent*, Intro., and Ross and Pugh 1953–4. There is a problem with widows' property: if the heir was a minor, I have assumed that the widow is credited with the full income to which the heir would eventually succeed. However, with reference to the nobility, Gray (1934: p. 613) claims that minors' lands were treated as crown lands and not taxed. This would explain the lack of return for e.g. Richard Brasebrugge (above, p. 50), but Gray gives no reference (cf. *Rot. Parl.*, IV, pp. 486–7) and it is not clear in any case that this would automatically apply to the gentry, who were more likely than the nobility to be mesne tenants and therefore to hold lands that could not be automatically considered crown lands during a minority. The two outstanding cases in Warwickshire are the widows of Roger Harewell and John Malory – in the latter instance the heir, Thomas, was not a minor but was probably abroad (below, n. 169). He would still have been liable for tax (*Rot. Parl.*, IV, p. 487) but his mother may well have had the bulk of the family property. Unfortunately it has not been possible to discover the size of jointure of either of these. It seems extremely improbably that the Harewells were relatively speaking any wealthier than they appear to be, judging by Agnes Harewell's return, but the Malorys may have been better off, a point to be remembered when categorising Thomas Malory as a 'poor knight' (below, n. 85). Even so, their previous and subsequent history does not suggest that the family was notably better off than the figure for John's widow would suggest. The only family property in Thomas' hands before the late 1430s seems to have been Shatwell, Leics. (Farnham, *Leics. Village Notes*, III, p. 226).

74 Crump 1924: p. 142; Hunnisett 1971: p. 206. Obvious comparisons with the tax returns, showing the inadequacy of I.P.M.s, can be made, e.g. for William Lucy (C.138/11/14; C.140/20/30) and Hugh Cokesey (C.139/122/36).

75 S.B.T. D.R.37 Box 73.

like with like, and here the results are less promising. An account with valor made for the Shirleys in 1413–14, covering most of the estate, gives a value *ultra reprisas* (the terms of the tax assessment) of about £300, while Ralph Shirley's income was listed in the tax returns as £100. But if one adds to this his mother's dower income, assessed in 1436 at £92, which seems to have been included in the valor, and the £40 recorded on the returns of another Ralph Shirley, presumably his heir, Ralph II, the discrepancy becomes less alarming.[76]

In the case of Humphrey Stafford of Grafton, however, the gap is disturbing. His valor of 1449, after expenses have been deducted, totals about £370, while his tax assessment is only £266, and the valor figure does not include annuities, which were to be taxed in 1436. In 1449 these came to over £70, although they were probably rather lower in 1436. There were no notable acquisitions between the two dates to explain the differences in the figures so this seems to be a serious case of under-assessment. Stafford was a commissioner in Worcestershire and may have used undue influence where his own assessment was concerned, but then so was William Mountford in Warwickshire. Perhaps the Worcestershire commissioners were more lax than those in Warwickshire. Stafford was, all the same, the most highly rated landowner in Worcestershire, and, as others have suggested, the figures probably do at least give us an indication of relative income, even though variation in practice between counties may make comparison of incomes drawn from more than one county hazardous.[77] It is not easy to believe that landowners, on receipt of their tax bills, would have allowed their neighbours to get away with serious relative under-assessment.

The lists of landowners by status for all three points of analysis are to be found in appendix 2 and the gentry of 1436 are mapped in figure 3. To allow for lack of evidence, particularly at the lower level, any gentlemen who surface between 1437 and 1439 have been included in the list for 1436, as has any member of the gentry known to be alive in 1433 who has left no further mark but is not known to have died before 1436. People known to be esquires in 1440 with no recorded title before that date have been counted amongst the gentlemen for 1436. As in the other cross-sections, minors and widows have normally been accorded the status of the previous head of the

76 Wright 1983: p. 71; Shirley 1873: pp. 389–94; Gray 1934: p. 632; Nichols 1795–1811: III, ii, pp. 708–9, pp. 716–7. Shirley acquired lands through his wife between the account and the tax return, which might well explain any discrepancy (Shirley 1873: pp. 43–4). It seems that almost all the jointure lands of Hugh's widow, taxed separately in 1436, were included in the account (*I.P.M.* 18 Hen. VI/65). The official total of values given on the account is about £20 less than the actual total of the individual figures.

77 Br. Lib. Add. Roll 74,168; *Cal. Fine Rolls 1430–37*, p. 260. For the Staffords' estate management, see below, pp. 00. Scholarly opinion is divided on the accuracy of the returns as far as the nobility are concerned (Gray 1934: pp. 611–12; Pugh and Ross 1953; Rosenthal 1964; Bean 1984).

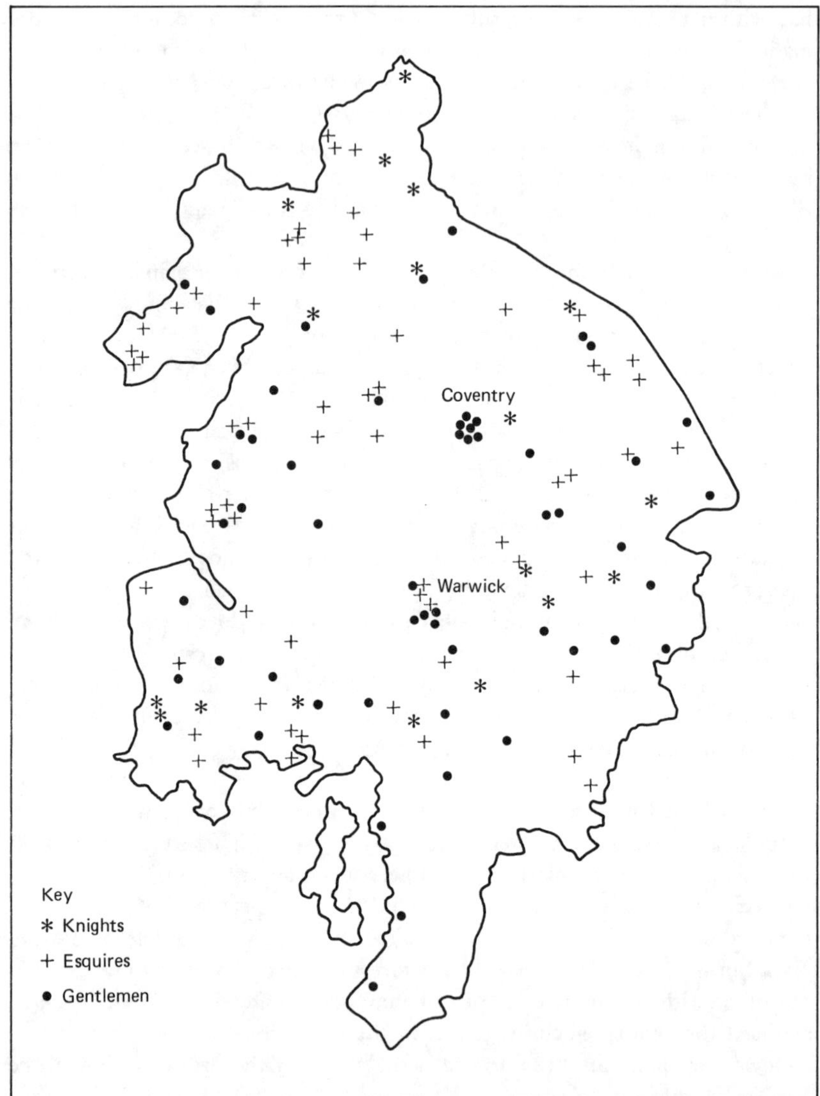

Figure 3 Distribution of Warwickshire gentry, 1436

family, but where there is a series of minorities, or a compound of sparseness of evidence and minorities – as, for example, in the case of John Rous of Ragley – status has had to be guessed.[78] In counting numbers of manors,

[78] *Cal. Pat. Rolls 1429–36*, p. 143; *Cal. Close Rolls 1429–35*, p. 88; C.139/14/13, /45/37 (this gives John I's age as seventeen in 1420, and the chancery rolls evidence shows him to be of age in

heirs have normally been credited with their widowed mothers' properties, unless the latter had remarried, in which case the present husband is counted a member of the Warwickshire gentry and the widow's properties are assigned to him. It cannot be emphasised too strongly that for esquires and above all for gentlemen these lists are not definitive; that there may be other titled gentry lurking amongst unread records; that, particularly in the 1410 list, especially where minor landowners are concerned, there are serious gaps in our knowledge of estates owned in other counties; that choices have to be made about how to use the sometimes contradictory information. They are merely a possible approach to the fifteenth-century understanding of status.

By this reckoning, in 1436 there were eighteen knights, fifty-nine squires and fifty-five gentlemen. The last figure should not be taken too seriously since at this stage it is heavily conditioned by the availability of evidence. The number of knights, however, can be usefully compared with numbers in the previous century. Comparisons are complicated by the fact that other historians have perhaps tended to be too exclusive in their definitions of county landowners and, unfortunately, the only readily available comparable figures for the fifteenth century, those for Derbyshire, are not precise, either chronologically or in terms of status. But checking these figures against those taken from the great council summons of 1324 shows that the number of men prepared to go to the trouble of receiving the accolade had declined significantly: in Warwickshire in 1324 there were forty-two knights, in Gloucestershire about fifty and in Nottinghamshire forty-three. The number of resident Nottinghamshire knights at this time was twenty-two; Saul, on rather more restrictive definitions of residence than those used here, suggests about twenty for Gloucestershire. There is no reason to suppose that Gloucestershire would have markedly more knights than Warwickshire – the counties have an identical number in the oath-lists of 1434 – and the broader parameters used here would presumably raise his number to somewhere between thirty and forty. In Staffordshire an incomplete list of 1337 records thirty-five knights, while the Staffordshire plea-rolls of 1341–51 produce sixty. Astill finds thirty-eight knights in Leicestershire in the second half of the century and Bennett, rather speculatively, about forty 'knightly houses of the first rank' (including some *armigeri*) on the basis of the 1379 Poll Tax returns.[79] So it appears that, while Edward III's military enterprises had kept the number of knights at a reasonably high level,

1431, so his failure to feature much before 1440 is puzzling). The first reference I have for Rous which accords him a title is from 1441, when he is called 'esquire' (*Cat. Anc. Deeds*, VI, C5242).

79 Wright 1983: p. 5; *Parliamentary Writs*, II, p. 640, 650–1; Payling 1987b: p. 107; Saul 1981: pp. 32–3; Hilton 1975a: p. 218; Astill 1977: p. 15; Bennett 1983: p. 81–2.

there had been a notable decline in the militarily less glamorous years that followed.[80]

This suggests that knighthood was no longer desirable for any but a small segment of committed fighting men. To find out whether this was so we must attempt to grasp what it meant to be a knight in 1436. The histogramme of all incomes in 1436 (figure 4) and the table recording average income, manorial estates in Warwickshire and geographical distribution of lands for all the gentry of 1436 (table 1) sum up the basis for much of the following discussion. It is evident that status and income were matched, in broad outline at any rate; since income was largely derived from land, status was also largely consonant with size of estate, especially at the upper levels of the hierarchy. Gray's calculations for all the counties for which detailed returns survive underline the correlation of knighthood and wealth, while also showing that it was no more than approximate. He found that twenty-seven of the sixty-nine people with incomes of £100 or more in 1436 were knights, and another four became knights over the next six years.[81] If some Warwickshire knights had relatively little land in Warwickshire, they had plenty elsewhere.[82] However, four of the knights whose incomes are recorded – Thomas Burdet, William Bishopestone, Edward Doddingselles and Ralph Neville – and probably at least two others – Nicholas Burdet and Thomas Straunge – had incomes significantly below the average. Neville, as the younger son of an earl, could hardly be denied the title,[83] but the first three had all undoubtedly earned it in warfare, or, in the case of those, like Thomas Burdet, who had been knighted before Henry V's reign, as members of military families who would later be available for war service. Straunge and Nicholas Burdet also belong in this category.

80 But cf. Saul 1986; ch. 1 for waning enthusiasm for knighthood from the early fourteenth century. For knights and war service in the fourteenth century, Powicke 1962: pp. 171–9; Saul 1981: pp. 48–51; Bennett 1983: pp. 163–8; Astill 1977: pp. 248–50, 274; Sherborne 1964. A relationship between numbers of knights and the quality of royal military leadership is implied in Waugh's figures for the thirteenth century (Waugh 1983: pp. 985–6) and this slightly weakens his interpretation of these (above, n. 32).

81 Gray 1934: p. 623. A point emphasised in Payling 1987b: pp. 36–9, which perhaps overstresses the comparative importance of a small number of knightly families (below, p. 147 for further discussion). His calculations from Carpenter, M. C. 1976 to back up his remarks about the percentage of the county's wealth held by the greatest families in Nottinghamshire do not work because, Warwickshire being what it was, the incomes of the leading Warwickshire families were drawn from the lists of more than one county.

82 No attempt has been made to give figures for manors in other counties, since there is no certainty of identifying all these without the survival of full estate accounts; again, I.P.M.s are unsatisfactory, as they are often incomplete and not infrequently fail to record land at all if it was in the hands of feoffees. Unfortunately, the fifteenth century produced nothing like the *Nomina Villarum* used so effectively by Saul (1981: pp. 224–7). Naturally, lands elsewhere have to be kept in mind in this analysis; for the greater gentry, number of Warwickshire manors must indicate extent of involvement in the county, not wealth or poverty.

83 *Dugdale*, p. 856.

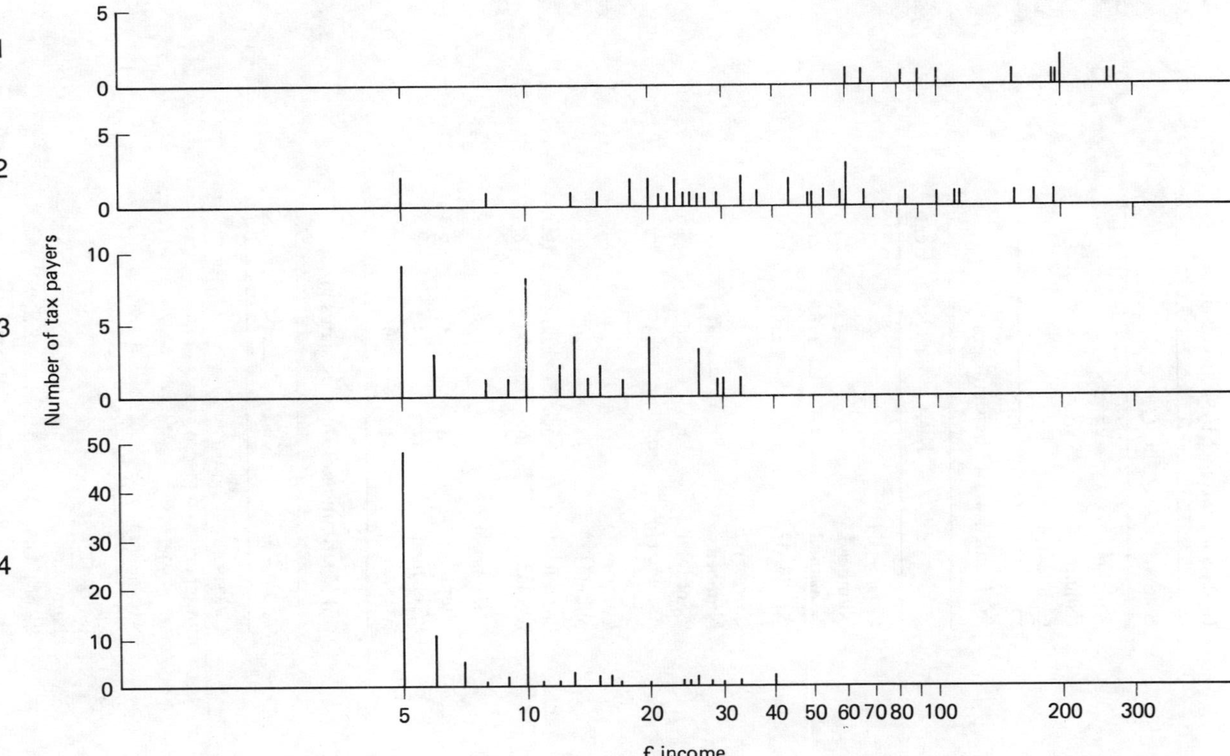

Figure 4 Distribution of incomes in Warwickshire, 1436: 1 Knights; 2 Esquires; 3 Gentlemen; 4 Non-gentle taxable population.

Table 1 Landed society in 1436

(i) Average incomes by status group

Status	Inc. (£)
Knights	155
Esquires	50
Gentlemen	13

(ii) Landed wealth by status group

	Kts.	Esqs.	Gents.
Category A			
Number	1	7	28
% of total	5.6	11.9	51.0
Av. inc. (£)	–	21	13
Category B			
Number	1	23	18
% of total	5.6	39.0	32.7
Av. inc. (£)	100	43	12
Category C			
Number	12	26	9
% of total	66.7	44.1	16.4
Av. inc. (£)	146	60	18
Category D			
Number	4	3	0
% of total	22.2	5.1	0
Av. inc. (£)	183	106	–

(iii) Distribution of lands by status group

	Kts.	Esqs.	Gents.
Category E			
Number	0	13	42
% of total	0	22.0	76.4
Av. inc. (£)	–	17	12
Category F			
Number	0	17	10
% of total	0	28.8	18.2
Av. inc. (£)	–	40	14

Table I (*cont.*)

	Kts.	Esqs.	Gents.
Category G			
Number	2	13	2
% of total	11.1	22.0	3.6
Av. inc.	60	58	–
Category H			
Number	5	6	1
% of total	27.8	10.2	1.8
Av. inc. (£)	166	57	26
Category I			
Number	11	10	0
% of total	61.1	16.9	0
Av. inc. (£)	162	93	–

Note: A – No Warwickshire manors
B – 1 Warwickshire manor
C – 2–4 Warwickshire manors
D – 5+ Warwickshire manors
E – Land in Warwickshire only
F – Land in 1 other county
G – Land in 2 other counties
H – Land in 3+ midland counties
I – Land in 3+ counties, one or more outside the midlands

All % calculations are correct to 1 decimal place.

All income calculations are correct to nearest £. NB incomes for the landowners of 1436 are incomplete; those for whom figures are available are indicated in app. 2.

Disputed manors are generally counted for both claimants; some may therefore be counted twice.

Leases are not normally counted, except in cases where the whole manor with lordship was held by crown grant.

It is clear in fact that knighthood at this stage still carried overtones that were primarily military. Almost every one of the knights of 1436 had served in France or was shortly to do so, sometimes receiving the accolade after going overseas;[84] the families of the 'poor knights' of 1436 were to produce no further

[84] *Dep. Keep.'s Rep.*, 44, p. 626 (Aston); *Dep. Keep.'s Rep.*, 44, p. 621, 48, p. 249; Br. Lib. Harl. 782 fo. 53, Cotton Roll XIII.7 (Bishopestone); *Dugdale*, p. 848 (Burdets); *Dugdale*, p. 1,103; *Cal. Pat. Rolls 1429–36*, p. 359 (Chetwynd); Br. Lib. Add. Ms 6667, p. 256 (Cokayn); *Dep. Keep.'s Rep.*, 48, p. 251 (Cokesey); *Cal. Pat. Rolls 1416–22*, p. 198; Nicolas, *History of the Battle of Agincourt*, p. 378 (Doddingselles); *P.R.O. Lists and Indexes*, Suppl. Ser., IX, ii, pp. 387, 398 (Hastings); *ibid.*, p. 411; Br. Lib. Add. MS 6922, Cotton Roll XIII.7 (Mountford); *Dugdale*, p. 476 (Peyto); Br. Lib. Stowe 440 fos. 32v., 34v. (Shirley); Nat Lib. of Wales Peniarth MS 280

knights for the rest of the century.[85] If there were fewer knights in 1436 than in the fourteenth century, it was because knighthood was increasingly recognised as something that depended on landed wealth as well as military prowess and so many of the greater gentry were now content with the title of esquire. Meanwhile the crown had become less assiduous about maintaining a pool of knights from whom fighting men could be drawn and the campaigning of Henry VI's reign, now a permanent rather than a seasonal form of soldiering, was less attractive to the gentry.[86] That there were as many as eighteen is due to the survival of many of the warriors of the great expeditions of Henry V's reign.

All the same, the careers of the knights show that by this time they were prepared to hold high local office, particularly those offices, such as sheriff, M.P. and commissioner for raising war finance and troops for offensive or defensive purposes, which might demand military expertise.[87] By contrast, in the fourteenth century a distaste among more prominent landowners for public office is indicated by the low status of M.P.s until the later part of the century, by the crown's need to demand the presence of belted knights at parliaments that were to levy taxes and by the presence on campaign of some prominent esquires who seem to have been happy to serve in a military capacity but reluctant to make themselves liable for peace-time office by being knighted.[88] That by the fifteenth century some sort of administrative service was now seen to be consonant with military dignity is readily apparent from the histories of some of the knights of 1436. The characteristic pattern was for military service to be interspersed with tenure of offices of this kind – but more rarely with appointment as J.P. – and for both types of service to be rewarded at the end of

mm.53, 68 (Stafford); *Cal. Pat. Rolls 1422–29*, p. 471, *1429–36*, p. 49; E.404/50/154 (Straunge); *Dep. Keep.'s Rep.*, 48, p. 269 (Trussell – if this is the correct William Trussell). This is merely a selection of the evidence for their military careers. Neville may also have served on campaign; there are problems of identification because of the number of men with this name (*Dep. Keep.'s Rep.*, 42, pp. 382, 410; 'Roles Normands et Français', p. 173).

85 *Dugdale*, pp. 343, 855 (Doddingselles and Neville), and p. 82 for Thomas Malory, a slightly later 'poor knight'. The Bishopestones died out with William (*Dugdale*, p. 701) and the Burdets, although they produced no more knights, probably moved into a higher income bracket after Nicholas' marriage (*Dugdale*, p. 848). There was a long minority in the Straunge family (Carpenter, M. C. 1976: App. 1, *sub nom.*) but their landed status suggests that they would in any case not have produced any non-military knights in the fifteenth century.

86 Allmand 1983: pp. 246–9; below, p. 120. The war retinue of 1414 is the only occasion when the Beauchamp retinue served in any sizeable numbers (Bod. Lib. Dugdale MS 2, pp. 277–81). Cf. Wright 1983, p. 81 for decline in numbers of knights. Note the paucity of mass knightings between 1426 and Edward IV's reign (Metcalfe 1885: pp. 1–2; Nicolas 1842: III, pp. vii–viii). For lesser men and knighthood, above, p. 41 and also e.g. the list of Warwick's men taken to France in 1414 (Bod. Lib. Dugdale MS 2, pp. 277–81), comparing with later status for those listed in app. 2. For the recovery of mass knighting, see below, p. 86.

87 For offices, below, p. 266 n. 17. For all these offices, no separate refs. will normally be given.

88 Saul 1981: pp. 45–7, 120–2; Wood-Legh 1931; Powicke 1962: pp. 174–5; Juriça 1976: pp. 217–39; Naughton 1976: pp. 15, 50; Illsley 1976; Coss 1974b: p. 9; Denholm-Young 1969b: p. 58.

the military career with exemption from all further office.[89] Naturally, extended absence on campaign, as in the case of the near-professional Thomas Straunge, precluded tenure of local office, but even he was rendering important administrative service in Ireland.[90] Interestingly, the greatest of all these men, William Mountford, was not only happy to serve as J.P., but went on holding this and the other major offices after receiving his exemption. His case seems to indicate that some of the greater gentry already saw office, if on an occasional rather than a permanent basis, as an essential attribute of the leadership of local society. There is also some indication that, even if military service was usually a prerequisite for knighthood, a knight's duties could already be seen to lie primarily in the official sphere. There is no evidence that Hugh Willoughby ever served as a soldier, but he had a long career of public office, rewarded towards the end by exemption, and John Culpepper's service to the crown also was purely as a local officer. Both were prepared to hold the office of J. P., one which seems to have been thought rather beneath the dignity of most knights.[91]

Knights tended also to have the most broadly distributed estates (see figure 5), although the group with the highest income was firmly anchored in the midlands. The scattering of their lands is connected with the fact that, as in Derbyshire and in fourteenth-century Leicestershire, they came mostly from the older families; longevity had given them time not only to reach this level of income but also to acquire the scattered lands which were likely to have been accumulated through successive marriages.[92] The length of the family's existence however was not necessarily related to the length of time it had existed in Warwickshire. For example, two of the knights, Sir John Cokayn and Sir Hugh Willoughby, although of ancient lineage, were new to Warwickshire,

89 Exemptions: *Cal. Pat. Rolls 1441–46*, p. 438 (Doddingselles), p. 175 (Mountford), *1436–41*, p. 136 (Peyto – given while still campaigning), p. 540 (Stafford – as for Peyto). Bishopestone, Burdet, Chetwynd and Shirley did not hold office after their periods of military service, although no formal exemptions for them have been found. This pattern continues later in the reign with an exemption after military service for Leonard Hastings (*Dep. Keep.'s Rep.*, 48, p. 346; *Cal. Pat. Rolls 1446–52*, p. 212), but under circumstances of diminished active participation in war.

90 *Cal. Pat. Rolls 1429–36*, p. 49.

91 Cf. exemptions in the thirteenth century: Waugh 1983: pp. 971–5. For Willoughby's exemption: *Cal. Pat. Rolls 1441–46*, p. 431. He did in fact hold office after this, although less frequently. His career pattern could, however, be explained by his Duchy of Lancaster connections (below, p. 00). Culpepper is not to be confused with the justice of the same name, who was not knighted and died in 1414 (Foss 1870: p. 180). For the status of J.P.s in general, see below, ch. 8.

92 Wright 1983: pp. 7–8; Astill 1977: p. 265. For marriage and its consequences for estates, see below, ch. 4. Despite the strictures about I.P.M.s (n.74, above), these can be used as a rough guide to lands outside Warwickshire, and *Feudal Aids* is a useful supplement for the early part of the century, as of course is the identity of the county in which people were listed and taxed in 1434 and 1436. In most cases no specific references have been given for these properties. For a detailed breakdown of landholding covering most of the century, see Carpenter, M. C. 1976: App. II.

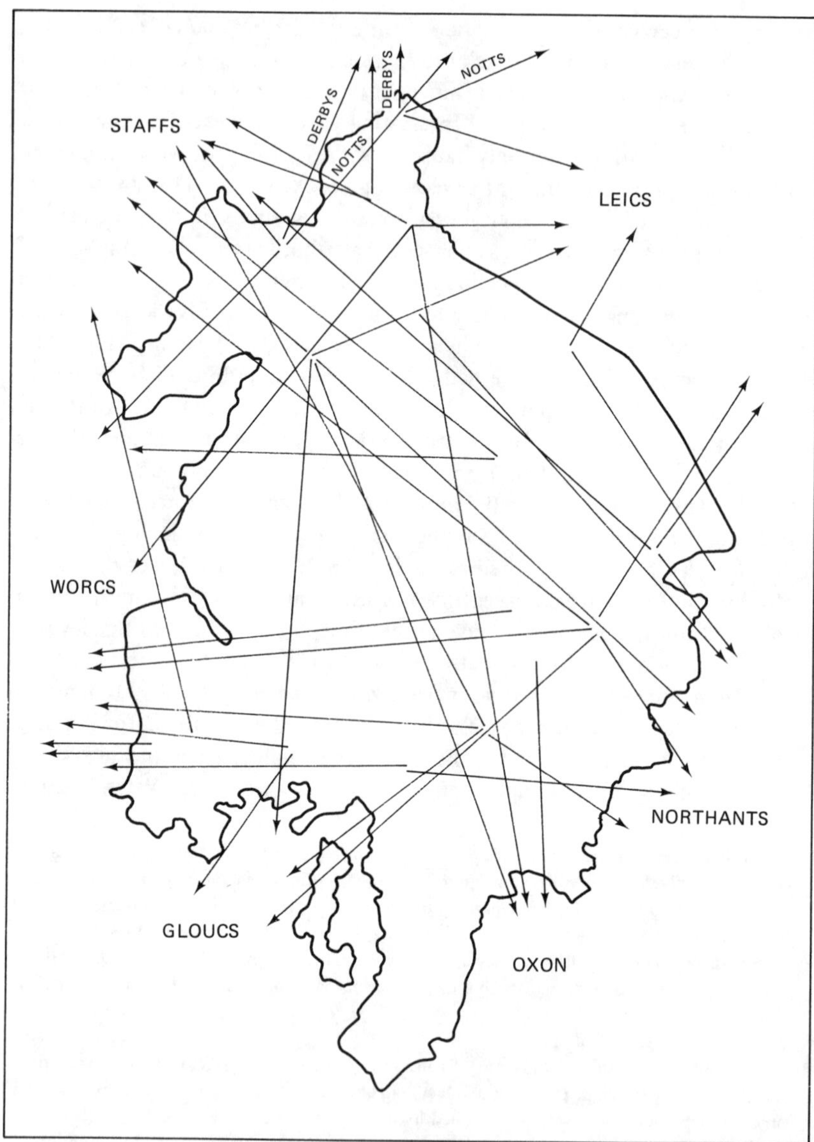

Figure 5 Neighbouring counties where Warwickshire gentry had estates, 1436. (Derbys. and Notts. are included for north Warwicks. families only. The arrows do not indicate precise places where lands were held.)
(i) Knights

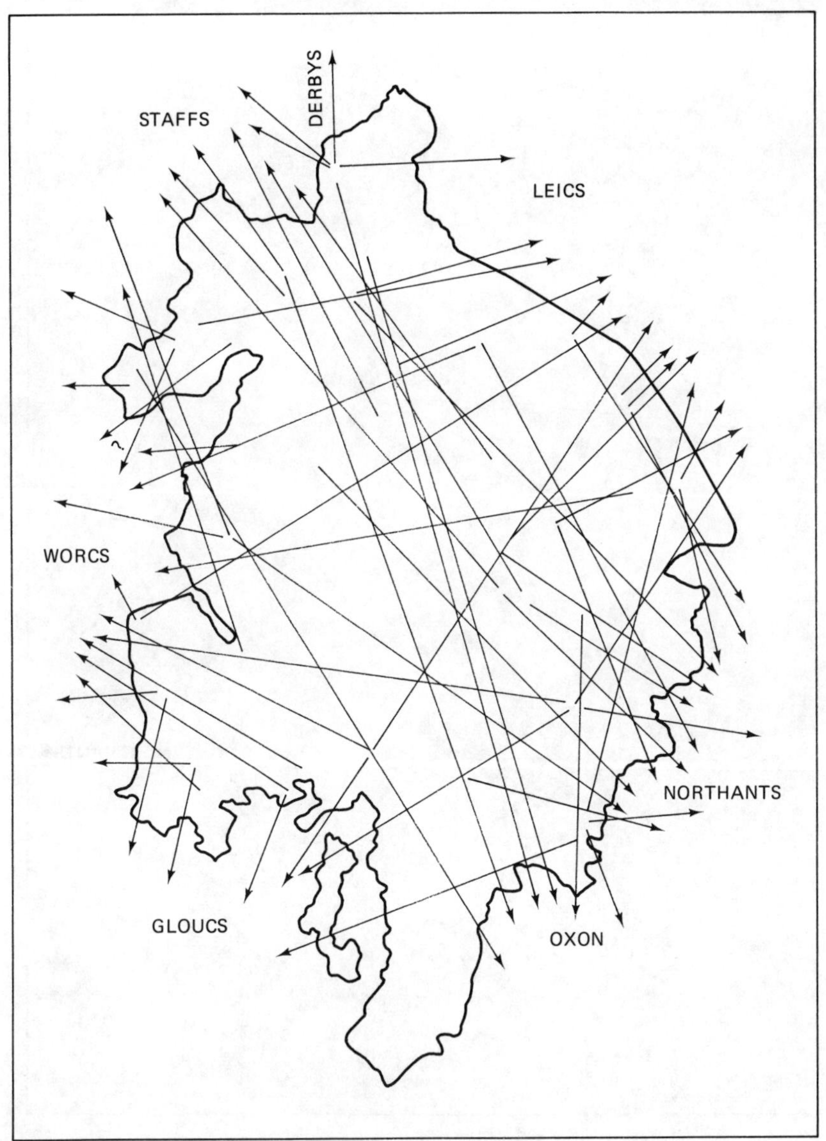

Figure 5 (ii) Esquires

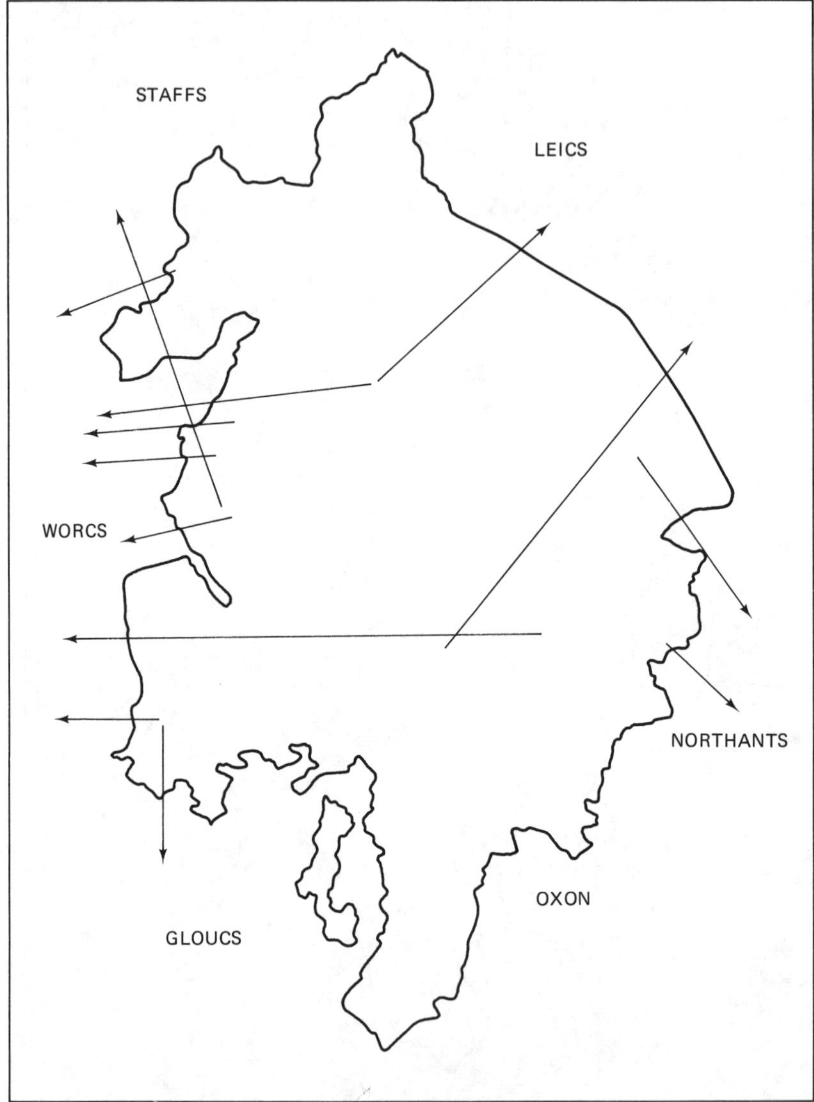

Figure 5 (iii) Gentlemen

where they were brought by marriage and inheritance. It could be argued that the knights were likely to constitute the most unstable part of local society, since the more a family set out to extend its properties the more likely it was to end up with a dispersed estate.[93] In general, too much should not be made of

[93] *Dugdale*, pp. 1,051, 1,120. Also the comments in relation to social mobility, below, pp. 116–19.

the knights' ancient lineage; by definition we are likely to know more about the history of the most prominent families. The fact that anything at all can be discovered about past generations of some of the minor families indicates that several of these also had survived over many generations.[94] Another attribute of ancient lineage was that they normally lived on good-sized manors, where they held franchisal rights and controlled most of the vill. The evident enhancement of status that came from dominance within the vill will be discussed in a later chapter.[95]

The knights of 1436, considered as a group, suggest that by this time there were two distinct, if overlapping, views of knighthood. The first was a purely military one and applied to those knights whose income and landed status did not qualify them for a place at the apex of local society. If they held high office, they did so as an aspect of their military duty. Secondly, there were the men who by every definition, wealth, income, lands, ancestry, service, were the leaders of local society. Interestingly, though, they still saw military duties as a significant part of this leadership. Not all of these had a substantial landed stake in Warwickshire; the societies where several of them were pre-eminent lay elsewhere. While they might reside in Warwickshire from time to time, their chief interest in the county was to ensure the continuance of the property they held there, since it was part of the landed power that made them so prominent in other parts of England. Of those who had several properties in the county, two, Sir John Cokayn and Sir Ralph Shirley, were actually more involved in other counties.[96] Moreover, Warwickshire lacked knights wealthy enough to vie with the lesser peerage found in some other counties. If there was a large gap in income between most of the nobility and most of the knights throughout England, it was particularly marked in this county.[97] The scarcity of knights committed primarily to Warwickshire and the absence of any really outstanding gentry families meant that the Mountfords, with their wealth and large number of Warwickshire properties, were unchallengeable as the foremost of the Warwickshire gentry in 1436.

94 E.g. the vastly obscure Comptons or the Lisles (*Dugdale*, pp. 549, 938). A similar point is made in Clark 1977: p. 125.

95 *V.C.H.*, III, pp. 28, 30, 260, IV, pp. 49–50, V, p. 42, VI, p. 126; C.139/32/18 (this point applies only to those whose principal residence was in Warwickshire). Cf. Derbyshire: Wright 1983: p. 7; also Astill 1977: pp. 8–9 and below, pp. 242–3.

96 For Shirley, see refs. in n. 76, above, for Cokayn, *Dugdale*, pp. 1,120–1. For comparative information on distribution of lands in other midland counties, see Astill 1977: pp. 6, 82, 265, and Wright 1983: pp. 12–14. These two views of knighthood are made explicit in a fifteenth-century text (Russell, *Boke of Nurture*, p. 192).

97 Cherry 1981a: Section B; Gray 1934: pp. 631–9; Pugh 1972: pp. 97–101 (which modifies Gray's figures in this respect). Partly this was a matter of exogamy (below, pp. 99–100, 123 n.101.), which inhibited the establishment of cadet branches of the nobility, as were found in Devon. But the wealthy Devon knights, several of them later ennobled, included commoners (Cherry 1981a: Section B).

If the greater knights, led by the Mountfords, sat at the apex of Warwickshire society in 1436, there were so few with reason to be permanently involved in Warwickshire affairs that they cannot have sat alone. An examination of the esquires will reveal which of them may be placed alongside the more prominent knights. Figure 4 and table 1 show them to be a remarkably disparate group. At one end are people like Edward Bromflete and William Lucy who on any reckoning were the equals of most of the knights: at the other those like Thomas Grene, one of only nine esquires designated on the tax-returns, and John Chetwynd who, like Grene, is designated esquire on the only slightly less exclusive oath-list. As far as distribution of property goes, the esquires do at least follow the pattern set by the knights, in that breadth of distribution correlates well with income and, as with the knights, generally speaking the older families were the wealthiest and had the most scattered estates.[98] Consequently, the esquires also mirror the knights in that amongst the wealthiest of them were some whose interest in the county was rather peripheral and that even those who had considerable Warwickshire properties, such as Thomas Ferrers, Roger Harewell and William Lucy, were extensively involved elsewhere (see figure 5). But as a body they do not have any obvious defining characteristics and it will rapidly become evident that there were several different ways of defining an esquire.

The problem is best approached through the extremes within the group. First we have six men – Robert Ardern, Edward Bromflete, Thomas Erdington, Thomas Ferrers, Roger Harewell and William Lucy – who in terms of land and wealth overlap with the knights. Moreover, Ardern and Lucy were sons of knights, Bromflete was closely related to a knight and Ferrers was the son of a member of the peerage.[99] The common factor was lack of military experience. Here, the only exception is Ferrers, who had served in France in 1417.[100] He held office only once, in 1447, and it may be that he had secured an exemption from knighthood and office which was not recorded in the Patent Rolls. Bromflete certainly had an exemption, acquired in 1442, and evidently lacked interest in all forms of public activity.[101] Roger Harewell's failure to be knighted is to be explained in different terms; clearly pre-eminent in every other way, he came from a family lacking a military tradition. Had his income assessment survived, John Catesby would in all probability have been in the same category.[102] Both belong to the group that was causing the government

[98] *Dugdale*, and *V.C.H.* under individual families for source of general points about tenure, family history etc. Also, Carpenter, M. C. 1976: Apps. I and II.

[99] *Dugdale*, pp. 926, 507, 1,135; S.B.T. D.R. 37 Box 60 (deed of 1426).

[100] *Dep. Keep.'s Rep.*, 44, p. 600.

[101] *Cal. Pat. Rolls 1441–46*, p. 96. He is rarely named in surviving deeds of other landowners and, interestingly, took the trouble to obtain another exemption in 1458 when all sorts of surprising people were being put into office (*Cal. Pat. Rolls 1452–61*, pp. 431–2 and below, pp. 481–2).

[102] *Dugdale*, pp. 809–10, 787–8.

so much trouble in its search for knights, in that they were relatively new families, wealthy but with a professional rather than a military background. Thomas Erdington, the only one of this group of outstanding esquires to be knighted later, was to follow a fairly new route to the accolade in acquiring it through membership of the king's military household without actually going on campaign, another indication that both service and military service were in the course of being redefined in relation to title. Interestingly, this service was rewarded with exemption from office, which makes his career very similar to those of the fighting knights.[103]

At the other end there are the esquires of very limited wealth, as low as some of the gentlemen. In the £29 and under group are Geoffrey Allesley, John Cotes, William Holt, Simon Malory, John and Robert Onley, Thomas Sydenhale and John Waldeve,[104] in the £20 and under group, Thomas Beaufitz, William Botener, John Chetwynd, Thomas Grene, Thomas Herthill, William Lisle, Robert Stokes, Thomas Waryng and Thomas Woodlow. Of these, Botener, Grene, Chetwynd, Holt, Sydenhale, Waldeve, Waryng and Stokes (who is listed in Staffordshire) are named as esquires in the 1434 list, while Holt and Grene belong to the tiny number of esquires designated on the tax-return, so there can be little doubt about their status. For all that, on other documents Stokes, Sydenhale and Waryng hover uneasily, along with Geoffrey Allesley, between the ranks of esquire and gentleman, and most of the others in this group with incomes of under £30 are rarely given any status at all.[105] Since with these men we are clearly dealing with the very bottom of the rank of esquire, by defining what entitled them to claim this status we may be able to understand what separated an esquire from a gentleman.

The most obvious characteristic is some form of service to the crown. Beaufitz (by virtue of his London offices),[106] Botener, Chetwynd, Cotes and Holt all held at least one of the major local offices, that is, escheator, J.P., sheriff or M.P., and Allesley was to join them in 1439 and Robert Onley in 1441. Indeed John Cotes' official standing bears no relation to his income unless one bears in mind that £30 of this was probably in the hands of his mother, Margaret Metley.[107] Chetwynd, Holt, Robert Onley and Waldeve could also be

103 *Cal. Pat. Rolls 1436–41*, p. 505, *1441–46*, p. 205.

104 Baldwin Mountford, technically in this group, has been excluded, as he is clearly an esquire as son and heir to William (*Dugdale*, p. 1,010).

105 E.g. *Cal. Fine Rolls 1437–45*, p. 175; K.B.27/738 Coram Rege rot.60 (Stokes); K.B.27/725 Coram Rege rot.62d.; S.B.T. D.R.37/959 (Sydenhale); K.B.9/224/89 (Waryng); K.B.27/658 Coram Rege rot. 113; *Dugdale*, p. 598 (Allesley). Thomas Herthill is listed amongst the esquires solely on the basis of the only known occasions when he was given any title at all, in 1438 and 1442 (S.B.T. D.R.37 Box 56 (deed of 1438), D.R.3/239, 240). For more on variant designations, see Carpenter, M. C. 1976: App. 1.

106 He was coroner of the City of London by 1441 and a Middlesex J. P. in the 1440s and 1450s (*Cal. Pat. Rolls 1436–41*, p. 516, *1441–46*, p. 474, *1446–52*, p. 591, *1452–61*, p. 671).

107 C.1/11/155; below, p. 127 n.116, p. 402 n.4, p. 103 n.27.

termed esquires by one of the definitions of the Poll Tax of 1379, for they had served the king in war. Holt, moreover, belonged to the king's esquires, a group that was always dignified with a title in royal documents, owing his manor of Aston to a royal grant.[108] Significantly, six of the eight minor esquires designated on the Warwickshire oath-list,[109] which was produced as part of an attempt to maintain the peace locally, were royal officers of some sort, suggesting that in some governmental minds 'esquire' and 'officer' were becoming synonymous.[110]

Grene, Lisle, Waryng and the rest of the esquires in this low-income group present something of a problem. Lisle seems to be a unique case and will be discussed later. The only possible qualification in the case of Herthill, John Onley and Woodlow was that they all served the earl of Warwick. Yet our present understanding is that by this time minor noble servants were more normally called gentlemen: that they constituted an important category of another group that was beginning to receive universally-recognised titles, the 'gentlemen of service'.[111] Again the problem seems to be governmental confusion, in this instance coming face to face with noble confusion. By the 1440s or indeed earlier esquires are being customarily designated on noble records, at least in the recording of indentures,[112] but earlier in the century the practice for non-knightly gentry had been both less uniform and more haphazard. The terms *armigeri, scutiferi* and *valletti* had been variously employed. For example, in a Warwick account of 1408–9 there are no *armigeri*, only *scutiferi* and *valletti*, nor are there any on an account of 1402–3. By 1417–18 *armiger* is in quite prolific use. Some of the men listed under 'fees of knights and esquires (i.e. *armigeri*)' are dignified individually as *armigeri* but others are not, while one of them is labelled *scutifer*, all of which seems to be a prime instance of confusion of official and personal status. The use of the terms themselves is inconsistent. Some of the *armigeri* in the early accounts seem too

[108] *Dep. Keep.'s Rep.*, 44, pp. 595, 614 (Chetwynd); *Colls. Hist. Staffs.*, o.s. 17, p. 53; *Cal. Pat. Rolls 1436–41*, p. 519 (Holt); Br. Lib. Stowe 440 fo. 61 (Onley); Bod. Lib. Dugdale MS 2, p. 279; Br. Lib. Cotton Roll XIII.7 (Waldeve); above, n.48 for Poll Tax reference.

[109] That is, the seven listed above and Richard Marbroke, a one-manor esquire whose income is unknown.

[110] *Rot. Parl.*, IV, pp. 422, 456. Sydenhale and Waldeve held minor offices (*Cal. Fine Rolls 1405–13*, p. 91, *1413–22*, pp. 151, 222, 298, 416, *1422–30*, pp. 6, 220); Marbroke was a king's esquire (*Cal. Pat. Rolls 1422–29*, p. 158).

[111] For all individual refs. to noble service and connections, see app. 3. The evidence for Thomas Herthill before 1436 is inferential: his younger son George served Warwick by 1432 and he himself was feed by the keepers of the Beauchamp lands in 1446 (*Dugdale*, p. 469 for their relationship). For gentlemen of service, see Storey 1982: pp. 93, 95; Morgan 1986: pp. 24–6; Thrupp 1948; pp. 240–1; Mertes 1988: p. 27. Onley may have served once on an exceedingly minor commission, as tax-collector for Coventry (*Cal. Fine Rolls 1413–22*, p. 29), but this was more probably a member of the Onley family of Coventry (*Wedgwood: Biographies*, p. 649).

[112] E.g. Br. Lib. Eg. Roll 2190, Add. Roll 17,209; S.C.R.O. D.641/1/2/17, 18, 231; Nat Lib. of Wales Peniarth MS 280, *passim*; S.C.12/18/45.

lowly to be afforded such a title. This is also true of Richard Beauchamp's Calais retinue of 1414, which consisted essentially of his peace-time affinity, and was divided into *milites, armigeri* and *valletti*. If the *valletti*, in contradiction to the late-fourteenth-century governmental identification of *vallettus* with 'yeoman', represent the group that was later to be called 'gentlemen' (and that is what some of them manifestly are), then some of the *armigeri* look more like *valletti*. Of particular note is the fact that some of the dubious esquires of 1436 are dubious *armigeri* in these earlier listings. Thomas Stokes, probably Robert's father, is called *armiger* in the accounts and the Beauchamp retinue list, while Thomas Woodlow is listed under *armigeri* in the accounts but is *vallettus* in the retinue. Even more confusion surrounds the use of *scutifer*, employed in the Beauchamp accounts for substantial esquires like Baldwin Straunge, doubtful esquires like John Waldeve and outright gentlemen like William Parys. Meanwhile the Common Pleas give Thomas Archer, an *armiger*, the title of *scutifer* in 1405 and equally on a deed and a recognisance of the same period the term is clearly meant to designate the group immediately below the knights.[113] Bishops' registers, moreover, among the earliest records to give full information on status, continue to use '*domicellus*', a term with strong connotations of domestic service, for both esquires and gentlemen well into the century and employ '*scutifer*' for an esquire in 1408.[114]

We lack even the comforting reassurance that in the early decades of the fifteenth century 'gentleman' was recognised to be the proper title for lawyers in the employ of the nobility. For most of the century they are rarely given anything beyond a descriptive title in the records of the nobility. As late as 1430, seventeen years after the Statute of Additions had ushered in the use of 'gentleman' for the lowest rank of gentry, as eminent a lawyer as Thomas Greswold could be called *domicellus*. This must indicate that, while professional service in both noble household and law courts was indeed being subsumed into the same category, the title of gentleman was not yet in common use to describe it. There are certainly gentlemen in the households of the countess of Warwick in 1420–21 and of Sir John Fastolf in 1431–2 but it may well be that even by 1436 the common usage for all such professionals outside the law-courts was to adapt the king's custom of calling his lesser servants 'esquire'. This would account for several of the marginal esquires revealed in the 1434 list and in other records. Indeed, so convinced was the clerk who drew up the Warwickshire election indenture of 1421 that 'esquire' could be applied to men who by

113 Br. Lib. Eg. Rolls 8770–3; Bod. Lib. Dugdale MS 2, pp. 277–81; C.P.40/579 rot. 53d.; Nott. Univ. Lib. Middleton MS Mi D 4004; *Cal. Close Rolls 1402–05*, p. 174. Both Stokes were of Stotfold, Staffs. (S.B.T. D.R.37 Box 40 (Stoke deed); K.B.27/615 Coram Rege rot.26d.). Parys is also *armiger* in a Common Pleas entry of 1410 (C.P.40/599 rot. 341). On *vallettus* in the previous century, see above, p. 00. Cf. Mertes 1988: pp. 26–31.

114 Worc. Dioc., Reg. Clifford, fo.8; Cov. and Lichf. Dioc., Reg. Burghill fo.195; below, n. 115. For bishops' registers and status, see above, p. 51.

1436 would certainly be called 'gentleman' that he used it for everyone, however insignificant, who was not a townsman.[115] We shall see that this does not hold good for all the professionals, but it seems to work for some, perhaps for those with a respectable, if not a large, quantity of landed wealth.

That leaves Grene, Sydenhale, Waryng and Malory from the low-income esquires, if we continue to put the case of William Lisle on one side. Malory was probably the brother of John, an indisputable esquire, and may have acquired the title by association.[116] The first three form an interesting group, to which John Waldeve should also be added. All four lived in the Arden, the region of late colonisation and small manorial fragments. These characteristics were especially marked in the heart of the Arden near Tanworth, where the four resided. We shall see that this area produced numbers of very petty gentlemen; it is therefore all the more likely that there would be an inflation of rank that would give rise to small-scale esquires.[117] Sydenhale was so marginal as to be called 'gentleman' on occasion, but of Grene's status there can be no doubt at all although his income was tiny and there is no record that he held any manorial lordship at all. He was, however, Alderman and Proctor of the Stratford Gild, to which many of the local gentry belonged, so his title was perhaps the outcome of a combination of office and standing amongst his Arden neighbours.[118] The distinctive social structure of the Tanworth region becomes very evident if we move a little further north to the area south of Tamworth, where there were some notably wealthy knights and esquires but few lesser men confident enough to aspire to any form of gentility. But William Lisle did manage to get himself accepted as an esquire in this area, sometimes at least, even though, despite being lord of three manors, he was allegedly in receipt of the extraordinarily low income of £10. It is indeed not impossible that the figure the tax commissioners recorded was an error, a point which should be borne in mind in making use of calculations based on these figures.[119]

[115] *Dugdale*, p. 527 (extraordinarily, Greswold is still given this title in the same source in 1458 (Cov. and Lichf. Dioc., Reg. Boulers, fo. 92)); K.B.27/646 Rex rot. 3 (note also William Cokesey, *domicellus* and attorney-general in 1391: W.C.R.O. C.R. 136/C307); Longleat MS Misc. IX, 6414; Thrupp 1948: pp. 240–1; C.219/12/5. For lawyers as gentlemen, above, n.70. Russell's 'Boke of Nurture' equates gentlemen with esquires (p. 187) and seems to rank the esquire among rather humble company (pp. 188–9).

[116] *Cat. Anc. Deeds*, IV, A8103; Mallory Smith 1985: p. 34; below. p. 300 n.70 for identification of Simon.

[117] For the Arden, see above, pp. 20–5 and below, p. 77.

[118] For Sydenhale, see above, n. 105; *Stratford Register*, pp. 8, 21. Sydenhale is not given the title of esquire on a deed on which three other esquires are designated (E.42/124). For refs. to Grene, see e.g. *Cal. Close Rolls 1422–29*, p. 204; S.B.T. D.R.37 Box 42/2466, 2484, 2499; K.B.9/257/50. The gild is discussed in Carpenter 1980a: p. 523, and below, p. 339.

[119] 'Gentleman' on four known occasions only, otherwise normally 'esquire', and the fourth reference may be to a younger William (Sims, *Calendar of Walsall Deeds*, p. 20; K.B.9/300/56; Nott. Univ. Lib. Middleton MS Mi D 4148, 6/173/24). His entry on the return comes between two other entries of £10, which may have caused the clerk's hand and eye to slip. It has been

Are the esquires of 1436 susceptible to any generalisations at all? On the whole, the evidence presented here suggests that in 1436 there was as much confusion about esquires as there had been in the Poll Tax schedule of 1379. In the latter, esquires had been classified as landowners of knightly level, lesser landowners of the level of franklins, and landless men 'in service or in arms';[120] we have met variants on all these themes amongst the esquires of 1436. However, if there was a single attribute which seems to have defined an esquire in 1436, in the royal view at least, it was service. Eighteen of them were sheriffs in this or another county before 1440, many of these also J.P.s. Another nine were J.P.s, another three were escheators or appointed to important local commissions. Excluding the king's own servants and Baldwin Mountford, only sixteen cannot be shown to have held office at all before the end of 1440 and of these Brasebrugge, Bromflete and probably Ferrers had deliberately excluded themselves from office, or were to do so, and Robert Onley was to hold multiple responsibilities from 1441 and was serving the king in a military capacity in 1436. Most of the other twelve were either very marginal esquires, or, like Richard Verney, on the way up and later to hold local office. The Fieldings, with their claim to imperial lineage, are a special case and John's son William, also an esquire, was to serve extensively as a local officer from the later 1440s. This second group could therefore be seen in relation to office as the pool of belted knights had been in relation to military service, that is available for this form of service and consequently dignified with the title.[121] Interestingly, a later writer gives some support for the idea that the title of esquire was originally conceived to indicate official status, since Camden thought that the title was at first 'a name of charge and office onely', not one 'of dignitie and worship'.[122]

So by 1436 there was a schema by which the knights fought and held local office, usually of a vaguely military kind, in the intervals of fighting, but were then allowed to retire, while the esquires bore the brunt of the local administration, taking both the less obviously 'military' offices and those which

retained in the calculations because there are too many other imponderables to start making individual exceptions of this kind and he was obviously not excessively wealthier, or he would never have been called 'gentleman' at all.

[120] *Rot. Parl.*, II, p. 58, translated in Dobson ed., *Peasants' Revolt*, pp. 107–8.

[121] Royal servants are Fillongley (*Cal. Pat. Rolls 1436–42*, p. 471, *1452–61*, p. 77), Greswold (n. 115, above), Marbroke (below, n. 159) and Repington (S.C.6/1038/1). For exemptions, see above, p. 61, and, for Brasebrugge, *Cal. Pat. Rolls 1467–77*, p. 564. This was not obtained until 1475, but he held no office earlier and may have bothered with an exemption at this point because political conditions were making the availability of numbers of officers essential for the king (below, pp. 516–22). The other esquires who held no local office are Folkesworth, Fielding, Grene, Richard Harewell, Herthill, Hubaud, Nicholas Middlemore, John Onley, Stokes, Richard Verney, Waryng and Woodlow. For Verney's later career, see below, chs. 4, 5, 9–12. For Robert Onley's military service, see above, n. 108. For reasons for excluding Baldwin Mountford, see above, n. 104. For the Fielding lineage, see below, p. 258 and for William's offices, e.g. *Cal. Pat. Rolls 1446–52*, p. 590.

[122] Camden 1610: pp. 176–7.

fell vacant for lack of knightly takers. Such a system, though without the military overtones, is clearly indicated in the sermon which opened the parliament at which the oaths of 1434 were ordained in which it was said that both knights and esquires had a duty to administer justice.[123] Esquires were quite frequently rising men and, whether rising or not, could greatly extend their generally more limited territorial influence through tenure of office, which gave them jurisdiction over other men's tenants. Local office may consequently not have seemed to them too much of a burden.[124] Given the fact that the lands of the middle-ranking esquires were more likely to be concentrated in Warwickshire than those of the greater ones, it was probable that the duties of local office would fall on them. Those of the more prominent esquires who kept out of office may well have felt that their lands alone brought them sufficient political weight without the burdens of office; after all most men in this category came from knightly families and had clearly avoided knighthood in order to avoid public duties of all kinds. Some of them were considerable local figures in whom reluctance to hold office did not betoken a lack of interest in local affairs. Extrapolating from status defined by service to the crown, the servants of the nobility could also be termed esquires.

In theory and, roughly speaking, in reality, the hierarchy of service reflected the hierarchy of wealth and territorial status, which is to be expected, since land and service had always been so closely linked. However, the equation rather broke down at the two extremes of the class of esquire. At one end were some very rich men, like Roger Harewell, who came from non-military backgrounds; at the other the rather meagre figures with strong traditions of office-holding, like Chetwynd and Cotes, and, yet further down the scale, the esquires in private service, for whom 'gentleman' was later to become the normal usage. Moreover, there are distinct signs that the title of esquire was beginning to be linked in some cases, even in the official mind, not so much with the office that was the consequence of land tenure as with the lands that might qualify a man for office. The obvious examples are the 'knightly' esquires, who did no service but had to be called something, and the petty esquires of the Arden, most of whom did not hold office. The honorific use of the title, even if not entirely new, could not become normal until esquires were named with greater regularity in both public and private documents, something which was only just beginning to happen. This perspective on status was thus a relative innovation in 1436. It can best be explored further through discussion of our last remaining group, the gentlemen.

The fifty-five gentlemen identifiable in 1436 clearly lie at the bottom of the local hierarchy, both financially and territorially (see table 1). Of the eleven

[123] Something of the sort is suggested by Saul for the fourteenth century, but the association of knighthood with office seems to have been weaker then (Saul 1981: pp. 256–7), and above, p. 60; *Rot. Parl.*, IV, p. 419, cited in Cooper 1983a: p. 449.

[124] For the thirteenth century, cf. Waugh 1983: p. 986.

with incomes significantly above the average, five – Boughton, Brome, Fulwode, Gower (his son and heir) and Shukburgh – were to reach the rank of esquire over the next ten years or so, as was John Rous, whose income is unrecorded, but whose estate was well above the average size for a gentleman.[125] Two other rich gentlemen – Wymondeswold and Norwood – were probably Coventry merchants, whom contemporary prejudice would be unlikely to raise above this rank.[126] Having established roughly where a gentleman lay in the hierarchy of wealth and landed power, we must ask what made a man a gentleman. This question has been given two distinct answers. Morgan and Storey believe that the rank was called into being largely for the dignification of a growing band of professional administrators and lawyers. According to Saul, on the other hand, they are the new landowners who crossed the divide between peasantry and gentry in the advantageous conditions after the Black Death. For Morgan also, insofar as there were country gentleman at all, they seem to have been men of the type favoured by Saul: 'Of course, the gentleman is there in landed society, developing a presence in the field of private enterprise as a "farmer" of leased-out demesnes'.[127]

The Warwickshire gentlemen show beyond reasonable doubt that a gentleman could be either a gentleman of service or a gentleman by tenure. Twenty-seven can be shown to have held some sort of manorial lordship, *not* just demesne leases as Morgan suggests and Saul implies, in Warwickshire or elsewhere, and a further three – Boughton (by marriage), Richard Dalby and George Herthill – were heirs to manorial lordships.[128] Twenty of these thirty manorial lords are not known to have had any professional employment, despite the fact that the evidence is biased towards the discovery of gentleman-lawyers, since the legal records are the main source for gentlemen at this time.

Two gentlemen, William Dixwell and Thomas Hayton, neither of them a manorial lord, appear to have been farmers, in both the medieval and the modern sense, of some substance, moving in gentlemanly circles.[129] If the evidence supports Saul's ideas to this extent, there must be serious doubts whether this is a 'new' class. As the next chapter will show, the evidence for the

125 K.B.27/723 List of Fines (Boughton); *Cat. Anc. Deeds*, IV, A10387 (Brome); S.B.T. D.R. 37 Box 50 (Botley deed-1443) (Fulwode); S.B.T. D.R.37 Box 76 (Tanworth rental-1446) (Gower); *W.F.F.*, 2608 (Shukburgh). For Rous, see above, n.78.

126 For Wymondeswold, this is inferred from his residence and connections (*Cal. Pat. Rolls 1422–29*, p. 430, *1436–41*, p. 106). For Norwood, *Colls. Hist. Staffs.*, n.s., I, p. 55. For landowners' prejudices about mercantile wealth, see Thrupp 1948: pp. 263–4.

127 Storey 1982; Morgan 1986: esp. p. 21; Saul 1981: pp. 25, 241–3.

128 *Dugdale*, p. 99 (Boughton – he married Allesley's daughter and co-heiress, but must have had some of her property, presumably in jointure, by 1436); *Dugdale*, p. 562; below, p. 220 (Dalby – co-heir to Hugh); *W.F.F.*, 2638 (Herthill). For the others, see Carpenter, M. C. 1976: App. II.

129 For Dixwell, see e.g. *V.C.H.*, VI, p. 63 (indicating the origins of the family); E.163/7/31 Part I; K.B.9/282/67 (a rather ungentlemanly crime committed in gentlemanly company); for Hayton, see e.g. *V.C.H.*, VI, p. 183; *Cal. Pat. Rolls 1413–16*, p. 336; *Cal. Fine Rolls 1437–45*, p. 322.

movement of successful peasants into the gentry is not very convincing and it will shortly be argued that it was not the class below the esquires that was new so much as the need to identify it. In the case of Dixwell and Hayton and in that of John Willenhale, a gentleman not known to have had either lordship or professional employment, superior connections seem to have been the determinant of superior status.[130] An insight into how this could come about is given by Richard Jefferies' portrait of Frank, 'the borrower', in the late nineteenth century. He is no more than a lessee, but as he acquires a growing number of leases he begins to put on the life-style of a gentleman and, having done so, gains the entrée to local society and is well on the way to acceptance as a gentleman. As it is said of him, ''pend upon it, he have zucked zumbody in zumhow.'[131] The need at this low level of gentility to buttress landholding with connections might explain why some lords of fragmentary manors were not styled gentleman at this time. The lack of records in which these families feature does of course reduce the probability of discovering a title for them, unless they used the Westminster law-courts, but it also suggests that they played little part in local society.[132] Of the gentlemen who had no manorial lordship or expectation of one, thirteen or fourteen and possibly one or two more were lawyers or administrators, or both.[133] Apart from the merchants, the categories of manorial lords and professionals cover virtually all the gentlemen of 1436, but they were by no means mutually exclusive, since wealth accumulated by service could then be invested in land. This was indeed the road to social advancement taken by most of the upwardly mobile figures of the time.[134]

If it seems that gentlemen were marked out either by tenure or by service of a non-official nature, there is evidence that some attempts were being made to incorporate them into the hierarchy of local office. As the quantity of local administration grew, it was inevitable that men below the rank of esquire would be holding local office. By 1440 Thomas Stretton had become a J.P., nine others

[130] E.g. *Cat. Anc. Deeds*, I, C366, 1305, III, D750, IV, A10387; *Cal. Close Rolls 1435–41*, p. 268.

[131] Jefferies 1880: I, pp. 82–99; a similar point is made about sixteenth-century gentility, Russell 1971: p. 17.

[132] These include the Tates of Coventry and Gilson manor, Coleshill, the Whitneys of Clifton upon Dunsmore, the Wittleburys of Stretton on Fosse, the Powers of Ruin Clifford and the Willicotes of Chelmscote in Brailes (*Dugdale*, p. 1,022; *V.C.H.*, VI, p. 66, V, p. 154; *Dugdale*, pp. 704–5; *V.C.H.*, V, p. 19).

[133] Lawyers are marked on the lists. For servants of the nobility, see app. 3. Crown servants are Brome (*Cal. Pat. Rolls 1429–36*, pp. 452, 453 etc.), Est (*Cal. Pat. Rolls 1422–29*, p. 35 etc.) and Stretton. He is not known for certain to be in the king's employ until made Clerk of the Works in 1456 (C.81/1371), but is likely to have been promoted from other service and was already the recipient of crown favour in 1435 and 1437 (*Cal. Fine Rolls 1430–37*, pp. 231, 323). He is included in the tables as a manorial lord because he had custody of a Warwickshire manor at this time (*ibid.*), but he had no other lordship beyond this temporary one.

[134] See below, ch. 4.

had been escheator or M.P. for Warwick borough and another eighteen tax-commissioner, coroner or under-sheriff, and this is likely to be an under-estimate, as the holders of the last two offices are rather haphazardly recorded. Excluding crown servants and those who held office later or in another county, only nineteen are not known to have had any local responsibility, while many officers and non-officers served as jurors.[135] Nevertheless, if a place for gentlemen was in the course of being found in the official hierarchy, the crown seems to have been only marginally aware of this fact. Their status was rarely indicated on appointments to office. Moreover, the oath-list of 1434, which, in its search for those who were most likely to influence the preservation of local order, seems to have tried to seek out the holders of the lesser offices, as well as a few noble servants, is woefully deficient in both lesser officers and gentlemen. Indeed the instructions for the commissioners were to take the oaths of knights, esquires and *yeomen*.[136]

At this point we can see very clearly the contradiction between local and governmental concepts of hierarchy. The crown on its part preferred to recognise only a hierarchy of service, defined in exceedingly exclusive terms, amongst landowners. Led by its own law-courts, it was perhaps grudgingly coming round to the opinion that lawyers also served and should be dignified. But minor landowners, whose service lay in a very minor capacity or was non-existent, could be left with prosperous peasantry in an undifferentiated body of yeomen, husbandmen and franklins, needing to be given some sort of title merely for the convenience of the king's courts. Unimpeachable 'gentlemen', identified from private records, may well turn up as 'yeomen' or 'franklins' in the records of the king's courts.[137] Local society on the other hand was beginning to realise that all local offices were now of sufficient importance that they should be given wherever possible to men who were not peasants. By the same token, tenure of such office could add a lustre to the name of the holder that raised him above the peasantry. Furthermore, extrapolation from the normal identification of office and tenure at a time when the royal government was so enormously extending its reach into the provinces would lead them to the logical conclusion that the mere possession of lordship gave a man a significant role in the king's administration. It seems that this process had now gone far enough for its significance to have percolated down to the least

135 Those who held no office were Astley, Blankame, Bradwell, Dixwell, Fulwode (a juror), Hayton, Herthill, Lecroft, Malory, Moreton, Henry and Robert Porter (both jurors), Rodborn, Rivell, Shukburgh (a juror; his father had held office), Somerlane (a juror), Verney, Walsh, Wymondeswold. For jurors, see K.B.9 indictments.

136 *Rot. Parl.*, IV, p. 456.

137 Above, pp. 45–6, 73. Legislation of the late-fourteenth and fifteenth centuries consistently failed to recognise the place of gentlemen in the social hierarchy (e.g. *Statutes of the Realm*, II, pp. 75, 113, 241, and above, n.136). For status in the records of the courts, above, n. 70 and Carpenter, M. C. 1976: App. I.

significant holders of manorial lordship, and for the title 'gentleman' to be recognised as the respect due to these men. Even the least of them was now a cog in the social system that provided the power on which the royal government was based.[138] But even at this stage local society itself remained a little hesitant about the claims to gentility of the 'farming' gentlemen, to judge by the case of the Spensers, who really *were* peasant yeomen made good, and were not recognised as gentlemen until long after they had acquired manorial lordship.[139]

In beginning to insist on the respect due to all the king's officers and to all manorial lords, lesser landowners were showing a far more mature awareness of the realities of local government than the king, enmeshed as he was in his ancient scheme of military service supplemented by high local office. It was surely this new definition of gentility, rather than the arrival of a new class of lesser landowners from amongst the peasantry, that produced the gentlemen of fifteenth-century England. Additional factors were the growth of the lay professions and the urgent need for all minor landowners to differentiate themselves from the richer peasants. That it was *gentil*, with its aggressively non-agricultural connotations, that was the term that was adapted to meet this need is itself important.[140] Moreoever, as Holt has pointed out, the title is by origin not a title of service but a title of status, which must add strength to the argument that it was designed initially for minor landowners and then rapidly adapted for professional men.[141] That it was adapted so quickly shows that even as a mark of tenure it had the connotations of service by tenure that have been put forward in this discussion.

Confirmation of the definitions of gentility suggested here comes from the statements produced in the mid fifteenth century to confirm and deny the Pastons' right to gentility. The issues that feature prominently are their ancestry, their relationship and association with people of 'noble blood' and other 'worshipful gentlemen', their tenure of judicial office, whether their line was sullied with menial agricultural toil and, most significantly in this context, whether they had manors, courts and bondmen.[142] It is also significant that the

[138] Above, pp. 42–3, 45; on the relationship of land and power, below, pp. 283–5. Morgan (1986: p. 19) suggests that yeomen came to be differentiated from the gentry chiefly by 'the exercise of rule', which fits with this interpretation if one extends 'rule' to include manorial lordship. By the late sixteenth century the identification of manorial rights and gentility was so close that owners of manors who wished to remain yeomen extinguished the rights. I am most grateful to Dr. John Morrill for communicating this point to me. Cf. in the seventeenth century 'a gentility of social function' (Morrill 1976a: pp. 18–19).

[139] Finch 1956: pp. 38–9; Jeayes ed., 'Catalogue of Spencer Charters', 1646; below, ch. 4. The Althorp reference makes it clear that the Spensers had a manor at Wormleighton long before they bought the former Mountford property in 1506.

[140] Above, p. 45.

[141] Thrupp 1948: pp. 305–6; Wagner 1972: pp. 117–8; Holt 1982: p. 117.

[142] *Paston Letters*, I, pp. xli–ii, II, pp. 551–2.

word that is continually stressed when assessing someone's worth or condition is 'livelihood', which in this period meant landed income.[143] The strong relationship between land and gentility is rendered all the more evident by the snobbish attitude to people involved in trade.[144]

As with the esquires, once there was an accepted connection between title and local standing, there could be considerable local variation. Twelve of the gentlemen of 1436 came from the Tanworth and Coventry parts of the Arden, the area most notable for fragmentary manors, just as Norfolk, with a similar tenurial geography, had an outsize list of notables in 1434.[145] The concentration of gentlemen here was also due to the fact that, again like Norfolk, it produced numbers of lawyers and administrators, many of them aspirant representatives of these minor families.[146] East to south-east Warwickshire had no less than sixteen gentlemen.[147] Here it was not tenure that inflated status but the lack of noble lands and resident knights. This group includes men like Dixwell, Duston, Hayton and Willenhale, whose claims to gentility were dubious on all counts and must have rested on their being men of some consideration in a region where there were relatively few.[148] For both esquires and gentlemen another important local determinant, one not confined to a particular region, could be the identity of the principal lord of the vill. If he were an absentee, or an ecclesiastical lord who failed to take a very active role in local politics, the holder of a minor sub-manor might find himself pushed into unexpected prominence. A good example from Warwickshire are the Rushtons of Studley, who held a subordinate manor of Studley Priory, holders of the main manor.[149] The effects of environment on status have been noted in England at a later date and we can actually see them at work in an election indenture of 1447; in this William Hore and Thomas Hore of Solihull are elevated to the unheard-of level of esquire, simply because there is no-one else of any sort of standing on the entire list. Such considerations could produce outright error, as when a local jury in 1483 made the understandable mistake of assuming that William Catesby II had been knighted.[150] If a collection

[143] *Plumpton Corresp.*, p. 11; *Paston Letters*, I, pp. xlii, 82, 154, 254, 350, II, p. 202.

[144] *Paston Letters*, I, pp. 135, 513–14, 541.

[145] Bradwell, Brome, Broun, Est, Fulwode, Gower, Hore of Elmdon, Hore of Solihull, Parker, Porter, Rushton, Walsh. For Norfolk, see Blomefield 1805–10 and *Cal. Pat. Rolls 1429–36*, pp. 404–7; also MacCulloch 1986: p. 26 on the density of gentlemen in the Norfolk-Suffolk 'wood-pasture' region.

[146] Baker 1981: p. 25, citing *Rot. Parl.*, V, p. 326–7.

[147] Astley, Blankame, Boughton, Campion, Derset, Duston, Hugh and Richard Dalby, Dixwell, Goode (but really Gloucs.), Hayton, Hore of Stonethorpe, Moreton, Shukburgh, Starkey, Willenhale.

[148] Above, p. 54.

[149] *V.C.H.*, III, p. 180.

[150] Wagner 1972, p. 127; C.219/15 Pt II/4 Pt II; K.B.27/900 Rex rot.5. The same error over Catesby was made by Wootton Wawen priory (King's College, Cambridge, WOW/505).

of neighbours could be as uncertain as this over a title that was not open to doubt, then the opportunities for self-elevation by neighbourly acclaim are obvious.

In fact the relationship with local geography and economy needs to be applied to all the lesser landowners in all parts of the county. Analysis of their geographical distribution (figure 3) shows that, outside the major towns, Coventry and Warwick, the resident gentry tended to proliferate in the wealthier areas, particularly the more prosperous parts of the Arden and the fertile areas in the east to south-east. This was not just a matter of these regions' ability to support a larger number of landowners. In the case of the greater figures with more widespread lands what mattered was whether their Warwickshire estates created enough wealth to permit their use as a main residence and to require their personal presence to protect them. Consequently, in the less prosperous area in the far north of the county, there were numbers of greater families with widely distributed lands who tended not to put their Warwickshire interests first, even if several of them were sufficiently involved in the county to qualify as Warwickshire gentry within the terms of this study. This meant that those who did so, like the Mountfords, and, eventually, the Ferrers of Tamworth and the Willoughbys, exercised a disproportionate amount of influence within the area. It is noteworthy that it was only when Thomas Bate and Richard Bingham were enjoying the Warwickshire properties of the Cokayns and the Willoughbys, as second husbands of widows who were not in possession of the main property elsewhere, that these estates played a large role in the families' affairs. In the case of the Willoughbys this role was to continue when the lands returned to the main line, but not in the case of the Cokayns. At a much lower level, the barrenness of the Dunsmore Heath area, which had few vills or resident gentry, may have enhanced the standing of the minor landowners like the Starkeys and the Dustons who constituted virtually the only gentry there.[151]

This analysis of Warwickshire society in 1436 shows that there were three different perceptions of status at the gentry level. The crown's remained based on service; it took cognisance of the greater royal servants only; it still made rigid distinctions between the soldiers – considered to be at the pinnacle of local society, even when they were actually minor figures compared with some of the esquires – and the mere officers. Henry V, who did take an interest in the lower ranks of the gentry, insisted on seeing all of them in terms of his military machine.[152] The nobility's understanding of the term was also based on service, in this case the service rendered to them. Lesser landowners themselves were increasingly apportioning status on the basis of a combination of service of any

151 Above, p. 19 and below, pp. 102–3; cf. Hughes 1987: p. 5.

152 Morgan 1986: p. 22. A good example of the crown's outdated definitions is in Saul 1983: p. 16.

kind and territorial position. At certain points their reckoning and the crown's were out. Knights were not always the most prominent local men; esquires did not fit neatly into the position of the middle rank, either as officials or as landowners; gentlemen barely existed at all in the eyes of the crown. The definition by service that was the closest either crown or nobility got to accepting this rank did not always match the gentlemen's own understanding of their status. If the gentlemen wanted to make a clear demarcation between themselves and those who soiled their hands with work, their royal and noble masters had yet to grasp the fact that this could be of considerable interest to anyone who wished to command the peasantry. Neither had crown or nobility yet realised that these lesser gentry were important people locally, and leadership of the minor gentry went by default to the greater ones.[153]

Since all three views of status were simultaneously in operation, it is hardly surprising that the historian should be confused; the records show that at least some contemporaries were also in a muddle. Confusion was accentuated by the fact that, while knighthood was a title of dignity, and hence, once bestowed, universally acknowledged, those of esquire and gentleman were titles of worship, often self-assumed, debatable and variable in meaning from area to area. It was even authoritatively stated at about this time that arms, the mark of gentility, could be self-assumed.[154] It would be wrong to assert that local landowners themselves were not individually clear about where they stood in local society, although one man's estimate of himself might not always coincide with the opinions of his neighbours. What is evident is that in 1436 the gentry had a shrewder grasp of their own worth and importance than either the crown or the nobility.

IV

If we now move back to 1410 (see table 2), the outlines of the pattern of 1436 are already clear, with the obvious distinction that, three years before the Statute of Additions, the term 'gentleman' has yet to come into use and is indeed barely to be found even by 1415.[155] There were ten knights, fewer than in 1436 because there had been little warfare over the previous twenty years, but the knights all came from families with knightly or military traditions – in

153 Below, ch. 9.

154 Storey 1982: p. 93; Thrupp 1948: p. 307; Morgan 1986: p. 18; Upton, *Essential Portions of Nicholas Upton's De Studio Militari*, p. 48.

155 App. 2; Storey 1982; p. 93. The only Warwickshire gentleman I have unearthed for 1413–15 is William Alstre (JUST 1/1524 m.25). As evidence for both esquires and gentlemen at this period is erratic, 1415 has been chosen as the *terminus ad quem* for both groups.

some cases both – and most of them were later to serve Henry V in France.[156] They were, as later, prepared to hold the higher offices, although their reluctance to be J.P.s was even more evident in 1410 than later, and those who eventually received exemption from office did so after actual war service under Henry V and his son. In the absence of information on incomes, and with the added problem that for some of these families we have no evidence from 1436 either, it is difficult to know whether there was a group of poorer, purely military knights. The lack of recent campaigns should mean that there were fewer of these than in 1436, but Thomas Burdet (still alive in 1436) was of only moderate means and Baldwin Straunge and Ailred Trussell may be presumed to have been of similar financial standing. It seems however that none of the three can have been knighted on campaign, since none is known to have been to war by the date of his knighthood. Territorially, the knights are little different from those of 1436.

The esquires, although very like those in the 1436 list, are smaller in number and rather more distinguished as a group. They included men whose fathers had been knights, or heirs of military families who were shortly to be knighted, mostly in Henry V's wars.[157] All except the very youngest of these must have remained esquires purely because of their lack of military experience. Another two were sons of knights who chose not to be knighted and there was one who was the grandson of a knight.[158] There were fewer esquires with a single Warwickshire manor, not because the number of esquires whose interests were peripheral to Warwickshire had gone up by 1436, but simply because the esquires of 1410 had more lands on average than those of 1436, as the table makes clear. All but two of the families of this rank in 1410 maintained their status until 1436 and over half of them held one of the greater local offices between 1390 and 1420. But before coming too firmly to the conclusion that an

[156] For the knights with military backgrounds or service, see *Dugdale*, p. 1059; Br. Lib. Cotton Roll XIII.7 (Brasebrugge); *Dugdale*, pp. 847–8 (Burdet); *Dugdale* p. 1,120 (Cokayn); *Dugdale*, pp. 504, 507 (Lucy); *Dugdale*, pp. 316–18; Br. Lib. Cotton Roll XIII.7 (Stafford: this is the father of Humphrey I (*Dugdale*, p. 316); the last unequivocal reference to *his* father, another Humphrey, dates to 1401 (*Cal. Pat. Rolls 1399–1401*, p. 417), and it is clear that Humphrey I's father was a knight by 1405–06, when he is referred to as 'the younger' and designated 'knight' (*Return: 1878*, I, p. 270). The *V.C.H.* (V, p. 151) misses out a generation, by omitting one of the Humphreys between Ralph and Humphrey I); the Straunges were perhaps a younger branch of the baronial family of Knokyn (*V.C.H. Bucks.*, IV, p. 264); Baldwin and his brothers all served as soldiers (above, n. 84; Br. Lib. Add. MS 24,704 No.36, Cotton Roll XIII.7; Bod. Lib. Dugdale MS 2, p. 277; *Gesta Henrici Quinti*, p. 167); *Dugdale*, pp. 716–18 (Trussell); *Dugdale*, p. 955 (Peche – widow). For exemptions, see above, n.89.

[157] Ardern (*Dugdale*, p. 928); Bermingham (*Dugdale*, p. 898; Br. Lib. Add. MS 24,704 No. 25, Eg. Chart. 146); Bishopestone, Doddingselles, Hastings, Mountford, Peyto, Shirley, Trussell of Bilton (for all these, n. 84, above).

[158] Richard Chetwynd (*Colls. Hist. Staffs.*, o.s., 12, p. 267); Thomas Stafford (*ibid.*, n.s., 11, p. 53); Roger Aylesbury (*Dugdale*, p. 830). Thomas Erdington was not knighted, nor it seems was his father, but he came of a family of ancient lineage (Hutchins 1861–74: III, p. 355) and his son was eventually to be a knight.

esquire was a more elevated figure in 1410 than in 1436, we should remember the automatic bias in the sources. At this time governmental records are almost the only source for evidence of status below the knights and the crown was most likely to give the title of esquire to those who best conformed to its own definitions, that is to its own household esquires, to sons of knights or aspirant knights and to some of its greater local officers.[159]

The list of untitled men has deliberately been drawn as widely as possible. It comprises untitled lawyers and administrators, anyone who was later to be titled and any other manorial lords. Not surprisingly, therefore, it constitutes both a more heterogeneous collection and a less imposing one than the esquires. Many of these men had not reached the level of esquire by 1436 and, of those who had, several were pretty marginal.[160] Few of them came from military families.[161] Three of the nine men in the group who held important local office were esquires before long, the remaining six were nearly all territorially too slight to have been given the title, most of them qualifying for office as lawyers.[162] Between 1416 and 1436 twenty-two of the untitled men of 1410, or their successors, were given the rank of gentleman. Interestingly, despite the

[159] 'Esquires of service' are Castell (crown: Roskell 1954: pp. 162–3, *sub nom.*); Catesby (lawyer and Beauchamp: Br. Lib. Eg. Roll 8769; app. 3); John Chetwynd (crown: *Cal. Pat. Rolls 1413–16*, p. 233); John and Thomas Harewell (Beauchamp: app. 3); Holt (crown: above, n.108); Hugford (Beauchamp: app. 3); Lillburne (Mowbray: app. 3); Marbroke (crown: *Cal. Pat. Rolls 1413–16*, p. 152); Onley (Bergavenny: app. 3); Seyville (crown: *Cal. Pat. Rolls 1401–05*, p. 23); William Purfrey (lawyer: K.B.27/613 List of Fines rot.4d.); Waldeve (Beauchamp: app. 3). None of the Comptons of Compton Wyniates is given a title after William in 1413–16 until Sir William, the successful servant of Henry VIII (below, pp. 240–1), except for Robert, 'gentleman' in 1467 and possibly 'esquire' in 1474, also referred to as 'venerabilis vir' in the 1450s and 1460s and Edmund, 'discretus vir' in 1489 (K.B.27/824 Coram Rege rot.69d.; S.B.T. E.R.1/61/138; *Dugdale*, p. 551).

[160] App. 2B. Those whose families were at the level of esquire or better before 1436 were Bellers, Botener, Clopton of Moor Hall, Cokesey, Cotes, Greswold, Greville, Hore of Wishaw, Malory, Metley, Middlemore, Onley of Bishops Tachbrook, Sauser (below, n. 162), Sydenhale, Waryng, Waver (Bod. Lib. Dugdale MS 13, p. 343), Whitacre (K.B.9/203/19), Woodlow (for all refs., app. 2 unless otherwise specified). Ralegh would undoubtedly be in this category had there not been a long series of minorities etc. (*Dugdale*, p. 529; *Cal. Pat. Rolls 1405–08*, p. 296; *W.F.F.*, 2643; S.B.T. D.R.37 Box 33 (deeds of 1423, 1442); *Cal. Fine Rolls 1445–52*, p. 153, *1452–61*, p. 282; *Cal. Pat. Rolls 1461–67*, p. 266; below, p. 111).

[161] Of the origins of William Clopton, untitled in 1410 but knighted soon after, I have been able to find little (*I.P.M.* 7 Hen. V/46; *Dugdale*, p. 860).

[162] Botener (Bod. Lib. Dugdale MS 13, p. 343); Greville (*Cal. Pat. Rolls 1416–22*, p. 298); Sauser (*Cat. Anc. Deeds*, vi, C6330). The major officers who were not esquires by 1436 or died before then without attaining this rank were Brome, Dalby, Gower, Metley (but his son Nicholas was an esquire in 1436), Thomas Purfrey (who must have been considered at least of 'gentleman' status from the offices he held), and Weston. All of these were probably lawyers (app. 2) and their lack of any sort of title in 1410 may reflect the uncertainty already observed over what to call lawyers. Sauser, as a non-manorial noble servant, should also belong to this group, and the use of 'esquire' in his case (twice only as far as is known) can only have been in an administrative sense: above pp. 69–70.

bias of the evidence towards 'official' gentlemen, particularly lawyers, only six of these soon-to-be gentlemen belong to this category, nearly all the rest being gentlemen solely by virtue of manorial lordship.[163] If the evidence for status in 1410 is heavily biased in favour of the crown's hierarchy of service, the bias itself probably reflects reality, in that esquires did not yet bother to identify themselves on deeds and almost no one felt the need to find a term for the lesser landowners, even for those who were later to be the minor esquires, unless that is they were also servants of the nobility. In this case, as we have seen, they might be given a title by their masters. However, the rapid move to identify all sorts of lesser landowners after the legislation of 1413 in terms that were universally acceptable, if still lacking consistency, shows that, if the statute was the catalyst, the will to dignify them was already there. If the statistical profile of the 'others' of 1410 is compared with that of the gentlemen of 1436, it is obvious that, allowing for the presence in the 1410 list of families that were clearly of escurial rank in all but name, these are essentially 'proto-gentlemen'.

By 1500 (table 3) the movement towards recognition of all levels of landed status was much more complete and the crown itself was beginning to catch up with it. The most striking development is the growth in numbers of gentlemen,[164] the reflection not so much of an actual growth (although this applies in the case of the 'professional' gentlemen) as of a more general willingness to apply the term to professionals[165] and above all to minor landowners. At the other end, the same convergence of tenurial and social status is evident with the knights. By 1450 the number of knights had sunk to twelve, the decline being due to the continuing identification of knighthood and military service at a time when enthusiasm for the war was diminishing and campaigning in France becoming a specialist activity for a smaller number of near-professionals.[166] In

[163] Ardern of Newbold (K.B.27/631 Coram Rege rot.35); Astley (*Cal. Pat. Rolls 1422–29*, p. 499); Brome (*Cal. Fine Rolls 1422–30*, p. 269); Dalby (app. 2); Derset (K.B.27/659 Coram Rege rot.46); Eton (*Cal. Pat. Rolls 1422–29*, p. 423); Fulwode (K.B.27/632 Coram Rege rot.47); Gower (*Cal. Close Rolls 1413–19*, p. 507); Greswold (K.B.27/626 Coram Rege rot. 57; later esq.: above, n.160); Hayton (K.B.27/672 Coram Rege rot. 38d.); Hore of Elmdon (K.B.27/632 Coram Rege rot.47); Hore of Solihull (K.B.27/626 Coram Rege rot. 57); Hore of Stoneythorpe (*Cat. Anc. Deeds*, II, C1834; *V.C.H.*, VI, p. 128); Lecroft (K.B.27/695 Coram Rege rot.19); Malory of Tachbrook (Nichols 1795–1811, III, i, p. 498); Sauser (*Cal. Close Rolls 1413–19*, p. 500; also esq.: above, n.162); Sydenhale (varies between 'gentleman' and 'esquire': above, n. 105); Ward (K.B.27/626 Coram Rege rot.57); Waryng (as Sydenhale); Willenhale (K.B.27/661 List of Fines); Wyncote (his ?son, Walter) (*Dugdale*, p. 712); atte Wode (K.B.27/699 Coram Rege rot.42d.). Also Brett (probably), Clopton of Clopton, Duston, Porter of Upper Ettington, Verney and Rous by *c*. 1436 (below, app. 1). The only known professionals, in this group of later gentlemen who were untitled in 1410, are Brome, Dalby, Eton, Gower, Greswold and Sauser. For these, see app. 2 and app. 3, *sub* Beauchamp of Warwick.

[164] To allow for gaps in the evidence, 'gentlemen' designated between 1501 and 1503 and those who have left no evidence after 1497 have been included.

[165] Storey 1982: pp. 97–109; Ives 1983a: pp. 1–2.

[166] For the military service of the knights of 1450, below, n.169 and *Dep. Keep.'s Rep.*, 48, p. 346 (Hastings) and Carpenter 1980b: p. 323 (Malory).

Table 2 Landed society in 1410*

(i) Territorial wealth by status group

	Kts.	Esqs.	Others
Category A			
Number	0	1	17
% of total	0.0	2.4	27.4
Category B			
Number	0	17	28
% of total	0.0	40.5	45.2
Category C			
Number	5	19	17
% of total	50.0	45.2	27.4
Category D			
Number	5	5	0
% of total	50.0	12.0	0.0

(ii) Distribution of lands by status group

	Kts.	Esqs.	Others
Category E			
Number	1	13	38
% of total	10.0	31.0	61.3
Category F			
Number	2	10	14
% of total	20.0	23.8	22.6
Category G			
Number	2	7	5
% of total	20.0	16.7	8.1
Category H			
Number	1	7	4
% of total	10.0	16.7	6.5
Category I			
Number	4	5	1
% of total	40.0	11.9	1.6

* For key, see table 1, above, p. 58.

Table 3 Landed society in 1500*

(i) Territorial wealth by status group

	Kts.	Esqs.	Gents.
Category A			
Number	0	12	46
% of total	0.0	19.0	55.4
Category B			
Number	4	19	31
% of total	40.0	30.2	37.3
Category C			
Number	4	26	5
% of total	40.0	41.3	6.0
Category D			
Number	2	6	1
% of total	20.0	9.5	1.2

(ii) Distribution of lands by status group

	Kts.	Esqs.	Gents.
Category E			
Number	0	14	59
% of total	0.0	22.2	71.1
Category F			
Number	0	18	17
% of total	0.0	28.6	20.5
Category G			
Number	1	9	6
% of total	10.0	14.3	7.2
Category H			
Number	9	15	0
% of total	90.0	23.8	0.0
Category I			
Number	0	7	1
% of total	0.0	11.1	1.2

* For key, see table 1, above, p. 58.

the middle years of the century representatives of several knightly families failed to receive the accolade. In some instances, as in the cases of Robert Ardern and John Cockayn III, there are perhaps special reasons, but whatever the particular circumstances, there can be no doubt that in both Warwickshire and Derbyshire at this time men whose families had traditionally filled this role, in many cases for generations, were failing to do so.[167] Only Leonard Hastings and Thomas Malory, of the new knights, had seen any active service.

Neither were they being replaced by other families, since service in war remained almost the only route to knighthood. Only Thomas Erdington II, William Bermingham II and William Catesby I came to the title by the new means of non-military service in the king's household. Catesby's elevation may be significant, as, unlike the other two, he was of a family whose traditions were legal rather than military. But he is a lone example, and we shall see shortly that it may represent less a change of attitude on the part of the crown than the extension of an existing policy related to the Duchy of Lancaster.[168] From the king's point of view the decline in the number of knights was potentially a disaster; leading local landowners who did not bother with the accolade were likely not to bother with local office either, leaving it to devolve to an even greater extent than before to less well qualified incumbents. The king could find himself with an official class consisting entirely of gentry of the second or even third rank, one of the principal dangers the crown had been trying to avert ever since the problems with knighthood began. He needed to persuade both himself and his leading gentry that office was in itself not an incidental burden of knighthood but a source of honour and power, worthy of the attentions of a knight and of the dignity of knighthood. If the actual number of knights in 1450 was in fact marginally greater than in 1410, only six of them had been knighted since 1436 and it is clear that the crown's definitions and its needs were now badly out of phase.[169] Even had there suddenly been a war, producing numbers of belted knights, there was no guarantee that these would have come from the tenurially powerful local families whose service in the shires was so badly needed, for increasingly the new members of the local elite would be from families lacking any sort of military traditions.

By 1470 this trend was beginning to be reversed. Two related developments were responsible, the one local, the other governmental. Locally, from the 1460s local office begins to be seen as consonant with the very highest social and tenurial status. No longer a burdensome by-product of knighthood or a reason

[167] Wright 1983: p. 9; below, pp. 115–16, 432–3, 459.

[168] *Cal. Pat. Rolls 1436–41*, p. 299, *1441–46*, pp. 205, 91; *Dugdale*, pp. 788–9,901. For their knighthoods, below, n.169. For knights and the Duchy of Lancaster, below, pp. 88–9.

[169] These were William Bermingham II (K.B.27/747 Coram Rege rot.33); William Catesby I (Shaw 1906: 1, p. 132); Thomas Erdington II (*Colls. Hist. Staffs.*, o.s., 12, p. 314); Leonard Hastings (*H.M.C. Hastings*, 1, pp. 20–1); Thomas Malory (*Colls. Hist. Staffs.*, o.s., 12, p. 316); Baldwin Mountford (B.R.L. 427014). Also Doddingselles, William Mountford, Neville, Peyto, Trussell and Stafford, for whom see app. 2. For military service of these, see above, nn. 84, 166.

for avoiding it, it became an essential attribute of local leadership. This is particularly marked with the commission of the peace, which grew steadily larger and for the first time was regularly led by a group of knights. Nor was this a departure confined to Warwickshire, for it has been observed, both in the late fifteenth century and in the early years of the following century, in Derbyshire and elsewhere.[170] The reason for this change of attitude lay partly in the continued growth in the importance of the office of J.P., the additional powers given in 1461 being perhaps the immediate catalyst, and partly in changes in local power structures that gave the leading gentry an enhanced sense of their local worth. These will be discussed at length in the concluding chapters of this study.[171] For these same reasons, the leading members of local society were increasingly willing to be knighted. Changes at the governmental end provided the knights from whom officers could be drawn. As the king began to grasp the importance to himself of the office-holding side of knighthood, he reintroduced the mass knighting ceremonies which had earlier been designed to provide a pool of fighting kings.[172] Following on from earlier practices, such service, like the military service of earlier decades, might eventually be rewarded with an exemption from further office, although this would not normally happen until old age.[173] Even if some of the knights made by the king, such as Henry Ferrers, Ralph Shirley III and Henry Willoughby, owed their titles immediately to their military prowess, they were clearly intended to continue to earn them as part of the king's official class. Others, like Richard Harecourt, William Trussell II of Bilton, Richard Bingham and Thomas Littleton, were very much the new type of knight, who had served the king as household men or justices.[174]

170 Wright 1983: pp. 104–5, 108–9; Arnold 1984; Hassell Smith 1974: p. 61; Clark 1977: pp. 17–18; Cooper 1967: p. 423; Zell 1977: pp. 125–6; Virgoe 1981, p. 79. For the Warwickshire commissions, *Cal. Pat. Rolls 1461–67*, p. 574, *1467–77*, p. 634, *1476–85*, p. 576, *1485–94*, pp. 503–4, *1494–1509*, p. 663.

171 *Proceedings before the J.P.s*, pp. lv–lvi; below, chs. 8, 13–16.

172 Nicolas 1842: III, pp. viii–xii; Winkler 1943: ch. 4, esp. p. 78, and p. 103. Although Winkler points out that there were a larger number of knighting ceremonies under Henry VI, her account and Nicolas' lists indicate clearly that the number of non-noble knights so created was falling rapidly; Wright 1983: pp. 10–11. Note that John Paston I is urged to take on the honour offered by Edward IV in 1461, the time when knighthood is beginning its recovery, because it will please his friends and discomfort his enemies, although he needs first to be reassured that Edward is secure on the throne (*Paston Letters*, II, pp. 235–6).

173 E.g. William Lucy K.B., 1487, frequent officer, exemption 1491, d. 1492 (Nicolas 1842: III, p. x; *Cal. Pat. Rolls 1485–94*, p. 342; *I.P.M. Hen. VII*, I, 835).

174 The knights of 1470 were Bermingham, Catesby, Erdington, Malory (above, n. 169); Richard Bingham, justice (*Cal. Pat. Rolls 1441–46*, p. 343; Nicolas 1842: III, p. viii); Henry Everingham, former royal servant, possibly knighted during Readeption (*Cal. Pat. Rolls 1446–52*, p. 43; *Cal. Close Rolls 1468–76*, p. 256); Henry Ferrers, royal servant, knighted at Tewkesbury (*Cal. Pat. Rolls 1461–67*, p. 78; *Wedgwood: Biographies*, p. 318); Thomas Ferrers, K. B. at creation of duke of York, but a knight from 1 Edward IV (*Dugdale*, p. 1,136); John Greville II (*Dugdale*, p. 707); Richard Harecourt, king's servant, knighted by king 1461 (C.81/1378/31; Nicolas 1842: III, p.

The result of all this was that service, landed wealth and status began once again to come into line at the top of provincial society, while knighthood came to be seen as an expression of local leadership in all its forms, no longer confined to the military sphere, a state of affairs which was to endure throughout the next century and beyond, except in the case of religious disqualification. In 1600 Thomas Wilson could write that knights were:

> cheefe men in their Countryes both for livinge and reputacions, though many of them knowe scarsly that Knighthood meanes, but are made Knights for the Creditt of their Contry and to induce them to live in a more honorable manner, both for their own Creditt and the service of their Prince and Country, then otherwise perhaps they wold doe ...[175]

The only well-endowed families which consistently failed to produce knights either in the late fifteenth century or in the following one were those which, like the Berminghams and the Brasebrugges, had abandoned all pretensions to local ascendancy. Conversely, poorer knights disappear; neither the Doddingselles nor the Trussells of Billesley were to produce a knightly member after the early fifteenth century.[176]

The changes overtaking knighthood meant that from the later fifteenth century the numbers of knights in England began to grow again, as they would have to if they were to furnish a pool of local officials. Already in 1470 their numbers had almost recovered to the level of 1436,[177] a significant fact if we bear in mind that the knights of 1436 had been a predominantly military caste and the lack of military opportunities between the two dates. The fact that there were so few knights in 1500 must be attributed to chance and to the policies of Henry VII, which between them had greatly reduced the number of leading

viii); William Harecourt (*Cal. Pat. Rolls 1467–77*, p. 12); Simon Mountford (*Register of Knowle*, p. 41); William Norreys, royal servant, knighted before battle of Northampton (*Wedgwood: Biographies*, p. 640); Edward Ralegh, a knight immediately after coming into his lands (*Cal. Pat. Rolls 1461–67*, p. 266; S.B.T. D.R.37 Box 34 (deed of 1464)); William Trussell of Bilton II, royal servant (*P.R.O. Lists and Indexes*, Suppl. Ser., IX, ii, p. 422; *Colls. Hist. Staffs.*, n.s., 4, p. 174); Richard Verney (B.R.L. Wingfield Digby MS A586); Henry Waver, Lord Mayor of London, knighted at Elizabeth Woodville's coronation (Nicolas 1842: III, p. viii). Ralph Shirley III and Henry Willoughby were knighted later, at the battle of Stoke, 1487 (Leland, *Collectanea*, IV, pp. 214–5) and Thomas Littleton at the Prince of Wales' knighting in 1475 (Nicolas 1842: III, p. ix), having been appointed justice in 1466 (*Cal. Pat. Rolls 1461–67*, p. 515). Wright, quoting Ives, observes that lawyers were increasingly likely to be knighted in this period (1983, p. 10).

175 Wilson, *State of England*, p. 23.

176 *Dugdale*, pp. 902, 1,059; above, n. 85 for the Trussells and Doddingselles. The latter family were burdened with a dowager for much of the later part of the century (Carpenter 1986b: p. 42 and below, p. 215), but their subsequent modest history indicates that the family's failure to produce any more knights had more to do with changes in the nature of knighthood. Some eminent men were still paying to avoid knighthood: e.g. John Ormond, probably brother of the earl of that name, who paid £12 10s in 1501 not to be made K.B. at the marriage of Prince Arthur (*Cat. Anc. Deeds*, VI, C6402).

177 See n.174, above.

gentry, the low point falling, fortuitously, more or less in that year.[178] Nevertheless the composition of the class in 1500 is further evidence of an unmistakable alteration in the status of the knight, in which administrative responsibility, territorial power and local standing had replaced military experience as the primary qualification, in the eyes of both government and locality.

An interesting gloss on the history of knighthood in the fifteenth century, as reconstructed here, comes from Frances Winkler's work on the king's knights under the Lancastrians. The developments revealed in her thesis correspond tellingly with those suggested here for knights in general. The biographies she gives show that in the earlier part of the century the knights made by the king performed a mixture of military and official functions, the official ones consisting largely of quasi-military duties, whether local, like those of the shrievalty, national or ambassadorial. As the war lost its central place in the life of the landed elite under Henry VI, these knights became an increasingly civilian body, serving the crown in an ever more civilian capacity, but, to emphasise the king's reluctance to recognise the new facts of life, their numbers dwindled.

There is however a striking exception to this pattern, the knights of the Duchy of Lancaster, who, right from the start of Henry IV's reign, include men from families with little or no military tradition and are evidently being expected to serve the Duchy in a non-military capacity, even if some of them were on occasion to be caught up in the king's wars.[179] Hugh Willoughby could well belong in this category. He was a non-military knight from the early part of the century, from a Duchy family, who served consistently as a J.P. in a period when it was unusual for a knight to do so.[180] With regard to the Duchy, kings had a clear conception of the need to dignify the greatest servants on their own estates, but it did not extend to grasping the fact that it was not just the gentry of the Duchy of Lancaster but of the whole of England who were rendering service of a non-military kind. When William Catesby was knighted by the king

[178] By chance, numbers of prominent families were in disgrace or had just lost the head of the family in that year e.g. Mountford of Coleshill (*Dugdale*, p. 1,012); Bermingham (*I.P.M. Hen. VII*, II, 528); Catesby (*Dugdale*, p. 789); Verney (*I.P.M. Hen. VII*, I, 656), while several men were knighted soon after 1500 e.g. Belknap, kt. by 1516 (PROB 11/16 fo. 122v.); Thomas Lucy, a minor 1500 (lands held by Hungerford), kt. by 1514 (*Cat. Anc. Deeds*, V, A12878); Throgmorton, K.B. 1501 (Nicolas 1842: III, p. xi); Aston, kt. by 1502 (K.B.27/962 Coram Rege rot.48). The other cause of the temporary lack of knights was Henry VII's policy of interpolating outsiders, mostly royal servants, into the county through confiscation, marriage and wardship (below, pp. 103–5, 131–2). Some of these, like Sir John Risley, had quite substantial Warwickshire lands (some of the Catesby properties in this case: *Cal. Pat. Rolls 1485–94*, pp. 209–10) but showed so little interest in the county that, even on the generous definitions used here, they cannot be counted as 'natives'.

[179] Winkler 1943: *passim. The Order of Chivalry* sees ambassadorial duties as an intrinsic part of the knightly occupation (p. 95).

[180] Above, p. 61. He also conforms to the pattern in receiving an exemption from office shortly before his death (above, n.91; Cameron 1970: p. 10; Payling 1987b: ch. 2).

in 1452, it was perhaps in recognition of his connection with the Duchy, since he was its tenant on two of his main estates. But Catesby's service was in the king's household rather than to the Duchy. If his knighthood may therefore indicate the first flickers of a policy of extending knighthood for civilian service beyond the boundaries of the royal estates, the knighting ceremonies of Henry VI's successors show that this was what was shortly to become the norm.[181]

A further result of the ending of the previous confusion over status between government and governed was the greater definition at each level of the gentry hierarchy. The esquires are a much more homogeneous group by 1500. While there are fewer outstandingly wealthy members of this class, and several of these or their descendants were to become knights before long,[182] the number of insignificant esquires has also dwindled and would be considerably lower were it not for the inclusion of six rather poorly endowed heirs and cadet branches of the Brasebrugge and Mountford families. Most esquires held the major local offices; those who did not tended to be political outcasts, like George Catesby, son of Richard III's councillor, or Thomas Mountford, son of Sir Simon, executed for treason in 1495, or royal servants, like William Cope, who were too much occupied with the king's business to be active in the shires, or the ones, like Richard Brasebrugge, who were obstinately fending off administrative burdens.[183] In sum, they begin to look very similar to esquires as defined early in the seventeenth century: the male heirs or descendants of knights and peers, the heads of ancient families who held this title by prescriptive right, and the local officers. Like their descendants of the sixteenth and seventeenth centuries, they would normally expect to hold local office, unless 'put by' for being politically unsound, which, after the Reformation, tended to mean being doctrinally unsound.[184]

Consequently, by 1500 the equivalent of the minor esquires of 1436 are more usually ranked as gentlemen, even if some, usually those from the older families, like Richard Cotes, William Holt and Richard Mountford of Church Bickenhill, are sometimes accorded the higher title.[185] The vast majority of gentlemen now belong in the one- or no-manor groups, the only real anomaly being Richard Cotes, who, as one of the co-heirs to the eight Hugford manors, ought to have been an esquire, but was presumably rated lower because of his financial difficulties and insignificant local career. In part this was due to the fact that 'gentleman', not esquire, was now universally understood to be the

181 For overlordship of the Catesby lands, see their accounts in S.C.6 and C.244/19/133.

182 Above, n.178 and for the Grevilles and Cokayns, *Dugdale*, pp. 706, 1,120.

183 For Catesby and Mountford, see above, n. 178; for Cope, *Cal. Pat. Rolls 1494–1509*, p. 133; for Brasebrugge, above, n. 176.

184 Wagner 1956: p. 5; Cliffe 1969: pp. 244–50; Hassell Smith 1974: p. 53; Zell 1977: p. 128. In keeping with this growing uniformity, by the seventeenth century 'esquire' had become much more of an inherited title, much less one to be assumed at will (Sayer 1979: p. 4).

185 E.g. K.B.9/408/3 (Cotes and Mountford); K.B.27/962 Coram Rege rot.8 (Holt).

proper title for lawyers and minor administrators, but it was also the result of recognition that it was the proper title for minor manorial lords as well. Once this was generally accepted, there was no longer any need for confused clerks, when they considered such men worthy of some sort of title, to call them esquires in the hope that this would do. If the gentlemen's place in the hierarchy of gentility was being given recognition, so was their role in the hierarchy of local office. Over the course of the century they had also gained acceptance of the right to bear arms. The full extent of this change can be appreciated from Selden's bemused comment on the witnesses in the Hastings–Grey dispute of Henry IV's reign who said that they were gentlemen but had no arms: 'the like whereof or any thing of that nature I have not elsewhere observed.'[186]

The move to define status by the linked criteria of peacetime office and service and tenurial position was recognised in a judicial decision of the late fifteenth century which, in interpreting the Statute of Additions, stated that the styles of esquire or gentleman could be earned by tenure of office.[187] It accounts to a large extent for the growth in the number of Warwickshire gentry families during the century: from 112 in 1410, to 132 in 1436 and 155 in 1500. Status continued to be defined in these terms in the following century, a definition accentuated by the enormous growth in administration occasioned by social, economic and religious change. This, and the availability of vast new areas of land after the Dissolutions, was then to produce a yet more spectacular rise in the numbers of gentry, along with a heightened association of status and public office, but the essential attributes are there by 1500.[188] All social hierarchies are blurred at the edges of status groups and classes,[189] but, after a long period of muddle, some measure of agreement on status had been reached by the later fifteenth century. This was above all because both government and locality were agreed that status and local office were closely linked and that even the least possessor of manorial lordship was by definition a cog in the royal administration. No social hierarchy or system of status designation is ever static and it is by no means suggested that this was how things were to remain over

[186] Wagner 1972: p. 122, 1956, pp. 78–80; Selden, *Titles of Honour*, p. 723. For Cotes' problems, see below, pp. 133–4.

[187] Cooper 1983a: p. 49. Unfortunately, no reference is given for this.

[188] E.g. Hassell Smith 1974: p. 53; Cliffe 1969: pp. 5–6; Zell 1977: pp. 133–6; Fletcher 1975: p. 128; Clarke 1977: pp. 125–32; Cornwall 1964–5; Laslett 1971: pp. 36–7; Smith, R. B. 1970: p. 66; Stone 1967: p. 38 (the base line of 1433 used here is presumably meant to be 1434 or 1436), 1966: pp. 23–5; Cooper 1967, and, above all, Hughes 1987: p. 27 (288 gentry families in Warwickshire in 1640: definitions much as those used here). Although Cooper's sensitivity to the many similarities between medieval and early-modern England is most welcome, I believe that the case he makes for continuity in ideas of gentility in 1983a, cannot be entirely sustained in view of the change in ideas of service suggested here.

[189] For later confusion, see e.g. Smith, R. B. 1970: pp. 65–6; Hughes 1987: p. 27.

the next centuries, only that by the later part of the fifteenth century a period of peculiar confusion over title and status was drawing to a close.[190]

As earlier remarks have indicated, some of these developments are reflected in the tables of wealth, land distribution and status (figure 4 and tables 1–3), although it cannot be stressed too strongly that these figures are highly fallible, particularly as regards distribution of lands in other counties, and that the small numbers involved, combined with the quantity of queries, make them statistically of rather dubious value. At least the figures for 1436 show that there was a rough equation of wealth with status, number of Warwickshire manors (although this must of course largely break down for the knights whose major land holdings were elsewhere) and, at all levels, with geographical distribution of lands. The anomalous figures for the gentlemen are due to the fact that the wealth of those at the bottom of both categories is inflated by the merchants. It would however be unwise to push the conclusions drawn from these figures any harder. Indeed, regarded as a whole, they tend to show a remarkable continuity in the characteristics of each group, and it is only by examining the career patterns and local activities of the families individually that changes in perceptions of status can be seen.

The crown's rather fumbling progress towards a better understanding of these developments can be seen to some extent in the lists produced periodically by its servants, starting with the rolls of arms of the early fourteenth century. Such lists remain purely military into the fifteenth century.[191] The 1434 oath-lists are an early attempt at a conspectus of local society with a view to recording local rather than military responsibility and, as we have seen, the Warwickshire evidence suggests they are far from satisfactory. During the course of the century there were efforts to discover the names of local notables under various headings. Lists of people with incomes of £10 or more were produced in the 1470s, for example. Richard III kept lists of prominent figures county by county, and Edward IV was said to retain in his memory detailed knowledge of very minor landowners.[192] Near the end of the century Henry VII's King's Boke was drawn up. This was primarily a means to discover potential knights for the purposes of fiscal distraints but it is far more comprehensive and reaches down to a much lower social and tenurial level than earlier distraints. The only fourteenth-century list which is comparably full is

[190] To indicate how concepts of rank and status keep changing: in the late eighteenth and early nineteenth centuries, using knighthood as a reward for service to the crown was a *novelty* (Beckett 1986: p. 115).

[191] Works cited above, nn.22, 49. The lists for the fifteenth century are discussed in Morgan 1986: pp. 18–19, 22. See also Saul 1981: pp. 30–4; Denholm-Young 1969a: pp. 89–120; S.B.T. D.R.503 fo.60v.

[192] Thrupp 1948: p. 237; Morgan 1986, p. 18; Horrox and Hammond eds., *Br. Lib. Harleian Manuscript 433*, III, pp. 234–39, and I, p. xxxv for the suggestion that kings probably routinely had such lists; 'Historia Croylandensis', p. 564. Note also William Worcestre's adaptation of an earlier list of Norfolk gentry (Virgoe 1981: p. 83, and refs., p. 87 n. 62).

that of 1344, in which the government was recording all possible sources of military service at the height of the Hundred Years War.

The fifteenth-century lists show that the crown was ever more aware of the need to record the names of its potential local servants. Fifteenth-century distraints, the last vestiges of the old military listings, on the other hand, seem to have been very selective and were undoubtedly being exploited for fiscal purposes only. The distrainees were usually allowed to escape with a fine, even in the later fifteenth century, when demand for knights was growing, and many of them were neither soldiers nor holders of the major local offices; in fact, these processes were effectively being used as an additional tax on landed incomes above the distraint level.[193] In keeping with this long-overdue move away from identification of status and military service, the Heralds became less 'registers of prowess' and registrars of military families than validators of the claims of all those families that bore arms in the heraldic sense. Since the early fifteenth century, bearing arms had been the chief qualification for gentility, but, by the end of the century, arms had lost their exclusive connection with military service. By 1580 so close had the connection of arms and land become that arms could be borne by anyone with a landed income of £10 a year or more. The final irony in this 'demilitarisation' of service and status was that the governmental absorption of the Heralds' organisation at the end of the fifteenth century meant that the crown's information on potential public servants came from the Heralds' lists.[194]

V

In summing up this survey of local status, attention should be drawn to two major themes, the one perhaps peculiar to Warwickshire and to other similarly-constituted counties, the other probably characteristic of all provincial societies at this time. To take the first, it is apparent that it was not only Warwickshire's geography that made her borders artificial but also the distribution of her greater residents' estates. Tenure of lands in another county, often in several counties, was characteristic of all the Warwickshire knights and greater esquires. The chapter on estates will show, in specific instances, how much of the income of a family with Warwickshire lands might be drawn from properties in other areas, but this phenomenon is immediately evident in the instance of, for example, the Hores of Wishaw (clear income of at least £50 but

[193] Huntington Lib. MS HM 19959 (I am most grateful to Dr. Morgan for lending me his microfilm of this manuscript); Saul 1981, p. 33. For distraint proceedings on this enquiry, see E.159/277 Recorda mm.11,11d., 12, 14, 46, 47; E.159/279 Recorda mm.4,43d., 46, 46d., 47d.; E.198/4/19–21. For earlier distraints, e.g. E.198/4/16; E.159/243 Communia, Easter, Mich., Trin. These refs. were mostly taken from Wright 1983: p. 149 n. 16, and Morgan 1986: p. 31 n. 25.

[194] Keen 1984: p. 139; Thrupp 1948: pp. 306–8; Wagner 1956, 1967: chs. 1, 3, 4.

only three Warwickshire manors) or, even more striking, the Erdingtons (income of at least £190, two or three Warwickshire manors). Figure 5 reveals very clearly the extent to which such families were unavoidably involved in the affairs of other parts of England and it is a consideration which must never be forgotten.

The second issue concerns the causes and consequences of the confused and contradictory notions of status that have been chronicled here. It should be no surprise that ideas of status were bound up with notions of the body politic, since the landowners who cared about status were all, the very least of them, participants in the political community, even if only by being represented in parliament. The failure for most of the century of both crown and nobility to grasp the centrality of the part played by all landowners in local rule, which can be seen in their faulty perceptions of status among the gentry, is very telling; it suggests a lack of close familiarity with the day-to-day life of the provinces which is hardly unexpected in people with such large-scale responsibilities, but could provoke misunderstanding and estrangement in times of crisis. If, for the gentry, status was ever more closely bound up with local office and possession of lordship over men, they were unlikely to accept the idea of a middle stratum of *mediocres* that was being floated by government, churchmen, judges and others at this time, which sought to separate all non-noble landowners, or sometimes just the lesser ones, from the peerage and herd them with the merchants. It was a notion that held good in parliament, where the political nation as a whole met the king, but not one on this evidence that lesser landowners would have been prepared to accept within the structure of provincial society.[195] The historian needs to avoid this mistake, recognising that if those who sat on the bottom rung of the gentry were increasingly being accorded a title by local society it was because it meant something in local terms.

However, if we are satisfied that it was indeed lordship that came to define gentility in the fifteenth century, in terms of separating the lowest of the gentry from those below them, we are left with the problem of the gentlemen who owed their dignity primarily to their professional status, the lawyers and administrators. As Hoccleve, an exemplary victim of this state of affairs, observed, 'Seruyse, I wot wel, is non heritage'.[196] Some of them were indeed lords of acres and of men, but in most cases that was not why they were eventually universally deemed to be gentlemen. One reason for the persistent use of the title for such men was that it continued to reflect the viewpoint of those who saw local society from above, the government and the nobility; it was the professionals amongst the minor landowners who were self-evidently of most immediate importance to *them*. Nevertheless, if their neighbours were also

195 Thrupp 1948: ch. 7.
196 Hoccleve, 'Regiment of Princes', p. 31.

happy to accord them the title, it must have meant something more than this. One reason was that gentleman-professionals rendering services to their employers could be readily subsumed into a scheme, increasingly recognised by both crown and locality, in which lordship was important precisely because of its connotations of service. But both the professional servants of crown and magnates and the lawyers could also be absorbed into a hierarchy viewed solely from below, in which what really mattered was local perceptions of local worth. With the administrators this was obvious, for their standing came from their masters, and it was enhanced by the fact that they were the intermediaries between the nobility and the vills where the nobility's lordships lay.[197] With the lawyers it was an aspect of the acknowledgement that anybody who served the law must be an influential local figure. Thus lawyers were the first group of laymen, to be joined eventually by the married clergy, doctors, schoolmasters and even estate-agents, to whom deference was due simply on account of their job.[198]

The ever-closer identification of land and status that accompanied the developments we have examined meant that loss of land was not only damaging in itself but could entail loss of status, a point made forcibly in the next century, when the identification was even more complete: '[A] gentleman that sells one acre of land sells one ounce of credit, for gentility itself is but ancient riches so that if the foundation shrinks the building must needs follow after.'[199] Be it noted that our analysis suggests that even in 1436 neither crown nor nobility would have been happy with this definition, although local terminology was already moving in that direction. Loss of an acre or two would have been a particularly urgent matter to the marginal landowners of an area like the Tanworth part of the Arden, who had few acres to spare. As the levels of the hierarchy grew more clearly defined, in respect of both terminology and criteria, the penalties for failing to maintain the position owing to a particular rank would be incurred more rapidly and more publicly, especially at the bottom end of the hierarchy. After all, if gentility was becoming a signification of the right to be accorded a place amongst the rulers of the shire, falling away from that status had also to be signalled immediately; the stakes were growing higher.

Such pressures were made the more intense by the uncertainties that remained for much of the century, despite the progress towards definition. The Sumptuary Law of 1363 allows for esquires with an annual income of 200 marks, a figure whose validity is borne out by the Warwickshire evidence and by the household expenditure of £80 to £100 of John Paston, described as 'a somewhat careful, even tight-fisted squire'. And yet it was stated in 1410 that a knight could live on little more than 100 marks a year and an esquire on little

[197] Mertes 1988: pp. 68–9; I owe this last point to Dr. John Morrill.

[198] Ives 1983a: *passim*; Holmes 1982; Reader 1966.

[199] Quoted in Clark 1977: p. 123.

more than 40, and distraints continued at the £40 level, which was presumably the basis from which the slightly higher figure of 100 marks was drawn.[200] Local variation, which continued into the next century, contributed further to the confusion. In poorer regions lower incomes might be expected at each status level.[201] The presence of other greater or lesser landowners could have a significant effect on the relationship of status to landed income. This would be especially true of esquires and gentlemen, since with them rank was not bestowed once and for all, as it was with knights, but largely self-assumed. If M. E. James is right, from the later fifteenth century the bestowing of honour became much more the exclusive preserve of the crown, while the development of the College of Heralds and the crown's efforts to knight its more eminent commoners were important parts of this process, but for most of the later middle ages honour was self-bestowed; even a knight could be made by any other knight. 'A man was . . . free to judge of his own ripeness in gentility, subject only to the opinion of his neighbours'.[202] While so much rested on the impression made on neighbours, local competition for status and for the lands and connections that were its prerequisite could be fierce. There is no doubt that status and the demands it made were potentially destabilising forces in the fifteenth-century polity. How destabilising this was can only be judged in the light of the examination of social mobility which follows.

200 *Statutes of the Realm*, I, pp. 380–1; Morey 1951: pp. 82–3; Myers ed., *English Historical Documents*, IV, p. 669.

201 Wilson, *State of England*, p. 24; Wright 1983: p. 9.

202 James 1986c; Thrupp 1948: p. 307, from which the quotation is drawn; Nichols 1863: pp. 208–13, which shows that knights were made normally by 'the king or his representative' by at least the early thirteenth century; above, p. 79.

4

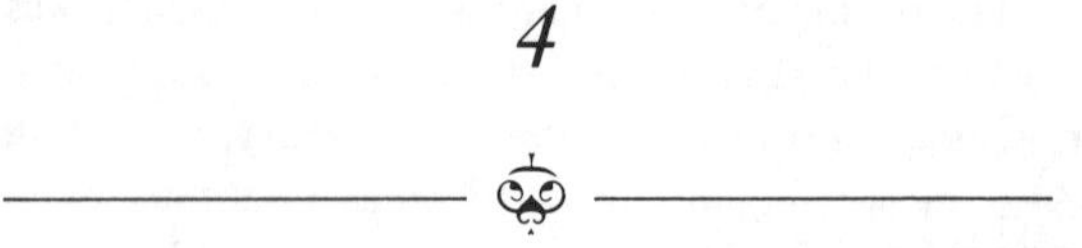

SOCIAL MOBILITY AND THE CREATION OF ESTATES

I

The openness of the county elites of England to intruders from below has recently been questioned in a work which takes as its starting-point the year 1540. This date is itself significant in indicating the still lingering belief amongst some historians of early-modern England that English society before the Tudors was more rigidly stratified than it was subsequently to become.[1] To a medievalist acquainted with the results of the Conquest, arguably persisting for a century or more, with the debate over the 'crisis of the knightly class' in the thirteenth century and with the steady stream of complaints about 'upstarts', foreign or otherwise, emitted by jaundiced contemporaries, this view has come to seem rather unreal.[2] Indeed, the orthodoxy of the moment for English society between the Black Death and the end of the fifteenth century is identical with the one the Stones set out to investigate for a later age: an 'age of ambition', a time when the ranks of landowning society were peculiarly open to wealthy newcomers, to prosperous peasants grown rich on the misfortunes of their social superiors, to merchants and lawyers.[3] Even those Tudor historians who stress the greater intensity of social mobility from the mid sixteenth century tend to find its first beginnings in this period. The issue is crucially important for a study of this kind. If the number of aspirants to gentility was growing, that could have a significant effect on competition for the adjuncts of gentility: royal office, noble protection and employment, and the marriage and land markets. If the society was unable to absorb social climbers there would be

[1] Stone and Fawtier Stone 1986: *passim*, esp. pp. 7–8; Stone, 1966; Mingay 1976: pp. 29–30, 39–50; Levine 1987: pp. 39–40; in contrast, see Cooper 1983a. For a rare general discussion of the problem for late-medieval England, see Bennett 1978.

[2] E.g. Holt 1982–5; Chibnall 1986: chs. 1–3; M. Paris, *Chronica Majora*, V, pp. 205, 229, 344–5; King 1970; Coss 1975; Carpenter, D. A. 1980; McKisack 1959: pp. 2–28, 436–8.

[3] Du Boulay 1970: chs. 3 and 4; Saul 1981: pp. 17–18, 25–7, 231–2, 241–9 (although he slightly modifies his views on p. 248); Campbell 1960: pp. 16–18; Postan 1972: pp. 174–5; Bolton 1980: p. 346; Bennett 1987a: pp. 32–7; and refs. on later social mobility cited in n.1.

intensification of local conflict. The Stones' thesis is that, while the 'openness' of aristocratic society in England has been exaggerated, the absence of legal bars to social advancement and the careful management effected by the elite itself ensured sufficient absorption of newcomers for stability and survival.[4] This chapter aims to test these propositions for the fifteenth century by examining the means by which landed and social status could be won and lost and then attempting to draw up a balance sheet of social movement for the century as a whole.

If gentility was equated with landed lordship and if the hierarchy of status to a large extent reflected the hierarchy of landowning, then the key determinant of social mobility must have been the availability of estates carrying lordship. Paradoxically for a period when lords' demesnes and peasant tenements were a glut on the market, estates of this kind were hard to find and increasingly expensive to buy. From the ending of the great assarting period in the later thirteenth century until the Dissolutions of the sixteenth there was no substantial source of supply,[5] although land of this kind became more readily available in the last two decades of the fifteenth century.[6] At the same time demand was increasing, as a growing band of lay professionals – lawyers and administrators – tried to invest their money in the estates that would give them the entrée to landed society.[7]

Whether the piecemeal acquisition of peasant land and leased demesne could be the passport to gentility is a subject we shall have to pursue in due course, but undoubtedly the only easy means to an estate was marriage. This meant that the fluidity of the county elite was heavily influenced by the accidents of birth and death. It also meant, as McFarlane pointed out, that in the pursuit of landed wealth the odds were heavily weighted in favour of the existing elite, since an heir was always an attractive proposition for an heiress.[8] Warwickshire heiresses went almost invariably to heirs of substantial estates. For example, in about 1435 Robert Ardern secured the heiress to Richard Clodesdale; William Bishopestone's two daughters and co-heiresses married respectively Thomas Palmer and William Catesby before 1444; at the end of the century, one of Nicholas Brome's daughters married Edward Ferrers, heir to Henry Ferrers of Flecknoe and Hambleton (Rutland) and great-grandson of the

4 Stone and Fawtier Stone 1986: *passim*, esp. ch. 12.

5 Bolton 1980: ch. 7; Raban 1982: pp. 177–8; McFarlane 1973: p. 56, 1981c: this last qualified by Smith 1984, although his conclusions fail to allow for the problems of later owners of some of Fastolf's purchased lands (*Paston Letters, passim*).

6 Below, pp. 131–4.

7 Above, p. 82.

8 McFarlane 1973: pp. 59–60. Sandra Raban makes the same point for the thirteenth century: 1985: pp. 260–1. On the likelihood of there being a male heir, see Rosenthal 1984. For the growing literature on 'love' and marriage, Dockray 1986, which has a full review (pp. 61–2).

last Lord Ferrers of Groby.[9] This pattern tended to hold equally good at the bottom of gentry society: John Barbour of Bishops Itchington, for instance, was able to marry one of his daughters and co-heirs to William Shukburgh, a much grander local figure, some time before 1432; in about 1492 the heiress of William Lecroft II married Henry Lisle's eldest son, John, another instance of an heiress marrying above her station.[10] As these examples show, heirs themselves had little difficulty in locating marriageable heiresses. In the more prominent families, even the younger sons, such as Henry, founder of the Ferrers of Hambleton, younger son of Thomas I, were sometimes able to marry property, their proximity to relative greatness making up for their lack of acres.[11] This was highly desirable from the point of view of their fathers and elder brothers, as it set them up without impoverishing the family estate, but again it helped cut out the striving newcomer.

Heiress-hunting, however, was not the easiest of occupations, as it might have to be done far from home. During the period between the end of the fourteenth century and the early sixteenth century only thirty-four Warwickshire estates of reasonable size came to a female heir and of these only six were really substantial and not subject to attempts to dismember them on the part of the present incumbent: Bishopestone, Brome of Baddesley Clinton, Burdet, Clopton of Moor Hall, Clodesdale and Hugford of Emscote. The habit amongst owners without sons of selling off their lands during their lifetime, as happened, for instance, with the Metley estates, had helped limit the selection.[12] Several that might have come to heiresses were settled in tail male, or at least allegedly so, or remaindered on the main line of the family, and passed in toto or in part to a male collateral, sometimes after damaging disputes. These included one of

9 *Dugdale*, p. 928; C.139/153/21/4; S.B.T. D.R.3/286. The other Brome daughter, however, married a newcomer, Thomas Marrowe, a London lawyer (S.B.T. D.R. 3/275–6; Ives 1983a: p. 468). Cf. Nottinghamshire: Payling 1987b; pp. 124–5.

10 S.B.T. E.R.1/61/409–11; Br. Lib. Add. MS 28,564 fo. 24; B.R.L. Wingfield Digby MS A642,643.

11 *Wedgwood: Biographies*, p. 318; and below, p. 102. On younger sons' success with heiresses, see also Payling 1987b: pp. 125–6.

12 Several of these estates were already in effect taken by the start of the period, through earlier marriages. The estates were: Allesley, Bagot, Beaufitz, de Bereford, Bishopestone (above, n.9), Botener and Everingham, Brome of Baddesley Clinton (above, n.9), Burdet (below, p. 251 n.26), Burdet of Huncote, Castell, Clodesdale (above, n.9), Clopton of Moor Hall, Cokesey, but his sister and heiress had married long before he died (Derbys.R.O. S.L. Croxall/T73), Fillongley, Freville, Hardwick, Hastang, Herthill of Pooley, Lecroft (above, n.10), Malory of Newbold Revel, Marbroke, Metley of Wolston and Hugford of Emscote, Mountford of Lapworth, Neville, Onley of Birdingbury, Spine, Sydenhale, Waldeve of Alspath, Waldeve, Whitacre and Hore of Elmdon, Woodlow, but already sold to Metley and Brome (*V.C.H.*, VI, p. 276; *Dugdale*, p. 469). For references for all these except Woodlow, see below, pp. 250–1 nn.25, 26; also n.25 for some smaller estates that came to heiresses. For the Metley lands, see below, n.33. On the tendency for landowners without direct heirs or with heiresses to break up the estate, see below, p. 224 and McFarlane 1973: pp. 55–6.

the greatest gentry agglomerations of the century, the Cokesey/Greville estate, of which the Greville part was held in tail male, while the Cokesey segment was divided among the heirs general, a group of Cokesey cousins.[13] Even some Warwickshire heirs were forced to seek heiresses outside the county, a situation replicated in reverse within the county, where we find heiresses marrying heirs from further afield; it was the heiresses' market, all they had to do was wait for the best offer, wherever it came from. Edmund Cokayn of Derbyshire, who married the heiress of Herthill of Pooley early in the century, was one such newcomer to the county by marriage. Others were the three husbands found in about 1417 for the heiresses to the large Freville estate, Roger Aston of Staffordshire, Thomas Ferrers I, younger son of Lord Ferrers of Groby, and Hugh Willoughby of Nottinghamshire. Ralph Neville, younger son of the earl of Westmorland, arrived at about the same time by marriage to the co-heiress to Ferrers of Wemme, and, at the end of the century, Neville's own granddaughter, the heiress to his son, married William Gascoigne of Yorkshire.[14] In every case, it had proved possible to attract an exceedingly well-qualified partner, sometimes from a long way away.

Such marriages beyond the county boundaries tended, however, to be confined to the higher reaches of local society. Amongst the lesser esquires and gentlemen, even heirs and heiresses married locally, sometimes positively parochially. This was literally the case with the marriage of the daughter and heiress of John Waldeve of Alspath to John Boteller also of Alspath, and figuratively so for the Lecroft–Lisle match already mentioned.[15] That the greater figures of the county should have had a broader choice of marriage partners is only to be expected, for they lived their lives on a broader canvas. Many of them had estates in other counties and it was often from these counties that their spouses were drawn. This is true for example of the Cokayns, whose main interests were in Derbyshire, and of the Shirleys, another Derbyshire family, which also had substantial properties in Leicestershire, and it holds good of several other families of this stature.[16] Equally, families of this kind would be more likely to attend the royal court, to be elected to parliament, to

[13] *Cal. Pat. Rolls 1494–1509*, p. 192. Other entailed lands included those of Harewell of Shottery and Bidford (*V.C.H.*, III, pp. 54, 260), Mountford of Monkspath (*W.F.F.*, 2648; C.1/164/52) and, allegedly, Aylesbury (*V.C.H.*, III, p. 199), Brett (*V.C.H.*, IV, pp. 6–7; C.1/344/12–16, /269/19–21) and Hugford of Emscote (K.B.9/378/43); also below, p. 249 n.20, p. 250 n.23. The question of growth in the practice of tail male at the end of the century will be discussed below, pp. 250–2.

[14] *Dugdale*, pp. 1,120, 1,135; Nott. Univ. Lib. Middleton MS Mi M 214; *Dugdale*, pp. 855–6.

[15] *Dugdale*, p. 948; JUST 1/1547 m.6d. For Lecroft and Lisle, see above, n.10.

[16] *Dugdale*, pp. 1,120, 620–2; Wright 1983: p. 44; see above, pp. 61–5. Also e.g. Nicholas Burdet, wife from Worcestershire (*Dugdale*, pp. 847–8), Philip Chetwynd, wife from Staffordshire (*Dugdale*, p. 1,101), William Catesby II, wife from Northamptonshire (*Wedgwood: Biographies*, p. 164), John Ferrers, wife from Staffordshire (*Wedgwood: Biographies* p. 319). See Carpenter, M. C. 1976: App. IIC for location of properties outside Warwickshire. Cf. Nottinghamshire: Payling 1987b: pp. 130–3.

use the Westminster law courts and to be in London on various kinds of business. In any of these ways they might meet a suitable family from another part of England with which to form a marriage alliance, or, if they were lucky, one with an heiress to dispose of.[17]

One way in which a family with widespread connections might go about the business of match-making is nicely illustrated by the story of Joan, daughter of William Muston of Cavell, Yorkshire. She was sent to stay with her uncle, Thomas Muston of Hunscote, Warwickshire, at least one reason for the visit being the hope that she would find a suitable husband; Thomas later complained that he might have had better offers from Warwickshire families than the one made by her eventual husband, Robert Marler, 'considering her good virtuous rewell and disposicion'.[18] If this has a distinct ring of Jane Austen about it, that is not surprising; 'love' may have loomed larger in negotiations by the time of *Pride and Prejudice*, but it is not likely that the process had changed much otherwise. Some Warwickshire marriages may well have come about through just the sort of informal contact that had brought Joan Muston to Warwickshire. Humphrey Stafford II and John Peyto, for example, were both married to members of the royal household, the former to the co-heiress of Sir John Fray, chief baron of the exchequer, the latter to the daughter of Robert Manfeld, esquire of the body. In neither case would contact have been readily made through their lands, and it seems reasonable to assume that the meetings had taken place within the royal entourage. This is particularly likely in Peyto's case, as at the time of the match (1453/4) his father, William, was himself moving in court circles because of his association with the duke of Somerset. Sometimes a marriage made further afield could itself be the basis of a subsequent one. Richard Archer of Tanworth, for instance, having married the widow of Thomas Lucy of Charlecote, a Shropshire heiress, found a widow from the same county to be his second wife after the first one's demise.[19] Often we can only guess at the web of family and tenurial connections through which marriages were arranged: only chance survivals like Thomas Muston's complaint to chancery give us a rare insight into the lives of the human beings behind the marriage indenture. Another instance is a letter of 1497 from Thomas, earl of Ormond, recommending the widowed William Littleton to Ormond's son-in-law as a match for the son-in-law's daughter. Ormond's knowledge of Littleton's availability and circumstances, on which he has evidently informed himself very fully, comes, as he explains, from the fact that he and Littleton have adjoining lands in Worcestershire. Then there is the story of the stingy bachelor, revealed to us, like the Muston case, through a

[17] For an example of a connection made through the law leading to marriage, see the alliances of Catesby and Palmer to the Bishopestone heiresses (above, n.9; Ives 1983a: pp. 383–4).

[18] C.1/66/402. Cf. similarly, Hanham 1985: pp. 267–8.

[19] *Wedgwood: Biographies*, pp. 792, 569–70; *Dugdale*, p. 477; *Dep. Keep.'s Rep.*, 48, pp. 390, 396; *Dugdale*, p. 781.

chancery petition, who was reluctantly persuaded into marriage by friends of the lady; she extracted a sizeable trousseau from him and promptly jilted him.[20]

Heirs and heiresses to attractive estates who were in the wardship of people outside the immediate family were perhaps the group most frequently married outside the county, since extracting a high price for them, rather than finding a suitable match or consolidating the family estate, would often be the guardian's principal concern. Sir John Fastolf's cynical dealings over Stephen Scrope show that these would often be won by the highest bidder.[21] William Peyto had a marriage in Derbyshire arranged for him while he was in wardship, although in this case the death of the bride forestalled the wedding. In the event, Peyto did marry into a Derbyshire family of more ancient lineage, but his bride was also the widow of a Warwickshire neighbour, who had her husband's dower lands, so on every count the match he made as an adult was an improvement on the one arranged for him in his minority.[22] On the other hand, if the wardship was vested in the family's noble patron, which it might well be, it could be the cause of a marriage nearer home, made within the lord's own following. This is almost certainly true of the Ardern–Clodesdale union that has already been mentioned. Robert Ardern, the son of Warwick's receiver, was in the earl's guardianship in 1420–1 and Clodesdale was another Warwick retainer.[23] The two estates fitted beautifully together, but without Warwick's assistance the Arderns might not have secured quite so desirable a match.

There can be no doubt, even if the lord's role has often to be inferred, that noble influence played a large part in the arranging of marriages. Numbers of matches were made within affinities, especially within the powerful and cohesive following of Richard Beauchamp. Often, as in the case of the Ardern–Clodesdale one, or of William Catesby I's marriage to the Bishopestone heiress, good lordship helped the favoured client secure a good marriage without searching beyond the county boundary. This can be seen both at the lower levels of local society – for example, the marriage of Thomas Herthill, a Warwick retainer, to the heiress of another, John Woodlow – and at the highest levels, notably in the Mountfords' coup in securing the heiress to the large Peche estate for William, the heir to Baldwin I. Here there was a two-fold link, as the fathers had in common not only the Beauchamp connection but also

[20] S.C.1/51/141(i); C.1/228/17–24. For similar indirect connections leading to marriage, see Payling 1987b: pp. 130–1. Another delightful story from chancery combines some of the ingredients of both Cinderella and Romeo and Juliet (C.1/187/13).

[21] *Paston Letters*, ed. Gairdner, I, pp. 153–6, II, pp. 113–15.

[22] *Dugdale*, pp. 472, 476; *Cal. Close Rolls 1413–19*, p. 483; Wright 1983; pp. 197–8.

[23] For Ardern's custody (and that of Ralph Brasebrugge, also from a family connected with the Beauchamps), see Longleat MS Misc. IX m.37d. Ardern's lands and marriage were given in custody to Lady Bergavenny in 1420 (*Cal. Pat. Rolls 1416–22*, p. 306), but the Longleat MS admits of no doubt that he was in the household of Warwick's countess as a ward 1420–1. For Ardern's marriage, see *Dugdale*, p. 928.

allegiance to John of Gaunt, whom they had both served in Spain. As we shall see, the benefits of these arrangements among neighbours worked both ways, adding strength to the lord's local following while providing rewards for his followers. But the lord's assistance could also be another means to the enlargement of the geographical scope of the marriage market, for his lands and connections were frequently wide-ranging. It was probably the Buckingham nexus that secured the Hexstall heiress from Kent for Henry Ferrers and the co-heiress to William Burley of Shropshire for Thomas Trussell of Bilton.[24]

This kind of favour, whose effects we have examined so far in relation to established families, was particularly important to the rising men, whose need to marry land was matched in many cases by their low value on the market.[25] Often ambitious lawyers and administrators had to be content with a widow. We shall see that as sources of wealth they were not to be spurned, but their great disadvantage was that their lands were normally only a temporary benefit. Even if they bore children to the new husband, any existing offspring would eventually inherit the wife's own lands (unless these were all female, in which case they might be trumped by the birth of a male heir), and any of the first husband's lands held in jointure would normally revert to his heirs on the death of the wife. The heirs of the first marriage might have to wait a long time for their inheritance but it was at least assured, while the heirs of the second were normally assured of nothing.[26] On the other hand, widows' very disadvantages made them easier to capture and, as independent holders of a jointure and in many cases executors of their husbands' wills, they were less amenable to control by the family that might spurn a rising careerist. A widow might prefer a dynamic, self-made man to yet another callow sprig of the aristocracy. The number of desirable widows captured by such men is striking: the widow of John Cokayn I by Thomas Bate, lawyer and crown servant, of William Cotes, father of John, by Edward Metley, lawyer and magnate servant, of Edward's son Nicholas, himself a lawyer, by Richard Hotoft, lawyer, of Thomas Straunge I by Thomas Middleton, later servant of Warwick the Kingmaker, of William Shukburgh by Thomas Stretton, crown servant, of Philip Chetwynd by

[24] *Dugdale*, pp. 701, 469, 1,009, 955; *Wedgwood: Biographies*, p. 318; S.C.R.O. D.641/1/2/17; Roskell 1983a: p. 344; *Cal. Close Rolls 1461–68*, p. 53; Rawcliffe 1978; p. 334. For noble connections, see app. 3 and for Herthill see above, p. 68 n.111. For the role of marriage in strengthening affinities, see below, p. 312. For similar evidence from a powerful affinity of the fourteenth century, see Walker 1986: pp. 103–8.

[25] Cf. Walker 1986: pp. 101–3 on the particular need that rising men rather than established families had for noble patronage in this respect.

[26] For jointures, see below, pp. 107–13. Arrangements (licit or illicit) could be made which would keep the second husband and his family in possession for longer, e.g. probably in the case of the Cotes and the Metleys (below, nn.27 and 116, and p. 67 n.107, p. 402 n.4). If there was issue of the second marriage, the wife's own estates in the jointure would remain with the second husband by courtesy until his death, even if this was long after hers, as e.g. in the case of the Lucys and the Archers (below, p. 109).

Thomas Littleton, lawyer, of Hugh Willoughby by Richard Bingham, lawyer, to name only some of the more notable examples.[27]

But the pursuit of widows tended also to be a more profitable enterprise when it was backed up by noble patronage. A lord could be particularly helpful here, both in the informal influence he could bring to bear on widows of his own men and more immediately if he had been named as executor or supervisor of the previous husband's will. Littleton and Bate probably owed their good fortune to the duke of Buckingham and it is clear that widows were desirable enough for any ambitious landowner to use his lord's agency to find one. Richard Archer amassed a large amount of land, some temporary, some permanent, by judicious choice of widows, but his first and best marriage, to the Lucy widow, was probably the fruit of the Warwick connection.[28] At a much higher level, in 1462 William Hastings rounded off his meteoric rise from esquire to baron during the political crisis of 1459–61 by marrying the widow of William Bonville. She was sister of Warwick the Kingmaker, who had just helped to place on the throne the heir to the houses of March and York, the Hastings' long-standing lords.[29] At the end of our period Henry VII, with his tighter control of the crown's feudal prerogatives, was able to find rich widows for several of his servants, both rising and established. Examples are Lord Fitzhugh's widow for Henry Willoughby, along with the wardship of her son, which brought him a large annual income, and the widows of Richard Burdet and Edmund Lucy for Hugh Conway and Richard Hungerford, both of them from outside the county.[30] In these cases the royal lord's motives may be presumed to be a mixture of wanting to reward his men cheaply and to infiltrate loyal men into Warwickshire society, but there could be a more benign side to such practices. In finding a husband for the widow of a client from amongst his other followers, the lord was not only rewarding a loyal servant but also having that care for the widow's heir which was part of good lordship.

27 *Wedgwood: Biographies*, p. 50; C.1/11/155; *C.A.D.*, IV, A6498; *Dugdale*, pp. 297, 359 (shows that Edward Metley had Cotes properties); and above, n.26 and p. 67 (Cotes and Metley); *Dugdale*, p. 34; *Stratford Register*, p. 81 (Middleton: the evidence for his marriage is given in full in Carpenter 1976, App. p. 36 n.75); S.B.T. E.R.1/61/409, 411; *Cal. Close Rolls 1447–54*, p. 513; *Dugdale*, p. 1051. For royal service, *Letters of Queen Margaret*, p. 140 (Bate) and above, p. 74 n.133. (Stretton). For lawyers, Nat. Lib. Wales Peniarth MS 280 m.94 (Bate); *Wedgwood: Biographies*, p. 472 (Hotoft); S.B.T. D.R.37 Box 107/9; *Coventry Leet Book*, pp. 77, 99; Norris 1897, p. 17 (Edward and Nicholas Metley); Foss 1848–64: IV, pp. 419–20, 436–40 (Bingham and Littleton). For lawyers and widows in general, see Ives 1983a: pp. 368–71. For the political connections of these men and their wives, see app. 3. For widows as executors, see below, n.41.

28 *Dugdale*, p. 781; above, n.19; and app. 3 and below, p. 109.

29 *G.E.C.*, VI, pp. 370–4; app. 3.

30 *Cal. Pat. Rolls 1485–94*, p. 373; *I.P.M. Hen. VII*, III, 455; Nott. Univ. Lib. Middleton MS Mi A1/2; Cameron 1970, pp. 11, 21; S.B.T. D.R. 37 Box 40 (deed of 1502); *Cal. Pat. Rolls 1494–1509*, pp. 400–1; Br. Lib. Add. MS 21,480 fos.110, 118; app. 3; and below, p. 574. For Henry VII's policies, see Bean 1968: ch.5, ii; Chrimes 1972a: pp. 209–12; *Prerogativa Regis*, pp. v–xlvi. Cf. also Wright 1983: pp. 41–2.

The professionals who were lucky enough to find heiresses, rather than having to make do with widows, almost invariably had their lords to thank. Littleton's widow is a case in point, for she was also co-heiress to William Burley and childless from her first marriage and she was to prove to be the founder of the family's fortunes.[31] John Throgmorton, lawyer and servant of Richard Beauchamp, was brought to Warwickshire by marriage in *c.* 1409 to the co-heiress of Guy Spine of Coughton, another Warwick retainer. This was a particularly convenient match, as it gave him lands in west Warwickshire that were most conveniently placed for the existing Throgmorton properties centred on Fladbury in east Worcestershire.[32] John Hugford II, Beauchamp servant and retainer and heir to a family with a long record of service to the house of Warwick, married Margaret, the heiress of Nicholas Metley, who died in 1437. Metley was an annuitant of William Lord Ferrers of Chartley, while both Ferrers and his father, Edmund, before him were part of the Warwick nexus, so it is more than likely that it was Beauchamp who found this heiress for his close servant. However, Hugford's problems with his wife's inheritance highlight the difficulties that might lie in the way of the less imposing heiress-hunter, for the advantages of the match were much reduced by Metley's plans to compensate himself for the lack of a male heir by selling much of his property for the good of his soul. Three manors, Baddesley Clinton and Wappenbury in Warwickshire and Woolsthorpe in Leicestershire, were willed away. Baddesley Clinton was sold to John Brome in 1438. Whether Hugford managed to stop the sale of the other two is unclear: he claimed that Metley died intestate and that the manors had thus come to Margaret; Robert Catesby, one of the executors, maintained that they had both been sold to him and Hugford had seized them after Towton. Either way, it was not an easy inheritance for Hugford.[33] As with widows, the crown's servants were particularly advantaged in finding heiresses under Henry VII, when the king's concern for his feudal rights and his active interest in the composition of local societies ensured good matches for

[31] *Wedgwood: Biographies*, p. 139; *D.N.B.*, *sub* Littleton.

[32] *Dugdale*, pp. 749–50; Bod. Lib. Dugdale MS 15, p. 163. For the Throgmorton lands in Worcestershire, *V.C.H. Worcs.*, III and IV, epec. III, pp. 356–8.

[33] *Dugdale*, p. 35; app. 3; S.B.T. D.R.3/612,226,228,229,789; and below, pp. 404–5, 492. Further material on the Catesby claim *ex inf.* Dr Carole Rawcliffe. The unnumbered document whose contents Dr Rawcliffe was kind enough to discuss with me will be referred to hereafter as P.R.O. Catesby Doc. Hugford still had these lands in 1484 (Br. Lib. Add.MS 28,564 fo.140: confirmed by the P.R.. Document). Woolsthorpe is now in Lincolnshire. There were two John Hugfords, one the brother of Thomas, still alive in 1478, the other the son and heir of Thomas, who married Margaret Metley and died in 1485 (C.P.40/868 rot.477; C.1/26/533; *I.P.M. Hen. VII*, I, 136). It was probably the former who was the Warwick officer in the 1430s but the latter may have been a Warwick servant from as early as 1446 (app. 3; D.L.29/645/10464: it is not clear whether the John Hugford the younger and the John Hugford feed in 1446 and still alive at the time of this account (1481–2), both mentioned in the account, are one and the same or uncle and nephew).

some of his men. For the Conways it was a double triumph, for not only did Hugh get Richard Burdet's widow but his younger brother Edward captured the Burdet heiress.[34]

So far the emphasis has been on marriage as a means to tenurial aggrandisement, but even established families did not always choose to use marriage to extend their property. While political connections could be the route to the uniting of estates, the family's priority might be to exploit the heir's marriage for political ends. Again, the evidence is inferential, but there are good grounds for supposing that this was the motive with respect to several marriages that were made when one of the partners was in a particularly vulnerable position. One such is the marriage in 1448 of Thomas Ferrers II, heir to Thomas I, to Anne, daughter of Leonard Hastings and sister of William. It was arranged at a time when the Ferrers' distant properties in Essex were under threat and needed protection from the most powerful local lord in that region, the Hastings' patron, Richard, duke of York.[35] Another is that of Simon Mountford, eldest son of Baldwin, the son and heir of William, to the daughter of Richard Verney. This match, made in about the early 1450s, was probably a response to the maturing of William's plans to disinherit Baldwin in favour of Edmund, his heir by his second marriage; some of the disputed property lay in south Warwickshire, where neither party had many friends, and the Verneys could provide a means of entry to gentry networks here, as indeed proved to be the case.[36] A final instance, from the many that could be cited, is the marriage arranged in February 1471 during the Readeption of Henry VI for Elizabeth, daughter of Sir Robert Harecourt. Harecourt, a Yorkist retainer, had recently been murdered by his old enemies the Staffords of Grafton, and his widow badly needed protection under the renascent Lancastrians. Elizabeth's husband was to be John, the heir of Richard Brasebrugge. Brasebrugge, while not directly connected with the earl of Warwick, who had just removed Edward IV and restored Henry VI, was friendly with men who were. More importantly, he was linked to Lord Sudeley, who played a leading part in the Readeption and whose other associates amongst Brasebrugge's neighbours provided several of Warwickshire's officials during the Readeption. For the Brasebrugges also the match was a good idea, for a marriage contracted with the daughter of a Yorkist martyr during the Readeption would prove useful insurance against the return of the exiled Edward IV. Moreover, under normal circumstances the Hare-

34 *Dugdale*, p. 850.

35 *H.M.C. Hastings*, I, p. 300; Carpenter 1980b: p. 40 n.72; app. 3. For this dispute and for York's protection of the Ferrers' interests, see below, pp. 172–3, 426, 454, 469.

36 *Dugdale*, p. 1,008. For the Mountford dispute, see below, ch. 12. Verney was already supporting Mountford by Michaelmas 1454 (K.B.27/774 Coram Rege rot.77d.). Ilmington, the second most important manor in dispute, lay in south Warwickshire (*V.C.H.*, v, p. 99).

courts as a family were by this time fairly well above the Brasebrugges' station.[37]

It could be argued that under Henry VII almost all the marriages of widows with male heirs to servants of the crown were made with political advantages in mind, since by this time failure to secure the protection of the royal entourage could be very damaging to the heir's prospects. An agreement of Margaret Beaufort and Roger Horton of Kingsbury made in 1502 shows the close interconnection of marriage and protection in this reign. In it Margaret is promised the wardship and marriage of Horton's son, while she herself promises to do all she can to recover the family's lost land.[38] An earlier agreement between Elizabeth Woodville and William Hastings, made in 1464, when Elizabeth was soliciting help from those about the king in obtaining her disputed jointure, and just before her success in obtaining the king's favours in every sense made such assistance redundant, shows that this was nothing new. By this treaty Elizabeth's heir was to marry Hastings' daughter and during the minority of his son-in-law Hastings was to benefit from any lands he was able to recover for Elizabeth, a clause which naturally gave him a vested interest in the success of the litigation.[39]

Even without such pressing concerns, there were plenty of reasons for marrying heirs to the daughters of political associates, friends and neighbours who had nothing to offer but their dowries. Marriage agreements were often complex and, despite all the recognisances and security clauses which they regularly featured, could lead to bad feeling and expensive litigation.[40] The need for tact, delicacy and mutual trust in the negotiation of terms is well-illustrated in a letter of William Catesby I concerning the agreement for his own second marriage. Once the marriage was made, the two families thus brought together would expect it to be a source of mutual support. The bride, if widowed, would often be her husband's executor and might well remarry. For all these reasons it might be better to match with known and trusted families, even if they had no heiress to offer. This is surely why Richard Brasebrugge who, as owner of a substantial estate, was well placed to find an heiress, married a daughter of Sir Hugh Willoughby, a powerful neighbour with whose family the Brasebrugges had extensive connections.[41]

37 Nott. Univ. Lib. Middleton MS Mi D 4558, 4558/1; *Wedgwood: Biographies*, pp. 420–21; app. 3. For politics and political affiliations at the time of Readeption, below, pp. 510–13. Dr Wright makes the perceptive point that social (? and political) eminence could be exploited to marry daughters off more cheaply (Wright 1983: p. 45).

38 Ussher 1881: pp. 205–6, cited in Rowney 1981: p. 388.

39 *H.M.C. Hastings*, I, pp. 301–2. This dispute was later to cause some bad feeling between Hastings and the Greys (below, pp. 511–12; also p. 489).

40 There is plentiful evidence of litigation related to marriage settlements in Early Chancery Proceedings (C.1).

41 S.C.1/51/147; S.B.T. D.R.10/518. For the Willoughbys, *H.M.C. Middleton* and for the families' connections, see below, pp. 298–9. The marriage took place *c.*1443. Almost any will made by an

A second argument against looking for an heiress was financial. Normally speaking, a jointure for the couple would be created at the time of the marriage. These lands, which would be held by the two for life, with reversion to the heir or heirs of their bodies, would consist primarily of land given by the husband's family, since the contribution of the wife's was usually a lump sum. But if the bride were an heiress, some of the lands she was due to inherit could go into the jointure, which meant that the dowry she brought might be correspondingly smaller. For example, in the settlement of 1473 between Nicholas Brome and his bride-to-be, Elizabeth, sister and heiress of Master John Arundel, there is no provision for any payment at all.[42] A family would have to set the immediate advantages of cash in hand for the present owner against the long-term prospects for his heirs and, understandably, often took the former course.[43] The sums paid in marriage portions could be large: Thomas Ferrers I received 450 marks for the marriage of his son to the Hastings daughter, in 1457 Richard Verney made £200 in marrying his heir Edmund to a daughter of William Fielding, in 1471 Robert Harecourt's widow paid 300 marks for the Brasebrugge heir.[44] Marrying the heir to the daughter of a noble house could be especially lucrative. There were sound political reasons for William Lucy I to marry a daughter of Lord Grey of Ruthin in the earlier part of the century and later for William Catesby II's marriage to a daughter of Lord Zouche, since in each case the noble family held lands near important properties of the gentry family – in Bedfordshire and Northamptonshire respectively – but we may suspect that these arrangements brought more tangible benefits as well. What these might amount to can be gauged from the price that Henry Willoughby was able to exact from Edward Grey, Viscount Lisle, when he agreed to marry his heir to Grey's daughter in 1489. Although Willoughby had yet to come into his full inheritance and may well have been short of cash and in a weak bargaining position, the price of his heir to a nobleman was no less than 700 marks.[45]

If an heir's marriage could prove more lucrative when his bride was not an heiress, heiresses themselves could be expensive and sometimes damaging to the family's interests. They too might command lump sums; in 1488 for example John Aston had to pay £300 for the daughter and heir apparent of

adult male in the period will show the wife being named as executor; also Kettle 1984: pp. 100–1 and (with dubious effect), *Stonor Letters*, II, p. 88.

42 McFarlane 1973: pp. 64–8; S.B.T. D.R.3/264–6.

43 Money from the heir's marriage could be vitally important in providing portions for daughters (Houlbrooke 1984: p. 74; below, p. 214 for provision for daughters).

44 *H.M.C. Hastings*, I, p. 300; S.B.T. D.R.98/122a; Nott. Univ. Lib. Middleton MS Mi D 4558/1. Also the table of marriage portions in Cooper 1976: p. 311.

45 *Dugdale*, p. 504; Roskell 1981b: p. 314; Nott. Univ. Lib. Middleton MS Mi D 4798, 4803. This sum was mistakenly given in Carpenter 1986b: p. 41 as 1,000 marks. The money proved very important in the years before Willoughby had control of his entire estate (*H.M.C. Middleton MS*, p. 122; below, pp. 111–12).

William Littleton in addition to providing a jointure worth sixty marks a year from the family lands. Worse still, after all this expenditure, by the time of his death nearly twenty years later Littleton had provided himself with a male heir.[46] It was these jointures, an unavoidable part of nearly all marriage settlements for the husband's family, and a not infrequent factor for the wife's, that could threaten the health of a landed family. Inevitably surviving marriage indentures are biased towards the greater families, leaving us with little information on the actual values of jointures among the lesser gentry, but it is safe to say that they were usually commensurate with the value of the estates of the two parties. Ten marks or even less seems to have been normal amongst the minor families, twenty marks or twenty pounds amongst the more prosperous, rising to forty or sixty marks or even beyond amongst the very great.[47] The precise balance between dowry and jointure varied and must have been negotiated, the stronger party coming out on top. For instance, although Henry Willoughby grew very rich from the Lisle match, the price was the tying up of a hundred marks worth of property in jointure for the couple.[48] In a similarly unequal match at a lower level, when Richard Archer married his grandson and heir, John II, to a daughter of Simon Mountford in 1467, in return for his jointure of twenty marks he obtained a mere eighty marks in cash from Mountford. For Archer the importance of this marriage was that kinship with the Yorkist Mountfords might help the family live down the death of John's father and Richard's eldest son, John I, executed in 1460, when the Yorkist lords took the Tower from the custody of Archer's lord, the duke of Exeter. Mountford was no doubt only too happy to exploit their need in order to get a good bargain for himself.[49] Similar circumstances may explain Nicholas Brome's rather unsatisfactory arrangements with John Arundel, for in 1468, not long since, Brome had seen his father murdered and he himself had used the Readeption to take revenge on the killer, and now needed friends in high places.[50]

[46] William Salt Lib. H.M. Aston Coll. 20/1; *Test. Vetust.*, pp. 467–8. See also *Test. Ebor.*, III, p. 240: money to be saved for the heir to finance a marriage that brings land.

[47] E.g. Fulwode/Herthill in 1438 (S.B.T. D.R.37 Box 56 (deed of 1438)), Lisle/Lecroft in *c.*1492 (above, n.10), Hore/Metley of Whitnash by 1505 (*Dugdale*, p. 348; *Cat. Anc. Deeds*, I, C1528) at the lowest level. Verney/Fielding in 1457 (S.B.T. D.R.98/122a), Brome/Marrowe in 1491 (S.B.T. D.R.3/275–6), Brasebrugge/Harewell in 1493 (*Cat. Anc. Deeds*, IV, A7247) and one of 16 marks for a younger son (Doddingselles/Malory) in 1434 (*Cal. Close Rolls 1429–35*, pp. 313–14), all in the middle range. Ferrers/Hastings in 1448 (above, n.35), Littleton/Fielding in 1479 (B.R.L. 351443) and one of 100 marks with a further £100 to be purchased (Willoughby/Fitzhugh, 1491) (*H.M.C. Middleton*, p. 122) at the top end. See also the table of jointures and marriage portions, Wright 1983: p. 207.

[48] Nott. Univ. Lib. Middleton MS Mi D 4798, 4803.

[49] S.B.T. D.R.503 fos.66v.–68; Scofield 1923: I, p. 93; below, pp. 474, 477.

[50] Below, pp. 510, 512; the Master John Arundel in question could be either the one who died in 1477, or the possible son of Sir Renfrey, who died in 1504. Both were well-connected, the latter being chaplain to Edward IV in 1479 (Emden 1957–9: I, pp. 49–50, 50–1).

The jointures required to secure heiresses could have disastrous effects on the heir's prospects, for heiresses all too often turned into widows, some of whom long outlived their husbands and, worse still, remarried, while remaining in possession of the jointure. Time after time an attractive marriage induced families into tying up a substantial part of the estate in this way. In at least thirty-nine instances during the century the husband or his family were prevailed upon to put into the jointure or to leave to the wife a large part of the estate, or its core, or both. The only reason that many heirs escaped the consequences of these rash compacts was the obligingness of their mothers in predeceasing their husbands or dying not long after them. Again, it was the desirable heiresses for whom the greatest sacrifices were made. Thomas Lucy's widow, a Shropshire heiress, retained much of the Lucy lands, including their residence at Charlecote, when Richard Archer married her in 1415; these were returned to the Lucys at her death in 1420 but her own lands did not come to the Lucy heirs until Archer's death in 1471. More dramatically, the price of Hugh Willoughby's marriage to the Freville co-heiress was no less than the settlement on her of a substantial part of the Willoughby lands; this was despite the existence of an heir by Hugh's previous marriage, who was thereby cut out of most of his inheritance. In 1442 Philip Chetwynd settled his two principal manors, Grendon in Warwickshire and Ingestre in Staffordshire, on himself and his wife, the co-heiress of William Burley; she, as a widow, was to prove such a happy windfall for Thomas Littleton. In 1465 Humphrey Stafford II's marriage to an heiress, who was also the daughter of a chief baron of the exchequer, obliged him to settle much of his land, including his central manor of Grafton, on himself and his wife.[51]

Other considerations could also encourage playing fast and loose with the heir's prospects. Again political benefits loomed large. Ironically, John Cokayn I, having gone through the experience of having to sue his widowed mother for her inheritance earlier in the century, proceeded in 1436 to tie up most of her lands, including his Warwickshire residence of Pooley in Polesworth, as the price of his earlier marriage with the daughter of Sir Hugh Shirley. Shirley's importance as a landowner in Derbyshire and north Warwickshire, where the

51 Bod. Lib. Dugdale MS 17, p. 50 (Lucy also made the handsome sum of £240 from the match, which was no doubt another reason for tying up his property); *Cal. Close Rolls 1413–19*, pp. 232–3, *1419–22*, pp. 84–5; *Cal. Fine Rolls 1413–22*, p. 331, *1471–85*, p. 28; Nott. Univ. Lib. Middleton MS Mi F 1; *Colls. Hist. Staffs.*, o.s., 12, p. 316; E.326/10798, 10852. For the longevity of Chetwynd's widow, see *I.P.M. Hen. VII*, II, 909. The Willoughby settlement was renegotiated in 1449 after Hugh's death, leaving Margaret with a much reduced life-interest in the Willoughby lands – thus most of them passed to Richard, Hugh's heir by his first marriage – and confining the Willoughby lands due to pass to Hugh's second family to some distant properties in Lincolnshire. It was Richard's death *s.p.* in 1471 that brought the whole estate to Margaret's children. Nevertheless Margaret was left with her share of the Freville lands for life (Payling 1987b: pp. 50–1, 1987a: pp. 152–4; *Dugdale*, p. 1,141 n.f.; *Inquisitiones Post Mortem Notts.*, p. 67).

bulk of the Cokayn properties lay – he was indeed a close neighbour at Newton Regis in Warwickshire – and his connections with the king must account for the sacrifices made by Cokayn on behalf of his heir.[52] John Brome of Baddesley Clinton, who as we shall see was a most meticulous manager of an estate put together in the course of a successful professional career, was prepared to hand most of it over to his wife in return for a politically advantageous match with that same Shirley family.[53] Early in the reign of Henry VII, Richard Burdet, heir to Thomas Burdet II, who had been executed for treason in 1477, settled a large part of his lands on his wife, the daughter of Simon Mountford. He could be persuaded into this course because it had been Mountford's about-turn that secured him these lands against the young heirs of his father's second marriage. He was doubtless relying on his powerful father-in-law to keep the other heirs at bay and to help the family regain respectability in local society.[54] It is only in the case of second wives like Burdet's that any sentiment at all seems to creep into these marriage settlements and provisions for wives, and it was a sentiment that could prove the heir's, and even the estate's, undoing. William Mountford and Thomas Burdet not only tried to disinherit their sons by their first marriages but also proposed to leave large parts of the estate to their much younger second wives;[55] while their older sons might contest the diversion of the inheritance, there was not much they could do about the settlements on the wives. Similarly John Holt was persuaded to give the family's only manor to his second wife for her life. His son protested in no uncertain terms about this alleged leading astray of his father and neither the Mountford nor the Burdet heirs allowed their fathers' dispositions to go unchallenged.[56]

If emotions reigned in these instances – the classic tale of an elderly man besotted with a younger second wife – all the other arrangements we have examined were hard-headed gambles in which a wife's life-expectancy was weighed against all the possible benefits of the match. Too often gambles failed and heirs were excluded from a large part of their inheritance, sometimes for lengthy periods. Some of these widows were remarkable for their longevity. Joan Chetwynd survived Philip by more than forty years, dying in 1504. John Cokayn's widow was still alive in 1459, John himself having died in 1438. William Greville's widow had Milcote, the family's main estate and residence

52 *V.C.H.*, IV, p. 20; C.139/87/40/5; Wright 1983: p. 33; below, n.57 for further complications in the Cokayn–Shirley relationship; Shirley 1873: *passim*, for the Shirley family's lands and importance; above, p. 88 n.180 for Hugh's royal connections. Wright (1983: p. 33) suggests that the Cokayn feoffment was made to protect the estate from royal wardship, but since, were this the case, the prophylactic measures presented a greater peril to the estate than the danger to be averted, this does not seem likely.

53 S.B.T. D.R.3/264–6.

54 *I.P.M. Hen. VII*, I, 802; below, pp. 536–9.

55 *Cal. Close Rolls 1476–85*, p. 35; *W.F.F.*, 2649; *Dugdale*, pp. 849, 1,010–11; below, ch. 9, esp. p. 464, pp. 535–6.

56 K.B.27/869 Coram Rege rot.96d.; C.1/53/205; below, ch. 9 and pp. 536–9.

in Warwickshire, from the very early fifteenth century until 1449, and her son John, who died in 1444, never had possession. The Ralegh family was crippled by successive dowagers and female heirs, who had most of the family lands from the death of William under-age in 1420/1 until the death of Edward Bromflete, husband of William's sister Joan in 1460. Even then the mother of the heir, Edward Ralegh, continued to hold some of the estates, including the central manor of Farnborough.[57]

Margaret, wife of Hugh Willoughby, in whom so much of the Willoughby property had been vested, died only in 1493, her husband having predeceased her in 1448. Her son Robert, who died in 1474, was kept out of all of his mother's lands and much of his father's, but that did not dissuade him from putting his main manor of Wollaton, Nottinghamshire, into jointure, almost as soon as he had inherited from his older half-brother, and his wife in her turn survived him until 1491. Both the Willoughby dowagers remarried and between them excluded Robert's son, the future Sir Henry, from his full inheritance until 1493, when he was already in his forties.[58] While Richard

57 Chetwynd-Stapylton 1892: pp. 106, 109; *I.P.M. Hen. VII*, II, 909; C.139/87/40/5; PROB 11/4 fo. 129v.; *Cal. Pat. Rolls 1399–1401*, p. 440, *1401–5*, p. 2; *Cal. Fine Rolls 1437–45*, p. 299, *1445–52*, pp. 151–2; *V.C.H.*, V, p. 200; *Dugdale*, p. 529; PROB 11/4 fo.146; S.B.T. D.R.37 Box 34 (deeds of 1423–54). The Cokayn genealogy is unclear. In 1435 Sir John's wife, on whom he settled some lands, was called Isabel (*W.F.F.*, 2581), and Dugdale, normally a reliable source, gives his wife as Isabel, daughter of Hugh Shirley (*Dugdale*, p. 1,120, confirmed by Br. Lib. Add. MS 6667, p. 88). At his death and in his will of June 1435, Cockayn's son and heir was named as John and in 1441 John, heir to Sir John of Pooley and Ashbourne, is said to be sixteen years old (*Cal. Close Rolls 1441–47*, p. 8; Br. Lib. Add. MS 6667, p. 256). However, in 1439, after Sir John's death, we have reference to Joan, widow of Sir John Cokayn the younger, daughter of Sir John Dabridgecourt, who is suing Isabel, widow of Sir John Cokayn, for debt (*Colls. Hist. Staffs.*, n.s., 3, p. 156; also the will of John Dabridgecourt (1415), in which he names his daughter, Joan, wife of John Cokayn knight: *Reg. Chichele*, II, p. 53), while in 1416 the same Sir John made a grant witnessed by his son and heir, John (*H. M. C. Rutland*, IV, p. 53). Nobody (except for Clark and Rawcliffe, very briefly, in 1983, p. 11) seems to have noticed any problems in relation to the Cokayns. The only possible solution seems to be that Sir John the younger, husband of Joan, was the heir in the 1416 grant, that he died *v.p.*, having married and been knighted, and that the next surviving son was also called John. Support for this comes from the second marriage of Ralph Shirley I, whose bride is described in 1419 as daughter and heir apparent of John Cokayn knight (Wright 1983: pp. 212, 231); this was presumably between the death of John the eldest son and the birth of John the eventual heir *c.*1425. The Greville descent is complicated by the fact that William, the founder of the family, chose to divide his lands among his sons, and let his first purchase and residence, Camden, Gloucestershire, go to a younger son, Lewis, from whom the Greville heirs male eventually descended at the end of the century. Confusingly, in his pardon for entering Camden without licence in 1402 and in other directives associated with Gloucestershire, Lewis is called 'son and heir of William', but this can only mean heir in the limited sense that he had been designated heir for Camden (*Dugdale*, p. 706; *Cal. Pat. Rolls 1401–05*, pp. 2, 157; *Cal. Close Rolls 1405–09*, p. 19; *Cal. Fine Rolls 1399–1405*, p. 185).

58 Cameron 1970; *Inquisitiones Post Mortem Notts.*, pp. 32, 67, 73; *I.P.M. Hen. VII*, I, 865, 725; above, n.51. Cameron's dates for the deaths of the widows are at variance with those in the I.P.M.

Bingham, Margaret's second husband, managed his wife's jointure with great scrupulousness, his care was not matched by Peter Legh, the second husband of Robert's widow. It was only the great wealth of the estate, particularly the Wollaton coal, on which Henry was relying heavily for his first will in 1489, that made it possible for Henry to have any independent existence at all until the mid-1490s, and his public life was severely curtailed until then.[59] In the case of the Straunge family, a rapid succession of deaths of male heirs early in the century was followed by the long widowhood of Elizabeth, wife of Thomas I, who had died in 1436. The consequence was that the family went completely into abeyance until 1490. It was only then that Elizabeth finally died, in possession of her jointure of the Straunges' three Warwickshire manors, including their residence of Walton Deyville, having outlived her son, Thomas II.[60] Even when the effects of jointures were less dramatic, a succession of dowagers, holding by jointure or in dower, could be a formidable burden on the heir. This can be seen very clearly in the complexities of marriage treaties, like those of William Littleton in 1479 and of his daughter in 1488, or of wills, like John Shirley's of 1485, in which various segments of the property are shown to be in others' hands and still to come to the head of the family.[61]

This being the case, we may well ask why some families replicated this mistake in each generation. The Willoughbys are one instance, another the Grevilles, who put Milcote manor into jointure again in 1499.[62] The answer is that often they had no choice. The owner of a small estate might find himself obliged to risk leaving a major part of his lands in the hands of his widow if he were to contract a marriage worthy of his standing. For example, throughout the century, the Rouses, a family hovering on the fringe of the county elite, put one of their two Warwickshire manors into jointure.[63] A wealthier family could be placed in the same position once a substantial part of the estate had become tied up in this way. Holding only a remnant of the property, the heir became a much less desirable commodity on the marriage market; if his mother had remarried, his value was diminished further, for his inheritance, when it eventually reached him after the step-father's attentions, might not be worth the having. The only way to negotiate a match commensurate with his dignity might then be the creation of a jointure from most of the rest of the estate. This would explain Robert Willoughby's superficially rather rash treatment of

59 For Bingham's administration of Middleton, see below, pp. 168–9; Cameron 1970: p. 15; *I.P.M. Hen. VII*, 1, 725; C.P.40/864 rot.251d.; *H.M.C. Middleton*, pp. 121–2. Henry held a major office only twice before 1493, as sheriff of Staffordshire in 1486 and of Lincolnshire in 1490 (*Lists and Indexes*, 9, pp. 79, 128).

60 *Dugdale*, p. 577; W.C.R.O. C.R.133/15; *I.P.M. Hen. VII*, 1, 599; *Cal. Fine Rolls 1485–1509*, pp. 4–5; above, n.27.

61 B.R.L. 351443; Wm. Salt Lib. H.M.Aston Coll. 20/1; Shirley 1873: pp. 404–5. See also the Vernon–Shirley marriage agreement of 1496 (Leics. R. O. 26D53/2552).

62 *V.C.H.*, v, p. 200.

63 *V.C.H.*, v, p. 191; C.139/56/51/2, /178/49.

Wollaton, as well as other instances, such as Thomas Straunge II's settlement on his womenfolk of most of the land he had, together with what was eventually to come to him from his mother. For John Greville II, settling Milcote in 1499, the problem was that the loss of the Cokesey inheritance to the heirs general had gravely diminished the property.[64] When there was no direct heir, or a female one on whose behalf no promises had been made to her husband's family, the holder could afford to be conscienceless in his provision for his wife. Thus, Hugh Cokesey settled his two Warwickshire manors of Willey and Hunningham on himself and his wife in 1441, shortly before his death, knowing that on her death the lands would go to his sister.[65] John Beaufitz tied up most of his property in his wife, quite probably to pay out his son-in-law, Robert Belyngham, who had abducted his daughter and heiress and, as a servant of Henry VII, had managed to make the marriage stick and to escape unpunished. Eleanor Beaufitz did not quite succeed in outliving her son-in-law, but she allowed him only a brief enjoyment of his ill-gotten property.[66]

There were ways out for the heir. Probably the least profitable was litigation. This did occur and could result in a new settlement,[67] but as a matter of principle it was a dangerous thing to do. To a large extent, this society rested on mutual trust and a willingness to carry out agreements, if not always in their true spirit, at least to the letter. Too many challenges to jointures and wills could in the long run undermine faith in the ordinary ways of doing business. No society could function if its members were in a perpetual state of enmity and litigation. In the short run families that became notorious for violating or contesting agreements were likely to experience difficulty in finding marriage partners or business associates of any kind. We shall see that people who acquired a reputation for unreliability of any kind were apt to lose their friends. A better way was to renegotiate the jointure with the widow. The Archers were expert at doing this, which was just as well as they had rather a lot of widows during the course of the century. In 1474 Nicholas Brome was able first to obtain the rest of the estate in return for allowing the main manor of Baddesley Clinton to his mother and, little more than a month later, to get Baddesley itself by paying her an annual rent of £20.[68] Whether it could be done depended greatly on the family's resources: what else the heir had to offer in exchange.

[64] W.C.R.O. C.R.133/16; *Dugdale*, pp. 72–3, 710, 706; *Cal. Pat. Rolls 1494–1509*, p. 164. On attempts to prevent widows remarrying, see Kettle 1984: p. 99.

[65] *V.C.H.*, VI, pp. 118, 260; C.139/122/36/4. She died in 1460, fifteen years after him.

[66] PROB 11/8 fo.161, /11 fo.173v.; *Cal. Pat. Rolls 1485–94*, p. 239. For the Belyngham abduction, see below, pp. 577–8.

[67] For examples of litigation: Willoughby (Cameron 1970: p. 15), Cokayn/Bate, Chetwynd/Littleton, Mountford (for all these, below, pp. 411, 431 and chs. 12–15), Fulwode (S.B.T. D.R. 37/949), Lucy (*Cat. Anc. Deeds*, IV, A8331), Harewell (*I.P.M. Hen. VII*, III, 217).

[68] S.B.T. D.R. 37/968–9, 982, Box 36 (memorandum of *c.*1500). Note also a *post mortem* settlement with the family of a previous wife (S.B.T. D.R.503 fos. 46, 46v.). For Brome, S.B.T. D.R.3/265–8. Below, pp. 432, 612 for the ostracising of consistent trouble-makers.

Because there was land to spare, Robert Throgmorton was able to rearrange the will of Thomas, his father, in 1474. The will seems to have been made on the assumption that Robert would continue with his father's policies of treating the more recent Warwickshire acquisitions as secondary to the older lands in Worcestershire, but it was precisely these new lands that Robert intended to make the centre of his agricultural and political ambitions. Since he proposed to go in for pastoral farming he also needed a more compact estate than his father had left him. Fortunately, by this stage the Throgmortons were sufficiently prosperous for Robert to be able to provide his mother with an annual income of 100 marks, with which she was to support herself and her three younger sons, provide dowries for her five daughters and pay her husband's debts, while Robert was to maintain and marry a sixth daughter, and that still left Robert with the lands and money he needed for his own ventures.[69] Heirs who were unable to make such wholesale rearrangements might still secure some sort of share in the dowry or jointure. Henry Willoughby, for example had an interest in Wollaton in 1489, two years before his mother's death.[70]

There is no doubt that marriage was a speculation and recognised as such, or that the dowry and the jointure were seen as venture capital in a business in which wealth, politics and the pursuit of land all played a part. Two Warwickshire agreements illustrate this very clearly. One, made in 1501, contracted George, son and heir of Robert Throgmorton, in marriage to Katharine, daughter and co-heiress apparent to Nicholas Vaux, a considerable landowner with some rather peripheral Warwickshire interests. Great care was taken to ensure that the couple inherited a reasonable competence soon after Vaux's death; what could not be written into the contract was that Katharine should remain heir to her father's lands, so it was agreed that in the event of Vaux producing a son the price he paid for the match was to rise dramatically, from £183 to an additional 1,000 marks.[71] The second is more interesting still. In November 1478 Richard Burdet, the son whom Thomas II had disinherited, was trying to recover his inheritance, his father having been executed without subsequent attainder in early 1477. Being landless he needed the means to pursue his claim in the courts and so he contracted himself in marriage to the daughter of John Shirwode, a Coventry merchant. This rather demeaning match brought him 200 marks with which to pay his legal expenses and the payment by the Shirwodes of his debts, as well as further advances; for the Shirwodes it was a gamble on Richard's success, which, if it succeeded, would give them an otherwise unattainable close relationship with a leading Warwickshire landowner. In the event, Richard double-crossed them; by his marriage to

69 Coughton Court, Throckmorton MS Box 72/5; below, pp. 181, 184, 185–6 for the Throgmortons' exploitation of their estates.

70 *H.M.C. Middleton*, pp. 121–2; Cameron 1970: p. 15; cf. *Colls. Hist. Staffs.*, n.s., 6, ii, p. 202.

71 *V.C.H.*, VI, p. 183; Coughton Court, Throckmorton MS Box 72/1. Vaux did in fact subsequently have a son (PROB 11/20 fo.9 *et seq.*).

the daughter of Simon Mountford, who had been given custody of the person and estates of the young heir of the second Burdet marriage, he had himself recognised as the Burdet heir, while the Shirwodes were left complaining about their wasted money.[72]

Any attempt to summarise the effects of the marriage market in making and breaking new and established families has to take account of the immense variety of aims that the parties might be hoping to fulfil. Although the system tended to favour the established families, the more ambitiously they speculated, the greater their chances of foundering. It was on these mishaps that the rising men might build their fortunes through marriage to a well-endowed widow. If we take the elite families over the period as a whole, most of them suffered to some degree from widows and on occasions this had serious consequences which could take the family partially or wholly out of local affairs for a time. The fall in status in mid-century of the Cokayn and Shirley families, although undoubtedly related to the decline of knighthood, cannot be entirely divorced from their problems with dowagers.[73] The Straunges all but disappeared for a large part of the century and had only just reappeared before they disappeared for good by becoming extinct in the male line. Elizabeth Straunge's jointure and Thomas II's minority removed them from the scene long before their actual demise.[74] The Willoughbys, a far greater family, had comparatively little impact on midlands affairs from the death of Hugh in 1448 until Henry's succession to the complete estate in 1493. Worst affected of all were the fortunes of the Chetwynds, excluded from their inheritance from 1442 until 1504, and of the Cokayns. Like the Chetwynds, John Cokayn III tried to use violence against his supplanter, Thomas Bate, but in his case, perhaps because he was innately unstable, perhaps because he was given no inducement to keep the peace, violence became a way of life. He was one of the men named in parliament in 1459 as a notable disturber of the peace – not, it seems, because of any Yorkist leanings – and time after time he turns up in the legal records as a perpetrator of violence. He had no public career at all and, it appears, few important friends. By 1494 he was hopelessly in debt and forced into a humiliating agreement by which his Derbyshire neighbours, the Fitzherberts, paid his debts and cancelled an obligation for £500, as well as overlooking other 'good dedys and kyndenes showed and done to hys [Fitzherbert's] grete costes and charges'. In return, the Fitzherbert daughter was to marry John's grandson and eventual heir, Thomas II; most of the Cokayn properties were to be held for Fitzherbert for the latter's lifetime and for five years after his death, before reverting to Thomas; and John himself was to be given a weekly dole of 26s 8d

72 C.1/54/378; *Cal. Pat. Rolls 1476–85*, p. 102, *1452–61*, p. 338; below, pp. 537–8.

73 Wright 1983: p. 9; above, p. 85. Also Richmond's comments on the effects on the career of Sir Roger Swillington, John Hopton's half-uncle, of having to find £200 a year for his mother (1981: p. 12) and below, p. 257 n.53 on the nobility and dowagers.

74 *Cal. Pat. Rolls 1485–94*, p. 346.

at the church porch of Etwall, Derbyshire (presumably rationed in this way to prevent him getting into debt again). Of this, 6s 8d was to be deducted until he had repaid yet another debt to the Fitzherberts.[75]

In this light it might seem that marriage served more to create opportunities for new men than to enhance the position of the old. It was certainly a significant force in this respect, not just in providing rich widows, but, perhaps more importantly, in making gaps in the local elite which could open the way to newcomers. But so far we have been concentrating on the matrimonial gambles that failed. Often they met with success. Some of the greatest families grew greater still through fortunate marriages. The Staffords of Grafton, the Mountfords, the Arderns, the Catesbys added to their lands in Warwickshire, the Berminghams, the Burdets, the Shirleys, the Lucys, the Purfreys of Shelford did so further afield, as did the Staffords of Grafton.[76] Moreover, the failures need to be put in perspective, for often they meant no more than a temporary eclipse. The Willoughbys eventually reaped the fruits of the Freville marriage, with Henry one of the most eminent men in the north midlands under the first two Tudors.[77] The worst mistakes and direst consequences could usually be surmounted if the family had started from a prominent enough position and managed to produce a competent heir at the right time; Thomas Cokayn II lived to restore the family's fortunes and to announce his achievement in triumphant doggerel on his memorial in the parish church at Ashbourne in Derbyshire, the family's principal seat.[78] Conversely, until they had crossed the invisible dividing-line between striving and respectability it was not easy for newcomers to acquire land so easily by marriage, much less large inheritances of the kind the older families could almost always obtain somewhere. They needed a noble protector or, later on, the patronage of Henry VII, although earlier in the century a favoured few might thrive by being in with Henry VI's courtiers. For most, widows would normally prove the limit of their marital aspirations.

Nevertheless, even when an established family's gamble came off, fortunate marriages were not always a guaranteed path to greater wealth and influence. The results of dabbling in the regional and national marriage markets, which we have seen to be a common practice amongst greater landowners, were not always beneficial. The more dispersed an estate grew, the harder it was to

[75] For the Chetwynd and Cokayn conflicts, see below, pp. 411, 431. For Cokayn's lawlessness, see also e.g. *Colls. Hist. Staffs.*, n.s., 3, pp. 187, 192–4, 196–7, 213 and n.s., 11, p. 54; K.B.9/421/74; *Rot. Parl.*, v, p. 368. His neglect by the nobility after the 1440s can be seen in app. 3, but note his powerful feoffees (perhaps mortgagees?) in 1475 (C.67/49 m.3). For the Fitzherbert settlement, see *I.P.M. Hen. VII*, II, 832, 942.

[76] For the Stafford of Grafton marriages, below, pp. 118–19. For the other marriages not already mentioned in the text, see Jeffs 1961a: p. 276 (Bermingham/Hilton), *Dugdale*, p. 847 (Burdet/Bruyn), p. 622 (various Shirley marriages), p. 54 (Purfrey marriages).

[77] Cameron 1970; below, ch.15.

[78] *Dugdale*, p. 1,121.

manage and defend. Problems with peripheral manors will be considered at greater length in the next chapter, but they are also relevant to the present discussion. It was not just that it was harder to exploit these properties at a distance. There was also the obligation on the new owner to build up local contacts if he was to make the lands safe from the encroachments of neighbours and from other claimants. The alliance of the Ferrers of Tamworth with the Hastings to protect their Essex lands has already been mentioned. Combining the entailed properties of the Ferrers of Groby with their share of the Freville inheritance had given them an estate scattered through eight counties. The fact that the Freville property had evidently been divided with economic equity rather than convenience of management in mind, despite some later adjustment,[79] did not make their circumstances any easier.

The Willoughbys, who got one of the other heiresses, had problems on a similar scale. If anything theirs were worse; the acquisition seriously unbalanced the estate since it included what were now two of their three richest manors, Middleton in Warwickshire and Gunthorpe with Lowdham in Nottinghamshire. Unlike Ferrers who, as a younger son, had as yet no fixed residence, the Willoughbys had an existing seat in Nottinghamshire, first at Willoughby, then at Wollaton. Moreover, in Middleton they had obtained only a subordinate member of Tamworth, which was suffering from prolonged neglect. It took the family many decades to turn Middleton into a proper second seat and to establish a political presence in Warwickshire, and much of this was owed to Richard Bingham, second husband of Margaret, widow of Hugh Willoughby, who lived with her at Middleton until his death in 1476.[80]

Families that were circumspect enough to prefer local brides might still run into unexpected difficulties. In the late fourteenth and early fifteenth centuries the Catesbys built up an estate along the Warwickshire/Northamptonshire border that was both compact and well-suited to the pastoral farming on which they were engaged by this time. In the early fifteenth century John II, second son of John Catesby I, was provided for with a marriage to the co-heiress of Mountford of Lapworth. This gave him Grandborough, which was close to the other Catesby properties, but also Lapworth and Bedsworth in Tanworth, much further to the west. Consequently, when John I's eldest son died and John II became heir to the Catesbys he found himself lord of a much less manageable estate. His response was to continue to concentrate on the eastern properties, abandoning the home farm at Ladbroke to make Ashby St Ledgers in Northamptonshire his main residence, but to do what he could with the detached estates. The older lands were consolidated and some of the more peripheral ones given to Robert, John II's younger brother, and his heirs. The marriage of John's own heir, William I, to the Bishopestone heiress made some

79 S.B.T. D.R.10/1316, 1317; Nott. Univ. Lib. Middleton MS Mi M 214; *Cal. Close Rolls 1441–47*, pp. 265–6, 313; C.139/174/34.

80 Nott. Univ. Lib. Middleton MS Mi M 214, 5/167/103; below, pp. 168–9.

sense of the lands to the west by bringing in the other main manor in Lapworth, along with some Gloucestershire properties that fitted quite well with other Catesby lands.[81] William seems to have taken more of an interest than his father in the new estates, for in 1460 he partially bought out Thomas Palmer, who had married the other Bishopestone heiress, and, soon after this, lodged a claim to the remaining manor in Lapworth, the one owned by John Brome of Baddesley Clinton. His claim succeeded and he may have been intending to enclose the whole township for cattle-raising, but his son, William II, abandoned any policies of this kind. Instead, he chose to exploit his connections with the Hastings power bloc, and then his almost unlimited opportunities under Richard III, to reinforce his holdings in the south-east midlands, acquiring property as far east as Bedfordshire and Buckinghamshire.[82]

Marriage could be made to yield geographically coherent estates, as it did for the Arderns and the Mountfords, but this could not be guaranteed. Those who were confined to the more localised market of the lesser landowners tended to be more successful in this respect: the union of the Boteller and Waldeve properties at Alspath has already been mentioned and, earlier in the century, Thomas Greswold and his nephew John achieved the notable coup of acquiring the two halves of the estate of the Hores of Solihull in two successive generations.[83] The dangers of heiress-hunting in the superficially more attractive national market are graphically exemplified in the history of the Staffords of Grafton. Their original and principal seat was at Grafton in east Worcestershire, but the extent and geographical spread of their properties were vastly increased by their success in finding an heiress in every generation from the late fourteenth to the late fifteenth centuries. First there was the Hastang heiress, who brought important Warwickshire properties, then Elizabeth Burdet of Huncote, from whom they got another Warwickshire manor, then the co-heiress to the Aylesburys, who added more land in Warwickshire and estates in Buckinghamshire and Northamptonshire, and finally the Fray co-heiress.[84] No attempts were made to integrate these diverse lands and there were major problems with arrears on the more distant ones, some of which were potentially amongst the most valuable on the estate. Humphrey II allowed his finances to get into a state of considerable disarray and it is quite conceivable that his neglect and the failure to make more enterprising use of the whole estate, even

81 Dyer 1981: pp. 18–21; Birrell, '*Status Maneriorum* of John Catesby', pp. 15–17; *Dugdale*, pp. 309, 312, 330, 332, 783, 787–8; S.C.6/1043/28; *Cat. Anc. Deeds*, III, A4363, IV, A6892, V, A12018; Roskell 1981b: pp. 310–11; below, pp. 191–2.

82 *Cat. Anc. Deeds*, III, A4419, 4575, 4776, 5360, IV, A8481, 9322–3, 9650; *Cal. Close Rolls 1476–85*, pp. 354–6; Horrox and Hammond eds., *Br. Lib. Harleian Manuscript 433*, I, pp. 137, 182, III, pp. 149–50; Roskell 1981b: pp. 311–12, 318; below, pp. 192–3. For the dispute over Lapworth, see below, pp. 502–3, 558.

83 K.B.27/747 Coram Rege rot.33d.

84 *Dugdale*, pp. 313, 316, 318; *V.C.H.*, VI, p. 40; *Wedgwood: Biographies*, pp. 792–3; Br. Lib. Add. Roll 74,168; above, p. 100.

under better management earlier in the century, originated in the belief that any financial problems could easily be solved by a fortunate marriage. For Humphrey II the knowledge that he was likely to inherit the large estate of the Staffords of Southwick seems to have destroyed all sense of reality.

Both Humphreys, father and son, were obliged by the need to defend their scattered holdings to maintain a high political profile, and a lot of effort had to be expended on the disputed Aylesbury lands. Eventually Humphrey II had to play some very high politics indeed to keep out his rivals for the Hook lands, which may have been all that stood between him and ruin. He committed himself wholesale to Richard III, and, his principal opponent having supported Henry Tudor, was quite unable to compromise with the new regime and died in the first rebellion of the reign. Those families like the Ferrers, the Willoughbys and the Mountfords which had spectacular success with heiresses early in the century but failed to seek them out in subsequent generations were acting with considerable wisdom. They chose to put political advantage and consolidation of property and local standing before haphazard accumulation. Generally speaking Warwickshire families seem to have acted with greater circumspection than the Staffords; even of those who participated in the national marriage market, relatively few seem to have married their heirs outside the midlands.[85]

II

Given the unpredictability of the marriage market, both the established families aiming for a coherent expansion of the estate and the newcomers trying to create a secure landed base would have to buy estates, and, as has already been observed, this was no easy matter at this time. So intense was the competition for estates that sales of reversions were not uncommon.[86] Until the last decades of the century it was the newcomers who were responsible for most of the purchases. Older families might occasionally buy a single manor, as the Catesbys did at Marston Waver in 1427, or add a piece to an existing estate, such as Les Hammes pasture, bought by Thomas Ferrers I in the 1430s, but their purchases were usually confined to lands for younger sons or for the church.[87] It is significant that families on the make tended to abandon

85 *Rot. Parl.*, VI, pp. 325–6; K.B.27/886 Rex rot.1d.; S.C.8/E.1310; K.B.9/337/6; C.P.40/840 rot.398; Baker 1822–41, I, pp. 352–5; C.140/163/3,7; JUST 1/1547 m.5–5d.; C.P.40/802 rot. 81; *Colls. Hist. Staffs.*, n.s., 4, pp. 203–4; *Wedgwood: Biographies*, pp. 204–5, 821; *G.E.C.*., XII, ii, pp. 683–4. For the Staffords in politics, see below, chs. 10–15 and for the management of their estates, below, pp. 162, 169–71. For a conspectus of marriages up to the 1470s, see Carpenter, M. C. 1976: App. VII.

86 E.g. *V.C.H.*., VI, p. 121; S.B.T. E.R.1/99 fo.92; William Worcestre, *Itineraries*, p. 48. Or even promises of first option, as a mark of favour (E.326/10341).

87 Bod. Lib. Dugdale MS 13, p. 304. Les Hammes was bought some time between 1432 and 1437 (S.B.T. D.R.10/2616, 2441). For purchases for younger sons and for the church, see below, pp. 219, 241.

purchase once they were established enough to command lucrative marriages. This was true of the Catesbys, assiduous purchasers in the late fourteenth century, when they still had their way to make, and later of the Throgmortons, whose last great purchase, the other half of their manor of Coughton, was made in 1449. Established families could also avoid purchase by reviving old claims, of which, as gentry of ancient lineage, they were likely to have a plentiful supply; this was a course pursued particularly by those in difficulties, such as the Peytos when they fell on hard times towards the end of the century and Robert Ardern in mid-century.[88] For new men purchase was a far more central issue, as it was often their only means of access to the status and power vested in landed society. Accordingly, if we are to assess the extent and nature of upward movement into and within Warwickshire landed society, we must first discover how the money that went into land was made.

Two methods can be disposed of rapidly. First, there is little evidence of Warwickshire families inproving their landed position with money won in the French wars. Two men are recorded as recipients of grants of land in France. One is William Bermingham I, who in 1419 was given lands in Falaise in tail male. The following year he was serving in the Falaise garrison, so he seems to have taken an active interest in this property, and it may have helped the family come through the difficult period when their main English estate, the manor of Birmingham, was taken from them. In 1428 William Bishopestone received a grant of land in France, but his career also exemplifies the hazards of this method of self-advancement, as he allowed the French to take Château Gaillard, where he was captain, and was imprisoned at Rouen for his negligence. The Burdets may have profited from the war, since they served long and loyally in France, but they are not known to have made any purchases during or after their time in France, and, since they were able to effect marriages to two heiresses and a widow in this period, they had little need to.

It is clear from Allmand's work that the French wars of the fifteenth century, unlike those of the fourteenth, were not a widespread source of profit. Those who were given lands in France might make a reasonable living from them but usually not more. For the rest, who went on expeditions or served in a garrison for a time, the war would be a lottery in which they might lose.[89] The petitions

88 *Cal. Pat. Rolls 1476–85*, p. 539–40; C.P.40/894 rot.41; *Dugdale*, p. 601; *V.C.H.*, v, p. 5; W.C.R.O. C.R. 1911/17. For the Throgmortons, see below, p. 128 and nn.103–4.

89 *Dep. Keep.'s Rep.*, 41, p. 774; Br. Lib. Eg. Ch. 146; *Actes de la Chancellerie d'Henri VI*, II, pp. 157–60, 359; *Roles Normands et Français*, pp. 91–2; McFarlane 1981c; Allmand 1983: pp. 69–80, 166–70, 246–9; Massy 1984. For the Burdets' war service, see *Dugdale*, p. 848; K.B. 27/635 Rex rot. 9; Allmand 1983, pp. 30, 267 n.87; above, p. 82. For the dispute over Birmingham, see below, pp. 377–8. For the debate on the economic and social consequences of the war in general, McFarlane 1981e; Postan 1973a,b. See Allmand's remarks on the use of smaller numbers of cavalry and commanders of lower status in the more defensive and less lucrative phases of the war after Troyes (1988: pp. 65–7, 71–2), and, similarly, Powicke 1969; also Pollard 1983, pp. 33, 69, 99–100, and pp. 120–1 on Talbot's profits. John Chetwynd may also have been given a

of Gilbert Hore and John Chetwynd for payment of their wages probably represent the financial experience of many campaigners under Henry VI; the fact that they were in distinguished company, from the duke of York down, cannot have been much comfort. Indeed the single occurrence in Warwickshire landed society directly attributable to the war was the decline of the Peytos in mid-century brought about by William's capture and ransom in the 1440s. He returned from France heavily in debt, being forced to mortgage his three Warwickshire manors in 1445–6 and 1451, and the family took a long time to recover; in 1487 William's grandson died 'not having entered, and having refused to enter, on his father's estate', a refusal which was probably due to reluctance to accept the family burden of debt. He seems, in fact, to have died at Fladbury, the Worcestershire residence of his brother-in-law, Robert Throgmorton. Here we have a real example of social mobility in both directions, for at the beginning of the century Peytos would probably have refused marriage with a Throgmorton, much less have been dependent on Throgmorton charity for their existence.[90] Given the small number of beneficiaries from the war, it would be a matter of chance whether there were any in a particular county, although the preponderance was likely to be higher in poor counties with a tradition of military service to the crown, like Cornwall and Cheshire.[91]

Secondly, in this county, well away from the London suburbs and home counties where London merchants tended to invest their wealth, merchants had no significant effect on the structure of local society.[92] A few of them might buy a single manor, like the Bristowes, who bought Whitley manor within the Coventry leet, or the Tates of Coventry, who acquired Gilson manor in Coleshill, but even these remained very much on the margins of gentry society, the Gilsons barely on the margins. The Bristowes owed such prominence as they had to the location of their property, since the political upheavals of the middle of the century made Coventry and its surrounds a peculiarly sensitive region, and to their epic confrontation with the town government and other local landowners later in the century.[93] Only one Coventry merchant managed to establish himself in a reasonably commanding position in landed society in

lordship in France, although the grant was rescinded a year later: the grant is to a 'Jean Cherwyn, écuyer anglais' (*Actes de la Chancellerie d'Henri VI*, II, pp. 372, 384; also Allmand 1983: p. 62).

90 *Actes de la Chacellerie d'Henri VI*, II, pp. 271–4; Pollard 1983: p. 80; Johnson 1988: pp. 56–9; S.C.8/153/7626–9; *Dugdale*, p. 477; *W.F.F.*, 2625, 2652; *Colls. Hist. Staffs.*, o.s., 11, p. 246; *Cal. Close Rolls 1441–47*, pp. 356, 369, *1454–61*, p. 456; *Cal. Pat. Rolls 1446–52*, pp. 257, 501; *I.P.M. Hen. VII*, I, 292.

91 Allmand 1983: pp. 246–51; Hatcher 1970: p. 145; Bennett 1983: ch. 9. Cf. McFarlane 1973, ch. 1, ii, for war and the nobility.

92 Thrupp 1948: chs. 5 and 6.

93 *V.C.H.*, IV, pp. 52–3, VIII, p. 87. For Coventry in the Wars of the Roses and the Bristowes' conflicts over enclosures, see below, pp. 497–8, 539–42. For the Tates, see above, p. 74 n.132.

this period. This was William Botener, who bought Withybrook manor in *c.* 1406, attained the status of esquire and became a regular J.P. But he failed to found a line and his daughter and heiress married into the landed gentry, so mercantile wealth was vested in this manor for a single generation only.[94] If one considers the likelihood of lines failing, it becomes apparent that a wholly improbable number of merchants would have to fight their way into the gentry for this group to have any lasting impact on landed society. It was probably more likely that mercantile property would pass to a gentry family, as happened with Emscote, which Robert Hugford bought off the mayor of Coventry in 1408.[95]

A more common source of new entrants to landed society was younger sons, although they can hardly be termed 'new men', and their lands were likely to come from marriage or gift rather than by purchase. More will be said on these when we come to consider the dispersal of estates, but they should also be examined in the context of social mobility. Some of the richer families, which could afford to give single manors to one or two of their cadets, chose to do so. Robert Catesby is an example mentioned already, another is Henry Ferrers, second son of Thomas I, who was given Flecknoe. At the end of the century there were three younger Mountford branches, at Church Bickenhill, Monkspath and Kington.[96] This policy was also pursued by some of the new families that had prospered, perhaps because, as comparative newcomers, they were less willing than more established families to see members of the family suffer the indignities of marginal gentility. For example, Thomas Hugford gave Princethorpe to his younger son William and Thomas Littleton provided handsomely for all three of his sons at his death in 1481.[97] Estates granted to younger

94 *Dugdale*, p. 215; *W.F.F.*, 2433; S.B.T. D.R.31 fo.429; *V.C.H.*, VI, p. 266; app. 2.

95 The manor was the property of the Rivells of Buckby, Northamptonshire, but at the time of the sale it was in the hands of William Attleburgh, mayor of Coventry, second husband of Joan Rivell (*Cat. Anc. Deeds*, IV, A8470; *V.C.H.*, VI, p. 166). Cf. Bennett 1987a: p. 32 on the close interconnections of administrators, lawyers and townsmen in this period; this must depend to a great extent on the degree of urbanisation (above, pp. 18–19 on the lack of urbanisation in Warwickshire).

96 *Cal. Close Rolls 1454–61*, pp. 324–5; Bod. Lib. Dugdale MS 15, p. 43; *I.P.M. Hen. VII*, III, 760; C.1/64/52 (see also below, p. 219); S.B.T. D.R.37/1050; for Catesby, see above, p. 117. The problem of younger sons is discussed at greater length below, pp. 211–21.

97 *Visitation Warwicks.*, p. 337; Dugdale's genealogy (*Dugdale*, p. 278) is clearly in error in interpolating an additional Thomas Hugford between Thomas and William, as John and William are both sons of Thomas (C.P.40/868 rot. 477), as is *Visitation Warwicks.* in interpolating Thomas between William and his son John (*I.P.M. Hen. VII*, III, 1151). William married as his second wife the daughter of a man from Princethorpe (*Visitation Warwicks.*), but was 'of Princethorpe' while his first wife, Alice Beaufo, was still alive, so it seems he was given the family manor of Princethorpe. It is improbable that he could have been escheator in 1452 without owning a manorial lordship (C.67/47 m.6; Baker 1822–41: I, p. 231; *V.C.H.*, VI, p. 243; *Cal. Fine Rolls 1452–61*, p. 17). For Littleton, see *Test. Vetust.*, p. 362 and below, p. 214.

sons could be protected by entail from passing out of the family; for instance, the Harewell manor of Shottery in Stratford reverted to the main Wootton Wawen line in 1452 on the death without direct heirs of the daughter of Richard, younger son of John I.[98] Usually, however, a cadet's substantial estates, if any, would come from a fortunate marriage. Since their marriage value was low, as they had little to offer for a jointure, they had to take what they could get where they could get it, so that most of those who managed to find an heiress had to go elsewhere to do so. An instance concerns the three younger sons of John Harewell I who were fortunate enough to marry the three Dicklestone heiresses of Gloucestershire.[99]

Over the course of the century, perhaps ten junior branches were established within the county on a permanent basis with a reasonable landed competence; more than arrived by war or commerce, but not a significant number.[100] Most younger sons, as we shall see, had to be content with a small annuity or a fragment of an estate, and this no doubt explains why they turn up so often as defendants in criminal cases. Humiliating dependency on an older brother or nephew was not conducive to encouraging respect for existing power structures, especially in the case of those who were too poor to marry and settle into domesticity.[101] Their best bet was undoubtedly to enter the professions. In 1505 John Harewell II left an annual income to his younger son William to support him in his education – 'that he may learn his grammar & after to Oxford or Cambridge to his sovestry & logic' – and thereafter in training for the law or the priesthood. It was, indeed, from the ranks of the professionals, younger sons and others, that most of the upward social mobility in fifteenth-century Warwickshire came.[102]

There was a variety of routes, but, as William Harewell's father realised, the first prerequisite was usually knowledge of the law. This was obviously essential

[98] C.139/145/9/2; below, p. 218.

[99] *Cal. Close Rolls 1422–29*, p. 10; *Dugdale*, p. 809.

[100] These were Robert Catesby (above, p. 117), Edmund Dalby (C.1/26/249; *Ministers' Accounts of St. Mary*, p. 44), Henry Ferrers (above, p. 122), Richard Harewell (immed. above), John Harewell of Whitley (Cooper 1936: p. 19), William Hore of Stoneythorpe (*V.C.H.*, VI, p. 128), Richard Littleton and the three Mountford cadet lines (above, p. 122).

[101] E.g. K.B.9/377/24, /383,92, /405/3; K.B.27/788 Coram Rege rot. 65; more refs. below, p. 221, n.118; Duby 1977d; and below, pp. 217–19 for more on younger sons; also *Calendar of Proceedings in Chancery*, I, pp. lxxii–vi. Cadet branches are generally thought to have been less profuse in southern and midland England, regions which were less isolated and therefore less endogamous than those further north. Note also the greater likelihood of finding resident kin (presumably unmarried in the case of siblings) in a gentry household in pre-industrial England than in the households of those below them (Houlbrooke 1984: pp. 51–3; Hughes 1987: pp. 39–40; below, p. 260).

[102] Cooper 1936: p. 19. For a general survey of the professions in the period, see Griffiths 1980b; for comparison of law and trade as avenues to upward mobility, Ives 1968: pp. 156–61; also Ives 1983a: esp. chs. 13–15 and pp. 374–7 for a comprehensive account of the legal profession (pp. 30–2 for the law and social climbers); and p. 51 n.70, above for other literature on professionals.

for the practising lawyers, either the minor attorneys or those who aimed at the higher reaches of the profession, but several, perhaps most, of those who went into royal or noble service had some training in the law. Expertise acquired in noble service could be transferred to the royal administration; this was probably true of John Brome of Baddesley Clinton, who may well have owed his entry into the king's service to his erstwhile master, Richard Beauchamp, and certainly true of John Throgmorton, who was appointed to an exchequer office in the hereditary tenure of the Beauchamps and continued to serve Richard Beauchamp thereafter.[103] An examination of the major purchasers of land in the first eighty years of the century, before the boom in the market, reveals that nearly all belonged to one or more of these categories: John Beaufitz, servant to Sudeley and to Edward IV; John Brome, lawyer and servant to Warwick and to Henry VI; Richard Dalby, who served various magnates, notably Buckingham and the dukes of Norfolk; Thomas Greswold, lawyer and crown servant; the Hugfords, close servants of all the holders of the Warwick lands; Thomas Littleton, lawyer, royal justice and initially employee of several noble families; Nicholas Metley, attorney of the duke of Norfolk and annuitant of the Ferrers of Chartley; Thomas Porter, servant of Warwick and possibly of Henry V; John Smyth, lawyer and servant to Edward Grey, Lord Lisle; John Throgmorton, lawyer and servant to Warwick and the crown; the Verneys of Compton Murdack, servants to Warwick.[104] If we include also the Archers who, although

[103] App. 3. The earliest reference I have for Brome in the royal service is from 1435 (*Cal. Pat. Rolls 1429–36*, p. 452), but he was already involved with exchequer personnel by 1429 and receiving favours by then (*Cal. Fine Rolls 1422–30*, pp. 269, 278). For Throgmorton, see Roskell 1954: pp. 224–5.

[104] For noble service, see app. 3. For lawyers, app. 2; above, n.27; Bod. Lib. Dugdale MS 15, p. 163 (Throgmorton). For crown servants, D.L.29/463/7542–62 (Beaufitz); above, n.103 (Brome); above, p. 70 n.115 (Greswold); above, n.103 (Throgmorton). It is not absolutely certain that the Thomas Porter who was valet of the bedchamber to the Prince of Wales in 1411 and, as such, received a grant of land in Warwickshire, was this one (*H.M.C. 15th Report*, p. 117), nor is the identification of the Thomas Porter(?s) who served Henry V and Henry VI and received various grants (*Cal. Pat. Rolls 1422–29*, pp. 73, 226) with the Warwickshire man or with the Prince of Wales' servant definite, although the royal servant was still alive in 1444, which would enhance his claims to be the Warwickshire man, since the latter did not die until 1448 (C.67/39 m.18; C.139/133/14). The Warwickshire man first surfaces for certain in 1426 as 'of Solihull' and as holder of Northamptonshire land that he had been granted by Richard Beauchamp's second wife, but he may have been in Westminster, serving the king, until then, leaving few traces in the local records (*Cat. Anc. Deeds*, iv, A9035, 9788; C.139/133/14). For more on Porter's origins, below, n.156. For land purchases, PROB 11/20 fo.161 (Beaufitz: *Dugdale* and *V.C.H.* do not record that the family owned any of his major properties before John's lifetime); *Cat. Anc. Deeds*, IV, A8371; S.B.T D.R. 3/226; *Dugdale*, pp. 971–2; *V.C.H.*, VI, p. 121 (Brome); *Dugdale*, pp. 541, 546; *Cal. Close Rolls 1447–54*, pp. 23, 328–9 (Dalby); Skipp 1970b: pp. 84–5; *W.F.F.*, 2518, 2538; S.B.T. D.R.37 Box 42/2474, 2480, 2484, 2494–5, 2501; B.R.L. 249975, 427016 (Greswold); *Dugdale*, p. 368: *WFF.*, 2590 (Hugford); *Colls. Hist. Staffs.*, o.s., 12, pp. 326–8 (Littleton); *Dugdale*, pp. 34–5, 294, 970; *V.C.H.*, VI, p. 276 (Metley); C.1/16/432 (Porter); *Dugdale*, p. 264; *V.C.H.*, v, p. 71, vi, pp. 176, 252 (Smyth); *V.C.H.*, III, p. 173; Coughton Court,

established at Tanworth in the thirteenth century, were still only of middle rank, and served the local nobility, notably the holders of the Warwick lands, for most of the century,[105] that leaves only three large-scale purchasers between 1400 and 1480 who cannot be included in the category of 'rising professionals'.[106]

Where did the money for purchase come from? The sums that could be earned in the law have been exhaustively analysed by Ives. The suits brought against defaulting clients by Henry Boteller, lawyer and Recorder of Coventry, in the Common Pleas in 1474–81 give some idea of the figures involved, while also revealing the problem of bad debts which is still a part of the barrister's way of life. At the other end of the legal profession, Thomas Littleton, as justice of King's Bench, was granted annuities in excess of £80.[107] Royal servants, if they were lucky, could supplement their official fees with the profits of sinecures, particularly custodies. John Throgmorton had a number of these between 1418 and 1438, the most lucrative being the temporalities of the see of Worcester in 1433, and they doubtless helped pay for the various pieces of land he bought in this period, culminating in the purchase of the two halves of Spernall manor in 1441 and 1443 and of the second half of Coughton in 1449.[108] Even though these men were likely to have had to settle for widows rather than heiresses, the widow's jointure could be a source of funds for buying land that would be permanently theirs. The Chetwynd lands may well have helped buy Tixall, Staffordshire for Thomas Littleton some time before 1470, Richard Archer's purchase of Botley in 1443 may have been at least partly financed by the succession of widows he married and Nicholas Metley's very substantial purchases may have owed something to the large jointure of his mother, the Cotes widow.[109]

The contribution of noble employment to territorial advancement, on the other hand, was usually of a different nature. The sums earned in such service were not normally large – mostly £5 to £20 a year – while a reasonable-sized

Throckmorton MS Box 35 (various grants to John and Thomas Throgmorton), Box 36 (deed of 1419), Box 52 (deed of 1427), Box 44/22–3, Boxes 48 and 49 (various grants to John); *W.F.F.*, 2662; below, nn.120 (Throgmorton), 160; below, p. 126 (Verney). Cf. in another county, the similar case of Bartholomew Bolney (*Book of Bartholomew Bolney*, pp. xxiii–vi).

105 *Dugdale*, p. 820; S.B.T. D.R.37/915, 939. For the Archers' origins, see below, p. 135.

106 These are Botener, Bristowe and Tate, all originally from Coventry (above, pp. 121–2) The Spensers did not begin purchasing until the 1470s and bought only on a small scale until the end of the century (Jeayes ed., 'Catalogue of Spencer Charters', 1532–37; below, p. 132). Cf. Bennett 1983: p. 202.

107 Ives 1983a: ch. 13, and pp. 142–3 on arrears of fees; C.P.40/852 rot.42, /856 rot.175d., /868 rot. 230, /874 rot. 274d., /878 roti. 288d., 466; *Foedera*, v, ii, p. 139.

108 *Cal. Pat. Rolls 1422–29*, p. 480; *Cal. Fine Rolls 1413–22*, pp. 255, 276, *1422–30*, pp. 38, 163, 225, *1430–37*, pp. 21–2, 116–17, 171, 304, 321, *1437–45*, p. 19. For purchases, above, n.104; below, n.120.

109 Above, nn.104–5 for all purchases and above, p. 103 n.27 for Margaret Metley's identity.

estate could cost well over £100,[110] although sinecures, as in the case of crown servants, could bring in lucrative windfalls. For example, in the 1430s the Verneys had custody of the Beauchamp park of Claverdon, with the right to fell 700 trees, to take the undergrowth and to exercise free warren.[111] Lords occasionally made presents of land, which may be how the Dalbys came into Brookhampton, their residence and first sizeable estate, given them by the duke of Norfolk, and how John Onley acquired Birdingbury, his only Warwickshire manor, by the gift of William Beauchamp, Lord Bergavenny in the early years of the century.[112] In the 1450s and later some minor gentry arrived from the north with their master Richard Neville, the new earl of Warwick, and were settled by means not entirely clear on small estates near Coventry.[113] The Verneys seem to have had help of a slightly different sort in buying the manors of Compton Murdack and Kingston that were the foundation of their prosperity. As far as can be deduced from the subsequent dispute with the executors of Richard Beauchamp, Beauchamp had helped the Verneys buy the properties from Robert Skerne, another member of his affinity, on condition that after Beauchamp's death they would alienate Kingston to the church of St. Mary's Warwick, where a chantry was to be built as Beauchamp's memorial. When the Verneys went back on the agreement they finally consented to pay £566 13s 4d for the manor. Considering that in 1461 Richard Verney was making £49 clear from it, this was a good bargain even at fifteen years' purchase, much more so at twenty, especially as they had also had help in buying Compton, which by the same date was yielding a clear £60.[114]

[110] E.g. £200 for Tilbrook, Beds. in 1480 (*Cat. Anc. Deeds*, IV, A8481), 250 marks and a life annuity of 10 marks for Woodloes in 1448 (W.C.R.O. C.R.26/1(2)/W24), £382 for a third of Middleton in 1495 (*Cal. Close Rolls 1485–1500*, p. 243). At fifteen or twenty years' purchase, even an estate yielding as little as £10 a year would be expensive. For the size of fees, see app. 3 and discussion below, p. 631.

[111] S.B.T. D.R. 98/722.

[112] *Dugdale*, p. 323; *V.C.H.*, v, p. 106 (but possibly purchased *t.*Ed.III: see below p. 220 n.116).

[113] Richard Clapham, John de Middleham, John and Robert Otter, John Shirwode. All came from families connected with the Neville estates in the north of England, mostly arriving soon after Neville's inheritance of the earldom of Warwick. Clapham and the Otters certainly, de Middleham probably, were connected with the earl. Clapham, originally 'yeoman of Warwick', and so probably a household servant there, served Warwick at Berkswell and had an estate in Alspath/Meriden; Shirwode seems to have acquired land in Coventry in the early 1450s and was also at Alspath soon after, the Otters and de Middleham may have lived in Warwick's household; Robert Otter married Clapham's widow, thereby coming into the Clapham estate. (Coles 1961: App. B, pp. 12, 17; *Cal. Pat. Rolls 1452–61*, p. 122; S.C.6/1038/2; K.B.27/810 Coram Rege rot.27; *Coventry Leet Book*, p. 255; *Cal. Pat. Rolls 1461–67*, p. 490; *Cal. Close Rolls 1461–68*, pp. 158, 106; C.67/41 m.10; C.P.40/852 rot. 339, /868 rot. 432; Wm. Salt Lib. H.M. Chetwynd Coll. Bundle 4 (agreement of 1484)). Thomas Otter, probably a member of the same family, seems to have been one of Richard III's imports from the north, but was following in a tradition already established by Richard's predecessor as holder of the complete Neville estate (Pollard 1977; *Cal. Pat. Rolls 1476–85*, p. 369, *1485–94*, p. 39). Also below, pp. 498, 552.

[114] S.B.T. D.R.98/477, 495a, 722, 504a. For Beauchamp and St. Mary's, see *Dugdale*, pp. 445–7.

Richard Beauchamp's role in this shows another benefit of noble patronage. With the scarcity of purchasable estates and the strong possibility that there would be residual claimants to those that reached the market, the lord could perform a valuable service by encouraging his men to sell to one another and then providing the influence to defend the transaction.[115] Many of the major purchases were made this way. Nicholas Metley seems to have obtained Wolston, Marston, Wappenbury with Eathorpe and possibly Weston under Wetherley through the Warwick/Ferrers connection, although in none of these cases is the descent clear. John Brome of Baddesley Clinton bought the reversion of Woodloes in 1448 from a family that, like his own, had a long tradition of service to the Beauchamps. Less eminent employers could also help their servants out: for instance, John Underhill, to whom Edward Belknap sold land in Whitchurch in 1499, had served Belknap's grandfather William as attorney in 1481–2, and may well have remained in the family's service. And professional services could of themselves provide openings in the land market. For example, Ralph Astley of Hillmorton, a lawyer who helped William Peyto raise the money for his ransom, was also able to buy some Peyto properties, which had presumably come on the market for the same reason. Sometimes noble influence in purchasing estates could take dubious forms, as when the Beauchamp nexus probably helped Thomas Porter extract the manor of Eastcote and Longdon from the senile Thomas Archer in 1427 and the duke of Buckingham sold the Verney of Great Wolford manor of Kites Hardwick to his servant, Richard Dalby, in 1447, when the heir to the family was in his charge.[116] Both these sales were contested and so were two of the three made by

[115] Connections with kinsmen and neighbours could operate in the same way (*Paston Letters*, I, pp. 38–9; *Stonor Letters*, II, pp. 144–5); these could themselves be part of a lord's network (below, pp. 312–18).

[116] For these purchases, above, n.104; for noble connections, app. 3; for Metley, Ferrers and Warwick, above, p. 104; for the Verney wardship see S.C.R.O. D.641/1/2/269–72; for the Belknap sale, below, n.141 and Northants. R.O. Temple (Stowe) Coll. Box 6/2; for Astley and Peyto, see Canterbury Dioc., Reg. Stafford, fos. 135, 135v.; W.C.R.O. L.4/36. The descent of Wolston, Marston, Wappenbury, Eathorpe and Weston under Wetherley, which were amongst Metley's purchases, is unclear. The *V.C.H.* implies that the only Metley property at Weston was the Cotes estate, held by Margaret as part of her jointure from her first marriage (above, pp. 67, 103 and below, p. 402 n.4 for this), but Metley must have had some property of his own here, as the Metley manor came to John Hugford but the Cotes were in possession of their part again at the end of the century. Cf. initial conclusions in Carpenter, M. C. 1976: App. II n.9, that the Cotes lost these lands for most of the century to the Metleys and their descendants. The same is true of Hunningham, where, as at Weston, both families had lands (*V.C.H.*, VI, pp. 118, 252; *Dugdale*, p. 298; *W.F.F.*, 2723; K.B.27/919 Coram Rege rot.33). However, it seems clear that Wolston and Wappenbury with Eathorpe came from Thomas Stafford of Baginton and Marston from Thomas Woodlow, both Warwick retainers (*Dugdale*, pp. 40–1, 294; app. 3).

John Brome: Lapworth and Woodloes.[117] Precautions could be taken, like Brome's grant of some of his lands in Lapworth and elsewhere to his father in 1426. This enabled him later to attempt to extract statements from his tenants to the effect that they had paid rent to his father's agents, thereby establishing a hereditary claim.[118] Nevertheless, without continued noble protection, while there was such competition for estates, purchasers were never likely to be safe. Brome lost Lapworth to the Catesbys after the fall of his Lancastrian protectors. Although he was adroit enough to hang on to his other two purchases under the new regime, as soon as the renewed upheavals presaging the Readeption began he was murdered by John Herthill, his rival for Woodloes.[119]

The major purchasers tended to take what they could where they could, unless, like the Archers, the Dalbys and the Verneys of Compton Murdack, they were trying to create a consolidated estate for pastoral-farming or cattle-raising. This is another important distinction between the old and the new families, for, until the boom in sheep-farming at the end of the century, established families had little incentive to exploit their estates; it was unlikely to be profitable without a great deal of effort and they did not need to generate further capital for land purchase. The Throgmortons and Catesbys are exceptional in this respect, for they continued to take an active interest in exploitation long after they had joined the leading families. This was no doubt why the Throgmortons acquired the other half of Coughton in 1449, enabling them to consolidate and ultimately to enclose.[120] Failing purchase, leasing was the best way to fill in gaps in an estate designed for pastoral farming. During the period up to about 1480, when the land market was stagnant, it was used most effectively by the Throgmortons, the Catesbys, the Dalbys, the Verneys of Compton Murdack and John Beaufitz. But there was competition even for leasehold and here again it was helpful to have a co-operative lord. The lay lords in Warwickshire, especially those with active interests in the county like Warwick and Buckingham, seem on the whole to have been rather reluctant to lease demesnes and pastures wholesale, perhaps regarding it as a diminution of lordship. There were some pickings to be had from them, but the main sources of supply were the lands of the great ecclesiastical institutions and, to a lesser extent, because it did not own much land in Warwickshire, the Duchy of Lancaster.

117 Below, pp. 458, 502–3. Carpenter 1986b: p. 44 is in error in saying that all three of Brome's purchases were contested: the dispute over Baddesley Clinton was wrongly inferred by both myself and Dugdale (*Dugdale*, p. 970) from S.B.T. D.R.3/612. This is a statement about a dispute over unspecified lands, headed in a later, probably sixteenth-century, hand, 'A case longinge ? [sic] to Baddesly'. However, P.R.O. Catesby Doc. makes clear that Baddesley Clinton was the one Metley property whose sale was not contested (above, p. 104; below, p. 492 n.21).

118 W.C.R.O. Z.131/5; *Cat. Anc. Deeds*, v, A10661.

119 *Dugdale*, p. 971; below, pp. 502–3, 510, 558. Cf. Bartholomew Bolney, a fifteenth-century lawyer, most of whose many purchases were made piecemeal (*Book of Bartholomew Bolney, passim*).

120 Below, ch.5. For the Throgmortons' purchase of the second half of Coughton, see Coughton Court, Throckmorton MS Box 35 (deed of 1449). Cf. Ives 1983a: pp. 343–4.

By and large the ecclesiastical estates were concentrated on the Warwickshire/Worcestershire and Warwickshire/Northamptonshire borders and around Coventry, so it tended to be families from these areas that did best out of leasing. The Throgmortons, aided by a tradition of service to some of the many institutions in Worcestershire, were able to lease land from Studley Priory, the abbey of Evesham and the bishopric itself. The local gentry in general had a greater share in the leases of the see in the second half of the century.[121] On the other side of the county the Catesbys were able to obtain leases from their neighbour the abbey of Combe, until relations soured in the 1460s, and in 1452/3 they were farming Braunston, Leicestershire from their then noble protector, the duke of Somerset.[122] John Beaufitz leased land near Coventry from the Hospitallers.[123] John Brome, because of his connections with the court, was able to supplement his land at Baddesley Clinton with an extra messuage obtained from the Duchy of Lancaster in 1443 on a thirty-year lease, although he lost it after the Yorkist victory, and his heir regained it only in 1469.[124] Even at the end of the century, when purchase was becoming easier, leasehold remained desirable, and consequently a possible cause of friction. This was all the more so in that so many families were now trying to make compact estates for sheep-runs; so, in 1495 Robert Throgmorton was in dispute with the Hospitallers over his lease of Balsall near Coventry, where he was grazing sheep. For this reason personal connection remained important in getting access to leases. For example, in 1484 John Archer II was given a perpetual lease of pastures in Alrewas, Staffordshire by Thomas Mountford, the heir of Simon, which he must have owed to the fact that he was married to Thomas' sister.[125]

The difficulties in building up compact estates for pastoral farming before the more expansive 1480s are highlighted by the fortunes of the Dalbys of Brookhampton and the Verneys of Compton Murdack. Both families were resident in southern Warwickshire, a region where there was extensive conversion from arable to pasture in this period.[126] Both were ambitious. So it was entirely logical that both should want to use the money and influence they

[121] Dyer 1981: p. 17–18, 1980b: pp. 109–11, 214, 379–80; Br. Lib. Add. MS 28,564 fo.31; *V.C.H.*, III, pp. 80–2; Coughton Court, Throckmorton MS Exhibition Box/9, Box 33 (Studley lease), Box 48 (grant of 1418, agreements of 1436 and 1437, deeds of 1426 and 1460). For lay lords and leasing, see e.g. S.C.R.O. D.641/1/2/269–72; W.C.R.O. C.R.895/8/1–21, C.R.623/1; S.B.T. D.R.37 Box 107; Br. Lib. Eg. Rolls 8477–8544 (Walsall, just over the Staffs. border). These show that there were some large-scale leases of demesne to be had but what there was tended not to go to the gentry. See also below, p. 167.

[122] *Cal. Pat. Rolls 1494–1509*, pp. 141–2; *Cat. Anc. Deeds*, IV, A8848, I, A1412.

[123] *Dugdale*, pp. 264, 965.

[124] D.L.29/463/7547, 7549; S.B.T D.R.3/261.

[125] STAC 1 Vol. 1/50/2, Vol. II/109/1–5; S.B.T D.R.37 Box 59 (deed of 1484). Archer was made Mountford's estate steward in 1495 (S.B.T. D.R.37, Box 60 (deed of 1495)).

[126] Above, p. 23.

had won in noble service to put together extensive pastures, for leasing or direct exploitation or both. Unfortunately their lands were in too close proximity for both families to be successful at a time when there was not much land on the market, especially as leasehold seems also to have been in short supply in this area. Dalby did marginally better than the Verneys in the matter of leases, obtaining a shared lease of the warren of Tysoe from his employer, the duke of Buckingham, who had the main manor, and a lease of Westcote, a subordinate hamlet of Tysoe, from the Oxford Hospitallers. The second of these though was soon disputed by and ultimately lost to Magdalen College Oxford. The Verneys had to make do with leases from St. Mary's Warwick, mainly of tithes, some of which involved them in a lot of conflict.

It is then hardly to be wondered at that these two ambitious families found themselves in dispute over both the ownership of estates – chiefly the lands of the Verneys of Great Wolford – and the right to leases, particularly over Cheping Kington, owned by the dukes of Norfolk and subsequently by the Howards. Conflict drew them both ever more urgently into noble politics, not necessarily with happy results. In the event the Dalbys, having no representative of Richard Dalby's ability to replace him when he died in 1477, had to give best to the Verneys, who had already gained the upper hand long before then. But the Verneys too seem ultimately to have suffered from the expense of litigation and from the damage to their lands and stock inevitable in such a prolonged conflict. When wool-growing became so profitable at the end of the century and much more land became available to support it, the Verneys took a surprisingly inactive role, when one considers how many years' experience they had over their newly-active neighbours. Sir Richard Verney, having risen from insignificant origins to knighthood, lived to see his son and grandson, both admittedly less outstandingly able men, fall back amongst the *mediocres* of the county.[127]

It was in the last two decades of the fifteenth century and the first two of the next that the pattern of land acquisition changed; no longer was it mainly new

[127] The Dalby–Verney dispute features prominently in the political sections (chs. 10–14). The major sources of leases in the far south were lay magnates, particularly Warwick and Buckingham. There are no detailed accounts for the Warwick lands here, but for Buckingham's, above, n.121. For the leases cited in the text, B.R.L. 168236; *V.C.H.*, v, p. 177; B.R.L. 437204; *Ministers' Accounts of St. Mary's*, pp. 136, 168. For Dalby's death, C.1/78/89, for the status of the Verneys, below, p. 216 and app. 2. An additional complication for Dalby was that he was a younger son, although he seems to have come into the whole estate in the end (below, p. 220). There are problems with the Verney genealogy, principally a tendency to confuse John Verney esquire, father of Richard, supervisor, receiver-general and auditor to Richard Beauchamp, 1–10 Hen.VI, escheator of Worcestershire in 1438 and elector in Warwickshire in 1432, with John Verney cleric, his son, dean of Lichfield and auditor of Richard Beauchamp in 1432–3 (Ross 1956, p. 8; *Dugdale*, p. 566; Sinclair 1987a: pp. 172, 356–7). A careful reading of the following makes the distinction clear: S.C.6/1303/13; Br. Lib. Add. Rolls 26,899–900, Eg. Rolls 8509–8521; W.C.R.O. C.R.895/12–16; Warwick Castle MS 485–8; Warwick Corp. Recs. W.19/5; Worcs.R.O. 899:95/94–102; *List of Escheators*, p. 180; C.219/14/1/3/2 (Warks.) (all John Verney the father); *Ministers' Accounts of St. Mary's*, p. 1 (although the same error is made here: see

families that were buying land and exploiting the agricultural market, now the established ones were quite as active. Partly this was because more lands were available for political reasons. In addition to the advantages to Henry VII's servants of his tighter control of his feudal rights, there was the fact that Henry meted out harsher treatment to his political opponents. Earlier in the century the gentry who rebelled, unlike the nobility, tended not to have the sins of the fathers visited on the progeny. The family of Robert Ardern suffered no more than temporary confiscation of part of their lands after Robert's rebellion in 1452;[128] the Malorys of Newbold Revel, if Thomas *did* commit treason in the 1460s, lost none of their lands and had reattained respectability by the early years of the sixteenth century;[129] neither the Ferrers of Tamworth nor the Catesbys incurred any permanent damage from active support of respectively the Yorkists and the Lancastrians, despite the fact that William Catesby I went as far as going into a brief exile in Scotland with the deposed Henry VI.[130] Even in the later years of Edward IV, when it became harder for the nobility to survive political miscalculation,[131] the Burdet family did not suffer for the alleged misdeeds of Thomas II.[132] Already under Richard III the climate began to change and a favoured few, led by William Catesby II, benefited from the massive confiscations of the reign,[133] but it was under Henry VII that for the first time in the century it became normal for the families of gentry rebels to suffer permanent loss of most or all of the family property.[134]

In Warwickshire this meant that the estates of three major families, the Catesbys, the Staffords of Grafton and the Mountfords, became available during this reign. Few of these properties went to native families, but the fact that they were given mostly to household men who were not resident in the

below, p. 174 n.119); Le Neve 1964: pp. 6, 44; S.B.T. D.R.98/459a; W.C.R.O. C.R.895/17 (for the cleric); B.R.L. 434595 (where both appear); S.B.T. D.R.98/722 (where the supervisor's relationship to Richard Verney is made clear). Once in the Walsall series the supervisor and receiver general is referred to as 'clerk' (Br. Lib. Eg. Roll 8518), but he is not designated as such elsewhere on this roll or on any other roll in the series, so it seems likely that whoever drew up the roll was momentarily confusing him with his son. Equally, in another account, of 1425–6 (Gloucs.R.O. D.184/M15/1), the supervisor and receiver general is referred to consistently as 'clerk', but the weight of the other evidence suggests that this too was an error.

128 *Dugdale*, p. 928; *Cal. Fine Rolls 1452–61*, pp. 67, 70–1, 82–3; *Cal. Close Rolls 1447–54*, pp. 459–60; S.C.8/89/4403.

129 Carpenter 1980b: pp. 41–2; *Cal. Pat. Rolls 1494–1509*, p. 663; below, p. 593. Field (1981–2; and see below, p. 612) makes a not entirely convincing case for Malory having been guilty of treason.

130 *Dugdale*, p. 1,136. For Catesby's exile, see below, p. 493.

131 Lander 1976b: pp. 153–5.

132 *Dugdale*, p. 849; *Cal. Pat. Rolls 1476–85*, p. 102; below, p. 536.

133 He had already begun to profit in the later years of Edward IV from his membership of the powerful Hastings nexus (below, pp. 527–8). His opportunities under Richard III included also access to some doubtful dealing in land. See refs. in nn.87 and 110, above and Horrox and Hammond, eds, *Br. Lib. Harleian Manuscript 433*, I, pp. 6, 65, 91–2, 125, 194, 285; also Williams 1975–6: pp. 46–7; below, pp. 549, 551–2, 554.

134 *Rot. Parl.*, VI, p. 276; *Cal. Pat. Rolls 1485–94*, *passim.*

county meant that there was more land available for leasing; these absentees were more than happy to lease out whole demesnes or even whole manors and sometimes even to sell these very peripheral properties.[135] The fortunes of the sheep-farming Spensers were founded on leases of this kind from the former Catesby lands, and subsequently on the purchase of a former Mountford manor nearby from William Cope, the household man who had it by the king's grant. Marriage of a Spenser daughter to Cope himself helped cement this mutually beneficial relationship, from which Cope got a steady income and the Spensers the land they needed to create their great sheep-runs across the Warwickshire/Northamptonshire border.[136] Henry VII's men might also get access to leases of confiscated lands that had remained in the hands of the crown; for example Robert Throgmorton was part of a consortium leasing the former Mountford manor of Hampton in Arden in 1499.[137]

Some of Henry's closer servants profited in other ways from the king's energy in exercising his rights over landed property. A good example is Edward Belknap, co-heir to the Sudeley lands, who was making extensive purchases in the late fifteenth and early sixteenth centuries and probably deriving a good deal of his capital from proximity to the king. He must have done particularly well from his brief but probably profitable appointment as Surveyor of the Royal Prerogative in 1508, with the duty to search out income owed to the king and the right to share in the profits.[138] But, however alluring the king's patronage might be in enlarging the family property, it was never safe to assume that even the king's more intimate servants were immune to Henry's eye for the main chance. For example, Henry Willoughby, who moved in circles very close to the king, obtained the custody of part of the Grey of Codnor lands in 1504 and then in 1508 was able to join with John Zouche in buying them, a purchase which made him one of the greatest men in the north midlands. But this is only half the story, for he actually paid rather more than he might have expected for them; before his death, Henry Grey of Codnor had already sold the lordship to Zouche's father, and Willoughby's daughter was married to the Zouche heir. On Grey's death, however, Willoughby and the other men with responsibility for Grey's lands had been prevailed upon to sell them to the king for the use of the duke of York. What Henry VII did, after establishing that the original sale

[135] *Cal. Pat. Rolls 1485–94*, pp. 96, 121, 209, 230, 275 (Catesby); *ibid.*, pp. 111, 140, 145, 150–1, 230–1, 250, 302 (Stafford of Grafton); *Cal. Pat. Rolls 1494–1509*, pp. 65, 73, 84–5, 133, 308, 340 (Mountford). All three were partially restored subsequently (*Rot. Parl.*, VI, pp. 491–2, 526; *Wedgwood: Biographies*, p. 793).

[136] Thorpe 1962: pp. 55–7; *Cal. Pat. Rolls 1494–1509*, p. 133; *Test. Vetust.*, p. 427; Finch 1956: pp. 38–9.

[137] Br. Lib. Add. MS 21,480 fo.38v.

[138] *Cal. Close Rolls 1485–1500*, p. 302; *Dugdale*, pp. 297, 522; *V.C.H.*, V, p. 70, VI, pp. 47, 249, 275; Beresford 1945–6: p. 93; *Cal. Pat. Rolls 1494–1509*, p. 591; also e.g. *Cal. Pat. Rolls 1494–1509*, pp. 280, 599. Cf. the benefits derived by the Vernons and others from their association with the crown in the later fifteenth century (Wright 1983: pp. 20–1).

was genuine, was to sell their own property back to Willoughby and Zouche, a privilege for which they paid £1,400.[139] Robert Throgmorton, who became one of Henry VII's more intimate associates towards the end of the reign, died in 1518, still owing £500 to a London alderman, for which he had reluctantly mortgaged property in Huntingdonshire. It is highly probable that this debt was the result of a recognisance made to Henry in 1502 for a debt of 500 marks, itself probably the outcome of paying for a royal grant.[140]

Lands were also becoming available at the end of the fifteenth century because of a greater willingness to sell on the part of the owners. Why this should be so is not entirely clear but it seems to be related to changes in the economy which will be discussed at some length in the following chapter. Much of the land reached the market as a result of consolidation for the construction of pastoral estates and a good deal of it was consequently in the main pastoral area south of the Avon. Numbers of families, old and new, were engaged in this exercise. Edward Belknap, for instance, sold his lands in and around Whitchurch in southern Warwickshire in the course of extending his property in the east and south-east of the county. The purchaser of his land at Crimscote and Alderminster near Whitchurch was John Underhill who already had land at Lower Ettington nearby.[141] Henry Willoughby was another of the consolidators of this time. In 1499 he sold Whitnash near Warwick to Benedict Metley, a grazier who was also engaged in consolidation. This manor had never been anything other than peripheral to the Willoughbys but the pastoral boom had now produced both a reason for selling it, in that cash was required for lands elsewhere, and a buyer. Willoughby had already sold a manor in Leicestershire to Thomas Kebyll in 1495 and in the same year he bought out the Botellers of Wood Hall, Hertfordshire, who owned the other main manor in Middleton, some of the £382 it cost having presumably come from the sale to Kebyll.[142]

Whether consolidation and exchange were the only economic causes of the growth of a more active land market is uncertain. The history of the Cotes family suggests that perhaps there were others. They were struggling throughout the century with the consequences of a long-lived dowager and a series of apparently rather mediocre heads of the family,[143] but it is only in this period,

139 *Cal. Pat. Rolls 1494–1509*, pp. 583–4; *Cal. Close Rolls 1500–09*, pp. 56–7, 133; *Cat. Anc. Deeds*, v, A13484. In 1510 Willoughby had debts 'which grow to a thousand pounds' (Smith, R.S. 1964: p. 15), and some at least of these may well have come from his dealings with Henry VII.

140 PROB 11/20 fo.9v.; *Cal. Close Rolls 1500–09*, p. 65.

141 Morrison 1932: p. 35; *W.F.F.*, 2774; Br. Lib. Add. MS 34,739 fo.4; above, n.138.

142 *Dugdale*, p. 365; Hoskins 1950a: pp. 74–5; *Cal. Close Rolls 1485–1500*, pp. 243, 275–6. For Metley, *Cat. Anc. Deeds*, II, B3080; S.B.T. D.R.31 Bushwood No.6; W.C.R.O. C.R.1908/76/4,7–9, /92, /93/1–2, /177/10; Br. Lib. Add. MS 47,677 fo.62v.; Ives 1983a: pp. 343–4 for Kebyll's own consolidation. Note that consolidation was going on earlier in the century too (above, pp. 117–18 for the Catesbys, and Richmond 1981: p. 26).

143 Above, pp. 89, 102. The last of the family to hold a major office was John I in 1441 and not even the Hugford marriage could return the family to office.

when marriage to one of the Hugford heiresses should have improved their prospects, that they began to sell off their properties.[144] Equally, it was only in the 1480s that the Peytos appear fully to have felt the financial effects of Sir William's capture and ransom in mid-century.[145] Perhaps the Cotes chose to sell their lands now rather than earlier because the plethora of would-be buyers, grown rich in the king's service or by wool-growing, or both, had pushed land prices up to a point which made it worth their while. However, the fortunes of the Peytos suggest that there may have been a more general inflation which made the position of families in difficulties, like the Peytos or the Cotes, untenable. Whatever the causes – and this problem will be considered again in the context of land exploitation – there is a clear-cut break in the pattern of land-purchases after about 1480. From that date a far greater proportion of landowners was speculating in land, agriculture and royal favour. As in the early thirteenth century, when there was a similar political climate, and perhaps in some respects a similar economic climate, both opportunities and pitfalls increased and as a result the openings for newcomers were greater than at any time in the century.[146]

III

The slackness of the agricultural economy for most of the century must be borne in mind when considering the role of agricultural enterprise and the piecemeal acquisition of land in lifting families into the ranks of the gentry. There are really two separate questions to be answered. The first is whether a prosperous peasant tenant could accumulate land from other tenants or from the demesne to the point where he might be judged a yeoman: still a son of the soil but one who could be asked to serve as juror and might be qualified to vote. The second concerns the ability of yeomen to climb into the gentry by means of agricultural profits alone. Studies of peasant families in this period do not suggest that even the more prosperous peasant tenants found it very easy to

[144] *Cal. Fine Rolls 1485–1509*, p. 78; *Cal. Pat. Rolls 1494–1509*, p. 592; *I.P.M. Hen VII*, II, 913; *V.C.H.*, VI, pp. 118, 249, 275; *W.F.F.*, 2723; K.B.27/919 Coram Rege rot.33. In 1484 John Cotes II was impleaded for debt by Edward Doddingselles II (C.P.40/890 rot.226d.), but not too much should be made of this, as disputes over complex recognisances and credit-raising mechanisms (below, p. 206) often ended up in the Common Pleas as pleas of debt. The Cotes themselves bought Whitchurch in 1512 (*V.C.H.*, V, p. 210), so it is possible that they too were selling to rationalise, or that the earlier sales had been to cope with a temporary financial problem.

[145] Above, p. 121. But William's death intestate in 1464 (*Dugdale*, p. 472; *Cal. Fine Rolls 1461–71*, p. 127) suggests there were already serious problems earlier on, although note that Dugdale (*Dugdale*, p. 477) attributed the rebuilding of Chesterton (below, p. 200) to John, not William, Peyto, which, if correct, would suggest that John had surmounted the effects of his father's ransom.

[146] Holt 1961a: *passim*; Painter 1943: *passim*; Raban 1985; and works on 'knightly class' above, n.2.

accumulate land permanently. It has been found that peasant holders of multiple tenancies tended to break up their enlarged holdings amongst their children in later life or at their deaths. It has also been observed that peasant lessees of demesne land were less well equipped than gentry lessees to increase their profits by improving the land, and that much of the demesne leased to peasants in this period was rented out piecemeal. Until the last decades of the century it is difficult to see that there could have been large enough profits to pay for the accumulation of large estates, since the market for agricultural produce was so sluggish. Instances have been cited in peasant studies of families that did make the transition from virgater to farmer, in both senses, of many acres, and we must probably assume that these were the origins of some of our Warwickshire yeomen, but known examples are rather few and far between. Indeed, the period between the late twelfth and late thirteenth centuries seems a far more promising one for prosperous peasants aspiring to gentility: sizeable tracts of land that might eventually be turned into lordships coming into the agricultural economy through assarts, high agricultural prices and less competition for land from rising lay professionals.[147] If more attention is given to the late-medieval 'kulak' than to his thirteenth-century forebear, this must be because we know more about him, but the Archers, for example, and some of the other gentry families of the Warwickshire Arden, are indubitable descendants of the 'kulaks' of the thirteenth century who prospered during the assarting of the woodlands.[148]

It was undeniably easier for peasants to accumulate land in the fifteenth century than it had been in the fifty years or so before the Black Death.[149] But to turn to the second of our questions – the ability of yeomen to break into Warwickshire landed society on agricultural profits alone – there are few signs that this was possible without additional aid. The increase in the number of gentlemen to be found amongst minor manorial lords during the century reflects changes in social practices rather than in social structure. In any case, this phenomenon has no bearing on the real barrier a yeoman had to cross, the acquisition of a landed estate carrying manorial lordship, which we have seen to be no easy matter without a great deal of money and a fair amount of protection. It is true that the occasional use of the term 'husbandman', 'grazier' or 'franklin' for minor lords could imply an agrarian origin to the wealth that had

147 E.g., amongst a vast literature, Dyer 1980b: ch. 14, 1984; Hilton 1975: pp. 40–1; Howell 1983, ch. 5; Harvey ed. 1984: *passim*; Harvey 1977: pp. 288–90; Hoskins 1957: pp. 141–7. Note Dyer's comments on problems in finding money for rent, attributable to the lack of a market (1980b: p. 216), and that he finds rather more accumulators in the less sluggish early sixteenth century (p. 315; below, pp. 153–6 for more on the economy); similar conclusions in Glennie 1988.

148 Roberts 1965: ch. 5. The ideological background to discussions of the medieval English peasantry is interestingly analysed in Gatrell 1982.

149 Miller and Hatcher 1978: pp. 53–7.

brought them their land and hence their status.[150] Moreover, on the other side of the divide, there were certainly numbers of yeomen and husbandmen leasing demesnes in Warwickshire and elsewhere, and we have seen that in Warwickshire one or two could aspire to a rather perilous gentility without even the possession of lordship over men.[151] But most of the yeoman lessees, such as John Lichfield, grazier, farmer of Kingston manor from the Verneys in 1437, or Robert Bonefaunt, Buckingham's farmer of the demesne at Great Wolford, remain obstinately plebeian throughout their lives.[152]

In theory a yeoman could build up a lordship piecemeal and there were certainly some small estates claiming to be manors, presumably because their lords had jurisdiction over their tenants, which seem to answer to this description. One such was Whateley in Kingsbury, identified as a manor in 1544, which seems to have originated in two virgates mentioned in 1236; another was the reputed manor of Marlbrook in Meriden, which consisted of only sixty acres of arable with another two hundred acres that were principally woodland.[153] Significantly, both were in the Arden, where the plethora of fragmentary manors and the remaining opportunities for assarting could make the creation of small-scale estates like this, by small-scale acquisition, a possibility.[154] Even so, none has been found to originate in the fifteenth century, although some certainly came into existence in the great assarting period of the thirteenth century.[155] Gentry known to be of yeoman origin, such as Thomas Porter, probably from a family of yeomen resident in Solihull and Edgbaston, and Thomas and John Greswold, offspring of another yeoman family from the Arden, had risen in most cases through the professions, notably the law.[156]

The Spensers, the one Warwickshire family of the fifteenth century to achieve a significant social rise solely by agricultural enterprise, did not really prosper until the boom in wool at the end of the century. They were able to acquire leases earlier, notably of Hodnell in about 1461 and of some of the

150 E.g. Thomas Andrewes, 'grazier' 1487, 'husbandman' 1497, 'esquire' 1487 and later (K.B.27/906 Rex rot.8d., /945 Coram Rege rot.44d.; *I.P.M. Hen. VII*, II, 45); John Gamul, 'gentleman-franklin' 1461 (C.P.40/802 rot.202), Thomas atte Wode, 'husbandman' 1443, but 'gentleman' 1436 and later (K.B.27/728 Coram Rege rot.5, /699 Coram Rege rot.42d.).

151 Above, p. 74; Dyer 1980b: ch. 8; Hare 1981; Du Boulay 1965; Harvey 1969.

152 S.B.T. D.R.98/473; S.C.R.O. D.641/1/2/269–72. Lichfield is variously called 'mercer', 'grazier', 'drover' (*Cal. Pat. Rolls 1422–29*, p. 248; *Cat. Anc. Deeds*, III, B3929, IV, A6986).

153 Holdsworth 1922: I, pp. 179–85; *V.C.H.*, IV, pp. 105–6, 152.

154 Above, p. 22.

155 Roberts 1965: ch. 5.

156 Porter is sometimes referred to as 'of Solihull' (e.g. above, n.104) and he is coeval with a Henry Porter of Solihull and Edgbaston, who usually has no title but is once 'husbandman' and occasionally 'gentleman' (K.B.27/700 Coram Rege rot.68, /682 Coram Rege rot.69d.; C.67/38 m.18; and above, n.104). The relationship is established almost conclusively by a petition concerning Thomas' son, Baldwin (C.1/41/302). For the Greswolds, Skipp 1970b: pp. 84–5.

Mountford lands at Wormleighton before the confiscation,[157] but they did not begin their rapid social rise until the opportunities for wool-growers and the freer market in land had greatly improved conditions for all pastoral farmers.[158] Moreover, we have seen that their earlier history reveals the degree of prejudice that existed against allowing gentility to people whose fortunes were based entirely on the profits of farming.[159] The Spensers' rise coincided with that of other graziers, such as Benedict Metley of Whitnash and Henry Smyth of Coventry, both of whom began to put together sizeable estates at the end of the century and in the early years of the sixteenth century.[160] It is only under favourable economic conditions like this that we should realistically expect yeomen to break into the ranks of the gentry on the strength of agricultural profits alone. Even in these instances there were extraneous factors, such as employment by the crown in the case of Metley, and the money that his father had made in the law in the case of Smyth.[161]

There can be no doubt that the real avenues to the acquisition of land and to social advancement lay through the professions. If there were better opportunities for aspiring yeomen at the end of the century these were also being taken by lawyers and administrators, who were in some ways better placed to exploit them because of the benefits they could derive from royal favour. Studies of social mobility in England over the next two centuries and more emphasise the exceptional character of the Spensers' rise and the degree to which the professions, including the crown's own servants, were the principal source of new entrants to the landed aristocracy. Where there was enterprise in estate exploitation it was as likely as not to come from the professionals, who often managed their newly-acquired lands with a keen eye for profit.[162] Nevertheless, the key to upward mobility remained the securing and retaining of estates, and for this some form of protection from whoever wielded the most power in the localities, whether king or nobility, was essential, even when land grew easier to find. Again it was the lawyers and administrators, not the farmers quietly

157 Br. Lib. Add. Ch. 48,701 (erroneously dated by Henry VI's regnal year, but a deed of Edward IV's reign). In the Mountford account for 1433–4 (S.B.T. D.R.37 Box 73) is recorded a rent of £6 10s 8d at Wormleighton from 'purselles'. One of the earliest notable Spensers was Robert Purcell alias Spycer of Bucks., who already owned a manor at Wormleighton in 1437 (Jeayes ed., 'Catalogue of Spencer Charters', 1646, 1652).

158 See works cited above, n.136.

159 Above, n.157; Jeayes ed., 'Catalogue of Spencer Charters', 1652; C.P.40/890 rot.226d; above. p. 76.

160 For Metley, above, n.142; *Dugdale*, pp. 55, 264, 365; Beresford 1945–6, p. 69; *V.C.H.*, VI, pp. 121, 176, 252; *Cal. Close Rolls 1485–1500*, p. 327; above, nn.104, 142; cf. Dyer 1980b: pp. 333–4.

161 *Materials: Henry VII*, I, p. 337, II, p. 310. For Smyth, see below, p. 187.

162 Stone and Fawtier Stone 1986: *passim*, esp. ch. 12 and pp. 122–9, 144–8; Stone 1966; Finch 1956: pp. 165–70; Aylmer 1974; pp. 259–67; Holmes 1982, 1979; Hughes 1987: p. 33. But note the reservations about the lower ranks of the law as an avenue of social advancement expressed in Brooks 1986: pp. 272–4.

accumulating wealth away from the hurly-burly, who were best placed to find and make use of this.

IV

Now that the means to upward mobility have been examined, we must make some attempt to assess the amount of movement into and within Warwickshire landed society as a whole. It is most important not to mistake changes in terminology for real social changes, and the dangers of this rather weaken the conclusions on movement into the gentry. Since the term 'gentleman' was in more general use by the end of the century, many of those who seem to have acquired gentility over the period had in actual fact merely taken to themselves the new-fangled name for people in their position. Movement within the gentry is summarised in table 4. The two groups, 'elite' and 'middle-ranking' families, have been distinguished in a rather rough and ready way. The elite comprises families assessed at £60 or more in 1436, or with what seems an equivalent amount of land, and, at the lower boundary of the group, status and office have also been taken into account. For example, the Trussells of Billesley, a rather marginal family, are taken out of the elite once they lose knighthood and office, while the Cokayns and the Arderns, because they start from a higher financial and tenurial position, are restored to the group once the reversal of the mid-century decline in their fortunes had begun. Since the object of the exercise as far as the elite is concerned is to evaluate the exclusivity of the families that dominated county affairs, no family with greater interests in other counties has been counted as part of the Warwickshire elite unless it was heavily involved in Warwickshire as well. This excludes the Culpeppers and, for most of the century, the Knightleys. The middle-ranking families are those with incomes of £20 to £50 in 1436, or equivalent estates, again excluding the poorest of these if they had little public responsibility, and, as with the elite, excluding families like the Malorys of Tachbrook for whom Warwickshire was secondary to interests elsewhere. Also included, despite their low income, are important public figures, such as William Donyngton, Recorder of Coventry, or Thomas Stretton, royal servant and J.P.[163]

The tables reveal what could be called a 'semi-open elite'. On the whole the rate of failure in the male line in both groups is remarkably constant and, predictably, this is far and away the major cause of families falling out of either of the groups. To these we must add the 'interruptions' through dowagers or temporary female inheritance that are notable amongst the greater families. Thus marriage to an heiress, or even to a dowager, was a significant means of advancement into the elite, especially during the first seventy years of the

[163] *Coventry Leet Book*, p. 134. For Stretton, see above, p. 74 n.133.

Table 4 Social mobility

Elite

(i) Stability of elite

	1410		1436		1470		1500	
	No.	%	No.	%	No.	%	No.	%
Number in group	*30*	*100*	*28*	*100*	*23*	*100*	*22*	*100*
Newcomers	–	–	9	32	10	43	12	55
From previous list	–	–	19	68	13	57	10	45
In next list	19	63	13	46	10	43	–	–
Failures	11	37	15	54	13	57	–	–

(ii) Origins of elite families

	1410		1436		1470		1500	
	No.	%	No.	%	No.	%	No.	%
Newcomers	–	–	*9*	*100*	*10*	*100*	*12*	*100*
Marriage[1]	–	–	4	44	3	30	2	17
Advancement[2]	–	–	5	56	5	50	6	50
Inheritance[3]	–	–	0	0	2	20	4	33

(iii) How elite families failed

	1410		1436		1470		1500	
	No.	%	No.	%	No.	%	No.	%
Failures	*11*	*100*	*15*	*100*	*13*	*100*	–	–
Male line ends	7	64	6	40	6	46	–	–
Interrupted	1	9	4	27	1	8	–	–
Decline	2	18	5	33	5	38	–	–
Move out of county	1	9	0	0	1	8	–	–

Middling ranks

(i) Stability of middling families

	1410		1436		1470		1500	
	No.	%	No.	%	No.	%	No.	%
Number in group	*28*	*100*	*35*	*100*	*36*	*100*	*36*	*100*
Newcomers	–	–	18	51	14	39	17	47
From previous list	–	–	17	49	22	61	19	53
In next list	17	61	22	63	19	53	–	–
Move up to elite	4	14	4	11	3	8	–	–
Failures	7	25	9	26	14	39	–	–

Table 4 Social mobility

(ii) Origins of middling families

	1410		1436		1470		1500	
	No.	%	No.	%	No.	%	No.	%
Newcomers	–	–	*18*	*100*	*14*	*100*	*17*	*100*
Marriage	–	–	2	11	0	0	5	29
Advancement	–	–	11	61	6	43	6	35
Inheritance	–	–	3	17	3	21	4	24
Decline from elite	–	–	2	11	5	36	2	12

(iii) How middling rank families failed

	1410		1436		1470		1500	
	No.	%	No.	%	No.	%	No.	%
Failures	*7*	*100*	*9*	*100*	*14*	*100*	–	–
Male line ends	7	100	8	89	12	86	–	–
Interrupted	0	0	1	11	0	0	–	–
Decline	0	0	0	0	2	14	–	–
Move out of county	0	0	0	0	0	0	–	–

1 In all tables this is rather an arbitrary classification: for several men, e.g., Littleton, Throgmorton, marriage and political advancement were inseparable.

2 In all cases, includes both territorial and political advancement.

3 Includes inheritance from a dowager.

century. This point is emphasised by the fact that the favours received by some of those whose rise is attributed to 'political advancement' included good marriages.[164] It is therefore apparent that there were openings amongst the elite but that they depended rather on biological accidents, and we have seen that the richest marriages tended to go to members of established families, some of them not even native gentry. In general people tended to marry at their own social level, unless there were pressing reasons to do otherwise.[165] The best prospects for new men at the apex of local society were therefore temporary: limited tenure of a widow's estate and, perhaps more important in creating a subjective sense of fluidity at the top, the temporary eclipse of some great families, which made room for others at the highest level of local politics and administration. It happened that in the middle of the century a number of important families were going through a sticky patch. The fact that this coincided with the crisis in national politics was not entirely fortuitous: the Arderns' misfortunes were

164 E.g. Metley, Throgmorton, Conway, Hungerford.

165 Above, pp. 97–100; Thrupp 1948: pp. 263–9; marriage within one's own class is firmly recommended by Caxton (Caxton, *Book of the Knight of the Tower*, pp. 168–9). Cf. Wright 1983: p. 44.

directly attributable to political miscalculation and those of the Malorys and Cokayns certainly owed something to the violence and uncertainties of local politics caused by the failure of the central government. The number of wealthy widows at this time, all of them taken by ambitious newcomers – Bingham, Denton, Littleton, Middleton and, earlier on, Bate[166] – was probably also no accident, in that it seems to reflect the climax of the speculative ventures with jointures, presaging a more cautious period to come.[167] It is the return of these jointures to the heirs that accounts for the large proportion of the elite arriving by inheritance at the end of the century.

An additional question, and one that has important implications for whether local landowners had a subjective sense that this was an open hierarchy, is how many of the new elite came from within the county. A glance at the list of successful widow-hunters is not encouraging, for they were none of them natives by origin. This is not unexpected. We must remember that rising men needed the protection of a patron in virtually all the undertakings that helped them on their way, and neither the king nor the lords of great estates had any reason to confine their favours to the gentry of the particular county where a perquisite had come to hand; the beneficiary was likely to be the follower who was next in line for a reward. Nevertheless, in each of the first two periods nearly half the newcomers to the elite came from the middle ranks of the native gentry. Most of them had made the journey by means of royal or noble protection and their own political adroitness, sometimes aided by the profitable marriages that these advantages could bring. By contrast the absence of recruits to the elite from the group below in 1500 is striking; apart from three former elite families which had recovered their position after a period of eclipse (Ardern, Chetwynd and Cokayn), all the newcomers came from outside the county. This is indubitably the outcome of Henry VII's policy of confining his favours to his own men, which had restricted the opportunities for native gentry unless they themselves were part of the royal entourage.[168]

By an irony probably not appreciated by the people concerned, it was only in this last period that a greater number of permanent places at the pinnacle of local society become available to newcomers. Here again we see the hand of the king, both his alacrity in confiscating the estates of three outstanding families – Catesby, Stafford of Grafton and Mountford – and his preference for granting these and the fruits of his tighter control of feudal prerogatives to his own men. As we observed when looking at the nature of upward mobility, opportunities and dangers multiplied at this time. However, the very reluctance of the king to

[166] John Denton married Philip Purfrey's widow, who had the family's main holdings in Warwickshire (*Dugdale*, pp. 54, 971, but note Dugdale's error in giving 'Thomas' for 'John' on p. 971); *Cal. Close Rolls 1468–76*, p. 256).

[167] Below, pp. 259–60.

[168] Newcomers from within the county: 1436 – Archer, Harewell of Bidford, Metley, Purfrey; 1470 – Brome, Greville, Hugford, Verney.

allow such windfalls into the hands of local families meant that, despite the need for a larger pool of potential holders of the major offices caused by the expansion of the commission of the peace, the elite was smaller in 1500 than it had been at any time in the century. Even the outsiders sufficiently committed to the county to be included in this group – Conway, Hungerford and Pudsey – can hardly be said to have placed Warwickshire amongst their foremost concerns. This contraction in the elite was to cause problems for the king in running the county.[169] It also exemplifies the paradox that the opening up of avenues to the top in this period was accompanied by a narrowing of opportunities, as these came to depend more and more on the king's favour.

An examination of the middling families shows that there were significant differences between them and the elite, both in means of entry and in subsequent fortunes. At this lower level marriage was a less certain path to success, unless there was a large number of heiresses, as happened, in this case quite by accident, at the end of the century. Once God and the rest of the family had been taken care of by the previous owner, the size of estate brought by the sort of bride who might be won at this level was not likely to be large. A good marriage would help, as it helped Thomas Greswold, and, while the elite might spurn a lawyer or administrator with little beyond his personal expertise, it was easier for a rising man to seem a promising match for the heiress to a small estate.[170] However, the real upward movement into the ranks of the *mediocres* would be through service or purchase of land, or, more often, both. Between 1410 and 1436 there were ample opportunities in both royal and noble service. In the next period the exclusiveness of the royal court tended to reduce possibilities there, although those able to gain access, like John Brome of Baddesley Clinton, did very well indeed out of it. In the final period, the king, who had become the controlling force in Warwickshire politics by his tenure of the Warwick lands, was the only significant source of preferment.[171]

Despite the fact that involvement in the affairs of the great was so promising a path into the middle ranks of the gentry, life at this level was usually less dangerous, the stakes being normally considerably lower. Political errors were more infrequent and the temptation to tie up a large part of the heir's inheritance as the price of a great heiress was weaker. It is worthy of note that, between the 1430s and 1470s, just at the time when so many of the elite families were going through difficulties of this sort, the middling landowners were experiencing a highly stable period. Those who foundered, or came close to doing so, like the Bromes, were suffering the effects of trying to fight their way into the elite. This stability was enormously important in ensuring continuity in local affairs at a very difficult time for the leading local figures and for local

169 Below, pp. 591–2.
170 Above, p. 118.
171 Below, section II.

society as a whole. All the more so when one considers that the simultaneous demise of a number of families was bound to necessitate a certain amount of manoeuvring for new associates and could give rise to a multiplication of land disputes.

It is therefore unsurprising that it is the middle-ranking families that exhibit the greater degree of continuity over the whole period. Only four of the thirty elite families of 1410 feature in each of the four surveys, while another four are represented at the beginning and the end but not at both the interim dates. For the middle ranks the survival rate is seven out of twenty-eight, with (significantly, since interruptions were usually the result of over-large jointures) only one interrupted survival. Particularly interesting is the fact that six of these eight middling families with a continuous or near-continuous history could be termed 'parish gentry', although these were parochial figures of a rather elevated kind.[172] The point can be emphasised by a comparison of the complete list of gentry for 1410 and for 1500, which shows that thirty-three of the original 115 families survived without significant interruption over this ninety-year period and that of these no less than seventeen – more than half – were parish gentry.[173] Several of these were of ancient lineage, a point which adds weight to the earlier observation that the apparently more ancient lineage of the greater families may owe more to the survival of evidence than to actual fact. Of the ten families that survived with interruptions, almost all were from the upper levels of the gentry.[174] It is clear that at the top of local society life was subject to all sorts of hazards which could put a temporary or permanent end to a familiy's presence amongst the elite or even to its existence, whilst, further down the scale, the only serious threat was failure to produce a male heir.

The greater stability among the middle ranks is emphasised by an examination of the origins of these families. This shows both the danger faced by the elite families of declining to the level of the *mediocres* and the extent to which the middling families drew their membership from among the native Warwickshire gentry. Despite the usual problems of inadequate information – for example, nothing has been found about the origins of William Broun, a very rich and fairly prominent esquire of 1500, not even whether his origins lay in

[172] Fulwode, Holt, Hubaud, Lisle, Middlemore, Walsh (*Dugdale*, pp. 737, 871, 938, 894; *Visitation Warwicks.*, p. 237; *V.C.H.*, III, p. 265).

[173] Clopton of Stratford, Compton of Compton Wyniates, Derset, Gower, Hardwick (perhaps rather more than 'parish'), Hayton, Hore of Solihull, Hore of Stoneythorpe, Waryng, Willenhale, atte Wode, Wyncote and the families listed in n.172 minus Holt (*Dugdale*, pp. 698, 549, 348, 712–13; *Visitation Warwicks.*, pp. 79, 341 (an inaccurate genealogy); Nichols 1795–1811: IV, ii, p. 643; S.B.T. D.R.37/920, Box 42/2491, 2513; *W.F.F.*, 2462; *V.C.H.*, III, pp. 63, 182–3, VI, p. 183; Davenport 1907, p. 26; B.R.L. 432058); app. 2; and below, pp. 254–7 for a discussion of the survival of lineages.

[174] Ardern, Catesby of Ladbroke/Lapworth, Chetwynd of Grendon, Cokayn, Greville, Holt of Aston, Lucy, Purfrey, Ralegh, Trussell of Bilton.

the county[175] – it is clear that a significant proportion could come from elite families, whether from those in decline or from cadet branches.[176] In 1436 five, possibly seven, of the eighteen new entrants to the group came from lesser Warwickshire families, some gentle, some lower still, while two were from elite families in decline and three were junior branches of elite families. In 1470 the tally is fourteen newcomers, six from lesser county families, a bumper crop of five declining elite families and three junior branches of these families. In 1500, of seventeen newcomers, six came from below, two from declining elite families and five from younger branches of elite families.[177] It will be observed that, even at the end of the century, when the new entrants to the top ranks were largely outsiders, the middling gentry remained almost entirely of local origin, a characteristic which must have lent force to their role as a stabilising influence. It would also act as a valuable safety valve in satisfying ambitious natives that, even if their entry to the elite were to be barred by outsiders, they could find a place amongst a group that was less powerful but still locally influential.

Turning now to the question of how easy it was to break into landed society from below, it has to be admitted that the evidence is so flawed as to be of very limited value. Not only do changes in usage obscure real social change – this makes assessment of the period 1410 to 1436, when 'gentleman' was coming more generally into use, particularly difficult – but also the gross lack of evidence for the origins of most of the families raised to gentility makes it very dangerous to offer any firm conclusions. Ideally, to obtain full answers to our questions, we would need a study which combined family reconstitution by means of manorial records and the sort of approach employed here. Of some gentlemen we know nothing beyond a couple of references. As far as origins are

175 Broun was said to have an income of 200 marks in *c.*1500, he was described as 'king's servant' in October 1485, was a J.P. and married the daughter and heiress of Henry Waver II (Huntington Lib., Calif. MS HM 19959; *Cal. Pat. Rolls 1485–94*, p. 11, *1494–1509*, p. 8; *Dugdale*, pp. 91–2).

176 Cadets of elite families of middling rank are not given as a separate category in the table but subsumed under 'marriage' or 'inheritance'. In 1436 they were Catesby of Hopsford, Chetwynd of Alspath and Mountford of Hampton (as an independent eldest son), in 1470 Hugford of Princethorpe, Mountford of Church Bickenhill and of Monkspath, in 1500 Burdet of Bramcote, Catesby of Marston Waver, Mountford of Kington and of Monkspath (the latter a different branch from that of 1470) and Ferrers of Baddesley Clinton (eldest son of a junior branch of Ferrers of Tamworth, but only fully established in Warwickshire by marriage to the Brome co-heiress).

177 Newcomers from below: 1436 – Botener, Brome, Greswold, Thomas Porter, Richard Verney and possibly Donyngton and Stretton, whose origins are unknown; 1470 – John Beaufitz, Henry Boteller, William Bristowe, Richard Dalby, William Verney, John West of Little Bromwich; 1500 – Boteller of Solihull, Clopton, Hardwick, Metley, both Smyths. For lawyers, see app. 2 and *Coventry Leet Book*, p. 283 (Henry Boteller); *Coventry Register*, p. 111, *Origines Juridiciales* . . ., pp. 248, 258 (Bristowe); *Cal. Pat. Rolls 1467–77*, p. 11 (West). Also possibly Beaufitz (*Early Records of Furnival's Inn*, p. 29; *Records of Lincoln's Inn*, i, p. 5). For noble service, see app. 3; for royal service, see above, n.104 and ch. 3, nn.121, 133, 159. Elite families in decline: 1436 – Cotes, Trussell of Billesley; 1470 – Ardern, Cokayn, Doddingselles, Peyto, Malory; 1500 – Catesby, Mountford of Coleshill. For younger branches of elite families, see above, n.176.

concerned, we are bound to know more about entrants to the ranks of the gentry from amongst the lawyers and administrators, since the records are biased in their favour, and there is no guarantee whatsoever that all the gentlemen of non-official origins have been picked up. For what it is worth, a count has been made of new arrivals amongst the gentry within each of the periods, 1410–36, 1437–70 and 1471–1500.[178] This has been done by counting the newcomers at the end of each period; the tally therefore does *not* include families that both arrive and disappear within the period and to that extent it is not a complete count.

Since the object is to discover how many men were able to break into gentry society within these periods, those who already owned at least part of a manorial estate, even if it was only later that they acquired a title to go with it, have not been included. It has already been argued in the previous chapter that in these cases the title seems to signify changes in the apprehension of gentility more than in the status of the person concerned. The men who are classed as genuine new arrivals within each period are all those who were given a title of gentility (some first surface as fully-fledged esquires) for the first time, not having possessed any manorial estate at the start of the period. However, to counteract the considerable weighting of the evidence in the earlier decades in favour of the discovery of gentry of service, for the period 1410–36 families which had no lordship in 1410 and significantly enlarged their estates within that time without being given a title of gentility have also been included. All the same this probably does little to rectify the bias towards gentility of service, since it is considerably easier to find a new lawyer in the records than to chart the piecemeal acquisition of land by a yeoman family. In all three periods, newcomers to Warwickshire from established families in other counties have been excluded as far as possible.

The count yields twenty new gentry families between 1410 and 1436, fifty between 1437 and 1470 and twenty-nine between 1471 and 1500. To a large extent this apparent growth must reflect the more universal use of the term 'gentleman'. This would explain the bulge in the middle of the century: more families were being dignified with the title for the first time in these years and correspondingly fewer later on. Many of the 'new families' of 1437–70 feature in the legal records as employees or political connections of leading Warwickshire nobility and gentry, the greater number who can be identified being directly attributable to the growth in litigation in this uneasy period. Nevertheless, we should not jettison any attempts to deduce social change from this evidence. The preponderance of gentry of service amongst those newcomers who can be identified is so great as to be more than simply the reflection of the nature of the records. Between 1410 and 1436 the totals are thirteen gentry of

178 App. 2 and Carpenter, M. C. 1976: App. 1 together give most of the information lying behind these figures. To allow for chance survival of evidence, a few years' leeway either side of the terminal dates has been given.

service, one merchant, William Botener, who had bought his way into the landed gentry, and a possible agrarian family, the Durants;[179] between 1437 and 1470, twenty gentry of service at a conservative estimate,[180] four merchants, only one of whom had acquired an estate, and perhaps five agrarian gentlemen;[181] between 1471 and 1500 seven gentry of service,[182] one grazier and two (Thomas Boteller of Hampton and Benedict Metley) for whom royal service and agricultural enterprise seem to be equally important.[183]

It would thus be over-cautious not to conclude that there really was an enlargement of the ruling class in this century caused by the expansion of the lay professions. This may well be why it has sometimes been assumed that the term 'gentleman' was created for the benefit of these professionals; because they

[179] The gentlemen of service are Betley, Brome, Broun, Campion, Colshill, Richard Dalby, Donyngton, Est, Greswold, Metley, Parker, Thomas Porter and Stretton. For these, see apps. 2 and 3 and refs. in n.177, above; also *Cal. Pat. Rolls 1422–29*, p. 35 for royal service of Est. For Botener, see above, p. 122. Although he already owned a manor in 1410, he has been counted a new entrant to the gentry in 1436 because his title, for which there is no evidence until 1433, seems to be related to his subsequent accession to office and more extensive mingling in gentry affairs (Bod. Lib. Dugdale MS 13, p. 343; *Cal. Pat. Rolls 1413–16*, 424). The Durants existed in 1410 (*Cal. Close Rolls 1409–13*, p. 315) but acquired their manor of Barcheston and a title between 1410 and 1436 (*Dugdale*, p. 601). However, their connection with Sudeley (app. 3) suggests that they may also have owed their title to noble employment.

[180] John Atherstone, John Basset, John Beaufitz, Henry Boteller of Coventry, John Boteller of Alspath, Richard Boteller of Solihull, John Brewes, John Brewster, William Bristowe, Richard Clapham, John Denbawde, Thomas Dey, John Gamul, Robert Hadley, Richard Hedley, Thomas Holden, Ailred Marshall, John Otter, Thomas Rastell, Thomas Ward. (app. 3 and C.P.40/852 rot.253d.; *Coventry Leet Book*, p. 283; *Coventry Register*, p. 105 (it is suggested here that this is John Boteller of Coventry, later steward of the town (*Coventry Leet Book*, p. 474), but this reference may be too early for the Coventry man); K.B.27/875 Coram Rege rot.46d.; *Coventry Register*, p. 111; *Cal. Close Rolls 1468–76*, p. 367; C.P.40/842 rot.380d., /852 rot.252d. (a series of suits by Thomas Dey for debts, which look like pursuit of defaulting clients); *Cal. Fine Rolls 1452–62*, pp. 67, 70, *1471–85*, p. 66; C.P.40/844 rot.246 (Robert Hadley, who seems originally to have been a merchant: *Cal. Fine Rolls 1461–71*, p. 49); Baker 1980: p. 196; S.B.T. D.R.10/2466, D.R.37 Box 42/2532; C.1/47/158; Horrox and Hammond eds, *Br. Lib. Harleian Manuscript 433*, III, p. 204).

[181] Merchants: John Chacom, Thomas Danyas (these two, for whom there is very limited evidence, appear in the early 1470s and may therefore be assumed to be established by c.1470), John Shirwode, John Wyldegrys (*Cal. Close Rolls 1468–76*, pp. 382–3; K.B.27/861 Coram Rege rot.36; *Cal. Pat. Rolls 1452–61*, p. 338; *Cal. Close Rolls 1461–68*, p. 59. Note that Shirwode may have owed his arrival (and his acquisition of a manor at Alspath) to his connection with Richard Neville: above, n.113). Agrarian gentlemen: Thomas Andrewes and John Spenser, and perhaps Henry Broun, William Overton and Peter Venables (*V.C.H.*, VI, pp. 183–4; C.1/152/8; K.B.27/828 Coram Rege rot.68). For Andrewes, see above, n.150; for Spenser, see above, n.157 and pp. 136–7.

[182] John Boteller of Coventry, William Broun, Baldwin Hethe, Degory Heynes, John Marmeon, Richard Palmer, John Smyth (app. 2 for lawyers; app. 3 for noble servants; Nott. Univ. Lib. Middleton MS Mi A 1/2 for Marmeon; for royal service, see above, n.175 for Broun; B.R.L. Wingfield Digby MS A639 for Hethe; *Cal. Pat. Rolls 1476–85*, p. 173, *1485–94*, p. 394 for Heynes).

[183] The grazier is Henry Smyth (above, p. 137); for Boteller of Hampton and Metley, Br. Lib. Add. MS 21,480 fo. 38v.; S.C.6/Hen. VII/868 (*sub* Wootton Wawen); above, nn.142, 160, 161.

were the social climbers *par excellence*, they tend to be far more visible than their more numerous landowning peers. As was suggested earlier, the gentility of the professionals should not be seen as empty titles but as a recognition of the power that their employment conferred on them.[184] While this meant that the numbers of gentry could grow even while estates remained in short supply, it put a considerable strain on landed society, for no lawyer or administrator was going to remain content to live on his fees and wages. A manorial estate would almost invariably be the summit of his ambition, but this was not an aim that could be very easily fulfilled, at least not without treading on others' toes.

V

This has been a long journey through the Warwickshire hierarchy; it is now time to sum up such discoveries as we have been able to make. It is possible that they do not apply to other counties. Susan Wright's work implies that conditions were not very different in Derbyshire, but counties have been found to differ markedly in the next two centuries where social mobility is concerned, and there is no reason to suppose that there would have been greater uniformity in the fifteenth. In particular, there may well have been more fluidity nearer London, with its more active land market and outsize number of rising professionals and wealthy merchants. It is also possible that areas where Duchy of Lancaster influence was strong, and crown patronage could consequently have a disproportionate impact on structures of power and landholding, developed differently. The peculiarity of the Duchy areas in the midlands will be a recurring theme of this study, and the policies of the crown in Nottinghamshire may well account for the greater rigidity of the landed elite that Payling has found in this county.[185]

[184] Above, pp. 90, and 93–4.

[185] Wright 1983; pp. 25–8; Everitt 1966: pp. 56–73, 1968: pp. 51–59; Thrupp 1948: chs. 5 and 6; Payling 1987b: *passim*, esp. ch. 3. The Duchy had an unusual degree of influence over land tenure and social structures in its main centres, simply because of its unusual size and wealth, even before it was in royal hands (Walker 1986: pp. 162–5, 240). However, it is noticeable that Wright, also examining a 'Duchy of Lancaster' county, seems to find no such entrenched elite, and, although Payling has some support in his figures for office-holders (below, pp. 274–5), closer examination of his lists and family histories (ch. 2 and apps.) reveals that his elite of twelve families was by no means as static as he suggests. Many, if not most, of these families were new and no less than a third either died out or went into temporary eclipse within his period of sixty-two years. His concentration on these families, to the exclusion of others such as the Makerells and the Meryngs, who seem to have been as important for at least part of his period, and his keeping all families rigidly within categories fixed by the tax returns of 1436 predetermine some of his conclusions. Equally, his use of fourteenth-century lists to show a greater concentration of power in a smaller number of hands by, and during, the fifteenth century (Payling 1987b: pp. 107–8) fails to convince, because he does not allow for the new families, replacements for those that died out, whose existence he himself demonstrates in describing the past history of his elite families (one third of which fail to figure in the fourteenth-century lists). However, this is not to deny that there may well have been differences between Nottinghamshire and Warwickshire.

As is almost invariably the case with social mobility, the conclusions for Warwickshire are contradictory, society looking more open from some vantage points than from others. It was quite possible for an established family to exist on its estates with no thought of enlarging them by marriage or political connection, until the male line became extinct. Only then would an opening for newcomers appear and it was likely to go to another elite family, perhaps one from outside the county. Luckily for ambitious social climbers, most of the greater families chose the path of speculation. Any family that wanted to do more than preserve its position had to be ready to gamble and adapt. The prices that might have to be paid were long-lived widows with large jointures, far-flung properties, the reversals of fortune risked by maintaining a high political profile and debts incurred in the generous expenditure that was the hallmark of a prominent local figure. The temporary or permanent eclipses that might result could open the way to newcomers. Significantly, the major families that survived most unscathed over the period – Bermingham, Brasebrugge, Doddingselles, Lucy, Trussell of Billesley for example – were mostly rather unadventurous and indeed undistinguished when their status and lands are set against their achievements. Most of them had existed over generations[186] and, granted that they had had the good fortune to produce male heirs, their durability may be explained by a reluctance to take risks in marriage or politics.

The dangers of playing for high political stakes are graphically illustrated by the Catesbys. They had been carefully consolidating their position and efficiently maximising their landed profits throughout the century. If William I's move into high politics by membership of Henry VI's household brought a brief shipwreck, he was careful to provide himself with a way back to respectability; this he did by keeping in with friends outside the increasingly exclusive court in the crisis years of 1458–61.[187] It was William II who exposed the family, but in doing so he gave it opportunities on a scale it had never enjoyed before. He was unlucky in that his master, Richard III, failed to survive, but it was the commitment to Richard that had taken the family to its greatest heights before bringing about its temporary ruin.[188] Henry Willoughby, who managed to emerge unscathed from his investment in the favour of the first two Tudors, might well have been dragged down in 1495. He would have joined Simon Mountford, an able and adventurous politician who finally over-reached himself and paid the penalty.[189] Quietism was therefore a virtue, particularly during the middle years of the century and under Henry VII, but it was not a virtue that was going to enhance a family's status. In the event, most

[186] *Dugdale*, pp. 898, 1,056–7, 343, 507, 716–8.

[187] Below, chs. 12, 13.

[188] Below, ch. 14.

[189] Below, ch. 15.

of the more enterprising families, old and new, played the game with considerable skill, even when setbacks occurred. The Willoughbys reconstructed their unwieldy estate on the basis of the two richest manors, Wollaton and Middleton, abandoning residence at the village from which they took their name, as its financial value fell and it became peripheral to the main geographical focus of their property.[190] The Hugfords extended their political connections into eastern Warwickshire to defend the Metley lands. They added strength to their political presence there by giving one of the older family properties in this part of the county to William, younger son of Thomas, who would be better placed to look after the family's interests there than the main line at Emscote.[191]

Like the Willoughbys, adventurous families had to be ready to relocate their main residence as the needs of new acquisitions and obligations dictated.[192] The Shirleys moved north from Lower Ettington in the far south of the county, their home since the Conquest, when their lands in the north midlands began to outweigh those further south. Had they not lost the Basset inheritance, acquired in 1423, to the duke of Buckingham they might have given more attention to their Warwickshire lands; as it was, this loss settled the matter in favour of their Leicestershire and Derbyshire properties.[193] The Throgmortons, under Robert, moved from Fladbury in Worcestershire to Coughton.[194] The Spensers were later to build an imposing mansion at Wormleighton, only to abandon it for Althorpe not long after.[195] The Littletons' wanderings were still more remarkable. They started at Frankley, Worcestershire, which came to Thomas through his maternal grandmother, whose name he took. The Chetwynd marriage took Thomas to the Chetwynd residences at Grendon in north Warwickshire and Ingestre in Staffordshire. The Burley inheritance, to which Thomas' wife succeeded in 1459, lay principally in Shropshire and Staffordshire, and it was in the latter county that Thomas made his own main purchase of Tixall manor. When he divided up his lands among his three sons at his death in 1481, the eldest, William, got Frankley, the patrimony, which was henceforth to return to its old role as the family residence, but as the centre of an estate consisting principally of the Burley lands inherited from his

190 Cameron 1970: p. 10, but he seems to date the removal to Wollaton rather too late: Hugh, Henry's father, already lived there (C.1/66/454) and is already described as 'of Wollaton' in 1417 (Derbys.R.O. D518/F.6); below, pp. 157, 161.

191 Above, n.97; below, pp. 330–1.

192 Note a similar adaptation by Thomasin Hopton, widow of John, on finding herself unexpectedly responsible for the interests of a young heir (Richmond 1981: p. 74; also p. 80).

193 *Dugdale*, pp. 619–23; Nichols 1795–1811: III, i, pp. 381, 385; *V.C.H.*, IV, p. 202; Shirley 1873: pp. 43–4, 51).

194 Above, p. 114.

195 *Dugdale*, p. 515; *V.C.H.*, V, pp. 218–20; Finch 1956: p. 39; Thorpe 1962: pp. 55–61.

mother.[196] This same flexibility will be evident again with regard to the focus of the gentry's religious interests.[197]

Warwickshire landed society in the fifteenth century can best be described as being in a rather limited state of flux. Estates were subject to a process of accumulation and dispersal; concentration of lands in a small number of families was inhibited by the fact that in this least isolated of counties so many heiresses went to outsiders. Some estates grew, usually by marriage or inheritance, occasionally by purchase: for example, those of the Archers, the Arderns, the Belknaps, the Littletons, the Throgmortons, the Verneys and the Willoughbys. Others broke up when the male line ended: for example those of Bishopestone, Brome of Lapworth, Freville. Others grew and were then dispersed: for example Brome of Baddesley Clinton, Cokesey/Greville, Dalby, Hugford of Emscote, Metley.[198] Only under Henry VII did an external agency take a hand in this dispersal, with the confiscation of the Catesby, Stafford and Mountford estates, all of which had been growing over the course of the century.

It has been calculated that between 1349 and c.1520 80 per cent of Warwickshire land changed hands, which certainly argues for a lack of exclusiveness in local society. However, given that the composition of all social groups is always subject to change, and allowing for the constant attrition of the landed classes by failure of the male line, this was a period of restricted social mobility amongst the gentry. In this respect it contrasts significantly with the thirteenth century, when it seems that many more families failed through debt or political error. While prices remained stable and the government failed to take much interest in the sums that could be raised through feudal prerogatives and fines, even indebtedness as serious as that resulting from William Peyto's ransom could be surmounted.[199] Usually the sale of a piece of land would be

[196] *Test. Vetust.*, pp. 365–6; *Cal. Close Rolls 1461–68*, pp. 53–4; *Colls. Hist. Staffs.*, o.s., 12, pp. 326–9; Roskell 1983a. Their original Warwickshire manor was Baxterley, in north Warwickshire; the *V.C.H.* has confused this with the Chetwynd lands (IV, p. 25).

[197] Below, ch.6.

[198] For Brome of Lapworth and Freville, see *V.C.H.*, V, p. 112; *Cat. Anc. Deeds*, III, A4262, IV, A7468, 8371, 9783; *Dugdale*, p. 1,135. For the Cokesey/Greville estate, *V.C.H.*, V, p. 200, VI, pp. 118, 260; *Cal. Pat. Rolls 1494–1509*, pp. 164, 173; above, p. 113. For the dispersal of the Dalby estate on Richard's death, see C.140/78/89/2 (although this I.P.M. may have been in error: below, pp. 534–5). By contrast, Payling finds a tendency towards concentration of estates in a smaller number of hands in Nottinghamshire in the Lancastrian period, attributing it principally to a higher level of endogamy amongst the elite than is found in e.g. Warwickshire (1987b: pp. 107–10; and above, nn.101, 185). But the influence of the Duchy of Lancaster may also have played a part and there may be some doubts about Payling's conclusions (above, p. 147 and n.185).

[199] Works cited above, nn.2, 146. For the figures on land changing hands, see Dyer 1981: p. 3. The association of inflation with instability and, by implication, the reverse, has been noted elsewhere: e.g. Russell 1971: p. 16.

enough to raise a large capital sum.[200] The cards were consequently firmly stacked in favour of existing landed families, which left little room for new ones. If the dangers to established families and the opportunities for new ones grew at the end of the century, it was not until the Dissolutions that land again became as readily available as it had been in the assarting centuries before and after the Conquest. Indeed, England's landed elite was never again to be as open as in the century after the Conquest.[201] Far from being the prelude to an explosion of social mobility in the following century, in terms of social stratification the fifteenth century must be reckoned one of the more rigid periods.

During the whole of the fifteenth century only four Warwickshire families, the Bromes, the Hugfords, the Throgmortons and the Verneys, reached the elite from the ranks of the lesser gentry without the benefit of a large windfall by marriage or inheritance such as was the making of the Littletons. Unless there was an unusually able and long-lived head of the family it was unlikely that the leap could be accomplished in less than two or three generations. The Bromes nearly made it in one but met disaster along the way; the Verneys, who rose so rapidly under Richard I, immediately fell out of the elite under his less distinguished successors. To rise so quickly both families had to take risks. The more circumspect Hugfords needed two generations, despite the advantage throughout the century of the patronage and protection of the holders of the Warwick lands, and had no sooner established themselves as a front-ranking family than they became extinct. The Throgmortons, the lasting success of the century, produced three able heads, in John, Thomas and Robert. These showed great astuteness in making use of lordship on their own terms, looking for heiresses and, above all, in continuing to accumulate and exploit their estates with the assiduity of parvenus long after the family was well established. Even so they could not be counted amongst the outstanding local families until the later years of the century, by which time they were already in the third generation and had survived several hazards along the way.[202]

Despite these strictures, there was social mobility in the sense that there were

200 See figures quoted above, n.110 and McFarlane 1973: p. 196; also the will of John Archer II, enabling the executors to raise the large sum of £200 by the sale of a single pasture (S.B.T. D.R.503 fos. 74v.-6).

201 Loyn 1962: pp. 29–36; Miller and Hatcher 1978: pp. 33–41; above, n.2. This conclusion is, interestingly, echoed by a Tudor historian: Clay 1984: I, pp. 142–6. Cf. Warwickshire in the next period (Hughes 1987: pp. 27–32).

202 For Thomas' marriage to the Onley heiress, see *Dugdale*, p. 323. John II, younger brother of Thomas, was executed by the Yorkists after Mortimer's Cross, while his son, Thomas' nephew, was taken fighting for the Lancastrians at Tewkesbury, but pardoned ('William Worcestre', Annales, p. 486; Warkworth, *Chronicle*, p. 19). Thomas and Robert also experienced considerable difficulties with the Onley inheritance in Buckinghamshire in the 1470s (below, pp. 525–6). For the careers of all three, see below, chs. 10–15, *passim*. It seems that this pattern of rising by stages is characteristic of movement into the elite in later centuries as well (Stone and Fawtier Stone 1986: pp. 39–40, 111–12, 283–4).

no formal bars to advancement and that it was evident that some people did manage to work their way up, while elite families also fell from grace, although their decline tended to be only temporary. The fact that sons of yeomen who had risen could find themselves able to exert about the same amount of influence, if in different ways, as sons of knights who had fallen, in the ranks of the middling gentry, can only have encouraged a belief in the flexibility of the hierarchy. If a lot of the room, especially amongst the elite, was for scions of wealthy families from outside the county, a steady trickle of natives raised themselves into and within local landed society. Most of these were professionals of one sort or another and it is certainly these men who made the greatest impact in terms of social mobility; it is difficult to see who else would have been equipped, for the whole process was so fraught with dangers and difficulties that it needed the protection and expertise that only these could command. Even patient agricultural accumulators like the Spensers needed friends to secure leases and purchases of land.[203] Although the problem of social mobility brings rising professionals into such sharp focus, we should not be misled into supposing that they were typical of the gentry: we have seen that they were if anything rather atypical. But their ambitions could not be ignored, for they had immense destabilising potential. This was in fact 'an age of ambition', in the sense that there was a growing number of social climbers, but it was not a time when ambitions were to be easily fulfilled. The strain that this state of affairs might place upon local societies is obvious.

Indeed if stability is a more notable feature of this society than change, it was a precarious stability; old and new families required vigilance, foresight and an instinct for profitable speculation. It was easier for the established families to gamble because they had more to fall back on in the event of failure. On the other hand, they often had to seek marriages further afield than the families with very localised interests, and this could be as dangerous as it was profitable. Moreover, like the aspirant parvenus, they were obliged to assume public responsibility and to participate in local politics if they were not to become backwoods squires, as the Doddingselles were to be after the death of Edward I in 1466.[204] Gentry families could do little about the ever-present possibility that the line would come to an end, but they could try to direct all the aspects of their fortunes that were amenable to earthly control.[205] That so many managed this complex and dangerous responsibility with such success indicates the high level of competence to be found amongst these landowners, and it should not surprise us if they expected an equal measure of skill from their royal and noble superiors.

[203] Thorpe 1962: pp. 55–6; above, p. 132.
[204] *Dugdale*, p. 344.
[205] But see the discussion of entail, below, pp. 248–52.

5

THE EXPLOITATION OF ESTATES

I

Warwickshire farming in this period has already been definitively surveyed by Christopher Dyer.[1] The object of this chapter is therefore less to give another overview of estate management than to add another dimension to our understanding of the gentry by asking what they expected to get out of their estates and how they expected to do it.[2] Estate records survive in reasonable numbers for five families: Brome of Baddesley Clinton, Catesby (with some for William Bishopestone, part of whose estates the Catesbys inherited in the mid-1440s), Ferrers of Tamworth, Stafford of Grafton and Willoughby. There is also a certain amount of material for the Archers, Mountfords, Shirleys, Throgmortons and Verneys of Compton Murdack, and enough evidence for some other families – mainly deeds, but also those I.P.M.s which include extents, and some references from legal records – to be a useful supplement.

Agricultural conditions in the fifteenth century, it hardly needs saying, were not favourable to landlords. Grain prices were low, wages high, and in mid-century even the hitherto quite buoyant market for the products of animal husbandry slumped. Peasant tenants, the balance of demography now tipping decisively in their favour, were refusing to pay dues and staging rent strikes. On many great estates, including the lands of the see of Worcester, which were concentrated in the west midlands, income and rent levels reached their nadir in the middle of the century, just when the profits of animal husbandry, which had to some extent compensated for the failure of grain revenues, were declining.[3]

1 Dyer 1981.

2 Also Carpenter 1986b: pp. 45–50 for a preliminary exploration. For a study of another gentry estate in the fifteenth century, see Richmond 1981: ch. 2.

3 Bolton 1980: ch. 7: he thinks the situation was particularly bad in the midlands (pp. 232–3); Hatcher 1977: ch. 3; Hilton 1975: pp. 66–7; Dyer 1968, 1980b: pp. 150–2, 188–9; Harvey 1977: pp. 157–8; Du Boulay 1966: p. 220; Dobson 1973: pp. 270–3; Bean 1958: pp. 41, 104; Hare 1981, 1985 (in some ways a corrective to the prevailing gloomy view); Rogers 1866–1902: IV, p. 328; Mate 1987: pp. 525–6.

It is probably safe to assume that the greater lords were in a better position to cope with these difficulties than the gentry. The nobility and the great ecclesiastical institutions tended to own the best land and the larger manors, where seigneurial authority was stronger and labour services, which could insulate against the effects of rising wages, more prevalent.[4] It was the gentry, moreover, who were now the major source of the king's extraordinary revenue. They could try to foist as much as possible of this on to their tenants, but the experience of 1381 had shown them the unwisdom of such a policy if carried too far.[5] The estate records show that the sums paid to tax-collectors were not large, but their cumulative effect must have been irritating, to say the least, particularly when they came with the regularity of the first half of the century, and gave an additional weight to the pressures of declining incomes.[6]

At what point the landlord economy took a turn for the better is a subject of some debate. It used to be thought that population, prices and profits all began to rise in the last three decades or so of the fifteenth century. Other studies, including Dyer's of the estates of the bishopric of Worcester which is of particular relevance for this area, have indicated that rents and income were rising from about this time.[7] This interpretation is now, however, under attack from two sides. First, late-medievalists are beginning to doubt whether all was as well as has been assumed. There is some particularly disturbing evidence from Kent suggesting that the real demographic crisis occurred precisely at the time of the alleged recovery. Kent may be atypical, being perhaps peculiarly susceptible to outbreaks of plague carried from London and the continent, but its experience may not have been unique. Dyer's studies of peasant demography in this period show that the improvement in the bishop of Worcester's income in this period was not matched by a demographic recovery amongst his tenants. Blanchard's work on the north midlands, another area with relevance for this study, suggests very patchy demand for land: the higher rents, concentrated mainly in some pastoral areas, he attributes to the boom in cloth exports and they may have been declining after 1500.[8] Secondly, Tudor

4 Kosminsky 1956: pp. 99–102, 108. For further discussion of this point, see below, pp. 167, 256–7.

5 Harriss 1975: *passim*, Maddicott 1975; Tuck 1984: pp. 203–4, 208–10.

6 E.g. 6s 8d from the Willoughby manor of Middleton in (probably) 1447–8 (Nott. Univ. Lib. Middleton MS 5/167/101); 3s 4 1/2d from the Stafford manor of Leamington in 1438–9 and 3s 4d from the same family's manor of Broadwell in 1450–1 (S.C.R.O. D.641/1/2/281,283); 4s from the Catesby manor of Lapworth in 1454–5 (S.C.6/1042/6). To these must be added the sums paid by their tenants, as any money paid to the king reduced the chances of the full sums due being paid to the lord. For the frequency of taxation, see Griffiths 1981: chs. 6 and 15.

7 Helleiner 1967: pp. 20–4; Hatcher 1977: ch. 5; Kershaw 1973: pp. 183–4; Du Boulay 1966: p. 220; Dyer 1980b: pp. 189–90.

8 Hatcher 1986; Mavis Mate, from unpubl. paper delivered to the Medieval Economic History Seminar at Cambridge (I must thank Dr Mate for allowing me to quote from this paper); Dyer 1980b: ch. 9; Blanchard 1970. Cf. also Mate 1987: pp. 531–5; Poos 1985.

demographers are beginning seriously to question whether the population began to grow before the 1520s.[9]

The detailed fortunes of the Warwickshire gentry at this time will be considered later, but some general pointers should be noted here. On the side of the pessimists there is the work of Phythian-Adams on Coventry.[10] If he seems to read the evident decline of the Coventry population in the early sixteenth century too far back into the fifteenth, the Catesby accounts for their Coventry properties lend him some support, showing problems with arrears and more particularly with decayed rents from at least the early 1440s, reaching serious proportions by 1481–2.[11] However, declining population, a problem probably experienced by most late-medieval towns, is not the same thing as economic decline, and it is clear that competition for pastures around Coventry was intense enough to cause a major eruption in the last three decades of the century.[12] Estate accounts for the Warwickshire gentry at the end of the fifteenth century and the beginning of the sixteenth do in fact suggest a buoyant economy in Warwickshire and elsewhere in the midlands, with low arrears, fewer vacant tenements, enclosure proceeding apace and a lively market in land.[13] The enclosure riots at Coventry may give us the key to this apparent prosperity, in that it could be confined to certain pastoral regions benefiting from the boom in the cloth trade at the turn of the century and perhaps also from the peasantry's increasing meat consumption. Demand for grazing land would have raised rents for pasture, while conversion and enclosure would also have intensified the slack competition for arable land.[14] The government commissions into enclosure of the early sixteenth century indicate concern for the effects of pastoralists on arable farming, as do the returns to some of these, which claim that people were being made homeless by the growth of sheep farming.[15] Pessimistic views notwithstanding, all the evidence seems to indicate that from about 1480 landlords in Warwickshire were having a much easier time than before.[16]

Even so, if there was a partial recovery towards the end of the century, the depression of the earlier years is not in doubt. It is probable that it was the gentry who suffered most, squeezed between the demands of the crown and the resistance of the peasantry. Meanwhile the higher living standards of the peasants inflated consumption patterns, forcing the gentry to find more money

9 Campbell 1981; Blanchard 1970.

10 Phythian Adams 1979; *passim*.

11 S.C.6/1039/2–8, /1041/19, /1042/3,4,5, /1043/26.

12 Reynolds 1980: pp. 76–7; below, pp. 539–42, 576.

13 Above, pp. 133–4 and below, pp. 185–7; *Domesday of Inclosures, passim.*

14 Blanchard 1970: pp. 433–4, 442; *Duchy of Lancaster's Estates in Derbyshire*, pp. 11–16; Dyer 1981: p. 20, 1983: pp. 210, 214; 1988a: pp. 36–7; Bolton 1980: p. 47. For instances of the effect of local economic conditions on rent levels, see Hare 1981, 1982: p. 19 (rise in rents in cloth areas of Wiltshire); Dyer 1980b: pp. 291, 331–39; Hatcher 1970: ch. 7.

15 *Domesday of Inclosures, passim.*

16 Below, pp. 171, 185–7, 195.

in a hostile economic environment.[17] We might therefore expect that it would be these lesser landowners, rather than their better-cushioned superiors, who would respond the more enterprisingly to the changed economic conditions.[18]

The agrarian economy of Warwickshire has already been outlined, its most notable characteristic being the distinction between the Arden and the Feldon, which should be borne in mind throughout the following discussion. The Arden was an area of variable fertility and mixed farming, with a fair amount of early enclosure and land held in severalty. The Feldon, the old grain-growing region, was undergoing depopulation through death and migration and, increasingly, was being turned over to pasture. Like other members of the gentry whose estates have been studied, the lesser landowners of Warwickshire tended to hold small manors or fragments of manors.[19] Few of the estates whose acreage is known would fit into Kosminksy's categories of medium or large manors. There were some exceptions, like the Doddingselles manor of Long Itchington, but mostly we are discussing small-scale enterprises, reliant on wage-labour and not necessarily able to outbid other employers, not even the more prosperous peasantry, in the competition for agricultural servants.[20] Those with widespread lands – and this includes most of the families which have left accounts (Catesby, Ferrers, Stafford, Willoughby) – were in a better position to emulate the greater lords and exploit the variability of local conditions by using parts of their estates for specialist activities like sheep-farming. On the other hand, they also had difficulties in managing these more far-flung estates from which most of the lesser gentry escaped.[21]

[17] Above, pp. 44–5; cf. Given-Wilson 1987a: pp. 120–1.

[18] A similar suggestion is made in Dyer 1981: pp. 34–5, in Britnell 1980 and, implicitly, in Carus-Wilson 1959. See also, McFarlane's assessment of the extent and limits of enterprise to be found among the nobility (1973: pp. 47–60, 217–27); Bolton 1980: pp. 221, 227 (but cf. pp. 225–6, 228); Bernard 1985: pp. 175–6; Rawcliffe 1978: pp. 49–50; Rosenthal 1965, 1976: pp. 70–1; Davies, R. R. 1968; Wright 1983: pp. 21–2; also Britnell 1977 for more general conclusions on the effects of the Black Death in stimulating flexibility in land management. But cf. Hare 1985, pp. 90–1 for evidence of continued enterprise on monastic estates.

[19] Above, pp. 19–25.

[20] Kosminsky 1956: p. 97; Saul 1981: pp. 210–24; Given-Wilson 1987a, pp. 120–1; C.139/32/18 (Long Itchington: 20 virgates, 100 acres arable, 20 acres meadow, 80 acres pasture). For instances of the size of gentry manors, e.g. *W.F.F.*, 2482 (Ardern manors of Park Hall in Castle Bromwich and Peddimore, together totalling 4 carucates arable, 100 acres meadow, 40 acres wood); *W.F.F.*, 2723 (Cotes manor of Weston under Wetherley: 300 acres arable, 12 acres meadow, 6 acres wood, 10 acres pasture); *I.P.M. Hen. VII*, III, 615 (Brome manor in Lapworth: 300 acres arable, 200 acres pasture, 40 acres meadow, 100 acres wood); *Dugdale*, p. 369 (Hugford manor of Newbold Comyn: 100 acres arable, 40 acres pasture, 24 acres meadow). Also Dyer 1981: pp. 14–15 on the problems caused by labour shortages and note that it seems to have been the Commons who were the most agitated about the growing costs of labour (Dobson ed., *Peasants' Revolt*, pp. 72–8). For confirmation from Essex of Kosminsky's conclusions about the lands of minor lords, see Britnell 1980.

[21] Dyer 1981: pp. 16–17. Rawcliffe points out the need for an able and alert staff on the estate of a great lord in this period, and the position of a gentry family with scattered lands was not wholly dissimilar (1978: pp. 49–50).

Not surprisingly, there is no evidence that any of the Warwickshire gentry families were using their demesnes to produce grain for the market. There were certainly home farms, to which we shall come shortly, but most of the demesnes and sometimes whole manors were leased out. The leased manors tended to be those more distant from the main residence or residences, or the less valuable, sometimes both. In the 1460s, for example, the Ferrers were farming out their Essex manors, which were valuable but distant.[22] By 1413–14 the Shirleys had leased out the manor of Lower Ettington in southern Warwickshire. Although it was worth over £30 and had been the family seat since the Conquests it had become peripheral to their interests, which were moving north into Leicestershire and Derbyshire.[23] In 1433–4 William Mountford had some of his south Warwickshire estates – Fenny Compton, Avon Dassett, Honiley and Blackwell – at farm, as well as his lands at Ullenhall which were much closer to his residence at Coleshill but worth only £6 a year.[24] A disputed lease of Belne, Worcestershire, allegedly made by Richard Burdet in 1476, runs against this pattern in that it concerned a valuable manor (leased at nearly £35 a year) lying not far from the core of the estate, but it belongs to a time when Burdet was fighting to establish his right to inherit and needed ready cash to finance his litigation. The fact that, most unusually for this time, the lease was to run from year to year indicates Burdet's intention to repossess himself of the estate as soon as he was in a position to do so.[25]

Farming of complete manors seems to have been less widely practised than farming the demesne, although the manor house itself was quite frequently leased. In some cases leasing of the residence reflected no more than the redundancy which was often the fate of these buildings, both now and later, on estates which had been absorbed by marriage or purchase.[26] This would be true for example of the houses at farm on Simon Mountford's south Warwickshire estates at the time of their confiscation in 1495.[27] The Willoughbys, on the other hand, found that their ancient seat of Willoughby, Nottinghamshire became redundant when the family acquired more substantial lands elsewhere. In 1406–7 most of the liveries from the estates in and around Willoughby were in goods bought for the lord, which suggests that the income from the manor was being put straight into supplying a household here, but by 1421–2 the whole manor was at farm.[28] This abandonment of residences may also denote a trend to reduce the number of residences in the face of rising

22 S.B.T. D.R.10/2465–6.
23 Shirley 1873: p. 393; above, p. 28. The manor was also leased out in 1454/5 (Shirley 1873: p. 45).
24 S.B.T. D.R.37 Box 73.
25 C.P.40/870 rot.333; Dyer 1980b: pp. 167, 171; above, p. 110 and below, pp. 536–9.
26 Stone and Fawtier Stone 1986: pp. 74–9.
27 S.C.11/683.
28 Nott. Univ. Lib. Middleton MS 6/170/35, Mi M 138C (1); above, p. 149.

costs.[29] Giving up direct farming probably encouraged such a policy: few manors were now producing crops which needed to be eaten if they were not to be sold and the rentier economy required less stringent and persistent oversight on the part of the lord. The disadvantage, as we shall see, was that peripheral estates which were rarely visited could pose serious problems of management.

Nevertheless, on the evidence of these families, the phrase 'rentier economy' does not imply a lack of energy in managing the estate. Several have left incidental evidence of the employment of receivers and auditors.[30] The Catesby, Ferrers and Willoughby account series reveal a centralised and yet flexible administration, capable of responding to the lord's needs, while the single Mountford receiver-general account for 1433–4 shows this to be another highly organised estate. It had two centres, one at Coleshill for the lands in the north, the other at Ilmington for the south Warwickshire properties. Comparisons with later valuations of the estate indicate that the income was all received at Coleshill, which was also the point of disbursement for most of the lord's expenses, including journeys further afield. Some at least of the costs of running other northern manors were met at Coleshill, so it was a highly centralised account. But when the household went south, purchases from Coleshill ceased, and there must have been another household account, probably based on Ilmington, the revenues for which were presumably brought, by Mountford himself or one of his more senior servants, from Coleshill.[31]

The Catesby estates, which were more dispersed than the Mountfords',[32] were organised in two main groups, one in Warwickshire, the other in Northamptonshire, unified by a single point of receipt in the household. The money that was not locally assigned was usually delivered direct to the lord or lady, although, while John Watson was clerk of the household, much of the cash came to his hands. Use of the same officer for several of the manors in each segment was a further unifying factor. Both groups were deployed to provide the Ashby St Ledgers household with goods or cash.[33] The Northamptonshire accounts show that from at least 1446 (the date of the earliest account) until about 1463, while the other manors were sending cash liveries to the household at Ashby or directly to a member of the family, Welton in Northamptonshire was being used as a purchasing centre for Ashby. Its proximity to Daventry and

[29] Personal communication from Dr Dyer; I would like to thank him for permission to quote his views. Compare a similar policy initiated by Edward of Buckingham in the early sixteenth century (Rawcliffe 1978: pp. 54–5, 86–9; *Account of the Household of Buckingham*, p. 5).

[30] For example, John Malory in 1437 (*Cal. Pat. Rolls 1436–41*, p. 12), Richard Burdet in 1476 (C.P.40/870 rot.168d.) and Alexander Culpepper in 1504/5 (*Dugdale*, p. 1,037). For a general discussion of administrative structures, Given-Wilson 1987a: pp. 104–7.

[31] S.B.T. D.R.37 Box 73; S.C.11/683; E.179/192/59.

[32] Above, pp. 117–18.

[33] S.C.6/949/15–18, /1039/2–8, /1041/19–21, /1042/1–14, /1043/1–32, /1117/16. NB some of these accounts are rather fragmentary, which may affect some of the conclusions on administration, but probably only to a limited extent, as the evidence is so plentiful.

to the main London road made it peculiarly suited to this role and its revenues were used to make purchases at both London and Daventry. Consequently the Welton accountant was often in surplus at the end of the account, as a result of spending more than was demanded in the charge, and this would be reimbursed to him by assigning his arrears from other estates to Welton.[34] By 1463 this policy had been abandoned, and all liveries were paid in cash, although the practice of administering the Northamptonshire lands as a single unit remained.[35]

On the Warwickshire estates local assignment continued. Here the centralisation was even more marked, a single officer acting as accountant for most of the more important Warwickshire properties. The first we meet is John Watson, parson of Radbourne, who was also clerk of the household and accountant for some of the Northamptonshire property, and was succeeded in turn, in some of his Warwickshire manorial offices, by two minor local landowners, Edmund Newnham and Henry Griffith. These two seem to have been in charge of a Warwickshire receivership, as opposed to the system of rendering money direct to the household practised under Watson.[36] Most of the assignments for purchase were made, for obvious reasons, on the Coventry lands, which accounted in tandem with Corley, so that the Corley arrears could make up for overspending on the Coventry account. In the early 1440s there was more extensive local assignment and the same system for reimbursing the accountant linked Radbourne, Hardwick and Ladbroke, all of them under Watson's authority.[37] But thereafter the only local purchases outside Coventry were coals bought for Ashby at Bedsworth and Lapworth.[38] Unlike Welton, Coventry remained a purchasing-centre until about 1480, apparently because in the 1460s William Catesby I began to take more interest in his Warwickshire estates beyond the Northamptonshire border region. It was at this time that he laid claim to John Brome's manor at Lapworth, with a view to bringing Lapworth more fully into the family's pastoral activities, and it seems that he established another, albeit secondary, residence there, for which Coventry was an obvious source of supplies.[39] But by 1480 his heir, William II, had abandoned this venture; Coventry was producing cash liveries only and new acquisitions were moving the focus of the estate eastward again.[40] William I's own acquisition, the Bishopestone lands, which had already brought him a

34 S.C.6/949/15 fos.1–42, /16,17.

35 S.C.6/949/15 fos.40–80, 96, /18. Cf. Postles 1981.

36 S.C.6/1041/19,20, /1042/2–14, /1043/2–27, /1043/31–33; also refs. in n.35, above. Unfortunately, like so many of the Catesby accounts, the receiver-general ones lack the top, so the identity of the receiver-general is not certain.

37 S.C.6/1039/2–7, /1041/19, /1042/2–5.

38 S.C.6/1042/1,3,11,13,14.

39 Above, p. 118; below, pp. 192–3, 502–3; S.C.6/949/15 fos. 106–111, /1039/2, /1042/10.

40 S.C.6/1039/6–8, /1043/26; above, p. 118 and below, p. 554.

second estate at Lapworth, were treated as a separate accounting unit while they were shared with Thomas Palmer, the husband of the other co-heiress, and only absorbed into the Warwickshire group after they had been formally divided in 1460. This division was probably a significant factor in William's decision to give some attention to the Lapworth properties as it left him with the Bishopestone manor at Lapworth and enabled him to make independent decisions about the management of his share of the inheritance.[41]

The administration of the Ferrers' estates was also adjusted to allow for changing needs, although the less complete survival of its accounts makes its organisation less clear than the Catesbys'. The earliest series is for the Tamworth lordship, the group of Warwickshire estates brought to the family in about 1417 by the Freville co-heiress. Revenues from these went to a single receiver, who passed them on to the lord. All the evidence suggests that Ferrers, second son of William Lord Ferrers, was still residing principally at his father's seat at Groby, Leicestershire and using his wife's estates purely as a source of ready money. There was no home farm at Tamworth at this time, two of the properties in the Tamworth lordship, Lea Marston and Stivichall, were used as a jointure for Thomas I's heir and his wife in 1448, and on several occasions liveries were made to Thomas I at Groby.[42] By 1464 the accounts have taken a different form; there is now a single roll for most of the Ferrers properties, both the Freville and the entailed Ferrers of Groby lands, to which Thomas I had fallen heir on the death of his older brother in 1445. But the roll excludes Tamworth, for which unfortunately no accounts survive after 1437–8. This may mean that Thomas II, who had succeeded his father in 1459, was residing more permanently at Tamworth and keeping a separate estate and household account, now lost, for this central manor. The accounts for Stivichall near Coventry of 1480 onwards lend credence to this interpretation, for they show that purchases for the household were made there – in 1488–9 almost its entire income was used for this – and surplus cash was handed direct to the lord more often, both of which must imply that Ferrers was residing not far away. All this fits with what we know of the Ferrers' political activities, for Thomas II, in contrast with his father, who retained a strong interest in Leicestershire affairs, was already fairly heavily involved in Warwickshire politics from 1460. The family then became even more committed to the county from about 1470, when Lord Hastings, their relative and patron, became a great power in the north midlands.[43] The organisation of the Ferrers estates, like that of the Catesbys, reveals yet again that adaptability to circumstances so characteristic of the successful gentry families.

41 S.C.6/1043/30, /1042/8,12; W.C.R.O. C.R.1911/15,16; *Cat. Anc. Deeds*, III, A4419.

42 S.B.T. D.R.10/2434–2436a, 2437, 2441–2, 2445, 2451, 2456–7, 2616; B.R.L. 437894; S.B.T. D.R.10/721; above, p. 105; below, pp. 215, 326. For deeds concerning Thomas' inheritance of the Ferrers of Groby entailed lands in the 1440s, Leics. R.O. DE 2242/3/31752.

43 S.B.T. D.R.10/2462,2465–8, 2474, 2478, 2482, 2486; *G.E.C.*, V, p. 358 n.c.; below, chs. 11 and 12.

In the case of the Willoughbys the changes are more striking still, since the estates underwent four major modifications as well as several minor ones. First the Freville lands were acquired and then they remained for a lengthy period in the hands of Hugh's widow and her second husband, Richard Bingham, along with part of the Willoughby inheritance. Meanwhile, under the lordship of Hugh and subsequently of Bingham, Middleton, the principal Warwickshire acquisition from the Frevilles, was being turned from a rather neglected subordinate member of Tamworth to a thriving estate in its own right. In Nottinghamshire the family was moving its main seat to Wollaton and away from Willoughby, which by late 1420 was already partly at farm.[44] The absence of full accounts for the whole estate between Hugh and Henry Willoughby is explained by the fact that it remained fragmented in the hands of dowagers for most of this period, but there is unfortunately an almost complete lack of more general accounts for the estates under Hugh, which makes it difficult to see what sort of supra-manorial organisation there was. It is evident, however, that the estate was less centralised than the Catesbys'. The group of Nottinghamshire properties centred on Willoughby was used to provide cash liveries direct to the lord, once Willoughby had ceased to be a residence, and a mixture of cash and locally purchased goods before. It was administered separately from the Nottinghamshire acquisitions of Gunthorpe with Lowdham, even under Hugh, when all the Nottinghamshire properties were united, and there must have been another separate acount for Wollaton, for which, unfortunately, no individual accounts have been found.[45] There seem also to have been separate local receiverships for Middleton and for the Leicestershire and Lincolnshire properties, although the existence of what seems to be a fragmentary receiver's account for the part of the estate held by Richard Bingham in right of his wife indicates that at this point at least there was a controlling central administration on these lands.[46] On the evidence we have, it is probable that, throughout the period up to Henry Willoughby's inheritance, all the estates that were not used as residences – which means for most of the time all except Wollaton and Middleton – were employed simply as sources of cash revenue, sometimes paid to an official, sometimes directly to the lord and lady, although there is the occasional record of a local purchase.[47]

Full receiver's and ministers' accounts survive from 1497 onwards, that is, well into Henry's tenure of the complete estate. Although these accounts reveal wholesale centralisation under a single official, the lesser holdings sometimes grouped locally, they also show a measure of flexibility and local independence.

44 Above, pp. 109–12, 149, 157; Nott. Univ. Lib. Middleton MS Mi M 138C (1); below, pp. 177, 168–9.

45 Nott. Univ. Lib. Middleton MS 6/170/35,39,47, 6/177/59,62, Mi M 138A,B,C (1),D,E,F (for Willoughby etc.), 6/170/37–8,40,45–6,48, 6/176/18, 5/167/98 (for Gunthorpe etc.).

46 Nott. Univ. Lib. Middleton MS 6/170/75, 77–83, 5/167/101–02, 6/170/68–70, Mi M 167–9, 6/176/8.

47 For refs., see nn.44–6, above.

In 1497–8 the receiver did not handle over £200 of the estate's income, the money being apparently disbursed locally by the accountant *in situ*. Since the largest of these sums were from Henry's residential manors of Wollaton and Middleton, or from the properties close to these, we may probably assume that the revenues were being used locally to supply Henry's households. Some of the accounts show that, while Henry was remarkably successful in collecting the full charge, he was prepared to take a fairly relaxed attitude towards the manner of its collection. Several accounts end with substantial *debita*, which are settled sometimes at the accounting stage and sometimes before the opening of the next account, disappearing between consecutive accounts without being cancelled.[48]

One other estate has left enough evidence to indicate how it was run, that of the Staffords of Grafton. This is a particularly interesting group of records because it puts before us an estate that was less than well managed. Whilst an impressive series of receiver-general accounts and valors for the whole estate running from 1448–58 indicate a high degree of centralisation organised round a single point of receipt for cash renders, regarded individually the family holdings seem not to have been well integrated.[49] Grafton and Upton, the old family centre, were managed as a unit but the more recent acquisitions for which accounts survive, all of them but Hanbury outside Worcestershire – that is Leamington and Broadwell in Warwickshire, Milton Keynes in Buckinghamshire and Blatherwycke in Northamptonshire – indicate the absence of any attempts to organise local receiverships or to unify administration on the lines of the other dispersed estates we have examined.[50] It is as if each new property were left to run as an independent unit as long as it rendered its cash dues to the receiver's coffers. The only other unifying factor was the lord himself, whom we find living with his lady at Milton Keynes in 1446–7.[51] It may be that the ever-growing embroilment in high politics of Humphrey Stafford I and his son, Humphrey II, helps explain the decline in the revenues of the more distant properties, as it gave them less time for personal supervision of the estate.[52] It is also evident that without a receiver-general of the calibre of John More, who was responsible for the outstanding run of estate accounts, the Stafford lands would be in danger of degenerating into a collection of miscellaneous, dispersed and undirected entities. This then is one example of a lord failing to meet the demands posed by growth and relocation of an estate.

48 Nott. Univ. Lib. Middleton MS 5/167/103, Mi M 139–42, Mi A 1/1,2.

49 Br. Lib. Add. Roll 74,168–78.

50 Br. Lib. Add. Roll 74,129, 74,146, 74,158–67; S.C.R.O. D.641/1/2/281–5.

51 Br. Lib. Add. Roll 74,129.

52 Above, pp. 118–19 and below, pp. 170–1.

II

Having examined the mechanisms of management, we may now turn to performance. The key indicators are investment, rent allowances, cash liveries, or their equivalent in kind, and arrears. All the records indicate active interest on the part of the owners and their servants, even by the Staffords, although we shall see that they alone of the families we are able to study failed to take their responsibilities as landlords sufficiently seriously. William Catesby I, for example, is recorded as being present at the audit on outlying manors on two, possibly three, occasions and from the 1450s there are references first to a Black, then to a White Book in which the household and other expenses of the Catesbys are recorded. Catesby himself took a hand in this on at least one occasion.[53] Rentals were periodically remade by all the lords for whom we have a number of estate accounts, as well as by others, such as the Archers and the Verneys of Compton Murdack.[54] As Dyer has observed, a new rental was an expensive business, so the assiduity with which they were renewed is all the more remarkable.[55] Often they were a response to a particular crisis, major or minor. The Ferrers have left a substantial series of rentals and extents for Stivichall and some of their other Warwickshire properties, starting from 1418–19, soon after their first entry, and running through to the 1450s, shortly before the death of Thomas I.[56] In their case it may be that prolonged absenteeism was the spur to this unusual degree of concern. On other estates we sometimes find a coincidence of mounting arrears and new rentals. For instance on the Willoughby manor at Middleton, by Michaelmas 1446 arrears had risen to over £11, a sum which included over £4 of bad debts, which had to be respited at the end of the account, and in that year a new rental was made.[57] Richard Bingham showed his seriousness about the stewardship of his wife's estates by seeing to the drawing up of at least two new rentals at Middleton, one in 1454, the other in 1472.[58]

The Catesbys renewed rentals on several of their properties in 1443–4 (in this case the reason was probably the acquisition of the Bishopestone lands), the late 1440s and the mid 1450s. In 1457–8 there were new rentals for the most problematic parts of the estate, Ladbroke manor and the lands in Coventry.[59]

53 S.C.6/1042/5,7, /1117/16.

54 For Ferrers, Willoughby, Catesby and Stafford, see pp. 163–4, 169–70; for Brome, see S.B.T. D.R.3/800; for Archer, see S.B.T. D.R.37 Box 76; for Verney, see S.B.T. D.R.98/465,504a; Warwick Castle MS Greville Ch. 263. There are also two earlier rentals for Compton Murdack (S.B.T. D.R.98/31a,126a).

55 Dyer 1980b: p. 164.

56 S.B.T. D.R.10/2432,2434–5,2436a,b,2437,2440–5,2455,2464,2334; S.C.12/16/45.

57 Nott. Univ. Lib. Middleton MS 5/167/101 (note that the right hand side of this document is so mutilated that it is difficult to be certain about the debts: they could be as high as £14).

58 Nott. Univ. Lib. Middleton MS Mi M 206–7.

59 S.C.6/1041/19,20, /1042/2,3,5; S.C.12/16/15,21,29,30.

In 1461–2 at Lapworth there was even more activity. William I returned from a brief exile in Scotland with the deposed Henry VI to find a fair amount of dilapidation around his estate, most notably at Lapworth. This manor had been confiscated and regranted and had probably been suffering neglect for many years before. Catesby himself and his steward supervised an examination of the tenants about their rents, a view of the animals in the park and the superintending of repairs. A new rental was prepared for the manor and for the lands at Henley and Beaudesert nearby, where difficulties had been mounting during the troubled 1450s, when Catesby had had little time to oversee his lands.[60] An examination of the records cited here demonstrates that renewal of rents, which often meant downward revision, did not invariably solve the problems of decays and arrears. But it could bring improvements, or at least halt the inexorable growth of arrears, even if only by the lord's settling for a more realistic sum, and it is important from our perspective as an indicator of the lord's responsiveness to the needs of his estate.

The subject of repairs brings us to another aspect of careful stewardship, the maintenance of buildings, which was the other characteristic response to vacant tenements and falling rents. Repairs of this kind are especially evident in towns, and are found on the Catesby holdings in Coventry and Henley (although in the latter case they rather gave up in the 1460s, perhaps unwilling to throw good money after bad) and those of the Ferrers in Tamworth.[61] Catesbys, Staffords and Willoughbys were all assiduous in repairing mills. These seem to have been alarmingly prone to breakdown, but, when in repair, could bring in rents of 20s or more a year.[62] Overall it is clear that being a rentier no more meant neglecting the estate than it did allowing a slack administration. There was continuous investment in all these estates. Building of all sorts is a constant theme in the accounts; sometimes just a few shillings were spent, sometimes several pounds, a sum equivalent to the entire cash livery of a small property. In 1444–5, for example, at Baddesley Clinton John Brome was responsible for repairs and rebuilding, costing some 25s, on the manor-house itself and on outbuildings around it, using his own quarry and tile-house on the manor to provide some of the raw materials.[63] In 1427–8 Hugh Willoughby built a new grange at Middleton, as part of the refurbishment of the estate.[64] In 1442–3 Humphrey Stafford I of Grafton spent over £10 on repairs at Blatherwycke to

60 S.C.6/1042/6,10,11; below, p. 494. Cf. Richmond 1981: pp. 67–8.

61 S.C.6/1039/2–8, /1041/19, /1042/2–4,10, /1043/1,7,8,11,14,19,26,27; S.B.T. D.R.10/2434–6,2436a,2437,2441,2457; B.R.L. 437894.

62 S.C.6/949/15 fos.8,13, /1042/2,3,5,6,10,14; Br. Lib. Add. Roll 74,129, 74,146, 74,168, 74,171; S.C.R.O. D.641/1/2/283 (the sum of 16d only); Nott. Univ. Lib. Middleton MS 5/167/101, Mi M 139. The Ferrers mills at Tamworth were particularly profitable and seem to have required little repair (refs. above, n.61).

63 S.B.T. D.R.3/800; below, n.215.

64 Nott. Univ. Lib. Middleton MS Mi M 168.

tenants' houses, to the water mill and to the houses on the manor site.[65] Manor houses and their outbuildings were tended even when farmed. In 1433–4, for example, William Mountford spent over £8 on substantial building works at Kingshurst, the residence at Coleshill from which the Mountfords had moved on when they came into the main manor there.[66] In 1466–7 there was substantial rebuilding on 'Master Catesby house' at the Northamptonshire manor of Braunston, despite the fact that it seems never to have been used for residence.[67] In 1467–8 the Ferrers spent over £5 on such repairs at their Essex manor of Ilgers Lachelees.[68]

Enclosure was another form of investment which was widely practised, even on more distant manors. Enclosure as an aspect of direct management will be discussed later, but it should not be seen in this rather limited light only. As a means of maintaining or increasing the value of lands, enclosure of pastures, arable and woods and the upkeep of boundary and drainage ditches and of palisades around parks were not to be neglected.[69] It is to be expected that references to 'closes' should occur with particular frequency on Arden estates – for example, on a property of Thomas Greswold at Yardley just over the Worcestershire border in *c*.1425, on land of the Fulwodes at Tanworth in 1456, on the Porter manor of Eastcote and Longdon in 1463[70] – and there is more information for Arden lands which have left fuller records. In 1417 Thomas Archer demised to Edward Metley a close in Tanworth called Newland (and therefore presumably a relatively late assart) consisting of arable, meadow, pasture and woods. Between 1443 and 1458 John Brome was enclosing arable fields, pasture and wood at Baddesley Clinton.[71] In 1447–8 William Catesby I spent nearly £5 in repairing the palisade of his park at Lapworth.[72] In 1454–5 Humphrey Stafford II was making closes at Upton, which lay in the Worcestershire continuation of the Arden.[73] The wetter soils in parts of the Arden made repair of ditches especially important on some estates, since a badly maintained ditch could lead to flooding of roads and of other tenements.[74] Particular energy in this direction was exhibited by John Brome and his son Nicholas at Baddesley in the 1440s and later, and by Richard Bingham at Middleton in the 1450s. Brome was also concerned with repairing ponds and mending flood-gates which had caused drainage problems, while Bingham was

65 Br. Lib. Add. Roll 74,146.
66 S.B.T. D.R.37 Box 73; *V.C.H.*, IV, p. 50.
67 S.C.6/949/18.
68 S.B.T. D.R.10/2465.
69 On the possible profitability of parks, see below, p. 180 n.157.
70 K.B.27/657 Coram Rege rot.36d.; K.B.9/284/7; C.P.40/868 rot.231d.
71 S.B.T. D.R.37/861,866; and below, p. 189.
72 S.C.6/1042/2.
73 Br. Lib. Add. Roll 74,174.
74 Above, p. 20; S.B.T. D.R.3/794.

making attempts to rectify the ruinous state of the enclosures separating his tenants' lands from the common fields.[75]

While enclosures in the south of the county were associated primarily with pastoral farming, it would be a mistake to assume that all active enclosers in any part of the county were intending to exploit their lands themselves. One very good reason for enclosing all types of land in all parts of the county was not just to maintain but to increase its rentable value and, like the rebuilding of ruinous tenements, it was often a speculative response to falling land values. The Archers are a particularly good example of 'rentier enclosers'. By the end of the fourteenth century they had created a substantial compact manor at Umberslade in Tanworth by piecemeal acquisition and engrossing in the waste and the common fields, and some of this they had enclosed. The estate probably already included sizeable pastures. But the evidence they have left, even allowing for the fact that the absence of estate accounts and the preponderance of rentals and deeds in the surviving archive must bias our conclusions, reveals a thriving rentier economy. That their tenants included a Coventry butcher lends weight to the theory that their profits were coming mainly from the pastoral ventures of others. However, the amount of land in the hands of John Archer II in a rental of 1498–9, the height of the pastoral boom, does imply some direct exploitation by then, but this was not incompatible with a continuation of the renting policy;[76] at this time Henry Willoughby was able to raise up to £25 from pastures and meadows at Middleton while still retaining a large part of them for his own use.[77] Even in the Feldon, where sheep-farming was becoming so important to the landlord economy, conversion to pasture and enclosure could be made with a view to renting out. This was how the Verneys of Compton Murdack exploited their closes at Kingston and Compton initially, drawing over £100 from them in 1461.[78] Agistment, or leasing the right to pasture animals, could be another valuable commodity in both Arden and Feldon, the more so as competition for pasture amongst tenants intensified. In 1447–8, for example, over £20 was being taken for this on the Catesby manor of Radbourne, a significant adjunct to the profits made at the same manor by the lord's own activities as a grazier.[79] A court roll of Richard Quatermayns, Oxfordshire landowner and retainer of Richard Beauchamp, indicates how helpful a lord could be in the process of engrossing as a preliminary to enclosure, for it shows that at his manor of Sherburne in Oxfordshire

[75] S.B.T. D.R.3/790–1, 794–6, 799–801, 803–5; Nott. Univ. Lib. Middleton MS Mi M 131/39/2,7, /40–47.

[76] Roberts 1965: ch. 5, 1968, pp. 103–10; S.B.T. D.R.37 Box 76 for Archer rentals. For examples of their leases, see S.B.T. D.R.37/861,866,1062, Box 46 (leases of 1460, 1479).

[77] Nott. Univ. Lib. Middleton MS Mi M 139–42.

[78] Hilton 1975d: pp. 169–71; *Ministers' Accounts of St Mary's*, p. 77; S.B.T. D.R.98/504a.

[79] S.C.6/1042/2. For profits from the sheep themselves, see below, p. 192.

Quatermayns had been able to consolidate his property by a series of exchanges with the earl.[80]

Investment in land, by lease or purchase, could also be made in order to rent out. We have seen that 'new men' were often zealous in this direction but we should not assume that these lands were all intended for their own use.[81] Lawyers and crown servants were unlikely to have thought it worth their while to sacrifice time from their jobs for the pursuit of the generally slighter profits of agriculture until the late fifteenth century when the profits of pastoral farming burgeoned. We do not know how Thomas Greswold, king's attorney and coroner in the King's Bench, managed the estate he created piecemeal in the Arden, but leasing is the most probable answer.[82] The Hugfords held a number of substantial leases, in Stratford, Milverton and Ullenhall, but it is quite likely that these too were mostly re-leased, in the same way that Robert Hugford had made a life lease of a manor in Worcestershire that he had at a low rent from his employer, Richard Beauchamp's father, Earl Thomas.[83] Similarly the Archers leased Aspley manor from the dukes of Norfolk and their successor, Lord Berkeley, only to lease it out themselves,[84] and the survey done for the Freville heirs in 1419–20 shows that the Frevilles had rented a pasture at Henley from the earls of Stafford at 17s and leased it out to John Harewell at 63s.[85] John Brome leased Le Waleys pasture in Baddesley Clinton from the Duchy of Lancaster and, although he spent money on enclosing it in 1443–4, he continued to lease out at least a part of it until 1447–8.[86] It was the willingness of the major landowners to rent their lands at well below their real value, either as a favour to a loyal follower or just out of lack of interest, which enabled the gentry to profit by leasing and re-leasing, and this may well be one area of significant difference between greater and lesser landowners in this period. The nobility could perhaps afford concessions or simply slackness which would have been ruinous to most of the gentry.[87] Many more examples of the renting out of newly acquired land could be cited. If the social climbers were more likely to be doing this than the established families, the numerous Arden deeds reveal a market in the buying and selling, leasing and re-leasing of pieces of land, which

80 Oxon L.R.O. Parker MS 1/i/5. For his service to Beauchamp, see Oxon L.R.O. Dillon MS 1/b/2,3.

81 Above, pp. 124–5.

82 Skipp 1970b: pp. 84–5; *W.F.F.*, 2518,2538; S.B.T. D.R.37 Box 42 (deeds of 1423 and 1440); B.R.L. 249975,427016; C.1/58/175; K.B.27/747 Coram Rege rot.33d. Cf. Dyer 1980b, p. 215.

83 *Dugdale*, p. 683; *Ministers' Accounts of St. Mary's*, p. xxxiii; Cooper 1936: p. 4; Dyer 1980b: pp. 171, 214 (the latter indicating that *c.*1450 some at least of the Stratford land was occupied personally by John Hugford); *Cal. Close Rolls 1409–13*, pp. 285–6.

84 *Dugdale*, p. 817; *Cat. Anc. Deeds*, IV, A10213; S.B.T. D.R.37/978.

85 Nott. Univ. Lib. Middleton MS Mi M 214.

86 D.L.29/463/7547; S.B.T. D.R.3/799–802.

87 Cf. for example Richard of York: Carus-Wilson 1959; Rosenthal 1965. But cf. a partial revision: Johnson 1988: pp. 64–5. Also refs. above, n.18.

was undoubtedly facilitated by the existence of so many small closes and in which nearly all the gentry of the area participated.[88]

In general the record of investment and maintenance by the Warwickshire gentry is impressive and no more so than on estates which were suffering from dereliction. The energy with which John Brome attacked the problems of Baddesley Clinton after it had been through a succession of owners has been described by Dyer.[89] In the same year that William Catesby I put so much effort into Lapworth and Henley he also undertook repairs to the manor house at Bushwood, the former Bishopestone manor at Lapworth, which he had obtained through his marriage. It is apparent that Catesby had become conscious not just of the immediate problems occasioned by exile and confiscation but also of the need to make a more positive use of the family's western properties.[90] The heirs to the Freville lands, which had been through a period of minorities and early deaths, had particularly urgent problems on their hands. Even at Tamworth, the centre of the estate, one of the burgages was described in the survey of 1419–20 as '*valde ruinosa*' and in his first years as lord Thomas Ferrers I was obliged to put a lot of money into repairs in town, manor and castle.[91]

More remarkable still is the Willoughby/Bingham rescue of Middleton from its neglected state. Between the death of Baldwin Freville senior, in 1400, and 1410 little money had been invested, houses on the peasant tenements had fallen into ruin, rent allowances had been allowed to grow, mills and demesne pastures had decayed and in 1406–7 drought had caused a drastic fall in all incomes from pastures and meadows.[92] By 1427–8, the next extant account, vacancies have almost disappeared and rent allowances remain low thereafter. At this time Hugh Willoughby was already enclosing pastures and building up stock on this manor which was to be his Warwickshire residence. In 1446–7 (the next account) there was a thriving home farm and extensive repairs to the water mill and mill dam were underway.[93] Under Richard Bingham, who did not hold Wollaton and resided permanently at Middleton, further progress was made. By 1454–5, the date of the single surviving account for Bingham, cash liveries had improved somewhat and, unusually for Middleton in the mid fifteenth century, the accountant was almost quit.[94] Moreover, we have other evidence indicating Bingham's care for the estate. His renewal of rentals and attack on the problem of untended ditches have been mentioned. In a court roll for 1454/5 it is reported that all the ditches on the lordship are now well

88 Above, p. 22. The Archer collection of deeds at the S.B.T. (D.R.37) gives the single best insight into this land market.

89 Dyer 1972: pp. 5,9.

90 Above, p. 118 and below, pp. 192–3 for William I's exploitation of these lands.

91 *Dugdale*, p. 1,135; Nott. Univ. Lib. Middleton MS Mi M 214; for repairs, above, n.61.

92 Nott. Univ. Lib. Middleton MS 6/170/68–9, Mi M 167.

93 Nott. Univ. Lib. Middleton MS Mi M 168, 5/167/101.

94 Nott. Univ. Lib. Middleton MS 5/167/102.

maintained '*et omnia bene*'. Three later rolls of 1465, 1472 and 1473 show Bingham still working away to improve hedges and ditches and to prevent flooding caused by neglect, almost to the end of his life.[95]

Meanwhile he was also consolidating the Willoughby lands by exchanges with other local lords, including John Boteller, the owner of the other main manor at Middleton, which Bingham's step-grandson, Henry Willoughby, was eventually to absorb.[96] It should be remembered, moreover, that this active, concerned landlord was for much of this time a justice of the King's Bench.[97] By 1497, the first extant account for Middleton after 1454–5, it had become a valuable manor, important enough to the Willoughbys to make the purchase of the Botellers' manor worthwhile. Rents were now worth over £60 and cash liveries totalled about £50. The growth in income was not due solely or even principally to the addition of the second manor, for this, judging by an earlier account, would have added only about £19 to the cash profits.[98] It seems that much of the remainder of the increase came from substantial increases in demesne rents, due partly to the rise in pastoral rents but also to the years of patient tending of the lands under Willoughby's step-grandfather.

An instructive contrast is afforded by the Staffords of Grafton, notably Humphrey II, who succeeded his father, Humphrey I, in 1450.[99] Uniquely amongst the families that have left substantial records, the Staffords did not on the whole respond to falling profits with increased investment and more attentive management. On the first Leamington account of 1438–9 there are already very serious problems, with arrears of over £35 outstripping the rents of about £34. Although arrears at Leamington totalled only 5s in 1459–60, there must be a strong suspicion of wholesale and ultimately inefficacious cancellation, since they had stood at over £30 in 1450–1 and had risen again to over £27 by 1475–6, the date of the last surviving account, when a debt of over £30 was left at the end of the account. Meanwhile rent allowances fluctuated at the high level of 70s to 80s. At Broadwell, for which there is a single account, for 1451, arrears stood at over £20 and rent allowances at over 26s, again a large figure in comparison with other estates, although on this account the official was able to acquit himself. Significantly on these two manors very few efforts were made to remedy the situation, almost no money being spent on repairs and apparently no new rentals being prepared. There was the same lack of restorative investment at Hanbury, Worcestershire, where a single account, for 1430–1, shows arrears totalling nearly half the charge. Indeed the Leamington account for 1450–1 specifically refers to a rental made as long ago as 1424–5,

95 Above, pp. 163–6; Nott. Univ. Lib. Middleton MS Mi M 131/42, 43–45, 47.

96 Nott. Univ. Lib. Middleton MS Mi D 4462, 4468; *Cal. Close Rolls 1485–1500*, pp. 243, 275–6; above, p. 133.

97 Ives 1983a: pp. 482–7.

98 Nott. Univ. Lib. Middleton MS Mi M 139, 169.

99 *Dugdale*, p. 318.

although the Leamington rental was eventually to be renewed in 1460. Because these estates lay in the wealthy south of the county, and because of the lack of investment, cash liveries were high – about £40–£60 for Leamington and over £50 for Broadwell – and the full implications for the Staffords' income of this neglect can only be seen by examining the accounts for Grafton and Upton, the core of the estate.[100]

Here there was more careful management; rentals were renewed, arrears mostly remained low until the 1460s, there was some rebuilding and repair on tenements and there was even some investment on enclosure of meadows at Upton. But here too expenditure on the estate was severely limited and the accounts for the whole estate in the late 1440s and early 1450s show how little was being ploughed back into the Stafford lands in general. The last two surviving accounts for Grafton and Upton, for 1468–9 and 1481–2, indicate what was likely to happen to the value of lands under these conditions. The accountant of 1468–9 was so inexpert as to have to render in English, and, despite a single attempt at financial stringency on the part of the auditor in 1469, arrears rose first to half the value of the liveries and by Michaelmas 1482 to double their value. This, it should be remembered, was at a time when this part of the west midlands was thriving and Humphrey Stafford was doing very nicely as a servant of the House of York, a fact which may explain why he failed to bother with his lands.[101]

Single accounts for Blatherwycke, Northamptonshire in 1442–3 and for Milton Keynes, Buckinghamshire in 1446–7, in giving a slightly different picture from the records mentioned so far, serve to underline the normal Stafford attitude to estate administration. Both have high arrears – £13 and more on a total charge of over £44 at the former and more than £38 on a charge of over £93 at the latter – and on both rent allowances are high – in excess of 78s and 118s respectively – but, exceptionally, the lord had responded by undertaking substantial repairs, mostly to the manor-house but also to mills and tenement buildings. But the unusual degree of care at Milton Keynes may be explained by the fact that Humphrey I was using it as a residence. Blatherwycke, for its part, was shared with Thomas Chaworth and his wife, sister of Humphrey's wife Eleanor, and Chaworth may well have had rather more stringent views on the upkeep of estates than his brother-in-law.[102] It has already been observed that the widespread Stafford properties seem to have had little administrative unity, the lord himself constituting the principal unifying force, and that the deterioration which eventually affected even the centre of the estate may have had a lot to do with both the Humphreys becoming

[100] S.C.R.O. D.641/1/2/281–5; Br. Lib. Add. Roll 74,158; above, p. 24.

[101] Br. Lib. Add. Roll 74,158–76, 74,178; N.R.A. 'Miscellaneous Deeds in the College of Arms', 508/1; below, pp. 511–12, 553.

[102] Br. Lib. Add. Roll 74,129, 74,146; *Cal. Fine Rolls 1452–61*, pp. 205–6.

increasingly part-time landowners and full-time politicians. Things might have been much worse without the work of John More, receiver-general when the estate was at its best in the 1440s and 1450s, and under whose auspices the splendid series of surviving accounts for the whole estate was produced. It might not be too fanciful to suppose that More introduced some order to the family economy but was unable to persuade his masters to take the condition of their lands seriously; once he had departed a rapid deterioration set in.

It is time now to take stock of these gentry rentier economies. Although Pollard concluded pessimistically, on the evidence of the Talbots' efforts at Whitchurch, that careful management could make a difference of only 10 per cent to estate revenue, the records of the Warwickshire gentry suggest that its effects should not be minimised.[103] The fact that they all owned smaller estates than the nobility may have enabled them to keep more effective control of their revenues than families like the Talbots. In any case, 10 per cent was a significant proportion of a gentry income, when demands on their finances were as great as ever and the economic trend was all down-hill. Nobody would pretend that this was an easy time for them, and, without the unremitting care so signally neglected by the Staffords, these landowners were likely to be in trouble. On the other hand, if the effort was put in the results could be gratifying. On the Catesby, Ferrers and Willoughby lands there are the isolated problems which have been referred to but no obvious decline. Most of these accounts come to an end in the mid-1480s, so they cover the worst part of the century, but the pattern is one of steady if fluctuating cash liveries, arrears that tend if anything to fall, without much evidence of wholesale cancellation (although the lack of consecutive accounts might obscure this), rent allowances staying mostly within reasonable limits and fairly stable rent levels, even occasional, if small, increments. The weaker performances, as on the Catesby lands at Coventry, are usually attributable to insurmountable local economic problems and there is no question of their reflecting a general decline in the condition of the estate.[104] Only the Willoughbys have left a series of records from the end of the century and these show that the estate was in an impressive state of health. Arrears were low or non-existent, most rents had not fallen noticeably from the earlier part of the century, and some, as at Middleton, had risen.[105] Willoughby may have been lucky in that his lands were well placed to exploit the boom in animal husbandry, but the evidence of the earlier decades on this and other estates shows that, even in the absence of favourable economic circumstances, and given enough care on the part of the lord, survival as a rentier was perfectly possible.

There were however two areas of particular difficulty common to most of the estates which can be studied. One was their reduced ability to discipline their

103 Pollard 1972.

104 Above, p. 155.

105 Nott. Univ. Lib. Middleton MS 5/167/103, Mi M 139–42, Mi A 1/1,2.

tenants. This accounts for quite a large part of the arrears and explains some of the cancellations. In the early part of the century and in some cases later on lords were still trying and failing to collect overdue payments from their tenants. Some of these were the profits of jurisdiction, such as heriots, amercements, and fines for licences to leave the manor, others were just long-unpaid rents. For example, in 1405–6 at Middleton a fine of over £4, which had been charged on the father of two fugitive villeins, was respited because the man had no property on which to distrain. On the same manor in 1406–7 all the tenants except three were freed from the common fine.[106] In 1428–9 on the Ferrers manor of Stivichall an unpaid heriot worth 10s was allowed and in the 1460s amercements worth 6s 9d on the same family's manor of Tettenhall, Staffordshire were listed as uncollectable, while various small fines at Lea Marston were respited.[107] Undoubtedly the decline of seigneurial revenues and peasant resistance to paying the old rents were a significant loss to landlords but, given that they were part of an irreversible trend, they can hardly be regarded as indicators of the health of a particular estate. Most lords continued to try to assert their authority, not without success. As late as 1480–2 Thomas Ferrers II was able to seize over £9 worth of grain from a tenant at Stivichall to pay for the repair of tenements that the man had burned, and some heriots were still collected on some manors, although there were now limits to what could be done.[108] When Robert Onley tried to claim in 1442 that some of his tenants at Birdingbury, in the more manorialised Feldon, were villeins he got nowhere. Nearly twenty years before, Humphrey Stafford I had had the same lack of success in proceedings against a Grafton tenant.[109]

Secondly there was the problem of politically sensitive rents and dues, which faced all landowners from the minor gentry to the greatest lords. There were tenants who were too powerful to be coerced. One such was Thomas Tyrell who by 1469 owed Thomas Ferrers II over £14, nearly three-quarters of the total arrears on the manor, for his land at Gyngioberdlaundrey in Butsbury in Essex. Since Tyrell was a powerful man in Essex, where the Ferrers had few connections – indeed he owned one of the other manors in the township – and, perhaps for this reason, was feed by Ferrers, the latter was hardly in a position to put pressure on him to pay. Reluctance to do so would have been intensified by the fact that this distant property was under threat from a rival claimant for much of our period and the Ferrers needed to rely heavily on local powers to

[106] Nott. Univ. Lib. Middleton MS 6/170/68.

[107] S.B.T. D.R.10/2465–6.

[108] S.B.T. D.R.10/2474. For heriots, see e.g. S.C.6/1043/15; S.B.T. D.R.10/2474 (both, interestingly, from the early 1480s). Note also the remarkable success of the Willoughbys and Binghams in extracting a customary levy from tenants at Gunthorpe with Lowdham, Nottinghamshire, in even the worst years for landlords (Nott. Univ. Lib. Middleton MS 6/170/38,40,45–6,48).

[109] K.B.27/732 Coram Rege rot.71, /654 Coram Rege rot.110d.

defend it.[110] At Middleton in 1446–7 more than £2 of the arrears of £11-plus was owed by gentry neighbours of Hugh Willoughby whom he would be reluctant to offend: William Lisle, who was perhaps capable of coercion, and William Mountford, who most certainly was not.[111] On the same manor, Richard Bingham's attempts to improve drainage in the 1450s and 1460s met resistance from Thomas Hore, lord of the neighbouring manor of Wishaw, and in 1472 from Henry Lisle, William Lisle's son.[112] The same manor reveals difficulties of a different but related nature earlier on, when in 1406–7 it was recorded that 4s 10d of amercements could not be collected because the tenants were outside the lord's jurisdiction and inside that of the earl of Warwick, a man whose authority was not likely to be questioned in this part of the world.[113]

That the problem of powerful tenants who withheld rents was widespread is not in doubt. As Dyer suggests, it is quite possible that they themselves were in financial difficulties, but we can show that this was evidently not always the case and our examples demonstrate that the need to weigh economic necessity against political advantage could on occasion work in the gentry's favour.[114] In 1460–1 William Catesby I failed to pay his rent for Radbourne Grange to the abbot of Combe, presumably because at that point he was in exile. The abbot re-entered, as he was entitled to do by the terms of the lease, initiating a dispute which went on until 1481. The fact that Catesby, who had repossessed himself of the grange, failed to pay his rent for part of this time must have had more to do with this conflict than with any poverty on Catesby's part.[115] In 1460, to take another instance, William Harewell made use of Buckingham's death and disgrace to take some of the duke's lands at Wootton Wawen, which he hung on to and which are listed on successive Buckingham accounts under overdue rents.[116] The Throgmortons, who gave the bishops of Worcester such a terrible time over rents for much of the century, were, as we have seen, one of the most successful families of the century; they were merely exploiting the fact that as servants and powerful neighbours they were simply not men that the bishop could afford to offend.[117]

Another aspect of the tendency for politics to impinge on estate management was the relationship with some of the more prominent estate officials, particularly those who could not be forced to make a proper discharge. The Verneys of Compton Murdack made life very difficult for their employers, the

110 S.B.T. D.R.10/2466; *I.P.M.* 16 Ed.IV/71.
111 Nott. Univ. Lib. Middleton MS 5/167/101.
112 Nott. Univ. Lib. Middleton MS Mi M 131/42–4. Cf. Richmond 1981: pp. 71–2.
113 Nott. Univ. Lib. Middleton MS 6/170/68.
114 Dyer 1980b: pp. 180–3.
115 *Cal. Pat. Rolls 1494–1509*, pp. 141–2; S.C.6/1042/13, /949/15 fos.83 *et seq.*
116 N.R.A. 'Calendar of MS at Merevale Hall, Warwickshire', Bundle 1/3; S.C.R.O. D.641/1/2/274–8; S.C.6/Hen. VII/868–9.
117 Dyer 1980b: pp. 180, 186, 379–81; above, p. 151.

earls of Warwick, in the 1430s and 1440s,[118] and in the later 1440s and 1450s one of this family, John Verney, rector of Ladbroke, was behaving in characteristic fashion towards William Catesby I.[119] Rather unwisely, and unusually, since the Catesbys usually employed tried and trusted servants and tended to avoid using local notables, Catesby had put Verney in charge of Ladbroke. It is probable that the motives for this were political, as the Verneys were looming large in Warwickshire politics at the time and Catesby himself was extending his Warwickshire connections. As other lords found, a politically useful employee was not always a reliable one.[120] In 1447–8 under Henry Wridde, an obscure local figure, Ladbroke had no arrears, the accountant having been acquitted the previous year, and its clear value stood at over £20. By Michaelmas 1449, after just a year of stewardship, Verney had turned inherited arrears of 40s 3/4d into a final debt of well over £12. By 1453–4 arrears were at nearly £10. At Michaelmas 1457 superintendence was returned to the Wridde family; whether Verney had paid up by this time is not known, but to have done so would have been uncharacteristic for a member of this family.[121] If he had not, Catesby was in difficulties; the arrears no longer lay on the accountant and could be recovered only through legal process, usually conducted in the Common Pleas.

In effect the lord of a powerful but inadequate or recalcitrant official had the choice of keeping him on in the hope that the money might eventually be extracted in the give and take of administration, at the risk of continually mounting arrears, or dismissing him and taking his chance in the courts. This would certainly be expensive and time-consuming and might well prove to be politically unwise when the employee was an important figure in local politics or in the employer's own retinue, as Edward duke of Buckingham found, when he pursued his officials through the courts and was rewarded by being betrayed to Henry VIII by his own household.[122] There is no record of Catesby suing Verney, nor is it probable that he thought it worth his while to tangle with this ambitious clan over a few pounds. Such sums could be collected while the official remained in charge if he was insignificant enough to be coerced, as we

118 Below, pp. 419–20.

119 *Ministers' Accounts of St. Mary's*, p. 1 for Verney, the brother of Richard, but note that this replicates the mistake in *Dugdale*, p. 566, where this John Verney and John Verney, supervisor to Richard Beauchamp, a layman and father of Richard and of John the cleric, are confused (above, p. 130 n.127 for a full discussion).

120 Below, pp. 416–22. That Catesby was cultivating Verney at this time can be seen from the fact that he presented him to Ladbroke in 1440 (*Dugdale*, p. 333).

121 S.C.6/1042/2–3,5,7. For the Verneys' attitude to obligations incurred in the course of service, see above, p. 126 and below, p. 419.

122 Rawcliffe 1978: pp. 55–65, 165–73, and cf. pp. 49–50; Harris 1986: ch. 4, 1969: pp. 146–50; McFarlane 1973: pp. 50–2, 223–7; Bolton 1980: p. 227; Maddicott 1970: ch. 1 (showing Lancaster's increased financial pressure on his estates, which may help explain the desertions from him at the end); above, n.18.

can see from the records of Catesby himself. In 1461–2, the year when Lapworth was taken firmly in hand, the bailiff there agreed to forego part of his salary until his arrears were paid off and he did indeed complete the payments eleven years later.[123] But the dilemmas posed by officials like John Verney and by important but recalcitrant tenants and neighbours are not to be minimised in any discussion of estate administration, applying as much to the greater landlords, particularly the nobility, as to the gentry. If land was above all a commodity which gave political power, to alienate powerful people in the course of turning it to profit was hardly wise. The same restraints could even apply to pressure on more lowly tenants in a period when lords were losing their jurisdictional control over them.[124]

All the difficulties confronting the rentier were intensified by distance. The personal attention which we have seen to be so vital to the process could be given much less readily to properties far away from the normal residence or residences. If the lands were conveniently placed in two geographical blocks not too far apart, the use of two residences could prove a solution, as it did for the Willoughbys and even for the Mountfords, with their much less dispersed properties, who by this means were able to draw together their north and south Warwickshire estates. William Catesby I seems to have embarked on the same course when he began to make use of his west Warwickshire estates in the 1460s. But it was not an appropriate strategy for the Ferrers, a family anchored firmly in the midlands, for whom residence in Essex would have had little point.[125] Yet the value of some of the peripheral manors meant that to expose them to the dangers of economic decline and, possibly worse, the greedy eyes of neighbours or counter-claimants, by failing to show sufficient interest, was perilous. Despite the problems with arrears, the Ferrers' Essex lands were bringing in over £40 of the £110 or so in cash liveries recorded on their incomplete account for 1467–8. Similarly placed were the Staffords, with their high levels of liveries from their outlying properties.[126] If much of the home manors' profits went straight into supplying the household, these distant lands were an invaluable source of cash in hand. Inevitably, however, there was more leakage from them, particularly if the manor was farmed out complete. In the late 1420s and early 1430s, for example, there were arrears and decayed rents of quite sizeable proportions on the Lincolnshire estates of Hugh Willoughby.[127] In 1413–14, when the Shirleys had yet to relocate themselves permanently in the north midlands, there were serious problems on their Nottinghamshire,

[123] S.C.6/1042/10, /1043/5.

[124] On tenants, see Harris 1986: pp. 124, 142, and the comment made in the nineteenth century: 'Landlords to maintain a political control over their tenants, sacrifice a large pecuniary interest' (Stone and Fawtier Stone 1986: p. 14). Also above, pp. 42–3, below, p. 269.

[125] For residences, see above, pp. 149, 157, 160.

[126] S.B.T. D.R.10/2465; above, pp. 169–70.

[127] Nott. Univ. Lib. Middleton MS 6/170/81–3.

Leicestershire and Derbyshire estates.[128] Moreover, it was on these distant properties that the question of controlling officials was likely to be at its most acute. It was sensible, in areas where the lord himself was too much of a stranger to have many friends, to use bailiffs or farmers like Tyrell who were influential local figures and would have a vested interest in defending the lands, but, as the Ferrers discovered, agents of this sort did not make the best accountants or tenants. The more compact the estate the easier it was to run, for no estate ran itself without constant supervision.[129]

III

In turning from the rentier economy to direct management we need to make an artificial but significant distinction between production for consumption and production for the market. The artificiality is due to the fact that agricultural goods surplus to household requirements might be sold even on an estate that was in no way geared to the market economy. This would apply especially to grains, which would not normally be grown primarily for sale at this time, and to the by-products of animal husbandry such as carcases from the annual cull of elderly animals and the skins of beasts that had died from disease, and occasionally surplus livestock might also be sold.[130] Nevertheless it is an important distinction to make, if we are to single out the families that were setting out to exploit the available sources of agricultural profit. The Catesby and Brome estates, which have left the fullest information on direct management, present the greatest difficulties in distinguishing goods intended for household consumption from those intended for the market and are best considered as complete units after a more general discussion of direct management on other, less well-documented estates.

To maintain a home farm at the family seat was a sensible course, for the farm could supply the household, obviating the need to arrange transport to and from markets – an important consideration when labour was scarce and expensive – and it insulated the lord against sudden price rises in bad years.[131] All the estates which have left enough records to allow us to judge maintained home farms of some sort, apart that is from the Ferrers, who may not have been residing more than intermittently at Tamworth until the 1460s or 1470s; by this time there are no extant accounts for Tamworth, which is where such a farm would logically have been.[132] In 1448–9 the Staffords were incurring harvest costs at Grafton, perhaps for the peas and oats whose harvesting at an

[128] Shirley 1873: pp. 389–94.

[129] For further comments on the need for careful supervision, at both gentry and noble level, McFarlane 1973: pp. 47–50; Sinclair 1987a: pp. 163–5; Crawford 1986: p. 9.

[130] E.g. S.B.T. D.R.3/802 (although these appear to be gifts rather than sales); S.C.6/1042/2–3; Br. Lib. Add. Roll 74,174–5. Also Mertes 1988: pp. 98–9.

[131] On home farms in general, see Mertes 1988: pp. 96–8.

[132] Above, p. 160.

unspecified manor is recorded on the general account for 1454–5. They were also keeping some of the demesne meadows there for their own use for most of the period for which accounts survive, and in 1446–7 they had enough animals to warrant the use of part of the rectory meadow. It was doubtless for this personal use that some of the enclosures at Grafton and Upton were made.[133]

We have observed the Willoughbys' establishment of a home farm at Middleton as soon as it became their Warwickshire residence. By 1427–8 Hugh Willoughby was enclosing his pastures, adding to his stock of animals and building a new grange. By the late 1440s, when we have a short series of accounts, part of the demesne pastures and most of the meadows were in Willoughby's use, and barley, oats, drage, peas and wheat were being harvested, although it was still necessary to buy grains, mainly barley and malt, for the household. By 1448–9 all the demesne pastures were in the lord's hands and by the following year there were enough animals to require the services of a 'keeper of beasts'. In 1454–5, although the account is less informative, the demesne pastures remained in the lord's use and some arable farming was going on.[134] The much less full general accounts of Henry Willoughby, which start in 1497, indicate almost nothing about arable farming at Middleton, but show that the family was still making use of its meadows and pastures there. These were being enclosed in 1501–2, and there was a similar use of pasture at their other and more important residence of Wollaton.[135] The Mountfords' home farm at Coleshill was used exclusively for animal husbandry. Their northern estates lay in good cattle country and in 1433–4 they bought twenty-three oxen at Coventry, the centre of the regional cattle-market, at what seems to have been a pre-fattening price. Some at least of these were kept in their park at Hampton and the slaughter of cattle and sheep from the lord's stock for the household at Coleshill and Ilmington is recorded throughout the year.[136]

On none of these estates is there any indication that the products were sold, although the cursory nature of the later Willoughby accounts may obscure a small profit from animal husbandry, and it is just possible that profits were recorded separately.[137] On other estates, which have left only passing references, mostly culled from the legal records, it is impossible to deduce the purposes of direct farming. However, the economic circumstances make it probable that throughout the century grains were grown purely for home consumption, and that until about the 1470s animals were usually kept for the same purpose. Periodically there are references to oxen in numbers which

133 Br. Lib. Add. Roll 74,160–8, 74,174.

134 Nott. Univ. Lib. Middleton MS Mi M 168, 5/167/101–2.

135 Nott. Univ. Lib. Middleton MS Mi M 139–43, Mi A 1/1,2.

136 S.B.T. D.R.37 Box 73; below, p. 182. The cattle bought at Coventry cost 6s 4d each, which comparison with the prices in the Brome accounts (S.B.T. D.R.3/799–805) suggests to be a pre-fattening price. Cf. Mate 1987: pp. 523–4 on direct exploitation to provide meat for households.

137 McFarlane 1973: p. 129 for the separate recording of casual profits, which could obscure them from view.

suggest they were being used for ploughing. In 1456, for example, Richard Fulwode had eight oxen in a close at Tanworth.[138] Richard Archer, also of Tanworth, left eight oxen and a plough in his will, and his wife Alice 'a yoke of small oxen'.[139] In 1461 Richard Dalby had twelve 'great yoked oxen' at his residence of Brookhampton in southern Warwickshire.[140] In his will of 1481 Thomas Littleton mentions ploughs, plough harnesses and plough oxen, and in 1516 John Brasebrugge left twenty-two oxen to his daughter.[141] There are also passing references to grains. In 1465 Richard Hotoft was robbed of quantities of wheat, barley and oats at Marston in east Warwickshire.[142] Some time in the 1470s or 1480s Elizabeth Malory, widow of Sir Thomas of Newbold Revel, sold over £7 worth of merchandise to a brewer of Coventry; this was presumably barley which was surplus to her requirements.[143]

While there is plenty of evidence of home farms on all types of gentry estates, both large and small, there was another and easier way of providing grain for the household, which was to lease the tithes of the parish where the lord's residence was situated. This may have been how the Verneys supplied themselves at Compton Murdack, where in the 1470s, and probably before, they held the tithes owned by St. Mary's Collegiate Church, Warwick. If, by the 1470s, the tithes were producing little grain, the supply would have been more substantial earlier in the century, before enclosure and conversion. Richard Verney was steward of all the church's properties in England and Wales in the 1470s, but he may also have owed the grant of the tithes to the family's connection with the church's patrons, the earls of Warwick.[144] The Mountfords furnished their large household at Coleshill by renting the tithes of Coleshill and of Church Bickenhill nearby and later of Kingsbury, another neighbouring parish. The account of 1433–4 records payments for winnowing and threshing the grain, although they were not obliged to harvest it themselves. Even then the size of the household necessitated the purchase of additional grains.[145] In 1444–5 Thomas Malory received part of the Stretton tithes from Axholme Abbey which owned the priory of Monks Kirby, the main lord of the parish of the same name, where Newbold Revel lay. Like the Verneys, he was quite literally reaping the rewards of a political connection, as he was feed by the abbey.[146] Tithes were valued enough commodities to be the cause of conflict, as they were in the late 1450s and early 1460s, when the tithes

138 K.B.9/284/7.

139 S.B.T. D.R.37 Box 90.

140 C.1/27/359.

141 *Test. Vetust.*, p. 366; PROB 11/18 fo.173v.

142 K.B.9/313/58.

143 C.1/60/102.

144 B.R.L. 437204; *Ministers' Accounts of St. Mary's*, pp. 167–8; for enclosure here, see below, p. 184. I owe the comment on the non-arable nature of the later tithes here to Dr Dyer.

145 S.B.T. D.R.37 Box 73; C.1/24/263.

146 S.C.6/1039/18.

of Alspath were just one of the elements in the great dispute between John Shirwode and Richard Clapham.[147]

Sheep and cattle were not the only livestock produced for home consumption. Foremost amongst the others were rabbits. Several of the gentry, including the occasional quite minor figure, had free warren on their lands, and others, like Richard Dalby, who farmed Buckingham's warrens at Westcote and Hardwick in Tysoe, had the opportunity of renting them.[148] They could be exploited in a variety of ways; the warren with the rabbits in it could be rented out, the rabbits could be sold (at the end of the century Henry Willoughby was doing both at Wollaton and making about £14 to £18 thereby) or the lord could use the rabbits to feed his own household, as Humphrey Stafford I seems to have been doing at Grafton in 1451–2.[149] Then there were fish-ponds, found in particular profusion in the wetter and moated parts of the Arden, and a vital means of supply for a diet built round so many fast days.[150] The high level of fish consumption can be deduced from the fact that, where records of household purchases survive, they almost invariably include dealings with fishmongers.[151] John Brome was active in the management of his ponds at Baddesley. Richard Verney went so far as to sell fish at Northampton fishmarket, although it was more normal for those who wanted to profit from their ponds to rent them out to farmers.[152] Alternatively, like warrens, fishponds could be leased from the greater lords on manors where they did not normally reside. In 1419–20 Ralph Brasebrugge obtained a life lease of the earl of Warwick's four large pools at Sutton Coldfield, at a rent of £10 or 120 breams a year.[153] In 1448 William Wyncote of Binton acquired a twenty-year lease of the abbot of Bordesley's fishery, islets and meadows there.[154]

For the very privileged few there were deer parks. Edmund Mountford made a park at Kingshurst in Coleshill in 1447–8.[155] Henry Willoughby had one at Middleton at the end of the century. Robert Throgmorton was accused at the Swanimote court of Feckenham Forest in 1499 not only of having made a park out of the common forest at Wyke but of compounding his felony by making a

147 C.1/29/367; and below, pp. 497–9.

148 Bailey 1988. For Dalby, see B.R.L. 168236. Most of the greater families had free warren at least at their main residence, for which see *V.C.H.*. Minor families with this right included Hubaud at Ipsley (C.P.40/852 rot.7d.). That 'free warren' could mean rather more than the right to take rabbits can be seen from C.P.40/723 rot.106d.

149 Nott. Univ. Lib. Middleton MS Mi M 139–43, Mi A 1/1–2; Br. Lib. Add. Roll 74,160.

150 Perry 1980: p. 62; Dyer 1980a: pp. 63–4, 1988b; above, p. 22.

151 E.g. Br. Lib. Add. Roll 74,129; S.B.T D.R.37 Box 73; the Catesby's accounts for Coventry (above, n.37); Nott. Univ. Lib. Middleton MS Mi M 138 F, Mi A2.

152 S.B.T. D.R.3/799–805; Dyer 1988: p. 32.

153 *Dugdale*, p. 914. However, in 1444–5, Henry, Richard Beauchamp's heir, was making some use of these ponds himself for his Cardiff household (Br. Lib. Eg. Roll 8534).

154 *V.C.H.*, III, p. 63.

155 *V.C.H.*, IV, p. 53.

deer-leap into the park, by which he had, perhaps unwisely, entrapped some of the queen's deer.[156] The special snobbery associated with the ownership of large parks is illustrated by Henry Waver I. In 1465/6 this arriviste ex-mayor of London, who had just completed his acquisition of the whole of Cestersover, with which he had rather a tenuous family connection, marked the supposed return of the Waver family to its own by imparking 500 acres of arable and pasture there. Since no crop was likely to thrive in the proximity of a herd of deer, turning part of the estate over to them was one of the most conspicuous forms of consumption there could be.[157]

If all these undertakings were primarily to supply food, others were first and foremost for profit. It was the mixed Arden economy which provided the greatest variety of outlets for gentry enterprise, as will become apparent when we look at Brome's estate at Baddesley Clinton.[158] A major source of cash, of course, was the woodland itself. Obviously, there was a vast domestic market for wood, but the industrial markets furnished by the Droitwich salters and the Birmingham metal-workers must have helped push up prices.[159] Sales of wood and undergrowth feature in nearly all the accounts for Arden properties: at Middleton, Lapworth, Corley, Bedsworth and Baddesley Clinton in Warwickshire, and, to a limited extent, Grafton and Upton in Worcestershire.[160] The value of woods could be greatly enhanced by enclosure and this was a common practice.[161] On the survey of the Freville lands of 1419–20, Middleton was valued particularly highly for its woods, which had been surveyed by Baldwin Freville in 1399–1400, and one of which was already enclosed. There seem however to have been no serious attempts to exploit them until the time of Henry Willoughby, who in 1498–9 was making in the region of £12 from the Middleton woodland.[162] The Archers were especially alive to the possibilities of their woods; two of their leases specify exactly how much wood might be taken from their land and in 1500 they commissioned a survey of the woods on the estate.[163] Enclosed woods can be found on other estates in the Arden, for example on the Porter lands at Eastcote and Longdon in 1463, on the Hubaud manor of Ipsley in the 1470s, at Pooley in Polesworth under Thomas Cokayn II in the early sixteenth century (albeit an enclosure made chiefly for hunting) and

156 Nott. Univ. Lib. Middleton MS Mi M 139; *Swanimote Rolls of Feckenham Forest*, p. 46.

157 *Dugdale*, pp. 90–1; *Cal. Pat. Rolls 1461–67*, p. 542. For more on Waver's sense of dynasty, below, pp. 200, 240. Dr Dyer points out to me that parks might be used somewhat more productively, for pasture, a comment exemplified by the Catesby's use of their park at Lapworth for cattle and at Ashby for swine (below, p. 192); see also Cantor 1970–1.

158 Skipp 1970a; Dyer 1981: pp. 25–9.

159 Above, pp. 18, 24.

160 S.C.6/1039/4–8, /1042/2–6,10,12,13, /1043/20,26; S.B.T. D.R.3/799–803,805; Br. Lib. Add. Roll 74,158.

161 Above, p. 165 and detailed discussion of Brome lands, below, p. 189.

162 Nott. Univ. Lib. Middleton MS Mi M 214,167,140.

163 *Cat. Anc. Deeds*, IV, A7587; S.B.T. D.R.37 Box 46 (lease of 1460); Smith, L. W. D. 1980.

on the lands of John Ardern, who also had some woodland in his park at Castle Bromwich at this time.[164]

Another profitable commodity in the Worcestershire part of the forest was salt-pits. Thomas Throgmorton I bought one of these in 1402, and in 1506 his great-grandson, Robert, acquired some more from Sir Charles Brandon.[165] Then there were markets and fairs. In the survey of the Arden geography, it was noted that the variety of the Arden economy was a stimulus to these; the profitability of Birmingham manor must have owed a lot to its income from its market and urban rents, and the lords of Birmingham took active steps to enhance this income.[166] At Coleshill, home of the Mountfords, there was an annual fair and a weekly market, which would have made a considerable contribution to the £34 and more it rendered in 1433–4. The bridge at Coleshill was probably built by one of the Mountfords in the fifteenth century, a sensible investment in a potentially very profitable part of their economy.[167] The gentry of the Arden were undoubtedly making good use of the region's possibilities; there is even a suggestion from a lease of the Archers of 1479 that convertible husbandry was being practised here.[168] It may well be that it was the very minor gentry and ambitious yeomen so characteristic of the area, who have left so few and so fragmentary records of their economic activities, who, spurred on by their closeness to the gentry breadline or by thoughts of social promotion, made the best use of the opportunities there.

Some of the greater Warwickshire gentry, on the other hand, both Arden landowners and others, were involved in projects considerably beyond the county boundaries. Simon Mountford, for example, had a share in a caravel. The Wollaton coal was vital to the finances of the Willoughbys. Ralph Astley of Hillmorton, a less substantial figure, but one who, as a lawyer, had property in London and its environs, owned two pubs, one in London and one in Hertfordshire.[169] But if there was a single venture that could be made to yield a profit throughout the century it was animal husbandry. It was the gentry who continued with pastoral farming when most of the greater lords had dropped out during the mid-century slump, and the gentry therefore who often took up the leases that became available as a result.[170] What could be done depended on

164 C.P.40/868 rot.231d., /852 rot. 7d.; *Dugdale*, pp. 1,121, 887.

165 Coughton Court, Throckmorton MS Box 50 (deeds of 1402 and 1506).

166 Above, pp. 18, 20–5; Holt 1985: p. 11; but note the sizeable income from the rural parts of the manor (Watts 1978–9: pp. 11–17). C.139/12/3 gives an idea of some of the sources of profit at Birmingham.

167 *V.C.H.*, IV, p. 50; S.B.T. D.R.37 Box 73; *Trans. Birm. and Mid. Inst.*, 42 (1916), p. 14. Also above, p. 30.

168 S.B.T. D.R.37 Box 46.

169 Dunham 1955, p. 38; *H.M.C.*., 11 (1887), III, p. 113 (ref. from Dunham 1955); below, p. 112. For more on the Willoughbys' coal, Nott. Univ. Lib. Middleton MS Mi M 139–43, Mi A 1/1,2; Smith, R.S., pp. 83–7, 97; Cant. Dioc., Reg. Stafford, fos. 135–6.

170 Dyer 1980b: pp. 150–2, 214–5, 1981: pp. 16–17; Wright 1983: pp. 19–21; Richmond 1981: pp. 44–6.

the nature and location of the estate. Wetter regions caused foot-rot in sheep but were suitable for cattle, which could be grazed on river pastures. Hence the Arden, particularly the western part, near Lapworth and Baddesley Clinton, was good cattle country. A reasonably well drained lowland estate however could be very well-adapted for sheep-farming; water meadows had the best grass, and lowland pastures were obviously better for breeding and for younger animals than exposed uplands.[171] Great lords, like the bishop of Worcester, could exploit their lands for specialist functions, moving the flocks between lowland and upland pastures according to their age and the time of year. This was recommendable because one of the best ways of ensuring the health of a flock and of increasing the milk yield of the ewes was to move the animals around. As Dyer has pointed out, some of the gentry had similarly scattered estates, if on a smaller scale. Whatever form of stock-rearing was undertaken – cattle-grazing, small- or large-scale sheep-farming – enclosed pastures on the home manors were essential, although the use of common and fallow grazing by sheep-farmers continued for a long time to come. A large flock or herd was likely to overburden the common pastures: by the second half of the century manorial court rolls show that the growing numbers of peasant animals were already proving too much for the available pasture. And the risk of disease, which could wipe out whole flocks and herds, grew when animals were intermingled.[172]

The full commercial possibilities of both sheep and cattle seem not to have been exploited to their utmost at this time. In the case of sheep, it was the wool that was the cash crop. Carcases and dairy products were mostly consumed in the household. With cattle also, dairying seems to have been of limited importance; these herds were there to satisfy the growing hunger for meat evident in England in the second half of the century, a development reflected in the number of graziers who begin to feature in records at this time.[173] Both sheep and cattle produced skins, for which there was a market at Birmingham and Coventry, but any profits made from these was purely incidental to the principal sources of cash. There was an enormous growth in animal husbandry towards the end of the century, but earlier on the record is more obscure. The best-recorded early pastoralists are the Catesbys and John Brome, who will be discussed later, but there is enough evidence, most of it incidental, to suggest that they were certainly not unique in the period up to the 1480s.

The mere act of buying or leasing a pasture, or even enclosing one, is not sufficient evidence, since this could be just one aspect of the rentier economy. We are looking for landowners who kept sheep or cattle in numbers, and if possible for evidence of commercial dealing in the products of those animals.

171 Thirsk 1967: pp. 179–88; Dyer 1980b: pp. 136–7, 1967–8: p. 120; *V.C.H.*, v, p. 108.

172 Dyer 1980b: pp. 136–8, 1981: pp. 16–17, 30–1; Thirsk 1967: pp. 182, 188.

173 Dyer 1981: pp. 17–20 and the discussion of and references to the Brome and Catesby estates, below pp. 188–93; Dyer 1983: pp. 210, 214, 1988, pp. 36–7.

For cattle-raising for profit the sources are slight. The western part of the Arden is where we should expect to find this, given the terrain, its proximity to markets and drove roads and its later history.[174] It was here, at Hampton in Arden, that the Mountfords were fattening cattle for personal use. But, apart from Brome and William Catesby I, no gentry lord from this area has left any indisputable evidence of commercial cattle-raising. A chancery petition from the 1440s of John Holt of Aston near Birmingham reveals that his tenants owned numbers of cattle, and in 1444 a drover was staying at Aston to collect cattle there. But, as Aston was en route between north Wales and Coventry, it may be that he was merely pausing to take some additional animals from the Holt tenants, although it is not impossible that he had come to deal on a larger scale with the lord.[175] In 1448 the Archers were renting land at Tanworth to a butcher from the neighbouring town of Henley in Arden and to John Boteller, possibly John Brome's associate in cattle fattening, but there is no evidence that at this stage they were grazing on their own account.[176]

We have rather more evidence for commercial sheep-farmers before the 1480s. While allowing for the huge appetites for meat of the landowning classes and their followers, any lord who owned a flock of much more than 100 sheep must be assumed to be selling the wool if nothing else. There is a solitary example from the north of the county; in 1443, some men from Derbyshire, probably at the instigation of John Cokayn III, stole more than 500 sheep, including ewes and lambs, valued at £50, from Cokayn's step-father, Thomas Bate, at the Cokayn residence of Pooley in Polesworth.[177] Further south, but still in the Arden, was Billesley Trussell, where the Trussells were sole lords. This village was already deserted by 1450, but whether the Trussells raised any flocks here is not known.[178] All other known instances, apart from the Throgmortons, who will be discussed shortly, come from the eastern and southern regions of the Feldon and from the adjacent parts of Leicestershire and, especially, of Northamptonshire. Western Northamptonshire, with the neighbouring south-east Feldon, was in the process of becoming one of the great pastoral areas of England.[179] In 1422–3 Richard Knightley was farming Preston Capes, Northamptonshire from the earl of Warwick and supplying the earl with 100 sheep for his household, which may have been Knightley's own animals.[180] In 1437 380 sheep worth £40 were taken at Stretton, Leicestershire from Joan, widow of Nicholas Metley.[181] In the 1470s, by which time the

[174] Above, p. 24.
[175] Above, p. 177; C.1/15/207.
[176] S.B.T. D.R.37 Box 76; for Brome and John Boteller, below pp. 189, 191.
[177] K.B.9/250/45. For the Cokayn-Bate feud, see below p. 411.
[178] Bond 1969–70.
[179] Finch 1956: pp. 38–9.
[180] Warwick Castle MS 373.
[181] K.B.9/230B/191.

movement to animal husbandry was gathering pace, the Verneys and the Peytos each accused the other of breaking into enclosed pastures at Kingston and Chesterton in southern Warwickshire, and about this time associates of the Verneys alleged also that the Peytos had been responsible for 100 of their sheep at Kingston being harried by dogs.[182]

The Verneys are indeed one of three families apart from the Catesbys for which there is rather more than incidental evidence of sheep-farming before the 1480s, the others being the Dalbys, also in southern Warwickshire, and the Throgmortons on the Warwickshire/Worcestershire border. This last family has left no direct record, but the composition of their estate is highly suggestive. First it was in an area where the bishops of Worcester were keeping some of their flocks until they abandoned sheep-farming in the middle of the century.[183] Secondly much of the Throgmorton land was enclosed before the early sixteenth century, and if the bulk may have been enclosed at the time of more widespread pastoralism, at the end of the century, Thomas Throgmorton was already in possession of an enclosed pasture at Coughton in 1454.[184] Thirdly the Throgmortons' acquisitions by lease and by purchase had provided them by the middle of the century with a very compact block of land, focused on Wyke in Worcestershire and Coughton and Spernall in Warwickshire. They also owned some Cotswold land which would have given them upland pastures.[185] It is probable that it was only under Robert, and therefore not until the last three decades of the century, when potential profits were higher, that the estate was fully reorganised for pastoral farming. Nevertheless, the family's sharp eye for a commercial proposition, from salt pits to episcopal offices and royal custodies, must make it possible that they were profiting from pastoral farming before.[186]

With the Dalbys and Verneys we are on firmer ground. We know that the Verneys converted their land to pasture, albeit initially for leasing purposes, in the first half of the century. At the same time Richard Dalby and his father, Hugh, were in the process of creating a compact estate based on Upton, Ratley and Tysoe, which lay along the pastoral area of the western slopes of Edge Hill, and on Brookhampton, which features in Rous' list of early depopulated settlements. Richard Dalby had a second group of lands not far away at Cheping Kington and Combrook, where he had an enclosed pasture in 1464.[187]

182 C.P.40/868 rot. 384; below, p. 533.

183 Dyer 1980b: pp. 136–7, 150–1.

184 *V.C.H.*, III, pp. 74–5; Tate 1943–4: pp. 95–7; Beresford 1945–6: p. 104; K.B.27/774 Coram Rege rot.38.

185 *W.F.F.*, 2603, 2662; Coughton Court, Throckmorton MS Exhibition Box, Boxes 35, 36, 48, 49, 52 (various deeds), 72 (agreement of 1474); *Cal. Pat. Rolls 1494–1509*, p. 64.

186 *Cal. Fine Rolls 1413–22*, pp. 255, 276, *1422–30*, pp. 38, 163, 225, *1430–7*, pp. 116–7, 171, 304; Dyer 1980b: pp. 156, 379, 380; above, pp. 129–32.

187 Hilton 1975d; Dyer 1981: p. 17; *V.C.H.*, V, pp. 144–5, 175, 177; *Dugdale*, p. 562; *Cal. Close Rolls 1447–54*, p. 23; C.139/93/49; C.140/78/89; S.B.T D.R.37 Box 36 (grant of 1392); Br. Lib. Add. Roll 16,556; C.1/28/482; Beresford 1945–6, p. 87; K.B.27/833 Coram Rege rot.67d.; above, pp. 129–30.

In 1461 he had at least 400 sheep at Brookhampton, and, if the Verneys began by leasing out their pastures, by 1479 Edmund Verney had over 200 sheep at Combrook and Brookhampton.[188] The probability that the lengthy Verney–Dalby feud was due to competition for pasture in southern Warwickshire has been discussed. Much of the conflict centred on the lease of Cheping Kington, conveniently placed for both lords, and on Dalby's attempt to wrest land he must have needed for pasture in Upton, Ratley and Kites Hardwick from Richard Verney's cousins, the Verneys of Great Wolford. The surprising failure of both families, in view of their head start, to take as prominent a part in the later pastoral boom as might have been expected may be attributed to the deleterious effects of their war of attrition, in trampled closes, stolen flocks and legal costs.[189]

From about 1480 animal husbandry became a very big business indeed. It is not just that we know more about depopulation and enclosure at this time because of the royal commissions;[190] litigation alleging breach of closes and depasturing grows apace, especially in the great pastoral region in the south; there are more specialist graziers, like Benedict Metley, Henry Smyth and the Spensers; and for the first time in the century, as far as we can tell, families, all of them pastoral farmers, made their way into the gentry almost entirely by the profits of agriculture. This was, furthermore, a period of land sales and consolidation, the land market galvanised by on the one hand the need to acquire and consolidate good grazing land and on the other the temptation to sell such land when it was valued so highly.[191] The number of families that have left records of consolidating, depopulating and enclosing and of ownership of flocks and herds – mainly flocks – in these years is large. They are concentrated principally but not exclusively in the Feldon, but Arden participants in the boom included the Throgmortons, the Middlemores, who in the 1480s had a hundred-acre pasture at Studley in the south-west Arden, and John Archer II, who in 1484 acquired a perpetual lease of all the pastures at Alrewas, Staffordshire, belonging to Thomas Mountford, Simon's heir. It is possible that, like earlier owners and lessees of pasture, these last two were in turn letting them out, although it should be remembered that in this period Archer was retaining more of his own pasture at Tanworth than his predecessors had done.[192]

With the Throgmortons the evidence is again inferential, but strong. Robert was indubitably enclosing demesnes and whole manors from at least the 1480s, and in the early 1480s he was litigating over enclosed pastures at Edstone and

188 C.1/27/359; C.P.40/870 rot. 274.

189 For this dispute, see below, chs. 11–14.

190 *Domesday of Inclosures.*

191 Above, pp. 133–4; Dyer 1981: pp. 10–11. For litigation, see K.B.9 files and K.B.27 and C.P.40 rolls for this period and, for some examples, the references to pastoral farming immediately below from these classes and below, pp. 533–4, 591.

192 C.P.40/887 rot.114d.; S.B.T. D.R.37 Box 59 (deed of 1484); above, p. 166.

Studley, both of which lay in amongst his properties in Warwickshire;[193] moreover, his dealings with his estates are instructive. Having come to an agreement with his mother in 1474, which enabled him to keep a compact estate in and around Coughton at the expense of the temporary loss of some of the Worcestershire lands, he consolidated further in 1496 by effecting an exchange with the abbey of Evesham. This gave him yet more land in Coughton, Alcester and Sambourn, including 300 acres of pasture, in return for some of his more westerly lands and the Gloucestershire lands which may previously have been used for upland pasturage. This transaction and the extensive enclosure that followed at the end of the fifteenth and beginning of the sixteenth centuries lend weight to the view that Robert was concentrating his efforts on one large enclosed sheep run near his home manor.[194] He was also leasing the lands of the Hospitallers at Balsall, which appear by now to have consisted principally of pasture.[195]

But there is no doubt that the really large pastoral ventures were centred on the eastern borders of the Feldon. It was here that the Spensers made their fortune, raising cattle, some of them sold to London, as well as sheep.[196] By 1486 John Spenser of Hodnell was in a position to sell 300 hoggerels to John Catesby of Althorp.[197] The Spensers are remarkable and exceptional for their single-mindedness in building up the family business before making their way into politics. It was surely their carefully accumulated wealth which attracted William Cope, a prominent royal servant, into marriage with the daughter of John of Hodnell. This match brought the family the benefits of proximity to Henry VII, in the form of the lands garnered by Cope in the royal service, without the dangers.[198] No less noteworthy is the family solidarity which ensured that when John of Hodnell died in 1496, at a delicate stage in the family fortunes, he could rely on his nephew, John of Wormleighton, to look after the inheritance of the underage heirs, even to the point of moving to Hodnell to do so, and then to relinquish it when they reached their majority.[199] No other family has left quite as much evidence for animal husbandry in these years as the Spensers, but they were certainly not unique in this part of the county. Amongst their competitors were Edward Belknap at Weston under Wetherley and elsewhere, the Doddingselles of Long Itchington, the Hugfords of Princethorpe, Richard Knightley at Napton, Nicholas Malory at Newbold Revel,

193 *V.C.H.*, III, pp. 74–5; Tate 1943–4: pp. 95–7; Beresford 1945–6: p. 104; *Domesday of Inclosures*, II, pp. 450–1; C.P.40/874 rot.339, /882 rot.276.

194 Coughton Court, Throckmorton MS Box 72 (agreement of 1474); *Cal. Pat. Rolls 1494–1509*, p. 64; above, n.193 for enclosure refs.

195 STAC 1 vol. I/50/2, vol. II/109/1–5.

196 Finch 1956, p. 39; *V.C.H.*, V, p. 220; Thorpe 1962: pp. 51–63; above, pp. 136–7; cf. Thomas Kebyll in Leicestershire, part of the midlands pastoral belt (Ives 1983a: pp. 348–51).

197 Thorpe 1962: p. 56.

198 *Test. Vetust.*, p. 427; above, p. 132.

199 PROB 11/11 fo.39; Finch 1956: pp. 38–9.

John Peyto I and II at Chesterton, Edward Ralegh at Farnborough, various Shukburghs at Shuckburgh and Napton, Thomas Lucy near Stratford and Henry Smyth, son of the Coventry lawyer, a dedicated engrosser and encloser, whose activities encompassed several parts of the county but were chiefly concentrated near the Leicestershire border.[200]

Before leaving the subject of animal husbandry at the end of the century, the Mountfords' failure to exploit these opportunities should be mentioned. John Spenser, who eventually acquired and enclosed the former Mountford manor at Wormleighton, adding it to the one he already possessed, claimed in his defence to the royal commissioners enquiring into enclosure that it 'was nevir good for corne'. An examination of local agricultural conditions suggests that he was right.[201] On the other hand, the fact that it was in general these southern pastoral manors that the family was unable to reclaim after Simon's confiscation implies that they were particularly valued for pasturage.[202] And yet, as far as the evidence will allow us to judge, no enclosures were made at Wormleighton until the time of William Cope, who was granted the manor after its confiscation in 1495. Equally, in 1484 the Mountfords leased out all their pasture in Alrewas in perpetuity.[203] Coleshill itself lay in well-watered country and its suitability for cattle is indicated by the fact that its meadows, all of them rented out, were valued at over £6 in 1495.[204] Although William did enclose Kingshurst in Coleshill with much of the Coleshill demesne and Edmund impaled Kingshurst park, there is no indication that their ambitions went beyond the raising of animals for home consumption that was already going on at Hampton.[205]

200 *Dugdale*, p. 522; *Cal. Pat. Rolls 1494–1509*, p. 599; Alcock 1977; C.P.40/878 rot.442; K.B.9/405/3; *V.C.H.*, VI, p. 243; *Cal. Close Rolls 1500–09*, p. 13; C.P.40/846 rot.484; W.C.R.O. C.R.1248/68/19; *V.C.H.*, VI, p. 176; S.B.T. D.R.98/527; Hilton 1975d: pp. 171–2 (this is, incidentally, not the plea of peasant tenants done out of their livelihood by an enclosing landlord but an assertion of his rights by the ambitious and successful lawyer, John Beaufitz); *Dugdale*, p. 515; Thorpe 1962: p. 57; *V.C.H.*, vi, pp. 182, 215; K.B.27/893 Coram Rege rot.109, /922 Coram Rege rot.40, /966 Coram Rege rot.26; Dyer 1981: pp. 19–20; *Dugdale*, p. 264; *V.C.H.*, VI, pp. 121, 176; Beresford 1945–6; Rous, *Historia Regum*, pp. 122–3; *Domesday of Inclosures, passim*; Bond 1982: pp. 153–4, 165–6 (pointing out that the large number of gentry enclosers at Burton Dassett may have got the idea from each other, and that enclosure was easier where the manorial structure was simpler i.e. Feldon rather than Arden, so that one man could more easily get control of the whole village). As late as 1481–2, William Belknap and John Norbury, joint heirs to Ralph Boteller Lord Sudeley, were making no attempt, beyond keeping in hand the main Warwickshire manor, Griff in Chilvers Coton, to exploit the possibilities of their estate, as William's heir, Edward, was eventually to do. It is clear from the account for that year that they were mostly in London and regarded these lands primarily as a source of cash (*Cal. Close Rolls 1485–1500*, pp. 302–3, 327; Northants. R.O. Temple (Stowe) Coll. Box 6/2).

201 Thorpe 1962: pp. 51–63.

202 S.C.12/22/89.

203 S.C.11/683; *Dugdale*, p. 515; Thorpe 1962: p. 51; above, p. 185.

204 Above, pp. 20, 182; S.C.11/683.

205 Bod. Lib. Dugdale MS 15, p. 45.

From William's I.P.M. of 1453 it is apparent that the lion's share of the Coleshill revenues came from rents; although the same return reveals the existence of 204 acres of demesne pasture at Monkspath in Tanworth, the low return from that manor both in 1433–4 and in the early years of the following century makes it highly improbable that it was being used for commercial purposes. Nor, on the limited evidence available, does the family seem to have been very active in exploiting the woodland on its substantial Arden estates.[206] Like the Staffords of Grafton they were apparently too active as politicians to be very conscientious farmers. Unlike the Staffords, though, they seem to have been in no danger of running into economic difficulties, judging by the incomplete surveys of their lands from the late fifteenth and early sixteenth centuries. We should not therefore make too much of their rather unenterprising attitude in suggesting a spiral of decline that would explain Simon's alleged treason.[207] What their case does show is that, with a large enough income (theirs was the largest of any family assessed in Warwickshire in 1436) and the conscientious management indicated by the account of 1433–4, agricultural enterprise was by no means essential to a family's survival.

IV

This survey concludes with a closer study of the efforts of John Brome and the Catesbys to exploit all the possibilities afforded by their estates. They have been left until last because their activities are so impressive and so well-recorded that each is best considered as a whole. Both, Brome in particular, have been written up by Dyer, so this discussion will concentrate on the aspects of their management to which he gave less attention, notably those which relate their estate management to their other concerns.[208] For Brome the evidence consists primarily of a series of *compoti*, court rolls and rentals for Baddesley Clinton, his principal manor and residence, acquired in 1438, mostly covering the period 1443–58.[209] Brome's care in refurbishing this neglected manor, discussed by Dyer, has already been referred to: enclosure, repairs, ditching, digging out of ponds and weeding are all mentioned, particularly in the early accounts.[210] Peas, oats and wheat were grown for home consumption and in 1444–5 the fields were being fertilised with manure from the farmyard.[211] Brome followed the precepts of good husbandry in taking his seed-corn from elsewhere, partly from Lapworth, perhaps from his own lands there.[212] We have already seen

[206] C.139/150/33; S.B.T. D.R.37 Box 73; S.C.12/22/89.

[207] S.C.11/683; S.C.12/22/89. Cf. the values in the sources in n.206.

[208] Dyer 1981: pp. 18–21, 1972. Also Birrell ed., '*Status Maneriorum*', Intro.

[209] S.B.T. D.R.3/789–91, 799–806. Most of the general statements below can be substantiated by reference to these; detailed references are given for particular instances only.

[210] Dyer 1972: p. 5; S.B.T. D.R.3/790–2, 799–805.

[211] S.B.T. D.R. 3/800; Dyer 1972: p. 6.

[212] S.B.T. D.R.3/800,801,805; Oschinsky ed., *Walter of Henley*, p. 325; *Cat. Anc. Deeds*, IV, A8371.

how he restored and exploited his fishponds.[213] Also on the estate was a quarry, which, like so much else in certain parts of the Arden, had to be drained, but could then be used both to supply stone for rebuilding on the manor and as a source of profit.[214] Similarly a tile-house, which first appears in an account for 1457–8, seems to have been intended primarily for his own rebuilding, but could nevertheless be turned to profit, as it was in that year, when the £2 from sales of tiles helped finance the £4 spent on repairing it.[215] Larger profits came from the Arden woodlands. Between 1443 and 1446 Brome spent more than £8 on enclosing woods and other lands and was rewarded by a rise in revenue from wood sales from 3s 10d in 1443–4 to £6 7s in 1451–2.[216]

But his main profit-making ventures were in the cattle trade. In 1448 he bought the reversion of Hydes Pastures, on the Warwickshire side of the Leicestershire border, of which he had possession by 1457, and in 1449 the estate of Woodloes near Warwick, to which he added more land at Woodcote, including perhaps 300 acres of pasture, in 1450.[217] At Baddesley he already possessed an estate with a high proportion of demesne land, most of it probably enclosed, which he consolidated with a number of purchases. Like the rest of this area of the Arden, it had the triple advantage of suitable pastures, proximity to the cattle market at Coventry and easy access to the drove roads from north Wales to London which passed through Coventry.[218] Moreover, Brome was an influential member of the royal household and it was the household that was his most important customer. The fact that the Lancastrians had a penchant for Kenilworth and Coventry meant that for at least part of the time his customer was on his doorstep.[219] It is not improbable that Hydes Pastures was bought with a view to using it as a staging post when it was necessary to take the beasts to London.

Henry VI's court seems to have constituted the profitable end of Brome's trade. The oxen, bought mainly at Coventry, normally cost about 10s to 13s each, and most of the more lucrative sales – about 16s to 19s a beast – were to household suppliers like John Boteller or Hugh Mayn, or to large-scale graziers like Benedict Lee, who may also have been selling at least part of his wares to the court.[220] Sales to lesser local figures could leave Brome with a loss,

213 Above, p. 179.

214 Dyer 1972: pp. 8–9; S.B.T. D.R.3/799–805.

215 Dyer 1972: p. 9; S.B.T. D.R.3/805. An extension to the hall and repairs had already entailed the use of tiles in 1444–5 and 1447–8 (D.R.3/800,802), so the tile-house may have been in use before it was refurbished.

216 S.B.T. D.R.3/799–803. This also involved keeping his tenants' animals out of the newly-enclosed wood (D.R.3/790–2).

217 Dyer 1972; p. 3, 1981, p. 18; *W.F.F.*, 2635; W.C.R.O. C.R.26/1(2)/W.24–6, XXVI–XXXI; C.P.40/887 rot.176.

218 Dyer 1972: pp. 4, 6, 8; above, pp. 23–4, 182.

219 Below, pp. 367–8, 458.

220 Dyer 1972: pp. 6–8; S.B.T. D.R.3/799–805.

particularly once the cost of the animals' keep is deducted.[221] The obverse side of these perhaps somewhat inflated prices was that Henry VI's household during his majority was a notoriously bad debtor. At Michaelmas 1443 over £86 was owing on oxen supplied to the royal household and it is probable that the other arrears of well over £90 charged on this account came principally from the same source. In 1445–6 Brome received over £80 of arrears, apparently all from the household.[222] If the debts appear eventually to have been paid, Brome's position in the treasury helping no doubt to set the exchequer wheels in motion, the position of unpaid money-lender to the crown was not likely to appeal to someone so patently anxious to accumulate money as effectively and speedily as he could.[223] The growing debts of the crown would partly explain why the venture was being wound down by 1456–7, when Brome was already beginning to rent out his demesne, ironically just as the court was moving permanently to Coventry, and by 1464 his conversion to rentier was complete.[224]

But there was another reason for the change of direction, in the increasing precariousness of Brome's position. By the mid to late 1450s it was clear that he stood or fell with the Lancastrian dynasty. The fact that two of his three major land purchases had been made in the face of rival claimants and that, of these, Woodloes was already under threat from the Herthills, servants of the Yorkist earl of Warwick, made it imperative for him that the courtiers should remain in power. His struggle with Warwick himself over the Beauchamp chamberlainship of the exchequer only reinforced this necessity.[225] The ensuing difficulties can be seen at an early stage. He had to allow John Mayell, one of the residuary heirs to Woodloes, whose friendship it would be unwise to lose in the face of the Herthill threat, to build up arrears of rent.[226] In 1450 he had been attacked by men from Warwick, probably acting under the orders of Richard Neville, and there may have been an earlier assault from one of his enemies in 1447–8 when it is recorded that enclosures were thrown down and pastures destroyed. Perhaps significantly in that year no purchases or sales of animals are recorded, and by 1456 Brome may well have felt that his political future was too uncertain to devote as much attention as before to his estate.[227] After 1461 he had lost the market for his cattle, had to pull himself up from political disgrace and was obliged to face the fact that the threat to two of his major Warwickshire

[221] For example, in 1445–6 he received only 7s–9s for some of them (S.B.T. D.R.3/801).

[222] Griffiths 1981: pp. 310–22 and ch.15; S.B.T. D.R.3/799, 801.

[223] Harriss 1957; above, p. 124.

[224] S.B.T. D.R.3/804,805; Griffiths 1981: pp. 777–85. The king's household was always liable to be unable to pay its creditors when the crown was in financial difficulties (Given-Wilson 1986, pp. 102–10).

[225] *Dugdale*, pp. 971–2; and below, pp. 458, 473.

[226] S.B.T. D.R.3/803; *W.F.F.*, 2660; *Dugdale*, p. 469.

[227] Below, p. 458; S.B.T. D.R.3/802.

properties had become very serious indeed. He had also lost the lease of the Duchy of Lancaster pasture at Baddesley Clinton, which was not to be restored until 1469.[228] Under these circumstances, that he had decided by 1464 to live off his rents alone is not to be wondered at. By 1485, however, in the generally improved conditions for graziers, there may have been a partial return to former policies, for there is some evidence that Brome's younger son was fattening cattle at Hydes Pastures.[229]

Nevertheless, while the venture lasted, it proved profitable. Brome's relations with John Boteller show how carefully the business was managed. It appears that for at least part of the time the two were operating a joint enterprise, in which Boteller sold animals to Brome, who fattened them and sold them back to Boteller, who in the meantime was renting some of Brome's other pastures at Baddesley for his own purposes.[230] Assuming that the arrears of Michaelmas 1443 represent the previous year's sales, between 1443 and Michaelmas 1452 Brome made a profit of nearly £130 from his sales of stock. Allowing for running costs this averages out at about £10 a year or more, a respectable income for a gentleman, according to the tax returns of 1436.[231] A marriage treaty of 1473 implies that the Brome lands, from which Lapworth had since been lost to the Catesbys, were worth almost £100 a year, while in 1436, before the acquisition of Baddesley, Woodloes and Lapworth, they had been valued by the tax commissioners at £36. Whilst all the figures from the tax returns are almost certainly rather too low, this still represents a large increase in income, which must have owed a lot to John Brome's tireless concern for his estate.[232] Nor should it be forgotten that in the midst of these commercial undertakings Brome was able to supply his own household at Baddesley with grains and meat; in 1451–2 he was also keeping sheep, probably at Woodloes, apparently purely for the purpose of home consumption.[233]

The Catesbys started from a higher social and tenurial level than John Brome but remained active exploiters of their estates for most of the century. In this they offer an interesting contrast to other families in the period up to about 1480, like the Ferrers, the Mountfords and the Staffords, or even the Willoughbys. These, once established in the upper echelons of local society, did not feel the need to do more than ensure that the estate was properly run and maintained, and the aspirations of the Staffords did not even go this far. The Catesbys maintained a home farm to grow grain at Ashby in the 1440s, when records for that manor survive, and may well have done so throughout the century. In 1402–3 there was still one at Ladbroke but by 1444–5 the centre of

[228] See below, ch. 13, esp. p. 502; above, p. 167.

[229] K.B.27/923 Coram Rege rot. 9d., /924 Coram Rege rot.50, /926 Coram Rege roti.57d., 67. For interesting comparisons with and sidelights on Brome's activities, see Mate 1987: pp. 524–7.

[230] S.B.T. D.R.3/799,800,803.

[231] This is similar to the figure suggested by Dyer (1972: p. 8).

[232] S.B.T. D.R.3/264. For a discussion of the accuracy of the 1436 figures, above, pp. 52–3.

[233] Dyer 1972: p. 11; S.B.T. D.R.3/803.

the estate had evidently shifted to the Northamptonshire manor.[234] Rents in kind from Bishopton in Warwickshire were also delivered to Ashby and later to Lapworth, when it became for a time a second residence.[235]

But the most striking fact about the estates, particularly under William I, is the way they were put to special uses integrated into an overall policy. As we have seen, the Catesbys' accounting system encouraged integration, but the practice went a good deal further than that. We have a good picture of how the estate was run in the 1440s and 1450s. Radbourne, a depopulated manor given over entirely to pasture, was employed for animal husbandry. A large breeding flock was maintained here to produce wool as a cash crop and to this were added growing numbers of cattle. Extra pastures were acquired by means of leases. Expenditure on enclosure, on a sheep house and on tar and pitch to stop foot-rot show the scale and seriousness of the operation. Radbourne's employees were fed with grain liveries from Ashby. Meanwhile sheep, cattle and cheeses were sent from Radbourne for consumption in the Ashby household and stock from Ashby, also for consumption, were sometimes pastured, probably for fattening, at Radbourne.[236] Lapworth, which had a park, provided venison for Ashby and occasionally pastured cattle driven from Radbourne, and Ladbroke contributed rabbits from its warren, swans and fish to the Ashby larder.[237] Ashby also had its own warren and produced swine from its park.[238] Until about the 1460s Radbourne's only cash crop was its wool, the profits of which, varying from about £20 to over £50, were sent direct to Catesby or his wife.[239] When two adjacent Northamptonshire estates were briefly used for pasturage in the late 1450s, their wool was sent to Radbourne, which was evidently being used as a central collecting point.[240] The Arden manors at this time were all being effectively exploited for their wood and there was some enclosure of woods leading to higher profits.[241]

In the 1460s and 1470s the enterprise becomes yet more impressive. This was the time when William I refurbished his west Warwickshire properties, successfully laid claim to John Brome's manor at Lapworth, which made him the owner of almost the entire village, and it seems established another residence here.[242] It was then that the Catesbys, like the Vernons in Derbyshire, expanded the scale of their cattle fattening and turned it into a source of profit as well as of food. Animals were bought at the local cattle

[234] S.C.6/1041/18, /915 fo.8, /949/16,17, /1043/15; Dyer 1981: p. 18.

[235] S.C.6/1042/8,12; above, p. 159.

[236] Dyer 1981: pp. 19–20; S.C.6/1042/2–7,13, /949/15 fos.83 *et seq.*, 98–111, /1043/10,24, /1117/16; Dyer 1980b: p. 138; Thirsk 1967: pp. 187–8; *V.C.H.*, VI, pp. 115–6, 198; S.C.6/1042/7; Birrell ed., '*Status Maneriorum*', Intro.

[237] S.C.6/1042/2,5,6,7; *V.C.H.*, V, p. 112.

[238] S.C.6/949/16.

[239] Refs. in n.236.

[240] S.C.6/949/15 fos. 32–4.

[241] For refs., above, n.160.

[242] Above, pp. 118, 164, 168.

markets, principally Coventry and Lichfield, and sold at Coventry and other midland markets, notably Banbury.[243] By this time much of the Warwickshire estate had been drawn into the business, particularly Lapworth, where enclosure was underway and much of the meadow was now retained by the lord for his own use.[244] The accounts show how animals were moved between manors, especially between Lapworth, Ashby and Radbourne, which had retained its role as the main stock manor. In 1475–6 Radbourne also received nineteen oxen from Marston Waver in Bickenhill, an Arden property somewhat to the north of Lapworth. There is evidence to suggest that manors were being used for specialist purposes: in the same year Radbourne received heifers with suckling and weaner calves from Ashby, which indicates that some at least were bred there and transferred for pasturage.[245]

The Catesbys seem to have gone in for the same joint enterprises with local graziers as John Brome, for Benedict Lee, a grazier of Warwick, and John Derby, presumably also a grazier, were selling cattle to Catesby and buying them from him.[246] In the early 1460s there are signs that some of the outlying estates were also being drawn into the family's pastoral activities; in 1463–4 hoggerels which had been bought for the flock were kept at Grandborough.[247] By this time sheep were being kept to sell for meat, as well as for their wool.[248] Animal husbandry was always a risky business because of the dangers of disease. In an account of Edward IV's reign serious losses from murrain are recorded and, probably for this reason, no shearing took place that year.[249] Nevertheless, as Dyer has shown, the value of Radbourne more than trebled after its conversion to pasture.[250] The large series of Catesby accounts shows that a combination of careful attention to the administration of rents and assiduous exploitation of the limited opportunities for profit could carry a lesser landowner triumphantly through the worst economic conditions of the fifteenth century.

V

The records for the estates of the Warwickshire gentry in the fifteenth century are not adequate for a general assessment of the economic fortunes of the class

243 Wright 1983: pp. 19–20; S.C.6 1042/13, /949/15 fos.83 *et seq.*, 98–111, /1043/10,24, /1117/16.

244 S.C.6/1042/12,13, /1043/5.

245 S.C.6/1043/10, /949/15 fos.83 *et seq.*, 98–111.

246 Refs. as in n.245. For Lee, K.B.27/830 Coram Rege rot.61d.

247 S.C.6/1042/12.

248 S.C.6/949/15 fos. 83, 106–11.

249 Dyer 1980b: pp. 137–8; S.C.6/949/15 fos. 98–111. The beginning of the charge on this account is missing, which might explain the absence of a figure for wool, but the charge begins in the middle of the sale of stock and in the previous account (fo.83) wool comes after the sale of stock on the charge.

250 Dyer 1981: p. 21.

as a whole and no other evidence is sufficiently reliable.[251] Had we a second set of tax-returns for the end of the period, relative if not absolute wealth could at least be compared. In the absence of these there is little point in trying to do complex calculations based on subsidy returns, as these tend to produce only the illusion of precision based on too many unknowns to be at all reliable. What we can do is decide how well, on the evidence before us, lesser landowners were likely to have surmounted arguably one of the worst periods for them in the agrarian history of England. The indisputable conclusion is that although most of them must have been under some strain, if they responded effectively, as most apparently did, they had nothing to fear. It is probable that the smaller landowners, nearer the base of the gentle hierarchy, struggling to provide for their families while sustaining a level of consumption superior to that of the richer peasants, lived closer to the margin of their income. Unfortunately, it is these people's farming practices about which we know least. However, from what we have been able to find out about them, it appears that they had a sharp eye for profit and many of them resided in the Arden, where the opportunities were particularly good.

For some of the richer families we do have some indication of wealth at the end of the period, although it would be unwise to compare these figures direct with those for 1436, as the latter almost certainly underestimate if not perhaps by an enormous amount.[252] Thomas Burdet for example was alleged in the 1460s to have lands worth 500 marks, that is well over £300 a year. If this was perhaps an exaggeration, in 1478 the inquisition into his lands after his execution valued the Warwickshire properties at more than £150, and the Worcestershire ones cannot have been worth much less.[253] This inquiry was performed by a specially appointed commission that was probably more careful about sending in an exact return than was usual with I.P.M.s. In 1499 Thomas Lucy's wardship was assessed at 500 marks a year, probably a true valuation since it was made under Henry VII.[254] In 1501 Robert Throgmorton promised that his heir would be left lands worth at least £254 6s 8d a year and his will shows that he had many other financial responsibilities.[255] In the later years of Edward IV John Rous II, owner of a moderate-sized estate, whose family had undergone various moments of crisis during the time of political upheaval, was able to make a loan of 400 marks, or more than £250.[256] For comparison we can cite the 1436 figures for the Burdets and the Lucys, £60 and £110 respectively. Both families had come into sizeable properties since then,

[251] But see Dyer's very convincing conclusions on the agriculture of the whole area in Dyer 1981: esp. pp. 34–5.

[252] Above, pp. 52–3.

[253] C.1/27/359; C.145/328/66.

[254] Br. Lib. Add. MS 21,480 fo.160.

[255] Coughton Court, Throckmorton MS Box 72/1 (Vaux marriage agreement); PROB 11/20 fo.9v.

[256] C.1/61/19. For the Rous family, see above, p. 54; Carpenter, M.C. 1976: App. II; *Cal. Pat. Rolls 1467–77*, pp. 246, 634 (heir's participation in Readeption).

but, while allowing for this and for underestimation in 1436, we cannot help but conclude that they had prospered. Simon Mountford, probably the wealthiest of all, could afford to be the king's creditor to the tune of £400 in 1468 and in 1475 he contributed no less than five lances and sixty archers to Edward IV's expedition to France.[257] An indication of how easy it was for a landowner to raise lump sums comes from evidence suggesting that Simon financed his war effort by mortgaging part of his property; there is no sign that this did his finances any lasting harm.[258] The kind of profit that could be made from animal husbandry at the end of the century can be estimated from the Spensers' purchases of the early sixteenth century: Wormleighton, Fenny Compton, which cost them £1,900, and Althorpe, which cost £800, and other lands whose price, like Wormleighton's, is not known.[259] Moreover, it should be remembered that prices were stable almost throughout the century; if they did begin to rise at the end, it was a barely perceptible increase, so that living costs, allowing for the inflations of fashion, would have remained generally stable.[260]

If there were difficult times earlier on, there were also bonuses in the form of the offices and annuities that have been examined in the previous chapter. There were also very unexpected windfalls, like the rent charge of over £25 payable to the Duchy of Lancaster on the Willoughby estate of Gunthorpe with Lowdham, which lapsed during the years of gross maladministration under Henry VI and had not been reimposed by 1465–6, the date of the last account for this property before the 1490s, when, inevitably, it had reappeared under the keen oversight of Henry VII.[261] But it would be a mistake to see these extras as the sole barrier between the gentry and ruin and to argue, as has been done for the nobility, that they were forced to go to war over the fruits of royal patronage or face financial disaster.[262] The Staffords, and probably also John Cokayn III and Robert Ardern, found themselves in a position where economic and political survival had become inextricably fused, but that was their own fault.[263] Only a family as rich as the Mountfords could afford to ape some of the nobility in neglecting to use several of the opportunities their estates offered, but they too seem to have taken the trouble to manage their lands with care. On the surviving evidence, the Warwickshire gentry as a group can be said to have been conscientious and even constructive lords; they knew what they had to do and they set about it with the intelligence and efficiency that we must increasingly recognise as the hallmark of their actions.

257 *Cal. Pat. Rolls 1467–77*, p. 106; *Dugdale*, p. 1,011.

258 *Cal. Close Rolls 1476–85*, pp. 232–3, 235; above, pp. 150–1 for further comments on this.

259 Thorpe 1962: p. 57; Jeayes ed., 'Catalogue of Spencer Charters', 1490, 1532–7.

260 Rogers 1866–1902: IV, *passim*; above, pp. 153–4.

261 Nott. Univ. Lib. Middleton MS 6/170/37,40,45–6,48, Mi M 139.

262 Bois 1985; p. 114; Storey 1966: pp. 19–20; implicitly, Given-Wilson 1987a: pp. 153–9 (discussed further below, p. 632 n.51). Cf. Lander 1969: p. 83 and McFarlane 1973: pp. 59–60, 177–86, 195–206.

263 See above, pp. 115–16, 118–19, 169–71 and below, chs. 6, 11–15.

6

EXPENDITURE AND DISPERSAL

I

So far the emphasis of this study has been on accumulation of land and of money. Dispersal of estates has been touched on only as an aspect of accumulation, a part of the price that had to be paid for heiresses. Yet this is only one element in the story; if we are to understand the mind of the late-medieval landowner we should look as closely at the demands on his lands and his purse, since these must have had a primary bearing on how he satisfied them. They took three main forms. First, there were his living expenses. What sort of lifestyle did a member of the gentry maintain? How much of his income did he spend on his daily needs? What does his expenditure tell us about his attitudes to his wealth, his lands and his social position? Secondly, there were his dealings with the rest of his family. How broadly was the family defined? Recognition of a family bond could take two forms, the one involving no more than remembrance of a relative in prayers or a small testamentary gift, the other, much more burdensome, necessitating the loss of part of the estate or its income to support a relative or provide a dowry for a daughter. This in itself will take us only part of the way, for the family might have different meanings at different times, a subject which will be explored further in the summarising chapter that concludes this first section. Thirdly, there was the salvation of the soul. In the hurly-burly of daily life this was not likely to be an ever-present preoccupation, but it was nevertheless a very real necessity, particularly to the rich and privileged, who knew all too well from the platitudes of religious discourse that they were doomed to pay for their earthly privileges with long periods in Purgatory and perhaps even with eternal damnation.[1] They knew also that in the struggle for existence and advancement they were likely to commit sins for which they would later have to pay. If the solution was, to quote B. L. Manning, to have resort to the 'spiritual bank with which any soul

[1] See especially Owst 1926, 1961; also Shepherd 1983; Aston 1983; Ozment 1980: ch. 2; Le Goff 1984.

might open an account', by setting up perpetual prayers and subventing acts of charity, it was one that amounted to yet another drain on the estate.[2]

That lords had to make choices in the management of their lands has already become evident; for example whether to offset an advantageous marriage against the loss of part of the property in jointure, or deciding between squeezing maximum profits out of the estate and retaining the loyalty of tenants, neighbours and officials. In this chapter we are dealing with a whole series of needs and obligations that could prove contradictory to the purpose of keeping the 'family enterprise' in good order.[3] How the gentry chose to resolve these conflicts may tell us a lot about their priorities, about the differences between the greater and the lesser families, the old and the new, and, thanks to the work of McFarlane, the gentry and the nobility.[4] The whole chapter, especially sections II and III, leans heavily on the evidence of wills. Problems in their use will be discussed in context, but a general caution should be entered at this point. On the whole surviving wills come from the greater families. Moreover, during this period wills grow in numbers and in length, especially from about 1480, and the inclusion of disposition of lands (that is, the will, properly speaking, as opposed to the testament recording bequests of personal property) becomes a more regular feature towards the end of the century. It is therefore necessary to give as much weight as possible to the evidence left by lesser families and to allow for the growth of source material over the century. Nevertheless, taking the majority of illustrative evidence from the end of the period, particularly the years 1480–1520, has proved unavoidable.[5]

II

Evidence for living-standards survives haphazardly. The best sources for consumption-patterns are household accounts, or details of purchases attached to ministers' or receiver-general accounts, but these are available for only a small number of families, most of them too confined to the upper echelons of gentry society to form an adequate basis for generalisations. Wills, particularly the fuller ones of the later years of the century, can give quite substantial information about plate, household furnishings, kitchen equipment and so on.

2 Manning 1919: p. 116.

3 Laslett 1971: p. 105. Also Wright 1983: pp. 29–30.

4 McFarlane 1973: esp. ch. 1, iv and v.

5 The bulk of surviving wills for the Warwickshire gentry are in the P.C.C. (Prerogative Court of Canterbury) wills in the P.R.O. (PROB 11), but there are some in private collections which do not feature in the Canterbury registers, sometimes because they were not proved or were superseded by a later will, and a few were proved in other sees, such as Worcester, Lichfield or York or in archdeacons' courts. All obvious sources of wills have been examined; why none have survived for, for example, the Burdets, or only one for the Catesbys is far from clear. Bean 1968: pp. 151, 243–4 for the reasons for the increase in numbers of wills.

This is one of the points at which care has to be taken not to confuse proliferation of evidence with proliferation of goods. The wills of widows are especially useful because they often include a very full listing of domestic items.[6] Legal records, listing goods stolen after forcible entry, can provide further information. The availability of records of building and architecture is even more unpredictable. A few houses built for the Warwickshire gentry during the fifteenth century are still standing in a state from which their original structure can be determined. In some cases the houses of the very minor gentry and greater yeomen have survived, but it is not always possible to know who actually owned them, especially in the multi-manored settlements of the Arden. The most useful sources for the identification and reconstitution of fifteenth-century buildings are Dugdale and the *Victoria County History* and, to a more limited extent, John Leland, the sixteenth-century antiquary, but one is mostly dependent on scraps of information.

How the gentry lived is not a matter of purely antiquarian interest for us any more than it was merely a matter of personal taste for them. It was as important to them as to any present-day upwardly-mobile middle-class family that they should live 'correctly'. Indeed it was rather more important because, as in all periods of material scarcity, political power, or 'worship', as they often termed it, was expressed visibly in physical grandeur. The close relationship of material and non-material greatness is well expressed in the petition of William Harecourt's widow, after his high living had landed her, as executor, with a large debt: 'the seid william was in his lyue a man of grete countenance and putte hym selue to grete costys and chargys as well in the kyngs seruice . . . as of other grete astates'.[7] But the degree of grandeur had to be very precisely calculated. *Largesse* was one of the major knightly virtues: Warwick the Kingmaker allegedly owed much of his popularity to the liberality of his kitchens and, at the other end of the social scale, Chaucer seems to remark with approval of his franklin that 'it snewed in his house of mete and drinke'. However, to step beyond the limits of acceptable consumption was not only financially unwise but politically unsound.[8] Each rank was expected to keep within its degree; it was the peasants' unwillingness to observe this basic rule that excited such hostility amongst the ruling class, leading to legislation that depicted very clearly the relationship between social position and material

[6] E.g. wills cited in n.36, below. Few married women left wills (Kettle 1984: pp. 94–5); I have found a single one (Elizabeth Norwood 1509: Worcs.R.O., Worc. Dioc. Wills, II, fos. 27–9), but in this case the testatrix was mostly seeing to her obligations, and disposing of her property, as widow of her first husband. Her present husband was named executor. On law and custom on distribution of personal property at death, see Kettle 1984: p. 93.

[7] Duby 1968: pp. 35–6; C.1/45/132. Also Bennett 1983: pp. 228–30; Starkey 1981: pp. 255–6. For more on the meaning of worship, see below, p. 245.

[8] Keen 1984: pp. 2, 154, 155; Stow, *Annales*, p. 421; Chaucer, *Complete Works*, p. 20, ll.331–60. Hospitality and degree in its use remained important beyond this period (Heal 1984; Stone and Fawtier Stone 1986: pp. 172–4, 211–4; Stone 1967: pp. 74–5).

consumption.[9] Sir William Stonor, who failed to observe these social niceties was warned 'ye may breke your howshold with your honour and worschep.' Margaret Paston rebuked her son for his extravagance on the grounds that, far from advancing the family politically, it would diminish them, in forcing her to break up her household and sell off her lands.[10] If 'worship' could be won by expenditure, it could equally well be lost by it.

The family residence was undoubtedly an important means for making a statement about the family position. It was after all the place where the family could put itself on show to the visiting world – from peasant tenants, come to pay a rent or beg a favour, friends and neighbours of equal or higher standing, through even to members of the nobility in the case of the greatest of the gentry. It was typical of ambitious men to rebuild the principal residence of newly-acquired estates. Examples are Richard II's favourite, Sir William Bagot, at Baginton, Henry VII's servant, Edward Belknap, at Weston under Wetherley, the manor he made the centre of an estate built up through purchase and inheritance, John Brome at Baddesley Clinton, John Shirwode at Alspath, the Throgmortons at Coughton, Richard Verney at Compton Murdack, Henry Waver I, London merchant and mayor, at Cestersover and William Broun, royal servant and husband of Waver's eventual heiress, at the same place.[11] Thomas Cokayn II, refounder of the family fortunes, celebrated by rebuilding Pooley Hall in imposing style.[12] One typical progression in the well-watered parts of the Arden and of the south-east was to rebuild a moated manor house of the thirteenth or fourteenth century on higher ground and in a grander style.[13] Although this was by no means confined to parvenus, it is noticeable that, while John Spenser embarked on just such a project at Wormleighton in the early years of the sixteenth century, building 'a fair Mannour house' there, the Berminghams, a venerable family which suffered from minorities and political reverses for much of the century, appear to have been content to remain in their moated manor-house, built probably in the thirteenth or fourteenth century.[14] Sir William Compton, who rose with such remarkable rapidity in the service of Henry VIII, achieved the ultimate in symbolic political statements in taking the stones from the manor at Fulbrook,

9 Above, pp. 44–5; Myers, *Household of Edward IV, passim*; Munro 1983: pp. 65–6; Scattergood 1987: pp. 269–70.

10 *Stonor Letters*, II, p. 98; *Paston Letters*, I, pp. 350–1, 353, 355, 358–9. Note also similar concerns in later centuries: Stone and Fawtier Stone 1986: pp. 172–4; Bonfield 1986.

11 *Trans. Birm. and Mid. Inst.*, 67 (1947–8), pp. 13–15; *Dugdale*, p. 297; *V.C.H.*, IV, pp. 13–16; *Trans. Birm. and Mid. Inst.*, 17 (1891), pp. 82–3; *ibid.*, 33 (1907), pp. 70–2; S.B.T. D.R.10/554; *V.C.H.*, III, pp. 75–81; Leland 1907–10: II, p. 50; *Dugdale*, pp. 564–5, 91–2. For the careers of most of these and of others mentioned in this chapter, see chs. 3 and 4 and associated appendices and Carpenter, M. C. 1976: Apps.

12 *Dugdale*, p. 1,121; *V.C.H.*, IV, p. 187.

13 Roberts 1962: p. 37, 1971–2; and refs. p. 22 n.17.

14 *Dugdale*, p. 515; *V.C.H.*, V, pp. 218–20; Thorpe 1962: pp. 59, 61; Watts 1978–9: p. 32.

once owned by Warwick the Kingmaker, the last man not of the royal house to hold the earldom, to build his glorious new house of Compton Wyniates.[15]

The grandeur and history of the owner would, however, normally be represented in rather more modest fashion. One obvious device was to cover the building in the heraldry of the immediate owner and sometimes that of previous owners and ancestors and of patrons, if they were great enough for the family to wish to advertise the connection. Edward Belknap had his arms carved in the wood at Weston, along with those of the Sudeleys, Mountfords of Beaudesert and Botellers/Pincernas to whom he had fallen a rather distant heir. John Boteller of Solihull, another new man, rebuilt Elmdon Hall, inherited from the Hores in the early sixteenth century, putting the arms of the Hores and the Botellers and those of their predecessors, the Waldeves and Whitacres, in the beams. William Broun, who rebuilt the gatehouse at Cestersover, emblazoned it with the Broun and Waver arms.[16] Alternatively, heraldry could go into the windows; in his new house at Chesterton, William Peyto emblazoned on the glass the arms of his family connections but also those of his patron, Beauchamp of Warwick. The arms of the Beauchamps were to be found in the windows of Richard Verney's new mansion at Compton Murdack, with those of his other patrons, Henry VI and Queen Margaret and the duke of Buckingham.[17] The tendency for new men – Belknap, Boteller of Solihull, Broun, Compton, Waver – to place so much emphasis on the past, sometimes spurious, of their families and on their links to previous owners should be noted, as it is a phenomenon to which we shall return.

It is the social climbers also who tend to provide the evidence for the building of pseudo-castles. John Rous, who had come into local prominence in the fourteenth century and enlarged his estate at Ragley, the family residence, had been pardoned under Richard II for crenellating his new house there. John Spenser received a licence to crenellate at Wormleighton in 1512. In 1465 Henry Waver I was permitted to crenellate at Cestersover.[18] At Baddesley John Brome and his son Nicholas erected a semi-fortified manor-house, surrounded by a moat, with a drawbridge and gatehouse and even gunports. The size and frequency of the windows give the lie to any idea that this was more than a fantasy castle. At Coughton the Spines began the gatehouse which the Throgmortons completed, and here too there was originally a moat and, again, enough windows to make the fortification less than serious. Thomas

15 Below, pp. 240–1; Leland 1907–10: II, p. 48. Similarly Hastings used lead from the confiscated Roos castles he had been given at Belvoir and Stoke Daubigny to build Ashby de la Zouche (Leland 1907–10: I, pp. 97–8).

16 *Dugdale*, pp. 297, 1,001–2, 91–2.

17 *Dugdale*, pp. 474–7, 564–5 (NB Dugdale thinks the rebuilding may have been done by William's son, John (above, p. 134 n.145). The heraldry, as well as the family's subsequent economic position, seems to make this unlikely.

18 *V.C.H.*, III, p. 29; *Dugdale*, p. 853; *V.C.H.*, V, p. 218; *Dugdale*, p. 91.

Cokayn II added a detached tower to his new house at Pooley. It is perhaps no accident that one of the most imposing and least useful of all fifteenth-century castles was that built at Kirkby Muxloe by Lord Hastings, the most successful social climber of them all.[19]

Nobody in fact wished to build himself a real castle any more, with all the discomfort that would be necessary to maintain a real defence against fifteenth-century artillery. The whole trend of building was not only towards greater grandeur but also towards more comfort. As Mark Girouard has shown, this was the time when lords began to build domestic chambers for themselves, where they could enjoy warmth, the clean air produced by a fire-place and a chimney, good light from large, glazed windows and privacy. This would often be done by adding an upper storey to the hall.[20] A contract with a builder drawn up in 1314 by Sir John Bishopestone, Sir William's ancestor, shows that even a moderately prosperous landowner could already be demanding such amenities. The centre of the house was still to be a hall – in this case forty foot long by eighteen foot wide – but there were to be downstairs chambers on either side, both with windows, one with a fireplace, and also 'an upper chamber, the length and width of the house, with two fireplaces'.[21] In 1448 Richard Fulwode made an agreement with his widowed mother on demarcation lines in their joint living quarters in the family residence. This shows that by this date an esquire of exceedingly modest tenurial and financial pretensions was residing in a house which had, in addition to the hall, a chamber above, another beneath, where a chimney was to be built before Mrs Fulwode would consent to go into occupation, a parlour, a chapel, a cookhouse, brewhouse, bakehouse and malthouse, an outer court and a gatehouse, albeit one with room for no more than a garret.[22] Indeed some landowners of Fulwode's social level or slightly below apparently considered a hall to be entirely redundant. For example, Solihull Old Hall, the seat of the Waryngs from at least 1505, but built in the second half of the fifteenth century, probably never had a hall, being what we would recognise as a two-storey house.[23]

Moving up the social hierarchy, we find the same desire for comfort, even if it is nevertheless combined at this level with the large hall and military frills with which a near-yeoman might dispense but which were still thought proper

[19] National Trust 1987, pp. 9, 42 (where, interestingly, the gunports are said to be similar to those of Kirkby Muxloe, even more of a fantasy fortification); *V.C.H.*, IV, pp. 13–15, III, pp. 75–8, IV, pp. 187–8; Nichols 1795–1811: IV, ii, pp. 623, 625.

[20] Girouard 1978: ch. 3. Some extraordinarily interesting evidence suggests extra rooms could be made to yield extra cash by boarding and sub-letting (*Colls. Hist. Staffs.*, n.s., 4, p. 141, n.s., 6, i, p. 145).

[21] *Trans. Birm. and Mid. Inst.*, 33 (1907), pp. 69–70.

[22] S.B.T. D.R.37/949. Similarly, a house owned by William Muston, a minor esquire, at Wellesbourne Mountford in 1417, with a hall, six chambers and other amenities (C.P.40/683 rot.406).

[23] *V.C.H.*, IV, p. 217.

for people with a standing to maintain. The Rous residence at Ragley, so improperly crenellated under Richard II, also had, besides the obligatory hall, all the amenities of five chambers, a cookhouse and a larder. John Brome's house at Baddesley Clinton, rebuilt after his acquisition of the manor in the 1430s, was more imposing still. The original house, as built by Brome, was probably four-sided, the hall filling the side that is now vacant. The other three sides consisted of private rooms and household offices, and there was an additional room at the end of the hall. By 1535 the amenities included a parlour and a great chamber, which may well date from Brome's time, and a 'new chamber', probably put in by Edward Ferrers, who had married Brome's granddaughter, the eventual heir to Baddesley. There were glazed windows here and at Bromesplace in Warwick, where a number of them were broken by assailants in 1450.[24] At Coughton Sir Robert Throgmorton was probably responsible for the timber-framed wings on either side of the gatehouse, erected in the early sixteenth century, one of which contained the hall. A separate and fully-glazed T-shaped building was built about the same time, probably to provide additional lodging-space. The whole led John Leland to declare a little later, 'Mr. Throgmorton hathe a fayre maner place moated at Coughton'.[25] At Pooley Thomas Cokayn II added a two-storey solar wing to the single-storey great hall.[26]

If the emphasis so far has been on building by new owners, or newly-prosperous owners, it is evident that older families were at least as keen to improve the comforts of their homes. Edward Doddingselles I was probably responsible for the rebuilding of Long Itchington manor, of which most has now disappeared, but which has been described as 'a timber-framed building of much distinction'. It had a large hall, estimated at forty-two foot by twenty-two and a half, with, it is thought, a solar and other private accommodation at the far end and a two-storey wing next to the hall entrance, containing household offices below and bedrooms above. In that he was replacing what was probably an earlier moated manor-house, Doddingselles' rebuilding shows that this practice was not confined to the rising families.[27] To take another old family, a little later, about 1500, the Brasebrugges entirely rebuilt Kingsbury Hall, probably on the site of an earlier castle. One of the chambers here contained a four-light window.[28] Even castles were now expected to be more commodious. In 1419 Tamworth castle contained six chambers as well as the hall, and the will of Thomas Ferrers II, dating from 1495, shows that amongst these rooms

[24] C.139/14/13; *Trans. Birm. and Mid. Inst.*, 17 (1891), pp. 82–7; Dyer 1972: p. 9; S.B.T. D.R.3/799–802, 805; Norris 1897: p. 135; National Trust 1987: pp. 42–3; S.B.T. D.R.3/628. On the political connotations of the hall, see James 1974: p. 183.

[25] *V.C.H.*, III, pp. 75–8; Leland, 1907–10: II, p. 50.

[26] *V.C.H.*, IV, p. 187.

[27] Chatwin 1960–1: pp. 7–8.

[28] *V.C.H.*, IV, p. 101; Chatwin 1947–8: p. 17.

was a great chamber, an amenity which owners of the grander houses were increasingly making use of, retiring there in search of warmth and privacy.[29] The estate records of the Mountfords and Catesbys show that they too were providing themselves with private chambers and guest rooms.[30]

Lawrence Stone has observed that in the great period of the English country house the builders who met insolvency, a not uncommon phenomenon then, were more often the new arrivals than the established families.[31] If the evidence is too slight to enable us to uncover the profligate builders of fifteenth-century Warwickshire, on the whole it would appear that the most assiduous were the rising professionals like Brome and Richard Verney who, like Stone's parvenus of a later period, had the greatest immediate need to stamp their authority on their newly-acquired lands. Older families, coming into a second residence by marriage, like the Willoughbys, or even the Catesbys, who had already reached a certain position by the fifteenth century, or their younger sons, like Thomas Ferrers I, obtaining an estate by a fortunate marriage, seem to have felt less need to do more than make repairs, extensions and improvements.[32] Those who were not disposed to exploit the economic potential of unused additional residences were content to allow them to go to ruin, as happened at Peddimore under the Arderns and Ansley under the Culpeppers. This did not betoken abandonment of the estate, only of the unwanted residence, as the Culpeppers' tigerish defence of their Warwickshire properties, even after they had virtually relinquished all contact with Warwickshire, as soon as these estates were placed under any sort of threat, shows very clearly.[33] In all this, as in most other respects, the Throgmortons are an exception, retaining the mores of a rising professional family long after John I had placed the family fortunes on a respectable footing. Half a century after the death of John, it was as vital for Sir Robert to make his mark at Coughton, which under him became the centre of the estate, as for John Brome at Baddesley Clinton.

The same dual purpose of comfort and display informed the furnishing of houses. We might expect the standard of living of most of these families to lie somewhere between that of the richer Worcestershire peasants, whose possessions have been listed by R. K. Field, and of Sir John Fastolf, one of the wealthiest landowners below the peerage in mid-fifteenth-century England, whose inventory survives amongst the Paston papers. Three of Field's families

29 Nott. Univ. Lib. Middleton MS Mi M 214; PROB 11/11 fo. 201; Girouard 1978: ch. 3; Meeson 1983; below, n.37 for the great chamber at Charlecote in 1496.

30 S.B.T. D.R.37 Box 73 (Mountford account); S.C.6/1039/2, /1042/6. Cf. Ives 1983a: pp. 354–6.

31 Stone and Fawtier Stone 1986: pp. 271–3.

32 S.C.6/1042/3,6, /1043/10 (Radbourne), /1042/10 (Lapworth); *Trans. Birm. and Mid. Inst.*, 27 (1901), p. 25; Nott. Univ. Lib. Middleton MS 5/167/101; B.R.L. 437894. For exploitation of unused residences, see above, pp. 157–8.

33 *Dugdale*, pp. 924, 1037; *Trans. Birm. and Mid. Inst.*, 53 (1928), p. 209; K.B.27/856 Coram Rege rot.28d.; *Cal. Close Rolls 1468–76*, p. 423. Cf. Stone and Fawtier Stone 1986: pp. 71–9.

owned several metal vessels and items of furniture and of these one had furnishings for a bed. Fastolf on the other hand, even in what appears to be an incomplete inventory, had an impressive number of jewels, beds, bed-clothes and bed-hangings, towels, clothes and items of table linen and of kitchen equipment.[34] Unfortunately there is no complete inventory for any of the Warwickshire families, save for that of Ralph Shirley III taken in 1518, and his income was probably not appreciably below that of Fastolf. An inventory for William Catesby II, made at the end of 1484, when he was probably at least as rich as these two, has a very full listing of clothes and some other easily moveable items and of weaponry, but appears to be less full on furniture and includes little domestic equipment or plate and no jewellery at all.[35] We can certainly not assume that the listings of goods in wills, even in those of widows, is complete; they are in any case biased towards the upper end of the hierarchy. It is evident though that families like the Catesbys, Crewes, Shirleys, Danets, Doddingselles, Harewells, Hugfords and Lucys were not stinting themselves; beds, other items of furniture, household and bed linen, hangings to mitigate the draughts in parlours as well as in bed-chambers are listed in substantial quantities. Bequests of items of clothing to the church for vestments and to servants and sometimes to relatives and executors are indications of well-stocked wardrobes. Some of the garments were furred, a necessity in the horrible English climate but one with strong connotations of fashionable privilege. As one would expect, the widows left particularly rich quantities of kitchen utensils.[36]

Lists tell us little about the life that was lived amongst these worldly goods, but a reference in the will of Joan Hungerford, widow of Edmund Lucy, to 'ij settelles in the parlour' gives an inkling of the comfortably domesticity that could be achieved in the new private rooms, and one of the few surviving inventories for the period, that of her former husband, reveals a hall, parlour, great chamber and withdrawing chamber, each well enough furnished to provide inner and outer warmth.[37] The embroidery of the owner's heraldry on hangings and coverlets provided self-advertisement to go with warmth and comfort: Gerard Danet, co-heir by marriage to the Hugfords of Emscote, had a

34 Field 1965: pp. 142–3; *Paston Letters*, I, pp. 107–14; McFarlane 1981c; also Astill 1974; Fowler 1940; Hanham 1985, pp. 326–39; Richmond 1981: pp. 130–1; Crawford 1986.

35 Shirley 1873: pp. 417–26; Tudor-Craig 1977; pp. 97–8. For the Shirley income, see above, p. 53.

36 For Shirley and Catesby, above, n.35; PROB 11/2b fo.108v. (Crewe), /20 fo. 7 (Danet), /12 fo. 108v. (Doddingselles), /10 fo. 66 (Harecourt of Maxstoke), /3 fo. 80, /17 fo. 52 (Harewell), /18 fo. 141v. (Hugford), /10 fo. 167; *Cat. Anc. Deeds*, v, A12393 (Lucy). Further evidence of a similar kind is to be found in other wills of the period. Also evidence from thefts of goods (K.B.9/301/58, /253/16). Cf. Ives 1983a, pp. 358–60. For furs, their costs and their use, see Veale 1966: chs.1 and 7 and *Statutes of the Realm*, I, pp. 280–1, 380–1. One problem with will evidence is that heirlooms, which could be valuable and large in number (e.g. *Stonor Letters*, I, pp. 145–7), being non-devisable, would not normally appear.

37 *Cat. Anc. Deeds*, v, A12393; PROB 2/12.

bed adorned with his badge of a greyhound's head.[38] Pursuing the theme of gracious living, there is not much evidence of book-ownership, and the works mentioned in wills are mainly prayer-books of one sort or another, although Goditha, daughter of Thomas Throgmorton and wife of Edward Peyto, owned a collection of devotional pieces, while a manuscript of mainly devotional works, which includes *Piers Plowman* and de Mandeville's *Travels*, appears to have been associated with William Clopton of Moor Hall.[39] But Thomas Littleton, not surprisingly, owned numbers of treatises and other works, which he left to the abbey and convent of Halesowen, and Gilbert Talbot, successor to Humphrey Stafford II in some of Humphrey's confiscated manors, owned a copy of *The Canterbury Tales* 'in paper prynt'.[40] Before we dismiss the Warwickshire gentry entirely as philistines of the first order, it is worth remembering that the Paston papers show that a gentry family would almost certainly have more acquaintance with reading-matter than this evidence suggests, although, being a family of lawyers, they may, like Littleton, have been more literate than most. William Catesby II, another lawyer, owned the books of law and prayer-books that we might expect, but also 'a boke of cronycles' and 'a boke callid liber de natura legis natur'', and he may well have had other volumes not listed here. When considering the amount of 'culture' found amongst the Warwickshire gentry, it is worth noting that Catesby owned 'a pair' or [sic] Organs'.[41]

A particularly notable feature of the wills of even relatively minor figures like John Beaufitz is the quantity of plate and jewellery listed.[42] That this was not just conspicuous display is hinted at by the schedule of possessions, mainly jewels and plate, delivered by Richard Bingham, husband of Hugh Willoughby's widow. It was attached to Hugh's will and probably represents goods left by Hugh. Some of the more valuable items have been handed to merchants in return for money, whether in loans or sales is not clear, and it may well be that financial surpluses were turned into valuables, which could then be used to raise capital at need, by selling or pawning. Hugh seems to have been particularly keen on this kind of investment, for provision in his will for his

38 For reference, see n.36; Butters 1968: p. 139.

39 E.g. PROB 11/20 fo. 7; *Cat. Anc. Deeds*, V, A12393; PROB 11/7 fos. 23v.–24; S.C.6/1042/3 (a purchase under the account for Shuckburgh of an unknown book for the wife of William Catesby I); *A Worcestershire Miscellany*, p. 15; Kratzmann and Simpson eds. 1986: pp. 35–48. I am most grateful to Dr Thorlac Turville-Petre for drawing my attention to the Clopton manuscript, for supplying me with this last reference and for allowing me to see some of his unpublished work on the manuscript.

40 PROB 11/7 fos. 23v.–24; *Trans. Birm. and Mid. Inst.*, 35 (1909), p. 83.

41 See references *sub* 'books' in *Paston Letters*, II, index; Tudor-Craig 1977: p. 98. Also Fleming 1987; Richmond 1981: p. 130; Ives 1983a: pp. 362–7; Bennett 1946–7.

42 PROB 11/8 fo. 161. Also wills and inventories in n.36 and e.g. PROB 11/7 fos. 23v.–24; Cooper 1936, p. 18; Nott. Univ. Lib. Middleton MS 5/168/44, Mi D 4800; *Dugdale*, p. 529; Ives 1983a: pp. 360–2.

daughters and younger sons was made almost entirely in items of silver, and the same goes for most of his legacies. More evidence that surplus cash was salted away in the form of silver comes from John Throgmorton's will of 1445, which refers to silver plate that the abbot of Northampton has in pledge.[43] It is evident in fact that credit was a major part of the gentry economy. Its extent can only be guessed at because historians are only just beginning to realise the huge importance of credit at all levels of society in medieval England.[44] As it operated among the gentry, it resembled rather the system which was alleged by inter-war Vienna to exist in Budapest, where the currency was supposed to amount to the sum of £5 which was continually passing round among the inhabitants of the city. So mutually dependent were landowners on each other's good will as debtors and creditors that an enormous premium had to be put on trust and honesty.[45] Credit was an inevitable accompaniment to an economic system built on land, since most agrarian income is collectable only at predetermined times of the year. It may well be that landowners tended to anticipate an entire year's income and that the debts whose payment was usually enjoined in wills were primarily the expenditure of the last year. This being so, a wise landlord would put away in durable form as much as he could in good years to tide him over the bad. As someone inscribed on a jug made in Richard II's reign, 'He that wyl not spare when he may he shal not spend when he would'.[46]

Nevertheless, it is clear that a very high percentage of profits went in immediate expenditure on maintaining a suitable standard of living. This, after all, was the purpose of the careful husbanding of resources – to enable the owner to live in an appropriately impressive style without getting seriously or permanently into debt.[47] In only one document, the Mountford receiver's account of 1433–4, can we see precisely what proportion of the receiver's income was spent on the household, and even in this instance we remain ignorant of the amount of money received and disbursed direct by the receiver's employers that failed to pass through the official's hands. In that year over £274 was received, and of this more than £250 was spent, of which about £30 went

43 *H.M.C. Middleton*, pp. 111–2; *Test. Ebor.*, II, pp. 131–4 (Willoughby appears from the will to have been buying up items of silver from his neighbours); PROB.11/3 fo. 248v. Also *Paston Letters*, I, pp. 171–2, 350–1, 417–8; Pugh 1986b: p. 84. Putting money into plate seems, on the evidence of *Test. Ebor.*, to have been a particularly northern phenomenon (e.g. also *Test. Ebor.*, II, pp. 110–14).

44 E.g. Faith 1984: p. 165; Wright 1983: pp. 22–5; Saul 1986: pp. 181–2; Hicks 1986a: pp. 25–7. Historians of Europe and of sixteenth-century England have been aware of this for longer (Duby 1968: pp. 252–8; Spufford 1976: p. 163; Sabean 1976: pp. 101–2).

45 *Stonor Letters*, I, pp. 114–15, 150–1, 155–6, II, pp. 23–4, 99–101; *Paston Letters*, I, pp. 353, 375–6.

46 A course urged on John Paston I (*Paston Letters*, I, p. 154); Alexander and Binski eds. 1987: p. 524; for wills, see below, p. 223.

47 Duby 1968: pp. 35–6. Cf. the Derbyshire gentry (Wright 1983: pp. 23–4).

on costs incurred in the management of the estate and most of the remainder on household expenses.[48] For the rest we have to be content with indications, such as the fact that in 1458 Thomas Greswold had in his house at Solihull £5 in gold and £3 10s in silver, the equivalent, taken together, of a decent annual income for a gentleman, according to the tax returns, and £100 worth of goods; that in 1432 Thomas Sydenhale, a lesser esquire than Greswold, had £10 and some silver plate; or that in 1499–1500 the entire income of £248 plus from the Wollaton coal, bar about £30, was delivered direct to Sir Henry Willoughby's wife for the use of the household.[49] The Willoughbys were peculiarly fortunate in having this sizeable annual windfall and it may have enabled them to put aside more cash, in the form of plate, than was usual.

Studies of great landowners have revealed a universally low rate of investment in the estate and there is no reason to suppose that lesser lords were acting any differently. Although their margin for error was considerably smaller than that of the greater nobility and they were consequently obliged to tend their estates more carefully than most of their superiors, with less spare cash they may have had to spend a higher percentage than the nobility on their households.[50] In any case, despite rising wages, farming and maintaining the estate remained low-cost enterprises so that even a careful manager like John Brome would not usually grow greatly out of pocket thereby. For example, in 1444–5, a year when a lot of effort was put into repairing and improving, he received about £150 from Baddesley Clinton while spending only about £25 on its entire running costs, excluding the purchase of cattle bought for resale. Of this sum only about £11 can be counted as investment in the sense that it was designed to bring permanent improvement to the estate, the rest being labour costs (over £4 10s) and the normal expenses of husbandry.[51] The Staffords of Grafton, who could be regarded as standing at the opposite end of the spectrum to the Bromes in their interest in estate improvement, invested considerably less. A valor of 1448–9, for example, shows that their lands were valued at over £420 before deduction of expenses, of which well over £350 reached the hands of either the Staffords or their receiver, while a total of just over £7 10s was invested in the estate in that year, all of it on repairs.[52] Only land purchases

[48] S.B.T. D.R.37 Box 73. Above, p. 158 for evidence that it was probably most of the income that was recorded.

[49] K.B.9/289/46; Cov. and Lichf. Dioc., Reg. Boulers fo.92; C.244/6/248; Nott. Univ. Lib. Middleton MS Mi M 142.

[50] E.g. McFarlane 1973: pp. 83–101; Postan 1967; Hilton 1975b, 1985a, pp. 127–8. However, the fact that the gentry may have been forced to exercise rather more care for the estate than the nobility may have led them to invest a rather higher proportion (above, pp. 155–6).

[51] S.B.T. D.R.3/800. This sum does not include the arrears of £80 charged on this account which Brome received at a later date (above, p. 190). See also Dyer 1972: p. 5.

[52] Br. Lib. Add. Roll 74,168.

obliged the gentry to expend really large sums on their estates and the return on these was measured as much in political as in economic terms.[53]

A fair amount of the gentry's income probably went on the wages and keep of household servants. Judging by the vast quantities of meat they consumed, some of these households must have been pretty large, but, again, only the Mountford account provides us with full information. There were apparently eighteen household servants, including a chaplain, in 1433–4 (the group listed below these are probably the agricultural servants, of whom some may also have been resident), and their wages alone cost William Mountford nearly £16. Another indication of the size of a gentry household comes from John Spenser's establishment at Wormleighton in the early sixteenth century. At this time he was wealthy but still had a long way to go socially and yet he was already responsible for a *familia* of sixty.[54] Wills yield some additional evidence, since servants were often named as beneficiaries. However, as they are either referred to *en masse* or singled out by name, they do no more than reveal the universality of servants' presence, sometimes in quite sizeable quantities, in gentry households.[55] Servants were needed not only to minister to their employers' needs or to accompany their womenfolk on journeys for protection (for example, in 1453–4, Janyn Smith rode from Grafton to Henwood with Joyce Middlemore, possibly the mistress of Humphrey Stafford II),[56] but to stand as another visible manifestation of their master's greatness, whether in the household itself or riding with him on his travels. In 1434, for instance, Sir William Mountford was at Coventry with his *familia* and in 1421 both Mountford and John Throgmorton I, on paying a visit to their lord's household, were accompanied, the former by three varlets and two boys, the latter by six varlets.[57]

Household servants who accompanied their lord or members of his family would normally be wearing his livery, as they were permitted to do by the legislation of 1390, a mark of the wealth and following he could command. The tunics carried to London from Coleshill and back in 1433–4 for Sir William Mountford were probably liveries. In 1453–4 63s 2d was paid by the Staffords' receiver to a London draper for a livery for William Stevens who was presumably a household servant. In their itinerations accompanied by liveried servants the gentry were of course merely aping the nobility, while being quite unable to aspire to the epic proportions of the great noble retinue, but that did

53 For the costs of these, see above, p. 126.

54 Above, n.48; *Dugdale*, p. 515; Finch 1956: pp. 38–9. For meat consumption, above, p. 182. Cf. the first duke of Buckingham's permanent domestic household of 100–200 (*Account of the Great Household of Buckingham*, pp. 2–3).

55 E.g. W.C.R.O. C.R.133/15; Nott. Univ. Lib. Middleton MS 5/168/53; PROB 11/11 fos. 39, 201; *Reg. Chichele*, II, p. 382.

56 Br. Lib. Add. Roll 74,173; also McFarlane 1973: p. 99.

57 Above, n.48; Longleat, Marquess of Bath MS Misc.IX fo. 75.

not make their gesture any the less significant; it was enough to impress equals and subordinates, and even an impression confined to the locality would mark a man as worthy of the attentions of a magnate or even of a king.[58] While households had this function of conspicuous display, a comment in the Paston letters shows that, as with most items of gentry expenditure, value for money on the part of the household was still demanded.[59]

What was bought for these households and where? Accounts give us some idea. The basic necessities, of grain (some of it malted for ale) and meat, had to be bought if there was no home farm, or if, as often happened, it was inadequate to supply a large household. For obvious reasons these were best bought locally, as the Staffords did for their household at Milton Keynes in 1446–7. In 1433–4 the Mountford receiver went to Stratford for barley and bought a lot of goods at Coventry and some at Coleshill. The Catesbys' use of Welton, with its proximity to Daventry, and of Coventry, as purchasing centres for the household at Ashby, and the later policy of supplying the Lapworth household from Coventry have been mentioned.[60] But the purchases of the lords who have left evidence – admittedly wealthier ones, with the exception of John Brome, and he was certainly not badly off – show that their consumption went well beyond the bare necessities of life. It has already been observed that fish for fast-days was a frequent item of expenditure, even on the part of lords like the Catesbys who had their own fish-ponds. Other items that feature with some regularity are almonds, raisins, eggs, butter, spices of various kinds, fowl, fruit (strawberries were bought for Henry Willoughby in July), mustard, shell-fish, ale, candles and wine. Those items not bought locally might be acquired at fairs, and both the Catesbys and the Mountfords made use of Stourbridge Fair, although the Catesbys also patronised the one at Rugby, much closer to home.[61] London was naturally also a place for the purchase of luxury goods, like the psalter brought from there for William Mountford.[62] Coventry was in itself a specialist market for cloth, of which the Catesbys made substantial use, even while they still wove their own from wool and flax.[63] If this suggests parsimony, it is evident that a wise lord followed contemporary precepts in achieving display without profligacy. Just as Margaret Paston seems to have

[58] *Statutes of the Realm*, II, p. 75; above, n.48; Br. Lib. Add. Roll 74,173. For noble retinues, see McFarlane 1973, pp. 102–21 and Holmes 1957: ch. 3; Mertes 1988; p. 133.

[59] *Paston Letters*, I, pp. 127–8.

[60] Br. Lib. Add. Roll 74,129; above, n.48; S.C.6/1117/16, /949/15 fos. 21–3; above, pp. 158–9.

[61] S.B.T. D.R.3/800, 805, D.R.37 Box 73; B.R.L. 437894; S.C.6/949/15 fo. 34, /1039/2,3,4, /1042/2 (Ladbroke fishpond); Nott. Univ. Lib. Middleton MS Mi M 138F; *Paston Letters*, II, index *sub* 'food'. Also refs. in n.60; Nott. Univ. Lib. Middleton MS Mi A2. Cf. *Account of the Great Household of Buckingham*, pp. 6–7, McFarlane 1973: pp. 95–100, and Mertes 1988: pp. 107–10, 114–17 for further discussion of consumption patterns and places of purchase, mainly among the nobility, and Richmond 1981: pp. 145–7 for another gentry family.

[62] S.B.T D.R.37 Box 73 (Mountford account); also e.g. S.C.6/949/15 fos. 21–3.

[63] S.C.6/1039/2,3,4, /1117/16.

been quite happy for her son Clement to appear in elderly and made-over clothing, William Catesby II paid nearly £9 in 1480–1 to have the clothes of his three younger children mended.[64]

Insofar as the evidence permits, we may conclude that the three needs of display, comfort and retrenchment were normally kept in successful balance. If fashion dictated that in the construction of houses comfort should begin to take precedence over naked and, literally, unadorned displays of military power, then following fashion was itself a significant aspect of making the world respect one's authority. The Staffords' neglect of their estates may well have been accompanied by over-extravagant expenditure which reduced the amount available for improvement – although there are no signs of such folly in the incomplete records of expenditure that we have – and it is quite probable that Robert Ardern and John Cokayn III, two other men who got into financial difficulties, had overspent on their households. So little was Cokayn to be trusted with money in his pocket that his eventual rescuer was obliged to confine him to a weekly allowance. Ralph Brasebrugge seems to have been fairly deeply in debt to various London tradesmen in the early years of the century, but there is no evidence that this had a lastingly debilitating effect on the family; his debts may well have been no more than a symptom of the credit system.[65] It does not seem that problems of debt were generalised amongst the greater Warwickshire gentry. Equally, while we remain almost entirely ignorant of their consumption patterns, there is no reason to suppose that the less wealthy families, having exercised such care in putting together their estates and, as far as we can tell, in garnering in the proceeds, would be any more likely to blow the lot than the greater families of whom we know more.

A more tempting avenue to self-destruction may have been litigation; this seems to have been the principal cause of John Paston I's difficulties and it put Richard Burdet into serious debt in the 1470s. As a temptation it was harder to withstand than extravagant consumption because it was so obviously justifiable in political terms. It involved the assertion of rights, so vital for a landowning family's survival. It was consequently peculiarly attractive to men who already felt themselves to be under threat. That did not make it any less undesirable if it led to compulsive use of the law, which was apt to be both expensive and destructive of friendship and trust. It is not improbable that Stafford, Ardern and Cokayn all owed their financial decline, as the second two certainly owed much of their political decline, to over-litigation rather than to material extravagance.[66] But they were exceptions. William Stonor's uncle warned him

64 S.C.6/1117/16; *Paston Letters*, I, pp. 41–2.

65 Above, pp. 115–16, 120, 169–71; below, p. 432; *Cal. Pat. Rolls 1408–13*, pp. 129, 251, 258. On credit in the gentry economy (which of course is not the same thing as real debt), see above, n.44.

66 *Paston Letters*, I, pp. 358–9, 361–2; C.1/54/378. For the costs of litigation, Ives 1983a: ch. 14 and Saul 1986; pp. 92–4. Clearly a large part was less in direct legal fees than in keeping an attorney to watch over one's interests at Westminster and, if necessary, in the expense of living in London

not to 'over wissh yow [over-consume?], ner owyr purches yow, ner owyr bild you; for these iij thynges wolle plucke a yongman ryth lowe', and went on to warn, 'Ner medyll not with no gret materis in the lawe'.[67] This warning covers the bulk of the expenditure that a landed family might make, and most of the Warwickshire gentry, greater and lesser, appear to have been able to avoid ruining themselves by it, even in the worst years in mid-century. The gentry's need to make a visible impression on those around them seems to have been a spur to more efficient management, in a period when both wages and peasant living-standards were rising, but not to have been a major threat to their survival.

III

The upkeep of younger members of the family was a more serious drain on the estate. On the one hand it was damaging to the family worship for younger sons and brothers who bore the family name to be seen living in penury, or for daughters to be seen to be marrying noticeably beneath them. Thus in 1517 John Fitzherbert left a sum of money to his younger brother Henry which was to enable his heirs male to purchase an heiress '[because] he ys a gentleman and ... I wold that the name shuld contynewe in worship according to our degree ...'[68] On the other hand, provision for these various family appendages was at the expense of the all-important senior line and the worst of it was that their numbers were so unpredictable. Thomas Throgmorton died in 1472 leaving three younger sons and five daughters; in 1417, when William Mountford made his first will, he had five younger sons, in 1485 John Shirley had no less than six, and each of the last two had numbers of daughters.[69]

It is therefore unsurprising to find that for purposes of subvention the family was defined very narrowly indeed.[70] It is rare to find relatives beyond daughters and younger sons provided for. Even eldest sons were often obliged to wait for their father's death to see any of their property and were likely to achieve an independence before then only through marriage, when the bride's

oneself: e.g. *H.M.C. Var. Colls.*, II, pp. 34 (douceurs for a replevin: over 30s), 44 (total litigation to date reckoned at nearly £80), 55–6 (writ of error and associated proceedings: over £12); *Paston Letters*, I, p. 489 (costs of Caister suit, including damage suffered, reckoned at over £1,300); Smith, A., 1984: p. 60. On persistent troublemakers and litigants and their tendency to lose their friends, below, pp. 432, 612, 622. Cf., similarly, the association of litigation and ruin in the thirteenth century on which see Carpenter, D.A. 1980: pp. 745–6.

67 *Stonor Letters*, II, p. 98, cited in Houlbrooke 1984: p. 49.

68 Wright 1983: p. 50. Similar beliefs expressed in the Paston family (*Paston Letters*, I, pp. 38–9, 44, 95).

69 Coughton Court, Throckmorton MS Box 72/5; B.R.L. Wingfield Digby MS A473; Shirley 1873; pp. 404–5. NB the plague, whose effects diminished the family's income, may have helped by diminishing also the number of siblings (Clay 1984: I, p. 148).

70 Cf. Hicks 1986b: pp. 90–2; Beauroy 1986.

family would demand a jointure for the young couple.[71] Bastard children might also receive support, as, for instance, from Thomas Straunge I and Nicholas Metley, both of whom died in 1436, and from John Cokayn III in the 1490s. Metley, having only a daughter to succeed him, was perhaps in a better position than many to dismember the estate in order to provide for illegitimate offspring, but Cokayn was able to make arrangements for both a son and a daughter, despite having a male heir and being atrociously in debt.[72]

Younger brothers, who were more likely to have been provided for already by their fathers than to be left to the care of an older brother, feature relatively rarely in grants and bequests. One instance when they do appear, which highlights the demands that children other than the heir could make on the estate, is the will of Ralph Shirley III in 1516. It results from his apparent failure, understandable in that it would have robbed him of forty-eight marks of annual income, to fulfil his father's will with respect to his six younger brothers. In the event his brothers had to settle for two marks less than the sum left them by their father, John.[73] That elder brothers did resent this diminution of their prospects on behalf of their siblings can be seen not only in this episode – one which was incidentally anticipated in John's will – but also from Henry Lisle's extraction of a promise from his son and heir John to grant his two younger brothers the income left them by their father. Another indication is Richard Brasebrugge's grant of land to his younger son, Simon, in which the concurrence of the eldest son is recorded in the deed. The resentment that a younger brother, wholly dependent on the charity of an elder brother, might feel is well expressed in the complaint of John, younger brother of Walter Ardern, who lamented his lack of means 'to leve upon lyke a gentilman' and asked for a grant of Peddimore, one of the Arderns' Worcestershire manors.[74]

Where a more distant relative is remembered in a will, there is usually a particular reason for it. Nicholas Metley almost certainly left substantial lands to his brother's sons because they bore the family name, which was otherwise about to die out so soon after Metley had brought it to unprecedented eminence.[75] Two other nephews remembered in wills, John Cokayn I, nephew of his namesake of Bury Hatley, Bedfordshire, and Ralph Shirley III's nephew,

71 Above, pp. 107, 109.

72 W.C.R.O. C.R.133/15; S.B.T D.R.3/258; *I.P.M. Hen. VII*, II, 832; *H.M.C. Rutland*, IV, p. 53; above, pp. 104, 115–16.

73 Shirley 1873: pp. 404–5, 410, 414, 416.

74 PROB 11/14 fo. 147v.; Nott. Univ. Lib. Middleton MS Mi D 4045; *Calendars of Proceedings in Chancery*, I, pp. lxxii–iii; the Ardern story is cited in Morgan 1986: p. 21; also Wright 1983, p. 47, and the provisions in the will of Thomas Culpepper (1428), although he had the additional problem of dealing with the children of two marriages (*Reg. Chichele*, II, pp. 382–3; Jeffs 1961a: pedigree between pp. 347 and 348). Despite the instances cited here, to allege that heirs' misbehaviour to younger brothers was a recurrent theme (Houlbrooke 1984: p. 42), seems, on the Warwickshire evidence, to be going too far (further discussion, below, pp. 217–21).

75 S.B.T. D.R.3/258; Norris 1897: pp. 15–17 for a brief summary of his career.

also Ralph, may well have been godchildren, since they bore their uncles' names. Perhaps, like little Lillyvick Kenwigs a few centuries later, they had been given these names with the deliberate intention of attracting their uncles' favour, although it must be said that godchildren in general do not figure largely in bequests.[76] In his will of 1489 Henry Willoughby made a grant to his cousin, John Marmeon, but Marmeon had been a faithful estate official and was now charged with the oversight of the will and of Henry's family in return for the small life-annuity he was to be left.[77] A study of the people named in religious dispositions shows the same strongly vertical conception of the family. Parents are often mentioned by name, and sometimes grandparents, otherwise there are usually only generalised references to ancestors, heirs and successors, although a wife's parents may sometimes feature. Occasionally, 'friends' appear as a group, along with the 'all Christian souls' who are almost invariably named as objects of prayers; sometimes a lord to whom the testator had been very close might be remembered, as Baldwin Straunge left Richard Beauchamp earl of Warwick 'unum grisium cursorem' in 1416, but there is no question of the family in the religious context being anything other than strongly nuclear and firmly vertical.[78] This is by no means the whole story,[79] but if bequests in wills and donations to the church are to be used as evidence of definitions of the family among the gentry, they admit of no doubt on this point.[80]

Nevertheless, as ever, we must make something of an exception for the successful professionals. On the whole they were rather more willing to spread their good fortune around the family. Doubtless they were impelled by a sense of obligation, as well as a desire to impress the members they had left behind and the reluctance of the *nouveaux riches* to be linked in any way to dingy poverty.[81] The bequests to his nephews of the lawyer, Nicholas Metley, are a case in point. Another example is Thomas Bate, royal servant and husband of the widow of John Cokayn I, who remembered various Bates in his will, while also leaving what was no doubt conscience money to assorted Cokayns, whom

[76] PROB 11/3 fo. 90; Shirley 1873: pp. 414–16. In contrast, see Bossy 1973. For Lillyvick Kenwigs, see Charles Dickens 1950: pp. 179–81, 686–91.

[77] *H.M.C. Middleton*, pp. 121–2; Nott. Univ. Lib. Middleton MS 5/167/103, Mi M 139–40, Mi D 4800.

[78] An examination of almost any of the wills of the gentry in the PROB 11 class will establish this point. The wills mentioning 'friends' are those of Alice Archer (S.B.T. D.R.37 Box 90), William Lecroft (C.1/147/16; *I.P.M. Hen. VII* III, 1147) and Joan Hungerford, widow of Edmund Lucy (*Cat. Anc. Deeds*, V, A12393). The projected Stafford of Grafton chantry, licensed in 1447, includes 'friends and kinsfolk' amongst the objects of its prayers (*Cal. Pat. Rolls 1446–52*, p. 108). The naming of 'all Christian souls' in prayers for the dead was normal (Wood-Legh 1965: p. 309). Cf. the different views in Bossy 1973: pp. 136–8 and the comments on them in Carpenter 1987: p. 69; also Reynolds 1984: pp. 3–4. For Straunge's will, see *Reg. Chichele*, II, p. 94.

[79] Below, pp. 239–40, 257, 260–1, 620–1.

[80] Below, p. 228.

[81] This may make the comments of the Pastons (above, n.68) less than typical.

he had deprived of a large part of their inheritance. Thomas Littleton was not content to find an heiress for his second son Richard and a place in his own profession of the law for his third son Thomas. He ensured in addition that each son inherited part of his property, although it meant breaking up the estate that he had so painstakingly accumulated. With both Bate and Littleton this atypical pattern is replicated in their disposition of *post mortem* prayers. Bate ordained prayers for his brothers and sisters in addition to those for his parents, probably conscious that they would be less able than he was to afford them for themselves. Littleton's chantry in Worcester cathedral perpetuated the memory of the two relatives by marriage who had done most to make his fortune: his father-in-law, William Burley, to whom his eldest son became co-heir, and his wife's first husband, Philip Chetwynd, whose lands Littleton had held in jointure for nearly forty years.[82]

The practical reason for the very restricted definition of family on the part of the older families was quite simple and lay in the inability of even the richer gentry, in contrast to most of the nobility, to provide for its members without doing grave damage to the estate, and the estate had to come first.[83] For the same reason the actual provision for those who could not be left unprovided for had to be on as small a scale as was practicable. As Susan Wright has pointed out, daughters were less of a burden than younger sons; relatively speaking the sum expended on a daughter's dowry would usually secure a larger income if she married an heir than if the same amount were invested in lands for a younger son.[84] There was also the fact that they were normally given lump sums rather than lands or incomes (although in at least two instances non-inheriting daughters were left land)[85] and that these sums, even those as large as the 400 and 500 marks bequeathed by Henry Willoughby to two of his daughters in 1493, could be raised with relative ease by the mortgage or sale of land.[86] The quantities of money at issue vary as much as the earlier discussion

[82] For Metley, above, n.75; PROB 11/4 fo. 129v., /7 fos. 23v.–24. For the careers of Bate and Littleton, above, pp. 102–3, 124, 149. Also the comments in Ives 1983a: pp. 410–12 and Allmand 1982: p. 172. Another example of a successful professional remembering the source of his wealth is Kebyll's institution of prayers for Richard Hotoft, whose lands he had obtained by rather indirect inheritance (Ives 1983a: pp. 332–35, 359–60). See also the generosity to various Throgmortons of Thomas Marrowe, serjeant-at-law, who was related to them by marriage (*Records of King Edward VI's School Birmingham*, p. xxix). For Littleton, cf. another successful lawyer, William Paston, and his younger sons (*Paston Letters*, I, pp. 44–5).

[83] McFarlane 1973: pp. 70–2; Given-Wilson 1987a: pp. 141–8. Cf. James 1974: pp. 21–6, where provision for the family is clearly related to economic resources and Cooper 1976: pp. 213–4. More on this, below, pp. 256–7.

[84] Wright 1983: p. 49; above, p. 126 for costs of lands. But note the difficulties encountered by the Pastons in disposing of daughters and, conversely, the financial sacrifice that the father of one of the Paston brides had to make to secure the match (Richmond 1985: pp. 31–6). Cf. also Richmond 1981, pp. 142–4.

[85] Nott. Univ. Lib. Middleton MS Mi D 3999; Shirley 1873: pp. 410–14.

[86] *H.M.C. Middleton*, p. 123; above, p. 195 for raising lump sums from landed property.

of marriage contracts would lead us to expect. Some time in the second half of the century, Thomas Hore of Solihull, a landowner right at the margin of gentility, decreed that his feoffees were to collect twenty marks for his daughter's marriage; several heads of families settled for £100 or marks, as, for example, John Harewell I in 1428, Thomas Straunge I in 1436 and William Chetwynd II in 1514; at the top end we have Henry Willoughby, William Mountford, who provided 500 marks for each daughter in 1417, and William Littleton, who showed that he believed in maintaining the family tradition of generosity towards all their children by leaving 550 marks for his only unmarried daughter.[87]

We have seen that the best way of disposing of a younger son was to find him an heiress or a profession, but we have seen also that heiresses were in a position to be choosy and so this could not be a realistic aim for everyone. As in the case of Henry Fitzherbert, cadets could be given lump sums to help them marry an heiress – for example, John Harewell I left £100 to his son John for his marriage and William Mountford bequeathed 400 marks to each son – but this was not a common practice.[88] If marriage to an heiress was the best way out of the younger son problem, heiresses were only likely to be attracted to one who already had some sort of competence. This would have been especially true of a county like Warwickshire where there was little endogamy and heiresses normally participated in a national marriage-market, a fact that we have seen to account for the lack of cadet branches in the county.[89] It must have been the lands due to come his way as second son of Lord Ferrers of Groby, even before he became heir male to the Ferrers, that secured one of the Freville heiresses for Thomas I.[90] But if the whole point of finding an heiress was to avoid giving away any land to a cadet, this may not have been a very attractive proposition. In the 1430s Edward Doddingselles I married his two younger sons into the Malory and Hugford families; for one marriage he had to put sixteen marks a year of land into jointure, for the other an unspecified amount from his Oxfordshire estates, and in neither case was the bride even an heiress. The Doddingselles were another of those families weakened by a long-lived dowager,[91] and in this instance the problem of a mother who survived until 1492, her husband having died in 1466, was accentuated by these two younger brothers; it may account in large measure for the low political and social status of Edward's heir.[92]

87 C.1/139/63; PROB 11/3 fo. 80; W.C.R.O. C.R.133/15; Wm. Salt Lib. H.M. Chetwynd Coll. Bundle 30; B.R.L. Wingfield Digby MS A473; *Test. Vetust.*, pp. 467–8; above, pp. 106–9 for marriage contracts.

88 PROB 11/3 fo. 80; B.R.L. Wingfield Digby MS A473; above, pp. 122–3 for further remarks on younger sons and pp. 97–105 for heiresses and the marriage market.

89 Above, p. 123 n.101. Cf. Cooper 1976; p. 215.

90 *G.E.C.*, v, pp. 356–8. Cf. Palmer 1984: pp. 29–30.

91 *I.P.M. Hen. VII*, I, 815.

92 *Cal. Close Rolls 1429–35*, pp. 313–4; *Cal. Pat. Rolls 1436–41*, p. 343; above, pp. 87, 144 n.177.

For these reasons, a profession might be thought a better destination for a younger son. Curiously, however, as Ives has shown, the law was by and large the province of first sons, perhaps because the outlay in training a lawyer and supporting him in the first stages of his career was as great as the cost of a reasonable marriage.[93] Nevertheless, some Warwickshire lawyers were younger sons; these include Thomas Harewell, younger brother of John I, and John Catesby of Althorp, the justice.[94] Younger sons are also found in royal and noble administration, a job for which a legal training was desirable but a full and expensively-acquired professional qualification not essential. John Verney, father of Richard, probably a younger member of the Great Wolford family, is an example from the earlier years of the century, Robert Greville, probably a cadet of the Milcote family, servant of Warwick the Kingmaker and of Lord Stanley, is one from the middle years.[95]

How many younger sons went into the church is not an easy question to answer. Again, there were financial problems. These, and indeed those of putting a son into the law, are summed up in the provision for his younger son, William, in the will of John Harewell II to which reference has already been made.[96] Harewell assumed that, whether he opted for the church or the law, William would require support at the rate of twenty marks a year until he was thirty. Bearing in mind that this was a family with strong professional traditions, we may wonder whether many families, particularly the less wealthy ones, or those with numbers of offspring, would be inclined to make such an outlay.[97] On the whole clerical brothers seem to occur in families that were in a general process of self-improvement through the professions, notably the Bates and the Verneys of Compton Murdack. Perhaps in these instances it was thought worthwhile to gamble the family's slender resources on the careers of all the sons, in the hope that success would bring the rewards that could never be achieved by retrenchment.[98] It may well be that it was only the nobility that could afford to have their cadets trained for the church as a matter of course, not least because they knew that they were almost guaranteed a high return. The exceptions amongst the gentry were those families like the Ferrers which had a niche for members who entered the church, in this case its own collegiate church at Tamworth. Interestingly, Hugh Willoughby, who had at least three younger sons to provide for, envisaged that all three would either go

93 Ives, 1983a: p. 33 and chs. 3 and 4.

94 *Coventry Register*, p. 80; *Dugdale*, p. 788, 809–10; Ives 1983a: p. 383.

95 For the Verneys, see above, p. 130; for Greville, see B.R.L. 168023; *Cat. Anc. Deeds*, I, B511, 512.

96 Above, p. 123 for previous discussion of the provision for William in this will.

97 Cooper 1936: p. 19. For the Harewells' professional traditions, see above, n.94 and app. 3.

98 PROB 11/4 fo. 129v.; S.B.T. D.R.98/479; Le Neve 1964: pp. 6, 44. Also Ralph Astley lawyer, who left money for a younger son to be supported at school (Cant. Dioc., Reg. Stafford fo. 136).

into the church, if a benefice could be found for them, or, failing that, would have to be furnished with marriage portions.[99]

One way out was to persuade an uncle or grandfather to provide for a child. This was doubtless a reason for asking a rich relative to act as godfather; if we are right in assuming this relationship between Ralph Shirley III and his nephew of the same name, it was a ploy that paid off, as the nephew was left four pounds a year for life, a sum that compares very favourably with the incomes of other younger sons, even those from wealthy families. After all the trouble that the Doddingselles had been through in attempting to support their cadets, it must have been gratifying for Margaret, widow of Gerard, to be able to record in her will in 1500 that her younger son Humphrey had been left various goods by his uncle, Master Henry Sharp.[100] William Lord Hastings left 100 marks for the marriage of his niece, daughter of Thomas Ferrers II, a case of one family profiting by a related one's advancement. In his will of 1528 Henry Willoughby provided lands worth probably forty pounds a year for his younger son Hugh, but expressed the hope that Hugh might be able to get his support from elsewhere, either through marriage or from his Egerton grandfather. Another possibility was to earmark the mother's lands for a younger son or sons, as was done by the Hubauds in the middle of the century and for Thomas Stafford, son of Humphrey I, who inherited part of his mother's Aylesbury properties.[101]

By and large, though, the burden fell on the head of the family and, this being the case, it is not surprising that the provision for cadets tended towards the niggardly.[102] Many had to be satisfied with a life annuity, entailed on the main line, no basis for contracting a profitable marriage, and mostly of a size that would hardly support an independent existence. That the younger Shirleys got only eight marks a year and in the event had to be content with six shows that even a great and wealthy family was not prepared to do more than mete out a minimum existence to its younger members, especially

99 Pantin 1955: pp. 22–5; Orme 1984; pp. 37–9, 66–9; Palmer 1845: p. 104; PROB 11/11 fo. 201; *Test. Ebor.*, II, pp. 131–3. Professor Brooke points out to me that a surprisingly small proportion of English bishops were noble in earlier periods, but it seems that the figure was higher in the later middle ages (refs. above); if the church had been unfashionable for the aristocracy before, this seems not to have been the case any more. It should be mentioned that even a cursory reading of the bishops' registers of Worcester and Coventry and Lichfield reveals a number of clergymen with the names of midland gentry families; without a full exploration, using extensive ecclesiastical records, many younger sons in the church may remain unidentified. One of John Hopton's younger sons became a priest (Richmond 1981: pp. 133–5, 140–1).

100 Shirley 1873: p. 415 (this is on the assumption that Ralph the nephew was a younger son); PROB 11/12 fo. 108v.

101 *Test. Vetust.*, p. 372; PROB 11/22 fo. 272; *V.C.H.*, III, p. 124; *Colls. Hist. Staffs.*, n.s., 4, p. 176; *V.C.H. Bucks.*, III, p. 433.

102 Cf. Wright 1983: pp. 46–50; Payling 1987b: p. 115.

when it had so many of them. Figures of ten pounds, ten marks, or less, recur among families as eminent as the Chetwynds, the Fieldings, even the Willoughbys.[103] In 1504 Henry Lisle, an esquire of moderate means, awarded his two younger sons as little as forty shillings a year each, and, as we have seen, still felt it necessary to extract a promise from his heir to allow these pittances.[104]

All these examples come from the late fifteenth and early sixteenth centuries, when the new stringency with regard to the dispersal of estates was restricting the freedom of the owner. It may be that another result was a movement from landed endowments to annuities at this time and therefore in general a harder time for younger sons.[105] Indeed in 1490 William Chetwynd I made the right to grant annuities to his younger sons a condition of the marriage settlement between his heir, William II, and Maud Ferrers.[106] It is certainly true that in the earlier part of the century most of the surviving evidence for the endowment of younger sons shows them being awarded grants of land, however pitiful, rather than annuities, but it cannot be assumed that there was a real change to annuities later on. The greater use of wills for the disposition of property in the later fifteenth century[107] and the survival of a larger number of marriage settlements from this period mean that we have information about annuities which usually we would otherwise encounter only through the accidental survival of accounts. Grants of property on the other hand are always likely to be better-recorded. Moreover, the terms on which the lands were granted were equally ungenerous throughout the century. They were normally for life or governed by a strictly circumscribed descent which prohibited alienation and enforced reversion to the senior line on the failure of the junior one. Within these limits a younger son of a reasonably well-off family might do quite well. Richard Harewell, younger son of John I, was given the manor of Shottery; in the 1440s Henry Ferrers, second son of Thomas I, had Flecknoe in Warwickshire and Hethe in Oxfordshire, both part of the entailed Ferrers of Groby estate, from his father; Robert Mountford I, William's second son from his favoured second family, was given Monkspath in the 1450s, and in the next century it was not only Hugh Willoughby but also his brother Edward who were left lands worth forty pounds a year, as was Edward Ralegh's younger son Anthony.[108] Hugh Willoughby seems to have found even this outsize portion

[103] Above, n.73; *Colls. Hist. Staffs.*, 12, p. 332; PROB 11/18 fo. 39; Nott. Univ. Lib. Middleton MS 5/170/81; Cooper 1976, p. 214.

[104] PROB 11/14 fo. 147v.; and below, p. 225.

[105] Below, pp. 259–60; McFarlane 1973; pp. 81–2; Wright 1983: p. 47.

[106] *Colls. Hist. Staffs.*, 12, pp. 330–2.

[107] Above, n.5.

[108] C.139/145/9/2; *Dugdale*, p. 307; C.139/174/34; *W.F.F.*, 2648; PROB 11/22 fo. 272; S.B.T. D.R.37/2132. Cf. Saul 1986: p. 25.

for a cadet inadequate, since he felt it necessary to increase his fortune by risking (and eventually losing) his life on overseas ventures, while Henry Ferrers' lands were only a stepping-stone to an heiress who was the real making of his fortunes.[109]

The land used for these purposes was almost never patrimonial and rarely lay at the core of the estate. Sometimes it was specially bought: John Aston, who died in 1483, had bought lands for his two younger sons, and Robert Throgmorton left lands and salt-vats purchased in Droitwich for his younger son Michael, but even this newly-acquired property was strictly entailed on Michael's heirs male with reversion to the senior line.[110] Those of the more substantial families which consistently provided for cadets or for eldest sons during their fathers' lifetime might make use of a particular property for this purpose. The Archers tended to reserve two Shropshire properties for this while Flecknoe fulfilled the same function in the Ferrers family and Monkspath for the Mountfords. The wisdom of using estates that were not of central importance to the family is illustrated by the later history of Monkspath. Having been given to John, Simon's younger son, on his marriage, as part of his jointure, it passed to John's widow after John had died during his father's lifetime; her subsequent remarriage deprived the Mountfords of all access to the property for the rest of her life.[111]

Although it is not always possible to know where they were charged, even annuities would normally be levied on outlying estates, since they reduced the amount of money available in and around the lord's residence.[112] A fortunate exception to all these rules was Robert Catesby, younger son of John Catesby I, the father of John II. When John became heir to his father through the death of his older brother, William, at a time when the family was accumulating lands with some rapidity, he was presented with a large, diverse and potentially unmanageable estate. Robert was the beneficiary of one aspect of the solution, which was to carve off parts, mostly those lying to the north of the main Warwickshire interests in and around Ladbroke, to make a permanent endowment for a younger branch, and so were founded the Catesbys of Hopsford, of whom Robert was the first.[113]

If the evidence for less prominent families is inevitably sparser, there is no reason to suppose that they were behaving any differently. The Hubauds'

109 *D.N.B.*, LXII, pp. 36–7; *Wedgwood: Biographies*, p. 318; *Dugdale*, p. 973; above, pp. 98, 122.

110 Wm. Salt Lib. H.M. Aston Coll. 39/1; PROB 11/20 fo. 9v. Cf. Naughton 1976: pp. 24–5.

111 S.B.T. D.R.503 fos. 57, 66; C.139/174/34; S.B.T. D.R.37 Box 48 (grant by William Ferrers of Groby, 1404); *W.F.F.*, 2648; *V.C.H.*, v, p. 168; C.1/64/52. Also above, p. 122 for the cadets of the Mountfords and the Ferrers. Cf. Wright 1983: p. 34.

112 E.g. S.B.T. D.R.37/2132 (Ralegh); Shirley 1873: pp. 414–16 (Shirley); Nott. Univ. Lib. Middleton MS 5/170/81 (Willoughby). Cf. Wright 1983, p. 34.

113 Above, p. 117; *Cat. Anc. Deeds*, III, A4363, IV, A6892, 7567.

use of a maternal inheritance has already been noted. The Hores of Elmdon pursued a similar policy. William, younger son of William I, was given Stoneythorpe, which had probably come to the family by marriage, although on what terms we do not know, and in 1450 Thomas gave lands in Solihull and Knowle, which he had from his mother, to his younger brother, the same William.[114] Robert, younger son of John Fulwode, alleged that he had inherited some fifty acres of the family lands at Tanworth in about 1450, and in 1502 Richard Fulwode, John's son and heir, left land in Nuthurst and Tanworth to his second son Lawrence, on condition that it was not alienated except to the heirs of the senior line.[115]

Towards the end of the century Thomas Shukburgh I tried to resolve the conflicting demands of his two families by the classic division into patrimony and acquisition. The old family manor of Upper Shuckburgh, from which they took their name, went to Thomas II, his heir by his first marriage, while the more recent acquisition of Napton was left to the sons of his second marriage, although, as it turned out, all he got for his pains was a protracted conflict amongst his heirs. The same principle seems to have governed the division of Hugh Dalby's estates; Richard, who got the lion's share, including Brookhampton, the single manorial estate, was only a younger son, probably the second. It seems that he was getting the spoils of his father's successful career in magnate service, while the much smaller patrimony went to the eldest son John.[116] Although it has been suggested by Susan Wright that amongst the lesser gentry primogeniture was less universal at this time,[117] the Warwickshire evidence, such as it is, gives no grounds for supposing that the patrimony would be divided at this level any more than at the summit of local society. The relative drain on family resources would be all the greater where there was less to draw on, and the fact that so many of the younger sons whose criminal propensities were noted earlier on came from very minor families – Hores, Greswolds, Dalbys and Starkeys, for example – suggests that it was these that were most

[114] The descent of Stoneythorpe is unclear, but it appears to have come to William Allesley, whose daughter married William Hore I of Elmdon, and thence to William's younger son, another William (*Dugdale*, p. 348; *Cat. Anc. Deeds*, III, C3053–4; *W.F.F.*, 2437), although Robert Willenhale and his wife had a life tenancy. In 1450 William received more of his mother's lands (S.B.T. D.R.37 Box 42/2508). The *V.C.H.* has a slightly different descent, but, similarly, through a female (III, pp. 127–8).

[115] *V.C.H.*, V, p. 169; PROB 11/13 fo.229v.

[116] *V.C.H.*, VI, pp. 216–7; *Dugdale*, p. 336; C.1/57/135–6; K.B.27/893 Rex rot.10; C.139/53/49. The origin of the Dalby estate in Brookhampton is obscure, but it seems in part at least to have been purchased by Hugh (*Dugdale*, p. 562; *V.C.H.*, V, p. 106); above, p. 116. In the end Richard got the lot, through John's death *sine prole* (V.C.H., V, p. 106). For patrimony and acquisition, see Holt 1972: pp. 12–13, and below, p. 258.

[117] Wright 1983: pp. 48–9.

reluctant to diminish the heir's already limited prospects by supporting their younger members.[118]

The pattern seems the same at all levels of gentry society: the interests of the heir were a priority to which the needs of other members of the family came a very bad second. It could of course be argued that the bias of the evidence towards official documentation and away from the recording of personal feelings produces an unbalanced account of the landowner and his family, although it must be said that the private papers we have do not put much of a dent in the interpretation given here. Some sense of personal emotion survives in, for example, the bequest made by John Cokayn of Bury Hatley to his son-in-law Edward Doddingselles I on condition that he be a good husband to Cokayn's daughter, and in the chancery petition of Hugh Willoughby's eldest daughter. She claimed that, as she was leaving Wollaton, at the conclusion of what must have been a very emotional visit, made shortly before her father's death, the latter, rather like King Lear, called the whole household together and declared that he had found more kindness in her than in all his other children and that, despite being married, she was to have as large a share of his goods as any of his unmarried daughters.[119] Her sisters' version of the story is not recorded.

The point was, however, that those who were swayed by personal feelings tended to run into trouble. Uxorious husbands of perhaps much younger second wives, like Thomas Shukburgh I, William Mountford and Thomas Burdet II, who tried to overturn the laws of inheritance for the children of the second marriage, or those like John Holt, who were tempted to leave them outsize dowers at the expense of the heir, let loose a flood of litigation that threatened to overwhelm the whole estate.[120] While greater freedom might be permitted in the disposition of goods, Hugh Willoughby's alleged act of special

[118] K.B.9/228/2/19,20, /230A/3, /245/33, /273/78; K.B.27/634 Coram Rege rot.17, /701 Coram Rege rot. 56d., /737 Coram Rege rot.77 (Hore); K.B.9/284/37, /313/31; K.B.27/821 Coram Rege rot.17d. (Greswold); K.B.27/730 Coram Rege rot.84, /769 Coram Rege rot.65d., /903 Coram Rege rot.5 (Dalby); K.B.27/720 Coram Rege rot.43d., /726 Coram Rege rot.107d., /822 Writs of Attorney, /873 Coram Rege rot.12; *Materials: Henry VII*, I, p. 110 (Starkey); and above, p. 123 n.101 for further comments on the criminal propensities of younger sons. See Jefferies 1979: p. 69. Cf. Hughes 1987, p. 35.

[119] PROB 11/3 fo. 90; C.1/66/454. In this context, the care taken by widows in the distribution of household goods, particularly amongst their daughters, is of interest (e.g. PROB 11/12 fo. 108v., /17 fo. 52, /10 fo. 167). Both the Paston and the Stonor papers reveal the existence of emotion, some of it running quite deep, but, with the exception of Marjery Paston's famous love affair with the low-born Richard Calle, it is all constrained by the overriding importance of the property: e.g. *Paston Letters*, I, pp. 43–4, 128, 206–7, 218–9, 251, 262, 293, 349, 350–1, 362, 379–80, 394, 458–9, 496, 541–2, 590–1, 621–2, 662–3, 665–6; *Stonor Letters*, I, pp. 97, 104, 110, 123–4, 157–9, II, pp. 6–8, 44, 86–90, 100–1. For the Calle affair, *Paston Letters*, I, pp. 341–3, 541, II, pp. 498–500. For similar conclusions on the heir's position, Wright 1983: pp. 31–2.

[120] *Dugdale*, pp. 1,010–11, 849; C.1/53/205. The Burdet and Mountford affairs are discussed at some length, below chs. 12–14.

favour to his daughter ended up in the law-courts, which is why we know about it. Generosity might be carried as far as tying up part of the estate for a few years to accumulate the necessary lump sums to find heirs or heiresses for the non-inheriting children, but it was unwise to take it further.[121] In nearly all gentry families, except perhaps the ones rising rapidly up the social scale, as long as the other siblings could be protected from social degradation, the land had to be put first if it was to survive in fit condition for the heir.

IV

While non-inheriting children could be fobbed off with a lump sum or a more or less adequate allowance, the demands of God were not so easily met.[122] This is a preoccupation whose importance to the gentry is for obvious reasons difficult to evaluate. It is highly improbable that days were spent agonising over the morality of a particular piece of business or political sharp practice. On the other hand, wills leave us in no doubt that when it came to their last hours these men and women were very conscious of the next world and the agonies it might bring them. The very fact that they were prepared to give sizeable sums of money and sometimes precious landed property to mitigate the pains of Purgatory and for the salvation of their souls must argue a seriousness in their attitude to the next world. Enough has been said to make it evident that by and large they were circumspect in the management and preservation of their property, making outlays only when they were sure of a return, which suggests that bequests to the church indicate extreme seriousness of purpose. In some instances, moreover, we have their own confessions, demonstrating their

[121] B.R.L. Wingfield Digby MS A473; Coughton Court, Throckmorton MS Box 72/5. Despite the argument about 'strict settlement' (below, p. 247 n.14), it does not seem that these priorities, or even the methods used to achieve them, changed much over the succeeding centuries: e.g. Stone and Fawtier Stone 1986: p. 46; Bonfield 1986. Corrodies, an underexplored phenomenon, in helping to provide support for the head in his old age, may have helped furnish a little extra for the rest of the family from the estate, particularly as the grantees seem generally to have been careerists who would usually have less land to play with. The corrody may indeed in some cases have been a substitute in old age for the employer's fee. The patron/employer would probably have put pressure on the institution concerned to grant the corrody, unless the grantee was an employee of the institution itself: e.g. John Archer from St Mary's York in 1459 (at the king's request: influence of Exeter/Percy?); a consortium with a strong Grey of Lisle air (below, pp. 530–1), including John Hugford, Thomas Beaufitz, John Smyth, Wiliam Raves, from Stoneleigh in 1477 (S.B.T. D.R.37 Box 91, D.R.18/A124).

[122] Further comments on the religion of the Warwickshire gentry are to be found in Carpenter 1986b, pp. 52–4 and 1987. Where possible, repetition of material in these articles has been avoided and the reader is referred to them for further discussion. The subject itself has a large literature. See amongst others, works cited in nn.1, 2, 78, above, and Pantin 1955; Knowles 1955; Thomson 1965, 1984; Dobson 1967; Owen 1971; Mason 1976; Wood-Legh 1965; Rosenthal 1972; Vale 1976; Kreider 1979; Saul 1980; James 1986e; Scarisbrick 1984; Bossy 1985; Tanner 1984; Richmond 1984; Heath 1984; Fleming 1984.

consciousness of wrongs done and duties neglected and their fear of the consequences *sub specie aeternitatis*.

The most remarkable of these is the will of William Catesby II made immediately before execution in the aftermath of Bosworth, in which almost every other sentence is an admission of wrong done, a plea for forgiveness or a request for prayers for his soul.[123] If this was a spectacularly remorseful end to a spectacularly ruthless career, there are other examples. John Throgmorton I died in 1445, having established his family's fortunes by a successful career in public and private service. He felt it necessary to confess that 'where I haue ben all dayes of my life in my countree Asterer [i.e. 'a stirrer'] in ye world as ye world asketh', he might have overstepped the bounds of moral behaviour and requested that restitution should be made to anyone who claimed either that he had failed to fulfil his obligations or that, having taken goods as the price of his 'labour', he had failed to do the job properly.[124] In 1500 Margaret Doddingselles, widow of Gerard, urged her son and heir to make restitution of a particular property for the sake of his father's soul.[125] Henry Willoughby, one of the most astute and successful politicians of the whole period, and not a man to sacrifice worldly benefits without sufficient cause, asked his heir and executors to restore any lands he had held improperly, to recompense anyone he had wronged and to request the forgiveness of all his victims. More than half a century before, his grandfather Hugh had expressed the same kind of anxiety on these issues. Walter Cokesey, in an extraordinary access of self-mortifying zeal even went as far as to leave money to recompense any tenants either he or his ancestors had treated extortionately or maliciously.[126] And all testators, virtually without exception, asked their executors to see that their debts were paid, although this could entail a heavy drain on the estate's finances.[127]

It cannot be assumed that these were merely words put into the testator's mouth by a priest or confessor. These landed proprietors and their wives were people who had a clear appreciation of their rights and their status, and would be unlikely to allow a man who was effectively an underling to do what he liked with what was their last reckoning with God. And the words had meaning, for the reckoning did mean the loss of part of the property for the heir; however bounded by convention the religious acts of the gentry, they were genuine sacrifices of worldly interest. Henry Willoughby's household account of 1509–10 shows that moral duties were remembered not merely in the presence of

[123] *Dugdale*, p. 789; Williams 1975–6: pp. 48–9.

[124] PROB 11/3 fo. 248v.

[125] PROB 11/12 fo. 108v.

[126] PROB 11/22 fo. 272; *Test. Ebor.*, II, p. 130; Cant. Dioc., Reg. Arundel I fo. 225–225v.

[127] E.g. Coughton Court, Throckmorton MS Box 72/5; S.C.6/1117/16 (payment of William Catesby's debts); S.C.6/Hen. VII/1108–9 (Lucy estates in guardianship: includes payment of debts). Cf. Ralph Lord Cromwell's attack of conscience in his will (McFarlane 1973: p. 49). Above, p. 206 for possible origins of some of these debts.

death but at other times as well, with sums, albeit small ones, being doled out periodically in alms and in various gifts to the church. A more dramatic instance of care for the soul in the midst of life is Baldwin Mountford's decision to become a priest in the moment of triumph, just as the succession of Edward IV finally assured him the undisputed inheritance of all his father's vast estates. Perhaps he felt the need to purge himself before it was too late of the sins he had committed in defence of his rights during the 1450s.[128]

It is clear then that the fear of what might come after death was real enough, at the end of life if not before, to demand preventative measures. The measures were equally obvious; if the rich stood in peril of being condemned for their wealth and the worldly for the means they had used to achieve prosperity, then both faults could be rectified by the sacrifice of those riches.[129] The trouble was that at this point earthly and heavenly needs verged on the near-irreconcilable. If a man's first duty was to maintain the integrity of the family estate, how could he justify taking it apart for a merely personal matter, even at a time when more and more emphasis in religious thought was being placed on the individual soul's relationship with its maker?[130] After all, might he not have to sacrifice personal preferences in the matter of marriage or of his younger children for the sake of the lands of which he was merely the temporary steward? Undoubtedly there were heirs who took this line and were unwilling, and perhaps in some cases unable, to fulfil the terms of their predecessors' wills. This tended most often to happen when the immediate heir was female and the previous owner had consequently failed to show the usual concern for the estate's integrity. For example, in 1408 John Brome of Lapworth ordained that his manor of Lapworth was to be used after his wife's death to found a chantry, while his lands in Henley and Studley were to be given to the Stratford gild on the death of his daughter without issue. But both properties were ultimately sold to John Brome of Baddesley by Brome of Lapworth's grandson and eventual heir, the family having manifestly failed to fulfil the obligations imposed on it. Similarly John Hugford, who married Nicholas Metley's daughter and heiress, prevented, or subsequently revoked, the sale of most of the Metley property that had been earmarked for the church.[131]

But there were also direct male heirs who failed to fulfil their father's or grandfather's wishes. If the most elevated of these was Richard II, who omitted to implement the wishes of his grandfather, Edward III, an almost equally

[128] Nott. Univ. Lib. Middleton MS Mi A2; *Dugdale*, p. 1,011.

[129] Ref. above, n.2.

[130] Ozment 1980: chs. 3 and 5; Pantin 1955: Part III, *passim*; Bossy 1985: pp. 45–9, 127. An illustration of how grants to the church could compete with other reasons for dismemberment comes from the Pastons, when an estate set aside for a chantry had to be used to secure John Paston III's marriage (Richmond 1985: p. 30).

[131] *Cat. Anc. Deeds*, III, A4262–3; S.B.T. D.R.3/258. For the subsequent fate of these lands, above, p. 104. Other instances of failure to fulfil wills concern Richard Archer and his wife (below, n.204).

famous example is John Paston II; his neglect of his father's tomb, for which his mother was constantly berating him, seems to be attributable to a combination of reluctance to spend the money that would be required to commemorate John I as he had wished and profligacy in other directions.[132] Robert Throgmorton implied in his will that he had failed to implement in their entirety either of his parent's wills, a neglect that was probably caused by his anxiety not to lose any of the lands that he was so carefully consolidating. In an effort to avoid the same fate himself at the hands of his heirs he charged that no man break his will under pain of the curse of the church. In 1504 Henry Lisle made his eldest son swear to have his father's wishes carried out 'as he shall aunswere afore the high juge of heven.'[133] Here we have the quintessence of the dilemma: no son wanted to inherit a diminished estate, but no father liked to contemplate extra years in Purgatory as a result of a son's neglect, and all sons in their turn, if they were fortunate, became fathers. Nor did a son wish to be punished himself for failures in respect of his father's will.

Some sort of a *modus vivendi* that would satisfy the needs of both generations had to be worked out; the fact that there are in the event so few examples of serious neglect by an heir indicates that this had been achieved. Indeed the Pastons' concern over the failure to do the right thing by John I and the talk in the countryside that their neglect occasioned are in themselves implications that this was an out of the ordinary occurrence. The basis for the accommodation was the belief, reinforced by sermons and religious writings, that heaven was organised very much like this world, with God taking the role of ruler, military leader and justice, and Mary and the 'company of heaven' acting as nobles and courtiers. It followed that God could be influenced in the same way as earthly rulers, by displays of military force, by visual representations of the greatness of the departed and his family and by offering bribes to the greatest judge of all or to the courtiers who acted as intermediaries. If they were channels of grace in one direction, they could also become conduits of 'interest' in the other. Consequently gifts to God need not represent a loss to the family but could be used to perform the dual function of depicting the grandeur of the testator and his line both on earth and in heaven; the house impressed only the neighbours, but the chantry could impress the numberless host of heaven as well.[134]

The most immediately obvious illustrations of this attitude to the next world are tombs and funerals. Specifications for funerals become more elaborate as

132 Given-Wilson 1978; Richmond 1984: p. 195; *Paston Letters*, 1, pp. 359, 380, 458, 510, 602; above, p. 210. Also the comments in Carpenter 1987: pp. 68–9. Margaret Hungerford overrode her husband's religious dispositions; like some other noble widows, she used her position to splash out on the church, but this was not normal behaviour for a gentry widow (Hicks 1986b, 1987; cf. Holmes 1957: pp. 35–8); also Hicks 1985a; pp. 126–7, 135–6.

133 PROB 11/20 fo. 9v., /14 fo. 147v.

134 Bossy 1985: p. 11; Owst 1926: pp. 201–2, 1961: pp. 78–85, 114–116; Shepherd 1983: p. 178; Le Goff 1984: pp. 5, 210–13; Keen 1984: esp. ch. 3; Haines 1975; Carpenter 1986b: p. 53, 1987: p. 68; Burgess 1987: pp. 845–53.

wills increase in length towards the end of the century, but there is no reason to suppose that such ceremony was new; the emphasis on lack of ceremony in the wills of McFarlane's 'Lollard knights' implies that it was as much in vogue a hundred years before.[135] The importance given to the attendance of paupers and priests, to the provision of robes and candles for the procession of family and attendants and to chanting and tolling of bells suggests that what was being envisaged was the last ride of a lord and his retinue, even if the livery of the outriders was now to be unrelieved black.[136] The ride over, the last earthly residence of the corpse was to be marked with a majesty suitable to his station. Monuments were being built, sometimes to specifications in wills, throughout the century, quite grand ones for relatively minor families. For example, in Newbold on Avon church there are the tombs of Geoffrey Allesley, who died in 1441, lord of Little Lawford in the parish, his wife, their daughter and heiress and her husband Thomas Boughton. John Harewell I, who died in 1428, was a man of greater standing than the Allesleys and Boughtons, but nevertheless a product of a family without knightly traditions. He was nevertheless commemorated by an altar tomb of marble with an alabaster effigy in full armour, placed in his parish church of Wootton Wawen. Joan, the widow of two lawyers, Nicholas Metley and Richard Hotoft, was commemorated by a marble gravestone with a brass.[137]

Greater figures, particularly those with a family chantry, college or other religious institution, might demand a grander commemoration still. In the 1460s Richard Willoughby, Robert's older half-brother, specified in minute detail how his and his wife's tombs were to look – he was to be 'hoole armyd except the hed of the best harnes and godelyest wyse wyth his helme undr his hed' – and what was to be written thereon. In 1495 Edmund Lucy ordered that a marble stone, seven foot by four, be placed over his grave in the family priory of Thelsford near Charlecote, on which was to be graven the arms of himself and his wife, their portraits and a suitable inscription to be chosen by his executors. The same year Thomas Ferrers II willed that he should be buried next to his wife in the collegiate church at Tamworth, which had been inherited from the Frevilles, along with the castle; here, from the later years of the century, numbers of Ferrers were buried. Over their graves were to be placed marble gravestones surmounted by brasses, on which they themselves, their

[135] McFarlane 1972: ch. 6; also Vale 1976: pp. 12–14.

[136] A selection of examples spanning the period, but with the inevitable bias towards the later part: PROB 11/2B fo. 108v. (Crewe – 1418), /4 fo. 129v. (Bate – 1459), /6 fo. 33v. (Archer – 1470), /6 fo. 201 (Lee of Marston – 1476), /11 fo. 177v. (Lucy – 1495), /13 fo. 148 (Ardern – 1502), /18 fo. 173v. (Brasebrugge – 1516). Also other wills cited in this chapter and Fleming 1984: pp. 44–5. Sometimes the attendants were to be clothed in white: e.g. Alice Thwaites (*Test. Ebor.*, IV, pp. 10–11); I have not come across any examples in Warwickshire.

[137] *Dugdale*, p. 97; *Trans. Birm. and Mid. Inst.*, 49 (1923), pp. 40–2; PROB 11/3 fo. 80; V.C.H., III, p. 204; *Dugdale*, p. 39.

children and 'our beasts' were to be depicted, with again a writing devised by the executors.[138]

The writing mentioned by both Lucy and Ferrers was an important aspect of the commemorative function of monuments, for it was the monuments that allowed the gentry to choose how to present themselves to posterity, both in the way they looked and in how they were described. That many chose to be represented in full armour is to be expected; even if they had never borne arms in battle, they remained a warrior caste and expected to be received into heaven as such. In 1525/6 John Ardern went so far as to leave his white harness, or armour, to Aston church 'for a George to wear it, and to stand on my Pewe'.[139] Richard Bingham on the other hand chose to be remembered in the robes of a lawyer, the profession that had made him.[140] It goes without saying that they would put their own arms and sometimes their ancestors' or those of related families on their tombs, but even the greatest were often happy to be depicted in the badges of their lords, showing that service to the right master generated reflected glory rather than degradation. Several had the Lancastrian *SS* collars, including Walter Cokesey on a brass, Thomas Erdington I (died 1434), Humphrey Stafford I (died 1450) and John Ferrers II, whose service to Henry VII is marked by the addition of a pendant Tudor rose. Others, like Thomas Erdington II (died 1467), had collars of suns and roses to show their service to the house of York. Thomas Crewe (died 1418), servant of Richard Beauchamp, had the Beauchamp arms on his brass and in the windows of his superb chantry in his parish church of Wixford.[141] Sometimes the lord is remembered in the inscription, as with Robert and John Hugford, whose careers were dominated by service to the earls of Warwick, or Thomas Straunge I, commemorated as 'late constable of the king in Ireland', or Edward Doddingselles II, whose gravestone was once marked with an inscription recording that he had been usher to Henry VII.[142] Thomas Cokayn II went further than anybody in enumerating in detail the achievements by which he wished to be remembered, in doggerel whose utter unmemorability as poetry is matched by its importance to the historian who wishes to understand the mind of the fifteenth-century landowner.[143]

138 Nott. Univ. Lib. Middleton MS 5/168/34; *Dugdale*, pp. 498–501; PROB 11/11 fo. 177v.; *Dugdale*, pp. 1,137–9; PROB 11/11 fo. 201. For tombs in general, cf. Fleming 1984: p. 51.

139 *Dugdale*, p. 928. On the growing popularity of the cult of St. George in the later fifteenth and early sixteenth centuries, see Barron 1985: p. 32.

140 *Dugdale*, p. 1,053.

141 *Trans. Birm. and Mid. Inst.*, 1884–5,p.71,47(1921), pp. 68–70 (slight doubts about identification here), 35 (1909), p. 75, 70 (1952), pp. 7–8, 1872, p. 7 (but ignore the quaint story); *V.C.H.*, III, p. 192 and illus.

142 *Dugdale*, pp. 279, 574, 346 (Hugford identification deduced from date of death for John; inscription of date of death on tomb that seems to be Robert's is apparently incomplete but there is no alternative possibility of the right period).

143 *Dugdale*, p. 1,121; Carpenter 1986b: p. 36.

In all the conspicuous display connected with religion it is not just the dead man who is remembered but the family in general. By this means the bequests of the head of the family could be justified to his posterity, and this point holds as true of prayers for the living and the dead as of physical displays. Not only could a family's past, present and future, all conceived in strictly linear terms, be remembered in prayers,[144] but a representation of the family that was at once physical and spiritual could be achieved through a chantry. Although prayers for the dead, often in perpetuity, continued to be ordained well into the sixteenth century, the foundation of chantries and collegiate churches was now past its peak. This was chiefly because, for families that could afford it, saturation point had been reached, but it was also the result of the barriers the law now put in the way of permanent amortisation of land for these purposes, especially under Henry VII and his son.[145] Nevertheless, several were still founded by the Warwickshire gentry during this period, usually when a family that had not so far possessed a chantry reached a peak of eminence where it felt bound to do so.

So, for example, in 1448/9 Thomas Erdington II established one in his parish church of Aston, where there had probably been an Erdington chapel since the time of Edward III. In 1447 the Staffords of Grafton were granted a licence to found a chantry at Bromsgrove, parish church of Grafton, which they renewed in 1476. Amongst their fellow licensees in the renewal was Thomas Littleton, who also gave property to the prior and convent of Worcester for perpetual prayers for his family at one of the altars of the cathedral. The Mountford chantry, which should have been established at Coleshill after William's death, probably proved abortive because of the protracted dispute over the inheritance.[146] For old families with their own foundations, like the

[144] Above, p. 213. Hicks' stark contrasting of the interests of the owner of the lands, in endowing chantries for his own salvation, and of the lineage that would lose the lands therefore needs to be modified, as it omits the concept of prayers and remembrance for the whole lineage (Hicks 1986b; also 1985a: pp. 126–7, 135–6, 1987).

[145] Carpenter 1987: pp. 57–8, 59–60 for more on this; also Fleming 1984: p. 39 and Hicks 1985a: p. 140. For the chronology of chantry foundation, see Vale 1976: pp. 22–3; Kreider 1979: ch. 3. Kreider points out that non-perpetual foundations were growing from about the middle of the fifteenth century, as the result of attempts to evade the mortmain legislation, and that licences became particularly hard to get under Henry VII. It is striking that a number of non-perpetual foundations in this reign and the next are given an endowment of eight marks a year, just above the normal minimum level for a chantry (Wood-Legh 1965: p. 203), or more: e.g. those of William Littleton (*Test. Vetust.*, pp. 467–8), Ralph Shirley III (Shirley 1873: pp. 412–3), Robert Throgmorton (PROB 11/20 fo. 9v.), Henry Willoughby (PROB 11/22 fo. 272). Some of these foundations made under the first two Tudors are for ninety-nine years, which seems to be an attempt to get round the legislation prohibiting perpetual grants. Where it seems clear that a perpetual foundation was hoped for, the institution has been treated as a chantry.

[146] *Dugdale*, p. 875; *Trans. Birm. and Mid. Inst.*, 1872, p. 2; *Cal. Pat. Rolls 1446–52*, p. 108, *1476–85*, p. 11; Worc. Dioc., Reg. Alcock fos. 102–04; PROB 11/7 fo. 23v.; B.R.L. Wingfield Digby MS A473. For the Mountford dispute, see below, chs. 11 and 12. Also the chantry certificates

Lucys at Thelsford or those that took over a residence with a religious institution attached, like the Ferrers at Tamworth, it was not necessary to do more than maintain their connections with these institutions, as the Lucys did throughout the century and the Ferrers when their interests began to move more fully into the county. It is worth noting that none of the Lucys seems to have felt the need to found a chantry at Thelsford until Edmund's donation of eight marks a year in 1495, perhaps because, as ancient patrons of a priory, they had not seen any point in adding this new and cheaper form of family commemoration.[147]

Chantry foundation was not, however, the prerogative of the greater families alone. At the end of the century William Lecroft of Coleshill, a one-manor gentleman, left lands to support prayers for seven years after his death, with the intention that a chantry should eventually be established in the parish church; perhaps the absence of a Mountford chantry was an encouragement to the lesser man. The Middlemores of Edgbaston, who were only a little higher than the Lecrofts on the ladder of local society, had their own chantry at Studley, their original home, founded in the mid fourteenth century but still attracting grants from the family in the early fifteenth.[148] Nevertheless, it was more usual for lesser landowners to ordain prayers by joining together in gilds and fraternities, like the ones at Coventry, Stratford, Knowle and Henley, or by joint foundations like the charterhouse, Bablake Hospital or the Collegiate Church of St. John the Baptist, all three in Coventry.[149] Henry Lisle managed to combine the personal and the institutional by giving his advowson of Wilnecote with its tithes to the gild at Stratford, in return for masses for his family.[150]

The location of the private chantries tells us much about the role they played in the creation of a family's identity. They marked their founders' arrival not only socially speaking but also in geographical terms; almost invariably they

excerpted by Dugdale (Bod. Lib. Dugdale MS 9, pp. 474–501) for more on chantries and religious gilds.

147 *Dugdale*, pp. 501, 505; *Cat. Anc. Deeds*, v, A12393; PROB 11/11 fo. 117v.; *Dugdale*, p. 94; PROB 11/11 fo. 201. Edmund Lucy's foundation was for six years only, but, bearing in mind that it was made at eight marks a year in the reign of Henry VII, it was probably hoped that it would become perpetual (see n.145, above).

148 C.1/147/16; *V.C.H.*, III, p. 186.

149 *Coventry Register, passim; Stratford Register, passim*; S.B.T. Stratford Corp. Records Div. XII (accounts); *Knowle Register, passim*; Cooper 1946: pp. 65–8; *Dugdale*, p. 189; *Cal. Close Rolls 1485–1500*, pp. 214–5, *1500–09*, p. 335; *Cal. Pat. Rolls 1494–1509*, pp. 419, 567; *Trans. Birm. and Mid. Inst.*, 1874, pp. 29–36, 1886, pp. 39–40. Cf. Burgess 1987: pp. 841–5. Burgess finds that his urban will-makers rarely put long-term provisions into their wills and suspects that much religious provision was made outside wills (pp. 855–6); this would apply much less to landowners, who, normally using lands rather than goods (below, p. 241), would have to make dispositions in advance when they tied up their estates (also below, pp. 248–9). In some grants, lesser men may have been acting as agents.

150 *Dugdale*, pp. 695–6; S.B.T. Stratford Corp. Recs. XII/192.

would be located in the parish church of the residential manor and they moved when the family moved. The Throgmortons, for example, were licensed in 1448 to grant lands for a chantry in Fladbury church in Worcestershire, the parish of their manor of Throckmorton. Although this step marked their achievement of a pre-eminence in their old home, by 1518 the focus had changed; by that year Sir Robert had bought lands to endow a chantry at Coughton, the more recent acquisition, to which he had moved his residence, and after 1448 there is no record of any further grant to Fladbury.[151] Similarly, the Littletons' first tangible expression in religious terms of their enhanced social position was Thomas' altar in Worcester cathedral, but once his eldest son William had returned to the family home of Frankley, now elevated to the position of centre of a large estate, the family's religious interests were transferred to Frankley parish church, where William established what was effectively a chantry.[152] In the 1470s the Brasebrugges moved their chantry from an old chapel at Kimberley near Hurley to Hurley itself, and by 1516 the new chantry seems in turn to have become less important to them than Kingsbury, the parish church of both the earlier foundations, which they were now rebuilding.[153] The Middlemores, first of Studley, then of Edgbaston, and the Shirleys, formerly of Lower Ettington, but now increasingly preoccupied with their property in the north and east midlands, seem to have abandoned completely their old family foundations during the course of the century, although the former family began to show renewed interest in Studley in the early 1530s. Families would go on insisting on their right to present to institutions in which they had apparently long lost interest, for the presentation remained a part of the property to be defended, but at that point their involvement stopped.[154]

Then there were those who founded a chantry at what had become the centre of a new estate created by the amalgamation, by inheritance or purchase, of new property with the old. One such was Thomas Cokesey, heir to both Cokesey (whose family name he had taken) and Greville. He established a chantry at Weston on Avon, the parish church of Milcote, to which the Grevilles had recently moved their residence from Camden in Gloucestershire. In doing so,

[151] *V.C.H. Worcs.*, III, p. 356; PROB 11/20 fo. 9v.

[152] PROB 11/7 fo. 23v.; *Worcs. Hist. Soc.*, 1909, p. 95; *Test. Vetust.*, pp. 467–8. This was another non-perpetual foundation of Henry VII's reign, at eight marks a year (above, n.145). Cf. the Hungerfords, another 'parvenu' family (Hicks 1985a: pp. 135–8, 1987 and Carpenter 1987: p. 71 n.73).

[153] *V.C.H.*, IV, p. 110–13; *Dugdale*, p. 1,062; Br. Lib. Add. Ch. 48.212; PROB 11/18 fo. 173v.; below, n.177.

[154] *V.C.H.*, III, p. 186; PROB 11/13 fo. 186; *Dugdale*, pp. 743, 619, 625–6; *V.C.H.*, V, pp. 82–3; for presentations to family institutions that were otherwise neglected, e.g. Cov. and Lichf. Dioc., Reg. Hales fos. 11v. (Astley of Norfolk to Astley of Hillmorton chantry in Hillmorton), 17 (Bermingham to Hospital of St. Thomas, Birmingham), 17v. (Ardern to chantry of Blessed Virgin Mary, Birmingham).

Cokesey seems to have neglected not only the Cokesey foundation at Kidderminster but the chantry established at Tetbury, Gloucestershire by his father, John Greville II.[155] By contrast, the religious dispositions of other families exemplify the extent to which their Warwickshire properties remained marginal to their main concerns. For example, the will of Thomas Culpepper of 1428 shows how firmly committed to Kent this family was and how little interest it took in its Warwickshire possessions. Hugh Willoughby's will of 1443 tells a similar story about his family's concerns in the north midlands and their lack of involvement with the Freville inheritance in Warwickshire at this stage.[156]

This study of the geographical location of a family's religious identity can be taken a stage further by examining the history of family burial places. Once a gentry line was firmly established in a particular residence, it would become normal for its members, especially the heads of the family and their wives, to be buried in the parish church of the manor, or sometimes in its associated religious house, as in the case of the Ferrers and the Lucys.[157] The older families nearly all had their mausolea: for example, the Cokayns at Ashbourne, Derbyshire, the Erdingtons at Aston, and the Staffords and their successors, the Talbots, at Bromsgrove in Worcestershire.[158] Once the burial place was fixed it was rare for a prominent member of the family to be buried elsewhere, unless forestalled by circumstances beyond his control. This did indeed happen to Robert Throgmorton, who had prepared a tomb for his use at Coughton but, in the event, died at Rome, on his way to the Holy Land.[159]

The history of the family burial place, which was naturally closely linked to that of the chantry, is a good index of the family's social and political position. Broadly speaking, the more confident the family of its local standing, the less likely were its members, particularly the males, to seek out the reflected glory of a social superior or of a religious institution by being buried away from the family residence. This identification of choice of burial place with acknowledgement of the location of family power can be seen clearly in the will of John Paston II; still worrying about his failure to build his father's tomb at

155 *Dugdale*, pp. 706–7; PROB 11/11 fo.134v.; *Trans. Birm. and Mid. Inst.*, 1884–5, pp. 58–71, 37 (1911), pp. 38, 55–6. For further evidence of the commitment to the new centre of Weston on Avon, see Sir John Greville's will (Worcs.R.O. 008.7/BA3590/1 fo. 44). The licence to alienate land for a chantry at Tetbury was granted to Greville and several others, so it is possible that he was merely acting as an agent for others in this instance (*Cal. Pat. Rolls 1476–85*, p. 181), but there was a Cokesey manor here, which gives some support to the idea that he was directly involved (*V.C.H. Gloucs.*, XI, p. 265), and John Greville and his wife were amongst the beneficiaries of the prayers. For problems with the Greville genealogy, above, p. 111 n.57.

156 *Reg. Chichele*, II, pp. 382–3; *Test. Ebor.*, II, pp. 130–2.

157 Above, n.147, but, for an exception, below, n.194.

158 *Derbys Arch. Jnl.*, 3 (1881), pp. 109–10, n.s., 1 (1924–5), pp. 140–2; *Trans. Birm. and Mid. Inst.*, 1872, p. 7, 47 (1921), pp. 68–70, 35 (1909), pp. 74–7, 81–2.

159 PROB 11/20 fo. 9v.

Bromholm, he urges that it be made, 'so that owre cousyns . . . have the more deuocion to that place and the rathere reste there bodyes there'.[160] The Throgmortons are a good illustration both of a family that grew great enough in its own eyes to make more of its burial place, and of the relocation that could follow on the enlargement of the estate. John I marked his achievement of an eminence greater than that of any of his forebears by adorning the graves of himself and his parents with marble, a retrospective enhancement of their status, while Robert moved the family mausoleum to Coughton.[161] Some of the rising families that managed to remain at the same residence established their burial place very quickly. One such was the Hugfords: all three members of the family to own Emscote – Robert, Thomas and John – were buried there, as was John Beaufo, who came into the manor by his father's marriage to one of John's daughters, and his wife and children. Even so, Margaret Metley, the heiress whose marriage to John facilitated the family's move from the status of 'professional' minor gentry, albeit of an elevated kind, to substantial landed status, chose to be buried not at Emscote but at Wolston, her father's residence, a fact which may well reflect a feeling on her part that she had married ever so slightly beneath her.[162] From at least 1428 the Harewells were buried at Wootton Wawen, acquired in the late fourteenth century. However, the sense of family identification with the place was not strong enough to prevent William and his wife early the following century requesting burial in the Friars Preachers in Warwick, where they had established a chantry.[163]

The close relationship between family advancement and using the parish church of the central manor as the family burial place can be seen in the history of the Verneys. Despite their earlier success, no member of the family considered Compton Murdack a fitting place for interment until 1523, when Anne, daughter of Richard II, the son of Edmund and grandson of Richard I, was buried there. She was followed in 1526 by Richard himself, who had built a new chapel there expressly for that purpose, the first of the family it appears to lavish any attention on the parish church. By contrast, Richard I was buried at St. Andrew's Priory, Northampton and Edmund in the Friars Preachers, Warwick. This delay in the creation of a permanent family religious centre at Compton Murdack lends weight to the other indications that too much dispersal of energy in conflict had hindered the full acceptance of the Verneys as pre-eminent in southern Warwickshire. Lack of confidence in their local standing held them back from being contented with a last resting place where the only lustre was their own. It was not after all until 1514 that Compton

160 *Paston Letters*, I, p. 507. Note also the kin attracted to Yoxford, one of John Hopton's two residences in Suffolk (Richmond 1981: pp. 74, 129–30).

161 PROB 11/3 fo. 248v.; above, n.159.

162 *Dugdale*, pp. 279, 39.

163 PROB 11/3 fo. 80; *Dugdale*, pp. 462, 809; Cooper 1936: pp. 18–19; PROB 11/17 fo. 52.

Murdack was known by its later name of Compton Verney.[164] The Littletons, whose delay in settling on a family religious centre has already been observed, followed the same pattern, fixing on the parish church of their residential manor only when they felt important enough in their own right not to need the prestige of a great religious institution.[165]

If one indication that a gentry family was not fully confident of its position in local society is a preference for the church of a religious order over that of the home parish, another is the tendency to gravitate to the burial places of greater families into which its members married. The most striking example is Thomas Ralegh (died 1404), who had married into the Astleys, a minor noble family, and chose to be buried in that family's long-established collegiate church at Astley. So chequered was the history of the Raleghs during this century that the first one to be buried at the residence of Farnborough appears to have been Edward I, who died in 1509.[166] If wives mostly followed their husbands, rather than the reverse, it can be shown that Thomas Ralegh is not an isolated instance. Although he came from an older family, Philip Purfrey, son-in-law of John Brome, was buried at Baddesley Clinton, which had quickly become the religious epicentre of the Bromes.[167] More remarkable still was the burial at Fladbury of Edward Peyto; his settling for a secondary residence of his brother-in-law, Robert Throgmorton, shows how far the relative positions of the fairly ancient Peytos and the very new Throgmortons had been reversed.[168] Sometimes, like Margaret Hugford née Metley, a wife who was a considerable heiress in her own right chose to have her body placed at her old home, especially if the family she had enriched was no greater than her own. Another such was Elizabeth, heiress to the Herthills of Pooley and wife of Edmund Cokayn, who remained at Pooley in a tomb adorned with the Herthill and Cokayn arms rather than be buried amongst the Cokayns at Ashbourne in Derbyshire.[169]

In the case of the eminent families with much less permanently focused local identities, notably the Cokeseys, Shirleys and Willoughbys, use of a variety of burial places reflected less a sense of social insecurity than the broad distribution of their lands and their ability to attract heiresses who changed the composition of the estate. As so often, chantry foundations and choice of burial

164 *V.C.H.*, v, p. 59; W.C.R.O. C.R.162/180; *Dugdale*, pp. 565, 569; Bridges and Whalley 1791: I, p. 455; Gover, Mawer and Stenton 1936: p. 252.

165 For refs., see above, n.152.

166 *Dugdale*, pp. 110–11, 529–30, 971; *Cal. Fine Rolls 1399–1405*, p. 265; PROB 11/4 fo. 146, /17 fo. 110; S.B.T. D.R.37 Box 34/2132. Farnborough features not at all in the will of Edward Ralegh's predecessor in the lands, Edward Bromflete (PROB 11/4 fos. 146–146v.).

167 *Dugdale*, pp. 54–5; PROB 11/5 fo. 251; Norris 1897: pp. 45–9.

168 *Dugdale*, p. 477; *I.P.M. Hen. VII*, I, 292; above, p. 121.

169 *V.C.H.*, IV, p. 197 (wrongly named Isabella here).

place went hand in hand, so that the Cokesey and Greville mausolea followed the path that has already been traced for their chantries.[170] The last Shirley monument that can safely be identified at Lower Ettington dates to 1327, and in the later fifteenth century Shirleys tended to be associated with and buried in the abbey of Garendon, a few miles distant from their Leicestershire residence of Staunton Harold. But Ralph Shirley I and his wife were buried in the college of Newark and Ralph II was interred at Brailsford, Derbyshire, which he had inherited from his mother.[171] Although Henry Willoughby was buried at Wollaton, his grandmother, the Freville heiress, and her second husband, Richard Bingham, were buried at the Freville manor of Middleton, where they had both lived. This in itself was a novelty, for Middleton had previously been a member of Tamworth, and Baldwin Freville I, owner of both properties, although he died at Middleton in 1400, was buried in the collegiate church of the principal manor. That Middleton retained its importance for the Willoughbys, even after its reuniting with Wollaton under Sir Henry, can be seen from the fact that Henry's daughter Dorothy was buried there, despite having married into the Fitzherberts, whose church at Norbury, Derbyshire, is full of family monuments, including that of Dorothy's husband and his second wife.[172]

It will be obvious by now that central to the whole issue of the location of chantries and burial places and therefore to the family's religious identity was the relationship with the parish church. As we have seen, it was in the church of the main residential manor that chantries were normally founded and members of the family buried. Almost every testator whose will has survived made some sort of grant to the local church, and those with more widespread lands, like the Archers, the Brasebrugges, the Lucys, the Raleghs, the Shirleys and the Throgmortons, to several. In 1492, for example, William Lucy left money to eight churches in the vicinity of Charlecote and in 1518 Robert Throgmorton was similarly generous to another five in Warwickshire, Worcestershire and Buckinghamshire, all of them linked to family manors. Even quite distant connections might be remembered if they were of sufficient import to the donor; in 1470, for instance, Richard Archer left money to Thelsford Priory because he had once been married to a Lucy widow and had for a time held part of the Lucy lands in his wife's right.[173] Churches received vestments, plate and

[170] Above, pp. 230–1.

[171] *V.C.H.*, v, p. 82; *Dugdale*, pp. 625–6; Shirley 1873: pp. 43–4, 49–50, 52, 410–4; Nichols 1795–1811: III, ii, pp. 787, 798.

[172] PROB 11/22 fo. 272; *Dugdale*, p. 1,053; *Trans. Birm. and Mid. Inst.*, 69 (1951), p. 26, 1882–3, pp. 6 –11. Bingham left Middleton church an antiphonal and a vestment (Nott. Univ. Lib. Middleton MS 5/168/53). He and his wife were, of course, resident there (above, p. 117).

[173] S.B.T. D.R.37 Box 90 (wills of Richard and Alice Archer – two for Richard, both being also in PROB 11/6 fo. 33v.); S.B.T. D.R.503 fos. 74v.–6; S.B.T. D.R.37 Box 90 (will of John Archer

sometimes books, as well as money. Robert Throgmorton ordered painted and gilded images of Our Lady and the Angel Gabriel for Coughton church. The spate of rebuilding of parish churches in the fifteenth century, particularly of chantry chapels, can be linked in large part to locally resident gentry.[174] Here again the phenomenon of the 'new family' is evident and building was often associated with the arrival of new owners, usually the rising professionals, and their decision to make the parish church the centre of their religious activities. We can see this, for example, in the case of the Bromes at Baddesley, the Spensers at Wormleighton, Robert Throgmorton at Coughton and Richard Verney II at Compton Murdack. Edward Ralegh, whose family had long held Farnborough, may be included in this category, since the family took most of the century to get back to its old residence, and Ralegh celebrated their return with generous patronage of the parish church.[175] The better off, whether well-established or arriviste, could feel the same need to improve the church of a newly-acquired secondary residence, as a means of notifying the neighbourhood that, newcomers or not, they were not to be trifled with. The Catesbys put windows with remembrances of themselves into the churches of Wootton Wawen and Lapworth and built a new tower at Ladbroke and provided it with a set of bells, while the Willoughbys made various additions to Middleton, including a west tower. But in neither case were the favoured churches to replace the old religious centre, at Ashby and Wollaton respectively.[176]

As the reference to the Willoughbys suggests, expenditure on rebuilding the parish or other local church was not confined to the social climbers. The Brasebrugges at Kingsbury, the Doddingselles at Long Itchington, the Mountfords at Coleshill, the Straunges at Walton were all engaged on it, as were the Ferrers at Tamworth, who, if 'new' in the sense of having married into Warwickshire society, were from a very ancient family.[177] Parishioners, neigh-

III); PROB 11/18 fo.173v.; *Dugdale*, p. 505; PROB 11/10 fo. 167, /11 fo. 177v.; *Cat. Anc. Deeds*, v, A12393; PROB 11/17 fo. 110; S.B.T. D.R.37 Box 34/2132; Shirley 1873: pp. 404–5, 410–14, 414–16; PROB 11/3 fo. 248v., /20 fo. 9v. Also, as earlier examples, the wills of Richard Clodesdale (1428), Thomas Straunge I (1436) (PROB 11/3 fo. 74; S.B.T. C.R.133/15).

174 PROB 11/20 fo. 9v. (Throgmorton). For others, refs. in nn.36,173 and elsewhere in this chapter.

175 *V.C.H.*, iv, pp. 17–18; *V.C.H.*, iii, p. 82; PROB 11/20 fo. 9v.; *Dugdale*, p. 565; PROB 11/17 fo. 110. Cf. Richmond 1987: p. 203. Nicholas Brome, a violent man (below, p. 512) is supposed to have built the tower at Baddesley in penance for murdering the parish priest (*Dugdale*, p. 972).

176 *Dugdale*, pp. 791, 813; S.C.6/1043/11, /1041/18, /1042/7. The gift of bells to Ladbroke church post-dates moving the residence permanently away from that manor (above, p. 117). For the Catesbys and Ashby church, S.C.6/949/15 fos. 34, 43, 63, /1039/4. For Willoughby, see *V.C.H.*, iv, p. 159. In this case there is no direct attribution to the Willoughbys, but it is difficult to see who else would have made the additions, if the dating is correct. Margaret Willoughby née Freville had a chapel for herself added to the manor-house at Middleton in the 1440s (Nott. Univ. Lib. Middleton MS 5/167/101).

177 *V.C.H.*, iv, pp. 110–11 (again, the dating is a strong indication of the identity of the builder); *Trans. Birm. and Mid. Inst.*, 79 (1960–1), p. 7, 1878–9, p. 64; *V.C.H.*, iv, p. 54; W.C.R.O. C.R.133/15,16.

bours – especially the lords of the lesser manors within the parish – and visitors were left in little doubt of the identity of the local benefactor and of the family to whom in that parish the greatest deference was due. His arms were to be found on stone and glass, his predecessors were as often as not buried in or near the chancel, perhaps in a family chantry heavily adorned with the family arms. At Grendon the Chetwynds put portraits of the family and its connections in the windows; at Charlecote, the cope left by Edmund Lucy was embroidered with the arms of himself and his wife.[178]

Given the relationship between the residence and the religious centre of the family, it is hardly surprising to find that in nearly all the gentry's religious dispositions there is a strong degree of localism. This began at the diocesan level, with north Warwickshire owing its allegiance and its donations to 'the mother church' at Lichfield and south Warwickshire to Worcester, but it went much further. Donations to churches in and around the family estates have been referred to, and this is a pattern that holds good for all levels of the gentry, from Fulwodes, Lecrofts and Spensers at the bottom of the pile, to Ferrers, Mountfords, Shirleys and Willoughbys at the top, applying equally to patronage of other institutions, like monasteries and gilds.[179] The monasteries that are still remembered are those with a special, usually a local, link to the family. Either they have a long-standing connection with the estate, like Thelsford or Pinley in the case of the Lucys, or Garendon with the Shirleys,[180] or, while lacking a formal bond of this sort, they still lie near the residential manor, like Merevale, patronised by Thomas Bate and the Brasebrugges, Combe by the Raleghs and Peytos, or Maxstoke by William Harecourt of Maxstoke.[181] There may also be a link of service or dependent tenure, as in the case of John Beaufitz with his neighbours, the Hospitallers at Balsall and Fletchamstead and Kenilworth Priory, or the Malorys with Axholme, owner of Monks Kirby Priory.[182] The exceptions to this rule, who received donations from much further afield, are the universally popular orders, the Carthusians and above all

[178] *Dugdale*, pp. 1,103–5; PROB 11/11 fo. 177v. Also e.g. *Dugdale*, pp. 296, 713, 791, 813, 876–7, 987, 1,019, 1,115; S.C.6/1043/11; *V.C.H.*, III, p. 64, iv, p. 55; *Trans. Birm. and Mid. Inst.*, 1877, p. 7.

[179] Hilton 1967: p. 9; PROB 11/13 fo.229v.; C.1/147/16; PROB 11/11 fos. 39,201; B.R.L. Wingfield Digby MS A473; Shirley 1873: pp. 404–5, 410–14, 414–16; Nott. Univ. Lib. Middleton MS 5/168/53; PROB 11/22 fo. 272.

[180] For the Lucys and Thelsford, above, n.147, for the Shirleys and Garendon, above, n.171. In the latter case the connection goes back a very long way indeed, since the de Ferrers, early benefactors to Garendon, were the Shirleys' overlords at Ettington and in Derbyshire from the time of the Conquest (*Dugdale*, p. 619; Nichols 1795–1811: III, ii, p. 787; *V.C.H. Derbyshire*, I, pp. 340b, 341a, 345b).

[181] PROB 11/4 fo.129v., /18 fo.173v., /17 fo.110, /10 fo.66; *Cal. Pat. Rolls 1429–36*, p. 64.

[182] *Dugdale*, pp. 264, 965; PROB.11/11 fo. 173v., /8 fo. 161; D.L.29/463/7541–62; S.C.6/1039/18, /1107/7.

the Friars, who were remembered in the wills of almost everyone,[183] and religious institutions in London, which tended to be favoured by some of the lawyers and crown servants, like Metley and Gerard Danet, both of whom elected to be buried in London, and John Throgmorton I.[184]

All this local generosity redounded to the credit, both earthly and heavenly, of the donor family, and the same motives can be seen at work more obviously in the provision of 'good works', particularly roads and bridges, in the neighbourhood of the centre of the estate. The Chetwynds, for example, may have been responsible for the provision of an important bridge across the River Anker at Grendon and Hugh Clopton undoubtedly ordered the building of a bridge at Stratford which stands to this day.[185] Money for repair of local bridges was left by Richard Archer, Thomas Bate, Thomas Ferrers II, Robert Throgmorton and several others, and for roads by, amongst others, Clopton, John Harewell I (including some for a road near an outlying property in Somerset), Metley and John Spenser of Hodnell.[186]

The instances cited here span the century, and, if allowances are made for increasing evidence, there is no indication that they were growing in number during the period. This is an important point because it is sometimes alleged that the focus of religious donations was changing in ways that indicate a weakening of belief in Purgatory and a move towards making charitable gifts in the expectation of more tangible earthly returns.[187] It should therefore be stressed that the evidence of the Warwickshire gentry does not support this interpretation. Prayers for departed souls were being ordained at all levels of gentry society well into the sixteenth century, even if lesser men could afford no more than an altar light, an anniversary or the prayers of a religious fraternity, or, at most, a chantry priest supported by a meagre annual income.[188]

183 A point which can be verified by reference to almost any of the wills in this chapter: also that of John Onley II of Birdingbury (PROB 11/2B fo. 433). The Carmelites in particular are mentioned by name in several wills e.g. John Harewell I and Edith Ruggeley (Cooper 1936: p. 14; PROB 11/3 fo. 193d.) and they were also the beneficiaries of William Botener's charity (*Dugdale*, p. 215).

184 S.B.T. D.R.3/258; PROB 11/20 fo. 7, /3 fo. 248v.

185 *V.C.H.*, IV, p. 75; *Dugdale*, p. 699.

186 PROB 11/6 fo.33v., /4 fo.129v., /11 fo.201, /20 fo. 9v.; *Dugdale*, p. 699; PROB 11/3 fo. 80 (Harewell – Cooper 1936: p. 16 for his ownership of Beer Crocombe, Somerset); S.B.T. D.R.3/258; PROB 11/11 fo. 39.

187 Carpenter 1987: pp. 67–8 for further discussion of this point. Also Jordan 1961: pp. 152–4, 1959: esp. ch. 6; Fleming 1984: pp. 45–6; Scarisbrick 1984: pp. 4–5.

188 Examples of bequests from lesser gentry etc.: Richard Boteller (the elder?) (*c.* early sixteenth century) (Bod. Lib. Dugdale MS 23 fo. 32v.), Hugh Clopton (d.1496) (*Dugdale*, p. 700), Richard Fulwode (d.1502) (PROB 11/13 fo. 229v.), Thomas Hore of Elmdon II (grant made before 1461) (S.B.T. D.R.37 Box 42 /2521), John Herward yeoman of Frankton (grant of 1436/7) (*Dugdale*, p. 281), Edward Hubaud (grant of 1497) (*Cat. Anc. Deeds*, I, B164–5), Richard and John Waldeve of Alspath (grants of 1403, 1408) (*Cat. Anc. Deeds*, I, B53, 58), Thomas Waldeve of Hurley (grant of 1479) (Br. Lib. Add. Ch. 48,212). Carpenter 1987: pp. 59–60.

Conversely, despite the lack of evidence from the less rich early wills, we can show that paupers were receiving grants throughout the century,[189] and, if there was perhaps an increase in enthusiasm for educational provision towards the end of the century, this was primarily a matter of fashion.[190] A reading of all types of grant in context makes it absolutely clear that their major function was, without exception, the same, to inspire memory of the departed donor, prayers for his soul and, perhaps most important of all, a healthy respect for his family.[191]

If merchants such as Hugh Clopton or rising yeoman farmers such as John Spenser were more enthusiastic about dispensing money on objects like education, bridges, roads and the poor, this was not because they were of a 'bourgeois' cast of mind, which led them to demand value for money in this world, not being content with less certain rewards in the next. Rather it was because, in the case of merchants, they had more goods to dispose of and therefore more money to expend, and, in the case of both merchants and yeomen, fewer lands. When acquisition of estates of any kind of size was so difficult, to compete with the gentry chantry-founders by using existing properties or buying additional ones was foolish and probably in most cases impossible.[192] It is in fact evident that at each level there was a clear conception of how the demands of heaven and earth could be satisfied but that the solution varied with social status. The growth of chantries had in itself been due in part to the gentry's need to have their own foundations, rather than merely play a part in their lords' much greater enterprises. Similarly the gilds and fraternities, which made possible the participation in religious foundations of townsmen, yeomen and minor gentry, were a response to the same aspiration manifested at a lower social and economic level.[193] Despite the formidable membership of some of these gilds – the Stratford one, for instance, started with the king and

[189] E.g. from Nicholas Metley (d.1436) (S.B.T. D.R.3/258); Thomas Mollesley (grant of 1451 – this is the famous 'Mollesley's dole' of Walsall; for the affecting but rather improbable story of its origins, Dugdale's correction and its actual purpose, *Dugdale*, pp. 347–8; *V.C.H. Staffordshire*, XVII, p. 266; Shaw 1798–1801: II, p. 73); Alice Digby (d.1496) (*Dugdale*, p. 1,013); Robert Throgmorton (d.1518) (PROB 11/20 fo.9v.); Thomas Slade (d.1530) (Bod. Lib. Dugdale MS 23 fo. 32; *Dugdale*, p. 1,001).

[190] See the grants of Hugh Clopton (n.188), Marjery Belyngham (*Dugdale*, p. 333), Edward Ralegh (PROB 11/17 fo. 110; S.B.T. D.R.37 Box 42/2132), Robert Throgmorton (n.189), John Spenser (PROB 11/11 fo. 39).

[191] Note particularly that Marjery Belyngham's endowment to send a Cistercian monk to Oxford was made specifically that he might say prayers for her and her ancestors.

[192] Above, pp. 97, 127.

[193] Dugdale 1817–30: *passim*; Pantin 1955: pp. 105–9; Vale 1976: pp. 22–4; Horrox 1981: p. 156; Wood-Legh 1965: p. 5; Carpenter 1987: pp. 60–1, 67–8, 70–1 and refs. to work on religious gilds, p. 60 n.26; also Westlake 1919: pp. 60–5; *English Gilds*, ed. Smith and Smith, esp. pp. 212–21, 232–6, 236–8. That type of donation and social status were related is to some extent backed up by Fleming 1984, but it is not clear that the number of wills can support the weight of his statistics. For literature on changing charitable ethics, see above, n.187.

included most of the leading nobility and gentry of the area – they were remembered almost exclusively by these lesser families when it came to bequests.[194]

The self-made professionals, as so often, follow a pattern of their own. Throughout the period they tend to leave fuller and more precise wills than their contemporaries. Thomas Bate's, for example, is unusually lengthy and detailed, in both its provisions and its funerary specifications, for a gentry will of the mid fifteenth century. In 1481 Thomas Littleton is one of the first of the gentry to specify the masses he wishes to have said for his soul and to name individual saints in the clause commending his soul to God. John Smyth's will of 1500 is an extraordinarily detailed and individual document. In 1520 Gerard Danet belies his expressed desire for a quiet funeral with a massively detailed exposition of how he is to be laid to rest, after commending his soul, uniquely, to four named saints.[195] In these instances we are meeting lawyerly precision and perhaps a more accentuated version of the generally-held belief that, since this world had been successfully managed by the careful deployment of interest, the same would hold good of the next. And when these men behave like merchants in expending considerably more in their wills than any of the other gentry, and when, also like merchants, they pay more attention to charitable projects like roads and education than is general amongst the gentry, they are not striking out on new paths that will lead eventually to the Reformation. On the contrary, they are manifesting a social unease that makes them spread their largesse around as broadly as possible and support projects where they do not have to compete with the established families.

The parvenus' unusual concern with ancestry and with the extended family surfaces again, and with particular prominence, in their religious dispositions. We have noted John Throgmorton I's pains to have his parents' grave marked with a tomb once he was in a position to do so. By the time John Smyth made his will, he had sealed an indenture for the construction of his tomb, complete with specified writing. The tendency of men of this type to take a wide view of

194 For example, by Clopton (*Dugdale*, pp. 699–700), Fulwode (PROB 11/13 fo. 229v.), Lisle (*Dugdale*, pp. 695–6), Middlemore (PROB 11/13 fo. 186), Spenser (PROB 11/11 fo. 39). Exceptions among the greater gentry are Richard Archer, who was of middling rank and had particularly close connections with the many lesser gentry in his part of the county (PROB. 11/6 fo.33d.; and below, section II) and the Lucys, closely associated with the Stratford gild; Sir William, exceptionally for a Lucy, was buried with his wife in Stratford parish church (S.B.T. Strat. Corp. Recs. XII/62, 84, 93, I/502, 518; *Dugdale*, p. 505). William Bishopestone and the Burdets, who had the most intimate connections of any of the greater families with this gild (S.B.T. Stratford Corp. Recs., I and XII *passim*), may be further exceptions, but have left no wills. In the case of Bishopestone and the Lucys it was clearly their own proximity to Stratford that produced this association, with the Burdets there is no obvious reason; Stratford lay in their part of the world but some miles away from their residence at Arrow. Also below, p. 339.

195 PROB 11/4 fo. 129v., /7 fo. 23v., /13 fos. 47v.–48, /20 fo. 7v. For their careers, above, pp. 102–3, 124, 146, 149 for Littleton, Bate and Smyth, and *Dugdale*, p. 280 and *Cal. Pat. Rolls 1485–94*, p. 275 for Danet.

the family in setting up *post-mortem* prayers has also been remarked on.[196] Gerard Danet's request that his arms be displayed at his funeral, with twelve scutcheons set about his corpse and on the pillars near his grave, is replicated nowhere else, notably not in the wills of any of the gentry from older families.[197] Paradoxically, or perhaps characteristically for parvenus, men of this type tended to show a greater loyalty to old institutions than the older families, sometimes to institutions with which their links were to say the least marginal. By this means they were staking their claim to an ancient lineage or acquiring for themselves the lineage that went with the lands they had bought. Henry Waver I's adoption of the Waver chantry at Monks Kirby is an instance of this.[198] The Pulteneys, a Leicestershire family who owed their position to the efforts of Sir John Pulteney, the mid-fourteenth-century mayor of London, did not neglect their connection with the Coventry White Friars founded by Sir John, and in the early sixteenth century they were still being buried there, although they had almost no links beside this one with Warwickshire.[199] In 1437/8 Thomas Greswold revived the de Oddingselles chantry at Solihull, founded under Edward I and now defunct, by granting rents to support a daily mass for himself, his parents – who were both equally plebeian – and his patron and employer, the king.[200] William Botener, Coventry merchant turned landowner, and scion of an eminent Coventry family that had a long history of patronising the city's institutions, almost entirely rejected the family traditions on moving to Withybrook, although he himself had maintained them while in Coventry. Once installed at Withybrook, he proceeded to keep to the traditions of his predecessors, the Castells, in nurturing the links with the abbey of Combe.[201]

The best example of all is Sir William Compton, who effected a meteoric rise in the service of Henry VIII from yeoman/fringe gentry origins to a wealthy knighthood. In his exceedingly expensive will of 1522 he ordered a burial in Compton church, referring grandly to 'my ancestors' who lay buried there, and decreed that a tomb be made for his father's grave, where his mother's body was to be placed, the tomb to be adorned with the family arms; all this to convince everybody that his ancestry was indeed noble. He also provided for the foundation of no less than two chantries at Compton, left a large sum of money for perpetual obits at seven different institutions, distributed vestments

[196] Above, pp. 213–14; PROB 11/13 fo.47v.

[197] PROB 11/20 fo.7v.

[198] *Dugdale*, pp. 90–1.

[199] *Dugdale*, pp. 186, 336–7; *Trans. Birm. and Mid. Inst.*, 1872, pp. 64–5.

[200] *Dugdale*, pp. 945, 947; *Cal. Pat. Rolls 1436–41*, p. 179. No member of the family is recorded as being buried there until 1537 (*Trans. Birm. and Mid. Inst.*, 49 (1923), p. 45) but the burial places of Thomas and his immediate successors are unknown.

[201] *Dugdale*, pp. 177, 193, 207, 214–16; *Cal. Pat. Rolls 1429–36*, p. 64. Botener made a grant to Holy Trinity, Coventry in 1407, before he moved to Withybrook (*Cal. Pat. Rolls 1405–08*, p. 374), and one to the Coventry Carmelites under Henry V (C.143/445/12).

to forty churches in the neighbourhood of Compton and left 200 marks to the poor. In short, he was behaving like a parody of a great gentleman of ancient lineage in the hope that he would be taken for one.[202]

What Sir William failed to realise was that the donations to the church of the older families were highly cost-effective. If the sums of money expended on funerals and immediate *post mortem* prayers and bequests are added up, they do not in most cases amount to very much, especially when the testator was leaving a direct male heir. Although it is not always possible to be precise about the figures, it can be said that the sums vary generally between £1 and £15. Apart from the merchants, who are a special case because of their plenitude of goods, the only people who consistently spent lavishly at this stage were the new men like Compton; his bequests, excluding the money for chantries and anniversaries, totalled about £200, those of John Beaufitz nearly £40, those of the normally careful John Spenser more than £42.[203] For men like this, the worship bought by these means took precedence over the integrity of the estate. Older families, who needed to maintain rather than create worship, confined their large outlays to building works on the parish church and the foundation of chantries, both of which brought in a substantial return in that they were a permanent reminder to the parish and the neighbourhood of the family's wealth and achievements. In this light church towers were probably the best investment of all because they could be seen and their bells heard from so far away. The established gentry tended also to confine the actual grants of land to the church to peripheral or specially acquired properties, the sort of land that younger sons had to be content with.[204] They were certainly generous when it came to saving their souls but with a carefully calculated generosity.

The visibility of religion in terms of both ceremonies and buildings has been stressed throughout this discussion, particularly because it made it possible for the gentry to accept and justify to themselves spoliation of the estate for the good of their souls. As in so many cultures, religion was an important aspect of conspicuous consumption. This is a point to be remembered when considering the extent to which the religion of the gentry at this time was becoming

[202] *Dugdale*, p. 547; *Test. Vetust.*, pp. 591–4.

[203] *Dugdale*, p. 699; *Test. Vetust.*, pp. 591–4; PROB 11/8 fo. 161, /11 fo. 39. Cf. the similarly expensive will of Henry VII's servant, Sir Hugh Conway (1517) (PROB 11/19 fo. 161; below, p. 574).

[204] E.g. Richard Archer (PROB 11/6 fo.33d.; S.B.T. D.R.37 Box 90 – will of 1471: see Carpenter 1987: p. 58: Archer's wife wanted her manor of Stotfold sold for charitable purposes (S.B.T. D.R.37 Box 90); instead he used Morton Bagot which the family was likely to lose to the Conyngesbys: below, pp. 493–4); George Catesby (*Cat. Anc. Deeds*, IV, A9814); John Harewell II (Cooper 1936: p. 19); Ralph Shirley III (Shirley 1873, pp. 410–16); Thomas Throgmorton, after readjustment (Coughton Court, Throckmorton MS Box 72/5); Robert Throgmorton (PROB 11/20 fo. 9v.). See also the properties in Shropshire, a county where he was little involved, given by Thomas Erdington in the 1450s (C.143/451/20, /452/10).

'privatised'.[205] Although this issue belongs more properly to the history of religious beliefs, it has importance for how the gentry saw their religious life in relation to their public pursuits. The evidence for private oratories is such that nearly all landowners of any standing whatsoever must have had them by this stage. If the Fulwodes were licensed for private worship in their own house as early as Richard II's reign and had a private chapel by the middle of the century, then few families at the level of knight or esquire can have been without such amenities.[206]

The emphasis in religious thought in the later middle ages on the individual Christian's responsibility for his soul,[207] and in private life on greater comfort and seclusion must both have encouraged the hearing of prayers at home, particularly in the inclement winter months. But this is not evidence that the gentry were cutting themselves off from the life of the parish. It was after all the parish church that was benefiting principally and increasingly from their attentions and, even if this meant that it was to some extent becoming an offshoot of their household, it was still the place of worship for the rest of the parish. There was little point in putting marks of the family's status in the church if nobody but the family was able to look at them. Moreover, any lord who failed to make frequent public appearances among his tenants at a time when tenants and king were subverting manorial authority would have been exceedingly unwise.[208] The church was the place where lord, family and servants could be viewed by the maximum number of his tenants, in the midst of the visible expression of the family's past and present grandeur. In a parish with more than one manor they would also be seen to advantage by the tenants

205 Richmond 1984: pp. 198–9; Bossy 1985: *passim*, esp. pp. 45–9, 127; also Carpenter 1987: pp. 65–6.

206 *Dugdale*, p. 782; S.B.T. D.R.37/949. NB Dugdale's own notes give the date of the licence as 1402 (Bod. Lib. Dugdale MS 12, p. 493). Other examples of families known to have had the right to private worship and/or private chapels include Ardern (Cov. and Lichf. Dioc., Reg. Burghill fo. 198v.), Astley (Cov. and Lichf. Dioc., Reg. Burghill fo.200), Brasebrugge (*Dugdale*, p. 1,059; Cov. and Lichf. Dioc., Reg. Arundel fo. 239), Brett (*V.C.H.*, IV, p. 6), Chetwynd (*Dugdale*, p. 1,103), Clopton of Stratford (*V.C.H.*., III, p. 262; Worc. Dioc., Reg. Carpenter fos. 82v., 137), Clodesdale (Cov. and Lichf. Dioc., Reg. Burghill fos. 157v., 195), Cokayn (*V.C.H.*, IV, p. 187; Cov. and Lichf. Dioc., Reg. Burghill fo. 148v.), Ferrers (Nott. Univ. Lib. Middleton MS Mi M 214), Harewell (*V.C.H.*, III, p. 260; Worc. Dioc., Reg. Clifford fo.8), Hugford (*V.C.H.*, VI, p. 166; Cov. and Lichf. Dioc., Reg. Burghill fo. 142v.), Littleton, at Frankley (*V.C.H. Worcs.*, III, p. 123), Lucy (PROB 11/10 fo.167), Mountford (*Dugdale*, p. 1,011), Purfrey (*Dugdale*, p. 54), Willoughby (*Dugdale*, p. 1,051; Nott. Univ. Lib. Middleton MS 5/167/101). Bearing in mind the haphazard survival of information, the density and social spread are impressive. Also Mertes 1987: pp. 124–6, 1988: p. 140 and Fleming 1984: p. 42.

207 Of particular interest in this respect is the early-fifteenth-century document published in Pantin 1976, because it was found among the Throgmorton papers; unfortunately there is no evidence as to its original provenance.

208 Carpenter 1987: pp. 65–6. See refs. above, pp. 43, 44–5. Also Ault 1970; according to Saul (1986: p. 159), licences for private worship were conditional on a specified number of days' attendance at the parish church.

of other lords; the family that had done most to adorn the church and left a clear reminder of its efforts by strewing its arms around the building put itself in the forefront when it came to winning the allegiance of all its tenants in the parish and indeed those of the other lords. When political power was in the last resort based on local military power, that was a very important consideration indeed.[209]

IV

The constantly recurring theme of this discussion has been the reconciliation of conflicting needs. The obligation to maintain the integrity of the estate conflicted with the need to expend the estate's resources on objects which were themselves necessary attributes of the worship that the estate conferred. Both imperatives could run against the personal inclinations of the head of the family to look after both his family and his soul. In this, as in so much else, the gentry followed similar paths to the nobility, but with less to play with and therefore less room for manoeuvre than most of their social superiors. Even so, more often than not, reconciliation was achieved. Expenditure on making a show on earth and in heaven was legitimate while it did no unnecessary damage to the estate, especially to the properties that were conceived to be its centre. Careful management of the estate's resources ensured that such outlays could be made without any adverse effects. Above all, as long as the major outlays were directed as much towards the honour of the family corporation, living and dead, as to that of the incumbent of the moment, many of the problems of conflicting interests disappeared. It is worth noting, therefore, that one of the few legitimate reasons for hiving off part of the estate was to prevent the holders of the family name falling into undignified poverty. It remains to conclude this first section by asking what exactly estate, 'family' and 'lineage' meant to the fifteenth-century gentry.

[209] Below, pp. 283–4.

7

CONCLUSIONS: LAND, FAMILY AND LINEAGE

A large part of this opening section has revolved around land, its significance and the uses to which it was put. It will be obvious already that landed property in this period was far more than an economic commodity. To a large extent the possession of land defined a gentry family as a political and social entity. Land might therefore be sacrificed for political or social benefits, particularly in marriage settlements. It might be pursued in expensive litigation that cost far more than the property was worth. Its income might be allowed to fall to avoid offending important tenants or officials. Expenditure of its profits alone did not make a family great; one that spent beyond its social position was regarded with contempt. That the purpose of land went far beyond pecuniary profit is apparent from Margaret Paston's comment: 'money is sone lost and spent whan yat lyfelode abideth'. That it was land alone that counted can be seen in the instructions in the will made in 1500 by John Smyth, a lawyer who had taken his family into the ranks of the gentry, to his son, Henry, who was fast growing rich in the livestock boom of the late fifteenth century. It seems that John had some doubts about the effect of his son's entrepreneurial instincts on the family's position. Henry was told that the money his father would leave him was to be used neither to settle his father's debts nor to buy sheep or cattle, but only to purchase land for himself and his heirs.[1] What land, above all land held in heredity, gave was political power, a stake, formal or informal or both, in the governance of the body politic, and that was what separated off the landed aristocracy, however meagre those at the bottom might be, from the rest.[2] As late as 1881 the earl of Derby listed the reasons that made people want to become landowners as 'political influence, social importance, power over the tenantry, residual enjoyment and sport', and 'rental income last'. The statement could apply equally well to this period.[3]

1 *Paston Letters*, I, p. 366; PROB 11/13 fos.47v–48. For 'livelihood, above, p. 77.

2 For development of this fundamental point, above, pp. 75–7 and below, pp. 282–6, 347–50.

3 Stone and Fawtier Stone 1986: p. 14. Also the remarks in Raban 1985: pp. 241–2, 253, 259, and Cooper 1985: p. 190.

If it was land that gave landowners their power, it was then their ability to handle friends, neighbours and superiors, and the income from the estate, enabling them to live at the level dictated by their power and influence, that gave them the all-important quality of 'worship'. Worship, a word in constant use in this period, was the quality a landowner expected to have if he used his resources properly. It defies modern definition, but can best be described as the worth or credit that was earned by living up to one's status as a landowner in all publically-visible aspects of live, from housing and food through litigation to dealing with the king or his officers. A man or family that lost its worship lost a large part of its existence.[4]

Land was something that produced complex and deeply emotional responses and the same applies, with perhaps even more force, to the words 'family' and 'lineage'. These have recurred periodically throughout this opening section in a variety of contexts but their meaning to a gentry family of the fifteenth century has yet to be defined. This might seem so obvious as not to require amplification, and yet studies of the same problems in other periods should warn us that it is far from obvious.[5] We have already seen that the notion of the family is in itself a variable commodity and lineage was no less so. Identity can focus on a place, on a name that may or may not take its origins from the family's hereditary residence, or on a sense of lineage that has more to do with pedigree than with either of these and, by this time, was best expressed in heraldry.[6] Then there is the question of where the living family, especially its head, stood in relation to the lineage. Implicit in much of the discussion so far has been the idea of 'stewardship'. The notion that the head of the family was no more than the temporary owner of property, for which he had to answer to the past and future of his line, has mostly found favour with historians of the pre-industrial English aristocracy.[7] It seems in general to hold good for the families that we have been studying. It would certainly account for their almost religious commitment to all their real property, except for that which might be disposed of by choice for their own purposes.

But within the limits of respect for the family estate, particularly its patrimony, they could still show individual preferences, such as those already discussed in their wills and other religious dispositions. Furthermore, steward-

4 Above, p. 198; usages of 'worship', 'worshipful', 'disworship' could be multiplied almost *ad infinitum*: e.g. *Paston Letters*, I, pp. xli (particularly good because ironic), 134, 154, 258–9, 350, 359, 366, 514, II, pp. 14, 120–1, 236, 551–2; *Stonor Letters*, I, pp. 97, 103, II, pp. 94–5, 98; Malory, *Works*, pp. 75, 466; Caxton, *Book of the Knight of the Tower*, p. 169; McFarlane 1973: p. 113. Rawcliffe and Flower 1986: pp. 158–9 for a partial definition.

5 Holt 1982–5; Duby 1977b; Painter 1961; Davies, R. R. 1987: ch. 5; McFarlane 1973: pp. 61–82; Bonfield 1983: *passim*, 1986; James 1974: *passim*, 1986c: pp. 325–6; Stone and Fawtier Stone 1986: esp. chs. 3 and 4; Thirsk 1964.

6 Wagner 1972: pp. 118–25, 1956, *passim*, 1967: chs. 1 and 2.

7 Stone 1979: pp. 28–9, 69–70, 409; Fleming 1984: p. 37; Cooper 1976: p. 300; Hicks 1986b: pp. 90–3.

ship of the estate was only one part, if a very important one, of aristocratic mores. These included other qualities, notably loyalty, that could lead the estate into serious jeopardy or even total destruction. And on occasion, as in the favouring of his wife or a particular child, the head of the family could show himself far from immune to the affections that are sometimes thought of as peculiar to the modern world. As we move from family matters into the political world, we shall come across more instances where the temporary incumbent chose to put his personal inclinations above his custody on behalf of the lineage. In some cases this was only a matter of giving preference to an equally pressing moral imperative, particularly loyalty to a lord, but in others, above all the preferential treatment of second wives and their families, the normal moral and legal norms were simply being set aside.[8]

To return to the lineage itself, there can be no doubt about the gentry's reverence for its past, and even for the past of long-defunct families of their 'contree'.[9] We know from the Plea Rolls that the gentry had long memories for claims sometimes going back 100 years or more and for the descents through which they were justified. Uncertainties could often be verified by reference to the family archive, at least for those that went back no more than 200 years or so.[10] One instance where we can see very clearly the consequences of a consciousness of past history is the Arderns' claim to descent from Turchil of Arden, the great tenant-in-chief of Domesday, from whom the earls of Warwick themselves had acquired much of their land. Here lineage was doubly beneficial; it gave them a certain equality with the greatest landowner of the locality, and even a superiority over almost all their neighbours, including the earl, since they could show that their name and hence their claims to distinction, having a Saxon origin, antedated those of almost everyone else.[11] The importance to this family of the name of 'Ardern' raises the question of the significance to the gentry in general of the survival of the family name and, related to this, of the descent in the male line. Exclusion of female heirs was not merely a ploy to preserve the family name, for descent to more than one heiress necessitated the dismemberment of the estate. It has been assumed by most historians that by the fifteenth century both nobility and gentry were normally settling their lands in tail male.[12] While this may be true for the nobility, there

[8] Above, chs. 4, 6; below, chs. 10–15; Baker ed., *Spelman*, II, p. 204. The subject is summed up below, pp. 627–8. See also the very interesting discussion of these problems, Hicks 1986b.

[9] See the remarkable antiquarian commemoration performed by Sir Thomas Erpingham (Virgoe 1981: p. 83).

[10] Clanchy 1979: pp. 138–47; *Paston Letters*, I, p. 46, II, pp. 551–2 (clearly family archives); for pedigrees in litigation, e.g. C.P. 40/651 rot.494, /868 roti.425–6; B.R.L. 357336; *Colls. Hist. Staffs.*, o.s., 17, pp. 143–5. A search for evidences going back a hundred years is mentioned in *Paston Letters*, I, p. 322.

[11] *Dugdale*, pp. 925–7, 932, 376–7; *Visitation Warwicks.*, pp. 176–81.

[12] Bonfield 1983: p. 2, 1986; Cooper 1976: pp. 199–201 (although it is not clear whether he is referring to gentry as well as nobility here; he certainly discusses both in the article). But note

must be serious doubts whether the gentry had already followed suit at this stage.[13] Moreover, whatever man disposed, God, in the shape of demographic imperatives, might dispose otherwise, leaving an estate settled in tail male with no heirs male to succeed.[14] As the people concerned, whether noble or gentle, must have been fully aware of these unpleasant facts of life, it behoves us to ask whether they pursued any strategies to circumvent them. If not, that might suggest that they were not as obsessed with male succession as the evidence on the face of it might lead us to believe.

Interestingly, remembrance of lineage was not always entirely accurate. Despite the formidable memory evinced in the Plea Rolls, when it came to recording genealogies for the Heralds in the sixteenth and seventeenth centuries, mistakes, some of them of considerable import, were made. While it was understandable that there should be faults in the family memory when it had to go back 200 years, those made in the sixteenth and early seventeenth centuries about ancestors of the fifteenth are more surprising. Historians working on earlier periods have shown that genealogies can be very revealing about the sense of lineage when they are in error or fail to tell the truth and this could hold equally true for the late middle ages.[15]

If the family's identity in relation to its past requires definition, we have yet to investigate fully its structure with respect to its present. It is not enough merely to examine wills and religious dispositions, valuable as these are in throwing light on the priorities of the head of the family, for, as any member of a moderately extended family knows, even quite distant relatives, or relatives with whom contacts have lapsed, can suddenly be drawn back into the family orbit in response to particular needs and circumstances. There is a whole series of ties that can, and could then, be activated periodically. Some historians, notably those of the sixteenth and seventeenth centuries, have assumed indeed that in medieval England, just as stewardship on behalf of the lineage circumscribed the individual identity of the incumbent of the land, so the extended family reduced the distinctiveness of the nuclear family.[16]

the caution of the leading authority, McFarlane (1973: p. 73) and of Milsom (1969: p. 147, quoted in Cooper 1976: p. 200 n.26), and cf. Houlbrooke 1984: p. 237.

13 McFarlane 1973: pp. 145, 273–4; Holmes 1957: ch. 2; Powell and Wallis 1968: pp. 463–5, 473; Given-Wilson 1987a: pp. 137–53; see below, pp. 248–52, for discussion of entail and the gentry.

14 McFarlane 1973: p. 145; Wright 1983: pp. 37–8; Bonfield 1983, 1986. The debate over the 'strict settlement' and the importance of demography, of only marginal relevance to this issue, may be pursued by reference to Bonfield's publications.

15 *Visitation Warwicks.*; *Visitation Worcs.* and see below p. 255 for comments on these. These are the earliest visitations of a midland county in print. For discussion of earlier pedigrees, see Duby 1977a, b.

16 Cressy 1986 (on varying notions of family); on kin, Stone 1979: pp. 69–70 and, more subtly, James 1974: esp. ch. 1. Cf. Houlbrooke 1984: pp. 19–20.

We must also return to the question of the heir's position relative to the other demands on the estate discussed in the previous chapter, as this is not only a valuable guide to the gentry's beliefs about the family but an indicator of whether these beliefs were changing. Studies of family settlements amongst the landed aristocracy from the twelfth to the nineteenth centuries reveal a remarkably consistent pattern, in which the heir's prospects take a normally unchallenged precedence, especially in the case of direct heirs male, while a variety of strategies are pursued to provide for daughters and younger sons and, before the Reformation, for the soul of the head of the family. The issue that has concerned historians is whether the heir's inheritance was given a stronger priority at some times than at others; McFarlane argued that the growth of the use and the entail put heirs in some danger between 1300 and 1500, but he subsequently modified these opinions to some extent, and it is worth examining their validity with respect to the gentry.[17]

The best starting point for our discussion is the exclusion of the female heir; if it can be shown that preservation of the family name was and remained imperative, we have a firm basis for further investigation. Unfortunately, certainty eludes us. It is clear that from *De Donis* in 1285 to Taltarum's Case in 1472 the law protected conditional gifts, including grants in tail male, and that thereafter it was possible to break an entail. But it is equally clear that the law did no more than provide a framework within which prevailing mores were the real determinants. This point is exemplified by the length of time that elapsed between Taltarum's Case and the appearance of a real threat to family settlements.[18] Of one thing there can be no doubt and that is that heads of families felt a strong need to bind the future. This is apparent in their wills, where heirs are made to promise to adhere to their fathers' wishes, and daughters' dowries are made conditional on their acceptance of a husband approved by their mother or elder brother.[19]

The pervasiveness of ambitions to tie up the estate beyond the immediate generation is best exemplified by the almost universal use of the entail at all

17 Holt 1983: pp. 211, 215–17, 1985: pp. 1–4; Painter 1961; Holmes 1957: ch. 2; Houlbrooke 1984: p. 235; Cooper 1976: pp. 200–33; Bonfield 1986; Beckett 1986: pp. 87–9; Stone and Fawtier Stone 1986: ch. 3; McFarlane 1973: pp. 61–82, 276–8 and, for modifications, pp. 61 n.1, 268–74; note also that in his original argument allowance was made for the effects of mortality in preventing the dispersal of estates (p. 79).

18 McFarlane 1973: pp. 63–4, 80; Wright 1983: p. 35; Baker ed., *Spelman*, II, pp. 205–6; Cooper 1976: p. 299. On the relationship of law and actual practice in a later period, see Stone and Fawtier Stone 1986: pp. 47–8, 51–2. An entail was broken as early as 1449 without it establishing a precedent (Payling 1987b: p. 266; Hicks 1986a: p. 31 n.50).

19 Above, p. 225 and e.g. PROB 11/11 fo.201, /20 fo.7 (stringent controls placed on the heir as well until he reaches the age of 23); *Test. Vetust.*, pp. 467–8. Also *Test. Vetust.*, p. 366 for binding a widow and PROB 11/9 fo.141v., S.B.T. D.R.3/176 and Cooper 1936, pp. 14–15 for other instances of control of heirs from beyond the grave.

levels of gentry society throughout the century. There would normally be a succession of settlements, almost invariably involving entail, each designed to deal with the successive episodes in the life of a generation within the family: the jointure on the marriage of the head, often made while he was still the heir, the jointure for the marriage of his own heir – or heiress(es) – and the settlement for his will. Each would build on the previous entails which bound the family as it existed, or was thought to be likely to exist, at that stage.[20] It is also clear that by and large posterity was ready to be bound. For example, a feoffment of John Throgmorton made in 1430 was still in force in 1474, when the last surviving feoffee granted the land back to Robert, John's grandson, so that he could reapportion the lands between himself and his mother. As all the feoffees were close associates of the family, there is little reason to doubt that new arrangements could have been made earlier on had Robert's father, who died in 1472, so wished.[21] But, however willing the family was to accept commitments to relatives or to God made by previous generations, entails could deal in a precise manner with the living family alone; descendants as yet unborn could be catered for only in general terms. How far were such settlements designed to surmount the uncertainties that might affect the lineage in the future?

In answer, it has to be said that, if the general use of entail is not in doubt, there can be no corresponding certainty as to the purpose of such arrangements. According to Susan Wright, it was normal for male collaterals to take precedence over direct female heirs amongst the Derbyshire gentry, at least where the patrimony was concerned. However, when it comes down to enumerating instances when this undoubtedly occurred, she has only four to offer, all but one from the last years of the fifteenth century or the early years of the sixteenth.[22] The Warwickshire evidence furnishes a small number of settlements on the eldest son in tail male, the earliest of these belonging to 1401, and a lease of 1415 to Emma Catesby, widow of John I, and her heirs male, as

[20] E.g. Br. Lib. Add. Ch. 24,216 (Duston, Palmer of Frankton, Hardwick etc., 1409); *Cat. Anc. Deeds*, III, A4359 (Catesby, 1427); S.B.T. D.R.10/518 (Brasebrugge, 1443); *Cal. Close Rolls 1454–61*, pp. 185–6 (Mountford, 1454); S.B.T. D.R.98/502 (Verney, 1460); S.B.T. D.R.3/530 (Brome, various deeds from 1460s, 1470s); S.B.T. D.R.37/1025 (Fulwode, 1484); and, from I.P.M.s selected across the century and from a variety of social levels within the gentry, C.138/4/50 (Ruggeley), /11/14 (Lucy), /50/85 (Ardern), C.139/53/49 (Dalby), /110/44 (Knightley), 150/33 (Mountford), C.140/20/30 (Lucy), /56/51 (Rous). This is a very small selection from a large quantity of evidence. Also, on the development of the entail and the use, Bean 1968: ch. 3; Naughton 1976: pp. 25–6; Jefferies 1979; Ramsay 1985a: pp. 73–81; below, n.49.

[21] Coughton Court, Throckmorton MS File of Deeds (deed of 1430), Box 35 (deed of 1430), Box 72/5. For links between the Throgmortons and the feoffees, see deeds in Coughton collection and e.g. *Cal. Pat. Rolls 1441–46*, pp. 237, 267–8, *1446–52*, p. 268; *W.F.F.*, 2603, 2610, 2614; *Cal. Close Rolls 1429–35*, pp. 226–7, *1435–41*, p. 346.

[22] Wright 1983: pp. 35–7, 43.

well as a greater number of arrangements that do not exclude the female heir.[23] In every case when property descended to a younger brother or his heirs, the previous owner had died without heirs.[24] This is all therefore rather inconclusive, but what is incontestable is that within our period in at least thirty-six instances the inheritance went to a female heir or heirs, almost invariably by direct descent. Unfortunately it is not possible in most of these cases to know whether there were any male collaterals, although it is certain that there were in two – Brome of Baddesley Clinton in 1517 and Metley of Wolston in 1436 – and probable, given the number of male branches in these families, that there was one at least for the Neville of Oversley lands in 1482 and for the Hore of Elmdon lands in the 1490s.[25] Four other estates were contested by heirs male in the 1490s. The claims were unsuccessful in the case of the Burdets (an estate which had been settled in tail male, all but one manor, and a settlement which was probably over-ridden by the connivance of the king), of the Hugfords and of the Aylesburys. In the fourth instance, the Porters of Ettington, the heir male was able to get the family property of Upper Ettington, while the

23 *V.C.H.*, IV, p. 259 (Hore of Wishaw, 1401); *Cal. Pat. Rolls 1401–05*, p. 2 (Greville, 1401); *H.M.C. Rutland*, IV, p. 53 (Cokayn, 1416); *W.F.F.*, 2584 (Willoughby, 1435); *W.F.F.*, 2596 (Culpepper, 1437); W.C.R.O. C.R.162/121 (Boughton, 1441); *Colls. Hist. Staffs.*, o.s., 2, p. 316 (Chetwynd, 1442); E.326/10798 (Stafford of Grafton, 1465); Northants.R.O. Fitzwilliam Coll. 1250 (Catesby, 1470); Derbys.R.O. D156M/48B,84 (Burdet, 1487 – to heirs male but remainder to heirs of the body in general), *I.P.M. Hen. VII*, III, 1157 (Brett, 1496 – a curious entail, by which the land may pass to daughters once the supply of sons is exhausted, but is entailed on heirs male thereafter); *V.C.H.*, V, p. 200 (Greville, 1499); *Records of King Edward's School*, pp. xxix–xxx (Marrowe, 1505 – a lawyer passing on to his nephew not the lands acquired during his career (these go to his daughter) but his London 'place', if he promises not to alienate it). For the lease in tail male (Combe Abbey to Catesby, of Radbourne Grange), see *Cal. Pat. Rolls 1494–1509*, pp. 141–2. For some of the entails not excluding heirs general, above, n.20. Cf. Payling 1987b: p. 113.

24 *Viz.*, Chetwynd of Grendon and Hastings (twice) (*Colls. Hist. Staffs.*, o.s., 12, pp. 265, 267; *Dugdale*, p. 53).

25 Allesley (1441: *Dugdale*, p. 99); Bagot (1407: *V.C.H.*, VI, p. 23; *Dugdale*, p. 231); Barbour (*c.* 1432: S.B.T. E.R.1/61/409,411: the status of John Barbour II, one of the heirs, is not clear; as he is treated on an equal footing with the co-heiresses, it is more likely that he was a brother or nephew than a son); Beaufitz (1487: *Dugdale*, pp. 965–7); de Bereford (*c.*1401–7: B.R.L.348026; *W.F.F.*, 2437; *V.C.H.*, IV, p. 259); Bishopestone (1444: *Dugdale*, p. 701); Botener (1436: *V.C.H.*, VI, pp. 265–6; *Dugdale*, p. 215; Shaw 1798–1801: II, p. 185); Brett (above, n.23, for ref. and evidence of collaterals); Brome (1517: *Dugdale*, p. 972); Burdet of Huncote (early fifteenth century: *Dugdale*, p. 289); Castell (1434: *Dugdale*, p. 215; *V.C.H.*, III, p. 265); Clodesdale (1428: *Dugdale*, p. 884); Clopton of Moor Hall (1444: *Dugdale*, p. 860); Cokesey (1445 and 1498: *V.C.H.*, VI, p. 118; *Dugdale*, p. 73; PROB 11/11 fo.134v.; *Cal. Pat. Rolls 1494–1509*, p. 164); Everingham/Lowe (1472: Shaw 1798–1801: II, p. 185; *Wedgwood: Biographies*, p. 307; *Cal. Close Rolls 1468–76*, p. 374; C.P.40/844 rot.462, /882 rot.327); Fillongley (*c.*1460: *V.C.H.*, IV, p. 71; *Dugdale*, p. 1,036; *Wedgwood: Biographies*, p. 325; Carpenter, M. C. 1976: app. 33 n. 37); de Flandres (1434/5: Bod. Lib. Dugdale MS 15, p. 123; Nichols 1795–1811: IV, ii, p. 643), Freville (1418–9: *Dugdale*, p. 1,135); Hardwick (1510: *V.C.H.*, VI, p. 152); Hastang (early fifteenth century: *Dugdale*, p. 313); del Hay (early fifteenth century: *Dugdale*, p. 888); Herthill of Pooley

hereditary lease of Lower Ettington went to the heir general.[26] It was also in this decade that a junior branch of the Grevilles, having inherited the Greville properties from Thomas Cokesey né Greville by entail, tried to contest the reversion of the Cokesey lands to Hugh Cokesey's right heirs, all of them claimants through the female line.[27]

It might therefore be possible to argue that it was only at the end of our period that settlement in tail male began to be a more accepted practice amongst the gentry, and that it was such a shift that caused the number of disputes in the 1490s between heirs male and heirs general. This would certainly fit with Susan Wright's evidence.[28] In one of the Warwickshire settlements of this period favouring a brother over a daughter, that of the Aylesbury lands, which was subsequently to lead to dispute, there was very handsome compensation for the daughter, considerably in excess of what she might have expected in dowry. This suggests that such a form of inheritance was not yet regarded as a normal procedure.[29] And, despite the existence of this deed executed by the previous owner of the lands, it was, as we have seen, the heir general who eventually triumphed. It may also be significant that the Year Books and other legal works of the fifteenth century are almost entirely silent on issues related to descent by tail male, which could be taken to imply that this was not a subject that came much before the courts, and that the only case where it does arise – quite coincidentally the Hugford one – dates also from the last years of the century. Indeed one discussion of various types of special tail refers to tail male as if it was just one of a number of possibilities

(1404, but lands not fully achieved until 1417: *V.C.H.*, IV, p. 20); Hore of Elmdon (*c.*1492–9: *Dugdale*, pp. 1,001–2); Lecroft (1490: *Cal. Fine Rolls 1485–1509*, p. 119; B.R.L. Wingfield Digby MS A642, 643); Malory of Newbold (1512/3: *Dugdale*, pp. 82–3; Bridges and Whalley 1791: I, p. 603); Marbroke (1438: *Dugdale*, p. 782); Metley of Wolston (1437: *Dugdale*, pp. 34–5; S.B.T. D.R.3/258); Mountford of Lapworth (early fifteenth century: *Dugdale*, p. 787); Neville of Oversley (1482: C.140/83/26; *Dugdale*, p. 856); Onley of Birdingbury (Throgmortons had land by May 1478: Coughton Court, Throckmorton MS, Jeayes 'Calendar', 179; *Dugdale*, p. 323); Spine (1412: *Dugdale*, p. 749); Sydenhale (*c.*1460–3: Baker 1822–41: I, pp. 371–2; Bod. Lib. Dugdale MS 13, p. 465); Waldeve of Alspath (last ref. to John, 1441: *Dugdale*, p. 985; K.B.9/240/105); Whitacre and Waldeve of Elmdon (by 1404 and 1406: *Dugdale*, p. 1,041; *V.C.H.*, IV, pp. 67, 257; below, p. 363).

26 K.B.27/918 Coram Rege rot.9, /939 Coram Rege rot.15d.; Br. Lib. Add. MS 34,739 fo.4; *V.C.H.*, V, pp. 79–80; C.1/461/10–16; *V.C.H.*, III, p. 199. For the Burdets, see below, pp. 00 and for the settlement in tail male, see *W.F.F.*, 2727. There is no evidence, apart from William's claim, that the Hugford estates were ever granted in tail male, and Thomas' will (1469/70: S.B.T. E.R.1/65/414) shows a clear preference for the heir general.

27 *I.P.M. Hen. VII*, II, 562, 651; *Cal. Pat. Rolls 1494–1509*, p. 192; *V.C.H.*, IV, p. 200; above, p. 250 n.25.

28 Wright 1983: pp. 43–4. Susan Wright suggests that the trend was in the other direction – in favour of female heirs – in the early sixteenth century, but she has little evidence for this. Cf. Payling 1987b; p. 114, and Houlbrooke 1984: p. 237, for similar conclusions to mine. A cursory reading of the I.P.M.s for Henry VII's reign confirms the impression that tail male was increasing at this time (e.g. *I.P.M. Hen. VII*, I, 335, 403, 677, 821, 1078).

29 S.B.T. D.R.37 Box 36 (deed of 1480).

open to landowners and certainly not the preferred form of settlement.[30] It must also be said that the disputes seem to be occasioned more by the male collaterals' belief that they had a case than by any significant change in the terms of inheritance. However, that in itself may indicate a changing climate of opinion.

One problem is that there could be varying opinions on how distant an heir of the appropriate kind might be preferred over a closer heir of the wrong sex. This is a point made by McFarlane in respect of the nobility: the more distant the heir male, the greater the chances of a closer heir general being preferred.[31] The same priorities can also be observed in the case of Nicholas Metley, who gave his nephews precedence over his daughter with regard to his less important properties only. It is also instructive that neither Metley nor John Brome of Lapworth was entirely successful in alienating a large amount of their land to God at the expense of their daughters; presumably it was a general prejudice in favour of daughters (as well of course as the ambitions of their sons-in-law) that helped preserve the lands for them.[32] Moreover, even at the end of our period, the Cokesey inheritance went by entail to the very distant heirs general; this despite the fact that it meant the dismemberment of the estate and of the large Cokesey–Greville accumulation that had made Thomas Cokesey and his father so powerful and that there was a much closer heir male available, who already had the Greville lands, ironically by tail male. Had Thomas Cokesey so wished he could by now have broken the entail and ensured that the estate retained its integrity; his failure to do so is very telling.[33] By contrast, Lawrence Stone suggests that by the eighteenth century 'a reservoir of nephews and cousins' and even more distant male relatives was being drawn on to keep the inheritance in the male line.[34]

The central question raised by the issue of settlement in tail male is the importance to the family of the preservation of the family name. If it was thought to be of overmastering importance, then even demographic accidents could be overcome by the simple process of insisting that the heir or indeed the heiress' husband took the name that went with the inheritance. From the eighteenth century this became common practice, sometimes producing those hyphenated names such as Plunkett-Ernle-Erle-Drax which feature in the 'Burlington Bertie' view of the English aristocracy.[35] Lawrence Stone con-

[30] *Reports des Cases*, 6–11; *Readings and Moots at the Inns of Court*, esp. pp. 172–4. Also *Littleton's Tenures*, Book 1, ch. 2 for a similar reticence on tail male. For the Hugford dispute in the Year Books, *Reports des Cases*, 11, Hil. 2 Hen. VII, p. 14 fo.12 and Trin. 2 Hen. VII, p. 3 fo.17, cited in Ives 1983a: p. 240 n.84.

[31] McFarlane 1973: pp. 72–3; also Holmes 1957: pp. 44–5 and Given-Wilson 1987a: pp. 142–3.

[32] Above, pp. 104, 224.

[33] Above, p. 251.

[34] Stone and Fawtier Stone 1986: pp. 70–1, 90–1.

[35] Stone and Fawtier Stone 1986: pp. 54, 80–9.

cludes, reasonably enough, that this practice had its origins in the 'demographic crisis' of the late seventeenth and early eighteenth centuries which threatened to extinguish numbers of families in the male line.[36] Since the nadir of the English population after the Black Death was reached in the fifteenth century it is worth looking for a similar response.[37]

A few examples can be found: both Thomas Littleton, born Westcote, and Thomas Cokesey, born Greville, took the name of the ancestor through whom they inherited substantial property, the maternal grandfather in the case of the former and the great-grandfather in that of the latter. Hugh Shirley's inheritance of the estates of Lord Basset of Drayton was conditional on his adoption of the name and arms of the Bassets.[38] This may in fact not be a very good example; although the estate was left to a gentry family, the demisor was a member of the nobility, and the sense of dynasty may have been rather better developed among the nobility than among the gentry, a subject to which we shall shortly return. A famous instance, the grant of the Hastings of Pembroke inheritance to William Beauchamp, younger son of Thomas earl of Warwick, on condition he take the arms and try to get the title revived, also belongs in this category. There were also the baronies, such as Ferrers of Groby or Bardolph, where the original surname was preserved in the title even after it had gone to a new owner.[39] All in all, however, neither nobility nor gentry made very strenuous efforts to keep their names alive, a point made all the more forcibly by the fact that it was the Cokeseys, one of the few families to insist on a name-change, who made and allowed to stand the entail that finally ensured both loss of name and destruction of estate.[40]

If lineage seems on the whole not to have been identified at any level of the aristocracy with a particular name, what did it mean? The one place where it was consistently recorded was in the family heraldry; it is worthy of note that, in the two examples offered immediately above, the survival of arms was reckoned to be as important as that of the family name. We have already seen plenty of evidence that arms were thought to be a significant mark of a family's position, and the heraldry that the gentry placed in their houses and religious foundations often recorded the history of the family and of its related branches with some thoroughness. Heraldry could indeed be regarded as the single most

36 Stone and Fawtier Stone 1986: p. 80.

37 Hatcher 1977: esp. pp. 26–7, and note that these figures apply particularly to landowners. Also Rosenthal 1984.

38 Note on *Test. Vetust.*, p. 365; *Dugdale*, p. 707; Wright 1983: pp. 35–6. An example from the previous century is Sir Andrew Sackville, who tried to ensure the preservation of the name through a bastard (Saul 1986: p. 26).

39 Jack 1965; McFarlane 1973: pp. 74–5.

40 A splendid counter-example comes from the shop-keeping classes, perhaps exemplifying the unusual concern with lineage seen already in the social climbers of the period: the Calle shop, home of the family of the despised Richard Calle, husband of Marjery Paston, was left in tail male, or, failing that, was to be sold if possible to a Calle (Richmond 1985: p. 34).

important source of memory of the lineage amongst the gentry. Its significance in the gentry mentality can be judged from the fact that, in the sack of the Blount manor of Elvaston, a tapestry with the Blount arms on it was, with heavy symbolism, quartered by the raiders.[41]

It is worth thinking about how exact a recollection of its history a gentry family, in comparison with the nobility, was otherwise likely to have. The acquisitions of the nobility from marriage or inheritance, if not always on the scale of the Nevilles' accession to the Montacute of Salisbury and Beauchamp of Warwick lands, were likely to be large. Even when their gains were less dramatic, as in the case of the Botellers and the Sudeley lands, increasingly at this time they were accompanied by a revived title, often identified with a particular place, that made it impossible to forget the origins of that particular access of wealth.[42] It is arguable that to the nobility of this period the real source of lineage came from the title, which is no doubt why they clung tenaciously to subordinate inherited titles, sometimes using them as courtesy titles for heirs.[43] An indication of how well-remembered the previous owners were comes from the way the crown sometimes referred to the accumulations of noble families; for example, after they had been taken into crown hands, the Warwick properties were known as 'Warwick and Spencer lands', showing that the separate identity of the Despenser inheritance that had come to Richard Beauchamp was far from forgotten.[44] With the gentry the story is somewhat different. We have seen how their estates were often built up piecemeal; even the acquisition of another estate by inheritance or marriage might add no more than one or two manors. If it brought more, it was highly improbable that the new property would approach the dimensions of a noble estate. Is it surprising that gentry families, acquiring bits and pieces over the generations, and with nothing beyond heraldry (still a very inexact science), the family memory and

[41] Above, pp. 200, 236; see e.g. *Dugdale*, pp. 296, 474–7, 564–5, 752, 791, 813, 987, 1,105; *V.C.H.*, III, p. 192, IV, p. 54; also the arms specified for Richard Willoughby's tomb (above, p. 227 n.138; *Colls. Hist. Staffs.*, n.s., 4, pp. 123–4.

[42] *G.E.C.*, XII, i, pp. 416–21. The institutions associated with the Sudeley lands and title were Winchcombe Abbey, near Sudeley itself, and Arbury Priory, near Griff in Warwickshire, and to both these Ralph Boteller showed a striking loyalty (Leland 1907–10: II, pp. 54–5; *Dugdale*, pp. 521, 523, 1,074–5; Dent 1877: pp. 119–20; Bod. Lib. Dugdale MS 13, pp. 176–7). For examples of the practice of elevating husbands to the heir's title in the fifteenth century, see *G.E.C.*, *passim*. For further discussion of this and the related issues discussed immediately below, see Carpenter 1986b: pp. 54–6.

[43] E.g. the earl of Stafford for Buckingham's heir and Lord le Despenser for Henry Beauchamp (*G.E.C.*, II, p. 389, XII, ii, p. 383; *Dugdale*, p. 414). Richard Beauchamp jousted in France bearing the arms of families absorbed much earlier, Tony and Hanslap/Mauduit (*Dugdale*, p. 407).

[44] E.g. S.C.12/36/15; *Cal. Pat. Rolls 1485–94*, pp. 6, 253, 375. Note John de Warenne's hope of preserving 'the Name, Honor, and Arms' of Warenne in precisely this way by ensuring that, in the event of there being no male heir, they would come to the royal house (Holmes 1957: pp. 41–2).

the family archive, if it were well-preserved, to commemorate the lineage, should have a somewhat truncated memory of their past? The Warwickshire and Worcestershire Visitations of the sixteenth and early seventeenth centuries reveal downright errors in the recording of fifteenth-century ancestors, often abysmal ignorance of the names of wives, even of those that brought important inheritances with them, and, in the case of the Worcestershire Visitation, made as early as the 1560s, a memory that rarely goes as far back as the fifteenth century.[45]

Problems in recording and remembering the family past would have been accentuated by the ways in which they managed the present. If there has been a single outstanding theme in this section it must be the need for adaptability amongst the gentry families. That meant taking risks, restoring and residing on estates that had been of limited importance to their previous owners, abandoning old residences, even to the point of redefining the patrimony, as for example was done by Shirleys, Throgmortons and Willoughbys. And with this willingness to change direction went a less than permanent commitment to the family religious centre of the moment, the place where previous generations were most likely to be recorded, in prayers and in heraldry, and on their tombs, for this too could be readily abandoned when it became necessary for the shape of the estate to change.[46] By contrast, the nobility often retained a continuing reverence for the religious foundations of others that had come with new lands; they too were a part of that memory of the great estate and title they had inherited and, except in the case of very minor acquisitions, it was unlikely that they would neglect or forget them. The seats of families whose estates they had absorbed and the religious foundations associated with these would as often as not be remembered, as the earls of Warwick retained a firm connection with the Despenser/Clare abbey of Tewkesbury after Richard Beauchamp had married the Despenser heiress, ensuring the continuance of the link between family and place. Gentry families, having less means and less reason to remember either their predecessors on an estate or their ancestors who had resided elsewhere, did not identify their lineage with a particular place or places as firmly as was normal with the nobility.[47] The magnates who behaved most like the gentry were those ambitious minor nobles who, in their willingness to go for everything and to adapt themselves to the consequences, took the same path of

45 E.g. *Visitation Warwicks.*, pp. 9, 29, 56, 73, 83, 125–6, 173, 309, 337, comparing with considerably fuller and more accurate genealogies in *Dugdale* to note errors and omissions, and *Visitation Worcs.*, *passim*. For some discussion of the earliest visitations, Wagner 1956: ch.11.

46 Carpenter 1986b: pp. 54–5; also Astill 1977: pp. 50–9.

47 Leland 1907–10; IV, pp. 159–61; Hicks 1980: pp. 126, 128, 142, 190, 196; Carpenter 1986b: pp. 54–5; Payne 1987; Hicks 1986c: pp. 19–20; Gransden 1982: pp. 253, 311; Mason 1984; *Rous Roll*, ed. Ross, pp. viii–xii; *Dugdale*, pp. 411–12. See also n.42, above, on Sudeley and the institutions he inherited. Similarly the monarchy (Rosenthal 1987).

self-advancement as the lesser landowners.[48] It is arguable that in this, as in their preservation of titles and in their earlier resort to tail male, the nobility at this stage had a more strongly developed sense of lineage than the gentry. This would not be wholly surprising; they had after all acquired the political experience that would foster a sense of self-importance rather earlier.[49]

In general, where the sense of lineage is concerned, it is the differences between gentry and nobility that strike more forcibly. In part this was a function of the fact that the nobility had been a political power for a good deal longer than the gentry, but it was also related to the greater margin of safety that most of the nobility possessed in dealing with demands on the estate, especially in this period. There was a large gulf, both tenurial and financial, between most of the gentry and most of the nobility. Even if noble families got into debt, it did not really matter as long as the debt was not owed to the crown. Tradesmen were unlikely to foreclose on such powerful and valued customers, nor was it normally in the interests of rulers to have their leading deputies in permanent financial difficulties, although some, like Henry VII, might be foolish enough to think so.[50]

Although the gentry too could surmount debt, they found it harder to fend off creditors, as the experience of some executors shows.[51] While sums could be raised by mortgages, even the larger estates could rapidly be attenuated by too many of these.[52] On the other hand, for all but the most meagre of the nobility, the loss of an estate or two, or its income, by mortgage, or indeed for family or religious purposes or in a dispute, was not a serious financial matter. We have seen that, given adequate care and watchfulness, the gentry could survive perfectly well, but the penalties for carelessness were generally more

[48] Hicks 1985a: pp. 135–8, 141–2, noting particularly his comparison of the family's incessant urge to minor new foundations, and lack of a 'single, imposing mausoleum' like those of the Montacutes, the Beauchamps and the Despensers; above, p. 230 n.152.

[49] A point reinforced by Benjamin Thompson's work for his Cambridge Ph.D. on wills in the fourteenth century; those of the nobility, in the specificity of endowments and religious dispositions, antedate gentry wills by up to a century. Bean's belief that the gentry led the way with the use (1968, pp. 115–22) has since been convincingly challenged, although Jefferies thinks they used entail to keep the estate together before they began to exploit the use (Astill 1977: pp. 71–2; Jefferies 1979; Palmer 1984: pp. 200–3).

[50] On noble indebtedness, see Bernard 1985: p. 174; Mertes 1988: p. 77; Bean 1958: pp. 104–8. On noble finances in general in this period, e.g. McFarlane 1973: ch. 1, iii and iv; Holmes 1957: ch. 4; Bean 1984; on the gap between nobility and gentry, Pugh 1972: pp. 96–100 (but somewhat qualified); Ross and Pugh 1953–4; Gray 1934; Given-Wilson 1987a: p. 121; above, pp. 65, 155–6, 214. A recent work has queried whether we should be as sanguine about noble finances as McFarlane and Holmes would have us be (Harris 1986: pp. 10–14; see also Pugh 1972: p. 106; and cf. Rawcliffe 1978: ch. 6). In fact, it seems implicitly to make this point about peers and creditors (Harris 1986: ch. 2). For Henry VII and the nobility, see below, pp. 594–5.

[51] Above, pp. 121, 198, 206.

[52] Notably the Peyto one (above, p. 121).

immediate and higher than they were for the nobility.[53] Consequently they, far more than their superiors, needed to be able to adapt, in order to exploit good fortune and to surmount ill fortune, and sometimes simply to make ends meet. If that meant relocating the family centre and consequently redefining its lineage, then they were prepared to do it.

Two groups among the gentry offer significant exceptions to this pattern, while helping to confirm it. The first consists of those families, like the Brasebrugges, the Doddingselles and the Lucys, that resided in the same place for generations, taking on little new land, meddling relatively little in politics and producing a string of sons to inherit the estate and the name.[54] While the latter circumstance was a stroke of good fortune, the quietism was apparently a deliberate choice and one that ensured an unadventurous family history. When the Lucys, unusually, ventured much of their land in jointure to secure the heiress of Hugford of Shropshire for Thomas I, they lost it to her second husband, Richard Archer, for several years.[55] But for the most part these families, with their unusual stability, do not conform to our picture of a typical gentry family. Nor do the other group, the parvenus, who, in lacking anything much of a past at all, set out to construct themselves one, with an exaggerated reverence for their own or others' ancestors.[56]

In one sense, however, all but the most backwoods of the gentry must be defined as 'rising men'; in politics and life-style they were all modelling

53 For the effects on the nobility of loss of part of the estate, see particularly the discussion of the consequences for the Talbots of the decline of the Blackmere revenues (Pollard 1968, ch. 9). Carelessness among the nobility seems to have been displayed less often in management of the property (see McFarlane 1973: p. 49) than in over-large jointures, although, even when these had not been given, a series of dowagers, which was just bad luck, could be as damaging (Archer 1984a, b). The Courtenays simply had a run of bad luck in the early fifteenth century: blindness, early deaths and minorities (Cherry 1979: pp. 92–7). Even the Hungerfords, assailed by all manner of political and financial disasters, managed to weather them to a surprising degree (Hicks 1986a,b; McFarlane 1973: pp. 126–8). There is little doubt that, in the absence of numbers of dowagers, the nobility had little to fear financially, except perhaps for some of the minor barons (Pugh 1972: pp. 99–100). Cf. the Langleys, more or less destroyed by a combination of misfortunes (Coss 1974b: pp. 14–19) and, in Warwickshire, e.g. the Arderns, Cokayns, Peytos and Malorys (above, ch. 4 and below, chs. 11–16; although they eventually recovered, they lost their pre-eminent place in local society for decades. For more on these contrasts, above, pp. 155–6; below, pp. 616–17. Cf., for a later period, Bonfield 1986: p. 343.

54 Carpenter 1986b: p. 55; *Dugdale*, pp. 1,056–9, 343–4, 502–5. A similar point is made by Stone and Fawtier Stone (1986: pp. 111–12) about the stability of later elite families that were of 'parish gentry' origins. Above, p. 148.

55 Above, p. 109.

56 Carpenter 1986b: p. 54; above, pp. 200, 213–14, 239–40. The Pastons are of course the classic case of a parvenu family (e.g. *Paston Letters*, I, p. 501 (John II hopes John III will have issue 'as honorable as euer was any off yowre ancestris', and the assertion of their gentility in relation to their ancestors (above, p. 76)). Also John Smyth, the lawyer, who leaves his *leases* to his lineal heirs, directing that, if the direct line ends before the leases run out, the leases are to be surrendered (PROB 11/13 fos.47v.–8).

themselves, however inadequately, on a prototype set by the greatest of the nobility. They were constantly trying to move upwards, while the foremost nobles had arrived and could concentrate on consolidating their position, rather than constantly restructuring to make some minor additions or raise their income by some small proportion. Only a really large windfall, usually from an heiress, would normally tempt the established nobility, and it was only an accession of these dimensions that would lead them to relocate the centre of their local power. Then they would take over the central residence of the new estate, complete with lineage and associated religious identity. Even then the original property and its lineage would be important enough to them to remain at the heart of their concerns, as Richard Neville showed in his simultaneous involvement in northern and midland affairs once he had fallen heir to both the Neville and the Beauchamp lands.[57] It was the effort to be like the nobility that forced the gentry in this respect to be comparatively unlike them in their attitude to lineage and estates.

Can we then define the sense of lineage of a gentry family of the fifteenth century? The answer is 'yes', if we match their flexibility in our use of the term. First, there was a memory that could go back hundreds of years to record ancestors, possibly fictional, from whom they wished to take their descent. Outstanding examples of this are the Arderns and Turchil, and the Fieldings, who claimed descent from the Hapsburgs; in 1414/5 John Fielding even went so far as to name himself 'Fielding alias Hapsburg', and Sir William, John's son, thought it worthwhile to spend time in drawing up the evidence of the family's supposed illustrious descent before going into battle at Tewkesbury, in case he did not survive (as it happens, he did not).[58] In each case there were obvious advantages in hanging on to these forebears, who gave them an inalienable superiority over almost all comers. Then there were memories that preserved claims to properties, the sort that feature in the Plea Rolls. Finally there was the family's sense of its immediate past, whose backward reach and accuracy were likely to vary in inverse proportion to the extent of its movement and of its appetite for new land.

If the sense of lineage was variable and circumscribed, what about reverence for the integrity of the estate? This and other studies leave no doubt that the patrimony, although it could be redefined from time to time, was almost invariably to be preserved for the heir, if direct and male; heiresses and collaterals might be less fortunate. The common resort to purchase to provide for younger sons and the church emphasises this point, as does the practice of settling even the less central properties on cadets in tail male with reversion to

57 Raban 1985: pp. 252–6; below, chs. 12, 13.

58 *Visitation Warwicks.*, p. 176; W.C.R.O. C.R.2017/ F.102 (inset between pp. 16 and 17), F.105/ 31; *Dugdale*, pp. 86–7.

the main line.[59] However, it was suggested by McFarlane that it was precisely in this period that the heir's prospects were put at risk by the instruments of the use and the entail, which enabled the current owner to pursue his own inclinations where alternative demands on the property were concerned. For McFarlane the salvation of the heir came at the end of the fifteenth century, in the shape of prospective in-laws who insisted on limitations on the owner's right of alienation being written into the marriage contracts.[60] Warwickshire certainly offers examples of such stipulations, the first of these dating from 1473 – Brome (1473), Shirwode (1483), an interesting example because of the relatively low social status of the family, Littleton (1488), Chetwynd (1490), Brasebrugge (1493) and Archer (1503) – but it may be legitimate to ask whether, as far as the gentry were concerned, their purpose was really the one that McFarlane suggested.[61]

As the discussion in the previous two chapters has shown, there is no evidence that direct male heirs had been in any danger from dismemberment of the estate; there was in fact an almost reverential attitude to their rights, which often cost their younger brothers dear.[62] But there was one danger from which there had been little attempt to protect the heir and that was outsize jointures for their mothers and step-mothers. These, as we have seen, were the single cause of serious loss of property to the heir. Is it significant or merely coincidental that the practice of insisting that a defined quantity of land descend to the heir followed immediately on a period when dowagers had been having a field day?[63] Once this stipulation was introduced, the heir and his wife were directly protected against the demands of any subsequent wives of the present incumbent and of any step-children that might result from a subsequent marriage. They were also indirectly protected against the consequences of existing jointures, since the father would be obliged somehow or other to square the obligations to his wife in his own marriage contract and those to his son in the latter's. Ironically the desire to limit the damage done by the jointures of the preceding generation did not prevent parents-in-law demand-

59 Above, pp. 217–21; Wright 1983; pp. 31, 46–50; Astill 1977: pp. 73, 76–7; Jefferies 1979 (maintaining the estate's integrity alleged to be the main purpose of the use); also Houlbrooke 1984: p. 235.

60 McFarlane 1973: pp. 78–82.

61 S.B.T. D.R.3/264; Northants.R.O. Temple (Stowe) Coll. Box 40/3 (an agreement between brothers but with a similar purpose); Wm. Salt Lib. H.M. Aston Coll. 20/1; *Colls. Hist. Staffs.*, o.s., 12, pp. 330–2; *Cat. Anc. Deeds*, IV, A7247; S.B.T. D.R.503 fo.79v. Also, from 1514, *Cat. Anc. Deeds*, V, A13104; E.40/13104. Susan Wright has an earlier example, from 1453 (1983: p. 31).

62 A point confirmed by Wright's findings for Derbyshire (1983: p. 31). A Langley marriage agreement of 1311, promising that three manors will descend to the heir, implies that the heir's prospects were *less* good at this date, before the growth of extensive entail, than later in the period (Coss 1974b: p. 11).

63 Above, pp. 107–13.

ing sizeable jointures for their own daughters;[64] how exactly all these conflicting demands were met is rather beyond the scope of the present enquiry, as it is a problem that barely begins to take shape before 1500, but it is one that would be well worth investigating.

Finally, what did 'family' mean in relation to the present? We have seen that, as far as subvention in this world and prayers in the next were concerned, the gentry family was very closely defined. Here the concept of the all-embracing extended family is highly inapposite. But it is apparent that family could mean different things at different times, for example in the case, cited by Astill, of a Leicestershire gentry family whose collateral branches came together to avenge the murder of one of its members.[65] A distinction needs to be made between the necessary limitations on generosity caused by the constraints of the purse, reflected in the limited sense of family when it came to endowing prayers, and the much more extended sense of family that could exist when it came to finding people on whom reliance could be placed and from whom help could be sought. Historians who have commented on the role of the kin in the creation of avenues of political and professional advancement are surely correct. An obvious instance is the career of Thomas Littleton, which owed much to the connections, as well as to the lands, of his father-in-law William Burley and of his wife's first husband, Philip Chetwynd.[66]

Furthermore, although the place of the wider kin in the medieval family should certainly not be exaggerated, the extended family could clearly have an important role in politics. This is a tricky subject, since so many of the gentry were inter-related, and J. C. Holt's warning against using such relationships as explanations of political groupings is clearly very much to the point.[67] That gentry households were more likely than those of their inferiors to contain kin beyond the nuclear family has already been observed. Making comparisons at the other end of the social scale, the financial gulf between nobility and gentry, which made for differences in the extent to which younger sons could be supported, and the tendency for heiresses to marry outside the county ensured that there would be few families with locally-resident cadet branches. Put together, these two factors meant that there were often numbers of unattached younger sons resident in the main household.[68] Whether both resident sons and such collateral branches as there were observed a consistent loyalty to the head of the family can only be determined after politics and political

64 See the agreements cited in n.61, above.

65 Cressy 1986; McFarlane 1973: p. 113; Astill 1977: pp. 102–3.

66 Below, chs. 9–16; Houlbrooke 1984: pp. 44, 46–7; Bennett 1983: chs. 8–10. For Littleton's career and family connections, see above, pp. 103, 124, 214 and Roskell 1981a: p. 190, 1983a: pp. 351–2.

67 Holt 1961a: pp. 66–9; also Davies, R. R. 1987: p. 127.

68 Above, pp. 99–101, 123 n.101, 150 n.198 and e.g. below, p. 580. For conclusions on the wider family, below, pp. 620–1.

connections have been examined.[69] To what extent kin beyond immediate collaterals, especially relatives by marriage, could be a significant source of political allies is a question the answer to which must also wait on the second section of this study.

The whole question of family and lineage where the gentry were concerned has to be put in the context of a world in which there were few certainties and the prizes went to those who were prepared to make life even more uncertain by taking risks. The weight of responsibility that could bear on a landowner is well summed up in a weary letter, written probably in the early to mid 1470s, from Robert Onley of Birdingbury and Weston Underwood to his daughter, the widow of Thomas Throgmorton. Onley assures his daughter that 'I know well that ye have gret trowbyll for your lyvelood. And for many other thyngis', and laments that he can help her less than he would like because 'I have had late both trowbyll and losse'.[70] This however is not to suggest a Hobbesian society lacking all trust and security. As we shall see, it was the ever-present dangers that forced landowners into mutual trust. And the process of settlement and entail, which was designed to bring an element of certainty to their dealings, required forethought and hence some measure of assurance that life would not be overful of upheavals. But any society based on land will be prone to dispute, even without the accumulation of possible sources of friction in all the aspects of gentry life that have been surveyed in this first section. For most of the fifteenth century there were too many professional newcomers with too little land to satisfy them. Throughout the century there was too small a margin between income and expenditure for even the wealthiest gentry families, caught as they were between the demands of the crown and the refractoriness of their tenants, to relax vigilance over their property and its income, and too little opportunity to acquire land without showing adventurousness and adaptability. And on top of all this there was, stretching across the middle of the century and beyond, a political crisis of massive proportions.

The first part of this study has shown how well most of them coped with these circumstances, whether by opting for a quiet life, which could certainly be done if the family had no ambitions, or by courting danger but skilfully guarding themselves as far as possible against the consequences, a theme that will recur when we come to examine local politics. In this context it is only

69 Below, chs. 9–16; Houlbrooke 1984: p. 53 (but cf. Houlbrooke 1984: p. 42, discussed above, p. 212). Cf. the over-pessimistic estimate of Lander 1986.

70 Coughton Court, Throckmorton MS Box 61 Folder 1/1. The letter probably refers to the dispute over Weston Underwood, Bucks., which the Throgmortons were to inherit through Margaret on Onley's death (below, pp. 525–6). Onley refers to Robert Throgmorton, Margaret's son and heir, as 'my son' but must mean his grandson. It is evident that Robert's father Thomas (died 1472) is dead (*Dugdale*, p. 749 for family details). I am most grateful to Mrs Clare McLaren Q.C. for permission to quote from the Throgmorton document.

logical that 'family' and 'lineage' should have been changeable commodities, to be defined in different ways as different needs dictated, but there can be no doubt of their central position in the mental world of the fifteenth-century gentry. As ever, at the root of both lay the land that made the family what it was and it was the land that lay at the heart of the local politics that are the subject of the second section of this study.

8

THE LOCAL OFFICERS

The local administrative officers of the crown are important to us for two principal reasons: first, the composition of the officer class tells us a lot about status and can also contribute to our evaluation of the rate of social mobility;[1] secondly it is enormously significant in the study of local power structures. Because of the devolution of power to the localities during the previous century, whoever held the local offices or could control the men appointed to those offices was potentially in a position of immense local authority.[2] This is a subject on which much more will have to be said in the context of political developments within the county.[3] For the present it suffices to perform a rapid survey of the offices that really mattered in local politics.

First and foremost among these was the shrievalty. Although the office had sadly declined since its great days of the twelfth century, and difficulties in accounting made it in many ways an unattractive post, the sheriff retained one key power. This was to administer locally all the writs sent out by the royal government and especially those of the central courts of law.[4] Since it was land that lay at the basis of all landed society and political power, the defence of that land and the rights that went with it were the fulcrum of local politics. From the late twelfth century, the official agency for this had been the king's common law. By this time a large proportion of the litigation concerning landowners, whether civil pleas in the Common Bench or in the plea side of the King's Bench, or crown prosecutions in the *Rex* side of King's Bench, was taking place at Westminster. However, no suit could proceed without the sheriff's co-operation. He it was who received and administered the writs that summoned to court the defendant, without whose presence no suit or prosecution could normally continue, called up the jurors, and if, as rarely happened, a case got as far as this, enforced the court's judgement. A non-co-

1 Above, p. 138.
2 Above, pp. 42, 44.
3 See especially below, pp. 354–8 nn.26–40, as well as comments here.
4 Cam 1930: ch. 1, 1950; Morris 1947; Jewell 1972: esp. ch. 7; Jeffs 1961a: Intro. and chs. 1–4.

operative sheriff was a disaster for a litigant, as some of the petitions to chancery, the only officially-constituted alternative to the common law, make only too clear.[5] Sheriffs could also be central figures at other times, notably in political crises, for they were the men with the power to raise the *posse comitatus*.[6] The Warwickshire shrievalty was a joint one with Leicestershire.

None of the other local officials at this time had as significant a role as the sheriff. Much of the work of the J.P.s was concerned with the minor crimes and disorder of politically insignificant peasants, and this aspect of their duties had yet to grow, as it was to do later, to the point where it acquired a political importance of its own. All the same, as the crown increasingly took over peacekeeping responsibilities at village level, these powers of arrest, imprisonment, taking security and indictment were already acquiring a political significance, even where the lower orders were concerned, for they were a matchless contrivance to harass the tenants and servants of an opponent. Moreover, when it came to dealing directly with an opponent from the gentry, the commission of the peace had a key role, and this was its almost unique powers to initiate criminal prosecutions.[7] As the Paston letters show very clearly, the commission could be suborned either to make untrue indictments or to refuse to entertain indictments for crimes that had undoubtedly occurred.[8] Although by this time cases where landowners were implicated would normally thereafter be removed by writ into the King's Bench,[9] in the initial stages the J.P.s were in a commanding position. Their powers to take security of the peace could also play a part in aggravating directly an opponent from the gentry in the conduct of a local dispute.[10]

The escheator, responsible for the discovery and collection of the king's

5 On the relationship of land and power, below, pp. 283–4. Morris 1947: pp. 63–4; *Statutes of the Realm*, I, p. 264; Blatcher 1936: Part II, ch. I, Part III, ch. 2, 1978: chs. 1–5; Hastings 1947: pp. 169–83, 197–208, 211–36; Harding 1973: pp. 98–115; Post 1980: pp. 46–8; Mills 1957; Condon, 'A Wiltshire Sheriff's Notebook'; *Select Cases in the Court of King's Bench under Edward II*, pp. lviii–lxvi. For a fuller discussion of the subject, see Carpenter, M. C. 1976; pp. 107–9 and 1980a: pp. 524–5. The presence of the defendant was not required for assizes of novel disseisin, but these could not establish an unassailable title (Palmer 1984: pp. 62,66). For petitions to chancery alleging non-cooperation by the sheriff, e.g. C./1/25/218, /11/206, /32/216. For other avenues to justice, see below pp. 350–1.

6 See refs. in n.4 and esp. Jeffs 1961a: ch. 1.

7 E.g. *Paston Letters*, I, pp. 301–2, 310–14, 323–4, 329–31; *Stonor Letters*, I, pp. 97–8 (other lower courts could be used in the same way: *Paston Letters*, I, p. 52); above, p. 42; Hanawalt 1979: pp. 50–2; Post 1983; *Proceedings Before the J.P.s*, intro. and esp. ch. 7; Putnam 1929, 1950b; Ainsley 1984; Harding 1960, 1973: pp. 86–98; *Rolls of the Warwickshire and Coventry Sessions*; Hale, *Pleas of the Crown*, pp. 92–8, 165–9; for sixteenth-century developments, see above, p. 43; below, p. 341 n.242. Prosecutions could also be initiated by private appeal or through indictment before the coroner or at the sheriff's tourn (Post 1976: pp. 21, 31–3; Cam 1950: pp. 153–63; Hunnisett 1961: p. 199; Baker 1979: pp. 23, 413–14, 429.).

8 *Paston Letters*, I, pp. 72–4, 161–2, 277–8, 559–60, II, pp. 476–7. Also refs. below, p. 354 n.27.

9 *Select Cases in the Court of King's Bench: Edward II*, pp. lviii–lxvi; below, p. 356 n.34.

10 E.g. C.244/100/7 and comments on this case (Dalby-Verney), below, pp. 495–7.

feudal revenues since the thirteenth century, was also a relatively minor figure compared with the sheriff, but unlike the J.P. his office was on the way down rather than the way up. Bean has shown how the kings' interest in these financial resources was declining; they had in any case been rendered increasingly redundant by the revolution that took place between 1215 and the mid fourteenth century, which defined the feudal incidents away while replacing them with taxation as the major source of royal revenue. When monarchs began to take a renewed interest in their feudal rights towards the end of the century, they tended to use *ad hoc* commissions and officials, so that the office failed to follow its erstwhile responsibilities into renewed prominence.[11] Nevertheless the escheator still had duties that could cause irritation if the appointee was not sufficiently amenable; if it was unlikely to be held by a man of real local stature, it was not an appointment that could be entirely ignored by local society.[12] Like the shrievalty, the escheatorship in Warwickshire for most of the period was held jointly with Leicestershire. There were also various local commissions; the more significant ones – those for example for loans, some subsidies, array, gaol delivery and special inquiries authorised by chancery – tended to be staffed by the same sort of people who sat on the commission of the peace, and often included the sheriff as well;[13] tax commissions were usually manned by very minor members of the gentry and substantial yeomen.[14]

There was one local office that had immense prestige attached to it but little local importance and that was the representation of the shire in parliament. To say that it was of minor importance to local affairs is not entirely true, as the knights of the shire were elected, effectively by acclamation, in the shire court, and to be able to control this gathering, nominally of the major landowners in the county, could be an acid test of a magnate's local influence. Nevertheless, once the man was elected he would have little impact on the rough and tumble of county affairs, beyond the presentation of the petitions of the county he represented.[15] Even so, the county would not wish to be represented to the rest of the nation by an insignificant local man. There were also M.P.s for Warwick and, after its incorporation in 1451, for Coventry.[16]

In this chapter three topics will be addressed; the status and, indirectly, the wealth of the holders of the major offices; secondly, the size of the officer class

[11] Stevenson 1947; Bean 1968: *passim*, esp. chs. 4 and 5; Ross 1974: p. 375; Chrimes 1972a: pp. 129–30, 208–11; *Prerogativa Regis*, pp. vi, x; Richardson 1941; on changes in the royal revenues, see Harriss 1975: *passim*.

[12] Below, pp. 355–6.

[13] E.g. *Cal. Pat. Rolls 1416–22*, p. 198, *1422–29*, p. 354, *1429–36*, p. 357, *1446–52*, pp. 299, 412, *1452–61*, p. 560, *1467–77*, p. 246, *1476–85*, pp. 50, 401, *1485–94*, pp. 180, 239 (*bis*), *1494–1509*, pp. 145, 194.

[14] E.g. *Cal. Fine Rolls 1405–13*, p. 91, *1413–22*, p. 28, *1422–30*, p. 220, *1430–7*, p. 106, *1461–71*, p. 112.

[15] On elections, see Edwards 1964. On petitioning, see Cam 1962a and Maddicott 1981: pp. 61–72.

[16] *Wedgwood: Register*, pp. 700–1.

and its exclusivity; and thirdly, the extent of political influence on local officers. This last theme will be dealt with only cursorily here, as it is a problem that can really only be considered properly in the context of the politics themselves. Table 5 and figure 6 contain the material on which the discussion of office and status is based.[17] As there were social and tenurial qualifications for nearly all local offices (although in the case of knights of the shire these were somewhat vague, and it is extremely unlikely that all the escheators had the statutory minimum income, set in the fourteenth century, of £20 a year), it is unsurprising to find marked differences in social levels between the offices.[18]

Table 5 shows very clearly that right through the period, allowing for the fact that at certain times there were very few knights to choose from, the offices with the real social prestige were the shrievalty and the position of knight of the shire. These were positions that knights were willing to hold even at the beginning of the century when they were still largely disdainful of the commission of the peace. Interestingly, the sheriffs were by and large more prominent men than the knights of the shire. Partly this was related to the fact that two representatives had to be found for every county at times when there was a real shortage of knights,[19] but it is apparent that men were being elected knights of the shire who would under normal circumstances have been considered too lacking in political or tenurial weight for the shrievalty; examples are Thomas Porter of Eastcote in 1430, before he became the major figure in the Warwick affinity he was to be in the 1440s, John Cotes in 1433 and Thomas Bate in 1441. Although this is not the place to consider the influence of politics on shire elections, it should be pointed out that all three were in the service of powers that were influential in Warwickshire at the time of their election, and that anyone – that is usually a magnate or the royal government – who took the trouble to become involved in an election might well want to ensure that the elected man would be biddable in parliament.[20] Sheriffs, on the

[17] The sources are as follows: for sheriffs, *Lists and Indexes*, 9, pp. 145–6; for M.P.s, *Return: 1878*, pp. 261, 262, 264, 266, 267, 270, 273, 275, 277, 280, 282, 285, 286, 288, 290 (no Warwickshire returns for these three), 293, 296, 298, 301, 304, 307, 309, 312, 314, 317, 320, 322, 325, 328, 331; *Wedgwood: Register*, pp. 699–700 (no returns for 1460–1, 1461–2, 1469, 1470–1; mostly inadequate returns for 1483–); for J.P.s, *Cal. Pat. Rolls 1399–1401*, p. 565, *1401–05*, p. 520, *1405–08*, p. 498 (no Warwickshire commissions listed in *1408–13* vol.), *1413–16*, p. 424, *1416–22*, p. 461, *1422–29*, p. 571, *1429–36*, p. 626, *1436–41*, p. 592, *1441–46*, p. 480, *1446–52*, p. 596, *1452–61*, p. 679–80, *1461–67*, p. 574, *1467–77*, p. 634, *1476–85*, p. 576, *1485–94*, pp. 503–4, *1494–1509*, p. 663; for escheators, *List of Escheators*, pp. 169–71 (a decreasing number of counties had escheators appointed under Henry VII from the 1490s (see *Cal. Fine Rolls 1485–1509* for this); what significance, if any, this had is not known; but see above, p. 265).

[18] *Statutes of the Realm*, I, pp. 266, 388, II, pp. 309, 342; Jewell 1972: pp. 33, 192; Morris 1947: p. 48; Saul 1981: p. 110.

[19] Above, pp. 85–6.

[20] For all three, see above, pp. 67, 102, 124 n.104, and below, pp. 272 n.27, 410, 425. The influence of politics on shire elections is discussed below, pp. 341–3. Although it does not invalidate the point made here about political influence and lesser status, mention should be made of Payling's

other hand, who had insufficient landed power and local status were likely to find themselves in trouble in the execution of their duties, however imposing the back-up from their patron. Nevertheless, as we shall see, particular political situations could produce relatively meagre sheriffs. The urban representatives in parliament need not detain us long; they were the local merchants or lawyers or carpet-bagging interlopers, most of them lawyers, we would expect.[21]

It was the commission of the peace that underwent the most interesting developments in this period. At the start of the century it was small in size and dominated by the nobility and professionals, whether lawyers, royal servants or the administrators of the nobility. This applies both to its Warwickshire members and to its external appointees. Consequently the native members were mostly somewhat minor figures,[22] and their appointment seems to have been owed primarily to their professional expertise or to their royal or noble masters' influence rather than to their local status. From the middle of Henry V's reign, and most particularly from the 1440s, the size of the commission began to grow, while the number of local men increased in proportion. At the same time, and especially from the end of the 1450s, the proportion of professional men (as defined above) fell, until circumstances at the end of the century caused it to rise again slightly. An aspect of this was a decline in the percentage of lawyers, or at least of people appointed for their legal expertise rather than because they were substantial landowners who happened to be lawyers; in fact the number of lawyers remained more or less constant, failing to grow with the size of the commission.[23] The obverse of all this was a marked increase, both relatively and absolutely, in the numbers of first the esquires and then the knights. What

suggestion that M.P. was often a man's first office, and that attendance at Westminster got the M.P. the attention which led to his being appointed to other offices (Payling 1987b: pp. 143–4; Saul 1981: pp. 127–8 cited in Payling 1987b: pp. 143–4, but cf. Clark and Rawcliffe 1983: p. 28). This theory works best in Warwickshire with lesser men, like Porter, or John Chetwynd and Nicholas Metley, but less well for others, notably the more eminent gentry, whose families would probably aleady be well known to the government.

21 For personnel, see *Wedgwood: Register*, pp. 700–1; McKisack 1932; Horrox 1981: pp. 158–60.

22 This description fits with Saul's account of developments in the commission by 1400 (1981: pp. 133–5).

23 Identifying these 'professionals' is obviously a difficult and somewhat subjective exercise; the rule of thumb has been to place in this category those like Henry Boteller or John Weston who are unlikely to have been appointed otherwise (and, as lawyers, who were exempt from, and may well not have met, the property qualification), and those, like Thomas Hugford or Thomas Crewe, who had enough land to qualify but were not among the most prominent of the gentry and were very closely identified with a noble patron. Problems arise in defining the position of Thomas Littleton and Richard Bingham, when both serve on the commission at a time when they were judges and substantial local landowners, that is the 1450s and 1460s for Bingham and the late 1460s onwards for Littleton (*Cal. Pat. Rolls 1441–46*, p. 343; *Feodera*, VII, p. 139; Foss 1870, p. 419). The policy has been to define each as a Warwickshire gentry appointee as long as two other royal justices were named on the commission; thus Bingham qualifies all through and Littleton until June 1478, from which date he was clearly appointed as the second justice rather than as a local landowner.

Table 5 Status of local officers

(i) Peace commissions

(a) Average numbers by period[1]

	1401–22	1423–39	1440–60	1461–77	1478–1500
Commission size	12	12	16	19	18
Native gentry	5	6	10	11	8
Native kts.	1	1	2	5	3
Native esqs.	2	5	7	5	3
Native gents.[2]	2	0	1	1	2
Professionals[3]	3	4	4	3	3

(b) Percentages by period

	1401–22	1423–39	1440–60	1461–77	1478–1500
Whole comm.	100	100	100	100	100
Native gents.	43.4	51.6	60.7	65.6	43.9
Others	56.6	48.4	39.3	34.4	56.1
Native gents.	100	100	100	100	100
Knights	15.2	16.7	16.2	43.7	35.8
Esquires	47.8	75.0	73.8	44.9	43.4
Gents./others	37.0	8.3	10.0	11.4	20.8
Professionals as % native gentry	63.0	66.7	44.8	30.4	32.9

(ii) Sheriffs[4]

	1401–22	1423–39	1440–60	1461–77	1478–1500
Total number	10	16	14	15	14
Knights	4	7	6	7	4
Esquires	4	9	8	8	10
Gents./others[5]	2	0	0	0	0
Percentages					
Knights	40.0	43.8	42.9	46.7	28.6
Esquires	40.0	56.3	57.1	53.3	71.4
Gents./others	20.0	0.0	0.0	0.0	0.0

(iii) M.P.s[6]

	1401–22	1423–39	1440–60	1461–77	1478–1500
Total number	29	22	18	6	6
Knights	11	8	4	2	3
Esquires	17	14	13	4	3
Gents./others	1	0	1	0	0
Percentages					
Knights	37.9	36.4	22.2	33.3	50.0
Esquires	58.6	63.6	72.2	66.7	50.0
Gents./others	3.4	0.0	5.6	0.0	0.0

Table 5 (*cont.*)

(iv) Escheators

	1401–22	1423–39	1440–60	1461–77	1478–1500
Total number	9	7	16	9	8
Knights	1	0	0	0	0
Esquires	6	4	11	6	5
Gents./others	2	3	4	3	3
Yeomen	0	0	1	0	0
Percentages					
Knights	11.1	0	0	0	0
Esquires	66.7	57.1	68.8	66.7	62.5
Gents./others	22.2	42.9	25.0	33.3	37.5
Yeomen	0.0	0.0	6.3	0.0	0.0

[1] All numbers in table 5 are rounded up or down to the nearest integer.
[2] In the early commissions, this includes men without title.
[3] These are 'native' appointees but they cut across thc esquire/gentleman division.
[4] Figures given for sheriffs, and for escheators, from Warwickshire only i.e. not Leicestershire appointees.
[5] This category applies to the early fifteenth century, when designation was more haphazard; the 'yeomen' category is for those for whom the title was consistently used later in the century.
[6] There are incomplete returns for some periods, especially the reign of Henry VII.

was happening was that the commission was becoming more obviously important, and attracting the attentions both of the local magnates (and of the crown when it was taking an interest in the county), and of all local landowners. Magnates and crown now thought it worth their while to get clients with political authority, rather than just a professional remit, on to it, while the gentry began to see quarter sessions as something they could not afford to ignore. The sessions were ceasing to be a mainly professional gathering for transacting the unimportant business of insignificant people and becoming an event of some political significance. As soon as the number of knights began to grow again and the knights themselves changed their attitudes to local office, it was inevitable that they would dominate the commission. This is what began to happen in the 1460s.

These developments did not occur in Warwickshire alone and no doubt the introduction of a property qualification in 1439 reflects the early stages in the office's growth in political stature throughout the country.[24] What had caused this is rather harder to see. The statute of 1461 that subordinated the sheriff's tourn to the J.P.s had an obvious effect in enhancing the social standing of the

[24] Above, p. 43 and p. 86 n.170; the pattern suggested here is very much in accord with that in Wright 1983: ch. 7, but below pp. 340–1 for some disagreement with her conclusion. *Statutes of the Realm*, II, p. 309. For these developments, cf. Virgoe 1981; pp. 75, 79–80.

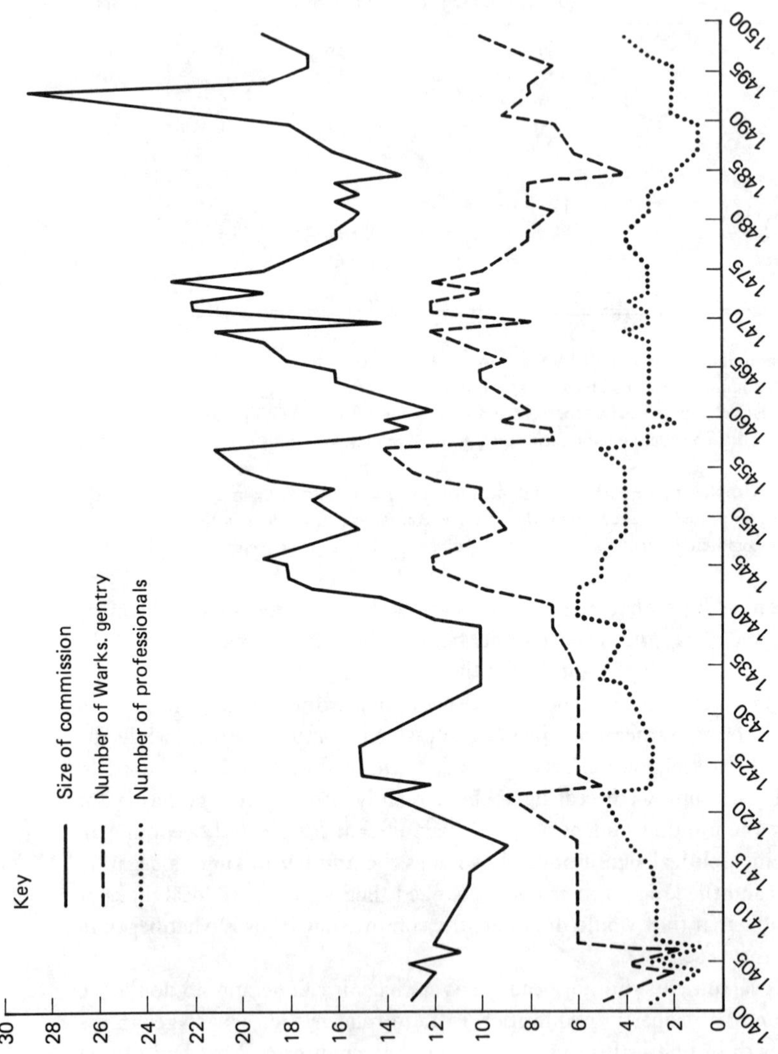

Figure 6 Justices of the peace 1401–99
(i) Overall size and composition of commission. (For years with two or more commissions, the average, normally rounded down, has been taken.)

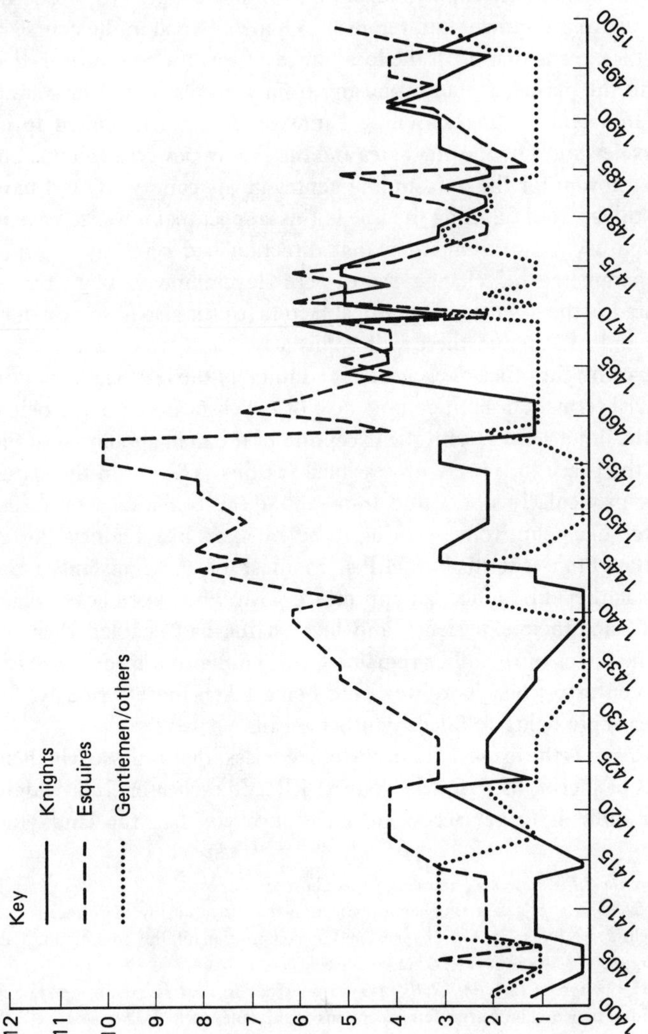

Figure 6 (ii) Gentry representation. (Years with two or more commissions have been dealt with as in figure 6 (i).)

commission, as figure 6 shows. This must presumably be attributed to the fact that more of the minor business concerning people's manorial tenants would now come before the sessions, with all the implications that could have for a lord's disciplinary powers over his tenants.[25] But the earlier rise in the status of the commission is less readily explicable and may indicate a growth, obscured from us, in the use of indictment and removal to King's Bench in the course of litigation. What is clear is that of all the local offices it was the commission that changed most in the period, metamorphosing from a professional administrative gathering to a body with real political muscle. At first, it tended to be dominated in its new form by the magnates and their more powerful clients, but then it became a forum for the outstanding gentry in the county. If, as I have argued, it was still far from fulfilling the role in this respect that it was to have in the sixteenth century, its movement in that direction had certainly begun.[26] Within these parameters of change there were developments that can be directly attributed to the influence of political factors (this is also to some extent true of sheriffs and M.P.s) and these will be discussed at a later stage.

This leaves us with the office of escheator, indubitably the least significant in social and tenurial terms. On both counts most of the escheators ranked below the holders of the other offices, with the exception of the men appointed to the commission of the peace for purely professional reasons. The fall in the status of the office is particularly noticeable from about the mid-1420s onwards. Although several, like John Rous, went on to be J.P.s, or, like Thomas Porter and Richard Boughton, sheriffs or M.P.s, in most of these instances the escheatorship was their first office, an apprentice post. They were never again appointed to it once their experience and local status had enabled them to outgrow it.[27] The status of the office remained low, failing to improve towards the end of the century, when its duties were being taken more seriously, for they were increasingly being fulfilled by other means.[28]

Our second theme is the exclusivity of the officer class: that is those who held the major offices of sheriff, M.P. for the county, J.P. and escheator. It is evident that it was not difficult to get access to office once you had the lands and

[25] *Proceedings before the J.P.s*, p. xxxvii; and comments above, p. 86.

[26] Above, pp. 85–6; below, pp. 340–1. For some indication that litigation by these means *was* growing, see below, p. 364 n.75. On changes in the composition of the commission, see *Proceedings before the J.P.s*, pp. lxxviii–lxxxiii.

[27] *List of Escheators*, pp. 170–1; *Cal. Pat. Rolls 1441–46*, p. 480; *Lists and Indexes*, 9, pp. 145–6; *Wedgwood: Register*, p. 699. There are a few exceptions to this rule, such as Thomas Bate, J.P. and M.P. before he became escheator (*Cal. Pat. Rolls 1441–46*, p. 480; *Wedgwood: Register*, pp. 699–700; *List of Escheators*, p. 170), but he was closely attached to the queen in this decade, a time when the court's influence over local appointments was growing through much of England, so this was an exceptional career as local officer (below, p. 410). These observations apply with much less force to the escheators of 1401 to *c*.1423, who were generally of a rather higher social and official level.

[28] Above, p. 265.

Table 6 The officer class

	1401–39	1440–60	1461–77	1478–1500
Total number	46	50	31	31
In previous period	–	22	24	18
Newcomers	–	28	7	13
Survive to next period	22	24	18	–
Percentages				
In previous period	–	44.0	77.4	58.0
Newcomers	–	56.0	22.6	41.9
Survive to next period	47.8	48.0	58.0	–

influence to justify appointment (see table 6). This is unsurprising, since the county elite and the rank below them, which were to some extent defined by office-holding in the survey of social mobility, were by no means impenetrable.[29] Given the earlier observations on the instability of the county elite it is not unexpected that only four families – Hugford of Emscote, Lucy, Catesby of Ashby Ledgers and Mountford of Coleshill – held a major office in Warwickshire in all the four periods into which the century has been divided for this analysis. This point adds force to the conclusion that the more eminent families that survived throughout the period tended to do so by keeping a low profile, which could mean avoiding office. We know also that it was acquiring the lands and the influence that qualified a man for office that was the real bar to social advancement.[30] That several of the newcomers to high office in this period were professional men is therefore also predictable, for they were the group best qualified to overcome these hurdles. Moreover, their own expertise or their political connections or both would be good reasons for appointing them.[31]

A pool of major officers that never fell below thirty in any one of the four periods of this analysis, while the number of gentry families of all levels was growing from about 100 to about 150, cannot be deemed exclusive. It was the growth in the size of the peace commission that was responsible above all for the increase in the number of families appointed to one of the important local

29 Above, pp. 138–44.

30 Above, pp. 97–130, 257.

31 E.g., in Period II, Thomas Greswold, Thomas Bate, Thomas Littleton, Richard Clapham and John Beaufitz, in Period III, John West and William Bristowe and, in Period IV, John Smyth, Thomas Marrowe and Edward Belknap: apps. 2 and 3. Above, pp. 137–8, 152 for professionals and social mobility.

offices. The expansion of the official class in the second period is especially marked, and so is the large number of newcomers to office. These were developments that were due first to the particularly rapid growth in the commission at this time and secondly to the political upheavals, which brought a wide variety of sometimes rather surprising people to office.[32] In the last two periods however – although really only from the mid 1470s – the officer class did shrink and the number of new recruits fall, while the number of gentry families was actually rising. Partly this was the result of the contraction of the peace commission, as the royal earls of Warwick got the county firmly under control, but under Henry VII it was also due to the diminution in the size of the county elite and to his related reluctance to trust local men. It is a remarkable fact that of the ten known new recruits to the officer class before 1500 under this king, only one, John Smyth, was from the county's native gentry, and he, as a Coventry lawyer, was hardly representative of the Warwickshire landowners as a body, while no less than seven had in some way been interpolated into the county by the king. Had we the missing parliamentary returns the number of new officers might rise, but this would not significantly affect the impression of a growing exclusivity engineered by the king.[33]

But it was only after 1485, and to a lesser extent in the 1450s, when known supporters of Warwick and York like Thomas Erdington and Thomas Ferrers were kept out of office, that men who might have wished to exercise such power were debarred from it.[34] The fact was that there was such a need for well-qualified officers, and so many Warwickshire families who were likely to be appointed to posts in other counties, that people were more likely to be trying to avoid office than to be excluded from it.[35] This is a rather different conclusion from the one reached by Payling for Nottinghamshire in the first half of the century, where he found a much more restricted and exclusive officer class. Here we seem to meet again the peculiarities of the Duchy of Lancaster counties; the restricted circle of officers is the result both of the crown's continuous reappointment of a small number of prominent men closely linked to the Duchy and of a more general policy of confining office-holding to a

32 Below, pp. 435, 481–2.

33 Above, p. 88 and below, pp. 574–92. Note also the lack of escheators under Henry VII (above, n.17).

34 Erdington, a known supporter of Warwick, had no office in Warwickshire betwen 1453 and the first Yorkist commission of the peace in December 1460 and no major office anywhere after 1446, having been sheriff and M.P. before (*Lists and Indexes*, 9, p. 145; *Cal. Pat. Rolls 1452–61*, pp. 122, 680; *Wedgwood: Register*, p. 699). The Ferrers had taken little interest in their Warwickshire lands (above, pp. 160, 176–7), but they were committed Yorkists for most of the decade and it is a fact that the family's first Warwickshire offices came with the Yorkists in December 1460, Thomas II being appointed to both the shrievalty and the commission of the peace simultaneously (*Lists and Indexes*, 9, p. 145; *Cal. Pat. Rolls 1452–61*, p. 680). For the political background to this, see app. 3 and below, pp. 454, 469, 485.

35 Cf. Nottinghamshire and Gloucestershire, according to Payling 1987b: pp. 199–200, and Saul 1981: pp. 161–3.

smallish circle, most of them associated with the Duchy. Both practices are characteristic of the tight hold kept by the crown on the Duchy areas for much of the century of which we shall see more in later chapters of this study.[36]

The fact that in Warwickshire avoidance of office was likely to be more common than exclusion from it is an important consideration when it comes to assessing the political influence to which the Warwickshire officers were subjected. This problem has been much debated both in local studies and in discussions of the Commons' role in parliament.[37] It is not difficult to show that most local officers were attached in some way or other to one or other of the major local powers, whether noble or royal.[38] It is equally easy, particularly in a study of this kind which does not have to rely solely on the records of the nobility for evidence of political allegiance, to demonstrate that the political composition of the officers, particularly the J.P.s, changes with the political complexion of the shire. This can be done especially effectively in times of upheaval like the 1440s or 1450s.[39] What is much harder is to decide what this means. Technically the choice of local officers was in the hands of the crown.[40] However, the government would have been exceedingly unwise to ignore the messages coming up from the shires about the local balance of power; these would have given a clear indication of who it was had the force behind him to put the king's commands into effect.[41] Moreover, for reasons that will become clear later on, to hold their affinities together the nobility had to be assured of the co-operation of the local officers.[42] There are two possible ways of

36 Payling 1987b: pp. 139–42 and App. V. On a rough calculation, Derbyshire, another north midland Duchy county, follows a similar pattern to Nottinghamshire (Wright 1983: pp. 97, 110: 1429–60, 16 J.P.s from 12 families, 1430–1509, sheriffs from 16 families; Warwickshire same periods: 37 J.P.s from 36 families, sheriffs from 31 families). Wright, however, finds less exclusiveness in Derbyshire than Payling in Nottinghamshire (Wright 1983: p. 110). Below, pp. 367–8, 518–20, 523–8.

37 E.g. (from a large literature) Wright 1983: pp. 93–4, 111–18; Bennett 1983: p. 37; Astill 1977: pp. 150–6; Saul 1981: ch. 4; Dunham 1955: pp. 29–36; Cherry 1979: pp. 84–6; McFarlane 1981d, 1973a; Jalland 1972; Roskell 1937: ch. 2, 1954: pp. 68–82; Edwards 1957; Richardson 1938, 1946; Rogers 1969; Williams 1925; also works cited below, p. 342 n.246.

38 Cf. officers from refs. in n.17 and app. 3; also pp. 349–50 below; the statement in Jeffs 1961a: pp. 180–2, that Richard Beauchamp and Richard Neville had little influence over the Warwickshire sheriffs is not correct (below, chs. 10, 12–13).

39 Below, chs. 11–12.

40 Jewell 1972: pp. 37, 146, 193; *Proceedings before the J.P.s*, p. lxxvii; Fortescue, *De Laudibus*, p. 55; Wilkinson 1929: pp. 34–70. For some idea of how sheriffs were actually made, see the list of possible sheriffs (C.81/1391/19), and for an exceptional and valuable insight into the influences that could lead to appointment, *Paston Letters*, II, p. 164, where John Paston I is told that 'Broun of your Inn' (the Warwickshire John Brome) is undertreasurer and Paston should approach him to be named escheator of Norfolk; similarly, *Letters of Margaret of Anjou*, p. 59. Also legislation of 1414, cited in Pronay 1974: p. 97.

41 *Paston Letters*, I, pp. 299–300, 589–90 for evidence of feed-back from the localities influencing appointment to the commission of the peace and other offices. For more on this, below pp. 347–51.

42 Below, pp. 288–9.

approaching the problem; one is to assume that the political masters of these men engineered their appointment, the other to assert that they would have been chosen regardless of influence because their local status made their appointment inevitable.

Clearly the truth has to lie somewhere between these two extremes, and it is equally evident that the explanation is likely to vary with circumstances. We may take it that the local powers who offered annuities and protection would prefer to attract men who were likely to hold office, both because their administrative responsibilities would enhance their lords' power and because, with or without office, they belonged to the group that had the greatest influence among the gentry. However, there were undoubtedly times when political circumstances simply made it impossible to appoint the obvious candidates to office; two such were the last years of Lancastrian rule, when some very odd people were named, and the Readeption and immediately after. Equally, the absolute domination of all the local offices by Richard Beauchamp's men, especially in the 1420s and 1430s, must be taken to be a politically significant fact, telling us not just that he could get the government to appoint his men, but that his power within the county was such that the king had very little option, for nearly all the members of the officer class were in some way connected with Beauchamp.[43]

Furthermore, politics can be shown to have changed the very structure of the commission of the peace, as much as the social and institutional agencies that have been referred to. If it grew in size most significantly between 1439 and the late 1450s, and again between 1461 and 1474, this was only partly the result of the factors that have already been mentioned. Once the commission had been 'politicised', intense local factionalism, as existed in these periods, invariably led to an enlarged commission, as the local powers fought to control it.[44] On the other hand, as the graph shows very clearly, strong unilateral control could cause the commission to shrink and its membership to diminish socially even after the move to a larger and socially more elevated commission was well-established. This is what happened in the 1430s, the hey-day of Richard Beauchamp, and again after 1474, when first Clarence's empire began to decline and then the earldom of Warwick devolved effectively to the crown. That is also why the professional element, having fallen in relative terms for most of the century, began to grow in the last years of the century, as Henry VII preferred to trust these men over substantial local gentry and began to run out of local appointees altogether.[45] At times of acute national crisis the impact of politics can be seen yet again, not just in the rather unexpected names that crop up among all the officers, but also in the sudden fall in the size of the peace commission resulting from the government's uncertainty about many of its

[43] For refs. for officers in these periods, above, n.17; Roskell 1954: p. 70.

[44] Below, chs. 11–13.

[45] Below, chs. 10, 13–15.

more prominent subjects. In the same context, the appointment of a politically or tenurially lightweight sheriff usually means that politics had been at work. This applies equally to Nicholas Ruggeley, pricked in 1430, when his master Richard Beauchamp was particularly anxious to consolidate his position, or to Henry Fillongley, a household man who had alarmingly few contacts in the county, chosen in 1458, when there were not many the government was prepared to trust, or to John Beaufitz, a servant of the crown, appointed in 1476, the year before Clarence's fall.[46]

It has to be concluded that it is impossible to be dogmatic about the relationship between politics and office-holding. We may take it that even those who were reluctant to assume office would probably not spurn responsibility if their lords were keen for them to be appointed. We may also take it therefore that, leaving aside the small number of prominent gentry that seem deliberately to have opted for isolationism and those with appointments in other counties,[47] failure to hold office spelled political exclusion either from the ruling local group or from an intrusive national government. But exactly how far the local powers could dictate the choice of officers regardless of the appointees' personal standing in the locality must have varied according to the power structure of each county, to the capacities of the local nobility and to the situation in which they found themselves. A wise magnate, unless under a great deal of pressure, would try to ensure that he could dominate the officers in his native counties without recourse to unsuitable candidates. Those who were tenurially too weak to implement the crown's commands or simply held in contempt by their fellow gentry would be little use to either the crown or their lord.

[46] Below, pp. 387–8, 481–2, 521; for Ruggeley's and Beaufitz's Warwickshire lands, see Carpenter, M. C. 1976: App. IIA.

[47] Of these, as we might expect in Warwickshire, there were a large number: Carpenter, M. C. 1976: pp. 45–6 and App. VA.

Part II

CHRONOLOGICAL

9

SOCIAL AND POLITICAL NETWORKS 1401–50

I

It is with social and political networks that the artificiality of the division between the structural and the chronological becomes most apparent. Social networks could well have been dealt with in the first section of this study, since they are likely to owe much to prevailing mores and social habits. They have however been placed deliberately in the part of the work that deals with more volatile aspects of the county's history because they were inseparable from political affiliations and therefore subject to the same kind of influences and responsive in the same way to changes in the political climate. Whether there were permanent networks amongst the gentry which outlived or even helped to mould particular power structures is a particularly important question, but it cannot be answered except within a chronological context; to presuppose the existence of such relationships is to evade the question all together.

The statement that social and political relationships were inseparable perhaps requires some justification. In trying to understand what ties of this kind meant to fifteenth-century landowners and therefore what governed their choice of associates, the work of sociologists and anthropologists can afford considerable help, not because it offers convenient reach-me-down rules but because it encourages the historian to stand back and consider the role of relationships of this sort within any society. The informal, non-institutional relationships found in all societies – relationships which may indeed coalesce around a formal institution, like a government department or a university – perform rather different functions at different times and within different contexts. In what has been termed a 'primitive government' they assume a very large role in both public and private life, to the point where trying to separate the public from the private is not only impossible but unreal. An obvious example here are those African societies held together largely by the sense of lineage.[1] At the other

[1] See e.g. Mair 1962; Gluckman 1965; Malinowski 1926, a classic study; for later comments on it, Gluckman 1965; also, on England in the earlier middle ages, Warren 1987: ch. 1, esp. p. 3.

extreme is the modern, 'developed' world, where public life and public institutions are so well grown and so deeply embedded at all levels of society and government that there are relatively few opportunities outside the environment of immediate families and friends for the free play of informal networks. Nevertheless, such networks remain important in the neighbourhood, in the work-place, in out-of-work activities and can still assume considerable significance in the functioning of local and national politics; and it is a truism that, did they not exist, there could be neither society nor government.[2] However, it cannot be denied that in most of the developed world choice of friends and associates, although conditioned by a multiplicity of influences, has very little to do with political advantage except in the case of professional politicians. When public and private lives do too obviously impinge upon one another, there are instant cries of 'corruption'.[3]

It is the issue of corruption that brings us to relationships of this kind in the fifteenth century, for there has sometimes been a tendency to assume that government in the later middle ages performed the same function in the same environment as government today, and therefore to label the larger role that private relationships then played within the body politic as a form of corruption. This is a problematical society to analyse because it represents a half-way house between the two extremes that have just been described. On the face of it there was a sophisticated governmental structure which raised money for the king by long-established methods and, most important for our purposes, provided a system of law and law-enforcement, running all the way from the king to the least villager or townsman. By its means, order was maintained, disputes dealt with and criminals punished. In practice, however, this legal system was only a very recent intruder into a web of private relationships that not only remained a more powerful, because more permanently present, element in people's lives, but was also absolutely essential to the running of the

[2] For the role of private relationships in the modern world, see e.g. Gellner 1977: pp. 4–6; Bourne 1986; and, a popular but perceptive study, Heald 1983. Bourne rightly points out that anthropologists make too much play with 'asymmetry' between patron and client and too little of reciprocity in these relationships (1986: p. 7) and he has some sensible things to say on the belief that the modern state precludes such relationships (1986: p. 8). Network analysis has become a fashionable occupation among anthropologists in recent years. Unfortunately, when anthropologists discover a new subject, they tend to become obsessed with taxonomy and definition; it should therefore be stressed that in this study the word 'network' is employed in the broadest possible sense, meaning any significant body of private relationships among a given group of people. Some concepts employed by anthropologists are very useful here, notably the idea of measuring the 'density' of a network by the degree to which all its members were connected with each other, and by how far they were linked by all the possible types of relationship open to them e.g., in this case, kinship, marriage, political allegiance, local office. For some of the principal recent work on networks, see Mitchell 1969, 1973; Boissevain 1974. Note most of these references are taken from Smith, R. M. 1979.

[3] Noonan 1984.

king's government.[4] Public order and private power were inseparable and this makes it essential to grasp the nature and importance of private authority in this period.

The relationship of land to power in this period has already been touched on briefly; it is now time to expound it at greater length.[5] If behind all governmental actions lies the threat of force, that force lay much nearer the surface in a world where the government's authority had not been internalised to the extent it is today, and where self-help was still a very real option. It was moreover a world where the government's coercive power was severely limited, not just by the absence of a standing army and a police force, but more significantly by the lack of modern communications that could rapidly supply force at the point where it was required. Thus whoever commanded the available manpower at the local level would, in the last resort, be the enforcer of the king's commands, the person whose presence guaranteed that the king's government could be carried on.[6] That meant the local nobility and gentry, whose lands gave them a readily-disposable army of tenants, which was why gentility could be defined by lordship over men.[7] An analysis of any of the little armies under the leadership of gentry or nobility named in the law-courts

4 For an excellent survey of historians' problems with this subject, see Harriss 1981: pp. xviii–xxiii; also McFarlane 1973: pp. 115–21; Baker ed., *Spelman*, II, pp. 84, 104, 141–2; for the *locus classicus* on the evils of 'bastard feudalism', intro. by Plummer to Fortescue, *Governance of England*. On the relationship between the public and the private in this system, in England and elsewhere, in both the middle ages and later, Carpenter 1983 and literature cited there; also Powell 1983a, b, 1984b; Wormald 1980, 1985: pp. 13, 137, 1986a; Clanchy 1983; Rawcliffe 1984; Palmer 1984, *passsim*; Du Boulay 1978; Davies, R. R. 1987: pp. 132–3; Roberts, S. 1983: pp. 5–6, 22–3; Green 1985: pp. 68–9; Whittick 1984: pp. 71–2; Hurstfield 1967. For similar points with reference to the earlier middle ages, see Reynolds 1984: pp. 20, 60–1, 220–1; for a recent interpretation stressing the role of the public, and the same sort of interaction with the private, well before the twelfth century, see Davies, W. and Fouracre eds. 1986: esp. Conclusion.

5 Above, pp. 47–8, 208, 244–5, 263.

6 On government and force, Weber, quoted in Taylor 1982: pp. 4–5, and Southall 1965: p. 120. For literature on government and force in late-medieval England, see above, n.4. Good illustrations of the power that came from locally-controlled force in the middle ages are to be found in Davies, R. R. 1978: pp. 67–70, Palmer 1982: p. 265, and, from the fifteenth century itself, *Procs. Priv. Counc.*, V, pp. 35–9, 57–9, and Storey 1966: p. 153, a superb example showing what happened when local force outweighed governmental force. Also Prestwich 1983: p. 110 and Cooper 1983b: p. 95 on the relationship of landed wealth and obligation to provide troops, Gillingham 1981: pp. 33–4, and Goodman 1981b: pp. 139–40. Note the excellent point in Davies, W. and Fouracre eds. 1986; p. 239: 'The more institutionally ambitious a state, by and large, the more systematically violent its methods'. This reliance on local power still obtained, if in varying forms, long after the fifteenth century: e.g. Fletcher 1986: *passim*, esp. pp. 372–3; Bernard 1985: pp. 39–40, 206–8; Brewer and Styles eds. 1980: *passim*; Stone and Fawtier Stone 1986: pp. 12–14; Roots 1968; also other works cited in Carpenter 1983: p. 213, n.49.

7 Above, pp. 73–4. Also Ferguson 1960: p. 117, quoting two fifteenth-century comments that equate respectively 'seignory' and 'noblesse', and lordship, 'seignory' and jurisdiction and governance (reference courtesy of John Watts).

reveals the extent to which the rank-and-file were drawn from the tenantry of the leaders.[8] An indication of the close relationship between lordship and military power is given in tenant leases of the sixteenth century, when the obligation to turn out for the lord was sometimes written into the contract, presumably because the weakening of manorial lordship had deprived the lord of automatically-rendered military services from his agricultural tenants.[9] There was thus, even in the operation of the king's government, a large measure of delegation to both official and unofficial powers and a heavy reliance on the sense of mutual solidarity and co-operation amongst landowners. The relationship of private force and neighbourly co-operation is nicely illustrated in a letter from the Stonor correspondence, in which Henry Makeney, proposing to enter a disputed manor in which Sir William Stonor also had some sort of interest, asks Stonor to send him 'a gode lad or ij that y be note bete owte ayene'.[10]

But this is only part of the story. We have seen already that the gentry's main preoccupations, as long as the dynasty lasted, were the security and extension of the family estate and, inextricably bound up with this, the preservation and enhancement of its social status. Although it was the king's law which provided the mechanisms for the maintenance of the land's integrity, not only could that law not operate without private force behind it, but the law itself was only used when private settlements had failed.[11] Normally speaking lands would be secured, litigation avoided, local equilibrium maintained by the operation not of public law but of mutual trust. The overwhelming importance of this quality in every aspect of the gentry's lives which took them outside the immediate family circle, from credit to marriage contracts and death-bed dispositions, has been continually stressed. In this world almost no private action, not even what to us would seem the most intensely personal matters of choice of spouse or partition of the estate amongst children, could be divorced from the public sphere into which a dispute about any of these decisions could bring them. Nor could they be separated from the role they played in creating and reinforcing associations whose effectiveness could prove crucial to a family's well-being, for it was on these associations that depended the family's capacity to defend its

8 E.g. K.B.9/245/33, /260/101, /265/78, /266/51, /379/5, /383/92, /387/10, /992/76.

9 Coward 1983: pp. 96–7; Goring 1975. The connection between magnate lordship over the gentry and access to military power can be seen very clearly in Warwickshire in Warwick's Calais retinue (Bod. Lib. Dugdale MS 2, pp. 277–81). Also Maddicott 1970: p. 45; Payling 1987c: pp. 183–4; *H.M.C. Rutland*, I, pp. 2–3; *Paston Letters*, I, p. 344; Sinclair 1987a: p. 160; Br. Lib. Eg. Roll 8481 (deaths recorded of tenants on campaign), for examples of tenants providing political/military support.

10 *Stonor Letters*, II, pp. 30–1; on the importance of cohesion amongst the governors to effective government, e.g. Fletcher 1986: esp. p. 144. See also *Paston Letters*, I, p. 323.

11 For a comprehensive view of the infinite complexities of the legal system and its use, see Palmer 1984: also works cited in n.4.

own while keeping out of the law-courts. If litigation became unavoidable, it was, as we shall see, the strength of friendship that could help a landowner through. All this is made very plain by the surviving correspondences, and it is in dealing with political and social relations that they really come into their own as evidence, for they enable us to look behind the mostly very formal sources to the processes that produced them. Extensive study of these collections rapidly makes it clear that this was a world where the personal connection, often made or activated at a dinner or in a tavern, was paramount; despite justified queries about the typicality of these families, particularly the Pastons, the cumulative evidence on this point is overwhelming. It reveals that the relationships between landowners, expressed usually in the bald form of lists of names on deeds or legal records or noble account rolls, could be built up by complex processes. And it demonstrates the importance of indirect connections – 'friends of friends' – whether made through a lord or another gentry family, at which we could normally only guess.[12]

Even without this rich vein of source material, it is often not difficult to see these private processes at work. A cursory reading of some of the rolls of the Common Pleas, which tended to be used by landowners for minor civil wrongs, reveals the multitude of complex private arrangements over inheritance, marriages, leases, mortgages, other bonds and a host of other matters that could go wrong. It was when this happened that they tended to end up in the public domain. A few examples from public and private records will suffice to show how vital it was to a gentry family to secure for itself a reliable network of friends and associates and also how closely private relationships and public affairs were interlinked. Purchase of estates was one possible hazard: that these were hard to come by has already been mentioned, and those that became available for purchase were more than likely to be encumbered with other claimants.[13] One way of finding a purchasable estate and then having some certainty of hanging on to it was to use friends and political associates; a vendor who moved within the same circles as the purchaser was more likely both to be persuaded to sell and to have relatives in the same network who could be discouraged from pursuing their own claims to the land. Indeed most major land sales – for example, Marston, Wolston and Wappenbury to Nicholas

[12] Below, chs.10–16; also Carpenter 1980a, 1983; above, n.4. See also Heers 1977: pp. 7–9 and Reynolds 1984: pp. 20, 27. A few examples from the correspondences: *Paston Letters*, I, pp. 19, 37, 116–8, 238–41, 243, 267–8, 350, 513, 538, 628, II, pp. 12–14, 44, 56, 67–8, 104–5, 202–3, 278–9, 390–1; *Stonor Letters*, I, pp. 97–8, 119–20, II, pp. 18–19, 76–7, 93–4, 128–9, 157; *Plumpton Correspondence*, pp. 3–4, 6, 33, 35, 46–8. These could all be replicated several times over, and more examples are given during the course of the discussion, below and in the following chapter. For indirect connections, e.g. *Paston Letters*, II, pp. 70, 98–9, 158–9, 196, 234.

[13] Above, pp. 97, 127–8.

Metley, or Compton Murdack and Kingston to the Verneys – seem to have been brought about by such means.[14]

Arrangements of this kind that owed nothing to the public sphere could nevertheless be very easily brought into it by the use of bonds, enforceable at common law, to ensure their observance.[15] For instance, in 1406 Hugh Willoughby made a bond to John Dabridgecourt not to try to recover Elvaston manor, Derbyshire, which he had just granted to the Dabridgecourts, unless an annuity payable to Hugh and his heirs was allowed to lapse.[16] Another instance is the indenture between the executors of the will of John Harewell I, all of them close members of the family, to ensure that its terms were properly carried out.[17] This was clearly an attempt to avoid the sort of complications that were discussed earlier.[18] Similarly, dealings with feoffees show the importance to landowners of preserving a secure system of private relationships and the rapidity with which the private could become public when the system broke down. The records of the court of chancery are full of cases caused by the failure of feoffees to carry out the instructions of the original feoffor or his heirs. Sometimes this was deliberate fraudulence, the loyalty of the feoffees undermined by a rival claimant, sometimes, perhaps more often, it was merely the result of confusion about the identity of the real heir.[19] In either case, success was likely to go to the party that had the closest links to the feoffees or that could bring the greater amount of pressure to bear on them.[20]

A modern parallel that may help us make some sense of this rather alien morality lies in the role played by the Mafiosi until very recently in Sicily. Here the rejection of the external public authority of the Italian government has led to a similar concentration of both public and private power in the hands of local forces. The resulting belief that real authority lies with the 'uomi di rispetto' who can compel obedience by the use of private force – the Sicilian equivalent of the medieval 'men of worship' – produces the same reliance on mutual aid rather than governmental directives for the maintenance of order and security.

14 Carpenter 1980a: pp. 522–3; above, p. 127 (where the Metley purchases are attributed to different political connections from those suggested in the article; both versions may well be correct); Smith, A. 1984: p. 60. Cf. *Paston Letters*, I, pp. 38, 410–12, II, pp. 115 (where sale and personal protection are explicitly combined), 224–5; *Stonor Letters*, II, pp. 128–9.

15 For examples of how the private could enter into the public sphere through bonds, see Powell 1983a: pp. 63–6.

16 Derbys.R.O. D518/E.4.

17 E.326/5531.

18 Above, pp. 224–5.

19 It is of course always difficult to establish precisely what is going on in these cases, but possible examples of fraud are C.1/28/537a (part of a case discussed below, p. 493), C.1/57/27, /58/175 (but these may be honest mistakes); in C.1/269/19–21 the feoffees certainly seem to be motivated by a quite understandable confusion.

20 See the Mountford case and the initial entry of Edmund as heir, allowed by the feoffee Thomas Greswold (below, p. 464).

It is of particular interest to the late-medievalist that this system, which, like that of late-medieval England, works largely by the use of latent rather than overt violence, changes its character when imported into the United States, where it meets a much more extensive and penetrating system of public order. There the Mafiosi become marginalised and their influence does indeed breed corruption, in the sense of encouraging strategies that go against prevailing norms; the violence becomes overt because it is the only way the Mafia leaders can sustain their authority, for they are no longer the men to whom unthinking obedience is due.[21] The purpose of this comparison, which should not of course be carried too far, is to suggest that societies like late-medieval England or modern Sicily, that in many ways look deceptively like our own, may have rather different conceptions of official morality and of the boundaries between the private and the public and that it behoves us to try and discover what these were and how they affected the way private relationships worked.

In the course of this discussion, I shall try to elucidate how the gentry chose their friends and associates and how networks of linked landowning families were structured. The first section of this study has made it clear that the gentry passed their lives in an intensely competitive atmosphere, where momentary inattention could bring a minor or sometimes a major disaster. Every time they dealt with their land they were putting it at risk. Thus, they had to be very well assured of the loyalty of those they involved in their transactions. In analysing local networks we are therefore asking some important questions about the nature of gentry society, about the kind of relationships in which they placed their trust when it really mattered. Their choice of associates can tell us a great deal about their sense of identity with respect to their family, their neighbours, their superiors, their locality and the world beyond their locality.

While the different elements of their lives were less rigidly separated than most people's are today, late-medieval landowners could belong to more than one type of group. There are the obvious divisions of family and neighbourhood, although, with the propensity for local marriage that has been noted, particularly amongst the middling and lesser families, these could easily overlap.[22] Then there were the links with the nobility. Perhaps it is time to abandon the term 'bastard feudalism', even in the shorthand, non-pejorative

[21] Hess 1973: *passim*, esp. remarks on pp. 11, 53, 70; Arlacchi 1983: pp. 99–117. In general, Mediterranean societies have been attractive objects of study for social scientists with an interest in patronage and networks becuase, as 'half-way houses', they tend to show in varying degrees a particularly interesting mingling of the public and the private. This also makes them of peculiar interest to the late-medieval historian. E.g. Boissevain 1974; Campbell 1964; Gellner and Waterbury eds. 1977. On the use of latent rather than overt violence, see Hess 1973: *passim*; Boissevain 1974: chs. 5 and 6; Maddern 1985: esp. chs. 3 and 4.

[22] Above, pp. 99, 101; Holt 1961a: p. 69.

sense in which it has been used since McFarlane's day,[23] but, whatever we call them, connections between nobility and gentry were an inescapable part of this society. It was the nobility, throughout the middle ages and beyond, who provided the essential connecting link between centre and locality by virtue of being the group with individually the greatest amount of force at their disposal. By the same token, and indeed as another aspect of their role as carriers of the king's authority into the shires, they were the immediate protectors of the gentry's landed interests, whether operating formally as the king's officials, or informally, either by the use of purely private influence, or by bringing such influence to bear on the legal system.[24] In exceptional circumstances, where there were no resident nobility, or a vacuum caused by, for example, confiscation or minority, a major gentry family could assume this role; a number did so in Cheshire in the late fourteenth and early fifteenth centuries, and the Vernons held a similar position in Derbyshire in the 1420s. But the subsequent history of both counties shows how natural it was for the nobility to be the local leaders, if they were available.[25] This was after all a strongly deferential and hierarchical society, the hierarchy expressed largely in terms of land ownership, and it was only natural that the nobility should take the lead in local affairs, as they were to do for centuries to come. Their directing role in the preservation of local peace is neatly summed up for us in the sermon that opened the parliament of 1433, which had been called at a time of concern about public order, when it was said that it was the duty of prelates, peers and magnates to seek peace and of knights, esquires and merchants to administer justice.[26]

The nobility for their part needed the gentry quite as much as the gentry

[23] McFarlane 1981a; Lewis 1964. Historians, myself included, have been at fault in not making clear that throughout the modern discussion of 'bastard feudalism' and, in relation to this, of 'feudalism', the words have been used merely as shorthand, a misunderstanding that prompted the remarks in Wormald 1985: pp. 7–8.

[24] On the role of the nobility (of which more in the following chapter), see Harriss 1981: pp. xvii–iii; Reynolds 1984: pp. 250–1,330–1; Given-Wilson 1987a: pp. 1, 166; Storey 1971 (but also comments in Carpenter 1983: p. 231); Wilkinson 1964: p. 336; Hoccleve, 'Regiment of Princes', p. 19. For the nobility's continuing local leadership, see e.g. Beckett 1986; below, pp. 347–51, 638, 643.

[25] Bennett 1983: pp. 22–40, 215–23; Wright 1983: pp. 66–70. Note that the drawing of the north-west into the polity under Richard II and Henry IV necessitated the emergence of noble 'brokers' (Bennett's appropriate word) between centre and locality, and that most of the Vernon power in Staffordshire dissolved on the arrival of an adult earl of Stafford/duke of Buckingham.

[26] See also the comment on the maintenance of 'justice', 'unity and concord' by Starkey, cited in Harriss 1981: p. xviii. On deference and hierarchy in the late-medieval-early-modern period, see Intro. to Fletcher and Stevenson eds. 1985: pp. 1–2; Bernard 1985: pp. 189–97; Hoccleve, 'Regiment of Princes', p. 17; Caxton, *Book of Knight of the Tower*, pp. 168–9. The sermon (*Rot. Parl.*, IV, p. 419) is quoted in Chrimes 1936: p. 97. For the circumstances of the parliament, Griffiths 1981: pp. 144–6. On land and hierarchy, see above, ch. 3; for more on the nobility and local administration, see below, pp. 347–51.

needed the nobility. We have seen that the combined landed power of the gentry easily outweighed that of the nobility.[27] That meant that to have at his disposal the potential military power of his own tenants alone was not enough, the magnate needed also that of a large number of his lesser neighbours if he was to be a political force in the areas where his lands lay. How the nobility turned lands into political power will be discussed in the next chapter; for our present purposes it is enough to note that it was their need to do so that made them ready protectors of the gentry's interests. Because the magnates needed to win the support of the gentry, the latter could best hope to rest those settlements and agreements which exposed property to dispute and litigation on firmer foundations by ensuring that they had the full force of the affinity of the local magnate behind them. This could be done either by involving its leading gentry members, or, better still, by getting the participation of the magnate himself. On the other hand, where a nobleman was too weak, untrustworthy, seldom in the region, or simply inadequate, it might be safer to rely on friends and neighbours. It cannot be stressed enough that this relationship between nobility and gentry was one of mutual co-operation and benefit, incorporating often a close personal tie. It could be expressed in as mundane a form as the gifts of fish made by William Catesby in the 1440s to his lords, the earl and countess of Shrewsbury and Lord Lovell, or, more elegantly, but probably with no greater force, in the words of Lady Sudeley to Thomas Stonor, her 'right trusty and entierly welbeloved frend'; having asked him to arrange the sealing of some deeds for her in his capacity as feoffee, she goes on to promise, 'yf ther be any thing that y may do for you in any mater in tyme comyng y wol do yt with all myn hert'.[28]

To use the sociologists' convenient if inelegant terms, we are dealing in horizontal and vertical relationships. But not all vertical relationships were between nobility and gentry, there were also those between the gentry of different social and tenurial levels and those between greater and lesser nobility. Thus rigidly distinguishing interconnections amongst the gentry from those between nobility and gentry is inapposite, especially since, as we shall see, they worked to reinforce each other. However, it is worth attempting to isolate the dominant influence – family, neighbourhood or lordship – binding together a particular network, because of what it may tell us about the political structure of the locality. There must be a qualitative distinction between a pre-existing local network which a lord takes over and one built initially around the lord. Equally, an apparent absence of local networks may be attributable to the effects of magnate influence, or may have more to do with particular local circumstances. The key question is how far the gentry were capable of managing their own affairs, of keeping the peace and offering mutual protection

[27] Above, p. 36.

[28] Carpenter, 1980a: pp. 520–31; S.C.1/46/39 (also *Stonor Letters*, I, p. 47); S.C.6/949/16.

amongst themselves, without looking automatically upwards for magnate leadership.[29] Clearly, there can be no proper answer until the course of local politics has been analysed, but equally there can be no discussion of politics until this preliminary ground has been covered.

Central to the whole issue of local networks is the definition of local identity. I have suggested in an earlier chapter that the 'county community' has been too readily assumed to be the entity that bound local landowners together.[30] There are both general and particular grounds for doubting whether the administrative unit should be given this all-encompassing role. First, it is normal for people to belong to a variety of groups, each defining itself in different ways and, in the case of the fifteenth-century gentry, the range of possible identities would increase further up the social hierarchy. The connections of some very minor landowners would probably not reach beyond their immediate environs, but a major landowner could have ties with his lesser neighbours, with more substantial neighbours over a wider geographical area, with the men of equivalent status he met at the county court and the sessions of the peace, with men of a variety of social positions from different parts of England with whom he shared allegiance to his lord, and with men from all parts of the realm he encountered at Westminster: in the law courts, the king's court or parliament. Moreover, none of these groups were mutually exclusive and any one might prove the most important at any one moment; someone who was a Warwickshire man first and foremost in one situation could see himself as primarily his lord's man in another. When sitting in the Commons as a Warwickshire representative he was in some senses both at once, with a duty to remit the desires and complaints of the county he represented and to bear in mind the wishes of the lord whose support had as often as not got him there.[31] Under certain conditions the county and the lord could almost become synonymous. Secondly, we have seen that Warwickshire itself was a rather artificial creation and that neither magnate nor gentry estates took much heed of the county boundary. It was therefore highly likely that ties fostered by geographical proximity, whether horizontal or vertical, would create groups that straddled the county boundary.

Behind attempts to define local identities lies the meaning of 'neighbourhood', which could have different meanings at different social levels. For neighbourhood to be defined primarily in terms of the county, the networks created by geographical proximity and political connection would have to coincide with the administrative framework. Whether they did so is of crucial

[29] This will be a constant theme: for interpretations stressing the horizontal, see below, n.260; also Reynolds 1984: p. 1.

[30] Above, p. 33 and refs. to literature on the county community there; also Everitt 1985a and 1985b: pp. 41–2; Williams, P. 1984: p. 137; Fletcher 1983: p. 152.

[31] Above, p. 275. The complexity and multi-layered quality of these relationships are stressed also in Reynolds 1984: pp. 3, 330–1, and Holt 1961a: p. 36.

importance to this study: since the county was the channel of public authority, any network that largely encompassed it would be enormously powerful. A lord whose estates were so distributed as to make it easy for him to build up a network of this kind around himself would be well-placed to gain control of the county and hence of the local administration. On the other hand, in counties devoid of resident nobility there might develop a set of relationships amongst the gentry that coalesced around the administrative unit without the leadership of a lord. Alternatively, without magnate leadership the county could become a vacuum, its landed residents looking outwards to noble affinities or other groupings in the neighbouring shires.[32] Whether there was or was not a county community in fifteenth-century Warwickshire is a question carrying enormous implications for the nature and location of authority in the county, but it is only one of the many types of localisms within a provincial society that needs to be examined.

For all that we need to differentiate between this society and our own in the use to which friends and associates were put, it is important, if we are to acquire some imaginative insight into the motives behind the structure of these relationships, to remember that these were nevertheless human beings, with some of the same preoccupations as ourselves, to whom the meaning of friendship may not be so dissimilar to ours. A fine exemplification of this point is found in a letter sent by Richard Harper, a fifteenth-century Staffordshire gentleman, to 'Master Baryngton'. Baryngton is about to pay a visit to London and Harper asks him to deliver a book that he has promised to another friend; then he requests that Baryngton speak up for him if he hears him (Harper) being criticised, 'as I late ded yow in your absence where ther was grete wordes spoken ayenst yow'; he warns Baryngton that the latter may be in danger of losing an office but says that he will be happy to lend his support to prevent this happening; finally he laments that Baryngton and his wife will be unable to visit the Harpers on their way to London. *Mutatis mutandis*, it is very easy to imagine a letter between friends and business associates of the present day touching on the same mixture of private and professional affairs.[33]

II

The analysis of gentry relationships is heavily reliant on deeds, although these may be supplemented with evidence of association in the receipt of royal patronage and in dealings with the law. The use of deed evidence raises considerable problems, starting with the haphazardness of their survival. There are a large number for the part of the Arden lying roughly between Solihull in

32 Cheshire is an obvious example of the former, with the king as absentee lord until the rise of the Stanleys (Bennett 1983: *passim*, esp. pp. 70–7); eastern Warwickshire follows the second pattern at times (below, pp. 299–300, 307, 313).

33 Rowney 1981: p. 395, quoting Br. Lib. Eg. Roll 2664 fo.2v.

the north and Baddesley Clinton in the south because of the survival of the Brome and Archer collections, and this must be remembered when evaluating the distinctiveness of this area.[34] Deeds for parts of the county where landowners were heavily involved in neighbouring counties have had to be sought in record offices outside Warwickshire, while evidence from legal records for areas of this kind will often be found in the judicial proceedings of other counties. Clearly, there is a limit to the number of documents that can be consulted in a study covering 100 years, but searches for evidence of Warwickshire men have been made in all the neighbouring counties, as well as in some more distant ones like Derbyshire where several Warwickshire men had lands. Because we are using an unknown proportion of the actual deeds produced, great care has to be exercised in determining the significance of a particular transaction and it is unwise to read too much into it without supporting evidence. However, at times one has no choice but to take the risk, particularly when tracing changes in local loyalties, and this applies quite as much to the political sections which follow as to the analysis of local associations.[35]

Nevertheless certain patterns give some encouragement in the use of deeds. In several cases there is a coincidence, sometimes very precise, of the arrival of a new landowner in Warwickshire, or the first appointment to a Warwickshire office of a landowner hitherto more involved in other counties, and the first appearance of that person on deeds involving significant numbers of important Warwickshire gentry. This is true, for example, of John Lord Beauchamp of Powick after his purchase of Alcester. Ralph Neville reappears on Warwickshire deeds on appointment to his first office in 1445, after a twelve-year gap in which we may assume his northern interests came first. William Catesby I is another first-time office-holder whose participation in Warwickshire deeds coincides with his appointment.[36] Cause and effect are rarely straightforward – Ralph Neville, for example, became an officer because of the connection with Beauchamp of Powick and it was the same connection that brought him more extensively into association with his neighbours[37] – but we can at least say that the chronology of deeds need not be entirely misleading.

The next problem is the uses to which the evidence contained in deeds may be put. It has already been suggested that the choice of personnel for transactions can never be regarded as in any way indiscriminate. After all, if the loyalty of even minor estate officials, tenants and lessees could not be always depended on, how much more care had to be taken in embarking on a course of

34 S.B.T. D.R.3 and D.R.37.

35 Cf. the similar use made in Cherry 1979: pp. 78–9.

36 For Beauchamp, see below, pp. 331–2; for Neville, *Cal. Pat. Rolls 1441–46*, p. 480; Coughton Court, Throckmorton MS Box 37 (deed of July 1445); for Catesby, *Wedgwood: Biographies*, pp. 163–4; *Cat. Anc. Deeds*, IV, A10387 (of which more below, p. 329).

37 Below, p. 412.

action which could put all or part of the estate at risk, especially as it might end up in the law-courts. Although minor local landowners would almost invariably be used as lesser witnesses to deeds, so that they could vouch for the validity of the document if it were called into question (a not infrequent occurrence in a land plea),[38] men of greater local weight would be more imposing witnesses and the presence of their names on the deed could deter claimants to the property. When it came to the choice of foeffees, marriage partners, fellow securities to the crown or the law-courts and executors, some guarantee of the good faith of the other participants was essential. The records of both common law and equity show all too clearly what could happen when things went wrong, when associates proved broken reeds, and, this being the case, it seems proper to take the evidence of association revealed in deeds very seriously as indicators of where the gentry believed their real friends were to be found.[39] That however does not answer the question of how such friends were made and defined. I have suggested already that the linkage between families and between groups could be complex and indirect; decisions have to be made about how to use the source material to describe and explain politics and political connections, without either neglecting the infinite complexities of gentry networks or pushing the evidence further than it will go.

There is one group of frequent participants in deeds whose role requires further discussion, and that is the lawyers, for some historians have suggested, not unreasonably, that they acted in a purely professional capacity and that their involvement therefore tells us nothing about their relationship with their clients.[40] Against this, it can be argued that this contention entails an anachronistic separation of the private from the public. There is little doubt that the lawyers retained by magnates, such as John Catesby II, Thomas Harewell and John Weston by Richard Beauchamp, earl of Warwick, were trusted servants whose relationship went far beyond the mere rendering of professional services. Even William Babington, John Cotesmore and James Strangways, prominent serjeants-at-law in receipt of Beauchamp's fee, came to his household to offer him advice.[41] For lawyers used by the gentry the question is less clear-cut. Henry Boteller, for instance, was employed by a

[38] Fortescue, *De Laudibus*, p. 77. See e.g. S.B.T. D.R.37 Box 76 (depositions of witnesses to the Archer sale of Eastcote to Thomas Porter), Box 73 (declaration of duke of York, 1455); C.1/14/24, /15/25.

[39] Above, pp. 106–8, 172–5, 284–6. However, associates could sometimes be drawn at random, notably in the possible use of people who happened to be in the King's Bench as pledges to pay fines (Powell 1979: pp. 227–31): the context and personnel of the transaction have to be taken carefully into account.

[40] The problem is discussed in some of its aspects in Ramsay 1985a: pp. 50–5 and 1985b: pp. 106–10 and Rawcliffe 1979: pp. 93–4.

[41] App. 3; Br. Lib. Eg. Roll 8773; Longleat, MS of the Marquess of Bath Misc. IX fos. 95v., 111; Sinclair 1987a: pp. 273–4. Note also Cotesmore's relationship to Richard Quatermayns, a Warwick client (Driver 1986: pp. 89–90; above, pp. 166–7).

number of Warwickshire men in the 1470s and 1480s, to some of whom he may have felt little beyond a professional obligation, and this may have been particularly true of those for whom his main function was to represent them, along with a large number of others, in the central law-courts.[42] But even in these instances, the case for professionalisation can be overstated. As Palmer's study of the Whilton dispute shows, any lawyer worth his salt had to be trusted to keep a constant eye on his client's affairs in the courts, and if he could be suborned by a rival he could do untold harm to his employer's interests. The Paston correspondence, where, if anywhere, we can see the fifteenth-century lawyer at work, lends weight to the view that no lawyer or legal agent could be anything other than a close associate of his clients if he was to be trusted to do his job properly. Several examples from Warwickshire show the existence of a relationship of trust between an attorney and his clients; for instance, in 1416 William Mountford was represented in his suit against William Boteller of Sudeley by Thomas Greswold, who by the following year was one of the feoffees to all Mountford's lands.[43]

It should be remembered also that a lawyer was usually himself a landowner and his practice often consisted largely of neighbouring families, with whom it would be difficult to have a purely professional relationship.[44] This would be all the more true if his clients were drawn mostly from the following of the lord whom he himself served.[45] Moreover, any group of people that is obliged to make frequent use of lawyers is likely to have a personal relationship with its legal representatives, whether these are the family solicitors of landed families or the directly-employed legal staff of great business corporations. Looking at the problem from the lawyer's point of view, there was every reason to cultivate the friendship of his clients, since the law was the great avenue of advancement and the support of his neighbours and his lord would greatly improve his prospects and security. If lawyers often served more than one lord, they were not alone in this and it need not present any serious barrier to finding political significance in their relationship to at least some of their patrons. Obviously a lawyer might be used as witness or feoffee by numbers of neighbours simply because he was a local man of worth who had the added advantage of knowing his way around the law-courts – as, for example, appears to have been the case with John Campion of Gaydon in southern Warwickshire – but that in itself is a

[42] A good indication of Boteller's clientele comes from a series of suits for debt, which appear to be essentially against defaulting clients (C.P.40/852 rot.42, /868 rot.230, /874 rot.274d., /878 roti.223d.,466, /882 rot.7d.; above, p. 125).

[43] Palmer 1984: esp. pp. 52, 131–2; *Paston Letters*, I, pp. 155, 169, II, pp. 245, 507–8, and the close relationship between Fastolf and his legal adviser, John Paston I (e.g. II, pp. 109–10, 112–13, 118–19, 128–9, 131, 133–6); JUST 1/1524 m.31; B.R.L. Wingfield Digby MS A473; Ives 1983a: ch. 6, esp. pp. 138–40, 143–5; *Colls. Hist. Staffs.*, 1934, II, p. 86 and *Plumpton Correspondence*, pp. 2–3, 5, 6–10, 22–4.

[44] Ives 1983a: ch. 6, esp. pp. 116–19; also the discussion of Greswold's circle, below, p. 310.

[45] Ives 1983a: pp. 100–3.

mark of trust and an important element in the constitution of a local network.[46] Not infrequently a lawyer achieved such a position because of his links to more important local landowners: an example is Hugh Dalby, also from south Warwickshire.[47] In conclusion, while mere representation of a client in court has not been taken as indicative of a significant relationship without supporting evidence, where deed evidence is concerned lawyers have been treated like any other participants.[48]

III

Since there were major changes in noble power structures after 1439, resulting from the Beauchamp minority, and we need to assess their effects on local networks, the discussion has been divided into two parts, with a break at 1439. The initial step entails simply tracing the identifiable groupings, noting their location and composition, before proceeding to a closer examination of their structure (see figure 7). For the moment the analysis will focus on horizontal links, that is, those among the gentry themselves, before moving on to vertical links with the nobility, even though this is an artificial distinction and many problems will only have been brought fully into focus when both dimensions have been explored.[49] Although it is not always certain that witnesses to deeds were actually present at the transaction,[50] and feoffees need certainly not have been, it is difficult to see that the necessary degree of trust could have been established without frequent personal contact amongst people who acted in association with one another. The realities of local topography must therefore loom large in the discussion, although it has not been possible to establish whether the difficulties of travelling in winter, noted by Fletcher in his study of seventeenth-century Sussex, produced any strong bias towards deeds executed in the summer months.[51] Clearly the quality of local communications could be a major determinant of the meaning of neighbourhood: where they were good, a neighbour might reside some distance away, where they were less good, neighbours could be very local indeed. Equally, enclosure of a locality by woodland or difficult terrain could strengthen the bonds of neighbours within that area, cut off as they were from ready access to the outside world, while in more open country relationships might be less concentrated and range across a wider geographical area.

46 Carpenter 1980a, pp. 517–18; *Stratford Register*, p. 40; below, pp. 302–3.

47 Br. Lib. Add. Roll 16,556; app. 3; below, p. 303, 306.

48 For tracing political allegiances, lawyers' associates, particularly those revealed by deeds, have been treated more circumspectly.

49 For two general discussions of the problem, each in its own way excessively pessimistic, see Houlbrooke 1984: p. 45; Lander 1986. See also Bennett's useful survey of such relationships in the north-west (Bennett 1975: pp. 64–70).

50 Cheney ed. 1970: p. ix.

51 Above, p. 29.

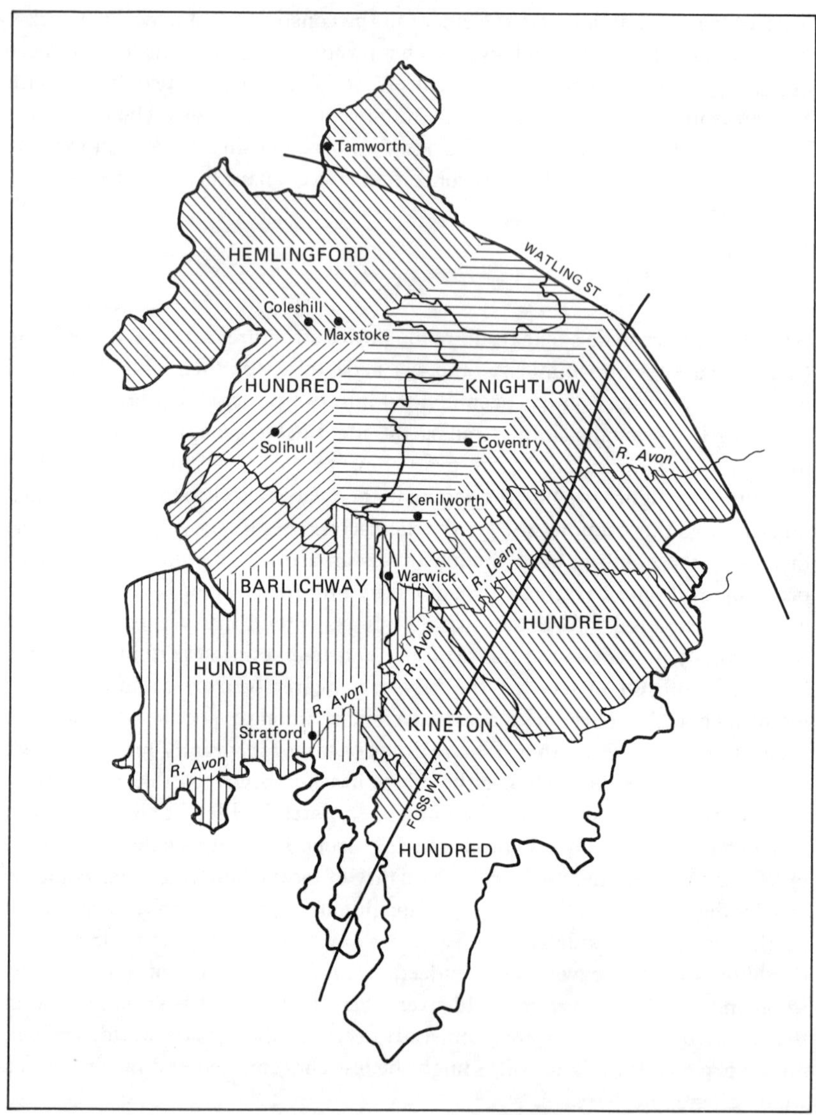

Figure 7 Location of networks *c.* 1401–50

The dictates of geography become immediately apparent if we start with the best-documented group, that in the heart of the Arden, centred on Tanworth, Lapworth and Solihull. One has to read only a few deeds to grasp the existence of a readily identifiable and strongly localised network, and further investigation merely confirms this pattern, a fact which suggests it is not just the abundance of evidence which produces the impression of local solidarity. The main figures here were of middling rank: Archer, Fulwode, Gower, Grene, Greswold, Marbroke, Sydenhale, Waryng, and also Aylesbury and Hore of Elmdon, who, as owners of estates in two parts of the county, turn up in other local groups.[52] Brome of Baddesley Clinton and Porter of Eastcote arrived in the late 1420s, when they acquired land here, and there were also a number of minor gentry and greater yeomen, such as the Benfords, the Birches of Solihull and Longdon, the Parkers of Tanworth and the Hores of Solihull. The only really eminent family in this area were the Catesbys, who, although involved to a limited degree with this network, had more important and pressing interests elsewhere.[53] Although the connections of some of these families stretched as far as Kenilworth or Alspath, which were also in the Arden but well to the east, the geographical limitations of the group are obvious and easily explained. Its members resided in an area that was still quite heavily wooded with somewhat marshy valley bottoms to the north and east. A local market at Solihull, one of the more populous places in the county (where, incidentally, several deeds are dated), and the existence of other natural meeting-places at Lapworth and Tanworth, where many of the area's more important figures resided, sufficed to discourage trips north to Coleshill or south to the market town of Henley in Arden.[54] The only north Warwickshire family that can be convincingly linked to this group are the Middlemores, and it is significant that, with their estates at Edgbaston to the north and Studley to the south, they were obliged to pass through or close to this area. The less important families here, with more completely localised interests, were more likely to have connections with similar families in east Worcestershire, particularly around Yardley, just over the border, than with Warwickshire landowners from further afield.[55]

Moving north, to the area bounded by Coleshill, Birmingham, Tamworth, Newton Regis and Atherstone, we encounter a rather different type of local identity. Although this area was also in the Arden and parts of it were badly drained, there was a network of roads extending from Coleshill, as well as Watling Street in the north-east of the region and major crossroads converging on Birmingham and Tamworth. Eastwards, towards the Leicestershire border, the forest itself began to thin out.[56] Because the region was less confined geographically, the associations of its resident landowners ranged over a

[52] Below, pp. 300, 304.

[53] E.g. S.B.T. D.R.37/828, 837, 846, 856, 872, 875, 878–9, 884, 888, 891, 901, 904, 906, 915, and selected deeds in Boxes 36, 37, 42 and 51; *Cat. Anc. Deeds*, I, C212, II, C1980, III, A4359, 4371, 4579, IV, A7556; E.42/124; S.B.T. D.R.3/219, 226; Bod. Lib. Dugdale MS 15, p. 67; *Cal. Fine Rolls 1422–30*, p. 49; K.B.27/636 Coram Rege rot.66, /637 Coram Rege rot.14. For status throughout this chapter, see above, ch. 3; for lands, Carpenter, M. C. 1976: App. II, *Dugdale* and *V.C.H.*, both *passim*. For the priorities of the Catesbys, see above, pp. 117–18.

[54] Above, pp. 20, 28–30; *V.C.H.*, III, p. 208, VII, p. 77; Rowlands 1987: p. 40.

[55] K.B.27/637 Coram Rege rot.14; S.B.T. D.R.3/226, D.R.37/879; *Calendars of Proceedings in Chancery*, I, pp. lxxii–vi; for Worcs. connections, above, n.53.

[56] Above, pp. 20, 30.

considerably wider area, often far beyond the county boundaries. However, this was not the only reason for the lack of parochialism in this part of the county. The region was dominated by very substantial landowners – Ardern, Bermingham, Brasebrugge, Erdington, Freville (succeeded by Aston, Ferrers and Willoughby), Mountford, Cokayn, Shirley and Culpepper – with relatively few men of middle rank – Lisle, Middlemore, Ruggeley, Mollesley, Stokes, Waver of Marston Waver, a little to the south (a family which ceased to exist soon after 1433)[57] and Hore of Wishaw, whose main interests were in Cambridgeshire[58] – and numbers of yeomen, few of whom had any pretensions to gentility. The latter tend to turn up as minor local witnesses on great men's deeds but do not have the close relationship with them that is evident between the major and minor figures in the Tanworth area. Most of the pre-eminent landowners were, as was characteristic of their type, possessed of properties in several parts of Warwickshire and in several other counties, and, this being one of the poorer parts of the county, there was not a great deal to keep many of them here. Indeed, those in the north-east corner of the county – Willoughby, Aston, Ferrers, Shirley, Culpepper, Chetwynd of Grendon – were at this time much more involved with their property and connections in other counties, having few known contacts with their Warwickshire neighbours. Even several of the middling families had lands in Staffordshire.[59]

The result was that in this part of Warwickshire, unlike the region to the south, there was a lack of families with strongly localised interests around whom a tightly-knit local group could coalesce. All the same, it is clear that there was a group of families, consisting primarily of those resident west of the Tame, that were in frequent contact with each other, although, as will become apparent later, this was by no means an exclusively local network. Coleshill's function as a major local centre for the north and north-west would have provided these families with a ready-made meeting point, even though the Mountfords, the lords of Coleshill, living their lives on a broader canvas, were associated only intermittently with them. The main local figures concerned were Bermingham, Brasebrugge, Erdington, Ardern, Lisle, Ruggeley (initially as Warwick's official at Sutton Chace and from 1422 as the owner of Dunton), Stanhope (owners of Dunton to 1422) and, from about 1419, Mollesley.[60]

57 *Dugdale*, p. 977. The last reference to Waver of Marston Waver dates to 1433 (B.R.L. 377534).

58 Jeffs 1961a: pp. 298–9.

59 Willoughby: Notts.; Aston: Staffs.; Shirley: Derbys., Leics.; Culpepper: Kent, Northants., Rut.; Chetwynd: Staffs. For all these, Carpenter, M. C. 1976: App. 11C. For the local economy and its effect on the number of resident gentry, above, pp. 20, 78.

60 E.g. *Cal. Close Rolls 1413–19*, p. 97; *W.F.F.*, 2487; B.R.L. 112349; B.R.L. Wingfield Digby MS A491, 496; S.B.T. D.R.18/A21,22, Stratford Corp. Recs. I/442; JUST 1/1514 m.48; E.326/6831; C.139/153/21; Bod. Lib. Dugdale MS 13, p. 325, 17, p. 38; Nott. Univ. Lib. Middleton MS Mi D 4139; S.B.T. D.R.37 Box 36 (Deed of 1409); Sims ed., *Walsall Deeds*, p. 16. For Coleshill, see Watkins 1983–4.

The appearance in this group of Baldwin Freville II in his brief period as an adult shows that he too should be considered a part of it.[61] Further east there were Repington from about 1421, Stokes, possibly Malory of Bramcote[62] and some more tenuous links with Cokayn and Shirley that probably owed more to magnate connections than to any sense of local solidarity.[63]

Moving down the Leicestershire border, we enter more open country, where there were no geographical barriers to the south, or eastwards into Leicestershire itself. Westwards, however, lay the parts of the Arden around Coventry, an area of late settlement dominated by ecclesiastical lands and by the Stoneleigh and Coventry liberties, where there were almost no nobility and few gentry.[64] Almost throughout this whole north-eastern area there is little evidence of extensive local inter-connections. The exception is Alspath, which lay to the west of Coventry and rather resembled Tanworth, in being a large Arden village, with numbers of sub-manors and consequently of minor gentry and substantial yeomen.[65] Even there the more important landowners, like John Chetwynd, tended to look elsewhere when they wanted to do business with more eminent families.[66] Between Coventry and the north-eastern border with Leicestershire, there were few gentry of any substance. Of those there were, Richard Hastings, the most important, was almost entirely absorbed by affairs in Leicestershire,[67] Henry Fillongley had almost no local ties at all except for those with his various noble employers,[68] and the Purfreys were not only heavily involved in Leicestershire but could easily find Warwickshire associates elsewhere. Within a radius of ten miles of them resided a number of gentry families whom the open terrain and the proximity of Watling Street

61 Nott. Univ. Lib. Middleton MS Mi D 4004.

62 Bod. Lib. Dugdale MS 15, pp. 69, 122, 17, p. 38; E.326/8627. Just one deed links Malory with this group (S.B.T. D.R. 37 Box 36 – deed of 1409).

63 E.g. Br. Lib. Add. MS 28,564 fo.59; W.C.R.O. C.R.136/C790; *Cat. Anc. Deeds*, VI, C5340, V, A11333; Bod. Lib. Dugdale MS 15, p. 69, 17, p. 38; B.R.L. Wingfield Digby MS A496; Ussher 1881: pp. 198–9. On almost all these deeds the greater gentry represent a particular magnate interest in north Warwickshire: see the discussion of these below, pp. 313–17.

64 Above, pp. 19, 21–2, 30, 54.

65 E.g. S.B.T. E.R.1/61/291; Wm. Salt Lib. H.M. Chetwynd Coll. Bundle 4 (undated deed of early fifteenth century); E.326/5491, 5514, 6508, 8952. For the characteristics of topography, manorial structure and landowning at Alspath, see *V.C.H.*, IV, pp. 150–2. Note that some of the manorial history here is not quite correct (see below, pp. 498–9).

66 E.g. *Cal. Close Rolls 1429–35*, p. 361, *1435–41*, p. 268; *Colls. Hist. Staffs.*, o.s., 12, p. 314.

67 *Cal. Pat. Rolls 1436–41*, p. 506; *Cal. Fine Rolls 1422–30*, p. 203; *H.M.C. Hastings*, I, pp. 7, 83–4; Leics. R.O. DE 2242/3/7, DE 1625/3 (in this last deed a Warwickshire man, Richard Hubaud, features, but only by virtue of his Leicestershire lands); Farnham, *Leicestershire Village Notes*, VI, p. 275.

68 *Cal. Pat. Rolls 1422–29*, p. 486, *1429–36*, pp. 295, 506, *1436–41*, p. 435, *1441–46*, p. 241; *H.M.C. Hastings*, I, pp. 7, 83–4; app. 3.

brought within easy reach.[69] Ease of communication meant also that Simon Malory, the brother of John of Newbold Revel, who lived at Chilvers Coton, which lay even further to the north than the Purfrey residence of Shelford in Burton Hastings, could choose to take his associates either from the north Warwickshire group or from his brother's connections well to the south.[70] It would indeed have been perfectly possible for a network running right down Watling Street, all the way along the Leicestershire border, to develop, and we shall see that early in the century this is precisely what happened, but, as it turned out, there was no force to hold it together over a longer period.[71]

By contrast, further south there was the largest network in the county. This covered an area from Monks Kirby and the southern suburbs of Coventry, east and south of the Avon, as far south as a diagonal line drawn roughly across the county from Lower Shuckburgh through Gaydon and Lower Ettington to the Gloucestershire border. The geographical spread of this grouping is explained by the fact that it ran through open rolling country and that it was bisected by the Fosse Way, which made for ready communication across a large area. Its density is attributable to the numbers of middling and greater gentry resident in the area and the fact that, in most cases, they gave their Warwickshire estates at least as much weight as their lands elsewhere. The lesser families were concentrated in the area between the Avon and the Leam, the greater ones due south of Warwick.[72]

There were in fact two differentiable groups here, but they were too extensively inter-connected to be considered entirely separate entities. The first, while extending as far north as Monks Kirby and Coventry, consisted largely of those middling families of the Avon-Leam region: Botener, Donyngton, Catesby of Hopsford, Stafford of Baginton (successors to the more eminent Bagots), Hore of Stoneythorpe (also in the Tanworth group because of their land at Elmdon), Waver of Cestersover, Stokes (the north Warwickshire family, who also had an estate at Stoke near Coventry), Cotes, Metley, de Merrington, Weston, Sutton – then Allesley and Boughton, the Suttons' successors at Little Lawford – Onley of Birdingbury, Leventhorpe (sold out 1433), Bellers (these last two being primarily Leicestershire families) and John Malory of Newbold Revel, one of the most important of the middling gentry of Warwickshire. The Knightleys, a more substantial family, can also be identified with this group,

69 Br. Lib. Add. Ms 28,564 fo. 59; C.139/110/44; WARD 2/1/3/2; JUST 1/1524 m.28; *Cal. Pat. Rolls 1413–16*, p. 391; *Cat. Anc. Deeds*, II, A2753, IV, A8180; Farnham, *Leicestershire Village Notes*, VI, p. 275; Bod. Lib. Dugdale MS 13, p. 343; Northants.R.O. Knightley Charters 150.

70 B.R.L. Wingfield Digby MS A485, 491; W.C.R.O. C.R.162/123; E.326/10762. For the relationship to John Malory, see *Cat. Anc. Deeds*, IV, A8103. The clerics named in the deed are nearly all from Malory of Newbold manors, so the deed must belong to this family; for Malory lands, K.B.27/900 Rex rot.5.

71 Below, p. 314.

72 Above, p. 54.

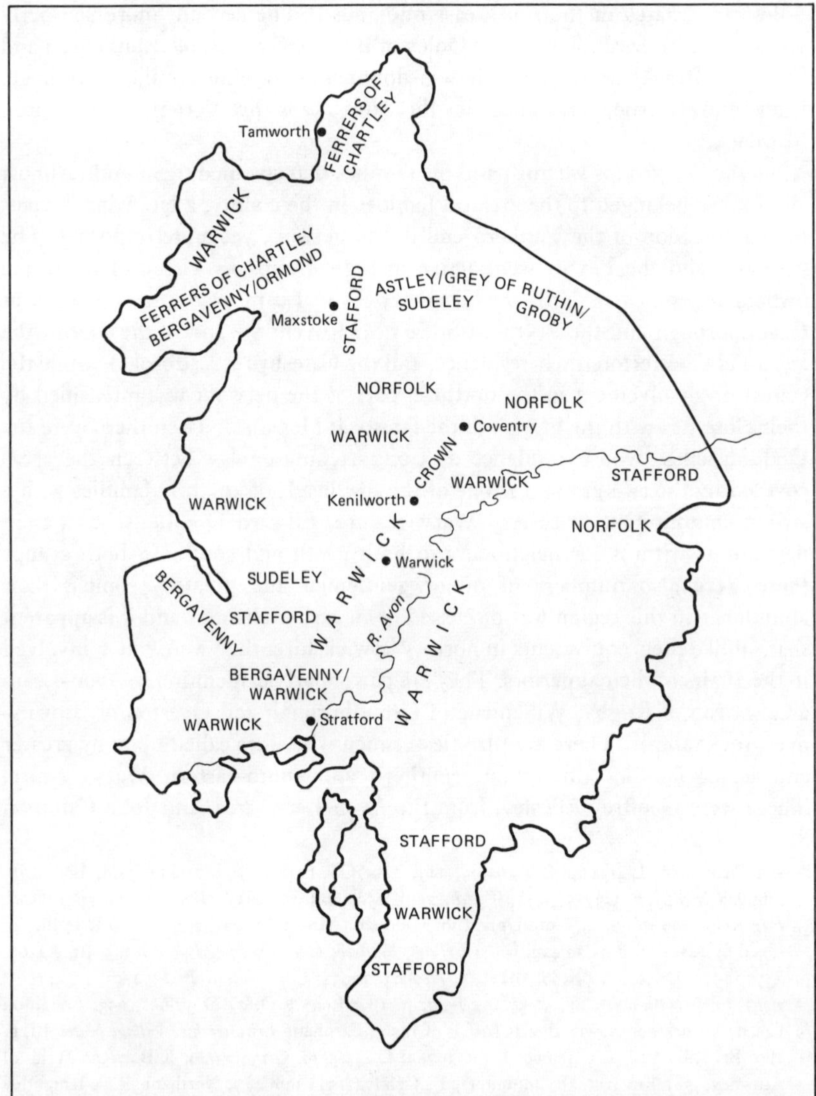

Figure 8 Major landed interests of the more significant local nobility *c.* 1401–72

although their interests in Staffordshire, Shropshire and Northamptonshire tended to engage them more, and there were also some minor families from the area near Dunsmore Heath, like the Dustons and the Dersets. The absence of the Staffords of Grafton from transactions in this part of the county, despite their extensive estates in eastern Warwickshire, emphasises the way this family neglected its affairs further east, even after these had been reinforced by the

Aylesbury estates in the south-east midlands.[73] The second, more southerly group included lesser figures like Onley of Bishops Tachbrook, Shukburgh and Dalby of Brookhampton, but it was dominated by elite families: Straunge, Lucy and Skerne, succeeded in the late 1420s by Verney of Compton Murdack.[74]

To the two groups we must add the families that spanned them both. Almost all of these belonged to the greatest families in the county, a fact which makes the composition of the southern end of the network yet more imposing. The Catesbys and the Peytos were active in both groups by virtue of being the owners of estates in both the Coventry-Avon-Leam area – the Catesbys at Grandborough and the Peytos at Sowe near Coventry – and to the south – the Peytos at Chesterton, their residence, and the Catesbys at Ladbroke – while the Catesbys' involvement in the northern part of the network was intensified by their close ties with the branch of the family at Hopsford. Then there were the Doddingselles, whose residence at Long Itchington lay between the areas covered by the two groups; as one of the few heads of knightly families with a strong commitment to eastern Warwickshire, Edward Doddingselles was in demand as witness for neighbours to both north and south. In both groups there were also numbers of minor gentlemen and greater yeomen; their abundance in this region was discussed in an earlier chapter, and it is apparent that, unlike their equivalents in north Warwickshire, they were much involved in the affairs of their superiors. They are particularly evident in the Avon-Leam area: Baron of Rugby, Willenhale of Grandborough and Overton of Brownsover, for example. There are three lesser men who were called upon by greater and lesser families throughout southern and south-eastern Warwickshire. These were Geoffrey Allesley, from the Avon-Leam area, and John Campion

73 E.g. W.C.R.O. L.4/32–4, C.R.162/65, 117, 119, C.R.1248/68/29, /71/44, /74/8; Bod. Lib. Dugdale MS 13, p. 343, 15, p. 71; *W.F.F.*, 2433, 2502, 2513; Sims ed., *Walsall Deeds*, p. 13; *Cal. Pat. Rolls 1429–36*, p. 64; Nott. Univ. Lib. Middleton MS Mi D 3961–2; S.B.T. D.R.37 Box 40 (deed of 1436), D.R.31 fo.429, E.R.1/61/466, /68/628; *Cat. Anc. Deeds*, I, C1305, III, A4363, 4377, 4573, D750, IV, A8180, 10411, V, A10893, 10934; *Cal. Close Rolls 1402–05*, pp. 472–5, *1413–19*, p. 516, *1419–22*, p. 57, *1441–47*, p. 169; Leics.R.O. 23 D 57/651, 653; Coughton Court, Throckmorton MS Box 45 (deeds of 1426); Farnham, *Leicestershire Village Notes*, III, p. 180; Br. Lib. Add. Ch. 48,660; E.326/10762; C.244/5/38; C.139/53/49; K.B.27/566 Writs of Attorney, /582 Rex (rot. 18: unnumbered); JUST 1/1514 mm.2, 7; Northants.R.O. Knightley Charts. 150–2, 164, 198; Magdalen College, Oxford Muns., Willoughby 604. For the history of Bagot-Stafford, see S.B.T. E.R.1/61 466. For Sutton-Allesley-Boughton, see *V.C.H.*, V, p. 155, VII, p. 189, for Leventhorpe, VI, p. 175. There were two branches of Knightleys, one with land in Staffordshire, the other, the main branch, in Northamptonshire (Baker 1822–41: I, p. 381). Also refs. n.74, below.

74 E.g. W.C.R.O. C.R.1248/70/30,48, /71/17, C.R.133/12,15; S.B.T. D.R.98/89a, 90, 90a, 94–5, 97, 112, 460, D.R.31 fo.390, E.R.1/61/410–11; *Cal. Close Rolls 1422–29*, pp. 258, 262, *1429–35*, p. 119; *Cat. Anc. Deeds*, I, C497, II, C2457, III, C3330, IV, A8342; C.139/53/49; Bod. Lib. Dugdale MS 15, pp. 69, 71–2; Magdalen College, Oxford Muns., Willoughby 603, 605. Also refs. n.73, above.

and Hugh Dalby from further south. Significantly the last two were certainly lawyers and it is probable that Allesley was as well.[75] Allesley's local eminence is attested by the fact that he acted as steward of the east Warwickshire properties of the Staffords of Grafton, since this family was unlikely to have chosen an ineffective man to safeguard its absentee interests; he was also feed by William Peyto.[76] In the far south of the county, a region rather devoid of gentry families and deficient in evidence – and it is not improbable that these characteristics are related – one can see inter-connections between the minor local families here and the families immediately to the north, mostly the lesser ones, that were involved with this great eastern and south-eastern network.[77]

Moving west across the Avon to complete the circle round the county, we come to the focal point of the power of the earls of Warwick, stretching west and south-west from the town of Warwick, the *caput honoris* and chief residence of the earls, into Worcestershire and northern Gloucestershire. Although this was the southern part of the Arden, it was less enclosed than the area to the north, for it was more accessible from the south and east, and had indeed been settled quite early, while the saltways provided easy communication with the adjacent parts of Worcestershire.[78] Nevertheless, it is clear that, as far as Warwickshire was concerned, this was a surprisingly self-contained area. This is unexpected because as an administrative, feudal and commercial centre Warwick was a natural meeting-place, and it was only just across the river from the southern wing of the large network in southern and eastern Warwickshire just discussed. It seems, however, that the Avon[79] and the woods to the west of the river discouraged frequent contact between east and west, and we have already seen that the Arden was something of a barrier to communication with the Tanworth area to the north. There certainly were some links with families to the east, but they were due largely to the influence of the earls of Warwick,[80] and the names that appear and reappear in the evidence for this part of the county are those of the gentry residing west and south-west of Warwick, together with Warwick townsmen, usually gild or borough officials, and, less often, those from Stratford or, occasionally, Henley.

This rather small corner of Warwickshire contained an outsize proportion of the county's elite, principally it seems because many of its families had done

75 See nn.73 and 74, above. For the Catesby families, Norris 1897: pp. 15–16 and *V.C.H.*, VI, p. 266. For ref. to Campion as a lawyer, n.46, above and for more on him, *Ministers' Accounts of St Mary's*, pp. 23–4; S.B.T. D.R.37 Box 73 (Mountford account).

76 S.C.R.O. D.641/1/2/281 (evidence for his being a lawyer); B.R.L. 295194. For Dalby, see above, p. 295.

77 S.B.T. 'Typescript Calendar of Gregory-Hood Deeds', 519, 552, D.R.31 fo.315; W.C.R.O. C.R.133/12; K.B.27/653 Coram Rege rot.26d; *Cal. Close Rolls 1399–1402*, p. 94.

78 See above, pp. 20, 29.

79 For the dangerous condition of the bridge over the Avon at Stratford until Hugh Clopton left money for a new one, *V.C.H.*, II, pp. 138–9.

80 Below, pp. 317–18.

well out of their connection with the house of Warwick, and it may be that for most purposes they felt they had enough neighbours of sufficient eminence without looking for associates further afield. This belief would have been strengthened by the cohesive effects of the Warwick connection.[81] The names that constantly recur in conjunction with each other are Hugford, particularly Robert, the first of the family to live at Emscote near Warwick, Aylesbury, Burdet, Harewell, Neville, Trussell of Billesley, Spine and their successors the Throgmortons, Crewe, Clopton of Moor Hall and, amongst the lesser figures, Brome of Warwick, Rody, atte Wode, Wyncote, Hubaud, Holt of Alcester, Sauser, Parys and Woodlow. To the major families may be added Stafford of Grafton and Cokesey, both families of some stature in eastern Warwickshire, but both conspicuous by their absence from almost all the surviving transactions involving gentry east of the Avon. In both cases, estates in Worcestershire made them much more closely connected with west Warwickshire landowners.[82] The Staffords indeed, if the deed evidence gives a true picture, after a flurry of activity early in the century, seem to have had little concern for developing a network of local associates around themselves. This seems to have been another aspect of that lack of interest in the minutiae of normal gentry life, already evident in their handling of their estates, which went with their increasingly grandiose political ambitions.[83]

Now that the groups have been delineated, they may be explored in greater depth. First, there is the question of the extent of interconnection. There are obvious links in the case of families like the Catesbys, the Hores of Elmdon, the Bishopestones, the Metleys and the Stokes, which had lands in more than one part of the county, and the same goes for the Bromes, once John of Baddesley Clinton began to buy lands away from the old family property in Warwick. However, widespread lands did not necessarily mean widespread associations;

[81] Below, pp. 312–13.

[82] E.g. *Cal. Pat. Rolls 1422–29*, p. 423, *1436–41*, p. 495, *1441–46*, p. 391; *Cal. Fine Rolls 1413–22*, p. 255, *1430–7*, pp. 21–2, 171, 321; *Cal. Close Rolls 1405–09*, p. 382, *1409–13*, pp. 82–3, *1413–19*, pp. 431–2, *1435–41*, pp. 346–7; *Cat. Anc. Deeds*, III, A4651, 4262, IV, A8467; *Colls. Hist. Staffs.*, o.s., 11, p. 226; W.C.R.O. C.R.611/575/4; S.B.T. D.R.41/71/247, 477–8, E.R.1/61/154, /99 fo.88v., D.R.37 Box 48 (will of 1417, deed of 1420), Stratford Corp. Recs. 1/473; E.42/122; *Stratford Register*, p. 84; Coughton Court, Throckmorton MS Box 35 (deeds of 1412, 1428, 1430, 1431 (two), 1436 (two)), Box 36 (deeds of 1408, 1412, 1419 (two)), Box 38 (deeds of 1426, 1427), Box 48 (deeds of 1422, 1426, 1432, 1437), File of Deeds (deeds of 1426, 1430), Box 52 (deeds of 1427, 1429 (two), 1439); Bod. Lib. Dugdale MS 13, p. 287, 15, pp. 77 (*bis*), 125; Br. Lib. Add. Ch. 42,389; Warwick Castle MS 114, 246, 477; JUST 1/1514 m.6d.

[83] *Cal. Close Rolls 1413–19*, pp. 431–2; N.R.A. 'Calendar Sutherland MS' in S.C.R.O. D.593/A/2/10/11; Coughton Court, Throckmorton MS File of Deeds (1430 deed). Note also that William Pullesdon, the Stafford auditor by Michaelmas 1450, was part of this network (Br. Lib. Add. MS 74,170; above, n.82). For the Staffords' tendency to neglect their immediate interests, above, pp. 169–71. In the very early years of the century, the plethora of Humphrey Staffords makes identification difficult, but, were more deeds to be assigned to this particular family, they would only emphasise their connections outside the area.

for example, the Mountfords seem to have had almost no interest at all at this time in fostering connections with families from south Warwickshire where they had not only substantial estates but also their second residence.[84] The analysis of individual deeds can reveal the multiplicity of types of connection that might bring people together from different parts of the county. For example, in 1408 a deed was executed at Solihull in which John Waldeve of Alspath and his wife gave their land in Solihull to a group of feoffees. Amongst the witnesses was John Hore of Solihull, obviously brought in as a minor local landowner. The feoffees included Waldeve's neighbour at Alspath, Robert Castell, and the vicar of Alspath, to whose ultimate benefit the transaction was probably intended. Another witness was William Lord Clinton, who, as owner of Maxstoke Castle, about three miles to the north of Alspath, was the magnate within easiest reach, and the other feoffees were Robert Hugford and Thomas Crewe, neither of whom lived particularly close to either Alspath or Solihull, but who were both important officials of the earl of Warwick, whom Waldeve also served.[85] Deeds of this kind, showing landowners from various parts of the county coming together for a variety of reasons, could be replicated endlessly, and they demonstrate how difficult it is to be precise both in defining local networks, since the groups are so often interconnected, and in establishing the circumstances that were needed to create such a network.

Nevertheless, some generalisations can be made both about the strength of links across the county and about the type of landowner most likely to provide them. The obvious answer to the second question is that it was usually the greater gentry, since more widespread connections went with more widespread lands, and the more eminent families were more likely to marry away from their immediate neighbourhood and therefore to acquire or inherit property further afield.[86] When minor gentry mixed with families out of their neighbourhood it was usually, as in the case of John Hore of Solihull in John Waldeve's deed, because a transaction was being carried out in their village or town by a landowner from another area. There is no doubt that there were certain key families, mostly from the upper echelons of local society, who played a large role in knitting the county together. One of these was the Archers, whose known connections ran right down the western side of the county, from Coleshill and Aston to Billesley and Arrow, and, on occasion, further north to

84 The one known exception is a deed of 1437 (Jeayes, 'Catalogue of Spencer Charts', 1646), in which Buckingham is among Mountford's co-feoffees; it could indicate therefore a growing interest in the south of the county, where Buckingham was a major landowner, in the wake of the duke's arrival as a force in the county (below, pp. 403–5), although the survival of this one deed could be entirely coincidental. The Mountfords certainly spent part of the year on their southern estates (above, p. 158).

85 E.326/6508. For all evidence of clientage, see app. 3.

86 Above, pp. 61–4, 66, 99–101. Cf. Wright 1983: pp. 56–7.

Amington and across the Avon to Chesterton. If their importance seems out of keeping with their status, it must be remembered that in the Arden they were comparatively a major family and evidently acted as the central point in the network of minor families around Tanworth. The connections of Thomas Crewe, who resided at Moor Hall in Wixford in the south-west, followed a similar pattern. The Mountfords' associates were still more widely distributed; in the south-west, the west and right across the north, as far south as Astley and Maxstoke. In the north-east, despite the absence of an identifiable local network, Thomas and William II Purfrey acted as links with the north Warwickshire group and the Avon-Leam section of the east Warwickshire network. William Peyto, as we have seen, was a vital link through most of eastern Warwickshire. In the south it was principally the Lucys and the Straunges, both living near the Avon, both equidistant from Warwick and Stratford, who provided the main links between the groups on either side of the river. The Lucys furthermore were involved to an unusual degree in the affairs of the Stratford gild, which would have brought them into frequent contact with the families west of the Avon, for whom Stratford was the local market, and with the other members of the gild, who tended to come from the south-western corner of the county. They also had connections with the Tanworth area through their family link with the Archers. But lesser men also played some role as 'brokers' between the local groups. Allesley, Campion and Dalby, links between the two sub-groups of eastern Warwickshire, have been mentioned. Dalby's connections went further, both east and west of the Avon. Nicholas Metley and his father Edward were well ensconced in both the Avon-Leam and the Tanworth groups. Two others have left less dense evidence but could also be mentioned: Thomas Stafford (the Avon-Leam area and west of Warwick) and Thomas Stokes (Avon-Leam and the far north). Although distribution of estates played an obvious part in drawing some of these men into more than one local network, the interesting thing is that all the lesser connecting figures were lawyers or noble servants or both and were evidently in demand as business associates because of their professional expertise and connections.[87]

It is difficult to say with any certainty whether there were some areas whose

87 The activities of all these 'brokers' can be traced in the deeds above, nn.53, 60, 63, 67–9, 73–4, 82. See also e.g. Bod. Lib. Dugdale MS 15, pp. 69, 122, 17, p. 42 (deed of 1401/2); *Reg. Chichele*, II, p. 94; *W.F.F.*, 2519 (*recte* Gower), 2539; E.326/6508; *Cal. Pat. Rolls 1422–29*, p. 127; *Cal. Close Rolls 1422–29*, pp. 339–40, *1429–35*, p. 119, *1435–41*, p. 199; *Rot. Parl.*, IV, p. 152; *Cat. Anc. Deeds*, III, A4545, IV, A6498, 6948; Westminster Abbey Muns. 14633–6; Nott. Univ. Lib. Middleton MS Mi D 4004, 4140. Richard Archer's first wife was William Lucy I's widowed mother (above, p. 109; *Cal. Fine Rolls 1471–85*, p. 28; *Dugdale*, p. 781). For the Stratford gild, see S.B.T. Stratford Corp. Recs. I and XII, and, for the Lucys and the gild, see above, p. 239. For service to magnates, see app. 3. For lawyers, app. 2, above, nn.46, 47, 76, and S.B.T. D.R. 37 Box 107/8,9.

links with the rest of the county were tenuous, because the whole situation was so volatile. Given the importance as brokers of a few key men, all it needed was for a line to come to an end, as happened to the Crewes, or for a family to reorientate itself politically, as Richard Dalby, son and eventual heir of Hugh was to do, for the county's political and social geography to undergo a metamorphosis.[88] Nevertheless, it is apparent that, volatility or no, in the first four decades of the century all the Warwickshire networks were to some extent interconnected. All the same, there are no *a priori* reasons for assuming that the Warwickshire networks were as closely connected with each other as they were with those in adjacent counties; indeed, what we have already seen of the structure of the county would lead us to assume rather the reverse. To take an extreme case, it has been pointed out that the gentry of the north-east dealt mostly with Leicestershire families; they were in fact part of a Leicestershire network from which their Warwickshire lands were divided by the artificial boundary of Watling Street. Even in the well-knit group to the south there was at least one family, the Trussells of Bilton, whose known associates at this time came almost entirely from Leicestershire, Northamptonshire or counties to the north of these,[89] and others, like the Malorys, the Knightleys and the Catesbys, who were substantially involved with landowners from these two counties, principally because they held lands there themselves.[90] The same goes for the ties of the gentry in the far south-west of the county with Gloucestershire, a situation accentuated by the fact that a sizeable detached part of Gloucestershire lay in the middle of the south-west of Kineton Hundred. The Grevilles, for example, who were later to be a potent force in Warwickshire politics, were at this time far more bound up with their Gloucestershire lands and connections.[91] The propensity for north Warwickshire families to own lands in Leicestershire, Staffordshire and Debyshire is reflected in the location of their associates, most obviously in the case of Cokayn and Shirley but in that of others as well, for example Ruggeley and

[88] Below, p. 405.

[89] E.g. *Cal. Close Rolls 1429–35*, pp. 57–8, *1435–41*, p. 345; Nichols 1795–1811: II, i, p. 243; Leics.R.O. DE 2242/3/7; JUST 1/1537 m.27 (essoins); *Colls. Hist. Staffs.*, o.s., 17, p. 26. For the Trussell lands, see *Cal. Fine Rolls 1461–71*, p. 95.

[90] *Cat. Anc. Deeds*, III, A6082, 6084; Nichols 1795–1811: III, i, p. 497; Leics.R.O. DE 2242/6/62–3; *Cal. Pat. Rolls 1405–08*, p. 139, *1416–22*, pp. 64, 259; *Cal. Close Rolls 1399–1402*, p. 144, *1419–22*, p. 105; Longleat, MS of Marquess of Bath 6414 (Richard Knightley – *sub* feodary's account); *Sir Christopher Hatton's Book of Seals*, pp. 177–8; *Cat. Anc. Deeds*, III, A4547, IV, A8287, 8361, V, A10893; WARD 2/1/3/2. For the lands of these families, see Carpenter, M. C. 1976: App. II. There were also some connections with Oxfordshire, to the south: e.g. Cant. Dioc., Reg. Stafford fo.135–135v.

[91] *Cal. Pat. Rolls 1401–05*, pp. 2, 155, 286, *1408–13*, p. 382; Gloucs.R.O. D.1086/T2/7, 8, D.149/T1014. Another example is William Bishopestone, who had lands in Gloucestershire (Carpenter, M. C. 1976: App. IIC).

Stokes.[92] The artificiality of the shiring of the Birmingham plateau is also very evident.[93]

The artificiality of the Warwickshire boundaries as a whole is particularly apparent in the way they cut across the great landed estates, which had such a pronounced influence on the location of networks.[94] To a large extent the great cross-border estates dated back to the time of Domesday, and these themselves in many cases followed the pattern of Anglo-Saxon estates, giving them a very ancient lineage indeed. This makes their failure to coincide with the shire boundaries wholly explicable in the light of the late and arbitrary shiring of the midlands. For example, the Honor of Robert of Leicester lay in Leicestershire and north-east Warwickshire, and the bishop of Worcester's much older estate in south-east Worcestershire and south-west Warwickshire.[95] If the baronial lands ran across the county boundaries, then those of their feudal tenants were likely to do so as well and this state of affairs would be emphasised by intermarriage amongst the tenants. Nowhere is this more striking than in the region between Worcester and Warwick, where two powerful Honors, those of the Beauchamps of Elmley, descendants of Urse d'Abitot, and of the successors of the count of Meulan at Warwick, were united in the middle of the thirteenth century.[96] In each Honor the lord had kept much of his land for himself, and the continuing political presence of the Beauchamps, as owners of both, encouraged interconnection between gentry families living near the two great bastions of Beauchamp power, the one in Worcestershire, the other in Warwickshire.

By the fifteenth century, then, it was normal for the gentry in the adjacent areas of Warwickshire and Worcestershire to own land in both counties, and the process continued, as marriages were arranged amongst the earls' following, most notably the alliance between the east Worcestershire Throgmortons and the west Warwickshire Spines.[97] Virtually all the gentry living west of Warwick were more likely to turn westwards, to Worcestershire or Gloucestershire, for associates, to families like the Wollashulls, the Vampages, the Washbournes, the Andrewes, the Tracys and the Wodes, with which they were linked by political and family ties, than to other Warwickshire gentry to the north or east of the Avon.[98] Although it would be an exaggeration to claim that

[92] For refs., above, nn. 60, 63; below, n.134; above, pp. 62–3.

[93] Particularly noticeable in the relations of the Berminghams with their lesser neighbours, drawn from the various counties on the plateau (e.g. *Cal. Close Rolls 1413–19*, p. 97; *Cal. Fine Rolls 1413–22*, p. 363; K.B.27/613 Rex rot.8, /654 Rex rot.19d.); above, p. 25 for the geography of the plateau.

[94] Above, pp. 30–2.

[95] Dyer 1980b: p. 8; Sanders 1960: pp. 61–2; above, pp. 27–8, 32–3.

[96] Sanders 1960: pp. 75–6, 93–4; *Beauchamp Cartulary*, pp. xviii–xlviii; above, p. 31.

[97] *V.C.H.*, III, *passim*; *V.C.H. Worcs.*, *passim*; above, p. 31.

[98] Refs. above, n.82. The Andrewes, although occasionally active in Gloucestershire, were primarily a Wiltshire family (Roskell 1954: p. 147).

these west Warwickshire families were wholly separate from the rest of the county, not least because the earls' principal residence happened to be the county's administrative centre, it is difficult to believe that they did not think of themselves as belonging first and foremost to a west midlands region – coinciding, incidentally, to a large extent with the diocese of Worcester – bounded by the geography of the Warwick estates, rather than to the county of Warwick.

So far we have concentrated on the forces that shaped local associations in and around Warwickshire, and we have yet to look at those which extended the boundaries of friendship well beyond a man's immediate locality. One of these was tenure of property in non-adjacent counties. Usually this had come about through marriage or inheritance and, since Warwickshire gentry were on the whole reluctant to marry their male heirs into families outside the midlands,[99] it tended to result from the movement of new families into the county, like the Rushtons, originally from Lancashire, or Ralph Neville, younger son of the earl of Westmorland. More rarely, a grant of an estate might extend a landowner's interests; an example is John Onley, originally of Buckinghamshire, given Birdingbury manor by his lord, William Beauchamp of Bergavenny.[100]

Another avenue to friendships well outside the county was service to the crown, in war or in government. John Brome of Baddesley Clinton, for example, had a strictly localised circle of associates, as befitted someone of his undistinguished parentage, until he joined the royal service in about 1429; thereafter he participated in transactions with people from many parts of England, some of them also government servants, including several from the exchequer, Brome's place of employment, among them the treasurer, Lord Cromwell.[101] The effects of war in bringing together men from all over England are neatly illustrated by the group of witnesses that attested John Marney's declaration after his release from captivity in Anjou in the 1420s. These included a number of west midland men – John Beauchamp of Powick, William Bishopestone, Nicholas Burdet and Ralph Neville – and others from various parts of the country, among them the duke of Suffolk, Lords Talbot and Scales, Sir John Fastolf, Sir John Montgomery and Sir John Salveyn.[102] Such connections were perhaps unlikely to survive the return to England, except when they brought together men whose residences were not too far apart, but, in the latter case, they could well be the initial step that brought families into a more long-lasting association. The Marney declaration itself may indicate the beginnings of the group that formed around Beauchamp of Powick after his

[99] Above, p. 119.

[100] *Dugdale*, pp. 856, 323; *V.C.H. Lancs*, VI, p. 420; above, pp. 99, 126.

[101] *Cal. Pat. Rolls 1436–41*, p. 100; *Cal. Fine Rolls 1422–30*, pp. 269, 278, *1430–7*, pp. 134, 196; *Cat. Anc. Deeds*, III, A4478, IV, A7468.

[102] *Cal. Close Rolls 1422–29*, p. 399. This is probably the Warwickshire Ralph Neville; a man of that name was in France in 1420–1, who could also be the Warwickshire one (above, p. 60 n.84).

purchase of Alcester in 1444, when he and Lord Sudeley (who was also concerned in the affairs of John Marney) were to become closely associated with the major families of south-west Warwickshire, including the Burdets and the Nevilles.[103]

Connections acquired through the law, particularly at Westminster, and by attendance at the royal court on legal, parliamentary or other business have already been mentioned in the context of marriage but are much harder to establish with certainty.[104] However, one obvious example is the world of Thomas Greswold, the lawyer and king's attorney, which ranged far beyond the very localised group of associates typical of an Arden gentleman of his status. Even so, he retained a partiality for associates from among the professional men of his home in west Warwickshire and east Worcestershire. The same kind of local loyalty was observed by Ives in examining the friends of Thomas Kebyll, a lawyer of rather similar social origins.[105] The Paston correspondence shows the full range of connections that it was open to a successful lawyer to exploit, from fellow-members of the Inn, through the entourage of the nobility, to the royal administration itself.[106]

Since the greater families were more likely to look outside the immediate locality for friends and associates, whether to other areas of the county, to other counties beyond the locality, or to contacts made in noble or governmental circles, it was the regions containing numbers of families of middle rank and below that were likely to contain the most effective local networks. Comparison of three contrasted areas emphasises this point. The Tanworth region is an archetypal local neighbourhood, drawing its strength from the dominance of middling and lesser families in an area lacking easy access to the outside world, where a complex tenurial structure and a thriving land-market constantly threw together all the local families, whatever their social level. Further north, there was undeniably a group of local landowners who customarily did business together, but its members, drawn mostly from the county elite, often had heavy commitments elsewhere, and there was too great a gap between them and the minor local gentry, with too few middling families to bridge it, for the gentry here as a body to have much in common with each other. Thirdly, in the east and south-east, the presence of numbers of middling families, mostly with strongly localised interests, most notably in the Avon-Leam region, provided the ballast that created an effective local network. It was able to absorb some very minor families, as well as several of the county elite, despite the fact that

[103] Below, pp. 331–2. This grouping is also in evidence in Fastolf's later use of Beauchamp of Powick as a feoffee (*Paston Letters*, II, p. 557).

[104] Above, p. 100.

[105] *Cal. Close Rolls 1435–41*, p. 40; *Cal. Fine Rolls 1437–45*, p. 44; K.B.27/626 Coram Rege rot. 57, /649 Coram Rege rot.28; and refs., above, n.53. For Greswold's origins, see above, p. 136; for Kebyll, see Ives 1983a: pp. 23–35, 115–19.

[106] See e.g. *Paston Letters*, I, pp. 155, 157–8, 160–2, II, pp. 56, 164, 173, 187, 247, 276, 507–8.

some of these, such as the Catesbys and the Knightleys, had more pressing concerns in the neighbouring counties of Leicestershire and Northamptonshire. When, quite fortuitously, numbers of these middling families disappeared temporarily or permanently in the second half of the century, the area as a whole lost much of its cohesiveness.[107]

Having looked at the range of horizontal links, we need to ask what, besides geographical proximity and common professional interest, brought them together, for on that may depend much of the strength and durability of the connection. Kinship was certainly an important factor, although the dangers in using it as an all-purpose explanation have been pointed out.[108] The participation of members of the family in family settlements was in any event bound to be encouraged because, as participants, they were subsequently obliged to warrant the transaction, so this was one way of inhibiting internecine feuding within the family.[109] It is not difficult to find examples of collateral branches acting co-operatively within the same network; for instance, the Harewells of Wootton and Bidford, the Catesbys of Ladbroke and Hopsford and the Chetwynds of Grendon and Alspath.[110] Once one moves further away from the centre of the family it becomes harder to separate kinship and neighbourhood, especially when dealing with relationships through marriage, themselves often the product of geographical proximity. The Cokayns and the Shirleys, for example, were connected by marriage but they were also neighbours twice over, as Derbyshire landowners, and as manorial lords in the same north Warwickshire village of Newton Regis.[111]

Marriage into a family outside the immediate locality did undoubtedly play a role in bringing together gentry who would not otherwise have been connected. Richard Archer's marriage to William Lucy's mother, for example, gave the Lucys links with the Tanworth network that would probably not have arisen in the normal course of their business.[112] At a lower social level, the marriage of Thomas Shukburgh I to Thomas Sydenhale's daughter provided a connecting link between the geographically very separate Tanworth and east Warwickshire

107 See below, p. 600.

108 See above, p. 260.

109 See above, p. 212; Astill 1977: p. 63.

110 E.g. *Cat. Anc. Deeds*, III, A4377, 4545, 4573, IV, A10411, V, A10934 (Catesby); *Cal. Pat. Rolls 1441–46*, p. 241; *Cal. Close Rolls 1429–35*, p. 119; C.139/115/27 (Harewell); *Cal. Close Rolls 1435–41*, p. 268; *Colls. Hist. Staffs.*, o.s., 12, p. 314; *Cat. Anc. Deeds*, II, A2753; Wm. Salt Lib. H.M. Chetwynd Coll. Bundle 7 (deed of 1427) (Chetwynd).

111 Wright 1983: p. 231; *V.C.H.*, IV, pp. 161–2; Roskell 1954: p. 168. It is noteworthy that some families were neighbours in more than one area; this may be the result of deliberate marriage policies rather than of pure coincidence; e.g. the Erdingtons and the Harecourts, both Leicestershire landowners (and Richard Harecourt of Saredon actually Erdington's lessee (possibly mortgagee) at Barrow) and neighbours in Dorset (Nichols 1795–1811: III, i, p. 64; *Cal. Close Rolls 1429–35*, p. 148; *H.M.C. Hastings*, I, p. 72; Hutchins 1861–74: III, p. 355).

112 Above, p. 306.

networks.[113] Marriage within local groups was not uncommon and was one of the things that added to a group's cohesiveness and durability. The east to south-east network is a particularly good example. Marriages linking Malory to Doddingselles, Purfrey to Knightley, Fielding to Purfrey and Bellers, Metley to Cotes, and Cotes to Shukburgh lent cohesion to the upper levels of this group, and those of Barbour to Newnham and Shukburgh, Sutton to Allesley and Dalby, and Dalby to Hayton did the same at the gentleman-yeoman level.[114] Marriage was perhaps especially important in this region, where the local network covered such a large area, for it helped bind more distant neighbours into the group, like the Purfreys and the Malorys of Chilvers Coton. Instances could be duplicated from elsewhere, notably the Tanworth region, most of them coming, as we would expect, from the less eminent families who more often married nearer home.[115]

Now that the possible influences on horizontal associations have been examined, it is time to bring in the vertical ties that have lain in the background for so much of this discussion. That lords did play a role in creating or strengthening links between gentry families within their entourage is beyond doubt. The fact is that the common thread running through many of these groups is not just neighbourhood but also service to a common lord. Since a lord's affinity was normally to be found in the environs of his estates, this is predictable, although the extent of localisation would depend on the compactness of the estate. Moreover, because of the lord's considerable role in the marriage market, matches which bound neighbours more closely together also intensified local commitment to the dominant magnate.[116] Between 1401 and 1439 there were two areas in Warwickshire where political allegiance was as important as neighbourhood in creating a sense of local identity; these were the

[113] It should be noted, however, that Sydenhale already had lands in Northamptonshire, which would have brought him into contact with this part of Warwickshire and may, of course, have been the origins of the match; *Visitation Warwicks.*, p. 345; W.C.R.O. C.R.1248/71/44; *Miscellanea Gen. et Herald.*, 2nd ser., 3 (1890), p. 318.

[114] *Cal. Close Rolls 1429–35*, pp. 313–14; C.139/110/44; *Wedgwood: Biographies*, p. 314; Nichols 1795–1811: IV, i, p. 287; C.1/11/155 (see *Cat. Anc. Deeds*, IV, A6498 for evidence that Metley's wife was called Margaret, and above, p. 67); *Dugdale*, p. 311; S.B.T. E.R.1/61/409–11; C.1/6/110; *Dugdale*, p. 99; Br. Lib. Add. MS 28,564 fo.17.

[115] Simon Malory married Sutton's other daughter (C.1/6/110), and William Purfrey II married one sister of John Chetwynd of Alspath, while John Malory of Newbold married another (Chetwynd-Stapylton 1892: pp. 84–5). A bond of 1412, involving Malory, Purfrey and Richard and John Chetwynd (*Cat. Anc. Deeds*, II, A2753), shows that these connections by marriage had real meaning. Marriages in the Arden include e.g. Benford-Hore of Yardley, Worcestershire (S.B.T. D.R.37 Box 56 (deed of 1446)), Greswold-Bromley, Greswold-Hore of Solihull (K.B.27/747 Coram Rege rot.33d.).

[116] Carpenter 1980a: pp. 514–17, 523–4, where the literature on the subject is also surveyed; also Maddicott 1970: pp. 59–65, and, published since then, Wright 1983: ch. 5; Cherry 1979: pp. 76–8, 79–80; Pollard 1979: pp. 47–56. See also *Paston Letters*, I, pp. 585–6, 603, II, pp. 98–9, 100–1. For the lord and the marriage market, see above, pp. 101–5 and cf. Walker 1986: pp. 103–8.

south-west and the north to north-west, the areas dominated by the estates and affinity of Richard Beauchamp, earl of Warwick, far and away the most powerful magnate with the most concentrated tenurial power in the county. In the south-west, every one of the families that has been named as a part of the local grouping, with the exception of the Nevilles, served Beauchamp and, in most cases, served him regularly and in several capacities. Thomas Crewe, for example, was attorney to his mother and councillor and chief steward to Beauchamp himself; Crewe's step-son William Clopton was retained for life; Thomas Burdet I was also a life retainer and an active servant and his son Nicholas was in Beauchamp's household in 1420–1; three generations of Hugfords, Robert, Thomas and John, served him in a number of ways throughout the period; so did John Throgmorton, whose father, Thomas I, had served both Beauchamp and his father, the previous earl. To the north, if the depth of connection is less striking, it is clearly there: notably in the case of William Mountford, but also with Ardern, Brasebrugge, Clodesdale, Erdington, Holt of Aston, Lisle, Ruggeley, Stokes and Waver of Marston Waver.[117]

It is evident that the force that created a local network across two adjacent counties could come as much from the lord as from local geography or the distribution of gentry estates. In the case of the Warwickshire–Worcestershire nexus, the centre of the Beauchamp power, it was lordship that to a large degree had created tenurial geography.[118] The families consistently linked across the county boundary share, almost all of them, a relationship, often a close one, to the house of Warwick. This relationship, as in the case of the Throgmortons, could give additional vigour to the links between the counties by helping to construct gentry estates that straddled the border.[119] Equally in north-east Warwickshire it was the absence of resident nobility for most of the period, as much as the Leicestershire interests of the local gentry, that produced the vacuum which allowed the nobility of west Leicestershire, Joan Beauchamp, Lady Bergavenny at Ashby de la Zouche and William Lord Ferrers at Groby, to draw landowners over the Warwickshire border into the Leicestershire networks in which they and their followers participated.[120]

117 For all these, see app. 3.

118 See above, p. 308.

119 For Warwick's connections outside Warwickshire, see Br. Lib. Eg. Rolls 8770–5; Longleat, MS of Marquess of Bath Misc. IX; S.C.12/18/45–6. This is by no means a complete list of records, but, taken in conjunction with n.82, gives enough information to illustrate this point. The connection extended into Gloucestershire: e.g. *Landboc de Winchelcumba*, II, pp. 505–11.

120 For Ferrers of Groby and Bergavenny connections in Leicestershire, see e.g. *Cal. Close Rolls 1405–09*, pp. 110–12; *Cal. Pat. Rolls 1422–29*, p. 486, *1429–36*, p. 27, *1436–41*, p. 446; *Cal. Fine Rolls 1413–22*, pp. 266–7, *1422–30*, pp. 203–4; JUST 1/1524 m.28; Leics.R.O. DE 2242/3/7, 44'28/187; *Test. Vetust.*, p. 227; Roskell 1954: p. 83; Ives 1983a: pp. 24–6; and nn.67–9, above. It seems that Lord Grey of Codnor also played an important role in this network (Roskell 1954: pp. 205–6; Wright 1983: p. 66).

When ties of neighbourhood and of political allegiance were so closely drawn we may well ask whether distinguishing between the two has any purpose or indeed any reality. But the question does have some point, for the answers may tell us a lot about the gentry's sense of their own worth and importance. It is clear, for instance, that magnate affinities could have considerable force in the moulding of local identities. For example, in the early years of the century there *was* a substantial local network in north-east Warwickshire, which ran right across the north of the county to encompass Lord Clinton at Maxstoke, William Mountford, John Cokayn, the minor Astleys at Wolvey Astley, William Purfrey I and John Malory of Newbold Revel, and revolved around the natural noble leader in the area, William Lord Astley of Astley. After Lord William's death in *c.*1417 his estates devolved to his son-in-law, Reginald Grey of Ruthin, for whom this Warwickshire/Leicestershire estate was exceedingly peripheral. Although Grey had thought it worth his while to summon some of Astley's Warwickshire followers to Ruthin in 1414, once Astley was dead the area no longer had a resident magnate with any reason for maintaining a political connection there, and both magnate affinity and local grouping rapidly lapsed together.[121] Similarly, the lack of any identifiable group up to 1439 either in the south-east corner of the county around Farnborough and Wormleighton or in the far south may be attributed as much to noble inertia as to lack of resident gentry; both the south and the north-east were to be transformed when they began to move into the forefront of magnate politics after 1439.[122]

A clear example of a change in localism under the impetus of magnate politics occurred within this period in the north to north-west. As ever, care must be taken not to confuse the appearance of deed evidence for a network with its actual emergence, but in this case there is an impressive conjunction of evidence showing the impact of Edmund Ferrers of Chartley in north Warwickshire. Until 1415 his associates had come almost exclusively from Staffordshire, although one or two, like Roger Aston or Richard Chetwynd, had, or were soon to have, lands in Warwickshire.[123] Between 1415 and 1422 Ferrers was mostly out of the country.[124] After his return, and more especially after he had inherited a claim to Birmingham manor on the death of Elizabeth Clinton in 1423, he is found on a growing number of deeds with Warwickshire landowners, often those with lands in Staffordshire who would have given him

[121] *W.F.F.*, 2404; W.C.R.O. C.R.136/C127, 149, 790; *Dugdale*, p. 67; E.326/6831, 9045, 10665, 10763, 10765; *Cat. Anc. Deeds*, v, A10668; Cant. Dioc., Reg. Arundel, I, fo.219 (the William Castley here is almost certainly William Casteleyn, linked with Astley and his associates). There seems to be no evidence for Astley's date of death. His last appearance as a J.P. is January 1414 (*Cal. Pat. Rolls 1413–16*, p. 424), while the next commission was issued in December 1417 (*ibid. 1416–22*, p. 461). His wife was a widow in December 1420 (W.C.R.O. C.R.136/C149).

[122] Below, pp. 327–9.

[123] Powell 1979: pp. 293–7; K.B.27/613 Rex rot. 30; *Cal. Close Rolls 1447–54*, p. 70; Leics.R.O. DE/170/45/1–3.

[124] *G.E.C.*, v, pp. 317–8.

an obvious entrée to Warwickshire society. Most were from north Warwickshire but some lived closer to Warwick. Significantly, some, such as Mountford, Erdington, Archer, Throgmorton and Straunge, were of the Warwick affinity, for it is clear that Ferrers was moving into the Warwick entourage.[125] In 1418 he had served under Warwick in France.[126] In 1420–1 he had already acted with Warwick as feoffee for Lord Clinton, the most important of the minor nobility of north Warwickshire, who had been consistently linked with Warwick and his men since the early years of the century. In 1431 Ferrers formalised this tie by marrying his daughter to Clinton's son and heir.[127] Thus, when we find evidence that north Warwickshire associates of Ferrers, like Mollesley and Repington, are acting with members of the Warwick affinity from 1421, and when deeds of the 1420s and 1430s indicate the growth of a solid north Warwickshire–Staffordshire network focused on Warwick and Ferrers, it is not unreasonable to conclude that we are watching the growth of a local group brought together largely by the ambitions of a local magnate.[128]

A cursory examination of the position in north Warwickshire of the earl of Warwick himself adds force to this interpretation.[129] Until about the 1420s, for all that he had lands and retainers in Staffordshire,[130] his gentry followers and their friends, in striking contrast with what was to follow, had little to do with the north midlands. The exceptions were those like John Cokayn or Ralph Shirley who had pressing concerns of their own there. The explanation of this state of affairs is probably that the two major powers in the west and north midlands, which, in the absence of an adult earl of Stafford,[131] were respectively Warwick himself and the king as duke of Lancaster, had achieved such full control of their own spheres that each was able to seal his area of authority off from the other.[132] So effective was this mutual exclusion that even between 1408 and 1414, when affairs in Staffordshire were getting badly out of hand, the mayhem did not percolate over the border into Warwickshire and remained

[125] Below, p. 377; *Cal. Close Rolls 1422–29*, pp. 186, 268, 326, *1429–35*, pp. 119, 125; K.B.9/203/18; B.R.L. Wingfield Digby MS A496; B.R.L. 351370; Jeayes ed., *Lyttleton Charters*, pp. 80–1, 82; Bod. Lib. Dugdale MS 15, pp. 13 (*bis*), 69, 122; K.B.27/681 Rex rot.21; Leics.R.O. DE 2242/3 (unnumbered indenture of 1431); app. 3.

[126] Wylie and Waugh 1914–29: III, p. 131.

[127] *Rot. Parl.*, IV, pp. 152–3; Wm. Salt Lib. Wm. Salt Orig. Coll. 45/5/57. For Clinton and Warwick, see e.g. *Cal. Close Rolls 1413–19*, p. 451, *1419–22*, pp. 28–9, *1429–35*, pp. 125, 131; B.R.L. Wingfield Digby MS A496; JUST 1/1524 m.32d.; E.326/6508, 6831; above, n.119.

[128] For refs., see above, nn.60, 125.

[129] For a fuller account, see below, pp. 373–92.

[130] S.C.12/18/45; Br. Lib. Eg. Roll 8773.

[131] Stafford's father, Earl Edmund, died at Shrewsbury in 1403; Stafford himself received livery in 1423 (*G.E.C.*, XII, i, p. 181; *Cal. Pat. Rolls 1422–29*, p. 75). His mother, who did not die until 1438, had some of his Staffordshire and Warwickshire lands (*Cal. Pat. Rolls 1436–41*, p. 233; S.C.R.O. D.641/1/2/14; Wm. Salt Lib. Wm. Salt Orig. Coll. M557; *Cal. Close Rolls 1402–05*, pp. 230–6, 237–40).

[132] Wright 1983: pp. 83–4; *V.C.H. Staffs.*; *V.C.H. Derbys.*; Powell 1983: pp. 286–8; below, pp. 364–8.

very much a Staffordshire-Derbyshire affair, the responsibility of the Duchy of Lancaster.[133] This situation can be illustrated from the known associates of Cokayn and Shirley at this time. The Derbyshire estates of these two north Warwickshire families had tied them closely to the Duchy, and in the early fifteenth century, except for the period when Cokayn came within the Astley ambience, both moved very much in Derbyshire circles, showing a distinct indifference to their Warwickshire neighbours. It was as if their allegiance to the Duchy were taking them right out of Warwickshire society.[134] The absence of a representative of the Staffords, the one noble family that could pose a threat to Warwick in north Warwickshire, by using its considerable landed power in southern Staffordshire, was another factor in preserving the barrier between Warwickshire and the north midlands, for it gave the earl of Warwick a sense of security about the north of the county which meant he could ignore what happened north of Tamworth. Although Hugh Erdeswick, one of the main protagonists of the north midlands war of the last years of Henry IV and the first of Henry V, may have been in Warwick's service by 1417, and the earl's connections with north Warwickshire were expanding under Henry V, Warwick seems to some extent to have remained detached from north midlands politics until a number of developments in 1422–3 forced him to take an urgent interest.[135]

First, the accession of the infant Henry VI may have made him afraid that the Duchy's control north of Warwickshire would weaken, allowing any conflict there to spill over into his own domain. Secondly, in 1423 the earl of Stafford, later duke of Buckingham, had livery of many of his lands.[136] Thirdly, in the same year, the dispute over Birmingham broke out, which forced Warwick to exercise his lordship in deciding the destiny of this strategically important and valuable estate, for, if he did not, someone else would. This was all the more urgent in that, shortly before, Joan Beauchamp had acquired the Botetourt inheritance, which included Bordesley and Haybarn near Birmingham.[137] With Ferrers moving into the area, just as John Lord Sutton, of Dudley Castle in the Staffordshire part of the Birmingham plateau,

133 Powell 1979: pp. 288–97; K.B.27/613 Rex roti.8, 30. Note that the first of these K.B. references does show the involvement of William Bermingham, but he seems to be a unique Warwickshire participant.

134 E.g. S.B.T. D.R.3/176; Jeayes ed., *Gresley Charters*, 392; *Cat. Anc. Deeds*, v, A11333 (the deed cited in this one); Jeayes ed., *Derbyshire Charters*, pp. 10, 11, 99, 171, 197, 198, 210–11, 222, 241, 251, 262, 270, 342; *Cal. Close Rolls 1413–19*, pp. 270–1, 527; *Cal. Fine Rolls 1413–22*, p. 427; Derbys.R.O. D779/T81–2, 86; Leics.R.O. DE 221/2/1/24/1. For their Duchy connections, see Shirley 1873: pp. 32, 37, 40–1 and Roskell 1954: p. 168. See also above, nn.63, 121.

135 Br. Lib. Eg. Roll 8773, *sub* expenses of council: an amibiguous entry concerning Perton (below, p. 368 n.90); Powell 1979: pp. 288–98. But cf. JUST 1/1514 m.48 for some early links with north Warwickshire.

136 Above, n.131.

137 Below, p. 373.

came into his lands,[138] the range of possible lords now being offered to the gentry of north Warwickshire and south Staffordshire made it dangerous for Warwick to ignore the north midlands where they met his Warwickshire interests. Much more will have to be said on the politics of north Warwickshire in the 1420s and 1430s, but this brief sketch of the political background to the growth of the gentry network in this part of the county shows the importance of taking the interests of the nobility into consideration when discussing relationships amongst the gentry.[139]

The nobility were also often the means of bringing together local groupings across the county. A neighbour, although potentially a rival, was probably a safer bet as an associate than a more distant landowner, since families living in close proximity were well-nigh obliged to rub along together, and, if they did not, other neighbours would feel impelled to force them into amity for the sake of local stability.[140] If therefore the choice of associate fell on gentry who were connected not by neighbourhood or by family, it was most likely to fall on those with a common political allegiance. For, beyond family and neighbourhood, the strongest guarantee of good faith was the ability of the common lord to preserve the peace and force his clients to honour their obligations to one another. This being the case, it is no surprise that in these years connections across the county are found most often among clients of the earl of Warwick, and that the key figures mentioned earlier who provided the links between the local networks came mostly from the earl's followers.

Many examples could be cited, from all over the county, of groups of local men, some of them clients of the earl, acting in conjunction with Warwick clients from other parts of Warwickshire, but a few will have to suffice. In 1414 William Waldeve, a household officer of the earl, enfeoffed his lands to Ralph Brasebrugge, Baldwin Freville and Nicholas Ruggeley, all of them neighbours, two of them Warwick clients, and to Thomas Crewe and Richard Curson, retainers of the earl from respectively south-west Warwickshire and Worcestershire.[141] In 1427 Thomas Archer made a settlement of his lands using his neighbours, Thomas Waryng, John Fulwode and Richard Marbroke, and fellow members of the Warwick affinity from outside the Tanworth area, William Mountford, Thomas Straunge and John Harewell.[142] In 1431 the

[138] *Cal. Close Rolls 1422–29*, p. 35.

[139] For a full analysis of politics in this area, see below, pp. 377–8, 388–92.

[140] Hassell Smith 1974: pp. 196–7; Sharpe 1983; Hay 1984: p. 8; *Paston Letters*, I, p. 340, II, pp. 4–5, 136–7, 197, 326; *Stonor Letters*, I, pp. 110–12, 122; Kail ed., *Political Poems*, p. 6, ll.161–4. A good example of an agreement reached apparently by such neighbourly intervention is Northants.R.O. Knightley Charters 265. See also an instance of a deed being given to a neighbour for safe-keeping: *Calendars of Proceedings in Chancery*, I, p. lxxiii.

[141] Nott. Univ. Lib. Middleton MS Mi D 4004.

[142] S.B.T. D.R.37/891.

witnesses to Thomas Straunge's feoffment of his lands were his neighbours William Lucy and Hugh Dalby, both connections of the earl, and several of the earl's other followers from further afield, Edmund Ferrers of Chartley, William Mountford, Thomas Burdet and Roger and Thomas Harewell.[143] There are also deeds that show beyond all reasonable doubt the affinity meeting to transact its members' business, the participants drawn from right across the county and beyond. One such is William Holt's feoffment of 1435 to Warwick himself, Edmund Lord Ferrers, John Throgmorton, John Catesby, William Wollashull of Worcestershire and Thomas Est of Warwickshire and Worcestershire.[144] Robert Ardern's feoffees of about the same time, who, like Holt's, included the earl himself, were drawn even more widely but were also dominated by men of the Warwick-Ferrers of Chartley connection.[145] In 1423 Richard Curson, one of Warwick's close servants, made a recognisance in which he was supported by the earl's most important clients and servants in the west midlands and elsewhere in England.[146]

It seems impossible not to conclude therefore that there were certain kinds of identity, whether bounded by a locality or by wider horizons, that were defined primarily in terms of lordship. While we might expect that a cross-county network would be created or strongly reinforced by a cross-county lordship, the fact that in this period the only real unity of this geographically, economically and tenurially diverse county came from the powerful and cohesive affinity of Richard Beauchamp, earl of Warwick should give us pause in contemplating the notion of the 'county community'. It also raises serious questions about the meaning of neighbourhood and locality to the local networks that were described earlier in the chapter. How much did these owe their existence to the magnate influence which has been detected in some of them? At the extremes such questions can be easily answered. The failure of the Astley network to survive Lord Astley's death must show its lack of real roots in existing gentry relationships: it was the artificial creation of a lord, but none the less effective during the lord's lifetime for that. Conversely in the Arden near Tanworth and in the Avon-Leam area there was a genuine sense of neighbourhood which cut across and outlasted magnate connections.[147]

143 *Cal. Close Rolls 1429–35*, p. 119.

144 *Cal. Close Rolls 1435–41*, p. 36.

145 C.139/153/21.

146 *Cal. Close Rolls 1422–29*, p. 127. For further examples, see e.g. *Cat. Anc. Deeds*, v, A10934; *Cal. Close Rolls 1429–35*, p. 361.

147 There are problems, however, with the Avon-Leam area's political identity. Certainly it does not seem to be dominated by Warwick retainers. On the other hand, there is a remarkable paucity of evidence for the political allegiances of even its greater figures; a paucity which originally led me erroneously to put part of the area under Mowbray influence (Carpenter 1980b: pp. 31–2, 1980a: p. 517) and which produced the bracing but generally deserved correction in Archer 1984a: ch. 6, although there may be more of a case than Dr Archer is prepared to admit for there being some Mowbray activity here in the 1420s (below, pp. 380–7).

The problem lies with localities that fall between these poles. The acid test is the ability of a network to survive the demise of local political leadership, or the disappearance of one or two key figures extensively linked with both lord and locality. West of Warwick, loyalty to the earls of Warwick must have been the primary unifying factor. To the south of the town the group is more mixed, for, although it consisted essentially of neighbours owing a common allegiance to the earl – Peyto, Lucy, Straunge, eventually Verney and, more distantly connected, Hugh Dalby – it was attached to the politically much more diverse network covering east and south-east Warwickshire. In the far north, especially the north-west, it has been shown that the group of local landowners, mostly very much a part of the Warwick affinity, grew in size and cohesion under the influence of Warwick and the Ferrers of Chartley, as the north became a more highly politicised area. Although the durability of these groups cannot be assessed until the effects of the disappearance of the Warwick hegemony after 1439 have been considered, the period before 1439 does give some indications. Where political connection led to neighbourhood marriage, a network born initially of magnate influence could grow into something that was part of the fabric of local society. That is certainly true of the core of Warwick power in west Warwickshire and Worcestershire, where the power of the local nobility

Unless we are to accept the existence of Saul's 'independent knights and esquires' (1981: p. 98), which, as an interpretation, seems to go right against the grain of everything we know about late-medieval society (and indeed of later periods), and especially of Warwickshire society, we may have to conclude that crucial evidence is lacking for the Warwickshire connection in east Warwickshire/Northamptonshire. Note that there are no extant receiver-general accounts for Richard Beauchamp beyond 1420–1 (Longleat MS 6414), and that thereafter we are dependent on ministers' accounts, and none has been found for Northamptonshire. The good series of receiver-general accounts (Br. Lib. Eg. Rolls 8770–3) ends in 1409–10 and the Lisle Valor of *c.* 1423–36 (S.C.12/18/45) irritatingly breaks off just before Northamptonshire. Thus our best chance of identifying the complete Warwick affinity comes earlier in the century, just when the existence of the Astley connection meant that the earl was least likely to have been active in east Warwickshire. It is also possible that Lord Grey of Ruthin inherited more of his father-in-law's connection than has yet been discovered; information on this has so far turned up entirely haphazardly. It is quite probable that John Malory, father of a Beauchamp man (app. 3), who *must* have had influential support to have been elected M.P. four times, and Edward Doddingselles, a fellow-defendant with Warwick in 1429 (JUST 1/1537 m.6), whose younger son married the daughter of Thomas Hugford (*Cal. Pat. Rolls 1436–41*, p. 343), both moved, even if only informally, from the Astley to the Warwick connection. Note that William Ralegh, a member of the east Warwickshire family related to the Astleys (above, p. 233; *Dugdale*, p. 529), was granted an annuity by Beauchamp from Bucks. in 1436 (C.139/123/28). Also that the widow of Ralph Brasebrugge (d.1395), father and grandfather of Warwick retainers, married Robert Goushill, a Mowbray servant who subsequently married the widow of Thomas Duke of Norfolk (*Calendar of Inquisitions Post Mortem 1–6 Henry IV*, p. 103; *Cal. Pat. Rolls 1399–1401*, p. 545), this being undoubtedly an area of potential Mowbray influence (below, pp. 380–1). But, even if Warwick influence here was greater than the evidence suggests – and this was probably not the case before the 1420s – the case for a group here held together by neighbourhood rather than by politics still holds, because of the numbers of middling and lesser families, few of whom were likely to have had a magnate affiliation.

had been binding the lesser landowners together for centuries,[148] and it was perhaps coming to be true of north Warwickshire in the 1430s and early 1440s, under the influence of Warwick, Ferrers and, eventually, of Buckingham. For those families that were not absolutely of the front rank but prominent enough to have estates on both sides of the county boundary, like the Harewells and, initially, the Throgmortons in the south-west, or the Lisles, Ruggeleys and Mollesleys in the north, a network that spanned their territorial interests, even one that was at first magnate-created, would be useful enough to outlast the magnate himself. All the same, networks in both the south-west and the north became weaker in the confused politics of the middle of the century.[149] Due south of Warwick, despite the pervasiveness of the Warwick affinity, there is little evidence of inter-marriage, although, in practice, that did not prevent this group having a surprising durability.[150] Most of the inter-linked families in this area, however, being of some substance, married away from their home base.

This analysis of gentry networks up to 1439 must conclude by emphasising the complexity of such groups. In none of them can neighbourhood, kinship or political connection be claimed as the over-riding linking element, although, in each, one or two of these three played a predominant role. Political ties could themselves be complicated and various. In Warwickshire at this time, especially in the 1420s and 1430s, almost all political affiliations went back ultimately to Richard Beauchamp. His affinity overlapped with those of Joan Beauchamp and Edmund Ferrers;[151] William Lord Clinton used Warwick, his clients and his associates as feoffees; Richard Lord Straunge, the only adult nobleman with estates in the far south of the county while Buckingham was a minor, was a Warwick annuitant. Clinton, Straunge and William Lord Astley tended to be involved with Warwick's men whenever they took part in transactions within the county.[152] As Warwick's interest in the north of the county grew, ties with north midlands magnates seem to have become more important to him, and his influence began to ramify through other affinities. Accordingly, in 1435 he acted as feoffee for Thomas Ferrers of Tamworth, second son of Lord Ferrers

148 Examples of marriages here, some of them between families known to have been linked to the house of Warwick, are: Throgmorton-Spine (above p. 104), the daughters of John Throgmorton to Russell, Gifford and Rous (*Test. Vetust.*, p. 248), Burdet-Bruyn (*Dugdale*, p. 847), Harewell-Washbourne (C.P.40/757 rot.337d.), Harewell-Clopton of Moor Hall (*Dugdale*, p. 809), Hubaud-Chaturley (*V.C.H.*, III, p. 124), Straunge-Clopton of Stratford (S.B.T. D.R.37 Box 48 (deed of 1420)).

149 Marriages among the Warwick-Ferrers of Chartley connection in north Warwickshire: Archer-Stokes (*Dugdale*, p. 781; S.B.T. D.R.503 fo.56v.), Brasebrugge-Willoughby (S.B.T. D.R.10/518), Chetwynd-Ferrers of Chartley (*G.E.C.*, v, p. 319), Cokayn-Bate (*Wedgwood: Biographies*, p. 50), Hore of Elmdon-Mollesley (*Dugdale*, p. 348), Lisle-Middlemore (*Dugdale*, p. 938), Mountford-Vernon (*Dugdale*, p. 1,008); below pp. 490, 599, 602–3, 605.

150 Below, pp. 329–30.

151 App. 3. More on this below, pp. 376–92.

152 For Astley and Clinton, above, nn.121, 127. For Straunge, S.B.T. E.R.1/67/591 (date clearly erroneous); Bod. Lib. Dugdale MS 17, p. 68; Warwick Castle MS B1.

of Groby, his first known transaction with the new owners of Tamworth, although they had been in possession since about 1417. The other feoffees, principally from Leicestershire and the north midlands, included some of Warwick's own men, but also people like Richard Hastings, William Trussell of Bilton and Elmesthorpe in Leicestershire, Thomas Fouleshurst of Leicestershire and Thomas Ferrers' brother-in-law, Roger Aston. All these had hitherto been involved with the Leicestershire nobility – Joan Beauchamp, Ferrers of Groby himself or the duke of Norfolk – and had played little part in Warwickshire or in the Warwick connection.[153] From the later 1420s Warwick was trying to find a place in his system for the young Buckingham,[154] although Buckingham was not to come fully into his own until 1438; it was then that he inherited his mother's estates, amongst them some of his Staffordshire properties and most of the Warwickshire ones, and bought Clinton's north Warwickshire lands.[155] When lords came together in this way, they could extend the range of their clients' possible connections; conversely, they themselves might make use of relationships among local landowners to cultivate ties in areas where they had lands but had previously taken little interest.[156]

When Richard Beauchamp died in 1439, the links between the local gentry networks and between the magnate affinities, in all parts of the county and around its peripheries, coalesced to a remarkable degree about this single nobleman. If we can establish what happened both to the local groupings and to connections across the county when he died and a series of minorities followed, we may have some basis for evaluating the relative importance of horizontal and vertical links in the lives of the gentry in the first half of the century.

III

Throughout the following discussion it must be remembered that we are dealing with a period of only ten years, as opposed to the four decades of the previous section. It is a period moreover in which the political balance within the county could change almost from year to year. There is less evidence and

[153] Bod. Lib. Dugdale MS 17, p. 66; app. 3; above, nn.67, 68, 120; below, p. 392 n.187. For a group of similar complexion from 1432, see Cov. and Lich. Dioc., Reg. Heyworth fo.28.

[154] Deduced from Buckingham's early connections in Warwickshire/Staffordshire, which include several Warwick-Ferrers of Chartley men (*Cal. Close Rolls 1422–29*, pp. 318, 326; Jeayes, 'Catalogue of Spencer Charters', 1647; Bod. Lib. Dugdale MS 15, p. 13).

[155] Bod. Lib. Dugdale MS 13, pp. 325–6; above, n.131; below, pp. 392–3.

[156] A good example is *Paston Letters*, II, pp. 100–1, 193, 234, 407 (Warwick and the Pastons), a relationship presumably activated in the 1450s by way of the Paston/Norfolk link; there were Warwick (Beauchamp trust) lands in East Anglia (Hicks 1981: p. 149), but Warwick had probably taken little interest in the area until the rapprochement with Norfolk which resulted from his move towards York; below, p. 455 n.46.

the dangers in using it are that much greater. The conclusions must be treated with caution and points where the material is particularly thin will be indicated.

When Richard Beauchamp died his son was a minor, who came into his lands some time in about 1444–5, and died not long after, in June 1446. He in his turn left an infant heiress who died under age in January 1449. This left the way clear for Richard Neville, son of the earl of Salisbury, to become earl of Warwick, as husband of Henry's sister Anne. There is much more to be said on the Beauchamp inheritance and on the uncertainty as to its ultimate destination, which was already apparent at the time of Richard Beauchamp's death.[157] For our present purposes it is enough to note that this was an extremely volatile decade in Warwickshire politics, especially at the magnate level, coinciding with a period of growing dissension in national politics. Had Richard Beauchamp's presence throughout the county been less powerful, the transition to politics without the earl of Warwick might have been easier; as it was, there was suddenly a large political kingdom to be fought over, and the efforts of a series of pretenders to stake out a piece of it for themselves had a profound effect on the relationships we have been examining.

The first point to establish is how well the local groupings survived the removal of Beauchamp's guiding hand. Thereafter we can move on to evaluate the effects of the interregnum on geographically more extended associations. One development that had far-reaching consequences was the unfortunate coincidence of the Beauchamp minorities with the demise or eclipse of several families which had played a pivotal role either within local groups or in linking groups together. Mostly this *was* no more than coincidence, but occasionally politics played a part in creating these gaps. In the Tanworth area, for example, William Catesby I is largely absent from deeds of this period, despite the enlargement of his Arden interests when he inherited part of the Bishopestone property in 1444. Partly this was due to a preference at this time for his east Warwickshire and Northamptonshire lands. Partly it can be attributed to the absence of deeds for the Catesbys' west Warwickshire properties in this decade, since they used their local connections here primarily to ensure that they had strong local backing for their own transactions and rarely acted for other Arden landowners. Nevertheless one pressing reason for neglecting west Warwickshire would have been the ending of the west midland following of the earls of Warwick that had made it worth the Catesbys' while to seek out friends there, and the fact that there were now powers of considerably greater import for the family in Northamptonshire and Leicestershire. Strongest amongst these were those focusing on the Duchy of Lancaster, with which the Catesbys had long-standing tenurial connections.[158]

157 There is no record of Henry receiving livery and he would not in fact have been of age until March 1446, although he had already been created premier earl in April 1444 and duke a year later, and he was active in Warwickshire from about 1445 (*G.E.C.*, XII, ii, pp. 383–5; below, p. 413).

158 *Cal. Fine Rolls 1437–45*, p. 300; Somerville 1953: pp. 563, 568–9, 570, 590; C.244/19/133; S.C.6/

It was however in the Tanworth area, notwithstanding the loss of the Catesbys and deaths or minorities in several families, that the local network survived best, and this is unsurprising since it was here that the densest and most independent group was found in the earlier period.[159] Its continuing vigour can be seen in the fact that even John Norreys, a courtier based in Oxfordshire and Berkshire, who had inherited the Marbroke property at Codbarrow and had otherwise little to do with Warwickshire, made use of the Tanworth group in settling this estate.[160] At the level of the minor gentlemen and greater yeomen it was flourishing as before. Amongst the middling landowners there was a significant gain in the arrival of John West of Solihull, legal colleague and then, or later, great-nephew by marriage of Thomas Greswold, who followed Greswold into this group.[161] As before, while the network extended as far east as Kenilworth, it remained a highly localised association, centred north of Henley, south of the Cole and west of the Blythe. If its links with north Warwickshire were on the increase, that was a development that had originated in the 1430s, attributable to the surge of magnate interest in the north of the county. As before, it was principally the Ferrers of Chartley affinity that fostered these links, although there was now no Warwick affinity with which the Ferrers following could mingle to form a political connection running the length of west Warwickshire. The Archers, who were linked to so many local families, were the main point of contact between the Tanworth region and the north, as their dispute with Thomas Porter of Eastcote brought them ever more closely into the Ferrers orbit.[162]

Further north the influence of the Ferrers affinity and its role in making a single unit of north-west Warwickshire and southern Staffordshire in this decade become very evident. Staffordshire families like Bagot, Aston, Erdeswick, Whitgreve and Vernon, which had been linked more or less formally to the Ferrers before, continued to develop the relationships nurtured since the 1420s with north Warwickshire landowners connected to the Ferrers. Among these were the Erdingtons, the Repingtons, the Ruggeleys and the Mollesleys, and Merevale Abbey, a religious house with which the Ferrers had close

949/15 fo.8, /1042/2 (and in all other Ashby and Lapworth accounts, for details of which, above, pp. 158–60).

159 E.g. S.B.T. D.R.3/237, D.R.37/915, 926–8, 930–1, 934, 937, 939, 942, 948, Box 42 (deeds of 1440–9), Box 46 (deed of 1446), Box 49 (deeds of 1443), D.R.503 fos.59–60 (Monkspath deed); *Cal. Fine Rolls 1445–52*, pp. 15, 65; B.R.L. 249975, 427016; see also n.163, below for connections to the north.

160 Jeffs 1961a: p. 164; *Dugdale*, p. 782; S.B.T. D.R.37/937, 948. He also features in other deeds cited in n.159.

161 *Cal. Pat. Rolls 1452–61*, p. 77; C.1/58/175. John Greswold, Thomas' nephew and West's father-in-law, was forty-four in 1458 (C.139/174/39), so it is quite possible that his daughter was already of marriageable age by the end of the 1440s. Refs. in n.159 for evidence of West's involvement in the Tanworth region.

162 For the Archers and the Porters, see below, pp. 382, 425–6, 430.

ties.[163] The Staffordshire wing of the group gained additional strength in 1439 from the marriage of Buckingham's retainer, Philip Chetwynd, to the widow of Edmund, Lord Ferrers. This match reinforced the close ties between the Buckingham and Ferrers affinities in Staffordshire and was a further episode in the mingling of the two affinities that had been going on since at least the late 1420s, initially under the auspices of Richard Beauchamp, and which had brought Cokayn, Mollesley and Ruggeley, for example, into the Buckingham circle.[164]

Within this cross-border grouping, the survival of the north Warwickshire network is readily observable, despite some notable absentees: the Berminghams' tenure of their manor of Birmingham was seriously in doubt, the Mountfords were seeking an ever larger stage, the Arderns and Cokayns were going through a difficult patch.[165] But Erdington, Repington, Ruggeley, Mollesley, Brasebrugge, Stokes and Lisle remained in association with each other and with their Staffordshire neighbours. By the end of the decade they had been joined by the Freville heirs to whom most of the family's Warwickshire land had fallen, Thomas Ferrers I and Hugh Willoughby (or, at least, his widow and her second husband), who were now beginning to play some part in Warwickshire affairs. Politically it had become a much more heterogeneous group, even more so than this sketch indicates, as we shall see shortly, but there are signs that its reclamation by the Warwick-Ferrers interest was not impossible.[166] What was emerging therefore was a local network that, having originally owed its identity to a large extent to the influence of a noble affinity, was achieving a life of its own.[167] It could be taken over by a magnate with

[163] E.g. *Cal. Fine Rolls 1437–45*, p. 175; *Cal. Close Rolls 1435–41*, p. 399, *1441–47*, p. 188; S.B.T. D.R.98/849, 850, D.R.10/518, 721, D.R.37 Box 42 (deed of 1448); Sims ed., *Walsall Deeds*, p. 17; Nott. Univ. Lib. Middleton MS Mi D 4145, 4764; Bod. Lib. Dugdale MS 13, p. 301, 15, p. 127; Warwick Castle MS B11; *Cat. Anc. Deeds*, III, D1175; Shaw 1798–1801: I, p. 147. For Ferrers connections outside Warwickshire, E.163/7/31 (and app. 3 for comments on identification of this list), *Colls. Hist. Staffs.*, n.s., 11, pp. 40–1; Pevsner and Wedgwood 1966: p. 353 (*recte* Robert, Lord Ferrers) and above, nn.60, 125, for some earlier connections with Warwickshire.

[164] *Dugdale*, p. 1,103; for Buckingham connections, app. 3; Nat Lib. Wales Peniarth MS 280; Wm. Salt Lib. Vernon Coll. A/7/15. For earlier intermingling of associates, see nn.60, 125, above.

[165] For these, above, pp. 115–16 and below, pp. 431–3.

[166] For the political complexion of the group, refs. above, n.163 and app. 3. Henry of Warwick maintained the family's link with the Ferrers of Chartley (app. 3) and William Repington's bequest of the reversion of his estates to Henry in 1446 suggests a meaningful link with at least one of the Ferrers-Warwick men of the earlier period (E.326/8627; and above, nn.60, 125, for refs. to Repington's associates before 1439), as does Mollesley's acting as an agent for Henry in 1442–3 (Br. Lib. Eg. Roll 8532; above, p. 298 for Mollesley's associates before 1439). John Ferrers, possibly the younger brother of William, was steward of the household to Henry. Although Richard Beauchamp feed a John Ferrers of Groby, the fact that the steward had a son called Edmund suggests he came from the Chartley family (*Cal. Close Rolls 1441–47*, p. 188; Bod. Lib. Dugdale MS 15, p. 255; C.139/96/3/18). Willoughby was in fact linked to Buckingham and to this north midlands circle as early as 1443 (*Test. Ebor.*, II, p. 134).

[167] The pattern of marriages here amongst the gentry continued with the Brasebrugge-Willoughby match of 1443 (above, n.149).

ambitions in its locality, as it began to be annexed in this period by the duke of Buckingham, but it could survive, it seems, without magnate leadership.[168]

Nevertheless, a look at the neighbouring region in the north-east reveals quite how much the geography of local association owed to the noble balance of power in this decade. It also puts a further gloss on the political complexity of the northern group. From 1440 the whole of north Warwickshire was more extensively exposed than before to influences from Leicestershire. The principal reasons for this are to do with Edward Grey, heir to the Astley estates as eldest son of Reginald Grey of Ruthin by his second wife, the daughter of William Lord Astley. He inherited the lands when his father died in 1440 and was subsequently able to rebuild the north-east connection that had lain dormant since the death of his grandfather, Lord William.[169] By 1441–3 he was linked to Malory of Newbold Revel and Erdington, two families that had been part of the earlier Astley connection, and possibly also to a third, Purfrey. During the 1440s he built up a very wide-ranging connection in central and north-eastern Warwickshire, encompassing Maxstoke, Ansley, Fillongley, Binley near Coventry, Coventry itself and the religious houses at Nuneaton, Arbury and Combe.[170]

Grey's presence in north-east Warwickshire was reinforced by the second source of his power, which came through his wife, the Ferrers of Groby heiress. Through her, on the death of Lord William in 1445, he obtained the title of Lord Ferrers of Groby and the properties that did not go to Thomas Ferrers, including the large Leicestershire estate.[171] When added to the Astley property,

[168] Below, p. 405.

[169] *G.E.C.*, I, p. 284, V, pp. 358–60; for the date of Astley's death, above, n.121; for the Astley connection, above, p. 314.

[170] E.326 /10717; Bod. Lib. Dugdale MS 15, p. 127; *Cat. Anc. Deeds*, VI, C4070; *Cal. Close Rolls 1435–41*, p. 478, *1447–54*, p. 17; *W.F.F.*, 2630; K.B.27/738 Coram Rege rot.99., /754 Coram Rege rot.105d.; Leics.R.O. DE 2242/3/31767(1), 40056; S.B.T. E.R.112/1/3; app. 3. The Purfrey connection is an indirect one, through William Purfrey II's participation in a Chetwynd deed with Erdington and Malory (*Colls. Hist. Staffs.*, o.s. 12, pp. 313–14), and rests to some extent on the family's earlier direct involvement with Lord Astley (above, p. 314).

[171] *I.P.M.* 23 Hen. VI/33, 36 Hen. VI/40; *G.E.C.*, V, pp. 354–60.

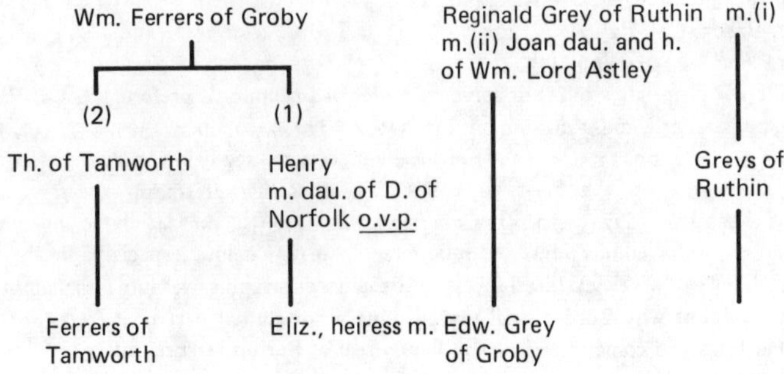

with its two centres at Astley in Warwickshire and Broughton Astley in Leicestershire, this gave him a concentrated power base in east Warwickshire and Leicestershire.[172] Meanwhile Thomas Ferrers, Grey's uncle by marriage, whose residence at Tamworth lay within easy reach of Astley, was becoming more involved in Warwickshire affairs from the late 1440s. This was perhaps because the addition of the Ferrers property of Tettenhall in Staffordshire to the Freville estates he already had in and around Tamworth gave him a reason for taking his responsibilities west of Leicestershire more seriously.[173] The Ferrers of Groby as a family were an integral part of the Leicestershire network; this also included Joan Beauchamp (now succeeded by her son-in-law, James Boteller earl of Ormond, and her grandson, the future earl of Wiltshire) and John Lord Beaumont.[174] Thus the arrival of Thomas Ferrers and Edward Grey in north-east Warwickshire during the 1440s meant that there were now two major figures in the region with connections that linked Warwickshire to Leicestershire.

This is reflected both in Grey's own associates – amongst these were Lord Beaumont, the Leicestershire families of Moton, Mulso and Ashby, and families like Trussell of Bilton and Hastings, which had lands in both counties[175] – and in the way connections stretching across the two counties gained strength in the 1440s. Since Lord Beaumont, who appears to have been one of the pivotal figures in Leicestershire at this time, was a major power on the Duchy of Lancaster estates in Leicestershire and a growing force at court, there was every reason for the gentry in the areas of Warwickshire that bordered on Leicestershire to make more of their connections with the neighbouring county and with Northamptonshire, to the south, another Duchy of Lancaster county.[176] An obvious example is Thomas Ferrers himself, a Leicestershire man who had moved into Warwickshire by marriage and who in 1448 married his heir, Thomas II, to the daughter of Leonard Hastings. This was a union of two families bestriding the county boundary, both of them linked to the Grey-Ormond-Beaumont nexus.[177] Thomas Erdington II, who

[172] W.C.R.O. C.R.136/C159.

[173] Above, pp. 105, 160. His first and, as it turned out, only office was sheriff of Staffordshire, to which he was appointed in 1447 (*Lists and Indexes*, 9, p. 127).

[174] Above, p. 307 and nn.67–9; *G.E.C.*, x, pp. 125–7; Jeayes ed., *Lyttelton Charters*, p. 87; *Cat. Anc. Deeds*, II, B2805; *Cal. Pat. Rolls 1461–67*, p. 112; *H.M.C. Hastings*, I, pp. 1–2.

[175] *Cal. Close Rolls 1435–41*, pp. 475, 478, *1447–54*, pp. 17, 172.

[176] Somerville 1953: pp. 563, 568. For some examples of Beaumont's preferment, *Cal. Pat. Rolls 1436–41*, pp. 509, 558, 569, *1441–46*, pp. 139, 348, 473, *1446–52*, pp. 42, 329, 457, 519, 590; *Cal. Fine Rolls 1445–52*, pp. 11, 190, 211. For local connections, see below, n.177.

[177] *H.M.C. Hastings*, I, pp. 1–2, 20–1, 44, 300; *Cal. Close Rolls 1441–47*, pp. 29, 91–2, 135, 261, 288–9, 313–17, 474, *1447–54*, p. 51; *Cal. Pat. Rolls 1446–52*, p. 124; above, nn.170–2. For further cross-border connections, see refs. cited in n.183, below, especially the St. George feoffment. This east Warwickshire/Leicestershire connection spills over into Northamptonshire, which is no doubt why Lord Lovell played quite a substantial part in it (refs. immediately above). Hastings had come into the main family seat at Burton Hastings after the death of his

had lands in Leicestershire but has left few traces in that county before this period, turns up on two major Leicestershire transactions of the 1440s, acting with members of the Beaumont and Ferrers of Groby families, and also plays a prominent part in an agreement over the Groby property in 1445.[178] Henry Fillongley, whose previous dealings in Leicestershire had tended to be related purely to his service to Joan Beauchamp and her family, was now linked to this complex network, which ran from central and north-east Warwickshire into Leicestershire and beyond.[179] The rise of new local powers had drawn together local groupings throughout the more easterly sectors of central and northern Warwickshire, and had made the political affiliations of the north of the county even more complex than they had become under the expanding authority of Richard Beauchamp. To appreciate the full extent of intermeshing amongst magnate followings in this region, one has to realise that Edward Grey's authority in north Warwickshire owed a lot to his close ties with the duke of Buckingham, which will be discussed in chapter 11,[180] and may have benefited also from a certain amount of co-operation with William Ferrers of Chartley, Lord Edmund's successor.[181]

But Grey's influence by no means ended there. In east and south-east Warwickshire there had been a certain amount of attrition amongst the gentry. Weston was dead, Botener was succeeded by first the Derbyshire Lowes and then the Leicestershire Everinghams, Metley succeeded by Richard Hotoft, to whom Leicestershire was more important than Warwickshire, the Cotes eclipsed by the Metley-Hotoft embezzlement of part of their estate, William Peyto in France, then a captive there, then financially crippled by his ransom,

older brother Richard's widow the year before, so he too was a newcomer to the cross-border families (*V.C.H.*, VI, p. 57).

178 *Feudal Aids*, III, p. 121; *Cal. Pat. Rolls 1441–46*, pp. 279–80; *H.M.C. Hastings*, I, pp. 73–4; *Colls. Hist. Staffs.*, o.s., 11, pp. 234–5; Leics.R.O. DE 2242/3/3176(1), 40056. Note also his annuity from Lord Lovell, granted in 1447, in the light of Lovell's association with this group (*Colls. Hist. Staffs.*, n.s., 4, p. 145; above, n.177). Even if, as was possible, this was merely part of a business deal, its significance, as a sign of some kind of relationship, cannot be ignored.

179 *Cal. Close Rolls 1441–47*, pp. 171, 474, *1447–54*, p. 17; B.R.L. 418917; *Cat. Anc. Deeds*, II, B3752; *Colls. Hist. Staffs.*, n.s., 3, pp. 159–60; E.326/10717; K.B.27/741 Coram Rege rot.17; C.47/10/26/8.

180 Below, pp. 401–5.

181 There was some overlap between the associates of both magnates, in Erdington, Colshill and possibly Malory. For Erdington, see app. 3; *Cal. Close Rolls 1441–47*, p. 188; S.B.T. D.R.37 Box 42 (deed of 1448); for Colshill, see app. 3 and deeds of this time, in which he features with Ferrers and Grey connections (W.C.R.O. C.R.162/121; S.B.T. D.R.37 Box 50 (deeds of 1443)). These last are for the conveyance of Botley in Ullenhall from the Malorys of Walton-on-the-Wolds to the Archers. Participants included Erdington, Thomas Malory, Colshill and Thomas Sydenhale (linked to Grey: below, p. 329); it could be that this transaction was effected by means of the links between the Ferrers and the Greys, but this may be to put too much weight on the evidence.

and there was a minority in the Knightley family after 1441.[182] The Avon-Leam network had consequently lost something of its cohesiveness. But it did survive and in surviving it became a vehicle for the ambitions of Edward Grey. Hotoft and Thomas Boughton, the successor to Geoffrey Allesley, both served him, and he can be linked to several other families from this region and from further south, such as Shukburgh, Derset and Hore of Stoneythorpe and even to the Porters of Upper Ettington, in the far south of the county. There is no doubt that these families were extensively enough connected to constitute a local network, the continuation in a somewhat weakened form of the east to south-east grouping of the previous period, and that Grey had taken over the leadership of this group.[183] His authority south of the Avon-Leam area would have been buttressed by the Ferrers of Groby property he had inherited in the adjacent county of Northamptonshire and possibly also by his family connections with the Greys of Ruthin, who were a considerable force in that county. That in 1444–5 every one of the local gentry feed by Axholme Abbey's dependency at Monks Kirby in east Warwickshire was linked in some way to Grey is sufficient indication of the dimensions to which his power in that part of the county had grown, for the abbey would have wished to ensure that its gentry connections belonged to the dominant local group.[184]

What had happened in eastern Warwickshire was that the arrival of a new magnate power had transformed the geographical scope of associations amongst the gentry. At last someone had been able to exploit the lack of natural barriers to association along the east Warwickshire border. Under Grey's political leadership the links between the gentry in the north-east had become sufficiently extensive for a local group to emerge for the first time since the death of William Lord Astley, and, through the Grey connection, it had become linked to existing groups that Grey had taken over further south. There was now a single network running from some way south of the Leam as far north as Astley

[182] Weston: *Cal. Pat. Rolls 1441–46*, p. 31 (could be a different John Weston): last known ref. to him is 1433: *Coventry Leet Book*, p. 144. Botener: last known ref. is 1433: Bod. Lib. Dugdale MS 13, p. 343; Shaw 1798–1801: II, p. 185. Metley: S.B.T. D.R.3/259; *Dugdale*, p. 34 – a comparison of Hotoft's tenure of office in Warwickshire and Leicestershire (*Cal. Pat. Rolls* and *Wedgwood: Biographies*, p. 472) quickly establishes the relative importance to him of the two counties. Cotes: above, p. 102; below, p. 401. Peyto: *Dugdale*, pp. 476–7; above, p. 121; below, p. 416. Knightley: C.140/110/44.

[183] W.C.R.O. C.R.136/C159, C.R.162/121; Br. Lib. Add. Ch. 48,660; B.R.L. 418917 (feoffment by William St George, of the Ormond circle in Leics., of Brandon manor in east Warks., which he had recently inherited: *H.M.C. Hastings*, I, pp. 1–2; *V.C.H.*, VI, p. 276); K.B. 27/724 Coram Rege rot.79d., /726 Coram Rege rot.60d., /729 Rex rot. 10d.; Magdalen College, Oxford Muns., Westcote 2; also refs. in nn.170 and 179, Botley deeds in n.181, and further discussion of Grey's activities, below, pp. 401–5.

[184] *I.P.M.* 23 Hen.VI/33. No Northamptonshire lands are recorded in Grey's I.P.M. (*I.P.M.*, 36 Hen.VI/40), but it does not seem that Thomas Ferrers got this estate (C.139/174/34; *Cal. Close Rolls 1441–47*, pp. 265–6, 313); Jack ed., *Grey of Ruthin Valor*, pp. 66–78; S.C.6/1039/18 (the gentry recorded here as associated with Axholme include Colshill, Malory and Boughton).

and Mancetter. The Avon-Leam group remained, if in rather a weakened form, but, where it had previously been politically multifarious, it had come under the sway of a single magnate. Grey's success in this respect can be measured by the fact that he was even able to command the services of Thomas Sydenhale, a resident of the Tanworth area, because of Sydenhale's family link with the Shukburghs.[185]

All the same, the network in east and south-east Warwickshire was less imposing and geographically less extended than it had been before, notably in the weakening of the links between its eastern and southern sectors. Although the evidence is on the flimsy side, there are indications that here too it was Grey's intervention and not just a series of accidents that was responsible. It is a striking fact that the Catesbys, so active in this area before and after the 1440s, have left few traces on documents concerning eastern Warwickshire in this decade. They reappear in force, however, in 1448, in a family settlement in which the participants include representatives of other major families from this area who are barely visible throughout the decade, such as Robert Catesby, William Peyto and Edward Doddingselles, as well as local figures, like Thomas Boughton, who had been associated with Grey. Moreover, some of the other participants, among them John Talbot Lord Lisle, William Lord Lovell and Thomas and William Tresham and prominent men from other parts of Warwickshire and Northamptonshire, can be identified as representing a faction that was antipathetic to the Greys of Groby and Ruthin at this time, one of uncertainty for Grey's power in Warwickshire.[186] Other deeds from 1448–50 seem to support the hypothesis that we are witnessing the resurgence of the east Warwickshire network in something approaching its full pre-1439 glory.[187] We can therefore conclude rather tentatively that Grey had not only taken over a thriving group of associates, but been so successful in turning it to his own purposes that he was able to exclude from it men he did not trust, particularly the major local gentry. It was only when Grey's power waned slightly at the end of the decade that the grouping in this area regained the level of cohesiveness and political diversity which had characterised it before Grey's arrival. If this hypothesis is valid, it is further evidence that horizontal and vertical links acted upon one another in ways that are neither straightforward nor predictable.

Under these circumstances it is perhaps not surprising that the ties of eastern Warwickshire with the area due south of Warwick, which had made the whole of eastern and south-eastern Warwickshire such a cohesive unit in the period up to 1439, grew somewhat threadbare in this period. This is particularly so when

185 K.B.27/726 Coram Rege rot.60d.; below, pp. 402–3.

186 *Cat. Anc. Deeds*, IV, A10387; for the political background, see below, pp. 422–4. Peyto's inaction in this period is of course also accounted for by his misadventures in France (above, p. 327). Note that in 1444 associates of Catesby, the Treshams etc. acted with Edmund Grey of Ruthin; as usual in local politics, nothing is straightforward (Northants.R.O. Fitzwilliam MS 660).

187 *Cat. Anc. Deeds*, III, A4289, IV, A9000; W.C.R.O. C.R.1248/70/32.

we consider that they had been forged to a large extent by Peyto, Doddingselles, the Catesbys, Hugh Dalby and Geoffrey Allesley, of whom the first three were perhaps excluded from the east Warwickshire network, and the second two dead and succeeded by men intimately connected with Grey and his close associate the duke of Buckingham.[188] Nevertheless the southern group survived. Verneys, Lucys and Peytos remained in association, despite the loss of their common allegiance to the earl of Warwick, and Thomas Middleton, who had married Thomas Straunge's widow, was absorbed into the group, while William Lucy maintained the family's tradition of forays across the Avon. John Campion remained a minor member of the group, the separation of the two networks of eastern Warwickshire confining his contacts more exclusively to this southern one. By the end of the 1440s there are indications that Richard Verney was taking this group westwards, to the new powers in the west midlands, Lords Beauchamp and Sudeley.[189]

West of Warwick there is no doubt whatsoever of the continued existence of a cohesive Warwickshire-Worcestershire network throughout the decade, whether the Warwick lands were in custody or in the hands of the adult heir. Some of the personnel changed, through deaths and minorities, but the continuity is obvious. The core, on the Warwickshire side, had originally comprised Throgmorton, Harewell, Burdet, Trussell of Billesley, Hugford, Bishopestone and Crewe/Clopton. It had already been somewhat modified since the early years of the century, to accommodate the deaths of some and the fading importance of others, and to incorporate additional figures, such as Neville and Hubaud, along with a larger Worcestershire ingredient.[190] In the 1440s the Harewell line at Bidford died out and there was a minority in the main Harewell family at Wootton, while Ralph Neville was at first less in evidence. But in their place came John Rous, head of a family that had recently emerged from a long series of minorities, and Thomas Littleton of Frankley in Worcestershire, a major landowner in north Warwickshire after his marriage to the Chetwynd widow in 1444, who remained for the moment firmly rooted in the west midlands.[191] These names and the familiar Worcestershire ones of Wollashull, Vampage and Bruyn continue to appear together, along with numbers of minor local gentry, although by this time the Hugford participation

188 C.139/93/49; *Dugdale*, p. 99; and below, ch. 11 for politics in southern Warwickshire in the 1440s. The successors to Hugh Dalby and Allesley were Richard Dalby (app. 3 and below, pp. 405, 417–18) and Thomas Boughton (above, p. 328).

189 *Cal. Close Rolls 1435–41*, p. 445, *1441–47*, p. 463, *1447–54*, p. 51; S.B.T. D.R.98/113, 115a, 116a, 117, 118, 479, 849–50, D.R.41/103, p. 86, D.R.37 Box 35 (deeds of 1440 and 1446); W.C.R.O. L.4/36.

190 See refs. above, n.82.

191 *Dugdale*, pp. 809–10; *Stratford Register*, p. 71; C.139/145/9; *Cal. Pat. Rolls 1416–22*, p. 3; *Cal. Close Rolls 1429–35*, p. 88; *Test. Vetust.*, p. 365; Chetwynd-Stapylton 1892: p. 109. For Neville, see above, p. 292.

in this group had become more occasional, as the former Metley lands turned their interests eastwards. As before, to the extent that the Staffords of Grafton had any local connections, they centred on this group. The ties of family and of traditional mutual support and trust fostered by the long-lived Warwick connection were enough to ensure the continued flourishing of the network even in the absence of the Warwick power itself.[192]

What changed, then, was not the group itself but its leadership, a subject that will receive much fuller attention in chapter 11. From Warwick's death until about 1445 the most powerful potential force in the region was Buckingham.[193] However, two other west midlands magnates soon came to the fore. As early as 1439 John Beauchamp of Powick, a native of Worcestershire, and his kinsman and long-standing associate Lord Sudeley, whose chief residence was at Sudeley in north Gloucestershire, had some authority here, as two of the keepers of the dower lands of Warwick's widow.[194] Sudeley was raised to the peerage in 1441, and in 1443 he inherited his mother's jointure, which included Sudeley Castle and two important estates in east Warwickshire.[195] He had been constable of Kenilworth since 1433 and steward since 1437 and his power was being immeasurably enhanced by his close ties with the Suffolk circle.[196] By 1439 he was linked with two men who were later to be part of his affinity in south-west Warwickshire, John Aylesbury of Edstone and John Throgmorton.[197] This was the beginning of a connection that was eventually to stretch across the county from south-west to north-east and was to play a significant part in Warwickshire politics later in the century.[198] For the moment it was largely confined to the north Gloucestershire/south-west Warwickshire region, although by the end of the decade it was beginning to percolate into south Warwickshire, courtesy of the Verneys,[199] and in 1441 John Beaufitz of Kenilworth had entered on what was to be a life-long allegiance to Sudeley.[200]

[192] E.g. Bod. Lib. Dugdale MS 15, pp. 77, 165, 217; Coughton Court, Throckmorton MS Box 35 (deed of 1449), Box 36 (deed of 1440), Box 37 (deed of 1445), Box 45 (deed of 1444), Box 49 (file of deeds – deed of 1446), Box 50 (deed of 1439); *Cal. Pat. Rolls 1436–41*, p. 495, *1441–46*, p. 344; *W.F.F.*, 2603, 2610, 2614; *Cal. Close Rolls 1435–41*, p. 346; *Cat. Anc. Deeds*, VI, C5242; Warwick Castle MS 116A,B,C, 117A,B; C.1/24/186; C.244/36/73; Jeayes ed., *Lyttleton Charters*, p. 87; C.244/36/43; Griffiths 1972a: pp. 152–3.

[193] Below, pp. 403–4, 411, 421–2.

[194] *G.E.C.*, XII, i, pp. 419–20; *Cal. Pat. Rolls 1436–41*, pp. 279, 360. For Sudeley and Beauchamp and their earlier connections, see *G.E.C.*, II, p. 47, XII, i, pp. 418–20; *Cal. Close Rolls 1422–29*, p. 399, *1435–41*, p. 123; Bod. Lib. Dug. MS 39 fo.65; Dent 1877: p. 115.

[195] *Cal. Pat. Rolls 1441–46*, p. 2; *Cal. Fine Rolls 1437–45*, p. 254; *Cal. Close Rolls 1405–09*, p. 221.

[196] Somerville 1953: pp. 560–1; Griffiths 1981: pp. 303, 343–4, 359; *Cal. Pat. Rolls 1436–41*, pp. 39, 407.

[197] *Cat. Anc. Deeds*, III, A4477; Coughton Court, Throckmorton MS Box 52 (deed of 1439); app. 3.

[198] Below, pp. 512–13, 601, 607–8.

[199] Above, p. 330.

[200] App. 3; also Thomas Harewell (see app. 3).

John Beauchamp of Powick, who was raised to the peerage in 1447, and, like Sudeley, had been absent in France for much of Henry VI's reign, began to hold local office in the west midlands in 1437.[201] From 1434 there is evidence that he was involved with families from the Worcestershire, Gloucestershire, Warwickshire region, not infrequently in conjunction with Sudeley.[202] He already owned one half of Alcester manor in south-west Warwickshire and in 1444 he acquired the other.[203] From 1445 he is consistently linked with the main figures in the Warwickshire–Worcestershire nexus, sometimes in conjunction with Sudeley, his influence clearly outstripping any that Buckingham might have had before his arrival.[204] It is especially noteworthy that the growth of his power actually coincides with the majority of the one nobleman who might have thought he had an absolute right to the allegiance of the gentry of this area, the new earl of Warwick. The effects of the intervention in this area of magnates heavily reliant on a power base in Gloucestershire – that is Sudeley and before him Buckingham, who had a major group of estates centred on Thornbury – can be seen in the greater preponderance of Gloucestershire men in this west midland network in the 1440s, notably the families of Tracy, Whittington and Poyntz.[205]

In summing up this survey of what happened to the local networks between 1439 and 1449, we can use the distinction made earlier between 'natural' neighbourhood groups and those created by magnate politics, even though it obscures the fact that this was a difference of degree rather than of kind. Of the first category, the Tanworth group survived rather better than its equivalent in the Avon-Leam area, and certainly a lot better than the extensive but loosely-connected network of east and south-east Warwickshire of which the latter formed a part. This was undoubtedly because the Tanworth area was both more confined geographically and, primarily because of its isolation, less exposed to political intervention. Of the groups where a common allegiance to the earl of Warwick or his associates was a significant binding force, the survival of that at the centre of Beauchamp power is not to be wondered at, given its long history. The continuation of the group south of Warwick is more surprising. It could be argued that the small number of prominent families here had little choice but to rely on each other, but, once their common bond with

[201] Br. Lib. Add. Ch.6835; *Cal. Fine Rolls 1437–45*, p. 3; *Actes de la Chancellerie*, II, p. 159 n.1; Dent 1877: pp. 116–17; Wylie and Waugh 1914–29: III, p. 354; and refs. in n.194, above.

[202] For associations of both 1436–9, see *Cal. Pat. Rolls 1436–41*, pp. 222, 289; Warwick Castle MS 116; Br. Lib. Add. Ch. 72,643; B.R.L. Wingfield Digby MS A527; *Cat. Anc. Deeds*, III, A4477; W.C.R.O. C.R.1248/70/55a. Both had some much earlier involvement with Warwickshire, including with men from this area (above, pp. 309–10; *W.F.F.*, 2519; also above, nn.194, 197).

[203] *V.C.H.*, III, p. 16.

[204] Above, n.192, for refs. Note also the marriage of John's heir Richard to the daughter of Humphrey Stafford I in 1446 (*Dugdale*, p. 769 n.1); this ended badly (Carpenter 1986a: p. 39).

[205] Above, n.192 and below pp. 412–20.

the earl of Warwick was dissolved, they could easily have been absorbed into the powerful affinities of Suffolk and his friends in the adjacent counties of Oxfordshire and Northamptonshire, and yet this apparently did not happen.[206] Most interesting of all is the continued strength, albeit in an altered form and under new and more divided magnate authority, of the northern group, born so recently under the aegis of Warwick and Ferrers of Chartley. It seems undeniable on the analysis so far that horizontal ties among the gentry, even if magnate-created, if they matched the gentry's needs, could with remarkable rapidity acquire a force which enabled them to outlast vertical ties with the nobility. Although incoming magnates could themselves exploit this situation, finding ready-made local affinities waiting for them, we shall see that it was not always possible to master a network that they had not created themselves.

If this troubled decade in some respects shows the strength of the ties that bound the gentry to each other, it also demonstrates how easily the groups could be reshaped by the dynamics of magnate politics. We have already seen how the introduction of new forces altered the political geography of the county in this period, most notably in the close ties that began to develop, on a scale not seen before, between northern and eastern Warwickshire and Staffordshire and Leicestershire. What happened to the rather tenuous county unity, so dependent on the most prominent members of the Warwick affinity? There is certainly evidence that links across the county within the following of Richard Beauchamp lasted beyond his death; the Verneys' to the Porters of Eastcote, the Lucys' to the Archers, Thomas Hugford's to William Mountford, for example.[207] What we do not have in these years, by contrast with the period before, is evidence of numbers of transactions showing a county-wide affinity in action. The death or temporary removal of pivotal members of the affinity like Thomas Harewell or William Peyto did not help, but they could have been replaced, as alternatives had been found earlier on to people like Thomas Crewe and John Harewell. More important was what was happening to the county politically at this time.

First, insofar as there was still a directing force behind the remains of the Warwick affinity, it consisted only in part of Warwick retainers like William Mountford and Thomas Hugford, for, this being one of the richest prizes to arrive on the patronage scene, there was strong courtier interest in the estate.[208] Consequently both Mountford and Hugford, especially the former, were brought into close connection with court circles. If these happened to

[206] On Northamptonshire, see below, pp. 408, 423–4; on Oxfordshire, see Griffiths 1981: pp. 336–7.

[207] S.B.T. D.R.98/89a, 849, 850, D.R.37 Box 50 (deeds of 1443); Warwick Castle MS B11; S.B.T. E.R.1/65/448; K.B.27/738 Coram Rege rot.34d., /756 Coram Rege rot. 4.

[208] *Test. Vetust.*, pp. 233, 240; *Cal. Pat. Rolls 1436–41*, pp. 279, 360, 367, 435, *1441–46*, pp. 268, 450, *1446–52*, p. 1; *Cal. Fine Rolls 1437–45*, pp. 77, 122. For more on these estates in custody, see below, pp. 400, 421.

include Warwickshire gentry from other parts of the county, like Thomas Littleton or Henry Fillongley, such contacts were unlikely to foster a sense of common identity as Warwickshire men, because their context was highly unlocalised.[209] Similarly, John Throgmorton's links with the court, which had existed ever since he was made Beauchamp chamberlain of the exchequer in 1419, began to assume a far greater role in his transactions in this period.[210] It could indeed be argued that his relationship with Sudeley, the king's butler, grew as much from their association at court as from ties of neighbourhood in the west midlands.[211] This was in any case a time when it was wise to cultivate court connections, as it was the period when the group around Suffolk was moving rapidly into the ascendant. Consequently, Warwick retainers who came into contact with this circle through the Beauchamp lands were all the more likely to distance themselves from their local roots. The only occasion for which evidence survives when the old Warwick affinity becomes visible again, as an entity located primarily in the west midlands, is in the series of recognisances of 1445–6 to raise the ransom money for Warwick's old retainer, William Peyto. It is probably not coincidental that this was also the one period in the decade when there was an adult earl.[212]

Secondly, no single magnate managed to pull together the localities that made up the county to create a political unit of Warwickshire, as Richard Beauchamp had done in the last two decades of his life. Under Beauchamp, despite the inevitable cross-border connections attributable to the existence of cross-border estates, the networks that existed within the county operated inside the county boundaries to a quite surprising degree. The only exception was the west midlands nexus that was very much the earl's private property. Where there was extensive involvement with the adjacent county, notably between the north-east and Leicestershire, this was essentially because there were too few gentry committed primarily to Warwickshire in these areas for a Warwickshire network to develop. It was the magnitude of the earl's control, first over west Warwickshire, finally over virtually the whole county, that determined that the gentry of Warwickshire would turn inwards, towards the area of Warwick hegemony, rather than outwards, to the adjacent counties where their interests would in many cases more naturally have taken them. After 1439 there was no such force to hold the county together and the unity

209 *Cal. Fine Rolls 1445–52*, p. 109; *Cal. Pat. Rolls 1494–1509*, pp. 99–102; *Cal. Close Rolls 1447–54*, p. 51; K.B.27/732 Coram Rege rot.25, /756 Coram Rege rot.4; *Cat. Anc. Deeds*, IV, A10387. It was in the 1440s that William's son Edmund embarked on the career in government that was eventually to align his father more closely with the court (*Cal. Pat. Rolls 1441–46*, p. 244, *1446–52*, pp. 1, 6, 27; below, pp. 408–9, 427, 448, 457).

210 Roskell 1954: p. 224; *Cal. Pat. Rolls 1436–41*, pp. 23, 553, *1441–46*, pp. 267–8; *Cal. Close Rolls 1435–41*, p. 476, *1441–47*, pp. 131, 218–19, 222–3, 229, 367; *Cal. Fine Rolls 1437–45*, p. 19.

211 *G.E.C.*, XII, i, p. 420.

212 *Colls. Hist. Staffs.*, o.s., 11, p. 246; *W.F.F.*, 2625; *Cal. Close Rolls 1441–47*, pp. 356, 369.

evaporated; links between east and west and north and south became more tenuous, while those with neighbouring counties, often fostered by magnate connections, flourished. Tensions between former clients of the earl of Warwick, which began to surface at this time, lent force to these tendencies.[213] Warwickshire seems on this evidence to have had little meaning as a county beyond the purely administrative one unless its discrete regions could be forced into a political unity.

IV

The discussion has revealed a variety of identities amongst the Warwickshire gentry in the first half of the century. One self-evident conclusion is that there were different identities at different social levels, those of the greater gentry being geographically much more extended than those of their lesser neighbours, unless these last were lawyers or servants of crown or nobility. For a very minor landowner, hovering between gentry and yeomanry, the link to the local knight or esquire was usually the only access to a wider political and social world. It was very much in the interests of the more prominent landowner to foster such relationships, for it was through them that he became a power in his immediate locality; if it were known that he was the man with the military power of the lesser men in his neighbourhood at his disposal, his standing with both nobility and gentry was likely to rise. For example, it was probably Thomas Erdington who helped raise the minor gentry members of Edmund Ferrers of Chartley's little army that took the field against Joan Beauchamp in 1431, and probably Thomas Boughton and perhaps Thomas Shukburgh who ensured the bribability of the jury that Edward Grey seems to have suborned in the Betley case in 1442.[214] This was doubtless why William Mountford, not noted for his condescension where insignificant neighbouring landowners were concerned, stood witness in 1426 for his tenant William Lecroft, a minor manorial lord, bringing along other eminent landowners to join him in the transaction, and why he acted as arbitrator between lesser landowners at Coleshill in 1446.[215]

It was by using such men as Mountford as a vehicle that a magnate could gain access to the landowning strength of a whole neighbourhood; in a sense the greater gentry also were lords of affinities, an essential connecting-point in the

[213] Below, pp. 406, 416, 425–8, 431.

[214] K.B.27/681 Rex rot.21, /726 Coram Rege rot.60d. For both these cases, see below, pp. 389–90, 402–3.

[215] B.R.L. Wingfield Digby MS A496; B.R.L. 431133; also e.g. *Dugdale*, p. 527; B.R.L. Wingfield Digby MS A473 for Richard Haversham, a minor Coleshill landowner, servant and associate of Mountford (S.B.T. D.R.37 Box 73 (Mountford account); Br. Lib. Eg. Roll 8503); the same account reveals Mountford exerting himself to get a writ for Lecroft; see also JUST 1/1514 m.39.

ascending hierarchy from neighbourhood to region to country. It was through their connections, and to a lesser extent through those of the middling gentry, that the influence of the affinity would percolate through a region.[216] That was why the magnates generally did not attempt to retain minor gentry beyond those who were employed on their administrative staff. It did mean, however, that, unless a lord's affinity was both well-organised and powerful enough to make both its head and its members the natural focal points for the rest of the county, it could be submerged by other forces in local society, for it would almost invariably be outnumbered by the rest of the local gentry. The Warwick affinity for much of the 1440s is a good illustration, for until the death of Duke Henry, and even beyond, it retained its identity, while lacking any directional force or real political clout.[217] The fact that political structures operated in this way makes it very difficult for the historian to evaluate their effectiveness and dangerous to do so simply by a head-count; a magnate with a compact estate, an eye for the right retainers and, above all, ability might have influence over circles well beyond his immediate following, influence exercised largely through the localised groups for whom the major retainers were the key to a wider world. We have seen that connections in far-flung regions – 'friends of friends' – made through the interlocking of noble affinities could be used to activate support in regions previously peripheral to a magnate's interests. Often it would be the gentry with the largest connection of their own who could best be used for this.[218]

Higher up the landowning hierarchy, other layers of identity were superimposed on the primary one of locality. The importance to gentry relationships of personal encounters at taverns and private dinners has already been mentioned. Then, as later, another favourite activity where the local elite could mingle was hunting.[219] One way of evaluating the relative significance of the various local identities is to ask under what circumstances the gentry would normally come across one another, since it was by such meetings, where they might seal deeds, discuss local and national affairs and simply pass the time of day, that the friendship and trust that created a local network would be built up. One obvious place was their own households. The Mountford account of 1433–4 shows that there were visits in that year from Ralph Brasebrugge, Robert Ardern, Richard Vernon of Staffordshire and Derbyshire and Robert

[216] Cf. Sir William Etchingham in fourteenth-century Sussex, who mingled in high society and also hunted with neighbours and friends (Saul 1986: pp. 63–4). Note that John of Gaunt, summoning a retinue for special occasions, such as war or parliament, sent letters not only to his retainers, but also to his receivers, to call anyone they could (Walker 1986: p. 5). See Hughes 1987: pp. 43–5, 50, 54 for similar points on the local identity of Warwickshire gentry in the seventeenth century.

[217] Below, ch. 11; Sinclair 1987a: pp. 301–2.

[218] Above, p. 321. A similar point is in Horrox 1986a. Cf. Walker 1986: pp. 160–1, 227–30, 255–64 and the more general discussion of this issue, below, pp. 621–2.

[219] Saul 1986: pp. 191–2; Richmond 1981: pp. 154, 182–3.

Whitgreve of Staffordshire, all of whom feature in deeds in which Mountford himself participated, and from Maurice Berkeley of Weoley, Worcestershire, who married Mountford's daughter.[220] Another point of contact were the riding retinue of Richard Beauchamp, and his households at Warwick, Elmley and Berkeley, as well as those outside the west midlands, although Warwickshire men not intimately concerned in the earl's affairs were much less likely to congregate at his more distant residences. Beauchamp's accounts give us occasional but invaluable glimpses into this world and into the comings and goings of his clients, friends and associates. An account for Warwick reveals the presence there in March 1423 of Mountford, John Baysham (a cleric who was Beauchamp's supervisor and receiver-general), John Throgmorton and other members of the earl's council, who had gathered together to draw up his general account. An occasion like this could be employed by the gentry to pursue their own concerns and could produce a deed like William Clopton's conveyance of 1419, in which Baysham, Throgmorton and two other Beauchamp officers, John Harewell and William Wollashull, took part.[221] Beauchamp's household accounts allow us to see also the sort of gathering of the affinity from which the transactions we examined earlier, involving men from several different parts of the county, could have issued.[222] For example, in March 1421 there were present at Berkeley Castle the earl himself, William Holt of Aston, John Throgmorton, John Harewell and Thomas Archer, a body of men who covered between them a large part of western Warwickshire.[223] It was noted earlier that some deeds show every sign of having been drawn up during a meeting of Warwick's councillors and principal retainers.[224] This is particularly evident, not surprisingly, in grants made by the earl himself, such as the one to George Herthill at Woodcote near Warwick in 1437, witnessed by Mountford, Peyto and Thomas Hugford, or Warwick's feoffment in 1408 of part of his lands to Robert Hugford and Thomas Crewe, dated at Warwick, or the grant of an annuity in 1423 witnessed by Mountford, Throgmorton, Harewell, Robert Poyntz, another retainer, '*et aliis*'.[225]

Meetings of the affinity or a significant part of it can be inferred from some of the deeds issued at Warwick, such as an agreement of 1402, witnessed by a group of the earl's prominent servants, William Bagot, Thomas Burdet, Ailred

[220] S.B.T. D.R.37 Box 73 (Mountford account); Atkyns 1712: I, p. 690; above, pp. 298, 314–15; Sinclair 1987a: pp. 169–70 for meetings of Warwick's council at Thomas Crewe's house.

[221] Warwick Castle MS 373, 485; *Colls. Hist. Staffs.*, o.s., 11, p. 226; Sinclair 1987a: pp. 187, 269–70.

[222] Longleat, MS of Marquess of Bath Misc. IX, *passim*; Warwick Corp. Recs. (consulted in W.C.R.O.) W.19/5; Sinclair 1987a: pp. 268–9.

[223] Longleat, MS of Marquess of Bath Misc. IX fo.76v.

[224] Above, pp. 317–18.

[225] E.R.1/65/448; *Cal. Close Rolls 1405–09*, p. 382; *Cal. Pat. Rolls 1446–52*, p. 22.

Trussell, Robert Hugford and Robert Brome.[226] The participation of citizens and officials of the borough in several transactions involving gentry from the areas south and west of Warwick, notably in the period of Richard Beauchamp's rule, shows how the town could be a place where neighbours and non-neighbours alike came together. The fact that in many cases the participants were Warwick's men – as were the town officials by definition – suggests that it was the business of the affinity, perhaps as much as their own, that had brought them to the town on these occasions.[227] Another affinity in action can be seen in a grant by William Lord Astley of November 1414, witnessed by John Cokayn, Giles Astley, Thomas Erdington, John de Astley and Thomas Purfrey.[228]

Another important point of contact was the religious and social gild. Mention has already been made of the main ones, at Coventry, Stratford, Knowle and Henley; there was also less well-recorded gilds at Birmingham and Aston Cantlow, the latter being eventually placed under the patronage of the lord of the manor, Edward Neville Lord Bergavenny, and a later one at the Warwick manor of Brailes founded by Richard Neville earl of Warwick.[229] Clearly these associations served different purposes for different people, but some of them played a significant part in bringing together the local gentry. The gild at Knowle, midway between Lapworth and Solihull, was a focal point for the numbers of minor gentry and prosperous yeomen resident in the area, and may well have helped in the development of the marked degree of local identity found there.[230] Coventry's Holy Trinity gild, on the other hand, for all its imposing membership, including royal, noble and gentry members drawn from throughout the county and beyond, seems not to have acted as a major social focus for landowners, except perhaps at great festivals, particularly Corpus Christi.[231] The Leet Book does not suggest that this large and prosperous town, patronised by the royal family, felt the need to put great efforts into cultivating local landowners.[232] Moreover the familiar north/south divide in Warwickshire is evident here as well: just as the diocese of Coventry

[226] W.C.R.O. C.R.611/575/4. Bagot, having blotted his copybook under Richard II, was now an ex-retainer, but the deed shows that not all links with the Warwick entourage had been severed (above, p. 313; Sinclair 1987a: pp. 297–8; also below, p. 362).

[227] E.g. B.R.L. Moulton and Keen Coll. 26 (deed of 1427); S.B.T. D.R.98/467; Northants.R.O. Knightley Charters 168 (dated at Weston under Wetherley in the Avon-Leam area, but the personnel consists of Warwick's clients and Warwick town officials); and refs. in nn.73, 74, 82, above.

[228] W.C.R.O. C.R.136/C790; above, p. 314.

[229] *Coventry Register; Stratford Register; Knowle Register*; Cooper 1946: pp. 65–8; *English Gilds*, pp. 211–21, 232–38, 239–45; *Dugdale*, pp. 837, 555; *V.C.H.*, III, p. 34; above, pp. 18–19.

[230] For literature on this subject, above, p. 238 n.193. For Knowle, see *Knowle Register* in conjunction with local families listed in app. 1.

[231] The affray which launched the Stafford–Harecourt feud took place at Coventry during Corpus Christi, and the town was evidently full of great figures at the time (*Paston Letters*, ed. Gairdner, II, pp. 88–90; below, pp. 427–8).

[232] *Coventry Leet Book, passim.*

served north Warwickshire and the north midlands, while Worcestershire served the west midlands, so the gilds of Coventry and Stratford tended to cater respectively for these two regions.

It was the Stratford gild that operated as a meeting-point for local landowners on a large scale, its members ranging from the king downwards and including the earl of Warwick and most of his family, as well as most of the local gentry, great and small, and many other men from further afield.[233] Indeed, insofar as it served the needs of the Warwick affinity, the dominant local force, the gild transcended its local role. For landowners from a wide radius around Stratford, marriage, or the acquisition of an independence in some other way, was almost immediately followed by entry into the ranks of gild members. A grant of 1429 to the gild from William Mountford, Thomas Mollesley, Richard Haversham and Thomas Waryng shows not only how far its reach extended beyond the town's environs, but also, in the participation of the first two, both of them Warwick retainers from well outside the immediate locality, how effectively it served as a social focus for the Warwick affinity.[234] It wined, dined and even breakfasted the gentry who were passing through, and observed obits for the dead. Some of the leading local men – notably Thomas Burdet I, William Lucy and William Bishopestone – were active on the gild's behalf; on one occasion the gild showed its gratitude to Burdet by hiring a harper in his honour.[235] Again and again the gentry entertained by the gild or engaged on the gild's business were the earl's men. Like the earl's household, the gild was a place where they could meet for many different purposes. When Bishopestone, Burdet, Lucy, Thomas Harewell and John Clopton of Stratford witnessed a deed for the gild in 1439, they could easily have seen to their own business at the same time, since these are amongst the names that turn up time and again in transactions from this area; all but Clopton were Beauchamp men.[236] It is not without significance that there was no gild of this standing at Warwick, that the Coventry gild seems to have had a much less localised function for its landowning members and that there is no evidence for gilds of any importance in the east of the county. All these points emphasise the fact that, as far as the gentry were concerned, Warwickshire's centre of gravity was the west where most of the Warwick estates lay. They also show that the town of Warwick, a lesser commercial centre than Stratford,[237] was not a place where the gentry were likely to gather, unless summoned by the earl, or bound there on business which could be done nowhere else – that is, anything to do with the county administration.

233 *Stratford Register*, *passim*; S.B.T. Stratford Corp. Recs. XII/212; Hilton 1975: pp. 93–4.

234 S.B.T. Stratford Corp. Recs. I/442.

235 S.B.T Stratford Corp. Recs. XII/20–50 (for Burdet's harper, No.26).

236 S.B.T. Stratford Corp. Recs. I/473.

237 Above, p. 18. Cf. Lewes, which declined after the Warenne family disappeared in 1347 (Saul 1986: p. 176). *Dugdale*, pp. 462–3.

This is now the place to consider the role of the administrative divisions of shire and hundred in moulding local identities. For all that this discussion has consistently stressed the fact that the forces that bound the gentry together served to pull the county apart, some discussion of this problem is unavoidable. For the minor gentry the hundred was the most obvious point of association, and surviving records show them coming together as hundredal jurors.[238] To some extent the very localised groups we have identified coincide rather well with the hundredal divisions, especially in east Warwickshire. There, particularly in the 1440s, when it extended as far north as the border with Hemlingford Hundred, the Avon-Leam group can be placed more or less in Knightlow Hundred, and the southern group in Kineton Hundred. However, the particularly close-knit group in the Tanworth region lay in both Hemlingford and Barlichway Hundreds, while Tanworth itself was in a detached portion of Kineton, and it is clear that local geography was a far more influential force here than any administrative division. In general, while it should be recognised that the meeting of the hundred or the hundredal jury could be a convenient occasion for the sealing of deeds, networks as local as these flourished because their members lived close enough to each other to meet in all sorts of different ways. Public business should not be given too large a role in their creation.

It was in bringing together men from different neighbourhoods that the administrative division could have played an irreplaceable part, and this brings us to the question of whether there was a county community in Warwickshire in the first half of the century. If there were 'jentilmen of the shire of Norffolk' in 1452, was there the same sense of common identity in Warwickshire at this time? Lacking the direct evidence of the Paston letters, we can only speculate, but we might usefully ask whether the sessions of the peace and the meetings of the county court could provide enough of a sense of unity amongst the middling and greater gentry to override all the fissiparious tendencies that seem to have been so powerful in this county at this time.[239] In the case of the sessions of the peace, this seems rather improbable. For much of the century the J.P.s, especially the small number of working justices, tended not only not to be drawn from the greater families, but to be dominated by lawyers. The bench at any one session would normally number only four or five,[240] although the presence on some occasions of juries from all over the county and all levels of the landowning hierarchy would certainly have played a part in enabling men from across the county to meet.[241] The fact is that quarter sessions were not going to

[238] E.g. K.B.9/196/1/2.

[239] *Paston Letters*, I, p. 64; also ii, pp. 120–1. For literature on the subject, see above, p. 29 n.33 and p. 33 and n.50.

[240] Above, pp. 267–72. For attendance of J.P.s at sessions, indictments in K.B.9 class and E.101/590/33. Cf. Wright 1983: p. 109.

[241] This can be established by a glance at any of the K.B.9 files, most of them coming from the quarter sessions: e.g. K.B.9/224/131, /246/18. For a county jury at an *oyer* and *terminer* session

be the major social and political event they were later to become as long as much of the maintenance of discipline over the gentry's social inferiors was still carried on in the manorial courts. Only when these courts had decayed still further and the plethora of Tudor economic regulation had usurped their function, and when to this was added the enforcement of religious discipline, would the sessions come into their own as the main agency for the regulation of the lower orders. Only then would they be more of an unmissable event. If other men were sitting in judgement on your own tenants in their capacity as J.P.s, then to be a J.P. and to attend the sessions where this happened and involve yourself in the intrigues around the bench became a matter of very great moment indeed. In the fifteenth century this process was still very much in its initial stages.[242]

This leaves us with the county court, an institution of far greater antiquity and still of some importance, despite its loss of most of its judicial authority, for it remained the place where the king's writs and proclamations were received, and representatives of the shire elected.[243] We have some knowledge of its composition at this time, albeit of a rather specialised kind, from the names on election indentures. Neither the Warwickshire indentures nor those from its neighbours offer much encouragement to the idea that there were county communities in this part of the world.[244] The Warwickshire records, unlike those cited by Maddicott, show that normally only about a dozen men from the shire attended, a handful of whom came from above the minor gentry level. In 1419 the number of those present from the shire was as low as four, in 1423 only six. In 1429 the only landowner of any substance who attended was Thomas Harewell, in 1447 there were no gentry of this level at all. The one comparatively well-attended election was in 1413, when the M.P.s for Henry

held at Warwick later in the century, K.B.9/164/1/10, 11. In fourteenth-century Leicestershire there was considerable attendance by jurors at assizes (Astill 1977: p. 193).

[242] Above, pp. 42–5, 86, and, of Tudor local studies, Hassell Smith 1974: chs. 3–5, 9–11, 14; Clark 1977: pp. 55, 114–15, 127–8; MacCulloch 1986: Part 3; Fletcher 1986: pp. 5–11, 43; 1985; Zell 1977: pp. 133–6. But note Hughes 1982; MacCulloch 1986: pp. 37–8; Zell 1977: p. 143.

[243] Maddicott 1978a, 1981; Palmer 1982: Part II.

[244] The discussion is based on the following documents (all C.219): 10/4 (Warks., Worcs.), 10/5 (Warks., Worcs.), 10/6 (Staffs., Warks.), 11/2 (Gloucs., Leics., Warks., Worcs.), 11/3 (Derbys., Warks.), 11/4 (Gloucs.), 11/5 (Derbys., Staffs., Warks., Worcs.), 11/8 (Derbys., Northts.), 12/3 (Warks.), 12/4 (Warks.), 12/5 (Northts., Warks., Worcs.), 12/6 (Warks.), 13 Pt. I/1 (Warks.), /2 Pt. II (Notts., Warks.), /3 Pt. II (Northts., Notts., Shrops., Staffs., Warks., Worcs.), 13 Pt. II/1 (Notts., Warks.), /2 Pt. I (Gloucs.), /2 Pt. II (Northts., Warks., Leics., Worcs.), 14 Pt. I/1 Pt. I (Gloucs.), /1 Pt. II (Northts., Shrops., Warks., Leics.), /2 Pt. II (Warks., Leics., Worcs.), /3 Pt. II (Derbys., Warks., Leics.), /4 Pt. II (Northts., Warks., Worcs.), /6 Pt. II (Warks., Worcs.), 15 Pt. I/1 Pt. III (Warks., Worcs.), /2 Pt. II (Northts., Staffs., Warks.), 15 Pt. II/4 Pt. II (Northts., Wark., Worcs.), /6 Pt. I (Gloucs., Northts.), /6 Pt. II (Warks., Worcs.), /7 Pt. I (Gloucs.), /7 Pt. II (Northts., Staffs., Warks., Leics., Worcs.). Payling 1987c: p. 175 notes that under normal circumstances only the more important electors would have been named, but that does not invalidate this point, as it is these men with whom we are dealing; also Roskell 1937: p. 22.

V's first parliament were chosen. Although only a dozen men from the county were present, they included several of the greater landowners: Mountford, Crewe, Brasebrugge, Straunge, Ardern, Holt of Aston, Archer, Metley.[245]

One reason for the low attendance of the greater gentry is that, having lands in more than one county, they were often electors elsewhere. For example, Crewe, Stafford of Grafton and Hugford are named in the Worcestershire indenture of 1410, Ardern, Gower and Throgmorton in that of 1414, Catesbys turn up in Northamptonshire, where Thomas Malory was also an elector in 1441, Knightleys in Northamptonshire and Staffordshire, Astons and Chetwynds in Staffordshire, Greville in Gloucestershire, Shirley and Cokayn in Derbyshire, and Archer in Shropshire. In 1432 Thomas Erdington I contrived to be an elector in both Warwickshire and Leicestershire. By the time we have allowed for these, for the M.P.s themselves and the sheriff, and for the Warwickshire men acting as sheriffs or being returned as M.P.s in other counties, the chances of there being a gathering of the worthies of the shire in the county court, for elections at least, are fairly remote. Of course this may have been a phenomenon confined mainly to the midland counties, where it was commonplace for landowners to own estates in more than one county, and this may explain why the evidence for fuller gatherings of both greater and lesser gentry at county courts has tended to come from more self-contained areas, like East Anglia.[246] It has been suggested, however, that the names of the lesser men were recorded only when there was a disputed election, and it may be that full indentures of this kind register less county-wide cohesion than local conflict.[247]

The gentry who did come to these meetings rarely represented the whole county. Notable absentees from the meetings held at Warwick are the northerners, whose failure to come to the county town has also been observed in the seventeenth century. With the exception of William Mountford, they are also rather unrepresented among the working justices of the peace, presumably for the same reasons.[248] While those who had more pressing interests in other counties, like Cokayn and Shirley, were likely to be involved in elections elsewhere, there seems no reason for the almost continuous absence of Mountford, Erdington, Ardern and Brasebrugge, still less for that of lesser men

[245] C.219/12/3, /14 Pt. II/1 Pt. II, /15 Pt. II/4 Pt. II, /11/2.

[246] For refs., see n.244. For indentures from other counties (not all noticeably different from Warwickshire's), Maddicott 1978a: p. 30; Edwards 1969: pp. 393–4; Rogers 1966: pp. 69–76; Bennett 1983: pp. 23–4; Virgoe 1966: pp. 194–6, 1973 (in this case the unusually large attendance made it impossible to complete the election), 1987: pp. 41–3; Payling 1987c: pp. 177–8; Roskell 1937: pp. 21–3. Astill 1977: pp. 192–3 finds similarly small numbers attending in another midland county. See also the discussion above, pp. 25–7. For some evidence drawn from the Paston letters on concepts of local identity in East Anglia, below, p. 347 n.3.

[247] Payling 1987c: pp. 176–85; note also the low social position of a high proportion of the men on one of Virgoe's large indentures (Virgoe 1981: p. 82; cf. Kishlansky 1986: esp. ch. 3). See, similarly, Wright 1983: p. 146.

[248] Above, p. 29.

like Lisle. The conclusion that they simply could not be bothered seems inescapable; perhaps the fuller attendance of the county elite as a whole in 1413 must be attributed to coercion, this being an occasion when the king, concerned about the state of order in the midlands, may have demanded that local societies give maximum endorsement of their representatives.[249] The one landowner from north Warwickshire who appears on the indentures consistently is Richard Haversham of Coleshill, a very insignificant gentleman, who, as an estate official of the family, may have been there to represent the Mountford interest. It is a fact that the representation of interests is a major feature of these records, echoing Palmer's conclusion that county courts in the thirteenth century were dominated by the stewards of the great landowners.[250] Thomas Crewe, who was Richard Beauchamp's steward, was regularly present, and so was John Barbour, another Beauchamp steward. Edmund Colshill, who was steward of Axholme some time before 1444–5,[251] and may well have acted in this capacity for other major landowners, appeared on several occasions. Lawyers and estate servants like Colshill, Geoffrey Allesley, Thomas Greswold, John Campion, John Beaufitz, who features from the time he became steward of Kenilworth, Edmund Starkey, John Onley and Nicholas Rody tend to form a largish proportion of the electors.[252]

There were also electors who could scarcely be termed Warwickshire landowners even by the broad definitions employed in this study, whose presence can only be accounted for by their professional duties. Richard Langham, a Leicestershire landowner who may have served the Ferrers of Chartley, was present on more than one occasion,[253] and in 1427 John Griffith was an elector. Although he owned the manor of Stockton in south Warwickshire his real interests lay in Staffordshire and his involvement in county affairs was virtually nil. It is more than likely that he was present as an official of another Staffordshire landowner with land in southern Warwickshire, the bishop of Lichfield.[254] There are indeed one or two exceedingly odd gatherings, this being one of them, and it is not without significance that it was this one that produced a disputed election.[255] Another highly unrepresentative meeting was that of 1447, comprising almost exclusively minor figures from Solihull and

249 For disorder in the midlands at this time, above, p. 315 and below, p. 365.

250 Above, n.215; Palmer 1982: ch.5; Payling 1987c: pp. 171–2; Roskell 1937: pp. 23–4; Driver 1963: p. 45; Maddicott 1978a: pp. 30–1.

251 S.C.6/1039/18.

252 Apps. 2 and 3 and above, pp. 124, 303. For Starkey, receiver of William Mountford, *Cal. Close Rolls 1441–47*, pp. 277–8.

253 C.219/12/6, /13 Pt. II/2 Pt. II. Robert Langham of Leicestershire was indicted of assault with Ferrers in 1423 (K.B.9/203/18).

254 C.219/13 Pt. II/2 Pt. II; *V.C.H.*, VI, p. 227; *Dugdale*, p. 341. A later member of the family certainly served the bishops and Stockton lay close to a group of manors in south Warwickshire owned by the bishops (S.C.6/Hen.VII/1846).

255 Below, pp. 385–7.

nearby, which proceeded to elect Edmund Mountford, who had shortly before held Solihull and the neighbouring manor of Sheldon by royal grant; one wonders why they all bothered to go to Warwick for the election, except to give it some outward show of propriety.[256] It has not proved possible to link deeds directly to known gatherings of the shire (or indeed of the hundred), as Bennett was able to do with the meeting of the Lancashire county court in 1414;[257] to establish whether any transactions emanating from such meetings have survived, although worthwhile, would require that all deed material be put on computer, an exercise best left to someone initiating a project of this kind in the micro-chip age. But there is at least enough evidence from the election indentures to suggest with some force that the county court was no more a recognised meeting-place for the Warwickshire gentry as a body than were the quarter-sessions.

V

It should be evident from this close study of relationships amongst the gentry in the first half of the century that there is no single heading which will subsume all the possible sources of identity that they might have. It has been emphasised that every one of these men had more than one, that the wider their horizons the more identities they had, and that the relative importance of these varied with circumstance, while all of them overlapped to some degree. However, three substantial conclusions emerge with some force. The first is that there were undeniably neighbourhood networks and that some of these show remarkable continuity. It was a continuity that depended to quite a large degree on the minor gentry and greater yeomen, who had in most cases no direct tie with the nobility, whose choice of associates could remain undisturbed by political upheavals, of which there were many in this period, particularly between 1439 and 1449. The most stable areas, in the sense of providing tried and tested partners over long periods for both major and minor landowners, were therefore those like the Tanworth and the Avon-Leam regions, where middling and lesser gentry proliferated. The area west of Warwick proved to be a unique case, where the dominance over a long period of a single noble family had produced a network that survived the eclipse of the family. Magnate politics could also have a similar, if less striking, effect in developing a sense of local identity elsewhere, notably in the north to north-west.

Secondly, if it was understandably the lesser figures to whom the local network meant most, there is no denying the attachment to their immediate locality of the more eminent gentry. Only a few, like the Staffords of Grafton

[256] C.219/15 Pt. II/4 Pt. II; *Cal. Pat. Rolls 1441–46*, pp. 244, 296.

[257] Bennett 1973, 1983, pp. 23–5; also suggested in Maddicott 1978a: p. 30 and, for an example, *Paston Letters*, I, p. 98.

and, to a much lesser extent, the Mountfords, disdained to cultivate friendships with their immediate neighbours, or, like Thomas Hugford, were too enmeshed in their masters' affairs to develop an intensive connection among their close neighbours.[258] Neglect of the locality would have been foolish, for the friendship of their neighbours gave them not only readily-available associates but also a reservoir of political support where they were most likely to need it and where they could, at need, channel it towards their noble masters. But what defined the '*patria*' of the more prominent gentry beyond their immediate environs is a more difficult question. In Warwickshire it could easily be an area comprising part of an adjacent county; to a man like John Throgmorton, Thomas Hugford, John Harewell or Thomas Crewe it must to a large degree have been the Warwick affinity, or that bit of it with which they were most often involved. For such men, particularly for Thomas Hugford, who lived in its shadow, the centre of the world must have been Warwick Castle, and it is hard to believe that this was not so even for William Mountford, the greatest of them all, in the period of Richard Beauchamp's rule. At this time, and especially between 1422 and 1439 when the earl's power was at its height, if the county had any identity which meant something to the gentry over and above its administrative purposes, it must have been inseparable from the connections coalescing round the earl. These seem to have been the only force which regularly brought the disparate neighbourhoods together. It is equally hard to see that even a knight of the shire between 1439 and 1449 would have had much sense of representing something that had any existence beyond the lines drawn on an administrative map; the gathering of electors that had sent him there would certainly have given him little additional cause to believe in its reality. It may well be that this lack of a sense of 'community' within the shire was common to all the midland counties, where the administrative boundaries tended to override the more powerful localisms of neighbourhood and tenurial structure.[259]

It follows from this that, thirdly, while horizontal relationships were often strong and lasting, this was a county where the nobility had a powerful part to play in the ordering of social and political relationships among the gentry.[260] It would nevertheless take an exceptional or an exceptionally lucky magnate to bring the localities of Warwickshire together and build them into a political unit through which he could direct to his own ends the administrative processes of the crown. Not the least of his difficulties was the fact that it could hardly be

258 The fact that Hugford was serving the Beauchamps in Glamorgan from 1436–48 (Sinclair 1987a: p. 350) would have reduced his involvement in Warwickshire affairs.

259 Cf. Astill 1977: ch. 3; Wright 1978: pp. 285–6, 1983: esp. pp. 4, 17, 44, 57–8, 62–3, 83–92, 146; Hilton 1975a: pp. 224–5; Hughes 1987: *passim*, esp. pp. 39–40, 42–50; Crouch 1986.

260 Cf. Virgoe 1981, pp. 83–4. For contrasting conclusions, Wright 1983: *passim*, esp. ch. 5; Walker 1986: chs. 4 and 5; Payling 1987c; pp. 184–5, 1987b: pp. 93–105; Saul 1981: ch. 3, 1986: pp. 156–7; Bennett, 1983: ch. 2; Maddicott 1978a; below, p. 618 n.7.

done without control of the neighbouring sectors of most of the counties around Warwickshire.[261] We must now begin to look at this issue, the point at which private relationships met public processes, the politics of Warwickshire in the fifteenth century.

[261] That this had long been the case is evident from the coalitions in and around Warwickshire formed under Stephen (Crouch 1986: pp. 81–6).

10

WARWICKSHIRE UNDER RICHARD BEAUCHAMP: 1401–39

I

The politics of Warwickshire were inescapably part of the politics of England: neither royal government nor locality could afford to ignore each other, and nor can the historian forget the fact that each inevitably impinged on the other. It is for this reason, by way of a preface to the analysis of Warwickshire politics in the fifteenth century, the structures that linked locality to polity will be briefly considered. This was a two-edged relationship concerning on the one hand enforcement and on the other response. To begin with the former, how centre and locality worked together would determine whether the king ruled or merely reigned. We have seen already that there was both an official and an unofficial chain of command, the one working through the king's appointed officers, the other through the exercise of privately-owned force and private networks of relationships. The two chains were interlinked and mutually reinforcing.[1] The fact that at the local level the officers *were* the private powers, an equation expressed in the very qualifications for office,[2] makes nonsense of any attempt to separate the two means of enforcement.

We have seen also that the nobility had a peculiarly important pivotal role between centre and locality. The area that a magnate might command, where he was 'a man of worship', delineated by the geography of his estates, was his 'contree',[3] and he would normally expect his authority over it to be recognised

1 Above, pp. 282–9; cf. Elton 1974: pp. 183–4.

2 Above, pp. 47–8, 266; cf. Kishlansky 1986: pp. 15–16.

3 *Rot. Parl.*, IV, p. 422. See the illuminating declaration by the duke of Norfolk, 1452 (*Paston Letters*, ed. Gairdner, II, p. 257: ref. courtesy of John Watts). 'Contree' had more than one meaning, amongst them 'county': for further examples of 'county', see *Paston Letters*, I, pp. 203, 259, 400, 543, and for examples of 'area' or 'region' see Leland, *De Rebus Britannicis Collectanea*, IV, p. 210, and *Procs. Priv. Counc.*, V, pp. 39, 58–9, and, less unequivocally (showing the confusion of administrative and political entities that followed from the mediatisation of government through the magnates), *Paston Letters*, I, pp. 154, 259, 264, 376 (*bis*), 377, 394, 525, II, p. 354.

by appointment to the commission of the peace in the counties that lay within it. But this in itself was more a public recognition of his private greatness than a means of conferring official authority. Nobles rarely sat at the sessions, but, without such recognition, a nobleman probably felt demeaned. Moreover, by being placed on the commission, in the event of there being a case in which he took an active interest, he could ensure his own presence on the bench, a fact which could be important to him in the pursuit or preservation of local dominion.[4] Paradoxically, it was in the fourteenth and fifteenth centuries, when the nobility had long ceased to be the king's official local agents in the ordinary ruling of the shires, that they really came into their own as royal deputies. During these centuries the royal government in the localities expanded enormously and, at the same time, was devolved to the local landowners, who exercised it with an almost unprecedented lack of supervision.[5] In consequence, this being a society in which everybody automatically looked upwards for direction, and in which political power came firstly from personal military might, it had to be the nobility, the men who on their own could raise the most powerful force, who held the key to local government.[6] This would remain the case until the gentry, whose tenantry, combined, could normally outnumber that of the nobility, were able to run their affairs more independently of their superiors. The analysis of networks has shown that in the first half of the fifteenth century this was not the case, in Warwickshire at least.[7] Naturally such a state of affairs held profound consequences for the nature and deployment of royal authority, and these will be explored in this and the following chapters, but it should not be assumed that it automatically gave birth to 'overmighty subjects', disruptive, incapable of discipline and doing the king's bidding only when it suited them. It must be remembered that without the king the nobility were nothing, for, leaving aside the favours he had to offer, the grand scope of their authority was only a reflection of his greatness. Unlike earlier times, when royal leadership in local rule had been minimal, if the king failed to exercise his power in the later middle ages the nobility found themselves increasingly rudderless and unable to function.[8]

4 Below, pp. 453, 476. Cf. Payling 1987b: pp. 218–9; Goodman 1981b: pp. 139–40. Another advantage of sitting on the commission was that the lord could get hold of the roll issuing from the sessions and take it into the King's Bench (Powell 1984a).

5 Above, pp. 41–2, 44.

6 Above, pp. 284 n.9.

7 Above, p. 36; below, chs. 12, 16–17 for later changes in gentry perceptions of their role. Cf. the advice to John Paston I: 'It is full nessessary to make zow strong be lord-chep and be oder menys.' (*Paston Letters*, I, p. 164); also Kail ed., *Political Poems*, p. 65, ll.33–4 (lords as shoulders and backbone of the body politic).

8 For the literature on 'overmighty subjects', see above, p. 283 n.4. Compare the treaties of Stephen's reign (for which see Davis 1967: pp. 111–14), by which the barons attempted to keep the peace in the localities without the king's help, with their helplessness in the face of monarchical failure under e.g. Edward II and Henry VI (Maddicott 1970; Phillips 1972; Fryde

Just as the real power of the nobility came from private rather than public resources, so even the authority of the gentry was not conferred by public office alone. Indeed, it could be said that tenure of office was the consequence rather than the cause of the possession of authority, starting with the manorial lordship that conferred ready access to physical force and was in many ways the mark of gentility.[9] Equally, those who held no office could still be significant local figures, by virtue of their lands and their connections, although it is probably true to say that, even if office was a burden, eminent landowners who were not appointed to it and had not secured an exemption were probably reckoned of little account by their neighbours. What made it possible for local officials to act was local recognition that they had behind them significant military force, both their own and that of the landowners they represented. In the earlier part of the century, when the status of the J.P.s was rather low, it was the backing of the rest of the shire, in conjunction with the king's commission, that really gave them their authority.[10]

Because local officials were so dependent on local powers for their effectiveness, whatever the overt mechanisms for appointing them, it simply was not possible to ignore the balance of power in the shires, and kings who did so, by listening too hard to favoured courtiers, were likely to find themselves with a number of ungovernable counties.[11] As long as local power structures were acknowledged in the appointment of local officials, there was no need for military might to be anything other than the unspoken force lying behind official administration; when they were not respected, or when a county was politically divided, royal government rapidly became the plaything of local politics and the local force that made government possible ceased to be implicit and became overt, as in the notorious case of the Bedford riot of 1439.[12] Alternatively, attempts to rule the shires without sufficient local support, even impressive royal commissions specifically set up to deal with disorder, like the *oyer* and *terminer* sent to Derbyshire in the 1450s, could simply fall flat on their face.[13] But it is important to stress that when government in the provinces

1979; Griffiths 1981). Cf. also Scotland, where noble power could be enhanced by the growth of royal power (Wormald 1986b: p. 192).

9 Above, pp. 73, 75–77.

10 For the status of J.P.s, see above, pp. 267–72, and for attitudes to tenure of office, see above, pp. 47, 60–1, 85–6.

11 For the official methods of appointment and comments, see above, p. 275 and refs. For some idea of the consequences of ignoring local feeling in the appointment of officials, see *Paston Letters, passim* for the 1440s and early 1450s, and Saul 1984 (but there may be an alternative explanation for the events in Gloucestershire in the 1320s, albeit one with similar implications for royal rule in the localities, explored in the as yet incomplete work of Julian Turner, but discussed in his Cambridge Univ. B.A. dissertation, 1983).

12 Maddern 1984: ch. 4; *Select Cases Before the King's Council*, pp. cxii–iii, 104–7; *Procs. Priv. Counc.*, v, pp. 35–9, 57–9; and see remarks above, pp. 287–9.

13 Wright 1983: pp. 135–6.

collapsed in these ways, it was because something had gone badly wrong, usually with direction from above, from nobility or king.[14]

So far we have examined only one aspect of the relationship between centre and locality, the downward hierarchy of enforcement, but there was another in the reverse direction, which was about response, and all vested powers ignored it at their peril. Just as the king had to sense the needs of his nobility if they were to be effective agents of his government, so the nobility had to listen to the gentry, without whom their local authority was nothing, the greater gentry had to keep close to the lesser gentry, and all owners of manorial lordship were wise by this time to pay at least some heed to what their tenants were saying.[15] Central to this issue, in terms of making the realm governable, were the magnates' readiness to take the comments and requests of the shires to the crown and the kings' willingness to listen to the magnates. Although parliament provided the gentry with access to the central government, only the king decided when and how often it met, and, with so much official business to get through, there was no guarantee that a private petitioner would make much headway.[16] The king's council and its offshoot, the court of chancery, were also means of access to the highest authority, but they took time, might require influence and, especially chancery, were rather uncertain in their outcome. Kings who left the complaints of the mass of their landed subjects to parliament were likely to be in trouble, as Henry VI was to find in 1449–50. Those who made themselves available to their nobility and through them to the rest of their landed subjects could respond with speed and flexibility.[17] One reason for the incessant harping on 'counsel' and 'natural advisers' in the political literature of late-medieval England was that, if the nobility were unable to get to the king, they could not show themselves to be the natural channels of communication between the centre and locality, with obviously damaging effects on their 'worship'. As one of Margaret Paston's correspondents wrote to her in 1461, 'it were expedient that the Kyng were infourmed of the demenyng of the shire'. In

[14] For contemporary comments on the vital role of the king's leadership for internal peace, see below, pp. 353–4.

[15] Rawcliffe and Flower 1986: pp. 157, 170–2; Walker 1986: pp. 194–6 on the consequences for Gaunt in Lancs. of not tending his retinue carefully enough. The results of ignoring tenants' responses were seen all too clearly in 1381 and 1450 (Hilton and Aston eds. 1984: *passim*; Griffiths 1981: ch. 21).

[16] Brown 1981; Myers 1981; Edwards 1979: pp. 44–65; on the links between parliament and the constituencies and their importance in linking government to subjects, see also the literature cited in p. 265 above, n.15, and Cam 1963b; Maddicott 1981. On how kings garnered information from the shires earlier in the middle ages, see Holt 1981. For contemporary comments on the importance of access, see e.g. the Cade rebels' manifesto and York's protestation of 1452: *Eng. Hist. Docs.*, IV, pp. 266–7, 269; Bishop Russell's draft sermon of 1483 in Chrimes 1936: pp. 172–3; *Four English Political Tracts*, pp. 34, 39; 'Modus Tenendi Parliamentum', pp. 87–8 (but see comment on its reliability, below, n.19).

[17] Griffiths 1981: pp. 304–10, 610–49. In contrast, Edward III (Maddicott 1981: pp. 80–2; Harriss 1975: Part II, *passim*) and Henry V (Harriss 1985c; Catto 1985: p. 86).

this case 'a testymonyall which is made by a greet assent of greet multitude of comouns' was to be conveyed to Edward IV, using John Paston I as intermediary, but whether the messages came via nobility or gentry, the king would do well to take notice.[18]

While it is not difficult to outline the structures of politics, the problems begin when we try to come to terms with the rules that governed their conduct. The fact that they were rarely explicitly articulated does not mean that they did not exist; it is almost invariably the norms of a society that are least often discussed, and the less literate and self-conscious the society, the less evidence it will leave of its most fundamental assumptions. But even this rather inarticulate society has left us some clear guidance on basic political and constitutional principles as starting-points for the present discussion, some of which have already been briefly alluded to in the previous discussion of the mechanisms of government.[19] For landowners, so dependent on the king's law for the preservation of the property without which they were nothing, the single most important attribute of kingship was justice. This meant in practice that the king should ensure the proper functioning of his legal system – how this was to be done is to be an important area of inquiry in these chapters – and that he

[18] Below, pp. 352–3; *Paston Letters*, II, p. 344. On the magnates' general responsibility to speak for the realm (although the author shows how the gentry and townsmen began to speak for themselves), see Harriss 1975: Part I, and note the expression of this view by the Commons in 1348 (*Eng. Hist. Docs*, IV, p. 443). Cf. Hirst 1978: p. 116).

[19] Although use has been made here of some of the medieval theoretical literature on the subject, its value is obviously limited by the fact that, except perhaps for the works in the 'mirror for princes' tradition (Harriss 1985a; Orme 1984, pp. 95–8, 100–3; Green 1980: ch. 5; Born 1928; *Paston Letters*, II, p. 392), it was in most cases unlikely to have been read by landowners and that its authorship – initially mainly clerical, then increasingly legal – is often all too obvious in the tendentiousness of certain sections. For example, the clerics' insistence on the importance of the church in the polity and their increasing emphasis in the fourteenth and fifteenth centuries on the duty of leading subjects to amend and, if necessary, depose a bad ruler, which has more relevance to the growth of conciliarism in the church, particularly after the schism, than to the realities of secular rule (Wilks 1963: pp. 220–4; Guenée 1985: pp. 81–6), and the emphasis in the *Modus*, a tract much used by lawyers, on the place of petitioning in parliament ('Modus Tenendi Parliamentum', pp. 27–30, 80–91). Equally problematical are the views of judges, used extensively by Chrimes in his important pioneering study (1936). It is for this reason that little use has been made of the works of Fortescue, except where he is obviously replicating the standard line. As he was writing to explain the defeat of his side in a recent political crisis, his views can be taken neither as representative nor as indicative of opinions generally held *before* that crisis (see the comments in Brown 1969: p. 117 n.1; Carpenter 1983: pp. 233–4; Ives 1982: pp. 190–1). Nevertheless, all these works and opinions, even if only at second hand, must have had some importance in moulding opinion. They are at their most useful for our purposes where they are at their most platitudinous, reflecting commonly-held beliefs, and where their views coincide with those implicitly or explicitly revealed by the governing class at times of political crisis. In general, the ideas expressed by lay landowners have been preferred as sources for this section, and for references for these in the fifteenth century I am most grateful to John Watts. The whole section is of course no more than a cursory survey of a vast subject, which has yet to come into its own.

should give to each of his subjects, especially his noble subjects, his due, rewards to the deserving, punishment to the undeserving. Both harshness and favouritism were to be avoided, and the obligation on kings to reward and support those most important to them had to be fulfilled without unbalancing the hierarchy of power and status, which was the crux of effective government.[20]

In his dealings with the nobility, the king's proper exercise of patronage was only one aspect of showing respect for that hierarchy, and not necessarily the most important. The single most stringent imperative was that the king recognise the unique position of the magnates as practical implementers of his policies and treat them accordingly. This he was expected to do in several ways: patronage which differentiated the greater from the lesser, the deserving from the undeserving; accessibility which enabled the nobility not so much to act as professional counsellors as to speak for the realm; willingness to listen to advice, particularly over military matters, since it was the magnates' power over men that would enable the king to raise his armies, and the magnates who would lead them into battle, with or without the king's overall generalship. A king who took advice from his greatest subjects would be protected from the twin evils of pillaging his subjects by wasting his own substance and consequently having to tax unnecessarily, and pillaging his subjects by misusing or failing to implement the laws that protected their landed property.[21] Although much less was written on the duties of the nobility, it must be assumed that they were expected to model themselves on the king in their dealings with their own social and political subordinates, showing the same respect for justice, the same ability to balance personal obligation against the need to eschew favouritism and the same respect for the hierarchy, and such writing as there is on the subject tends to make these points.[22] We shall see that these were indeed the

[20] Wilks 1963: p. 162; Guenée 1985: pp. 41–2; Hoccleve, 'Regiment of Princes', pp. 91–2; Griffiths 1975: pp. 204–5; *The Libelle of Englyshe Polycye*, pp. 45–6; *Eng. Hist. Docs.*, IV, pp. 274, 409–12; Chrimes 1936: pp. 8–9, 14–20; *Four English Political Tracts*, pp. 58–61, 72–8, 124–8, 133–9, 146–9, 186; Harriss 1985a: pp. 11–12; Kail ed., *Political Poems*, p. 1 11.10–12, 14–15; Condon 1986a: p. 241; Wilkinson 1964: pp. 120, 134; Fryde 1979: p. 14 (where the noble attitude to justice and favour is well summarised).

[21] Stevenson, *Wars of the English*, II, ii, pp. 442–3, 447, 451; *English Chronicle*, pp. 86–90; Hoccleve, 'Regiment of Princes', pp. 145, 173–4, 175–8; Malory, *Works*, p. 1 ll.32–6; Chrimes 1936: pp. 39–40, 151–2, 171–5; Kantorowicz 1957: pp. 191–2, 362; Brown 1969: pp. 104, 117; Treharne 1969: pp. 56–8; *Four English Political Tracts*, pp. 32, 122, 142, 146–51, 183–5, 192–6, 198–9; Harriss 1975: pp. 129–30, 514; Harriss 1985a: pp. 15–16; Kail ed., *Political Poems*, p. 1 l.19, 11 l.72, 12 vv.11,12, 16–17, 22–4; *Aquinas: Selected Political Writings*, pp. 8–10 for the well-known king/tyrant distinction in relation to property; also Fortescue, *Governance*, p. 117; refs. in n.16, above. This series of ideas is endlessly reiterated in the major documents of the political crises of the fourteenth and fifteenth centuries: e.g. *Eng. Hist. Docs.*, III, pp. 525–6, 527–39, IV, pp. 409–12, 266–7; Wilkinson 1948–58: II, pp. 190–7, 244, 1964: pp. 180–2; *Rot. Parl.*, V, pp. 179–81.

[22] *Eng. Hist. Docs.*, IV, p. 1,132; *Rot. Parl.*, IV, p. 419 (quoted in Chrimes 1936: p. 97); Chrimes 1936: pp. 171–2; Harriss 1985a: p. 7; Kail ed., *Political Poems*, p. 13 ll.129–30.

qualities required in a successful magnate politician. Any king or magnate who failed to make use of his most powerful landed subordinates, or was unable to do so, was going to find power difficult to exercise.

Integral to the preservation of the social hierarchy that made government possible was the maintenance of the landed hierarchy that underlay it, and this returns us to the king's first attribute of justice. Where king and nobility were concerned, this was less a means of developing a sense of mutual need, for the need was self-evident on both sides, than the single most important aspect of the king's obligation to see to the well-being of his lieutenants. Since 1215 that had meant that rulers were expected to observe the laws that they themselves had imposed on their subjects. That did not mean, however, that they should abandon flexibility in the use of the law when law itself proved too rigid, for justice was always to be tempered with mercy. Moreover, the occasional piece of malpractice might be allowed to pass in the interests of effective government or to enable the king to reward a diligent servant.[23] The king was also supposed to see that all his subjects observed the law towards one another. In his capacity as umpire between his nobility, it was the personal respect that the king could command that mattered, much more than the mechanisms of the law, but his ability to enforce justice on all depended on his capacity to use all the weapons that law and executive power offered him. That was why he was in the theoretically paradoxical position of being under the law but subject to the restraint of God alone, for disputes among partisans could be regulated only by one who stood above partisan affairs. Time and time again the commentators on the late-medieval body politic stress precisely that quality implied in this corporeal metaphor: the oneness, the unity that is greater than the sum of its parts, all of it stemming from the *iusticia* of the ruler. Justice was linked to peace and it was only by leadership of the highest order that internal peace could be maintained.[24]

[23] Again, Aquinas is the *locus classicus* (*Selected Writings*, pp. 55–71); also e.g. *Eng. Hist. Docs.*, IV, pp. 409–12, esp. c.16; Hoccleve, 'Regiment of Princes', pp. 100, 108, 112, 120–5; Chrimes 1936: pp. 8–9, 46–9, 53–60, 122 n.1; *Four English Political Tracts*, pp. 58–61, 128–33, 139, 200–2; Wilks 1963; pp. 207–9, 217; also, Carpenter 1983: pp. 209–14 and refs. in n.20, above.

[24] Kern 1948: p. 170; *The Libelle of Englyshe Polycye*, pp. 45–6; *Eng. Hist. Docs.*, IV, p. 274; Hoccleve, 'Regiment of Princes', pp. 101–3; Chrimes 1936: pp. 14–20, 61, 122 n.1; *Four English Political Tracts*, pp. 73–5, 165, 196–200; Harriss 1985a: pp. 10, 11–13, 16–18; Kantorowicz 1957: *passim*; Guenée 1985: pp. 86–8; *Aquinas: Selected Writings*, pp. 2–7, 28–31, 40–2, 70–1; Kail ed., *Political Poems*, pp. 1 l.21, 9 v.2, 13 ll.129–30, 52 v.9, 64–9 (sustained analogy of a kingdom and the body); desire for consensus exemplified in council regulations framed during Henry VI's minority (Wilkinson 1964: pp. 246–7); concern expressed in council in late 1453 that lack of consensus and the king's incapacity lead to the king's orders being disobeyed, with particular anxiety about the failure of law (Griffiths 1984: pp. 77–9). For the classic Bractonian position on the king and the law, see Kantorowicz 1957: pp. 147–64; also Treharne 1969: pp. 49–54 (which includes a rejection of the authenticity of the *addicio*, which does allow for direct action against a tyrant, as a Montfortian interpolation) and pp. 59–78 on the impossibility of making solutions to the problem of bad kings work; see Tierney 1963 for a survey of the historiography of the *addicio* (but I am not convinced by his conclusions).

It is not easy for us to appreciate the reasons for the endless harping on this theme unless we grasp how many pressures there were for disharmony and how very vulnerable landed wealth was to the consequences of division.[25]

So much is self-evident from both the written statements and the high politics of late-medieval England. Moreover, there is already enough work on 'low politics' to enable us to go a little further in exploring what really governed political attitudes and relationships. It is clear that the obligation on the nobility to protect the lands of the gentry had an altogether different dimension from the king's duty to safeguard noble interests; it was the means above all others by which the nobility secured the gentry's allegiance. They themselves had no choice but to give theirs to the king – unless, that is, the king had entirely forfeited it and an alternative candidate was found – whilst the gentry could, if only to an extent heavily delimited by the geography of tenure, decide between the claims of local magnates to their services and support. In the previous chapter we saw how the nobility could lend their reinforcement to the network of loyalties on which the security of gentry lands depended so much; but when private arrangements broke down and moved into open conflict, it was not enough to have a following among the gentry, for at this point influence over the administration of the law became an inescapable necessity. Without it, any magnate would find it hard to attract any sort of following; the private affinity provided the means to manage the public authority, which in turn reinforced the private affinity. The completeness of this circle gave a considerable advantage to the nobility who had inherited a network of clients.[26] Whether and how a newcomer could break in is a question that these chapters will attempt to answer.

The intermingling of private and public has already been stressed in this study, and its permeation of every aspect of local administration cannot be overplayed. As was implicit in the previous chapter, we need to jettison the notion of a powerful administration continually impeded by recalcitrant local powers, substituting for it a series of processes of self-regulation of immense complexity and antiquity, into which the king's institutionalised power had been relatively recently absorbed. It follows that there is scarcely a governmental measure that can be assumed to be determined by disinterested bureaucratic procedure. Reading the fifteenth-century correspondences or Palmer's account of the Whilton dispute it does not take long to discover this truth.[27] From top

[25] Above, section I, *passim*.

[26] Carpenter 1980a: pp. 524–7, 1983: pp. 216–26,. 1986a: pp. 25–6. On the local basis of affinities, see the literature cited above, p. 4 n.15; also above, pp. 287–9, below, pp. 423–4.

[27] E.g. *Paston Letters*, I, pp. 96–8, 116–18, 142, 238–41, 249–50, 299–300, 559–60, 567–8, 577–80, II, pp. 12–14, 22, 44–5, 56, 72–4, 104–5, 234, 390–1, 426–8, 535–7, 559–60; *Stonor Letters*, I, pp. 97–8, 121, 130, II, pp. 51–2, 82–3, 88, 123, 126–7, 143; *Plumpton Correspondence*, pp. 33, 35; *Colls. Hist. Staffs.*, n.s., 6, i, p. 100. Palmer 1984: *passim*. Also, from a large literature, Baker ed., *Spelman*, II, pp. 89–92; Blatcher 1935–6, 1978: pp. 56, 59 and ch. 5; Powell 1979: pp. 163–5;

to bottom, a hidden hand could lie behind the bureaucratic processes; not invariably, but often enough to alert the historian to the dangers of taking official documents at their face value. With the royal government assuming an ever-growing part in the operation of lordship, this was beginning to apply almost as much in cases concerning the peasantry as in those where the parties were all landowners.[28]

Most obviously, the J.P.s and sheriffs who were the local executive officers of the legal system cannot be assumed to be acting with the impartiality we would expect of their modern counterparts. Not only were they bound to consider their own position in matters concerning other landowners, they could also be subjected to more direct pressures, notably those that were sometimes brought to bear on J.P.s at the sessions. These were rarely as dramatic as the events at Bedford in 1439, but the accounts of the nobility not infrequently record the dispatch of a prominent servant to the sessions, as, for example, William Clopton was sent by the earl of Warwick to attend those at Worcester in November 1417 and the following January a number of councillors were despatched to another sessions where they were to speak to the sheriff and deputy escheator. Moreover, since these were essentially amateur officials, they might fail to do their duties out of sheer negligence, ignorance or overwork; this was particularly true of sheriffs' failures to return the writs without which pleas in the Westminster courts could not proceed.[29]

If revelations of this kind no longer occasion much surprise among historians, it is as well to remember that they may apply equally to procedures that seem on the face of it more immune to private manipulation. Take, for example, the Inquisition *Post Mortem* that was performed on the death of a tenant-in-chief to discover and value the lands held in chief. These normally resulted in the declaration of all or most of the settlements that governed the estate's ultimate destiny. The family had a vested interest in the land being declared free of royal lordship and in the undervaluing of the lands of heiresses and underage heirs to keep down the cost of custody and marriage. The widow would want to ensure her full dower or jointure, while the heir would be anxious to see that she did not defraud him. The feudal lord, who could well be the dead man's patron, would want to ensure that the king did not usurp any rights he might have over the land, and any nobleman could have an interest of a general kind in the fate of an estate that lay close to his own. The king, for his part, would want the jury to find that the lands were not held in trust, whether

Hanawalt 1979: pp. 57–63; Hastings 1947: pp. 169–83, 211–36; Harriss 1957: works cited above, p. 283 n.4, p. 285 n.12.

[28] Above, pp. 284–8; Clayton 1985: p. 141 (an article that takes a rather lurid view of late-medieval disorder). For the downward extension of royal justice, see above, pp. 42–3, 45.

[29] Br. Lib. Eg. Roll 8773; Condon, 'Wiltshire Sheriff's Notebook'; and see refs. above, n.27. For the mechanisms involving local officials that were important to landowners and some of the difficulties these could cause, above, pp. 263–5.

this was the actual case or not.[30] In 1417–18 Warwick sent for a copy of the I.P.M. of his feudal tenant and servant Alan Straunge, and in 1420–1 he was overseeing the inquisition into the lands of Ralph Brasebrugge I, another client who held of him in fee.[31] In 1446 Buckingham sent men to the Staffordshire I.P.M. into the lands of Henry duke of Warwick.[32] There was also a further, more sinister, side to these enquiries: where the inheritance was in doubt, the verdict of the jury on the identity of the heir could be a crucial weapon in the judicial armoury of the claimants.[33]

Then there was the procedure by which cases were taken from lower courts into the King's Bench. There is considerable obscurity about precisely how and why this was done,[34] but we have some indications. One is in the Plumpton letters, when Sir William Plumpton is informed that 'your writts and *certiorare*' – i.e. *certiorari*, the normal removing writ – 'are labored for'.[35] Another comes from a chancery petition, in which the plaintiff, claiming to be unjustly indicted, says that as soon as he was informed of the prosecution he laboured for a *certiorari* concerning all the indictments laid against him.[36] 'Labouring' was the word most commonly used to describe actions of this kind that kept the right side of malpractice. Juries, for example, were laboured by the parties in a suit or by their lords, which meant not so much seeking to exert improper pressure on them as ensuring that they were familiar with the case of either party, although it could, of course, easily spill over into what we would call 'leaning' rather than labouring, especially if a powerful lord took a hand.[37] A box of legal papers in the Archer archive contains lists of jurors in pleas in which the Archers were involved, indicating their interest in knowing who was to decide their future. Attached to one of the lists are comments on the

30 *Paston Letters*, ed. Gairdner (3 vol. edn), I, pp. 53–5, quoted in Crump 1924: p. 142; Bean 1968: *passim*, esp. chs. 3 and 4; *Paston Letters*, I, pp. 141, 157–8, 160–2, 515–16, 598–9, 614–15, II, pp. 19–20, 24–5, 104–5, 219–20, 437, 475; *Stonor Letters*, I, pp. 104–5, II, pp. 119–21; *Plumpton Correspondence*, p. lxxxvii; C.1/174/58; Rowney 1983: p. 53 for the uses of the office in securing benefits.

31 Br. Lib. Eg. Roll 8773; Longleat, MS of Marquess of Bath 6414 *sub* Kingsbury.

32 S.C.R.O. D.641/1/2/56. Debates over the succession to Henry (below, p. 421) may have prompted him to do this.

33 E.g. in the conflict for Birmingham, below, pp. 377, 391; also Smith 1984: p. 64, Pollard 1968: pp. 54–5, the manoeuvres attending the Berkeley I.P.M. (Sinclair 1987b: pp. 36–7), the importance of the verdict of the I.P.M. after John Hugford's death (below, p. 575), and Paston, Plumpton and Stonor refs., above, n.30, and above, p. 285.

34 Maddern 1985: pp. 111–15; Post 1976: pp. 240, 277; Baker ed., *Spelman*, II, p. 141.

35 *Plumpton Correspondence*, p. 35.

36 C.1/64/1152.

37 Carpenter 1980a: p. 525. An example of labouring by a noble lord is the duke of York's letter to the jury in the early 1450s on behalf of Thomas Ferrers I (Br. Lib. Stowe MS 141 fo.6; and more on this case below, p. 469). For other examples of uses of the terms, see e.g. *Plumpton Correspondence*, pp. 29–31; *Paston Letters*, II, pp. 67–8, 75, 119–20; McFarlane 1973: pp. 114–18. An example of the use of outright threats against a jury comes from 1475 (K.B.9/946/66).

proposed panel, including the statement '... I pray put out all them of Kenelworth for Sir the baylly of that hundurd loues not me Sir asfor John Montefort & them of rouynton [Rowington] lette the be on at my gypparde'.[38]

Labouring might be necessary to secure both the serving of a writ and its return with a desirable endorsement and again it could occur on either side of the dividing line between the acceptable and the unacceptable. A good instance of the latter is the case of the unfortunate John Brewster, deputy sheriff of Warwickshire, charged in 1455 with serving an *exigent* summoning Richard Archer on pain of outlawry to pay a fine for an offence against Baldwin Porter. First he was told – by a fully ambulant Archer – to return that Archer was too sick to attend. When he refused he was eventually persuaded by a combination of excuses and blandishments to receive a *supersedeas* overriding the *exigent* from the hands of the Archers' messengers, although it should only have been handed over in open court. The sheriff himself having been hauled up in court, no doubt at the instigation of the Porters, Brewster was obliged to tell his sorry story. He was let off but his superior officer was fined 100 shillings. The Mountford account of 1433–4 gives some idea of the detailed management of all aspects of the legal processes that went on behind the scenes: copies of writs were obtained for friends, 'regards' were paid to sheriffs (the equivalent of the modern bottle of whisky passed at Christmas between business associates), two men were despatched to Coventry to search for evidences concerning a disputed property.[39]

An indication of the vast range of options open to a litigant can be gathered from a petition made in 1481 by Richard Bothewater and his wife Ellen concerning lands late of John Edmonds in Solihull and Kings Norton, Worcestershire. An inquest found Ellen heir to the lands, but the feoffees of Edmonds' brother managed to get a commission to make further enquiry. However, finding that this too was going against them, they brought its proceedings to a halt by announcing their intention of entering a plea on the issue. The feoffees then decided that their best hope was to give someone of greater importance a vested interest in their case, so they offered to sell the land, first to Thomas Littleton, one of the commissioners, then to John Hugford, a man of considerable local standing. Both refused, so the next ploy was to persuade John Gower, a local landowner, to enter the lands. Having forged a deed of entail to Gower, they were able to sue a novel disseisin against Bothewater (this must have been either on the original entry after the I.P.M. or

[38] S.B.T. D.R.37 Box 83. The comments refer to a jury of 15 Henry VII. Another reason for knowing the names of the jury was to be able to bring an action of attaint against them for a false verdict if the case went the wrong way. That this action could be brought was in itself a form of implied threat to the jurors (Baker 1979: p. 117); also on juries, see Green 1985: pp. 68–9; Powell 1988.

[39] K.B.27/778 Rex rot.44; S.B.T. D.R.37 Box 73; for the Archer–Porter dispute, see below, chs. 11–15; on *supersedeas*, FitzHerbert, *Natura Brevium*, pp. 588–98.

for subsequently expelling Gower) and won their case. This single insignificant episode shows how much care has to be exercised in handling judicial and administrative material, when, as in most cases, we have only the outward forms of the processes and no idea of the circumstances described here in which they were undertaken. What is more, we do not even know whether the version told by Bothewater represents the truth.[40]

The essence of the fifteenth-century constitution was that it had bias and favouritism built into every aspect of its practical working – that was inherent in the very personal nature of politics, at the highest and the lowest levels – but that if these went too far the system broke down. Moreover there were well-understood boundaries between the acceptable and the unacceptable in the conduct of law and politics, an unwritten code, which it is our job to break.[41] No landowner who wished to retain the respect of his neighbours could afford to neglect the whole-hearted pursuit of his interests, and yet all landowners knew full well that if any one of them overreached himself the delicate local equilibrium could be destroyed and they could be set on the downward path that ended in destructive violence. A society where wealth and power were based on land could hardly afford to indulge in such irresponsibility without overwhelming cause. At each level king and nobility had to exercise discretion to contain the conflicting ambitions of their subordinates.

In the earlier part of this study we have examined some of the realities of local society that could well cause gentry to step outside accepted norms of behaviour and nobility to offer excessive support to favoured followers: the competitiveness of the hierarchy, the scarcity of estates that favoured established families and put difficulties in the way of the growing band of newcomers trying to break in, the enormous potential for conflict in a landed society. Such tensions could not be contained unless there was a generally-felt willingness to avoid conflict if possible and, if it was not possible, to be bound by the rules. Like the king the nobility were expected to give special attention to the needs of their own clients and servants; failure to do so branded the lord as worthless, which was why, for example, John of Gaunt went on protecting Wycliffe long after he had abandoned any enthusiasm for his beliefs.[42] Yet, perhaps even more than the king, the magnate had to be open to the needs of the society beyond his affinity. The supreme authority of the monarch gave him a certain latitude in the exercise of bias before reaction set in; failure on a nobleman's part to respond to the needs of all local landowners would lead to a swift

40 S.C.8/E.1308. For Hugford, see below, p. 528. This one may have belonged to the Gloucestershire branch of the family (Davenport 1907: p. 27), but the lands at issue were in Worcestershire, and the Warwickshire man's importance at the time makes it more likely that the document refers to him.

41 See the initial exploration in Carpenter 1983; a similar point on uncovering norms is made in Roberts, S.1983: pp. 19–23.

42 McFarlane 1952: p. 102.

challenge from the other local powers, to whom the aggrieved parties would immediately turn. It has been constantly emphasised that the gentry were shrewd and experienced men; they expected a lot of their leaders and would be quick to identify the idols with feet of clay. On the other hand, a magnate who could find his way around the system would be in a position to command the services of the local gentry, both to enhance the protection that he was able to offer, and to ensure the wide-ranging authority that made him indispensable to the king in his 'contree' and by extension a man whom no ruler could afford to ignore.

The constitution of late-medieval England was well understood and, once the issues of public finance and local autonomy had been resolved in the first fifty years or so of the fourteenth century, not really a matter for dispute; there is a remarkable, indeed platitudinous, unanimity about the views expressed by both theoretical writers and practical politicians.[43] Thus, unlike the period from Magna Carta to c.1360, when the rules themselves were in doubt,[44] political divisions at national and local level arose in this period when the rules were broken. This body of rules has already been referred to as a 'code'. Its basic features – the supreme importance of justice and protection of landed property, the unthinking acceptance of the role of private relationships in the public sphere – are not hard to make out. What we know very little about is exactly how it worked when it came to the nitty-gritty of daily business. To go beyond this rather broad outline, especially to explore the mores of politics at the local level, and to find out what governed political behaviour, can only be done by taking a close look at the politics themselves. This is where the local study comes particularly into its own, in allowing us to put a manageable segment of the body politic under the microscope and to examine the preoccupations of its constituent figures as individuals and their dealings with one another as a group. By seeing how the concerns that we have been looking at in the first section of this work were pursued in the daily interaction of local politics, we may be able to discover some of the ground rules that determined the precise nature of the interlocking of the elements of the constitution. The intention is to dissect the nature of local power: how it was created and used, in whose interest it operated, whether local equilibrium was maintained, and, if so, how, and, moving on to a broader canvas, how nobility and gentry, both groups having urgent reasons to seek favour and to prohibit favouritism, saw their role within the body politic. The local perspective of this study means that the view from the bottom to the top will predominate over that from top to bottom. In particular the relationship between nobility and king will not be

[43] See the works cited above, nn.20–4, the numerous translations of the platitudinous *Secreta Secretorum (Three Prose Versions* and *Secreta Secretorum: Nine English Versions*) and Genet 1984. For discussion of two exceptions, Langland and Fortescue (who is only a partial exception), see Carpenter 1983: pp. 233–4.

[44] Much the best and the fullest account of this is Harriss 1975.

very extensively examined, although it is obviously inescapable insofar as it had a profound influence on the conduct of politics throughout the kingdom.[45]

II

The location of noble power within the county has already been described in outline and is mapped in figure 8.[46] Essentially there was a clear division between east and west: a line drawn roughly down the middle would divide the area where the earls of Warwick were dominant from that where neither the earls nor any other noble family had much in the way of land. Around Coventry, and to a lesser extent in the south-eastern corner near Wormleighton, the church was the major landowner. Over most of the eastern part of the county early settlement followed by extensive subinfeudation meant that magnate influence was fairly minimal. Of those that there were, Lord Astley was dead by 1420 and the Stafford/Buckingham lands were held by the underage Earl Humphrey from 1403 to 1423 (most of them in fact by his mother until 1438).[47] East Warwickshire was therefore peculiarly exposed to power wielded from its eastern neighbours, particularly from Leicestershire, since the gentry of the area bordering on Leicestershire tended to own estates in that county, often rather larger ones than they had in Warwickshire. The principal potential forces over the border were the Ferrers of Groby, the Mowbrays of Norfolk and, after 1420, when she acquired the Botetourt lands, which included Ashby de la Zouche in Leicestershire, Joan Beauchamp Lady Bergavenny.[48] In the far south of the county the most powerful noble was again Stafford/Buckingham, although Richard Beauchamp had one of the manors at Brailes and obtained the other through the Despenser heiress in 1423.[49]

Even the earls of Warwick could be said to have regarded Warwickshire as being on the periphery of their area of authority, since the county where they were truly unchallengeable was Worcestershire,[50] were it not that they could hardly avoid the problem of mastering the county from which they took their title, whose county town was their own *caput honoris*. The danger was that if they neglected Warwickshire someone else would step in and run off with the commanding following in west Warwickshire, which, adjunct or not to the Worcestershire affinity, was central to the earls' political power. Since the Warwickshire and Worcestershire clients were so closely interlinked, the earls

45 There is some discussion of this area in Harriss ed. 1985, esp. Harriss 1985a, c, and there is much more in Powell 1989.

46 Above, pp. 30–2.

47 Above, pp. 30, 314, 315.

48 Above, pp. 299–300, 307, 313. For fuller refs. on the Botetourt lands, see below, n.111.

49 *G.E.C.*, II, pp. 388–9; *G.E.C.*, XII, ii, p. 382; *V.C.H.*, V, p. 21; above, pp. 31–2.

50 Map in Carpenter 1986a: p. 27, and below, figures 11 and 12.

could not possibly afford to allow alien influences to be brought to bear in western Warwickshire. But, if their hold over west Warwickshire was to be secure, they really needed to extend their authority into the areas of the county where they had little lands or influence; if they failed to do so they could not guarantee any of their men proper support in disputes which ended in the law-courts.[51] Here there were two major problems. One was the earls' relatively slender tenurial hold on the north to north-west, which made them vulnerable to pressure exercised from south Staffordshire and north Warwickshire. Fortunately for Richard Beauchamp, the only candidates here, until Buckingham came into his Staffordshire lands and bought the Clinton estates in north Warwickshire, were the rather minor Ferrers of Chartley, who were eventually to throw in their lot with him. Clinton himself, who had the key stronghold of Maxstoke until it was sold to Buckingham in 1438, was too unimportant to be a threat and quite willing to be an ally.[52] John Sutton of Dudley, a castle on the Warwickshire/Worcestershire/Staffordshire border, was also underage until 1422, and he also was too insubstantial a figure to pose any threat unless backed up by a more powerful force.[53]

For the moment it was in eastern Warwickshire that the real problems lay, and yet the very absence of nobility here made it easier than it might have been. If this region could be ruled from Leicestershire, it could equally well be controlled from the earl's estates further south in Northamptonshire and Oxfordshire, or indeed from west Warwickshire. The close connections between the gentry south of Warwick, most of them Warwick's men, and those to the east could certainly expose the Warwickshire affinity to political influences from eastern Warwickshire, but they also acted as a channel by which Beauchamp's authority could permeate into that part of the county where he had least direct control.[54] Men like John Cotes, Edward Metley and Hugh Dalby may well have owed their first contacts with the earl or his father to their links with gentry living closer to the town of Warwick who served the Beauchamps, like the Straunges and the Lucys. Similarly, in the early years of the century, the connections stretching across north Warwick to Lord Astley, by way of Lord Clinton and other Warwick clients, brought the Malorys and other north-eastern families into the Warwick sphere, even if only indirectly.[55] What happened in the area around Coventry, the segment of east Warwickshire that lay between the north-eastern and eastern networks, would depend after 1399 on the earls' relations with the king, who was now lord of both Kenilworth

51 Above, pp. 284–8.

52 Above, pp. 32, 315, and, for Maxstoke's strategic importance, see p. 30.

53 *Cal. Close Rolls 1422–29*, p. 35. For the strategic importance of Dudley Castle, see above, p. 29.

54 Ross 1956: pp. 20–2 for a list of the estates, which is, however, partially in error in its differentiation of the Beauchamp and Despenser inheritances; see above, pp. 307, 313, 325–9, for local networks in east Warwickshire and relations with adjacent counties.

55 Above, pp. 300–3, 314.

and Coventry, and, as duke of Lancaster, a formidable power in Leicestershire.[56]

The young Richard Beauchamp, who succeeded his father, the former Appellant, in 1401 came into a difficult inheritance. His father had died less than two years after his restoration and the two years of confiscation and exile, from 1397–99, had seen a certain amount of desertion among his followers, or at least acquiescence in the lordship of Richard II's grantees, Despenser and Holland. Most notable were the conversions of William Bagot into an intimate servant of the king and of the less well-known John Russell, a former Beauchamp client from Worcestershire, into an active supporter of Richard's 'tyranny'.[57] As in any period of political upheaval, old scores had been settled and opportunities taken that were bound to be reversed after the coup of 1399.[58] All in all, it is not surprising that the first few years of the century in the west midlands were rather disturbed: there were two murders in 1400, one of them, in which the victim was a servant of John Russell, being very probably the legacy of the last years of Richard II's rule.[59] Russell was also involved in the major local dispute of these years, between William Lord Clinton and Clinton's widowed mother, Elizabeth, who had married Russell during the years of Richard II's ascendancy and contrived to obtain an outsize dower from the Clinton lands, including Maxstoke.[60] An assault in Derbyshire pepetrated in June 1401 by Beauchamp men from Warwickshire and a former servant of Clinton may also relate to this issue.[61] Bagot's dispute with William Holt over Aston may be another legacy of the last years of the previous king; Holt was rescued by the king, his mother having been protected at an earlier stage in the affair by the king's father, John of Gaunt.[62]

Warwick did not receive livery until February 1403, and his mother's jointure lands, including significant parts of the midland estate, not least Elmley Castle, did not come his way until March 1407,[63] so it is not altogether

56 Above, pp. 27–8.

57 *G.E.C.*, XII, ii, pp. 377–8; Dugdale 1675–6: I, p. 397; *Cal. Pat. Rolls* 1396–9, pp. 200, 336, 429; Post, 'Ladbroke Dispute, pp. 297–8; *Colls. Hist. Staffs.*, n.s., 11, pp. 45–51; Barron 1968; Sinclair 1987a: pp. 46–8. Some officials of Earl Thomas served the new owners of his lands during the period of confiscation (Warwick Castle MS 481; S.B.T. D.R.37/617; Sinclair 1987a: pp. 296–8). There is also useful material on the Beauchamp estates in this period in Richard Williams' Cambridge University B.A. dissertation on Earl Thomas, esp. good on Russell.

58 Notably in the Ladbroke manor dispute (Post, 'Ladbroke Dispute').

59 K.B.9/185/1/44, /186/74; Wylie 1884–98: I, pp. 119–20; Sinclair 1987a: pp. 297–8.

60 K.B.27/558 List of Fines d.; C.P.40/567 rot.490; *Cal. Close Rolls 1396–99*, pp. 359, 360, 433, *1399–1402*, pp. 2–3, 193, 280, 286, 393.

61 K.B.9/191/32. Deduced from the identity of the defendants; the victim was John Knivton of Derbyshire.

62 S.C.8/85/4228; *Cal. Close Rolls 1405–09*, p. 267; *Cal. Pat. Rolls 1399–1401*, pp. 9, 207; JUST 1/1514 m.47. Holt's mother was Bagot's sister, which was presumably the basis of a rather fragile claim (*Visitation Warwicks.*, p. 19).

63 *Cal. Close Rolls 1402–05*, pp. 35–6, *1405–09*, pp. 182–6.

surprising that he was not really in control of events, unable even to prevent attacks on his tenants at Pattingham in south Staffordshire without the king's assistance.[64] This early instability, which led to allegations that the Warwickshire roads were 'infested with bands of ruffians', climaxed in 1406 in the most shocking event of these years, the murder of Alan Waldeve, a north Warwickshire landowner, by his neighbour and Warwick's close associate, William Mountford.[65]

Nevertheless things were beginning to settle down. Henry IV, trying hard to heal the wounds left by the events of 1399–1400, secured an early settlement of the Clinton-Russell affair.[66] In 1406 Warwick was making efforts to protect his tenants at Pattingham[67] and by 1407 he was well enough established in Warwickshire to be able to effect an arbitration between Holt and Bagot which forced Bagot to accept the loss of Aston.[68] By 1408 he was secure enough to undertake a pilgrimage to Jerusalem from which he did not return until the spring of 1409.[69] Like his master the king, to whom he was performing loyal service in these early years, Warwick could be said to be in control by about 1407, and no doubt the headway that each of them made had been a help to the other; certainly the more settled atmosphere in national politics after the defeat of the conspiracy of 1405 must have made it easier to keep the peace at the local level.[70] Thereafter, unlike Henry IV, Warwick did not have ill-health and a recalcitrant heir to contend with. His accounts show that he had successfully reconstituted the Warwick affinity[71] and, more significantly, deeds indicate that he had already re-established the house of Warwick as the natural focal point of relationships among the gentry of Worcestershire and west and south of Warwick.[72] In this, especially in Worcestershire, he was greatly assisted by

[64] *Cal. Close Rolls 1402–05*, p. 36, *1405–09*, p. 279; S.B.T. D.R.37 Box 107/17; Br. Lib. Eg. Roll 8772 *sub* 'foreign expenses'; S.C.8/78/3862.

[65] Wylie 1884–98: I, p. 197; *Cal. Pat. Rolls 1405–08*, p. 327; *Cal. Close Rolls 1405–09*, pp. 220–1; Sinclair 1987a: pp. 158–9. In 1401 Waldeve was in dispute with a group of men who included Bagot, and by February 1408 Bagot was sufficiently restored to Warwick's favour to be among the earl's fellow defendants in a different suit, with Mountford as a co-defendant, while Mountford was acting as Bagot's auditor by Mich. 1402 (JUST 1/1514 mm.37, 48; C.P.40/567 rot.560d.), so this plea could be the origin of the quarrel with Mountford (but see below p. 364 for more on Bagot and p. 365 for an alternative possible cause).

[66] For refs., see above, n.60. For Henry's attitude to rule in his early years, see Brown 1972, and McFarlane 1972: pp. 59–77.

[67] S.C.8/78/3862 and above, as in n.64. But the affair continued until 1410, when a Loveday between Warwick's council and his Pattingham tenants was arranged (Br. Lib. Eg. Roll 8488).

[68] *Cal. Close Rolls 1405–09*, p. 267; *Dugdale*, p. 872.

[69] Wylie 1884–98: III, pp. 178–9.

[70] Wylie 1884–98: I, pp. 285, 454, II, pp. 13 n.2, 18, 232. Sinclair 1987a: pp. 84–90; McFarlane 1972: pp. 74–7; Warwick was generally well looked after by the king (Sinclair 1987a: pp. 46–52, 86–7).

[71] Br. Lib. Eg. Rolls 8770–2.

[72] Above, pp. 313, 317–18, 319.

the close relationship with his uncle, William Lord Bergavenny, who held some of the Warwick lands in west Warwickshire and east Worcestershire in tail male, was a major force in south Wales as lord of Abergavenny and of inestimable worth to Henry IV against the Welsh rebels, and a thoroughly experienced soldier, royal servant and politican.[73] The deeds of this period also show how the Astley connection across north Warwickshire linked up with the Warwick affinity to form a cohesive network from east to west.[74]

Even allowing for loss of evidence, Warwickshire seems to have experienced a period of peace between 1406 and 1413[75]. It is the assize rolls, not the King's Bench records, which tell us about conflict among the gentry in this reign (a fact which may support the view that King's Bench litigation grew later on),[76] and, although these reveal a fair amount of litigation, most of the cases disappear between one assize and the next, indicating settlement out of court. This is invariably a sign that the local powers are able to make their presence felt among the lesser landowners. In the Holt–Bagot case this is almost certainly what did happen, for an assize on the case was heard shortly before the arbitration was arranged. Indeed, so effectively were all the parties reconciled by February 1407 that Warwick, Bagot and Holt were then among a group of mostly north Warwickshire defendants, nearly all connected with the earl. Another of these defendants was the duke of York, who was later to hold the manors of Solihull and Sheldon when they came into royal custody; he may already have had some sort of interest in them, as there appears no reason otherwise for his activity in the north of the county, where he seems to have been an effective prop to Warwick, at a time when the earl's power had yet to attain its later eminence. He it was who helped Warwick in the Holt-Bagot arbitration.[77]

73 Wylie 1884–98: I, pp. 124, 371, 374, II, pp. 173, 296; McFarlane 1973: pp. 190–2; *Cal. Fine Rolls 1399–1405*, pp. 135–6; Bod. Lib. Dugdale MS 17, p. 51; Westminster Abbey Muns. 14633–4, 14639; above, p. 31.

74 Above, pp. 313–14.

75 The King's Bench indictment files for Henry IV's reign are thin, particularly in the later years of the reign. The proceedings of early Henry V stretch back into the previous reign but are, as one would expect, fuller on more recent events (Powell 1979: pp. 246, 285–317); see below, p. 394 and app. 4.

76 Above, p. 272. But also app. 4 for problems in dealing with legal sources.

77 JUST 1/1514 m.47; above, n.68. JUST 1/1514 m.48 seems also to be linked to this affair, as the plaintiff against Warwick, York etc., John Drayton, impleaded Holt for disseisin of Aston in 1401 (m.37d.). Confusingly, he was also a defendant in an assize with Holt and others in 1402 (m.41). Hugh Despenser's widow had Solihull and Sheldon from 1401 to 1414, when they were granted to York (see *V.C.H.*, IV, p. 219 for this complicated descent). For other disputes concerning Warwickshire landowners, see JUST 1/1514 mm.26, 37, 39d., 40d., 44d., 45d., 47d., 48, 50, 50d., /1515 m.7d.; K.B. 27/574 Rex rot.3 (if the Richard Archer mentioned here is indeed the Tanworth man), /594 Coram Rege rot.10d. In the sampled Common Plea rolls there is the same story of a limited number of disputes, which seem to be settled soon after

We have seen that the county escaped most of the more sensational violence that beset Staffordshire and Shropshire at the end of the reign, despite the fact that there were plenty of links between the counties through landowning, and through the connections of some north Warwickshire families with Edmund Ferrers of Chartley, one of the villains of the affair.[78] Even so, Warwickshire was not without its own small-scale battles at this time. Between 1412 and 1414 a dispute involving, on one side, the Chetwynds of Grendon and Alspath, John Malory of Newbold and William Purfrey, and, on the other, James Pulteney of Leicestershire led, it was alleged, to an assault on Pulteney at Misterton, his Leicestershire residence. In 1413 Thomas Burdet I and his son Nicholas embarked on their fairly sensational careers with a series of violent crimes in Worcestershire, all of them probably related to their feud with the prior of Worcester. Significantly, however, both affairs were settled quickly, the Burdets' by an arbitration manifestly under the auspices of the earl of Warwick.[79]

The same speed of response is evident in the much more threatening disputes over the inheritance of Mountford of Beaudesert which surfaced a little later, during Henry V's reign. The parties to the dispute were three of the most prominent gentry in the county, William Mountford, Baldwin Freville and John Catesby, and a minor nobleman, William Boteller Lord Sudeley of Gloucestershire. It may indeed have been this affair that had already led to the death of Alan Waldeve at Mountford's hands, for Waldeve had acted as attorney in Ireland to Baldwin Freville senior, father of one of the rival claimants to Mountford. As it happened, all four protagonists were retained by or in some way connected with Warwick, and the unusual speed and finality with which the cases were resolved suggests that the earl had a hand in their rapid and apparently peaceful progress through the courts. By 1418 the affair was over, Mountford having won against Catesby but lost to Sudeley and

they appear in the records (C.P.40/567 rot.586d., /579 rot.348 (possibly collusive suits), /599 roti.309, 341).

78 Powell 1979: pp. 286–317; Leics.R.O. DE 170/45/3; *Cal. Close Rolls 1447–54*, p. 70. The closest Warwickshire came to involvement in the disorder to the north and west was the prosecution of William Bermingham and Clinton for illegal giving of liveries at Lichfield and Shrewsbury respectively; both may have been acting in anticipation of the death of Elizabeth Clinton, in whose inheritance each had an interest (K.B.27/613 List of Fines, /615 Rex rot.34d.; below, p. 377).

79 *Cal. Pat. Rolls 1413–16*, p. 111; K.B.27/615 Rex rot.29d.; K.B.9/113/1; C.260/130/24; *Cat. Anc. Deeds*, II, A2753; K.B.9/202/43, 44; *Early Treatises on the J.P.s*, pp. 68–9; *H.M.C. Lechmere*, p. 303; Rawcliffe 1984: p. 41. Warwick published the award, on either side among the arbitrators was a Warwick man, *viz.* John Barton (Longleat, MS of the Marquess of Bath 6414; Roskell 1954: pp. 150–1) and Thomas Harewell, and the prior was bound over to Ailred Trussell, another Warwick retainer.

Freville, who proceeded to divide the inheritance between them, and nothing more was heard of it for nearly sixty years.[80]

Nevertheless, close examination makes it clear that throughout the reigns of the first two Lancastrians Warwick was very much a junior partner in the central midlands to the duke of Lancaster. The determination to be master in those parts of England which contained large crown estates is absolutely characteristic of Henry IV.[81] His command of Shropshire and Staffordshire,[82] which turned out in practice to be too domineering, seems to have been matched in Leicestershire. The Warwickshire shrievalty was held jointly with that of Leicestershire, and it is striking that on ten out of the thirteen occasions on which joint sheriffs were appointed under Henry IV the appointee was a Leicestershire man, and hence a native of a county where the Duchy of Lancaster was the dominant landowner. Moreover, of the three Warwickshire sheriffs, one, Robert Castell, was a servant of the Prince of Wales. The consistent appointment of sheriffs over whom he could exercise little control can only have been damaging to Warwick's authority in Warwickshire, particularly in the east, where his lack of lands meant that he could offer little practical protection to attract clients, other than the influence he could exert over the local officers. There is a similar story with the escheators in the first years of the reign.[83] Equally, the commission of the peace was by no means dominated by Warwick's men under Henry IV. Not only did the number of east Warwickshire men on the commission stay relatively high for much of the reign, but the presence of Thomas Rempston and Hugh Shirley, both of Leicestershire (although Shirley also had estates in Warwickshire), and both Duchy of Lancaster men, indicates how much weight Henry IV was able to

[80] K.B.27/617 Rex rot.23, /619 Rex rot.21, /861 Coram Rege rot.80 (case called into King's Bench on error, 1476); JUST 1/1524 mm.31, 32; *Dugdale*, p. 786; *V.C.H.*, IV, p. 53. For Boteller's connections with the Warwick affinity, see *Cal. Close Rolls 1413–19*, pp. 431–2; *Records of Henley in Arden*, pp. 9–10; *Calendar of Inquisitions Miscellaneous*, 7, pp. 234–6 (last two refs. are a good example of 'political' facet of I.P.M.s (above, pp. 355–6)). In this case the indefatigable John Barton (see n.79) was sent by the earl to Warwick to keep an eye on the assize (Br. Lib. Eg. Roll 8773 *sub* expenses of council). Mountford may have been persuaded to accept the verdict by the grant of 40 marks a year and the stewardship of Warwick's household in 1417/8 (*Dugdale*, p. 1,011). For Waldeve and Freville, see *Cal. Pat. Rolls 1396–99*, p. 530. For the descent of the Mountford lands, see *Dugdale*, pp. 786, 799, 1,007–8, and for the reopening of the case in 1476, see below, p. 517. For another possible cause of the Waldeve–Mountford enmity, see above, n.65.

[81] Bennett 1983: pp. 214–15; Wright 1983: pp. 83–4; Tyldesley 1978; ch. 8; Powell 1979: pp. 286–91, 300–17; Archer 1984a: pp. 82–3; Cherry 1979: pp. 93–4; Given-Wilson 1986: pp. 226–8; McNiven 1987: pp. 149–53, 185–6, 222; Payling 1987b: pp. 150–73, 1987c: p. 170. Note also his refusal to treat the Duchy as anything other than private property (Kantorowicz 1957: pp. 370, 403). It was Prince Henry who had Cornwall and Chester (Harriss 1985b: p. 168), but both father and son were active in both (Tyldesley 1978: ch. 8; Bennett 1983: pp. 18, 213–14).

[82] Powell 1979: pp. 286–308.

[83] *Lists and Indexes*, 9, p. 145; Roskell 1954: pp. 162–3; *List of Escheators*, p. 169.

exert from that county.[84] The paucity of Warwick's connections with north Warwickshire at this time, compared with the following decades, except for those made indirectly through Lord Astley, emphasises how restricted his sphere of influence still was, consisting as it did essentially of Worcestershire and south-west Warwickshire. It was, as far as we can be certain, in these counties alone that he himself was appointed J.P.[85]

Under Henry IV Warwickshire was undoubtedly part of the large area of authority in the midlands of the Duchy of Lancaster. The king and members of the royal family were frequently in the midlands, sometimes at Coventry or Kenilworth; Kenilworth was an important arsenal and was used as a residence for Henry's children both before and after his accession. Parliaments, particularly difficult ones, were summoned to Coventry. King and Prince of Wales were also to be found at Worcester, used as a base for some of the expeditions against Glendower. The Earl Marshal was imprisoned at Baginton, near Coventry.[86] To the king, the earl of Warwick was clearly a lesser allied nobleman who helped the duke of Lancaster rule the midlands, and this relationship with the crown held good even after it had become apparent from at least 1408 that Warwick was much more the Prince of Wales' man than the king's. It was Henry IV's determination not to be gainsaid in any area where he could expect his estates to make him the ruling magnate that precipitated the revolt in Staffordshire against his heavy-handed authority. Equally, his retreat from public life, which began in about 1409, produced the vacuum that led to disorder in his later years in those parts of England – Staffordshire, Shropshire, Leicestershire and the Duchy of Cornwall – where he had refused to surrender his power to anyone outside his immediate family.[87]

84 *Cal. Pat. Rolls 1399–1401*, p. 565, *1401–05*, p. 520, *1405–08*, p. 498; Archer 1984a: pp. 132–40. There are no recorded commissions for Warwickshire between 1409 and 1413, and there could well be at least one missing. If so, it might show Warwick's influence growing towards the end of the reign. For Rempston and Shirley, see Somerville 1953: pp. 136, 563; Shirley 1873: pp. 32–4. Rempston was also employed by the Earl Marshal, Thomas Mowbray, another of the potential powers in east Warwickshire until his execution in 1405 (Br. Lib. Add. Roll 16,556; below, p. 382). Gaunt had recruited extensively in Warwickshire, often amongst the families of Warwick's men (Walker 1986: p. 32, and *ibid.*: App. 1 for other Lancastrian retainers in and around Warwickshire).

85 For Warwickshire, see n.84, above; for Worcestershire, see *Cal. Pat. Rolls 1399–1401*, p. 566, *1401–05*, p. 521, *1405–08*, p. 499, *1408–13*, p. 486. This assumes that there are no missing commissions for other counties.

86 Wylie 1884–98: itinerary in IV, pp. 287–302; see also Wylie 1884–98: I, p. 368, II, pp. 49, 246, III, pp. 118, 326, 328, IV, pp. 158–9, 160, 176, 180, 229, 253; Wylie and Waugh 1914–29; I, pp. 190–1; McFarlane 1972: p. 90; Taylor, 'Chronicle of John Strecche', pp. 141–2; refs. in n.81. On the growth of Duchy power in the north midlands, see Walker 1986: pp. 224–51.

87 McFarlane 1972: p. 103; and see his restricted itinerary, Wylie 1884–98: as cited n.86; Sinclair 1987a: pp. 84–90; Payling 1987b: pp. 244–7, 1987a: pp. 140–2; McNiven 1985: esp. pp. 770–1; Powell 1985: pp. 54–5. There is more on this in Powell 1989. Interestingly, Simon Walker's work on John of Gaunt shows that Henry IV's father ran into almost identical difficulties in the localities, particularly in Lancashire, because of a combination of enormous potential power, enough to repel most local rivals, and lack of close personal supervision (Walker 1986: ch. 4). On Warwick and Prince Henry, see Harriss 1985c: p. 33, and below, n.89.

It is unsurprising to find that Henry V remained as uncompromising about this as his father. The hearings of the itinerant King's Bench early in the reign demonstrated beyond doubt that wherever the king was the dominant landed power he expected his word to be law, from the Duchy of Cornwall through the midlands to the Welsh border.[88] There were however inevitable changes. First, Henry V was a wiser man than his father and understood that it was sensible to accommodate a wider circle of local landowners if violent factionalism of the sort produced by the rule of Henry IV's friends in Shropshire and Staffordshire was to be avoided. Secondly, he was about to invade France, where he was to spend a large part of the reign. This was another reason for reconciliation and for broadening the basis of local power, since he would be in no position to deal with division at home, nor would he want a divided army in France. But absence in itself was bound to force upon him more delegation to local powers other than his own in the areas of the principal royal estates. It simply was not possible to be duke of Lancaster and Cornwall and earl of Chester while leading an army abroad as king of England. And Warwick, as an old friend and a valued servant, was an obvious man to trust.[89]

One way and another there was thus a relaxation of the royal grip on the midlands from Henry V's accession. The Staffordshire commission of the peace, for example, became much less the private preserve of Duchy officials. Not only were newcomers brought in, as the commission was enlarged, but in the nomination of Hugh Erdeswick, the initial leader of the opposition to the Duchy officials that had led to the débâcle of the last years of Henry IV, the new king showed that he recognised the need to accommodate a broader spectrum of local interests. Furthermore Warwick himself was placed on the commission, apparently for the first time, and this coincided with a more general movement on his part into the north midlands: by 1417 he seems to have had some sort of association with Erdeswick and other Staffordshire gentry,[90] and under Henry V

[88] Powell 1979: *passim*, 1985: pp. 55–72; Tyldesley 1978: ch. 8; Payling 1987b: pp. 142–3; Somerville 1953: pp. 176–89; Cherry 1979: pp. 93–5; Griffiths 1974: pp. 76–9, 1972b: p. 150. Henry V was also fond of Kenilworth (Taylor, 'Chronicle of John Strecche', p. 184; Harvey 1944: p. 97; Wylie and Waugh 1914–29: III, p. 270; Stow, *Chronicle*, pp. 344–5).

[89] Powell 1979: pp. 285–317, 1985: pp. 68–71; Sinclair 1987a: pp. 90–113; Powell and Wallis 1968: pp. 453–4. Note that annuities charged on the Duchy were almost halved under Henry V (Harriss 1985b: p. 169).

[90] *Cal. Pat. Rolls 1413–16*, p. 423, *1416–22*, p. 459; Powell 1979: pp. 285–99; Br. Lib. Eg. Roll 8773 *sub* expenses of the council. The entry refers to a gathering of Erdeswick and other Staffordshire esquires at Sutton Coldfield, Warwick's manor, along with at least two of Warwick's councillors 'for the matter of Perton' (Staffordshire), which he was negotiating to buy from about that time (Sinclair 1987a: p. 190). It is possible that they were there simply as local witnesses, but the wording seems to imply that they were actually Warwick's esquires. In 1421 the Burdets were bailed by a group from north Warwickshire with interests in Staffordshire and Derbyshire (Cokayn, Stanhope, John Chetwynd), another indication of the movement into the

north Warwickshire representatives, most of them connected with Warwick or Ferrers of Chartley, become more evident among Warwickshire officials, especially on the commission of the peace. Significantly Warwick was brought in to arbitrate in the dispute between Erdeswick and Ferrers that had torn Staffordshire apart.[91] The death of Lord Astley some time between 1417 and 1420, leaving a successor for whom Warwickshire came a bad third to Wales and Northamptonshire, almost obliged Warwick to direct his attention northwards, since most of Astley's more prominent associates had been in some way connected with the earl and he was therefore Astley's natural successor.[92] Another indication that the geographical scope of Warwick's authority within the shire was growing by royal licence comes from the shrievalty: of the nine sheriffs pricked under Henry V, only four came from Leicestershire, and one of the Leicestershire appointees, John Salveyn, was in fact the son of Warwick's treasurer at Calais.[93] An assize roll entry of 1429 shows that by that date the earl's links with east Warwickshire and Northamptonshire were well established.[94] In 1417 the death of Lord Berkeley, to whose heir he was married, broadened his responsibilities still further, taking them into the southern part of Gloucestershire, where he was to make Berkeley Castle one of his main residences.[95]

The listings of Warwick's forces for 1414 and 1417, the only occasions when he took a sizeable midlands contingent to France, demonstrate how his authority within the midlands had grown, including as they do men from major families from all parts of Warwickshire, as well as from Worcestershire, Staffordshire and Oxfordshire.[96] Denuding the region of nobility and gentry with the landed power to enforce the peace might have created problems in local administration, and it is noticeable that in the middle years of the reign the Warwickshire commission of the peace was almost entirely lacking in represen-

north of the Warwick affinity's connections (K.B.27/634 Rex rot.3). Note also that Thomas Stanley served under Warwick in France in 1416 (*Cal. Pat. Rolls 1413–16*, p. 403, cited in Powell 1979: p. 299) and Warwick's purchases in Staffordshire (Sinclair 1987a: pp. 52–3).

91 *Cal. Pat. Rolls 1413–16*, p. 424, *1416–22*, p. 461. However, one of these new officials was John Cokayn, who in this reign becomes extensively involved in Warwickshire as an official for the first time, the connection being, in all probability, that he was Henry V's man (Wylie 1884–98: IV, p. 40 n.4; *Cal. Fine Rolls 1413–22*, p. 22; *Cal. Pat. Rolls 1416–22*, pp. 198, 461; for ref. to Cokayn as M.P. in 1420 and 1421(2), see above, p. 266 n.17); Rawcliffe 1984. pp. 40–1, citing *Colls. Hist. Staffs.*, o.s., 17, p. 51; Powell 1979: pp. 285–99.

92 Above, p. 314.

93 *Lists and Indexes*, 9, p. 145. For Salveyn and Warwick, see Longleat, MS of Marquess of Bath 6414; *Test. Vetust.*, p. 203.

94 JUST 1/1537 m.6; and see below, pp. 374–5.

95 Sinclair 1987b: pp. 36–7; Longleat, MS of Marquess of Bath Misc. IX.

96 Bod. Lib. Dugdale MS 2, p. 277; Br. Lib. Cotton Roll XIII.7, Add. MS 24,704 Nos.25, 35–7; E.101/51/2.

tatives of the nobility.[97] Even so, the advantages of being able to remove to France disruptive elements like Edmund Ferrers, Erdeswick, and, eventually, the Burdets probably far outweighed any difficulties of this kind.[98] The practice of allowing wilfully violent and litigious landowners to make a new start in France was brought to a fine art by Henry V, and William Mountford's departure for the wars in 1417 must have taken a great deal of the heat out of the dispute over the Mountford inheritance.[99]

All in all the peace of Warwickshire was impressively maintained in these years, whether or not king and earl were in England. The big cases – the Mountford affair, the Burdets' conflict with the abbey of Evesham, the Berminghams against Joan Beauchamp, widow of William Lord Bergavenny, over the Botetourt lands and Joan against Nicholas Burdet – were resolved, usually by a combination of judicial decision and arbitration, often accompanied by the use of war service to remove at least one of the parties.[100] The smaller cases tend to appear once in the judicial records, then disappear, having presumably been settled out of court in the interim.[101] The only conflicts that refused to go away were the series of collisions between Thomas Greswold, the rising lawyer from the Arden region, and various neighbours, notably the Hores of Elmdon and Solihull. These were a reflection of the social and tenurial conditions around Tanworth; intermingled lands, too many minor landowners and pushy newcomers and, as everywhere at this time, too few estates to cater for them. Greswold was at the start of a successful career and running into opposition while trying to acquire lands by purchase and marriage.[102] Given these circumstances and the propensity for violence of the younger Hores, the lack of serious disruption at the heart of the Arden is in fact rather remarkable,

97 *Cal. Pat. Rolls 1416–22*, p. 461.

98 Powell 1979: p. 298, 1985: pp. 71–2; *G.E.C.*, v, p. 318; K.B.27/635 Rex rot.9.

99 Br. Lib. Add. MS 24,704 No.35; above, pp. 365–6. Powell discusses the rehabilitation in France of lawless members of the aristocracy under Henry V at some length in Powell 1989.

100 *Cal. Pat. Rolls 1416–22*, p. 147; *Early Treatises on the J.P.s*, pp. 71–2; K.B.27/634 Rex rot.3; *Cal. Close Rolls 1413–19*, p. 500; *Colls. Hist. Staffs.*, o.s., 17, pp. 78–9; McFarlane 1973: p. 119 (but McFarlane is, for once, in error in stating that the dispute ended there: below, p. 388). For the settlement of the Mountford dispute, see above, p. 365. William Bermingham, one of the Botetourt clamants (below, p. 389), clearly did not accept the settlement (Nott. Univ. Lib. Middleton MS 5/168/33: undated and wrongly attributed to 35/6 Henry VI. The petitioner's wife's name makes it clear that this is William I (died 1427: below, p. 378)).

101 E.g. K.B.27/608 Coram Rege rot.13d., /612 Coram Rege rot.27, /626 Writs of Attorney d., /661 Coram Rege rot.22, /631 Coram Rege rot.66, /631 Coram Rege rot.35, /637 Coram Rege rot.15d. For litigation and settlement, see Powell 1983a and 1984b: pp. 38–40.

102 K.B.27/636 Coram Rege roti.9,66. Greswold had married the daughter and co-heir of William Hore of Solihull, thereby alienating other branches of the Hore family and their relatives with claims to the lands (K.B.27/747 Coram Rege rot.33d. and below, p. 430). For the violence of the Hores, see below, p. 396. See also Skipp 1970b: pp. 84–5. For the characteristics of the Arden, see above, pp. 21–3.

and by the end of the reign Greswold had been fully absorbed into the dense network of Arden gentry.[103]

The Beauchamp household and estate accounts of 1417–18 and 1420–1 show very clearly how it was possible for Warwick to be simultaneously a soldier in France and a nobleman of mounting local importance at home, despite being continuously absent from England from 1417 to 1421. He had an able staff at home, men like John Baysham, John Throgmorton and John Harewell. His council was active, whether he was there or not, in the matters of the Berkeley inheritance and Perton manor, which he was arranging to buy, and a host of other affairs. Sometimes, tellingly, it acted *per preceptum domini* even when the earl was in France, and we know that his officials, such as John Throgmorton in 1417–18, went to consult him there. Whether he was at home or abroad, his household was a place where his men could meet, and where, one assumes, difficulties between them could be ironed out, either informally by peer-group pressure, or formally by the earl's council. Indeed William Worcestre's account of Warwick's building activities shows that, despite the fact that he was doing the king's business abroad for much of his adult life, he never ceased to be closely concerned about his affairs in the west midlands.[104]

If the history of Warwickshire under Henry V is typical, and if Henry was as good at getting the best out of the rest of his nobility as he was with the earl of Warwick, then the outstandingly successful combination of foreign conquest with peace at home is readily explicable. What the king had achieved in his relations with Warwick was a delicate balance between acknowledgement and profitable use of a great nobleman's local authority and refusal to surrender any part of his own that really mattered. If Warwick was now a greater force in northern and eastern Warwickshire than he had been under Henry's father, that was in no way detrimental to the king's hegemony in Staffordshire and Leicestershire, where he had no intention of sharing power. Indeed the greater freedom given to the earl had made him a more effective enforcer of his royal master's commands, and where their spheres were allowed to overlap to a limited extent, as in northern and eastern Warwickshire, if either failed or was for some reason unable to act, the other could step in. The disastrous consequences of Henry IV's withdrawal from public life could consequently be avoided. It seems that this combination of co-operation and firmness character-

[103] K.B.27/636 Coram Rege rot.66, /637 Rex rot.13; S.B.T. D.R.37 Box 42 (deed of 1423); above, pp. 220–1. For the local network, see above, pp. 296–7.

[104] Br. Lib. Eg. Roll 8773; Longleat, MS of the Marquess of Bath 6414, Misc.IX; N.R.A. 'Calendar Sutherland MS' in S.C.R.O. D.593A/2/10/11; Sinclair 1987b: pp. 36–40, 1987a: pp. 187–95; Pugh 1971: pp. 189–91; Worcestre, *Itineraries*, pp. 218–21. For a full account of his service in France, see Sinclair 1987a: pp. 93–113; on the capacity of magnate councils to cope with their lords' business, see Rawcliffe 1979.

ised all Henry V's dealings with his nobility and it proved a remarkably effective recipe.[105]

In 1422 there was a massive change of gear. Most obviously, the single directional force within England was lost, and power devolved from an unusually vigorous and energetic adult to a council of regency. As far as Warwickshire was concerned, even more momentous was the elimination of an active duke of Lancaster.[106] Henry IV's later years had shown that the king could not hope to play the role of magnate in the localities without the persistent personal supervision which the nobility were used to providing, and the succession of a baby was to make this more evident still. Furthermore, as the war lost much of its glamour and financial attractions, becoming a permanent defence of the French kingdom without royal leadership, rather than a series of outstandingly successful campaigns under a charismatic king, many of the warriors of the previous reign began to return home.[107] This meant that powerful figures like John Mowbray, the second duke of Norfolk, and Edmund Ferrers of Chartley were much more closely involved in local politics than before. Where men like Ferrers were concerned, who had been persuaded abroad to neutralise their violent instincts, this was not a happy prospect for their neighbours.[108] Removing the unruly to France was an option that tended to disappear as the unattractiveness of the war began to outweigh the disadvantages of outlawry and recognisance at home.

The new circumstances on the national scene coincided with new developments in and around Warwickshire. The death of Warwick's Berkeley father-in-law had already extended his interests into Gloucestershire, even though these lands were to be the subject of litigation for decades to come. In 1422 Richard earl of Worcester, son and heir of William Beauchamp of Bergavenny, died. While this had little immediate effect on the balance of magnate power in the west midlands, for William's widow, Joan, had been left in possession of most of the Bergavenny lands, including those entailed on the Warwick line, it enabled Warwick, who himself had just been widowed, to marry Worcester's widow. Since Worcester had died without a male heir, with her came the large and most conveniently situated Despenser estates. These, centred on Tewkesbury, fitted beautifully with the existing Warwick lands, to form an unrivalled core of influence in south-west Warwickshire, southern Worcestershire and north Gloucestershire. With most of the Berkeley lands remaining in Warwick's hands until his death, Gloucestershire was now to become an integral part of his local empire.[109] That empire was to receive few challenges

105 Harriss 1985c.

106 Somerville 1953: pp. 201–28. For the arrangements for the minority, see Griffiths 1981: ch. 1.

107 Allmand 1983: pp. 241–6.

108 Archer 1984a: pp. 207–11; *G.E.C.*, v, p. 318.

109 For the composition of the Warwick lands, see below, fig. 11, p. 449; above, p. 31; Sinclair 1987b; *G.E.C.*, I, pp. 28, 29 n.a., XII, ii, p. 382; *Cal. Close Rolls 1409–13*, pp. 144–6, 161;

from elsewhere. Although Buckingham had livery of his lands in 1423, he was still very young and inexperienced and did not have complete control of his Staffordshire and Warwickshire properties until 1438.[110] The withdrawal of Duchy of Lancaster influence in Staffordshire, Leicestershire and the area around Coventry meant that there could be little doubt that the greatest single power in the midlands was now the earl of Warwick.

However, one new power arrived on the Warwickshire scene in the early 1420s and that was Joan Beauchamp. In about 1420 she made a significant and permanent addition to the lands she had in dower, and, unlike her dead husband's estates, these were not doomed, for lack of a male heir, to revert to the earls of Warwick on her death. They were in fact to descend to her daughter, who had married James Boteller earl of Ormond, and to become the foundation of a new noble sphere of influence in and around Warwickshire. The property acquired by Joan was the Botetourt inheritance, to which brief reference has already been made. These lands had been bought by Hugh Burnell, who may himself have been linked with Warwick, and had certainly had some influence in the county, being consistently appointed to the peace commission, and from him they were purchased by Joan. They included some strategically significant properties, notably Bordesley, Haybarn, Mere, Handsworth and Clent, and Weoley castle and Northfield manor, which remained in the disputed possession of the Berkeleys of Weoley. All these were in the border region between north-west Warwickshire and south-west Staffordshire, where Warwick might consider himself especially vulnerable were he to maintain his movement northwards into Staffordshire. And east of Warwickshire was Ashby de la Zouche, which was to be the centre of an extensive Leicestershire connection which enabled Joan and her heirs to influence affairs in Warwickshire from the other side of the county. Joan, dubbed 'a second Jezebel' by a contemporary, would prove a formidable opponent should she refuse to play second fiddle to her nephew by marriage, and she still had the Bergavenny lands scattered among the Warwick estates in the Warwick heartland in Warwickshire and Worcestershire.[111]

Nevertheless, it was the earl of Warwick who would henceforth be dictating

Carpenter 1986a, pp. 26–7. In order to keep the Despenser lands in the family, Warwick needed a son, where Worcester had had only a daughter (McFarlane 1973: p. 193). Luckily, his wife was able to supply him with one.

[110] See above, p. 315.

[111] *Cal. Close Rolls 1405–09*, pp. 204–5, 244–5; *Cal. Pat. Rolls 1416–22*, pp. 305–6, *1461–7*, pp. 549–50; *Colls. Hist. Staffs.*, o.s., 11, pp. 222, 226–7; *W.F.F.*, 2504–5, 2516; B.R.L. 357336; *G.E.C.*, x, p. 125; *V.C.H.*, VII, pp. 58, 62–3, 68; *The Ancestor*, 8 (1904), pp. 173–9 (where it is suggested that Burnell may have suffered an infatuation for Joan, in which case one can only sympathise); Pearson 1902: pedigree; Jeayes ed., *Lyttelton Charters*, pp. 72–4; Adam of Usk, quoted in McFarlane 1973: p. 119. For Burnell, see Sinclair 1987a: p. 252; *Cal. Pat. Rolls 1401–5*, p. 520, *1405–08*, p. 498, *1413–16*, p. 424. For Joan and the Leicestershire networks, see above, p. 313; for Weoley and Northfield, see below, pp. 388–9.

the course of events over much of the midlands, and for the first time his authority was untrammelled, as the heavy hand of the first two Lancastrians was lifted across England and Wales.[112] He became a J.P. in every one of the counties bordering on Warwickshire, except for Leicestershire, where his estates were too few to warrant appointment.[113] His power over Warwickshire is well illustrated by the change in the balance between Warwickshire and Leicestershire sheriffs, which shows a complete reversal of the pattern of the early years of Lancastrian rule; from the accession of Henry VI until Warwick's death in 1439 there were five from Leicestershire and thirteen from Warwickshire.[114] During the 1420s the membership of the commission of the peace maintained its shift towards north Warwickshire at the expense of representatives from east Warwickshire and in the 1430s the commission began to be dominated by men from west of Warwick, where the earl was supreme. From February 1422, even before the death of Henry V, with the arrival of William Mountford and Thomas Mollesley, almost every new J.P. was Warwick's man, often his close servant.[115] Warwickshire knights of the shire are more consistently the earl's men than before, especially in the 1430s.[116] The incomplete valor, datable to c.1431, gives some idea of the earl's power at its peak, listing annuitants from Worcestershire, Northamptonshire, Staffordshire, Leicestershire and from all parts of Warwickshire.[117] In 1435, on his aunt's death, he was to inherit the entailed lands of the Bergavenny inheritance, which consolidated his hold over the core of his domain in south-west Warwickshire and Worcestershire.[118] There is evidence suggesting an increase in contacts with the gentry of east Warwickshire at the end of the reign of Henry V and in the early years of the minority: that the first indications of connections with Richard Knightley come in 1417–18, with John Cotes and John Onley of Tachbrook in 1420–1, and with William Peyto in c.1423–4 may be entirely fortuitous, but it does fit with the growth of Warwick's authority right across the midlands at this time. It would moreover make sense in the light of his increasing ability to influence events in the east of the county,

[112] I have to thank Dr Powell for pointing out that this was a general phenomenon, not confined to the midlands; cf. Wales: Griffiths 1974: pp. 81–5.

[113] *Cal. Pat. Rolls 1422–29*, pp. 563, 567, 568, 571, 572, *1429–36*, p. 624. The only county where appointment was not virtually immediate was Staffordshire, where he had to wait until 1430. Warwick seems also to have been recognised as the most important non-royal lay magnate on the minority council (Brown 1969: p. 109).

[114] *Lists and Indexes*, 9, p. 145.

[115] *Cal. Pat. Rolls 1416–22*, p. 461, *1422–29*, p. 571, *1429–36*, p. 626.

[116] For Warwickshire M.P.s 1401–39, see above, p. 266 n.17.

[117] S.C.12/18/45. For dating, see editors' note in McFarlane 1973: p. 197 n.3. Ross (1956, p. 16) dates it to *c*.1439, which is not possible because John Catesby, named on the valor, died in 1437 (*Cat. Anc. Deeds*, IV, A10411, 7131); see also Sinclair 1987a: pp. 332–4 for clients from the north midlands and Leicestershire.

[118] Above, n.109 for refs.

through his ascendancy over Warwickshire local officers and his lands in Northamptonshire and Oxfordshire.[119]

But if freedom brought power it also brought heavy responsibilities. Warwick may have been perfectly happy to extend his authority into Staffordshire but he really had very little choice. In the vacuum left by the Duchy of Lancaster, he could not afford a struggle for control there that would have unleashed the well-known fury of Edmund Ferrers against the inexperienced and untried Sutton of Dudley and Buckingham, and could do incalculable damage to the earl's estates and clients on the Warwickshire/Worcestershire/Staffordshire border. At the southern pole of his empire, if he wanted to hang on to the Berkeley estates he had to show himself an effective lord of the Berkeley political inheritance, not least because he needed the Berkeley affinity on his side.[120] The change in the geography of the Warwick sphere of influence was thus in some sense inexorable. The compact area of authority comprising Worcestershire and the adjacent parts of Gloucestershire and Warwickshire gave way to a more unwieldy one: Worcestershire, most of Gloucestershire, as much of Staffordshire as was necessary to preserve the peace of north Warwickshire and the western half of Warwickshire. To this it was necessary to add eastern Warwickshire, once it became clear that the absence of effective Duchy of Lancaster rule was going to open Leicestershire up to more extended magnate influence. This may have seemed especially urgent after the return to England in 1423 of the duke of Norfolk, whose considerable interests in that county could easily spill over into eastern Warwickshire.[121] What it came down to was that, to protect his enlarged following, Warwick needed to control the administration of Warwickshire, Worcestershire and Gloucestershire and to have some purchase on events in other adjacent counties. And this had to be done while he was continually in and out of France. As under Henry V, he had to rely on his council to carry out his instructions effectively in his absence; fortunately they showed themselves by and large as efficient and reliable as ever.[122]

119 There are problems in disentangling John Onley of Bishops Tachbrook from his namesake of Birdingbury, both in east Warwickshire. The Birdingbury man was certainly the Bergavenny servant. The proximity of Tachbrook to Lighthorne, the manor from which the Warwick man's annuity was paid, is the reason for assuming that the Tachbrook man was Warwick's servant. Either way, the first evidence for Warwick being connected with a John Onley – and, since both came from east Warwickshire, the point is made, whichever of the two it was – is from 1417–18. Richard Knightley's uncle, John, had already served Warwick, and Peyto's father had been linked to him (*Dugdale*, p. 474; for other refs., see app. 3); also above, p. 318 n.147.

120 Sinclair 1987b, 1987a: pp. 278–9.

121 Archer 1984a: chs.2 and 5. Note the number of Mowbray overlordships in east Warwickshire (*V.C.H.*, esp. VI), which, although probably of little political worth alone, when combined with the direct power that came from the Leicestershire estates, could make the duke a force in east Warwickshire, especially among the many families that had lands in both counties (above, pp. 299–300, 307). For Norfolk and east Warwickshire, see above, p. 318 n.147, and below, p. 380.

122 Sinclair 1987a: chs. 4 and 6.

It was on this necessity to extend his power base that was built the elaborate system of alliances with all the magnates who were involved in the county's affairs whose evolution has already been described.[123] Some of them, notably those with the Beauchamps of Bergavenny and Lord Clinton, were not new, but the breadth and complexity of Warwick's political connections in the 1420s and 1430s are altogether novel. The north-east he could leave to Joan Beauchamp and other minor Leicestershire nobility, as long as he remained on good terms with them; he would in any case have had great difficulty in making any impression here.[124] Further south he could exploit his own lands and office in Northamptonshire to reinforce the links with the gentry of eastern and south-eastern Warwickshire which were being forged by the interconnections of the large east Warwickshire network and the Warwick affinity. This could be done specially effectively with those, like the Catesbys and Knightleys, who had lands in both counties. In the far south he had his own lands, a close connection with Richard Lord Straunge, owner of two manors here, and property in Oxfordshire. In the north, as we have seen, rapprochement with the Ferrers of Chartley and their friends was followed by the absorption of the young Buckingham.[125]

As a system for extending Beauchamp's authority into all the regions where he needed to be effective it was remarkably complete, but it was not without internal tensions. First, although the involvement of so many political networks was a source of strength, in that the overlapping of associates would tend to neutralise conflict, if serious divisions arose there would be some hard choices for Warwick about whom to support and an urgent need for reconciliation before his alliances broke down. Secondly, it would have to adapt to changes in the tenurial position and ambitions of his client nobility. It was in fact this second weakness that was to put the whole system under the most considerable strain. To add to Warwick's problems there was the fact that for almost the whole period from 1422 until the earl's death in 1439, despite the remarkable success of the minority council in neutralising conflict, there was no single undisputed central authority that could step in, as Henry V had done, to deal with conflict that had got out of hand. Until his death in 1435 Bedford was the nearest substitute, but he was not the king, and he was abroad for much of the time. Throughout the period Warwick had to negotiate with very little external

[123] Above, pp. 314–21 and Carpenter 1980a: pp. 517–18, but there is an error here in the discussion of the relationship with Norfolk (above, p. 318 n.147).

[124] Note that in 1426–7 William Ferrers of Groby, a major figure in Leicestershire (above, p. 313), was either employing or in contact with Richard Archer and William Mountford, of the Warwick-Ferrers of Chartley connection in west and north Warwickshire (Br. Lib. Add. Roll 65,954).

[125] Above, pp. 374–5, 317–19; app. 3 for Straunge. Cf. Rowney 1983: p. 50 on Warwick, the Ferrers and Buckingham, a statement allegedly based on Carpenter, M. C. 1976, but, except in its reference to Warwick's close relations with Ferrers, unsubstantiated.

support a series of episodes that threatened to break his local order apart, and for much of this time he too was absent in France.[126]

The first serious outbreak came only a year after Henry VI's accession. In September 1423 Elizabeth Clinton, Lord William's mother, died. Part of her inheritance was the large and very valuable manor of Birmingham. Its importance was enhanced by its position at the conjunction of Warwickshire, Worcestershire and Staffordshire on the Birmingham plateau, where Warwick was exposed to power exercised from Staffordshire, and at the centre of communications to the north-west.[127] Birmingham was contested by the heir male and two heirs general. Unfortunately for Warwick the heir male was William Bermingham, who, if not under the earl's direct patronage, was certainly connected to people who were, and the heirs general were George Longville, a Buckinghamshire esquire, and Edmund Ferrers, now assuming a position of importance in the Warwick affinity.[128] In 1422 Ferrers was in fact feeing as his attorney in the case John Cotesmore who was retained as a lawyer by Warwick himself.[129] It is quite likely that Warwick did not mind too much who succeeded to the manor, as long as the new owner was well-disposed to him, but he was likely to mind very much indeed if the outcome of the dispute was a conflict which split his north Warwickshire following apart and left in possession of the manor someone who in the course of the dispute had become a confirmed enemy.

Two days after Elizabeth's death, Ferrers and a small army, mostly from Staffordshire, but including significant figures from north-east Warwickshire, entered Birmingham and threw William Bermingham and his family out. A couple of months later, the I.P.M. on Elizabeth obligingly found for the two heirs general, Ferrers and Longville; their verdict probably owed quite a lot to the fact that it is clear that Elizabeth herself intended the heirs general to succeed her. In May 1424 Bermingham retaliated with assaults on servants of Ferrers at Smethwick in south-west Staffordshire. Meanwhile the Warwickshire J.P.s had lost no time in indicting Ferrers and his accomplices for the disseisin of the Berminghams. The speed of action and the fact that the presiding J.P.s were William Mountford and John Weston, two of Warwick's most important officers, must suggest that the earl was far from happy about what Ferrers had done. There is indeed every indication that he embarked rapidly on a course of damage limitation. He was in England for most of 1424,

126 On the achievements of the minority, see Wolffe 1972.

127 *Cal. Pat. Rolls 1436–41*, p. 503; C.139/12/36. On Birmingham's economy and strategic importance, see above, pp. 18, 30. William de Bermingham seems to have had the manor in late 1399, on what basis is not clear (K.B.27/554 Coram Rege rot.1).

128 B.R.L.112349; *Cal. Close Rolls 1413–19*, p. 97; Br. Lib. Add. MS 24,704 No.35; above, pp. 314–15 and n.78. Powell 1979: p. 298 for the suggestion that Ferrers' failure in Staffordshire under Henry V led him to focus his ambitions in Warwickshire on his return from France.

129 Longleat, MS of Marquess of Bath 6414 (*sub* lawyers' fees), 66.

the year in which the process of conciliation began, with the bailing of Bermingham by Thomas Erdington. Erdington's loyalties were owed to both Warwick and Ferrers, but he had been named as surveyor of Elizabeth Clinton's will and was thus identified with the anti-Bermingham camp. In 1425 Bermingham agreed to pay a fine for the offence against Ferrers of the previous year.[130]

Most significantly, the case disappears from the records for some years, a clear indication that a settlement had been achieved. Unfortunately we do not know what form it took. The absence of a Warwickshire I.P.M. for Bermingham and his failure to feature in deeds or to hold office in the 1420s may indicate that Ferrers had won. This conclusion is probably confirmed by the fact that Ferrers was suing Elizabeth's executors for a bag of evidences concerning her lands in Warwickshire and elsewhere in 1427, since he was unlikely to be trying to recover the deeds of property he did not yet own, and above all by the fact that it was Ferrers and then his widow who presented to Birmingham church in respectively 1428 and 1436.[131] On the other hand, it is possible that Ferrers did not come into possession of the manor until Bermingham's death in 1427; it was in 1427 that Ferrers and his wife did homage for Birmingham and later that year Bermingham's widow was suing both heirs general for her dower in the manor, which she could only do if Bermingham had at some point established seisin.[132] It is probable that a compromise had been effected, by which Bermingham had the manor for the rest of his life and it was thereafter surrendered to Ferrers.[133] The settlement and its subsequent enforcement can only have been achieved under pressure from the earl of Warwick.

The precipitating factor in the next major crisis may well have been the earl's departure overseas. In March 1425 his appointment as Captain of Calais, made originally in July 1423, was confirmed and thereafter he was more frequently abroad. He was certainly in England for at least part of 1425, and was to return periodically, but he could give much less sustained attention to local affairs.[134] In November 1425 there was an affray at Joan Beauchamp's manor of

[130] K.B.9/203/19; C.139/12/36; *Cal. Fine Rolls 1422–30*, p. 50; K.B.27/654 Rex rot.19d., /657 List of Fines; *Reg. Chichele*, II, p. 268. Ferrers' force included John Ruggeley, abbot of the north Warwickshire house of Merevale, and William Charnels esquire of Bedworth in north Warwickshire. Warwick was certainly in England January to March, July and November 1424 and it does not seem that he went to France that year (*Feodera*, IV, iv, pp. 111, 114; *Procs. Priv. Counc.*, III, pp. 133, 138, 143, 145–7, 154, 163).

[131] *Colls. Hist. Staffs.*, n.s., 6, i, p. 163; Cov. and Lichf. Dioc., Reg. Heyworth fos.21v., 34.

[132] Leics.R.O. 26 D 53/1584; *Colls. Hist. Staffs.*, o.s., 17, p. 116; *Cal. Fine Rolls 1422–30*, p. 171. On the impossibility of the widow suing for dower without earlier seisin, see Palmer 1984: pp. 37–8.

[133] However, in 7 Hen. VI William Bermingham II, described as 'lord of Birmingham', made a grant of a wardship that was subject to the lordship of Birmingham (Shaw 1798–1801: II, p. 177).

[134] *G.E.C.*, XII, ii, p. 380; Sinclair 1987a: pp. 116–20. He attended council and parliament in April and May 1425 (*Procs. Priv. Counc.*, III, pp. 169, 170; *Rot. Parl.*, IV, pp. 261, 262). He received

Snitterfield involving some of her servants and, on the other side, a force led by Warwick's annuitant Hugh Cokesey and Cokesey's brother-in-law, Lord Talbot, in which Talbot's brother William was killed. It is highly probable that it was related to the Talbot-Ormond feud in Ireland, for Ormond was Joan's son-in-law and heir by marriage to her Botetourt lands. This conflict had reached a new pitch two years before when Talbot appealed Ormond for treason in the Court of Chivalry. The precise nature of Warwick's involvement is more puzzling. Snitterfield was situated among the core of the Warwick lands in south-west Warwickshire, and there can be no doubt that Cokesey's little army was composed essentially of Warwick's servants and tenants. The question remains under whose authority they were acting. One interpretation could be that in the earl's absence his affinity had got out of hand and was being used against his wishes to pursue the private quarrels of some of its leading figures. That Joan had hitherto been an ally of the earl lends some credence to this theory. However, there are more powerful arguments against it. First, such disobedience, especially on the part of the Hugfords, who had a representative in Cokesey's force, would have been altogether out of keeping with the normal pattern of relations between Warwick and his following. Secondly, there is every sign that steps were taken to ensure that Joan's men were quickly brought to justice and that Cokesey and his friends escaped, and only the earl would have had the local power to manage this.[135] Thirdly, Talbot had been put on the Warwickshire commission of the peace in July 1423, which must indicate that he was on good terms with Warwick. Furthermore he had married Warwick's daughter shortly before the affray, and among William Talbot's supervisors to his will was Warwick's official, John Baysham.[136] In sum, it is most probable

additional authority in France at Christmas 1425, when he was given custody of Normandy under Bedford (*John Benet's Chronicle*, p. 180).

135 *Cal. Close Rolls 1422–29*, pp. 317–18; K.B.9/224/323; *Cal. Pat. Rolls 1422–29*, p. 423; Pollard 1968: pp. 225–6; Harcourt 1907: p. 380; *Rot. Parl.*, IV, p. 198; *G.E.C.*, X, p. 125. Besides Hugford, Nicholas Rody and tenants of manors owned by the earl and of the town of Warwick were involved. Joan's forces were indicted soon after before Mountford, Weston and the Harewells (the latter clearly seeing their commitment to the Warwick affinity as overriding their loyalties to Joan), while there is no record of an indictment of the Talbot forces, and the fact that Joan felt impelled to appeal to parliament suggests that she could get none made. An additional cause of the dispute may have been that the Talbots, although not direct losers, had been one of the families that had burnt their fingers in their dealings with Hugh Burnell, while Joan had been the chief beneficiary of Hugh's dispositions of his lands (*The Ancestor*, 8 (1904), pp. 174–80; *Cat. Anc. Deeds*, III, C2398).

136 *Cal. Pat. Rolls 1422–29*, p. 571; *G.E.C.*, XI, p. 703; *Reg. Chichele*, II, p. 326 (for Baysham, see above, p. 371); also Pollard 1983: pp. 51, 109 n.29, 114 for association of Talbot and Warwick in France and pp. 80–1 for links with Warwick's retainers. In 1426, Warwick's servants, Throgmorton and Robert Andrewes (for whom see Roskell 1954: p. 147) acted as sureties for Talbot (*Cal. Pat. Rolls 1422–29*, p. 350). Baysham's relations with the earl were less than cordial at this time, but this does not dent the argument that Talbot was well in with the Warwick entourage as a whole (Sinclair 1987a: pp. 163–4).

that Warwick had himself authorised, if not initiated, the attack, with the aim of giving support to his new son-in-law, and of using the Talbot-Ormond feud to bring pressure on Joan.

It seems that Joan had been inspired by the acquisition of the Botetourt lands to try to extend her influence beyond the Warwickshire–Worcestershire region, where she was a useful adjunct, into areas where she was most unwelcome, or perhaps to insist on her position as a more senior partner in the area west of Warwick; it was after all here that the affray took place. And, as we shall see, there are signs that Joan, having carved out a secure position in Leicestershire, was beginning to think about using it to infiltrate eastern Warwickshire. Perhaps, had he been in England, Warwick could have restored his position locally and nationally without resort to violence, but, unable for the moment to return, he may have felt that a show of force was necessary to emphasise that he was still the dominant power over most of the midlands. Moreover, the events just described must be seen against a background of deteriorating relations among the nobility. Government by consensus was no easy matter for people used to the strong leadership without which the proper functioning of the body politic was almost impossible. By the end of 1425 things were bad enough for Bedford's calming influence to be required.[137] His return produced a general lowering of tensions, and in November 1426 the parties in the Snitterfield affray made mutual recognisances. In May 1427 a commission was set up to investigate Joan's complaints.[138] No more was heard of this particular episode, which is remarkable in itself, when one considers that a member of a noble family had been killed and the bad feeling that was to be engendered in later less happy times by deaths of this sort. This, however, was not the end of Warwick's troubles with Joan and her friends.

The fierce response of the Warwick affinity to Joan's ambitions may be explained to a great extent by the fact that his own fortunes were reaching a low ebb in the mid 1420s and he could not afford to allow any challenges to his power. In 1425 he had lost both the Berkeley suit and the precedence dispute with the duke of Norfolk and it was not long before he was to face what looks like a concerted assault from Leicestershire on his control of east Warwickshire, almost certainly spearheaded by Joan Beauchamp, possibly with support from other Leicestershire nobility. Among these may have been the duke of Norfolk, whose Leicestershire lands spilled over into east Warwickshire, in the form of some directly held estates and numbers of overlordships.[139] In 1427 the earl was again fulfilling his duties abroad for much of the year and was once again less able to defend himself against defiance at home. It may be significant that it was

137 Roskell 1965: pp. 187–8; Griffiths 1981: pp. 73–81; *Rot. Parl.*, IV, p. 296, V, pp. 406–7.

138 *Cal. Close Rolls 1422–29*, pp. 317–18; *Cal. Pat. Rolls 1422–29*, p. 423.

139 Sinclair 1987b: pp. 45–6; Roskell 1965: pp. 185–6. Gloucester may well have been behind both reversals (Roskell 1965: p. 192 and below, p. 387). For evidence of Joan's ambitions elsewhere in the county, see below, pp. 381–7.

in that year, in July to be precise, that the duke of Norfolk received his only appointment to the Warwickshire commission of the peace. Those in charge of royal policies may have intended no more than to use Norfolk to plug the gap left by Warwick's absence, but Norfolk's acceptance of the office can only mean that he had decided to pursue his interests across the border into Warwickshire. This was the one time in his adult life when he was in England for an extended period and therefore the one time when he was likely to take a real interest in the localities where his lands lay. There was a family tradition of connections with east Warwickshire, and in the 1420s Norfolk was linked not only with Hastings but also with Nicholas Metley and possibly with John Leventhorpe of Leicestershire, who had a manor at Brownsover in east Warwickshire.[140] Joan Beauchamp, whose activities in Leicestershire had hitherto been quite acceptable to the earl, but who was now showing alarming signs of independence, had come into association with Norfolk and Lord Ferrers of Groby, one of the pivotal families of the Leicestershire network, whose heir had married Norfolk's sister. In 1429, when Norfolk named his general attorneys in his will before going abroad, they included Joan's regular associate, Richard Hastings, suggesting that quite a close collaboration had sprung up between the two magnates by then. Warwick was no doubt less than happy about this association between his principal magnate rival of the moment and an ally who was fast becoming a nuisance.[141]

As ever, the regular intermingling of east Warwickshire landowners and Leicestershire families made that part of the county peculiarly vulnerable to the attentions of the Leicestershire nobility. This was especially true of those like William Purfrey, William Trussell of Bilton and Richard Hastings who had

140 *G.E.C.*, XII, ii, p. 381; *V.C.H.*, V, VI. For Norfolk's presence in England, see Archer 1984a: ch. 5, although Dr Archer does not pursue the question of whether Norfolk tried to establish a secure local power base in the period. For earlier Mowbray connections in east Warwickshire, see app. 3 (Hugh Lillburne and Hugh Dalby). For Leventhorpe, Southwell and Norfolk connections, see *Reg. Chichele*, II, pp. 473–4, 527–30, and for Leventhorpe's links with east Warwickshire/Leicestershire gentry, see e.g. C.139/110/44; Northants.R.O. Knightley Charters 150. (However, Dr Harriss points out to me that Leventhorpe was very much a Beaufort man, which would cut across the Beaufort/Bedford/Warwick versus Gloucester/Norfolk division that seems to be developing in this period (below, p. 387)). It is for these years that the account of Hugh Dalby's expenses in Norfolk's plea over Caludon survives (E.101/514/17); the lawyers employed by the duke included John Chetwynd and Nicholas Metley, as well as Joan's man Bartholomew Brokesby (for whom see e.g. Ives 1983a: pp. 24–6; Roskell 1954: p. 157). Dr Archer has minimised the importance of their employment, seeing it as a purely professional relationship arranged by Dalby in his capacity as Norfolk's man of affairs (1984a: pp. 292–3), but, coming at this juncture, it might show both further connection on Norfolk's part with Joan and some extension of his influence among the affinities of Warwick and Ferrers in eastern and central Warwickshire. See also, above, p. 318 n.147.

141 *G.E.C.*, V, pp. 357–8; C.139/60/43/26; above, p. 313; *Cal. Pat. Rolls 1429–36*, p. 27; *Cal. Close Rolls 1435–41*, pp. 323, 327; *North Country Wills*, p. 37; above, n.140.

lands in Leicestershire.[142] Connections across the county border acquired still more force when, in the mid-1420s, a union was effected between the Astleys of north-east Warwickshire and west Leicestershire and the Ferrers of Groby, through the marriage of Edward, eldest son of Reginald Grey of Ruthin by his second wife, the Astley heiress, to the heiress of Groby. Norfolk himself was linked to both these families: the marital connection with the Ferrers of Groby and both personal and family ties with the Greys of Ruthin. Since the Greys were amongst the leading landowners in Northamptonshire, this group of magnates was well placed, should they so wish, to exert pressure along the whole of Warwickshire's eastern border.[143] It is not inconceivable that Joan Beauchamp decided that the time was ripe to exploit the power of this circle by urging Norfolk to try and make a dent in Warwick's local armoury in a part of the county where the earl's influence had to be largely indirect.

In fact 1427 was a bad year for Warwick. It was then that he managed to upset the Archers, the principal family in the Tanworth region, on two separate occasions; first by failing in his duty as lord to arbitrate between them and two minor gentry also from the Tanworth region, and secondly by being unable to prevent – possibly authorising – a blatantly fraudulent conveyance of their estate at Eastcote and Longdon in the Arden to Thomas Porter, another Warwick client.[144] This transaction occurred as Thomas Archer, the head of the family, lay dying. He was no sooner dead than Richard his heir revealed more cracks in the Warwick affinity by getting into a wrangle with Hugh Cokesey over part of the jointure given to Thomas Archer and his first wife, who was Cokesey's great aunt.[145] This was one dispute that Warwick was able to settle without it ever reaching the law-courts, but another in that year, between the Hugfords and Richard Stafford, also a member of the earl's affinity, did get as far as the King's Bench, and it is further evidence that all was not well within his following.[146] Part of the trouble may have been that a growing sense of

[142] Above, p. 307. Note also Norfolk's connection with the Duchy of Lancaster man, Thomas Rempston, who had been sheriff of Warwickshire and Leicestershire, (above, n.84 and Archer 1984a: pp. 341–2) and the strength that links with the Duchy of Lancaster could give him in both counties, especially while there was a lack of royal direction. Rempston was also connected with Joan and her affinity (*Cal. Pat. Rolls 1441–46*, p. 241).

[143] *G.E.C.*, V, pp. 358–9; Archer 1984a: pp. 180–2, 343–5; *H.M.C. Var. Colls.*, VII, p. 332. For the Grey of Ruthin lands, see above, p. 328. For Grey-Ferrers genealogy, see above, p. 325 n.171. One of the negotiators for the Ferrers-Grey marriage was William Mountford, which indicates the difficulties in drawing clear-cut factional lines when all groupings were so much intermingled (*ibid.* and above, n.124).

[144] K.B.27/663 Coram Rege rot.67; S.B.T. D.R.37 Boxes 83, 76; S.B.T. D.R.37 Box 42/2506, 2507; above, p. 127.

[145] S.B.T. D.R.37 Box 60. The antiquarian notes on the Archer family (S.B.T. D.R.503 fo.46v.) erroneously date the agreement to 1438.

[146] K.B.27/667 Coram Rege rot.80d. Stafford was the heir of Thomas Stafford of Baginton, Thomas being Warwick's retainer and the owner for life of land that was subsequently due to go to Warwick (S.B.T. E.R.1/61/466).

insecurity made him over-anxious to placate the Ferrers of Chartley, his staunchest and most vital allies in north Warwickshire: in the arbitration that he had neglected to perform, both the Archers' opponents were close connections of the Ferrers, and Warwick's uncharacteristic dilatoriness could have been occasioned by fear of offending either of the parties. But neither the delay in arbitrating nor Warwick's apparent inability to protect the Archers from the designs of Thomas Porter can have done much for his worship in west Warwickshire, particularly when one remembers how influential the Archers were in the Tanworth region.

In September 1427, while Warwick was in France, there seems to have been an open challenge to his lordship in east Warwickshire.[147] What exactly lay behind the two episodes of that month is not clear, and we must be careful not to place more weight on the evidence than it can stand, but there are good enough grounds for deducing an attempt by Joan Beauchamp, quite possibly with the help of the duke of Norfolk, to discredit Warwick's authority here, where his lack of estates meant he could least well defend himself. The first grew out of a quarrel between Richard Atherstone abbot of Combe and the Astleys of Wolvey Astley, a younger branch of the family of Lord Astley.[148] The issue was suit of court by the Astleys' tenants at the abbot's view of frankpledge at Wolvey. An earlier dispute between Combe and the Astleys over grazing rights had been settled by arbitration in 1413/4, but it may still have rankled, and both affairs show how easy it was for the minor frictions of landowning to turn into major arguments. On 4 September 1427 the abbot sent his servant Baldwin Metley to levy a distress on the defaulting tenants at Wolvey. The Astleys and their servants set on him, stole his hat and, which was rather more serious, cut off his hand. There were also alleged to have been other attacks on the abbey and its employees. Subsequently, Giles Astley, the head of the family, and his three sons announced to all and sundry that they intended to kill the abbot and succeeded in putting him into such a state of fear that he was unable to levy any amercements at all.

Although the perpetrators were indicted three months later, the abbot claimed that the J.P.s, having promised to arrest the Astleys and take security from them, were too frightened to do so. It is quite possible that the commission was evincing reluctance rather than fear, since its leading member in Warwick's absence was Norfolk and there are grounds for arguing that he, or at least his friends, had a vested interest in the case. With this in mind, the abbot's adversaries are an interesting group. First there was Thomas Blankame, who was undoubtedly a servant of Joan and subsequently of her son-in-law and

147 *G.E.C.*, XII, ii, p. 381.

148 For what follows, see JUST 3/68/10/3; K.B.27/680 Rex rot.9; *Cal. Close Rolls 1422–29*, p. 358; *Rot. Parl.*, IV, pp. 365–6; *Dugdale*, p. 67. The presiding J.P.s at the indictment were Warwick's men, John Weston and John Harewell (app. 3, and above, n.135 and below, n.182 for Harewell's relative loyalty to Joan and Warwick).

heir to the Botetourt lands and Leicestershire affinity, the earl of Ormond.[149] Secondly there were the Astleys. As relatives of the senior Astleys, they were connected to the Greys of Ruthin, and Giles Astley had acted as witness for both William Lord Astley and William's son-in-law and heir Reginald Grey.[150] Furthermore in 1428, when Katharine Astley, Giles' widow, another of the accused, appeared at the gaol delivery proceedings at Warwick, one of her securities was William Bosville of Marston (probably Marston Jabbett near Wolvey), who had gone to Ruthin, with Giles and some other local gentry of the Astley connection, to witness a deed of Grey concerning the Astley lands.[151] It would be wrong to suggest that there was a united front of the interlinked leading magnates of east Warwickshire and west Leicestershire – Norfolk, the Ferrers of Groby, the Greys and Joan Beauchamp – against the earl of Warwick, not least because Reginald Grey had participated in an indenture with Talbot only a year before.[152] Nevertheless, it is not impossible that, with or without Grey of Ruthin's connivance, part of the old Astley connection was being mobilised to exploit the Astleys' feud with the abbot. The purpose of this piece of maintenance was to demonstrate that Joan Beauchamp was now able to use her power in Leicestershire as a springboard for an attempt to disturb Warwick's rather fragile rule in east Warwickshire; it is exceedingly improbable that so intimate a servant as Blankame would have acted with the Astleys without Joan's approval. It is also not impossible, although harder to substantiate, that it was Norfolk's influence that helped put this network at Joan's disposal.

Looked at from Warwick's point of view it was a serious blow to his standing in this area and in the county in general. The J.P.s who had presided over the indictment of the Astleys but subsequently failed to take any further steps to restrain them were both his own men.[153] If they had feared to take proper action against manifest disturbers of the peace that was bad enough; if they had chosen not to do so, suborned by parties unwilling to submit to Warwick's lordship, that was far worse. The abbot found it necessary to appeal to the king in parliament and it was the royal government that ordered the sheriff to arrest the Astleys and take security from them, initially without success. While it was later to become more commonplace for kings to help out ineffective earls of Warwick in this way, this is a unique instance under Richard Beauchamp of a

[149] For Blankame and Joan's family, app. 3 and K.B.27/682 Coram Rege rot.69.

[150] Wm. Salt Lib. Wm. Salt Orig. Coll., Huntbach MS 387/2/37a; W.C.R.O. C.R.136/C149, 790; E.326/9045.

[151] JUST 3/68/10/1; E.326/9045.

[152] *Cal. Close Rolls 1422–29*, pp. 273–4. It might be significant that Thomas Waweton, the speaker in the parliament of 1425 where Warwick lost to Norfolk and Gloucester did rather well, was attached to the Greys of Ruthin (Roskell 1965: pp. 185–6, 370).

[153] Note also that two other J.P.s, Mountford and Cokayn (the Derbyshire knight, not the justice), had been linked to Lord Astley and may perhaps have had a slight reluctance to bring his relatives and their one-time associates to justice (above, p. 314).

Warwickshire landowner not known to be on bad terms with the earl having to turn to a higher authority for protection, and Warwick must have considered it thoroughly demeaning.[154] He may have been more than demeaned, for there is some evidence that the natural protectors to whom the abbot would have looked, and who therefore must have failed him, were in fact Warwick and Edmund Ferrers of Chartley.[155] Furthermore, Edmund Colshill, the under-sheriff at the time, who was later sued by Katharine Astley for conspiracy, with the abbot as co-defendant, was the abbot's auditor and also an associate of the Ferrers.[156] Whichever way one looks at it, the ruling magnate of Warwickshire and his most trusted ally were shown by these events to be ineffective in east Warwickshire, a state of affairs that can have pleased neither.

Proof of guilt by association is always dangerous, and some of the interpretation suggested for this affair may require modification, but, whatever lay behind it, this was not a happy episode for Warwick, and it was soon followed by a worse one. On 22 September there was an election of knights of the shire at which William Mountford and John Malory were returned, but, shortly after, Warwick's retainer, William Peyto, arrived with a mob of Warwick townsmen and substituted Peyto's name for Malory's on the indenture. This he did with the connivance of that same under-sheriff, Edmund Colshill, who played such an equivocal part in the Astley affair. It seems that the county court had elected a candidate inimical to the earl of Warwick and its decision had been forcibly overturned by the earl's own men.[157] Lying behind a reluctance to elect Warwick's chosen candidates that was unusual at this time may have been a certain amount of resentment in east Warwickshire, regardless of political standing, at the way the last election, the previous year, had gone. Normally one of the representatives came from this part of the county, but in 1426 both had been from the area west of Warwick. This was perhaps an indication that Warwick was already rather uncertain about his standing further east, since an

154 *Rot. Parl.*, IV, pp. 365–6; *Cal. Close Rolls 1422–29*, p. 358. For later occasions when the king stepped in to support a weakening local power, see below, pp. 502, 508, 518.

155 See the abbot's feoffment of Wolvey of 1430 to the earl of Stafford, with Warwick, Ferrers, Mountford, and Vernon, a Ferrers retainer (above, p. 323), as witnesses from outside the immediate locality (Bod. Lib. Dugdale MS 15, p. 13). It is also possible that Baldwin Metley, the chief victim, was related to Nicholas Metley, the Ferrers of Chartley retainer of 1436. Although the advowson of Combe was owned by the dukes of Norfolk (C.139/60/43/26), which might weaken the hypothesis that Norfolk was happy to see the abbot worsted, there is no evidence of any other connection or of any attempt to defend the abbey under the second duke.

156 K.B.27/677 Coram Rege rot.57; C.P.40/723 rot.225; app. 3. Colshill came from Binley outside Coventry and was thus a neighbour of the abbey.

157 K.B.27/677 Rex rot.5. The dating in the legal record, as opposed to the election indenture, is clearly wrong and should read Matthew Apostle *and Evangelist*, not just Apostle: this is all the more evident from the fact that the saint's name is spelt *Mattheus* i.e. the normal spelling for *ap. et ev.*, not *Mathias*, the normal spelling for *ap.* (See Cheney 1970: p. 56). See Payling 1987c: pp. 176–7 and above, p. 342 n.247 for comments on elections of this type and Edwards 1984 for an indication of how this sort of situation could arise.

election was an acid test of a magnate's local worth and he may have wanted to avoid any resistance to his authority after the setbacks of 1425. He may also have wanted to secure more support in the Commons after the defeats in the parliament of 1425–6.[158] If Joan Beauchamp and possibly Norfolk wanted to exploit the weaknesses in Warwick's position exposed by the Astley-Combe case while the earl remained abroad, this was an ideal moment; any sense of grievance felt by the gentry of east Warwickshire over the choice of representatives could be used to show that Warwick no longer had the power to foist any officer he cared to name on this region.

The indenture for the disputed election survives and it is odd enough to warrant the judgement that this was more than just a matter of local resistance to the earl's candidate.[159] First, while elections for county and borough were normally carried out simultaneously, and the bulk of the names on the indenture tended consequently to be those of Warwick burgesses, in this instance no men from Warwick were present at all. The townsmen who should have been there must have been the rent-a-crowd that arrived with Peyto, and the absence of numbers of the earl's tenants ensured that the gathering could more easily be dominated by those who owed him no allegiance. Secondly, John Malory, the M.P. whose election was contested, resided at Monks Kirby in east Warwickshire, a township within easy reach of Leicestershire, which was under the overlordship of the dukes of Norfolk, the founders and patrons of Axholme Abbey which now owned the priory of Monks Kirby.[160] Thirdly the composition of the court at the election is highly suggestive; those present were almost entirely from east Warwickshire and included people like John Griffith of Staffordshire, Ralph Bellers and Richard Langham of Leicestershire and Thomas Boughton of Bedfordshire (who had yet to come into his wife's Warwickshire estates) whose connections with the county were either minimal or non-existent. Several of the more important electors – even William Lucy, the only one who can be linked with any certainty to the earl of Warwick – were associated with Joan Beauchamp, Norfolk, the Greys of Ruthin or their associates.[161] Malory himself, certainly no enemy to Warwick or his friends in the mid-1420s, had nevertheless been part of the Astley connection which someone, it seems, was now trying to resurrect as an antidote to Warwick in

158 *Return: 1878*, I, p. 312; Roskell 1965: pp. 185–6. For refs. to M.P.s 1400–39, see above, p. 266 n.17.

159 C.219/13 Pt. II/2 Pt. II.

160 *V.C.H.*, VI, pp. 174–5; *Cal. Pat. Rolls 1396–99*, p. 77; E.326/B9066. Thomas, Earl Marshal, Norfolk's brother, had taken refuge in Monks Kirby priory after his rebellion, causing the prior to flee after his discovery (*Cal. Pat. Rolls 1405–08*, p. 33).

161 K.B.27/669 Coram Rege rot.22; JUST 1/1537 m.27; Br. Lib. Add. Ch. 48,673; Farnham, *Leics. Village Notes*, I, p. 262, VI, p. 275; Ives 1983a: pp. 24–6. Also app. 3 and S.C.11/25 and discussion of electors above, p. 343. Lucy had married Grey of Ruthin's daughter (*Dugdale*, p. 507).

north-east and east Warwickshire.[162] The returning officer, who originally placed Malory's name on the indenture, was none other than Richard Hastings, friend of Joan and soon to be attorney to Norfolk. To deny this election political significance would be to take scepticism too far. When Peyto arrived with his crowd from Warwick, perhaps in response to an urgent summons from Mountford, and when he persuaded Colshill to carry the illegally amended return to Westminster, both men were acting on behalf of the absent earl, to ensure that the county bowed to his will; perhaps also to indicate to the nobility of Leicestershire and Northamptonshire that within Warwickshire their preferences were subordinated to his. East Warwickshire was not to be thought of as an adjunct of the power of the east midlands nobility but as an inextricable part of the rule over the west midlands that belonged to Richard Beauchamp.

Nevertheless the events of the mid 1420s show that this point had yet to meet with universal acceptance. Significantly it was between 1426 and 1428 that, almost uniquely in the period 1422–39, there were two consecutive appointments to the joint shrievalty from Leicestershire, both of them incidentally connected with Joan Beauchamp.[163] This was the culmination of a period in which Warwick had been put on the defensive both locally and in national politics. He was not only being threatened by Lady Bergavenny, and perhaps by Norfolk, in his own 'contree', but had been worsted by Norfolk over precedence and by Lord Berkeley, apparently aided by Gloucester and Gloucester's ally, Norfolk, over the Berkeley inheritance. Meanwhile Gloucester's power had been growing apace since the departure of Bedford in March 1427, to the benefit of Norfolk. Finally, Warwick had quarrelled with Bedford over the Captaincy of Calais, which he lost in 1427. Moreover, despite his affinity's show of strength at the election, the verdict was that the original nominees had been properly elected, and it was Malory, not Peyto, who sat in parliament.[164]

It is probable that Warwick was coming to realise that he could not maintain proper control of the greatly enlarged local power base that had been his since 1422 while he was forever crossing over into France. It was one thing to run a relatively small area of influence at a distance, in the absence of many of its more unruly elements and with the full backing of an active king, it was quite another to act as lord of a large part of the midlands in the face of numbers of rivals, with a vacuum, and at this point open hostility, at the centre of government. Recognition of the size of the task he had set himself may well

162 Nott. Univ. Lib. Middleton MS Mi D 3962; Bod. Lib. Dugdale MS 15, p. 13; and above, p. 314.

163 *Lists and Indexes*, 9, p. 145: these were Hastings (app. 3) and Thomas Stanley (S.C.11/25, on the assumption that this one and the sheriff are the same).

164 Sinclair 1987b: pp. 45–6, 1987a: pp. 116–21, 285; K.B.27/677 Rex rot.5; *Return: 1878*, 1, p. 314; Br. Lib. Add. Roll 17,209 (Berkeley in Norfolk's war retinue 1422–3); *Letters of Margaret of Anjou*, pp. 34–43; Rawcliffe and Flower 1986: pp. 176–7. I am grateful to Dr Harriss for his helpful comments on this period.

have been the deciding factor in persuading Warwick to accept the position of king's governor in 1428, thereby committing himself to a continuous period of residence in England.[165] He appears to have made the right decision. For four years from 1428 every sheriff of Warwickshire and Leicestershire was a native of Warwickshire and a client of the earl. From 1429 until the end of Warwick's life every single Warwickshire M.P. was indisputably attached to either Warwick or Ferrers.[166] The level of conflict within the county fell rapidly. Not only is there no further evidence of resistance on the part of rival nobility, there are indications that the affinities of Joan and the Ferrers of Chartley were prepared to co-operate.[167] Perhaps because all parties were drawing closer together, it was possible at some point probably in the 1420s or early 1430s for Warwick to settle the potentially divisive dispute over part of the Botetourt inheritance involving Joan and Maurice Berkeley of Weoley in Worcestershire, an arbitration that proved more durable than most of the subsequent settlements in this long-running affair.[168]

It is worth pausing to look at the region which contained the two estates at issue, Weoley Castle and the adjacent manor of Northfield, for we have here an outstanding example of the preservation of stability in the face of considerable tension, which tells us much about the quality of Richard Beauchamp's rule at its height. They were situated in the Birmingham plateau, and it was here, where Worcestershire, Staffordshire and Warwickshire met, that Warwick had become particularly open to attack once he had decided to extend his sphere of influence into the northern regions of Warwickshire and Worcestershire and into southern Staffordshire. This situation was acentuated by the fact that it was a region where communications were limited by hills and difficult terrain and the roads and bridges were commanded by a few key points, among them Weoley itself and Birmingham, also the subject of a prolonged dispute. It was also the area where the majority of the Botetourt lands were to be found. Their descent was complicated, with a proliferation of potential claimants, besides the Berkeleys of Weoley who were the principal protagonists at this time. Fortunately the Freville heirs, who represented one of the lines with a claim, that is Ferrers of Tamworth, Aston and Willoughby, seemed for the moment to have accepted Joan's purchase of the lands from Hugh Burnell, but Berkeley

165 *G.E.C.*, XII, ii, p. 381.

166 *Lists and Indexes*, 9, p. 145; above, p. 266 n.17. There is also some indication that Joan may have been trying to extend her power in Derbyshire; if so, this too was squashed, in 1434 (Wright 1978: pp. 312–16).

167 *Cal. Close Rolls 1429–35*, pp. 57–8; B.R.L. 351370. See S.C.11/25 and Ives 1983a, pp. 24–6 for some of Joan's men outside Warwickshire. In 1430 Blankame turned evidence against Katharine Astley, suggesting that, if Joan had had any interest in the Astley case, she had now abandoned the family (C.260/137/16).

168 C.1/19/6, 7b; the affair resurfaces at intervals from *c.* 1444 (below, chs. 11, 12, 15).

had apparently never agreed.[169] Another possible source of conflict was that another crucial strongpoint in the region was Dudley Castle, the residence of John Sutton Lord Dudley, who was on the side of Joan's son-in-law, Ormond, against Talbot in Ireland and, according to the Bermingham claim, the rightful overlord of Birmingham manor.[170] The Bermingham family furthermore also claimed to have some rights in the Botetourt lands.[171] Further north, in central and southern Staffordshire, were the main estates of the Ferrers of Chartley, the Berminghams' chief rivals for Birmingham.[172]

Remarkably, amidst all these possibilities for conflict, the only element that proved to be uncontainable was the resurgent ambition of Joan Beauchamp. Cut short in her empire-building in east Warwickshire, she turned to the north-west, where her new lands gave her rather more purchase than she had had on the other side of the county. Unfortunately this could not help but bring her into direct confrontation with the Ferrers of Chartley. The predominance in north Warwickshire and Staffordshire of the interlinked affinities of Warwick, Ferrers and Buckingham had been recognised in 1430 when all three were named on the Staffordshire commission of the peace.[173] What happened thereafter between Joan and the Ferrers only makes sense as the response of the vested local power to an intrusive newcomer. Again it was Warwick's absence that allowed things to get out of hand; in April 1430 he accompanied the king to France for his coronation and he remained abroad until February 1432.[174] Although the Ferrers and Begavenny affinities were still in amicable association as late as 1430,[175] the two leaders were soon to find themselves in violent confrontation. On 17 March 1431 Joan travelled with her entourage from her Worcestershire manor of Harvington, apparently making her way to one of the Botetourt manors, either Bordesley, which lay just east of Birmingham, or Handsworth to the north. Either way she had to go through Birmingham, on which almost all the local roads converged. When she reached the town, Ferrers set upon her with a large force and she and her retinue passed a night

169 Above, pp. 29–30, 373; for a full guide to the claimants, see pedigree acting as frontispiece to Pearson 1902, and Shaw 1798–1801: II, pp. 245–6. Neither Berkeley nor his part of the lands feature in the quitclaims etc. to Joan (*Cal. Pat. Rolls 1416–22*, pp. 305, 306; *W.F.F.*, 2504–5, 2516; B.R.L. 357336).

170 Griffith 1940–1; *Cal. Pat. Rolls 1436–41*, pp. 502–3; for Sutton of Dudley's precise role in the Birmingham affair, which does not become apparent until later, see below, p. 406 n.23.

171 Nott. Univ. Lib. Middleton MS 5/168/33. This may well be the cause of William I's earlier dispute with Joan Beauchamp (*Colls. Hist. Staffs.*, o.s., 17, pp. 78–9).

172 *I.P.M.* 14 Hen.VI/33.

173 *Cal. Pat. Rolls 1429–36*, p. 624. Ferrers was serving Buckingham as a justice in Wales in 1432 (*Marcher Lordships*, p. 76).

174 *G.E.C.*, XII, ii, p. 381; Sinclair 1987a: p. 129; Griffiths 1981: p. 57.

175 Above, nn.141, 142.

surrounded by this threatening multitude until the mediation of Thomas Greswold and others enabled her to leave the next morning.[176]

As in the case of the Snitterfield affray, when Warwick was also out of the country, it seems likely that, while the earl himself would probably not have sanctioned the use of overt violence had he been in England, he was not sorry to see Joan worsted. Amongst Ferrers' force was Thomas Erdington I, who was feed by Warwick at the time and is unlikely to have undertaken anything that was entirely against his master's wishes. There are already signs in 1430 that Warwick was not feeling particularly friendly towards Joan, when the sheriff of Warwickshire, Nicholas Ruggeley, who was employed by Warwick and connected with Ferrers, had declined to pay a royal annuity to Joan's intimate servant Henry Fillongley.[177] As in the Snitterfield affair, what happened subsequently also suggests the guiding hand of the earl. At the coroner's inquest Joan's men were named as the murderers of one of Ferrers' men who had died in the affray; the coroner happened to be one of Warwick's servants. Even before this verdict was delivered Joan was sued for the forfeit of a security of £1,200 to keep the peace that she had made some years earlier. She seems to have found local channels of redress closed to her and was able to proceed only by a suit in Common Pleas, by a hearing before the royal steward and by petition to chancellor and parliament.[178]

After his return to England in early 1432 Warwick remained there almost continuously until August 1437,[179] and his ability both to command and to calm is immediately apparent. In Michaelmas 1432 he sued Joan over the abduction of a ward. Since the alleged offence had occurred no less than ten years before, we may take it that this was a warning shot across her bows rather than a serious piece of litigation.[180] If so, it worked, since the following July she was prepared to humiliate herself in parliament over the Birmingham affray, in return for the pardoning of the sums forfeited by her friends on her securities, and of £200 of the £1,200 she herself had pledged.[181] The new commission of the peace issued

[176] K.B.27/681 Rex rot.21; K.B.9/228/2/89. Joan was involved in an earlier affray at Birmingham in 1429, which may be connected (*Rot. Parl.*, iv, pp. 410–11; K.B.27/681 Rex rot.5). Several of Joan's men were said to be 'of Harvington' – often a means of indicating that that was the most recent address – and Bordesley and Handsworth are logical destinations for a group passing Birmingham on its way from Harvington. In Carpenter 1980a (p. 530) the conclusions about her journey are faulty, in that they assume she came from the other Harvington, in south-east Worcestershire, not the Bergavenny property near Chaddesley Corbett (*V.C.H. Worcs.*, III, p. 40). Ferrers' army was said to be 1,000 strong, but this seems improbable. That Ferrers could ambush her at Birmingham suggests he was in possession of the manor then. For the roads at Birmingham, see above, pp. 29–30.

[177] C.1/12/73; *Lists and Indexes*, 9, p. 145.

[178] K.B.9/228/2/89; K.B.27/681 Rex rot.21; C.P.40/683 roti. 291-d.; C.1/7/228; *Rot. Parl.*, IV, pp. 445–6; S.C.8/295/14702.

[179] Sinclair 1987a: pp. 129–32; *G.E.C.*, XII, ii, p. 381.

[180] K.B.27/686 Coram Rege rot.46d., /688 Coram Rege rot.62.

[181] *Rot. Parl.*, IV, pp. 410–11.

in October 1433 signalled and sealed Warwick's triumph. Buckingham, who was still very much the earl's junior partner, replaced Norfolk, who had died in 1432, and the new gentry appointees, Throgmorton, Thomas Hugford and Nicholas Metley, were all clients of Warwick or Edmund Ferrers or both. With Warwick's feed man John Chetwynd replacing John Malory the following year on Malory's death, the earl's control of the commission was now virtually complete. How little Warwick needed henceforth to conciliate the east of the county can be judged from the fact that for five years Metley was to be the only representative of this part of Warwickshire on the commission.[182]

Two events in 1435 made Warwick's position even more assured. The deaths of both Joan Beauchamp and Edmund Ferrers removed, in the former case, an irritant whose lands passed in large measure to the earl, and in the latter an ally who had not always been easy to handle.[183] The Ferrers had already been made somewhat redundant to Warwick's management of north Warwickshire by the close intermingling of its clientage with the earl's in Warwickshire and with Buckingham's in Staffordshire.[184] The marriage of Ferrers' widow soon after to Philip Chetwynd, annuitant of Buckingham and uncle of John Chetwynd, Warwick's feed man, was a logical conclusion to what had gone before.[185] That was no doubt why there was no longer any marked enthusiasm for defending the claims of the Ferrers family to Birmingham. The verdict of Ferrers' I.P.M. pronounced him the owner, but when William Bermingham II seized the manor soon after Chetwynd's marriage, and was in turn disseised by Chetwynd and his wife, the jury in the subsequent assize of novel disseisin returned a verdict in favour of Bermingham. The special commission named for the assize, both lay and judicial members, was overwhelmingly biased towards the Warwick affinity, which leads one to conclude that, even though the assize was heard during the earl's last absence in France, it was the verdict that he wanted. Although the assize bypassed the issue of right, the Berminghams' claim to the manor was never challenged thereafter, not even when Chetwynd's patron Buckingham was very much in a position to do so over the next few years.[186] The Ferrers' claims to Birmingham were, it seems, now considered defunct. Their usefulness to Warwick had given them their chance to make them good, their redundance after Edmund's death took it away. The harmony obtaining in

182 *Cal. Pat. Rolls 1429–36*, p. 626, *1436–41*, p. 592; *G.E.C.*, IX, p. 606. Although the Harewells were feed by Joan also, John was very much Warwick's man and Thomas Harewell has left more evidence of involvement with Warwick than with the Bergavenny affinity in these years (*Cal. Close Rolls 1429–35*, p. 119; Coughton Court, Throckmorton MS Box 35 (deed of 1431); above, n.135).

183 *G.E.C.*, I, p. 26, V, pp. 318–19.

184 Above, pp. 320–1.

185 *Dugdale*, p. 1,103; *Colls. Hist. Staffs.*, o.s., 12, pp. 267, 314.

186 *Cal. Pat. Rolls 1436–41*, pp. 502–3; B.R.L. 112349; C.260/143/27; *G.E.C.*, XII, ii, p. 381. Of the commissioners, John Cotesmore (Br. Lib. Eg. Roll 8773), William Peyto and Thomas Hugford had served Warwick, the latter very closely.

the last years of Richard Beauchamp's rule and the ease with which he was now able to hold his coalition of local magnates in a balanced unity is well-illustrated by the feoffment made by Thomas Ferrers of Tamworth in 1435. Ferrers' feoffees included Warwick himself and prominent clients and associates of the earl, of Joan Beauchamp and of Thomas' own family, the Ferrers of Groby, and friends and relatives of Norfolk and the Greys of Ruthin. That Ferrers was prepared to surrender an estate to a group of this complexion, apparently untroubled by fears that the feoffees would fall out with one another, is cogent evidence that Warwick's governance of much of the midlands had now been accepted on his own terms.[187]

Richard Beauchamp, having been appointed lieutenant-general and governor of France and Normandy, left England in August 1437, never to return.[188] If the records suggest that, as before, in the absence of the earl the level of conflict in the area rose, there was this time none of the serious violence and tension that had marked his previous periods abroad. Since he died in April 1439 there is no way of knowing his future intentions, above all how his relations with Buckingham would have evolved, as the latter began to throw off the role of junior partner.[189] In May 1437 Buckingham had been given the stewardship of Tutbury on the Staffordshire/Derbyshire border, an enormous enhancement of his power in the north midlands and an appointment confirmed for life in August of that year. Had he lived, Warwick would for the first time have had to deal with a rival power of equal rank exerting authority from Staffordshire over north Warwickshire.[190] Buckingham's claims to equality with Warwick, or even superiority in this part of the world, received substantial reinforcement in 1438, when he came into his mother's lands and

[187] Bod. Lib. Dugdale MS 17, p. 66; above, p. 321 n.153; The Warwick men were Lord Greystoke (Longleat, MS of Marquess of Bath 6414), perhaps Thomas Stanley (Bod. Lib. Dugdale MS 2, p. 277; E.368/220/108: the usual problems of Stanley identification; the same man may have served Joan as well: S.C.11/25), John Boyville and Ralph Brasebrugge. The Bergavenny men were Richard Hastings and perhaps Stanley, the Ferrers of Groby men, Fouleshurst and John Doreward (Leics.R.O. DE 2242/3/7, 3176(1), 40056). The appointment of John Bate, brother of Thomas (above, p. 103), to be Dean of Tamworth, the Ferrers' collegiate church (Cov. and Lichf. Dioc., Reg. Heyworth fo.64) in 1436 could emphasise this intermingling of north Warwickshire and Leicestershire affinities, as Thomas may well have been in Buckingham's service by now (app. 3). See above, pp. 307, 313 for traditions of association between the Ferrers of Groby and the Bergavenny affinities; also C.P.40/647 roti.305, 381, 535d. for the use by Joan and her clients of William Weldon, Buckingham's official by early 1435 (S.C.11/25; Br. Lib. Eg. Roll 8624; Rawcliffe 1978, p. 199), and *H.M.C. Hastings*, I, p. 77 for evidence of an arbitration *c.* 1433 between Erdington, a Warwick–Ferrers man and the Leicestershire Lawrence Berkeley (for whom see below, p. 403).

[188] *G.E.C.*, XII, ii, p. 381.

[189] *Ibid.* Sinclair implies that Warwick was already rather unhappy about the condition of his estates (and therefore also of his political position locally?) in 1436–7 and (perhaps because of this?) reluctant to accept the lieutenant-generalship in France (1987a: p. 131).

[190] Somerville 1953: p. 539 (already given d.p., 1435); and above, pp. 27–8.

bought most of the north Warwickshire estates of Lord Clinton, including Maxstoke Castle, one of the key strategic points in north Warwickshire. The same year he was also given custody of the royal manor of Atherstone in the north-east of the county.[191] There can be little doubt that he was systematically accumulating lands with a view to becoming the dominant power north of Coventry.

Whether he and Warwick could have come to some accommodation over their respective spheres must be open to question, especially as there was now the new factor to consider in the adult Henry VI, and his possible policies in Staffordshire and Leicestershire as duke of Lancaster. Another new ingredient was Edward Grey, heir to the Astley estates and eventually to the Ferrers of Groby lands. Even in early 1439 Grey's ambitions in east Warwickshire were beginning to be evident with disruptive effects, and later, if not now, they were to be underwritten by Buckingham.[192] Whether Warwick's governance could have coped with Buckingham and Grey can never be known, but it can be said with some certainty that by the 1430s, and indeed before, he had established a viable and adaptable system by which he was able to weld together the diverse regions of Warwickshire into a political whole under his exclusive control. He was to be the last holder of the Warwick lands until Edward IV to bring off this considerable feat.

III

An examination of internal order in Warwickshire between 1422 and 1439 reveals much about kingly rule and local society. It cannot be emphasised too strongly that the lack of an adult king for most of this period put immense burdens on nobility and gentry. If disputes were endemic in this landed society, then the various expedients for resolution, whether by private settlement, litigation or a combination of the two, were absolutely dependent on everyone's confidence in the king's ability to put his weight behind the system when necessary. This is clearly evident from the contrast over much of England between the later years of Henry IV, when ill-health rendered the king's capacity for leadership distinctly weak, and the reign of Henry V, once he had dealt with the legacy of his father's last years, even though the latter was only in England periodically thereafter. Legal records are a notoriously unreliable guide to the state of order, but they do have their uses as indicators of levels of tension. When numbers of cases reach the courts it is fair to assume that local society is failing to absorb the conflict inevitably engendered by this competitive hierarchy; when disputes continue over several years or give rise to

[191] Above, p. 315 n.131; *Cal. Fine Rolls 1437–45*, p. 19; above, pp. 30, 321.

[192] The Cotes–Hotoft dispute: below, pp. 401–2.

violence, we may conclude that the relationships that normally served to resolve them are under stress or failing to function.

In this light the pattern of litigation revealed in the King's Bench records in the period 1401–39 (figure 9) is very instructive.[193] As the narrative of events has indicated, it fluctuates to some degree with the earl of Warwick's movements between England and France, one of the worst years being 1427, when he was abroad. But this is only part of the story. The level of recorded conflict as a whole is considerably higher from the later 1420s than it had been at any time since the early years of Henry IV. This rise is really too great to be attributed solely to better recording of cases, the result of an increase in the number of indictments from the lower courts being taken into King's Bench, or from a possible increase in appetite for King's Bench litigation.[194] Furthermore, although there was little violence, the amount of litigation increased from 1434 onwards, which cannot be accounted for by Warwick's absence because he was mostly in England until late 1437. The logical explanation for the steady growth in recorded disputes from the mid 1420s, which was reflected in concern expressed in parliament in 1425–6 and 1433 and on the part of the council in 1437,[195] is that it became progressively more difficult to keep order in the localities as the minority continued and the nobility's energy for managing a leaderless kingdom, while also hanging on to the kingdom of France, began to run out. In a sense the country could be said to have been running on auto-pilot since September 1422, guided through its leaderless years by the great reservoir of loyalty and unity built up by Henry V and by the vast and cohesive royal/Duchy of Lancaster affinity nurtured by Henry and his father.[196] But this could not go on for ever (not least because the faithful and experienced old guard was dying off), which is probably one of the main reasons why the nobility pushed Henry VI into his majority as soon as it was feasible. The problem gained an additional dimension when Bedford's death in 1435 removed the one universally respected leader. By 1439 it was probably already becoming evident that hopes for a royal leadership that would restore unity and stability were at best misplaced.[197]

193 The graph is confined to King's Bench litigation because the records survive virtually complete and have been examined *in toto*, although they are very unsatisfactory for Henry IV's reign (above, n.75). For the problems in using this material statistically, see app. 4.

194 App. 4. This includes all recorded conflict, not just King's Bench cases, but the steady rise is evident, although with fluctuations, in the King's Bench records alone (see figure 9).

195 *Rot. Parl.*, IV, pp. 296, 421–2, V, pp. 406–7; *Procs. Priv. Counc.*, V, pp. 83–4.

196 Brown 1972; McFarlane 1972: pp. 59–77; Harriss 1985c; Powell 1985; Catto 1985; Somerville 1953, biographical appendices, pp. 347–654. That consensus could still be achieved, even as late as the 1430s, is shown in Virgoe 1980.

197 Griffiths 1981: pp. 232–4, 329–33. For the corpus of Henry V's servants, see works cited immediately above; some of their life histories can be traced in *G.E.C.*, Somerville 1953: pp. 347–654 and Roskell 1954. It will be apparent that this study takes the traditional view of Henry VI and not that advanced by Wolffe 1972 and 1981. Some of the arguments against the novel

Looking at the period from Warwick's point of view, we can see that on the one hand he was given opportunities that neither of his earlier royal masters would ever have allowed him. On the other hand he could expect no help at all from the centre in making use of them and, as it turned out, not a little hindrance from ambitious rivals who were as unfettered by royal direction as he was. A situation in which he, as one of the foremost warriors of the kingdom, hardly dared leave England for fear of what could happen behind his back was good neither for the earl nor for the hopes of the English in France. If other soldier-magnates were experiencing the same problems, needing constantly to look over their shoulders while looking after the king's affairs in his second kingdom, their failures are hardly surprising. Despite all these obstacles, Warwick's achievements in the west midlands are impressive. It is evident that Warwickshire was never an easy county to master as a whole. It could be done only by a coalition with other nobility, exploiting a variety of power bases within Warwickshire and in the adjacent parts of the neighbouring shires to which the regions of this very uncentralised county looked. Allies had to be managed, their ambitions held in check, their conflicts with each other resolved. Those who showed signs of wanting to become more independent actors had to be restrained before they could build their own empires using the parts of Warwick's own affinity that had become commingled with their own. Disputes among the gentry which could tear these intermingled affinities apart had to be resolved without undue favouritism, and yet Warwick had always to be mindful of the needs of his real friends and avoid sacrificing their interests to those of his allies.

What is striking about these years is not just that the major crises were resolved, on the whole without gross or uncontrollable violence, but that, although the number of cases reaching the courts rose, a whole series of minor disputes entered the records only to disappear almost immediately, almost certainly to be settled out of court.[198] Conflicts that were later to resurface again and again either failed to reach the courts at all, like the Porter–Archer dispute over Eastcote and Longdon, or sank without trace after a single appearance in the records, like that between the Burdets and the Charnels over Bramcote in north-east Warwickshire.[199] Local conditions which could give rise to incessant

interpretation are outlined in Carpenter 1982: pp. 732–4, and more will be said in my forthcoming textbook, *The Wars of the Roses*. See also Lovatt 1981 and 1984.

[198] E.g. K.B.27/659 Coram Rege rot.83d., /653 Coram Rege rot.32d.; Br. Lib. Add. Roll 17,760; K.B.27/664 Coram Rege rot.84d., /665 Coram Rege rot.3, /667 Coram Rege rot.80d., /677 Coram Rege rot.36d., /676 Coram Rege rot.49, /688 Coram Rege rot.43, /693 Coram Rege rot.4; K.B.9/228/2/22; K.B.27/712 Coram Rege rot.25d.; K.B.9/230B/236, /228/1/8; K.B.27/699 Coram Rege rot.42d., /738 Coram Rege rot.98, /705 Coram Rege rot.90d., /706 Coram Rege rot.74. For the implications of cases disappearing from the courts, see Baker, *Spelman*, II, pp. 91–2, and Powell 1983a: pp. 58–60.

[199] See below, chs. 11–15; K.B. 27/691 Coram Rege rot.28d.

litigation, like those in the Tanworth region, which have been described at some length, or the very similar ones in and around Alspath, did not yet produce uncontainable conflicts. Certainly the Alspath area had its quota of disputes;[200] there was also a continuous series of outbreaks, some of them violent, near Tanworth, centred mainly on the ambitions of rising men, particularly Thomas Greswold and Thomas Porter, and the violent instincts of the Hores of Solihull. None of them, however, got completely out of hand, not even the confrontation in 1434–6 between the Hores and the Porters, which comes closest to indicating that the peacekeeping mechanisms were beginning seriously to falter.[201] And, unlike so many conflicts in the Arden later on, none was drawn into other disputes or converted into a pawn in local factionalism.

It can be said that the problems encountered by the historian in trying to pin down the nature of magnate loyalties in this region, even at times of crisis, show not just the inadequacies of the evidence but how little true factionalism there was, and how normal it was for the nobility, other things being equal, to co-operate with each other. If, as has been suggested, the duke of Norfolk may have welcomed some of the attempts to undermine Warwick's authority in the east of the county, and if, at the back of these efforts, there may have lain the abrasive figure of Joan Beauchamp, neither Norfolk nor Joan was in any way isolated from the earl and his followers. They could not afford to be, for their own friends and associates had to live co-operatively with neighbours of a broad spectrum of political affiliations. Hence it was almost impossible under normal circumstances for there to be an outright breach between any of the nobility. Usually they would manoeuvre within a framework of options, committing themselves to a particular stance for no longer than was necessary to gain a particular end. In the mid 1420s, when foremost among Norfolk's designs was the worsting of Warwick in the precedence dispute, the duke may have looked for other ways of discomfiting the earl as long as they did not lead to open hostilities, but once Warwick had shown he could defend himself and his followers it was more sensible for Norfolk to climb down in east Warwickshire.

That the gentry, apart from mavericks like the Hores and the Burdets, had as much interest in local order as the nobility is undeniable. In fact they had rather more, as should already be apparent from the first section of this work. It was their lands that were more likely to suffer and they could afford far less than the nobility to lose part of their year's income under the trampling hooves of a raiding party.[202] Undoubtedly the gentry networks described in the previous

[200] K.B.27/653 Coram Rege rot.32d.; K.B.9/230B/236; K.B.27/738 Coram Rege rot.98, /706 Coram Rege rot.74. Above, pp. 22, 136, 146–7 for local circumstances that were conducive to conflict.

[201] K.B.27/660 Coram Rege rot.15; Br. Lib. Add. Roll 17,760; K.B.27/663 Coram Rege rot.67, /701 Coram Rege rot.74; K.B.9/228/2/20; S.B.T. D.R.37 Box 83 (Archer v. Marbroke, 1437); K.B.9/230A/3, /245/33.

[202] Above, chs. 5 and 6, *passim*.

chapter played a large part in preventing, containing and resolving disputes; if everybody participated in the business of everyone else then each and every one had an interest in preserving an atmosphere of friendly co-operation. This must have been especially true of the Tanworth area, where complexity of tenure gave rise both to conflict and to the absolute necessity of seeking a quick resolution, and it was the strength of the network here that ensured that the regular succession of disputes did so little damage. All the parties in the major disagreements – Archer, Greswold, Hore of Elmdon and Solihull, Waryng, Parker, Birches, Middlemore – except perhaps for the intrusive Thomas Porter, were interlinked.[203]

However, although the importance of gentry networks in the preservation of local stability cannot be minimised, where there was an active magnate the gentry were likely to look to him for leadership, a point that has already been made evident in the study of these networks. Just as the nobility found it easier to work together when they had the security provided by the superior power of the king, so in this period the gentry needed a lord or group of lords on whom they could rely to force them into amity. It was in a sense an essential precondition for taking the risks that would carry them across the boundary between co-operation and conflict which they might need to cross in pursuit of their aspirations. Without such security it was impossible to reconcile the contradictory obligations of defending and augmenting the family honour and safeguarding local stability. The sudden surge of dissension in 1427, when Warwick's control was called into question, showed the dangers that could follow when local leadership wavered. Even the heart of the western Arden, where the nobility exercised so little direct control, owed its independence to a great extent to the fact that Warwick's dominance of west Warwickshire made it an uncontentious area. Once this situation changed after Warwick's death, this area too began to be drawn into the world of politics beyond its boundaries.

Enough has been said to show that Richard Beauchamp's rule was far from benign. It brooked no opposition, it allowed the Berminghams and later the Ferrers of Chartley to fall victim to his willingness to sacrifice their interests in the cause of local equilibrium. Other instances, in which the earl's need to favour his own intimates did possible injustice to their adversaries, could be cited.[204] Against all this it must be said that it worked, and, if it left victims behind, there were not enough of them to generate the sort of reaction that turned Shropshire and Staffordshire into arenas of civil war under Henry IV.[205] Between 1401 and 1439, under three very different types of rule, Beauchamp

[203] Above, pp. 296–7.

[204] E.g. Throgmorton v. Neville (Coughton Court, Throckmorton MS Box 35) and Cotes v. Hotoft (below, pp. 401–2, and Carpenter 1980a: p. 527).

[205] Powell 1979: *passim*.

was able to harness his own considerable abilities, his lesser associates' dependence on his support and protection and the natural desire of all landowners for a peace that could be reconciled with their own individual aspirations, to bring to Warwickshire a degree of stability that it was not to know again until the last years of Edward IV.[206]

[206] He was also, be it noted, running his administration, and even reforming it, again often from abroad, and experiencing only one major hiccup (for full details, see Sinclair 1987a: ch. 4).

11

THE INTERREGNUM: 1439–49

I

On Richard Beauchamp's death the king and the local magnates had to face the question of how Warwickshire and the other counties where he had been pre-eminent were to be ruled in the minority of his son. No minority rule could possibly encompass the breadth of governance that Beauchamp had commanded from 1422 to 1439, but there was no reason why it should be required any more. The reigns of the first two Lancastrians had shown that, given firm and reasonably amicable leadership in the areas to the north and east of the county, Warwickshire could be put under an effective divided rule that exploited the Beauchamps' power in the west midlands without necessarily obliging or allowing them to move very far north or east of their natural sphere of influence in Warwickshire, immediately south and west of Warwick. We have seen that the natural candidate for the job in Staffordshire and Leicestershire and, by extension, in north and east Warwickshire was the duke of Lancaster. However, once it had become clear that Henry VI was not the sort of king who could provide leadership, these sectors were open to competition. There were a number of candidates in Leicestershire and Northamptonshire, while in Staffordshire Buckingham was the only obvious one, especially as he already controlled the Duchy estates there. The drawback of them all was that none had the undisputed authority of a king that had made possible the harmonious division of the county between Richard Beauchamp and the first Lancastrian kings earlier in the century. Alternatively, one nobleman could try to recreate Richard Beauchamp's wholesale control of Warwickshire from a different tenurial base. Either way, the lack of direction from the throne was going to make it exceedingly difficult to find a workable solution for a county that required the active involvement of more than one magnate if an equilibrium was to be achieved. What happened in Warwickshire between 1439 and 1449 is not at all easy to follow. Loyalties could change from year to year, and the composition of political groups consequently becomes rather more elusive than before. The involvement of magnates from outside the county in what turned out to be a free-for-all over the Beauchamp political inheritance makes it particularly difficult to decide what was going on because so little work has been done on Warwickshire's neighbours. The attempt at a narrative which follows should therefore be regarded as by no means definitive.

Looked at from the perspective of the spheres of influence contained within its boundaries, Warwickshire after 1439 presents a rather different shape. West of Warwick, the core of the former power of the earls remained, the estates now in the hands of a group representing the old affinity of Richard Beauchamp and the nascent power of the courtiers who were rapidly congregating around the vacuous person of Henry VI. The wealth of the estate was bound to attract people such as the earl of Salisbury, senior representative of a family long favoured by the Lancastrians, and rising household men such as John Norreys and Lord Say. However, lest we are tempted to date political divisions too soon, it should be pointed out that it was to the duke of Gloucester that the profits of Henry Beauchamp's lands were paid during his minority. In the administration and custody of the estates during the minority there was a strong element of continuity from Richard Beauchamp's day, but there was no guarantee that the affinity could still function as a political entity.[1]

If any one man was going to succeed to the overall control of Richard Beauchamp, it could only be Buckingham. He now had substantial estates in north Warwickshire, and these, together with his large Staffordshire lands and the stewardship of Tutbury, gave him unrivalled control over the north midlands, the more so as Duchy influence was retreating rapidly throughout the area. With Richard Beauchamp and Edmund Ferrers dead, it was Buckingham above all who was able to pick up the pieces of the disintegrating Duchy hegemony in the north midlands. He also had lands in east and west

1 In May 1439 keepers to the use of Warwick's executors and of Isabel, Warwick's widow, were appointed: York, Salisbury, John Beauchamp of Powick, John Norreys (had the Warwick arms on his house (Sinclair 1987a: p. 307 n.52) but no earlier evidence of association with the Beauchamps and very much a courtier) and four Warwick retainers including Throgmorton. In December new keepers were appointed for Henry's minority should Isabel die, and their position in the minority was confirmed in 1443: Ralph Boteller of Sudeley, Beauchamp of Powick, Norreys and the same Warwick retainers minus Thomas Hugford and plus William Mountford and William Muston. Warwick's executors were in charge of the Beauchamp trust lands (for which, below, p. 444): Cromwell, Tiptoft and five Warwick retainers including Throgmorton. Gloucester was granted the minority revenues of both Henry's and Isabel's lands (after her death) in 1440 (*Test. Vetust.*, p. 233; *Cal. Pat. Rolls 1436–41*, pp. 279, 360, 367, 435, *1446–52*, p. 268; *Cal. Fine Rolls 1437–45*, pp. 122, 171; *Lists and Indexes*, 9, p. 158; Sinclair 1987a: pp. 301–3). For further comments on the keepers etc., see Carpenter, M. C. 1976: p. 127 n.6. For the Nevilles and the court, see Griffiths 1981: pp. 278, 343, 1968: p. 593, Storey 1966: pp. 114–15, and, on their long-standing ties with the dynasty, see Brown 1972 and McFarlane 1972: pp. 70–5.

Warwickshire and, now that the Berkeley lands that Warwick had saved from Lord Berkeley had descended to the earl's daughters by his first marriage, he was a greater force in Gloucestershire than the heir of Warwick himself. He was thus almost as well-equipped as Warwick had been to exercise the rule from within and outside the county that was essential for the mastering of Warwickshire as a whole. Nevertheless, it should not be assumed that Buckingham was necessarily concerned about the rule of Warwickshire *per se*; in all probability, Warwickshire was more important to him as an adjunct to his own power in Gloucestershire and above all in Staffordshire.[2]

Initially, it was not Buckingham but Edward Grey of Groby who was the new and divisive force in Warwickshire politics from 1439. He obtained the Astley estate on his father's death in 1440, and the Ferrers of Groby lands, with their extensive Leicestershire political connection, eventually fell to him on the death of Lord William in 1445. In addition to the landed power in north-east Warwickshire and Leicestershire that these properties gave him, he could hope for support from Northamptonshire, as long as he remained on good terms with his Grey of Ruthin relatives.[3] If he could square the duke of Buckingham, who had the manor of Atherstone in north-east Warwickshire from the king and a group of estates centred on Rugby in east Warwickshire in his own right, he could hope to be the dominant power all the way down Warwickshire's eastern border. In fact, in April 1440 he became Buckingham's annuitant and the fruits of their co-operation are already evident by 1440–1, when Richard Hotoft, a Leicestershire esquire who had married the widow of the east Warwickshire landowner Nicholas Metley, was serving both Grey and Buckingham. It was on behalf of Hotoft and from his native habitat of Leicestershire that Grey's first steps in Warwickshire politics seem to have been taken. Since the early years of the century the Metleys had been holding on to a large portion of the inheritance of the Cotes of Hunningham in east Warwickshire by increasingly dubious means. On Metley's death and his widow's remarriage, which delivered the Cotes lands to Hotoft, John Cotes, deciding that enough was enough, raided Hotoft's lands in Leicestershire, assaulted his wife and made off with 380 sheep. The offence took place at the end of 1437, but Cotes was an annuitant of the earl of Warwick – it was presumably Warwick who had been instrumental in keeping the peace between the Cotes and the Metleys, since both families were connected with him – and he escaped indictment until April 1439 when Warwick lay dying in France. Presiding over the sessions in Leicestershire at

[2] Rawcliffe 1978: app. A; also p. 66 on his use of Stafford and Maxstoke as residences; *G.E.C.*, XII, ii, p. 382; Payling 1987b: pp. 178–87; Wright 1983; chs. 5 and 6; Storey 1966: ch. 11.

[3] *G.E.C.*, V, pp. 358–9; and above, pp. 325–6, 393 and genealogy, p. 325 n.171.

which Cotes was brought to book was Grey's father-in-law, Lord Ferrers of Groby.[4]

Grey was soon to have a more direct entry into Warwickshire politics, his opportunity coming from a dispute at Coventry which began in 1438. It is a classic case of its kind from more than one point of view. First, most of the chief protagonists, including William Betley, the principal actor, were the rising professionals whose efforts to establish themselves among the landed gentry were potentially so destabilising. Secondly, we are not likely to find a better example of deliberate intervention by a magnate in a small-scale dispute for the sole purpose of political profit. The lands at issue were held by Betley's wife and came from her first marriage. Betley was a lawyer, and it was this marriage, it appears, that enabled him to join the landed proprietors of Coventry. It is not improbable that Grey was involved from the first, and there is evidence suggesting his presence in the affair by 1439–40,[5] but it is in 1440 that he begins to emerge as the prime mover. In that year a new claimant appeared. He was William Burgeys of Melton Mowbray in Leicestershire, and his family was connected in various ways with the Astleys of Patshull, cousins of Grey through his mother, with Grey himself and with Grey's father's family, the Greys of Ruthin.[6] Initially, it was the Astleys who were putting their weight behind Burgeys, but by 1442 and even before there can be little doubting Grey's pre-eminent role. In that year a jury found for Burgeys, but it was subsequently alleged that the jurors had been deliberately chosen to favour Burgeys over Betley, and had moreover been bribed. The probable force behind both these

4 K.B.9/230B/191; K.B.27/713 Coram Rege rot.29, Rex rot.21. There is a discrepancy of date between these two K.B.27 entries. The Rex entry shows that Joan had married Hotoft by December 1437. Edward Metley married Cotes' widow, apparently keeping much of the Cotes land in dower or jointure, which she still had in 1436 (C.1/11/155; E.179/192/59; above, p. 103 n.27). Since it was the widow of Nicholas Metley, Margaret's son by the second marriage, who was under attack, it is probable that the dispute started when Nicholas failed to hand the land over on Margaret's death. It is just possible that the episode relates not to the Cotes lands but to the destiny of the Metley inheritance (above, p. 104, below, pp. 404–5), for this was in contention at this time and Cotes was involved with their sale to perform Metley's will (P.R.O. Catesby Doc.). According to Leland (1907–10: II, p. 43), Warwick's last illness was a long one, so his impending death may well have been known at the time.

5 C.1/12/60; K.B.27/714 Coram Rege rot.103d. John Norwood, the original claimant, features in a deed of 1441 with some of Grey's associates (B.R.L. 418917). In 1439/40, in the course of the dispute, Betley was bound not to attack the sheriff or his deputy (C.1/11/206, /9/189); the sheriff in question, Lawrence Berkeley of Leicestershire, was concerned in a deed of 1445 of William Burgeys, the claimant that Grey put up to Betley's lands (*Cal. Close Rolls 1441–47*, p. 343; and below, p. 403), while the deputy, Thomas Sampson, allegedly embezzled writs during the case and was one of the bribed jurors (see below, p. 403), so both may have been acting for Grey from the start. For Betley as a lawyer, see app. 2.

6 *Cal. Close Rolls 1441–47*, p. 343, *1447–54*, pp. 17, 172; *Feud. Aids*, III, p. 105; *I.P.M.*, 8 Hen.VI/40. For ref. to Astley pedigree, see above, p. 325 n.171. For evidence that Reginald Grey was taking a certain amount of interest in Warwickshire, see C.P.40/723 roti.106d.,209d.

alleged improprieties, not least because the embracery bill ran into several hundred pounds, is Edward Grey. He was certainly extensively involved with these men by the following year and was by then heavily implicated in the affair himself. The names of the jurors show how much headway Grey had already made in Coventry and eastern Warwickshire.[7] These were not just venal officials but men like Henry Boteller of Coventry, the future Recorder, who was to serve Grey and his family for the rest of the century, and Thomas Boughton, a connection of the family since at least 1432, who in 1441 had come into the lands of his well-connected, east-Warwickshire father-in-law, Geoffrey Allesley.[8]

Since east Warwickshire, particularly the Avon-Leam area where the Allesley lands were, was the centre of a dense network of relatively minor families like the Allesleys and the Metleys, and their successors, the Boughtons and the Hotofts, Grey had found an excellent foothold in east Warwickshire landed society. The evolution of this grouping to become the focus of Grey's power along the east Warwickshire border, and a potent link between the gentry of east Warwickshire and the Leicestershire groupings in which Grey and his grandfather-in-law Lord Ferrers of Groby participated, has already been described.[9] Grey's nascent power in Warwickshire began to be recognised in the appointment of local officials; the sheriffs of 1439–41, Lawrence Berkeley and Thomas Ashby, were both Leicestershire men, both connected with Grey through their associates in Leicestershire, while in March 1442 Boughton was appointed to the commission of the peace, as in July 1443 was Grey himself.[10]

His penetration into Warwickshire was apparently undertaken with the full support of the duke of Buckingham, the only magnate who was tenurially in a position to dictate what happened in east Warwickshire. In 1443 the securities for the bailing of Burgeys included Grey and William Weldon, Buckingham's auditor since 1435.[11] Buckingham was in the meantime making himself a force elsewhere in the county. He was fortunate in that a group of wardships came his way at this time which materially strengthened his hand in areas where he was already a leading landowner. These were Verney of Great Wolford in the far

7 K.B.27/718 Coram Rege roti.109d.,110d., /724 Coram Rege rot.79d. (Betley disseised by a group which includes a man named Robert Edwardservant Grey), /726 Coram Rege rot.102, /727 Coram Rege rot.82, /729 Coram Rege rot.22; below, p. 410.

8 For Boteller, see above, p. 125; *Dugdale*, p. 99; Br. Lib. Add. Ch. 48,660. For Allesley's connections, see above, pp. 302–3. An indication of the strength of the links that were being formed is that in the 1480s Henry Boteller was still acting as feoffee in Coventry for Burgeys (*H.M.C.*, xv, x, p. 146), as, apparently, was Edward Grey's son.

9 Above, pp. 325–9.

10 *Lists and Indexes*, 9, p. 145; *Cal. Close Rolls 1435–41*, pp. 382–3,478, *1441–47*, p. 343; *Cal. Pat. Rolls 1441–46*, p. 480.

11 K.B.27/729 Rex rot.10d.; Rawcliffe 1978: p. 199.

south of the county and Trussell of Billesley and Burdet in west Warwickshire/east Worcestershire.[12] In the region where Warwickshire, Worcestershire and Gloucestershire met he had acquired or was acquiring the services of families which had traditionally looked to Richard Beauchamp: Bruyn, Skull, Stafford of Grafton and Vampage.[13] On the other side of the county, annuities to Reginald Moton of Leicestershire, Thomas Trussell of Bilton and Richard Hotoft gave him access to the powerful Leicestershire network in which were involved not only Grey and his grandfather-in-law but also other Leicestershire magnates, such as Joan Beauchamp's heirs at Ashby de la Zouche, the Botellers of Ormond, and John Lord Beaumont, a rising star at court.[14] By late 1443 Grey was associated with the duke of Norfolk and his affinity, the son of the man who seems to have been infiltrating east Warwickshire in the 1420s from his estates in Leicestershire. It is not impossible that Norfolk hoped to use Grey as an avenue for repeating his father's attempts at expansion westward. That would fit with the fact that the feed men of Monks Kirby, which was under Mowbray patronage, were all linked to Grey, and also with subsequent events in the early 1450s.[15] A clear indication both of the close links between Buckingham and Grey at the time, and of their joint control of east Warwickshire, comes from the dispute over the Metley lands, which broke out at the end of the 1430s. This was between Hotoft and his wife, the widow of Nicholas Metley, and Robert Catesby, who had bought two of the estates – one in east Warwickshire, one in Leicestershire – to be sold under Metley's will, a sale rejected by the Hotofts. Both claimants were from east Warwickshire, Hotoft was already under the lordship of Buckingham and Grey, and Catesby made haste to put himself under Buckingham's protection. The result was an

[12] S.C.R.O. D.641/1/2/269-72. This was also a time when there was a minority in the family of Harewell of Wootton Wawen in south-west Warwickshire, where Buckingham was overlord (E.179/192/59; C.139/145/9; *V.C.H.*, III, p. 198), and it was in 1437 that Buckingham, apparently uniquely in his career, took an interest in the affairs of the alien priory of Wootton, with which the Staffords had an old family connection (*ex. inf.* Benjamin Thompson; I am most grateful to Dr Thompson for permission to quote from his work on alien priories, part of which appears in his Cambridge Ph.D. thesis, completed 1989).

[13] S.C.R.O. D.641/1/2/233 (Richard Bruyn: same family as Warwick's officer, Maurice Bruyn?: Br. Lib. Eg. Roll 8770), D.641/1/2/17; Rawcliffe 1978: p. 221; above, pp. 308–9, 313 for earlier connections of Worcestershire men with Warwick.

[14] Rawcliffe 1978: p. 234 (but not Reginald *Morton*, as it says here; see original: Nat. Lib. Wales, Peniarth MS 280 fo.36); above, pp. 299–300, 307, 313.

[15] S.C.6/1039/18; C.244/40/45 (my thanks to Dr Lucy Moye for guidance on Norfolk's associates in this recognisance); Archer 1984a: ch. 2; note also that Melton Mowbray, Burgeys' home, was the duke's central estate in Leicestershire; he may possibly have been the William Burgeys who took advice of William Paston in 1444. If so, this would strengthen the case for connecting him with the Norfolk affinity (*Cal. Close Rolls 1441–47*, p. 343; *Paston Letters*, II, pp. 517–19). It may be significant that John Brome was serving Norfolk as auditor in 1445 (Griffiths 1980b: p. 114); above, p. 328.

arbitration, made in about 1442–3, on the orders of Buckingham, by a panel led by William Ferrers of Groby, Grey's father-in-law.[16]

Buckingham himself was doing well elsewhere. As far back as 1434 he had joined Warwick and the duke of Bedford in protecting Bramcote, a manor in north-east Warwickshire owned by the Burdets. In 1440, now sole surviving feoffee, he was obliged to act on their behalf again, and by 1442 the estate had been passed to a new group of feoffees representing very much the old Warwick and new Buckingham interest in west Warwickshire and Worcestershire.[17] As the guardian of the Burdet lands from 1442 Buckingham had a particular obligation to protect them, but his defensive measures were doing him a lot of good in the old centre of Warwick power. In the south of the county he had retained Richard Dalby, Hugh's heir, some years before, and the link with the Verneys of Great Wolford had been formalised in 1438.[18] It must be said, however, that, even though he was the leading noble landowner in the far south of Warwickshire, there is little further evidence that he was much concerned at this time over what happened here. It was in fact in north Warwickshire that he was best able and probably most anxious to make an impression. His close ties with the Ferrers of Chartley connection gave him an excellent foundation. After the marriage of the Ferrers widow to Buckingham's retainer Philip Chetwynd, the Staffordshire affinity of the Ferrers, which overlapped heavily with Buckingham's own following – Mollesley, Whitgreve, Vernon, Erdeswick – was probably closer to Buckingham than to William, the new Lord of Chartley.[19] Connections with the Cokayns which dated to the late 1430s were perhaps more vital to Buckingham's ambitions in Derbyshire than in north Warwickshire, but the relationship with Thomas Bate, who had the Cokayn properties in Warwickshire from about 1441, was certainly a significant gain. Between 1441 and 1443, when Grey's representation on the commission of the peace was growing, Thomas Bate and another Buckingham retainer, Humphrey Stafford of Grafton, also found their way on to it.[20]

Despite the apparently inexorable progress of Grey and Buckingham to a

16 P.R.O. Catesby Doc.; above, pp. 104, 401.

17 K.B.27/691 Coram Rege rot.28d.; K.B.9/240/104,105; C.1/31/149: records feoffment to Maurice Bruyn, Thomas Littleton, John and Thomas Hugford, Humphrey Stafford I of Grafton, Thomas Burdet I, John Throgmorton, John Vampage, William Tracy, William Wollashull etc., made before Burdet's death in 1442 (S.C.R.O. D.641/1/2/270). For the Worcestershire men in this group and their connections with Warwick, see above, pp. 308–9, 313, 404 n.13.

18 App.3; S.C.R.O. D.641/1/2/17.

19 For Whitgreve, Vernon and Erdeswick, see E.163/7/31 Pt.1 (Ferrers, and for reasons for attributing this to Chartley, see Carpenter, M.C. 1976; app. p. 106) and Rawcliffe 1978: pp. 221, 224–5, 222 (Staffords). Also Chetwynd settlements of this time (*Cal. Close Rolls 1435–41*, pp. 266,268; *Colls. Hist. Staffs*., o.s., 12, pp. 314–15, 316–17). He was also connected with Hugh Willoughby by 1443, although this relationship may have been more important in the context of Tutbury (*Test. Ebor*., II, p. 134).

20 For Bate and the Cokayn lands, see below, p. 411; *Cal. Pat. Rolls 1441–46*, p. 480; Wright 1983: pp. 65, 67–72, 99–100.

position of unassailable authority in Warwickshire, their advance did not go uncontested. It is by no means clear whether Buckingham himself was prepared to give Warwickshire the sustained attention that would have been required to build such a new power structure. He was apparently much preoccupied in Derbyshire and, of all the midland counties, Staffordshire must always have had the principal claim upon him.[21] It is apparent moreover that William Ferrers of Chartley was deeply resentful of the way things were going. He was probably not happy about his mother's remarriage: if the ground had been prepared by the interpenetration of the Ferrers and Buckingham affinities, this match with a retainer of Buckingham can only have caused intense anxiety. Buckingham had once been equal with the Ferrers of Chartley as a junior partner in the Warwick coalition but was now assuming the role of natural successor to Warwick's midland empire. The fact that Ferrers' mother took a sizeable portion of the family lands with her would have done nothing to allay these fears. Buckingham's takeover of one part of his following may have been matched by Grey's of another, including some of the Ferrers men from the north-east, the centre of the old Astley connection that Grey was apparently reactivating.[22] And while Chetwynd and his wife were enjoying the Ferrers jointure, not only were they not taking any steps to make good the Ferrers claim to Birmingham, but in 1442 William Bermingham II was able to get a reversal of the two I.P.M.s – those of Elizabeth Clinton and Edmund Ferrers – that had been major weapons in the Ferrers' legal armoury.[23]

There are indications that Ferrers' immediate response to events was to undertake the defence of William Betley against Edward Grey. While there is no direct evidence for this, it would have been the obvious course, and Betley's case could have been pleaded to Ferrers by Edmund Colshill, a friend of Ferrers who lived near Coventry and had done business with Betley at an earlier stage. In 1439–40 Betley was receiving the help of another old associate, Thomas Stretton, who became very firmly linked to Ferrers between 1441 and 1443.[24] Stretton was another of those rising professionals with destabilising aspirations and he was to end his career as Clerk of the King's Works.[25] He,

[21] See n.20, above; Rowney 1981: pp. 39–68.

[22] *Colls. Hist. Staffs.*, o.s., 12, p. 314; above, p. 391.

[23] *Cal. Pat. Rolls 1436–41*, pp. 502–03; K.B.27/723 Rex rot. 4-d. (there seems to be a misleading scribal error on the dorse, 'John Sutton' being written for 'John Vampage', who was prosecuting the case for the king); above, p. 391; it is in this episode that John Sutton of Dudley's claim to be overlord of Birmingham to the Bermingham tenancy surfaces (above, p. 389); it was upheld. Bermingham presented to Birmingham church in 1444 (Cov. and Lichf. Dioc., Reg. Catterick, fo.42v.).

[24] K.B.27/669 Rex rot.24; C.1/11/206, /9/189; *Cal. Fine Rolls 1430–37*, p. 231; Sims ed., *Walsall Deeds*, p. 17; *Cal. Pat. Rolls 1441–46*, p. 52. In Michaelmas 1442, Burgeys in his turn alleged embracery in the plea with Betley, against a jury of Coventry men; Stretton, and even Ferrers, could have lent a hand here (C.P.40/723 roti.485–6).

[25] *Coventry Leet Book*, p. 199; *Cal. Pat. Rolls 1452–61*, p. 286.

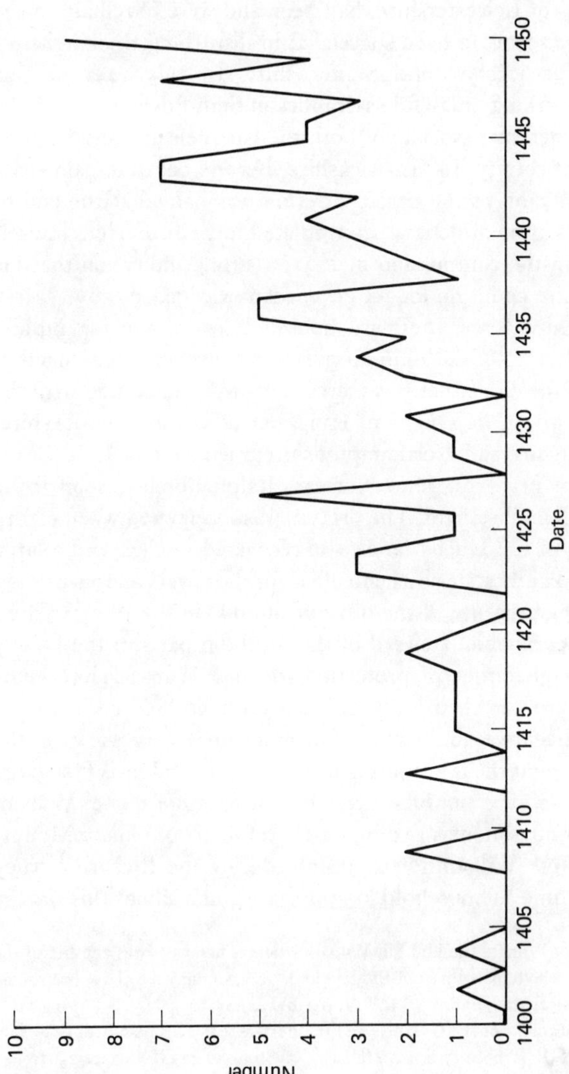

Figure 9 Conflict in Warwickshire (drawn from King's Bench records) 1400–50 (see important comments in appendix 4)

like Betley, had done well out of marriage to a widow and in his case also it may have been his marriage that drew him into this conflict.[26] Ferrers had another good reason for resisting the progress of the Buckingham–Grey juggernaut, for the family against whom Buckingham and his new friends were protecting Bramcote, the Charnels of Leicestershire, had been and were to remain in the Ferrers entourage.[27] He seems to have succeeded in disturbing Buckingham's hegemony in both Warwickshire and Staffordshire. In July 1441 he was ordered to desist from making unlawful assemblies in Staffordshire, and in the same year Richard Archer, an associate of both the Charnels and the Ferrers, was made sheriff of that county. In Warwickshire, Ferrers began to gain some influence on the commission of the peace; Stretton was named at the end of 1439 and, although this appointment was terminated in 1443, Ferrers himself had achieved a place on the commission in 1441, a strong indication that his standing in Warwickshire could no longer go unacknowledged.[28]

Then there was a third force, the royal household, now growing rapidly under the nominal leadership of the adult king. It was household men, together with other members of the circle that was increasingly to be identified with the court, that were being given the Duchy of Lancaster offices in Warwickshire, Staffordshire, Leicestershire and Northamptonshire; men such as Lord Beaumont (created Viscount in 1440), John Norreys, Ralph Boteller, soon to be Lord Sudeley, and William Tresham. The process was accelerated when Henry V's feoffment of much of the Duchy lands was recovered in 1442 and a large part of the Duchy's midland estates was enfeoffed for the royal colleges in 1443 and again in 1449.[29] The presence of the duke of Suffolk on the Warwickshire commission of the peace as chief steward of the northern parts of the Duchy from early 1439 was a guarantee of protection to those Warwickshire landowners who chose to throw in their lot with the royal household.[30] This must have been a strong incentive to William Bermingham II, in view of the continued uncertainty about the fate of his principal manor, and he is first given the appellation 'king's esquire' in July 1439, but he was not alone. William Catesby, Philip Chetwynd, Thomas Erdington II, John Holt, William Mountford and his son Edmund, William Peyto, Ralph Shirley and Richard Verney all feature for the first time as household knights or esquires about this time, a

26 His wife was the widow of William Shukburgh. William's heir, Thomas I, was another of the east Warwickshire gentry who took the part of Burgeys and Grey, so there may have been some quarrel between the two over the jointure (S.B.T. E.R.1/61/409,411).

27 Above, n.17; C.1/14/24, /15/25. For the Charnels and the Ferrers, e.g. K.B.9/203/18; Bod. Lib. Dugdale MS 15, p. 122; S.B.T. D.R.37 Box 59 (charter of Stotfold, 1438), Box 42/2503.

28 *Cal. Close Rolls 1435–41*, pp. 422–3; *Lists and Indexes*, 9, p. 127; *Cal. Pat. Rolls 1436–41*, p. 592, *1441–46*, p. 480.

29 Somerville 1953: pp. 206, 211, 339–40, 560, 563, 568, 569, 570, 576, 586, 590; Williams 1984–5: pp. 29–30; Griffiths 1981: pp. 340–2, 307, 337, 298. For a discussion of recent moves to see the growth of the household in Duchy areas as a seriously-designed policy, see below, pp. 475–6.

30 *Cal. Pat. Rolls 1436–41*, p. 592, *1441–46*, p. 480.

reflection of the rate at which the household was growing.[31] And just as the arrival of Buckingham, Grey and Ferrers and their men as guardians of the peace reflected their nascent power in the county, so the appointment of Bermingham and Verney to the commission must be attributed to the local influence of the household, and the same may be true of Thomas Greswold, coroner and attorney in the King's bench since 1422.[32]

The influence of the royal household in Warwickshire was particularly strong at this time because of the court connection with the Warwick lands.[33] Several of the members of the household recruited from Warwickshire in these years had been attached to Richard Beauchamp. William Mountford, Warwickshire sheriff in 1441–2,[34] managed to hold himself altogether aloof from magnate politics in Warwickshire, thanks to the independent power he was able to exercise as the greatest of the local men with responsibility for the Warwick lands. Had he decided to throw in his lot with Buckingham, the combined influence of the two of them, at Coleshill and Maxstoke, would have delivered north Warwickshire safely into Buckingham's hands. But instead Mountford, while retaining his links with other north Warwickshire landowners, chose to move towards the court. By 1444 he and Edmund, his eldest son by his second marriage, who proved to be very much his father's favourite, were well-ensconced there.[35]

None of these local factions was self-sufficient, as a glance at the groupings discussed in the previous chapter makes plain. The household men in particular cut across the principal noble camps in 1439–42.[36] Further indications of confusion and division in local allegiances can be deduced from the fact that William Betley was acting as attorney in the King's Bench for the Warwick executors, of whom the most active senior figure was Thomas Hugford.[37] While Grey may have felt that he was gaining valuable local esteem by supporting an attack on the legal representative of the major west midlands estate, Buckingham was probably not so pleased. A confrontation with the core of the old Warwick affinity, particularly when some of them, amongst them

[31] Bermingham, Catesby, Holt, Shirley and Verney *ex inf.* Dr G. L. Harriss (to whom thanks); *Procs. Priv. Counc.*, V, p. 121; *Cal. Pat. Rolls 1441–46*, pp. 205, 244, 175, *1436–41*, p. 136.

[32] *Cal. Pat. Rolls 1436–41*, p. 592, *1441–46*, p. 480; K.B.27/646 Rex rot.3.

[33] See above, pp. 333–4, 400.

[34] *Lists and Indexes*, 9, p. 145.

[35] *Cal. Pat. Rolls 1436–41*, p. 359, *1441–46*, pp. 75, 244; K.B.27/732 Coram Rege rot.25. See below, p. 427 for Mountford and his sons. Rowney 1983: p. 50 alleges that Mountford was drawn to Buckingham at this time through the Ferrers of Chartley–Chetwynd connection, but there is no evidence of this until 1450 (see below, pp. 456–7).

[36] Erdington: traditionally linked with the Ferrers of Chartley; Betley: King's Bench official; Chetwynd: retained by Buckingham; Bermingham: identifiable with neither Ferrers nor Buckingham; Mountford: associated with both; Richard Hotoft: Duchy of Lancaster official serving Grey and Buckingham (app. 3; K.B.27/718 Coram Rege rot.110d.; Somerville 1953: pp. 569, 570, 589).

[37] K.B.27/737 Coram Rege rot.95.

Hugford, were helping him protect Bramcote for the Burdet heir, was probably the last thing he wanted. He may have been in an equally anomalous position when the feud over the Botetourt lands reopened in the early 1440s, with Maurice Berkeley of Weoley now confronting Joan's heir, the earl of Ormond. Buckingham may have been giving some help to Berkeley, but Ormond was getting support from much the same group of former Warwick men as was also engaged with Buckingham on Burdet's behalf.[38] William Ferrers was also being placed in a somewhat contradictory position. By 1442 he had decided that his best means of self-defence was to join forces with John Beauchamp of Powick and Ralph Boteller of Sudeley, who were rapidly rising to power in south-west Warwickshire.[39] These two drew heavily for their support on the former Warwick affinity, mostly those from the area west of Warwick, and on other gentry from this region. Yet, while the Burdets and their feoffees for Bramcote came from precisely the kind of family that was being attracted to Beauchamp of Powick and Sudeley, Ferrers himself was linked with William Charnels who was trying to take Bramcote away from the Burdets.[40]

In fact, it does not look as if by the end of 1443 anyone amongst the rival nobility had managed to do more than carve out for himself one part of the county, a situation reflected in the balance between the parties on the commission of the peace.[41] Grey's was undoubtedly the largest and best-organised segment, but that was no bar to his being thrown into the Marshalsea in early 1443, possibly on the recommendation of someone at court, until he had found security towards William Betley. Nor did it prevent Thomas Boughton, one of Grey's Warwickshire associates, being summoned to chancery, presumably on the same matter, at the end of the year.[42] Considering the advantages he had started with, Buckingham had really not done terribly well. Not one Warwickshire sheriff of the 1440s can be unequivocally linked with him, and only one of the M.P.s, Thomas Bate, and he may have owed his second election, in 1449, more to the favour of the queen.[43] In 1444 the death of Philip Chetwynd deprived Buckingham of his direct ascendancy over the

38 K.B.9/246/18; C.1/15/207. This was a series of attacks on John Holt, for whom Ferrers, Sudeley and Ormond's son, the future earl of Wiltshire, stood feoffee. The attacks, by Thomas Hore of Solihull, were said to have been instigated by Berkeley, and among Hore's men were several from the Berkeley properties of Weoley and Northfield, so there seems little doubt that one at least of the issues was the Ormonds' right to the Botetourt estates. John Newhay of Nechells in Aston, prominently involved on Berkeley's side, was employed by Buckingham about this time (Nat. Lib. of Wales, Peniarth MS 280 fo.51). But see below, p. 415.

39 Above, pp. 331–2; *Cal. Pat. Rolls 1441–46*, p. 52; and see n.38, above. Ferrers had been associated with Beauchamp of Powick before, both having participated in one of the Chetwynd deeds in 1439 (*Colls. Hist. Staffs.*, o.s., 12, p. 314).

40 For the Beauchamp and Sudeley following, see above, pp. 330–2.

41 *Cal. Pat. Rolls 1441–46*, p. 480.

42 K.B.27/729 Rex rot.10d.; C.244/39/150.

43 *Wedgwood: Register*, pp. 18, 40, 63, 85, 112, 141; *Letters of Margaret of Anjou*, p. 140; *Cal. Pat. Rolls 1441–46*, pp. 409–10.

clients he shared with William Ferrers of Chartley, which may well account both for Ferrers' more adventurous policies from about this time and for Buckingham's difficulties later on with one of these men, Sir Richard Vernon of Staffordshire and Derbyshire.[44] In 1443 Buckingham was unable to prevent Thomas Bate and John Cokayn III, both his feed men, coming to blows over the Cokayn jointure, a fact which was symptomatic of his growing inability to control his affinity.[45] In part, his failure in Warwickshire was due to his acceptance of the office of Captain of Calais in 1442, which resulted in periodic absences, although none of them very prolonged, from late 1442 onwards.[46] But it is fair to ask whether he would have taken the job on had he really believed himself capable of reconstituting Warwick's rule in the midlands.

By 1444 he had had to retreat from the old Warwick heartland of Worcestershire and south-west Warwickshire in the face of the advance of Sudeley and Beauchamp of Powick. Their acquisition of Humphrey Stafford of Grafton I, Buckingham's newly-feed deputy at Calais, must have been especially galling. In 1444 Sudeley and Beauchamp made common cause with Ormond's heir, the future earl of Wiltshire, and once this had happened the defection of Stafford was all too likely, for he was a neighbour of Beauchamp at Grafton and of Ormond at Milton Keynes in Buckinghamshire. His lack of commitment to the management and protection of his lands beyond Worcestershire would have made an alliance with a family which could keep an eye on his valuable Buckinghamshire properties an attractive proposition.[47] Once Ormond and his son had decided to make a foray into Warwickshire politics, they would be reluctant to allow Edward Grey a free hand in the deployment of the Leicestershire connection, in which they themselves participated, to subvent his Warwickshire ambitions. By 1444 Ormond and Ferrers of Chartley, having both come to the conclusion that Sudeley and Beauchamp were the most promising allies, found themselves on the same side. From that moment attacks on Ferrers or his associates were unlikely to do Grey much good in Leicestershire, where Ormond's credit seems to have been at least as good as his.

44 Chetwynd-Stapylton 1892: p. 106; Wright 1983: pp. 69–70.

45 K.B.9/250/45, /258/4.

46 Rawcliffe 1978: pp. 20–1; *G.E.C.*, II, pp. 388–9.

47 K.B.9/246/18 and above, n.38 for the emergence of this group. Ormond owned Great Linford and Newport Pagnell, Bucks., Botetourt estates which were next door to Milton Keynes (B.R.L. 357336). Above, pp. 330–2 for the Sudeley–Beauchamp network and pp. 162, 169–71 for the Staffords of Grafton and their lands. Stafford is not known to have been feed by the Ormond family before 1448–9, but was absorbed into the Sudeley-Beauchamp group at an early stage. There is also evidence that Sudeley was already beginning to take an interest in the north of the county as early as 1443 (below, pp. 491, 601 for his later influence there), but the same evidence shows that even at this date it was quite possible for a man (Hugh Willoughby in this case) to name both Sudeley and Buckingham as overseers of his will: yet another warning against assuming the clear delineation of faction (*Test. Ebor.*, II, p. 134).

Although Grey remained a formidable power in east Warwickshire, at least until the late 1440s, he appears to have reached the limits of expansion about 1444. Perhaps his overfondness for extra-legal methods had brought him also to the edge of Buckingham's patience, for his annuity from the duke was not being paid in the late 1440s.[48] The marriage of Thomas Littleton to Philip Chetwynd's widowed second wife in 1444 can have done little for Buckingham's cause, even though he may have helped to bring it about, for Littleton was already linked to Beauchamp of Powick at this time and was later to become involved with the earl of Wiltshire.[49] As throughout this decade, these changes in the local balance of power were reflected on the commission of the peace. In early 1444 John Rous, one of Beauchamp of Powick's new associates, was appointed, while in 1445 Thomas Boughton, Grey's nominee, came off, to be replaced by Ralph Neville, another Sudeley-Beauchamp man.[50]

By this stage, however, a much more fundamental change was on its way, with the approaching majority of Henry Beauchamp, heir to the Warwick estates. The manoeuvres of the lesser magnates and Henry's treatment by the government give every reason to believe that he was expected to recreate his father's rule at its height. Thus in 1444 he went one better than his father, in getting the stewardship of Tutbury that had earlier been granted for life to Buckingham.[51] This must imply that, once Henry was of age, Buckingham was to be expected to subordinate his interests to Henry's in north Warwickshire and possibly even in Staffordshire. To the neutral observer, as a policy it seems foredoomed; no adult heir of the Staffords could acquiesce in the earl of Warwick having control over Tutbury, especially as the grant was made in heredity – even Richard Beauchamp seems not to have demanded so much in Staffordshire – and the Beauchamp estates were no match for Buckingham's in that county.[52] But there is a straightforward explanation for what seems a wholly misconceived stratagem, and this is that there was no policy at all behind the grant; rather it was just another example of the indiscriminate generosity that was the reward of anyone who could nobble the king or his intimates. Henry was being groomed as a court nobleman, which was why William Mountford, his single most pre-eminent retainer, had become a courtier by

[48] Rawcliffe 1978: pp. 232–3; S.C.R.O. D.641/1/2/272. Boughton came off the commission of the peace in 1445 (below, n.50), signalling perhaps the retreat of Grey's influence, and for more on this, see above, p. 329.

[49] Chetwynd-Stapylton 1892: p. 109; K.B.27/742 Coram Rege rot.83d.; above, pp. 102–3. William Burley, the father of Chetwynd's second wife, was Buckingham's retainer (Rawcliffe 1978: p. 208; Roskell 1983a: p. 351). Above, pp. 330–2 for Littleton's link with Beauchamp. Littletons and Ormonds were later neighbours in Worcestershire (above, p. 100) and may already have been so now.

[50] *Cal. Pat. Rolls 1441–46*, p. 480.

[51] Somerville 1953: p. 540.

[52] Rawcliffe 1978: p. 191.

1444.[53] As such, Henry had as much right to the benefits of the Duchy of Lancaster lands as any other member of the Suffolk circle.

In Warwickshire itself, the coalescence of Beauchamp of Powick, Sudeley, Wiltshire and Ferrers of Chartley made all four available as lesser aides to Henry, just as Joan Beauchamp, Wiltshire's grandmother, and Ferrers' own father had been to Henry's father. Since the former Warwick affinity was now divided to a large extent among these lords, a coalition of this sort was crucial to its reconstitution, but, as long as Beauchamp, Sudeley and Wiltshire were themselves linked to the court, the alliance was a very natural one.[54] That left the problem of how Buckingham and Grey were to be fitted into this new dispensation. It also left the problem of how to conciliate Buckingham for the humiliating loss of Tutbury. To this second question the government's response was entirely typical, in that it combined the inflation of honours with a solution that offended both noblemen. First, Buckingham was elevated to a dukedom in September 1444, but that annoyed Henry, even though he had already been made premier earl, so in April 1445 he too was made a duke. And that in its turn engendered a dispute over precedence between the two, while reopening the precedence issue between Warwick and Norfolk that had been resolved in Norfolk's favour, under less than amicable circumstances, back in the 1420s. The solution can have satisfied no one but Norfolk: at first Henry had to cede precedence to Norfolk in return for being placed above Buckingham, and eventually parliament came up with the somewhat farcical compromise that the two lesser dukes were to alternate precedence over one another.[55]

But in other respects Henry was doing quite nicely; between 1444 and 1446 he was well on his way to reconstituting his father's affinity. For the moment at any rate he was seemingly happy to make common cause with Beauchamp of Powick and Sudeley as the price of the recovery of the core of the affinity, the Worcestershire–south-west Warwickshire connection, where these two were now firmly in control.[56] The role of the court in restoring Henry to the former glories of his house is made very clear if one looks at his connections and those of his major supporters.[57] The Warwickshire officers of 1444–6 show how

53 Note the grants he was receiving (*Cal. Pat. Rolls 1441–46*, pp. 83, 286, 372, 400; *Cal. Fine Rolls 1437–45*, p. 249). He was already present at a meeting which, with the exception of Gloucester, was very much a household affair, in 1442 (*Rot. Parl.*, VI, p. 429) and was named as councillor at a very young age in 1441 (thanks to John Watts). See also Sinclair 1987a: p. 301, on the former Warwick men who moved into court circles at this time.

54 Griffiths 1981: pp. 290, 303; *G.E.C.*, II, p. 47 (but Beauchamp of Powick was evidently not of the innermost circles, at least not at the end of the decade, since he was an acceptable treasurer after the fall of Suffolk (*ibid.*)); above, pp. 323–4 for the Ferrers of Chartley and Warwick links.

55 *G.E.C.*, II, p. 388, XII, ii, p. 383.

56 Br. Lib. Add. Ch. 73,201.

57 See ref. in n.56, above, the full list of his annuitants and officers (E.368/220/108), and refs. showing household connections of Mountford and Erdington, two of Henry's own men (above, n. 31).

rapidly Henry, with the assistance of the royal household, was able to take control of the county. The sheriffs were Robert Harecourt of Leicestershire, son of a Warwick retainer, friend of Mountford and the duke of Suffolk, and Thomas Erdington II, king's knight and former feedman of Richard Beauchamp.[58] Mountford was added to the commission of the peace in April 1444 and Duke Henry himself replaced Buckingham in February 1446, possibly after some resistance on Buckingham's part.[59] The M.P.s of 1445 were William Mountford and Henry's annuitant, Thomas Malory of Newbold Revel.[60]

However, as his father had found, coalitions were likely to be full of tensions. For Henry at this time these were largely related to William Ferrers of Chartley and his following. Ferrers seems to have suffered from the double disability of being rather an ineffective man himself and inheriting an affinity that had too many aggressive, not to say unstable, spirits in it. Foremost among these were the Charnels, still intent on recovering Bramcote from the Burdets. Ferrers had the choice of failing in his lordship by abandoning them or doing his duty as a lord and so confronting all the magnates who stood behind Thomas Burdet II and his feoffees, that is Duke Henry, Beauchamp of Powick, Sudeley and Ormond and his son the future earl of Wiltshire. Unfortunately the Charnels were receiving enthusiastic support from the Archers, who were old friends of both the Charnels and the Ferrers. The Archers too were at odds with Duke Henry's clientage, for their arch-enemy, Thomas Porter, whose purchase of Eastcote and Longdon they still refused to accept, was assuming a prominent position in the new Warwick affinity.[61]

It is also clear that the manoeuvres with the dukedoms had done little to persuade Buckingham and Grey to accept the new regime. One of Henry Beauchamp's first acts as an adult had been to force Grey and William Burgeys to seal recognisances to him, which can only have been to warn them off further

58 *Lists and Indexes*, 9, p. 145; Bod. Lib. Dugdale MS 2, p. 277; *Dep. Keep.'s Rep.*, 41, p. 698; *Cal. Pat. Rolls 1416–22*, p. 362; K.B.27/732 Coram Rege rot.25; E.404/69/176 (cited in Storey 1966: p. 58).

59 *Cal. Pat. Rolls 1441–46*, p. 480. Instructions had been sent out to place Henry on the commission the previous July, just before the issuing of a new commission (C.81/1370/35) but no steps had been taken then, perhaps because of reluctance on Buckingham's part.

60 *Wedgwood: Register*, p. 63; and below, n.66 for evidence on the Malory–Duke Henry link.

61 C.1/14/24, /15/25; above, p. 127. Porter was associated with Hugford and Mountford in 1444, and even with Ferrers of Chartley himself (which suggests the Archers could have expected only rather half-hearted support), and in the same year he negotiated a loan of 100 marks from Coventry for Duke Henry (S.B.T D.R.98/850; K.B.27/731 Coram Rege rot.7d.; *Coventry Leet Book*, p. 207). Another sign of division within the Ferrers following and in the former Ferrers–Warwick nexus is the dispute in 1445 between two of Ferrers' north Warwickshire associates, William Repington and Thomas Stokes, and the fact that of these two Repington was Henry Beauchamp's man (K.B.27/738 Coram Rege rot.60). For Ferrers and Archer, see above, p. 323. Henry had other difficulties in the north Warwickshire/Staffordshire part of the Warwick 'contree': in 1441–2 some sort of feud had broken out with John Sutton of Dudley, which had still to be settled a year later (Br. Lib. Eg. Roll 8530, 8532).

attacks on William Betley, who was after all attorney to the executors of Henry's father.[62] In 1446 it seems that another step was taken to keep Burgeys and his protectors in line, when Viscount Beaumont, Wiltshire and some of the latter's men impleaded Burgeys for a forcible entry in Leicestershire.[63] Nor was Buckingham escaping the attentions of the new powers. In 1444 William Mountford and a group clearly bearing the stamp of the household and the Ormond/Wiltshire connection entered a plea in the King's Bench against William Draycote, Buckingham's constable and steward at Maxstoke.[64] It is not clear whether Buckingham responded to all this pressure: in the same year there was an attack by Maurice Berkeley of Weoley on John Holt of Aston and his feoffees, an imposing group comprising Beauchamp of Powick, Sudeley and Wiltshire, in which Berkeley was abetted by a minor employee and tenant of Buckingham from Maxstoke. Although this might be taken to be a sign that Buckingham had decided it was his turn to take the initiative in this losing battle for local supremacy, Berkeley was in fact indicted soon after by J.P.s of all political persuasions, including Buckingham's feed man, Thomas Bate, and Grey's servant, Thomas Boughton. What seems more likely, and ultimately more damaging to Buckingham, is that he was beginning to lose control of his clients, who were embarking on ventures of their own, regardless of the damage this could do their lord.[65]

When Henry Beauchamp himself began to run into difficulties, it is therefore unsurprising that the root cause was essentially his failure to absorb Buckingham and Grey into the power-structure he was constructing around himself. The trouble was that these two were the obvious focal points in eastern and south-eastern Warwickshire, and if they received no support, indeed positive hindrance, from the leading local magnates, it was far from clear where authority in this area would lie. The situation in some ways mirrored that of the 1420s, when it appears that Richard Beauchamp was confronting his aunt Joan over the issue of who ruled east Warwickshire. But in this case, Henry Beauchamp having apparently made no move to assume responsibility himself, if obstacles were put in the way of Buckingham and Grey, a dangerous vacuum could easily develop in much of east Warwickshire. The results were predict-

[62] C.P.40/756 rot.333; above, n.37.

[63] K.B.27/741 Coram Rege rot.17 – here called William Melton of Groby, an alias of William Burgeys, and further confirmation of his connection with Grey, who had Groby by now (*Cal. Close Rolls 1441–47*, p. 343). In May and October 1447 the same plaintiffs received quitclaims from Burgeys himself and from Thomas Astley, Grey's relative and one of Burgeys' supporters in the Betley case (above, p. 402) – the latter acknowledged by Edward Grey of Groby – of land that had once belonged to Burgeys' father John. This implies first that this was the property that had been the subject of the plea, secondly that Grey still maintained some sort of connection with Burgeys and thirdly that Henry Beauchamp and his courtier friends had found a common enemy in Burgeys and his friends (*Cal. Close Rolls 1441–47*, p. 474, *1447–54*, p. 17).

[64] K.B.27/732 Coram Rege rot.25; app. 3.

[65] K.B.9/246/18; and above, n.38 for details concerning the implications of the attack.

able; a number of serious divisions among the local landowners, and a failure of magnate rule that was ultimately to enable one family, the Verneys of Compton Murdack, to do substantial harm to the nobility who had been unable to control them.

A prolonged period of disorder and confusion began in 1444, with an episode that inflicted quite serious damage on Henry's own affinity. Katherine Peyto, the wife of William, one of the major landowners in eastern Warwickshire, was subjected to a series of attacks on her dower lands in Gloucestershire and Northamptonshire. The perpetrators were, in the case of the Gloucestershire assaults, a number of men from the Worcestershire-Gloucestershire-west Warwickshire region, among them Thomas Burdet, John Rous, Nicholas Gifford of Gloucestershire, Robert Russell of Worcestershire and Thomas Throgmorton, most of them of the Beauchamp of Powick–Sudeley connection, and, in Northamptonshire, Thomas Malory. The first group may still have seen themselves more as Beauchamp of Powick and Sudeley men than as part of the renascent Warwick affinity, but in terms of tenurial power Henry was indubitably their natural lord and some of their closer associates were already feed by Henry or soon to be so. Indeed, Russell claimed as justification for one of the attacks that he was acting as 'feedman to the Abbot of Pershore and so to my lord of Warrewk'. Malory was Henry's annuitant. All in all, there are good grounds for characterising the assailants as Duke Henry's men; unfortunately so was William Peyto, who had been retained for life by Henry's father and subsequently awarded a much larger annuity by Henry himself.[66] He was almost certainly a prisoner in France at the time of the attack – this was no doubt why that particular moment was chosen – and his ransom was to be organised soon after by the old Warwick affinity.[67] Accordingly, on every count Henry was showing himself to be a lord of little worth, both in failing to protect Peyto's lands and family just when they needed it most, and in allowing one part of his affinity to inflict damage to another. To emphasise his insufficiency, Katherine Peyto appealed directly to him, and, getting no response, was forced to take her case to chancery.[68]

But the real troubles of Henry's brief adulthood began with the entry on the scene of the Verneys of Compton Murdack. This was an ambitious family, who, in grasping long before most other landowners that the best path to agricultural

[66] C.1/15/77, 78. For a full discussion of the reasons for dating this petition to 1444, see Carpenter, M. C. 1976: p. 136 n.1. Although there is no evidence for an exact dating of the connection between Henry and Malory, since the time-span of Henry's adulthood is so short and Malory could hardly have been elected M.P. in 1445 (above, n.60) without Henry's support, we may reasonably suppose that the link was established by the time of the petition; Katherine Peyto certainly thought that Henry had the authority to deal with Malory.

[67] *Dugdale*, p. 477, but the date given here needs to be corrected by Pollard 1983: pp. 60–1; *Colls. Hist. Staffs.*, o.s., 11, p. 246; *W.F.F.*, 2625; Jones 1982: pp. 55–6; Pollard 1968: pp. 186–8; above, p. 334.

[68] C.1/15/78.

profits was by conversion to pasture, came face to face with their equally opportunist neighbour, Richard Dalby. The histories of these two families have already in part been told;[69] it remains to put them in their political context. Dalby was a servant of Buckingham,[70] and the Verneys were, nominally at least, under the lordship of Duke Henry, so the ingredients for a confrontation were there already. Unfortunately for Dalby, it occurred just when the divisions in eastern and south-eastern Warwickshire released the Verneys from the control of anyone at all. The origins of the quarrel lay in the fact that there was too little spare land here for both families to be able to build up the extended pastures required for large flocks.[71] In 1444 and 1445 Dalby was able to obtain two leases; the Verneys were probably happy about neither and the second, the lease of Cheping Kington, which came indirectly from Dalby's other lord the duke of Norfolk, was disputed by the Verneys later on and almost certainly unwelcome now.[72] The final straw, it seems, was the sale in February 1445 of part of the lands of Richard Verney's cousin, William Verney of Great Wolford. This took place while William was in Buckingham's wardship and could legitimately be seen by the Compton Murdack branch as unprincipled exploitation of a position of trust to benefit one of Buckingham's servants. They could also reasonably claim that, in the event of their cousins disposing of any property, especially in circumstances in which estates were in short supply, they should have had first refusal.[73] Up until then, and even immediately after, Dalbys and Verneys seem to have been on reasonably amicable terms, or at least to have had friends in common.[74]

The breach came in about May 1445, when Dalby was accused of abducting the daughter of a tenant of John Withynale of Northamptonshire from the latter's house. Dalby's later suit of conspiracy against his accusers shows that the prime movers in the case were the Verneys of Compton Murdack. Dalby's fellow-defendants came mostly from south-east Warwickshire, with two from Northamptonshire and a couple of others from further afield. Amongst the local men accused with him were William Derset, whose brother Thomas had been

69 Above, pp. 127–30, 184–5.

70 Above, pp. 124, 127.

71 Above, pp. 129–30.

72 *V.C.H.*, V, p. 177; C.1/28/482; K.B.27/818 Coram Rege rot.117. Cheping Kington, a Mowbray manor, was at this time in the hands of Margaret, widow of Sir John Grey, heir by his first marriage of Reginald Grey of Ruthin; she was sister of the second duke of Norfolk who had died in 1432; Grey's first wife had been Constance, widow of the Earl Marshal (Archer 1984a: pp. 143, 181–2; *G.E.C.*, IX, p. 605, VI, p. 159).

73 *Cal. Close Rolls 1441–47*, p. 296; S.C.R.O. D.641/1/2/269–72.

74 Although Dalby was nothing like as well-connected as his father, he had links with the Greys of Ruthin, which brought him into contact with William Lucy, Duke Henry's annuitant, the Greys' relative and Richard Verney's friend (*Cal. Close Rolls 1435–41*, p. 445: Dalby and Lucy acting with Sir John Cressy, a close connection of the Greys (*Wedgwood: Biographies*, p. 235); above, p. 107 for Lucy and the Greys; S.B.T D.R.98/113, 118, 479 for Lucy and the Verneys).

on the jury bribed by Grey in the Betley case, and William Weldon, Buckingham's auditor, who had stood bail for some of Betley's opponents in company with Edward Grey himself.[75] On the face of it, this was then a fairly straightforward case of Warwick forcing a confrontation with Buckingham and Grey over the rule of south-east Warwickshire by unleashing the fury of the Verneys against Richard Dalby and his associates from the Grey and Buckingham circles. Since Dalby had been linked with the Greys of Ruthin not long before, and since it was Buckingham who leapt to his defence, and William Verney, Buckingham's erstwhile ward, who bailed him from the Fleet in June 1445, there is much force in this interpretation.[76] However, what the affair also revealed was that all was far from well within Grey's own following in east Warwickshire. One of Dalby's fellow-defendants, John Scarburgh of Welford, Northamptonshire, also entered a plea for false indictment in this case, the defendant being one Thomas Sampson. Now Sampson, far from being a tool of the earl of Warwick, had, as under-sheriff, actually taken a considerable part in the discomfiture of William Betley on Grey's behalf.[77] Furthermore, he was one of that group of men, all of them with some sort of affiliation to Grey, who were being feed by Monks Kirby Priory. Another of the priory's feed men was Thomas Malory of Newbold Revel, who, while maintaining some sort of link with Grey, was also a none-too-reliable annuitant of Duke Henry. Moreover, in his attack on the Peyto lands in Northamptonshire, he had assaulted the bailiff, who was another of Dalby's co-defendants.[78]

If all this seems to show that Grey's affinity in Warwickshire was beginning to fall apart, there are signs that the disunity was spreading into Leicestershire and Northamptonshire. Amongst the men impleaded by Dalby for conspiracy was Thomas Mulso of Northamptonshire.[79] Both Withynale and John Waldgrave, the tenant whose daughter was allegedly abducted, were connected with Thomas and with other members of the Mulso family. The whole affair may indeed have originated in Mulso protecting Withynale, getting the Verneys to

75 K.B.9/94/1/9; K.B.27/737 Coram Rege rot.78d., /739 Coram Rege rot.60, /742 Coram Rege rot. 102, /741 Rex rot.28, /744 Coram Rege rot.13d.; above, pp. 402–3. There is confusion in the accusations, some alleging that the abduction took place at Brookhampton, Dalby's residence, the K.B. indictment naming Northamptonshire as the scene of the crime.

76 In July 1445 Dalby was issued with a royal protection because he was going overseas in Buckingham's retinue (*Dep. Keep.'s Rep.*, 48, p. 365); C.244/45/78; K.B.27/742 Coram Rege rot.88; for Dalby and the Greys, above, n.74.

77 K.B.27/770 Coram Rege rot.96d. Scarburgh and Sampson were in dispute over land in Northamptonshire, which doubtless accounts for their being on opposite sides in this case (K.B.27/774 Coram Rege rot.86). Scarburgh (or a predecessor of the same name) had himself been directly connected with Reginald Grey of Ruthin much earlier in the century and was to be linked with the Greys or their associates in the 1450s (Westminster Abbey Mun. 14633; *Test. Vetust.*, p. 279; *H.M.C. Hastings*, I, p. 143). For the Betley case, see above, p. 402.

78 For Grey and Monks Kirby, and Grey and Malory, see above, pp. 325, 328. John Derset of Sibertoft was the man assaulted by Malory (C.1/15/78).

79 K.B.27/742 Coram Rege rot.102, /744 Coram Rege rot.13d.

help him and in so doing giving them an opportunity to embarrass Richard Dalby.[80] But the Mulsos had a history which linked them with Buckingham, with Buckingham's auditor William Weldon, who had been a leading figure on the side linked with Grey in the Betley and the Dalby cases, with Grey himself, and with Grey's relatives, the Greys of Ruthin.[81] Without more knowledge of Northamptonshire and Leicestershire politics (both counties would amply repay close scrutiny) it is impossible to speculate further on what exactly was going on here, but it is evident that, whatever it was, it was not a display of unity on the part of the Buckingham–Grey nexus. The root cause of the disarray may have been a general uncertainty about the capacity of these two lords to act effectively in east Warwickshire and its neighbouring counties once Henry Beauchamp had arrived on the scene.

But the disunity now overtaking east Warwickshire was not confined to the followers of Grey and Buckingham; Henry Beauchamp, his affinity in this part of the world already disturbed by the outbreak of the feud between Malory and the Peytos, was having his own troubles with the Verneys. Although he almost certainly protected them against any retaliation by Dalby, which, as their lord, he was bound to do, there must be serious doubts about his role in the initiation of the dispute.[82] By the time the Verneys launched themselves at Richard Dalby they were already thoroughly embroiled with their own master over arrears of pay, tenure of lands and offices granted them by Henry's father and their alleged promise to grant their manor of Kingston to the collegiate church of St. Mary's Warwick that was to be the grand memorial to Richard Beauchamp.[83] Since one of the disputed estates, in Tamworth and Sutton Coldfield, had been the subject of a Verney family settlement witnessed by leading clients of Duke Henry in late 1444,[84] we may suppose that the breach did not occur until later, probably in early 1445. We may also assume that it was

80 *Cal. Close Rolls 1429–35*, p. 109, *1441–47*, p. 437.

81 *Cal. Close Rolls 1429–35*, p. 109, *1435–41*, p. 475, *1441–47*, p. 437 (in which one of Thomas Mulso's feoffees is Thomas Waweton, who figured prominently on the Grey side in the Bedford riot of 1437 (Maddern 1985: pp. 212–40; see also above, p. 384 n.152)); *Colls. Hist. Staffs.*, o.s., 17, p. 143; Cov. and Lichf. Dioc., Reg. Heyworth fo.28. A further complication is that in 1448 Verney himself was appointed supervisor of Cheping Kington manor by the widow of John Grey of Ruthin, Edward of Groby's step-brother, and relative by marriage of Norfolk twice over, even though her husband had presumably authorised the original lease to Dalby (S.B.T D.R.31 fo.317, D.R.98/642a; above, n.72).

82 Both Dalby's suit against the Verneys and Mulso, and Buckingham's against Richard Verney and Withynale had to wait until immediately after Henry's death, to come to court (K.B.27/742 Coram Rege roti.88, 102).

83 S.B.T D.R.98/477, 722. Beauchamp records suggest the dispute had been building up over some years (Warwick Castle MS 489 *sub* respites; W.C.R.O. C.R.895/8/20). For the agreement that the Verneys appear to have broken, see above, p. 126. Curiously, John Lichfield, the Verneys' tenant at Kingston, whom Henry had evicted, was another of the bribed jury in the Betley case (above, p. 403). The implications of this are anyone's guess.

84 S.B.T. D.R.98/850.

Henry who decided to have the showdown with the Verneys rather than vice versa; the Verneys would have had little to gain by deliberately precipitating a breach with the political connection which was at that moment validating their deeds. Perhaps we can go further and suggest that the Verneys, knowing that Henry was eager to bring things to a head with them, deliberately chose this juncture to go after Dalby in the hope that Henry would be forced by his obligations as lord to renounce his own process against them. Indeed, an award between Henry and his troublesome servants was due at midsummer 1445, almost precisely the moment when Verney's pursuit of Dalby began. Henry's council failed to make the award, examplifying that mixture of rashness and indecision that seems so characteristic of his brief adult career, and in 1446, shortly before his death, he was suing Richard Verney and his brother, the dean of Lichfield, for libel.[85] One would dearly like to know what they said.

It is indicative of the malfunctioning that had overtaken all the Warwickshire affinities in the mid-1440s that between 1444 and 1446 there were numerous disputes among Warwickshire landowners, several of them, like the Malory–Peyto and Dalby–Verney cases, revealing serious dissensions within the affinities themselves.[86] Henry himself seems to have been quarrelling with at least one other prominent retainer beside the Verneys, for he failed to pay Thomas Erdington the £10 annuity granted him by Earl Richard. As Erdington was also a royal retainer this was not the most intelligent thing to do, but perhaps Erdington was being made to pay for the fact that he was a friend of the Verneys.[87] The root of the whole problem was that Henry Beauchamp had been given responsibilities he was too young and too inexperienced to handle. These brought him into confrontation with the spheres of interest that had been established by others while he was still a minor, required him to ignore new gentry loyalties that had developed in the same period, and were backed up by a royal court that was now beginning to attract considerable resentment.[88] Since Henry had the formidable weight of the court and at least part of his father's old following behind him, it was very difficult for anyone else to acquire the authority to ensure the stability that Henry himself was unable to provide.

It was in fact Henry's premature death in June 1446 that made it possible for a more workable set of arrangements to be brought about. First the question of succession to an estate settled in tail male on the extinction of the male line had

85 S.B.T. D.R.98/477; K.B.27/740 Coram Rege rot.43d. For the Verney genealogy, above, p. 130. The date of 1445 for the award deduced from the date when the dispute seems to have begun and that of Henry's death, 11 June 1446 (*G.E.C.*, XII, ii, p. 384).

86 K.B.27/738 Coram Rege roti.34d., 43d., 66d., /742 Coram Rege roti.20d., 83d., 88, 88d., besides those already mentioned.

87 B.R.L. 347934–7; S.B.T. D.R.98/849–50.

88 Griffiths 1981: pp. 301–22.

to be resolved. At this point the deeper motive behind John Beauchamp's territorial and political penetration into Warwickshire becomes apparent. He thought he had a claim as heir male to the Warwick estates and earldom, and immediately after Henry's death he persuaded Thomas Hugford, the most important of all the Warwick estate officials, to present it.[89] But despite his own influence with the court, he was up against mightier powers there. The wardship and marriage of Henry's infant heiress Anne were given to Queen Margaret, who sold them to Suffolk soon after, and the farm of her lands, granted initially to Beauchamp of Powick and Sudeley, had eventually to be shared with Suffolk and the girl's maternal grandfather, Richard Neville, earl of Salisbury. Neville's daughter had married Henry, while his son and heir had married Henry's sister, who would become heir to Henry's daughter should she die childless.[90] It was doubtless the power of the Neville clan and of its court connections that protected the succession of Henry's daughter; if the estates were held not to have been settled in tail male, Salisbury stood to be grandfather, or, better still, if Anne were to die, father-in-law to the Warwick heiress. The following December, a council meeting at which Salisbury, Sudeley and Suffolk were present elected to set Beauchamp of Powick's claim aside.[91]

Once the succession question had been settled and a long minority was in prospect, the way was open for a division of the political spoils. Now more than ever the Warwick affinity was led from court.[92] This situation did no harm at all to the prospects of Beauchamp and Sudeley, both of them feoffees of the Duchy of Lancaster lands, in company with other courtier notables such as Beaumont, William Tresham and John Norreys.[93] The Beauchamp–Sudeley leadership of the former core of the Warwick domain in south-west Warwickshire and Worcestershire remained as firm as it had been since about 1444 and began to spread across the Avon into the area south of Warwick that Richard Beauchamp had also dominated. It may well have been the Verneys of Compton Murdack who led their neighbours under this new lordship, for they

[89] Warwick Castle MS FP/1; below, pp. 439–46 for a full explication of the descent of the Beauchamp lands.

[90] *Cal. Pat. Rolls 1441–46*, p. 436, *1446–52*, p. 1. Suffolk was still acting as guardian in 1448 (*1446–52*, p. 202). For the relationship with the Nevilles, *G.E.C.*, XII, ii, pp. 384–5; for the Nevilles and the court, see above, n.1. Leland (*Collectanea*, I, ii, p. 622) says that the Lords Beauchamp [of Powick?] and of St. Amand were the heirs male, although the latter seems not to have made a claim.

[91] C.81/1546/14; below, pp. 439–40. I owe this reference to Dr G. L. Harriss.

[92] See n.90 above and e.g. James Fenys' appointment to the Beauchamp shrievalty of Worcestershire (*Lists and Indexes*, 9, p. 158).

[93] Somerville 1953: p. 210. Significantly for Warwickshire, the jointure of Queen Margaret included Kenilworth and the Honors of Tutbury and Leicester (Somerville 1953: pp. 208, 340).

were always of an independent caste of mind.[94] The alliance in Warwickshire between Sudeley and Beauchamp of Powick and the Ormond family was consolidated by Sudeley's increasingly close identification with the court, where Beauchamp was also well-favoured and Ormond and his son, the future earl of Wiltshire, were becoming major powers.[95] This coalition of interests can be seen at work in 1447, when Maurice Berkeley of Weoley was punished for his previous attacks on Ormond and his friends by a posse of gentry coming predominantly from the area of Sudeley and Beauchamp influence on the Warwickshire-Worcestershire border, amongst them associates of both Ormond and Wiltshire.[96]

The strength of this faction began to squeeze Buckingham out of southern Warwickshire, as he had already been forced to retreat from the west Warwickshire-Worcestershire region. And even in north Warwickshire, as long as William Mountford's considerable local authority was reinforced by backing from the court, Buckingham was becoming rather redundant.[97] It seems that for the moment he was content to be so. If, during the earlier 1440s, he had been prepared to risk a confrontation with Henry Beauchamp and his allies, by 1447 he appears to have been thoroughly reconciled to the Sudeley–Beauchamp–Wiltshire coalition and to the principal members of Henry VI's household.[98] Duke Henry's death gave him a much freer hand in Staffordshire, which was where his real concerns in the midlands lay, and if Tutbury was now in the hands of the queen, at least that kept it away from a rival magnate. In the face of the growing dissension among the Duchy retinue, Buckingham was fully occupied in keeping order in the north midlands.[99]

The retreat of Buckingham's ally Edward Grey from east Warwickshire was also accomplished peaceably. His succession in 1445 to the Ferrers of Groby land and title may have persuaded him that it was in his best interests to concentrate his energies on Leicestershire, at least until he was well enough established as the heir of Groby to launch another thrust into east Warwickshire. We have seen already how his client Thomas Boughton was removed

94 Above, p. 330. The Verneys' relationship with the Greys of Ruthin, which becomes apparent at this juncture (above, nn.74, 81), may have been another effort to cut the ground from under Dalby's feet, since it linked them with the two noble families who seem still to have been on Dalby's side i.e. Grey and Mowbray.

95 Griffiths 1981: pp. 303, 337; *G.E.C.*, XII, ii, p. 734; and e.g. *H.M.C. Hastings*, I, pp. 1–2; K.B.27/756 Writs of Attorney d. It was apparently about this time that Humphrey Stafford of Grafton I moved firmly into the Wiltshire camp (*Cal. Fine Rolls 1445–52*, p. 109; Br. Lib. Add. Roll 74,168).

96 K.B.27/746 Coram Rege rot.118d.

97 Edmund Mountford's tenure of the two royal manors in north-west Warwickshire, Solihull and Sheldon, would have made the family a formidable force in north Warwickshire, had they not been lost almost instantly to James Fenys Lord Say (*Cal. Pat. Rolls 1441–46*, pp. 244, 296).

98 E.g. *Cal. Pat. Rolls 1446–52*, p. 78; *Cal. Close Rolls 1447–54*, p. 51.

99 Wright 1983: pp. 84–5, 68–75, 125–7; Storey 1966: pp. 150–3; *H.M.C. Rutland*, I, pp. 1–2; Somerville 1953: pp. 208, 539–40.

from the Warwickshire commission of the peace in 1444; Grey himself came off in March 1449, but not before his position in Leicestershire had been recognised by appointment to the commission there in June 1448.[100] As a Leicestershire magnate who was just beginning to settle into a large new estate, Grey would have been ill-advised to offend Ormond, another Leicestershire nobleman, by refusing to accept the rule of Ormond and his associates in Warwickshire.

How the vacuum in east Warwickshire left by Grey's departure was filled has to some extent already been discussed.[101] The leading figures seem now to have come from Northamptonshire rather than Leicestershire, and behind them was some forceful backing from the court and the Duchy of Lancaster, itself a substantial landowner in Northamptonshire. Foremost among them were John Talbot Lord Lisle, Shrewsbury's eldest son by his second marriage (Lisle's mother being one of Richard Beauchamp's heiresses from the Berkeley marriage), William Lord Lovell, William Catesby, the Treshams of Northamptonshire and William Peyto, who at the time of his capture in France had been in the service of Lisle's father. The networks of east Warwickshire reformed around this group, arguably perhaps more comprehensively than in the days of Grey's hegemony. Participating in them was Thomas Boughton who had played such a large part in Grey's Warwickshire affairs.[102] In view of the fact that William Tresham was shortly to be murdered while riding amongst the people of Lord Grey de Ruthin, it may well be that the move into Warwickshire was the last step in a progress that had given much of Northamptonshire to this group at the expense of the Greys. Tresham, whose control of the Duchy offices in Northamptonshire would have made an excellent basis for such a takeover, would have been an obvious target for assassination.[103]

An interesting indication of the possible strength of this connection comes from the muster rolls of 1443 and 1449 of Edmund duke of Somerset, who had married another of the daughters of the Berkeley marriage, and was to be much involved with the Talbots in the years to come; already in 1445 William Peyto was serving Somerset as well as Shrewsbury in France.[104] Among Somerset's

[100] For ref. to his succession to Groby, see above, n.3; *Cal. Pat. Rolls 1446–52*, pp. 590, 596.

[101] Above, p. 329.

[102] Griffiths 1981: pp. 258, 341, 498 on the growing influence of Margaret and her entourage in the Duchy midlands and on some of the personnel of this deed; *Cat. Anc. Deeds*, IV, A10387; Kingsford 1913: pp. 364–5. Note that Thomas Sydenhale, one of the jury in the Betley case, (above, p. 403), was Catesby's estate official, which would have helped give Catesby an entrée to Grey's erstwhile supporters (S.C.6/1041/19, /1042/1, 2, 34); see also above, p. 408; below, p. 439; Pollard 1968: pp. 224–5.

[103] Jack 1961: pp. 32–3; Stevenson, *Wars of the English*, II, ii, p. 769; Somerville 1953: p. 586; Avrutick 1967: pp. 208–9.

[104] Griffiths 1981: pp. 572–3 and ch. 24; *Dugdale*, p. 477; Jones 1982: pp. 52, 55–6, 258–9; Pollard 1983: p. 80 for Peyto, and p. 63 for the association of Shrewsbury and Somerset; E.101/54/11.

war retinue are men drawn from an impressive range of midland connections, including those of Buckingham, the Ferrers of Chartley, the household and Richard Beauchamp. Also listed is William Burgeys, which might well support the hypothesis that Grey of Groby, as well as his Grey of Ruthin relatives, was suffering from the advance along the east Warwickshire border of this group of men linked to the Duchy and the court.[105] While it has frequently and rightly been pointed out that wartime and peacetime retinues rarely overlapped, a nobleman like Somerset was likely to create an exception. Since his landed power in no way matched his title, and he was heavily dependent on the rewards he could garner from the court both for his own income and for the means of recruiting a following, fruitful relationships could be forged through war service. Peyto's service was certainly to continue beyond this French campaign. Furthermore, the Beauforts and the Talbots did have some lands in Warwickshire (including east Warwickshire), Leicestershire and Oxfordshire to buttress an extension of their influence from the Duchy areas of Leicestershire and Northamptonshire. By early 1449, when Anne Beauchamp was dead, they may have been initiating more purposeful designs in this part of the midlands, in the expectation of obtaining part of the Beauchamp inheritance.[106]

Instability in Warwickshire towards the end of the 1440s came less from opposition to the new *status quo* than from tensions within it, and there was now neither a Richard Beauchamp nor authoritative royal leadership to resolve them. There were first the families of the Ferrers of Chartley affinity that were unable to accommodate themselves to a power structure in which Ferrers seems to have been incapable of looking after their interests. The Ferrers connection undoubtedly remained a force in north Warwickshire and Staffordshire right up to the end of the decade, and it was not just the party of the politically dispossessed, for it included men like Thomas Erdington, Richard Vernon and John Norreys, none of them negligible figures and all of them linked to the royal household.[107] However, one has the sense that the affinity had developed

[105] E.101/54/5, 11; Jones 1982: p. 169 n.2.

[106] Carpenter 1980a: pp. 519–20 and literature cited there; Astill 1977: pp. 249–52; Pollard 1983: pp. 89, 99–101; Cooper 1983b: p. 96 n.48; Gray 1934: p. 615; Jones 1981: p. 81, 1982: p. 169 n.2; *Dep. Keep.'s Rep.*, 48, pp. 390, 396; K.B.27/762 Rex rot.35; *I.P.M.* 3 Hen.VI/18, 32 Hen.VI/29, 38/9 Hen.VI/58; *G.E.C.*, XII, ii, p. 381; *V.C.H.*, VI, pp. 259–60; Pollard 1983: p. 76 for Shrewsbury's limited connection in England, the result of absence on war service, which would have made him also reliant on his war retinue; for the Warwick partition, below, p. 442; for later developments, below, pp. 461–2. Cherry 1981b: p. 126 shows John earl of Somerset possibly using men recruited for service in France (including Philip Chetwynd) in the Courteney-Bonville feud. Cf. the Mowbray retinue (Archer 1984a: pp. 317–30).

[107] E.g. *Cal. Pat. Rolls 1446–52*, pp. 277–8; S.B.T. D.R.37 Box 42/2503; Bod. Lib. Dugdale MS 13, p. 301; Virgoe ed., 'Ancient Indictments Referring to Kent', pp. 215, 224–5; Griffiths 1981: pp. 612, 641–2; Kingsford 1913: pp. 364–5; above, pp. 323–4. Note also that in 1448–9 the Ferrers affinity supplied both the sheriff and the escheator in Staffordshire, in Thomas Ferrers of Tamworth and John Archer (*Lists and Indexes*, 9, p. 127; *List of Escheators*, p. 153).

into a grouping that existed despite rather than because of its noble leadership. Consequently the Ferrers men who did have reasons to be discontented were likely to find themselves without effective support from their lord.

Foremost among these were the Archers. They had seen Thomas Porter, the man who had deprived them of part of their lands, rise to a prominent position in Henry Beauchamp's affinity. In the process he had forged an alliance with William Mountford that gave him ready access to powerful protection in Warwickshire and the government, should the Archers try to recover their property.[108] Then there were the Charnels, whose claim to the Burdet manor of Bramcote had been stifled time and again by Thomas Burdet's patrons, now the unrivalled powers within the county, and by William Ferrers' reluctance to offend any of these. In the late 1440s Ferrers was taking much the same line with these clients as before, offering some help, but apparently unable or unwilling to risk a confrontation with the major powers in the county, his nominal allies.[109] In 1448 he and most of his principal associates did act as feoffees for Richard Archer when the latter recovered Eastcote and Longdon from the Porters, probably taking it by force while Porter was dying or as soon as he was dead, and Archer must have hoped that feoffees of this stature would be sufficient to warn off Baldwin, the Porter heir. But his faith would have been shaken by the fact that Ferrers and part of the Ferrers affinity were acting for Porter's widow in a deed of the following year.[110] Nor was Ferrers able to prevent the manoeuvre of the same year by which official procedures were exploited to preserve the Porter lands for Baldwin, the heir. On 24 May 1449, in response to chancery petitions from both sides, a commission was issued to investigate the entry on Thomas Porter's lands at Eastcote and Longdon. The proceedings, which survive among the Archer papers, make it clear that the blatant fraudulence of the original sale was about to be exposed by Archer's neighbours, among them, it seems, the very people who had witnessed it.[111] In no time at all the lands were seized by the crown on the grounds that Thomas Porter had failed to render his account as escheator in 1446–7. It was however only the properties at issue that were taken, not the rest of Baldwin's inheritance, and they were granted out to a group whose identity and subsequent dealings with Baldwin Porter allow for no doubts but that this was a

[108] Above, p. 414 and n.61.

[109] For an earlier example of vacillation, see above, n.61. Ferrers' continuing link with the major powers can be seen in e.g. Jeayes ed. *Berkeley Charters*, pp. 299–300; *Cal. Pat. Rolls 1446–52*, p. 246; Rawcliffe 1984: p. 54; C.139/138/22.

[110] Archer certainly had the lands by July 1448 (feoffment, ref. in n.107, above). The assumption of force comes from his indictment for attacks on Baldwin Porter at Eastcote and Longdon in January 1448; Thomas Porter died the following May (K.B.9/285/68; C.139/133/14); Bod. Lib. Dugdale MS 13, p. 301; Cov. and Lichf. Dioc., Reg. Booth fos. 61–3v.

[111] C.1/16/432, /17/40; *Cal. Pat. Rolls 1446–52*, p. 270; S.B.T. D.R.37 Boxes 76, 83.

ploy to keep them safe from Richard Archer.[112] Two other disputes of 1448–9, and possibly a third, were connected with the Porter–Archer affair, which was clearly having a seriously divisive effect on north and west Warwickshire.[113]

These were Ferrers' declining years. He seems at all times to have lacked his father's force of character and during the later 1440s he was rather losing control of his following.[114] His ineffectiveness as a leader may well account for the presence among his associates in these years of some of the other losers of north Warwickshire; perhaps he was the only local magnate sufficiently desperate to be prepared to take on the more hopeless cases. 'Loser' is too strong a word for Thomas Ferrers of Tamworth, but he had been an absentee for a long time and was starting from scratch in Warwickshire at a time when his well-established position in Leicestershire was being weakened by disagreements with Edward Grey over the Ferrers of Groby inheritance, to which Thomas was heir male and Edward heir general.[115] Thomas Ferrers was certainly not without friends, but he did lack friends in Warwickshire. His exposed position was demonstrated in September 1449 when two of Buckingham's leading servants from Staffordshire, with a mob of allegedly over eighty men, set upon his son and heir, Thomas II, at Coleshill and then moved on to Tamworth itself where they attempted to force their way into the castle to get at Thomas senior. The cause of this assault is unknown, but it appears to have been part of a continuing feud between Buckingham and the Ferrers of Tamworth, perhaps occasioned by no more than Buckingham's determination to let them know that he would brook no rival powers on the north

112 *Cal. Fine Rolls 1445–52*, p. 109. The grantees were William Mountford, Wiltshire, Humphrey Stafford of Grafton I and Littleton i.e. all four connected with the Warwick-court interest now increasingly led by Beauchamp, Sudeley and Ormond, while Littleton was also Baldwin Porter's brother-in-law (*Dugdale*, p. 983). One of the keepers' mainpernors was Richard Broun of Knowle, who played an increasingly active role in the dispute on the Porter side (below, n.113 and pp. 451–2). See also the joint plea of 1450 by three of the grantees and Baldwin Porter (K.B.27/756 Coram Rege rot.4).

113 Archer v. Broun (K.B.27/750 Coram Rege rot.65d.); Birches and Henry Porter v. Broun (K.B.27/749 Coram Rege rot.50d.); although this may possibly be related to a plea on defaulting feoffees (C.1/13/219), in which case it is probably not connected with the Porter–Archer affair; Draper v. Archer (K.B.27/754 Coram Rege rot.107d.).

114 Although able to arbitrate between Vernon and Gresley in Staffordshire in 1447, he himself had to submit to arbitration in a dispute with Richard Vernon in 1449–50 (*H.M.C. Rutland*, IV, p. 29; Wm. Salt Lib. Wm. Salt Orig. Coll. 45/5/57).

115 For his Leicestershire connections and interests, see *H.M.C. Hastings*, I, pp. 18, 73; *Cal. Close Rolls 1441–47*, p. 261; Bod. Lib. Dugdale MS 17, p. 66; above, pp. 160, 326–7. For his Warwickshire connections, see S.B.T. D.R.37 Box 42/2503: the Thomas Ferrers on this document *could* be a member of the Chartley family, but this is improbable because of the known Archer connection in 1448 of the Tamworth man (S.B.T D.R.10/721) and because of the Tamworth family's connections with the Ferrers of Chartley group, including the Archers, later on (below, pp. 451–4). For the Ferrers of Tamworth v. Grey, see *Cal. Close Rolls 1441–47*, p. 313; Leics.R.O. DE 2242/3/31757(2), /30304(2), /31767(1), /40056; and for the problems with the Essex lands, see above, pp. 105, 172–3, 175; below, p. 469.

Warwickshire/Staffordshire border. Whatever the cause, the episode must have been humiliating in the extreme.[116]

Another of William Ferrers' less happy associates of this time was Baldwin Mountford, eldest son of William, who had by now taken the place of his father in the north Warwickshire-Staffordshire network. William, on his part, had aligned himself with the royal household and with local nobility with strong household connections, like Wiltshire and Beauchamp of Powick.[117] That he intended to disinherit Baldwin in favour of Edmund, eldest son of his second marriage, whom he had been pushing into a privileged position at court, must have been known by now. It was surely the main reason for the policy he had been pursuing since 1439 of exploiting his custody of the Warwick lands to get himself and Edmund under the protection of the court.[118] That left William Ferrers of Chartley as the ineffective guardian of the interests of Baldwin Mountford, another north Warwickshire landowner in difficulties.

That several of William Ferrers' connections – such people as Robert Harecourt of Oxfordshire, John Norreys and Thomas Erdington[119] – were themselves in the royal household reveals the other major source of division in Warwickshire in the late 1440s, namely dissension among the courtiers themselves. It is a mistake to see this group as a coherent entity with a single purpose. After all they too were an affinity, with plenty of contradictory allegiances among them and a supremely ineffectual leader. It is highly probable that the mounting hysteria of politics in these years accentuated any disagreements. The fact that Erdington, Vernon and Norreys maintained their links with William Ferrers while other Ferrers clients were at odds with household men like William and Edmund Mountford implies a measure of disunity. Norreys indeed, who was specifically singled out as an obnoxious courtier in a lampoon of the late 1440s, was very intimately concerned with Ferrers' affairs at the time.[120]

It is the disunity at the apex of rule that seems to account for the single most shocking outbreak of violence in Warwickshire in the 1440s, the murderous affray between the Staffords of Grafton and the Harecourts at Coventry at the time of the Corpus Christi fair in late May 1448. The best description is in the Paston letters:

> on Corpus Christi Even last passed, be twene viij. and ix. of the clok at a[fternon], Syr Umfrey Stafford had browth my mayster Syr James of Urmond [i.e. Wiltshire] towa[r]d hys yn . . . [and] reterned from hym toward hys yn, he met

116 *Colls. Hist. Staffs.*, n.s., 3, pp. 195, 201; S.C.8/111/5528. Thomas Ferrers did serve as Staffordshire sheriff 1447–9, but he only served the second term because John Hampton, the chosen sheriff, managed to evade the office (Rowney 1981: p. 47).

117 Above, pp. 412, 415; S.B.T. D.R.37 Box 42/2503.

118 Above, pp. 333–4, 408, 409; below, p. 448.

119 For refs. for the Ferrers connection, see above, p. 324 n.163; for Harecourt, see below, p. 428.

120 *Excerpta Historica*, ed. Bentley, p. 162; above, n.107.

> with Syr Robert Harcourt comyng from hys moder towards hys yn, and pass[ed Syr] Umfrey; and Richard, hys son, came somewhat be hynd, and when they met to gyder, they fell in handes togyder, and [Sir Robert] smot hym a grette st[r]oke on the hed with hys sord, and Richard with hys dagger hastely went toward hym. And as he stombled, on of Harcourts men smot hym in the bak with a knyfe; men wotte not ho hyt was reddely. Hys fader hard noys, and rode toward hem, and hys men ronne befor hym thyder ward; and in the goyng downe of hys hors, on, he wotte not ho, be hynd hym smot hym on the hede with a nege tole . . . that he fell downe; and hys son fell downe be fore hym as good as dede. And all thys was don, as men sey, in a Pater Noster wyle. And forth with Syr Umfrey Stafford men foloed after, and slew ij men of Harcowrttus . . . and mo ben hurt; sum ben gonne, and sum be in pryson in the jayll at Coventre.

Besides Harecourt's two men, Richard Stafford, Humphrey I's younger son, had been killed and Humphrey himself wounded. The original cause of the dispute is not known, although the writer notes that it was 'of a nold debate that was be twene heme for takyng of a dystres, as hyt is told'.[121] The important point is that, even though he had seen little favour in recent years, Robert Harecourt had been on intimate terms with the court and that the Staffords of Grafton were themselves well connected with court circles at this time, through their ties with the Botellers of Ormond, Sudeley and Beauchamp of Powick. The latter's son and heir had indeed been with the Staffords at the time of the assault.[122] A conflict between two major midlands families with friends in common within the royal household had been allowed to fester without resolution until it ended in open riot and murder. That in itself is sufficient condemnation of a government that by 1449 had lost all sense of where it was going.[123]

II

Taken as a whole, the decade from 1439 to 1449 shows the difficulties of maintaining order in the localities when there was a failure of direction from the centre. The crisis in the midlands was particularly acute for two reasons: first, because the region had become accustomed in the first two decades of the

[121] *Paston Letters*, ed. Gairdner, II, pp. 89–90; K.B.9/259/70; *Colls. Hist. Staffs.*, n.s., 3, p. 186 (a rather different version, implying malice aforethought: one of the problems considered in app. 4). It is possible that the John Norwood, probably the man who features elsewhere in the Paston correspondence, who sent this account to Viscount Beaumont, was the Coventry man (see above, p. 402 n.5), but there is no evidence to substantiate the connection.

[122] E.404/69/176, cited in Storey 1966: p. 58; *Cal. Fine Rolls 1445–52*, p. 109. For Buckingham's direct links with the court in the late 1440s, see *Cal. Pat. Rolls 1446–52*, pp. 78, 180–1; Griffiths 1981: pp. 358–9; *Feodera*, v, i, p. 178; *Rot. Parl.*, v, pp. 188–96, 216 (some of the duke's men among those excluded from the Resumption, 1449 and from the king's presence in the parliament of Nov. 1450: see Rawcliffe 1978: Apps. B–D for these).

[123] A parallel failure with two families close to the court was soon to be evident on a much larger scale with much more devastating results, in the Percy–Neville feud (Griffiths 1968).

century to decisive royal intervention by way of the Duchy lands and, secondly, because of the absence for most of this period, when the full effects of the incapacity of the adult king were making themselves apparent, of an adult earl of Warwick. Nevertheless, that the real problems lay with the central government can be deduced from the fact that it was during Henry Beauchamp's brief adulthood that a level of instability was reached that was to be surpassed only at the end of the decade, when a national political crisis was giving rise to disorder all over the realm. Henry's difficulties, it may be recalled, had been in large measure the result of over-generosity to this courtier nobleman, which gave him more power than he could cope with, and churlishness towards Buckingham, which fatally weakened the man best able to act as prop to Henry in the midlands. They were therefore the direct consequence of the government's mishandling of affairs.

The incidence of overt conflict and violence in Warwickshire recorded in the King's Bench continues to rise throughout the 1440s (see figure 9), an index of the inability of the local magnates to find a working equilibrium that would enable the gentry to live in reasonable harmony with one another. Within the county only two successful arbitrations are known to have taken place in this decade and that was early on. It was then that Buckingham's influence in both east Warwickshire and the Warwickshire-Worcestershire border region was strong enough to force compromises on Robert Catesby and Humphrey Stafford I of Grafton over the manor of Hopsford in Withybrook, east Warwickshire and on Catesby and Hotoft over the Metley lands. The second mediation, taking place when Buckingham and Grey were beginning to get into difficulties, was by no means easily accomplished.[124] The arbitration to be performed by Duke Henry's council between Henry and the Verneys could only be made once Henry was dead, and it would be difficult to think of a more damning indictment of a lord's authority than that.[125] More striking even than the level of conflict is that so much of it took place between families with similar political allegiances, a phenomenon that becomes especially noticeable among the affinities of William Ferrers and Edward Grey as their influence faded.[126]

Across the county it is evident that all the stresses and strains inherent in a landed society were no longer being neutralised as before. For example, there was the ever-present problem of the rising man, particularly the one with access

[124] *Colls. Hist. Staffs.*, n.s., 3, p. 139; *W.F.F.*, 2609; above, pp. 405–8; P.R.O. Catesby Doc. The Catesby–Stafford arbitration was performed by William Tresham and John Vampage, both Buckingham retainers (Rawcliffe 1978: p. 221).

[125] S.B.T. D.R.98/495a, 496, 497.

[126] Refs. in nn.61, 86 above. Also Ruggeley v. Repington (K.B.27/756 Coram Rege rot.53d.); abbot of Combe v. Astley (K.B.27/748 Coram Rege rot.44d.); Holt v. Porter of Eastcote (K.B.27/759 List of Fines d.); Verney v. Basset (K.B.27/767 Coram Rege rot.7d.); Hotoft v. abbot of Combe (K.B.27/756 Coram Rege rot.55d.). For the link between the Grey connection and Combe, B.R.L. 418917.

to the courts of law. Thomas Greswold's move from east Worcestershire into the Tanworth region had set up tensions which, until 1439, were largely contained,[127] but from 1439 the tempo rose as Greswold became locked in combat with numbers of neighbours. Prominent among these was Thomas Hore of Solihull, apparently claiming to be the dispossessed heir to the lands in Solihull that Greswold had acquired by marriage.[128] It has been observed that this family was far from innately peaceable, and they undoubtedly belonged to that breed of landowner whose violence and litigiousness would be an ever-present threat to local order, but the fact remains that up to 1439 their criminal propensities had usually been kept in check.[129] After 1439 Thomas Hore became a sort of free-lance troublemaker, making himself available to Maurice Berkeley of Weoley for strong-arm tactics against John Holt and to others. As time went on, it became not uncommon for men like Hore, who felt they had nothing to lose and therefore no reason for restraining their instincts in the interest of local stability, to make common cause, a development that is a clear indication of the failure of local and national leadership to absorb or restrain them.[130]

Another newcomer to the Tanworth region was Thomas Porter and, like Thomas Greswold's, his intrusion was not the source of serious trouble until this decade. It could certainly be argued that conflict had been avoided at the expense of the Archers' legitimate claim to their land, but the development of an open split between the two families in the 1440s was avoidable and ultimately damaging to any prospects of settlement. It resulted from the growth of the Porters' relations with the ruling powers of the county and through them with the court, which left the Archers isolated politically and the Porters isolated from the Arden network.[131] Other new men, like Betley and Stretton, were also becoming the focus of conflict, their aspirations giving rise to uncontrollable tensions. When one sets this against the rise of professional men, such as John Catesby, father of William, or indeed Richard Verney's father, earlier in the century and the way they were able to find lands and a position in local society without causing serious rifts in local society, the contrast is instructive.[132]

[127] Above, p. 396.

[128] K.B.9/230A/3, /241/26, /253/16, /277/76; K.B.27/717 Coram Rege rot.88d., /747 Coram Rege rot.33d. As a leading King's Bench official, Greswold had every opportunity of pursuing his opponents through the courts, so it is likely that a higher proportion of his complaints reached the courts than was normal (see app. 4 for more on these and similar problems). An indication of the influence Greswold could call on comes from the indictment of Hore in 1439 (K.B.9/230A/3) which was actually made before the duke of Suffolk in his capacity as steward.

[129] Above, p. 396.

[130] C.1/15/207; K.B.9/246/18; and below, p. 477 for more on similar types in the next decade.

[131] Porter's isolation can be deduced from the solidity of the support for Archer before the chancery commissioners (above, n.111 for refs.) and the lack of local deeds bearing Porter's name.

[132] Catesby a lawyer, Verney a professional estate official (apps. 2 and 3 for both). For their careers, see above pp. 117, 130. If Verney's agreement with Richard Beauchamp, by means of which he

Even marriage to a well-endowed widow, probably the safest way into a landed position,[133] was causing serious problems. The difficulties encountered by Betley and perhaps by Stretton come immediately to mind. Far more damaging to local peace were the marriages of the widows of Philip Chetwynd and John Cokayn I to Thomas Littleton and Thomas Bate, which were followed by ferocious and sometimes violent conflict with the heirs, John Chetwynd and John Cokayn III.[134] The court had a hand in the discomfiture of John Chetwynd, which can have done nothing to reconcile him to his loss. Although a long-standing servant of the crown, he not only had no support against Littleton but was excluded from a share in the household bonanza.[135] The cause of his shabby treatment was almost certainly that his opponent was a friend of Wiltshire and therefore of the inner circles of the household, but, had the government possessed either more sense or more capacity for leadership, the very fact that both parties were connected with the court should have provided an avenue to quick settlement. The Cokayn–Bate conflict should never have occurred at all, seeing that they had a common lord in the duke of Buckingham.[136] In these cases also comparisons can be made with the earlier part of the century. Edward Metley's marriage with the Cotes widow, which apparently gave him a large share of the Cotes lands, had not led to any ructions with John Cotes, perhaps because both were connected to the earl of Warwick. It was only the greed of Metley's son Nicholas and of Nicholas' widow and her second husband Richard Hotoft, amid deteriorating political conditions, that gave rise to open dispute after over thirty years of apparently amicable sharing.[137]

Another source of tension inherent in landed society, that had failed to cause any serious trouble up to 1439 but became a major problem thereafter, were the

bought his land (above, p. 126), did eventually lead to conflict, it was only after Beauchamp's death that it did so.

[133] Above, pp. 102–3.

[134] For the marriages, above, pp. 102–3; for Bate v. Cokayn, above, p. 411; for Littleton v. Chetwynd, K.B.27/742 Coram Rege rot.83d.; *Colls. Hist. Staffs.*, n.s., 3, pp. 175–6, 181–2.

[135] *Cal. Pat. Rolls 1413–16*, p. 233, *1422–29*, pp. 15, 538–9; *Dep. Keep.'s Rep.*, 44, p. 563; *Procs. Priv. Counc.*, III, p. 294. He may have lost a grant made in 1447, but the office in question, a Shropshire one, is more likely to have been held by John Chetwynd of Oddeston, Leicestershire, who had lands in Shropshire; the Leicestershire Chetwynd could not be the recipient of the earlier grants, however, because he was still a minor in 1427 (*Cal. Pat. Rolls 1436–41*, p. 190, *1446–52*, p. 106; Chetwynd-Stapylton 1892: pedigree at end of vol.; *Cal. Fine Rolls 1422–30*, pp. 159–60). Some indication of the preferential treatment Littleton was getting can be gained from the fact that he received the special protection of being described as a servant of the chancellor when his suit with Chetwynd reached the chancellor's court, although his connection went no further than the fact that most of his early practice as a lawyer seems to have been in chancery (C.244/47/120; Foss 1870: p. 419; app. 4 for the benefits enjoyed by the chancellor's servants).

[136] App. 3. However, some attempt at a compromise in Derbyshire seems to have been made by late 1446 (Jeayes ed., *Derbyshire Charters*, p. 28).

[137] Above, pp. 67, 102 and p. 402 n.4.

'criminal gentry'. This study should already have shown that they were less common than has sometimes been supposed, but undeniably they did exist.[138] Thomas Hore of Solihull is a prime example. Usually, as with Hore's feud with Greswold over the Solihull estate, there was some real grievance underlying the descent into a life of crime, but it was characteristic of these men to pursue their ends with an unnecessary and undiplomatic degree of aggression and in the process to lose the goodwill of their neighbours and other associates. After this, having put themselves in a position where they were unlikely to proceed further through the mediation of friends, they were almost obliged to use even greater violence, increasingly finding their only allies among those in the same position as themselves. We have seen that the circumstances of the 1440s were not propitious for confining the perverse energies of men like Thomas Hore, and it was in this period that Robert Ardern of Castle Bromwich in north Warwickshire went so spectacularly to the bad. He was the son of a wealthy knight who had served Richard Beauchamp and was himself in wardship to Beauchamp. Later the earl and a distinguished body of men from the Warwick affinity acted as his feoffees. Ardern became sheriff of Warwickshire in 1437 while still in his twenties and, with the earl of Warwick behind him, looked all set for a distinguished career.[139] But it was then that he plunged into a downward spiral of violence, which began with murder and went on to debt, land sales, compulsive litigation – resurrecting ancient claims in the hope of re-establishing his income – and yet more debt, most of it arising apparently from penalties incurred under the criminal law and from the costs of litigation.[140] From this time on, despite his family's standing and the close connection with the earl of Warwick, he features on a very small number of deeds, and it is fair to assume that he was kept at arm's length by other landowners as soon as he ceased to be respectable; he was not after all showing himself to be the sort of man you would want to call as witness or, worse still, to have as feoffee. Curiously, in the midst of this disastrous career, he represented the county in the parliament of 1449–50. The incentive for Ardern to stand may well have been the immunity from arrest for debt that the position offered but that does not explain why his fellow landowners wished him to do so. He was elected by a very oddly constituted county court and it could be that nobody wanted the job of voting yet another tax, in the teeth of mounting opposition to the government's

[138] Carpenter 1980b, and literature cited there pp. 42–3; also Bellamy 1973: chs. 1–3; Waugh 1977; Hanawalt 1975.

[139] *Dugdale*, p. 928; Longleat, MS of Marquess of Bath Misc. IX m.37d.; C.139/153/21; *Lists and Indexes*, 9, p. 145; above, p. 101 n.23.

[140] K.B.9/232/1/80; K.B.27/740 Coram Rege rot.77; *Cal. Close Rolls 1435–41*, p. 349; C.1/26/139; Bridges and Whalley 1791: 1, p. 128; C.1/11/295, /114/48; *Cal. Close Rolls 1441–47*, p. 475, *1447–54*, pp. 189, 198–9, 419; K.B.27/738 Coram Rege rot.66d., /756 Coram Rege rot.44; W.C.R.O. C.R.1911/17.

policies at home and abroad, and that he was pushed into it by the few friends he still had, most of whom were closely identified with the court.[141]

Again, there are telling contrasts with the earlier period. Thomas Burdet I and his son Nicholas were from a similarly elevated background, if rather less wealthy, and were equally prone to violence, although in their case it took the form of unrestrained conflicts with their landed neighbours. For the Burdets, and for many like them, it had been possible to make a fresh start in France. This policy was attempted with Ardern, who accepted protections twice in the course of the 1440s, once to go to Berwick, once for Aquitaine, but on both occasions failed to go.[142] It is undeniable that the war had become a much less attractive proposition by now, but its lack of allure was due partly to the king's failure to provide military leadership, and one cannot help feeling that even in the 1440s Henry V would have got Robert Ardern to France. Had this option not been available, more authoritative local control and a less volatile political climate in the midlands would have made it easier to halt Ardern's self-destructive career.

In summing up Richard Beauchamp's successful career, the point was made that the gentry required both freedom and security, but could be persuaded to sacrifice their liberty to pursue their personal interests at will, in the cause of collective security. What went wrong at this time has to be set against these remarks. The essence of whether local political structures worked or not lay in whether they could absorb discord, while ensuring that people like John Cotes or Richard Archer, whose interests might have to take second place to the common need for local peace, remained unalienated. As long as the gentry trusted the magnates to maintain this peace, and as long as the magnates were satisfied that they had the king's reasonably impartial support in their endeavours, even the occasional victim might feel that it was better to knuckle under and to take what was offered rather than risk an upheaval that would benefit no one. Meanwhile the 'respectable' gentry as a body, whether victims or victors, would have a common interest in restraining the unruly and would be reluctant to exploit the violent instincts of the 'criminal' types. Between 1439 and 1449, however, this ceased to be the case. The ever-present sources of instability easily got the upper hand over the forces for stability, even though it was stability that really mattered to landowners.

If the nobility received little help from the king, their own efforts were far from impressive. It has been emphasised that the only way to control Warwickshire as a whole was to weld together the four or five regions into which it divided naturally; in the vacuum left by the Beauchamps of Warwick the only man who could have done this was Buckingham, but, even between

141 C.219/15 Pt.II/7 Pt.II; B.R.L. 427016, 249975. His fellow M.P. was the king's retainer, William Catesby. The indenture is witnessed by rather minor gentry. For the background to this parliament, see Griffiths 1981: pp. 286–7, 306, 318–19.

142 *Cal. Pat. Rolls 1441–46*, pp. 181, 220. For the Burdets, see above, pp. 365, 370.

1439 and 1442, when there was no-one else to put up a serious challenge anywhere in the county and he had the sledgehammer force of Edward Grey behind him, he failed to take his opportunity. In his favour it could be argued that a pincer movement from north and south Warwickshire, which was what Buckingham was best positioned to exploit, was not likely to work because so many important landowners had properties spanning the Warwickshire-Worcestershire-Gloucestershire borders. This meant that no magnate without some authority in Worcestershire and north Gloucestershire could readily win the allegiance of the majority of the gentry who formed the Warwickshire elite. From this point of view it was the earls of Warwick who were perfectly placed, since the centre of their own power coincided with the lands of these families.

All the same, Buckingham failed to make the best of what he had, failed even to build an effective power base in the areas of the county that should have been his. His trump card, the new lands in north Warwickshire, which made him the obvious lord for the numbers of north Warwickshire families who had lands in his power base of the north midlands, was never very effectively played. This was true even of the period when he had the Tutbury stewardship and indirect control of the Ferrers of Chartley connection through Philip Chetwynd. He never managed to win over William Mountford, whose support would have enabled him to run north Warwickshire and could also have been used to good effect in south Warwickshire, where the Mountfords had their other main block of estates. The coincidence of their landed interests made the Mountfords Buckingham's most natural allies in the county, as the next decade was to show, but his inability to exploit it in the 1440s is of a piece with his apparent disregard of affairs in southern Warwickshire. This was itself a grave mistake, given that this was a part of the county where he was territorially superior to any rivals. Buckingham also failed dismally in east Warwickshire. Although this would never be an easy region to control from within the county, as even Richard Beauchamp had found, Buckingham was the one magnate with enough landed power there to make a serious attempt. Instead he allowed Grey a free hand; a policy which seemed at first to be bringing a quick return but was ultimately bankrupted by Grey's lack of judgement which provoked resistance that reverberated against both Grey and Buckingham throughout Warwickshire.

The next decade would show whether Warwickshire as a whole could be controlled by anyone apart from the earl of Warwick. The next three decades would show whether Richard Beauchamp's achievement had been wholly exceptional; perhaps Warwickshire was no more than an 'administrative expression' that would normally have to be run by a coalition of interests. If this was indeed the case, then without the leadership from the crown that would be essential to ensure that differences among the coalition partners were rapidly ironed out, and equally without the part that the crown as duke of Lancaster had to play as a partner in the coalition, the county was doomed to become a cockpit of warring factions. Between 1439 and 1449 no long-lasting equilibrium could be achieved. The instability of power structures is strikingly mirrored in the composition of the commission of the peace. With the arrival of each new power, new names were added to it and sometimes old ones removed. As the number of magnates with a stake in the county increased, the commission grew in size. The surviving records of the sessions show a larger number of J.P.s presiding than before, and they tend to be of a variety of political backgrounds, as if all parties were anxious to see that no single group dominated the proceedings.[143]

Such a situation could be exceedingly dangerous, for any loss of faith in the prospects for local peace could tilt the balance towards unrestrained local conflict. How this could come about, and with what consequences, is something that will be discussed at greater length in the context of the mid-century crisis. On the other hand, for those gentry who were reckless and skilled enough to take the risks, the very divisions among the nobility provided unparalleled opportunities for self-advancement by playing the nobility against each other. One suspects that many of the other midland counties, all of them also artificial creations, were as divided as Warwickshire at this time, and it was in Derbyshire, and probably also in Staffordshire, that the Vernons were exploiting the lack of unity to their own advantage.[144] In Warwickshire the chief beneficiaries were the Verneys of Compton Murdack. They went into the 1440s a minor serving family, owing everything to the earl of Warwick and committed to handing over one of their two manors to their master for his collegiate church. They emerged with a seat on the J.P.s' bench, to give them local standing and protect them against the consequences of their uninhibited pursuit of their own interests, and an overwhelmingly influential say in who ran southern Warwickshire. In the meantime they had brought mayhem to the Warwickshire affinities and, having started on equal terms, risen far above their main rival, Richard Dalby. If they were temporarily persuaded into a cessation of hostilities with Dalby in the late 1440s by the temporarily united front among the leading Warwickshire powers, they were nevertheless poised to exploit new divisions as soon as they arose.

For a final assessment of the effects on Warwickshire society of this period of intermittent crisis we return to the relationships studied in the previous chapter and in particular to the role of the middling and minor gentry within the local networks. At an early stage in this inquiry it was asked whether the very minor gentry should really be treated as part of local landed society; in the light of the politics of this decade, and of the whole period up to 1449, the answer must be that they should. Time and time again they played a vital part in the course of a dispute, whether as troops in private armies, to which as often as not they

143 See e.g. K.B.9/238/54, /241/26, /245/33, /246/18, /250/72, /255/1/1, /260/101 and the record of attendance of J.P.s (E.101/590/33); see also above, p. 267.

144 Wright 1983: pp. 69–75; above, pp. 25–7.

brought their own tenants – those men whose judicial subordination gave even these minor lords their gentility – or as jurors, as in the Betley case, or as witnesses, as in the inquiry into the Porter-Archer conveyance.[145] Equally, for newcomers, both gentry with newly-acquired lands like Thomas Greswold, or magnates with political ambitions like Edward Grey, the quickest path to local acceptance was by way of the local networks that in many cases owed their permanence and stability to the minor figures with more localised interests.[146] The vertical ties that ran down through local society from the nobility had to percolate through to the lowest landowning levels if effective lordship was to be exercised. But since the nobility seem generally to have been reluctant to forge links with the lower reaches of the landowning hierarchy themselves, men such as William Mountford, John Throgmorton and William Peyto, who commanded such regard from their lesser neighbours, assumed even greater prominence in their lords' affinities than they would otherwise have had.[147]

It was moreover the strength of the local groupings, which owed so much to those middling and minor families who were less likely to have a direct affiliation with the nobility, that enabled Warwickshire society to withstand the shocks of the 1440s. As long as it remained possible for families to sustain their relationships with each other in an atmosphere of mutual trust, no amount of local or national division was going to tear the locality apart. As long as the interweaving of local connections, even while it bred discord among the noble affinities, continued to make the restriction of conflict the gentry's priority, there would be a bedrock of stability underlying the periodic waves of conflict. It has been shown that this was the case during the 1440s, when the local networks proved surprisingly resilient;[148] these years cannot have been a very enjoyable experience for all but a few ambitious and ruthless families, but they were survivable, given reasonable common-sense and circumspection. Whether the same could be said of the still more uncertain 1450s and 1460s remains to be seen.

145 Above, pp. 402–3, 425.

146 Above, pp. 332–3, 344.

147 Above, pp. 304, 306, 335–6.

148 Above, pp. 323–33.

12

THE PERIOD OF CRISIS I: WARWICKSHIRE UNDER THE KINGMAKER: 1449–61

I

The year 1449 was a watershed for Warwickshire, in that it saw the end of ten years of minorities and the arrival of the Kingmaker, Richard Neville, earl of Warwick, but it also marks a significant change in the nature of English politics in the fifteenth century. In October, the surrender of Rouen signalled the end of English rule in France and the next year there followed retribution on the men held responsible for this failure, Suffolk and his fellow courtiers.[1] For the whole of the ensuing decade there was never any certainty about who was to have the rule of England, and, once confrontation had degenerated into open conflict in 1455, security became an even scarcer commodity. Nor did a great deal of certainty arrive with Edward IV in 1461; it took him four years to deal with the north and to capture his predecessor, who, as a crowned and anointed monarch, was not a rival to be taken lightly. Within two years of achieving this measure of security he was facing a deterioration in his relations with the earl of Warwick which led eventually to Edward's hurried departure in 1470 and the Readeption of Henry VI. With the death of Warwick at Barnet, of Prince Edward at Tewkesbury and of Henry VI soon after and the birth of two healthy sons to Edward IV, all doubts about the future should have been at an end, but Richard of Gloucester's appalling mishandling of his brother's legacy put the body politic back into ferment all over again.[2] We shall see that it is quite clear that Henry VII did not feel safe until 1499, when he decided to execute Clarence's son, the last earl of Warwick, and it is arguable that neither the Tudors nor their subjects believed in the future of the dynasty until Henry

[1] Wolffe 1981: pp. 219–38.

[2] Wolfe 1981: chs. 13–16; Ross 1974, 1981, both *passim*; important comments on Edward IV's first reign in Wolffe 1976: p. 372, and, on the whole period, 1450–1509, McFarlane 1981f: pp. 244, 256.

VIII had succeeded peacefully and dissociated himself from the unpopular policies of his father's later years.[3]

Accordingly, apart from a period of just over a decade from 1472 to 1483, at no time during the second half of the fifteenth century could landowners assume that the rule of England, and therefore of its shires, would remain in the same hands for any length of time. From 1449 to 1460 the question was who would control the king, thereafter it was who would be king. We have seen both in broad outline and in the detailed analysis of local politics how difficult it was for a landowning society to function without complete trust in the royal authority that was the ultimate guarantor and protector of its landed rights. How much everybody looked upwards for direction is readily apparent: the gentry to the magnates and the magnates to the king. Since the gentry themselves were constantly obliged to look ahead in their family settlements, marriage policies and search for security, this prolonged period of uncertainty was bound to force them to re-examine their usual modes of action. The local upheavals of the 1440s had already made some of them less wedded to particular noble followings and more prepared to change lords if it meant better protection. From 1449 the lack of leadership which had afflicted the parts of the midlands that Richard Beauchamp had formerly controlled, and that was likely to become evident whenever and wherever magnate direction was weak, grew into a malaise running the length and breadth of England. In the 1450s both king and nobility failed the gentry, the king by being even more useless than before, the nobility by becoming too enmeshed in their personal battle for survival to give the localities the direction they expected. From 1461 to 1471 (with perhaps a brief period of respite in the mid 1460s) and 1483 to 1499 lack of leadership was still the problem but it stemmed less from lack of royal direction (although we shall see that this was a major problem under Henry VII) than from a general failure of confidence on the part of both nobility and gentry in the future of the regimes.

In the light of all this, we should expect to find a much more fluid pattern of local alliances and political affiliation, and this does indeed prove to be the case. For this reason there will be no separate discussion of social and political networks, as for the previous period, because so much of the analysis of the course of local events in the second half of the century depends on the evidence of such associations: to consider them on their own would merely lead to repetition. The dangers of an interpretation that is so dependent on documentation implying allegiance are all too obvious. However, not only is direct evidence of political affiliation increasingly scarce, especially from 1461 onwards, but the constant upheavals meant that a lesser landowner's attach-

3 See the debate on Henry VII's last years (cited below, p. 595 n.158); also Scarisbrick 1968: ch. 1; Arthurson 1981: *passim*. Interestingly, a chronicler writing in *c.* 1490 listed lords, knights and gentlemen killed in England 1447–89, implying that there had been a period of continuous crisis since 1447 (*Chronicles of London*, p. xlvi).

ment to the lord with whom he was retained, or who paid him an annuity, could be a very nominal affair indeed. The best indication that it had some meaning, leaving aside the extreme case of rebellion, is that a landowner was prepared to make use of a political connection to which he belonged in dealing with his lands; in these troubled times it can be seen as a particularly telling piece of evidence. In such cases the relationship became self-reinforcing, since the clients were acquiring a strong vested interest in the continuance of the affinity. Even so, in the prevailing atmosphere of doubt any lord who showed signs of weakness or miscalculation was likely to be rapidly abandoned, or at any rate to find his men looking round for alternative lords. When the consequences of mistakes had become so incalculable, there was very little room for error on anybody's part. The nobility were left struggling on the one hand with their own doubts about the future of the government and the threat of nemesis if they made a serious mistake in their dealings with the crown and its attendants, and on the other with demands from their followers that were almost impossible to meet under the circumstances. The pressure this placed on them further reduced their effectiveness as protectors and local leaders. How these problems were resolved – whether they were capable of resolution – will emerge from the following four chapters. A further chapter will attempt a synthesis of the main issues brought into focus by the political narrative, in which the effects of these years on local society will be assessed fully.

II

When Richard Neville became earl of Warwick and received his share of the Beauchamp inheritance in July 1449 he did so as a member of a family which had a long history of allegiance to the Lancastrian regime and had yet to be alienated from Henry VI's court, a fact which must be remembered in unravelling the tortuous history of these lands. The division of the Beauchamp and Despenser estates left by Henry Beauchamp has been analysed at some length by Michael Hicks.[4] The heirs to the Beauchamp of Warwick lands were Richard Neville and his wife Anne, who was Henry Beauchamp's sister and eventual heir, and the three daughters of Beauchamp's first marriage, to Elizabeth Berkeley, and their husbands, *viz.*, Margaret and the first earl of Shrewsbury, Eleanor and Edmund duke of Somerset, and Elizabeth and George Neville Lord Latimer, Warwick's own uncle. The heirs to the lordship of Bergavenny and the associated lands in England and Wales that Richard Beauchamp had inherited from his aunt Joan in 1435 were, in right of their wives, Richard Neville and another uncle, Edward, husband of Elizabeth, daughter and heiress of Richard Beauchamp earl of Worcester. The latter was

4 Hicks 1979b, 1981. I owe my thanks to Dr Hicks for a lengthy discussion of the subject, especially the point that the division was made with more regard to mutual convenience than to strict law; otherwise he bears no responsibility for the views expressed here.

the son and heir of Joan and her husband William Beauchamp Lord Bergavenny. Edward Neville and his wife were also the parents of George Neville, Richard and Anne Neville's co-heir to the Despenser estates that had been acquired by Richard Beauchamp earl of Warwick through his second wife; as she had previously been married to Richard Beauchamp earl of Worcester, George was her other direct descendant (see figure 10 for all these).[5]

The whole inheritance was riddled with anomalies. All three constituent estates had been settled in tail male, the entails having come to an end for lack of male heirs. In the case of all three estates the exclusion of the half-blood should have applied, since, in the light of his I.P.M., Henry Beauchamp seems to have had livery of most of the properties. This would have given the inheritance more or less complete to Anne, Richard Neville's wife, as Henry's only full sibling, and yet this turns out not to be what happened. Moreover, grants of 1453 and 1456 imply that, contrary to Henry's I.P.M., some of the Despenser properties in England never left the hands of the feoffees of Isabel Despenser, Richard Beauchamp's widow. Furthermore, a settlement by Richard on Isabel and himself made in 1423, on their marriage, remaindered a large number of Beauchamp properties on Beauchamp's right heirs if there was no heir male. Most of these were in the midlands, the heart of the Beauchamp estate, and they included the vitally important Elmley Castle, and several other Worcestershire estates, all of great strategic importance to an earl of Warwick. The remainder on the right heirs seems to have meant that he expected all four daughters to inherit, whether of the full or the half blood to Henry. There was also the matter of the sizeable trust set up by Richard Beauchamp to support a second son, which was otherwise to be used for charitable purposes and then divided amongst all his heirs. Among these lands also there were some valuable estates and some that were of considerable geographical significance to anyone with an eye on the midlands empire that Beauchamp had run.[6]

This is not the place to go into the details of the partition, which are extraordinarily complex, but some things are clear (see table 7 for an outline). One is that this was essentially a division amongst nobility who were either intimates of the court or at least well-connected there. The earl of Salisbury's position in this respect has already been mentioned, and it must not be forgotten that the younger branch of the Nevilles, to which Richard and his father the earl of Salisbury belonged, owed their rise, initially in rather fraudulent circumstances, almost entirely to the Lancastrian kings. The status

[5] Hicks 1979b: pp. 117–19; Storey 1966: app. 4, esp. pedigree on pp. 232–3; *G.E.C.*, I, pp. 24–8, VII, p. 479; for the Despenser marriage, above, pp. 31, 372.

[6] *G.E.C.*, XII, ii, p. 374, I, p. 26; *W.F.F.*, 2097; S.C.8/32/1575; *I.P.M.* 24 Hen. VI/43; *W.F.F.*, 2683; Dugdale 1675–6: I, p. 396; *Cal. Pat. Rolls 1436–41*, p. 359; Br. Lib. Add. Ch. 72,684; *H.M.C. Var. Colls.*, I, pp. 47–9; Hicks 1981; *W.F.F.*, 2539. For more refs., and comments on Henry's I.P.M., see below, n.9. For the strategic importance of some of the lands, see above, pp. 29–30 and Carpenter 1986a; pp. 26–8.

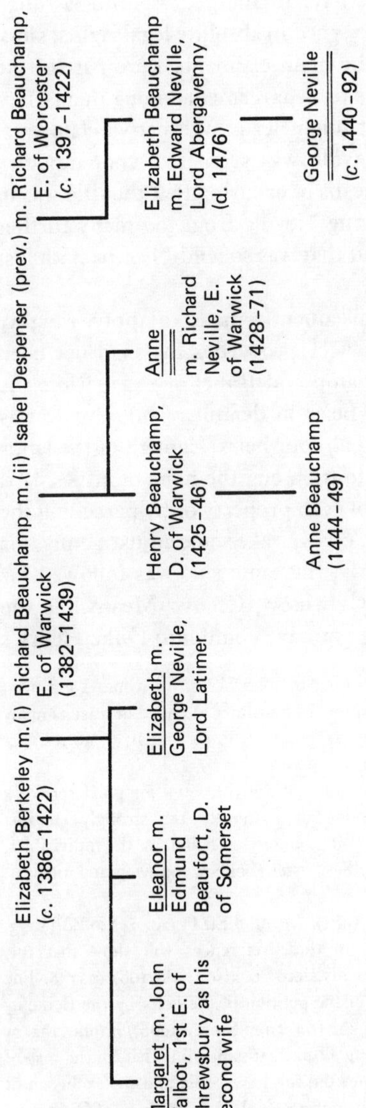

Figure 10 The Beauchamp heirs (from Storey 1966: pp. 232–3). The Beauchamp heirs are underlined once, the Despenser heirs twice.

of Shrewsbury and Somerset in relation to the court needs no elaboration. It was these ultimate heirs to the Warwick estate who had almost certainly been behind the stifling of John Lord Beauchamp's quite tenable claim to the title and lands of the earldom in the mid 1440s.[7] What emerged was thus a rough and ready division that paid relatively little regard to absolute legal rights; since nobody's claim was indisputable and all the main claimants were part of the same political clique, they preferred to come to an agreement among themselves rather than risk self-defeating conflict that might let in alternative claimants. The grant of the earldom to Richard Neville was seen in a contemporary political poem precisely in these terms; a means of ensuring that the title was in the hands of a courtier family and of gagging Neville from too many further claims on the inheritance: 'The Ber is bound that was so wild / For he hath lost his Ragged staff.'[8]

The exclusion of the half-blood was consequently made to apply, roughly speaking, only to those Beauchamp of Warwick properties that had not been put into the settlement on Richard Beauchamp and Isabel of 1423, while the remainder in this deed to Richard's right heirs in default of heirs male was observed and the lands were divided among all four heirs. Enough of the lands that fall into this category were divided in four among the heirs of all Richard Beauchamp's children, either by a division of each property or by parcelling the manors out among the heirs, to suggest that, give or take some adjustments, this was the basis of the distribution. Apparently, the same rule was followed for some at least of the dower lands of Henry's widow, Cecily.[9] Meanwhile the Despenser inheritance, parts of which may not have come into Duke Henry's

7 Griffiths 1968: pp. 594–5; above, pp. 420–1. According to John Watts, to whom I am most grateful for this information and for permission to quote it, Salisbury attended at least as many council meetings in 1449 as Wiltshire and Sudeley. *G.E.C.*, XII, ii, p. 374, II, p. 46 n.f.; for Shrewsbury and the court, see below, p. 460 n.64.

8 *Cal. Pat. Rolls 1446–52*, pp. 235–6 (note that the grant of the title was 'for good service'); *Excerpta Historica*, pp. 161–2; *John Benet's Chronicle*, p. 195 for the strongly curialist atmosphere in which the title was confirmed. In divisions among co-heiresses, the indivisibles, presumably including titles, normally went to the eldest sister (Pollock and Maitland 1968: II, pp. 274–5).

9 *W.F.F.*, 2683; C.P.25(i)/291/65/15 (ref. from Hicks 1981); *I.P.M.* 7 Ed.IV/20, 44, 20 Ed.IV/73; *Cal. Pat. Rolls 1446–52*, pp. 37–8. Comparison of these references will show that this explanation does not cover all the complexities of the division. See also Hicks 1981: p. 138. The wording of the livery of Cecily's dower lands and of the petition of the heirs by the Berkeley marriage (*Cal. Pat. Rolls 1446–52*, p. 451; E.404/67/226 (ref. from Storey 1966)) implies that at least some of Cecily's dower was to be divided among all four. It is possible that, in the case of both the Beauchamp and the Despenser lands, Henry did not have seisin and the exclusion of the half-blood therefore did not apply (*Sir Christopher Hatton's Book of Seals*, p. 166), but the I.P.M.s of Henry and Cecily suggest this was not the case (*I.P.M.* 24 Hen. VI/43, 28 Hen. VI/19), and Henry must have had seisin of anything Cecily held in dower. The I.P.M.s, however, may not be entirely reliable; for example Henry's I.P.M. lists lands known to have been in his mother's feoffment which was still in force after Henry's death (*I.P.M.* 24 Hen. VI/43; *Cal. Pat. Rolls 1436–41*, p. 359; Br. Lib. Add. Ch. 72,684). They may indeed have been 'massaged' by

Table 7 The Warwick inheritance

Estate	Held by Duke Henry	Held by feoffees	Destination
A *Beauchamp*			
(i) Feoffment of 1423, incl. Elmley, other lands in Worcs. and in Staffs., Gloucs.	No, but cf. I.P.M.	Yes	Divided among all four heirs
(ii) Others, incl. Warks. lands	Probably but some not in I.P.M.	No	Most to Neville alone
(iii) Cecily's dower lands	Yes	?Some	Most divided among all four
B *Despenser*	Some, but probably not all those in I.P.M.	Some	Divided between the two heirs, Geo. and Rich. Neville
C *Bergavenny*			
(i) Hastings	Some	No	Divided between Edw. and Rich. Neville
(ii) Entailed Warwick	No	Yes	In Beauchamp Trust (*q.v.*)
D *Beauchamp Trust*	No	Yes	Stayed in trust but under control of Neville

hands at all, remaining in the hands of the feoffees, was not held to be liable to the exclusion of the half-blood and was partitioned between the two heirs, Richard Neville's wife and Neville's cousin George.[10]

interested parties (above, pp. 355–6). For instance, the one group of manors to which Neville's right was never in doubt, the Warwickshire ones of the Beauchamps, are not included in Henry's I.P.M., while the Despenser lands, to some of which Henry certainly did *not* receive livery (above, n.6), mostly were.

10 Hicks 1979b: p. 117, although, as is evident from the text, I would not entirely agree with Dr Hicks' comments on the distribution and how it was done. George did not in fact get his half, except briefly after Warwick's fall in 1470 (Hicks 1979b: p. 117, and Pugh 1971: p. 194).

The legal position of the Bergavenny inheritance is even more obscure. There seems little doubt that, according to the terms of the original entail by William Beauchamp, both the Hastings of Pembroke properties – these included the lordship of Abergavenny itself – and the Beauchamp of Warwick lands that William had been given were to pass to the Warwick line when the male heirs of William's line were extinct. This occurred in 1435, when William's widow died, having had the lands for life, leaving a daughter married to the earl of Ormond and the grand-daughter, daughter of Richard earl of Worcester, married to Edward Neville. There was, however, a limitation on the Warwick heirs who were to inherit the Hastings part of the property; the entail said that these were to revert to the earl of Warwick and his heirs male for ever. Curiously, Edward Neville claimed that they should have passed to him and not to Richard Beauchamp in 1435, but he did have a possible claim to the Hastings lands once the Warwick male line was also extinct, and one that was apparently sufficiently tenable for him to obtain some of them and to style himself, and be summoned as, Lord Bergavenny. Perhaps, since the parties concerned were uncle and nephew, this is another case of a bargain being made to avoid the consequences of litigation.[11] But the Beauchamp of Warwick lands that had been entailed on William and reverted to Richard Beauchamp when Joan died were treated differently. These were now virtually all in the Beauchamp trust, a group of properties from various sources which was treated by all the holders of the Warwick earldom from 1449 onwards as their private property. This was despite the fact that these lands alone were never claimed by anyone to have been in Duke Henry's hands, making them the one part of the estate to which the exclusion of the half-blood could not possibly apply, and that the intention was that they be divided up among all four of Richard Beauchamp's daughters in the event, which did indeed come about, of there being no second son.[12]

Inevitably there were anomalies and disagreements. Richard Neville continued to style himself Lord of Bergavenny and the lordship of Abergavenny seems to have passed into the hands of the crown custodians, along with almost all the rest of the Warwick estates held by Richard Beauchamp, on the attainder of the duke of Clarence in 1478.[13] Equally some at least of the lands of Isabel's jointure in the Warwick lands that had gone to the other heirs were being treated by Henry VII as part of the Neville/Warwick estate.[14] The widow of Lord Latimer retained some sort of interest in the Beauchamp trust, apparently

[11] *G.E.C.*, I, pp. 26, 29, 30; *Cal. Pat. Rolls 1446–52*, pp. 264–5; *Excerpta Historica*, p. 7. For the history of the Hastings lands in Warwickshire, see e.g. *V.C.H.*, III, pp. 36–7, 181.

[12] Hicks 1981.

[13] *G.E.C.*, I, p. 32 n.a., XII, ii, p. 386 n.c.; *Cal. Pat. Rolls 1461–67*, p. 426; *H.M.C. Var. Colls.*, I, p. 47. Br. Lib. Add. Roll 74,169 implies Warwick owned the lordship of Abergavenny in 1449. Note that the Warwick estate did not come complete to the crown in 1478, as Richard of Gloucester had a small part of it (Hicks 1980: App. IIc).

[14] *W.F.F.*, 2729; *V.C.H. Worcs.*, IV, p. 14; refs. in n.9.

with the co-operation of John Hugford, the sole surviving trustee, even though her indisputable right to an eventual share in them had been consistently disregarded.[15]

As it turned out, the really serious conflicts over the inheritance were between Richard Neville and his wife's three half-sisters and their husbands. First there was the division of the Beauchamp of Warwick lands. Here it was not only the value that was at stake but also the coherence of the estate that Neville was finally able to secure. This point, of small interest to Richard Beauchamp when he contemplated division among his daughters if his line should end, could hardly be ignored by Neville if he saw himself as political heir to Beauchamp. The initial division into four parts of each of the Worcestershire properties must have been particularly unacceptable, since it was in this county alone that the earl of Warwick could command unquestioning obedience. The application of some form of pressure by his co-claimants to secure this partition may be deduced from the fact that Neville was granted the Warwick earldom, to which he had no rights if the exclusion of the half-blood was not to apply, almost immediately after the licence to enter was granted to all four heirs. His continued acquiescence in a settlement formalised in Trinity 1450 may have been the price of the new patent of March 1450, issued soon after he came of age, which seems to have given him a stronger title to the earldom.[16] Some time between then and 19 December 1456, probably during the period of Yorkist rule, and perhaps after Somerset's death at St Albans, Neville seems to have managed to obtain a rearrangement on better terms for himself. It was probably at this time that he ensured full control of the Worcestershire properties, but how far he was able to do the same with the other divided estates is not clear. The rearrangement cannot have been very radical or it would have been rejected by the victorious Lancastrians in 1459–60, and it may simply be that Neville relinquished some manors completely in return for sole ownership of others.[17] As long as he retained control of the trust

15 *Test. Vetust.*, p. 358.

16 *W.F.F.*, 2683; Coughton Court, Throckmorton MS Box 59/8; *Cal. Pat. Rolls 1446–52*, pp. 262–3, 235–6, 324; Powell and Wallis 1968: pp. 493–4. For Warwick's right to the title, see above, n.8.

17 *Sir Christopher Hatton's Book of Seals*, pp. 165–6 (implies that Warwick had had lands which, in the eclipse of Yorkist power, the other heirs were now able to claim). By the time of Warwick's confiscation in 1459 it seems that nearly all the partitioned manors were owned by him in their entirety (*Cal. Fine Rolls 1452–61*, p. 268; Storey 1966: p. 260 n.11: but, contrary to Storey, the entry remains ambiguous, even in the original: C.60/267 m.6). I.P.M.s of the other co-heirs (n.9, above) do not make mention of fragments of Warwick manors, neither do subsequent listings of the Warwick lands indicate partitioning (D.L.26/69 (ref. from Hicks 1981); *W.F.F.*, 2729). The confirmation in 1466 of the fine of 1450 (*W.F.F.*, 2683) does not damage this argument, for the fact that this settlement was confirmed does not mean that it dealt with *all* the lands that were now in Neville's hands. See also S.C.8/1394B, which suggests some earlier tension over the Worcestershire properties.

lands, he had a viable midlands estate, even if he had to reconcile himself to the loss of some west midlands properties and, rather crucially, of Drayton Basset on his exposed north-western flank on the Birmingham plateau.[18]

More fiercely divisive were the matters of the Beauchamp hereditary chamberlainship of the exchequer, which will be discussed shortly and to which Neville's rights were exceedingly dubious, and of the custody of George Neville's half of the Despenser lands. As this included lands in south Wales which fitted well with Neville's estates in the west midlands it was a highly sensitive matter. Here again there seems to have been a *quid pro quo*, this time to the earl of Warwick's advantage. The grant to Warwick and Anne of their half coincides with the licence of entry to the four Warwick heirs, and the grant of the custody of George's half followed the next May. All this suggests that Warwick's agreement to the form of the partition was tied up both with his acceptance of the settlement of the Beauchamp lands and with the Despenser custody. As he owned the other half of the Despenser lands himself, and his co-holder was his own cousin, his prior right to it would have been hard to dispute. When Somerset took the custody for himself two years later, Warwick's fierce reaction is therefore readily explicable.[19]

It is important to remember that these were disagreements between a group of favoured people over spoils to which their rights were generally speaking rather dubious. Richard Neville's progressive alienation from the court in the early 1450s was entirely unexpected, and its unexpectedness helps explain some of the peculiarities of Warwickshire alignments in these years. A brief review of the situation in Warwickshire in the late 1440s will reveal more clearly the choices that were open to the new earl of Warwick. If he was to reconstruct Richard Beauchamp's following he had to be accommodating to the whole spectrum of local connections amongst which the Warwick affinity was now distributed. The fact that there were serious divisions within and among the local affinities did not make his task any easier. His own position made the local magnates with court connections the more natural allies. This was fortunate as these were Wiltshire, Beauchamp of Powick and Sudeley, who between them controlled a large part of the former Warwick affinity and were in the process of acquiring the services of William Mountford, a pivotal client for anyone who wanted to reassemble the Warwick connection in north Warwickshire. There was one former power in the Warwickshire–Worcestershire region with which he did not have to concern himself very much: once the lords of Bergavenny had lost most of their lands in this region, on their reversion to the main Warwick line, they took little part in affairs here. Insofar as Joan Beauchamp had a political heir in Warwickshire, it was the Botellers of Ormond and

[18] See I.P.M. refs., above, n.9. Rowney 1983: p. 67 n.6 is in error on Drayton Basset for this period.

[19] *Cal. Pat. Rolls 1446–52*, pp. 262–3; *Cal. Fine Rolls 1445–52*, p. 157; Storey 1966: pp. 239–40; below, p. 466.

Wiltshire, who had inherited her Botetourt lands on the Warwickshire peripheries.[20]

The duke of Buckingham, the only Warwickshire magnate of comparable standing to the earls of Warwick, had on the face of it relatively little to offer the new earl, being neither very closely attached to the court at this time nor a particularly active lord in Warwickshire or Worcestershire. But what he did have was territorial strength at the opposite poles of the area Neville would expect to influence were he to try to rebuild the Beauchamp empire at its height, that is Staffordshire and southern Gloucestershire. He also had potentially massive influence on north Warwickshire, where the vulnerability of the earls of Warwick to invasion of the county from the north midlands had been underlined by Neville's loss of Drayton Basset on the Warwickshire–Staffordshire border. Buckingham and his erstwhile ally Edward Grey also had links, some direct, some indirect, with several of the men in the Wiltshire-Beauchamp-Sudeley ambience. Then there was the small number of men connected with the Suffolk circle – and therefore at this stage with Richard Neville – who were nominally subject to the lordship of William Ferrers of Chartley, but, unlike their lord, had been unable to find a *modus vivendi* with the Wiltshire group.[21] Prominent among these in terms of nuisance value were the Archers and the Charnels, the latter having a long-running feud over Bramcote with prominent members of the Wiltshire circle, while the most eminent in real terms was Thomas Ferrers. For him the stumbling block in making overtures to Wiltshire and the rest may well have been the lasting dissension with Edward Grey over the entailed lands of the Ferrers of Groby, for Grey himself was beginning to be indirectly linked to the Wiltshire nexus through the duke of Buckingham.[22] There is every sign that by the late 1440s Buckingham was coming to terms with this grouping and, even if his relationship with Grey had cooled for the moment, it was soon to be revived. In the meantime he himself was getting involved in some sort of confrontation with Thomas Ferrers, so there were good reasons for Ferrers to keep clear of all the leading powers in the county.[23]

There were a number of obvious courses open to the new earl of Warwick. First it would be sensible to come to an agreement over north Warwickshire with Buckingham. As it seems that the duke had regained the stewardship of Tutbury since Henry Beauchamp's death, his position in the north midlands was particularly powerful; even without the office, he remained far and away

20 Above, pp. 330–3, 410–24, 444; Clark 1977: pp. 14–15. Although Edward Neville Lord Bergavenny retained some interests in the west midlands (e.g. servants: see app. 3), the family's local offices for the rest of the century were virtually all in Kent.

21 Above, pp. 424–8, esp. n.107.

22 Above, pp. 408, 425–6 and below, p. 469.

23 *Cal. Pat. Rolls 1446–52*, pp. 78, 180; *Cal. Close Rolls 1447–54*, p. 51; Jeayes ed., *Berkeley Charters*, p. 186; Pollard 1968: p. 58; above, pp. 422, 426–7.

the greatest figure in the north Warwickshire–Staffordshire region, and it is clear that he was spending a fair amount of time here in the early 1450s.[24] Secondly Warwick needed to establish with Wiltshire, Sudeley and Beauchamp of Powick the sort of relationship that Richard Beauchamp had enjoyed with his lesser allies; in view of their connections with the old Warwick affinity this was an absolute necessity. The fact that it was now they who were the established power, and Warwick the aspiring newcomer, would make this a far from straightforward task. Thirdly, if the north of the county was to be left largely to Buckingham, there was no particular reason to give any help to people like Thomas Ferrers, Richard Archer and William Charnels, despite their indirect links with the court, all the more so when support of the last two was liable to lead to confrontation with the Wiltshire group.[25] Thomas Ferrers was best left alone for fear of offending Edward Grey, probably still the major force in east Warwickshire, or at any rate potentially the major force there, until Warwick had decided whether he would aim for more direct control of the area or leave it to Grey and Buckingham. In theory Warwick held a trump card in his negotiations with Buckingham, in that William Mountford, as a successful court politician, was more likely to seek Warwick's help than Buckingham's at this juncture. Mountford was now elderly and if his plan to settle most of his inheritance on his younger son Edmund was to succeed he would need powerful assistance of an immediate kind. This was no doubt why he had decided in about 1449 to throw in his lot with Wiltshire and his friends, seeing them as the most influential group in the county, and this was another reason for Warwick to keep on good terms with them.[26]

While it is easy in retrospect to see what Warwick should have done, there were major difficulties at the time. The single overriding question was whether it was indeed possible for two great noblemen like Warwick and Buckingham to divide a region between them without acrimony. Warwickshire had never been ruled in this fashion before; the only power-sharing had been between Richard Beauchamp and the Duchy of Lancaster, which was not a partnership of equals. Possibly a king of Henry V's calibre could have compelled co-operative rule on two noblemen of this stature, but under the prevailing conditions of Henry VI's majority there was to be no direction of the kind that would be required. Secondly there was the new earl's own ignorance of the area. This should not be underestimated. He was young, inexperienced, a northerner and linked with

[24] S.C.1/63/305, although no steward is listed in Somerville 1953: p. 540 between Henry Beauchamp and Richard Neville; for most of this time the Honor was part of the Queen's dower (p. 208). For Buckingham in the midlands, see Rawcliffe 1974: pp. 316–18, 1978: p. 66; Rowney 1981: chs. 1 and 2; Alcock 1978: pp. 196–7; *Account of the Household of Buckingham*, p. 12.

[25] Above, pp. 408, 425–7.

[26] Above, p. 426 n.112.

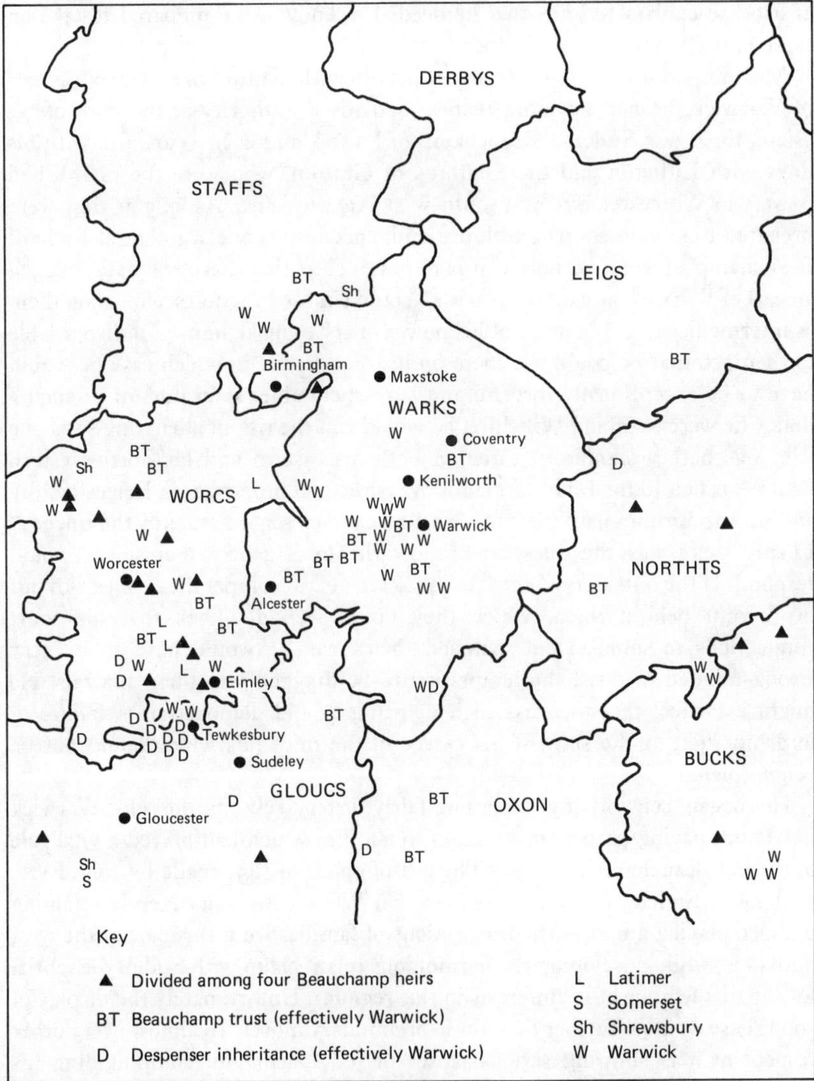

Figure 11 Division of the Warwick inheritance in and around Warwickshire 1449–50

the court and he needed instruction on the nature of midland politics.[27] Since the courtiers under Henry VI had not shown any willingness to listen to or learn about the needs of the localities, one wonders whether there was anybody

[27] Note Warwick's self-exculpatory comment during deliberations over the protectorate some four years later: '[he] sayd he [was] yonge of age and yonger of discrecyon and wysdome ...': Griffiths 1984: p. 80: no doubt an excuse, but one with substance.

at hand to explain to him what he needed to know as he prepared to take on these entirely new responsibilities.

Most important of all, unlike any of his fifteenth-century predecessors as earl of Warwick, he had no more than a mediatised authority at the core of his estate, for it was Sudeley, Beauchamp of Powick and even Wiltshire, with his links with Littleton and the Staffords of Grafton, who were the established powers in Worcestershire and south-west Warwickshire. As long as they were prepared to remain content with pre-eminence in this one segment of Richard Beauchamp's former authority, it is not even clear that these magnates needed an earl of Warwick any more. Warwick could choose to acquiesce in using them as intermediaries at the heart of his power or try to make himself indispensable to them, so that he could use them on his own terms, in which case he would have to be exceptionally forceful and supremely able. If in pursuit of such a policy he were to offend Wiltshire, he would run the risk of alienating someone who was both a significant force on both his eastern and his north-western flanks – as heir to the Botetourt lands Wiltshire had properties in Leicestershire and on the Birmingham plateau – and an ever-closer intimate of the queen.[28] Finally there was the question of how the local gentry themselves would respond. If the outsiders of the late 1440s wanted to compel the new earl to put his weight behind them, which they might well do given that his court connections to some extent matched their own, he would have to be very strong-minded to resist the temptation to be dragged into their quarrels. He might even feel that to resist such demands would demonstrate a failure of lordship right at the start of his career in the midlands which could not be contemplated.

He began sensibly by retaining fairly extensively in the old Warwick heartland, paying particular attention to families which had played a vital role in the old Beauchamp affinity.[29] The gift of goods of 1451 made by John Eyre, probably a Sudeley connection, shows that Warwick was not merely retaining but also playing a part in the transactions of families from this part of the west midlands, while developing the harmonious relationship with Sudeley essential for the furtherance of his interests in this region.[30] Unfortunately the display of good sense went no further than these preliminary moves. In almost every other respect he was showing serious lapses of judgement and compounding his errors by falling out with the other Beauchamp and Despenser heirs over their

[28] Griffiths 1981: p. 290; above, p. 373.

[29] App. 3.

[30] *Cal. Close Rolls 1447–54*, p. 410. This is probably the John Evers/Euer/Eyuere who features on several Sudeley deeds e.g. *Cal. Close Rolls 1468–76*, p. 307; W.C.R.O. L.1/85. He may have come from the Yorkshire family of that name (*Test. Ebor.*, III, pp. 222–5, with thanks to Dr Horrox); alternatively, there was a Robert Ever/Eure of Leicestershire who married the heiress of Malory of Bramcote, the right part of Warwickshire for a Sudeley connection (Mallory Smith 1985: pp. 29–30).

combined inheritance. First, he made a number of mistakes in his dealings with those men connected with Ferrers of Chartley or with the Suffolk circle, or both, who had felt themselves to be victimised by the ruling powers of Warwickshire in the late 1440s. A letter of June 1450 from Warwick to William Ferrers shows that a friendship had developed between them, and a number of acts of aggression on the part of some of Ferrers' clients during 1450 and 1451 indicate their hopes that the new earl would provide them with the protection they had lacked for some time. Ferrers' death later in 1450, leaving most of his midlands estates with his widow, who died in 1471, although she remitted much of her dower in 1455, and as heir an underage daughter, whose lands were in the keeping of Sudeley, would have made this a still more urgent necessity. So would the fact that she was married to Walter Devereux of Weobley, Herefordshire, who had little time for his inherited responsibilities in the north midlands.[31] It is possible that Warwick himself was actively encouraging them, although this would have been exceedingly foolish, as it would have brought him into confrontation with men whose friendship was of far greater importance to him; it is more probable that he allowed himself to be drawn into their disputes.

The episode in which Warwick's direct intervention is most evident is the conviction in January 1451 of Richard Broun of Knowle for forging documents to land owned by the Archers. The verdict was given at Tamworth, the home of Thomas Ferrers, another of these outsiders, and the names of the jurors, preserved among the Archer papers, reveal a combination of Warwick retainers (some with court connections), associates of the Archers and the Ferrers of Tamworth, and future supporters of Warwick and his clients. The fact that this coalition of interests was drawn from all parts of the county suggests that it was a powerful guiding hand that had assembled them.[32] On the assumption that it was indeed the earl's that had been at work, the jury is evidence of impressively widespread support for the new earl, but the case had most undesirable implications. It may well have been related to the Archer–Porter conflict, and Broun himself was one of the securities for the men into whose protective custody the Porter lands at issue had gone. These custodians, it should be remembered, were all important associates of the Wiltshire/Ormond group, indeed they included Wiltshire himself, and amongst them was William

[31] W.C.R.O. C.R.136/B1. The letter has been printed in *Notes and Queries*, 12th ser., 5 (1919), p. 120. It is dated 8 June and the contents show that the year must be 1450. For further discussion of the dating, see Carpenter, M.C. 1976: p. 195 n.1. For Ferrers' death and his heirs, *G.E.C.*, v, p. 320; *Cal. Fine Rolls 1445–52*, pp. 159, 188; *Cal. Close Rolls 1447–54*, pp. 206, 384–6, 454; *W.F.F.*, 2657: *Colls. Hist. Staffs.*, o.s., 11, pp. 248–9; *Cal. Fine Rolls 1471–85*, p. 2.

[32] K.B.27/753 Coram Rege rot.39. For the list of jurors, kept by the Archers, S.B.T. D.R.37 Box 82. Below, n.119 for ref. to the jury accused by Edmund Mountford of corruption. Common to both juries were Erdington, Everingham, Middleton, Edward Doddingselles and John Shepey. For further connections, see Br. Lib. Add. MS 28,564 fo.23 and app. 3 under Richard Neville.

Mountford, the man above all others that Warwick should have been trying to befriend at this time.[33] Warwick had in fact already nailed his colours firmly to the Archer mast the year before by standing feoffee to John I, Richard's son and heir, and persuading his father, the earl of Salisbury, to join him. The witnesses included Richard and William Vernon, and Henry and Thomas II Ferrers, all old friends of the Archers and of the Ferrers of Chartley connection in general.[34]

Warwick's hand may also be seen in events concerning Thomas Malory of Newbold Revel. A year before this verdict he had embarked on his startling criminal career, allegedly by lying in wait near Combe Abbey to murder the duke of Buckingham. There followed a series of attacks on the property of Combe and on the duke of Norfolk's park at Caludon nearby. The background to the whole affair has been a source of constant interest and speculation because of the possible identification of the Newbold Revel man with the author of the *Morte Darthur*. Its origin probably lay in a property dispute with Combe, which held several estates close enough to the Malory estates at Monks Kirby for friction of this kind to have arisen. The advowson of Combe was owned by the duke of Norfolk, who had married Buckingham's half-sister, his marriage having been granted to the duke's mother; in the plea against Malory over Caludon, the owners of the park (presumably co-feoffees) were named as Buckingham, Norfolk and Buckingham's relative John Stafford, archbishop of Canterbury. By July 1451, the properties of the abbey of Axholme at Monks Kirby were in receipt of Malory's attentions. This was an institution very much under the protection of the Mowbray family, and it had been closely connected with Edward Grey's affinity in the 1440s. Whatever its origins, the dispute was thus having the effect of resuscitating the Buckingham–Grey interest in east Warwickshire, in which Norfolk may also have played a part in the previous decade.[35]

Indeed, if the conflict was originally between Malory and Combe and then between Malory and Norfolk, Buckingham may have felt obliged to intervene to show that he and Edward Grey were still capable of bearing the rule in eastern Warwickshire. Subsequent events suggest strongly that Malory was hoping, and Buckingham expecting, that Warwick would step in on Malory's side, which was in itself a major reason for Buckingham to do so on the other. In 1448 and 1450 Malory was doing business with Robert Harecourt, who was enjoying the protection of the Warwick-Ferrers of Chartley-court connec-

[33] Above, pp. 425–6; *Cal. Fine Rolls 1445–52*, p. 109. Nicholas Westcote, brother of Thomas Littleton, Porter's brother-in-law and one of his protectors, was helping to preserve the lands at issue in 1453 (*W.F.F.*, 2653; Jeayes ed., *Lyttelton Charters*, p. xv; above, p. 426 n.112).

[34] S.B.T. D.R.37 Box 53. For links between these, see above, pp. 323–4.

[35] Carpenter 1980b: pp. 36–8 and refs. there; *Cal. Fine Rolls 1430–7*, p. 117; *G.E.C.*, IX, p. 608; *D.N.B.*, LIII, p. 454; above, pp. 325–9, 385 n.155, 386, 405–9.

tion.[36] In this context, the events associated with Malory's arrest in 1452 are highly suggestive. No commission of arrest was issued until July 1451, nearly a year after the final act in a run of misdeeds which, if true as alleged, were remarkable by any standard. This would seem to indicate that Malory was receiving protection from somebody. Then, although the commission was made out to both Warwick and Buckingham, the arrest was effected by Buckingham alone, and he took sixty men from Staffordshire to do it, a fact which implies fear on his part of considerable resistance. And all the subsequent processes, which would normally have been carried out at Warwick, took place in the north of the county, well within the sphere of Buckingham and Grey influence and out of Warwick's. Thus Malory was indicted at Nuneaton in Grey territory and imprisoned not in Warwick gaol but at Coleshill in the house of the sheriff, William Mountford. Mountford, for reasons that will be discussed, had by this time aligned himself firmly with Buckingham, while Coleshill was almost next door to Buckingham's castle of Maxstoke. Furthermore, although it was rare for a nobleman to sit at the sessions, the indicting J.P.s were led by Buckingham. Also among them were Thomas Bate and William Bermingham, the first already feed by Buckingham and the second soon to be so, and Thomas Greswold who was sole surviving feoffee to William Mountford's will. There can be little doubt that Buckingham was taking a close interest in the restraint of Thomas Malory and not much more that the man whose intervention on Malory's behalf he feared was Richard Neville. Ironically, it was because he was placed in custody in a private house rather than a castle that Malory was able to escape, and the commission for his re-arrest made no bones about the fact that it was Buckingham's and Grey's authority in east Warwickshire that he had been flouting. The net effect of Malory's efforts had been not only to draw Buckingham and Grey together again but to help Grey recover much of his former influence in eastern Warwickshire, buttressed now, if not before, by the duchy of Norfolk.[37]

For another of these acts of aggression by the outsiders of the late 1440s we must go back to early 1450. In February of that year Thomas Ferrers I and II allegedly attacked Buckingham's servants at Tamworth. In all probability this was retaliation for the assault the younger Ferrers had suffered at the hands of

[36] K.B.27/750 Coram Rege rot.48d., /754 Coram Rege rot.61d.; see below, pp. 454–5 for Harecourt and this group.

[37] Carpenter 1980b: pp. 37–8. For Grey in Warwickshire *c.* 1449–54, also *Cal. Pat. Rolls 1446–52*, p. 299; K.B.27/766 Coram Rege rot.64; C.1/27/268; W.C.R.O. C.R.162/227. There is evidence to suggest that Grey and Buckingham may already have been moving closer to Wiltshire etc., in the feoffment of early 1452 by Richard Hotoft, servant of Grey and Buckingham, of his main Warwickshire properties of Wolston and Marston to Thomas Throgmorton, who served Sudeley as well as Warwick, and John Brokesby, of the Leicestershire family traditionally associated with Wiltshire and his family (C.P.40/764 rot.332d.; app. 3, and Ives 1983a: pp. 24–6 for noble connections, and below, pp. 456–7 for more on this). In 1452–3 Buckingham was selling red wine to Grey (*Account of the Great Household of Buckingham*, p. 19).

two of the duke's men at Coleshill the year before and the riot in Tamworth itself that followed. The timing, however, is instructive.[38] The Ferrers were soon to be linked with Warwick in the Archer feoffment, were to help bring in the verdict against Richard Broun in the case heard at Tamworth less than a year later, and, most significant of all, in November 1452 were to acquire the earl, as well as the duke of York, as feoffees to the Essex lands at issue between them and the Greys. They would have been eager to have Warwick's encouragement in molesting Buckingham because of their own difficulties with Buckingham's friend Edward Grey. As they had not yet relinquished the family link with Viscount Beaumont, they could reasonably expect that Warwick, himself linked to the court, would see them as natural allies in north Warwickshire.[39] It is perfectly possible that up until then the earl had given them no encouragement whatsoever, but his subsequent willingness to be associated with the Ferrers of Tamworth in the Archer feoffment can only have been interpreted on all sides as public acknowledgement of the Archers' and the Ferrers' right to his protection. The presence on the deed of the Vernons, another of those Ferrers of Chartley families with court connections that were on uneasy terms with Buckingham, can only have strengthened the impression that Warwick was forming a united front with this group, and that this was being done in a deliberate effort to undermine the authority of Buckingham and Grey in northern and eastern Warwickshire.[40]

Confirmatory evidence for those who believed this to be Warwick's intention would have come from developments later in 1450 in the Stafford–Harecourt feud, which had begun with the murderous affray in Coventry in 1448. The Staffords had made no progress at all in finding redress through the lawcourts, a point which lends credence to the view that, despite his recent lack of favour, Robert Harecourt was still well in with the court.[41] Significantly the Staffords decided to take the law into their own hands the moment Suffolk went into exile, as it happens on the day he was waylaid at sea by the *Nicolas of the Tower* and beheaded. On that day, 2 May, a small army led by Humphrey Stafford II took revenge on their behalf. The force included Richard Beauchamp, son and heir of John Beauchamp, himself one of the victims of the assault at Coventry, Thomas Burdet, and enough men, both gentry and tenantry, from south-west Warwickshire to show an impressive solidarity behind the Staffords at the centre of the Warwick estates. The army rode to Stanton Harcourt, the Harecourts' Oxfordshire residence, and laid siege to the bell-tower of the parish church to which Harecourt and his men had fled on the approach of the attackers. Arrows were shot into the tower and an attempt was made to smoke

38 *Colls. Hist. Staffs.*, n.s., 3, p. 201; see above, p. 426.

39 He, like Warwick and York, was one of the Ferrers' feoffees in 1452 for part of the property disputed with Grey (*Cal. Close Rolls 1454–61*, p. 324; C.139/174/34).

40 Above, pp. 410–11, 427; Wright 1983: pp. 67–70.

41 K.B.27/751 Coram Rege rot.72; see above, p. 428.

the besieged party out by lighting a fire under the bell-chamber. When this failed, Stafford and his force withdrew, leaving a trail of devastation behind them.[42] In remarkable contrast with the lack of expeditiousness after the Coventry affray where the Staffords were the victims, within three weeks a commission of *oyer* and *terminer* had been issued. Its members consisted largely of Suffolk's former friends, with an admixture of Warwick and Ferrers of Chartley men.[43] When Harecourt himself eventually appeared in court in February 1451, having at long last been outlawed for his part in the Coventry business, he was bailed by William Vernon, Walter Blount (a friend of Queen Margaret at this time), Thomas Seyntbarbe of the royal household and John Norreys, a friend of Suffolk and William Ferrers, who had been a member of the *oyer* and *terminer* commission into the affray at Stanton Harcourt.[44] Harecourt himself had been retained by Warwick by Michaelmas 1451.[45] Thus, all appearances suggest not only that the Harecourts were receiving protection from the remnants of the Suffolk circle, now regrouping round Somerset and the queen, but that Warwick was still to be identified with this faction, both at court and in Warwickshire.[46]

It was also becoming apparent that the divisions among the courtiers themselves, which had allowed the dispute to get out of hand, were far from being resolved. If Harecourt's interests were being looked after by men like Norreys and Lord Moleyns, the latter a member of the commission into the Stanton Harcourt affray, where did that place Wiltshire, Sudeley and Beauchamp of Powick, all of them courtier nobility and principal protectors of the Staffords of Grafton and their associates? What confused the situation further was that Warwick's concern for friends of the household like Harecourt, or their associates, such as Malory, Archer and Ferrers, was carrying him in precisely the opposite direction to the one he needed to be taking in local

[42] K.B.9/266/51; Storey 1966: p. 58; above, p. 428. An interesting sidelight is the fact that Wiltshire, one of the Staffords' patrons, became part-owner of The *Nicolas of the Tower* in 1450/1. Did he have inside knowledge, communicated to the Staffords, of the fate that awaited Suffolk that day (Pearson 1902: note on pedigree preceding article)?

[43] *Cal. Pat. Rolls 1446–52*, pp. 386–7. The members from the Suffolk circle were Robert Hungerford Lord Moleyns (Griffiths 1981: pp. 587–91), John Fortescue (Griffiths 1981: p. 662), John Norreys (*Excerpta Historica*, p. 162), Richard Quatermayns (Driver 1986: pp. 94–5), and Thomas Danyell (Griffiths 1981: p. 309). Norreys was also associated with the Ferrers (above, p. 427) and married his daughter to Harecourt's heir (*Wedgwood: Biographies*, p. 421). Robert Scotsbrook, Drew Barantyn and Richard Quatermayns, who were also on the commission, had been part of the Oxfordshire affinity of Richard Beauchamp, as had Harecourt's father (S.C.12/18/46; *Dep. Keep.'s Rep.*, 41, p. 698; Oxon. L.R.O. Dillon MS I/b/3). Harecourt himself was steward of Warwick's Oxfordshire estates in 1456 (*H.M.C. Var. Colls.*, I, pp. 47–8).

[44] K.B.27/759 Rex rot.8; Wright 1983: p. 73.

[45] Oxon. L.R.O. Dillon MS I/b/10.

[46] Griffiths 1981: pp. 261–2, 361–2, 693–7. Particularly interesting in this context is the very warm letter of about this time from Warwick to Sir Thomas Tuddenham, Suffolk's notorious henchman in East Anglia (*Paston Letters*, ed. Gairdner, II, p. 117).

politics. It was not terribly wise to offend Buckingham and Grey vicariously through the Ferrers of Tamworth and Thomas Malory when Warwick was barely established in his new lands and certainly not in a position to take charge of north and east Warwickshire. It was the height of folly to be seen to stand behind those associates of the Ferrers and Malory, the Archers and the Harecourts. In doing so, he was setting himself on a collision course not only with the Wiltshire-Beauchamp-Sudeley connection, another noble faction that he could hardly afford to offend at this stage, but with the fulcrum of the old Warwick affinity which lay largely under the protection of this group of lords. Paying annuities to the Staffords of Grafton or Thomas Burdet, as he was doing, was a waste of money if Warwick and his friends were seen to be assisting the Harecourts. Nor would the espousal of the Archers' cause go down well with Thomas Burdet or the Hugfords or with Burdet's other feoffees for Bramcote, as long as the Archers were known to be close to the Charnels, who were quite unprepared to renounce their claim to the manor. Already in early 1450, in an ominous sign of dissension at the centre of Warwick's affinity, one of these feoffees, Thomas Hugford, an intimate servant of the present earl and his predecessors, was party to a plea against Thomas Hore of Solihull, an associate of the Archers. Like them, Hore had a long-standing grudge against the Porters.[47]

But the most serious consequence for Warwick of these ill-judged early manoeuvres was the loss of William Mountford. That this was likely to be the logical result of continued support for the Archers against the Porters has already been observed. This had been made abundantly clear by the plea against Thomas Hore involving Thomas Hugford; the other plaintiffs apart from Hugford were Baldwin Porter and the custodians of his lands, Wiltshire, William Mountford, Humphrey Stafford of Grafton I and Thomas Littleton, a group representing virtually all the parties that Warwick was antagonising in 1450–1. Since Thomas Hore was a long-time friend of the Archers and long-time enemy of the Porters, it is evident that in this particular suit the core of the old Warwick affinity was ranged against the Archers and their circle. It was however precisely the men like Hugford and Mountford, most of them resident in the area of his greatest territorial strength, that Warwick needed to cajole away from their present subservience to Wiltshire, Sudeley and Beauchamp. He had shown his grasp of this point by the annuities he had granted to several of them between 1450 and 1452, and yet those to whom he gave his practical help were the enemies of his annuitants: the Archers – and by extension the Hores and Charnels – and the Harecourts.

There were already danger signs in 1450, indicating that Buckingham was prepared to take Mountford under his wing, but the immediate cause of

47 For Hore and the Archers, see e.g. S.B.T. D.R.37 Box 42/2503, Box 50 (John Malory to Richard Archer etc., 1443), Box 76 (Hore's statement on Archer's behalf in the Porter case). For Hore and the Porters, see above, p. 396.

Mountford's estrangement was more direct. Apparently Warwick quite simply made a mistake. Knowing that the Mountfords of Coleshill were an essential family to retain, in January 1451 he gave a life annuity to Baldwin, William's heir by his first marriage whom William was intending to disinherit.[48] This extraordinarily misconceived step may have been urged upon him by the Archers and the Ferrers of Tamworth who were friends of Baldwin.[49] William's response was instant and all too predictable; he looked round for another local magnate who could be relied on to help him put into effect his intentions against Baldwin, the obvious one being his neighbour Buckingham. The decision to place himself under the protection of the duke had been taken by July 1451 when Mountford obligingly used his own house to detain Buckingham's enemy Thomas Malory.

The results of this error of judgement were of the first importance. Above all, it ranged Warwick and Buckingham almost irrevocably on either side in the Mountford affair, Warwick protecting Baldwin, Mountford's heir in law, and Buckingham Edmund, the heir preferred by Mountford, and locked them into a confrontation over control of north Warwickshire. It would be an easy matter for this to extend into the rest of the county, for Buckingham had lands in south Warwickshire, the location of some of the disputed Mountford property,[50] and Buckingham and Grey were already at odds with some of the other Warwickshire families associated with Warwick. Furthermore, William Mountford was in the course of extending his influence south into the part of the Arden around Alspath and Berkswell, which meant that Warwick had lost an ally who was now even more powerful than he had been under Richard Beauchamp.[51] This was particularly serious as it was precisely here that Warwick himself was infiltrating his own followers from the north of England.[52] And, now that Buckingham was at Maxstoke, Mountford had become far more important to Richard Neville than he had ever been to Richard Beauchamp. Finally, in placing himself on the opposite side to William Mountford, Warwick found himself at enmity with a well-connected courtier who had moved in the circles which had almost certainly been responsible for securing him his share of the Warwick estate. Looked at from the perspective of 1449 it was far more probable that William Mountford would have become Richard Neville's man

48 App. 3. Anstis, *Register of the Garter*, II, p. 141, for Buckingham's earlier connection with Mountford and also confirmation of the connection with the Beauchamp/Wiltshire circle (reference courtesy of John Watts).

49 Above, pp. 425–8, 451–5.

50 Notably Ilmington (*Cal. Close Rolls 1454–61*, p. 185). For this manor's importance to the Mountfords, see above, p. 158.

51 See his close connections with the Chetwynds of Alspath and with John Boteller also of Alspath from 1448/9 (earlier in the case of Boteler) and the links with other local men that these brought (C.244/37/16; *Colls. Hist. Staffs.*, o.s., 12, pp. 322–3; *Cal. Fine Rolls 1445–52*, p. 264; B.R.L. 418912; *Cal. Close Rolls 1468–76*, pp. 367–8).

52 Above, p. 126 n.113.

than that he should end up with Buckingham. He had after all failed to seal any sort of alliance with the duke in the 1440s, when his association with the Warwick estates, with Duke Henry and with the court had been sufficient to secure his position without recourse to a nobleman whom he may have regarded as too uncomfortably close to be an ideal lord.

In being drawn into conflict with Buckingham, who was moving towards the court at this time, Warwick was taking only the latest in a series of steps that would sever him irrevocably from the royal entourage. It was all too typical of the court affinity that its members should fall out over the semi-illicit division of the Warwick lands. The initial issue was the hereditary chamberlainship of the exchequer. This was claimed by the Berkeley heirs, that is Richard Beauchamp's daughters by his first marriage and their husbands. As it went with Hanslope in Buckinghamshire, of which they held three quarters and Warwick only a quarter, their case was not unreasonable. Some time in 1450 they gave the office to John Brome of Baddesley Clinton.[53] Brome, as a former Warwick man and a member of the royal household, should, like Mountford, have been an obvious recruit to Warwick's affinity.[54] Instead in July 1450 he was subjected on two consecutive days to attacks on his property at Warwick and Baddesley by men from Warwick who were led by one of the town bailiffs and were almost certainly acting under the orders of the earl. There were further attacks in August.[55] On 6 December, soon after York's arrival in London had led to Somerset being put into protective custody in the Tower, Warwick received a grant of the chamberlainship, and the next day Brome was forcibly ejected from the office. In January 1451 on Somerset's release the Berkeley heirs petitioned successfully for the return of the office.[56] The next year there were two more attacks on Brome's property by men connected with the earl of Warwick, the first by a Warwick townsman, the second by Richard Herthill, younger brother of Warwick's steward John Herthill. The Herthills had their own axe to grind in that they claimed to be heir to Woodloes manor near Warwick which had recently been sold to Brome.[57]

[53] Storey 1966: p. 235; E.404/67/226, /70/1/47 (cited in Storey 1966); *I.P.M.* 24 Hen. VI/43; Griffiths 1981: pp. 675, 695, for Buckingham's good relations with the court.

[54] App. 3; *Cal. Pat. Rolls 1446–52*, p. 60, *1452–61*, p. 65. He had already been appointed to the chamberlainship by Duke Henry in 1446, an appointment confirmed during the minority of Henry's daughter (*Wedgwood: Register*, p. xliv; *Cal. Pat. Rolls 1446–52*, p. 60) and in August 1450 he was appointed to the Beauchamps' hereditary shrievalty of Worcestershire while the office was in royal hands after the death of Cecily, Henry's widow (*Cal. Fine Rolls 1445–52*, p. 144).

[55] K.B.27/766 Coram Rege rot.59; S.B.T. D.R.3/628.

[56] Storey 1966: p. 235; Wolffe 1981: p. 244; *Cal. Pat. Rolls 1446–52*, p. 409; E.404/70/1/47, /67/226.

[57] S.B.T. D.R.3/628; K.B.27/768 Coram Rege rot.19; app. 3; *Cal. Pat. Rolls 1452–61*, p. 122; *Dugdale*, pp. 469, 971–2. Note that Dugdale is wrong about the origins of the dispute, which were clearly about Herthill's claim to be heir to an estate which Brome had bought, not about a mortgage (see S.B.T. E.R.1/99 fos. 92, 92v., 94; *Dugdale*, pp. 971–2).

Despite these events, there was to be no final breach with Somerset until the more acute dissension over the custody of the Despenser lands in 1453, and Warwick had not yet broken with the court. When Robert Ardern of Castle Bromwich took part in one of the abortive risings in York's favour in March 1452, his action had no bearing on Warwick's own political position. It was rather the last desperate throw of a man now almost entirely isolated from his peers and neighbours who was probably also in a condition of gross indebtedness and had little to lose.[58] In the same month in which Ardern rebelled, Warwick was still well enough respected by all sides to act as intermediary between York and Somerset at Dartford.[59] What he had done in his mishandling of Mountford and Brome was not yet to cut himself off from the court but to lose any chance of winning the loyalty of two men, Brome and Mountford, who could have been immensely useful to him and came from families that had traditionally served the earldom.

Because of this series of unlikely political realignments, the situation in Warwickshire between 1451 and 1453 is confusing in the extreme to the historian and may have been almost as unintelligible to the participants. His connections with Wiltshire and Buckingham notwithstanding, Mountford seems to have contrived to remain something of a free agent in these years. Take for example the case of William Peyto and his neighbour John Hathewick of Harbury. It was in 1451–2 that Peyto, a client of both Somerset and Shrewsbury, was in conflict with Hathewick.[60] Since Hathewick had recently managed to secure the south Warwickshire manor of Oxhill against rivals who were connected with Edward Grey and his family,[61] it is not surprising to find that Peyto's securities for his good behaviour towards Hathewick included men from east Warwickshire and Leicestershire who were connected with Grey. Nor is the presence on Peyto's side of William Mountford's favoured son Edmund unexpected, since both Peyto and Mountford were well-connected at court and, if the Mountfords were moving towards Buckingham, they were as

58 K.B.9/270/34; Griffiths 1981: p. 698; above, p. 432.

59 *The Brut*, II, p. 520. Note that Warwick was rewarded by the crown after Dartford: a sign of closer proximity to the court, or last-ditch efforts to win him over? (*Cal. Pat. Rolls 1446–52*, pp. 523–4: my attention drawn to this by John Watts).

60 K.B.27/762 Coram Rege rot.30d., /796 Coram Rege rot.20d.; *Cal. Pat. Rolls 1452–61*, p. 231; app. 3.

61 It is probable that Hathewick was successful in his claim to Oxhill, as he owned only one other Warwickshire property and yet was made a Warwickshire J.P. in 1444 (*Cal. Pat. Rolls 1441–46*, p. 480). For the dispute, which broke out again in 1454–6, see C.139/163/37; K.B.27/845 Coram Rege rot.81 (which also implies Hathewick's earlier ownership); *V.C.H.*, V, p. 125; Baker 1822–41: I, p. 353. One of the claimants, Constance Cressy, was Edward's sister, and her executor, Thomas Billyng, also involved in the plea, was connected with the Greys of Ruthin (*Wedgwood: Biographies*, pp. 235, 76; above, p. 417 n.74); the other claimant was Eleanor, mother of Humphrey Stafford II: as a follower of Wiltshire, he also was part of the group linked to Mountford (above, pp. 411, 426 n.112).

likely as not to be found in company with associates of Edward Grey.[62] What is odd is that amongst Peyto's securities was also William Mountford's son-in-law, Maurice Berkeley of Weoley, who barely a year before had once more been in conflict with the Ormond family, this time with Wiltshire, over the entire Botetourt inheritance.[63] By 1456–7 Berkeley was himself feed by Buckingham, and one reason for Berkeley's unexpected involvement in Peyto's affairs could be that Peyto's securities were drawn essentially from the Buckingham–Grey nexus, which Mountford was in the process of joining. But then one is left asking how it was that Berkeley was part of a group that was looking after the interests of Peyto, a man closely linked to the earl of Shrewsbury, when he was locked in unresolved conflict with the earl of Wiltshire, the brother-in-law and political associate of Shrewsbury's heir.[64]

If Berkeley seems rather an odd person for the Mountfords, with their attachment to Wiltshire, to consort with, so are some of the others who form a recognisable group around the Mountfords at this time. Among them was Peyto, but there was also Thomas Chetwynd[65] who, like Berkeley, had good reasons for being antagonistic towards Wiltshire and his friends, since Thomas Littleton, Wiltshire's feoffee and regular associate, was keeping Chetwynd out of his inheritance.[66] To make matters still more complicated, Littleton was also a feoffee of Peyto and in his dispute with Chetwynd was receiving Buckingham's assistance.[67] None of this prevented three of the Mountford group, namely Berkeley, Peyto and Purfrey, being placed on the commission issued in 1453 to arrest Richard Herthill and Richard Clapham, one of the servants Warwick had brought from the north, for molesting John Brome, who was himself a client of the earl of Shrewsbury.[68] Also on the commission was Henry Everingham, who had succeeded William Botener at Withybrook in east Warwickshire. He also may well have been Shrewsbury's man and he was later to be Peyto's feoffee, so his inclusion would make perfect sense, were it not that

[62] *Cal. Pat. Rolls 1452–61*, p. 231. William Purfrey and John Pulteney of Leicestershire, two of Peyto's securities, were connected with Grey (Baker 1822–41: I, p. 353; Br. Lib. Add. MS 48,054; W.C.R.O. C.R.162/22; app. 3). Another security was John Boteller of Alspath, for whose connection with William and Edmund Mountford, above, n.51.

[63] Atkyns 1712: I, p. 690; K.B.27/756 Writs of Attorney d.; C.P.40/757 rot.303; B.R.L. 357336.

[64] S.C.R.O. D.641/1/2/23; *G.E.C.*, XI, p. 705; Pollard 1968: pp. 58–60, 77–8, 198–201: Pollard downplays Shrewsbury's involvement with the court and that of his heir, seeing the latter more as a conciliator and identifying him with Buckingham (1968: ch. 3), but this may be open to doubt, in view both of his dealings with Somerset and Wiltshire and of doubts about whether Buckingham was really so 'moderate' (below, pp. 466–7; Jones 1982: p. 14 n.1; S.C.1/44/42; *John Benet's Chronicle*, pp. 195, 212–4; Pollard 1983: pp. 63, 81–2).

[65] Refs. above, nn.51 and 60.

[66] Above, p. 431; Nat. Lib. of Wales, Peniarth MS 280 fo.107; *Cal. Close Rolls 1447–54*, p. 246. For Littleton and Wiltshire, e.g. *Cal. Fine Rolls 1445–52*, p. 109; *H.M.C. Hastings*, I, pp. 1–2; *Cal. Pat. Rolls 1461–67*, pp. 549–50.

[67] *Cal. Pat. Rolls 1446–52*, p. 501; Nat Lib. of Wales, Peniarth MS 280 fo.107.

[68] *Cal. Pat. Rolls 1452–61*, p. 122; above, n.57; app. 3.

he was also retained by Warwick. What does seem clear, however, is that despite the resurgence of Edward Grey there was still quite a substantial remnant of that Shrewsbury–Somerset network that we saw coming to the fore in east Warwickshire in the late 1440s – Peyto, Everingham, Catesby – and that it was linking up with other local men who were moving in the same direction, like Mountford and Brome. Shrewsbury's and Somerset's acquisition of part of the Warwick estate in the midlands would have encouraged them to pursue their forays into Warwickshire. Further incentive may have come from the queen's power, courtesy of her Duchy dowry, in Tutbury and Leicestershire and at Kenilworth.[69] If there was no lack of dissension between and within the groups coalescing around the various court noblemen active in Warwickshire, that did not make them any more amenable to Warwick's influence as he began to distance himself from some of the leading court figures in the locality.

At the risk of becoming entirely opaque, both the Shrewsbury connection and the extreme fluidity in local politics can be explored further through the next stage in the Dalby–Verney feud, which began in the middle of 1452, intertwined on this occasion with a dispute between two branches of the Dalby family. Dalby was now less closely attached to Buckingham. In 1451 he had become feodary to Shrewsbury and in 1454 was to follow his father into the employment of the duke of Norfolk.[70] Verney himself in the interim had probably already married his daughter to Simon Mountford, Baldwin's son and

[69] For the Shrewsbury/Somerset connection in east Warwickshire, see above, p. 329; *W.F.F.*, 2644; *Cal. Pat. Rolls 1452–61*, p. 159; E.326/11094; W.C.R.O. L.1/79; Shaw 1798–1801: II, pp. 185, 268; app. 3. Henry Everingham was almost certainly related to Thomas Everingham of Newhall, Leicestershire (*Cal. Pat. Rolls 1452–61*, p. 159; Br. Lib. Add. Ch.48,675), but doubts have been expressed whether the Leicestershire Thomas was the one connected with Shrewsbury and Somerset (Pollard 1983: pp. 76, 99; Jones 1982: p. 183 n.2, but cf. Pollard 1968: pp. 58, 222–4). In view of the fact that there is copious evidence that the Leicestershire Thomas and Henry were involved closely with the Lancastrians right up to the end, and that they were both feoffees for Peyto (e.g. Br. Lib. Add. Ch. 48,675; K.B.9/298/2; *Paston Letters*, ed. Gairdner, III, p. 143; Griffiths 1981: pp. 341, 370 n.65; below, p. 482; *Cal. Pat. Rolls 1452–61*, p. 159; *H.M.C. Hastings*, I, pp. 1–2, 346), it seems probable that the Leicestershire man is the Somerset/Shrewsbury one. Everingham may well have been related to Maud Everingham, recommended as prioress of Nuneaton by Queen Margaret in 1448 and deposed in 1465 (*Letters of Margaret of Anjou*, pp. 163–4; *V.C.H.*, II, p. 69). There is some evidence that Mountford was already protecting Somerset's interests in Warwickshire as early as 1449, which, in view of the Mountford involvement with the court, would be unsurprising (C.244/61/61). For Brome and Somerset, see C.244/60/21; above, p. 458.

[70] K.B.27/768 Coram Rege rot.61, /769 Coram Rege rot.69; K.B.9/270/66; app. 3. The new outbreak may have been precipitated by a quitclaim by William Verney to Richard Dalby of the lands at issue in Upton and Tysoe in February 1452 (Bod. Lib. Dugdale MS 13, p. 469). The involvement of Dalby and of William Verney can be deduced from the fact that one of the defendants is from Great Wolford and that in the second indictment (below, n.73) Dalby is said to have incited the accused to act. Dalby seems no longer to have been Buckingham's feodary by now, but was still leasing lands off him in 1456–7, in itself a significant relationship in this region where leasehold land was in short supply (B.R.L. 168236 *sub* Tysoe; above, p. 130).

heir. There can be little doubt that Baldwin saw this match as a means of gaining an ally in south Warwickshire, for it was here that Ilmington, one of the estates of which his father hoped to deprive him, was to be found, and this was an area where the Mountford family had seemingly never troubled to find friends, even though it contained several of their properties. As it turned out, the Verneys were to be important allies for Baldwin and Simon in the years to come.[71] In view of Warwick's progressive estrangement from Somerset, with whom Dalby's masters the Talbots were becoming closely linked, and of Warwick's commitment to Baldwin Mountford, it is possible that Richard Verney was already making overtures to the earl. In consequence, when accomplices of Richard Dalby and William Verney were indicted in October 1452 for assaults on the property and persons of another branch of the Dalby family, it is no surprise to find Richard Verney presiding over the sessions. What is altogether extraordinary is that the other J.P. should be John Brome, for Brome was also connected with Shrewsbury and Somerset and had no reason to love the earl of Warwick or his friends.[72] When a further indictment was made in December, this time implicating Richard Dalby directly, the presiding J.P.s were Verney, Thomas Bate, who was feed by both Warwick and Buckingham, William Bermingham, a household retainer later to be feed by Buckingham, and Thomas Greswold, who, as we shall see, was very much tied up with Edmund Mountford at that time.[73]

It would be a brave historian who would draw any hard and fast conclusions about the structure of Warwickshire politics in the early 1450s from all this. It seems safest to say that everybody, the new earl included, was still feeling their way, and that few permanent enmities and likewise few immutable friendships had yet emerged. In this respect Warwickshire was a microcosm of the national scene, where lack of leadership was leading to proliferating disputes, and factions were forming but had yet to harden into irreconcilable divisions.[74] Deeds of 1450–2 show just how fluid local affiliations still were. In 1452 for example William Bermingham gave Birmingham manor in trust to Buckingham (by whom he was feed by 1456–7), Thomas Littleton (who might resent Buckingham on account of his connections with Maurice Berkeley, the enemy of Littleton's patron the earl of Wiltshire, but made use of Buckingham's protection against the Chetwynds and was to receive a life annuity from him in 1453) and Thomas Erdington (in receipt of a life annuity from

[71] *Dugdale*, p. 1,008. For Verney's part in Mountford's case, see below, p. 467 and for the Mountfords and south Warwickshire, see above, p. 305.

[72] Below, p. 466; app. 3; K.B.9/270/66. For a discussion of the Talbot–Beaufort relationship and of Shrewsbury's ties with the court, see above, p. 460 n.64, and Pollard 1983: pp. 81–2, 134.

[73] K.B.9/270/66; app. 3; below, p. 464.

[74] Note also e.g. Sudeley and Shrewsbury's heir performing an arbitration between Ferrers of Chartley and his retainer Sir Richard Vernon in 1450 (Rawcliffe 1984: p. 54). Positions may have hardened earlier in the north and south-west (Griffiths 1968; Storey 1966: ch. 13; Cherry 1981), but it could well be that equally detailed study would reveal a similar complexity at this stage.

Warwick by 1453–4).[75] This deed probably indicates an attempt by Buckingham to bring more of north Warwickshire into his affinity, one that was to fail in the case of Erdington. To take another example, the following year Sudeley granted some property to his son and heir Thomas and to Thomas' new wife who was Shrewsbury's daughter. The witnesses included William Catesby and John Brome, both clients of the Talbots, but also a representative from Sudeley's own affinity, who in this case was Thomas Throgmorton, the life annuitant of the earl of Warwick.[76]

Out of this melting-pot of conflicting allegiances would eventually come the hardened positions of 1454 onwards. From 1450 to 1453 people and events took unexpected turns: Warwick moved away from the court, Buckingham towards it; Warwick cultivated Ferrers of Chartley men, apparently as much as anything because of their court connections, and in doing so managed to alienate the members of the former Warwick affinity who were now most closely attached to the household; some household men or their friends, like Thomas Ferrers, Robert Harecourt and Thomas Erdington, began to move towards York.[77] Nationally, as York began to demand his political rights and the inability of the court to offer a proper substitute for kingship grew ever more evident, there were some equally surprising developments which in their turn accentuated the confusion at the local level.[78] The Nevilles should never have been driven into opposition to the Lancastrian crown. York was feeing Wiltshire until 1453, and he and Viscount Beaumont, one of the most notorious of the courtiers, stood feoffee for Thomas Ferrers at the end of 1452 for estates that York was soon to be actively defending against Edward Grey.[79] The gentry's usual capacity for manoeuvring skilfully in conditions of uncertainty ensured that there would be no clear pattern to Warwickshire politics in these years. Warwick's own retainers and annuitants were in many cases only reliable up to a point. Thomas Throgmorton might stand bail for Henry Somerlane, the bailiff of Warwick who had led one of the attacks on John Brome, but Thomas Burdet, a life annuitant of Warwick and a neighbour of Throgmorton, was placed on the commission to arrest Richard Herthill for his part in the attacks on Brome. On the commission with him was Henry Everingham, another life annuitant of

75 Bod. Lib. Dugdale MS 15, p. 76; app. 3.

76 *G.E.C.*, XII, i, p. 422; W.C.R.O. L.1/79; app. 3. An additional complication is that someone – presumably the Verneys, despite their 'Yorkist' leanings, and by exploiting Norfolk's connection with York – was able to use the *oyer* and *terminer* commission against the alleged Yorkist rebels in 1452 to get Dalby indicted of the Withynale abduction that had started the Dalby–Verney dispute back in 1445 (K.B.9/94/9; above, p. 417).

77 For their household connections, direct or indirect, see above, pp. 426–7, 453–6. For Ferrers and Harecourt, *Dugdale*, p. 1,136; *Cal. Pat. Rolls 1461–67*, pp. 29, 34. Erdington held no office between 1453 and the first 'Yorkist' commission of the peace, issued in December 1460 (above, p. 274). Cf. Richard Quatermayns in Oxfordshire (Driver 1986: pp. 95–6).

78 Griffiths 1981: chs. 22 and 23.

79 Br. Lib. Eg. Ch. 8773–4; *Cal. Close Rolls 1454–61*, p. 324; above, p. 447; below, p. 469.

Warwick, who, like Brome, was linked to the Talbots. Thomas Bate was also a life annuitant of Warwick but was feed by Buckingham as well.[80]

Facts like these speak for themselves of Warwick's inability to impose his will on the county, and this became all too apparent when the first real test of his lordship arrived at the end of 1452. This was the I.P.M. into the lands of William Mountford which would determine which of his sons was to win the first round in the succession dispute that inevitably followed William's death. The inquest was performed by a commission led by Buckingham and Grey and wholly dominated by clients of these two and the court, and it predictably found Edmund heir to all the lands that his father had hoped to leave him. Thomas Greswold, as sole surviving feoffee, let Edmund and his mother in; there is no evidence that Warwick had made any attempt to win his friendship. Ominously the one manor at issue outside Warwickshire, Remenham in Berkshire, was immediately enfeoffed by William's widow to the group who were to be the main prop of her son and herself for the rest of the decade, Buckingham, Somerset and Wiltshire. If these three had not yet come together in Warwickshire, where an outright break with Warwick had still to occur, they were evidently well on the way to taking up this position. More ominously still, the first named feoffee was no less a man than the king, a fact which must mean that, even if his options remained open for a while, Warwick was well on the way to reaching the point of no return with the court, with which Buckingham, as this evidence shows, must be increasingly identified.[81]

Edmund had recently regained custody of the two crown manors of Solihull and Sheldon in north-west Warwickshire, and all the Mountford manors at issue save one were in the north. Together Edmund and Buckingham were now in a position to dominate north Warwickshire from Coleshill, a meeting-point for the north Warwickshire gentry, and Maxstoke, the central stronghold of the area, and one of Buckingham's principal residences.[82] Warwick was left with

[80] Above, p. 461; K.B.27/765 Rex rot.4d.; *Cal. Pat. Rolls 1452–61*, p. 122; app. 3.

[81] *Cal. Pat. Rolls 1452–61*, p. 58; *Lists and Indexes*, 9, p. 145; C.139/150/33/2,4; B.R.L. Wingfield Digby MS A473; Lambeth Palace Lib. Kempe's Register fo.302; Westminster Abbey Muns. 4532. The gentry members of the I.P.M. commission were Thomas Boughton, servant and associate of Grey, John Brome, William Bermingham the sheriff, a member of the royal household and, not long after, of Buckingham's affinity, and, perhaps surprisingly, a sole representative of the earl of Warwick, John Rous (but he had been part of the Beauchamp of Powick connection in the 1440s: above, pp. 330–2). For evidence that Grey, Buckingham and the Wiltshire group may have been coming together earlier, see above, n.37. Related to the Mountford incidents of this year is the indictment of Simon Mountford in 1452 earlier that year for an entry on William Mountford's land in Staffordshire, in which, according to Rowney, the jury was 'packed' with Buckingham tenants (K.B.9/270/56; Rowney 1983: p. 63). For accounts of the Mountford dispute, see Griffiths 1980a; Carpenter 1983: pp. 219–25.

[82] These were granted in July 1452 (*Cal. Fine Rolls 1445–52*, p. 264), but, as before, were lost soon after, this time to the king's half-brothers (*ibid.*, *1452–61*, p. 30 and above, p. 422 n.97 for his earlier tenure). The other manors in dispute, apart from Coleshill and Ilmington, were Monkspath and Ullenhall near Tanworth, Kingsford near Solihull and Kingshurst in Coleshill. They

some allies of dubious worth and limited connections, like the Archers and Thomas Malory, and the possible support of old Warwick families from south-west Warwickshire if he had not offended them too far already. Even here there was an undesirable wedge of Buckingham-Mountford influence, centring on Edmund's estate at Ullenhall on the northern perimeter of the area and on Buckingham's at Wootton Wawen, which was well within Warwick's power base west of Warwick. What is more, the way events were moving in national politics, Warwick stood in some danger of permanent estrangement from Sudeley, Beauchamp and Wiltshire, which would do serious damage to his chances of harnessing the support of men from the traditional centres of Warwick power in this area and in Worcestershire, such as Thomas Throgmorton, Humphrey Stafford II and Thomas Burdet.[83]

The Warwickshire officers of 1450–2 give a good indication of Warwick's failure to make any real impact in Warwickshire.[84] None of the sheriffs was retained by him, while two of them, William Mountford and William Bermingham – sheriff in 1452–3, by which time Warwick's relations with the household were becoming strained – may be termed distinctly inimical to his interests. He himself was not placed on the commission of the peace until May 1452 (that is if we assume there are no missing commissions between July 1449 and then). Neither the new commission nor the one it replaced was dominated by Warwick's men, not even if we count dubious ones like Thomas Bate. Nor was there a preponderance of members from the core of the Warwick estates in south-west Warwickshire. John Brome, who probably owed his appointment in 1449 to the Berkeley heirs, remained a J.P. even after he had broken with Richard Neville.[85] Judged by the commission of 1452 Warwick was just one, and not even the most important, of several magnates with a stake in the county.

If a disproportionate amount of space appears to have been given to these first few years of Richard Neville's rule in Warwickshire, the justification is that it was at this time that the pattern of politics was set for the rest of the decade. The mistakes that Warwick made now and his inability to assert his authority over the county from the beginning were to dog him right through to 1461. Furthermore, it is worth paying some attention to the maze of cross-factional allegiances that grew out of the rapid permutations in local politics. They would

were all Mountford manors, as opposed to the Peche properties; many of the latter were in southern Warwickshire, but some in the north. The Peche lands had belonged to William's first wife, and even he could not contemplate willing them away from the heirs of her body. For the strategic significance of Coleshill and Maxstoke, see above, p. 30; also Watkins 1983–4. For Buckingham and Maxstoke, see above, n.24.

83 Humphrey I was killed by the Cade rebels in June 1450 (Griffiths 1981: p. 612).

84 *Lists and Indexes*, 9, p. 145; *Cal. Pat. Rolls 1446–52*, p. 596, *1452–61*, p. 680.

85 Brome became a J.P. in 1449, just as the division of the inheritance was being made (*Cal. Pat. Rolls 1446–52*, p. 596; above, p. 445).

provide the context for later events and they show an adaptability on the part of the gentry to complex and changing circumstances that was to give rise to significant developments later on.

In 1453 things were quieter in Warwickshire and the year was chiefly remarkable for the crystallising of parties in national politics. Almost simultaneously York's relations with Somerset entered a yet more vituperative stage and Warwick's own final estrangement from the leader of the court faction occurred. The cause, as with the earlier tension between these two, was the Warwick inheritance, this time the custody of George Neville's half of the Despenser lands. This was taken from Warwick and given to Somerset in June, and in July the two were at war in Glamorgan and Morgannock, two of the lordships at issue.[86] York himself is supposed to have broken with Wiltshire the previous March over the lieutenancy of Ireland,[87] and, as far as Warwickshire is concerned, by the end of 1453 the main political lines for the rest of the 1450s had been set: by November Buckingham, Wiltshire and Somerset, having already acted jointly as feoffees for Edmund Mountford's lands in Berkshire nearly a year before, had joined forces to protect his main inheritance in Warwickshire.[88] In national politics too the factions were separating out. In the crisis of January 1454 the nobility and their forces gathered in London; on the king's side were Buckingham, Wiltshire, Bonville, Beaumont, Poynings, Clifford, Egremont and Exeter and on York's were March, Norfolk, Warwick and, surprisingly at this juncture, Henry VI's half-brothers, the earls of Richmond and Pembroke.[89] Although some positions, notably those of the two young Tudors, were to change, noble politics, as long as the Somerset regime lasted, had now gone beyond the stage when the normal processes of adaptation and give and take were possible. It is from this time that Buckingham must be treated as a committed supporter of the court. It may well be that, as a late arrival, whose first loyalty had always been owed to the king, and who had never been particularly intimate with the queen, he had no great enthusiasm for the coup staged by Margaret's party at the end of 1456,[90] but it is always a mistake to see the court affinity as a single entity and Buckingham's recorded distaste for what happened then does not make him a neutral. He had staked too much

86 Storey 1966: p. 239; *Cal. Fine Rolls 1452–61*, p. 34; E.28/83 (cited in Storey); the dispute may have been aggravated by the fact that York and Somerset were fighting for control of south Wales (another pointer to Warwick's political sympathies at the time) (Griffiths 1974: pp. 85–6).

87 Storey 1966: pp. 104, 140.

88 K.B.27/773 Coram Rege rot.52d.

89 *Paston Letters*, II, pp. 296–8. Salisbury's two younger sons had been knighted by Henry VI along with the two young Tudors in 1452, perhaps in a last attempt to mend fences with the Nevilles (Winkler 1943: p. 98), and it may be that a relationship was formed then that was still in being two years later.

90 *Paston Letters*, II, pp. 164–5; Rawcliffe 1978: pp. 24–6. I owe this point about Buckingham's contrasting relations with king and queen to John Watts.

on Edmund Mountford's victory for neutrality to be an option in a climate where the old mode of magnate politics was for the moment dead. He may well have allowed himself to be drawn into similar positions in other counties, such as Staffordshire and Derbyshire, where he became the determined defender of the Vernons' interests from 1454.[91]

It was also in 1453 that Warwick's fortunes in Warwickshire reached their lowest point before the Lancastrian takeover of 1456. The election for the parliament of 1453 revealed the extent of his local eclipse. Almost uniquely, neither of the M.P.s was a member of the Warwick affinity. One, Henry Fillongley, was a household man close to Wiltshire, the other, Thomas Boughton, Edward Grey's man.[92] There was a ray of hope later in the year, however, when Edmund Mountford and his mother were indicted for the entry on the Mountford estates that Greswold had allowed after William's death. The J.P.'s who presided were Richard Verney, who from now onwards was to put himself as steadily behind his Mountford in-laws as he ever put himself behind anybody, and, happily for Warwick, Thomas Bate, who must have decided that at this juncture it was more useful in Warwickshire to be Warwick's man than to be Buckingham's, and this was a good sign in itself. Furthermore, if Baldwin and Simon Mountford are to be believed, Greswold actually allowed them to enter Coleshill in December 1453, another development suggesting that there was a sense that Warwick was now the coming man.[93]

His fortunes took several further strides forward at the end of 1453, when it became impossible to conceal Henry VI's insanity any longer. A series of council meetings followed in October and November, and on 23 November Somerset was imprisoned. It may well have been these developments that persuaded Greswold to allow Simon Mountford's entry into Coleshill, if that is indeed what he did. From late 1453 until late summer of 1456, with the exception of the short period from York's dismissal as Protector until the first battle of St Albans – February to late May 1455 – the power of the court was in abeyance.[94] In this there were serious implications both for the body politic as a whole and for the structure of power in the localities. York's only way of justifying his objections to Somerset, and therefore his only practicable mode of

91 Wright 1983: pp. 73–4. See also Griffiths' comment that Buckingham 'never faltered' in his support of Henry VI (1981: p. 798). For Buckingham's alleged neutrality, see Rawcliffe 1974: pp. 66–9 (but qualified in Rawcliffe 1978: p. 25); Pollard 1968: pp. 82–5. For counter-evidence, showing the duke's relationship with Somerset, see *Six Town Chronicles*, p. 141; *John Benet's Chronicle*, p. 212.

92 *Wedgwood: Register*, p. 207. That 1450–53 was the nadir of York's career also is made clear in Johnson 1988: ch. 5.

93 K.B.9/270A/74; K.B.27/774 Coram Rege rot.119. Carpenter, M.C. 1976: p. 207 is in error on the identity of the J.P.s at the sessions.

94 Griffiths 1981: pp. 720–1, and ch. 23, *passim*.

self-defence, was to stand as restorer of the body politic.[95] To all landowners, noble and gentle, with the exception of those committed unconditionally to the most intimate court circles, this meant a return to a situation in which compromise superseded conflict and relationships across political boundaries became as viable at all levels as they had been before, while the law ceased to be the plaything of faction. There had to be obvious exceptions: in York's case it was Somerset, in the Nevilles' something had to be done about the Percies and the duke of Exeter: arguably this had become essential for the implementing of any kind of rule in northern England.[96] In Warwickshire the claims of Baldwin and Simon Mountford had to be advanced. But were York and his allies to go any further in pursuit of their own interests and the creation of an exclusive clique, their acts would prove self-defeating, for, in acting like the courtiers, they would immediately forfeit the good will of the uncommitted majority of landowners. The return to the norms of government signalled by York's appointment as Protector entailed also the restoration of the power of the territorial magnates, both in council and, where they had been usurped by authority wielded from the court, in the localities. This was less significant for Warwick's rule in the midlands, where his failure so far had been due more to his own inexperience and to the lack of leadership from the crown than to outright competition from entrenched courtiers. Nevertheless, he at last had the freedom and the right sort of direction to make something of his political inheritance.

Warwick's use of the period when court rule was in abeyance shows the sort of management that was required to restore stability to the realm and the growing sophistication of the man on whose shoulders the main responsibility for re-establishing a viable order in the region rested. He gave his support to those he felt deserved it. In the case of the Archers, for whom in January 1454 he again acted as feoffee,[97] this was not such a good idea, since it was through standing by the Archers and their friends that he had risked alienating the old core of the Warwick affinity. But we shall see that he had undoubtedly realised by now that it was with this second group that his future lay. Naturally the issue that he wished above all others to see settled in favour of his own friends was the Mountford inheritance. By July 1454 Baldwin was in possession of Coleshill, which he enfeoffed for its protection to his son Simon and to

95 An ideological position discussed but given little credit in Griffiths 1981: ch. 22, but see Pugh 1986a: pp. 118–19 on York's rule in Normandy. For an unequivocal contemporary statement of the Yorkist position on the law, 'Verses on the Yorkist Lords', in *Political Poems*, ed. Madden, p. 331, ll.21–4 and 'Poem on the Battle of Northampton', ed. Madden, p. 335 ll.7–9. This large and very important issue has a central place in the work being undertaken for his Cambridge thesis by John Watts. I have found our discussions of it very useful.

96 Griffiths 1981: pp. 720–38; Cherry 1981: pp. 133–4.

97 S.B.T. D.R.37 Box 53 (feoffment of John Archer, 1454). This is a draft copy, the donor's name not filled in, but comparisons with Archer's feoffment of 1450 in the same box establish the identity of the donor.

Warwick's servant Richard Clapham. To keep Edmund out permanently the manor was remaindered to an imposing body of Yorkist sympathisers: these included the earls of March and Pembroke (the latter still sympathetic to York at this juncture), and Warwick himself and his wife.[98] Steps were also taken to preserve Thomas Ferrers' property from Edward Grey. In November 1452 a servant of Grey had persuaded Robert Castleford, one of Ferrers' feoffees, to release two Essex manors for the jointure of Grey's eldest son on his marriage to Elizabeth Woodville. In January 1455 Castleford was prevailed upon to disavow the release, and it was probably now that York, as feoffee to Thomas, wrote from Sandal Castle to the assize jury in Essex. This jury, drawn from a region where he was the pre-eminent magnate power, was instructed to come rapidly to a verdict, and, by implication, to make sure it was a favourable one for Thomas. If there were dangers here in the risk of a confrontation with Edward Grey, they were probably felt to be worth the protection of a man who was a considerable landed power in north Warwickshire and Staffordshire, where Warwick needed friends, an annuitant of Warwick and a close relative of York's indefatigably loyal retainers, the Hastings. Assisting the Ferrers had in the changed circumstances in north Warwickshire become a sensible option.[99]

In every other respect compromise was preferred to favouritism. It is greatly to the Yorkists' credit that such patronage as became available in Warwickshire in 1453–4 went not to Warwick's closest associates but to those through whom the numbers of gentry not yet firmly committed to either side, especially the substantial families linked to Wiltshire, Beauchamp and Sudeley, could be won over. As soon as Somerset was safely in prison, part of Robert Ardern's confiscated Warwickshire lands was given into the custody of Thomas Greswold, who, as sole feoffee of William Mountford, had a crucial role to play in determining the ultimate destiny of the lands. This grant may indeed have been a bribe to allow the senior Mountfords to enter Coleshill. Greswold's good will was also worth having because of his intimate involvement with the Tanworth network, especially with lawyers and crown servants there. As a means of influencing this tightly knit group, he was a good alternative to the rather compromising Archer connection.[100] The grant to Greswold may in fact signal the moment of Warwick's decision to distance himself from the Archers.

At the same time strenuous efforts were made to win over Thomas Littleton and his associates. Littleton was becoming a very powerful man. He had his own Worcestershire lands, the Chetwynd properties in north Warwickshire and

98 *Cal. Close Rolls 1454–61*, p. 185.

99 S.B.T. D.R.37 Box 73 (declaration of duke of York); Br. Lib. Stowe MS 141 fo.6; Carpenter 1980b: p. 40 n.72. Although Ferrers is not known to have been an annuitant of Warwick before 1455 (app. 3), the chances are that he was already connected (above, pp. 451, 453–4).

100 *Cal. Fine Rolls 1452–61*, p. 67. For Greswold's connections in the Tanworth area, several of them fellow lawyers like John West, above, pp. 295, 323. He lost some of the Littleton properties the following year (*ibid.*, pp. 82–3).

Staffordshire he held by marriage, his share in the custody of the Porter lands and the promise of half the Burley estate, which his wife was to inherit on her father's death. He was also Recorder of Coventry, an office he had held since 1448, and had the legal expertise which made him such a valuable annuitant.[101] His position is reflected in his participation in a significant number of transactions in the 1450s involving families from all parts of Warwickshire and various other midland counties.[102] Although he was closely linked to the earl of Wiltshire, which might have led to his being politically incapacitated in the years of Yorkist rule, he had a connection with the Yorkists through his father-in-law, William Burley, who had served York for many years and was speaker in the post-St Albans parliament,[103] and he himself was not the sort of man to stake a promising career on over-enthusiastic support of a particular faction. In February 1454 the rest of Robert Ardern's Warwick lands were given into Littleton's custody.[104]

To appreciate quite how wisely the distribution of Ardern's lands was made, we must look again at the history and geography of the north-west Warwickshire border region, which was where most of Ardern's properties were. This was the point where north Worcestershire, south Staffordshire and north Warwickshire met – the Birmingham plateau and beyond – where Warwick's territorial weakness, now accentuated by the loss of Drayton Basset, enabled magnates like Wiltshire and Buckingham, who were territorially stronger in the immediate area or its environs, to wield more direct authority. The area had always been a problem for the earls of Warwick, whether they were trying to create a midlands hegemony on the scale of Richard Beauchamp's under Henry VI, or merely fearful of incursions into their centres of power in Warwickshire and Worcestershire. The vital function of particular places here in controlling communications within the area and into north Wales and the north-west has been discussed. As military confrontation became a real possibility in national politics, access to long-distance routes along which armies could pass would assume ever greater significance, and in 1454 on the Birmingham plateau nearly all of them were in the hands of Warwick's enemies: William Bermingham the royal retainer at Birmingham, Maurice Berkeley, Buckingham's retainer, at Weoley, John Sutton of Dudley, a successful trimmer but for the moment a firm Lancastrian, at Dudley, while Edmund Mountford and Buckingham between them controlled the routes to the north.[105] Warwick needed friends in

[101] *Coventry Leet Book*, p. 235; above, p. 104. In the 1450s Littleton was patronised by four west midlands magnates, Wiltshire, Buckingham, Norfolk and Clinton (app. 3), as well as by the Duchy of Lancaster (Somerville 1953: p. 472).

[102] E.g. *Cal. Pat. Rolls 1446–52*, p. 501; *Cal. Close Rolls 1447–54*, p. 181, *1454–61*, pp. 189, 456; *Colls. Hist. Staffs.*, n.s., 4, p. 156, o.s., 11, p. 236; S.B.T. D.R.98/89,803; and below, p. 607 n.35.

[103] Roskell 1981a: pp. 189–90, 1983a: pp. 350–1; Storey 1966: p. 172.

[104] *Cal. Fine Rolls 1452–61*, p. 70.

[105] Above, pp. 29–30, 361. For Berkeley and Buckingham, see above, n.64, for Sutton of Dudley, see *G.E.C.*, IV, pp. 479–80.

north-west Warwickshire and by putting Ardern's estates into the hands of Greswold and Littleton he was doing more than winning access to the connections of two important local figures; he was also demonstrating a readiness to offer his patronage to all who were willing to take it. This was likely to do him more good here, and elsewhere in the county, than a grant to an established client would have done.

The person that Warwick really needed in this region, just as Richard Beauchamp had needed his grandmother, Lady Bergavenny, until he had been able to replace her with Edmund Ferrers of Chartley, was Wiltshire. The apparent absurdity of a rapprochement between the two earls begins to diminish when one remembers that the quarrel between Wiltshire and York was still very recent and that there were other good reasons for Warwick, York and Wiltshire to forget old enmities. Wiltshire could not count on the king recovering his wits and had no guarantee of ever re-attaining his privileged position at court. Indeed the uncertainty about when and whether the protectorate would end was a major factor in inviting hesitancy on all sides, Yorkist, Lancastrian and neutral. It was not in the interests of the Leicestershire–Northamptonshire connection for Wiltshire and York to remain at odds, for national faction was producing unwelcome division among this network, which included Wiltshire himself and his courtier colleague Viscount Beaumont, and the Yorkist Hastings, Mulso and Ferrers of Tamworth.[106] Thomas Littleton, the beneficiary of the patronage of the Yorkist government, was closer to Wiltshire than to any other magnate, while the only other notable grant in Warwickshire during York's first Protectorate, apart from the custodies of the Ardern lands, went to Thomas Burdet, a Warwick annuitant but also a member of the Wiltshire circle in south-west Warwickshire.[107] In 1453/4 a

106 Above, pp. 373, 389–90; also e.g. *Cal. Close Rolls 1454–61*, pp. 324, 49; Br. Lib. Add. Ch. 48,675; *Test. Vetust.*, p. 279; *H.M.C. Hastings*, I, pp. 300–1; Jeffs 1961a: pp. 254, 288; Johnson 1988: pp. 19, 105, 120, 228–41; Williams 1984–5: p. 30; Farnham, *Leics. Village Notes*, III, p. 141; K.B.9/94/1/2; Leics. R.O. Winstanley MS DG5/2. York was feeing Wiltshire as late as 1459–60, while York's annuities to Shrewsbury in the 1440s and connections with e.g. William Tresham and Thomas Palmer (Johnson 1988, as above) show how the whole Northamptonshire and Leicestershire connection cut across court/outsider lines in the late 1440s and 1450s (above, pp. 325–9, 423–4, 460–3). Note also that in November 1460 York was prepared to use the hitherto impeccably Lancastrian Sutton of Dudley on an embassy to France, even after St. Albans and Blore Heath, where Dudley had fought against him (*Colls. Hist. Staffs.*, o.s., 9, ii, p. 67; *Paston Letters*, ed. Gairdner, III, p. 25). For uncertainty about the political future and resulting cross-factionalism, see the revealing document published by Griffiths (1984: pp. 74–7, 79–81), although it is interesting to note that Beaumont was the only magnate to speak unequivocally on the part of the queen, which suggests that he was no longer prepared to compromise very far. Wiltshire was put on a loan commission in the south-west by York's government (Cherry 1981: p. 134), an act which becomes less 'extraordinary' (Cherry's word), when put in this context. There were probably similar problems in many other regions e.g. the Gloucestershire–Shropshire one, where there had been a York–Talbot alliance (Pollard 1968: pp. 235–6).

107 *Cal. Fine Rolls 1452–61*, pp. 80–1.

settlement was reached between Wiltshire and Berkeley over the Botetourt lands. This was significant not only because it is symptomatic of the atmosphere of compromise which made it possible for such accommodations to be made, but also because the division was distinctly favourable to Wiltshire, leaving him with everything but the estates at Weoley and Northfield that the Berkeleys had never relinquished. As the bulk of the properties were in or near the Birmingham plateau this may be further indication that Warwick was hoping for a working alliance with Wiltshire which would make this region secure.[108]

An examination of the Warwickshire officers between late 1453 and 1456 offers more evidence that compromise was one of Warwick's major priorities and that, even after St Albans, Wiltshire was among the courtiers to whom friendship was being offered. Most strikingly, all the sheriffs appointed in this period were from Leicestershire, which can only indicate that Warwick was prepared to share power in Warwickshire with other political connections, amongst them the earl of Wiltshire's, since his own influence over the Leicestershire gentry was minimal. If two of the sheriffs were members of the Hastings family, in between came Thomas Berkeley who was indirectly connected with Wiltshire, as were the Hastings themselves. In June 1454 a new commission of the peace for Warwickshire was issued which is conspicuous for the absence of any attempt to purge it of interests hostile to Warwick. Thomas Littleton was a new appointee and John Brome was not removed. The only new J.P. who was unambiguously Warwick's man was Baldwin Mountford. As his recent recovery of his inheritance had made him the premier knight in the county, his right to a place on the commission could hardly be gainsaid. Even so, in July he was removed in favour of Thomas Burdet and not restored to the commission until late 1455.[109]

Under these conditions a whole series of settlements became possible. As early as May 1452 Norfolk and Malory had agreed to an arbitration of their

[108] B.R.L. 357336. The collusion of Wiltshire and Buckingham to advance the interests of Edmund Mountford may have been the immediate occasion of the arbitration, for Berkeley was feed by Buckingham by 1456/7 (above, n.64), but the less antagonistic political atmosphere must have helped. Note that Wiltshire was party to the indenture for raising a navy to defend Calais in April 1454, which suggests a measure of co-operation with the Protectorate (Griffiths 1981: p. 732). For the Berkeleys of Weoley, see Rudder 1779: p. 698.

[109] *Cal. Pat. Rolls 1452–61*, p. 680; *Lists and Indexes*, 9, p. 145. For the Hastings and Wiltshire, above, pp. 313, 325–7. Berkeley married the daughter of William Brokesby, a member of a family closely attached to the Botellers of Ormond and Wiltshire and, before that, to Joan Beauchamp, their predecessor in their Leicestershire lands (Nichols 1795–1811: II, i, p. 413; Ives 1983a: pp. 24–6). As recently as May 1453 Bartholomew Brokesby, head of the family, had agreed to marry his son and heir to a daughter of Leonard Hastings (*H.M.C. Hastings*, I, pp. 300–1). The same Yorkist restraint with regard to the appointment of officers has been observed in Staffordshire, but with a different emphasis (Rowney 1983: pp. 54–5).

differences, and in May 1454 Malory was released on the security of a group of mainpernors who came almost without exception from the affinities of two of the magnates who had had him gaoled, Norfolk and Grey.[110] Since Grey had remained loyal to the crown while Norfolk flirted with the Yorkist opposition, this transaction can only be indicative of a general mood of compromise in east Warwickshire, in which the appointment of Leicestershire sheriffs would have played a part. A grant of October 1453 by the Mowbrays' abbey of Axholme, the owner of Monks Kirby and one of the objects of Malory's earlier aggression, suggests that some cohesion had already been restored to the area by then, for it was witnessed by Malory, Leonard Hastings and other east Warwickshire landowners connected with Warwick, Grey and York.[111] In 1457–8 Axholme's dependency at Monks Kirby was feeing two of these witnesses and performing the obsequies of a younger member of the Malory family, while employing Edward Grey's servant Thomas Boughton as steward.[112] The cumulative effect of all this evidence is to suggest that eastern Warwickshire, or at least the parts bordering on Leicestershire, had settled down again under the rule of Grey and possibly also of Norfolk.

Amongst the other successes of these years was, it appears, a compromise between John Brome and William Catesby over Lapworth manor, bought by Brome earlier in the century. As a result the conflict engendered by this sale was delayed into the next decade.[113] Some time between 1454 and 1456 efforts were made to get a permanent settlement to the Mountford dispute itself by means of an arbitration performed by York, Thomas Bourchier archbishop of Canterbury, Salisbury, John Tiptoft earl of Worcester and Viscount Bourchier. The division, which left Edmund with Coleshill, while Baldwin had to be content with the strategically and economically less important manor of Ilmington in south Warwickshire, may well have been unacceptable to both Warwick and Baldwin, but it speaks well for York's intentions of bringing an even-handed peace to the country.[114] Also about this time Richard Dalby and Richard Verney agreed to put themselves under the arbitration of the abbot of Kenilworth. Apparently the abbot succeeded in making an award and the land at issue was awarded to Verney in exchange for an annuity to be paid to

[110] K.B.27/764 Coram Rege rot. between 52d. and 53d., /772 Rex rot.35d.; *Paston Letters*, II, p. 117; *Cal. Pat. Rolls 1446–52*, p. 236; app. 3.

[111] Bod. Lib. Dugdale MS 9, p. 335; above, n.106; app. 3. William Mountford, named as a witness, was dead. Possibly an error for Baldwin or Edmund: see orig.: Reg. Boulers fo.54.

[112] S.C.6/1107/7.

[113] *Cat. Anc. Deeds*, III, A4500; above, pp. 127–8.

[114] *Dugdale*, pp. 1,010–11. For the dating of this arbitration, see Carpenter, M.C. 1976: p. 212 n.1 and Griffiths 1980: p. 11 n.23. It may well be that the conveyance of Ilmington by Baldwin, dated June 1454 and later overridden under duress by Simon, was made immediately after the arbitration (*Cal. Close Rolls 1454–61*, p. 429).

Dalby.[115] The Porter–Archer conflict disappears from the legal records after Baldwin Porter had made a release of all actions to John Archer and his associates in April 1456,[116] and it is highly probable that the *quid pro quo* was a promise by the Archers to leave Eastcote and Longdon alone.

In fact most of the major disputes died down within this period and fewer minor ones surfaced than in the preceding years. If Simon Mountford and Richard Clapham used the opportunity of Warwick's presence in the county in May 1456 to abduct a servant of Buckingham's constable at Maxstoke, as was later alleged, it cannot be said, his support for Baldwin Mountford aside, that Warwick was inciting his followers to open conflict in these years.[117] That he had learned the dangers of assisting trouble-makers like the Archers can be gauged from the fact that it was now that Richard Archer sought out the protection of the Nevilles' arch-enemy, Henry Percy Lord Poynings, while his son and heir John began to gravitate towards the duke of Exeter, who was on equally bad terms with Warwick and his family.[118] Warwick had apparently realised that he must give priority to his relations with the old Warwick families like the Hugfords, the Burdets and the Porters and therefore abandon the Archers, the Charnels and their like. His reward was the restoration of peace to the shire and the establishment of a much wider political base for himself. As early as 1454 the jury that Edmund Mountford accused of corruption, and presumably the one which had given the verdict on the family lands to Baldwin earlier in the year, encompassed a broad spectrum of eminent landowners from all parts of the county. Most of them were Warwick's feed men, but we have seen how little he could rely on the support of many of these earlier on.[119] In

[115] Dalby's petition to chancery (C.1/28/481, 482) mentions an arbitration of about six years before by John Holygrave, abbot of Kenilworth (succeeded by John Yardley in 1458: *V.C.H.*, III, p. 89). The petition itself can be dated by Dalby's claim that he was granted the farm of Cheping Kington seventeen years before, as he later said that it was demised to him in 1445 (K.B.27/818 Coram Rege rot.117). Dugdale's papers include a copy of what could well be a related agreement of 1458 for an arbitration between William Verney and Dalby (Bod. Lib. Dugdale MS 13, p. 469), although it would mean that William Verney had changed sides by then.

[116] Br. Lib. Add. Ms 28,564 fo.23.

[117] K.B.9/284/53; S.C.R.O. D.641/1/2/23. As this indictment was probably the means of imprisoning Simon to force him to release his lands to Edmund's feoffees, its veracity may be questionable (below, pp. 476–7). For evidence of Warwick's presence in Warwickshire, see below, n.120.

[118] *Cal. Pat. Rolls 1452–61*, pp. 240, 352; *Wedgwood: Biographies*, p. 18; S.B.T. D.R.37 Box 91 (writ of duke of Exeter); Griffiths 1968: pp. 606–20. Note that the writ querying whether Richard Archer had really gone to the siege of Berwick with Poynings, thereby qualifying for judicial immunity for his period of service (*Cal. Pat. Rolls 1452–61*, pp. 240, 352), was issued shortly after the Battle of St. Albans had put the Yorkists back into power (C.244/79/41).

[119] K.B.27/774 Coram Rege rot.77d. The jurors included Richard Verney, Simon Mountford's father-in-law, Erdington, Everingham, John Shepey, William Repington, Edward Doddingselles, Thomas Middleton, William Harewell, Ralph Greville (a witness for the senior Mountford line in 1454: *Cal. Close Rolls 1454–61*, p. 186) and Thomas Stretton. Several of these

May 1456 Warwick sat at the Warwick sessions with Littleton, Bate, Hugford, Boughton and Verney, each of whom in some respects represented a different political faction in the county and the region.[120] In June, when John Lord Clinton, who was later to fight for York, conveyed lands at Olton and Solihull to Thomas Greswold, he used a body of witnesses who demonstrate impressively how far enmities had been laid aside; the most eminent of them were Baldwin and Simon Mountford, Thomas Erdington – all three very much identified with Warwick – William Bermingham, of Buckingham's affinity and the royal household, Baldwin Porter, traditionally the enemy of the Ferrers of Chartley men with whom Baldwin Mountford had been linked before, and John Greswold, nephew and associate of Thomas.[121]

The great achievement of these years in Warwickshire and perhaps in the country at large had been to restore a level of co-operation and mutual trust which made it in most landowners' interests to return to normal standards of political conduct.[122] This meant setting aside mutual antagonism, even at the cost of disregarding their own short-term aspirations, in the long-term cause of preserving the peace. The way in which, as it seems, as committed a courtier as Wiltshire could be absorbed back into the political mainstream shows that it was still possible at this late stage, even after the drawing of factional lines in the preceding two years, for the normal politics of give and take to be restored. Once confidence no longer existed either in the possibility of compromise or in the continuance of local harmony, it had to be every man for himself, for victory would go to whoever got the first blow in. This is what happened when the queen's affinity pushed its way into power towards the end of 1456, emphasising its abandonment of any pretence of being a national government by moving its capital to the Lancastrian centre of Coventry, while Warwick fled the country for Calais.[123]

Before considering the consequences of this coup, we should examine an interpretation that has recently been gaining ground, although it owes its origins to a suggestion made by Jeffs a long while ago, that the growth of the

were in the jury that had given the verdict against Richard Broun in 1451 (above, n.32). The entry is marginated for Staffs: clearly an error.

120 K.B.9/282/67.

121 S.B.T. D.R.37 Box 42; *Cal. Pat. Rolls 1452–61*, p. 526. For Greswold, see C.139/174/39. Note also the chancery recognisance of early 1456 by Robert Harecourt, who was moving over to the Yorkists, and Bermingham, a Buckingham/household man, for John Delves (C.244/80/173).

122 For evidence on the pursuit of consensus at national level under York, see Johnson 1988: pp. 135–6, 158–9, 161–2, 170–1, 175; Brown 1969: pp. 113–14. There was still some attempt to win over court nobility as late as 1460 (Johnson 1988: p. 204). York was also able to put sufficient governmental weight behind Buckingham to enable the latter to deal with the long-running Vernon–Gresley feud in Derbyshire (Wright 1983: pp. 126–7). In this context, in Warwickshire, it is worth noting the unusually full and representative attendance at the county court that chose representatives for the post-St. Albans parliament (C.219/16/3 Part II (no numbering within the file); cf. above, pp. 341–2).

123 Griffiths 1981: pp. 773–85, 797–809; Scofield 1923: I, p. 24; Johnson 1988: p. 177.

court affinity, both in the 1440s and more especially in the 1450s, was a serious attempt to resuscitate the Lancastrian retinue after its demise during the minority. As a policy it is sometimes held to account for the choice of local officers at the end of the decade, a point which will be considered later.[124] It seems in fact that the retinue held together remarkably well during the minority, attenuated solely by the deaths of its ageing members, and that it was only in the majority that it really fell apart. Here the reasons are not difficult to seek: principally the favouritism that concentrated too many offices in too few hands – sometimes even non-residential hands – and the lack of leadership from the nominal head of the affinity, the king, that led to other powers, like Buckingham in Staffordshire and Derbyshire, and Cromwell in Nottinghamshire, stepping in, and the retainers themselves falling out with one another.[125] Margaret does indeed seem to have tried to rebuild a following for the crown, and her Duchy lands in and around Warwickshire must have been a major part of the foundation for this policy,[126] but it was very much a personal following for her and her son, rather than the private part of a national royal affinity that the Duchy had been in its great days. Its members were too much tarred with the brush of Margaret and her associates, mostly too divorced from landowners in the localities to constitute an effective local power base for the crown. It could not be otherwise, given the previous history of the reign, the number of people who had to be excluded, the desperate quality of the circumstances and the very fact that this supposedly national government was cowering in its private Duchy stronghold in and around Coventry and the Tutbury region.[127] The highly partisan nature of the new dispensation is seen all too clearly in what happened in Warwickshire immediately thereafter.

Almost at once Simon Mountford was indicted for an abduction allegedly perpetrated the previous May. The sessions was presided over by Buckingham, Littleton, Bermingham, Bate and Boughton, a gathering that shows the fragility of the cross-factional links that Warwick had fostered, once the county had come into the hands of a faction wholly dedicated to the advancement of its own

[124] Jeffs 1961a: pp. 146–67, 255–6; Morgan 1987: pp. 35–41, 50–3; Payling 1987b: pp. 187–8; Johnson 1988: p. 185; below, pp. 481–2. Curiously, Morgan sees this as an innovation, but, if it was a policy at all, it was obviously an attempt to reconstruct the powerful Lancaster-crown affinity of the earlier part of the century (above, pp. 366–8; Pugh 1972: p. 108).

[125] Pugh 1972: p. 108; Payling 1987b: pp. 178–87; Wright 1983: chs. 5 and 6; Storey 1966: ch. 11; Somerville 1953: list of Duchy officers; above, pp. 329, 408, 422, 435; similarly in Wales (Griffiths 1974: pp. 81–5); and on the movement of Oldhall from the Duchy to the duke of York, see Pugh 1986a: p. 116.

[126] Note particularly the propaganda efforts at Coventry (*Records of Early English Drama*, pp. 29–37); for Margaret's lands, see above, p. 461.

[127] Griffiths 1981: pp. 803–4; Storey 1966: p. 192; Morgan 1987: p. 44; below, pp. 481–2. An instance of this state of affairs is *Paston Letters*, II, p. 176. A revealing indication of the clear perception that the queen was now ruling is in Oxford University's change of patron, from York to the Prince of Wales, in 1457 (Storey 1987: p. 321; see also Crawford 1985: pp. 49–50; Wolffe 1981: pp. 302, 305–10, 316–17; Ross 1974: p. 20; *John Benet's Chronicle*, p. 225; *Coventry Leet Book*, pp. 285–92, 300–1; C.81/1375; *Paston Letters*, II, p. 143.

interests. The same sessions saw the indictment of John Shirwode, who was probably also a client of Richard Neville.[128] Simon and his father were then incarcerated, as they afterwards claimed, until they had agreed to make over their lands to Edmund. The releases began that December and were virtually complete in November 1458. In all these transactions the leading figures were Buckingham, his eldest son and the earl of Wiltshire.[129] Predictably in the renewed atmosphere of recrimination and conflict the Porter–Archer affair re-opened. Unfortunately for the Archers, their abandonment by Warwick did not make their case any more acceptable to the new ruling powers in Warwickshire, for whom Baldwin Porter's relationship to Littleton and Littleton's to Wiltshire were the most significant factors in the case. In January 1457 the opponents of both Archers and Charnels joined forces, when Thomas Burdet, Baldwin Porter, Richard Broun and several others allegedly maintained Burdet's feoffees for Bramcote against John and Richard Archer on a charge of making false documents. In April 1457 Richard Archer was indicted before Littleton for an offence against the Porters committed as long ago as 1448. On 10 October John Archer retaliated with a bill against the Bramcote feoffees and their maintainers, but four days later the Archers were silenced in a quitclaim of Eastcote and Longdon to Baldwin Porter. This was presumably forced from them as the price of having the other pleas dropped.[130] It should be remembered that John Archer was himself closely attached to the Lancastrians by now, was indeed to lose his life in their service.[131] But he did not happen to serve the Lancastrians who were in power in Warwickshire, and the case gives some indication of the amount of internecine feuding that was going on in the late 1450s. Partisan rule of this sort was too good an opportunity for anyone with the right connections to miss, especially for natives of Warwickshire while the court was at Coventry.[132] At the same time, as the queen's affinity ceased to be in any way representative of the body politic, there was no authority in the country that could impose peace on warring parties. This meant that there was complete freedom for people like John Cokayn III who had no sense of restraint and no inhibitions about the use of violence in the pursuit of their ends.[133]

128 K.B.9/284/53, /285/49.

129 *Dugdale*, pp. 1,010–11; *Cal. Close Rolls 1454–61*, pp. 185–6, 364–5, 429, *1468–76*, pp. 367–8; Westminster Abbey Muns. 4537 (Remenham quitclaim, March 1459). Simon and other Mountford friends were still being sued in the Common Pleas by Buckingham and Wiltshire in Hilary 1459 (C.P.40/792 rot.394 (ref. taken from Rawcliffe 1974)).

130 K.B.9/285/68 (this may well have been related to Archer's probable seizure of the lands at issue in that year: above, p. 425); K.B.27/786 Coram Rege rot.114d.; *Cal. Close Rolls 1454–61*, p. 253.

131 'William Worcestre', 'Annales', II, pp. 481–2.

132 See e.g. the pleas of John Norreys, Warwickshire landowner and courtier (K.B.27/784 Coram Rege rot.54, /785 Coram Rege rot.11d.).

133 Griffiths 1981: ch. 24; for Cokayn and some others like him, *Rot. Parl.*, v, p. 368, above, pp. 411, 430, 431–3 and below, p. 622.

Yet paradoxically it was just at this time that the Warwickshire gentry begin to demonstrate the depth of their understanding of the importance to them of local stability. This is a complex subject and it should be prefaced with a reminder of two important points about local politics that have emerged from the study so far. First, the weaker the authority of the local nobility and the more divided they were themselves, the greater the gentry's freedom of manoeuvre. This was very evident in the 1440s, most particularly in the case of the Verneys. Secondly in the three years preceding the Lancastrian revanche, as in the earlier 1450s, in order to re-establish the sort of cross-factional politics to which they were accustomed, the gentry had grown used to operating within a series of compromise positions where they chose to ignore most of the causes of disunity. When the queen seized power, although some of the gentry took the opportunities that were offered to pursue the private quarrels that had had to be renounced as the price of peace, that did not mean that any of them, apart from a few wild spirits typified by John Cokayn III and Robert Ardern, wanted to live in an atmosphere of permanent division.[134] If this study has shown anything conclusively, it is that the lives of the gentry were essentially premised on stability of some sort being the normal state of affairs. For their normal mode of life to be viable at all, they had to remain on reasonably friendly terms with their neighbours, their business associates and all those friends of friends who comprised the networks on which they drew in all their dealings with their property. People like Thomas Burdet and Thomas Littleton were having their cake and eating it: they defended the family worship by refusing to renounce the quarrels whose loss was perceived as disworship, while assuming that deep local divisions could be avoided. But nearly everyone else was in a similar position. The point was that it could be done as long as all the conditions that we have seen to be necessary for compromise and conflict to co-exist were present: essentially faith in the ability of king and nobility to impose peace when necessary. Now they existed no longer.

Unfortunately for both gentry and nobility, it was much more difficult for the magnates to prevent the formation of permanent factions when they were in a state of open confrontation. As Richmond has shown, as politics moved ever more decisively to the battlefield, more of the nobility chose to commit themselves to York or to Lancaster.[135] Arguably, they had no choice, for Margaret's rule had shown that neutrality was not an option that was open to the nobility; according to her lights, anyone not for her was against her. Consequently, every magnate wanted to ensure that he had the whole of his affinity on his side, so that it was there to be called on if an army had to be

[134] The problems are highlighted particularly by the divisions in the Leicestershire–Northamptonshire network (above, p. 471), where the leading figures had included York and Hastings and also Wiltshire, Beaumont and the father of Shrewsbury, the three lords specifically singled out for hostile comment by the Yorkist lords in 1460 (Johnson 1988: p. 203).

[135] Richmond 1977: pp. 74–9.

raised, and that through his affinity he could have access to all the military manpower of his 'contree'. But this of course was impossible in a county like Warwickshire where all the affinities were so closely intertwined and had become even more so over the previous few years. If neutrality was not an option for the nobility, it was almost the only one open to the gentry. Furthermore, the nobility, with their widespread lands and, in most cases, their substantial financial cushion, could surmount a certain amount of local disorder. For the gentry, whose interests tended to be concentrated in one or two places, and whose resources were almost always stretched to cover all their obligations, prolonged local upheavals were likely to be an unmitigated disaster. They could acquiesce neither in the single-minded and ultimately divisive pursuit of claims of the sort that was the hallmark of the later progress of Edmund Mountford's affairs nor in pressure to make them choose one side or the other in the national conflict.[136]

However, the gentry did hold one trump card, for if they chose to ignore the magnates' call for loyalty and ultimately for military assistance there was very little their noble leaders could do to coerce them, since they now needed the gentry more than the gentry needed them. The gentry may well have come to believe in the mid-to-late 1450s that they were better off without the nobility. What the nobility had given them hitherto was a local leadership which prevented feuds turning into factionalism. Now the magnates were positively demanding factionalism and, as far as their role in preserving the gentry networks across local divisions was concerned, it could be argued that the gentry were beginning to find that they could do it better themselves. There had always been a strong element of horizontal bonding in these networks, even if in Warwickshire and its surrounds it was the nobility who had usually had the main role in their formation and development. There is substantial evidence that it was at this time that the horizontal began to take precedence over the vertical in the forming of local associations, with profound consequences for the nature of local politics.

The transactions of 1457–9 reveal the existence of a remarkable network encompassing Warwickshire and at least parts of most of the counties around, which went right across local and national political divisions to embrace anyone whose fortunes were not linked inextricably with those of the court. To give just a few examples, in 1457 there was a transaction involving Thomas Erdington, William Harecourt of Maxstoke, a member of the Stanton Harcourt family, Richard Hastings, the younger brother of William, and Thomas Everingham, almost certainly a relative of Henry and quite probably his brother. All were from families that had traditionally been interlinked, but the

136 McFarlane noted the difficulties for the nobility in opting out and almost reached the position set out here on the gentry, choosing in the end to reject it (1981f: pp. 245, 256–7). Richmond also proposes a parting of the ways between nobility and gentry, but not in the way suggested here; I would not agree with him that gentry were forcing reform on nobility (1970: pp. 690–91).

first two were now Warwick retainers, the third was the duke of York's man and the fourth a retainer of Shrewsbury and follower of Viscount Beaumont and was later to be attainted for his Lancastrian sympathies by the victorious Edward IV.[137] The same year Richard Verney arranged a marriage alliance with the Fieldings. The Mountford business having gravely compromised his position, he was in all probability deliberately attaching himself to a family connected with the Greys of Groby, who were coming out firmly on the Lancastrian side. Involved in the feoffment for the marriage settlement were Thomas Littleton, the client of Wiltshire, John Brome, household man and associate of the Beauforts and Talbots, Henry Boteller, friend of Edward Grey and Sudeley (the latter being now firmly aligned with the queen) and Recorder of Coventry since Michaelmas 1455, other people from the Grey connection, and two of Warwick's sympathisers from southern Warwickshire.[138] In 1458 John Wode of Worcestershire died, naming Sudeley overseer of his will and leaving a group of feoffees led by Warwick which consisted almost entirely of Warwick or Sudeley men, of whom Thomas Throgmorton was in the service of both.[139] When John Hugford, son of Thomas, requested a chancery commission for a land plea, he asked that Thomas Boughton, Edward Grey's man, be named as a commissioner.[140] In 1457 Warwick himself indicated his appreciation of the need to regain this gentry middle ground which so many of his foremost clients were occupying by ordering the grant of various offices to Richard Beauchamp, son and heir of John Beauchamp of Powick, Sudeley's close associate and, like Sudeley, now a firm Lancastrian.[141] None of these cross-factional linkages would have been out of the ordinary before the 1450s, but the fact that they could be effected under the conditions of the late 1450s, in the teeth of the magnate influence which would in former days have brought them about, must show a weakening of the magnates' authority over the gentry and would have had serious effects on magnate ability to raise a military force from the shires.

Most remarkable of all is the fact that in December 1457 William Catesby, who was close enough to the queen to be one of the beneficiaries of the confiscations of 1459, and even went temporarily into exile with Henry VI, used Thomas Hugford and, of all people, Baldwin Mountford as witnesses to a

[137] Leics. R.O. DG5/2; *Colls. Hist. Staffs.*, n.s., 17, between pp. 186 and 187; Pollard 1968: pp. 222–4; K.B.9/298/2. For the Everinghams, see above, n.69.

[138] S.B.T. D.R.98/89, 122, 122a; *Coventry Leet Book*, p. 283; app. 3; Griffiths 1981: p. 801. Sudeley's commitment did not stop him losing his office of chief butler to Shrewsbury, an all-too-typical concentration of benefits amongst a small clique within a clique in this period (*Cal. Pat. Rolls 1452–61*, p. 428).

[139] PROB 11/4 fo.100.

[140] C.1/26/533.

[141] *Cal. Pat. Rolls 1476–85*, p. 97; Griffiths 1981: p. 801.

deed.[142] It is in fact apparent that amongst the Warwickshire gentry Edmund was not regarded as the legitimate heir to the Mountford estates. The forced conveyances of 1456–8 to Edmund's powerful protectors relied for their other participants almost exclusively on household men who had no links with the county at all. Of all these courtiers only Henry Fillongley came from Warwickshire, and he had been so long absent and was so wholly identified with Wiltshire and the queen that he could not be described as a member of the local society. Only three local witnesses were used, of whom one was Edward Grey's younger brother and only one, Richard Brasebrugge, shows signs of being a willing convert to Edmund's cause. As he lived rather close to both Coleshill and Maxstoke he probably felt he had little choice.[143] More pressure was probably applied to Humphrey Willingham of Mollington, one of Baldwin Mountford's manors in south Warwickshire, who witnessed the same deed as Brasebrugge. He had been a witness for Baldwin's enfeoffment of Coleshill to his Yorkist feoffees and remaindermen in 1454 and was one of the jurors impleaded by Edmund later that year. In September 1456 he was in Warwick gaol, probably for showing too much loyalty to Baldwin, and it was no doubt this experience that persuaded him to act as witness for Edmund two months later.[144] Baldwin Mountford actually remained a J.P., at any rate in name, until the commission was radically restructured in November 1458.[145] In contrast to Baldwin Mountford's appearance on Catesby's deed, Edmund Mountford does not feature on a single known Warwickshire document apart from his own, even though, as a household officer, he must have been resident in the county most of the time while the court was at Coventry.

The Warwickshire officers of 1458 to 1460, when events were moving rapidly towards violent resolution, reveal the gentry's unwillingness to commit themselves to Henry VI and probably also the government's consequent reluctance to trust them. The sheriffs of 1458 and 1459 were Henry Fillongley and Edmund Mountford. Their appointment was not part of a deliberate policy of household management of the shires, related to the hypothetical reconstruction of the royal affinity, for their lack of local connections would seriously have reduced their effectiveness, but was simply due to the fact that they were the

[142] Hannett 1894: p. 223; Roskell 1981b: p. 313; S.C.6/1042/10 (confirms the story of his exile which Roskell doubts); *Cal. Pat. Rolls 1452–61*, pp. 542, 581.

[143] Above, n.129. For Fillongley's career, see *Wedgwood: Biographies*, p. 325; also *Paston Letters*, II, pp. 178–9, 187–8; *Paston Letters*, ed. Gairdner, III, p. 30, and C.244/84/236. Insofar as he had connections in Warwickshire they were with the Buckingham–Edmund Mountford circle (Gloucs. R.O. D.1086/T103/7). In September 1459 Brasebrugge stood witness for Buckingham's feoffment of Staffordshire and Warwickshire lands; no other lesser landowner with leading interests in Warwickshire was involved (Wm. Salt Lib. Wm. Salt Orig. Coll., misc. copies of docs., Beck 116).

[144] *Cal. Pat. Rolls 1452–61*, p. 343; above, nn.98, 119.

[145] *Cal. Pat. Rolls 1452–61*, p. 680.

only local landowners who were in the crown's confidence and willing to take the job on.[146] This point is emphasised by the commissions of the peace of November 1458 and July 1459, which were gravely attenuated, with reduced gentry membership and a total absence of gentry representatives from west of Warwick. To fill this gap John Beauchamp of Powick had to be drafted in from Worcestershire. In 1458 the government was reduced to appointing John Willenhale, an utterly obscure gentleman from south-east Warwickshire who probably failed to meet the property qualification. Although the following year Richard Verney, having been removed in 1458, presumably because of his identification with Baldwin Mountford, was reckoned trustworthy enough to be restored to the commission, and Willenhale could be taken off, the commission was not greatly strengthened as a result. Thomas Littleton and William Catesby had both come off in November 1458, perhaps because with resources so thinly stretched they were more urgently needed elsewhere, perhaps also because, as the final confrontation approached, they were thought to have been too catholic in their choice of associates to remain J.P.s in the county that was the seat of government.[147]

But if the government found it difficult to drum up support in the late 1450s, so did the earl of Warwick. It was understandable that his clients should look round for alternative protectors. If even Thomas Erdington and William Harecourt, who had very little to do with the court, were consorting with Thomas Everingham,[148] it is hardly surprising that others went much further. Thomas Throgmorton found his way to the service of the Prince of Wales in 1457, presumably through the Sudeley connection, and sat on commissions of array against the Yorkist rebels in Worcestershire in 1459 and 1460.[149] Thomas Burdet, Henry Everingham and John Rous all defected, although in the case of Everingham his rather nominal link to Warwick must always have taken second place to what appear to have been long-standing loyalties to the Talbots.[150] Not

[146] Jeffs 1961a: pp. 146–67, 255–6; *Lists and Indexes*, 9, p. 145; above, pp. 475–6. Revealingly, one of Fillongley's very few local connections 1457–60 was with Edmund Mountford's close aide, John Boteller of Alspath (C.244/84/236; above, p. 457 n.51).

[147] *Cal. Pat. Rolls 1452–61*, p. 680; C.P.40/792 rot.394. For Littleton's and Catesby's appointments elsewhere, see *Cal. Pat. Rolls 1452–61*, pp. 673, 681. Cf. similarly Suffolk (Richmond 1981: p. 111) and the manoeuvres of Richard III when faced with the same problem of insufficient reliable officers (Horrox and Hammond eds., *British Library Harleian Manuscript 433*, I, p. xxxv).

[148] Above, p. 479.

[149] *Cal. Pat. Rolls 1452–61*, pp. 335, 558, 566. His brother, John, was indeed executed after fighting for the Lancastrians at Mortimer's Cross ('William Worcestre', 'Annales', II, p. 486).

[150] Burdet was appointed to the earls' of Warwick hereditary shrievalty of Worcestershire during the Coventry parliament and his annuity was paid from the confiscated Warwick lands, as was Everingham's, by royal command. Rous was on the anti-Yorkist commission of array (B.R.L. 168023; *Cal. Pat. Rolls 1452–61*, pp. 587, 560; *Cal. Fine Rolls 1452–61*, p. 252).

only was Richard Verney appointed J.P. in 1459, but he too served on a commission of array, in his case in Warwickshire, in that year.[151]

The reasons for seeking the protection of the court in Warwickshire are graphically exemplified by the steps taken in 1458 by Boulers, the royalist bishop of Coventry, to retrieve the stolen property of Thomas Greswold, the royal servant. He ordered that a demand be made in services at the parishes where the theft had taken place for the return of the goods and for the denunciation of the perpetrators if they were not returned. That this should be done on behalf of a layman was most unusual. It was doubtless not unconnected with Greswold's responsibility for the Mountford property and his earlier wavering between the two sides.[152] The complete eclipse of Warwick's power in the county is evident from the attacks on his property in 1459, from Somerset's attempt to waylay him at Coleshill the same year and, above all, from the very fact that Henry VI could use Coventry as his capital.[153] It could be said that both government and opposition found themselves hamstrung by the gentry's determination to wait, hoping to ride out the storm while avoiding attacks from either side. It may well be that the final confrontation took so long to come because so many landowners were unwilling to allow it to come at all. The Loveday of 1458 could have been forced on the nobility by their own followers.[154]

It may therefore be legitimate to ask how it was that either side could muster the requisite forces to bring the confrontation about. One important answer that has recently been offered is that it was the towns that supplied many of the troops.[155] Also significant is the fact that most of the major participants on either side were landowners in the northern or Welsh marches. The lords of the Welsh marches had undiluted control over the inhabitants of their lordships and could raise a large army without difficulty. T.B. Pugh has suggested that it

151 *Cal. Pat. Rolls 1452–61*, p. 560.

152 Above, pp. 464, 467, 469; Cov. and Lichf. Dioc., Reg. Boulers, fo.92; for Boulers, see Davies, R.G. 1982: p. 60. My thanks to Benjamin Thompson for guidance on the unusual nature of this procedure.

153 *Six Town Chronicles*, pp. 147–8; K.B.9/313/57, 58; Scofield 1923: 1, p. 34; *Historical Collections of a Citizen of London*, pp. 204–5. It was also at this time, in 1458, that the Lancastrian 'society' wedding of the year took place at Maxstoke: Buckingham's daughter to the second earl of Shrewsbury's eldest son (Alcock 1978: pp. 196–7; Cov. and Lichf. Dioc., Reg. Boulers fo.93v.).

154 Griffiths 1981: pp. 805–8. McFarlane noted the surprising slowness of the onset of war (McFarlane 1981f: pp. 237–8). In this context John Watts has some very interesting ideas on the Nevilles' position from 1455, raised in his Cambridge B.A. dissertation and to be developed in his Ph.D. thesis, the crux being that the Nevilles may have hoped to return to their normal position of loyalty to the Lancastrian crown once Somerset had been killed at St. Albans; the fact that Warwick was let into Calais *after* Margaret had come to power is hugely significant and would repay thorough investigation (Harriss 1960). See also details which lend support to John Watts' ideas (Johnson 1988: pp. 174–5). I am most grateful to him for allowing me to quote them here.

155 Goodman 1981b: pp. 145–8, 202–3, 219–20; *Coventry Leet Book*, pp. 282–3, 308–19.

was Buckingham's promises of military support that finally enabled the queen to take the initiative against her enemies in 1459. Although he makes this point with reference to Buckingham's gentry affinity, particularly the midlands sector, more important still to Margaret was the fact that he was one of the greatest of the marcher lords.[156] Margaret also made extensive use of manpower from the Palatinate of Chester, where the king was almost as absolute a lord as the marchers were within their lordships, and the Welsh marches may have been an important recruiting ground for her throughout this last period. Similarly the northern lands from which a large part of Margaret's army came were used to a more unitary lordship and therefore less constrained by the fears of breaking apart local groupings crossing political lines that beset regions further south. The north was also a more turbulent region, much of it already a war zone, whose inhabitants were probably less inhibited about taking their quarrels into the battlefield. Like their enemies, the Yorkists had access to forces from the Welsh marches and the north.[157]

Once the queen had launched her attack, the behaviour of her troops and the absence of magnanimity in the treatment of the defeated Yorkists may have led to the size of her forces diminishing, so that the Yorkists did not need an especially large army and could defeat her with only a 'fragment of [a] ... faction'.[158] And the Yorkists' progress had a momentum of its own. It is very noticeable that as soon as they began to make headway in 1460 and again in early 1461 the waverers and backsliders in Warwickshire rushed to find the nearest reasonably loyal follower of Warwick to act as feoffee or witness, hoping to ensure that they had a bolt-hole into the ranks of the new powers should these succeed in establishing themselves.[159] In this light, the deed evidence as a

[156] Pugh 1972: p. 106 (but the Lancastrians *were* able to raise some men from Staffordshire and Derbyshire (Griffiths 1981: p. 820), and may well have owed this to Buckingham rather than to influence over the Duchy (above, pp. 466–7)); Rawcliffe 1978: pp. 25–6; Harris 1986: p. 142; Pugh, *Marcher Lordships*; Davies, R.R. 1987: pp. 313 (on the large role of Marcher lords in earlier upheavals) and 398–9. For lordship in the Marches, see Davies, R.R. 1978: Part II, *passim*. Griffiths (1981: p. 778) suggests that large numbers of midland gentry 'turned out' 'to protect their royal patrons', but, apart from those mentioned here, and allowing for missing evidence, there really seems very little substantial fact to support this statement. Cf. Rowney 1983: pp. 64–5 on the lack of Staffordshire support for Buckingham and Sutton of Dudley when it came to fighting.

[157] Griffiths 1981: pp. 820, 866, 870–4, 1974: pp. 85–6; Stow, *Annales*, p. 404; Morgan 1987: p. 51; Goodman 1981b: pp. 27–30, ch. 2, esp. p. 49, pp. 200–1; Ross 1976: p. 136; Storey 1972: pp. 129–34; Tuck 1985b; Maddicott 1970: pp. 57–8; James 1986a; Bean 1958: pp. 34–5; Pollard 1975–6: p. 65.

[158] Griffiths 1981: p. 872. The quotation is from Lander 1969: p. 95.

[159] Notably (and predictably) Richard Verney, who had been tarred with the Warwick-Mountford brush as late as early 1459, and had Burdet, John Greville and Thomas Middleton (app. 3 for all these) witnessing a settlement in September 1460 and by December 1461 had feoffees who included Simon Mountford, John Hugford and William Harewell (C.P.40/792 rot.394; S.B.T.

whole in the last years of Lancastrian rule is highly suggestive. Few deeds involving Warwickshire landowners survive for 1459. This could be more than coincidence, for it might indicate that in the extreme uncertainty of that year few landowners were prepared to make such an open show of friendship to one another, for fear that some of their associates could be disgraced shortly after. But a situation in which the ordinary practices of landowning life were inoperable could not continue indefinitely, and by 1460 the gentry must have been desperate for any way out of the crisis. It is probable that increasingly the majority were hoping that if there was to be a solution it would be a Yorkist one, if only to get rid of the queen, and this may explain why, despite all the reasons for neutrality, when it came to the final showdown at Towton the Yorkists were able to raise such a large army, even if it was still smaller than the Lancastrian one. If effective royal authority was desired and welcomed because it brought stability, the converse must also have been true: the ultimate step of deposition could be taken, or at least allowed to happen, if the monarch himself brought nothing but instability.[160]

In this context it is worth looking at the failure of much of the 'new' royal affinity to respond to the crisis of the Lancastrian dynasty, in marked contrast to its loyalty to Henry IV, a point which emphasises the radical difference between the artificiality of Margaret's rapid creation and the deep ties which bound the retinue to the earlier Lancastrian kings.[161] It has been suggested that the main reason was the lack of substantial rewards, but, as often with a 'patronage' explanation, this seems only to go part of the way. The real point was surely the loss of confidence in the king, both as leader of his own affinity, and as director of the affairs of the realm. Neither grossly partisan politics nor gross uncertainty could in the end be acceptable, even for some of the beneficiaries, since both ran counter to the conditions required for the normal conduct of gentry affairs. This applies equally to the realm as a whole. If the reactions of the Warwickshire gentry to the events of the 1450s are examined, it becomes apparent that it was only certain types who participated directly in the national confrontation; failures like Robert Ardern, people who in the course of their own business had committed themselves too far in one direction like Thomas Ferrers II, John Archer or Edmund Mountford, and the utterly loyal retainers like William Hastings and perhaps Henry Fillongley, who seems to

D.R.98/502, 123e). The first transaction was also Burdet's point of re-entry to the Warwick affinity. Another to cover himself in this way was John Spenser, for whom see below, p. 607 n.37. Cf. Richard Quatermayns in Oxfordshire (Driver 1983: pp. 96–7). Coventry itself, the Lancastrian capital, was also doing some rapid turn-abouts (*Coventry Leet Book*, pp. 308–19).

160 This point is made in general terms in Davies, C.S.L. 1977: pp. 80–1; Goodman 1981b: pp. 50–1.

161 Payling 1987b: pp. 150–73, 194–8; Wright 1983: pp. 83–5.

have died with Wiltshire at Towton.[162] Mostly the gentry kept well clear. That was why there was so little overt support for York, even as enthusiasm for the reigning dynasty waned. The 1450s had been an entirely unsatisfactory decade for them, but most had come through, and in coming through had learned some valuable lessons which might be put into effect in the years to come.

[162] Also William Catesby (above, p. 131), although it is not clear in which of these categories he belongs, probably the second, as he was an able politician; above, pp. 105, 131, 432, 459, 474; *Wedgwood: Biographies*, p. 602; *Paston Letters*, ed. Gairdner, III, p. 30; *G.E.C.*, VI, pp. 370–1. As he fades from view after May 1460, Fillongley may have met his end at Towton, as it was there that his master, the earl of Wiltshire, died. He was certainly dead by Michaelmas 1463 (Griffiths 1981: p. 874; E.372/262 *sub* Warwicks.). It is of course quite possible that other participants have been missed (recently-discovered ones are Robert Catesby's sons and John Hugford at Towton, respectively for Henry VI and Edward IV: P.R.O. Catesby Doc.), but the search has been extensive and it does not seem that any major figures have been omitted.

13

THE PERIOD OF CRISIS
II: WARWICKSHIRE UNDER THE KINGMAKER AND THE DUKE OF CLARENCE 1461–78

I

In 1461 Warwick found himself without rival in and around Warwickshire. Buckingham had died at Northampton in 1460 and his son of plague in 1458; the heir was an infant grandson, who was not to come into his lands until 1473. The family estates in England were in the hands of the duke's widow, who in 1467 was to marry Walter Blount, a Derbyshire landowner who had eventually gone over to the Yorkists in the late 1450s. The dowager duchess seems to have spent a good deal of her time at Maxstoke, which meant that this particular north Warwickshire citadel was no longer the threat it had been in the past.[1] Warwick's northern flank was further secured by his appointment to the stewardship of Tutbury for life and to other Duchy offices in Staffordshire and Derbyshire, while Tutbury itself was granted in 1464 to the king's younger brother, the duke of Clarence, whose political interests were to move steadily closer to the earl's over the decade.[2] Warwick also had a grant of the crown manor of Atherstone in north Warwickshire which had formerly helped reinforce Buckingham's power there.[3] The senior branch of the Mountfords had won an outright victory with the defeat of the Lancastrians and Edmund's exile with Henry VI and the queen. Although Baldwin promptly retired into the priesthood, his son and heir Simon had been formally retained by Warwick since at least 1456 and had been very much under his protection before

1 *G.E.C.*, II, p. 389; Rawcliffe 1978, p. 27; *Cal. Pat. Rolls 1467–77*, p. 367; *Cal. Fine Rolls 1461–71*, pp. 11, 62; *G.E.C.*, II, p. 389; Alcock 1978: p. 197; above, p. 455.

2 Somerville 1953: pp. 540, 542; Hicks 1980: pp. 172, 43–51.

3 *Cal. Pat. Rolls 1461–67*, p. 186. He also had the royal manor of Fulbrook in south Warwickshire (*ibid.*). Buckingham had lost Atherstone in the 1451 Resumption (Rawcliffe 1978: p. 193).

then.[4] The confiscation of the lands of the earl of Wiltshire had left the disputed Botetourt estate in the hands of the crown, apart from Weoley and Northfield which remained with the Berkeleys. All the properties in the region of the Birmingham plateau, an area which had been so problematical for Warwick, went to the earl's own servants, Thomas Erdington, Fulk Stafford and Walter Wrottesley, and Berkeley himself moved in circles close to Warwick.[5] Throughout north Warwickshire, the area where he had been most under threat in the 1450s, Warwick was now unchallengeable.

Where north Warwickshire met Leicestershire he had gained from Wiltshire's removal. Wiltshire's lands and most of the Roos and Beaumont properties had passed to the newly-ennobled William Hastings, Warwick's own brother-in-law, from whom for the moment the earl had nothing to fear.[6] Edward Grey had died in 1457 and most of his lands had remained with his widow Elizabeth, who had married Sir John Bourchier, while some were shared with Grey's second son, another Edward, later Lord Lisle,[7] and both Grey and Bourchier were closely associated with Warwick.[8] If there were certain tensions among some of his associates in the north and east of the county over continuing problems with the Ferrers of Groby inheritance and its division among the Ferrers of Tamworth, the heirs male, and the Greys of Groby, the heirs general, there is no sign that these were seriously troubling the unity of

[4] *Dugdale*, pp. 1,010–11; *Wedgwood: Biographies*, p. 602; Griffiths 1980a: pp. 6–7; above, pp. 468–9, 474–5. Baldwin and Simon claimed that Edmund had quitclaimed the disputed land to them 'before the goyng of the seid Edmond Mountfort into the North with the . . . pretensed kynge'; i.e. presumably before going into exile or possibly to Towton, rather than during the northern campaign of Wakefield to St Albans II, when Edmund had every reason to believe he might win (Griffiths 1980a: p. 14; B.R.L. Wingfield Digby MS A590), but I have not found such a quitclaim, one which the senior branch would surely have kept.

[5] *Cal. Pat. Rolls 1461–67*, pp. 112, 186, 217, 297–8, 485; for Wrottesley's and Stafford's relations with Warwick, see Coughton Court, Throckmorton MS Exhibition Box (grant by Warwick), Gloucs. R.O. M.15/8, Br. Lib. Eg. Roll 8536, and below, n.54. *Cal. Pat. Rolls 1476–85*, p. 379. For Berkeley and the Warwick affinity, see Warwick Castle MS 118B. For Warwick's previous problems with the area around the Birmingham plateau and attempted solutions, see above, pp. 447, 470–3.

[6] *Cal. Pat. Rolls 1461–67*, pp. 103–4, 352, 354; *G.E.C.*, VI, p. 373. Hastings is described as a member of Warwick's council by Wedgwood (*Wedgwood: Biographies*, p. 616 n. 1), but his only known appointment to Warwick, a life stewardship of the Warwick properties in Leicestershire, Rutland and Northamptonshire, was not made until 1468, when it was clearly an honorific office granted in the hope of political advantage in the face of the oncoming storm (*H.M.C. Hastings*, I, p. 302). But Hastings was clearly much involved with Warwick's closest connections well before (e.g. *Cat. Anc. Deeds*, VI, C6437; B.R.L. 495218; *Inquisitiones Post Mortem: Notts.*, p. 63; Leics.R.O. D 611/196; C.140/30/53).

[7] *G.E.C.*, V, p. 360; *W.F.F.*, 2674: JUST 1/1547 m.4d.; *Cat. Anc. Deeds*, I, B104; *I.P.M. Hen. VII*, II, 802; E.326/11024. From 1468 some of these lands began to be granted to Grey by Bourchier and Elizabeth (see refs. cited here).

[8] App. 3.

Warwick's following across the north of the county.[9] In the south-east and south, with both Buckingham and Edward Grey Lord Groby gone, there was no magnate in a position to create any sort of following. Warwick's custody of the Latimer lands, which he obtained when his uncle and co-heir to the Beauchamp inheritance, George Neville, was declared insane, gave him additional authority in Northamptonshire to buttress his hold over east Warwickshire. His success in exploiting it can be seen from the intermingling of the two affinities under Edward IV.[10] In the area to the south and west of Warwick the problems of the 1450s had disappeared. The mediating power of Wiltshire, Sudeley and Beauchamp of Powick had all but gone; Wiltshire was dead, his line attainted, and the second two were now rather elderly and had lost their vital protection from the court. They were probably less ready to take an independent line in the earl of Warwick's home territory under the new dispensation;[11] it was now Warwick, not his rivals, who was basking in the favour of the court. Even though several of the grants of confiscated Warwickshire lands made in the 1460s, particularly those in the eastern part of the county, went to people who were closer to Edward IV than to Warwick, it is a striking fact that so many of the crown affinity in Warwickshire in the 1460s were the earl's men or members of retainers' families.[12]

Warwick was now a great national figure, whose responsibilities went far beyond the midlands. He was the king's foremost adviser, playing a particularly prominent role in foreign affairs, lord of the vast Neville estate in the north of England, and from 1461 to 1465 the man chiefly responsible for clearing up the

9 Elizabeth Grey (née Woodville and soon to be queen), widow of John, the eldest son of Edward of Groby, was trying to get some of this inheritance – as well as some of the Grey/Astley inheritance – for her dower, and in 1464, in marrying her son to Hastings' daughter, made the pursuit of these lands part of the agreement. The marriage did not take place, as Elizabeth acquired a far more formidable protector soon after, so the agreement probably did little damage to the Hastings' relationship with the Ferrers of Tamworth (C.1/27/268; *H.M.C. Hastings*, I, pp. 301–2; *Cal. Close Rolls 1461–68*, p. 179; Lander 1976e: p. 107; above, pp. 106, 325 n. 171, 469). There was a similar agreement between Ferrers and Sir John Stanley the same year, involving apparently both the Ferrers of Groby land and the Ferrers of Tamworth residual claim to the Botetourt lands (for which, above, p. 388) (Leics.R.O. DE 2242/3/30304(1); below, p. 504 for resolution of part of this claim).

10 *Cal. Pat. Rolls 1461–67*, p. 71; *G.E.C.*, VII, pp. 479–80; *Test. Vetust.*, pp. 360–1; K.B.27/836 Coram Rege rot.61d; Northants.R.O. Fitzwilliam MS 559; Hicks 1980: p. 48, 1986c: pp. 28–9.

11 *G.E.C.*, XII, ii, p. 734, II, p. 47, XII, i, p. 421; *Cal. Pat. Rolls 1461–67*, p. 72; Richmond 1977: pp. 80–2.

12 *Cal. Fine Rolls 1461–71*, p. 49; *Cal. Pat. Rolls 1461–67*, pp. 198, 199, 369, *1467–77*, p. 45. The Warwick clients in Edward's service were John Beaufitz (D.L.29/463/7542–62; *Cal. Pat. Rolls 1461–67*, p. 189), Richard Clapham (*Cal. Close Rolls 1461–68*, p. 101), Thomas Erdington (*Cal. Pat. Rolls 1461–67*, p. 186), Henry Ferrers (not in Warwick's service, but brother of long-standing annuitant) (*Cal. Pat. Rolls 1461–67*, p. 78), William Harecourt (probably) (*Trans. Birm. and Mid. Inst.*, 47 (1921), p. 70, 49 (1923), pp. 52–3); William Hugford (D.L.29/463/7552–62), Simon Mountford (but his loyalty to Warwick was waning by the time of this grant in 1469: below, pp. 503–11) (*Dugdale*, p. 1,011).

Lancastrian resistance there.[13] Even so, much would be expected of him in the midlands. Until 1465, when the Lancastrians were finally defeated and Henry VI brought captive back to London, doubts remained about the regime's future and it was the job of the king's immediate supporters to help him convince the country at large that he was here to stay.[14] They had one great advantage in this task, in that landowners had to put their faith in the new regime if they were to restore the co-operative *modus operandi* which alone made existence agreeable or even possible. No one apart from the Lancastrian exiles could have welcomed a return to the conditions of the 1450s. As long as Edward IV and the Yorkist nobility were prepared to be conciliatory, local equilibrium could be restored, and once this was achieved Edward IV would have established his right to rule. Nevertheless, success depended a great deal on whether king and magnates could offer the direction which would persuade lesser landowners to sink their differences in the cause of general peace.

Between 1460, which saw the first return of the Yorkists, and 1465 the signs are in some respects encouraging. In the mid-to-late 1450s, although horizontal linkages amongst some of the gentry may have grown in strength, the more localised networks, which depended so much on the existence of trust between neighbours, seem to a large extent to have disappeared, at least as far as the more prominent families were concerned. In the atmosphere of permanent mistrust engendered by the growth of confrontational politics and the failure of the noble affinities, the greater gentry, despite their determination to ignore political differences, had tended to be circumspect about doing business with their neighbours. A neighbour who might turn into an enemy was a dangerous ally, especially when there was so much local division and so little effective superior power to hold it in check. Many deemed it more politic to take their associates from any part of the county and almost any political faction as long as, for one reason or another, they seemed reliable. But it seems that the networks were re-establishing themselves in the early 1460s, especially in areas where they had often been dominated by the nobility. This in itself was an indication that the role of the local nobility in validating local transactions was being restored and that landowners were regaining their faith in groupings that had for the last few years been too divided politically to be relied on for dealings with their property.[15]

Evidence for much of the county is unfortunately sparse, but there can be no doubt that groups were re-emerging in the Warwickshire-Worcestershire-Gloucestershire region[16] and in parts of the north Warwickshire-Staffordshire region. In this latter area the network that had grown up around Richard

[13] Ross 1974: chs. 3–6.

[14] Ross 1974: pp. 45–63.

[15] Networks will be discussed at greater length in ch. 16 below.

[16] E.g. *Cal. Close Rolls 1461–68*, pp. 323, 188; *Cal. Pat. Rolls 1461–67*, p. 379; *Cal. Close Rolls 1476–85*, pp. 273–4; *Colls. Hist. Staffs.*, n.s., 4, p. 139; N.R.A. 'Misc. Deeds in Coll. of Arms',

Beauchamp, Buckingham and the Ferrers of Chartley and had remained a recognisable entity in the 1440s had virtually ceased to exist in the 1450s. Partly this was due to the death of William Ferrers of Chartley in 1450 and the passing of much of his Staffordshire and Warwickshire land to his widow who did not die until 1471,[17] but the group had survived both the Beauchamp minorities and William Ferrers' rather ineffective leadership between 1435 and 1450. The real reason for the failure of the group to function as a focus for the local gentry was probably that the whole area was so divided until the late 1450s. Then, by the time Buckingham and Edmund Mountford had dealt with their rivals in north Warwickshire and put an end to local division, they were too closely identified with the court to be trusted as leaders of a local network. In any case their methods had been too divisive for the new dispensation to work.

The network's reappearance from 1460 was due both to the restoration of peace and to the emergence of more convincing leadership. If Warwick was the greatest of the magnates with influence here, more direct lordship seems to have been provided by Hastings and, above all, by Sudeley. In the 1460s, perhaps because he was no longer a free agent west of Warwick, Sudeley began to exploit the power that could be exercised from his lands in north-east Warwickshire and his offices at Kenilworth. Another incentive for the re-establishing of the north midlands connection was that the number of families with a stake in the counties to the north who were active in north Warwickshire was growing. Much of this intermingling of north midlands families was due to the decision of two major north midlands landowners, the Ferrers of Tamworth and the Willoughbys (in the person of Richard Bingham, second husband of Hugh's widow), to involve themselves more heavily in Warwickshire affairs. The grouping also to some extent encompassed the north-east Warwickshire/Leicestershire connection, of which the Hastings had been a part before they were ennobled, and which William Lord Hastings was now in a position to lead.[18]

In the period 1460–4 these networks have a clear political identity, for they were becoming the natural points of contact of the affinity of the earl of

Part II, 508/13: S.B.T D.R.41/20 fo.47 (for dating to *c.* 1464, Bod. Lib. Dugdale MS 13, p. 55); Br. Lib. Add. Ch. 8441; Derbys.R.O. D156M/15; E.326/10798, 10852; C.244/97/192, /101/7.

17 Above, pp. 314–15, 320, 323–5, 451.

18 E.g. *Cat. Anc. Deeds,* VI, C6437; *H.M.C. Hastings,* I, pp. 25, 74, 295–6; B.R.L. 249983, 610247/46–7; B.R.L. Wingfield Digby MS A586; *Colls. Hist. Staffs.*, o.s., 11, p. 239, n.s. 6 II, p. 218; C.244/89/25, /93/43,53,80, /97/18; C.P.40/820 rot.293d.; S.B.T. D.R.37/982, D.R.503 fo. 57; Nott. Univ. Lib. Middleton MS Mi D 4148–9, 4465; *Trans. Birm. and Mid. Inst.*, 1884–5, p. 87; Leics.R.O. DG 5/5; Gloucs.R.O. D1086/T.103/9; Bod. Lib. Dugdale MS 13, p. 98 (from 1481 but shows clearly Sudeley/Hastings links); app. 3; above, pp. 117, 160, 299–300, 307, 325–8. Note that Sudeley's deputy at Kenilworth, John Beaufitz (D.L.29/463/7549–62), was in his affinity (app. 3). For Hastings' influence, see above, p. 488. There are signs that Walter Devereux of Ferrers may have had some influence here, despite his mother-in-law's tenure of the Ferrers' Warwickshire lands until 1471 (above, p. 451; Leics.R.O. DE 170/102–3).

Warwick and his client nobility. The connections focusing on the earl went further than this, for transactions involving families from different parts of the county or from the adjacent parts of the surrounding counties show that the single most important common factor among the participants was allegiance to the earl of Warwick. Examples are Richard Verney's feoffment of *c.* 1461, or the deed of 1464 in which Mountford, Edward Grey, Thomas Burdet, William Berkeley of Weoley and Richard Clapham participated.[19] In these years all the sheriffs, the known M.P.s and most of the J.P.s were in the earl's service. Some of them, such as Thomas Ferrers II, John Greville and Thomas Erdington, were entirely new to Warwickshire office, or had been excluded on political grounds for many years, and it was to Richard Neville that they owed their elevation to a position which might be onerous but brought immense authority.[20] The county as a whole, nominally at least, had come under the authority of a single man as it had not done since the hey-day of Richard Beauchamp.

There, however, the comparisons with the earlier period end, for it was one thing to be acknowledged lord of Warwickshire, quite another to make that lordship effective, especially over the gentry, who had grown used to ordering affairs without too much noble intrusion. In this respect it must be said that Warwick's record in the early 1460s is not impressive. There was bound to be some quite serious disorder early on, for it was only to be expected that the upheavals of 1460–1 would be exploited by the victors of the moment, particularly those whose enemies were connected with the losing party. It was true that some of these opportunistic acts could safely be ignored, as the victims were not in any position to register an objection. This applied to William Harewell's appropriation of Buckingham lands at Wootton Wawen, to John Hugford's seizure of Robert Catesby's lands at Wappenbury and Woolsthorpe while the Catesbys were temporarily disgraced by their support of the Lancastrians, and to William Repington's laying claim to the fishery of the abbey of Merevale, a house that had been under Buckingham's protection.[21]

[19] S.B.T. D.R.98/123e; Warwick Castle MS 118B.

[20] *Lists and Indexes*, 9, p. 145; *Wedgwood: Register*, p. 332; *Cal. Pat. Rolls 1452–61*, p. 680, *1461–67*, p. 574; above, p. 274 n.34.

[21] N.R.A. 'MS at Merevale Hall', Bundle I/3; S.C.R.O. D.641/1/2/274; S.B.T. D.R.3/258, 259, 612; C.P.40/802 rot.333. The Hugfords allegedly seized the land 'after the northe felde' i.e. presumably Towton (S.B.T. D.R.3/612). In his notes and his book, Dugdale gives the battle as Northampton (*Dugdale*, p. 970; Bod. Lib. Dugdale MS 13, p. 34), probably a misreading of this document. P.R.O. Catesby Doc. is categorical on this point. Dugdale is also in error in alleging that it was Baddesley Clinton that was seized (above, p. 128 n. 117). For the background to the case, above, pp. 104, 404–5. In June 1462 an alleged account of Metley's testament was given that was largely favourable to the Catesbys, and was presumably elicited during the course of their attempts to recover their land (S.B.T. D.R.3/258). For the Catesbys' position at this time, see below, p. 493. For Repington and Merevale, see C.P.40/802 rot.127; Nat Lib. of Wales, Peniarth MS 280 fo. 99.

But there were other conflicts that had to be resolved as quickly as possible. The earl of Wiltshire's feoffees, amongst them Thomas Littleton, had taken Bordesley from Thomas Erdington, to whom the king had given this former Wiltshire property. Erdington was Warwick's annuitant, and this flagrant act of defiance to both king and earl had to be dealt with quickly, as indeed it was, in November 1461.[22] Then there were the disputes involving John Hathewick and various other claimants over Oxhill in Warwickshire and Dodford in Northamptonshire which had broken out again in 1461. Too many prominent landowners – Hathewick, Eleanor Stafford, widow of Humphrey I of Grafton, William Purfrey II and various important feoffees – were involved for the conflict to be allowed to continue unabated.[23] The same could be said for the attempt of Thomas Conyngesby, a Worcestershire lawyer, to seize the Archer property of Morton Bagot, which had come to Richard Archer through his third wife. Doubtless Conyngesby had been prompted to choose this moment to lay claim to Alice's inheritance by the political disgrace and execution of Richard Archer's heir John I in 1460. However, Archer, even after the family's loss of Warwick's support during the 1450s, remained an important man in the Arden, and in the early 1460s he was well able to raise influential assistance elsewhere. Indeed, he had effectively been absorbed back into the Warwick connection, which was all to Warwick's credit, especially as it meant that the Porter–Archer affair went into abeyance for more than two decades. But that made it all the more imperative that attacks on the Archers should be dealt with promptly.[24] Equally, when the abbot of Combe claimed ownership of Catesby land at Hodnell in June 1461 while William Catesby was in exile, he found that his advantage was only short-lived, for Catesby soon returned to a royal pardon, secured by no less influential figures than Lord Stanley and Warwick's own mother, and was not slow to rebuild his circle of influential friends. In fact by 1463–4 he had possibly switched allegiances sufficiently to go north with Warwick on one of his campaigns against the remnants of the Lancastrians.[25]

[22] C.P.40/802 rot.125.

[23] JUST 1/1547 m.5; Baker 1822–41: I, pp. 352–3; above, p. 459.

[24] K.B.27/805 Coram Rege rot.80d., /808 Coram Rege rot.93; S.B.T. E.R.1/62/228, 229; below, n. 30. The Conyngesbys claimed that the manor had been settled for life on Archer and his wife Alice, who had already been married, and that they were the eventual heirs; the dispute seems to have broken out because the feoffees released the manor at Richard's request to be sold for masses for his and Alice's souls (*V.C.H.*, III, p. 135). Eastcote and Longdon were still nominally in the king's hands in Michaelmas 1461 (S.C.6/1089/2), but John Archer seems to have had them again by 1469 (S.B.T. D.R.37 Box 42/2526). For the renewed outbreak of the dispute, see below, p. 558.

[25] K.B.27/805 Coram Rege rot.74, /808 Coram Rege rot.45; S.C.6/1042/10 *sub* Lapworth, /949/15 fo. 40 (a tantalisingly ambiguous entry, which could refer to the costs of men going north 'to the lord Warwick' ('*domino Warr*'), or could be an error for '*domini warr*' i.e. 'by the lord's warrant', in which case the men might or might not have been going to serve in the northern campaigns); P.R.O. Catesby Doc.; 'William Worcestre', 'Annales', II, p. 491; *Cal. Pat. Rolls 1452–61*, pp. 542, 550.

These were the relatively minor disputes of 1461, while there were several others that are not worth individual mention but did their part in adding to the general turbulence.[26] Those that have been cited here were handled with varying degrees of expeditiousness. The question of Oxhill and Dodford seems to have been settled, for the moment at least, by 1463, when Hathewick's tenure at Oxhill was confirmed in an assize of novel disseisin. Meanwhile the Dodford plea was resolved at about the same time in favour of Eleanor. Hathewick was apparently connected with the Warwick affinity, a fact which must have helped him in his suit, and he immediately enfeoffed Oxhill to three of its key members, Thomas Hugford, Thomas Throgmorton and Thomas Burdet.[27] This is all the more remarkable in that the chief claimant was Eleanor Stafford, Humphrey II's mother, and all Hathewick's feoffees, of whom a fourth was Thomas Littleton, had a much longer history of friendship with the Staffords of Grafton than they had with Hathewick; all but Hugford were in fact Stafford's neighbours. Despite their support of Hathewick, Humphrey Stafford remained on good terms with them, notably with Throgmorton, who was employed as his auditor at this time.[28] The conclusion of this case must therefore be seen as a triumph for the peace-keeping powers of the Warwick affinity, the contending parties reconciled by the overall authority of the earl.

By contrast, the Archer–Conyngesby affair dragged on until at least 1464, ending temporarily at Warwick assizes that year in a compromise verdict, which probably pleased neither party. Conyngesby managed to inveigle Warwick into it on his behalf.[29] This was a mistake, as Archer's friends by this time included several of Warwick's friends, annuitants and servants.[30] More unfortunate still was the handling of the dispute between William Catesby and the abbey of Combe. Within two years of his pardon, granted in December 1461, Catesby had gathered around himself an imposing body of connections, some of them Warwick's own men.[31] There was therefore every reason to make peace between him and the abbot as soon as possible, and very little reason to suppose

[26] Carpenter, M.C. 1976: app. 148.

[27] JUST 1/1547 m.5; *Cal. Close Rolls 1461–68*, p. 188; Baker 1822–41: I, pp. 352–3. For Hathewick's connection with the Warwick affinity, see the mainprise he made in 1463 with various close servants of the earl (C.244/97/31).

[28] E.g. *Cal. Fine Rolls 1445–52*, p. 109; K.B.27/762 Rex rot.12 (the Burdet/Charnels case, and above, chs. 9, 11–12); C.1/24/57; S.B.T. E.R.1/61/185; *Cal. Pat. Rolls 1446–52*, p. 386; *Colls. Hist. Staffs.*, n.s., 4, p. 139; E.326/10852; *Cal. Pat. Rolls 1476–85*, p. 11; N.R.A. 'Misc. Deeds in College of Arms', Part II, 508/13.

[29] The verdict was that Archer was to get damages for part of the charge against Conyngesby but was to be arrested for false accusation on the others (K.B.27/808 Coram Rege rot.93). The Conyngesbys did in fact have the manor in the early sixteenth century, despite Richard Archer's instructions in his will of 1471 to sell it for religious purposes (*V.C.H.*, III, p. 135; S.B.T. D.R.37 Box 90; PROB 11/6 fo. 33d.).

[30] B.R.L. 610247/47a; S.B.T. D.R.37 Box 82 (plea of William Cumberford).

[31] *Cal. Pat. Rolls 1461–67*, p. 120; C.67/45 m.39; K.B.27/808 Coram Rege rot.45; *Cat. Anc. Deeds*, III, A4460.

that some judicious leaning on both parties by the earl would not produce the desirable outcome. Instead nothing was done until November 1466, by which time a fair amount of violence had been exercised on both sides.[32] Equally, despite intervention by Lord Stanley and by William Catesby after his return to favour, Warwick was unable to engineer a successful arbitration of the Hugford-Catesby of Hopsford dispute over the Metley lands. Significantly, in view of what was to be revealed about Warwick's control of his affinity, the main stumbling block appears to have been his inability to get Hugford to agree to the arbitration. Also noteworthy is the fact that both parties were reduced eventually to appealing to an outside power, Catesby to the queen and Hugford to the Commons. This also we shall see to be a characteristic outcome of Warwick's attempts to rule the shire in this decade.[33]

It was however the three really serious conflicts that erupted in 1461 that were ultimately to be most damaging to Warwick's local reputation. First there were two in which his intervention was specifically requested and failed. In October 1461 John Rous broke into a close of Thomas Burdet at Arrow and depastured it. This was the first of a series of attacks on Burdet's property which, according to Rous' account, were reciprocated with interest. The feud was between families that were neighbours and had been interlinked for a long time, and both parties were associated with the major local magnates, Warwick and Beauchamp of Powick. Both had defected briefly from their allegiance to the earl in 1459–60, so he had no reason to favour either of them. The scene should have been set for a rapid arbitration, and this is precisely what was demanded of the earl at some point in the early stages of the affair. But he was apparently unable to settle it, and in January 1463, amidst spiralling violence on either side, one of Thomas Burdet's servants was murdered. About 1464 both sides were reduced to appealing to the chancellor. This was Warwick's own brother, and these petitions, which the earl's negligence alone had rendered necessary, must have been galling in the extreme. Perhaps worse was the knowledge that some of the gentry from the core of the Warwick affinity were prepared to stand by Burdet, despite his apparent defiance of the earl's peace.[34] During the course of 1465, the year when Warwick returned from the north and was able to give some attention to his southern estates,[35] the conflict did die down, but by that time the damage to his local standing and to confidence in his ability to re-establish local order had been done.

Worse still was his failure to deal with Richard Verney. By 1460 Verney had

[32] K.B.27/805 Coram Rege rot. 79d.; JUST 1/1547 m.2; *Cat. Anc. Deeds,* IV, A8848.

[33] P.R.O. Catesby Doc.

[34] K.B.27/810 Coram Rege rot.73, /814 Coram Rege rot.61d., /815 Coram Rege rot.35; K.B.9/302/21; C.1/27/349, 407, /28/271; the stance of the local gentry is shown by Burdet's securities for a series of recognisances made before the chancellor later in the year (C.244/97/24,197). For the earlier relations with the earl of Rous and Burdet, above, pp. 450, 482 and app. 3.

[35] Below, p. 503.

contrived to get himself on what turned out to be the losing side but typically had managed to make rapid adjustments as soon as he realised which way things were going. In this his close relationship and earlier assistance to his son-in-law Simon Mountford had been of considerable use, enabling him to acquire Simon and a number of other Warwick men as feoffees by the end of 1461. Chancery recognisances of 1463–4 in which Verney was involved show how well he had infiltrated himself into Warwick's following by that time.[36] Consequently, right from the start of Yorkist rule, he was in a surprisingly strong position with regard to Richard Dalby, who had never shown his father's capacity for making powerful friends. Of Dalby's three lords, Buckingham and Shrewsbury were disgraced and dead, and Norfolk, although he had at least ended up on the right side, had never had much local power and died in late 1461. Despite the arbitration of *c.* 1456, Verney had no intention of remaining at peace with Dalby – the Cheping Kington lease seems especially to have rankled[37] – and he now had a wonderful opportunity to attack him before Warwick had time to impose order on the county. If we are to believe the petitions of Richard Dalby and his wife, and they are very circumstantial, for much of 1461 the Verneys, notably Richard and his eldest son Edmund, were perpetrating the most appalling series of acts of aggression against the Dalbys. They ambushed and assaulted Dalby and his wife as the two were returning from church at Cheping Kington and on another occasion attacked Mrs Dalby as she was on her way to church, knifing one of her servants in the churchyard. They threw Dalby's servants out of the manor. They stole fish and rabbits from Dalby's servants and so threatened them at harvest that they were unable to work. They refused to perform their part of the award made by the abbot of Kenilworth in the 1450s. In December 1461 they took a large number of sheep and oxen from the Dalbys' residence at Brookhampton and left them unsheltered in the pound, 'being than a grete snowe', without food or drink, while the under-sheriff, Edward Durant, refused to receive Dalby's writ of replevin, with the result that many of the animals died.

Much of this violence occurred while Dalby was away in the north with the fourth duke of Norfolk, and hence with the earl of Warwick, fighting the king's enemies. It was therefore logical that Dalby's wife should go to the earl, presumably while he was visiting Warwickshire, to get a letter instructing Verney to cease his molestation of her family. Verney treated this missive with the contempt due to an unacceptable suggestion from a social inferior. The fact that the venal under-sheriff, Edward Durant, was connected with Sir John Bourchier, Warwick's councillor, and with John Hugford, Warwick's close servant, cannot have given the Dalbys any great faith in the earl's ability to curb their dangerous antagonists. Although Verney was in Warwick gaol in October

[36] Above, pp. 467, 484 n.159; C.244/97/26, 28, 31; E.159/242 Recorda Hil. mm.43, 44.

[37] K.B.27/818 Coram Rege rot.117; for the arbitration, above, pp. 473–4.

1461, whence he was released on making security of the peace, and although a commission of arrest for the Verneys, of a distinctly Warwick complexion, was issued in April 1462, it seems to have proved impossible to restrain them. In this case also the final throw was a petition to Warwick's brother the chancellor, but in 1464, despite securities made in 1463, Verney was still molesting Dalby. In May 1463, in a desperate search for alternative and better protection, Dalby had become feodary to the king's own mother. Even allowing for the pardonable exaggeration of a petitioner, Dalby's plaint is strongly indicative that Warwick was already showing the helplessness in the face of prominent members of the Warwickshire gentry that was soon to become still more evident: 'Sir Rich is a comon oppressor of ye kyngs lieges and of so grete myght and power in yat countree that yor seid besecher is not of power to justifie w[t] hym by ye kynges lawes'. The most that Warwick could do was to keep him off the commission of the peace, but that does not seem to have made it any easier for Dalby to secure Verney's indictment by the other J.P.s.[38]

In the first few years of the Yorkist regime, in cases involving important members of his own affinity, where he himself had been appealed to, Warwick's authority had once proved ineffective and once been flouted. But the affair that was to prove his undoing in Warwickshire and reveal devastatingly the absence of unity at the heart of his following has yet to be touched on. It was really a series of cases, all centring on the township of Alspath or Meriden near Coventry. The geography and tenurial structure of this part of the Arden, similar to that near Tanworth, have been described. Most important in this context is that, like the Tanworth area, it produced numbers of very insignificant gentry. Hitherto, the proliferation of these families and the complexities of tenure had not given rise to the numbers of minor conflicts that were almost endemic near Tanworth.[39] It was Warwick himself who was responsible for the heightening of tension in the area, by bringing retainers from northern families south with him and settling them in Alspath and on his own manor of Berkswell to the south of Alspath: John Shirwode at Alspath and Richard Clapham at Berkswell.[40]

The Coventry region itself, having been rather a backwater since the days of forceful Duchy of Lancaster rule under the first two Lancastrian kings, had assumed a greater political importance than ever before in the 1450s, when the court moved to the town. Once the campaigns of 1459–61 had shown that control of the midlands was one of the deciding factors, Coventry was to remain in the forefront of royal concerns, for Warwickshire was on or near many of the

[38] C.1/27/359, /28/481–2; *Cal. Pat. Rolls 1461–67*, p. 202; C.244/100/7, /97/28, 31; *Sir Christpher Hatton's Book of Seals*, p. 266. For Durant and Bourchier, see app. 3, for Durant and Hugford, see P.R.O. Catesby Doc. (counsel to Hugford at the arbitration with Robert Catesby: above, pp. 404–5). There is no record of any indictments of Verney for these trespasses etc.

[39] Above, pp. 22, 77.

[40] Above, p. 126.

main highways through the midlands. The importance of the Coventry-Kenilworth axis was accentuated by royal interest in exploiting the political potential of the Duchy of Lancaster and Kenilworth's role as a military arsenal.[41] From Edward IV onwards, kings took care to let the citizens of Coventry know that he was also their lord.[42] Inevitably the rise of Coventry's strategic importance had led to a growing political involvement in the Coventry area, not just on the part of the earl of Warwick, but also from the Mountfords, for whom Alspath, just down the road from Coleshill, was a natural outlier,[43] and from Sudeley in his capacity as Constable of Kenilworth. It was Sudeley who really exercised the greatest influence on the Coventry-Kenilworth area through the local connections of his deputy John Beaufitz and through his link with Henry Boteller, Recorder of Coventry since Littleton relinquished the job in 1455.[44]

Already in the 1450s there had been signs that the newcomers to Alspath were not being properly assimilated, when one of these, John Shirwode, had been sued by John Boteller of Alspath for one of the fragmentary estates in the township. Shirwode claimed to have bought it of Richard Waldeve, a previous owner, while Boteller insisted he had inherited the property by marriage to the heiress of Waldeve's son John. The verdict went Boteller's way, but, because it was eventually given in the first months of Edward IV's reign, Shirwode was determined to make the most of the fact that he was connected with the earl of Warwick, while Boteller had lent considerable assistance to Edmund Mountford under the previous regime. Consequently when the prior of Maxstoke – another 'non-person' in this early period because he had enjoyed the duke of Buckingham's patronage – leased some land at Alspath to Boteller in December 1461, Shirwode entered it and threw Boteller out.[45]

Elsewhere in Alspath far worse things were about to happen. Richard Clapham and John Shirwode, their mutual links with Warwick notwithstanding, fell out over the Alspath tithes, owned by the prior of Coventry, and over another of Alspath's small manors. This estate, known as Gerard Seyntluce, had an exceedingly complicated descent, and it was also claimed by John Boteller and the Chetwynds; it may indeed have been the latter family's main property at Alspath.[46] In March 1462 Baldwin and Simon Mountford agreed

[41] Above, pp. 17, 27–8; Goodman 1981b: pp. 26–53, 160, 183.

[42] E.g. *Coventry Leet Book*, pp. 314–16, 322–7, 328–32, 340–1, 370–1, 383–4, 391–4, 408, 420, 423–4, 432–5, 535–7, 550, 589; *Trans. Birm. and Mid. Inst.*, 1876, p. 31; above, p. 27.

[43] Above, p. 457.

[44] App. 3; D.L.29/463/7542–62; *Coventry Leet Book*, p. 283.

[45] JUST 1/1547 m.6d.; K.B.27/808 Coram Rege rot.74d. Shirwode had already attacked the prior in September, even before the lease was made (K.B.9/313/22). For Boteller and Edmund Mountford, see above, p. 457 n.51 and for Maxstoke and Buckingham, see *Dugdale*, pp. 998–9.

[46] Bod. Lib. Dugdale MS 13, p. 26; C.1/28/376, /29/367; K.B.27/810 Coram Rege rot.27; S.B.T. D.R.10/554; Wm. Salt Lib. H.M. Chetwynd Coll. Bundle 4 (descent of Alspath and Stanley/

to arbitrate between Clapham and Shirwode. This made eminently good sense, in view of Coleshill's proximity to Alspath and of the fact that the Mountfords were prominent members of the Warwick affinity to which these two lesser men were also attached. Unfortunately the arbitrators acted with outstanding incompetence, leaving Shirwode with the impression that he had won and Clapham apparently in considerable confusion about the outcome. Yet another petition to the chancellor was made.[47] The chancellor himself may not have been entirely inclined to impartiality, since his own servant, Thomas Shirwode, probably John's son, had allegedly been threatened by Clapham.[48] By 21 September Simon Mountford himself was no longer an impartial arbiter but an opponent in a law-suit with Clapham. New arbitrators, John Brome of Baddesley Clinton and the abbot of Kenilworth, neighbours of both parties, were brought in to decide between Clapham and Mountford. Again the arbitration failed; Clapham claimed that a 'false award' was made and that on his way home to Berkswell from Kenilworth, where the arbitration had taken place, he was attacked by a number of men at Mountford's instigation. Two more chancery petitions from Clapham followed.[49]

One may well ask where, during all this messing about with failed arbitrations, was Warwick, the one man who had the authority to bring the whole affair to an end. The answer is that he was losing control of an affinity whose acute divisions were emphasised during the next two years, as accusation was followed by counter-accusation and Shirwode and Clapham continued to wrangle over a broad spectrum of issues. By May 1463 the rifts within the earl's following had deepened alarmingly. By then at the very latest Simon Mountford had taken up John Shirwode's case against Richard Clapham and three distinct conflicts – Shirwode versus Boteller, Shirwode versus Clapham and Clapham versus Mountford – had come together.[50] If enmity between Clapham and the senior Mountfords seems improbable after all they had been through together in defence of Simon's interests in the 1450s, it should be remembered that these same Mountfords had no cause to love John Boteller

Chetwynd agreements of 2 Ric. III, 1 Hen. VII). The *V.C.H.* (IV, pp. 151–2) is confused on the manorial descent at Alspath.

47 C.1/28/376; K.B.27/808 Coram Rege rot.87.

48 *Cal. Close Rolls 1461–68*, p. 158; S.B.T. D.R.10/554. However, for doubts concerning people named as 'servants' of the chancellor in chancery records, app. 4; even so, as he was probably a member of a Yorkshire family that was closely linked to the Nevilles (above, p. 126 n. 113), in Shirwode's case it may be that we can take the appellation at face value.

49 C.1/27/174, /28/375.

50 C.1/28/375; K.B.27/808 Coram Rege rot.87, /810 Coram Rege roti.20d., 27, /817 Coram Rege rot.15d., /808 Coram Rege rot.74d., /815 Coram Rege rot.64d., /827 Coram Rege rot.26; K.B.9/307/80; *Cal. Pat. Rolls 1467–77*, p. 331. Note however that as late as 19 May 1463 Mountford and Clapham were acting as joint securities for Burdet (C.244/97/197).

after his efforts on Edmund's behalf in the same period, and Shirwode may well have been able to exploit past rancour to win Simon over to his side.[51]

A fourth affair had already been absorbed into Mountford's own dispute with Clapham, that between Richard Verney and Richard Dalby, for among the men named as ringleaders in the ambush of Clapham when he was on his way home from the arbitration at Kenilworth was Richard Verney. Verney and Mountford were both involved in making securities for Thomas Burdet in 1463 and were neighbours in southern Warwickshire, relatives by marriage and friends of long standing. Verney had presumably been drawn into this business on Mountford's side because he had been antagonised by Warwick's efforts to protect Richard Dalby and Clapham was one of the earl's closest servants.[52] In August 1464 a commission was issued for the arrest of the men who had actually attacked Clapham, but not for Mountford and Verney who had been behind the assault. As in the case of the earlier commission for Verney's arrest, it was dominated by Warwick's men. During 1464 the dispute moved another step further, when, it was later alleged, a false accusation was made against several yeomen from Coleshill, presumably Mountford's servants or tenants, leading to their indictment for an assault near London. The people said to have been responsible for the accusation were Clapham, John Boteller of Alspath, the abbot of Kenilworth, John Hugford, one of Warwick's leading retainers, and various minor gentry and yeomen from Alspath, Kenilworth and the neighbourhood.[53] Thus most of the area west of Coventry and much of Warwick's affinity had been drawn into an ever more divisive conflict which the earl was proving incapable of controlling. We can assume that Warwick was more likely to favour the side which included Clapham and the Hugfords and can be almost certain that he had been trying to protect Richard Dalby against the Verneys. If this is so, the man who was supposed to be in charge of Warwickshire was rapidly alienating Richard Verney, one of the leading gentry in the south of the shire, and Simon Mountford, the greatest non-noble landowner in the county.

In fact the whole affair bit deeper than this, for it is apparent that Mountford and Verney were closely tied in with some of the earl's most eminent and closest clients, men like Walter Wrottesley, his councillor and steward, who was to follow him into rebellion in 1470, William Berkeley of Weoley, another rebel of the Readeption, Richard Middleton of Northamptonshire, a life annuitant, possibly brother of Thomas of Walton Deyville, also a life annuitant, Thomas Muston, for whom the earl stood feoffee, the Otters of Yorkshire and

[51] Above, p. 457 n.51. Boteller had been close enough to the family to be William's auditor by 1443 (C.244/37/16).

[52] C.1/28/375; C.244/97/24, 26, 197; for Mountford and Verney, see above, pp. 105, 467.

[53] *Cal. Pat. Rolls 1461–67*, p. 349 (the commissioners were Ferrers, Erdington, John Greville, John Molle (linked with Clapham: *Cal. Pat. Rolls 1467–77*, p. 331) and the sheriff, William Harecourt (*Lists and Indexes*, 9, p. 145)); K.B.27/827 Coram Rege rot.26; K.B.9/307/80.

Warwickshire, who were also to rebel on Warwick's behalf, and Edward Grey, later Lord Lisle, another of Warwick's councillors. Some of these no doubt set out to put some distance between themselves and Mountford when he became embroiled in his feud with Clapham, but the fact remains that in 1464, when the conflict was reaching its fiercest, several of them were still prepared to act as securities for Mountford. It could be argued that this was deliberate policy on Warwick's part, to refuse to acknowledge division in his following and to get his own councillors to stand surety for the men who were on the aggressive against other close servants. But there are good grounds for believing that what was really happening was that his affinity was splitting apart and that, if he was trying to limit the damage, he was not being successful. First, we must remember that Mountford's and Verney's connections in the Warwick affinity extended also to Thomas Burdet, which meant that all three of the major figures who were showing themselves not to be amenable to the earl's authority were interlinked. Secondly, to emphasise this point, Edward Durant, the under-sheriff who had acted corruptly for Richard Verney in 1461, was rendering similar services to Thomas Burdet against John Rous' fellow defendants in late 1463 or early 1464. Durant himself was associated with both the Bourchier-Grey and the Sudeley connections, not to mention John Hugford. If Hugford was apparently siding with Warwick's more loyal servants by the end of 1464, he too may have been wavering before then. In the light of all this evidence, it does not look as though Warwick was deliberately deploying his closest followers to restore unity to his affinity, but rather that he had lost control of the actions of most of his more substantial clients and was in the process of losing control of the whole country.[54]

[54] C.244/97/28, 31, 45, /99/16, 27, 39, 115, 137, /100/8; E.159/242 Recorda Hil m.43. For Wrottesley, *Colls. Hist. Staffs.*, n.s., 6, ii, pp. 216–9, 222–3, 226, 229–30, 233, 237 and above, n. 5; for Berkeley, see Hicks 1980: p. 48; for Middleton, see Horrox and Hammond eds., *British Library Harleian Manuscript 433*, II, p. 93, and *Cal. Close Rolls 1435–41*, p. 477, *1461–68*, p. 323 for evidence of the relationship to Thomas; for Muston, below, n. 82; for Durant and Hugford, above, p. 497. For other political affiliations mentioned here, see app. 3. *The Coronation of Richard III*, p. 373, suggests that the Richard Middleton named in Harley 433 as an annuitant of Warwick was a member of the Westmorland family. The issue is complicated by the numbers of Middletons in the north, most of them linked with the Nevilles (Coles 1961: Apps.). The Northamptonshire man was both of Northamptonshire and of Northumberland, so he could easily be one of the Middletons retained by the Nevilles (the Middletons of Belsay, Northumb. had a Neville connection and a Richard and Thomas of the right generation: *ex inf.* Dr Rosemary Horrox); not only was he probably related to Thomas, a life annuitant of Warwick, he was pardoned after the Readeption, and may well have been the Richard Middleton in receipt of an annuity from the neighbouring counties of Beds. and Bucks. under Richard III (C.67/46 m.20, /48 m.6; Horrox and Hammond eds., *British Library Harleian Manuscript 433*, I, p. 92). Durant was alleged to have a bad name for dubious practices of this kind (P.R.O. Catesby Doc.). There is a different version of the same episode involving Durant in S.C.8/6863B, which suggests either a different corrupt under-sheriff or a simple error, but Durant's role in the Dalby affair would seem to support the case against him.

And there is another aspect to the story, which is the role of the crown in all this. It is a striking fact that from about 1463, when Warwickshire begins to be seriously disturbed, the nature of the *corpus cum causa* files changes; increasingly they deal with peace-keeping securities between prominent gentry and nobility and a lot of their business in the 1460s relates to Warwickshire. It is impossible to be categorical on this point, because the sources may reflect no more than a reordering of records, and there are clearly other aspects of royal policy on internal order to be reckoned with. In effect, however, they seem to reveal a situation in which the king has become aware that Warwick is not coping – this must after all have been painfully obvious from the chancery petitions – and is stepping in himself to impose a truce on the parties. The same thing seems even to have been happening at the lowest social level, for Edward found it necessary to deal personally with a rising in Gloucestershire in 1463, which Warwick had initially attempted to quell.[55] What happened soon after confirms that Warwick was indeed losing control of at least part of his midland hegemony.

In 1465 the temperature rose still further. To make sense of the next stage we need to look at a new element. By early 1465 William Catesby was in a position to make an attempt on the manor of Lapworth that had been bought many years before by John Brome of Baddesley Clinton. Brome seems to have been less adept than Catesby at burying his Lancastrian past and presented a good target for a man who was now once more eminently respectable. A decade earlier the Catesby claim had briefly reared its head and been settled by compromise.[56] In early 1465 Catesby opened a new campaign, collecting statements and quitclaims from tenants at Lapworth to bolster his case against Brome. His master-stroke was a quitclaim by John Hancokkes, a descendant of one of the earlier feoffees of the manor, made to a group of Catesby feoffees of whom the foremost was the earl of Warwick. The earl had been persuaded to take the part of this former protégé of the court, perhaps feeling that he owed something to this erstwhile Lancastrian for the military help he may have given against his former allies in 1463–4. One of the witnesses to another of these transactions was Simon Mountford, which indicates that Mountford had yet to break irrevocably either with his lord or with Catesby, but the break came soon after.[57] In looking round with what must have been some urgency for a

[55] The whole subject of how and how successfully Edward kept the peace would repay careful investigation. Some preliminary comments on his use of the council, bypassing the normal legal processes, most notably in the second reign, are offered in app. 4; see also Barnes ed., 'Chancery *Corpus Cum Causa* File, 10–11 Edward IV'. For the Gloucestershire rising, see Hilton 1975: pp. 71–2; K.B.9/33/21; Kingsford 1913: p. 356.

[56] Above, p. 473. For the connection between Catesby's farming activities at this time and his claim to Lapworth, above, pp. 192–3.

[57] *Cat. Anc. Deeds,* III, A4251–2, 4256–7, 4274, 4381, 4402, 4406, 4513, 4537, 4547, IV, A8410, 8424. Note that Warwick is named as feoffee on only one deed, on all the others the feoffees are identical save for the omission of the earl. For Catesby's service with Warwick, see above, p. 493.

protector in face of this mounting threat, Brome found Simon Mountford, with whom he may already have established cordial relations during the failed arbitration of 1462 between Mountford and Clapham. As Brome's co-arbitrator, the abbot of Kenilworth, was already to be found on Clapham's side, both attempted arbitrations – the Mountfords' between Clapham and Shirwode and this one – had ended with the peace-makers themselves taking up partial positions, a fact which does not speak well for the cohesiveness of Warwickshire society at this time.

On 31 July 1465 at 5.00 a.m. a substantial force, aided and abetted by Simon Mountford, raided Clapham's and Boteller's lands at Alspath and in the course of the ensuing brawl murdered John Walker, probably one of Clapham's tenants or servants. For Warwick details of the personnel in this raid must have been horrifying. They included Shirwode, Simon and some younger Mountfords, Henry Frebody, another of the minor gentry from the Alspath area, and a host of lesser figures from an exceedingly broad radius east, south and west of Coleshill, and they demonstrated that Simon Mountford was on the way to becoming the greatest power in this part of central and north Warwickshire. To cap it all, Richard Verney and John Brome were also implicated, showing that almost every substantial member of the Warwickshire gentry who had found himself directly or indirectly up against the earl had come together under Mountford's leadership. Moreover, Mountford's securities in the early months of 1465, the period leading up to the incident, show him to be on disturbingly good terms with several of the major gentry from other parts of Warwickshire, some of them fellow-members of the Warwick entourage. It is not likely that this represents further attempts by the earl to use the affinity to bridle Mountford's aggression, for by this time he can hardly have been willing to use his closer associates any more to bail out this increasingly tiresome retainer.[58]

Long-distance control of Warwickshire from northern England had been seen to be unworkable, and now that the north was settled Warwick had the leisure to deal with the county. His triumphal entry into London with the captive Henry VI on 24 July was followed immediately after by the removal of Mountford from the commission of the peace, and on the same day and again on 28 August an imposing commission of *oyer* and *terminer* led by Warwick himself and packed with his well-willers was issued to deal with the rebellious gentry. Warwick seems indeed to have taken their resistance to his authority to be literally treasonable, for that was one of the words used in the commission to

Mountford had shown himself friendly with Catesby in 1463, on his return from exile (K.B.27/808 Coram Rege rot.45), and this deed must represent one of the last dealings between the two before the break with Warwick and the alliance with Brome made such associations impossible. It is also worth noting that in September 1464 Brome and Catesby had been on sufficiently good terms for the one to grant the other a twelve-year lease (Northants.R.O. Spencer MS 1246).

58 K.B.9/311/10, /313/26; K.B.27/916 Rex rot.6; C.244/99/27, 39, 45, 115, /100/8.

describe their crimes.[59] On 31 August the commission sat at Warwick, led by Warwick himself, and proceeded to hand down indictments of most of the principal malefactors. It is evident that Warwick had decided that the time had come to take Warwickshire in hand. He also went on the offensive against Richard Verney, who was in the Marshalsea by October 1465 and remained there until the following January, while Verney's son made a security of the peace before the Warwickshire J.P.s in April 1466.[60]

His point made, the earl, as in the 1450s, reverted to compromise rather than confrontation. Conditions in the mid-1460s were particularly favourable to such measures; the years from the capture of Henry VI until the breach with Warwick were the most tranquil of Edward IV's first reign, and it was now that the king himself was able to settle the issue of the Botetourt lands, if only partially, and to secure the confirmation of the fine of 1450 recording the division of the Warwick lands.[61] In July 1466 Warwick was in Warwickshire again. The previous month Walter Wrottesley, his councillor, acted as feoffee for John Brome for a number of properties, including the disputed manor of Lapworth. Even if he had remained friends with Mountford when the latter's relations with Warwick were deteriorating earlier on, it is improbable that such a loyal retainer as Wrottesley would act against his master's wishes now that an outright act of defiance had occurred. As Mountford was a witness to this transaction, we may guess that Warwick was not only abandoning his support for Catesby's claim to Lapworth but at the same time trying to mend a few fences with Mountford himself.[62]

Verney and Brome were in fact found not guilty with respect to the Alspath affray in two separate hearings in 1466 and early 1467, and all this may have helped create an atmosphere in which Brome and Catesby could accept arbitration for Lapworth in late 1465, and again in September 1466. The arbitrators named in 1466 give an interesting hint of where neutrality in Warwickshire was now thought to lie, for, although they were all three in some way connected with Warwick, as a group they were closer to Sudeley. This shows how far Warwick had failed to make himself the overall master of Warwickshire, the magnate to whom anyone wanting to bring local conflict to

59 Scofield 1923: I, p. 382; *Cal. Pat. Rolls 1461–67*, pp. 574, 489–90, 491. The other members included Thomas Billyng (one of Catesby's feoffees: n. 57), Thomas Ferrers, Thomas Hugford and Thomas Muston. The treason charge was made possible by the statutes of 1381 and 1394 which had made riot treasonable (Bellamy 1984: p. 56; *Statutes of the Realm*, II, pp. 20, 89). Warwick was having similar troubles in Staffordshire (*Colls. Hist. Staffs.*, 1934, ii, pp. 82–6, 90–1).

60 K.B.9/313/26; K.B.27/916 Rex rot.6, /818 Coram Rege rot.117, /823 Rex rot.19; C.244/103/14.

61 C.145/323/53; *Cal. Pat. Rolls 1461–67*, pp. 549–50; *H.M.C. Hastings*, I, pp. 2–3; Leics.R.O. DE 2242/3/30304(1) and above, n. 9; *W.F.F.*, 2683: Hicks 1979b: p. 117 (but these were not necessarily 'territorial concessions': above, p. 445 n. 17); and above, p. 445; there was also a Shrewsbury–Lisle agreement in 1466 (Pollard 1968: p. 61).

62 K.B.9/334/118; S.B.T. D.R.3/260.

an end would automatically turn. Sudeley was particularly well placed to assume this role as he was closely linked to several of Warwick's more intimate clients, including the Throgmortons and the Hugfords. In November 1466 arbitrators were named for the Combe–Catesby affair. These were Justices Needham and Danby, who were also the alternative arbitrators for Lapworth should the first mediators fail to reach agreement.[63] It was also in 1466 that the Bramcote dispute was finally settled, when William Charnels made a quitclaim of the manor to Thomas Burdet.[64] If 1467 was consequently a quieter year, the efforts to end the Lapworth dispute were not yet bearing fruit. In 1466–7 Catesby continued to amass declarations about his rights to the estate – some of them ambiguous enough to be of dubious value – while John Hancokkes, despite the pressure of a suit from Brome, repudiated a grant he had made to him two years before. Brome was also suing Richard Fulwode, another of the local men who had made a statement in Catesby's favour, and it is evident that the combination of Mountford's friendship and Warwick's conciliatory approach was giving him a new-found confidence.[65] In August 1467 at Warwick assizes he was found to have unlawfully disseised Catesby's feoffees to the manor and its associated lands, and responded by immediately suing an attaint against the jury.[66]

Conciliation was also the order of the day in the Alspath affair, but again with somewhat equivocal results. Not only were Brome and Verney exonerated, but all three leading men on the Mountford side, that is Mountford himself and these two, seem to have eluded the attentions of Warwick's *oyer* and *terminer* commission. Mountford was apparently never indicted at all, while the indictments of Brome and Verney were called into the King's Bench but not used until Henry VII found them in the files and processed them through the courts to make a bit of extra cash.[67] Most of the King's Bench proceedings arose out of the *visu corporis* of the murdered man or on the appeal of his widow, neither of these actions being potentially as effective as the commission, and throughout 1466 and 1467 they were producing a stream of 'not guilty' verdicts or pardons.[68] However, not even this *de facto* acquiescence in the crimes of Mountford and his accomplices could bring peace to the area. Warwick himself cannot be exonerated from responsibility for a counter-attack

63 K.B.27/818 Coram Rege rot.35, /821 Rex rot.6d.; *Cat. Anc. Deeds,* IV, A9012, III, A6055, IV, A8420, 9613, 8848. The arbitrators were Thomas Throgmorton, Beaufitz and Henry Boteller; as well as having in common allegiance to Sudeley, the first two were of the Warwick affinity, the third connected to Grey and Bourchier, Warwick's councillors (app. 3).

64 *W.F.F.*, 2680: for its earlier history, see above, chs. 11–12.

65 *Cat. Anc. Deeds,* V, A10642, 10451, 10661, III, A4399, IV, A8068, 8410; K.B.27/825 Coram Rege rot.54.

66 JUST 1/1547 m.11; K.B.27/826 Coram Rege rot.71d., /827 Coram Rege rot.35.

67 K.B.27/916 Rex rot.6. Also the Rex sections of e.g. K.B.27/907, /908.

68 K.B.27/818 Coram Rege rot.35 *et seq.*, /821 Rex roti.6d., 9d., /822 Coram Rege rot.88d.; also E.159/242 Recorda Hil. m.43.

at Solihull in April 1466, when two of Mountford's servants were assaulted, for, although the abbot of Kenilworth was the leading defendant in the case, and was probably not readily amenable to the earl's control, there were others, such as Richard and William Clapham and another minor servant of the earl, who were or should have been.[69] In July came a counter-attack, when an attempt on Richard Clapham's life was made by a body of men gathered from several parts of the midlands, a worrying indication of the breadth of support that Mountford could now muster.[70] Towards the end of the year Mountford went on the offensive again. In late 1466 his servants or tenants impleaded the men who were supposed to have had them falsely indicted two years before, among them the abbot of Kenilworth, John Boteller and John Hugford.[71] In Easter term 1467 Mountford accused an assorted body of mostly minor gentry from various places in central and southern Warwickshire, some of them defendants in other suits in the case, of maintaining the case of the widow of the murdered man. As Warwick's steward, John Herthill, and two of his other servants, John Hugford and Richard Clapham, were among the accused, Mountford may have been responding to another instance of direct intervention by the earl.[72]

Several aspects of this affair should have made it particularly disturbing to Warwick. The first is the geographical spread of the places from which the protagonists came; it is almost as if a minor civil war were being fought out in Warwickshire. Mountford himself had friends throughout the county, some of them men of considerable local stature, and he and Verney had been particularly adroit at winning over the leading figures of southern Warwickshire, where Mountford himself was a not inconsiderable landowner and had made some useful connections during the family's travails in the 1450s.[73] On Clapham's side also there were gentry from other areas in the county, even if they tended to be lesser men like Thomas Shukburgh, Edmund Starkey and Robert Compton. Mountford may have been guilty of deliberate stirring up of trouble south of Coleshill to enlarge his area of influence and embarrass Warwick further, but if Warwick was doing the same to hit back at Mountford he should have known better.

Secondly, as far as Alspath was concerned, not only did most of Warwick's efforts to be conciliatory go unrewarded, but they were taken by Mountford as a signal that any amount of disruption would meet with impunity. At this point it does seem that the earl was trying to use his affinity to restore harmony to the county. The men named as securities for the chief defendants in the Alspath affray at Michaelmas 1465 and Easter 1466, most of them from the more

69 K.B.27/821 Coram Rege rot.17d.

70 K.B.9/322/23, /327/49, 334/116. And see C.244/97/202, /99/125 for evidence of Mountford's connection with Derbyshire through the Vernons (for which see below, p. 508).

71 K.B.27/822 Writs of Attorney; above, p. 500.

72 K.B.27/824 Coram Rege rot.69d.

73 For Mountford's connections, see refs. above, nn. 49, 50, 52–4, 58, 70, and C.244/97/24, 28, 31, 197, /99/27, 33, 39, 45, 64, 115, 137, /100/8; and above, pp. 157, 474 n.119.

eminent Warwickshire gentry, consisted of people from eastern and southern Warwickshire who were likely to be friendly towards Verney, and two clients of Warwick who had never wavered in their loyalty towards him, Thomas Throgmorton and John Ferrers I, eldest son of Thomas II. Neither had acted as security for Mountford or his friends in the period when his relations with Warwick had been deteriorating. Although other securities made by Verney and his son in 1466–7 make it clear that he was on good terms with the Ferrers and with other gentry of north Warwickshire, there is no reason to construe this as indicative of a division between Warwick and the landowners of north Warwickshire, any more than Thomas Throgmorton's co-operation with the defendants shows him turning against his master. Rather, it suggests a determined attempt to reabsorb the troublemakers into the earl's following and reunite the north Warwickshire wing of the affinity, which, apart from Mountford, had taken little part in the whole affair, with the central and southern segment, which had given Mountford most of his support. This was buttressed by the series of securities to the king that the Verneys and some of the lesser defendants were obliged to make in chancery in 1466–7. It is noteworthy that several of the securities in chancery and King's Bench were connected in some way with Sudeley, whom we have already seen to be a powerful force for compromise in the shire. That he was at his strongest in the area near Coventry, the centre of the trouble, and in the north among Mountford's neighbours would have added to the pressure he could bring to bear on both sides.[74] And yet, as we have seen, in the face of remarkable

74 K.B.27/818 Coram Rege rot.35 *et seq.*; C.244/102/104, 115, 159, 186, 251, 252, /103/14, 43. Throgmorton came off the commission of the peace in March 1466, which could be taken as an indication of the earl's displeasure at his showing signs of friendship for the men for whom he was shortly to stand security, but this is not likely. His appointment in Warwickshire, where the Throgmortons had rarely been J.P.s, seems to have been no more than a temporary stop-gap while Mountford, Verney and others were unavailable for political reasons (*Cal. Pat. Rolls 1461–67*, p. 574). To emphasise the extent to which the securities of late 1465–67 mark a sustained attempt to overcome the divisions within the county and the Warwick affinity, John Peyto, one of the south Warwickshire securities for the Mountford group, acted as witness for Thomas Shukburgh, one of Clapham's allies, almost exactly at the moment he was standing security for Verney and Brome (W.C.R.O. C.R.1248/68/30). The Sudeley men involved in these securities included Throgmorton and Walter Ardern for the Mountford group, and Edward Durant and William Bristowe for a man to whom Verney had made security a little while before, who was probably a friend or servant of Richard Dalby (C.244/100/7, 104/118, 122; see refs. immediately above and app. 3). With reference to north Warwickshire, it should be noted that here too there was a dispute, between Walter Ardern and his younger brother John, that had to be settled by appeal to chancery, in 1466, and by an arbitration probably performed under the authority of the king (*Calendars of Proceedings in Chancery*, I, pp. lxxii–vi). An indication of how the north was slipping away from Warwick is that in 1466 the reversion of two of the Botetourt manors near Birmingham, all of which had been in the tenure of men connected to Warwick (above, p. 488), was given to Sutton of Dudley, a man who, whatever his immediate local allegiances, was consistently loyal to the reigning monarch virtually throughout his long life (E.159/257 adhuc brevia directa m.12; *G.E.C.*, IV, pp. 479–80).

forebearance, not to say appeasement on the earl's part, Mountford continued to do just as he pleased.

Thirdly, although nearly all the leading participants on either side were in some way linked to Warwick, there can be no doubt that it was his most intimate servants – Clapham, the Hugfords, John Herthill and others – who were the object of Mountford's attacks. Unfortunately, although the leading men on Mountford's side tended to be from the outer circles of the affinity or even from right outside the Warwick nexus, they were on the whole more important as landowners. To be an effective lord, Warwick could therefore either punish those who were making life so unpleasant for this inner core of his affinity or impose peace on both sides. In managing to do neither while attempting rather feebly to do both he was doing his cause no good at all and demonstrating that he needed the assistance of the king and of an elderly minor nobleman, Lord Sudeley, to keep his own affinity in order.

By 1468 Warwick had effectively given in to Mountford. In January Hugford, Clapham and the rest were pardoned the alleged false indictment of Mountford's men, but less than three weeks earlier Warwick had allowed Hugford to be taken off the commission of the peace and Mountford, Verney and Burdet to be restored.[75] This was Burdet's first local office since he had betrayed Warwick in 1459, and, as he was a friend of Mountford and Verney and had passed the intervening years in persistent troublemaking, the earl can hardly have looked with a friendly eye upon him. Behind these surprising concessions there probably lay two motives. First, although there was no open quarrel until the following year, it is likely that Warwick's relations with the king were sufficiently strained for it to be necessary to see to some rapid accommodations within the county; if Warwick was heading for a confrontation with Edward IV, the last thing he wanted was internecine fighting within his own affinity.[76] Then, in Derbyshire Mountford and Warwick were actually on the same side in the conflict between the Greys of Codnor and the Vernons, which was now beginning to assume very serious proportions. The eventual alignments which crystallised in 1468 were Grey and Hastings on one side and Warwick, Clarence, Shrewsbury, Vernon and Mountford on the other. Vernon and Mountford were connected by marriage and their families had been closely associated earlier in the century. Since the Derbyshire business was rapidly becoming a trial of strength between the king on Grey's side and Warwick and Clarence on the Vernons', Warwick could not afford to alienate Mountford over a piece of defiance in Warwickshire.[77]

75 *Cal. Pat. Rolls 1467–77*, pp. 49–50, 634.

76 Ross 1974: pp. 114–25.

77 Wright 1983: p. 78; Ross 1974: p. 119; *Cal. Close Rolls 1468–76*, p. 26; *Dugdale*, p. 1,008; above, pp. 314–15, 320 n.149, 323–4. By 1469 both Mountford and Vernon were feeing Henry Boteller, Recorder of Coventry, which would have made another link between them (Wright 1983, p. 78;

But the net effect of all Warwick's exertions was largely self-defeating, for conciliation in the face of such gross provocation continued to be taken for weakness. In July 1468 for example Edward Ralegh, a south Warwickshire landowner who had been a security for the Mountford party since early 1465 and had helped bail Verney and Brome in 1467, joined a minor Coleshill gentleman in raiding the earl's manor of Berkswell. Almost certainly this was yet another episode in the Mountford–Clapham affair, since both aggressors were connected with the Mountford side and Berkswell was Clapham's residence, but on this occasion it was not only the earl's manor that was raided but his own house that was entered. The insult was accentuated by the fact that no indictment was secured until the following January.[78] In the same year Richard Dalby, another of those whom Warwick had vainly been trying to defend against the friends of Simon Mountford, again came under attack, this time from a different quarter. In October William Verney of Great Wolford made another sale of the land at Upton, Ratley and Kites Hardwick in southern Warwickshire, whose purchase by Dalby had been the original cause of the dissension with the Verneys of Compton Murdack back in the 1450s. The buyer was Richard Harecourt, of the Oxfordshire family, to whom the neighbouring manor of Shotteswell had been granted by the king on its confiscation from Wiltshire. As the land had been purchased long before by Dalby, William Verney had no right to make this sale.[79] Nevertheless Harecourt impleaded Dalby on a charge of forging documents – these were presumably the real deeds recording the earlier sale – and it was probably Harecourt's proximity to the king that apparently prevented Dalby from holding his own.[80] It is far from clear that Warwick by this time had any effective control over any of the major gentry of south Warwickshire, and he may have declined to lend any further assistance to Dalby, on the grounds that it was better to allow further despoliation of this unfortunate esquire than to risk alienating the whole area.[81] The following February there was more proof of his impotence south of the Avon when William Lucy had the impertinence to

C.P.40/878 rot.466, where Mountford is said in 1481 to owe Boteller £20 6s 8d of an annuity of 26s 8d a year = 15 years+). Edward actually issued the commission for Derbyshire from Coventry in February 1468, and the fact that he troubled to visit this royal town when he was generally concerned about the midlands may have seemed ominous to Warwick (C.81/1380/2, 6). It may also be significant that in 1468 Edmund, son of Richard Verney, was issued by Lord Stanley, steward of the royal household, with letters of protection against purveyance (*Dugdale*, p. 565).

78 K.B.9/327/46.

79 *Cal. Close Rolls 1468–76*, p. 31, *1447–54*, p. 23; for the earlier history of the land, see above, pp. 127, 417; *Cal. Pat. Rolls 1461–67*, p. 198.

80 K.B.27/836 Coram Rege rot.71; Shaw 1906: I, p. 135; *Cal. Pat. Rolls 1467–77*, p. 85.

81 The securities for Verney and Brome and their associates (above, n. 74) had included Richard Boughton, John Peyto, Harecourt, Edward Ralegh and Verney's son Edmund. Clapham's supporters from this part of the county were very minor figures (above, p. 506).

enter Hunscote manor, the property of Warwick's client Thomas Muston, which had been enfeoffed to Warwick himself and his councillor and intimate servant Walter Wrottesley.[82]

The consequences of failing to protect his closest followers in the hope of ensuring a general peace and of then being unable to achieve that peace were made all too shockingly plain in November 1468. John Herthill might have hoped that, as Warwick's steward, the Yorkists' victory in 1461 would have given him the chance to make good his claim to Woodloes against the disgraced Lancastrian John Brome.[83] On the contrary the only real threat to Brome had come from the equally discredited William Catesby, and when Brome took part in attacks on the core of Warwick's affinity, among them Herthill himself, he got off to all intents and purposes scot free. In the course of 1468 Herthill must have come to realise that Warwick was not going to help him regain Woodloes for fear of offending Brome's powerful friends, notably Mountford and Verney,[84] and he finally took the law into his own hands and murdered Brome as the latter heard mass in the church of the Carmelites in London.[85]

Although Warwick's authority in the county was wearing fairly thin by now, from March 1469, when the dispensation to marry his daughter to the duke of Clarence came through, he was in no position to do anything about it, for his mind had moved to greater matters.[86] All he could do was hope that if it came to conflict with the king his local support would hold. In actual fact over much of the midlands it stood up remarkably well. It was possible to execute Rivers outside Coventry in August 1469 and his widow's appeal shows that several of Warwick's midlands followers, including Edward Grey, John Hugford, Thomas Stafford, the brother of Humphrey II, and William Berkeley of Weoley, had followed him into rebellion. Moreover, the capture of the king soon after also took place in the midlands, at Olney in Buckinghamshire, Warwick's own manor. John Herthill was also named as one of the rebels in April 1470, and in mid 1470 William Harecourt, another of the earl's servants, was involved on his master's side.[87] The single Readeption commission of the peace for Warwickshire, issued in December 1470, although weakened by the removal of Mountford, Verney and Burdet and of Edward IV's officers, Henry Boteller, John West and Thomas Littleton, had a reasonably respectable representation

[82] K.B.9/324/25; *Colls. Hist. Staffs.*, n.s., 6, ii, pp. 217–37.

[83] Above, pp. 128, 458.

[84] In March 1468 Brome gave all his Warwickshire lands to trustees who included William Harewell, a Warwick annuitant of consistent loyalty, who was to be an active supporter of his master in the Readeption, and this must be strong evidence that Warwick was not taking Herthill's claims seriously any more. (S.B.T. D.R.3/530/1; *Dugdale*, p. 810).

[85] 'William Worcestre', 'Annales', II, p. 519; Bod. Lib. Dugdale MS 13, pp. 33–4; K.B.27/835 Coram Rege rot.52.

[86] Hicks 1980: p. 45.

[87] Ross 1974: p. 132; *Dugdale*, pp. 143, 148; K.B.27/836 Coram Rege rot.61d.; *Cal. Pat. Rolls 1467–77*, p. 218; E.404/75/1/35.

of the local gentry, certainly more so than the equivalent commissions of the last years of the Lancastrians.[88]

The only nobleman in the Warwickshire area who had been associated with Warwick to defect before the final days of the Readeption was Hastings.[89] His departure was entirely predictable but at least he failed to take with him his brother-in-law and Warwick's annuitant Thomas Ferrers. Ferrers' readiness to stand by Warwick is all the more remarkable in that throughout the 1460s and into the Readeption he remained in contention with Edward Grey the younger and Sir John Bourchier over the Grey of Groby lands. And yet, as Grey and Bourchier nailed their colours ever more firmly to Warwick's mast during the Readeption, Ferrers continued to serve as a J.P.,[90] perhaps encouraged to do so by the fact that his brother Henry was serving Clarence on the Tutbury Honor.[91] Even Simon Mountford was ready enough to recognise realities. He had been retained by Hastings in 1469, presumably in the hope that he would act as a focus for anti-Warwick sympathies in Warwickshire. The king too had specially favoured him when visiting Coventry in 1468 and had made him a grant of the lieutenancy of the Isle of Wight in 1469/70. But transactions of the Readeption show that Mountford was prepared to come to terms with the rest of the north Warwickshire landowners, most of whom had remained loyal to Warwick.[92]

On the whole the county was remarkably undisturbed for much of this time of crisis, a repetition of the local response to the crisis of 1457–60. As in the 1450s, this cannot be attributed to a lack of legal evidence resulting from fear of entering a plea while an adversary was protected by the victors of the moment, for subsequent reversals of fortune could and did open the way to prosecutions. There were two major acts of revenge during the Readeption, the Staffords' murder of Robert Harecourt, for which they had waited more than twenty years, Humphrey II having prepared for the first opportunity by building

88 *Cal. Pat. Rolls 1467–77*, p. 634. Cf. the Lancastrian commissions of 1458–61, above, p. 482.

89 Hicks 1980: ch. 2.

90 K.B.27/844 Coram Rege rot.79 (reference kindly supplied by Dr L.S. Woodger); C.P.40/844 rot.457d.; C.1/27/268–9; above, p. 105; *Cal. Pat. Rolls 1467–77*, pp. 245–8, 634; *Colls. Hist. Staffs.*, n.s., 4, p. 175, 6, ii, p. 226; K.B.27/836 Coram Rege rot.61d.; K.B.9/330/10; above, p. 469. The sides in the Ferrers–Grey dispute divided unpredictably: if Bourchier had every reason to oppose Elizabeth Woodville on this issue, so did Hastings on the Ferrers' behalf, which all goes to show that there is no predictable relationship between private quarrels and stances in national politics (see refs. immediately above, Woodger 1974: p. 280, and Hicks 1980: p. 40). See also other dealings with these lands, above, n. 9.

91 Somerville 1953: p. 543.

92 App. 3; E.404/73/3/92; *Dugdale*, p. 1,011; Nott. Univ. Lib. Middleton MS Mi D 4558; *Cal. Pat. Rolls 1467–77*, pp. 245–7, 634. Mountford had good reason to keep quiet during the Readeption, the renewed threat from Edmund (Griffiths 1980a: pp. 7–8, 16–17; *Dugdale*, p. 1,011; below, n. 115). Mountford's retainer may also have been related to attempts to settle the Grey of Codnor–Vernon dispute (above, p. 508).

himself a niche within the Warwick affinity,[93] and Nicholas Brome's of John Herthill, his father's murderer.[94] There were also some attacks on Hastings' estates, which, luckily for Warwick, did nothing to shake the loyalty of the Ferrers of Tamworth, but otherwise little of note.[95] Surviving deeds of 1470–1 show the gentry's usual ability to make the best of a bad job by ensuring the continuance of friendships and associations across factional lines. Even Robert Harecourt's widow hastened into an alliance with the Brasebrugges, whose connections with Sudeley and the Ferrers made them a good source of protection against any more aggression from the Staffords. Simon Mountford's participation in the marriage settlement showed that, despite his nominal connection with Hastings, he had had the same idea.[96]

In the north and around Coventry, Sudeley's contribution was of immense importance, both in providing officers and in the preservation of local stability.[97] It may well have been Sudeley above all who was responsible for ensuring that Coventry gave Warwick and Clarence its full support.[98] Warwick and the king between them had done their best to deprive him of his power in western and central Warwickshire, the former by taking his Kenilworth offices in February 1468, presumably because he was so anxious about the area in and around Alspath, the latter by appropriating Sudeley Castle in February 1469

93 K.B.9/992/76; *Cal. Close Rolls 1468–76*, pp. 102, 109; Br. Lib. Add. Ch. 73,925; Coughton Court, Throckmorton MS Box 49 (deed of 1468); E.326/10852. *Paston Letters*, I, p. 361 is revealing on Harecourt's unsuccessful attempts to protect himself during the Readeption. It seems that it was the king himself who had protected the Harecourts against the Staffords throughout the 1460s (e.g. *Cal. Pat. Rolls 1461–67*, pp. 29, 34, 278, 346, 570, *1467–77*, p. 625; *Feodera*, V, ii, p. 144; Lander 1976: p. 315; Br. Lib. Stowe MS 440 fo. 68 for Robert's services to and favours from the king), and an indication of the importance to Edward of the family comes from a letter written after Barnet (S.C.1/60/15). That Edward protected the Staffords in their turn against retribution from the Harecourts in the 1470s is therefore all the more remarkable, especially in view of Thomas Stafford's hand in the death of Richard Woodville (above, p. 510), which was no doubt what helped the Staffords evade prosecution for the Harecourt murder from the Readeption government. It strengthens the evidence for believing that Edward was deliberately trying to win the family over in the 1470s (below, p. 524 and for the full context, see Carpenter 1986a: pp. 34–5). Note also that Harecourt's widow was persuaded by someone to withdraw her appeal for her husband's death (*Colls. Hist. Staffs.*, n.s., 6, i, p. 97).

94 *Dugdale*, pp. 971–2; Bod. Lib. Dugdale MS 13, pp. 33–4.

95 C.P.40/842 rot.350, /844 rot.95.

96 Leics.R.O. DE 221/1/2/7; Nott. Univ. Lib. Middleton MS Mi D 4148–9, 4558; B.R.L. 610247/47; app. 3; above, p. 105. See *H.M.C.*, XI (1887), iii, p. 113, cited in Dunham 1955: n. 14 p. 38, for efforts to win Mountford over to the Readeption government in October 1470.

97 App. 3; Nott. Univ. Lib. Middleton MS Mi D 4238, 4558/1; S.B.T. E.R.1/61/638; C.P.40/840 rot.132; Bod. Lib. Dugdale MS 15, pp. 123, 125.

98 Ross 1974: pp. 129–30, 132, 154; *Coventry Leet Book*, pp. 362–4, 369–70. A nice gloss on this is the payment to one John Holme in 1471 for changing the arms in the window of the Trinity Gild from those of Henry VI back to those of Edward IV (*Trans. Birm. and Mid. Inst.*, 1891, p. 25).

and giving it to Gloucester later that year.[99] Luckily for Warwick, since Sudeley remained a firm supporter of the Readeption right up to the end, the loyalty to Sudeley of John Beaufitz, now the earl's deputy at Kenilworth, and of Henry Boteller, the Recorder of Coventry, survived their lord's loss of office. While Boteller was taken off the commission of the peace as a precautionary measure, since he had been a servant of Edward IV, there is no indication at all that these two set out to oppose the Readeption government. Beaufitz, who was not to become J.P. until after the Readeption, had served Warwick as well as the king, and, although he had been commissioned to take rebels' lands in early 1470, he was content to take out a pardon from the new regime in January 1471.[100] It was just as well they were so co-operative, as Simon Mountford had already shown that he was at least as great a power as Warwick west of Coventry, and Sudeley may have made a major contribution to keeping Mountford quiet both in the Alspath region and further north.[101]

If Warwickshire did not give the earl of Warwick serious cause for concern during the Readeption, this was not because he had come any closer to bringing the county under his authority but because Edward IV had made no attempt at all to do so. Within Warwickshire even Hastings had been as much the earl's man as the king's for most of the decade.[102] The Warwickshire gentry really had no choice but to accept the new regime of 1470–1 for there was no one else to turn to. The commissions of array that Edward IV issued between Barnet and Tewkesbury show how few people he felt he could trust in either Warwickshire or Worcestershire until the Lancastrians had been decisively defeated. Even so Warwick may have had difficulties in raising men in Warwickshire, while, by contrast, Hastings is supposed to have been able to muster 3,000 men at Leicester, presumably in his own right and on behalf of the Duchy of Lancaster, during the Readeption campaign. Nor must it be forgotten that it was at Warwick itself that Edward declared himself king on his return in 1471 and outside Warwick that Edward was able to persuade his wayward brother to return to his allegiance. Once the Lancastrian defeat had occurred, both counties came very meekly under his obedience again.[103]

To sum up, from 1461 to 1471 Warwickshire should have been as completely subject to Richard Neville as it had been to Richard Beauchamp under Henry

[99] Somerville 1953: p. 560; *Cal. Close Rolls 1468–76*, pp. 51, 102; also Carpenter 1986a: p. 44 n. 41. There is some evidence that Warwick and Edward were competing for Coventry's loyalty as early as 1464 (*Coventry Leet Book*, p. 332).

[100] Ross 1974: p. 166; *Cal. Pat. Rolls 1467–77*, pp. 634, 218; C.67/44 m.6; app. 3.

[101] Above, p. 503 and note that Mountford was one of the men asked to affix his seal to declarations concerning the disputed common lands around Coventry made by Coventry's citizens in 1472, indeed, the only layman asked to do so in the capacity of local lord (*H.M.C.*, 15, x, p. 155; below, pp. 539–42 for the enclosure disputes).

[102] Above, n. 6.

[103] *Cal. Pat. Rolls 1467–77*, p. 284; Fabyan, *Chronicles of England and France*, p. 657; *Historie of the Arrivall*, pp. 8–11; Hicks 1980: p. 106; Carpenter 1986a: pp. 31–2.

VI, rather more so in fact because of the complete absence of rival powers. That it was not requires some explanation. Undoubtedly many of Neville's problems were due to the fact that he had so little time to give the midlands, especially in the early 1460s, when he was almost permanently in the north and the foundations of his later difficulties were laid. On the other hand, Richard Beauchamp had been abroad for much of the time when he had so successfully exercised such vast responsibilities. Neville also had the advantage of rather better direction from the crown than Beauchamp had enjoyed under Henry VI, even if Edward IV's rule was as yet nothing like as forceful as it was to become during the second reign.[104] The truth was that Neville was greatly inferior to Beauchamp as leader and political manager, although rather surprisingly he seems to have been not only more hesitant but perhaps less ruthless in the discharging of his local responsibilities, in Warwickshire at least.

There is every indication that from 1461 to 1464 the Warwickshire gentry were initially ready to fall back into old habits of deference to the nobility. They would pursue their private interests as far as they could, but were willing to accept that the price of peace was acquiescence in the magnate direction which would impose conciliation upon them if that seemed best to the noble ruler of the 'contree'. After 1461, once Warwick had shown that he was not the man to restore to the county a political system that would allow both for the conflict endemic in such a competitive society and for its necessary containment, two things happened. First some of the gentry could see no reason to renounce the disruptive pursuit of their own ends; if the county was to be disordered anyway it might as well be disordered with some benefit to themselves. Simon Mountford wanted to extend his power over a broad radius around Coleshill, John Brome wanted to defend Lapworth against William Catesby and not be forced to surrender it for the sake of local harmony, Richard Verney wanted to put paid to Richard Dalby's pretensions for good. Secondly the experience of all the gentry in the previous decade had shown the dissident gentry that they had nothing to gain by going to another nobleman for maintenance against the Warwick affinity; they had learned in those dangerous years that it was possible to manage without the nobility. It is clear that the group from all over the county that Mountford gathered around himself had no noble leadership. Hastings, Mountford's lord from 1469, could never have raised that much support in Warwickshire in the 1460s. The only magnate who could have dared challenge Warwick in this way was Sudeley, and his closest supporters were either uncommitted or acting as intermediaries between the embattled parties.[105]

By 1464 Warwick's failure was evident and it was therefore equally evident

[104] Wolffe 1976: pp. 371–2.

[105] Notably Richard Bingham and others in the attempted Brome–Catesby arbitrations of October 1465 and 1466 (above, n. 63) and Throgmorton as a security for Mountford's allies in 1466 (above, n. 74).

that this earl of Warwick, with all his advantages, was not going to be the focus for the networks of associated gentry from all parts of the county that his predecessor Richard Beauchamp had been. In particular, although it showed few signs of disloyalty, the north Warwickshire-Staffordshire grouping had minimal connections with landowners to the south,[106] while the northern connections of Warwick's affinity in south Warwickshire were confined almost entirely to the offices and fees that some of them held on the Buckingham estates.[107] As so often, the county was fragmented, but now the split was between north and south rather than between east and west as it had tended to be before. Almost all the known linkages between north and south came through Simon Mountford, a major landowner in both areas, whether he was obliging Warwick's more reliable men by participating in their transactions or putting together his own affinity to do down some of Warwick's most faithful clients.[108]

Until the renewed outbreak of civil strife towards the middle of 1469 there was no reason for Mountford and his friends to moderate their behaviour for fear of stirring up uncontrollable local dissension; even if the local framework proved ineffective, Edward IV's kingship was turning out to be an adequate restraint of gross local disorder over much of the country, as his response to events in Derbyshire and East Anglia demonstrates.[109] There can be no comparison with the 1450s. It is apparent that, Warwick's invocation of the grievances that had led to Henry VI's deposition notwithstanding, he could not hope to make the sort of general appeal to the country that had been possible for the duke of York. The gentry were not sufficiently desperate to withdraw their support from the crown *en masse*, as in the 1450s. The battle was very much Warwick's personal one with the king and the Woodvilles.[110] It was therefore only in the Readeption, when they lost the security of an authoritative king and when political control at all levels was so firmly in Warwick's hands, that the Warwickshire gentry could be prevailed upon to display a solid allegiance to Warwick and Sudeley. Even then neither Mountford nor Burdet, respectively councillor (in name at least) and life annuitant of the earl, could be trusted sufficiently to be used as local officers. Once Warwick had been defeated at Barnet, loyalty quickly gave way to self-preservation. Between Barnet and Tewkesbury Richard Beauchamp of Powick and his father Lord John went

[106] For refs., see above, nn. 18, 97 and below, pp. 601, 608; also comments above, p. 507.

[107] *Viz.* Clapham, Dalby and Hugford (S.C.R.O. D.641/1/2/186, 274–6). William Harecourt and Hastings were north Warwickshire members of the Warwick affinity employed by the dowager duchess of Buckingham (S.C.R.O. D.641/1/2/25, 274–5; S.C.6/1117/11).

[108] S.B.T. D.R.3/260, D.R.37 Box 82 (plea of William Cumberford); *Cat. Anc. Deeds*, IV, A8424; Derbys.R.O. D156M/15; and above, n. 73 for all refs. to Mountford's allies against Clapham etc.; more on this, below, p. 608.

[109] Ross 1974: pp. 119, 399–400.

[110] Hicks 1980: pp. 46–7.

over to Edward, together with Richard's brother-in-law Humphrey Stafford. Simon Mountford was sufficiently emboldened by Warwick's defeat to fight for his king at Tewkesbury.[111] In the 1460s, as they built on the lessons of the 1450s, some of the Warwickshire gentry had shown themselves to be remarkably self-assertive. Beyond occasional interventions to rescue Warwick from the consequences of his inability to cope with his own affinity, the king had so far done nothing to harness the new-found independence of the gentry. Should he do so, an entirely new structure of local power might emerge.

II

In 1471, on Warwick's death and Edward's return to the throne, Warwick's place in the midlands was taken by Edward's brother the duke of Clarence. As actual owner of the Honor of Tutbury he was an even more hugely powerful figure in the region than Richard Neville himself. But in 1474 he lost Tutbury and in 1477 he was arrested, to be condemned in parliament and executed the following year. I have discussed Clarence's record as earl of Warwick and his failure and fall at some length in a recent article and there seems no reason to retraverse this ground in detail.[112] Instead, the main points of the article will be summarised here, drawing particular attention to Clarence's brief period in power in the context of the developments in local politics that have been observed so far.

In 1471 Clarence was in much the same position as Richard Neville in 1461: no obvious rival and vast tenurial and financial resources with which to make himself ruler of a large part of the midlands. As in 1461 it is highly probable that the gentry were at first only too willing to let Clarence prove himself as an effective local leader, hoping that national strife was at last at an end and there could be a return to the normal pattern of local politics. The re-emergence of the south-west Warwickshire-Worcestershire network under Clarence's leadership in the early years of his rule demonstrates as much. The only difference was that the gentry now had twenty years' experience of fending for themselves and were therefore likely to be less patient with noble failure, and perhaps less ready to compromise their own ambitions at the command of the nobility for the sake of order in the neighbourhood. Had they not lived through decades of upheaval and shown that they could take most kinds of conflict in their stride as long as there was some kind of reasonably effective national government? Only in times of acute national crisis, as in the second half of the 1450s and the Readeption, had it proved necessary to be circumspect in stirring up trouble. When circumspection no longer seemed necessary, there now seemed much less

[111] Carpenter 1986a: pp. 31, 35; Stow, *Annales*, p. 425.

[112] Carpenter 1986a. More detail will be found there, and the names of the members of affinities referred to in general terms in the article will be found in app. 3. Footnotes are given only where new information has been added.

need to rein in their aggressive instincts. For example, soon after Clarence's arrival, John Greville II and his son Thomas Cokesey, who between them had become a very powerful force in the Warwickshire-Worcestershire-Gloucestershire region, came into a head-on collision with the Staffords of Grafton, who apparently resented their growing power. It was clearly going to require extremely assertive noble intervention to bring them and similarly-minded gentry to heel.[113]

This was something that Clarence was quite unable to provide. In the early 1470s, for the first time in the entire century, the most disordered part of the region was the corner of Worcestershire and Warwickshire where the earl of Warwick's estates and affinity had always been concentrated. Undoubtedly his job was made harder by the weakening of the controlling influence of Sudeley (who was soon to die and seems in any case to have been in prison at this time)[114] and of John Beauchamp of Powick, since it was through these two that much of the Warwick power here had been filtered since the 1440s, but there was really no excuse for his utter feebleness. And in the long term the removal of the intrusive presence of these two minor lords should have restored Clarence to the sort of authority exercised by Richard Beauchamp. In the north of the county things were little better. Here also Sudeley left a gap that Clarence was unable to fill. With his land and connections in the north midlands Clarence should have been able to maintain the network in north Warwickshire and the north midlands that had flourished in the 1460s and even managed to function through the Readeption, but there are firm indications that it was already becoming seriously divided as early as 1472–3. In and around Coventry, where Sudeley's removal from his Duchy offices and subsequent total displacement had left a real gap, things were if anything worse.

Faced with Clarence's manifest inability to manage, it is not to be wondered at that others began to see possibilities for themselves. Foremost among them was Simon Mountford, the first to attempt to cut a swathe across Clarence's political territory. Building on the following he had already raised around Coventry, he set about pursuing the long-dead family claim to the Sudeley lands, a part it seems of a grand design to recreate a similar political nexus. This would run from Sudeley Castle in Gloucestershire, through Kenilworth, where he eventually succeeded to Sudeley's former office of constable in 1474, up to Coleshill. It would include along the way his own south Warwickshire manor of Ilmington and two of Sudeley's manors in south-east Warwickshire which lay conveniently close to other Mountford properties. He was stopped in his tracks by the king, who kept Sudeley Castle for himself, or at least for Gloucester until 1478, and made sure that Mountford was not found heir to the other Sudeley

[113] This is the principal dispute referred to in Carpenter 1986a: p. 33, where full refs. will be found. For more on the west midlands network in this period, below, p. 603.

[114] Sudeley is said to have died in gaol (Alcock 1977: p. 181). See also Carpenter 1986a: p. 30 and p. 44 n. 41 for confusion concerning the exact timing of the stages in Sudeley's discomfiture.

estates.[115] However, from 1475 Mountford's association with Edward Grey, who acquired the estates of Thomas Talbot Lord Lisle that year, gave the two of them together an almost identical power base to Sudeley's. Most of the new Lord Lisle's lands were in Gloucestershire, but he also had a share in the Grey of Groby estates in north-east Warwickshire, in much the same area as the Sudeley properties in this part of the county. To quite a large extent Grey did indeed take over the Sudeley following. With Mountford's lands in the south, south-east and north, and his Kenilworth offices, the two were able to make substantial inroads into Clarence's authority.[116] Clarence's overtures to them failed to meet with any significant response, both being astute enough politicians to grasp that the real force in Warwickshire politics by then was the king.

Edward IV's influence throughout the region had been felt in two ways. First he had intervened frequently in 1471–4 to prop Clarence up and to rein back over-assertive gentry like Mountford, just as he had done for Richard Neville, but now on a much larger scale, using commissions, the council and other methods.[117] By 1474 he had decided to go a stage further and took Tutbury away from Clarence, keeping it himself but leaving the stewardship with Hastings as the basis for the recreation of the defunct Lancastrian retinue in the north midlands. When joined to Hastings' landed power in Leicestershire and to the Duchy offices the Lord Chamberlain held in that county and in Northamptonshire,[118] this had the effect of creating a continuous band of influence through the north and east midlands. Using this Hastings was able to

[115] In dealing with Mountford the king was probably also able to exploit the fact that he had allowed Edmund Mountford to return from exile in 1474 and, notwithstanding the terms of the reversal of his attainder, there was always the danger that he would resuscitate his claim to the Mountford lands (Carpenter 1986a: p. 32; Griffiths 1980a: pp. 8–9 (but this omits the pardon, which dates his return to 1474, not 1475), 18–19; also *Dugdale*, p. 1,011 and *Cal. Close Rolls 1468–76*, pp. 180, 367–8, showing that Edmund still had the deeds of release made by Simon and his father Baldwin in 1456–9 (above, p. 477) and that he had already made an attempt on the manors during the Readeption, when he had, ominously, referred to himself as 'of Coleshill'), and below, p. 535.

[116] Earlier foreshadowings of the Grey-Mountford-Stafford of Grafton-Berkeley of Weoley links in the 1460s can be seen in Warwick Castle MS 118B and in C.244/99/27, 39, 115, 137. For Grey and the Sudeley connection, see below, pp. 530–1. Further to the confrontation with Willoughby in the north Warwickshire/south Staffordshire region engendered by this expansion of Lisle's power (Carpenter 1986a: pp. 36–7) is Leland's mention of a fight at which 'Willoughby was sore woundyd' (Leland 1907–10: II, p. 103).

[117] The signet letter for the afforcing of the commission of the peace in September 1474 (Carpenter 1986a: p. 33), issued significantly at Kenilworth, shows that it was intended as a centrally-directed *oyer* and *terminer* commission and was specifically issued to deal with riots and other disturbances in Warwickshire and Leicestershire (C.81/1385/9).

[118] For Hastings' Duchy of Lancaster offices in Leicestershire and Northamptonshire, Somerville 1953: pp. 564, 586, 590; and note his role in the east Warwickshire/Leicestershire network in the previous decade (above, p. 491). For his retinue, see Dunham 1955, the classic account, although this now has to be considerably modified (see below, n. 119).

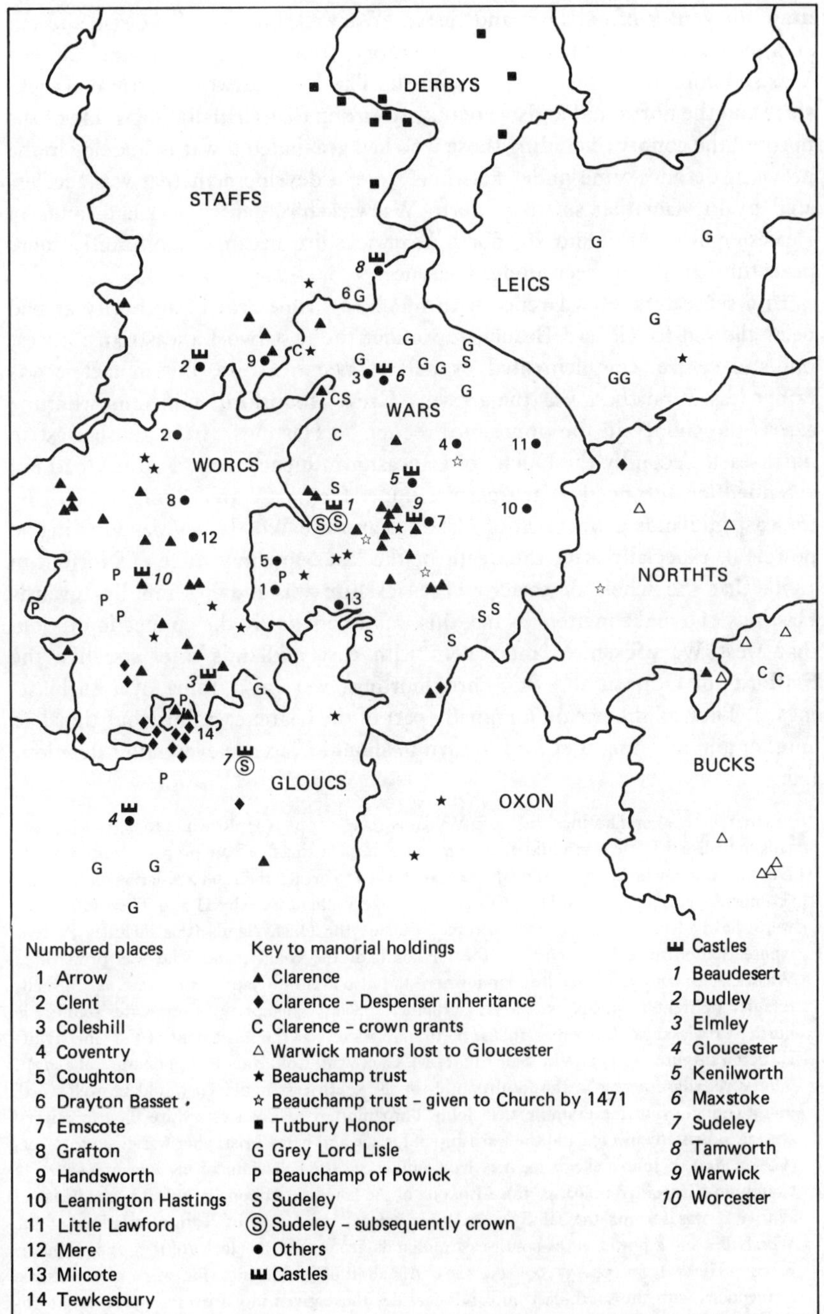

Figure 12 Clarence and the midlands 1471–78 (from Carpenter 1986a: p. 27)

draw the gentry of northern and eastern Warwickshire into his circle and cut another swathe through Clarence's territory, this time through much of east Warwickshire and right across the north. The links between north Warwickshire and the north midlands were now so strong that virtually the whole of the north of the county, including those who had gravitated towards Sudeley in the previous decade, came under Hastings' rule, a development that was accelerated by the fact that so many north Warwickshire gentry also had lands in Leicestershire. As it did so, north Warwickshire became significantly more peaceful than it had been under Clarence.[119]

In a sense this left Clarence with much the same area of authority as had been allowed to Richard Beauchamp under the first two Lancastrians: a west midland centre, complemented by half of Warwickshire, but in fact it was rather less. First there was the growing Grey–Mountford connection running across the county in the opposite direction to Hastings', from south-west to north-east. Secondly the Duchy of Lancaster influence from Tutbury had not extended far into north Warwickshire under Henry IV and Henry V. Thirdly the east midlands connection of Hastings and the Woodvilles was growing so powerful, especially after the death of the last Mowbray duke of Norfolk in 1476, that the whole of eastern Warwickshire was moving rapidly towards Hastings. To make matters worse, this was so obviously the connection to join that west Warwickshire landowners with east midlands interests, like the Staffords of Grafton and the Throgmortons, were also going over to Hastings.[120] They might remain nominally part of the Clarence affinity but they had another and now mightier lord to turn to should Clarence even falter, let alone fail.

119 Further material on Hastings' rule is in Williams 1984–5: pp. 31–7; Rowney 1984. But Rowney fails to realise that the north midlands retinue was not Hastings' private property but the king's Duchy retinue, which is no doubt why he was allowed to breach the 1468 legislation on retaining (Dunham 1955: pp. 52–66). His private clients, like William Catesby II and Thomas Ferrers, were mostly from Hastings' own 'contree', outside the Duchy lands (this includes Ferrers, whose Staffordshire lands were in the far south of the county, and who was primarily a Warwickshire and Leicestershire landowner, and also a close relative) and were *not* formally retained (Wright 1983: pp. 75, 78–81; Carpenter 1986a: p. 36; app. 3). For greater stability in north Warwickshire, Carpenter 1986a: p. 36; one result was the settlement of the Chetwynd–Littleton dispute in 1477 (Wm. Salt Lib. H.M. Chetwynd Coll. Bundle 4 (indenture of 1477)).

120 The Woodville interest in the local politics of the south-east midlands would be well worth investigating. Note for example that John Throgmorton of Gloucestershire died in Rivers' service in Brittany in 1472 and the wardship of his son and heir Christopher was given to Rivers (C.81/1385/14). John's allegiance may have influenced the behaviour of his cousin, Robert, of Coughton (Carpenter 1986a: p. 36). Also, one of the Lucys, traditionally linked to the house of Warwick, was serving the family's kin by marriage, the Greys of Ruthin, relatives of the Woodvilles and a power in the south-east midlands, from 1468–80 (Jack 1961: p. 222; *Dugdale*, p. 507; Hicks 1980: pp. 35–6, 145, 149). An additional reference for west Warwickshire connections with the south-east midlands, besides those given in Carpenter 1986a, is Northants.R.O. Fitzwilliam MS 249. A very revealing piece of evidence of the way the wind was thought to be blowing in the west midlands is that in January 1477 Hastings was made steward

Within his diminished 'contree' he did indeed continue to fail. It is difficult to see how, in the face of Hastings' rising power, any but the ablest could have succeeded.[121] From about 1474 Edward, while continuing to intrude in local affairs in the interest of Clarence's affinity, a policy which further devalued Clarence's worship, began to recruit quite extensively in Warwickshire to the royal household. He was also, as throughout the 1470s, paying particularly careful attention to Coventry and its environs, for he did not want it to defect again as it had done in 1470.[122] Moreover, by 1476 Edward's efforts had ensured that his brother was surrounded in Warwickshire by a ring of hostile castellans, or at any rate castellans who would put their loyalty to their king before any sense of obligation to the duke. At what point Edward decided to pull Clarence down is unknown and probably unknowable, but he could not ignore the events of early 1477. Within a short space of time Clarence's client Thomas Burdet was denounced for treason and the west midlands flared up again, as the Clarence affinity even in this bastion of Warwick power began to fall apart, and, to cap it all, in a last desperate attempt to show who was the master in west Warwickshire, Clarence indulged in the most appalling act of illegality in the case of Ankarette Twynho, abusing a legal system that Edward IV was publicly committed to upholding. All this at a time when, according to the Croyland continuator, Edward was greatly exercised about the amount of disorder that had arisen since the return of his army from France. In June 1477 Clarence was arrested and in February 1478 executed.[123]

Obviously, he failed because he was hopelessly inadequate to the task, but the circumstances of his failure are of particular interest. They show that certain members of the gentry, like Simon Mountford, Thomas Cokesey or Robert Throgmorton, were ready to go their own way if a magnate showed any weakness at all, a strategy of self-preservation which would have been wholly foreign to the gentry before 1450 and had only gradually been learned over the previous twenty years. Then they demonstrate that a determined king could exploit the gentry's growing sense that they themselves, not the magnates, might be their own best security. By 1478, when the Clarence lands came into crown hands, to stay there permanently as it turned out, Edward and his household nobility between them controlled most of the midlands. The effect

of the Worcestershire lands of the largely absent Lord Bergavenny, a responsibility which should naturally have fallen to Clarence or one of his close associates (*H.M.C. Hastings*, I, pp. 271–2).

121 Some arbitrations were performed by the duke, although one at least, in 1475, between the Verneys and Clarence's own collegiate church at Warwick, failed (Hicks 1983; B.R.L. 437204; C.P.40/870 roti.55d., 56; below, p. 535).

122 Note Edward's frequent presence in Warwickshire and nearby, especially in the difficult years 1473–4 (C.81/1384/1, 26, 27, /1385/9–14; *Dugdale*, p. 148). For an additional instance of royal interference in southern Warwickshire, in early 1476, Magdalen College, Oxford Muns., Westcote 46.

123 Hicks 1980: p. 141; 'Historia Croylandensis', p. 559.

on Warwickshire had been to complete that split between north and south that had already begun to emerge during the 1460s. Here, the decisive factor was the rebuilding of the Duchy of Lancaster affinity in the north midlands under Lord Hastings. That left the rest of Warwickshire, roughly speaking everything from Coventry southwards, directly under the command of the *de facto* earl of Warwick, the king of England.[124]

[124] Hastings' influence, however, went further south in the east of the county, into the part bordering on Northamptonshire, encompassing e.g. Boughton and Catesby (app. 3, Carpenter 1986a: p. 36, and below, pp. 527–8). For a gloss on the royal takeover of the Warwick hegemony, see the striking list of new members of the Stratford gild in 1478/9: includes the Prince of Wales, Rivers, John Alcock, bishop of Worcester (below, p. 541 for his connection with the Prince's council) and Thomas Littleton, the royal justice (S.B.T. Stratford Guild Recs. XII/90; above, p. 339 for the close relationship of the Warwick affinity and the gild).

14

THE PERIOD OF CRISIS III: WARWICKSHIRE UNDER THE CROWN 1478–85

I

From 1478 Warwickshire politics become still more closely enmeshed with those of its neighbours. There are two main reasons for this. The first is that the absorption of the Warwick estates by the crown left Hastings free to continue to treat north Warwickshire as the southern end of his north and east midlands power bloc. Hastings' rule in the midlands, whether subvented by the Duchy lands in Staffordshire and Derbyshire or by his own in the east midlands, remained one of the central supports of the king's increasingly interventionist rule. Now that south Warwickshire was directly under the king *in loco* earl of Warwick, the division between north and south within the county that had been perceptible ever since Clarence's loss of Tutbury in 1474, and even before, was to become an established fact in Warwickshire politics. Edward was happy to leave to Hastings the north of the county, which was consequently drawn ever more closely into the affairs of the other counties where the Lord Chamberlain was active. Even after Hastings' fall the north midlands connection endured and if anything became stronger, largely because in the nine years of Hastings' rule north Warwickshire had become almost inextricably bound into north midlands networks. With so many major landowners of north Warwickshire naturally facing north rather than south, there was no reason for it to be anything else as long as the king was content for his control throughout the north midlands to be exercised through intermediaries like the Lord Chamberlain or his successors.

The second reason is that at the same time the rest of the county was coming closely under the authority of the crown, as the Warwick affinity was absorbed into the fast-growing royal household.[1] Particularly influential was the part of the household that had as its focus the Woodville power in the Welsh marches

[1] Morgan 1973; Hicks 1979a; for a fuller account of the royal household, see Horrox 1989.

based on their control of the Prince of Wales' council in the march.[2] For some families who had lands in both the west midlands and the south-east midlands, the original landed base of the Woodville–Grey nexus, the route to the Woodvilles was bilateral, direct in this region and through the king in Warwickshire.[3] This applies for example to the Throgmortons and the Staffords of Grafton.[4]

The fact that Warwickshire is even more than hitherto a 'geographical expression' in this period makes tracing the course of county politics even more than usually hazardous. Up to 1485 Susan Wright's work on Derbyshire offers substantial help for the north midlands but there is much less guidance for Henry VII's reign.[5] Elsewhere, and in the north midlands after 1485, judging the significance of events and associations tends to become a matter of intelligent guesswork. At certain points the enterprise grows too foolhardy for anything more than speculation to be offered and a warning must be offered against placing too much faith in some of the more lightly-founded conclusions of these last two narrative chapters. It is hoped that eventually similar studies of other midland counties will give rather more substance to some of the detail. Despite these considerable reservations, the outlines of the events and developments in Warwickshire in the last decades of the century are clear enough for the general conclusions to stand firm.

In the period up to the death of Edward IV, the most striking development is the steady advance of Hastings and the king to a position of unchallenged control over the whole of Warwickshire and apparently over large parts, if not the whole of, the counties on which Warwickshire adjoined. Even before Clarence's fall Edward had retained or favoured Beaufitz, Richard Boughton, Thomas Cokesey, son and heir of John Greville II, Thomas Ferrers and his brother Henry, Thomas Littleton, Simon Mountford, Thomas Shukburgh, Humphrey Stafford of Grafton and William Trussell II of Bilton.[6] Afterwards he proceeded to take into his service virtually all Clarence's west midlands retainers and officers who were not already in the crown affinity. These included John Hugford, who became an esquire to both king and queen, William Catesby II and Edmund Verney. In 1482 he received back into his favour William Hugford, brother of John, who had been a royal officer since 1461 but had proved too enthusiastic a supporter of Warwick during the Readeption.[7] William Berkeley of Weoley was given a number of offices on

[2] Hicks 1979a; Lowe 1982.

[3] Hicks 1979a; Coughton Court, Throckmorton MS, Typescript Calendar, 179; K.B.27/873 Coram Rege rot.58d.; *I.P.M. Hen. VII*, I, 249.

[4] Carpenter 1986a: p. 36.

[5] Wright 1978; 1983: *passim*.

[6] Carpenter 1986a: pp. 34–5; D.L. 29/643/10438; Stow, *Annales*, p. 428; K.B.27/852 Coram Rege rot.71d.; *Cal. Pat. Rolls 1476–85*, p. 168.

[7] *Carpenter* 1986a: p. 41; *Cal. Fine Rolls 1471–85*, p. 43; C.81/1521/41 (cited in Hicks 1984: p. 26; note that this does not necessarily imply that Hugford fought for Richard Neville as Hicks

Warwick and crown lands around the Birmingham plateau in Warwickshire, Worcestershire and Staffordshire which he may already have held under the duke.[8] Richard Beauchamp of Powick, who had succeeded his father John in 1475, had his offices on the Clarence lands in Worcestershire and Gloucestershire confirmed, and indeed all Clarence's officers in Worcestershire seem to have been similarly favoured.[9] By Michaelmas 1480 the king was paying fees from the Beauchamp trust lands to Catesby, John Ferrers I, the heir of Thomas II, and William Hugford, and by 1481–2 to Humphrey Stafford, all of whom may have been feed under his predecessor.[10] John Ferrers' uncle, Henry, had been the king's man since 1461, despite his subsequent service to Clarence, and was to remain so. Although his main landed interests lay elsewhere, he owned a single manor in Warwickshire and was an important local figure as steward of Cheylesmore, the royal manor which was the principal lordship in Coventry.[11]

In the north of the county and in the east as far south as the Avon, most of the leading landowners were retained by Hastings. By the end of the reign he had sealed indentures with Mountford, John and Ralph Shirley, William Trussell of Bilton, John and Thomas Cokayn, John Wistowe of Tamworth, Henry Willoughby, Nicholas and Thomas Ruggeley, John Aston, Richard Boughton and John Burdet. The Ferrers, while never formally retained by Hastings, remained close to him.[12] Although several of these families were rather peripheral to Warwickshire and were evidently of interest to Hastings as Leicestershire or north midland landowners, the net result of retaining on this scale was that almost no-one of any importance beyond a line drawn diagonally across the county roughly from Middleton in the north to Lawford in the east was outside the Hastings affinity. We shall see that the Hastings connection in Warwickshire did in fact extend a good deal further even than this.

It is evident that in the part of Warwickshire he reserved for himself Edward for his part did not aim for blanket coverage of the greater gentry. A notable absentee from the royal affinity for instance was Robert Throgmorton. There may be a particular reason for his exclusion, for in defending the Buckinghamshire property of Weston Underwood he was due to inherit from his mother,

suggests); *Cal. Pat. Rolls 1476–85*, p. 311. Hugford had been given his Kenilworth office in 1461 (above, p. 489) and did in fact keep it after 1471 (D.L.29/463/7549–62), and he was feed from the Beauchamp trust manor of Snitterfield by 1480–1 (refs. in n. 10, below).

8 *Cal. Pat. Rolls 1476–85*, pp. 35, 96; *Cal. Close Rolls 1476–85*, p. 255; D.L.29/642/10422, /645/10461.

9 D.L.29/644/10458–9, /645/10461–3; *Cal. Pat. Rolls 1476–85*, p. 97; *G.E.C.*, II, p. 47; *Dugdale*, p. 766 puts his death in 1475, and see n. 88, below.

10 D.L.29/645/10464; S.B.T. D.R.5/2870.

11 *Cal. Pat. Rolls 1461–67*, p. 78, *1485–94*, p. 18; Hicks 1980: p. 217; Somerville 1953: p. 543; *Cal. Fine Rolls 1485–1509*, p. 308.

12 App. 3; Dunham 1955: pp. 119–20. The branch of the Ruggeley family to which Thomas belonged remained in Staffordshire and seems to have come from a younger son of Nicholas I (B.R.L. Wingfield Digby MS A507; *Colls. Hist. Staffs.*, n.s., 4, p. 197).

the daughter of Robert Onley, Throgmorton seems to have offended the duke of Gloucester. Presumably the subsequent and otherwise rather curious cold-shouldering of a man who was not only a major west midland landowner but was to do sterling service under Henry VII was out of deference to the king's brother.[13] While allowing for personal preferences of this kind, a comparison of the retainers of the king and of the previous earls of Warwick shows clearly that, apart from some rewards to minor officers like Thomas Ward and Thomas Frebody, Edward's retaining was highly selective.[14] It had no need to be anything else; as long as his authority was sufficient to prevent the growth of any affinity capable of challenging him in Warwickshire, the whole area was bound to look to him or to Hastings, his *alter ego* further north. Unlike the nobility, Edward did not have to engineer control of the local officers by securing the allegiance of the majority of the gentry qualified to be officers, for he himself appointed them. Once he had eliminated the potential mediatising powers, they could only be his men.

The king's following in Warwickshire between 1478 and 1483 was therefore a very loosely organised affair; it extended eastwards from its core in the old Warwick heartland through the links that Edward's own retainers had with the rest of the local gentry and through Hastings' retainers and associates. In the north and north-east of the county Hastings was undoubtedly the fulcrum of most local networks. This can be seen in transactions in which he himself participated, such as the grant of 1480 by John Vernon to Hastings, John Ferrers, Nicholas Montgomery, Humphrey Stanley, Nicholas Agard and Edmund and William Vernon, in which every participant besides Hastings himself was his retainer or related to his retainers. But it is also evident in deeds in which he took no part and in those in which Hastings' men were merely the leading figures. For example, in 1480 a grant to Henry Willoughby and Henry Lisle was witnessed by Richard Brasebrugge and Humphrey Stanley; Lisle and Brasebrugge were not retained by Hastings but were brought together with

[13] This is a fascinating and tantalising affair. It was between Throgmorton's mother, the heiress of Robert Onley of Birdingbury and Weston Underwood, and Robert Neville of Gayhurst, Buckinghamshire. Also involved were Gloucester, who had lands in this area, and an unnamed 'lord' of the Nevilles, possibly Lord Zouche, the latter being the overlord of the manor and one-time employer of both Onley and his son-in-law Thomas Throgmorton. However, the unknown lord could well have been Gloucester: in one letter Neville addresses this anonymous figure as 'right honourable and high and mighty prince and especial good lord' (modern spelling), a mode of address which suggests a royal duke. Alternatively, Neville could have had two protectors, Gloucester (by inference) and another unnamed lord, possibly Zouche. What seems clear is that Gloucester switched from protecting the interests of the Nevilles to attempting to get the manor for himself from both parties and lost to the Throgmortons (Coughton Court, Throckmorton MS Box 13/659, 660–2, Box 53, Box 55 (recovery of 1478), Typescript Calendar, 179; *V.C.H. Bucks.*, IV, p. 498; app. 3; above, p. 261). I am most grateful to Dr Horrox for her assistance in my efforts to sort this out; it is not her fault that I largely failed. I hope that a future student of the south-east midlands will do better.

[14] *Cal. Pat. Rolls 1467–77*, p. 258; *Cal. Fine Rolls 1471–85*, pp. 156, 285; D.L.29/643/10438.

Stanley, a Hastings retainer from Derbyshire, by friendship with another Hastings retainer, their fellow north Warwickshire landowner, Henry Willoughby. To give another example, in 1481 William Brasebrugge was drawn into the Hastings circle through his north Warwickshire associates Willoughby and Thomas Ferrers, both of them Hastings men.[15] These transactions and others like them, together with the list of Hastings retainers, show that he had fallen heir to two local networks: the Warwickshire-Leicestershire one, of which his acquisition of the Wiltshire and Beaumont estates had made him the leader, and, through the Tutbury offices, the north Warwickshire-Staffordshire one, now extending increasingly into Derbyshire. This latter network was in effect the revived Duchy of Lancaster one that, in the period of royal decline and inaction after 1422, had been partially taken over at various times by Richard Beauchamp earl of Warwick, Lord Ferrers of Chartley, Buckingham and others. Now it was back to the strength of its great days under the first two Lancastrian kings.[16]

Furthermore, as in the later days of Clarence, Hastings influence percolated down the eastern border of Warwickshire to the area adjoining Northamptonshire. Among his retainers was Richard Boughton, among his other associates the young Nicholas Malory, heir to the ne'er-do-well Thomas, and, most famously, the younger William Catesby, who had succeeded his father in 1476.[17] It was Catesby who was the focal point for the groupings that spread across eastern and south-eastern Warwickshire into the neighbouring parts of Northamptonshire. Catesby's connections among the gentry included other clients of Hastings who were neighbours or near-neighbours, like Boughton and John Denton, a Leicestershire landowner who held the Purfrey estates through his wife. There was also his own circle of friends in Warwickshire and Northamptonshire, such as John Hugford, who had the former Metley lands in east Warwickshire in right of his wife, John Spenser of Hodnell, and Everard Fielding of Leicestershire and east Warwickshire. Catesby was moreover heavily involved with the Latimer connection, which stretched from east

[15] N.R.A. 'Trusley Old Hall MS', 5222, consulted in Derby City Lib.; Nott. Univ. Lib., Middleton MS Mi D 4474; C.P.40/878 rot.304d.; Dunham 1955: pp. 116–20.

[16] Ives 1983a: pp. 24–8, 94–7, 100; Dunham 1955: pp. 119–20. Also e.g. *I.P.M. Hen. VII*, II, 123, 497 (undated but almost certainly belonging to these years: see Ives 1983a: p. 335); *Cal. Pat. Rolls 1476–85*, pp. 152, 275; *H.M.C. Hastings*, I, pp. 3, 19, 101, 296–7; *Cal. Close Rolls 1476–85*, pp. 86, 193–4; PROB 11/7 fo. 76v.; N.R.A.: 'Trusley Old Hall MS', 5220–2, consulted in Derby City Lib.; Derbys.R.O. S.L.Croxall T6; E.159/259 Mich. – recogs. for shrievalty of Thomas Entwysell; for Hastings in Leicestershire, Williams 1984–5: pp. 32–6; above, p. 491.

[17] Br. Lib. Harl. 3881 fo. 19. Ralph Wolseley, who submitted to Hastings' arbitration *c.* 1481–3, was Thomas Malory's sole surviving feoffee by 1480, while in 1481 a chest of Malory deeds was delivered to William Catesby II (*Colls. Hist. Staffs.*, 1934, ii, p. 81; K.B.27/900 Rex rot.5; E.40/14705; *Cal. Fine Rolls 1471–85*, p. 175). For Catesby and Hastings, see e.g. *Cal. Pat. Rolls 1476–85*, p. 233; *Cal. Close Rolls 1476–85*, p. 174; *Cat. Anc. Deeds*, IV, A6469, 9178; Fuller 1662: II, p. 286.

Warwickshire into Northamptonshire and was another of the many affinities to include Hastings among its personnel.[18] The advantages that were accruing to Catesby from his position as Hastings follower, royal annuitant and sought-after associate, can be gauged from the annuities and other rewards he began to accumulate from the east Warwickshire and Northamptonshire nobility towards the end of the reign: Lord Zouche, Buckingham, Lady Latimer, Edward Grey Lord Lisle and Hastings' brother Ralph.[19] A document of 1481 is a telling indication of the strength of Hastings' and Catesby's influence in the south of the county and indeed elsewhere in Warwickshire. This is the sale to Catesby of Oxhill manor in south Warwickshire by John Hathewick, in which Hastings, Boughton, Hugford and Richard Knightley took part, while the witnesses were Simon Mountford, Ralegh, Richard Verney, Robert Throgmorton and John Peyto.[20]

Even so Hastings and Catesby did not have everything their own way in east Warwickshire. John Hugford, to whom all the offices on the Clarence lands at Warwick had fallen, was becoming a very powerful local figure, both by reason of these offices and because he was the sole surviving Beauchamp trustee, while his wife's estates had made him into an influential figure in east Warwickshire. Rather surprisingly in view of the fact that his main residence, not to mention his most important offices, were at Warwick, Hugford's known associates in this period tended to reside in east Warwickshire or in south Warwickshire east of the Avon. Hugford's part in the sale of Oxhill has been mentioned. In 1479 he was involved with Catesby and other local landowners of a minor sort in a grant concerning land in Napton; in 1481, with his brother William, another east Warwickshire landowner, and Richard Boughton he witnessed the agreement of 1481 which concluded the conflict between Catesby and the abbot of Combe. Also at some point in this period Hugford stood feoffee for Thomas Straunge II of Walton Deyville in south Warwickshire, with a number of other gentry from southern and eastern Warwickshire.[21]

[18] *I.P.M. Hen. VII,* I, 23; *Cal. Close Rolls 1476–85*, p. 193; W.C.R.O. C.R.162/78, C.R.133/16; *Dugdale*, pp. 54, 971 (Thomas for John here, in error); *Cal. Close Rolls 1476–85*, p. 195; *Cal. Pat. Rolls 1494–1509*, p. 142; *Cat. Anc. Deeds,* V, A10990, IV, A6433; K.B.27/884 Coram Rege rot.45; *Cal. Pat. Rolls 1476–85*, pp. 233, 241; Northants.R.O. Spencer MS 867; Ives 1983a: pp. 108–9; Halle, *Union of Lancastre & York*, 'Edward V', fos. 13–13v. For Hastings and the Latimer connection, see *Cal. Close Rolls 1476–85*, pp. 223–4; *Test. Vetust.*, p. 360; Northants.R.O. Spencer MS 867, 870; above, n. 16. For the Latimer connection in general, see above, p. 489. Hugford was also associated with it, which gave him a link with Hastings and a double link with Catesby.

[19] *Cat. Anc. Deeds,* III, A4306, IV, A9650, 7459, 9178, 6600; S.C.R.O. D.641/1/2/26 *sub* payments by warrant; Rawcliffe 1978: p. 226; Magdalen College, Oxford Muns., Westcote 3, 41; Roskell 1981b.

[20] *Cat. Anc. Deeds,* IV, A8407.

[21] *Cal. Pat. Rolls 1476–85*, pp. 135–6; Hicks 1981: pp. 141–2; D.L.29/645/10464; *Cal. Pat. Rolls 1494–1509*, p. 142; W.C.R.O. C.R.133/16, C.R.2026/3; Northants.R.O. Spencer MS 867, 1533, 1662; above, p. 104.

In the south of the county and west of Warwick the old Warwick connection was centred firmly on the king. There are signs that Richard Beauchamp of Powick had hopes immediately after Clarence's fall of converting the Worcestershire part of the west midlands network, with which his father had been so intimately linked for so long, into a personal following of his own. More will be said on this point later; in the upshot he failed, partly because the king did not want a rival at the core of the Warwick earldom, partly because the Woodvilles were keen to annex Worcestershire to their empire along the Welsh marches.[22] As a result Worcestershire seems to have been run by two branches of the royal affinity; that linked directly to the king, and that serving the Prince of Wales in the marches.[23] As *de facto* earl, the king possessed the shrievalty of Worcestershire, and this alone gave him a head start over anyone intrepid enough to want a say in the county's affairs. His appointees to the office, it need hardly be said, were all household retainers.[24]

Looking at the Warwickshire networks in this period one cannot help but be struck by how they all in the end lead back to the king, directly, or through the Woodvilles and Greys or Hastings, just as, earlier in the century, they had all led back to Richard Beauchamp. For the king's own retainers and annuitants, like Hastings, Catesby, John Hugford, Cokesey, Mountford and Stafford of Grafton, and their associates, this is entirely predictable, but it applies equally to someone like Robert Throgmorton, who seems deliberately to have been rejected by the king. Throgmorton was a pivotal figure in the Warwickshire/Worcestershire border region and, whatever personal feelings kept him out of the king's favour, it was not desirable that he should be excluded from the grouping dominated by the royal affinity. In fact Throgmorton was not only as closely linked as ever to the men in his immediate neighbourhood retained by the royal earl of Warwick, he had as well those rather unexpected connections with the Woodvilles in the south-east midlands.[25] Time and again, tracing a Warwickshire landowner's connections, one ends with the king, and there is here a noticeable contrast with the court of Henry VI, powerful though that was; under Henry the courtiers became cut off from their localities, under Edward it was the durability of the local ties of the household men that made them such invaluable servants to the king. Loosely organised it might be, but ultimately the king's affinity was all-embracing.

Once assured of incontestable authority, Edward was not unwilling to allow

22 Below, pp. 542–4.

23 Deduced from major figures on the commission of the peace (*Cal. Pat. Rolls 1476–85*, p. 578); Hicks 1979a: pp. 75–83.

24 *Lists and Indexes*, 9, p. 158. Note also how the stewards of the bishops of Worcester in the later fifteenth century are nearly all linked to the royal household, a fact which Dyer attributes to the succession of Italian bishops, but which probably has more to do with the dominance of Worcestershire by the king (Dyer 1980b: pp. 156–8).

25 *Cat. Anc. Deeds*, V, A10990; Coughton Court, Throckmorton MS Box 35 (deed of 1478); *I.P.M. Hen. VII*, II, 562; Br. Lib. Add. Ch. 73,769, 58,315; above, n. 4.

local figures the freedom to build their own smaller empires within his system. These, however, were carefully constrained. Buckingham was ruled out entirely in Warwickshire, as he was almost everywhere else, for he would only have been an unacceptable rival to Hastings in north Warwickshire and to the king himself further south. Edward Grey Lord Lisle and his step-father Sir John Bourchier were treated with similar firmness but allowed slightly more licence. Until almost the end of the reign Grey was not permitted to hold office in Warwickshire; it was Gloucestershire, where he had inherited many of the Berkeley lands by his marriage to the Lisle heiress, that Edward saw as Grey's legitimate sphere.[26] The belt of authority that Mountford and Grey had constructed in the later years of Clarence survived just long enough to help condemn the duke at the parliament of 1478.[27] Grey's usefulness to Mountford was at an end as soon as it was clear that Hastings and Catesby were going to leave room neither for the reconstruction of the Astley connection across northern Warwickshire, nor for the rebuilding of the Grey of Groby affinity of the 1440s and 1450s in the east and south-east of the county. The point was reinforced by the withholding from Grey of office in Warwickshire. There is no record of any links between the two from 1478 to 1489; although we must allow for missing evidence, the absence of almost all the indirect connections which became evident in the mid-1470s strengthens the presumption that their ways had parted.

Nevertheless Grey was able to build up a following on a more limited scale. During the Clarence period he had established a link with John Hugford, and this persisted. Moreover, both Grey and Hugford, the latter particularly, established connections with the remnants of the Sudeley affinity which had survived the death of its lord and the dismembering of his estate. Hugford probably owed his eminence among these men to some extent to the fact that he was the king's most important estate official in the west midlands, which was where the main Sudeley properties, Sudeley and Beaudesert Castles, both of them now owned by the king, were to be found. But he was also the brother of William Hugford, parker of Kenilworth under Sudeley and then under Edward IV, which gave him access to the Sudeley affinity based on Kenilworth, and he was a substantial landowner south of the Sudeley estates centred on Chilvers Coton in north-east Warwickshire. Grey's advance to the leadership of part of the Sudeley affinity was a natural conclusion to his family's well-established ties with that connection. Henry Boteller, the Recorder of Coventry, had divided

[26] Hicks 1979a: pp. 80–1; *Cal. Pat. Rolls 1476–85*, p. 560; *G.E.C.*, VIII, p. 59. For further indications of Buckingham's exclusion from local authority, see his absence from peace commissions in nearly all the counties where he had major estates (*Cal. Pat. Rolls 1476–85*, pp. 560–3, 573, 576; Rawcliffe 1978: app. A). Edward was even prepared to hold Gloucester at length, here and elsewhere (Hicks 1986c: p. 17, and on Edward's jealousy of his and his family's authority in general in these years, see Hicks 1986c: p. 21).

[27] Carpenter 1986a: p. 37.

his primary allegiance between Sudeley and the Greys, and the proximity of the Astley/Grey estates around Nuneaton to Sudeley's properties at Chilvers Coton had brought the families together, notably in their patronage of Arbury priory in Chilvers Coton. Grey was accumulating other clients at this time, among them John Smyth, a well-connected Coventry lawyer who was to serve the family into the next century. Then there were Grey's links with the Lucys of south Warwickshire, who were related by marriage to the Greys of Ruthin, of whom Grey's father had been a cadet, and with Richard Brasebrugge in north Warwickshire, probably another tie inherited from Sudeley.[28] As we might expect from the connections with Boteller and Smyth, Grey, like Sudeley, was influential in the Coventry region, sufficiently so to head the commission of muster for the forces sent by the town to the Scottish wars in 1481.[29]

All the same, as long as Grey was denied access both to local office and to the favour of Hastings and the king, who were the real powers in Warwickshire, his inability to promote the interests of his clients in the county was bound to restrict his influence. By the end of the reign the king was showing signs of being willing to change his mind about Grey's role in Warwickshire, but it was only in the next reign that he was to come into his own in the county. That he had extensive ambitions in the midlands can be seen both from his activities during the Readeption and from the chancery petition he and the other heirs to Richard Beauchamp (including Gloucester, as husband of one of Richard Neville's daughters) made towards the end of the reign, requesting that they be granted the lands of the Beauchamp trust. From the fact that the pledges were both Grey's associates it may be deduced that he was the leading spirit in its instigation.[30]

The most widely-connected landowner in Warwickshire in Edward's later years was not a nobleman but a knight, Simon Mountford. He remained constable of Kenilworth and an active J.P.[31] and he alone of all the Warwickshire landowners was connected with substantial families in all parts of the county. As a north Warwickshire resident retained by Hastings, it is not surprising that he is to be found among the northern network, but he was also

[28] *Cat. Anc. Deeds*, I, B140–2, 1496, II, B2404, 2410–12, 3528; *V.C.H.*, IV, p. 176; S.B.T. D.R.18/A124; *I.P.M. Hen. VII*, I, 249; W.C.R.O. C.R.136/C310–12, C422, C.R.2026/3; E.101/516/8; E.326/6810; C.P.40/878 rot.206; C.67/53 m. 11; K.B.27/918 Coram Rege rot.9; D.L.41/34 fo. 76; Nott. Univ. Lib. Middleton MS Mi D 4798; *Dugdale*, pp. 602, 523, 1,075; *H.M.C.*, XV, X, p. 146; Carpenter 1986a: p. 37; *V.C.H.*, VI, p. 27; Northants.R.O. Temple (Stowe) Box 6/2 (which shows the surprising continuity of the Sudeley connection after his death and the division of the estate); app. 3; above, pp. 107, 417 n. 74 and 520 n. 120 on Lucy and the Greys.

[29] C.81/1390/19.

[30] *Cal. Pat. Rolls 1476–85*, p. 576; C.1/66/376; *Colls. Hist. Staffs.*, n.s., 7, pp. 286–7; Hicks 1981: p. 141. Grey's claim was as husband of Elizabeth, grand-daughter of Margaret, one of the co-heiresses of Beauchamp's Berkeley marriage (*G.E.C.*, VIII, pp. 59–60; above, p. 439).

[31] Somerville 1953: p. 560; K.B.9/350/48, /354/2, 4, /362/35, 44.

connected with gentry of south-west Warwickshire like Hugford and John Greville. He maintained the ties with the Coventry region he had built up in the 1460s, continuing to retain Henry Boteller until the latter's death in 1490. He was linked by marriage with the Archers, the leaders of the tightly-knit Tanworth group, and retained the wide-ranging collection of associates in eastern and southern Warwickshire, where he was a by no means negligible landowner, built up in the 1460s. In effect, if Mountford's connections are studied in detail, it becomes apparent that, apart from John Hugford, whose influence was largely derived from royal patronage, he was the only native of Warwickshire who could act as a focal point for all the networks in the county. In particular, it was Mountford alone who provided a permanent link between north and south,[32] a state of affairs exemplified by the feoffment he himself made in 1480 of three of his manors, one in north Warwickshire, two in south Warwickshire. The witnesses to this transaction came from the north, the south-west, the east and Coventry, and their only common characteristic was that they were all Warwickshire gentry and all friends of Simon Mountford.[33]

Why did the king allow a member of the gentry to accumulate so extensive a personal connection? The very fact that Mountford was no more than a knight, albeit a very powerful one, made it permissible. It was easy for Edward to cut him down at will; a magnate given such liberty would have been a far more challenging proposition. The essence of Edward's rule in Warwickshire was that it allowed free enterprise as long as the king himself could be certain that the Buckinghams and the Edward Greys, who might have got in the way of the free play of royal power, were held firmly in check. In fact, the system could not function without people like Mountford, for the groupings of which he was the focus provided the cohesion amongst the local gentry for which the nobility had formerly in large measure been responsible. If Edward was too distant and too burdened with other business to undertake the detailed management required, and unwilling to let the nobility, apart from Hastings, whose own concerns must have made him a frequent absentee, fulfil this function on any but the most localised scale, it had to be done by the major gentry. His policies in Warwickshire were accordingly based on a combination of close control and considerable laissez-faire. The acid test was whether the local groupings, having in common only the often rather tenuous connection with the king, could be made to co-operate to the extent necessary for the establishment of a stable society.

32 *Cal. Close Rolls 1476–85*, p. 123; *Cat. Anc. Deeds*, IV, A8407; S.B.T. D.R.37/1007, Box 40 (deed of 1478), D.R.503 fo. 66v. *et seq.*, D.R.41/71/283–4; *Cal. Pat. Rolls 1494–1509*, p. 142; C.P.40/864 rot.7d.; Bod. Lib. Dugdale MS 15, pp. 66, 182; W.C.R.O. C.R.133/16; *I.P.M. Hen. VII*, III, 760; Northants.R.O. Spencer MS 1488–9; below, p. 603.

33 *Cal. Close Rolls 1476–85*, p. 233.

The first indications were hardly promising. Clarence's fall released a flood of disputes, the result of the temporary vacuum and of expectations in some quarters that whoever succeeded him might be persuaded to take a partisan position. Between mid-1477, when the duke's position was already seriously under threat, and the end of 1479 twenty disputes are known to have broken out in Warwickshire. Meanwhile, the Throgmortons' struggle to hold on to Weston Underwood in Buckinghamshire, probably in the teeth of the duke of Gloucester, came to a head, and in Worcestershire Richard Beauchamp became embroiled in a bitter feud over the offices he had acquired after Clarence's condemnation.[34] None of these conflicts was entirely without importance and most of them were not new, which in itself must have been profoundly depressing for the king, for it showed that any failure of local control was liable to bring renewed upheaval in cases that he might well have supposed to be dead and buried.

The most recent of these was a confrontation between John Peyto and Richard Verney over a close claimed by both that lay between their manors of respectively Chesterton and Kingston. This was one of a growing number of conflicts over pasture and enclosure in the last three decades of the century, of which the Coventry one was the most considerable, which were the consequence of the expansion of pastoral farming, especially in southern Warwickshire, at this time.[35] This particular one had begun under Clarence and had led to a commission for the arrest of Verney.[36] A verdict in Verney's favour at Warwick assizes in July 1477 was followed immediately by an entry on Verney's land in Worcestershire, while each side accused the other of entering and depasturing the close at issue, and two of Verney's associates, probably servants or tenants, claimed that Peyto had set dogs on their sheep. The participants were not confined to these two; John Spenser of Hodnell, the rising grazier from south-east Warwickshire, was involved on Peyto's side, as were Peyto's feoffees, some of whom were very important indeed, and limitation of the conflict was therefore an urgent matter.[37] Another dispute in south-east Warwickshire, between two branches of the Shukburgh family, had similarly

[34] Hugford v. Bristowe (K.B.27/865 Coram Rege rot.55d.), Archer etc. v. Boteller (C.P.40/868 rot.327), Mountford etc. v. Waldeve (C.P.40/864 rot.7d.), Holt v. Holt (K.B.27/869 Coram Rege rot.30), Bergavenny v. Clapham (K.B.27/867 Coram Rege rot.10), Neville v. Curson of Exhall (C.P.40/868 rot.384), Mountford v. Ralegh (*ibid.* rot.381), Bermingham v. Baker (*ibid.* rot.382d.), St. Germain v. Shukburgh (K.B.27/869 Coram Rege rot.13d.), Hardwick v. Berkeley (C.P.40/868 rot.94), St. Germain v. Clinton (C.P.40/874 rot.457), Bermingham v. Bermingham (*ibid.* rot.545). This list excludes debt cases. For the cases discussed in more detail (none listed here), above, pp. 525–6 and below, pp. 533–45.

[35] Above, pp. 185–7; below, pp. 539–42, 591.

[36] Carpenter 1986a: p. 33.

[37] C.P.40/841 rot.327, /864 rot.253d., /868 roti.77d., 250d., 251, 384.

destabilising potential, since the feoffees of one of the parties included Hastings and Catesby.[38]

In the same part of the county in late 1477 the quarrel that had begun in the 1460s between the Dalbys and Richard Harecourt of Shotteswell broke out again. This was over the land that William Verney had sold long before to Dalby, then resold to Harecourt. Late in 1471 it had died down, as Dalby apparently accepted a fait accompli; he was doubtless encouraged to do so by his imprisonment in Warwick gaol at the hands of the Verneys, father and son, on what was probably a charge fabricated by Edmund Verney in his capacity as escheator.[39] However, on Dalby's death in 1477 it seems that his family and friends determined that an injustice that had been acceptable to an elderly and probably infirm man could no longer be allowed to stand, and they proceeded to break into some of the property.[40] Within two years the same group reopened the feud with the Verneys, who had apparently regained possession of the land in question.[41] There is evidence that towards the end of Dalby's life Edward IV had forced him into a compromise that would bring to an end this long-running saga. It would have been a relatively simple matter to exert pressure on both parties: Dalby was serving the crown at the time and was about to lose or had already lost his sole remaining noble employer, the duke of Norfolk, who died in 1476, while Edmund Verney was one of the king's household esquires. On the evidence of Dalby's I.P.M., made in November 1480, it appears that on his death the disputed lands were to go to the Verneys, that the arrangement broke down, perhaps because Dalby's widow refused to surrender Kites Hardwick, which, according to the I.P.M., she was holding with her second husband for life, and that in retaliation the Verneys seized the other, non-controversial lands of Dalby's estate. The delay in the performance of the I.P.M., perhaps engineered by one of the parties, meant that it was only then that the disseisin came to public notice.[42] In the meantime the Dalbys had responded by taking more than 200 sheep from Edmund Verney that had been

38 The plea is between Hastings and Catesby, plaintiffs, and Thomas Shukburgh, defendant, but it concerns Shukburgh property recently enfeoffed to a group that included associates of the first two (W.C.R.O. C.R.1248/68/35 and nn. 16–18, above), and was followed not long after by a dispute over the Shukburgh property between the heirs of the family (C.P.40/868 rot.592, /890 rot.452). For more on this, see above, p. 220.

39 Above, p. 509; K.B.27/836 Coram Rege rot.36d.; C.1/64/131. The episode must date to 1472–3, as it was then that Verney was escheator; he held the office again in 1480–1, but by then Dalby was dead (*List of Escheators*, p. 171; n. 40, below).

40 C.140/78/89; C.P.40/864 rot.481d. Edmund Bushell, one of the defendants, was an old associate of Dalby (e.g. K.B.27/843 Coram Rege rot.75). *Dugdale*, pp. 96, 562, misdates Dalby's death.

41 C.P.40/870 rot.274.

42 C.1/64/131; *Cal. Pat. Rolls 1476–85*, p. 91; *G.E.C.*, IX, pp. 608–10; C.140/78/89. Dalby's property, including the land at Kites Hardwick etc. contested with the Verneys, had been given to feoffees dominated by associates of Edward IV, Gloucester and Hastings, *viz.* Catesby, Morgan Kidwelly (Gloucester: Ives 1983a: p. 60), William Wyville (connected by marriage with Hastings' retainer Thomas Entwysell: Ives 1983a: pp. 101 n. 52, 454), William Essex (King's

pastured on the Dalby properties which were probably in Verney hands; these could well have been the Dalbys' own sheep of which they were repossessing themselves.[43]

Elsewhere in the county an arbitration between the Verneys and the Dean of Warwick that had been performed by Clarence failed to stick, trouble broke out between John Bourchier and a younger branch of the Astley family from which the Grey/Bourchier lands in Warwickshire had come, and the seemingly interminable Mountford affair surfaced again, Simon accusing Edmund (who had returned and been pardoned in the 1470s) of fabricating documents to Coleshill and Ilmington.[44] These were probably the genuine quitclaims made by Simon and his father under duress in the 1450s, which had been kept safe for Edmund and probably delivered to him on his return from exile in 1474.[45]

These were the more serious of the relatively minor affairs, but there were two others which easily outweighed them in consequence and in the size of the threat to local stability they posed. First there was the dispute over the Burdet inheritance, which threatened to become as divisive as the Mountford case. It originated similarly in an attempt to disinherit the heirs of the first marriage in favour of those of the second. In this instance, it was the adult Richard Burdet who was to lose the bulk of his lands to his infant half-brothers. Richard Burdet was at an even graver disadvantage than the older Mountfords had been, for his mother's marriage had been dissolved and he was referred to as 'bastard' and, like any other illegitimate child, on occasion given his mother's name of Waldeve. This was in fact a quite extraordinary affair; if the story told later by one of the witnesses before a chancery commission is to be believed, it would appear that Thomas, having presumably fallen for the woman who was to be his

Remembrancer: Horrox and Hammond eds. *British Library Harleian Manuscript 433*, I, p. 271). After Dalby's death, his original estates were seized by Edmund Verney and friends, while the disputed land went to Dalby's widow and her second husband. However, the later history of the lands makes it clear that it was the disputed property, not Dalby's own inheritance, that the family lost (*V.C.H.*, v, pp. 106, 145; *Dugdale*, p. 562). Kites Hardwick etc. came to the Danvers at the end of the century, either by sale from William Verney or by marriage to Verney's co-heiress. Either way, the property must previously have been restored to the Verneys of Great Wolford (*V.C.H.*, v, p. 145 n. 47; *Dugdale*, p. 541). Thus the only possible conclusion, if the I.P.M. is to be believed, would be that, perhaps after pressure from the king, Dalby's estate was enfeoffed to a group of king's men, that at his death they were to release the disputed land to the Verneys, that for some reason Dalby's widow was able to hang on to these, and that in retaliation the Verneys seized what was legitimately Richard Dalby's. Both parties petitioned against the verdict of the escheator William Bristowe that Brookhampton, which was in fact held of the dukes of Norfolk, whose land the king was in the process of embezzling, was held of the king, a finding presumably reached to please Edward IV (Bod. Lib. Dugdale MS 15, p. 131; Ross 1974: p. 248; and below, p. 539 on Bristowe).

43 C.P.40/870 rot.274.

44 B.R.L. 437204; C.P.40/868 rot.383d., /870 roti.55d., 451, /868 rot.382; above, pp. 488, 325 n. 171.

45 *Cal. Close Rolls 1468–76*, pp. 367–8; Carpenter 1986a: p. 32; above, p. 518 n. 115. There was also some further dispute over Remenham, Berks., another of the properties at issue, *c.* 1478–82 (below, p. 584 n. 107).

second wife, and wanting to rid himself of both his first wife and the son born of the union, set about both projects with a fairly remarkable strategy. First he ordered a priest to share a bed with himself and his wife, the intention being that she would be left alone in bed with the priest every morning when Burdet got up early to go hunting and lay herself open to charges of adultery. The virtuous wife, however, foiled his plans by getting out of bed as soon as her husband had done so. Then Burdet resolved to kill his young son Richard. The boy was rescued by a servant, who stole into his bedroom at Arrow by night and rushed the half-dressed child to the abbey of Alcester nearby, the abbot being his godfather.[46]

The inheritance dispute had begun on Thomas Burdet's execution for treason in 1477, an event which had helped precipitate Clarence's fall. It has very tentatively been suggested that Thomas' decision to deprive his eldest son, finalised in early 1477, may have encouraged Simon Mountford to denounce him to the king, for by dying when the newly-constituted heirs were so young Burdet left a rich wardship. This, along with the marriage of the heir, came to Mountford in 1478, undoubtedly as a reward for his part in the parliament which condemned the duke.[47] The king was bound to be concerned about the fate of these estates, situated as they were on the Warwickshire/Worcestershire border at the heart of the Warwick earldom, and could similarly not avoid an interest in the future of a family which had been for so long in the following of the earls.[48] Since he did not propose to confiscate the estates – Edward seems always to have been more reluctant to use attainders against rebellious gentry than against the nobility[49] – the choice of guardian was bound to be significant. Simon Mountford was a sensible grantee; the families of Mountford and Burdet had been interlinked, Simon was much beholden to the king for the grant of Kenilworth and therefore likely to prove loyal, and the wardship was some compensation not only for his efforts against Clarence (and possibly for providing evidence against both Burdet and Clarence) but also for Edward's steadfast refusal to let him have the Sudeley inheritance.[50] Whether the irony

[46] *Dugdale*, p. 849; K.B.27/877 Rex rot.19d.; Derbys.R.O. D156M/84. The material in this office on the case is very full and I hope some time to publish it. The divorce had apparently taken place between 1464 and 1466 (*Dugdale*, p. 849 n. b: the dating is confused). According to Stow's touching story, Burdet later repented his treatment of his eldest son and asked his pardon as he passed him on his way to execution (*Annales*, p. 430).

[47] Carpenter 1986a: pp. 38–9; *Cal. Pat. Rolls 1476–85*, p. 102; *Wedgwood: Register*, p. 444; C.145/328/66. A bond by Mountford to Hastings, made the day after the grant of the wardship, may well be connected, especially as Thomas Hore of Solihull, a participant in the deed settling the lands on the younger sons (assuming it *is* the same Thomas Hore, which seems probable), was also involved (*Cal. Close Rolls 1476–85*, pp. 123, 35).

[48] App. 3; above, chs. 9–11, *passim*.

[49] This observation is based chiefly on what happened in Warwickshire. Below, p. 574 for comparisons with the county under Henry VII.

[50] E.g. *Cat. Anc. Deeds*, IV, A8424; Warwick Castle MS 118B; S.B.T. D.R.37/998; Carpenter 1986a: pp. 31–2, 34–5, 39; above, p. 517.

of his helping to disinherit an older son was lost on Mountford cannot be known.

However, like Simon and Baldwin Mountford before him, Richard Burdet was not prepared to take his father's dispositions lying down. In December 1477 he initiated a series of attempts to take the Warwickshire properties, which continued into 1480. For these he was indicted at four separate quarter sessions between early 1477 and early 1480 and in all but the last Mountford was one of the presiding J.P.s[51] Converseley in Worcestershire, in spite of his father's arrangements, Richard was himself in possession, apparently even before his father's death; here a highly respectable and representative group of J.P.s was busy indicting Thomas' designated heir, Nicholas, and his mother for unlawful entries. Richard was also suing them in the Common Pleas for the same entries.[52] By November 1478 Richard was in such financial straits resulting from litigation that he was forced to sell himself in marriage to a daughter of John Shirwode of Alspath to raise the funds necessary to carry on with the case.[53]

But, not long after, his fortunes improved. Mountford may have been made rather anxious by the fact that Worcestershire society was as unenthusiastic about the disinheritance of Richard Burdet as Warwickshire had been about his own back in the 1450s. Nor does it seem that the Warwickshire gentry were overwhelmed by the justice of Nicholas Burdet's claim, for, he complained to the king, although the Warwickshire J.P.s ordered that he be restored, 'the . . . justices in that parte wer disobeyed and yor shirrif ther also', and Richard was holding on to the lands 'wyth force and be grete mayntenauns and supportacyon'. The protectors of Nicholas' interests were reduced to appealing to king and council on his behalf. Moreover, the Shirwode family, which was providing financial assistance for Burdet, were old allies of the Mountfords from the 1460s, and Simon was probably unhappy about making enemies in the area west of Coventry where they resided and where he had established himself so effectively in that decade.[54] Most important of all was the fact that rather unwisely Nicholas' representatives sued successfully to have the wardship rescinded in November 1478, on the grounds that all the lands were already in the hands of feoffees.[55] Thereafter Mountford had no further interest in protecting the claims of the younger sons. What he did instead was almost immediately to marry Richard to his own daughter, something which he would presumably have done with Nicholas had he retained the wardship. This

51 K.B.9/346/51, /350/48, /354/2, 4, 6.

52 K.B.9/351/76; C.P.40/868 roti.69d., 434d.

53 C.1/54/378; above, p. 114.

54 Derbys.R.O. D156M/49; for Mountford and the Alspath region, above, pp. 498, 503, 517–18.

55 *Cal. Close Rolls 1476–85*, p. 102. Mountford was himself on the commission that investigated the matter but was presumably outvoted by his fellows – unless he had already decided to switch his interests to Richard's.

produced howls of unavailing fury from the Shirwodes, who had spent their money in vain (and whom Mountford had offended all the same) and radically altered Richard Burdet's position.[56] In 1479/80 he became a member of the Stratford gild, a clear indication that he had joined the respectable landed gentry, and in the last indictment he had to suffer, made in April 1480, Mountford took no part at all. In late 1480, doubtless financed by Mountford, Burdet initiated a suit in the Common Pleas to establish his legitimacy.[57]

At first the king seems to have been none too happy about Mountford's sudden change of sides. In May 1482, by which time Nicholas Burdet was dead and his claim had passed to his younger brother John, Edward issued a commission of arrest for two bastards of the Stafford of Grafton family who had made an entry, undoubtedly on Richard Burdet's behalf, on John's and his mother's possession of Arrow, the Burdet residence.[58] On the other hand the king had to take into account the warning signs that a dim view was being taken locally of John Burdet's claims. After the indictment of April 1480 Richard seems to have escaped local prosecution altogether, and we must assume that it was Simon Mountford's influence that was keeping his son-in-law out of the quarter sessions.[59] Then, in April 1480 Seckington, a Burdet manor in north Warwickshire, was taken from John by Humphrey Stanley and Henry Lisle 'by the labur and storyng of on Richard Burdet Bastard'. Stanley, like Mountford, was retained by Hastings, and Lisle was part of the north Warwickshire network whose leadership Hastings had assumed. To protect John against Richard Burdet was therefore to risk alienating a large segment of the royal affinity;[60] the very fact that John had to resort to petition and that there is no record of an indictment for this offence suggests how far local opinion was now ranged on Richard's side.

It must have been clear to Edward that, with the support that Mountford could command, it was going to be very difficult to get his way without a show of force.[61] The membership of the commission of arrest for the men who had disseised John Burdet bears out this state of affairs, for it was somewhat deficient in weight and, in order to give it some strength, the king was obliged to appoint Robert Throgmorton to his first-ever Warwickshire office and only

[56] C.1/54/378; above, pp. 114–15. Richard's son and heir Thomas was said to be fourteen at Richard's death in 1492 (*I.P.M. Hen. VII*, I, 802). This must be an overestimate, as the marriage could not have taken place before Mountford's loss of the wardship in late 1478, but it does indicate an instant change of plan on the part of both Mountford and Burdet.

[57] *Stratford Register*, p. 166; K.B.9/354/6; C.P.40/874 rot.121. This last plea has every appearance of a put-up job: only one acre of land is in question and the defendant instantly puts Burdet's legitimacy at issue, thus opening the way to a decision on the root of the claim.

[58] *Cal. Pat. Rolls 1476–85*, p. 319.

[59] All further litigation on the younger claimants' behalf was by private plea, or, even more indicative of powerlessness, by petition to the king (above, n. 54 and below, n. 60 for refs.).

[60] S.C.8/E.1209; Dunham 1955: pp. 116–20; Carpenter 1986a: pp. 35–6; above, pp. 525–7.

[61] Refs. above, nn. 32–3.

his second office of any sort.[62] Sensibly, Edward, who differed from his predecessor in having a shrewd awareness of the state of the localities, decided that curbing Mountford's ambitions by clipping his wings in the Burdet affair was not worth a divisive local conflict in which the royal government would have been the main focus of resentment. Richard Burdet's claims had already been substantially reinforced in January 1482, when, after some delay, the bishop of Worcester sent his answer on the question of Burdet's legitimacy back to the Common Pleas where the suit had begun, declaring that Burdet was indeed legitimate.[63] Richard was left in possession of the whole estate except for Seckington in north Warwickshire, and, if we can believe John's later claim, Luddington and 100 marks of land at Arrow, which John got after an arbitration. If John, as it proved, was far from resigned to his loss, at least his recruitment by Hastings in 1482/3, as soon as he was old enough, absorbed him into the local society of north Warwickshire.[64]

The other major conflict of these years was potentially even more serious and took rather longer to settle. Strictly speaking, it was a mingling of several conflicts, all of them revolving around the common pastures within the Coventry leet. It need hardly be said that Edward continued to take Coventry's affairs very seriously indeed after Clarence had gone. He had no intention of allowing the city to slip from his control and in the commissions of the peace issued after Clarence's death he significantly increased the representation of J.P.s from Coventry and its surrounding area. The foremost recipient of his trust at this time was one of the main protagonists of the dispute, William Bristowe, a lawyer who was lord of Whitley manor within the Coventry leet. In 1479 he was appointed J.P. for the first time since making the mistake of sitting on the Readeption commission, and later that year he became escheator.[65] He showed his worth to the king in this office by bringing in at least one dubious verdict that suited the government.[66] There is evidence from the same year that he was linked either directly or indirectly to Hastings, which would be unsurprising since he had been Sudeley's man and, in taking charge of north Warwickshire, Hastings had taken over the Sudeley affinity here.[67]

62 *Cal. Pat. Rolls 1476–85*, p. 319.

63 C.P.40/874 rot.121; Worc. Dioc., Reg. Alcock fos. 68–68v. On Edward's awareness of the state of the localities, see 'Historia Croylandensis', p. 564.

64 Seckington seems not to have been at issue thereafter: John had it in 1493 and it had not been put at issue when the case reopened under Richard III (K.B.9/401/28; *W.F.F.*, 2727; below, pp. 556–7); Derbys.R.O. D156M/49–50, 84; Dunham 1955: p. 120. It does not seem very probable that Richard would have surrendered 100 marks of land at Arrow, as John claimed, so John's account of the arbitration may have to be taken with a pinch of salt. John must have been about 14–17 when retained (above, n. 46 for dating of Burdet divorce).

65 *Coventry Leet Book*, pp. 419–21, 425–6, 428–9; *Dugdale*, p. 148; *Cal. Pat. Rolls 1467–77*, p. 634, *1476–85*, p. 576; *List of Escheators*, p. 171; *Register of Coventry Guild*, p. 111.

66 Above, n. 42.

67 E.159/256 Mich. – recogs. for shrievalty of Richard Boughton, Hastings' retainer; above, pp. 491, 512.

From 1470 to 1473 Bristowe had been embroiled in a bitter feud with Coventry over his enclosure of pastures lying within the leet between Coventry and Whitley. By 1473 Henry Boteller, the Recorder, had been drawn in, both as the lessee from the city of some of the land at issue and as the representative of the citizens. In that year a compromise was made and the affair largely subsided, only to re-emerge with far greater ferocity in the uncertain atmosphere after the death of Clarence.[68] Boteller and Bristowe continued to fight over the pasture held by Boteller, but Bristowe's dispute with the town took a new turn.[69] By this time Coventry itself was divided, possibly (but by no means certainly) along the classic lines of merchants against crafts. The mayor and Recorder led one side, while one of the city chamberlains, a fiery character named Laurence Saunders, was the leader of the other. One of the chamberlain's jobs was to supervise the use of the common pasture in the leet, and Saunders, who had clearly decided that he had a special mission in this respect, had got it into his head that the mayor and Recorder were deliberately allowing a number of outsiders and 'ffrankeleyns of ye fforreins', amongst them the prior of Coventry, Bristowe and even Henry Boteller himself, to overuse the pastures while the citizens went short. This was a complex affair on which, thanks to the Coventry Leet Book, we are very well informed, and this is not the place to go into either the dispute or its causes in detail.[70] In the present context our interest in the affair lies in its impact on county politics. From 1480 onwards there was a series of appeals to the Prince of Wales who as earl of Chester was lord of Coventry.[71] It is highly probable that the responses of the Prince's council were prompted by the king, but by September 1481, for reasons that will soon be apparent, Edward had become directly involved. The king could hardly fail to be concerned right from the start, considering the importance to the crown of both the location of the dispute and the main protagonists, to whom must be added the prior, who by the end of 1480 had decided to have a whole series of issues out with the commonalty as a whole.[72] Since the town was later to decide that the next Recorder after Henry Boteller was not to be of counsel with the prior, it appears that once the latter had intervened it began to feel threatened from within.[73] The relationship between priory and town had

[68] Carpenter 1986a: p. 32; *H.M.C.* xv, x, pp. 144–6, 151–2, 153–6; *Coventry Leet Book*, pp. 349–50, 376–81. Above, pp. 18–19 for an account of Coventry and its surrounding area.

[69] K.B.9/360/80; JUST 1/1547 m.1; K.B.27/866 Coram Rege rot.7d., /886 Coram Rege rot.2 *et seq.*

[70] *Coventry Leet Book*, pp. 430–1, 436–40; Harris 1894. Harris linked this dispute to tensions between a mercantile oligarchy and the crafts. Although Saunders was indeed a dyer, hence a 'craftsman', the divisions seem more complex. I hope to explore the dispute at greater length at a later stage. Gill 1930: pp. 61–74, another account, deals with it purely in class terms.

[71] *Coventry Leet Book*, pp. 425–6, 428 n. 3, 432, 433–4, 436–40.

[72] *Coventry Leet Book*, pp. 443–8, 454–74.

[73] *Coventry Leet Book*, p. 525.

never been easy, and this new factor heightened the explosiveness of the whole situation.[74]

At first the king's response, if we may take it that his was the guiding hand behind the Prince's council, was largely favourable to Bristowe, a policy in keeping with his use of the man at this time. Saunders was certainly given very short shrift and was made to humble himself before both Bristowe and the mayor.[75] But it is evident that Edward was not very favourably disposed towards the town either, and had probably not yet forgiven it its support of the rebels in 1469–71. In the midst of the conflict, in April 1481, a request arrived in Coventry for troops for Scotland. The town responded by providing sixty men, after an offer of 200 marks in lieu had been refused by the king. Then Edward not only rejected the town's choice of leader – significantly Edward Bristowe, William's brother, which suggests the king's enthusiasm for this family was cooling – but sent Rivers along to see whether the town could provide any more troops. Coventry wrote a grovelling letter to the Prince, offering 100 archers *in toto*, and the reply reassured the town that both the Prince and his father now approved its efforts. But then the expedition was delayed and the troops kept in readiness at Coventry at great expense to the town.[76]

Lammas day (1 August) was approaching, the time for the opening of the commons, which had always been the moment when this dispute over grazing was most likely to erupt. Under these conditions of strain on the town's economy and food supplies things were more tense than usual. At least the new prior was favourably disposed to the town, but Bristowe was being as difficult as ever, refusing to open his meadow, and it was felt necessary to send word to the Prince, who promised to come to Coventry.[77] On 23 August he and some of his council arrived and on the 25 John Alcock bishop of Worcester, a Woodville protégé, Rivers, Lord Dudley, John Hugford, William Lucy (chosen probably as an impartial local landowner with Coventry connections) '& many other Gentils of Warr[wik]shire' went 'with many of ye Cite' to view the ground in dispute and take evidence from the older residents. These claimed to have been put out of the common pasture by Bristowe's father. A temporary compromise was agreed on, but, immediately after the lords had departed, an attempt to tear down Bristowe's enclosure led to a riot.[78]

74 *V.C.H.* VIII, pp. 2–3; Davis 1976; Coss 1974a; Coss ed., *Early Records of Medieval Coventry*, pp. xvi–xxix.

75 *Coventry Leet Book*, pp. 432–43.

76 *Coventry Leet Book*, pp. 370–1, 478–81, 483–9, 500; above, pp. 498, 512–13.

77 *Coventry Leet Book*, pp. 489–90.

78 *Coventry Leet Book*, pp. 490–2; *H.M.C.*, XV, x, pp. 154–5. Lucy had been on the Coventry muster commission earlier that year and had been an executor of Sudeley, the latter having been patron of Henry Boteller the Recorder, of Bristowe (both of them also Sudeley executors) and of other gentry in and around Coventry (C.81/1390/19; E.101/516/8; app. 3). For Alcock, see Evans 1915: p. 201 n. 2. Cf. very similar events on Whitley common in 1525 (Phythian-Adams 1979: pp. 254–5).

This was the point when the king's intervention, although still nominally exercised through the Prince, became rather more overt. Although he expected the offenders to be dealt with firmly, he accepted the town's protestation that the riot had been primarily Bristowe's fault and thereafter put himself firmly behind Coventry while beginning to lose patience with Bristowe, who was forced in the end to make his peace with the town.[79] By contrast with the year before, when a new demand for troops arrived in 1482, Coventry was permitted to buy itself off with a mere £20.[80] Once freed of the threats posed by Bristowe, the prior and the king, Coventry was able to put Saunders firmly in his place.[81] The whole business had taken Edward longer to deal with than perhaps he would have liked, and initially he had shown some misjudgement in allowing his lingering hostility to Coventry to lead him into giving too much trust and support to a troublemaker like Bristowe, but it shows that the king was capable of flexibility when he knew he had been wrong. Having made up his mind to be firm but friendly with Coventry and to discourage Bristowe, he was able to restore order while reducing Coventry to a gratifyingly cringing servility which he had the good sense not to abuse.

It is this readiness to adjust to circumstances, even if it entailed radical changes of policy, and to listen to the messages coming up from below that is so characteristic of Edward's rule of the county. It can also be seen to good effect in the delicate matter of the Master Forestership of Malvern Chace which became a major issue in 1480. Although the office and lands in question were in Worcestershire and rather closer to Wales than to Warwickshire, the outcome of the dispute had considerable significance for Warwickshire. This was because the main protagonist was Richard Beauchamp of Powick, and the question underlying the whole affair appears to have been whether he was to be allowed to recreate or even extend the sphere of influence that had been his father's in the west midlands in his prime.[82] Soon after the fall of Clarence, Beauchamp purchased the Forestership from Nicholas Hanley of Worcestershire, together with Halle manor and Hanley's lands in Hanley, Welland and Upton-on-Severn. It was Clarence's death that gave him the opportunity to do so, for the duke had held the overlordship of both office and lands, and, with the offices on the Clarence estate Beauchamp already possessed, which had been immediately confirmed by the king, he now had a very solid block of power around Hanley Castle in west Worcestershire.[83] By this time he may have had

79 *Coventry Leet Book*, pp. 492–501, 504–10.

80 *Coventry Leet Book*, p. 505.

81 *Coventry Leet Book*, pp. 510–13.

82 Above, pp. 410–28, 446–65.

83 *Cal. Close Rolls 1476–85*, pp. 187–9, 269–71; Br. Lib. Add. Ch. 73,695; *Cal. Pat. Rolls 1476–85*, p. 97; D.L.29/644/10458.

in his service Roger Harewell of Worcestershire, a cousin of the Warwickshire family and one of those household servants of Clarence who had betrayed the duke to the king,[84] and it was natural for Beauchamp to assume that he would succeed to at least part of Clarence's west midland authority. Once the king had the Warwick lands, Beauchamp was the only nobleman with lands in all three west midland counties, Warwickshire, Worcestershire and Gloucestershire.

At first Edward was apparently quite happy for Beauchamp to do so. In December 1480 a new settlement of the office and lands on Beauchamp was made, for which the attorneys to deliver seisin were the king's valets (one of them in fact Nicholas Hanley), and both office and lands were remaindered to the king.[85] But the sale was already being contested by John Hugford of Dixton, Gloucestershire, uncle of the Warwickshire John Hugford, and by two other members of the Hanley family. These sold them to a group of feoffees clearly representing the interests of the Woodvilles in the Welsh march. The connecting link here may be that the Warwickshire Hugford was in the queen's service. During 1480 there were suits involving Beauchamp and all the interested parties, but the real issue must have been the Woodvilles' refusal to tolerate the concentration of so much power along the Welsh border in the hands of a nobleman outside their circle.[86] Eventually Edward came round to their view, and in June 1482 he issued a commission for an enquiry into wastes committed by Beauchamp in the lands pertaining to his offices on the former Clarence estates 'for want of due execution of his office'. The commissioners included John Savage, who was one of the claimants to the Forestership from the Woodville camp, and other trusted officials of both king and queen. They also included Roger Harewell, which must have been a bitter blow to Beauchamp.[87]

It would be a mistake to assume that this shows Edward being led by the nose by his wife, for he himself had every reason to veto Beauchamp's efforts to take over any of the royal authority in the west midlands, and indeed the incumbents of the local offices in Worcestershire from 1478 to 1483 reveal a

84 *Cal. Close Rolls 1476–85*, p. 188; Nash 1781–2: I, p. 77; Carpenter 1986a: p. 40. Harewell was one of the witnesses to the grant of the office to Beauchamp.

85 K.B.27/934 Coram Rege rot.24. A related grant provides interesting information about the means of conveying livery of seisin, with the symbolic blowing of a horn to mark the transfer (Worcs.R.O. 705:139/4/14).

86 *Cal. Close Rolls 1476–85*, pp. 269–71; C.P.40/864 rot.332, /874 roti.87, 90d., 92, 267d., 568; Hicks 1979a: pp. 75–83. For the Gloucestershire Hugfords, see Atkyns 1712: I, p. 210. The Woodvilles' proprietary attitude to their power along the march is made clear in Lowe 1980–2.

87 *Cal. Pat. Rolls 1476–85*, p. 319. For the royal connections of some of the commissioners, see Horrox and Hammond eds., *British Library Harleian Manuscript 433*, III, p. 200 (for Savage), Hicks 1980: pp. 167–8 (for John Twynho), *List of Escheators*, p. 181 for Thomas Lygon (Worcestershire escheator almost throughout this period and therefore presumably acceptable to Edward IV, the effective ruler of Worcestershire through the Warwick estates).

determination to prevent the growth of any such power.[88] Although he was called to order by the commission, Beauchamp's interests were not entirely subjugated to the whims of the Woodvilles. The Forestership and its lands did not go to the Woodvilles and in January 1483 an arbitration was arranged between Beauchamp and the Hanleys, to be performed by a body consisting largely of lawyers and household men.[89] It must have declared in Beauchamp's favour, for the following May one of the Hanleys quitclaimed the Forestership and the lands to Beauchamp, and the case was to all intents and purposes closed until the accession of Henry VII enabled the remnants of the Woodville feoffees – who had apparently been acting all along for Richard Croft, one of their number – to reopen it.[90]

Taken as a whole Edward IV's rule of Warwickshire stands up well to examination. Gradually the outbreak of instability that had accompanied Clarence's fall was brought under control. Cases either disappear from the records or come to arbitration or are settled in some other way. The Dalby–Verney dispute for example at last came to an end after troubling the Warwickshire peace for nearly forty years, both sides, as it seems, eventually accepting the settlement probably made before Dalby's death. It is highly likely that pressure from the king was used to force the Dalby family into acquiescence, for both John Beaufitz, who was involved in the Verney recovery of the disputed property, and Edmund Verney were Edward's men.[91] The king and his household certainly played a large part in more formal compositions. We have already seen one instance of this in the Coventry affair. In 1479 Edward had a notable success in bringing to an end the Grey–Ferrers conflict, another long-running and extremely divisive feud.[92] He himself acted as arbitrator, as he did also in the settlement of the dispute between Thomas Stafford, Humphrey II's brother, and Edward Woodville over Dodford manor

[88] Above, p. 529. It seems that Edward IV was ready to allow Beauchamp on to the commission of the peace in Worcestershire, which argues a typical lack of vindictiveness and will to compromise (*Cal. Pat. Rolls 1476–85*, p. 578: listed as 'John', the accuracy of the calendar being confirmed from the original (C.66/540 m.22d., /548 m.20d.), but John had died in 1475 (above, n. 9)).

[89] Br. Lib. Add. Ch. 73,696. For details on some of the arbitrators, Ross 1974: p. 323; *Wedgwood: Biographies*, pp. 435–6, 436–7; Hicks 1979a: p. 77; Ives 1983a: pp. 473, 476; *Coventry Leet Book*, p. 493.

[90] *Cal. Close Rolls 1476–85*, p. 303; below, p. 575. A chancery petition of Richard Beauchamp made under Richard III, although it is unspecific about dates, states that Thomas and Roger Hanley disseised Beauchamp of office and land and then granted them 'for mayntenance' to the same group of feoffees that sued Beauchamp in the Common Pleas in Michaelmas 1480 (comparison of names shows that 'the lord Richard' referred to here was Richard Grey, the queen's younger son: Hicks 1979a: p. 61 for a useful genealogy of the family) – although they must later have transferred their title to Croft – and that Beauchamp subsequently re-entered; all this seems to have occurred under Edward IV (*Calendars of Proceedings in Chancery*, I, p. cxii; C.P.40/874 rot.90d.).

[91] K.B.27/882 Coram Rege rot.69d.

[92] B.R.L. 610247/50; *I.P.M. Hen. VII*, II, 144.

in Northamptonshire. This was part of the inheritance in Warwickshire and Northamptonshire that had been fought over by John Hathewick, the Staffords and various other claimants, from one of whom Woodville had bought the manor. In 1481 the king decreed that Thomas and his mother were to keep the manor while he himself would recompense Woodville with a grant of lands worth £50 a year. Since Woodville's heirs presumptive who witnessed the agreement consisted of almost the entire Woodville clan, from the queen and the princes down, the arbitration shows that, far from being putty in the hands of his wife, Edward was able to put himself above factional politics. He had special reason to do so in this case, since his own concerns were at stake, for Humphrey Stafford was an influential member of the royal affinity in the west midlands. In all his dealings with Warwickshire he had the wisdom to act magnanimously. For instance, when Simon Mountford and the king confronted one another directly over a tenement at Sutton Coldfield which was on the Warwick estate, Mountford lost neither the Constableship of Kenilworth nor his place on the commission of the peace. Doubtless pliability here helped him sort out the renewed outbreak over the Mountford lands, confined this time to those in Berkshire, that seems to have occurred between 1478 and 1482.[93]

Edward was able to combine his powers as king, duke of Lancaster (acting through Hastings in the north midlands and the queen in Northamptonshire) and earl of Warwick to bring peace and effective rule to 'greater Warwickshire' and probably to much if not all of the midlands.[94] By 1481 the only serious threat to local stability was the Coventry business and that was never allowed to go far beyond the boundaries of the leet. By 1483 Warwickshire was as peaceful as it had been at any time in the century. The secret of Edward's success was his almost perfect instinct for when to be firm, even harsh, and when to retreat gracefully. It has been emphasised throughout this study that the gentry had always been in two minds about whether they preferred peace, which could only be bought at the price of restriction of their individual freedom of action, or freedom which could so easily develop into self-defeating disorder. Edward gave them in many respects the best of both worlds by providing a framework of stability and within it the freedom to arrange their affairs as suited them best, as long as the use of their freedom did not jeopardise local order or the king's well-defined but generally relaxed view of his own prerogative. Under Edward IV, Warwickshire was as well run as it had been in the later years of Richard

93 Baker 1822–41: I, pp. 353–4. Early in the reign of Henry VII, Woodville was given the £50 a year owing from the settlement 'out of regard to Edward, late king of England' (*Materials: Henry VII,* I, pp. 562–3). D.L.29/642/10422; Horrox and Hammond eds., *British Library Harleian Manuscript 433,* III, p. 204; Griffiths 1980a: pp. 9 and 13 n. 46.

94 Somerville 1953: p. 238 for the queen and Northamptonshire. Since 1467 she had also had Kenilworth and, as holder of Kenilworth, had numbered Beaufitz among her servants (Somerville 1953: pp. 238–9; Myers ed., 'Household of Queen Elizabeth Woodville', p. 225).

Beauchamp of Warwick, in fact rather more stable, but the detailed direction of the shire was a lot more distant and easy-going.

Thus to cavil at the failure of Edward or his agent Hastings to draw the gentry into a single close-knit affinity is beside the point, for the essence of Edward's rule was to allow a loosely-structured local society to function within a firmly-delineated royal authority.[95] The losers were the major nobility, like Buckingham and perhaps Grey, for whom a role commensurate with their power and family traditions could not be found, and it was men of this type who were to prove the undoing of Edward's heirs. But, if one can generalise from Warwickshire at the end of Edward's reign, it is entirely untrue to suggest that his government was founded on a small household clique. On the contrary, the king's affinity in some form or other embraced the whole county, and it is clear that, even where the Woodvilles' interests were engaged, the affairs of Warwickshire landowners were administered in a remarkably non-partisan fashion. In the last years of his reign Edward had reached the enviable position of being powerful enough to dictate his own terms to the localities and secure enough to be able to run them in a relaxed and trusting fashion.

Certainly there were grievances, which in retrospect can be seen as 'causes' of the tragedy of 1483, most notably those felt by the small number of magnates like Buckingham who had not been fully absorbed into Edward's order either in Warwickshire or elsewhere. It was particularly unfortunate that these could identify the Woodvilles as a common enemy and that, while the king's affinity was utterly loyal to the king, much of it seems to have shared this antipathy to his wife's family.[96] But it was only Edward's early and unexpected death leaving an underage heir under the Woodvilles' control that gave the losers of Edward's later years a chance for revenge and turned dislike of the Woodvilles into an urgent political issue. Then it was only Gloucester's monumental stupidity that allowed a crisis at the centre of government to go beyond the

[95] Cf. Wright 1983: pp. 78–81.

[96] Ross 1974: pp. 330, 335, 424–6, 1981: ch. 2 (but cf. pp. 105–7 for some recognition of the household's role in the shires); Morgan 1973; Richmond 1986: pp. 182–6; cf. Lowe 1980–2, p. 569 (but this may over-stress division within the household), Crawford 1975: p. 157 on East Anglia, Arnold 1984: pp. 123–7 on the West Riding, Horrox ed. 1986: Intro. on the north. Hicks' work (1979a) suggests that the Woodvilles were allowed a broader licence – perhaps too broad a licence – than is implied here, but it is difficult to believe that the major acts of 'injustice' e.g. towards Buckingham and the Mowbray heirs were not initiated by Edward (cf. Lowe 1980–2: pp. 567–73, which is generally more favourable to them: too favourable?). Dr Horrox, to whom I am most grateful for several discussions on the subject, does not believe that there was a substantial Woodville affinity separate from the royal one, and she emphasises the extent to which the whole of the midlands and the south were drawn into Edward's affinity by the end of the reign. These issues are discussed in her book (Horrox 1989). Morgan, whose work seems to be the origin of the often-quoted assertion that Edward's power was too narrowly based, seems in fact to have changed his mind on this issue (Morgan 1987: pp. 64–7). 'Historia Croylandensis', p. 562 stresses the omnipresence in the realm of Edward's servants in the years after Clarence's fall.

question of the governance of the minority and become a debate about the succession.[97] Finally, one cannot emphasise enough that, as Henry VII was later to grasp, it was the *first* succession of a new dynasty that was the real danger point; once a hereditary right to rule had been established the moment of the crown's passing became much less fraught.[98] Hence comparisons with the minority of 1422 are inapposite. The events of 1483 are a very inadequate verdict on Edward's rule. In early 1483, if the rest of central and southern England was in the same condition as Warwickshire, the Yorkist dynasty was successful, accepted and set to go on indefinitely.

II

It is now clear that without Richard III's usurpation there would have been no Tudor dynasty. In 1483 the cause of Henry Tudor was dead, but by seizing the throne from Edward's heirs and having them murdered Richard alienated most of Edward IV's vast midland and southern affinity and turned Henry into the Yorkist claimant. Many of Henry's earliest and most loyal supporters came from the rebellious ranks of Edward IV's former household.[99] In the second reign of Edward IV Warwickshire had passed from magnate control to complete subjugation to royal command. The question for Richard III was whether he could maintain this authority, while the crown affinity that was so central to local rule was in such turmoil, or would hand the county back to the nobility. Were he to take the second course, could he hold the balance between the competing ambitions of the unleashed nobility?

As far as north Warwickshire and the north midlands were concerned he had little choice. The dominance that Hastings had enjoyed on the king's behalf had to be replaced as soon as the Lord Chamberlain was gone, and Gloucester was far too enmeshed in more pressing concerns to do the job himself. More cogent still was the fact that the price of Buckingham's support throughout the coups of 1483 had been to surrender to him all the responsibility from which he had been debarred by Edward IV, which included the traditional Stafford rule of the north midlands. The destruction first of the Woodvilles, the rulers of the

97 Ross 1981: ch. 4.

98 A more apt comparison than the more usual one with 1422 is with 1413–15, which, the age, experience and outstanding abilities of the new king notwithstanding, was by no means a straightforward period for the dynasty (Harriss 1985c: pp. 34–8; Powell 1985); for Henry VII and the succession, see below, pp. 594–5. Cf. Ross 1974: pp. 423–6, and 1981: pp. 35–43.

99 An interpretation implicit in Ross 1981: pp. 105–19 and Chrimes 1972a: ch. 1; see also McFarlane 1981f: p. 241; Bennett 1985: pp. 47–50, 62, 153; Wolffe 1976: pp. 372–3; McKenna 1979: p. 502; Williams 1984–5: pp. 36–7; Hanham 1975: p. 196; Davies, C.S.L. 1987: pp. 2, 5–11. Note also that Edward felt safe enough in 1482 to contemplate inviting Henry to return to England (Jones 1986: pp. 29–30). Again I must thank Dr Horrox for her confirmation of this view, for which there is greater factual support in her book (Horrox 1989); there is a brief reference in her introduction, Horrox and Hammond eds., *British Library Harleian Manuscript 433*, I, p. xxvi.

Welsh marches, then of Hastings gave Buckingham access to just those regions which he must have felt belonged to him as of right. It is highly probable that it was he who urged both courses on Gloucester and not improbable that he encouraged him to seize the throne to ensure that he lost neither region when the king came of age in a short time.[100] The report in the Stonor correspondence that 'All ye lord Chamberleyne mene be come my lordys of Bokynghame menne' may not be literally true but it correctly reflects the fact that it was Buckingham who succeeded to the Tutbury stewardship and to the lordship of men and region that went with it.[101] Initially at least the Hastings affinity in the north midlands seems to have gone over to its new master, and it is difficult to see what else it could have done, more especially as it was really a royal affinity. But Buckingham's rebellion in October 1483 ended his period of control in this area as swiftly as it had begun, and it does not seem that he had penetrated far into the local society of the region before he was removed from it.[102] It has been pointed out that 'Buckingham's rebellion' was really one of a series of revolts by Edward IV's former household to which Buckingham lent his name and leadership but with whose rank and file this nominal leader had few links.[103] Consequently, when Thomas Ferrers came off the next Warwickshire commission of the peace after the rebellion, the cause of mistrust is far more likely to have been his close connection with Hastings than any allegiance to Buckingham.[104]

Once Buckingham had gone, there was no attempt to put another magnate in his place over the whole north midlands, and the slighting of Maxstoke may mean that Richard had no intention of replacing him.[105] An obvious candidate would have been Edward Grey. Grey had been one of Richard's earliest supporters, rewarded with a viscountcy.[106] He was also given the confiscated lands of his nephew the marquess of Dorset in Warwickshire and some of the lands in Leicestershire, which meant that he now had full ownership of the former Astley properties which he had previously been sharing. However, Broughton Astley, the principal Leicestershire estate that Dorset's family the

[100] For the most up-to-date account of the usurpation, see Ross 1981: ch. 4, but cf. Horrox 1989; also Green,'Historical Notes of a London Citizen', pp. 587–8 for a contemporary suggestion of Buckingham's involvement in the death of the princes. Griffiths 1972b: p. 162 for Buckingham and the Welsh march.

[101] *Stonor Letters,* II, p. 161, discussed in Wright 1983: p. 80. Bennett emphasises the extent to which Richard was able to establish a military monopoly (1985: p. 43); replacing Hastings in the Tutbury region, where the king could call on so many Duchy tenants, was clearly crucial to this.

[102] Wright 1983: pp. 80–1, 107.

[103] Ross 1981: pp. 105–15; Wright 1983: p. 80; Bennett 1985: pp. 47–50, 62. This is another point that is amplified in Horrox 1989.

[104] *Cal. Pat. Rolls 1476–85*, p. 576; Ross 1981: p. 118 on the lack of midlands involvement in the rebellion.

[105] Jones 1987: p. 137.

[106] *G.E.C.*, VIII, p. 60.

Greys of Groby had inherited from the Astleys, went not to Grey but to William Catesby. The king's favours to Grey otherwise went no further than allowing him to seize Chaddesley Corbett in Worcestershire and Kibworth Beauchamp in Leicestershire, two of the Beauchamp trust manors that Grey had sued for late in Edward's reign.[107] After Buckingham's rebellion, Maxstoke Castle, no longer the key strongpoint in north Warwickshire since its dismantling, was retained by the king. Its constableship was given to a member of the north Warwickshire gentry, Henry Willoughby, here assuming prominence in Warwickshire for the first time.[108] As Willoughby was to seal a marriage alliance with Grey soon after Henry VII's accession,[109] it is not unlikely that the two were already acting in consort under Richard, and their combined authority may have helped the king bring north Warwickshire to order after Buckingham was gone.

All the same, it is hard to see how the north midlands as a whole could have been brought into line in the long term without a replacement of the stature of Hastings who was acceptable to local sentiment, and, as with the rest of England south of the Humber, Richard III may have been running out of people he could trust.[110] It is significant that some of the major desertions immediately before and during Bosworth came in this part of the midlands. The Stanleys, with one branch at Elford in Staffordshire, spring to mind; Elford may in fact have been the place where Henry Tudor spent the night of 18 August 1485, four days before Bosworth. In Warwickshire itself, the Stanleys are said to have met Henry secretly at Atherstone in the north-east of the county the night before the battle. On 18 August Henry had sent his troops south from Lichfield to Tamworth, the residence of the Ferrers, whose heir was married to a daughter of John Stanley of Elford.[111] John Hardwick of Flanders in north Warwickshire and Lindley in Leicestershire, another more distant

107 Horrox and Hammond eds., *British Library Harleian Manuscript 433*, III, pp. 144, 150; *I.P.M. Hen. VII*, II, 908, III, 1160; Hicks: 1981, pp. 141, 145; above, p. 325 n. 171 for the Astley/Grey family. For the alleged plot against Richard, involving Lisle and Dorset, Hanham 1975: pp. 37, 106, 119: in view of Grey's career under Richard and his rewards from the Dorset confiscation, it seems improbable.

108 Horrox and Hammond eds., *British Library Harleian Manuscript 433*, I, p. 193.

109 Nott. Univ. Lib. Middleton MS Mi D 4798.

110 Ross 1981: pp. 119–24; Pollard 1977; Bennett 1985: p. 81. The instructions to the northerner Marmaduke Constable as steward of Tutbury illustrate both Richard's awareness of the need to keep the region under firm control and his deep unease about it (Wolffe 1970: pp. 131–2, cited in Rowney 1984a: p. 45). Dr Horrox suggested to me that it was Richard's mistrust that kept out an obvious alternative candidate, the earl of Shrewsbury (below, p. 567 for his later power here). Williams (1984–5, pp. 39–40) suggests many of the Leicestershire landed classes were 'flocking' to Henry.

111 *Wedgwood: Biographies*, p. 799; Ross 1981: pp. 216 n. 21,218 n. 29, 236–7; Palmer 1845: pp. 98–9, app., pp. lx–lxiv; *Visitation: Warwicks.*, p. 7; but cf. Hanham 1975: p. 134 on the Atherstone meeting. For the Stanleys of Elford, see Irvine 1953: p. 46. For other help to Henry on the part of the Stanleys just before Bosworth, see Bennett 1985: pp. 92–3, and, from others, Hanham 1975: p. 21. On Richard and the Stanleys, see Jones 1986b.

Hastings connection, is supposed to have led Henry to the most suitable site for his army on the battlefield itself. As early as March 1485 Richard was having to instruct his tenants on the former Warwick manor of Sutton Coldfield in north Warwickshire not to accept liveries from anyone and to be ready to do service to their king.[112] Cumulatively these facts suggest not just that Henry had the support of individual landowners but that the whole of north Warwickshire and Staffordshire was unlikely to stand in his way. Richard's concern about the area is evident from the large sum of money – over £100 – spent on repairing Kenilworth, the crown's major stronghold in the central midlands, between 1483 and 1485.[113]

If Richard was able to name a stronger commission of array for Warwickshire at the end of his reign than the commissions into traitors after Buckingham's rebellion, the only gentry landowner from north of Coventry on the list was Simon Mountford, who was always too much of a free agent to be integrally bound up with the Hastings nexus.[114] Henry Baker, a minor Coleshill gentleman, was Warwickshire escheator in 1484–5 and is recorded as dying on 22 August, the day of Bosworth, which may well mean that he fought there for Richard. It could possibly indicate that Mountford did so as well, managing somehow to avoid attainder afterwards. But the fact that Mountford was on Henry VII's first commission of the peace for Warwickshire, issued barely a month after Bosworth, suggests that he had kept his hands clean.[115] The list of local notables from late in the reign in Harley 433, apparently designating reliable men who might be appointed to local office, is sadly deficient in north Warwickshire gentry.[116] Some sense of Richard's failure here comes from his retaining of William Bermingham III, a north Warwickshire man largely shunned by his neighbours, of whom it was alleged in 1491 'since birth he has been a lunatic once in every month, enjoying lucid intervals'.[117] The king had one prominent and firm supporter in north Warwickshire in William Berkeley, who, although resident at Weoley in north-east Worcestershire, had a number of offices on crown properties in the north of the county. Berkeley fought at

[112] Nichols 1795–1811: IV, ii, p. 646; Nott. Univ. Lib. Middleton MS Mi D 4241, 4243; *Dugdale*, p. 322 n.f. The Hardwick story puts an interesting perspective on Dadlington's claim to be the site of the battle, for Hardwick owned land there and could therefore have been particularly knowledgeable about the terrain (Br. Lib. Add. MS 6046 fo. 21; Richmond 1985a: pp. 18–20); Br. Lib. Harl. MS 433 fo. 210v.

[113] D.L.29/463/7564, 7566. Rowney (1981: p. 153) names six Staffordshire men who may have fought for Henry at Bosworth and only one for Richard.

[114] *Cal. Pat. Rolls 1476–85*, pp. 393, 489. Bennett makes the point that Henry's progress between Stafford and Lichfield slowed down considerably, to give his supporters, many of them local, time to arrive (1985: pp. 91–2).

[115] *I.P.M. Hen. VII*, III, 1149; *List of Escheators*, p. 171; below, p. 563.

[116] Horrox and Hammond eds., *British Library Harleian Manuscript 433*, III, p. 238. But cf. Horrox 1986: p. 99 for a more optimistic opinion on north midlands support for Richard.

[117] *Cal. Pat. Rolls 1476–85*, p. 478; *I.P.M. Hen. VII*, III, 1150.

Bosworth and was subsequently attainted. His decision to stand by Richard may well have been influenced by the fact that he feared that Thomas Boteller of Ormond, his chief rival for the Botetourt lands, would be favoured by Henry Tudor.[118]

To the south Richard did rather better in winning over the Warwickshire gentry. Catesby brought with him part of the east Warwickshire-Leicestershire-Northamptonshire connection that had gathered around Hastings, particularly those for whom he himself had been the immediate focal point. These included Richard Boughton, sheriff in 1484–5 and supposedly killed while on active service on Richard's behalf two days before Bosworth, Everard Fielding of east Warwickshire and Leicestershire, Thomas Kebyll the Leicestershire lawyer, and Geoffrey St. Germain, one of the post-Bosworth attaintees, who, like Boughton, was heir to some of the Allesley estate in east Warwickshire.[119] Catesby became a considerable power here during the course of the reign, receiving the majority of Buckingham's south Warwickshire properties, most of them in the east of the county, and acquiring by royal grant or by more dubious methods numbers of other properties in Leicestershire and Northamptonshire.[120] Since Catesby was feed by Buckingham, Richard may have hoped initially that the two of them could rebuild the connection from north to south-east midlands that Catesby had established with Hastings. Afterwards the king's hopes for a north midland partner for this favourite household esquire may have centred on Thomas Lord Stanley, another of the major landowners who feed Catesby. The vanity of such expectations, if Richard did entertain them, is summed up in the bitterness of Catesby's will made just before

[118] Horrox and Hammond eds., *British Library Harleian Manuscript 433*, I, p. 191; *Rot. Parl.*, VI, p. 276. Although there is no clear evidence that Ormond was acting treasonably before Bosworth (but Dr Horrox has some indirect evidence), he was immediately fully restored by Henry VII and remained close to the king throughout the reign, while Berkeley's attainder clearly acted in Ormond's interests (*G.E.C.*, X, pp. 131–2; and below, pp. 574, 588). Note that Berkeley was of Weoley, not Weobley, Herefs., as stated in Horrox and Hammond eds., *British Library Harleian Manuscript 433*, IV, p. 16.

[119] *Dugdale*, p. 99; Horrox and Hammond eds., *British Library Harleian Manuscript 433*, I, p. 75, III, p. 235; *Cal. Pat. Rolls 1476–85*, pp. 400, 489; *Rot. Parl.*, VI, p. 276; *V.C.H.*, V, p. 155; Ives 1983a: pp. 63–4, 109. St. Germain is otherwise a very shadowy figure; he came originally from Northamptonshire (Bridges and Whalley 1791: I, p. 85; Horrox and Hammond eds., *British Library Harleian Manuscript 433*, III, p. 130) but may have had some connection with Shilton near Withybrook in east Warwickshire (*V.C.H.*, VI, p. 213); he died on 23 August, the day after Bosworth, which suggests his participation, and his daughter later made a successful appeal against his attainder on the grounds that he had fought against his will (*I.P.M. Hen. VII*, I, 13; Bennett 1985: p. 130). Bennett suggests Boughton was killed by the Stanleys (1985: p. 95). Among the attaintees after Stoke were members of the Malory family of Litchborough, Northamptonshire (*Rot. Parl.*, VI, p. 397), and it is not inconceivable that they were also represented at Bosworth, escaping the consequences of the first offence but not of the second.

[120] Horrox and Hammond eds., *British Library Harleian Manuscript 433*, III, pp. 149–50; above, pp. 118, 131.

execution after Bosworth: 'My Lords Stanley, Strange, and all that blood helpe, and pray for my Soule, for ye have not for my Body as I trusted in yow'.[121]

In the rest of the county Richard was able to slip more or less smoothly into the shoes of his brother, the royal earl of Warwick. There was no question now of his sharing power with anyone here. Nor was there any chance that he would endorse Edward Grey's efforts to get the Beauchamp trust wound up and the lands, most of them in the west midlands, distributed among the heirs, as he himself had hoped to do when he and Grey were petitioning Edward IV as two of the joint heirs. It was far too convenient to the royal custodian of the Warwick lands to have the trust properties at his disposal by means of the fraud that had now lasted nearly fifty years.[122] Even as far north as Coventry Richard seems to have found the security that eluded him further north. He was able to strengthen himself here by following the example of his father-in-law Richard Neville and interpolating a retainer from northern England into the area west of Coventry. This was Thomas Otter of Berkswell, who had been preceded by relatives at Alspath and Warwick. After the Buckingham rebellion Otter acquired additional lands to the north, which gave the king a little more purchase on that part of the county, and an estate in south Warwickshire.[123]

In the far south and south-west Richard received the loyalty that was due to him as earl of Warwick. The only major landowner in this area he found it necessary to take off the commission of the peace was Thomas Cokesey, and in 1484 even Cokesey was considered reliable enough to be placed on a commission of array in Gloucestershire, and, soon after, his office at Henley in Arden, a crown manor in Warwickshire, was confirmed. So dependent was Richard on the gentry from this part of the county for his local officers that in 1484 he was obliged to appoint Robert Throgmorton a J.P., despite the hostility that he had probably felt towards him since the Weston Underwood affair in the 1470s.[124] John Hugford and his son-in-law Humphrey Beaufo, who now shared the major offices on the Warwick estates in the county, including those at Warwick Castle, performed loyal service. Hugford also provided a useful link

[121] *Cat. Anc. Deeds*, IV, A10182; *Dugdale*, p. 789. In August 1484 Catesby was made steward of the former Buckingham manor of Rugby, in east Warwickshire, now in Stanley's possession (Bod. Lib. Dugdale MS 13 p. 386).

[122] Hicks 1981; above, pp. 444–5, 531, 549.

[123] *Cal. Pat. Rolls 1476–85*, p. 369, *1485–94*, p. 39; Horrox and Hammond eds., *British Library Harleian Manuscript 433*, I, p. 264; S.C.11/827. For John Otter of Yorkshire and Warwick, see above, p. 126, and for Robert of Yorkshire and Alspath, who married the widow of Richard Clapham, see *Cal. Pat. Rolls 1467–77*, p. 292; C.P.40/868 rot.432; Wm. Salt Lib. H.M. Chetwynd Coll., Bundle 4 (deed of 1484). After the Buckingham rebellion Otter got William Brandon's manor of Weston in Bulkington; he was also given the Holt manor of Aston at farm, although by what right the king had this is unknown. It seems that Thomas Ward, Edward IV's Kenilworth official, also supported Richard (*Materials: Henry VII*, I, p. 77; above, p. 526).

[124] *Cal. Pat. Rolls 1476–85*, pp. 576, 398, 483. For Throgmorton, Gloucester and Weston Underwood, see above, n. 13.

between the Catesby group on the east Warwickshire border and some of the old Warwick affinity in west Warwickshire. Beaufo himself is another who probably died at Bosworth.[125] Humphrey Stafford was committed wholesale to Richard, for fear of losing the lands he had by royal grant and the Stafford of Southwick inheritance. This was contested by three men, of whom one had certainly joined the Tudor cause and another may have done; Stafford's loyalty had to be unquestioned.[126] In the area south of Warwick, another part of the county where the earls had traditionally been without rival, Thomas Straunge II was favoured by the king, and he too died on the day of Bosworth, presumably fighting for Richard III. Another to die on that day was John Clopton of Stratford, which lay at the junction of these two areas of Warwick hegemony.[127] Richard Beauchamp of Powick seems also to have stood by Richard as far as Bosworth, although, like his brother before him, the king was apparently less than convinced of Beauchamp's reliability.[128]

On the face of it, Richard III's position in Warwickshire seems not to have been too precarious. If neither the north of the county nor the north midlands as a whole were very reliable, at least Catesby was able to carry much of the east. In the old Warwick region habits of allegiance to the king as earl of Warwick were now so ingrained that they produced a ready acquiescence in the change of leadership, one that was to be evident again, with few exceptions, on the accession of Henry VII. It is probably necessary to differentiate between Edward IV's directly-recruited affinity, which displayed remarkable loyalty to his sons' cause, and those who came to him in the affinity of a household

[125] *Cal. Pat. Rolls 1476–85*, pp. 393–4, 401, 489, 502, 576; *Dugdale*, p. 278; above, p. 528; *I.P.M. Hen. VII*, I, 131. Note that he was Humphrey Beaufo esquire, not Sir Humphrey Beaufort, as in Ross 1981: p. 215.

[126] *Rot. Parl.*, VI, pp. 325–6; 'Historia Croylandensis', p. 568. Willoughby de Broke was already with Tudor (*G.E.C.*, XII, ii, p. 683), while Colshull died before Bosworth but the favour shown to his family by Henry implies possible support before he came to England (*Wedgwood: Biographies*, pp. 204–5; *Rot. Parl.*, VI, p. 325). Also above, pp. 118–19; Chetwynd-Stapylton 1892: p. 108. Stafford had the Botetourt manors, confiscated from the Botellers of Ormond, of Mere, Handsworth and Clent, which were located in and around the Birmingham plateau and consequently not far from his main estates in Worcestershire (above, p. 524 n. 6).

[127] Horrox and Hammond eds., *British Library Harleian Manuscript 433*, I, p. 147; *I.P.M. Hen. VII*, I, 868. The editors of Harley 433 equate Thomas Straunge of Warwickshire (he also had lands in Westbury, Bucks.) with the yeoman of the crown under Edward IV, but the royal officer is probably more likely to have been a member of the Shropshire family, as the grant received by the Thomas Straunge of the Harley MS came from the Shropshire issues (Horrox and Hammond, eds., *British Library Harleian Manuscript 433*, IV, p. 191, III, p. 198) and there is no evidence at all that the Warwickshire man served Edward IV in any kind of official capacity.

[128] *Cal. Pat. Rolls 1476–85*, pp. 398, 490, 513, 519, 560. Assuming that he was the J.P. referred to as John Beauchamp of Powick earlier on (above, n. 88), Richard was taken off the Worcestershire commission of the peace (*Cal. Pat. Rolls 1476–85*, p. 578). He was later accused of forging deeds to the property in dispute with the Woodvilles (above, pp. 542–3) on the day of Bosworth, which suggests that he was settling his lands before going into battle, perhaps on Richard's side (K.B.27/937 Coram Rege rot.38).

nobleman or along with a noble estate that had come into royal hands. As far as retainers of the household nobility were concerned, their acceptance of Richard's usurpation was probably conditional upon their lord's assent. Hastings had patently not agreed to it, and this, after their initial submission, may account for unease among some of his former followers in the north midlands, which was in any case the area where Hastings' clients had essentially been Edward IV's. Where allegiance was given to the king as earl of Warwick it seems that Edward IV had almost done his work too well and that the part of Warwickshire where the earls had always been most powerful was now firmly bound to the office of king regardless of who filled it.

Over most of Warwickshire Richard III's difficulties were therefore more long-term than immediate. The overriding problem was that Edward's rule had been so outstandingly successful in his last years that there was no particular reason for supporting Richard, except in the case of a small number of disgruntled nobility, unless he could offer substantial inducements. The motive for giving him positive assistance could only be greed, or, put more subtly, the hope of getting rewards or favour on a scale that would normally have been unobtainable. But Richard himself was clearly unwilling to abandon his brother's policies of discouraging the renascence of local magnate empires, so he was likely to reach the point where he was prepared to give nothing more to some of his major allies fairly quickly, and this was certainly what happened with Buckingham.[129]

Then there would be problems in holding the balance between the aspirations of his allies. For example, although Edward Grey was one of the first to come over to Richard, not only did he not ever achieve the position in the north midlands he might have wanted, but at first his ambitions in Warwickshire had to be subordinated to Buckingham's.[130] The confiscated lands that might have helped Richard resolve these conflicting needs and win over unenthusiastic locals to broaden the basis of his rule were not on the whole used wisely. Even if it was fears about the loyalty of the whole of southern England after the Buckingham rebellion that dictated his policies, his extreme reluctance to hand out land to local men – except to Catesby, who was doing rather too well – and his well-known preference for northerners can only have reinforced the feeling that the king neither trusted nor cared for most of landowning society south of the Humber.[131] The benefits that came to Thomas

[129] Ross 1981: pp. 113–14; Harris 1986: pp. 24–5; and see Bennett 1985: pp. 55–8 on the weakness of Richard's situation from the first and pp. 68–70 for the fact that his supporters tended to be 'men of dubious value'. Sutton's attempt to show that Richard had all the kingly virtues (1986) only emphasises how it was the circumstances of the usurpation that were his undoing. See also Richmond 1986 on this (pp. 182–3) and for a generally pessimistic view of Richard's support throughout the country (pp. 172–80).

[130] Above, nn. 106–7. Cf. East Anglia (Crawford 1975: pp. 200–1) and the comments in Horrox ed. 1986: Intro., pp. 6–7.

[131] Horrox and Hammond, eds., *British Library Harleian Manuscript 433*, III, pp. 144, 145, 148, 149, 150; above, n. 110.

Otter, one of the northern imports, have been mentioned. An excellent opportunity to make overtures to north Warwickshire was missed when the two Culpepper manors there, confiscated in late 1483, went to Charles Pilkington, one of Richard's northerners.[132] Although all the holders of offices and fees on the Warwick lands in the county and on other crown properties in south Warwickshire eventually had their grants confirmed, many must have felt that their loyalty was getting them precious little when there was a lot to be had.[133]

Another aspect of his problems in offering the tangible benefits that were the only justification for his usurpation was that he found it hard to keep order, for implicit in his usurpation was the promise that those who had suffered under Edward IV would find a remedy under the new dispensation. Indeed, according to Robert Catesby, one of the aggrieved claimants to resurface in the reign, Richard positively invited the reopening of disputes.[134] This, although inevitable if Richard was to convince enough of his subjects that it was worth having him as king, was particularly unfortunate in the light of Edward IV's major achievement in settling conflict. Moreover, as on earlier occasions, once the framework of local government and society was splintered, it was every man for himself; to sacrifice personal interests to the general need for peace was under these circumstances positively to invite attack. An added complication was that Edward's rule in his later years had worked not only by means of the king's own ability to curtail disputes but by an interlocking of the various circles of the royal affinity that inhibited the emergence of overt enmities, just as Richard Beauchamp earl of Warwick's affinity had operated under Henry VI. Thus, for example, Hastings and the Woodvilles may not have been on over-friendly terms but this did not prevent them or their associates doing business together.[135] The successive coups of 1483 made it much harder to maintain good relations where grounds for enmity already existed.

A good example is the Ferrers–Grey dispute, which had apparently been settled for good in 1479. In the divisive atmosphere of 1483, Edward Grey, his case strengthened by his early approach to Richard and the Ferrers' close relationship to Hastings, felt able to reopen the whole affair. It is most likely that this was the main ground for the Ferrers' lack of enthusiasm for Richard. In 1484 both parties had to be forced into peace-keeping bonds, both promising

132 Horrox and Hammond, eds., *British Library Harleian Manuscript 433*, III, p. 154; Ross 1981: pp. 84–5. Dr Horrox has pointed out to me that Pilkington did have some connections both with Hastings and with the north midlands, so he was not a complete outsider.

133 Above, nn. 123–4; *Cal. Pat. Rolls 1476–85*, pp. 390, 407; Horrox and Hammond eds., *British Library Harleian Manuscript 433*, I, pp. 140, 191; D.L.29/463/7563–6; S.C.6/1068/9. There is no record of the confirmation of any of the annuities on the Beauchamp trust lands except for that to John Ferrers I, although this does not mean they were not confirmed. William Hugford seems to have lost his Kenilworth office some time between 1475 and 1482 (D.L.29/463/7562–3).

134 P.R.O. Catesby Doc.; below, p. 558. This was presumably his interpretation of Richard's declaration about righting injustices (Ross 1981: p. 173).

135 See refs. to groups, above, nn. 16–18, 25; Ross 1981: pp. 39–40.

not to leave London or its environs, which suggests that matters were getting quite badly out of hand. If the bond itself shows that Richard was following his brother's practice of forcing antagonistic landowners into amity, the circumstances and conditions of the bond were exceedingly unpropitious for a king whose support was crumbling rapidly. It was in any case near-impossible to exercise Edward IV's rigorous discipline when it was the king who was on the defensive, desperate for all the help he could get. Another litigant to seize his opportunity was Richard Beauchamp of Powick, who predictably exploited the fall of the Woodvilles and his position as councillor to the king to demand releases from his opponents in the dispute over the Malvern Forestership.[136]

In fact, almost every major conflict in Warwickshire under Richard III entailed the reopening of old wounds. In the case of Bristowe and Henry Boteller and of the Burdet claimants, both affairs that had been settled very recently, it was perhaps to be expected that a change of rule, however it was accomplished, would invite a new initiative from the losing party. Bristowe was very much taken under Richard's wing, probably because the king hoped to take the place Sudeley had held as patron of the minor gentry of Coventry and its environs. In January 1484 Richard himself was named as remainderman in a deed concerning the lands at issue between Bristowe and Boteller that seems to have been designed to protect them for Bristowe. The witnesses were former Sudeley men, including John Beaufitz, who was still receiver of Kenilworth.[137] Bristowe, who was now king's attorney in the Common Pleas, instituted an appeal against the verdict in Boteller's favour that had been delivered in 1482, while the rulers of Coventry played their part in the humiliation of Boteller. After a showdown over his allegedly overbearing behaviour as Recorder, he was forced in January 1485 to take an oath before the mayor and fifteen other citizens to accept the conditions they had made about his future tenure of the office. It is inconceivable that the town could have done this without the authorisation of its royal lord, who had a large role in the appointment of the Recorder.[138]

John Burdet was also seizing his opportunity. The fait accompli, reinforced by the verdict on Richard Burdet's legitimacy, had left Richard with almost the whole estate. It seems that soon after Richard III's accession John was able to get the process underway on the last two indictments of his half-brother, made in 1479 and 1480, for Richard was outlawed on these counts in late 1483.[139] But this was another instance where Richard III failed to balance the demands on

[136] C.81/1392/18–9; *Cal. Close Rolls 1476–85*, p. 388; *Calendars of Proceedings in Chancery*, I, p. cxii; P.S.O.1/57/2917 (ref. to Beauchamp as councillor, with thanks to Dr Horrox).

[137] *Cal. Close Rolls 1476–85*, p. 361; *Coventry Leet Book*, p. 507; app. 3; Horrox and Hammond eds., *British Library Harleian Manuscript 433*, II, p. 168.

[138] C.P.40/887 rot.174; K.B.27/886 Coram Rege rot.2; *Coventry Leet Book*, pp. 520–1. For the appointment of the Recorder, see *Coventry Leet Book*, pp. 157, 525–8, 537 and refs. above, p. 410 n. 43.

[139] K.B.27/896 Rex rot.4.

his favour. Apart from the fact that he had a grievance against Edward IV's government, John Burdet was not an especially promising candidate for royal patronage. He was a north Warwickshire landowner who had been retained by Hastings, so his loyalty could be in doubt, and in assisting him the king would be alienating Richard Burdet's father-in-law, Simon Mountford, a far more important north Warwickshire man, who still had the constableship of Kenilworth.

In the event the king managed to offend both parties. Having given John Burdet the chance to re-open the case, he seems later to have come down on Richard Burdet's side. It is highly probable that he had already changed his mind about whom to support by late 1483 and that it was this that was the occasion for John Burdet's extraordinary outburst at Gloucester at that time. According to the account of the Conways, who inherited Richard Burdet's claim, John 'rayled upon kyng Rychard and spake ungoodly wordes of kyng Rycharde', whereupon the mayor put him 'in warde and duraunce' and sent word to the king of what Burdet had done. This, it must be remembered, was a time when the king was dealing with rebellions and was likely to come down hard on behaviour of this kind. He sent for Richard Burdet and told him what had happened; 'and theruppon the saide Rycharde Burdette made great labour to kyng Rycharde knelyng uppon his knees' to have John spared and released, which he accordingly was (all of which argues for good relations between the king and Richard Burdet and confirms that it was indeed the king's favour that had secured Richard's position against John). Friends of John then 'laboured' to Richard to give his half-brother something to live on, and he was granted Bramcote and Compton Scorpion. A fine of July 1485 confirmed this settlement. Later, when petitioning Henry VII, John Burdet claimed that he had lost his lands after participating in Buckingham's rebellion; it seems probable that this was merely a way of dignifying the railing of a disappointed man and attracting the new king's approval. Whatever the immediate motive for John Burdet's actions, it is apparent that the king had blundered in this affair also, alienating Richard by letting John reopen the case and John by subsequently deciding to transfer his support to Richard. John seized Luddington, one of the disputed estates, immediately after Bosworth and may well have fought against Richard III, for the king's removal would have been his only hope of getting more of his inheritance restored.[140]

If these two conflicts, and even possibly the Ferrers-Grey one, their resolution being so recent, might well have broken out again under any new king, Richard handled all but the Coventry affair indifferently, and showed some misjudgement even in this case; Henry Boteller was a widely-connected man and probably not someone that many people would have wished to see

[140] Derbs.R.O. D156M/84, 47, 49; *W.F.F.*, 2727: *Dugdale*, p. 849; Horrox and Hammond eds., *British Library Harleian Manuscript 433*, II, pp. 45–6; D.L.29/463/7563–6.

bullied in his old age. And it is worth remembering that John Hardwick, who, according to the story, so obligingly showed Henry Tudor the way on the battlefield of Bosworth, was married to Boteller's daughter.[141] Moreover, there were other conflicts that had been settled so long before or so comprehensively that it can only have been the usurpation, with its promise of rewards for whoever could ingratiate himself with this uncertainly-based regime, that brought them back to life. So the Warwickshire peace was troubled yet again by Brome versus Herthill, the Herthill interest now represented by the husbands of John's daughters, Porter versus Archer, now running into its fifty-eighth year, Brome versus Catesby and Catesby versus Hugford. There was, it must be said, a determined attempt to get these under control, and arbitrations were arranged for the first two in May 1484 and early August 1485, while the council attempted, albeit unsuccessfully, to settle the Catesby–Hugford case.[142] William Catesby and his circle played a large part in the private arbitrations, and it may be that he was using his influence in the Tanworth region to contain the conflicts. Even so, the fact that Nicholas Brome was emboldened to seize Bromes manor at Lapworth from Catesby in late July 1485 indicates a failure of Catesby authority in the area; he had after all been paying much more attention to his properties further east.[143] It also suggests that the writing was already thought to be on the wall for this particular regime.

The history of Warwickshire under Richard III probably reveals rather less well than other parts of the country the difficulties he had to contend with. South of Maxstoke the county remained reasonably docile, and even in the north Richard had the support of Mountford and possibly of one or two others. It is therefore all the more telling that we can still see so clearly in his treatment of the county what went wrong in his rule of England. There is the fear which led him to place so much reliance on northerners from the end of 1483, the cause of so much of the antagonism to his rule. This is particularly evident in his handling of north Warwickshire but can also be seen in his churlishness towards almost all the landowners elsewhere in the county. So frightened was he even in the securest part of his Warwickshire domain that, according to Leland, he rebuilt part of Warwick Castle so as to be able to fire guns from it.[144] Above all we can see the roots of his fear, the almost insuperable problem he had in persuading the midlands and the south that there was any reason for him to be king. He could not go on handing out rewards indefinitely, nor does he seem to have been ready to do so; he could not allow the losers of long-dead conflicts to think that they could all get a reversal of judgement if they stuck by him.

141 *V.C.H.*, IV, p. 108.

142 C.P.40/887 rot.176; W.C.R.O. C.R.26/1(2)/W.28; S.B.T. D.R.37 Box 73 (bond of 1485); *I.P.M. Hen. VII*, III, 615; P.R.O. Catesby Doc.

143 *I.P.M. Hen. VII*, III, 615; above, pp. 117–18, 159.

144 Leland 1907–10: II, p. 40.

Although we cannot be sure of who fought at Bosworth, it seems that only a very small number of the Warwickshire nobility and gentry had been given a reason for going into battle on Richard's behalf, at a place that was on their doorstep. Of the rest, nearly all were apparently careful enough to be wholly non-committal during the campaign to escape the attentions of the suspicious new king and even, like Grey, Mountford and Throgmorton, to be amongst the earliest appointees to office under Henry VII. The paucity of support for Richard in Warwickshire can be gauged from the fact that so few of the county's landowners bothered, even as a precautionary measure, to take out pardons in the first year of Henry VII's reign. Richard III, by his usurpation and subsequent rule, had put himself in a position where large numbers of his landed subjects were, like Lord Stanley, prepared only to stand by when the king was challenged and await the outcome.[145]

[145] *Cal. Pat. Rolls 1485–94*, p. 503; *Lists and Indexes*, 9, p. 146; Ross 1981: pp. 218, 222. On Richard's support during the reign and at Bosworth, see also Bennett 1985: pp. 56–77, 95; for a possible additional source on opposition to Richard III, see Condon 1986b. Warwickshire gentry pardoned Aug. 1485–Aug. 1486 were Ralph Shirley, Thomas Cokesey, John Underhill, Henry Boteller (C.67/53 mm. 1, 2,7, 11).

15

THE PERIOD OF CRISIS IV: WARWICKSHIRE UNDER THE CROWN 1485–99

I

Thanks to Edward IV and Richard III, Henry Tudor was in a remarkably strong position for one who had taken the throne by force with such a flimsy title. Unlike Edward IV he had few rivals with claims much more credible than his own, and, of these, Edward of Warwick, Clarence's son, the only real Yorkist contender, was in his custody. He had also managed to kill his predecessor on the battlefield, which meant that he did not labour under the terrible burden of Edward's first reign in having an anointed and crowned opponent to deal with. Like Edward he did have a kingmaker, in Henry's case Lord Stanley, soon after promoted earl of Derby, but this one was married to the king's mother, his most loyal subject. Furthermore, as we shall see, it had become much harder for magnates like the Stanleys to carve out petty kingdoms in the localities, the result of habits of obedience to the monarchy instilled into the gentry under Edward IV and of the decline in the gentry's instinctive reliance on the nobility that had been evident since the 1450s.[1] Henry had become king because Richard III had turned against himself the vast royal affinity which had taken over the midlands and the south in the later years of Edward's rule, or at least had made it indifferent to his fate. There was consequently a predisposition to be loyal to the man who had removed the usurper with the help of some of Edward's closest servants and married Edward's daughter.[2]

But he also had problems. The holocaust of leading landowners between 1483 and 1485, while minimising the threat of local particularism, deprived Henry of men who could take charge of a whole region on the king's behalf, as Hastings had done for Edward. Particularly vulnerable were those areas such as

[1] For more on this, see below, ch. 16.

[2] For a summary of Henry's position in 1485, see Chrimes 1972a: pp. 52–67; also Condon 1979: pp. 113–14; above, p. 547, n. 99.

the north midlands and the south-west where recent upheavals had left a vacuum.[3] And Henry himself it must not be forgotten was exceedingly inexperienced, almost entirely ignorant of conditions in England, and nurtured in an atmosphere of suspicion and insecurity. If we can see with hindsight that he should have had a far easier time than Edward IV in the 1460s, he himself was not aware that he was the founder of the Tudor dynasty, and the series of rebellions at the start of his reign can only have reinforced his sense of vulnerability.[4] What went wrong in Warwickshire and elsewhere in the first dozen years of the reign was the outcome of his mishandling of some very real problems.

The part of Warwickshire that presented the most serious difficulties was the north. There can be no doubt that, for the first ten years of the reign at least, the whole of the north midlands was in a state of crisis, perhaps worse than any it had experienced even in the middle years of the century.[5] The fundamental cause was Henry's failure to achieve a distribution of power that could form the basis of an equilibrium. Throughout the century stability in the region had depended to a large extent on the king's performance as duke of Lancaster. Under Henry VII the consequences of royal failure were graver than ever before. As long as the houses of Warwick and Buckingham lacked adult representatives, there was no magnate with sufficient personal power to reduce the region to order without systematic royal back-up. Furthermore, the years of rule from Hastings and the king had accustomed gentry and lesser nobility to look primarily to the king or his deputy for leadership. Now that north Warwickshire had been drawn so firmly into the north midlands, any disorder in Staffordshire, Derbyshire and Leicestershire was quick to spill over the county boundary. Henry's mistake was to hand over his authority in the north midlands to local powers but to be too mistrustful to let any single magnate have the ascendance he needed to master the region.

Power was particularly dispersed in the period up to 1494. James Blount, who seems to have been singularly ineffectual and wholly lacked the stature of most of his predecessors, was made steward of Tutbury.[6] The Savages were given the bulk of the Derbyshire offices, to the fury of the Vernons.[7] The Stanleys had the lion's share of royal power in the region. The earl of Derby and his wife Margaret Beaufort had custody of the Buckingham lands, and Humphrey Stanley, a member of the Elford family, was appointed to various royal offices in Staffordshire and was steward of the Buckingham estate in that

3 Hicks 1979a: pp. 73–4; Ross 1981: pp. 109–10 for the south-west.

4 Chrimes 1972b: pp. 70–2, 1972a: pp. 68–80.

5 Cf. Wright 1978: pp. 334–37 for Derbyshire. For a map of the midlands at this time, see above, figure 12.

6 Somerville 1953: p. 540.

7 Somerville 1953: p. 551; Wright 1983: pp. 85, 140–1.

county.[8] Derby was also chief steward of the northern parts of the Duchy of Lancaster, which included Warwickshire and the north midlands, whilst holding other offices on royal estates in north Warwickshire and Staffordshire.[9] His heir Lord Straunge had managed to seize Shenstone in Staffordshire, one of the Beauchamp trust manors, on the death in late 1485 of John Hugford, the sole surviving Beauchamp trustee.[10]

In addition to these there were other magnates with a stake in the north midlands. Henry Grey Lord Codnor had been a subordinate cog in Hastings' great north midlands machine and was being extensively used by Henry VII in the first years of the reign.[11] The earl of Shrewsbury was just beginning to transfer his chief interests from Shropshire to his newer property of Wingfield in Derbyshire.[12] In north Warwickshire itself Edward Grey Viscount Lisle was granted the stewardship of Kenilworth with other offices on Henry's accession and quickly confirmed on the commission of the peace in Warwickshire; he must have hoped that he was at last being allowed to realise his ambition of constructing a sphere of influence across the county boundary into Staffordshire.[13] The duke of Bedford, Henry's uncle, had the royal manors of Solihull and Sheldon restored to him and was given, amongst many other estates, the lordship of Sudeley and the confiscated lands of William Berkeley of Weoley. These included Weoley Castle with Northfield manor in north-east Worcestershire near the Warwickshire boundary. His servant Edmund Mountford got some of the offices on the Warwick lands in the same region: north Warwickshire, north Worcestershire and south Staffordshire. Mountford was also an official on the dower lands of the duchess of Buckingham, who was now married to Bedford. This made the latter potentially highly influential in what had always been a sensitive area.[14] His position was enhanced by the fact that the steward of his lands in Nottinghamshire, Derbyshire and Warwickshire was Henry Willoughby, who was growing into a substantial force in this region.[15]

Meanwhile, Simon Mountford, the only north Warwickshire landowner who had any real links with the rest of the county, who had shown himself

8 Rawcliffe 1978: pp. 35, 55, 216; *Materials: Henry VII*, I, pp. 11, 60, 95; Jones 1987: p. 132. An indication of Humphrey's status in the area is that he was master of the gild of St. Mary at Lichfield (*Gild of St. Mary, Lichfield*, p. 11). For the pedigree of the Stanley family, see above, p. 549 n. 111.

9 Somerville 1953: p. 422; *Materials: Henry VII*, I, pp. 77–8.

10 *I.P.M. Hen. VII*, I, 200.

11 Dunham 1955: p. 119; *Cal. Pat. Rolls 1485–94*, pp. 69–70, 280, 285, 353, 484, 490, 496–7.

12 Bernard 1985: pp. 140–1, 163.

13 D.L.29/463/7567; Somerville 1953: p. 561; *Cal. Pat. Rolls 1485–94*, p. 503.

14 Thomas 1971: pp. 259, 261–4, 279; *Materials: Henry VII*, II, p. 407; *Cal. Pat. Rolls 1452–61*, p. 116 for his earlier tenure of Solihull and Sheldon; Rawcliffe 1978: p. 210 (note that the biography on p. 227 is of Sir Edmund, not of Sir William as stated); PROB 11/10 fo. 82-v.; *Cal. Pat. Rolls 1485–94*, p. 167; *G.E.C.*, II, p. 390.

15 Thomas 1971: p. 288; for Willoughby, see below, pp. 563–70, 572.

consistently willing since 1478 to follow the lead of any king who held the Warwick lands, and who might therefore have been an invaluable tool in promoting cohesion among the Warwickshire gentry, was relegated to the outer circles of royal favour. The very benefits showered on his half-uncle Edmund, now basking in the return to power of his master the duke of Bedford, were both an insult and a threat, for Edmund's previous behaviour had suggested that as far as he was concerned the Mountford affair was still far from over. Deprived of his life grant of the constableship of Kenilworth, although an active local officer, Simon received little compensatory reward.[16] In north Warwickshire in general the fragmentation of power in the north midlands among a number of people with strongly vested local interests had serious repercussions. It was clear that there was going to be an almighty struggle for mastery in this region, from which the county could not keep aloof. Indeed, since all the north Warwickshire landowners of any stature except for Mountford looked primarily to the north, and Mountford himself was stripped of the capacity to lead north Warwickshire into a closer union with the south, this part of the county would inevitably become a recruiting ground for the contending parties in the north midland counties.

Exactly what happened in this region between 1485 and 1499 is not known and can only be guessed at in a study of Warwickshire, but some attempt to make sense of events is essential; although only on the fringe of the region, north Warwickshire was heavily involved in what went on. The chief beneficiary of the vacuum in north Warwickshire was Henry Willoughby, who was able to enlist the services of several resident north Warwickshire families, while his lands in Staffordshire and Leicestershire put him in a position to recruit north Warwickshire landowners whose main estates were in these neighbouring counties. In 1486 Willoughby made a marriage alliance with Edward Grey and in 1488 another with the widow of Lord Clinton. Clinton still had some lands in north Warwickshire and had been interested enough in these properties to pay annuities to Willoughby, Mountford and William Lecroft of Coleshill.[17] Although it would be some time before he came into his mother's and grandmother's dower lands,[18] Willoughby had evidently decided that this was the moment to force himself into a position of power in the region, and these marriage alliances were undoubtedly preparatory steps in this direction. Being retained by the king in 1487 would have given him any encouragement he

[16] He did receive a life grant of the stewardship of Castle Bromwich but can hardly have thought it adequate recompense for the loss of Kenilworth (*Materials: Henry VII*, I, p. 222; Somerville 1953: p. 560). For his local offices, *Cal. Pat. Rolls 1485–94*, pp. 40, 73, 180, 239 (*bis*), 276, 280, 286, 319, 348, 357, 503. For Edmund and Simon since 1461, see above, p. 511 n. 92, p. 518 n. 115.

[17] Above, p. 549 n. 109 for ref. for Grey marriage; *H.M.C. Middleton*, p. 121; *I.P.M. Hen. VII*, I, 331.

[18] Above, p. 111.

needed.[19] He already had the friendship of the other major powers in north Warwickshire, Bedford, Derby and Margaret Beaufort, and amongst his earliest allies from the north Warwickshire gentry was William Trussell constable of Maxstoke (probably William Trussell II of Billesley). Trussell had been appointed constable of Maxstoke by its custodian Margaret Beaufort and, like Willoughby, was a servant of Bedford. By 1489 Willoughby was in close association with Thomas Slade of Maxstoke, also an officer on Bedford's north midland estates. Another of Willoughby's friends in north Warwickshire was John Ardern, who by 1488 was retained by Derby's heir Lord Straunge.[20]

In November 1485 Willoughby initiated a sustained show of strength in Staffordshire and Derbyshire. His first exploit was the abduction and forced marriage to his younger brother Richard of the heiress to the Derbyshire family of Stathom, Jane Sacheverell, who had been widowed at Bosworth. Clearly this was meant to be the first of a series of matches, in which the Grey and Clinton marriages also featured, designed to turn the Willoughby family into a large north midland corporation. She was precontracted to William Zouche, and the circumstance that made the abduction feasible was that Lord Zouche, the head of the family, had kept faith with Richard III until the end and was now disgraced. In this escapade Willoughby was accompanied by a small group of Nottinghamshire and Derbyshire landowners and, from north Warwickshire, by Simon Brasebrugge, eldest son of Richard. But if his accomplices show that he was already attracting some local support, this was one coup that Willoughby was unable to pull off, and the following May the Willoughbys agreed to a divorce between Richard and Jane.[21] This was, however, only a temporary hitch. In October 1487, as sheriff and therefore returning officer of Staffordshire, he managed to intrude his friend William Trussell of Maxstoke as M.P. for the borough of Stafford, a virtual pocket borough of the dukes of Buckingham, along with Henry Lisle, an old associate in north Warwickshire. In the process Sir Hugh Peshale, a Staffordshire knight of some eminence, was deprived of his seat here.[22]

By 1488 Willoughby's ambitions had brought him up against Henry Grey of Codnor, the immediate cause of the collision being in all likelihood that both Zouche and Sacheverell were retained by Grey. It was probably at this time that Grey and Willoughby came into confrontation in a number of affrays, some of quite considerable gravity, in various parts of Nottinghamshire. One of these

19 *Cal. Pat. Rolls 1485–94*, p. 176.

20 *Cal. Pat. Rolls 1485–94*, p. 79; for Trussell and Willoughby, see immed. below; Thomas 1971: p. 288; *H.M.C. Middleton*, pp. 121–2; Nott. Univ. Lib. Middleton MS 5/167/103; below, p. 567 for the indictments for illegal retaining; below, n. 31 for ref. for Ardern and Straunge and n. 24 for ref. for Ardern and Willoughby.

21 Cameron 1970: pp. 15–16, 1978; Nott. Univ. Lib. Middleton MS Mi D 4151; *H.M.C. Middleton*, p. 120; *G.E.C.*, XII, ii, pp. 946–7.

22 *Colls. Hist. Staffs.*, 1928, pp. 273–4; Rawcliffe 1978: p. 82. For Peshale, see Rowney 1981: pp. 169–70.

took place in Nottingham itself at the time of the sessions.[23] In January 1488 Willoughby gathered a sizeable force, which included members of the Aston family of Warwickshire and Staffordshire, John Ardern of north Warwickshire, Ralph Shirley of Warwickshire, Leicestershire and Derbyshire, Everard Fielding of north-east Warwickshire and Leicestershire, and other gentry and yeomen from Nottinghamshire, Derbyshire, Leicestershire and Staffordshire, and with it launched attacks on Grey's lands and his servants or tenants in Nottinghamshire and Derbyshire. Some of Grey's assailants featured among the principal defendants in the Sacheverell affair, their loyalty to Willoughby surviving his slight setback in its denouement, and the presence of Richard Bagot of Staffordshire among the accused shows that at least one of Grey's own followers had been persuaded that Willoughby was now the better bet.[24] Indictments in Nottinghamshire and Derbyshire followed, Grey himself presiding over the Nottingham sessions. Meanwhile, to emphasise the growing divisions and disorder in the north midlands, in Leicestershire there was dissension among what had once been the all-pervasive Hastings retinue, when in 1487 and 1491 two members of the Staffordshire branch of the Ruggeley family made attacks on the property of John Hardwick, who, like them, had been attached to the Lord Chamberlain.[25]

As things moved from bad to worse, the king, despite his apparent concern with maintaining order in his realm at this time, did very little, although he can hardly have been pleased at Willoughby's attacks on Grey of Codnor, whom he was using on special commissions in Warwickshire and elsewhere.[26] In mitigation it could be said that by 1488 he had barely come through the initial phases of mopping up resistance after Bosworth and coping with the first serious Yorkist challenge that ended at Stoke, and may have had little attention to spare for internal disorder even of this magnitude. Moreover, the landowners

[23] *H.M.C. Middleton*, pp. 118–20. Note that here Willoughby's opponent is said to be Edward Grey Lord Lisle, but, although the depositions refer only to 'Lord Grey', it is clearly Grey of Codnor. The editor is confusing this with the earlier confrontation with Lord Lisle (*H.M.C. Middleton*, pp. 155–7, and Carpenter 1986a: p. 37).

[24] K.B.9/377/16, 42; K.B.27/914 Rex rot.5; C.244/139/24; *Colls. Hist. Staffs.*, n.s., 11, p. 59 (for Bagot); Cameron 1978: p. 84 for Grey's retainers; for further evidence of Willoughby's growing influence in the north midlands and north Leicestershire, much of this exercised among the former Hastings affinity, Leics. R.O. DE 170/45/60.

[25] K.B.9/388/12. For connections with Hastings, see Dunham, *Hastings*, p. 120, and above, p. 550 n. 112.

[26] K.B.9/377/22; *Cal. Pat. Rolls 1485–94*, pp. 280, 285, 353. For Henry and order, see *Select Cases in the Council of Henry VII*, pp. lix–lxi, 2. The only concrete evidence of action in this region is that Blount and another north midlands landowner were made to promise to keep the peace in July 1486: not a very encouraging sign given that Blount was the king's chief officer here (*Select Cases in the Council of Henry VII*, p. 14). Cameron 1978: p. 83 takes a very favourable view of Henry's treatment of Willoughby over the Sacheverell affair, but neither the events he recounts (notably p. 84) nor Willoughby's subsequent behaviour seem entirely to support his conclusion that Henry was acting promptly and effectively.

of the north and east midlands had proved most loyal at Stoke itself, and he was probably reluctant to offend any of them.[27] One intriguing possibility is that, faced with the problem of restoring order to the north midlands in the midst of a larger political crisis, he toyed in the early months of 1488 with the idea of restoring Clarence's son, Edward of Warwick, hoping that the return of the ancestral lord of a large part of the midlands might act as a unifying focus. The evidence for this is a lease of 1488 in which Edward features with Edward Grey of Lisle and Henry Willoughby. This is the only known deed of Edward, and it came at a time when Henry might well have contemplated his restoration. Furthermore the association of Grey and Willoughby makes sense in the context of the need to establish an effective ruling order in north Warwickshire and the north midlands, for a triumvirate of Warwick and these two could well have made an attempt to get Warwickshire, at least, fully under control. If Henry did indeed toy with such a policy, the opposition of the Stanleys, who would not have wanted a potential rival of this stature, and his own interest in keeping the Warwick power in the west midlands for himself would have been enough to dissuade him.[28]

How the Stanleys and Margaret Beaufort responded to the mayhem on their doorstep is hard to judge. The evidence can be read to suggest both support for and hostility towards the aggression of Henry Willoughby.[29] It may well be that Derby himself was too preoccupied by his vast new responsibilities further north to give much attention to the midlands.[30] Nevertheless the indictments of Warwickshire men for livery offences committed in September and October 1488, although irritatingly uninformative for the most part, suggest that the

[27] Chrimes 1972a: pp. 68–79; Polydore Vergil, *Anglica Historia*, pp. 22–3; Bennett 1987b: pp. 83–4, 136. Midland landowners' particularly strong representation on this campaign is due to the fact that Henry moved north and east from Coventry to meet Simnel's threat (below, p. 576).

[28] Sims, *Walsall Deeds*, pp. 24–5. The land in question was Bascote in Long Itchington, which had been given in trust to Henry Lisle by Thomas Mollesley of Moxhull in 1451 for the town of Walsall to use for charitable purposes (*Dugdale*, pp. 347–8 and above, p. 238). Hicks makes the point that Edward was, nominally at least, treated as heir at first (1979b: p. 125), but he was already fifteen in 1485 (Chrimes 1972a: p. 51), and, apart from this deed, there is no evidence that Henry intended to let him have livery on coming of age; also below, p. 592. It is possible that this was part of a policy of giving Warwick more public exposure after Stoke, to avoid another Simnel (Bennett 1987: p. 107).

[29] The Babingtons were consistently associated with Willoughby's opponents at this time (Wright 1983: p. 243; Cameron 1978: p. 89; *H.M.C. Middleton*, p. 120; K.B.9/377/16) and by mid 1495 Thomas Babington seems to have regarded Derby and his heir as 'his gud lordes' (*H.M.C. Var. Colls.*, II (1903), pp. 28–56, esp. p. 35, where the sense is ambiguous but 'his' seems to be Babington); Hugh Peshale, the knight whose election to Stafford borough had been interfered with by Willoughby, was a Stanley man (above, p. 564; Bennett 1987: p. 172). However, there is the evidence of the livery indictments (below, p. 567) to suggest that Stanleys and Willoughbys were on good terms at this time.

[30] Coward 1983: pp. 13–14; Jones 1986b: pp. 30–1.

reason for the prosecutions was that the king wanted to curb the use of Warwickshire as a whole, particularly central and southern Warwickshire, as a recruiting-area for Willoughby and his allies, and that among these allies were the Stanleys.[31]

Then there is the evidence of the earl of Shrewsbury's activities. It was Shrewsbury who was the newest force in the north midlands, and his chosen means of entry was the connection of Hales, the aged bishop of Coventry and Lichfield. In October 1488 he was made steward of the bishopric in Staffordshire and Shropshire. In September 1488 he had been prosecuted for distributing liveries at Lichfield, and five of his illegal retainers were from families with traditional ties with the bishopric.[32] Two of them, John Harecourt and Hugh Egerton, were also retained by Shrewsbury's uncle, Henry Vernon, who was to be a close ally throughout the reign.[33] The Vernons were in conflict with the Savages over the Duchy offices in the High Peak in Derbyshire, and in the late 1480s the Savages were apparently still under the protection of their close relatives the Stanleys.[34] It seems therefore that in 1488 the lines of a possible confrontation were being drawn between Willoughby, Grey of Lisle, the Stanleys and the Savages on the one hand and Shrewsbury and the Vernons on the other. Shrewsbury's almost immediate indictment for the livery offence by a panel of J.P.s strongly representative of the Stanley interest lends support to this hypothesis.[35] The hostility between Grey of Codnor and Willoughby on the other hand seems to have been subsiding, perhaps because Grey had come to the conclusion that he would have to live with this ambitious knight.

31 K.B.9/380/41(i); Cameron 1974: p. 30. Most of the liveries in question were given to and by men in central and southern Warwickshire. Amongst the alleged donors were Edward Grey, Henry Willoughby, Simon Mountford (soon to be linked again with Grey: below, p. 569) and George Lord Straunge, Derby's heir. Amongst the users of 'le Eglesfote' of Straunge was John Ardern, who participated in Willoughby's activities against Grey of Codnor later that year (above, n. 24), which is strong evidence that Willoughby and the Stanleys were still allies.

32 K.B.9/379/5; Rowney 1981: pp. 157, 164. Amongst the recipients of the Shrewsbury sign were the following men from families with traditional ties with the bishopric: Thomas Ruggeley, Thomas and John Harecourt and William and John Mitton (Rowney 1981: pp. 157, 233–47, 437–42; S.C.6/Hen.VII/1846; Wm. Salt Lib. Wm. Salt Orig. Coll. 335/1). Another recipient was a canon of Lichfield. For Hales, see Emden 1957–9: II, p. 856.

33 Wright 1983: pp. 77, 249–50; *H.M.C. Rutland,* I, pp. 15–16.

34 Wright 1983: pp. 107–8, 140–1; *H.M.C. Var. Colls.* II, p. 28; C.54/350 m.8d.; Ives 1981a: p. 306.

35 K.B.9/379/5. The J.P.s included Humphrey and George Stanley, William Wilkes, attorney to the Stanleys of Elford (Rowney 1981: p. 152) and Hugh Peshale (above, p. 564 and n. 29), but this cannot indicate that the Stanleys and Willoughby were already moving apart because the indictment coincided almost exactly with the granting of the Warwickshire liveries, which furnish very cogent evidence for the association of Stanleys and Willoughbys at this juncture (above, n. 31). It merely emphasises the complexities of north midlands politics at this time, as does the fact that the family of Hugh Egerton, the man retained by both Shrewsbury and Henry Vernon, were apparently clients of the Stanleys (Ives 1969–70: pp. 349–50).

Significantly, in Warwickshire, unlike Staffordshire, the prosecution of the livery offences was delayed until January 1489, a fact which implies a lack of urgent royal interest in controlling the destabilising activities of the Stanleys and their friends. By this time the king was becoming aware that the north midlands was getting badly out of hand and beginning to have the leisure to do something about it. In May 1488 he had already forced Willoughby and Grey of Codnor into mutual recognisances and in July 1489 he took recognisances from some of his Tutbury tenants in which they promised to observe the statutes on livery and maintenance and to serve no one but the steward. As the recognitors included Hugh Erdeswick and Richard Mynors, who had received liveries from Shrewsbury, the inference that Henry was trying to dampen the aspirations of potential rivals in and around the Duchy lands in the north midlands is obvious.[36] But the effects of his intervention in restoring order seem to have been rather minimal.[37]

It was about now that there was perhaps another shift in the politics of the north midlands. In the course of 1489 Willoughby threw in his lot with Shrewsbury and the episcopal connection now under Shrewsbury's control. In April of that year Shrewsbury was named supervisor in Willoughby's will, acting with some of Willoughby's most active allies.[38] More evidence that Shrewsbury, his associates from the episcopal affinity and Willoughby were now operating together comes from July 1489, when there was a large-scale affray at Lichfield, in which three yeomen and a chaplain, all of Lichfield, were killed. Their assailants included various Lichfield clergy, among them two of the vicars of the cathedral, one of the men retained by Shrewsbury the previous autumn and a member of the family of another of his retainers; also Baldwin Brasebrugge, of the north Warwickshire family, who had accompanied Willoughby in the attacks on Grey, John Marmeon, Willoughby's cousin and receiver, and yeomen and others from Middleton (the Willoughby residence in Warwickshire) and from other places in north Warwickshire. The presence also of John Charnels of north Warwickshire and Leicestershire and John Burdet of Bramcote shows how rapidly Willoughby's following in the north of the county was growing.[39]

36 *Select Case in the Council of Henry VII*, p. 17; Rowney 1981: pp. 156–7, 160 (numbers of household men in Staffs.); Cooper 1983b: pp. 81–2; Chrimes 1972a: pp. 188–9 (refers to a statute of 3 Hen. VII allowing the removal of local officials for unlawful retaining, but Throgmorton served out his full time as sheriff).

37 Cameron takes a much more sanguine view of the effects of Henry's intervention; there *is* some evidence of conciliar discipline (1974: p. 30), but, as so often, and as in the Sacheverell affair (above, n. 26), the examination on the ground shows all was nothing like as well as it appears to be from the central standpoint.

38 *H.M.C. Middleton*, pp. 121–2.

39 *H.M.C. Middleton*, pp. 121–2; K.B.9/383/92; Nott. Univ. Lib. Middleton MS 5/167/103. For the background to this unrest, see Kettle 1985: pp. 160–1.

In August a commission to investigate the riots was issued. It comprised James Blount, the steward of Tutbury, at least one representative of Willoughby's previous victims, connections of the Stanleys, and officers of the Buckingham estates which Derby and his wife controlled, and it was this commission that was responsible for indicting the perpetrators in September.[40] It seems then that the alliance of Willoughby and Shrewsbury had for the moment provoked the Stanleys into retaliatory action. Probably they felt that Willoughby's ambitions required restraint; in any case, if Willoughby was now consorting with the Vernons, which he could hardly fail to do if he was co-operating with Shrewsbury, the Stanleys could not stay with him while they still defended the interests of the Savages.[41] Willoughby also had the good will of Edward Grey, and by 1489 Grey had renewed the tie with Simon Mountford. Mountford may well have felt that his position had been so undermined under Henry VII that he had no choice but to take his chance with these rising powers of north Warwickshire.[42] All in all Willoughby was by this time in a position of unparalleled pre-eminence in north Warwickshire, and, as far as can be judged, was riding very high in the region to the north.

In the meantime, as tended to happen at a time of open confrontation, notable people were getting caught between the two sides. It has already been suggested that the response of the Stanley connection earlier on may have been somewhat mixed. What Bedford thought about the escapades of Willoughby, Slade and Trussell, all of them his servants, is unknown; perhaps he was too busy elsewhere to take much notice, but one would have expected Edmund Mountford, another servant, to bring the state of north Warwickshire to his attention.[43] The Ferrers of Tamworth were closely related by marriage to the Stanleys of Elford, but in 1490 they made a marriage alliance with the Chetwynds, whose head, William I, was to be murdered by the Stanleys in 1494. The Staffordshire families traditionally linked to the bishop of Lichfield, among them Stanley of Elford, Wolseley, Harecourt, Ruggeley of Beaudesert and Aston, were split right down the middle. So was the Duchy of Lancaster affinity as reconstituted by Hastings. That the king was distinctly uneasy about the north and north-west midlands can be seen from the fact that in the latter part of 1489 he convinced himself that William Berkeley of Weoley had committed treason at the time of Stoke, although he was eventually persuaded

40 *Cal. Pat. Rolls 1485–94*, p. 318; Stanley connections were Nicholas Montgomery, who was also linked to Willoughby's earlier victims, the Zouches and Sacheverells (Wright 1983: p. 91; Jeayes ed., *Derbyshire Charters*, 1916), and William Wilkes (above, n. 35). Ministers of the Buckingham estates were William and Richard Harper (Rawcliffe 1978: pp. 201, 205).

41 Above, n. 34.

42 *H.M.C. Middleton*, pp. 121–2; *Cal. Close Rolls 1485–1500*, pp. 115–16; S.B.T. D.R.37/1041.

43 Another source of confusion was that about this time the Stanleys were quarrelling among themselves (Shaw 1798–1801: 1, p. 354).

otherwise.[44] Yet still he failed to intervene, perhaps hoping that the Stanleys and his mother between them would bring the region to order.

What happened in the north midlands between 1489 and 1493 is, to say the least, obscure. The major realignment was the Stanleys' *volte face* in the Vernon–Savage dispute, which had occurred by March 1494. The precise dating of this change of heart is unclear. Some of the cross-factional deeds and associations that have been referred to may be explained by earlier wavering on the Stanleys' part.[45] For example, if the Vernons were now the Stanleys' friends, that made it much easier for Henry Willoughby, even after the Stanley-dominated commission of August 1489, to co-operate with both Vernons and Stanleys. There seems indeed to have been a growing consensus among all parties in this period that it was better to share power than to risk humiliation and disgrace in an outright struggle for control of the area.[46] All the same, the consequences of the lack of an undisputed authority throughout the region were fully brought home to the king in 1493. If he could manage to ignore the earlier series of riots and affrays, he could hardly turn his back on the murder of the heir to one important north midlands gentry family by the head of another. This occurred in February 1493 when John Burdet of Bramcote killed Thomas Cokayn I 'in his passage to Polesworth Church, as the tradition is'. The occasion of the murder was a dispute between the two families over Bramcote, the manor that had been energetically and eventually successfully defended by the Burdets against the Charnels for much of the century.[47] It was one of Burdet's few remaining properties, and he had surely felt impelled to go as far as this in defying the Cokayn claim because it had become clear that he stood no chance at all of getting any more.

The history of the Burdet properties since Bosworth[48] is rather hard to

[44] *Colls. Hist. Staffs.*, 1917–18, p. 262, o.s., 12, pp. 330–2, n.s., 6, i, pp. 138–9; S.C.R.O. D.W. 1744/9A; Rowney 1981: pp. 230–63, 441; S.C.6/Hen.VII/1846; Wm. Salt Lib. H.M.Chetwynd Coll. Bundle 4 (obligation of 1485), H.M.Aston Coll. 39/7, Wm. Salt Orig. Coll. 335/1; Dunham 1955; pp. 116–20; K.B.27/913 Rex rot.22. Note also that Richard Wolseley was one of the J.P.s who indicted Shrewsbury for illegal retaining (above, n. 32) and that William Chetwynd I was married to a daughter of the Egertons, one of the families linked to the bishopric (*Colls. Hist. Staffs.*, 1917–18, p. 278).

[45] *H.M.C. Var. Colls.*, II, pp. 34–5; C.244/142/96 (recog. of March 1494 by Edward Stanley not to harm Sir John, Christopher or Richard Savage). One problem for us and for the Stanleys is that in the Pilkington–Ainsworth dispute, from which much of our knowledge of their dealings comes, they were appealed to by both sides from the very beginning (*H.M.C. Var. Colls.*, II, pp. 30–1). However, bond evidence (also above, n. 34) seems to show conclusively a move by Stanleys and Savages from co-operation with one another to mutual antagonism.

[46] Possible evidence of a movement towards co-operation comes from 1493: settlements for the Cokayn–Fitzherbert marriage (above, p. 116), which involved Thomas Babington, who, like Fitzherbert, had been linked with the Zouches etc., and Henry Willoughby and some of his close associates (*I.P.M. Hen. VII*, II, 942; above, n. 29).

[47] *Dugdale*, p. 1,121 (where the murder is misdated to 20 Hen. VII); K.B.9/401/28; above, chs. 11–13.

[48] For the story of the dispute between 1477 and 1485, above, pp. 436–9, 556–7.

disentangle, both because of the conflicting accounts given by the rival parties later on and because neither version is very specific about dates, but the story goes something like this: John had taken Luddington after Bosworth (or, as he claimed, Richard had sold the manor to him), and John's agents had recovered it by fine against Richard in Hilary 1487. John also asserted that a compromise had been arranged, apparently under the king's auspices, by which he surrendered his rights to Arrow in return for a guaranteed title to Luddington, which he still had on the death of Richard in 1492. Richard left an underage son who died *c.* 1497, while his widow remarried, her second husband being the king's servant, Hugh Conway. As the king was far more emphatic about his rights in the west midlands than in the north, it clearly suited him much better to disregard John's claims to all the Burdet lands in south-west Warwickshire and Worcestershire, which included Luddington, and leave in possession a minor whose wardship could be given to reliable guardians and a widow whose husband was his own man. Conway, according to John Burdet, appealed to the king and managed to get the settlement of Luddington overturned on the technicality that Richard's wife, who had joint tenure with her husband, had not been party to the recovery.[49] The effect was to leave John Burdet out in the cold, his last remaining properties lying in north Warwickshire, just the area where there was the greatest chance that litigation could turn to violence. The culmination in homicide of the dispute with Cokayn over Bramcote was therefore very much the king's responsibility, particularly since the duke of Lancaster of all people should have been able to restore peace between two men who had both been part of the Tutbury connection in the days of Hastings.[50]

In the same month, if later allegations are to be believed, disorder in the region took on a more sinister aspect, when Sir Humphrey Savage, a younger member of the family that the Stanleys had been assisting not long before, had the treasonous conference with Perkin Warbeck's ambassador for which he was later attainted in the treason trials of 1494–5.[51] It would seem that the king was

49 Derbys.R.O. D156M/47, 48A,B, 49, 50, 84; *I.P.M. Hen. VII*, I, 802; *Cal. Pat. Rolls 1494–1509*, p. 41; *Dugdale*, p. 849. There appear to have been two arbitrations under Henry VII, since Sir John Guildford is named as arbitrator in one document but is not listed as arbitrator in another one. There is, however, confusion, for, while the Guildford arbitration is explicitly stated to have taken place soon after Henry VII's accession, the other was performed by, amongst others, Thomas Frowyk, named here as serjeant, who did not achieve that rank until after Richard was dead, although it is clear that this was a settlement between John and Richard (Derbys.R.O. D156M/50, 48A; Ives 1983a: p. 463). The last reference to Thomas III is from February 1497 (where he is incorrectly said to be son of Robert Burdet) (*Cal. Close Rolls 1485–1500*, p. 287). For Henry VII and the southern parts of Warwickshire, see below, pp. 574–9. For more on the Burdet–Conway marriages, see above, pp. 103, 105. Conway was also closely attached to Sir William Stanley, whose friends Henry would, at this stage, still have been disposed to favour (Jones 1988: p. 17).

50 App. 3.

51 Rowney 1981: p. 471; *Rot. Parl.*, VI, p. 504; Archbold 1899: p. 593. For a discussion of the real extent of the conspiracy, see below, pp. 583–7.

aware of this meeting, for in September two of his household men, Robert Belyngham of Warwickshire and William Vampage of Worcestershire, made an assault on the Warwickshire college of Knowle and its guardian, demanding money on the grounds that 'Ye have goodes in your kepyng of that false traytor Sir Humfrey Savages wherby ye aide hym wherfore ye shall be brought into warde afore the kyng like false traytours as ye are.'[52] A release on security made in King's Bench the year before shows that Savage was connected with Simon Mountford's son Henry, who was also implicated in the Warbeck conspiracy and actually took part in the invasion of 1495, and, worryingly for the king if he already knew about the conspiracy, with other eminent north midland families.[53] We do not know whether Henry yet had any inkling of the full extent of the alleged conspiracy within his household or of the implication of Derby's brother, Sir William Stanley, and Simon Mountford, with the immense repercussions this had for the north midlands.[54] Even without this information, the murder of Cokayn and the knowledge of Sir Humphrey Savage's treason must have been enough to make him think long and hard about the state of this part of England.

His solution, implemented in May 1493, was on the face of it a sensible one. The Stanley influence was substantially strengthened when Humphrey Stanley replaced James Blount, who had died in 1492, as steward of Tutbury. Stanley was furthermore to be made sheriff of Staffordshire the next November. The rest of the Duchy offices in the north midlands were shared out between the connections of Shrewsbury, Willoughby, Vernon, Savage, the bishop of Lichfield and the Stanleys.[55] Earlier in the year Willoughby, who had now succeeded to all his lands, was at last appointed to the commission of the peace in his home county of Nottinghamshire.[56] The king must have hoped that an even distribution of power, combined with the grant to the Stanleys of the additional ascendance that would enable them to lead the rest, would at last give the north midlands a chance to settle down. But he had reckoned without the Stanleys' capacity for abusing their authority.

Stanleys and Chetwynds were engaged in a dispute whose cause is unknown but may have been the Chetwynd manor at Alspath to which a branch of the

52 K.B.9/405/3. For Vampage and Belyngham as crown servants, see *Dugdale*, p. 218 and below, pp. 577–8.

53 K.B.27/923 Coram Rege rot.38. For Mountford and the rebellion, see below, p. 584.

54 It seems that he first heard the full details *c*. December 1494 (Arthurson 1981: p. 45).

55 Somerville 1953: pp. 540, 549, 550, 555, 557, 560; *Cal. Fine Rolls 1485–1509*, pp. 153, 182; *Lists and Indexes*, 9, p. 128. The other new officers were Thomas Gresley, brother-in-law of John Ferrers I and thus related by marriage to the Stanleys of Elford (Rowney 1981: p. 462; above, p. 549), Nicholas Montgomery (above, n. 40), Hugh Egerton, linked to the bishop of Lichfield, to the Chetwynds and to the Ferrers (above, n. 44; Rowney 1981: p. 462), Roger Vernon, Ralph Shirley III, connected with Willoughby (K.B.9/377/16; Nott. Univ. Lib. Middleton MS 6/173/24) and Ralph Longford, connected with the Stanleys (Jeayes ed., *Derbyshire Charters*, 1603).

56 *Cal. Pat. Rolls 1485–94*, p. 496; above, p. 111.

Stanley family had inherited a claim.[57] What followed on 21 June 1494 is vividly described in the petition of Alice Chetwynd, widow of William I. William was lured out towards Stafford by a forged letter and set off in the company of two servants and his son. On Tixall heath near Stafford he was surprised by the household servants of Humphrey Stanley and murdered. As the deed was being done, Stanley himself rode by saying he had come to hunt the deer 'where no deer was seen these xi years before.' Afterwards Stanley boasted about the murder at Lichfield and elsewhere. All his misdeeds, so Alice claimed, were done in the name of the king; as sheriff of Staffordshire, she alleged, Stanley was beyond prosecution.[58] There seems certainly to have been some truth in the last statement; were it not for Alice's petition and her own appeal of murder, we would not even know of Humphrey's complicity. The sole crown prosecution is the coroner's inquest, where Stanley's name fails to feature and an entirely different version of the episode makes it look as if the Stanley side was doing no more than defending itself against attack from the Chetwynds.[59]

Another murder had been added to the growing list of outrages in the region. What is more, on this occasion the murderer was abusing the king's own authority, not only as sheriff but also as steward of Tutbury, for among Stanley's accomplices was Nicholas Agard, whose family had an unbroken tradition of service to the Tutbury lordship for most of the century.[60] There were ominous signs of a return to the bad old days of Henry VI, when offices on royal estates had become the playthings of local politics. The reorganisation of 1493–4 had manifestly failed to work, primarily because the Stanleys could not be trusted not to misuse the power that the king had given them for the purpose of restoring the king's peace. What made it even worse was that Chetwynd himself was, like Stanley, an officer on the Buckingham estates in Staffordshire of which Henry's own mother had custody and, most serious of all, also a household servant of the king himself.[61] And elsewhere in the north midlands there were no signs of improvement. During 1494 the Savage–Vernon conflict increased in ferocity and, it seems, the Willoughbys broke with the Stanleys again.[62] By the end of the year, if not before, the king was fully apprised of the scope of the Yorkist conspiracy and of the horrifying degree to which it had

57 Wm. Salt Lib. H.M. Chetwynd Coll. Bundle 4 (obligation of 1484). For the Alspath manors in general, see above, p. 498 n. 46.

58 *Colls. Hist. Staffs.*, o.s., 12, pp. 333–5. As Rowney says (1981: p. 334), it was possibly meant to look like a hunting accident.

59 K.B.9/402/7; K.B.27/935 Writs of Attorney rot.1. The Staffordshire version could be true, but it is in a standard form alleging self-defence (Milsom 1981: p. 423, where it is suggested that this was often an 'edited version' of the real occurrence), while the petition of William's widow is full of telling circumstantial detail.

60 K.B.27/935 Writs of Attorney rot.1; Wright 1983: p. 90.

61 *Colls. Hist. Staffs.*, 1917–18, p. 278.

62 *H.M.C. Var. Colls.*, II, pp. 34–5. For Willoughby and the Stanleys in 1494, see below, p. 580.

supposedly penetrated his own household. The accusations made by Henry's spies and the Yorkist informer against Sir William Stanley and Simon Mountford, whether true or not, can only have been an additional spur to do something about the Stanleys and about the north midlands where the Stanleys were proving such unreliable royal deputies.[63]

Before discussing Henry's eventual solutions, we must go back to 1485 to see what was happening in the rest of Warwickshire before 1494, for it was in that year that the crises in the north and south of the county came together in one major confrontation. From Coventry southwards the king kept a far firmer and more direct eye on events. Already in the distribution of the spoils of 1485–6 he had shown himself readier than Edward IV to confiscate the lands of gentry rebels and to give them to household men with few connections with the area. A large body of lands formerly owned by William Catesby and Humphrey Stafford of Grafton in east and west Warwickshire and east Worcestershire came by and large into the hands of outsiders like John Risley, David Owen, Edward Poynings and Gilbert Talbot.[64] The Botetourt lands confiscated from the earl of Wiltshire in 1461 were returned to his heir, Thomas earl of Ormond, whose activities were concentrated primarily in Ireland, in the home counties and about the king's person. Although the lands lay mostly to the north of the enclave of the earls of Warwick that was now the king's, previous events had shown that they could exert considerable influence on what happened in the west midlands.[65] The lands of Thomas Straunge II, who had probably died at Bosworth for Richard III, were not taken, but on the death of his widow in 1491 the custody of half of them went, albeit temporarily, to Henry's intimate servant Richard Empson.[66] Richard Burdet had not so much joined Humphrey Stafford's rebellion in 1486 as helped Stafford evade capture for a time afterwards.[67] Burdet was not punished, but by 1496, and probably earlier, the marriage of his widow to Hugh Conway, one of the king's household knights, had taken place. The subsequent marriage of Conway's younger brother Edward to Burdet's daughter, who became his heir on the death of his young son in *c.* 1497, completed the process of transferring the Burdet lands to a household family.[68]

There is no doubt that in central and southern Warwickshire, unlike the

63 Above, n. 51, and below, pp. 583–7 for a fuller discussion.

64 *Cal. Pat. Rolls 1485–94*, pp. 209, 230–1, 275, 111, 140, 145, 250, 404.

65 *Rot. Parl.*, VI, pp. 296–7, 340; *Cal. Pat. Rolls 1485–94*, pp. 122, 125, 356, *1494–1509* (numbers of commissions, including J.P. in Essex); Ellis 1985: pp. 72, 75–6, 86–7; above, chs. 11–14.

66 *Cal. Pat. Rolls 1485–94*, pp. 346, 380; above, p. 553. The Straunge heirs were able to get a traverse on the verdict on the principal manors, held by Thomas' mother at her death in 1490, and these were returned to the family, but it took from 1491 to 1499 to do it (*Cal. Close Rolls 1485–1500*, p. 166; K.B.27/922 Rex rot.5, /949 Rex rot.10; Baker ed., *Spelman*, I, pp. 212–14).

67 K.B.9/138/72.

68 K.B.27/938 Coram Rege rot.16; *Cal. Pat. Rolls 1485–94*, p. 226; *Dugdale*, pp. 847–50; above, pp. 103, 105.

north of the county, Henry meant to be the undisputed ruler, and, apart from the single deed that has been discussed, there is no evidence that he intended to restore Edward of Warwick. In this part of the county he retained or favoured most of the major gentry, especially those from the traditional areas of Warwick power. Among his more notable clients were Thomas Cokesey, Robert Throgmorton, William Lucy and his heir Edmund, Edward Ralegh, the greatest of the gentry of south-east Warwickshire after the demise of the Catesbys, William Hugford, another east Warwickshire landowner, and William Littleton, heir of Thomas, whose estate was mainly in east Worcestershire.[69] After some initial hesitation over whether to treat John Hugford's brother William as heir to what was now one of the most important south Warwickshire estates, or to allow John's three daughters and their husbands to inherit, the verdict went decisively in favour of the daughters. Retaining one of the husbands, Gerard Danet, not long after ensured the king's influence over at least part of the lands.[70] John Hugford's pivotal offices on the Warwick estate were given to Thomas Brereton, another outsider and crown servant, while Edmund Brereton, a yeoman of the crown and presumably relative of Thomas, was made parker of Henley, the former Sudeley manor that went with Beaudesert Castle.[71] Edward Belknap, the eventual heir to the bulk of Sudeley's remaining property in Warwickshire, was also the king's man, becoming increasingly influential at court over the course of the reign.[72] Further west, Richard Croft and his fellow plaintiffs – Woodvilles and other former courtiers of Edward IV – now riding high on the victory of the Yorkist cause under Henry Tudor, were rewarded in July 1486 for six years of litigation with a verdict against Richard Beauchamp over the Forestership.[73]

69 *Cal. Pat. Rolls 1485–94*, pp. 140, 210, 78; *D.N.B.*, XXXIII, p. 374; *Materials: Henry VII*, ii, pp. 372, 391; *Cal. Close Rolls 1485–1500*, p. 237. Gerard Doddingselles was also retained at some time as a gentleman-usher to the king (*Dugdale*, p. 346; above, p. 227).

70 K.B.9/378/43; *Cal. Pat. Rolls 1485–94*, p. 275. In 1485/6 William Hugford demised Emscote to the duke of Bedford and other feoffees, which implies that those closest to Henry VII were at that time prepared to take his side against the heiresses. The I.P.M., held in August 1486, eight months after John Hugford's death, was, however, to find in favour of the heiresses and probably in early 1488 the justices in exchequer chamber rejected William's appeal against its verdict. He was still challenging the heiresses' right in 1491 but held none of the land at his death in 1493 (Bod. Lib. Dugdale MS 15, p. 74; *I.P.M. Hen. VII*, I, 27, 136, II, 913; K.B.27/918 Coram Rege rot.9; *I.P.M. Hen. VII*, III, 1151; Ives 1983a: p. 240; above, p. 251 n. 26). Note that if Nicholas Catesby's deposition was true, the Hugford estate lost some of the disputed Metley properties in 1485 (P.R.O. Catesby Doc., and above, p. 492).

71 *Materials: Henry VII*, I, pp. 43–4; *Cal. Fine Rolls 1485–1509*, p. 29; *Cal. Pat. Rolls 1485–94*, p. 8; *Rot. Parl.*, VI, p. 368. The Breretons have proved elusive; they were presumably from the Cheshire family, but I have yet to find a connecting link with the main branch (see *Letters and Accounts of William Brereton*, where the family is discussed).

72 *Cal. Close Rolls 1485–1500*, pp. 302, 327; *Cal. Pat. Rolls 1485–94*, p. 376, *1494–1509*, pp. 154, 280, 459, 591, 626–7; Chrimes 1972a: p. 130.

73 K.B.27/934 Coram Rege rot.24.

Thomas Cokesey's unctuous letter describing his capture of Humphrey Stafford shows how anxious the gentry of southern Warwickshire were to please the king.[74] Stafford's treason in early 1486 was in itself an acid test of Henry VII's authority in the old Warwick region, for it was an attempt by a well-connected west midland landowner to raise this area in the name of Edward of Warwick.[75] Its substantial failure was a triumph for the new king.

Once in command here Henry showed no disposition to let the region slip from his fingers. It has already been suggested that the indictments of January 1489 for illegal retaining in Warwickshire were intended primarily to put paid to any ideas landowners to the north may have had of using the centre and south of the county to raise additional troops for their violent confrontations. They were also a clear warning to south Warwickshire landowners like Robert Throgmorton, who was indicted for retaining as sheriff, that the only retaining here would be done by the king.[76] In 1493, when central and southern Warwickshire became infected with the disorder that had become normal and been largely ignored in the north, the king himself came to Kenilworth and subsequently issued an afforced commission of the peace for Warwickshire. This contained no less than twenty-one external appointees, most of them from the royal household.[77] This policy, contrasting starkly with the laissez-faire attitude further north, worked well for the first few years. It had the inbuilt advantage that since 1478 the south and south-west areas of the county had manifested a predisposition to obey a royal earl of Warwick. At Coventry, the older centre of royal power in the county, the story was the same. A serious riot between the townsmen and the prior's men, which had occurred shortly before Bosworth, was dealt with effectively in Henry's first few months, and thereafter, as the Leet Book shows, the king kept a close watch on the town, was indeed there on an early progress when he first heard about the rising that was quashed at the battle of Stoke. If Laurence Saunders continued to trouble the peace of Coventry, the rulers of Coventry and the king between them were able to contain his aggression.[78] Although south of Coventry there were numbers of disputes, by and large they were kept within manageable proportions, and most tend to disappear from the records quickly, indicating that they were dealt with by out-of-court settlements.[79]

74 K.B.9/138/9.

75 K.B.9/138/1–84, /371/2, 16–19.

76 K.B.9/380/41(1); above, p. 567.

77 K.B.9/405/3; *Coventry Leet Book*, p. 550; *Cal. Pat. Rolls 1485–94*, pp. 503–4; below, p. 579.

78 K.B.9/368/30; K.B.27/897 Rex roti.3–4, /913 Coram Rege rot.38d.; *Coventry Leet Book*, pp. 535–98; *Records of Early English Drama*, pp. 67–8, 556 (note).

79 Hugford v. Cotes (above, p. 00), Shukburgh v. Spenser (K.B.9/377/7), Catesby v. Knightley (K.B.27/901 Coram Rege rot.81d.), Straunge v. Clinton (C.1/82/54; K.B.27/903 Coram Rege rot.5), Belyngham v. Beaufitz (below, pp. 577–8), Brome v. Hugford (K.B.27/902 Coram Rege rot.13), Hubaud v. Hubaud (K.B.9/377/24), Cotes v. Danet (K.B.27/906 Coram Rege rot.12 – 'Daret' in K.B. roll, but almost certainly Danet), murder instigated by Thomas Cokesey (below,

The problems with southern Warwickshire were in fact less to do with disorder than with a growing division between north and south, and, coming to much the same thing, between the king's particular friends and those he relegated to the outer circles of his affinity. Just as Simon Mountford, the only north Warwickshire landowner consistently to have dealings with landowners from the central and southern areas of the county was neglected, so were his fellow officials from outside the far north. He and some of the more important gentry from these parts, Ralegh, Throgmorton, Nicholas Brome, John Smyth of Coventry, were hardworking J.P.s who rarely stepped out of line.[80] Two at least of the leading gentry from this area fought for Henry at Stoke. For all this the gentry of central and southern Warwickshire received few rewards, and, judging by the king's almost exclusive choice of Leicestershire men for the shrievalty in the 1490s and of his close servant Richard Empson for the Recordership of Coventry in 1493, precious little of Henry's trust.[81] Meanwhile they saw outsiders make off with the bulk of royal grants, and the king's more intimate servants, whether outsiders like Robert Belyngham or north Warwickshire men like Henry Willoughby, not only going unchastised for their misdeeds but apparently being positively rewarded for them.

It was Belyngham, a member of the royal household, who had recently rendered the king signal service at Stoke, who was responsible for the most outrageous piece of conduct. In 1487 he abducted the heiress of John Beaufitz, using men from the royal/Warwick manor of Berkswell, of whom at least one was a royal officer. This case has been cited as an instance of Henry's swift response to blatant illegality, but it turned out to be rather the reverse. While it is true that Belyngham was indicted with great rapidity before an afforced commission of the peace, he kept the spoils of his crime, for the marriage was not dissolved. Moreover, within a few months of being acquitted Belyngham was one of the jurors for the inquest that handed down the indictments for illegal retaining, and amongst those that he helped indict was the king's

p. 578), assaults etc. by Everard Fielding (K.B.9/388/8), Brugge v. prior of Coventry (K.B.9/392/9), Knightley v. Hayton (K.B.27/921 Coram Rege rot.83), Lucy v. Lucy (C.1/145/38; *Cat. Anc. Deeds*, IV, A8331).

80 K.B.9/377/7, 22, 24, /378/43, 379/13, 383/32, 386/9, /388/8, /393/12, /403/31. An interesting gloss on Henry's relations with these men is that Nicholas Brome was allowed to keep the disputed manor of Lapworth while the Catesbys were disgraced (but below, p. 592 for what happened when George Catesby was restored), but, with characteristic determination to defend every royal right, had him sued in Common Pleas for trespassing in the king's park at Lapworth (the Catesby park?) (C.P.40/930 roti.21d., 160).

81 *Lists and Indexes*, 9, p. 146; *Coventry Leet Book*, pp. 537, 547; Horowitz 1982. Although it seems that Henry initially put much trust in Throgmorton, he held no major office after his second spell as sheriff ended in 1487 until he was made a J.P. at the end of 1490 and had no grant after 1487 (*Lists and Indexes*, 9, p. 146, *Cal. Pat. Rolls 1485–94*, pp. 210, 503; Polydore Vergil, *Historia Anglicana*, p. 6). Throgmorton and Edmund Lucy were at Stoke (Vergil, *Historia Anglicana*, pp. 22–3).

eminently reliable and law-abiding local officer, Robert Throgmorton.[82] It is worth remembering that, as Belyngham was the king's man, his marriage to the heiress of a moderately prominent and well-connected landowner in the Coventry region cannot have been displeasing to Henry, and in April 1494 the seal of royal approval of the match was given when Belyngham was appointed to the Warwickshire commission of the peace. In 1492/3 the confiscated Stafford of Grafton manor of Hopsford, another estate within reach of Coventry, had been granted by Henry to William Vampage, the household official involved with Belyngham in the raid on Knowle in search of Humphrey Savage's goods that may well have been authorised by the king. It is far from improbable that Henry VII had encouraged his men to settle in this area, which had always been so important to the crown's interests in the midlands, and that Belyngham's marriage to the Beaufitz heiress had consequently been blessed, perhaps even designed, by the king.[83] The wills of Belyngham's parents-in-law reveal that they remained much less enthusiastic about him. From his father-in-law he received a silver cup worth ten marks, hardly a substantial sum, and the promise of the repayment of a substantial debt, from his mother-in-law, who made him overseer of her will – it would have been unwise to name anyone else in view of his relationship with the king – nothing at all. In neither will is Belyngham's relationship to the testator even mentioned.[84]

The only newcomer or close servant of the king to be absorbed into the circle of southern gentry was Thomas Brereton, who was another regular J.P. and was feed by Mountford.[85] It must have seemed to these men and to their associate Simon Mountford that to gain the king's attention you had to do something wrong; Thomas Cokesey, referred to by Leland as 'a ruffelar', the most successful of the southerners in terms of royal favour, was easily the most violent. In 1490 he was accused of inciting poachers to break into the park at Inkberrow in Worcestershire, paying one of them to murder a labourer who was in the park; in 1494 he was indicted for preventing the sheriff of

[82] K.B.9/377/22; Ives 1978: pp. 26–30; K.B.9/380/42; K.B.27/907 Rex rot.7d. Belyngham had captured Simnel at Stoke (Leland, *Collectanea*, IV, p. 214). Throgmorton himself was one of the sworn jurors for the indictments on the livery statutes, so it would be a mistake to make too much of local divisions as revealed by this inquest, but Belyngham's acting as juror on a case of so much interest to the king clearly shows that he had attained local respectability, in the king's eyes at least. Curiously, as Bennett notes in his rather fanciful version of the story (1987: p. 108), one of Belyngham's accomplices was Rowland Robinson, who was to be attainted in the November parliament for his part in the battle of Stoke and was later associated with Warbeck (*Rot. Parl.*, VI, p. 398; Arthurson 1981: pp. 29–30). It may be that the attainder of Robinson (who was nevertheless available for trial next year: *Cal. Pat. Rolls 1485–94*, p. 239) was as far as the king was prepared to go in expressing his displeasure at the abduction. Belyngham should not be confused with the Robert Belyngham esquire killed at Dixmunde in 1489: the abductor was still alive in late 1496 (Leland, *Collectanea*, IV, p. 247; PROB.11/11 fo. 173v.).

[83] *Cal. Pat. Rolls 1485–94*, p. 504; *Dugdale*, p. 218; above, p. 572.

[84] PROB 11/11 fo. 173v., /8 fo. 161.

[85] *I.P.M. Hen. VII*, III, 760; S.B.T. D.R.3/282–4; above, n. 80.

Gloucestershire restoring the abbot of Tewkesbury to property of which he had been disseised.[86] By 1493 the full administrative weight of the county, both active J.P.s and the small number of Warwickshire sheriffs, was being carried by gentry from the centre and south of the county and by Simon Mountford, whose links with the Willoughby circle were growing distinctly frail. Meanwhile the king's trust and favour were going primarily to the more unruly elements in the north, and the number of Warwickshire gentry with ready entrée to the court was growing ominously low. It was not a good basis for unity and stability.[87]

Towards the end of 1493 things began to come to a head. In September Belyngham made the raid on Knowle in search of Humphrey Savage's goods, apparently on the instructions of the king, and in October he followed it up with attacks on the property of two of the Warwickshire gentry, at Bubbenhall and Weston under Wetherley in east Warwickshire. For these last two offences he was indicted with some rapidity before Throgmorton and Brereton, but on the first, understandably enough, nothing was done for the moment.[88] In 1494 the tensions came out into the open. Henry Willoughby was the catalyst. He was one of the heirs to the Botetourt lands that had lately been restored to Ormond.[89] While, throughout the period of confiscation, Edward IV had steadfastly refused to listen to the cases of the alternative claimants,[90] the upheavals of the early years of Henry VII had clearly convinced Willoughby that it was worth a try. Although William Bermingham III, one of the other claimants, quitclaimed his rights to Ormond in June 1494,[91] Willoughby was able to persuade both his co-heirs to the claim inherited through the Frevilles to join him. These were John Aston, who had already taken part in Willoughby's earlier adventures, and Thomas Ferrers of Tamworth.[92] In March 1494 Ormond was disseised of Bordesley, one of the manors at issue, on Willoughby's orders, and in May a substantial force went to the same place to make

86 Leland 1907–10: IV, p. 20; K.B.9/387/10, /389/93, /402/86; *Cal. Pat. Rolls 1485–94*, pp. 140–1, 159, 254; Leland, *Collectanea*, IV, pp. 214, 255; *Dugdale*, pp. 707, 710.

87 There are in fact not many surviving transactions in which Mountford is named in this period, but there *are* a number for the northern group and he features in none of these, a fact which must be taken seriously because all the other northern gentry of any stature – almost all of them lesser figures than Mountford – do appear from time to time. Leland, *Collectanea*, IV, pp. 185–257 shows that the only Warwickshire men found regularly within the court were Cokesey, Willoughby and the newcomer, Conway.

88 K.B.9/405/3.

89 For reference to a pedigree showing all the claimants, see above, p. 389 n. 169.

90 *Cal. Pat. Rolls 1461–67*, pp. 112, 217, 221, 223, 297–8, 330, 485, 549–50; E.159/257 Mich. brevia directa m. 12; above, pp. 488, 507 n.74, 553 n.126.

91 *Cal. Close Rolls 1485–1500*, p. 226. The release was made by his uncle, Fulk, on William's behalf, presumably because of William's incapacity (above, p. 550); for the Bermingham claim to the inheritance, above, p. 389.

92 This account of the attacks is based on K.B.9/405/3. For Aston and Willoughby, see above, p. 565.

an attempt on the life of Ormond's receiver. On 21 July a plea of disseisin brought by Ormond for Handsworth, Staffordshire, another of the manors, had to be postponed when the jury failed to appear. The probable reason is suggested by another episode, at Warwick on 16 July, when Willoughby and a host of allies made an intimidatory demonstration to prevent the jury sitting in the assize of novel disseisin concerning Bordesley.[93]

The indictments reveal the imposing range of support Willoughby could now muster. As well as his co-claimants Aston and Ferrers, he could command, from among his older allies, the services of Trussell, Henry Lisle and his son John, and various Brasebrugges and Arderns and, as new recruits, William Littleton, perhaps drawn in as Aston's father-in-law,[94] some of the younger Mountfords, William Holt of Aston, Thomas Ward of Castle Bromwich, Henry Est of Yardley in east Worcestershire and Witton in north Warwickshire, Ralph Wolseley of Staffordshire and Robert Fitzherbert of Derbyshire. It must have been about now that Willoughby's second break with the Stanleys occurred, for in May 1494 a rent at Old Swinford, another of the disputed Botetourt properties, was demised for life to John Savage.[95] The Stanleys had undoubtedly turned against the Savages by this time, and the lease, which was in effect a legal ploy, shows that Savage and Willoughby had begun to act in concert; putting a friendly lessee into the property made another legal action, over ejectment of the lessee, available to the lord in the event of dispossession.[96] Ormond himself, Willoughby's principal enemy of the moment, was consistently linked with the Vernons and the Talbots,[97] so we may assume yet another readjustment of north midland factions, essentially Willoughby and the Savages versus the rest. Willoughby must have felt very confident of his position in the region and with the king to risk such relative isolation from the other major forces there.

These disseisins in north Warwickshire and Staffordshire might be thought bad enough in themselves, particularly when one takes into consideration the accompanying violence and contempt for legal processes, and the strategic significance of the area where most of the lands at issue lay. The fact that they showed both that Willoughby had managed to turn north Warwickshire almost into a private kingdom and that factional fighting in the midlands was as bad as ever underlined the gravity of the situation. Moreover, although Willoughby

93 K.B.27/935 Coram Rege rot.37; B.R.L. 504042; K.B.9/405/3.

94 Wm. Salt Lib. H.M. Aston Coll.20/1.

95 Nott. Univ. Lib. Middleton MS 6/173/31; B.R.L. 357336.

96 Milsom 1981: pp. 161–2; above, p. 570.

97 B.R.L. 357338, 347140; K.B.27/935 Coram Rege rot.37d.; *Cal. Pat. Rolls 1494–1509*, p. 257; *Cal. Close Rolls 1485–1500*, pp. 111, 264–5, 279; *Cat. Anc. Deeds*, II, C2550, IV, A7720, 7754. For what it is worth, this interpretation is reinforced by the fact that Ormond was paying Sir William Stanley an annuity in 1485–6 (B.R.L. 347140), which could be used to support the idea that Willoughby and the Stanleys were now at odds, but the fluidity of north midlands politics at this time enjoins hesitation in the use of evidence of loyalties in 1485–6 for those of 1494.

remained close to the king, Ormond and his family moved in the innermost circles of the court, while the value to Henry of his support in Ireland, which Perkin Warbeck was constantly threatening to use as the springboard for an invasion, cannot be overestimated.[98] The feud was threatening to divide the inner core of Henry's household, but its most serious immediate consequence was that it split the county apart.

We are in the fortunate position of knowing what occurred at the Warwickshire sessions of 15 July 1494, when an attempt was made to get an indictment for the assault at Bordesley on Ormond's receiver. The irregularity of the proceedings led to their being brought up again at a later sessions, where the malpractice at the earlier meeting was reviewed. On 15 July the J.P.s were Robert Throgmorton and two recent appointees who rarely sat at this time, the king's servants, Robert Belyngham and Edward Belknap. The conduct of the sessions suggests that they attended at Henry Willoughby's behest. Indictments were drawn up against the Willoughby faction and against two husbandmen of Butlers Marston accused of assaulting the vicar of their parish. On this second count Edward Ralegh and Edmund Verney, both south Warwickshire gentry, gave evidence. Belknap and Belyngham from the bench and Henry Willoughby from the floor set about getting both indictments quashed. Belyngham, having first denied that the attack on the vicar had taken place at all, announced that the prosecution had been set up by Edmund Verney and his son Leonard and that he proposed to have it set aside, whereupon Ralegh told the jurors that it seemed to him that under the circumstances there was no possibility of doing justice. On the other matter, both Belyngham and Belknap advised that nothing should be done for fear of causing 'multam tribulacionem inter generosos patrie illius'.

But it was Henry Willoughby, who had the strongest vested interest in its being thrown out, whose words were directly recorded by the clerk in English: 'Sires remembre we are neyghbours and warrewykshire men and this mater hath ben inquered of afore this tyme and the mater of trouth founden and if ye fynde eny more or othirwise then hath ben aforetyme founden ye shall cause warre amonges us duryng oure lifes.' Whether men like Simon Mountford, Throgmorton and Ralegh would really have seen either Willoughby or Belyngham as a 'Warwickshire man' must be open to doubt, but, as must be evident from everything that has been said about this society so far, Willoughby, in emphasising the need to avoid a permanent state of war among neighbours, had undoubtedly put his finger on an extremely sensitive point.

98 *Cal. Pat. Rolls 1485–94*, pp. 56, 122, 356, 367, 368, 464, *1494–1509*, pp. 388, 419; *Rot. Parl.*, VI, p. 340; Cooper 1874: pp. 37–8; *Cat. Anc. Deeds*, III, C3273; Arthurson 1981: *passim*; Ellis 1985: pp. 69–77, 86; *Reign of Henry VII*, ed. Pollard, I, p. 47; Polydore Vergil, *Historia Anglicana*, p. 6; *Select Cases in the Council of Henry VII*, pp. 2–3; Leland, *Collectanea*, IV, p. 236 (and pp. 185–257 ('Herald's Relation'), *passim*). In 1493 there was a risk that Ormond might even support Warbeck (*Reign of Henry VII*, ed. Pollard, I, p. 95).

The clerk incidentally was so disconcerted by all this that he went on recording the proceedings in English for several sentences more. The sessions failed to produce any indictments, and, judging by Willoughby's comments at the sessions, this was not the first time that he and his allies had managed to avoid indictment on this count. The next day Willoughby and his allies were responsible for the intimidatory riot at Warwick that has already been mentioned. No doubt most of them had been present in the town the day before to ensure that things went their way at the sessions.[99]

The sessions and the riot may well have been the last straw for the gentry outside the Willoughby circle, which essentially meant the southern gentry plus Mountford. Willoughby himself had failed to realise that the split between north and south, between favoured and unfavoured, had become so great that the foundation on which his plea had rested, the need for neighbourliness, carried rapidly diminishing force. Although throughout the century clear splits within county society had always been inconceivable because of the way groups of associates overlapped, by 1494 north Warwickshire and the rest of the county (if we make Simon Mountford an honorary southerner) had grown so far apart that most of these restraints had gone. It seems clear that the respectable backbone of the county felt it was time the newcomers and the other criminals under the king's protection were taught a lesson. After all Belyngham had been able to misuse his powers as J.P. because Henry VII had responded to his earlier misdeeds by placing him on the bench.

At the next quarter sessions, on 30 September, there were a large number of indictments, chiefly of the Willoughby circle, and the J.P.s were drawn from those 'southerners' who had been administering the county with for the most part small reward: Mountford, Ralegh, Throgmorton, Brereton and Brome. Indictments were made against the rioters of 16 July, and Mountford was apparently sufficiently alienated from his northern neighbours to agree to the prosecution of younger members of his own family. This time the J.P.s were successful in proceeding against the assailants of the vicar of Butlers Marston, and the mishandling of the previous sessions was recounted at length. But the full wrath of the J.P.s was reserved for Belyngham, whose performance as J.P. had probably finally exhausted the patience of the established Warwickshire families. He was indicted for the petty offence of causing flooding at Fenny Compton nearly eighteen months before (this may well have been Mountford's particular contribution, as he owned one of the manors there) and for the attack on Knowle to seize the goods of Sir Humphrey Savage in the king's name. This is a true index of the exasperation of these respectable gentry towards the king's favoured servants, for Belyngham had almost certainly been carrying out the king's orders. Early in 1495 Willoughby's forces were indicted for the

99 K.B.9/405/3. For evidence of Belyngham's connection with the Willoughby circle at this time, see C.P.40/930 rot.40d.

dispossession of Ormond at Bordesley and, soon after, the complete documentation was despatched to the king: the earlier indictments of Belyngham, the report of the mishandled sessions and of the subsequent sessions of September and January.[100] Henry can hardly have failed to be aware by now that something was seriously wrong.

The king had allowed his closest servants to behave like Henry VI's and with much the same results: they were hated by outsiders and divided amongst themselves. Not only did the Willoughby-Ormond dispute represent a division amongst his more intimate household, but the all-pervasive Reginald Bray, perhaps the closest of all Henry's advisers at the time, was linked both to Ormond and to at least two of the gentry of central and southern Warwickshire.[101] No doubt they had sought his friendship with a view to getting access to the king. Archbishop Savage, now the chief defender of the Ainsworths in the feud in the north-west with the Pilkingtons, which had been one of the main factors in splitting the Stanleys from the Savages and the Savages from the Vernons, was another influential royal councillor, while the Vernons were close to Ormond, who was also a strong force in royal councils. The Stanleys' proximity to the king needs no further elaboration. It is not improbable that there were similar divisions in the king's following elsewhere in England. And on top of all this he was threatened with a Yorkist invasion and, as he himself believed, with a related conspiracy within his own household.[102] It was his insecurity that made it almost impossible to discipline the more violent of his servants. Henry Willoughby, for example, was to produce well over a 100 troops for the king in the crisis of 1497, and Humphrey Stanley was also to have an important role in their defeat. The importance of the Savages in Worcestershire and Gloucestershire, where John IV held most of the offices on the Warwick estates, as well as being life sheriff of Worcestershire, meant that they too were almost exempt from royal control.[103]

It is against this background that we must now investigate the treason trials of January and February 1495. Of the fact of the attempted invasion at Deal by Warbeck's forces in July there can be no doubt, nor that among the leaders of

100 K.B.9/405/2, 3. The writ calling the indictments into King's Bench actually predates the final sessions recorded on the indictment sheet, which must have been added at the last minute, but the earlier indictments of Belyngham were added at the end of the sheet even after that.

101 Condon 1979; *Calendar of Milanese State Papers*, p. 299; above, n. 98; PROB 11/11 fos. 134v., 177v.

102 For the Vernons and Ormond, above, p. 580; for the conspiracy of 1493–5, above, pp. 571–2 and immed. below.

103 *H.M.C. Var. Colls.*, II, pp. 31–40; Chrimes 1972a: pp. 102 n. 7, 109; Ives 1981a: pp. 306–7, 1978: p. 41 (with reference to Willoughby's position in 1502); Arthurson 1981: pp. 588, 630, 705, 1987a: pp. 20–1; *Great Chronicle*, p. 277; Cameron 1970: p. 18. See also the particular role of Belknap and Willoughby in the defeat of the rebels at Blackheath in 1497 (Alcock 1977: p. 181) and the comments by Chetwynd's widow on Humphrey Stanley's proximity to the king (*Colls. Hist. Staffs.*, o.s., 12, p. 334).

the rebels who met their end here was Henry Mountford, younger son of Simon.[104] Equally, Ian Arthurson has shown that Henry VII had every right to feel insecure even ten years after Bosworth.[105] If these Yorkist pretenders and their foreign paymasters seem with the benefit of hindsight very improbable, so did Henry Tudor and his foreign-backed force in 1485. On the evidence of the midlands, in his first ten years Henry was not making a notable success of ruling England, and his failure may have generated substantial internal support for an invader. That said, it must be admitted that there are implausibilities concerning the alleged fifth column within and outside the royal household from whom the most eminent defendants came. Sir William Stanley, the king's chamberlain, and Simon Mountford were two of the outstanding casualties. It is perfectly possible that they were both guilty; Michael Jones has observed that Sir William, unlike the rest of his family, did not receive the rewards he might have expected on Henry's accession,[106] while Mountford shared the grievances of the other 'southerners' of Warwickshire. In his case these would have been more acutely felt, for Willoughby was manifestly displacing him as leader of north Warwickshire. Then, the advancement of his half-uncle Edmund at court and in Simon's part of Warwickshire would have excited both envy and anxiety, and he, of all the 'respectable' Warwickshire gentry, could have demanded recognition of his pre-eminent position in local society. The death of Edward Grey in 1492, leaving an underage heir who did not get livery until 1502, made Mountford's situation more uneasy, for Willoughby's need of Grey in the late 1480s had enabled Mountford to keep in touch with the Willoughby circle through his renewed link with Grey. In any case, by 1495 Willoughby's standing in north Warwickshire was so assured that he had no further use for Grey's heir or for Mountford himself.[107]

But if both men, and perhaps others named in the conspiracy too, had reason

[104] For the conspiracy in general, *Rot. Parl.*, VI, pp. 503–4; *Chronicles of London*, pp. 203–7; *Six Town Chronicles*, pp. 164–6, 172; *Paston Letters*, ed. Gairdner, VI, p. 153; Archbold 1899; *Dugdale*, p. 1,012; Arthurson 1981: pp. 42–55; Madden, 'Documents Relating to Perkin Warbeck', pp. 171–8; *Paston Letters*, II, p. 473.

[105] Arthurson 1981: *passim*, 1987b: pp. 4–5, 10–11.

[106] Jones 1988: pp. 20–1: he gives more credence to Stanley's role than I do.

[107] *Cal. Close Rolls 1485–1500*, pp. 115–16, 183; *Cal. Pat. Rolls 1494–1509*, p. 3. An interpretation stressing Simon Mountford's rivalry with Edmund in relation to 1495 is Griffiths 1980a: pp. 9–10. Regard for his heirs is the only possible serious motive for Simon's alleged treason: in the early 1480s Ormond, brother and heir of Wiltshire, Edmund's earlier protector, had had dealings with Edmund over Remenham, Berkshire, one of the manors at issue and the only one that Edmund managed to secure, when it was again the object of litigation with Simon. Simon might therefore have been toying with treason in the years before Edmund's death in March 1494, fearing that, with Ormond's proximity to the king, the whole inheritance was again in danger (Westminster Abb. Muns. 4545–6, 4551–2, 4554 (not all of these are dated, but they all seem to belong to the same period; and see above, p. 545); PROB 11/10 fos. 83, 83v.; *I.P.M. Hen. VII*, III, 1055; above, p. 574). There is, however, no evidence at all that Edmund was extending the scope of his claims after Henry VII's accession. Thus, for Simon to commit

to grumble – according to Polydore Vergil, Stanley had engaged in, and was prepared to admit, a certain amount of loose talk – one cannot help questioning whether they had done anything more.[108] Characteristically participants in treasonous plots or rebels in ill-supported causes had tended to be outright incompetents like Robert Ardern, or, at the least, erratic politicians like Humphrey Stafford II. Mostly they rebelled because they had nothing to lose or because they had manoeuvred themselves into a corner from which the only way out was rebellion.[109] Stanley and Mountford, even under the existing dispensation, had a great deal to lose. Both had trod their way through the political morass of the previous forty years with supreme skill.[110] Is it really conceivable that, coming to the end of their active lives, they would get themselves enmeshed in a badly-organised conspiracy and invasion in favour of an exceedingly dubious candidate?[111] Neither could remotely be classed as a committed Yorkist of the kind that might support the cause of York under any guise. Mountford in addition had male heirs, whose inheritance he was putting at risk, and he served Henry faithfully right up to the moment of his arrest. Mountford did not deny the charges brought against him, but may have hoped that bowing before the storm in this way would help save something for his heirs.[112]

The only direct evidence of the conspiracy, as it seems, was the confession of Sir Robert Clifford, one of the conspirators, whose statement was to all intents and purposes the price of a general pardon, and the reports of the spies sent by Henry into the Netherlands.[113] The evidence of such a 'supergrass' would nowadays be treated with extreme caution by most courts, and the same caveat should be entered in respect of the spies, who, notoriously and at all times, will sacrifice truth to the need to get a story for their masters. Henry himself however would have been disposed to believe them; there were deep divisions amongst his closest servants and he was a naturally suspicious man, so why should he not find credible the allegation that his chamberlain and the steward of his household, Lord Fitzwalter, were closet Yorkists? Why not believe that

treason because there was a relatively slight chance of losing his lands, seems to be to try a cure that was infinitely worse than the disease.

[108] Polydore Vergil, *Historia Anglicana*, pp. 75, 77. Dudley's petition (Harrison, *Petition of Edmund Dudley*, p. 89) implies that Sir William was unjustly executed.

[109] Above, pp. 118–19, 432–3, 459, 553, 576.

[110] For Stanley, see Coward 1983: pp. 9–15.

[111] Stanley was probably in his fifties (*D.N.B.*, LIV, p. 81), Mountford, whose first known appearance in the records dates to 1453, probably about the same age or slightly older.

[112] *Dugdale*, pp. 1,008, 1,011–12.

[113] Arthurson 1981: p. 45. According to Vergil (*Historia Anglicana*, p. 75), it was Clifford's statement alone that implicated Stanley. See also *Great Chronicle of London*, p. 256. Interestingly, he had already been pardoned once, in 1484, on condition he act as informer (C.244/136/92: ref. kindly supplied by Dr Horrox). For the intimacy of Clifford and of the other informer, William Barley, with Warbeck, see Génard, 'Marguerite d'Yorck et la Rose Blanche', pp. 14, 19, 22 and Polydore Vergil, *Historia Anglicana*, pp. 69, 73.

Simon Mountford was a traitor when his son, who was presumably already with Warbeck's forces, so patently was? So perhaps the explanation, as far as Stanley and Mountford are concerned, and possibly others too, is that Clifford's confession and the spies' stories fed Henry's paranoia, already growing in the atmosphere of unease at home and abroad. In the still more serious emergency of 1497 Henry was again convinced, not necessarily with good reason, that some of his innermost servants were about to betray him.[114]

But there may be another explanation for the executions of 1945. Henry was faced with a two-fold crisis. First there was the serious disorder in the shires. How far this went will not be known until similar internal studies have been done for other parts of England in this period, but we do know that the north midlands was in a state of turmoil and that south Warwickshire, where the king had an excellent chance of achieving complete dominance, had been mishandled to the point where the locals were turning against the royal household. We may guess from the Pilkington–Ainsworth feud that the north-west, the centre of Stanley power, was similarly disordered.[115] Secondly there was the division within the household itself, which is also highlighted by the Pilkington–Ainsworth affair, and we have seen that divisions at the centre and in the localities fed on each other. The safest response would have been a conciliatory and bipartisan one. The course of events in Warwickshire throughout the century makes it perfectly clear that, faced with a crisis of this sort, magnates and rulers did best when a minimum show of displeasure was combined with forced compromises and the restraint of the more unruly elements. This latter policy was especially imperative when the chief offenders had been exploiting a favoured position with the king or ruling local magnate.[116]

But this was not Henry VII's way of doing things. He was by nature and training suspicious, and to him landowners tended to be enemies to be reduced to servitude rather than natural allies. Furthermore, to exercise restraint over his closest servants or to punish them would be to admit that he had made a mistake, and, in contrast to Henry V and Edward IV, that seems to have been something that he was usually loath to do.[117] What is more, by giving his trust to so few, he had put himself in a position where it was difficult to take a firm line with men like Willoughby and the Savages, for they had become crucial to his survival.[118] Eventually he was to evolve a solution of a kind, which was to put almost everyone under bonds; that way he could live with his all-

114 Arthurson 1981: pp. 220–40, 389.

115 *H.M.C. Var. Colls.*, II, pp. 28–56.

116 Above, chs. 10, 14.

117 The exception is his adaptability in financial matters (Chrimes 1972a: ch. 6), but a certain inflexibility in his handling of men is implicit in much of the reign (see in particular Chrimes 1972b: p. 72, the perceptive account in Condon 1979, Hicks 1986d: pp. 61–2 and Cameron 1972), notably in the last years (for refs. to these, n. 155).

118 Above, n. 103.

encompassing suspicion, discourage his intimates from over-abuse of the law, except that which he himself demanded, and remain secure, while achieving the delegation of power to local society without which he could not rule.[119] But for the moment he had to handle his acute difficulties within the self-imposed limits of his policies at this time.

His only option accordingly was to make examples, and those singled out had to be sufficiently imposing and respectable to scare everybody else, but far enough from the king in terms of favour to show that he had no intention of recognising the primary role of his intimates in the destabilising of the provinces. Stanley and Mountford were perfect candidates. They came from the right areas, for between them they could act as an example to the north-west, the north midlands (notably the rest of the Stanley interest there), and to both north and south Warwickshire, while Stanley's pre-eminence in the household made him and Fitzwalter an awful warning to the rest of Henry's entourage.[120] At the same time Mountford certainly, and even Stanley, compared with the rest of his family, were not among the real favourites of the king. The removal of Mountford may have been prompted by Henry Willoughby, to whom Mountford's assiduous concern for enforcing the peace, even against members of his own family, would not have been sympathetic. It also helped alleviate the immediate pressures on Henry, in providing confiscated lands to give to the earl of Kildare, attainted in 1495, whom the king was shortly to restore to favour and to a position in which he would be crucial to Tudor rule of Ireland.[121] Perhaps there was a conspiracy, or perhaps Henry believed there to be one, or perhaps he knew perfectly well that there was none at all; whichever of these versions is true, it furnished an ideal opportunity for the king to do something about the midlands, and perhaps about other parts of the kingdom, without the radical revision of policy that would have been the best solution.

If this is a true assessment of at least some of the rationale of the treason trials, it can be shown to be in conformity with the king's handling of the crisis in Warwickshire. Here there were only rather minor gestures in the direction of conciliation, while the full thrust of the strategy was as before, to mistrust the local men who were not close to him and to reward outsiders and condone the actions of his favourites. Appeasement of local susceptibilities went as far as removing Belyngham from the commission of the peace and ensuring that

119 Refs. below, n. 155.

120 On Henry's fears about his household and its subsequent reorganisation, see Starkey 1987b: pp. 75–6. According to Coventry annals printed by Dugdale (*Dugdale*, p. 149), Sir (*sic*) Henry Mountford and another conspirator were executed at Coventry, something which would have rammed the message home.

121 Ellis 1985: pp. 76, 80–2, 85–105; Arthurson 1981: pp. 54–5; *Cal. Pat. Rolls 1494–1509*, pp. 84–5. In fact Kildare's restoration coincides with the grant of the Mountford lands (August, 1496). Polydore Vergil lends some support for the 'example' theory, especially as far as Stanley was concerned (*Historia Anglicana*, pp. 75, 77–9).

henceforth the major local offices were exercised by and large by the more law-abiding local gentry.[122] But the king continued to exert little discipline over his closer servants, and he made no effort to deal with the crux of the problem, north against south, ins against outs. Indeed, the continued concentration of administrative responsibility in the hands of the unfavoured and the southerners (usually the same people) can only have sustained the sense of disunity. Henry's paranoid attitude where his authority in central and southern Warwickshire was concerned extended as far as his own servants there. Thus, in 1496 Gerard Danet, an esquire of the body, was placed under a bond of £500 not to come within a thousand paces of the king, which must have made it rather hard for him to do his job.[123]

Henry dealt with the pressing problem of the Botetourt lands along predictable lines; Ormond was closer to him than Willoughby, and Henry had to ensure that Ormond would offer no support in Ireland to Warbeck, so Ormond won. It could well have been argued that the significance of the bulk of the estate in controlling the Birmingham plateau and communications to the north-west merited a different solution. It might have been better for the king for these lands to be in the hands of local men like Willoughby, Ferrers and Aston, than be returned to a family that was now rarely in the area, but that was not the point as far as the king was concerned.[124] In September 1494 the parties had been persuaded to agree to an arbitration. Comparison of the names of the arbitrators and of Ormond's feoffees and other associates shows the verdict to have been a foregone conclusion.[125] During the course of 1495–6 nearly all the claimants to the Botetourt estates took part in a series of quitclaims to Ormond, in return for which the Freville heirs, Willoughby, Ferrers and Aston, were given a lump sum of money.[126]

It has to be said that the immediate effects were entirely satisfactory. Willoughby himself is much less in evidence in the law-courts after 1495, no doubt chastened by his failure to get the Botetourt lands and even more by the

[122] *Cal. Pat. Rolls 1485–94*, pp. 503–4, *1494–1509*, p. 663; *Lists and Indexes*, 9, p. 146.

[123] Arthurson 1981: p. 389. Rowney (1981: p. 337) says that Humphrey Stanley lost office after 1496 because of the king's disapproval: he ceased to be Buckingham steward of Staffordshire at some time between late 1495 and late 1497, but he remained in his Duchy offices (Rawcliffe 1978: p. 216; Somerville 1953: pp. 541–2, 546, 548).

[124] It should be said in Henry's defence that this decision was in conformity with his usual policy (seemingly a continuation of Edward IV's), illustrated by the history of the Botetourt lands under both kings, of not disturbing established inheritances which had come into question through confiscation and regrant. The failure to get this message home soon enough had encouraged the renewed claims to the Botetourt lands. For Ireland and Warbeck, see above, p. 581. Ormond had taken the trouble to offer annuities from the Botetourt lands to leading local figures in the west and north midlands, but most of these men were close to the crown, and the crucial fact was the earl's own absence from the area (B.R.L.347140).

[125] B.R.L.357335–6; above, nn. 97, 98; below, n. 126.

[126] K.B.27/934 Coram Rege rot.23, /935 Coram Rege roti.30d., 34, 35d., 37d., 38; E.326/12684; *Cal. Close Rolls 1485–1500*, pp. 264–5; *Colls. Hist. Staffs.*, o.s., 12, p. 177; B.R.L. 357340.

chastisements of 1495. On the other hand, since by 1495 the king had otherwise let him have everything he wanted, he had much less cause for violence. Edward Grey and Mountford were gone from north Warwickshire and Grey of Codnor died not long after, the Stanleys were perhaps more vulnerable and warier about exploitation of their official power after Sir William's fall, while Shrewsbury was not yet a major force in the area.[127] Willoughby's earlier crimes, and the fact that he was allowed to get away with them, had made him a man of enormous power in north Warwickshire and the north midlands, and, having acquired more north midland property in 1492 through his new wife, the widow of Lord Fitzhugh, he now set about the peaceful business of obtaining the estate of the childless Henry Grey of Codnor.[128] Accordingly, when Shrewsbury and the Vernons came emphatically to the fore in the early years of the sixteenth century, Willoughby was well placed to maintain his own pre-eminence.[129]

In general both Warwickshire itself and the region to the north were less violently disturbed after 1494, and it must also be admitted that Henry's tolerance of the misdeeds of his men in the north midlands brought them solidly to his side in the crisis of 1497. Willoughbys, Stanleys, Savages, Vernons and Arderns all stood by him.[130] All the same, the problems that had been apparent in the king's handling of both north and south Warwickshire before 1494–5 remained. In the north midlands he continued to delegate to local powers while leaving them all with insufficient authority to do the job properly, and this made for further instability.[131] In 1496 two of Willoughby's closest associates in Warwickshire, Martin Ardern and Baldwin Brasebrugge, were in dispute with one another.[132] The same year the Zouches turned the tables on Willoughby by abducting his daughter. The matter was settled by an arbitration performed by Margaret Beaufort, perhaps the only magnate with any effective power in the region, and much of hers came from her unique position as the king's mother.[133] In 1498 Humphrey Stanley, while still the royal steward of Tutbury, was assaulted, allegedly with murderous intent, by a sizeable gathering of north Worcestershire and Staffordshire landowners, among them John Aston and William Littleton.[134] This was possibly revenge for the murder of William Chetwynd, or perhaps an occasion for the settling of

[127] *G.E.C.*, VIII, p. 60, VI, p. 132; Bernard 1985: pp. 140–1, 146.

[128] *Cal. Pat. Rolls 1485–94*, p. 373; Cameron 1970: pp. 11, 14, 21; above, p. 103.

[129] Somerville 1953: pp. 541, 552, 553; Bernard 1985: p. 146; Cameron 1970: pp. 17–20, 1972: p. 27.

[130] Arthurson 1981: apps. D and E.

[131] Somerville 1953: pp. 541–60.

[132] *Colls. Hist. Staffs.*, n.s., 10, i, pp. 94–103.

[133] Nott. Univ. Lib. Middleton MS Mi D 4805; Jones 1987: pp. 137–40. For another north midland arbitration by Margaret, this time at Coventry, see Cooper 1874: pp. 229–30 (with thanks to Dr M.K. Jones).

[134] K.B.9/415/76. The assailants included John Egerton, a relation by marriage of the Chetwynds (above, n. 44).

several scores with an official who had exploited his position and since become vulnerable. It was nevertheless an attack on the king's official and symptomatic of a lack of respect for royal law-enforcement which had become endemic in the region. Also in 1498 John Ardern's wife was raped at his residence in north Warwickshire. In the same year there was yet another murder involving a Warwickshire landowner, when servants, some of them of gentry status, of Sir Thomas Boteller of Warrington in Lancashire, who had property at Exhall near Coventry, murdered Ardern's servant. John Aston joined Boteller in going bail for the defendants, which implies yet more division among the former friends of Henry Willoughby.[135] Other feuds in the north midlands continued, while new ones began: Stanhope–Meryng, Empson–Plumpton, Aston–bishop of Lichfield (a dispute over an office in the bishop's gift, indicating, as several of the others do, that old friendships were failing to hold), Willoughby–Cokayn, Egerton–Vernon.[136]

It has not proved possible to establish whether any of these affairs were connected, or to trace the evolution of power structures in the north midlands between 1495 and the end of the century. Without more knowledge of the condition of the counties north of Warwickshire at this time, one can only say that the evidence of deeds and other transactions suggests a lack of fundamental division.[137] But there can be no doubt that there remained an absence of leadership, which was likely to continue until the king either took direct command himself, as Henry IV and Henry V had done, or, like Edward IV, allowed a leading magnate to concentrate in his hands all the power of the Duchy of Lancaster in the king's name. This Henry VIII was to do on his accession, when he handed the stewardship of Tutbury to the earl of Shrewsbury.[138] Edward of Buckingham came into his lands in 1498, but this was one nobleman Henry VII was not prepared to put in charge of the north midlands, although annuities to some of the more prominent gentry of the area were already charged on his estate and were to continue to be so.[139] In south Warwickshire, as in the north, the same policies remained in force with much the same effects. Although there was understandably more subservience to the king after the bloodletting of 1495, there was no real solution to the problems

[135] K.B.9/420/27, /419/32; K.B.27/950 Rex rot.4. The murder took place at a different Ardern residence, one near Coventry.

[136] Cameron 1972, 1970: p. 17; K.B.27/939 Coram Rege rot.54; *Colls. Hist. Staffs.*, 1939, p. 77; K.B.27/955 Coram Rege rot.50; Ives 1969. However, for some evidence of rapprochement here, see Leics.R.O. 26D53/2552. It may have been continuing failure to deal adequately with the problem of order, rather than an abstract hope for reform, that led to legislation on juries, starting 11 Hen. VII (Blatcher 1978: pp. 91–2).

[137] For example, collate these disputes with the personnel of transactions of the period listed in Wright 1983: pp. 211–33, 235–45.

[138] Somerville 1953: p. 541; Bernard 1985: p. 146.

[139] Rawcliffe 1978: app. B and pp. 227–31; Harris 1986: pp. 155–8; Rawcliffe 1980: pp. 115–18; app. 3.

that had caused the unrest. The dominance of outsiders in matters that were likely to be particularly sensitive to the native gentry was perpetuated. Simon Mountford's lands for example went entirely to these, the main recipients apart from Kildare being Simon Digby and Richard Pudsey, both king's esquires, William Cope, the king's cofferer, and Bray.[140] It was at this time that the Conways got the Burdet lands.[141] Richard Hungerford, another newcomer in the king's favour, married Edmund Lucy's widow some time between 1495 and 1498 and became effective head of the family until his death in about 1508.[142]

The effects of the continued neglect of the gentry of southern and central Warwickshire after 1495 become evident under close scrutiny. There remained a number of disputes and disturbances in the south-east of the county and in Gloucestershire. These were often related to the growth of pastoral farming in southern Warwickshire, most of them to do with Edward Ralegh,[143] while Belyngham added his usual quota.[144] However, the disagreements of these years were fairly run-of-the-mill and none is known to have had any widespread repercussions. The problems were less to do with local order than with the king's ability to rule the shire effectively. Not surprisingly he was running out of local officers. This was particularly true of the north of the county, where there was no one to replace Mountford, after his lands had gone to outsiders, but it was now beginning to be the case further south. In view of Mountford's connections with families in central and southern Warwickshire, Henry may well have wanted to avoid relying as heavily as he had before on the main group of J.P.s, almost all of them on friendly terms with Mountford. Indeed a generalised anxiety on the king's part about the local response to Mountford's fall may explain the accelerated movement of newcomers into the county that has been referred to. The use of Leicestershire sheriffs became yet more pronounced: between November 1496 and November 1501 the only Warwickshire sheriff was Richard Pudsey, who hardly counts as a native, and, even in 1501, the Warwickshire man chosen was Edward Belknap, a close servant and a fairly recent arrival.[145] From 1496 to 1502 almost all the new appointments to

140 *Cal. Pat. Rolls 1494–1509*, pp. 65, 73, 85, 133.

141 Above, p. 574.

142 Br. Lib. Add. MS 21,480 fo. 39; *I.P.M. Hen. VII*, III, 56; K.B.27/951 Coram Rege rot.35; *Cal. Pat. Rolls 1494–1509*, pp. 400–1. The last reference to Hungerford is from February 1508 (*Cal. Close Rolls 1500–09*, p. 335); Thomas Lucy was calling himself esquire and independently active in November of that year (E.40/15380).

143 K.B.27/955 Rex rot.2d., /956 Coram Rege rot.8d. (*bis*), /969 Coram Rege rot.47d., /970 Coram Rege rot.48d.; above, pp. 185–7; also, in 1496 the Hugford heirs took back the Metley lands that Nicholas Catesby had seized in 1485 (above, p. 575 n.70); the case went to the chancellor but its outcome is not known.

144 K.B.9/411/7; K.B.27/941 Coram Rege rot.110.

145 *Lists and Indexes*, 9, p. 146; *Cal. Pat. Rolls 1494–1509*, pp. 154, 280, 591; *Cal. Close Rolls 1485–1500*, p. 302.

the commission of the peace – Hugh Conway, Thomas Marrowe (married to one of the co-heiresses to Nicholas Brome), Richard Hungerford – were newcomers to Warwickshire. The exception was Robert Fulwode, a minor esquire of the Arden, whose appointment smacks of desperation in the search for a local landowner whom the king did not need to fear. Although Henry provided himself with an additional potential officer in 1496 by partially restoring George Catesby, he was understandably reluctant to appoint him to office. The restoration incidentally furnished yet more grounds for local antagonism to the government, for it allowed Catesby to keep the disputed manor of Bromeslands in Lapworth, which can have done little to placate Nicholas Brome, who had been rendering loyal service.[146] Luckily for Henry, Edward Belknap, after his misguided attempt to manipulate the sessions in 1494, was able to establish himself with the local gentry, which meant that one at least of the king's few friends in the south of Warwickshire was trusted by the natives.[147]

But if we remember that the rule of the shires, however strict, could not operate otherwise than by consensus, since the only military force available to make it work was the local landowners', it must be said that by 1502 the king was stretching the loyalty of large parts of Warwickshire to breaking-point. In the last analysis, the root cause of the government's difficulties in all parts of Warwickshire and to the north of the county was identical, namely the king's inability to learn to delegate in a way that would make his rule effective. In north Warwickshire and the north midlands he deputed too much and too little, allowing local forces too much freedom and yet failing to give anyone enough power to act as sub-ruler for the king; in Warwickshire further south, where he had no need to mediate his own authority, he failed to trust the local men who seem to have been only too eager to help him rule.[148]

By 1502 he had apparently finally recognised the need for change. The executions of Perkin Warbeck and Edward of Warwick in 1499, the latter probably owing as much to the impossibility of letting the Warwick lands out of the king's grasp as to any treasonous activities, may have made Henry feel secure enough to take the risk. The death of Prince Arthur in 1502 brought his line to the brink of extinction, and made him face up to the possibility of a

[146] *Cal. Pat. Rolls 1494–1509*, p. 663; S.B.T. D.R.3/275–6; *Cal. Fine Rolls 1485–1509*, p. 358; *Cal. Pat. Rolls 1494–1509*, pp. 40–1; *Rot. Parl.*, VI, pp. 491–2; Northants.R.O. Ashley MS 71; *Cat. Anc. Deeds*, IV, A7433; *V.C.H.*, V, p. 112. Doubtless the decision not to endorse Brome's tenure was heavily influenced by the fact that Catesby had married Empson's daughter (W.C.R.O. L.6/1674). For more on Marrowe, see above, p. 98 n. 9.

[147] *Cal. Close Rolls 1485–1500*, p. 302; *Cat. Anc. Deeds*, II, B2981; S.B.T. D.R.3/275–6, 283–4; W.C.R.O. C.R.959; *I.P.M. Hen. VII*, II, 508; C.142/37/135.

[148] For the suggestion that Henry became even more repressive after the scare of 1497, see Condon 1979: pp. 130–1.

minority after his own death, with all the horrors that were still remembered from 1483. He was forced to take stock of the situation.[149] In Warwickshire that date marks a sudden change. There had to be a new commission of the peace, as Arthur had been on the previous one, and it brought in numbers of home-grown gentry: John Greville, Henry Smyth (son of John), Nicholas Malory, Edward Doddingselles II. More followed, including some northerners, whose exclusion from Warwickshire office, even while they were permitted to make hay with the king's law, had helped bring about the separation of north from south: John Burdet, John Ferrers II and, above all, Henry Willoughby. Whereas between February 1499 and June 1502 there had been no more than five native gentry on the commission, on that of July 1507, the last of the reign, there were twelve.[150] Furthermore, from 1502 to 1507 every sheriff was a Warwickshire man and two, Henry Lisle and Willoughby, were northerners.[151] From the late 1490s, and with increasing tempo in the early years of the following century, the two parts of the county were beginning to be drawn back together again, sharing the responsibility of office, and meeting more often in the execution of that office, and the county was handed back to its native leaders. It was to be some time, however, before the remeshing of north and south was reflected in the pattern of local associations.[152]

In some respects the reabsorption of the gentry of north Warwickshire into the ranks of the local officers was made possible because the king was taking some very tentative steps towards implementing the same delegatory policy further north. He seems at last to have grasped the need for a single ruling power there, and in 1504 George Talbot was made steward of Tutbury, while simultaneously the Vernons, his relatives and close friends, began to get a tighter hold on most of the offices in the Peak. The placing of the entire Stanley family, apart from the king's mother, under recognisances at this time may have been partly to indicate that Stanley power was henceforth to be reined in outside the north-west. For the first time since Hastings' death there was something approaching an overall controlling power in the

149 Chrimes 1972a: pp. 92, 93. See also above, n. 28.

150 *Cal. Pat. Rolls 1494–1509*, p. 663; for similar conclusions for the West Riding, see Arnold 1984: pp. 132–3.

151 *Lists and Indexes*, 9, p. 146.

152 E.g. *Cal. Close Rolls 1500–09*, pp. 273, 309; *I.P.M. Hen. VII*, II, 508; WARD 2/39/146G/4; W.C.R.O. C.R.1248/70/49; S.B.T. D.R.10/1409 fo. 83; *Dugdale*, p. 928; Northants R.O. Spencer MS 873 (the king by whom the document is dated is indecipherable – either Henry VII or Henry VIII – but, despite the 'VII' written into the deed by another hand, the personnel clearly date it to 1 Hen. VIII); Nott. Univ. Lib. Middleton MS 6/173/54; C.142/37/135. On the importance of office in fostering communal identity, see above, p. 340. It was also in this period, or at least just before, in 1501, that the Brome–Catesby affair could finally be settled, Catesby getting Bromeslands in return for a payment to Brome (*Cat. Anc. Deeds*, III, A4263; E.40/14710; above, n. 146). Below, p. 605.

region.[153] As the Talbot–Vernon connection began to get a hold on the north midlands, the danger of north Warwickshire being drawn into a bitter and protracted dispute for control of the counties to its north began to recede. Henry VII's problem had always been that, if you give your servants licence to riot at will, as he had to all intents and purposes done in the north midlands, you cannot then place them in office alongside more orderly but less favoured men and expect the local administration to work. The failed sessions at Warwick in 1494 had shown as much. As peace was restored to the north, it became possible to admit Willoughby and his circle to the place they should have had long before in the running of Warwickshire. Conversely, it was also in this period that a home-grown south Warwickshire landowner, Robert Throgmorton, at last penetrated to the inner circles of the court.[154]

But if local society regained some of its independence, albeit a heavily-controlled one, there was a price to pay. Henry had at last realised that he had to use the local powers, whether magnates or gentry, but that did not make him any more trusting of them. After the rebellions of 1495–9 and the death of his eldest son he was probably even more suspicious than before. And so emerged the infamous practice of placing almost every person charged with responsibility under bond to the king, including some of his closest advisers;[155] neither Willoughby nor Throgmorton, for example, escaped.[156] This way the king had the worst of both worlds, losing some of his immediate authority in the shires, while greatly intensifying the atmosphere of mistrust around him. The confessions of Flamanck and Edmund Dudley give some notion of what it was like to live in this environment. Neither of them has to be wholly true to suggest how uneasily Henry's head lay in the last period of his reign. It is worth noting that it was Hugh Conway, as treasurer of Calais, who voiced the treasonable opinions about the succession contained in Flamanck's Information, one of Henry's oldest supporters and the very same man who was put into Warwick-

[153] Somerville 1953: pp. 541, 552–3, 555; Coward 1968: pp. 179–80; Condon 1979: pp. 113–14; the Stanleys seem even to have been to some extent on the retreat in the north-west (*H.M.C. Var. Colls.*, II, pp. 38–56). The consequences of this can perhaps already be seen in the arbitration effected by Shrewsbury in Derbyshire just before Henry's death and his own elevation to the stewardship, which gave him yet more authority in the region (Derbys.R.O. D10052 fos. 125–7; Somerville 1953: p. 541; also Wright 1978: p. 297; *H.M.C. Var. Colls.*, II, p. 41). Note also the number of important local figures involved with Shrewsbury and Vernon in feet of fines in Derbyshire between 1498 and 1500 (*Derbyshire Feet of Fines*, pp. 99–100).

[154] He was granted a wardship (*Cal. Pat. Rolls 1494–1509*, p. 495), was in transactions with servants of Henry (*Cal. Close Rolls 1500–09*, pp. 158, 209), became a J.P. in Worcestershire in 1497 and was not only an officer in both his two main counties of residence, but also employed on commissions outside them (*Cal. Pat. Rolls 1494–1509*, pp. 263, 437, 488, 666).

[155] Elton 1958, 1961; Cooper 1959; McFarlane 1966; Lander 1976c; Rawcliffe 1980; Arthurson 1981: pp. 546–7 and Chrimes 1972a: pp. 307–14.

[156] *Cal. Close Rolls 1500–09*, pp. 65, 77, 130, 207 (*bis*), 306, 337, 361, 84, 104, 132, 133, 134, 289, 296, 310.

shire to secure the king's interests there.[157] Henry was indeed fortunate not to die until his son was old enough to make a show of repudiating the policies of his father's last years;[158] had Henry VIII not been of age in 1509 the events of 1483 could well have been repeated.

This treatment of Henry VII may be judged over-harsh, but it is a necessary corrective to the conventional picture. It is significant that it is a local study, exploring the actual process of rule, that has highlighted the king's frailty. It is especially important to emphasise the truly terrible crisis of order in the north midlands in the first ten years of the reign, because this has been revealed only by a systematic study of the legal records, something that has been rather neglected for the latter end of the fifteenth century, and further investigation may well uncover similar crises elsewhere. Once the internal politics of the reign have been given the attention hitherto focused on those of Henry's predecessors, this could turn out to be a notably disordered period, at least until the late 1490s, and one in which the king's survival was in doubt throughout; Henry VII certainly thought that this was so.[159]

If the conventional view of Edward IV and Henry VII has been somewhat reversed, Edward being judged to have had the better understanding of what was really required in a king, this is a conclusion that has been reached through the close study of the actual practice of kingship by both kings and of its results. Henry had a lot of things in his favour in 1485: not only the absence of realistic rivals to either his throne or his authority, but the fact that the consequences of the failure of Henry VI and the success of Edward IV had made England easier to rule than perhaps at any time since the later years of Edward I. This issue will be considered further in the next chapter, but there can certainly be no doubting that in the west midlands the royal earl of Warwick had no rivals and that the north midlands had grown accustomed to firm leadership from the Duchy of Lancaster. The contrast can be seen by comparing the effects of failure of leadership in the north midlands under Henry VI and under Henry VII. Whereas in the former reign it allowed local powers to dictate the course of events, in the latter it led to confusion, for none of the contending parties could manage without the king.

On this evidence, with all his advantages, Henry badly misjudged the

157 *Letters and Papers*, I, pp. 231–40 and comments on dating in Chrimes 1972a: p. 308 n. 1; Harrison, 'Petition of Edmund Dudley'; Halle, *Union of the Two Noble Houses*, 'Richard III' fo. 13v.; Jones 1988: p. 17. The atmosphere of unease and suspicion can be seen in the dealings recorded in Henry's household book of 1499–1505 (Br. Lib. Add. MS 21,480).

158 Elton 1958, 1961; Cooper 1959; Chrimes 1972a: pp. 309–13; Scarisbrick 1968: pp. 11–12; Lander 1976c: pp. 297–300.

159 A similar point, suggesting that the reigns of Henry and Edward IV may differ more in the kind of work done on them than in actual fact, is made in Wolffe 1976: pp. 369–73. Bernard's categorical statement (1985: p. 5) that there was no unrest in the midlands at the time of the Warbeck conspiracies is symptomatic of the current ignorance of local politics under Henry VII. Also Chrimes 1972b: pp. 68–70, words which require little modification seventeen years later.

situation. It has become abundantly clear over the course of this study that the working of the body politic rested on the basis of mutual trust between centre and localities, between king and landowners, even if some kings, like Henry V and Edward IV, were perfectly prepared to strike terror into the hearts of men who abused that trust. This was something Henry VII never grasped. He thought he could dictate to the gentry who lay within his sphere as earl of Warwick, he thought he could let his favourites run loose if that gave them the power to withstand challenges to the royal government. He offended local susceptibilities unnecessarily, he failed to see that local societies, like kings, normally wanted stability, and that it was unwise to curb too harshly those who were already keeping the peace or to allow free rein to his servants who were failing to do so. Having finally grasped the need to delegate, he did not understand that delegation could only be based on the same mutual trust, and engendered further hostility by the use of bonds to protect him against those to whom he had handed power. He survived because he was naturally tenacious and rather good at winning battles and had the good fortune to rule at a time when it was becoming easier for a king to make mistakes and keep his crown.[160]

[160] An alternative view, not dissimilar to the one expressed here, if rather more emphatically stated, has however already been put forward in Lander 1980: ch. 10, esp. pp. 355–61 and is implicit in much of Arthurson 1981 (see esp. the contemporary comment, cited p. 65) and 1987b, hinted at in Chrimes 1972a and put rather more explicitly in Chrimes 1972b: pp. 82–3; also Bacon's comment, quoted in Davies, C.S.L. 1977: p. 103; and Davies, C.S.L. 1977: p. 114, and Condon 1979: p. 115. But all except Lander and Davies ultimately reach a generally favourable verdict. For the more conventional estimation, even in the current revisionist upgrading of Edward, e.g. Ross 1974: pp. 332–41, 420–5 and the astonishingly old-fashioned Grant 1985. This theme will be pursued further in my forthcoming book on the Wars of the Roses. On Henry's success as a soldier, see Arthurson 1981: p. 215 and 1987a.

16

POLITICS AND SOCIETY *c.* 1449–1500

It is time to draw up a balance sheet, to assess the gains and losses of Warwickshire society in these troubled years and to investigate the long-term effects on local society of living in conditions of political uncertainty for the best part of half a century. The obvious starting-point is the networks that bound landowners together in neighbourhoods within the county; did they survive and were there still forces capable of linking them together across the county? If we replicate more briefly the survey done in chapter 9, we find a situation of greatly increased complexity, in which it has become much harder to find a recognisable pattern. This is due only to a limited extent to diminishing evidence, although the Archer collection becomes noticeably less dense towards the end of the century. The real problem is that the extreme volatility of politics for much of the period forced the major gentry families, who throughout the century provide the bulk of the evidence, into an almost continual process of political readjustment. In a county like Warwickshire, where the nobility had hitherto played such a dominant role, this tended, at least in the first part of the period, to mean moving between groupings associated, however briefly, with a particular magnate. The net result was that few local networks formed by the inter-relationships of the more eminent gentry retained a fixed identity, or even an existence, for long. Since the evidence is inevitably patchy, it is not easy to trace their development or to be very certain about their composition at any one point. Under these circumstances, indications of the survival of localised groupings, however sparse and sporadic, must be taken very seriously.

The evidence for the early 1450s suggests that, in the expectation of the restoration of normal politics under the new earl of Warwick, there was a general return to the local networks that had played such a large part in political and social relationships in the time of Richard Beauchamp. This can be seen in all parts of the county. If the political complexion of some had changed – in south-west Warwickshire, for instance, Beauchamp of Powick and Sudeley took a lead that would have been wholly out of the question in Richard Beauchamp's time[1] – the structure was essentially the same. For example, the ties that the new earl made with north Warwickshire immediately after his accession to the title, through the Buckingham affinity and the remains of the Ferrers of Chartley following, were entirely in keeping with those that Richard Beauchamp had established in the 1420s and 1430s.[2] The principal innovation throughout the county and its penumbra was that in none of these groupings, not even that in his home territory in the west midlands, was Neville pre-eminent. No doubt he was intending with time to make himself so, but as it happened he was not given the time during the 1450s, and by the 1460s, as will become apparent, things had changed.

In east Warwickshire the situation had always been more volatile. This state of affairs was due to the absence both of geographical features defining the neighbourhood and of a dominant magnate, and to the existence of a number of middling gentry families whose loyalties seem to have been more to each other than to a particular local power. Despite the existence of a dense local network in the Avon-Leam area, the boundaries of neighbourhood, defined in terms of local groupings, had been continually subject to change, as a succession of magnates brought their authority to bear on the area. Consequently, the most stable period had been in the 1420s and 1430s, when Richard Beauchamp's ascendancy west and east of the region had enabled him to make it part of his massive midland nexus. Here, in the early 1450s, there was a return to the situation of the 1440s, when Edward Grey had enjoyed extensive support and had helped build a network that crossed the border into Leicestershire. However, Grey's power was now tempered by other forces, notably the Somerset and Shrewsbury connection, and there is also some evidence for Grey's master Buckingham taking a more direct interest in the area, perhaps for the first time. Throughout the decade this part of the county, more than any other, registered fluctuations in local power structures. Its political shape changed constantly. At times, as when Grey was exerting significant influence, it looked eastwards to Leicestershire; at others, the influence of Warwick pulled together the whole of the south of the county, across the Avon; at still others, the interests of the Verneys of Compton Murdack drew together the more eastern parts of Knightlow and Kineton hundreds.[3]

[1] E.g. *Cal. Close Rolls 1447–54*, p. 410; Warwick Castle MS 819; W.C.R.O. L.1/78–81; S.B.T. Stratford Corp. Recs. 1/501–3, D.R.37/966; Hilton 1975: pp. 68–9; C.1/24/57 (case from mid-1450s, but feoffment probably belongs to previous decade); above, pp. 466–66.

[2] E.g. above, pp. 450–7; S.B.T. D.R.31 fo.45/15, fo.53/3; Nott. Univ. Lib. Middleton MS Mi D 4764; Bod. Lib. Dugdale MS 15, pp. 75–6; Br. Lib. Add. MS 28,564 fo. 23.

[3] Above, pp. 452–3, 460–3, 473; and e.g. Bod. Lib. Dugdale MS 9, p. 335; Leics.R.O. DE 2242/6/64, DE 220 (sub-section of DG 12)/58; Northants.R.O. Spencer MS 833,838; *H.M.C. Hastings*, I, p. 143; *Cat. Anc. Deeds*, III, A4369, IV, A6380; S.B.T. D.R.37 Box 40 (deed of 1453), D.R.98/89, 122, 122a, 502, 505; K.B.27/766 Coram Rege rot.64, /774 Coram Rege rot.77d.; C.P.40/757 rot.339, /756 rot.333; C.1/10/223, /27/268; W.C.R.O. C.R.162/227; *Cal. Close Rolls 1447–54*, p. 410; S.C.1/51/147.

It was from about 1454 that the local networks became increasingly fluid and ill-defined, even in areas as cohesive in previous times as the Warwickshire-Worcestershire region. Partly this was simply a question of the gentry shopping around for the most attractive protection of the moment, but it also had to do with more fundamental problems. The well-knit local groupings that faced divided loyalties as the decade progressed were increasingly unable to function. For instance, in the south-west from late 1456 it was highly dangerous for any landowner to place much reliance on a local group that was divided between Warwick and the two Lancastrian lords, Sudeley and Beauchamp of Powick, and the number of feoffments where the witnesses and feoffees are primarily men from this locality diminishes rapidly. Similarly, in north Warwickshire, where the gentry generally owed allegiance to Buckingham and to Warwick, evidence of association among the gentry becomes much sparser towards the end of the decade. What made loyalties even more complicated here was that some of Buckingham's men were closer to the royal household than others, and that there were strong ties with Leicestershire, where the network was even more divided.[4]

The responses of the gentry to this extremely unfortunate situation, which have been touched on in the course of the narrative, are highly instructive and merit further exploration. We have seen that by 1459 there may have been a widespread reluctance to embark on landed settlements until the situation had clarified. It was noted then that such a state of affairs could not possibly be allowed to continue over any length of time, and it is clear that until Margaret's revanche produced the acute divisions of that year the gentry did not intend that it should do so. The neighbourhood was still the essential source of reliable associates, even more so when political loyalties were so subject to change; as far as possible, gentry families continued to associate with neighbours, and with other families with which they had long-standing ties, even though this might mean crossing the boundaries of magnate divisions. This was most easily done when rapprochement was the order of the day among the nobility, notably in the period of Yorkist rule from late 1453 until late 1456, but it could also be effected almost in despite of the nobility. It could even be argued that the suspension of hostilities, the curious 'phony war' between Margaret's seizure of power and her attack on the Yorkists, owed a lot to the unwillingness of the gentry of much of England to take sides.[5]

Such reluctance can be deduced from the sort of arrangements that were being made by the Verneys, which brought together Sudeley and Beauchamp and some of their clients with associates of Warwick, Edward Grey and Buckingham; or that of John Wode of Worcestershire, where Warwick and Sudeley and their men intermingled; or of Thomas Erdington, which used the

4 Above, ch. 12 and pp. 490–1, and app. 3.

5 Above, pp. 467–75, 479–83.

north Warwickshire-Leicestershire network to bring together followers of York, Warwick and Shrewsbury. In these transactions, despite the dangers of using local networks at a time of acute division, ties of neighbourhood managed to override political faction.[6] In a deed of William Catesby executed in 1457 local loyalties united men from two distinct parts of the county – east Warwickshire where Catesby resided when in the county, and west Warwickshire, where the land in question lay – whose political loyalties conflicted to an astonishing degree with Catesby's own.[7] The defence of Thomas Burdet's manor of Bramcote against the Charnels by a body of feoffees formed before Richard Neville arrived, deriving principally but not exclusively from the south-west, continued throughout the decade, crossing all manner of political divides.[8] Under these circumstances, members of the gentry who had a foot in both the main camps could be especially prized friends, and we begin to see them taking on an ever more important role, locally and, more importantly, in the cross-county transactions that will be examined shortly.[9]

Evidence for the continuance of local groups at the level below the one we have been discussing is variable. There is a surprising amount for central Warwickshire, where the lack of gentry in the Coventry region had usually encouraged local men to look further afield for their associates.[10] On the other hand, the Avon-Leam group, comprising both greater and lesser gentry families, had become rather attenuated with the demise of some families and the misfortunes of others. Indeed, in the whole of eastern and south-eastern Warwickshire evidence for the doings of the many small-scale gentry is distinctly sparse after about 1453.[11] However since co-operation among their superiors continued to a greater or lesser extent throughout the decade, it would be rash to assume that there was some sort of crisis of mutual confidence in this area. Around Tanworth, where lesser gentry were the norm, there really was internal division, as the Porter–Archer conflict split the region and brought it for the first time fully into the mainstream of Warwickshire politics.[12] Nevertheless, there can be no question that this strong local network survived, and this would seem to be the key to the whole problem of local cohesion in the 1450s; that however acute local division might be, it was overridden, or at least

[6] Above, p. 478 and e.g. C.244/80/173; S.B.T. D.R.37 Box 90 (will of Alice Archer, 1458), E.R.1/61/385; *Cal. Pat. Rolls 1452–61*, pp. 360, 523; *W.F.F.*, 2660; *Colls. Hist. Staffs.*, o.s., 12, p. 323.

[7] Above, pp. 480–1.

[8] Above, pp. 408, 456, 477; K.B.27/762 Rex rot.12, /779 Coram Rege rot.73, /786 Coram Rege rot.114d.; *Cal. Pat. Rolls 1452–61*, p. 523.

[9] Below, pp. 606–7.

[10] E.g. *Colls. Hist. Staffs.*, o.s., 12, pp. 322–3; *Cal. Close Rolls 1454–61*, pp. 189, 381; Bod. Lib. Dugdale MS 15, p. 125; Wm. Salt Lib. H.M. Chetwynd Coll. Bundle 4 (deeds of 27–32 Hen. VI); C.244/84/236; Gloucs.R.O. D 1086/T.103/7; S.B.T. D.R.10/1187; above, pp. 299–300.

[11] The bulk of the evidence for them is in n. 3, above, but see also e.g. K.B.27/766 Coram Rege rot.11d.; C.P.40/756 rot.29d.; Jeayes ed., 'Catalogue of Spencer Charters', 1652, 1654.

[12] Above, pp. 296–7, 318, 323, 344, 425–6, 429–30, 451–2, 456, 477.

put in perspective, by the more pressing requirement of the safety of the estate. This could mean ignoring the antagonism of noble lords, or trying to remain on good terms with neighbours who were themselves at odds with each other. It is a pattern of behaviour that we have already witnessed in the troubled 1440s, and it was all the more imperative in the more seriously disrupted 1450s. Despite failures in some families that had played a significant role in local networks, particularly the Avon-Leam, this was a relatively stable period for the middling ranks of Warwickshire society, who had been one of the main forces for stability in local networks up to 1450, a state of affairs which helped the gentry in their efforts to carry on as before.[13]

With the Yorkist victory (and even before, when they were periodically in power in 1460) and the expectation of a return to normal politics, the gentry again showed their willingness to revert to their traditional practice of taking most of their associates from neighbourhood groupings led by the nobility. This was especially true of the south-west, with its traditions of subservience to the house of Warwick,[14] and the north. Here the Warwickshire-Staffordshire network that had been the dominant grouping since the 1420s came under the leadership of Hastings almost as soon as the Yorkists looked close to victory. It had emerged under Richard Beauchamp and the Ferrers of Chartley but acquired a life of its own which made it available to any magnate able to win the landowners' confidence. An indication of how ready the gentry still were to accept noble direction is the way Sudeley's influence extended in Warwickshire, as it became apparent that neither Warwick nor Hastings was intending to give a large amount of their time to the county. Sudeley can be found playing a substantial part not only in the affairs of the south-west, where we would expect this, but also in central Warwickshire, where he was constable of Kenilworth and, most surprisingly, in the north, in conjunction with Hastings.[15]

As in the hey-day of Richard Beauchamp, Warwick's influence became strong enough to begin to percolate through to the east of the county. Nevertheless, because noble leadership over most of the county remained weak compared with what it had been in the first half of the century, local networks

13 See e.g. S.B.T. D.R.37/954–5, 957, 958, 959, 963, 966, 974, Box 42/2519; *W.F.F.*, 2661; *Cal. Fine Rolls 1452–61*, p. 67; C.1/18/32; K.B.27/762 Coram Rege rot.45, /786 List of Fines and Coram Rege rot.114d; above, pp. 142–3, 344.

14 Above, p. 490 n. 16 for refs. from the early 1460s and, for later in the decade, above, pp. 494–5, 500 and e.g. W.C.R.O. C.R.26/1(2)/W.27; Coughton Court, Throckmorton MS, Jeayes, Calendar, 176, Box 49 (deed of 1468); *Cal. Close Rolls 1468–76*, pp. 99, 102, 109; Br. Lib. Add. Ch. 73,925; W.C.R.O. L.6/141; Warwick Castle MS 127A; S.B.T. D.R.37 Box 48 (deed of 1460), Box 51 (deed of 1468).

15 Above, pp. 507, 512–13 and p. 491 n. 18; for the Coventry region and Sudeley, see also e.g. C.244/94/34, /97/16, 45, /102/186, /104/122. For more on Sudeley, see the refs. to Throgmorton's associates, below, n. 19, and C. 244/104/118, 122. In these, and in the Kenilworth region evidence, the interpenetration of the Sudeley and Grey affinities (above, pp. 530–1, and app. 3) can already be seen.

in east Warwickshire lacked any obvious political complexion. But the existence of groups here is not in doubt, despite the hiatuses in numbers of leading families. As before, they straddled the Northamptonshire and Leicestershire borders. Here also there was some Sudeley influence, and an interesting group of deeds dealing with the Sudeley-Norfolk manor at Fenny Compton shows how far such unity as existed across the southern parts of the county, and indeed beyond, was now due to the Sudeley-Warwick connection. In the sector near the Leicestershire border Hastings was already making his presence felt, principally through the Leicestershire connection, as he was to do with much greater force in the following decade. Sir John Bourchier, who, as heir to the Grey interest, was the obvious leading magnate here, seems to have been able to do very little.[16]

And this brings us to the most striking feature of Warwickshire affairs in the 1460s, which is the failure of the nobility. Much has been said on this in the narrative of events, but it is clearly reflected in the deed evidence. Only in the north of the county, the least disturbed area in the decade, did magnates, in this case the combined leadership of Hastings and Sudeley, take a leading part in the nurturing of local identity. Even they were apparently unable to exercise any control over the activities of Simon Mountford, the greatest of the local landowners, although he was nominally Hastings' retainer by the end of the decade. Central Warwickshire came increasingly under Mountford's rule, a relationship strengthened by Mountford's tie with Henry Boteller, who had extensive local connections, thanks to his professional employment, his annuity from Sudeley and his position as Recorder of Coventry. Because Simon never severed his links with many of his old associates in the Warwick affinity, he became effectively a fifth column within it, attacking some of his nominal lord's closest servants.[17] The effects of the increasing division within the Warwick affinity were felt in the south-west as well, many local figures associating with Thomas Burdet and John Brome at times when these two were on significantly

[16] *Cat. Anc. Deeds*, VI, C6437; Nichols 1795–1811: IV, i, pp. 368–9; S.B.T. D.R.98/508; W.C.R.O. C.R.1248/68/30; Bod. Lib. Dugdale MS 15, p. 73; Leics.R.O. DG5/5; Northants.R.O. Fitzwilliam MS 1414, 559 (the Henry Grene who features in these two deeds with Warwick etc. was a friend and relative of Catesby: *Cat. Anc. Deeds*, III, A4369; above, p. 329 n. 186), 679, Spencer MS 846, 851, 1244, 1654; K.B.27/818 Coram Rege rot.35, /824 Coram Rege rot.69d.; C.244/97/31, /100/7, /102/115, 159, /103/14; *H.M.C. Hastings*, I, pp. 2, 25, 295–6; above, n. 15. For the Sudeley-Warwick-Norfolk group, W.C.R.O. L.1/82, 85, 95. For Bourchier, see above, p. 488 n. 7 and p. 506.

[17] Above, pp. 498–508; also e.g. *Cat. Anc. Deeds*, IV, A8424; K.B.27/808 Coram Rege rot.45; Jeayes ed., 'Catalogue of Spencer Charters', 1654; S.B.T. D.R.3/260, D.R.98/123e, D.R.37 Box 82 (extract from plea roll Mich. 7 Ed.IV), D.R.18 Series C/W.4/12/4, D.R.503 fos. 66–8, E.R.146/6, D.R.41/71/284; Warwick Castle MS 118b; Derbys.R.O. D156M/15; C.244/97/24, 26, 197, /99/27, 33, 39, 115, 125, /100/8. For Boteller, see above, pp. 530–1 and app. 3; also e.g. *Cat. Anc. Deeds*, IV, A8420; E.326/4461; C.140/30/53; C.244/94/34; *I.P.M. Hen. VII*, III, 1144; *H.M.C. Lothian MS*, p. 55. For some of his clients at this time, refs. in p. 125 n. 107. For the link with Mountford, see p. 508 n. 77 and *I.P.M. Hen. VII*, III, 760.

bad terms with some of those closest to the earl.[18] The most cohesive network within this part of Warwickshire, according to the evidence we have, was that created by the Throgmortons for their personal needs, encompassing neighbours and relatives by marriage. It was this grouping, formed around this one family, that had the best connections with the adjacent parts of Worcestershire and Gloucestershire which had for so long been under the shadow of the earls of Warwick.[19] In east to south-east Warwickshire, Simon Mountford began to acquire a circle of friends, some of them known to have been attached to Warwickshire magnates, their one common political factor being their link to him.[20]

The same pattern is repeated under Clarence; much of the county shows its willingness to put itself under his direction until that direction is seen to be failing and then the gentry begin to go their own way. In the north, little changed after 1470–1; Hastings' grant of the Tutbury stewardship under the king in 1474 ended the hiatus caused first by Sudeley's disgrace and death, following hard on the temporary exile of Hastings himself, and then by subsequent uncertainty about whether Clarence would be an effective leader here. The area could then be rapidly knitted into the extended network of Hastings and the king, encompassing the north and north-east midlands.[21] The way Clarence's following fell apart further south has been described. There were internal divisions which the duke was unable to curb, but, as in the 1460s, much of the lack of unity was due to the individual decisions of members of the gentry, notably Robert Throgmorton, to find themselves a security that was not wholly dependent on the protection of a rather suspect magnate. In east Warwickshire we can already trace the beginning of the powerful connection led by William Catesby II in conjunction with Hastings that was to bring the whole region together, as it had not been united since the greatest days of Richard Beauchamp.[22]

From 1478 until the end of the century, local groupings, in continuing to mirror developments in local power structures, remain in a fairly constant state

18 *Cal. Pat. Rolls 1461–67*, p. 379; *Cal. Close Rolls 1461–68*, p. 188; *Cat. Anc. Deeds*, IV, A8424; W.C.R.O. C.R. 26/1(2)/W.27, C.R.26/XXXIII; Derbys.R.O. D156M/15; S.B.T. D.R.3/260, 530; C.244/97/28, 192, 197, /99/16, 27, 115; above, pp. 495, 500–1, 502–3.

19 E.g. *Cat. Anc. Deeds*, I, C331, IV, A8420; *W.F.F.*, 2677; *Cal. Close Rolls 1461–68*, p. 323, *1468–76*, pp. 99, 289–90; K.B.27/809 Rex rot.20d., /818 Coram Rege rot.35; E.326/10852; S.B.T. D.R.37 Box 51 (deed of 1468); W.C.R.O. L.1/85; Coughton Court, Throckmorton MS Box 72/5, Box 49 (deed of 1468). For his family, see *Test. Vetust.*, p. 248; *Cal. Close Rolls 1468–76*, p. 231.

20 Above, pp. 506–7.

21 Carpenter 1986a: pp. 32–3, 35–6. Also, for the south-west, Bod. Lib. Dugdale MS 13, p. 523, and, for the Hastings connection in north and east Warwickshire, see Bod. Lib. Dugdale MS 15, p. 299; Northants.R.O. Knightley Charts. 249; Wright 1978: p. 393 and Derbys.R.O. D410M Box 3/276.

22 Above, pp. 518, 520, 527–8.

of flux. The split between north and south, which had threatened in the 1460s and become evident from 1474, as Hastings' power in the area grew and Clarence's waned, hardened.[23] Once the king had taken over the Clarence lands, there were two major forces in Warwickshire, one in the north and one in the south, both ultimately with the full authority of the crown behind them. There was consequently little room for any other magnate influence, except of a rather subsidiary nature. The kings' determination that this should remain the case from Coventry southward can be seen very clearly in the way Edward IV put a stop in this part of the county to the ambitions of Edward Grey, and Henry VII to those of the Stanleys.[24] As far as more prominent gentry families are concerned, the local groupings dissolve increasingly into two large networks, one within a band across the county north of Coventry, the other covering the rest of the county.

For the last years of Edward IV's rule, this statement has to be qualified, for the substantial group associated with Catesby and Hastings down the eastern border enabled this region to retain something of a separate identity and provide a link between the far north and the rest of the county.[25] The old neighbourhoods survived as far as the minor gentry families were concerned, as they continued to associate in the same sort of groupings that had been evident before, but by and large this was no longer true of the *mediocres* and the elite of local society. A survey of the surviving evidence for the period from the fall of Clarence to the end of the century suggests that, for these, especially the elite, it was almost as normal to have dealings with men from other areas within one of the two main divisions of Warwickshire as it was to associate with more immediate neighbours.[26]

[23] Above, p. 523.

[24] Above, pp. 530, 566–7.

[25] Above, pp. 527–8.

[26] For the north, north-east and east 1478–85, see above, pp. 525–8; for central and southern Warwickshire, above, pp. 528–32 and refs.; for the north under Henry VII, above, pp. 561–74, 580 and refs.; for central and southern Warwickshire under Henry VII, pp. 574–82 and refs.; also, for this region from 1478–*c.* 1500, e.g. *I.P.M. Hen. VII,* II, 245, 913; *Cal. Close Rolls 1476–85*, pp. 232–3, 412, *1485–1500*, pp. 192, 302; *Cat. Anc. Deeds,* II, B2981, III, D798, IV, A8407, 9791; C.P.40/878 rot.206; WARD 2/38/146E/3; PROB 11/9 fo. 141d.; C.P.40/930 rot.358; S.B.T. D.R.3/273–6, 282–4, D.R.37/1022, 1027–8, 1031, 1041, 1050, 1070, Box 51 (deed of 1493), Box 60 (indenture of 1495), D.R.98/125a, 456, 529, 605, D.R.18/A353, D.R.10/505, E.R.1/61/324, /67/599; W.C.R.O. C.R.133/16, C.R.959, C.R.712/18, 19, L.1/99, C.R.26/1(2)/W.29, C.R.1248/71/29, C.R.456/31, C.R.1908/85; Northants.R.O. Spencer MS 867, 1533; *Dugdale*, p. 505; Br. Lib. Add. MS 34,739, p. 3, 28,564 fo. 186, Add. Ch. 42394(2); Coughton Court, Throckmorton MS Box 72 (marriage indenture, 1501), Jeayes, Calendar, 179. For evidence of local groupings (mostly, but not invariably, at a lowish social level), e.g. Northants.R.O. Spencer MS 1533, 1534, 1592, 1660; S.B.T. D.R.41/70/284a, D.R.10/554, D.R.37/1022, 1027–8, 1035–8, 1050, Box 33 (deed of 1481), Box 36 (deeds of 1480, 1481), Box 42/2536–8, Box 56 (deeds of 1495, 1507); Bod. Lib. Dugdale MS 15, pp. 66–7, 182; W.C.R.O. C.R.162/78, C.R.1908/76/8, L.1/99, 107, C.R.136/C422; Coughton Court, Throckmorton MS File of Deeds (deed of 1495), Box 35 (deed of 1478); N.R.A. 'Misc. Deeds in Coll. of Arms', Part II, 649/1. Of particular interest is

It is particularly noticeable that all the more prominent gentry of the Tanworth region, which had always been the most distinct locality, were extensively involved with families to the south and east. This development is all the more striking, in that, although the area had been moving towards greater absorption into the affairs of the rest of the county, it had tended to look to the north. Its reorientation south can be explained only by its being within the part of the county that the king had marked out for himself. The principal north Warwickshire figure to maintain contacts with this area was Simon Mountford, a point which emphasises his eventual isolation from most of his neighbours.[27] Another even more surprising change was the virtual disappearance of any strong local network south-west of Warwick, as the *caput honoris* of the former earls of Warwick ceased to be the heart of this great west midlands affinity and the affinity itself merged into the greater Warwick/household nexus stretching across southern Warwickshire.

It must be said that there was not necessarily any permanence about these arrangements. There are signs, even from the very limited amount of research I have carried out after 1500, that in the early decades of the sixteenth century a stronger sense of locality was reasserting itself among the more prominent gentry in the areas from Coventry southwards, along with a reforging of some of the links between north and south. This may have been a response to the growth of stability in the north and the lightening of the king's hold on the south.[28] It was also possible because, partly coincidentally and partly as a result of less stringent royal intervention, several major local families were coming back into their own again. For example, George Catesby was restored to some of the family estates in 1496. Furthermore, one or two of Henry VII's interpolated families, like the Conways, were beginning to establish themselves in local society.[29] It must indeed always be remembered that the disappearance, temporary or permanent, of a number of prominent families in an area could immediately diminish the strength of the local network, and this is certainly the main reason for the progressive weakening of the formerly powerful Avon-Leam group throughout this half-century. Here too, in the early years of the sixteenth century, there are signs of a reversion to former conditions, as families that had been in eclipse for one reason or another, like

that the remnants of the Sudeley connection still held together to bind both local groupings and cross-county connections (app. 3 for this, and above, pp. 530–1 and below, n. 43).

27 See refs. in n. 26, above, espec. to Archer collection (D.R.37) in S.B.T. and above, p. 600 n.12.

28 E.g. *Cal. Close Rolls 1500–09*, p. 273; *Cal. Pat. Rolls 1494–1509*, p. 604; Jeayes ed., 'Catalogue of Spencer Charters', 1491; W.C.R.O. C.R.162/180; *Cat. Anc. Deeds*, V, A13262, 13285, 13498; S.B.T. D.R.37 Box 40 (deed of 1502), Stratford Corp. Recs. II/83; C.P.40/950 rot.419d.; *I.P.M. Hen. VII*, III, 217; *Dugdale*, p. 589. Note too that Simon Digby was beginning to take on the mantle of Simon Mountford, at least in the north of the county and near Coventry (*Cat. Anc. Deeds*, VI, C4194; S.B.T. D.R.18/A23; Nott. Univ. Lib. Middleton MS 6/173/54); above, pp. 590–4. Also p. 593 n. 152.

29 *Rot. Parl.*, VI, pp. 491–2; above, n. 28.

the Malorys, the Knightleys and the Boughtons, began to return to full participation in local affairs.[30]

The patterns that have been traced in studying the local groups are replicated in this half-century with respect to the linkages between such groups. As with local networks, a return to normal conditions, in which magnates largely determined connections between groups, was soon stifled by the growing abnormality of local and national politics, and new structures began to appear. There are signs that Richard Neville was attempting to reconstruct Richard Beauchamp's great county-wide connection, and even succeeding, until about the mid 1450s. Then the effects of the confrontational style in national politics began to make it impossible for him to exploit the multiple alliance system, or even to give the area the time that was needed for such an enterprise.[31] By about 1456 Warwickshire seems to a large extent to have lost not only its neighbourhood identities but also any secure channel through which the gentry could find reliable associates in other parts of the county. The response of the greater gentry, whose horizons had always extended beyond their immediate localities, was to place much greater emphasis on the personal ties of friendship and kinship that had always played a part within all the Warwickshire networks; now, for the first time in associations among the gentry of different neighbourhoods, the horizontal began to take precedence over the vertical.[32]

This, however, was still a deferential society and so it was only natural, in the absence of adequate noble leadership, that people should look to prominent gentry as guarantors of their dealings. The emergence of such figures as leading local brokers across the county is one of the most striking features of the mid fifteenth century. Even in the early years of Richard Neville's rule, it can be seen in the group that coalesced around William Mountford. This was politically a very complex group, and its formation was a response to divisions among the magnates which failed to correlate with the pattern of loyalties among the gentry.[33] As the gap between the factions of the nobility and the political identities of the gentry widened, the role of gentry of Mountford's type became pivotal. As has been suggested, it was the men who had connections with antagonistic magnate factions who were most attractive to other gentry looking for a neutral position. Thomas Littleton assumed an increasingly

30 Carpenter 1980b; *Cal. Pat. Rolls 1494–1509*, p. 663; *The Ancestor*, 2 (1902), pp. 5–6; *Cal. Fine Rolls 1471–85*, p. 99; *Lists and Indexes*, 9, p. 93; K.B.27/900 Coram Rege rot.12; *Dugdale*, p. 100; *I.P.M. Hen. VII*, 1, 23, 56; *Cal. Pat. Rolls 1494–1509*, p. 395. For earlier loss of personnel in this area, above, pp. 327–8, 600.

31 *Colls. Hist. Staffs.*, o.s., 12, p. 323; above, ch. 12.

32 E.g. the alliance of Richard Verney and his relatives by marriage, the senior Mountford line (above, p. 467); the collection of feoffees used by Verney in 1457, which cut through local factions (above, p. 480) and the group of Burdet feoffees, established in the 1440s under the Beauchamp of Powick-Sudeley regime in south-west Warwickshire (above, n. 8).

33 Above, pp. 459–62.

prominent position in the 1450s. His land made him a natural associate of gentry in both the Warwickshire-Worcestershire area and the north of the county where it bordered on Staffordshire. His legal expertise and links with government circles made him a desirable friend of both nobility and gentry. His connections with noblemen in opposed political camps drew the gentry of all political persuasions to him as they tried to avoid the consequences of open conflict. His share in the custodies of the Ardern and Porter lands extended his territorial power and brought him into contact with other parts of the county.[34] He was a feoffee for Wiltshire, for William Peyto, for Beauchamp of Powick, for Thomas Burdet's disputed manor of Bramcote and for Richard Verney. Littleton, more than any other landowner, became in this decade the focal point for links between different parts of the county.[35] Thomas Throgmorton had a similar but more localised role in the same decade, his qualification being that he was equally trusted by Warwick and Sudeley.[36] At times of *volte face* in national politics, one can observe local families moving rapidly into association with whatever eminent member of the gentry had access to the new dispensation.[37]

If, in the 1450s, the more prominent gentry had been obliged to an ever greater degree to find their own ways of maintaining ties with families of like status across the county, it is not to be wondered at that their experience helped determine their responses in the 1460s. But now the cause was not just Warwick's failure to show himself an effective leader for the whole, or even part of the county. Nor was it the lack of any possible noble alternative, for Sudeley's influence was growing throughout the county.[38] The essential reason that Simon Mountford became the single most influential landowner in Warwickshire was that Warwick's inability to contain him or to offer a convincing alternative cross-county linkage left the field to this ambitious knight. As in the 1450s, a movement through most of the county to re-establish the Warwick affinity as the natural point of contact faded away.[39] In this instance, there is no doubt but that the Warwick affinity remained far and away the most powerful following in all parts of Warwickshire, but Mountford was able to establish his own circle within it. Men not known to be connected with

34 Above, pp. 469–70; also *Paston Letters,* II, pp. 148, 164, 294.

35 *Cal. Pat. Rolls 1452–61*, p. 159, *1446–52*, p. 501; *H.M.C. Hastings,* I, pp. 1–2; Warwick Castle MS 116A; S.B.T. D.R.98/89; above, p. 00. For Bramcote, see above, n. 8.

36 E.g. *Cal. Pat. Rolls 1452–61*, p. 360; *W.F.F.*, 2660; PROB 11/4 fo. 100; N.R.A. 'Misc. Deeds in Coll. of Arms', Part II, 508/5, 12, 751/7; *Cal. Close Rolls 1447–54*, p. 426, *1454–61*, p. 188; W.C.R.O. L.1/79; K.B.27/765 Rex rot.4d.; Br. Lib. Add. Ch. 73,501, 73,561.

37 Above, p. 484 and two very telling Spenser deeds: in June 1459 Wormleighton is settled with the help of Buckingham; in October 1460 hurried recourse is had to York, March, Rutland, Wenlock, Simon Mountford etc. (Northants.R.O. Spencer MS 1652, 1654).

38 Above, ch. 13.

39 Above, pp. 450–1, 490–2; see also e.g. Bod. Lib. Dugdale MS 15, p. 73; Leics.R.O. D 611/196; C.244/99/16,137.

Warwick were drawn to it, notably from eastern Warwickshire, where lordship had always been weak and changeable. In the south and south-east of the county Mountford could exploit not just the proximity of his own estates, which were the basis of his influence, but also the family connection with the Verneys, which had been created a decade and more before with the purpose of protecting these southern estates against the rival family claim.[40] If the allegiance of the northern sector of the Warwick affinity remained firmer – probably because Hastings and Sudeley, its local leaders, had little interest in supporting Mountford's ventures[41] – Mountford was himself a northerner, and it was he who to an ever greater degree provided the links between north and south Warwickshire.[42]

From 1474, when the two areas became still more distinct, and indeed from the time of Sudeley's fall from grace, Mountford's position as chief broker, eventually virtually the only broker, between north and south becomes yet more apparent.[43] But Edward IV's method of ruling Warwickshire encouraged the emergence of connections focused on the more prominent gentry, as long as they were contained within his and Hastings' all-embracing control of the whole county. The other major groupings of this sort have been referred to; those of John Hugford, based largely on his influential position with most of the local nobility, and of William Catesby.[44] It was Catesby who in 1483 showed that gentry of his type had now reached the point where they too could be significant arbiters of a region's political destinies. From the late 1470s to the end of the period various members of the gentry continued to take on this role, left vacant by the merging of the Warwick connection with the crown affinity, of bringing the diverse neighbourhoods of the county together. Robert Throgmorton's family and landed connections for example linked the south-west to the south-east and the adjacent south-east midland area.[45] Henry VII's more interventionist attitude towards the localities made him rather more reluctant to allow even members of the gentry so much freedom, especially in

40 Above, ch. 13 and p. 105.

41 Although Mountford was retained by Hastings in 1469 (above, p. 511), there is no evidence at all that Hastings was offering him any assistance in Warwickshire.

42 Above, pp. 515, 517–18, 531–2, 577 and n. 17; C.244/102/104, 251; Derbys.R.O. D156M/15.

43 Above, n. 27; although the Sudeley connection, mostly of minor gentry, linking the south-west to the Kenilworth/Coventry region and the east, showed a surprising durability, coalescing around Edward Grey and John Hugford and to some extent retaining a life of its own (above, p. 531 n. 28; and e.g. PROB 11/8 fo. 161, /13 fos. 47v.–48; *Dugdale*, p. 602; Northants.R.O. Temple (Stowe) Coll. Box 6/2).

44 Above, pp. 527–8, 530–1.

45 For Throgmorton, see above, p. 529; also e.g. *Cal. Pat. Rolls 1485–94*, pp. 210–11; *Cal. Close Rolls 1485–1500*, pp. 233–4; *Dugdale*, p. 505; Cooper 1936: p. 19; *Cat. Anc. Deeds*, IV, A9791; W.C.R.O. C.R.959; S.B.T. D.R.3/275–6, 283–4, 286, D.R.98/456, Stratford Corp. Recs. II/83, D.R.37 Box 40 (deed of 1502); B.R.L. 324030; PROB 11/4 fo. 14; *Cat. Anc. Deeds*, I, C1230; *I.P.M. Hen. VII*, II, 29, III, 217; N.R.A. 'Misc. Deeds in Coll. of Arms', Part II, 649/1, 751/8. Also Carpenter 1986a: p. 36 and above, n. 19 for his family connections.

the central and southern parts of the county. This may help explain the fall of Simon Mountford and certainly accounts for the king's development of the bond as a restraining mechanism when he began to allow more independence to local landowners towards the end of the reign. Even so, it was under Henry VII that Henry Willoughby grew into an ever more powerful focal figure in north Warwickshire and the north midlands, where the king ruled with a somewhat lighter hand.[46]

Throughout this difficult half-century, it is difficult to envisage Warwickshire as a county, for the absence of a force that could bind together its distinct segments left each area generally more involved with affairs in the adjacent counties than with those of other parts of the county. This was particularly true after the separation of north from south. Although each of the two main divisions retained a unity within itself, they had little in common with each other, and the north in particular was closely enmeshed in events in the north midlands. This separation of north from south was still to be apparent nearly two centuries later.[47] Geographically and economically it had always been on the cards, but, as long as the county had been dominated by the Warwick estates and earldom, the major political division, east from west, had reflected the composition of the Warwick lands rather than geographical and economic conditions. This radical reconstruction of Warwickshire regionalism is in itself testament to the destruction of the force that had once shaped the county's politics and society.

Indeed, the major theme to emerge from this survey is the retreat of noble influence from its once paramount place in politics in and around Warwickshire. Significantly, in this fifty-year period, the only magnate-centred network to attain a local leadership comparable to that exercised automatically by almost all the magnate affinities in the previous half-century was Hastings', which was to a large extent a branch of the royal affinity. There was nothing sudden about this development; it could not be, for the gentry learned only by trial and error that the old modes of conduct in local affairs were becoming inoperable. This remained a firmly hierarchical society; time and again the gentry showed their willingness to revert to their more traditional deference to the nobility, only to be let down by them. In the 1450s they were faced with the problem for the first time; the magnates were put under pressures which made them unable to fulfil their duties towards the shire. For lengthy periods they could not co-operate with each other, and therefore could not work with the overlapping political groups that were the normal fabric of local affairs. They could not give their 'contrees' the detailed attention which alone could secure a stable political following; consequently they could not guarantee the local peace, which, as far as the gentry were concerned, was really the main reason for their existence.

46 Above, ch. 15.

47 Above, p. 29.

Furthermore, the magnates' need for political and, in the end, military support grew ever more acute as they themselves were increasingly forced to take sides. This obliged them to demand that the gentry also declare either for or against them and to pursue divisive tactics as a shortcut to local predominance, in place of the patient nurturing of trust for which they now had too little time. Buckingham's and Warwick's handling of the Mountford affair is symptomatic of the new style of magnate politics.

For the vast majority of the gentry these tactics could only be wholly unacceptable. They certainly shared with the nobility a belief that management of their affairs had to be rooted in co-operation. On the other hand, where the nobles might feel that, once uncertainty and division had been introduced at the highest level of government and politics, they had nothing to lose by ensuring that the divisions worked in their favour, the response of the gentry was very different. For both nobility and gentry, co-operation across factional divisions had been the norm; now that this was for much of the time impossible for the nobility, the gentry saw no reason to change habitual modes of conduct if they could avoid it. As they began to realise, there was no reason why national division should automatically be reflected at the local level, if they for once chose not to follow the noble lead. This was the obvious course for most of the gentry, for they stood to lose far more than the nobility in uncontainable internal conflict; it was *their* local networks, on which they relied for their landed security, that were being rent apart by the magnates, it was *their* property that was likely to suffer most from localised violence. If crown and nobility had decided to change the rules of politics, the gentry were by no means obliged to follow suit.[48]

In opting not to abandon the politics of consensus the gentry forced themselves to find new ways of doing things; normal methods used in abnormal times required radical readjustments. In this they had two great advantages: that the single most important virtue that their training and way of life imposed on them was adaptability, and that the nobility, as desperate suitors for their assistance, could more easily be ignored. They began to learn how to adapt in the 1450s; thereafter, although still for the most part prepared to submit themselves to noble leadership again, they already had an alternative mode of conduct if the nobility should fail them again. If after 1461 there was never again a national political crisis on the scale of that of the 1450s, there was still most of the time sufficient uncertainty, punctuated with rapid changes of direction, for the nobility to continue to find it hard to fulfil their traditional role in the localities. And, as always, some of the nobility were less well-equipped to do so than others. But now, in contrast to former times – the 1440s, for example – if the nobility wavered, the gentry could look after themselves, and a magnate who failed lost control of his 'contree' not to another magnate

[48] Above, pp. 478–86.

but to the gentry he should have been leading. Once the gentry had made that psychological shift from automatic deference towards noble leadership, their combined landed power, easily outweighing that of the nobility, made it more than possible for them to direct their own affairs.

Until the 1470s there is no evidence that the monarchy was doing anything to exploit this fact, but thereafter it becomes clear that Edward IV and his successors were more than ready to intervene in Warwickshire politics. This had great advantages for them; like all rulers in the premodern world, they were obliged to rely on local force for the subvention of their rule, but under these conditions they could use both nobility and gentry much more on their own terms. The nobility were vulnerable because they could no longer count on local support if the king turned against them, the gentry because, however great they became in local terms, individually they could be readily cut down to size, as Simon Mountford was eventually to be. But the emergence of people like Mountford, as focal points of neighbourhood groupings and as brokers across the county, is itself symptomatic of a fundamental change in local power structures.

Like Mountford, they might owe their attractiveness chiefly to the size of their estates, or, like John Hugford or Thomas Littleton, it might have more to do with their noble or governmental connections, or, in the case of William Catesby II, it could be due to a combination of both. But whatever the source of the power of these individual members of the gentry, the result was the same, in bringing them a connection that owed little or nothing to the magnate affinities. Where men like this had previously been the conduits through whom the influence of the local nobility had flowed down to the meanest of the gentry, they were now much more their own men. This was true even of those like Hugford or William Catesby II who were cogs in the royal affinity that had subsumed the leadership of the earl of Warwick, and whose greatness was in large measure due to their links with a higher authority. Catesby made his independence abundantly plain when he chose to take his part of Hastings' political machine over to Richard of Gloucester in 1483.

The full implications of these conclusions, in relation both to the rest of the country and to longer-term political developments, will be considered in the concluding chapter, but it should be stressed that this was not a sudden or an immediately decisive process. Any magnate who was still prepared to lead was likely quite literally to acquire a following, and royal leadership in Warwickshire was in itself in large part based on the tenurial and political inheritance of the earls of Warwick. The real change in this period was that the gentry had learned to manage without such guidance. The dominance of the crown in the county was itself only possible because the gentry were now experienced enough in the independent management of their own affairs to be able to accommodate the rather loose direction which was all that any ruler, however dirigiste, could offer them amidst all his other responsibilities. The umbilical cord that had made the gentry look first to the magnates for direction had been cut, in the face of a crisis that showed them that accepting that the nobility would dictate the terms of local politics worked only as long as these were also the terms of the gentry. Even allowing for the inferior quality of rule offered by Henry VI, there is a sharp contrast between the early 1440s, when, with the Warwick lands almost intact and effectively under the supervision of the crown, the county became a battle-ground for noble factions, and the period from 1478, when, even at times of acute local division, the nobility had little influence over events.

The gentry may have emerged from the crisis with their power enhanced but this period should by no means be seen as an easy one for them. Most of the normal mechanisms for maintaining local stability were found to be wanting. That meant for a start that the potentially disturbing elements – the ambitious, the disappointed and the criminal – were much less amenable to restraint. John Herthill was a frustrated man whose dissatisfaction led him to murder. The recklessly unbridled careers of Robert Ardern, John Cokayn III and Thomas Malory have already been discussed. A more unstable society found it harder either to curb or to reintegrate them, with deleterious effects for both the criminals themselves and their victims.[49] For the ambitious – Thomas Cokesey, the 'ruffelar', Simon Mountford, Henry Willoughby, for instance – the circumstances were remarkably propitious. First, they could call on the warring nobility to aid their cause and, as in the 1440s, the lords were not in a position to turn down such a request. Then, increasingly, they found that there was no one, apart eventually from the king, with the authority to put a stop to their activities.

But for those on the receiving end of their attentions life was less pleasant. In earlier years management by the local magnates, even at its most divisive, as in the late 1440s, had generally succeeded in protecting the gentry against the worst consequences of their own intense competitiveness. From 1450 that security was wanting. Beyond injury and local destabilisation, the lack of security threatened a whole way of life – one which relied on planning ahead and keeping aggression in equilibrium with the desperate necessity of mutual tolerance and co-operation. In these circumstances of acute uncertainty about the future at both local and national levels, the flexibility and adaptability that we have seen to be the hallmark of all successful gentry families had to be exercised as perhaps never before. It was this instinct for manoeuvring in the interests of self-preservation that helped break down the magnate leadership of

[49] Above, pp. 115–16, 432–3, 452–3, 459, 477; Carpenter 1980b: *passim*; also literature cited there. An important article published since then is Field 1981–2. I hope shortly to re-examine the Malory situation in the light of this and other recent work; although Field rightly points out that I missed a reference that could put a different gloss on Malory's position in the 1460s (Field 1981–2: pp. 452–3 n. 3; Nichols 1795–1811: IV, i, pp. 368–9), the situation with regard both to Malory and to contemporary politics bears further examination.

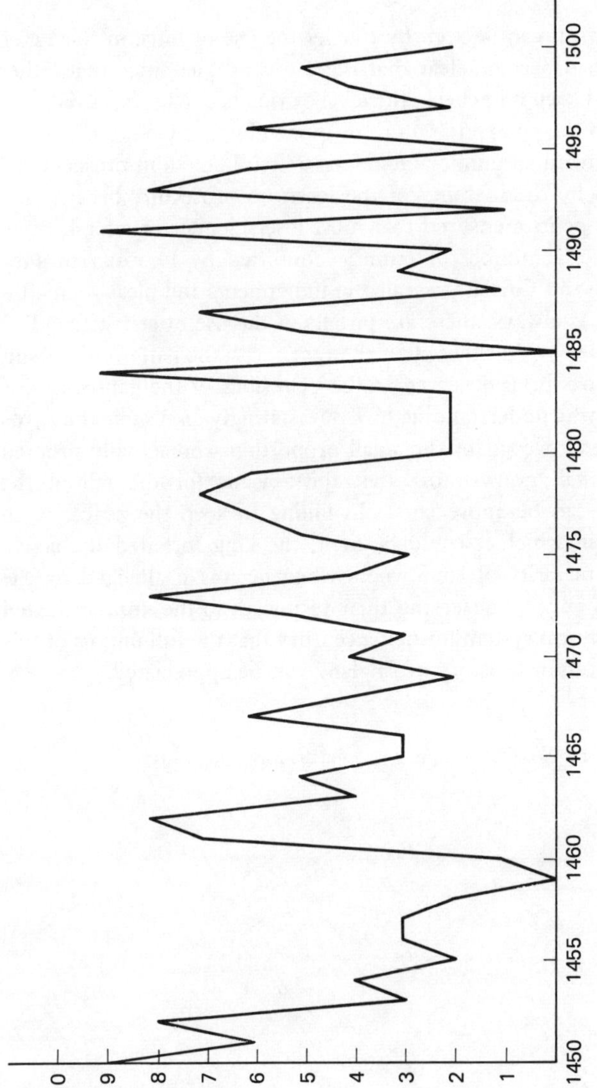

Figure 13 Conflict in Warwickshire (drawn from King's Bench records) 1450–1500 (see important comments in appendix 4)

local networks. If the gentry coped, essentially by realising that their own instincts for finding ways of keeping the peace, developed over hundreds of years of neighbourly rubbing along together, had to take precedence over their equally instinctive deference to noble leadership, it was not an easy lesson to learn.

That they did learn it can be seen by tracing the use of force in the 1450s (figure 13); once it had become clear that there was no guarantee that either king or nobility could keep it in check, the level of violence fell substantially, to rise again only when the complete failure of monarchy in 1459–61 presented claimants of all sorts with an unmissable opportunity. The fall in prosecutions cannot be explained by the inability of the losers to prosecute, because the volatility of national politics ensured that most losers sooner or later became winners; for example, a number of crimes committed by Lancastrian supporters between 1459 and 1461 are revealed in indictments and pleas soon after the Yorkist victory. As always, there are pitfalls in the use of statistics culled from the judicial evidence[50] but these figures fit well with the pattern of pursuit of compromise that has been observed in the behaviour of the gentry at this time. It is indeed only by understanding how devastatingly disruptive the 1450s were to all landowners, except for the small proportion who actually profited from the governmental 'gravy-train', that the reasons for the fall of the Lancastrian dynasty can be appreciated. In failing to keep the peace, or to create a framework in which it could be kept, the king forfeited the active support of the vast majority of landowners when he was challenged by the House of York. It is only by observing their responses to the unprecedented strains put on the political system for half a century that the full import of this period for the constitutional history of England can be appreciated.

[50] But see similar evidence in Wright 1983: pp. 137–8 for the period from 1455.

17

CONCLUSIONS

In bringing into focus the main themes of this study, we shall attempt to answer some of the principal questions that have been asked along the way. The logical starting point is the nature of a gentry society in the fifteenth century. It seems clear that we must include in it all landowners with pretensions to gentility, however insignificant they might appear. Although there was an undeniable hierarchy among the gentry, the fact that local studies have tended to concentrate on the county elite has exaggerated the distance between these and the lesser local figures. Landowning society had several levels, each one acting as a connecting link between those above and below it. As ever, misunderstanding comes from the two-dimensional view: failing to appreciate that local leaders looked downwards for political support as well as upwards to the world of lord and king for protection. Although it was always the great who represented the shire in parliament, they *were* nominally the representatives of all its inhabitants, and, if they took notice of their own interests alone, they would be in trouble from men who, even if at a lower level, shared in their power and in their way of life.[1]

All the gentry were differentiated from those below them by their life-style and aspirations and above all by the fact of their lordship over men or, in the case of professionals without manorial lordship, their participation in the world of lordship. However limited their horizons, their access to political society brought them into a wider world than that of their inferiors.[2] Certainly, as at the boundaries of all social groups, the distinctions between the most meagre of the gentry and the greatest of the yeomen should not be too emphatically drawn, especially in the case of the small number of non-professional gentry

[1] Cam 1962a,b; Edwards 1970; Stone 1967: p. 28 for the role of middling gentry as links between greater and lesser in the seventeenth century. Given-Wilson suggests a two-tier system, of 'county' and 'parish' gentry (1987a: pp. 70–3), but it was evidently more complex than this.

[2] Laslett 1971: pp. 27–30. In seventeenth-century Warwickshire younger sons of minor gentry were not normally considered gentlemen (Hughes 1987: p. 35), but this was not the case in the fifteenth century.

who did not have lordship over men. And equally, all landowners, particularly those on the fringe of the yeomanry, would spend much of their lives in the company of substantial yeomen, not to mention their own peasant tenants. Nevertheless, anybody who thought he was a gentleman had proclaimed himself a member of the group defined primarily by the lordship that produced the force that was the fulcrum of government and politics. By about the 1420s, at the lowest levels that tended to mean anyone who called himself a gentleman. If he could convince his neighbours and his betters that he belonged there, then, whether he held office or not, and even if his overt authority went no further than keeping the king's peace amongst his own tenants, he was a part of the world that wielded political power.

Having defined the base of gentry society, can we decide on the boundary at the top? Here, there is a firm legal distinction finalised in the fifteenth century, but it is everywhere evident that gentry and nobility had a lot in common.[3] However, it is equally clear that there were real differences of scale in estates, income and political horizons, and points at which quantitative differences became qualitative ones. The nobility had greater resources when it came to fulfilling the wants common to all landowners, or to risking part of their estates in an advantageous match or a hazardous political enterprise. Their lands and responsibilities made them more aware of the condition of the country as a whole and conversely more complacent about crises of order in one or two of the regions where they had lands. When they looked upwards in the hierarchy of deference, it was straight to the king. Their greater wealth and the fact that their tenurial interests were rarely concentrated in one locality meant that they could afford to make mistakes – like Edward Grey of Groby's over-enthusiastic entry on Warwickshire politics in the 1440s – or contract obligations – such as the Beauchamp trust – that could ruin a gentry family.[4] On the other hand, they were so exposed that serious political errors, such as being on the wrong side in a national political crisis, which a gentry family might survive, could bring instant disaster.

In the world of political manoeuvres the gentry's position gave them paradoxically both more and less freedom than the nobility. Their freedom to choose their masters, albeit limited by geographical determinants, contrasted with the nobles' unavoidable obligation to serve the king. On the other hand, the tenurial and financial gulf between them and most of the nobility made the price of error that could lead to the loss of an estate considerably higher. Moreover, while the nobles, despite making use of the law-courts, would normally look to the king to intervene personally in a major internecine feud, the gentry relied on a more complex interweaving of public and private

3 McFarlane 1973: pp. 274–5, but see also pp. 6–8; Powell and Wallis 1968: pp. 284–5, 463–5; Wormald 1986b: pp. 181–2. Note the caveat in Bernard 1985: p. 176. On similarities in the next century, see MacCaffrey 1965: p. 52.

4 Above, pp. 156, 214, 256–7; Given-Wilson 1987a: p. 66.

processes. In this the king's law, the king himself, the magnates and their own peers and neighbours all played a part. We have seen that some of the distinctions between the gentry and the nobility, notably in the matter of land acquisition, may have contributed to a distinct sense of family and lineage; it was quite possible for other differences of degree to become differences of kind. The time might come when these differences could bring a real parting of the ways.

Nevertheless, with respect to their landed position, their status and the demands on their pockets, the needs of the gentry were essentially the same as those of the nobility. Both groups also had in common the problem of balancing these often contradictory obligations against each other. Where they differed was again in the scale of the problem. The gentry's smaller incomes to cope with similar demands required, however, that they pay much closer attention to the details of all aspects of their daily lives, from estate management to provision for their souls. The constraints on both their public and their private lives meant that the greatest virtue that a member of the gentry could have was adaptability combined with careful and unwavering concern for minutiae. This is not to deny that a careless magnate could find himself in trouble,[5] but, except in times of acute national political crisis, the penalties for magnate failure were less immediate and severe. This was only fitting, for magnates had to be free to give at least some of their attention to the king's business – counsel, war, diplomacy – which might take them away from their estates for extended periods of time. This is another aspect of those differences that could part nobility and gentry under circumstances like those of the 1450s.

What is remarkable about most of the Warwickshire gentry families is that they rose so well to the demands made on them throughout the century. The fact that those who failed, like Robert Ardern, John Cokayn III, Thomas Malory and Humphrey Stafford II, seem to have dealt inadequately with most aspects of the management of their affairs emphasises the way in which the strands that made up a gentry family's concerns were inextricably interlinked. Stafford is a particularly good example, for it was his reluctance to attend to detail, either in estate management or in building a secure localised power base, that first obliged him to revolt against Henry VII and then ensured he would be unable to raise the country around him against the king. Why, within these broad distinctions between the survivors and the failures, some were more successful than others is not always clear, except that personal ability was almost invariably the key. It seems evident that a family like the Verneys, experiencing a meteoric rise, might well sink back if it did not produce heirs equal to the founder of the family fortunes. But there seems no good reason for the Archers' failure throughout the century to hold office in Warwickshire. Perhaps they were content with the unofficial power their leadership of the

[5] Above, p. 257.

Tanworth area gave them; perhaps they were too often in trouble. Whatever the reason, their history shows how difficult it is, in the absence of revealing private documents, to be certain about the gentry's aspirations and achievements.[6]

The actual balance of power between gentry and nobility in the localities has been shown to be a complex matter. As long as the authority of the government was mediated by the financial and technological constraints common to all pre-modern rulers, accentuated by the peculiar conditions of late-medieval England, the greatest landed powers had to be the leaders of local society. But how, and how firmly, that leadership manifested itself would depend on the variables of magnate ability, tenurial structure and the balance of forces within the body politic. In weighing the horizontal against the vertical in relationships among the gentry, we are not contrasting complete noble control with complete gentry freedom, but dealing with a continuum of change.[7] In the first half of the fifteenth century noble leadership was strong in most parts of Warwickshire. Noble authority was lent added force by the fact that, in the absence of gentry who stood not far behind the minor nobility, there was such a gulf in the county between peers and lesser landowners.[8] Where it was weak, as in the Tanworth region and at times in the east of the county, this tended to be due to absence of interest on the part of the nobility. When interest asserted itself, noble direction of local networks and local politics became unequivocal. But this did not mean that horizontal linkages were not strong, especially among the middling and lesser gentry, or capable of helping to direct the course of local affairs; they could, for example, provide a ready-made network for noble ambitions in north and east Warwickshire or a stable local environment in the face of divisive magnate politics.

Furthermore, however dominant the magnate direction in Warwickshire, the fragmentation of the county made it almost impossible for a single nobleman to control it and hence to have the huge political advantage of monopoly of the local administration. Because of the local society's susceptibility to leadership from above, it was not difficult for someone with enough tenurial power, like Sudeley, Beauchamp of Powick or Grey, to break in, by taking over existing networks or even, as in the case of Edmund Ferrers of Chartley and Richard Beauchamp in north Warwickshire, helping to create new ones. Entry could be

[6] For the Verneys, see above, p. 151. John Archer I was M.P. for two boroughs in the 1450s (clearly the result of the Exeter connection), and Richard was sheriff of Shropshire in 1430 and of Staffordshire in 1441. This was before the feud with the Porters really blew up, and it could be this and the family's subsequent behaviour that led to their falling out of the *cursus honorum* (*Wedgwood: Biographies*, p. 18; *Lists and Indexes*, 9, pp. 118, 127; above, pp. 425–6).

[7] Cf. Saul 1981: pp. 97–105; Maddicott 1978a,b, 1981; Virgoe 1981: p. 83. It might be suggested that Wright 1983 and Walker 1986 assume too readily that the historian must opt *either* for an independent gentry *or* for a wholly subservient one, but then so does the work against which they are arguing, Carpenter, M.C. 1976.

[8] Above, p. 65; Saul 1986: pp. 63–4, 72.

had with particular ease at times of weak or absent lordship. It was progressing beyond the lordship of a segment of the county that presented the real problems. It has been argued here that this could really only be achieved by someone who started with a west Warwickshire-Worcestershire-Gloucestershire power base, for this would guarantee the allegiance of the dominant west midland families, although lands in north Warwickshire would also be necessary. Both the men who achieved complete mastery, Richard Beauchamp and Edward IV, had these advantages, even though Edward's supremacy over all the nobility meant he had an easier time than Beauchamp in managing his coalition partners. It was coalitions that were the key to the rule of the county, which was why, without firm royal and noble leadership, it could easily become a focus for internecine feuding.

If Beauchamp and Edward were both equally successful in their handling of Warwickshire, there are contrasts in the way that they recruited among the gentry that tell us a lot about the management of affinities. While both made sure of the allegiance of most of the leading local figures, the king, from his more authoritative position, had less need either to secure the services of all such men – he could for example afford to neglect Robert Throgmorton – or to involve himself in the details of the gentry's lives. Neither did he have the time for this, so he was content to allow people like Simon Mountford and John Hugford to act as intermediaries between local networks and himself. If leading gentry members of successful affinities had always played a role of this sort,[9] particularly as links between minor gentry and the lord, magnate politics demanded that the lord concern himself more directly with the business of the county. He was after all, unlike the king, competing on equal terms with his peers for local dominance. Whether the king could in fact exercise authority through such a loosely organised affinity before the changes of the middle of the century[10] is a question that can only be answered from another county, as the royal estate in Warwickshire did not really exist until the Warwick lands came to the crown in 1478. What is certain is that a magnate could not. In the early 1440s Buckingham's success in extending his clientage among the greater gentry of Warwickshire and its penumbra did him little good because of his failure either to recruit lower down the social scale or to concern himself in the details of the life of the local gentry.[11] In the 1450s this policy was taken to extremes in a belief that securing the prospects of Edmund Mountford would bring the rest of Warwickshire over and it proved remarkably counter-productive. Interestingly, Simon Walker's work on John of Gaunt implies that a similar neglect to involve himself closely in local affairs (in this case due to his

[9] Above, pp. 335–6.
[10] Below, pp. 633–8.
[11] For more on this, see Carpenter, M.C. 1976: pp. 69–70, 106; Given-Wilson 1986: pp. 255–6.

special position as the king's uncle and the claimant to Castile) undermined Gaunt's efforts to rule his 'contrees'.[12]

The study of the gentry's way of life and of their dealings with the nobility is a precondition for an attempt to answer those larger questions about the mores and political ideology of landowners that were posed in the opening chapter.[13] The importance of the 'personal' interpretation of late-medieval politics is inescapable. Personal dealings and responsibility were constant, powerful motivators, encompassing even the making good of financial losses incurred in the course of public or private office.[14] The world of the gentry in the locality was a small one, where inability to get on with other participants would bring swift retribution. But, at the start of this study, it was suggested that, informing and growing out of these dealings of individual men and women, there must have been certain attitudes and beliefs which become apparent from a close examination of the aggregate of these individual lives. In a sense the first part of the study has focused on individual experiences and the second on collective ones: taken together, what can they tell us about landowners as a group?

The starting points have to be the family and the land. Much of this discussion has been couched in terms of families and of family ambitions. Yet the notion of family itself could be a very variable one.[15] On the whole, and in spite of all the latent conflict within the family, the wider kin acted as a reservoir of supportive relationships. Close collaterals might be regular associates, while more distant relatives, particularly kin by marriage, would tend to come into their own at times of crisis. Examples of this are Richard Verney and the Mountfords in the 1450s and some of the groups accused of violent crimes in the first years of Henry VII.[16] Since marriages were potentially so conducive to property disputes, it was unlikely that families would intermarry unless they had a great deal of faith in one another and therefore not at all unlikely that they would turn out to be political allies. The role of the kin was bound to be significant in politics, given the mutual reinforcement of marriage and affinity that is a constant all through the period. But it was when conventional political forces failed, as in the two periods cited, that it was most likely to come into its own, as one of the most

[12] Walker 1986: chs. 4 and 5. Neither Walker, nor Morgan in his reference to the Yorkist affinity (1987: p. 56), seems quite to realise how unusual affinities of this type were; below, p. 631 for comments on this; also, their lords were possessed of lands so widespread that the creation and nurturing of a strong localised following along the lines of that of an ordinary magnate was no easy matter. Arguably, because their power owed less to local authority, it was not even necessary. For Gaunt, see Pugh 1972: pp. 107–8.

[13] Also above, p. 359.

[14] Above, p. 42. Davies, C.S.L. 1977: p. 46 points out that the kingdom was still in some sense seen to be the personal property of the king.

[15] Above, pp. 260–1.

[16] Above, pp. 467, 564–7, 580; cf. Mertes 1988: pp. 164–5. Also the group of thirteen Cheshiremen, related by natural and affinal ties, who may have fought together at Blore Heath (Gillespie 1987: pp. 80–1).

cogent of the horizontal links that enabled the gentry to sustain themselves when thrown back on their own devices by nobility or crown.

In the context of political morality, however, the influence of the immediate family was more profound. There is no doubt that the incumbent of the moment was held to have a responsibility to his close relatives and to the past and future of his line. There can be equally little question that where these interests clashed the lineage took precedence over the living family, even if it meant self-deprivation for a while to fulfil the will of the last owner. This was an imperative that could only be disregarded with propriety if the incumbent was not a direct male heir, or if the wishes of his deceased father or older brother threatened the health of the lineage.[17] One does not want to overdo the concept of stewardship and make the mistake of contrasting a 'medieval' sense of temporary ownership with a 'modern' one of absolute right, but its moral force among medieval landowners is inescapable.[18]

The real responsibility of the living family lay indeed in its duty to the land that was the basis of the family's wealth, and, even more important, the source of the family's political power. To an overwhelming degree, this governed the gentry's expectations of the world, both public and private, beyond the immediate family. Their desperate need for stability, a characteristic common to all privileged classes, applies particularly strongly to landowners, whose livelihood could so easily be destroyed. This was especially so in a period when they themselves had such ready access to the forces of destruction, and perhaps, for the reasons that have been given, was even more characteristic of the gentry of this time than of the nobility. Also required was some certainty about the future; an environment which allowed them to think carefully ahead about their property.

Stability was to a large extent guaranteed by the interlocking of networks and affinities, the groupings within which they set about dealing with their lands. This was an ever-present defence against the formation of real faction and an incitement to the settlement of local conflict. The analysis of political and social relationships has done no more than scratch the surface of a complex set of overlapping relationships about which we still know very little. It is clear that, for political structures and groupings at all levels at this time, 'faction' is a very inadequate term. Politics were highly fluid; in choosing their allegiances, politicians had a spectrum of options within a more permanent framework delineated by their more long-standing friendships. That framework itself was by no means unalterably fixed, for it could bend, break or be rebuilt as circumstances changed. Relationships that had become moribund or had never been used, often those based on estates in other counties that had long been left to their own devices, could be activated at need. When the nobility did this, the

[17] Above, pp. 224–5.

[18] Stone 1979: p. 71; above, p. 245 n. 7.

gentry in the areas in question could be drawn for the first time into active service on a particular magnate's behalf.[19] Normal political life had therefore to include both great loyalty and great flexibility, for without either of these order and stability were unrealisable.

More can be learned about the ground rules of political behaviour by looking at the abnormal, the fortunes of the 'criminal gentry'. These men, notable for their consistent brushes with the law, can often be seen losing their friends as their conduct and position deteriorate. Allowing for the dangers of an argument from silence, especially when deeds survive so haphazardly, there can be little doubt that this was what happened to men like Thomas Malory, Robert Ardern and John Cokayn III, all of whom started out from positions of privilege, moving in the most respectable local circles. A particularly fruitful approach is to compare their behaviour with that of their equals who remained within the local 'establishment'. It is apparent that it was not so much the crimes they committed – the Harecourts and Staffords for instance murdered while contriving to remain respectable – as the disproportion of ends and means in their acts. Late-medieval landowners were undoubtedly readier to use and to countenance violence than the members of political societies in the modern developed world, but these men were too violent too often, in the pursuit of ends that were dubious or not worth the use of this ultimate sanction, for that was what violence was. It was therefore to be used only as a last resort, but only if there was no alternative and if an immediate process of damage limitation could be set in motion. It followed that those who were best placed to use it for carefully-calculated ends were the men with the best access to the local powers and that they were thus the least likely to need it. Consequently, open force was not employed in the normal course of gentry affairs as frequently as one might suppose.[20]

Equally, as the Mountford case demonstrates to perfection, there was an unspoken but well understood boundary to the use of personal influence within the law. Although it may look to us as if no holds were barred in the normal interplay of law and private processes, it can be seen from this case that Edmund Mountford's side finally overstepped the limits and paid the penalty, which was the denial to Edmund of local acceptance of his forcibly-assumed position. Again, what is noteworthy here is not so much what Edmund and his allies did – compare the dealings over Birmingham manor under Richard Beauchamp – as the way in which it was done and perhaps above all the circumstances, with the use of the increasingly unpopular power of the court.[21]

19 Above, pp. 321, 325–7; cf. Davies, C.S.L. 1977: p. 54.

20 Also the remarks in Maddern 1985: *passim*, and, for another late-medieval 'criminal', see Virgoe 1972–3.

21 Carpenter 1983: pp. 219–25 (and the discussion there of the case's significance in dealing with contemporary opinion on law, justice and disorder); also contemporary horror at the murder of Nicholas Radford and its aftermath (Cherry 1981b: p. 136), and the clear and apparently

As in evaluating attitudes to violence, in breaking the code of attitudes to private pressure on public processes, the historian, like the gentry he is studying, has to judge each case on its merits before attempting to generalise. What can certainly be said is that there *were* such unwritten codes of behaviour (it would indeed have been very strange had there not been) and that they undoubtedly had an effect in limiting upheavals in local society.

Much of this unwritten law can be summed up in the idea of 'reason'. This is a word whose range of meanings would be well worth exploring; they included equity – both in the technical legal sense and in the oft-repeated concept of doing unto others as you yourself would be done by – justice, conscience and consistency.[22] In general it was only the criminal or the men with their way to make who, oblivious of such rules, deliberately set out to stir things up by litigation or more direct methods. This did not mean that the rest of the gentry lived quiet lives, as Richmond has suggested was the case with John Hopton, for there were too many possibilities for litigation in the landed society, too many rights to be defended.[23] No land owner worth the name could afford to neglect challenges to these, nor, through failing to make the right friends, could he risk putting himself in a position where he was known to be easy game.[24]

The forces for instability have been dealt with at some length in this study: criminal gentry; rising professionals; landed rights, a source of contention even in the daily routine of agriculture, aggravated by complex tenurial structures; changes in the composition of local networks due to deaths or minorities; inheritance, wills and other aspects of internecine family feuding; competition for a pre-eminent place in politics and society. The professionals, it is clear, were one of the most frequent causes of conflict, not least because the estates they required to seal their rise into or within landed society were so hard to come by. To that extent the Pastons, of untypical of the gentry as a whole, represent an important element in local society in this period, especially of those areas like East Anglia or the Tanworth region of the Warwickshire Arden

approving connection made by Knighton between the kidnapping by the Folvilles of justice Willoughby and his partiality as a justice (Stones 1957: p. 134). It is the nature of the boundary that renders Barbara Hanawalt's comparison with white-collar crime inapposite (Hanawalt 1975), for, where the latter is committed in the full knowledge that it is illegal, if socially acceptable, many of the processes used in conflict and litigation (above, pp. 282–6, 354–8) were not in fact regarded as such. See also the illuminating observations on this subject in Noonan 1984: p. 266, and Wormald 1985: pp. 115–16.

22 Carpenter 1983: pp. 211–13, 236–7; George Ashby, *Poems*, pp. 34–5; *St. German's Doctor and Student*, pp. 97–119; Ives 1983a: pp. 163–4, 397–8. For one of innumerable instances of the morality of reciprocity, see *Paston Letters,* II, pp. 109–110.

23 Richmond 1981: esp. pp. 256–8; but note the doubts cast on Hopton's quietism in Carpenter 1982: pp. 730–1. Another example of a 'stirrer-up' with his way to make is Sir John Fastolf (McFarlane 1981c; Lewis 1958: both showing that it could be counter-productive).

24 Carpenter 1983: pp. 225–6.

which produced numbers of families of this type.[25] But, even if the established families were generally more reluctant to make trouble deliberately, it is evident that, on the face of it, the family's obligation to place the family's needs above all other considerations could only lead to unmitigated strife.

That, however, was only part of the story. The other part was that intense local feuding meant destruction of property and in the end too much uncertainty for any of the normal business of the gentry to be carried on, for all of it was presaged on mutual trust. In this respect, the Tanworth region is an admirable microcosm of the gentry world: the greater the proximity and the competition, the greater the possibility of conflict and consequently the more urgent the need to find ways of living in peace. The networks within which the business of the gentry was carried out, complex and malleable as they were, offered the context for the achievement of harmony.[26] If the values of landowning society were based on mutual emulation and the pursuit of worship, they had, even more firmly, to be posited on neighbourly good relations. We come therefore to the issue of individualism versus collectivity. Only a small number of misfits failed to understand that these were not mutually exclusive categories. It was not a question, either for them or for us, of setting altruism against self-interest, since it was self-evidently in everyone's interest to establish a means of mutual forbearance. This it was that lay behind the search for local consensus and the avoidance of competition in parliamentary elections that has been observed in both this and the sixteenth century.[27] This was also why no conflict could ever be settled for good by a legal verdict, unless the losing side was prepared to accept that decision, and why most disputes were best terminated by arbitration or some other kind of informal settlement.[28]

If consensus was as important as personal interests, what mattered was drawing the line between the single-minded pursuit of individual ambitions and the maintenance of collective security; there had to come a time for everyone when these did become incompatible ends. It was then that the good sense of the gentry asserted itself in the realisation that the law of diminishing returns had set in. That was the whole point of these unwritten rules about political behaviour, for they were the basis on which local societies made their collective decisions on whether it was time to call a halt to conflict. But it was

[25] Above, pp. 77, 146–7; for East Anglian lawyers, *Paston Letters* (either edn), *passim* and Richmond 1981: p. 181.

[26] Cf. Wright 1983: pp. 123, 135–6. In countries where the government was weak, private processes were able to do the job largely on their own (e.g. Brown, J.M., 1977a; Wormald 1980a, 1986a,b).

[27] Payling 1987c: pp. 176–7; Kishlansky 1986: esp. ch. 3; also MacCulloch 1986: p. 108 on dispute settlement in the sixteenth century; Palmer 1984 on the dangers and consequences of prolonged litigation.

[28] Powell 1979: pp. 318–32, 1983a, 1984b; Baker ed., *Spelman*, II, pp. 91–2; above, section II, *passim*.

therefore only when there was general confidence in the ability of local society to absorb tension and conflict that individual ends could be pursued right up to the point of what might be termed mutually assured destruction. Thus, the competitiveness of the gentry could only really assert itself when control from above was at its strongest. This is one aspect of the paradox that the shires could best manage their own affairs with the degree of independence that they all craved if they were absolutely confident of the crown's determination and ability to step in and knock heads together if things got out of hand.[29] We have seen again and again that, once belief in the continuation of local stability had been destroyed, all incentives to mitigate personal ambition for the sake of the general good disappeared.

In different ways these imperatives had also to apply to the nobility as much as to the gentry; they needed to believe in the king to be able to play their part in the management of the shires. Equally, both in the direction of the shires and in their dealings with each other, they had to balance individualism against the general good. Moreover, nobility, as well as gentry, had to observe the niceties of political behaviour. They might, as part of the greater privilege that went with their greater responsibilities, be permitted a freer hand in the excercise of force; it is evident that violence was an accepted means of indicating authority, that there was indeed a hierarchy of violence that reflected the hierarchy of land and status.[30] Nevertheless, they too were constrained from disproportionate and unnecessary resort to arms. In fifteenth-century Warwickshire they rarely involved themselves directly in this, and those, like Edward Grey and Henry Beauchamp in the 1440s, who seemed to be flinging their weight around too freely, tended to find it counter-productive. These inescapable facts of life – unwritten rules concerning the use of the law and of force, the conduct of disputes and individual and collective needs – must add up to a political morality. It was a morality common to all landowners and it had its basis in the necessities of their everyday lives. There is no question here of 'whitewashing' either nobility or gentry, merely of asking more complex questions about their motivation and achievements than has hitherto been the norm. Most particularly, to ask how they measured up by the standards of their day, having tried to deduce those standards from observed behaviour and its consequences.

An illustration may be offered here, in the obvious contrast between two of the main protagonists of this story, the two earls of Warwick, Richard Beauchamp and Richard Neville. Richard Beauchamp had an almost total understanding if his job, while Richard Neville was much less competent. Their contrasting abilities have been a major feature of a large part of this work and account for much of the contrast in Warwickshire in the early and middle years of the century. Beauchamp, because he understood the rules so well, was

[29] Maddicott 1984; Harriss ed. 1985; Jones, W.R. 1974; Carpenter 1983.
[30] Maddern 1985: ch. 2; Gray ed., *Late Medieval Verse and Prose*, pp. 105–6.

able to get almost everything he wanted in the shires; when he faltered in national affairs, as over the Norfolk precedence issue, it was perhaps because under Henry VI, even in the minority, the rules were beginning to be bent in ways which he found difficult to cope with.[31] Why Neville ultimately broke all the rules of magnate politics is another question. On the face of it he does seem to have been a classically 'greedy' nobleman, his huge grants from Edward IV insufficient to gratify his appetite. But he might be looked at another way, as one who, like the Percies under Henry IV, in climbing so high had put himself in an impossible position, from which he could only fall. His only option was to turn the king into a complete puppet, but this was not only unacceptable to Neville's peers but not much use to Neville himself in the long run, since he, like all the others, needed an effective king to keep the kingdom stable and his own interests inviolate.

Control of the ruler was really an unmixed blessing only to nobles like Somerset, who had little land and was heavily dependent on crown grants, especially after the loss of his French estates, or Suffolk, whose landed base was substantial but neither massive nor too far from the royal residences at Westminster and in the Thames valley. Suffolk's estates may have suffered at times from the disorder under Henry VI but his grants and control of the judicial processes must have more than made up for this.[32] For Neville, whose lands were enormous, widespread, a long way from normal royal itinerations in many cases and, worst of all, horribly exposed to Scots raids, a puppet king, unable to keep order and in need of constant supervision, was really more of a liability than an advantage. If we add to this the fact that, as this study has shown, he was finding at least part of his vast domain beyond his control, we might surmise that in 1469 he was panicking in the face of pressures with which he could no longer cope. He seems to have suffered from an unfortunate combination of charisma, which beguiled the world – and perhaps the man himself – into thinking that nothing was beyond him, and abilities which in no way measured up to these expectations. That verdict would not exonerate him from an unfavourable judgement – above all, that charismatic personality or not, he put his own needs of the moment above the needs of the kingdom as a whole – but it would be a different sort of judgement, taking due account of the expectations of his own contemporaries and assuming that most human beings are impelled by more complex motives than plain greed.[33]

31 I must thank Dr Sinclair for an interesting conversation on this; from our different approaches, we both seem to have come to similar conclusions about him.

32 Jones 1982: pp. 17–18; Johnson 1988: p. 157; Virgoe 1980; for the Percies, see Bean, 1959.

33 Cf. Ross 1974: pp. 70–1. For Warwick's career, see Kendall 1957, which is full, if fanciful; on his charisma, see Halle, *Union of Lancastre and York*, 'Henry VI', fo. 186, 'Edward IV', fos. 16, 19, 29; *Historical Collections of a London Citizen*, p. 220–1; *Historie of the Arrivall*, p. 21; *V.C.H.*, v, p. 175; Gransden 1982: pp. 292–3; Johnson 1988: p. 195; *Paston Letters*, II, p. 210; above, pp. 514–15. Warwick may also have felt that his estates were at risk if he lost influence with the king (Hicks 1979b: pp. 117–18).

The same considerations could be applied to other major actors on the late-medieval political scene. A prime example of someone who in the end put his personal quarrel with the king and his personal ambitions above the requirements of the rest of political society is Thomas of Lancaster under Edward II, and it is worth noting that he was abandoned by most of his peers as a result.[34] And that was why Richard of York had to stress that all he aimed to do was to reform the body politic, for, had he been perceived as a would-be governmental dictator or, even worse, a pretender to the throne, he would immediately have placed himself in the same category as Thomas or indeed as the court favourites whom he was trying to dispose of. Again, neither 'altruism' nor 'self-interest' are apposite words here: it was not in York's interest to be seen in an unfavourable light (as he found out in 1460), while it was very much in his interests and in those of the rest of landowning society for the body politic to be amended and confidence in the crown to be restored.[35]

It may be objected that this interpretation of late-medieval land owning motives and ideologies, while taking issue with the present very materialistic interpretation, is itself too materialist, in that it argues that their roots lay in the preservation of the estate. But this is not necessarily so. First, taken in its most limited sense, such materialism can readily lead to notions that put the greater above the individual good, at least for the privileged classes, as in the issues of individualism and collectivity that have just been discussed. Secondly, in the middle ages it had a less limited and material form in the idea of stewardship. The incumbent of the moment might well be obliged to sacrifice his present wealth and power to the souls of his predecessors, and his marital choices, his preferences among his children, and his inclinations in general, to the health of the estate and the lineage, in the present and the future. Thirdly, there were all the other virtues, particularly loyalty, that were part and parcel of the landowning mentality, which mostly helped keep property intact but, taken to extremes, could destroy it.[36] There were levels of motivation, the key to their differentiation being the weight given to individual ambitions and desires. At one level, there were those men, loosely dubbed the 'criminal gentry' here, for whom the pursuit of personal needs outweighed all other considerations, even at times the stability which protected their own lands. Then there were the vast majority, for whom material ends and political morality meshed. These people, seeing well beyond their material needs of the moment, would be aware of the sacrifices that might have to be made of their immediate interests for the sake of the lineage or of local security. Finally there were those for whom loyalty to a

34 Maddicott 1970: *passim.*

35 On York's public career, Johnson 1988 (see e.g. pp. 85, 191–2) and Griffiths 1981: chs. 22–5; John Watts is approaching his career along these lines, in his Cambridge B.A. dissertation and in his Cambridge Ph.D. thesis, now completed.

36 Keen 1984: pp. 11, 81, 185; Hoccleve, 'Regiment', p. 87 ll.2,404–5. Also James 1986c: pp. 325–6, 361–2 on the relationship of lordship, friendship and politics to morality.

lord or a cause, or to the memory of a husband's over-generous religious dispositions, overrode all other considerations: these included Hastings, who was lucky (until 1483) and the Hungerfords, who were not.[37]

This examination of political beliefs and motivations can be no more than a preliminary look at an enormous and almost unexplored problem, and more penetrating inquiry will require the development of a new and more sophisticated vocabulary.[38] But this initial discussion should enable us to take further the exploration of the constitution, the framework within which those beliefs operated, which was sketched in at the start of the political narrative.[39] Perhaps the most important thing to emphasise is that the whole system depended on the co-operation of king and nobility. Since the work of McFarlane it should be unnecessary to make this point. It should now be equally unnecessary to make the related point that this was not a society where it was assumed that 'the king's peace really was the norm and that justice emanated from the centre to the localities'. But to alter the perspective in which this governmental system, so deceptively like our own, is viewed, has not proved easy: rulers are still regularly praised for taking a stick to the nobility or blamed for failing to do so, patted on the back for initiating stringent enquiries in the localities or condemned for failing to so so. Once the necessary adjustment of vision has been made it becomes apparent that what looks like leniency might sometimes, but not invariably, be good sense, what seems to be forceful intervention could on occasion be foolhardy stirring up of trouble.[40]

We have seen that virtually all landowners had a vested interest in the perpetuating of internal peace and that the dual chain of command, formal and informal, from king to locality could work effectively only if every link in it had confidence in the others. If each element in the complex mixture of public authority and private might, that is king, nobility and gentry, did its job properly, and if each individual retained a proper respect for the rights of others, the rights and interests of all the members of the governing classes could be protected. But it is evident that the king had to be the nodal point of both the public and the private threads whose interplay made government at all levels possible. The key element in enabling public and private, individual and group to function co-operatively was direction from above and, in the last resort, only the king could give this. That was why a non-king like Henry VI was such a complete disaster; the magnates might well contribute to the mayhem that ensued, but it was the king who undermined the confidence of both nobility and gentry and hence of the shires.

37 Hicks 1985a, 1986a,b.

38 But attempts at exploration are already underway, notably in Powell's important study of Henry V's reign, Powell 1989.

39 Above, pp. 347–60.

40 Quotation from Clanchy 1974: p. 75. It is Clanchy who has written most forcibly on this subject: for his work and others', see above, p. 283 n. 4.

While this placed a great deal of responsibility on the king, it is arguable that ruling in a fairly passive mode was not that difficult. Kings, unlike the nobility, did not normally have to compete for the loyalty of their subjects, for it was unthinkingly theirs unless they did something to forfeit it. As long as he adhered to the theoretical imperatives to take counsel and provide peace and justice and respected the rules of political conduct that have been discussed here, particularly the sanctity of landed property, the king's rule would be acceptable, even if 'peace' and 'justice' consisted of little more than leaving the nobility to get on with the job. Ruling more actively was more difficult and required more careful thought about how far the unspoken limits could be stretched or breached. Since the nobility, who did not have the automatic obedience of their inferiors, had perforce to be more aggressive about their handling of their 'contrees', they would have to exercise the same discretion as the more interventionist rulers.

First a balance had to be struck between freedom and security. Ultimately all but the wildest of the gentry would have agreed that it was the second of these that mattered more, but it was necessary that the localities be run in a way that avoided too much loss of freedom and the sacrifice of too many legitimate-seeming aspirations. Kings, in particular, got the best out of their nobles by carefully weighing accommodation against discipline, but the same rules applied to the nobility in their dealings with the gentry. There was a fine line between laissez-faire and interventionism in the ruling of the shires, and we shall see that it may well have been redrawn during the course of the century, but to rule well, as Richard Beauchamp, Henry V and Edward IV did, was to tread that line successfully. It was particularly urgent not to allow a large number of locally important people to be alienated either by excessive interference or by excessive negligence from either the crown or the ruling magnate. This is what happened in Staffordshire and Shropshire under Henry IV, in Warwickshire in the early 1440s under the impact of Buckingham and Grey and in the late 1450s, under Buckingham and the locally resident court, and over much of the north midlands under Henry VII. The effect was always to make a region at best unco-operative and at worst ungovernable.[41] By contrast, Richard Beauchamp's rule ensured that its victims, like the Bermingham family, remained in the minority. If his obligation to look after his own meant that he could not be friends with everyone, he could at least avoid making too many enemies by the blatant over-use of favouritism. Secondly, and really inseparable from this balancing act, was the need of both king and nobility to listen to the people they were trying to govern. It is apparent that crown and magnates, even as diligent a nobleman as Beauchamp, were often

[41] Powell 1979: ch. 6, 1985: pp. 68–9; Harriss 1985c: pp. 45–50, 1985e, p. 202; see also Carpenter 1983: pp. 226–37.

ignorant of the daily trivia of gentry life.[42] Given their responsibilities in other parts of the realm, not to mention in other realms, it was unavoidable. This would apply to the crown even in areas where it was a major landowner. Crown and nobility, no less than the historian, had to be aware that there was a view from below as well as their own from above, although in some senses the nobility partook of both, for they were both the governers and the governed.

Mostly this governmental system, compounded of royal direction and landowning co-operation, worked. Even when things went wrong, as in the central three decades of the century, there were, as in any viable society, 'fail-safe devices' to prevent conflict causing social breakdown.[43] In the case of late-medieval England, these consisted of the habits of co-operation, the interlocked networks and affinities and the general acceptance of behavioural norms, all of which we have examined. So strong were these that even the reintegration of the earl of Wiltshire into a Yorkist-dominated polity could be contemplated in the 1450s and, at lower political levels, it was almost always possible to reabsorb disputants into the mainstream of local society, provided nothing had happened to create and perpetuate large-scale local division. There were undoubtedly different levels of stability. Warwickshire was at its most peaceful in times like the periods *c.* 1413–35 or 1478–83, when both local and national leadership were strong, or at least reasonably effective. When either or both of these was ineffective, as in the 1440s and 1450s, or in north Warwickshire in the first decade or so of Henry VII, disorder could get dangerously close to being out of hand. Moreover, there was always likely to be adjustment, leading to a certain amount of conflict, in periods like the 1440s and 1480s when numbers of families failed, either temporarily or permanently. If these coincided with weak or divisive rule from crown or nobility they could give rise to more serious upheaval. And yet, all through, the collective need for peace provided the motivational force for the maintenance of some sort of stability, while the complex overlapping networks provided the means. If this study has been correct in suggesting there was a fundamental change in the conduct of local affairs in the second half of the century, it occurred precisely because landowners were looking for ways of preserving their normal way of life under abnormal conditions.

In all this, patronage, except in the broadest terms of access to the favour that made the system work, was no more than a side issue to the central criterion of good government, which was the maintenance of internal stability and of the security of estates. A clear illustration of this is the fact that Richard Beauchamp, the only nobleman to win control over the whole of Warwickshire, did it with very little in the way of royal grants to pass on to his followers. There

[42] Above, pp. 93, 335–6; Lander 1969: p. 166 (a good instance of the government's astonishing ignorance of the country it was trying to rule).

[43] For refs. to literature, see above, p. 2 n. 7.

was indeed very little royal patronage to be had in Warwickshire except when the Warwick estates were temporarily or permanently in royal hands.[44] When patronage, in the sense of grants, became central to politics, as in the 1440s, it was a sign that it was being badly mismanaged. Even then it was no more than one aspect of the king's mishandling of the realm and not the most significant.[45] Similarly, it is a commonplace that, except in unusual affinities like John of Gaunt's or those of the northern marcher lords, which existed primarily for military purposes, the size of the tangible reward that the retainer could exact from his lord was not large.[46] Neither, for all the importance of 'labouring' and suing, should royal patronage conceived more generally as favour be used as an all-purpose tool for the analysis of politics. The essence of the political morality that has been elucidated from this study was the requirement of balancing personal intervention against the dictates of an even-handed justice.[47] Too much concentration on patronage in all its forms is another aspect of that reluctance to take discussion of political motivation beyond the immediate personal needs of the participants that has somewhat stunted the political history of the period.[48]

Much more significant to the success of the monarchy was whether the king could make use of the potential military power of his great subjects, for it was this that enabled him to rule, and if necessary to defeat his internal enemies. They would give him their support if they trusted him and their co-operation would enable the king to protect the interests of all his landed subjects. It was not money but landed security that would ensure the allegiance of political society. This fact of life was cogently summed up by a Florentine observer, when he said of Henry VII: 'The king is very powerful in money, but if fortune allowed some lord of the blood royal to rise and he had to take the field, he

[44] Carpenter 1980a: p. 519. There may have been more grants from the crown lands in France (for some of these, see above, pp. 120–1), but in Beauchamp's heyday, under Henry VI, not many of his west midland men were serving there. Similarly, the Courtenays ruled Devon in the late fourteenth century by dint of their large estates rather than patronage until misfortune overtook the family (Cherry 1979: esp. pp. 88–9). Note also the surprisingly small number of favours secured for his men by John of Gaunt (Walker 1986: pp. 94–100). See the apposite remarks in Virgoe 1981: pp. 83–4.

[45] Griffiths 1981: part II.

[46] Carpenter 1980a: pp. 519, 531; Pugh 1972: pp. 101–9; cf. Bean 1958: p. 91; Walker 1986: chs. 2 and 3; Holmes 1957: ch. 3. Also n. 12, above on the distinctiveness of Gaunt's affinity. However, the size of annuities does seem to have fallen between the fourteenth and fifteenth centuries (Walker 1986: pp. 107–8; Holmes 1957: ch. 3; Pugh 1972: p. 101). If this is true, it would be worth investigating why. Given-Wilson has recently suggested that retainers' financial rewards were larger than has been supposed, but nearly all his examples are taken from the fourteenth century and see comments in n. 51 below (1987a: pp. 155–6).

[47] Above, p. 358; for an excellent series of suing letters, see *Letters of Queen Margaret*.

[48] Similar remarks in Carpenter 1988.

would fare badly owing to his avarice; his people would abandon him.'[49] All of this must put a very different gloss on the importance of the king's finances. It might be necessary to avoid unacceptable financial demands (although it is clear that the definition of 'unacceptable' varied according to political circumstances and the ability of the king),[50] but a ruler could not hope to buy over landowners whom he had alienated by trampling over their deepest convictions about the sanctity of landed property and all that went with these. The fate of Richard III, who had done just this in disinheriting the heirs of a successful and respected king, despite all the blandishments he could offer to southern England, makes this very plain.[51]

The clear exception to the rule that royal patronage and favour were relatively unimportant in the late-medieval polity occurs in those parts of England that were dominated by the Duchy of Lancaster. The growing body of work on some of these areas is gradually revealing their peculiarities.[52] Even under John of Gaunt the sheer size of his lands, his close proximity to the throne and the impossibility of devoting adequate time to his local responsibilities, rendered the Lancaster affinity atypical.[53] After 1399, all these causes of abnormality were reinforced, with the addition that the Duchy was now run by the most powerful man in England, who had at his disposal a vast reservoir of patronage beyond the Duchy lands and offices and all the non-Duchy appointments to the local administration. It is not surprising therefore that in these areas the distribution of crown patronage should have been so important, for it was the easiest way that a king, with little time to spare to act as magnate but a lot of rewards to offer, could fulfil his duty in the localities as duke of Lancaster. The importance of crown patronage in these parts explains the meteoric rise of individual figures, often professionals, like William Babington of Nottinghamshire.[54] This, and the king's need for officials he could trust and to whom, as absentee lord, he could delegate extensive power, could account for the possible concentration of landed wealth and authority in the hands of a few that has been observed in Duchy counties.[55] All the same, even in and around

49 *Reign of Henry VII*, ed. Pollard, I, p. 135. Also *Boke of Noblesse*, p. 81, '. . . for it is saide that an empyre of roiaume is bettir without tresoure of golde than without worship'. Similar sentiments in Hoccleve, 'Regiment', pp. 145, 147. There must be similar doubts about the relationship between money and power where the nobility are concerned: see e.g. Maddicott 1970: pp. 22–3, showing the huge value of Thomas of Lancaster's estates, despite which he was deserted by his retinue when it mattered (pp. 295–7).

50 Harriss 1985b,d; Given-Wilson 1986, esp. chs. 2 and 3.

51 Ross 1981: pp. 111–12; above, pp. 554–5. Given-Wilson is trying to argue for a circle of purchase between taxpayer, king, nobility and gentry (1987a: pp. 153–9); some at least of his premisses are dubious (e.g. that late-medieval England was like France) and the notion as a whole is out of keeping with the fundamental importance of land as the source of political power.

52 Powell 1979; Wright 1983; Walker 1986; Payling 1987b.

53 Walker 1986: *passim*, and comments above, n. 12.

54 Payling 1987b: pp. 63–5.

55 Payling 1987b: chs. 2–4 (but see comments above, pp. 56 n.81, 147).

the Lancaster estates, in the last analysis it was good government, not patronage, that counted. This fact is evident from the failure of the retinue in the north midlands, powerful as it was, in the later years of Henry IV. It can also be seen in the lack of loyalty to Henry VI shown by Duchy retainers in the same region, although the retinue had been restored after the minority, because the king had failed in his duties to the locality, as both lord and monarch.[56]

Over-emphasis on patronage as the key factor in the late-medieval constitution owes a lot to a misconceived extrapolation from the better-known polity of Tudor England, a misconception that was possible because so little was known about the late-medieval constitution. It is apparent from local studies of Tudor England that royal grants played a far larger part in securing the allegiance of the nobility than in the previous period. Above all, in allowing the magnates to assume a role as channels of royal largesse, grants had a vital role in giving them the means to recruit affinities in their localities. A crucial point to remember here is that after the Dissolutions there was much more to go round. Until then, even in the later years of the fifteenth century, when there was more permanently confiscated land available, grants would have been wholly insufficient to fulfil this function. It appears indeed to be arguable that successful 'patronage politics' of this sort were in themselves only a temporary phenomenon, enduring only as long as there was enough for most of the seekers after favour to be satisfied.[57] But the existence of manna on this scale gave rise to a court-centred politics, continuing into the time of competition for diminishing resources, which is not found in late-medieval England before the end of the fifteenth century. However, there were other and more profound reasons both for the more centralised nature of sixteenth-century politics and for the related rise of patronage as a significant element in the constitution.

Local studies of Tudor England depict a world that is manifestly not the same as the one described in this book, but one which we have seen to be already evolving from the 1470s. The very fact that the magnates' real use to the gentry in the sixteenth century was to be augmenters rather than defenders of gentry estates, even though the security of lands was still a family's first priority, shows how the balance of power had changed. Local power was now shared far more evenly between king, magnates and gentry than it had been in the late middle ages. If the nobility still had the landed predominance that made them vital to the crown's security, the actual control over the enforcement mechanisms on which the security of estates depended had become the

56 Powell 1979; Payling 1987b: pp. 178–98; Wright 1983: pp. 84–6; above, pp. 422, 476.

57 Stone 1967: chs. 3 and 8, and p. 116; Ives 1969; Smith, R.B. 1970: pp. 133–42; Loades 1974: p. 132; Russell 1971: pp. 205–7; Hassell Smith 1974: *passim*, and see summary, pp. 340–1; James 1974: ch. 2; Fletcher 1975: esp. p. 240; Elton 1976; Clark 1977: *passim* and see chs. 8 and 10 on what happened when patronage ran out; Davies, C.S.L. 1977: p. 242; Calnan 1978: *passim*; Ives 1979: pp. 3–7; Williams, P. 1981: ch. 3 and pp. 371–4; Starkey 1987: pp. 90–2; Sharpe 1986, 1987: pp. 248–57; MacCulloch 1986: part III; Gunn 1988: pp. 226–7.

prerogative of the crown and the local gentry. In practice, since none of the gentry were able to challenge the crown, that meant that the royal government was in a stronger position to intervene unasked in the localities and its rule could be more direct. That left the nobility with a diminished role in the lives of the gentry, which they could augment by lobbying at court on behalf of their clients for the judicial favours which increasingly only the crown could offer and then, from the 1530s, for grants. Direct intervention can already be clearly seen in Edward IV's general commissions of *oyer* and *terminer* and Henry VII's use of special commissions to seek out royal rights and of his council learned and other intimates, and in the very fact that the enormous growth in the royal affinity meant that many local officials were the king's own men; in the following century it is everywhere evident.[58]

Until this had happened, politics could not become court-centred, just as patronage could become an issue only when the king's powers were being misused by a dominant group at court. In a sense in the later fifteenth century the localities began to return to the conditions of the twelfth and thirteenth centuries, when local officials were either crown servants, or closely supervised, or both, but with the difference that the scope of royal government had enormously increased since then.[59] Direct intervention went as far as using confiscated lands to interpolate the king's friends into the shires, rather than following the normal late-medieval practice of eventual return to the heirs. Under Edward IV the newer practice dates to the beginning of the reign but was largely confined to the nobility, under Henry VII, as the history of Warwickshire shows, it was extended to gentry lands.[60]

The most contentious parts of this work concern the means by which this change was brought about. One argument would be that it was simply a matter of the enlargement of the crown estate and the diminution in the number of noble families; once this and the corresponding growth of the royal affinity had occurred, the way was open to a more direct rule of the shires, the king acting as local nobleman.[61] There is much force in this, not least because we can see the

58 Stone 1967: ch. 5, sections II and III; Williams, P. 1981: pp. 440–51; Smith, R.B. 1970: pp. 158–9; Davies, C.S.L. 1977: p. 312; Mingay 1976: p. 52; James 1986b,c,d; Hassell Smith 1974: esp. chs. 2–4, 8–9; Clark 1977: esp. chs. 1–4; MacCulloch 1986: chs. 2 and 7; Calnan 1978, *passim*; Loades 1974: pp. 79–80; Ross 1974: pp. 397–9 (see also the numbers of commissions of this sort, into the king's rights etc. in *Cal. Pat. Rolls 1467–77* and *1476–85*); Chrimes 1972a: pp. 149–52, 209–15; Condon 1979: pp. 131–4; Virgoe 1981: p. 81; Lander 1949: pp. 129–33, 1976a: p. 37; Bellamy 1965: pp. 136–9; Avrutick 1967: p. 42.

59 Morris 1927; Green 1986: chs. 6–7; Warren 1987: chs. 3, 5–7; Carpenter, D.A. 1976; Putnam 1950a. For the change to a more devolved form of government, see above, p. 44, below, p. 636.

60 Above, p. 131; see Lander 1976b.

61 Chrimes 1972b: p. 115; Hicks 1978: pp. 102–3. On the general decline in numbers of nobility under Henry VII, see Loades 1974: p. 102 and Condon 1979: pp. 112–15; on the growth of the crown lands, see Wolffe 1970. McFarlane (1981f: pp. 259–60) has some support for the old 'demoralisation' theory to account for noble inertia, but on the Warwickshire evidence there

first two Lancastrians acting with similar dirigisme in the Duchy environs.[62] But it does not entirely hold water. First, there are areas, like Kent or the north-east, which experienced the same developments but were not dominated by crown lands. In the latter case the crown was able to use the bishopric of Durham as a surrogate royal estate, but that in itself tells us a lot about changing power in the provinces, for the bishop had been an almost independent authority in the middle ages.[63] Secondly, the nature of local politics did not change when, during the course of the sixteenth century, the crown shed a large part of its estate, and creations restored the number of peers to something nearer to earlier levels.[64] Against this, however, it might perhaps be argued that it was the intervening years of royal ownership that had inculcated new modes of conduct. But, most cogently, it is not at all evident that kings could have got away with permanent confiscations of noble land for most of the later middle ages. If the conclusions advanced here about the vital role of the nobility in binding together gentry networks before the mid-century crisis are correct and hold good in essence for the rest of the country, it is easy to see that confiscations would have caused enormous local antagonism. The lives of the gentry would have been badly dislocated, local loyalties put under severe strain, and the new nobility could find it impossible to establish themselves, while the resentful gentry provided a ready-made army for the dispossessed should they wish to return.

An obvious instance are Richard II's grantees at the end of his reign or the beneficiaries of the Lancastrian confiscations in 1459.[65] There was good reason for Henry IV and V, or Edward III before them, to restore the heirs of convicted traitors, for they knew that these men would be able to pick up the smooth running of the shires where their immediate forebears had left off.[66] But what if this close tie between nobility and gentry was beginning to wear thin? Then a new man might be inserted with greater ease. Already Edward IV was doing this on a large scale in the early years of his reign, and, if some of his new nobility did not survive the Readeption, they all kept going for virtually the whole of the first reign, and others, most notably Hastings, were able to establish themselves on a long-term footing.[67] Subsequently grants of this kind

seems to have been little of this until Henry VII's reign, and then Henry's policies were the effect not the cause of the growth in royal authority.

62 Above, pp. 366–8; for comments on the Lancastrian affinity under Henry VI, see above, pp. 475–6.

63 Clark 1977: chs. 1 and 2; James 1974: ch. 2; Scammell 1966; Dobson 1973: pp. 183–202, 222–38; Tuck 1985b.

64 Miller 1986: chs. 1 and 7; Bernard 1985: pp. 178–80; Virgoe 1978.

65 Tuck 1973: pp. 191–4, 215; Griffiths 1981: pp. 825–6, 860–2, 871; Johnson 1988: pp. 193–4.

66 McFarlane 1972: pp. 75–6; Harriss 1985c: pp. 35–40. Prestwich 1980: pp. 149–50; Tuck 1985a: p. 103. Also Thomson 1972: p. 246.

67 Ross 1974: pp. 72–83, 310; *Historie of the Arrivall of Edward IV*, pp. 8–9 and the comments on this in Morgan 1973: p. 11. But cf. Pugh 1972: pp. 91–3, with which I would not entirely agree (esp., see above, p. 515).

become a commonplace. To make it easier for kings to rearrange tenurial structures, it became possible for them to manipulate the law of landed property – just about the most dangerous thing they could do with regard to their landed subjects – and to bring dangerous members of the nobility down. Both policies were practised on a scale that had not been seen since the days of Edward I and before. Similarly, from about the 1470s kings could terrorise their nobility in a manner not seen since the days of Edward I and his predecessors.[68]

The crux of this argument is therefore that structural modifications in the body politic were required before the changes that have been depicted could occur. They arose from the gentry's overpowering need of security and stability, and the potential differences in their interpretation of these and the nobility's. It seems logical that those changes discussed and summarised in the previous five chapters should have occurred when a crisis lasting several decades brought the differences out into the open. While it may well be that withdrawal into neutrality was the gentry's normal response to crises of this kind, there was none of such combined magnitude and duration at any other time in the middle ages, except perhaps for Stephen's reign. Significantly, that too may have brought about major changes in relationships among the landed classes.[69] In the crisis of the fifteenth century the symbiotic relationship between nobility and gentry, which had successfully fought to keep royal intervention at bay since the early to middle decades of the fourteenth century, was broken.[70] Royal government was henceforth increasingly able to interpolate itself between the two into the shires. Rulers could break landowners of any sort who stepped out of line because the localities consisted no longer of a mutually-supporting web of local interests but of a body of landowners who for their security looked first to the crown. The nobility could no longer assume the

[68] Hicks 1980: ch. 4, 1979b: p. 127; Harris 1986: ch. 8 and Concl.; Ross 1974: p. 245; Chrimes 1972a: pp. 147–52, 154–6, 207, 310–4; Hicks 1979a: pp. 74–83; Lander 1976c; Loades 1974: pp. 125–7; Scarisbrick 1968: pp. 362–5; Williams, P. 1981: pp. 235, 339–50; Jolliffe 1963; Holt 1965: ch. 4; McFarlane 1973b; for refs. to confiscations and regrants, see above, nn. 60, 65–7. Neither Edward III nor Henry V was above interfering in the descent of estates if it suited him (Davies, R.R. 1978: pp. 57, 285; *Rot. Parl.*, IV, pp. 135–40; Wylie and Waugh 1914–29: III, p. 280), but I would argue that it had to be done more discreetly and on a smaller scale (contrast Richard II's efforts and his fate, below, p. 637).

[69] The *locus classicus* for gentry neutralism in the face of division is the Civil War: see in particular Morrill 1976b: ch. 3. Hughes, writing about the same period in Warwickshire, has significantly similar conclusions to those advanced here (1987: pp. 336–7). For the possible consequences of Stephen's reign, see Stenton 1961: pp. 234–57; Palmer 1980–1.

[70] How far back this state of affairs dates is at the moment unknown. The decline of the curial sheriff and the near-collapse of the eyre had occurred by the end of the thirteenth century (Carpenter, D.A. 1976: above, n. 59; Maddicott 1986; *Civil Pleas of the Wiltshire Eyre*, pp. 21–8; Cam 1963a), but Edward I's rule was undoubtedly exceedingly forceful in its attitude to the law and to law enforcement (Sutherland 1963: *passim*; McFarlane 1973b: pp. 266–7; Prestwich 1980: ch. 1; Harding, ed., 'Proceedings from the Trailbaston Roll of 1305').

support of the gentry in a crisis, once it was the crown that directed the administration of justice in the localities, and therefore the crown that guaranteed the security of gentry estates.

Extending Clanchy's illuminating use of the medieval coinages of 'law and love', 'love', or self-regulation, which had been the norm for most of the later middle ages, had by the end of the century been replaced by 'law', or the predominance of a centralised public authority.[71] Neither was intrinsically superior to the other, for each had advantages and drawbacks for landowners (the drawbacks of 'law' were becoming painfully evident by the end of Henry VII's reign), but they were different. The validity of this interpretation can only be tested by further local studies of England in both the fourteenth and the fifteenth centuries, combined with examinations of the precise working of royal power in the same period. In this context the real litmus-paper reign is that of Richard II, which cries out for constitutional treatment, especially an examination of the king's dealings with the localities, for it is apparent that, even in the 1380s, Richard was trying to establish the kind of rule by 'law' that was to be the norm by the sixteenth century. To determine whether Richard failed because of his own undoubted inadequacies, or whether the nature of the constitution at the end of the fourteenth century doomed all such attempts to failure would be a major step in the validation or rejection of this hypothesis.[72]

If it is accepted that some sort of change along these lines took place between the late fifteenth and the early sixteenth centuries, it remains essential to evaluate its full significance. One professional historian has written wisely about the historian's need, almost obligation, to find large-scale transformations within his chosen period,[73] and the charge could certainly be levelled against this piece of work that it has found 'the rise of the gentry' in yet another century. But that in itself is in a sense a corroboration of the conclusions advanced here, for the rise of the gentry took place over many centuries, and in each of them the development took a different form. In the thirteenth century, when one can first speak of gentry, as opposed to knights, they began to make themselves felt in local and national politics; in the fourteenth they began to assert their own values in parliament and, in so doing, won control of local government; in the fifteenth they began to diverge from the nobility in the management of the localities; many more changes were to follow over the succeeding centuries.[74]

71 Clanchy 1983; Carpenter 1983.

72 The full import of Richard's policies and the extreme reactions to them become obvious as soon as one studies them with power politics and the constitution, rather than patronage, in mind. For an illuminating conceptual essay dealing with the last years, see Barron 1968. See also Given-Wilson 1986: pp. 264–7, 1987b; Walker 1986: pp. 189–93; Virgoe 1971; Davies, R.R. 1971; Tyldesley 1978; Cherry 1979: pp. 90–2; Saul 1984: p. 33; and Keen 1973: pp. 299–300 for a very 'royalist' appreciation of the problem.

73 Hyam 1974: p. 142.

74 Treharne 1946–8; Harriss 1975: *passim*; Mingay 1976.

At the same time it was the power of the nobility that remained the dominant force in the body politic, arguably into the twentieth century, or at least almost into it.[75] George Bernard has warned us against facile assumptions about the decay of noble power under the early Tudors, and it is important to reiterate his conclusions in a study which traces comparative decline in magnate authority within the body politic, for words like 'decline' and 'crisis' with respect to the nobility can only be relative.[76] It has already been observed that the nobility could not but be the chief agents of effective government until the present century; there could no more be a government that relied entirely on the gentry than there could be gentry networks that operated entirely independently of the local nobility. The fierce reaction of successive sixteenth-century governments in the face of noble opposition is sufficient indication of their awareness of the vast military power of the nobility.[77]

What is proposed here is not the old cliché that Tudor rule was based on the gentry, but that the cliché may have contained a certain truth, in suggesting that the balance in the shires between king, magnates and gentry, and in the body politic between king and magnates, altered in the later fifteenth century. This is not to deny that there had been gentry before who had assumed the role of the nobility, but they had done so in areas where there was a lack of noble power; they had performed it as if they were nobility, working with a mediated royal authority, and had quickly given place to any magnate who appeared on the scene.[78] The government of the localities could not be anything but a co-operative venture among all three major elements in the constitution, and rulers who forgot that, whether late-medieval, Tudor or Stuart, soon found themselves in trouble,[79] but it could be done in different ways, and from the later fifteenth century, for a century or more to come, the crown undoubtedly had the whip hand.

How did this affect the gentry's perception of themselves? Arguably, it could be said to have made them into more of a county community, for they were less subject to the noble 'contree' and more directly answerable to the government through the administrative unit of the county, and this state of affairs would become more marked as the volume of government grew massively in the sixteenth century. Against this we must set the growing doubts among Tudor and Stuart historians about the meaning and usefulness of the phrase, especially as it is Warwickshire that has been the subject of the most effective demolition so far. There is also the awkward fact that the one period in the century when

75 A point made in Hexter 1961. See also Beckett 1986.

76 Bernard 1985: esp. pp. 1–5; Williams, P. 1981: pp. 111–13, 127–9, 428–37; Davies, C.S.L. 1977: pp. 320–1; Cooper 1983b: p. 95; MacCulloch 1986: chs. 2 and 7; Stone 1967: p. 349.

77 Williams, P. 1981: pp. 339–50.

78 Above, p. 288.

79 Bernard 1985: pp. 206–8; Loades 1974: pp. 180–1, 224–45; Russell 1971: pp. 137–9, 285–341; Davies, C.S.L. 1977: pp. 201–7. Cf. Scotland (Wormald 1985: pp. 158–60).

Warwickshire was a real unit was when it was wholly subject to the Beauchamp affinity. The north/south divide evident in the sixteenth century emerges towards the end of the fifteenth, and it is apparent that it was the Warwick estates, running all the way down the western part of the county, that had earlier on prevented the Arden-Feldon division from separating north and south politically and socially. When the 'contree' of the earls of Warwick ceased to be the focal point of Warwickshire, there was little to hold the two parts of the county together.[80]

However, again we must remember that we are dealing not with absolutes but with relative change; it is scarcely conceivable that Warwickshire in the seventeenth century, or indeed in the sixteenth, was not more aware of its identity as a county than it had been in the fifteenth, when it had been so dominated by a single west midland noble family. In all areas at all times there were many different kinds of local identity, varying in strength from area to area and possessing different force at different times, and it is apparent that the 'county community' can easily become a substitute for serious thought about the complexities of local identities in any period. Nevertheless, it seems unexceptionable to argue that greater royal intervention, combined with a greater awareness among the gentry of their own power and importance, is likely to have led to a more developed sense of county identity.[81]

Related to this is the resurgence of knighthood in the later years of the century and the increasing equation of knighthood and office. One explanation that has been mentioned briefly was that this too may have been to some extent a product of the gentry's altered self-perceptions.[82] The example of those members of the gentry who, in the absence of the nobility, emerged as local brokers in mid-century and apparently wished to mark themselves out by knighthood[83] may have been followed by all the pre-eminent gentry in the county, as noble influence retreated. Moreover, if they saw themselves as the leaders of the lesser landowners of the county, they might come to believe that they had an obligation to represent their fellows by serving in all the major local offices, including the commission of the peace. It seems that they had rejected the latter office earlier in the century, on the grounds that most of the gentry on

[80] Hughes 1987: esp. p. 55, but cf. p. 51; and see refs. in ch. 2, above, nn. 33, 34, 50.

[81] MacCulloch actually suggests a contrary development for Suffolk (1986: pp. 105–09): from county community in the fifteenth century, to noble power which crossed county boundaries in the early sixteenth, until the later part of the century, when the county community re-emerged as noble power foundered. This sounds very improbable as far as the fifteenth century is concerned because of the enormous power of the nobility in East Anglia at that time, and his interpretation of the fifteenth and early sixteenth centuries is too much conditioned by the availability of Paston material (which in any case by no means establishes unequivocally the existence of a county community); when it ceases he tends to assume that the county community disappears.

[82] Above, p. 86.

[83] Above, pp. 606–9.

the commission were representing the interests of their local lords, and that this relatively lowly job could therefore be left to the lords' lesser retainers. Once the nobility began to cede local leadership to the knights, these could see membership of the commission, now representing the interests not of the magnates but of the county's landowners, as an essential part of their responsibilities. As the commission grew in importance, so this perception of its role would grow. Put differently, as long as the nobility had the real power in the shires, it was enough to be known as the servant of the local magnate; once this authority had begun to be ceded to the king and the greater gentry, knighthood might become an indicator of personal stature, and office a dignity reflecting service to the king and the locality.

This interpretation should not be pushed too hard, for there are other more obvious reasons for both the reappearance of knights and their greater willingness to serve in local office, especially as J.P.s.[84] It does however arise naturally from the weakening of magnate dominance of the shires and the emergence of leading gentry figures in this period. This last was a phenomenon by no means confined to Warwickshire, and it was often men of this sort, like Simon Mountford in Warwickshire and Henry Willoughby in the north midlands, Sir John Scott in Kent or Sir William Parr in the north-west, who, as royal servants and men of some local standing, acted as vital channels of royal authority in the shires. It was their local leadership that made them so useful to the crown in its direct administration of the shires. Arguably, the royal affinity could not have functioned without pivotal local figures of this kind, who could undertake the local management for which the king had insufficient leisure. Simultaneously the increase in royal control of the shires made the avenues of advancement to such eminence more restricted.[85]

One other aspect of the gentry's self-image should be mentioned, and that is the process that M.E. James has called 'the nationalisation of honour'. Over the course of the sixteenth century, the crown's definitions and court values replaced the verdict of the locality and provincial values in attributing status in landed society.[86] What this meant for the gentry – that is the crown's role in conferring knighthood and the development of the College of Heralds to authenticate status and lineage – has been discussed with reference to status,[87] but it also has a place in the present context, for these developments too were related to the centralising of politics and to the crown's closer ties with the gentry.

The question that must now be asked is how typical Warwickshire was. In some ways it has already been answered, in that this concluding chapter has been concerned primarily with issues germane to the whole of England. But that

84 Above, pp. 85–6, 269, 272.

85 Ross 1974: pp. 310, 325–6; above, p. 141.

86 James 1986c.

87 Above, p. 95.

is clearly not enough, for if Warwickshire is entirely untypical the conclusions lose most of their force. It could be objected first of all that this county is unusual in the number of noble families who had some sort of interest in its affairs, even if this was often peripheral to their real concerns in an adjacent county; above all it was untypical in forming part of the concentrated west midland power base of the house of Warwick. This is certainly true, although there must have been other counties of a similar type. Moreover, the lack of gentry of sufficient stature to stand up to the nobility, or to aspire to the rank, may have helped to enhance the magnates' local authority in the first part of the century, although again Warwickshire cannot have been unique in this respect. Thirdly, its fragmentation made it different and may have meant that the mingling of affinities that has been shown to be one of the major causes of the readjustment of relationships between nobility and gentry in mid-century was more extensive than elsewhere. It may well be, however, that all midland counties were like this to a greater or lesser degree; although Susan Wright's work does not address this problem directly, it seems reasonable to infer from it that Derbyshire affinities were of this kind.[88] Fourthly, the crown became the leading landowner in the county in the middle of the transforming process whose outlines have been suggested. Again there would be other counties like this, such as Worcestershire, where the preponderance of the Warwick lands was greater still, or perhaps some of the regions where there was a concentration of York lands. In general, even if the parameters of development proposed here are accepted in outline, there must be differences between localities determined by geography, economy and tenurial structure; it is certainly not suggested that all counties were as subject to magnate influence or as lacking in communal unity as Warwickshire seems to have been for much of the century. Nor would it be maintained that, even if there were structural changes of the kind suggested here in all areas of England, occurring some time between the later fifteenth and later sixteenth centuries, they took place in the same way and according to an identical timetable.[89]

On the other side, it may be suggested that Warwickshire's experience was far from untypical. First, it was a county that was neither on the peripheries of royal government, nor, more important, subject to the heavy-handed lordship that was common to both of the marcher areas, or to the violence that was part of the way of life on the northern march.[90] It is these two regions that must always be regarded as exceptional until they were tamed by Tudor centralisation and the union of England and Scotland. Secondly, it can be argued from what we know of the history of royal government in the late middle ages that it was everywhere as mediated in some form as it has been shown to be in

88 Above, p. 345 n. 259; also the reviews of Wright 1983 by Hicks (1985b) and by Carpenter (1988).

89 For variations in local characteristics and some causes, see Mingay 1976: pp. 57–8; also above, p. 345 n. 260.

90 Above, pp. 483–4.

Warwickshire, and that some time in the late fifteenth century it began to become more interventionist everywhere in England.[91] Tudor local studies show the many local variations in timing of the advance of forceful royal government in the shires, but so far they all show the same story, whose origins in the fifteenth century have been traced here.[92] Finally Warwickshire's very fragmentation helps sustain the case that what happened there happened in other counties, for so many of the Warwickshire landowners, nobility and gentry, had substantial estates elsewhere, and it is hard to believe that they behaved fundamentally differently in these other areas. It is worth remembering that many of the major nobility involved in the crises of the fifteenth century had lands in Warwickshire.

This explanation of the growth of a more authoritarian style of rule in the late fifteenth century is not advanced as a complete and watertight answer. It is however offered in the hope that late-medieval historians will now concern themselves with the problem; for too long the field has been left to Tudor historians, who have been too unfamiliar with the late-medieval polity to put forward more than a rather crude outline.[93] There is an undeniable difference between the late-medieval and Tudor constitutions and, related to this, in the structure of power in the late-medieval and Tudor localities that needs to be explored through a more 'constitutional' approach to late-medieval politics and political society.

Although one of the principal themes of this work has been the inadequacy of a political history that goes no further than the preoccupations of the individual constituents of society, it is nevertheless with these that we started and with these that we should conclude. This has been a story with a large cast, and some attempt has been made to bring back to life their hopes and fears. We should ask finally what the developments that we have followed meant to a member of the Warwickshire gentry born in say 1410 who lived long enough to experience most of the events of the century. To make sense of change going on around you is never the same as taking the olympian view of the historian, and to our representative Warwickshire man it must have seemed at times as if nothing would ever again approach the settled world of his childhood and youth under Richard Beauchamp. In particular, while we might be complacent about the

[91] Refs. in p. 44 n. 39 and above, nn. 57, 58, 68; also Hicks 1979a and Horrox ed. 1986: Intro., and 1986a.

[92] Refs. above, nn. 57, 58. Fletcher (1975: pp. 23–4) finds this process occurring surprisingly late in Sussex, but, as his study starts later than the others cited here, it is possible that he is really talking about noble power relative to other counties rather than about the local dominance which was so often the norm in the late middle ages.

[93] But see Condon 1979 (although the emphasis on Henry VII in this excellent essay obscures both the continuities with Edward IV's reign and the structural changes that may have facilitated the policies described), and Harriss 1981: pp. xxv–vi. For a view of the problem from Tudor England that still stands up rather well, see MacCaffrey 1965, pp. 53–4. For an unusual, if eccentric, Tudor perspective, see Starkey 1986.

way the locality dealt with the crisis of the 1450s, he and his fellow landowners must have been in a state of near-constant worry punctuated with bouts of genuine terror, as rumours of one sort or another filtered down from confrontations in court or parliament or encounters on the battlefield.[94] It was fear that drove him and his fellows to find their solution, with all its implications.

By the end of his life he would be aware of the royal presence far more forcibly than ever before and correspondingly less conscious of the magnate influence that had permeated the county in the earlier part of his life. And yet, while there is no doubt that he would have experienced considerable temporary upheaval and, growing out of this, long-term change, his immediate preoccupations would have changed little, remaining those concerns with the family and the land that were described in the first part of this book. If in the following century religion was to bring readjustments even to some of these, nineteenth-century novels show us in many ways very much the same rural world of squire, parson (albeit a married and often better-educated one) and obedient tenants depicted here, with the same deferential attitude to the nobility who remain the real power in the land. Family and land are still at the heart of all their doings, however tinged with romance matrimonial politics may now have become.[95]

Looked at from a long perspective, provincial life in the fifteenth century was certainly part of 'the world we have lost', lost perhaps as recently as the early years of this century,[96] but it was also a period of significant changes which had profound effects on both local and national politics in the centuries to come. In deciding which of these views is the 'real' one, much depends on the historian's own perspective, whether he himself is looking upwards from a local standpoint or downwards from a governmental one. If downwards, he is likely to think of himself as a political historian and see almost daily upheaval; if upwards, he may well be a social historian, and, if his history no longer leaves out the politics entirely, he will be more interested in continuities. Both views are of course necessary. 'Localism', which has become such an issue in the historiography of the seventeenth century, seems to introduce a problem – the relative importance of national affairs in the local context – which does not exist. Most local concerns could easily become national ones, since the final arbiter in all disputes could only be the king, while national politics and policies could not but affect

94 Armstrong 1948.

95 Best exemplified in Trollope's Barchester novels and, in Jane Austen, in *Pride and Prejudice* (where note the deference shown to Lady Catherine de Bourgh and the extraordinary effect on this squirarchical/professional world of the appearance of Darcy, who is no more than a very rich connection of Lady Catherine). Cf. also the account of the seventeenth-century constitution in Sharpe 1986: remarkably like the one described in this study and, similarly, Beckett 1986: ch. 11.

96 Perhaps not entirely lost even now: seen on a Stratford billboard, August 1988: 'J.P.'s Son Stabbed in Revenge Attack' (*ex inf.* Benjamin Thompson).

the shires, for the nation was after all the sum of its localities.[97] How the national and the local affected each other could only depend on circumstances. To do justice to both the life of the locality, where it was daily concerns, mostly unchanging and often of minimal import, that mattered, and the life of the nation, where kings might rise and fall, but all power depended in the end on what happened in the shires, we must be conscious of both, of locality and polity.

97 Morrill 1976b: pp. 21–31, 1984: pp. 157–8; Fletcher 1986: pp. 361–3, 1983: pp. 153–4; Williams, P. 1984: pp. 138–40; Hirst 1978: pp. 105–6, 1981: pp. 92–4; Sharpe 1986: pp. 335–6; Hughes 1987: pp. xii, 220–54, 1981. Recent discussions, including some of those cited here, are tending to take the same 'two-way' (Hirst's word) view of the relationship. By the same token, the idea that the late-medieval nobility were not interested in court politics seems inappropriate; we cannot deduce this from their failure to attend parliament since, normally speaking, they had other means of getting access to the king.

Appendix 1

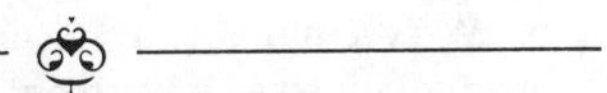

DIRECTORY OF WARWICKSHIRE GENTRY 1400–1500

This list is intended to assist the reader in following the activities of a large number of people and as an indication of the sort of numbers one is dealing with in studying all levels of political society. Thus, it includes virtually all gentry – and a few non-gentry, such as the Birches and some of the Benfords, and some members of gentry families who were themselves untitled – to have any kind of interest in the county in this period, although it remains somewhat selective with regard to families, such as the Botellers of Warrington, which had substantial holdings elsewhere and very little in Warwickshire. Nevertheless, some figures are listed who do not qualify for inclusion in the cross-sections listed in appendix 2 but were in some way involved in county affairs; Ralph Astley, for instance. Also listed are some members of branches of Warwickshire families, such as some of the purely Leicestershire branch of the Purfreys, whose sphere of activities was in other counties but who were on the periphery of Warwickshire affairs by virtue of their relatives' membership of county society. Unlike appendix 2 the list contains almost all members of Warwickshire families, not just the heads, although in the case of those, such as the Longvilles, who rarely turn up on Warwickshire records for most of the period, information is far from complete. The first date usually indicates entry on local affairs, the participant being probably somewhere between about fourteen and twenty-five years old, although in some instances, notably where there are surviving I.P.M.s and wardships, people turn up in the records at a much earlier age. However, in the case of families that acquired Warwickshire land, Conway for example, the date is of the family's arrival in the county. Similarly, the date of sale is given for families that disposed of their Warwickshire lands; for example, first John II Langley, then John III. Members of the more obscure families, however, are not necessarily picked up at an early stage in their lives. Moreover, the first date does not necessarily indicate the acquisition of gentility which, especially in the case of the minor men, not infrequently comes some time after a first appearance in the records: on this, reasonably full and accurate information up to 1472 is to be found in Carpenter, M.C. 1976: App. 1. In some cases, the separation of successive generations carrying the same christian name, especially in the case of more obscure families, is necessarily speculative. The appellations I, II etc. are those used in the text. Thus, in families which consistently used the same christian names, such as the Staffords of Grafton, the very early generations which hardly figure in the story at all are identified as 'sr., jr.' Under 'residence' the names of other counties are given where it is necessary to indicate that these were as, or more, important to the families concerned. An incomplete place-name under this heading – e.g. just 'Newbold' or 'Coton' – indicates inadequate information, while the naming of 'Warwickshire' as residence means that nothing more is known about the family's place of residence other than that it was in some sense in the county. *in the 2nd column indicates recorded activity before 1400, in the 3rd column, the same after 1500.

Name	1st	Last ref. or death	Residence
John Abell	1427	c. 1461–2	Tanworth
Richard Abell	1481	1481	Tanworth
Thomas Agard	1492	*	Ditchford Frary
Thomas Aldryche	1477	1499	Shustoke
Thomas Aleyn	1461	1488	Hurley
Geoffrey Allesley	1401	1441	Little Lawford
William de Alstre	1415	1415	Warwickshire
John Aluff	1483	1483	Arbury
John Andrewes	1465	1489	Sawbridge
Richard Andrewes	1487	1487	Warwickshire
Thomas Andrewes	1465	*	Sawbridge
John Appleby	1450	1470	Fenny Newbold
Henry Archer	1408	?1469	Tanworth
John Archer I	1441	1460	Tanworth
John Archer II	1465	*	Tanworth
John Archer III	1491	*	Tanworth
Richard Archer	1415	1471	Tanworth
Thomas Archer	*	1428	Tanworth
Henry Ardern	1499	*	Park Hall in Castle Bromwich
John Ardern	1466	*	Park Hall
Martin Ardern	1488	*	Park Hall
Ralph Ardern	*	1420	Park Hall
Robert Ardern I	1420	1453	Park Hall
Robert Ardern II	1494	*	Park Hall
Robert Ardern	1412	1419	Newbold
Robert Ardern	1438	1446	Snitterfield
Thomas Ardern	1457	1458	Warwick
Walter Ardern	1454	*	Park Hall
Richard Ashby	1475	*	Coventry
Edward Astley	1427	1448	Wolvey Astley
George Astley	1427	1475	Wolvey Astley
Giles Astley	1414	1430	Wolvey Astley
Ralph Astley	1407	1445/6	Herts., Hillmorton
Thomas Astley I	*	1429/30	Leics., Astley

Name	1st	Last ref. or death	Residence
Thomas Astley II	1447	1484	Leics., Astley
Thomas Astley	1475	*	Hillmorton
William Astley I	1427	1482/3	Wolvey Astley
William Astley II	?1493	*	Wolvey Astley
John Aston I	1467	1483	Heywood, Staffs., share in Freville inheritance[1]
John Aston II	1483	*	Heywood, Staffs., share in Freville inheritance
Robert Aston	*c.* 1417	1465	Heywood, Staffs., share in Freville inheritance
Roger Aston	1402	1449	Heywood, Staffs., share in Freville inheritance
John Atherstone	1449	1479	Atherstone
Reginald Attleburgh	1449	1449	Attleborough
William Attleburgh	1406	1457	Coventry
John Aylesbury I	1438	1480	Edstone
John Aylesbury II	1461	1492	Edstone
Ralph Aylesbury	1480	*	Edstone
Roger Aylesbury	*	1420	Edstone
Henry Badley	1490	1495	Coleshill
William Bagot	*	1407	Baginton
Henry Baker	1468	1485	Coleshill
John Banham	1449	1468	Warwick
John Barbour I	*	1432	Bishops Itchington
John Barbour II	1432	1446	Bishops Itchington
William Barbour	*	1410	Newbold on Avon
Thomas Baron	1402	1424	Rugby
John Basset I	?*	1410	Little Alne
John Basset II	1446	1482	Little Alne
Thomas Bate	?1438	1459	Pooley in Polesworth
John a Batre	1482	1498	?Berkswell
William a Batre	1489	1489	?Sheldon
John Beaufitz	1439	1488	Balsall
Thomas Beaufitz I	1419	1426	Warwickshire
Thomas Beaufitz II	1423	1458	Middlesex, ?Fenny Compton[2]
Thomas Beaufitz III	1472	1485	Warwickshire
Humphrey Beaufo	1460	1485	Oxon. (Emscote)

1 For analytical and mapping purposes they have been treated as a north Warwickshire family, as their interests spilled over into Warwickshire from Staffordshire and they held Pinley in Coventry, as well as part of Henley in Arden further south (S.B.T. D.R.10/1316–7).

2 Seems to have had property at Fenny Compton (W.C.R.O. L.6/92) and has accordingly been entered there on map, fig. 3.

Name	1st	Last ref. or death	Residence
John Beaufo	1485	*	Emscote
Edward Belknap	1491	*	Weston under Wetherley
William Belknap	1473	1484	No Warks. residence, although inherited substantial Warks. lands from Sudeley
James Bellers	1406	1421	Leics., Brownsover
Ralph Bellers	1428	1441	Leics., Brownsover
Thomas Bellers	1450	1472	Leics., Brownsover
Robert Belyngham	1487	1498	Balsall
John Benford	1446	1489	Tanworth
William Benford I	1402	1454	Tanworth
William Benford II	1495	*	Tanworth
Edward Bermingham	1499	*	Birmingham
Thomas Bermingham	1473	1492	Birmingham
William Bermingham I	*	1427	Birmingham
William Bermingham II	1428	1478	Birmingham
William Bermingham III	1480	1500	Birmingham
Thomas atte Berne	1427	1427	Tanworth
Thomas Berton	?1415	1430	Coventry
William Betley I	1423	1457	Coventry
William Betley II	?	by 1481	Coventry
Richard Bingham	1451	1476	Middleton
William Bingham	1463	1477	?Wishaw
John Birches	1415	1456	Solihull
Richard Birches	*	?1465	Solihull
Richard Birches	1417	1440	Longdon in Solihull
William Birches	1403	1438	Solihull
William Bishopestone	1408	1444	Bishopton
Thomas Blankame	1427	1436	Wolvey
William Blayston	1491	1491	Warwick
Richard Blyke	1425	1464	Shrewley
John Bonde	1416	1466	Nuneaton
John Bonherry	*	1428	Warwick
Thomas Bonour	1446	1446	Warwickshire
William Bosville	1410	1427	Marston Jabbett
Henry Boteller	1441	1490	Coventry
John Boteller	1407	1444	Exhall nr. Coventry
John Boteller I	1439	1452	?Solihull
John Boteller II	1477	*	Solihull
John Boteller I	1427	1479	Alspath
John Boteller II	1481	1485	Alspath
John Boteller	1481	*	Coventry
Richard Boteller I	1451	?1496	Solihull

Name	1st	Last ref. or death	Residence
Richard Boteller II	?1491	*	Solihull
Robert Boteller	1450	1463	Alspath
Thomas Boteller	?1481	*	Alspath/?Solihull[3]
William Boteller	1489	1493	Coventry
William Botener	*	1436	Coventry/Withybrook
Edward Botreaux	1417	1417	?Weston under Wetherley
John Botreaux	1412	?1436	Alcester
John Botreaux	?1468	1493	Salford
Thomas Botreaux ?I	1428	1444	Alcester
Thomas Botreaux ?II	1464	1500	Warwickshire
William Botreaux	1431	1445	?Alcester
John Boughton	1480	*	Little Lawford
Richard Boughton	1457	1485	Little Lawford
Robert Boughton	1452	1452	Little Lawford
Thomas Boughton I	1431	1460	Little Lawford
Thomas Boughton II	1477	1495	Little Lawford
William Boughton	1464	*	Little Lawford
John Brachet	1476	1476	Astley
John Bradwell	1431	1441	Little Bromwich
Richard Bradwell	1422	1425	Warwickshire
John Brandewode	1496	1496	Little Bromwich
Baldwin Brasebrugge	1477	*	Hurley in Kingsbury
John Brasebrugge	1471	*	Hurley
Ralph Brasebrugge I	*	1420	Hurley
Ralph Brasebrugge II	1420	1435	Hurley
Richard Brasebrugge	1435	*	Hurley
Simon Brasebrugge	1477	*	Hurley
William Brasebrugge	1474	1490	Hurley
Richard Bray	*temp.* Hen. VI		Stretton on Dunsmore
Edmund Brereton	1485	*	?Henley in Arden
Thomas Brereton	1485	*	?Warwick
Guy Breton	*	1405	Marston nr. Wolston
Henry Breton	1484	1489	Tamworth
John Breton	1417	1462	Tamworth
Richard Breton a/s Tamworth	1444	1444	?Tamworth
William Brett I	1401	?1470	Ansley
William Brett II	1475	1496	Ansley
Thomas Brewer	1491	1491	Warwickshire
John Brewes	1449	1485	Barton in Henmarsh
Thomas Brewes	1474	1496	? Same

3 There may be two Thomas Botellers, one of Alspath, the other of Solihull and Hampton in Arden.

Name	1st	Last ref. or death	Residence
William Brewes	1476	1476	Barton in Henmarsh
John Brewster	1410	1471	Warwick
Edward Bristowe	1451	*	Coventry
John Bristowe I	1420	1448	Coventry
John Bristowe II	1476	1488	Coventry
Thomas Bristowe	1413	1455	Coventry
William Bristowe	1459	1484	Coventry
John Brome	*	1408	Lapworth
John Brome I	*	1435	Warwick
John Brome II	1426	1468	Baddesley Clinton
John Brome III[4]	1480	*	Little Packington
Nicholas Brome	1469	*	Baddesley Clinton
Robert Brome	*	1406	Warwick
Thomas Brome	1468	*c.* 1469	Baddesley Clinton
Edward Bromflete	1422	1460	Farnborough
Henry Broun	1463	*	Napton on the Hill
John Broun I	1407	1433	Napton on the Hill
John Broun II	1410	1431	Napton on the Hill
John Broun	1481	1481	Coventry
Richard Broun	1439	1459	Knowle
William Broun	1485	*	Cestersover
John Brugge	1482	1495	Stratford on Avon
William Brysaldoun	1452	1452	Coventry
John Burdet	1477	*	Arrow/Bramcote
Nicholas Burdet I	1412	1441	Worcs., Arrow
Nicholas Burdet II	1477	1481	Arrow
Richard Burdet	1476	1492	Arrow
Robert Burdet	1401	1401	Baddesley Clinton
Thomas Burdet I	*	1442	Arrow
Thomas Burdet II	1442/3	1477	Arrow
Thomas Burdet III	1492	1497	Arrow
John Burgh	1415	1471	Leics., Wixford
John Bury a/s Marchall	1419	1419	Barton in Henmarsh
Nicholas Bury a/s Marchall	1477	1477	Barton in Henmarsh
Richard Bury a/s Marchall	1423	1427	Barton in Henmarsh
Thomas Bury a/s Marchall I	1429	1431	Barton in Henmarsh
Thomas Bury a/s Marchall II	1477	*	Barton in Henmarsh

4 Called 'III' because, although not of Baddesley Clinton, he was a younger son of that family (*Dugdale*, p. 971).

Name	1st	Last ref. or death	Residence
William Bury a/s Marchall	1449	1492	Barton in Henmarsh
Ralph Bushbury	1455	1455	Blyth
William Bushbury	1426	1426	Blyth
Edmund Bushell	1469	*c.* 1495	Dry Marston in Pebworth, Gloucs.[5]
John Bushell	1436	1436	Dry Marston
Robert Bushell	1400	1435	Dry Marston
Thomas Bushell	1435	1435	Dry Marston
William Bushell	1476	1479	? Dry Marston
William Bynyngton	1445	1445	Binton
John Campion	1416	1463	Gaydon
William Cantlow	1482	1482	? Nether Whitacre
Lewis Cardian	*	1416	Oxhill
Robert Castell	1400	1434	Withybrook/Alspath
George Catesby	1477	*	Lapworth
John Catesby I	*	1412	Ladbroke
John Catesby II	1407	1437	Lapworth/Ladbroke
Nicholas Catesby	1465	*	Hopsford in Withybrook and Bubbenhall
Robert Catesby	1405	1467	Hopsford in Withybrook
Thomas Catesby	1483	*	Marston Culy/Waver
William Catesby sr.	*	1408	Ladbroke
William Catesby I	1428	1476	Lapworth/Ladbroke
William Catesby II	1467	1485	Ladbroke
John Chacom	1473	1475	Coventry
William Chambre	1457	1473	Warwick
John Chetwynd	*	1449	Alspath
Philip Chetwynd	1427	1442	Grendon
Richard Chetwynd	*	1415	Grendon
Robert Chetwynd	1454	1454	Alspath
Thomas Chetwynd	1450	1450	Alspath
William Chetwynd sr.	*	1404	Grendon
William Chetwynd I	1451/2	1494	Alspath
William Chetwynd II	1490	*	Alspath
Richard Clapham	1453	1470	Alspath
Thomas Clapham	1454/5	1484	Alspath
William Clapham	1454	1480	Alspath
John Clinton	1477	*	Herefs., Barton on the Heath
Richard Clinton	?1403	1436	Warwickshire

5 Included because of their proximity to southern Warwickshire and extensive involvement in the region's affairs.

Name	1st	Last ref. or death	Residence
Thomas Clinton	1406	1415	Amington
Richard Clodesdale	1401	1428	Saltley
Hugh Clopton	1469/70	1496	Stratford on Avon
John Clopton I	1413	1467	Stratford on Avon
John Clopton II	1475	1485	Stratford on Avon
Thomas Clopton I	1453/4	1491	Stratford on Avon
Thomas Clopton II	1480	*	Stratford on Avon
William Clopton	1498	*	Stratford on Avon
William Clopton	*	1419	Moor Hall in Wixford
Edmund Cokayn	1435	1478	Pooley
John Cokayn I	*	1438	Pooley
John Cokayn II	1413	1419	Pooley[6]
John Cokayn III	1435	*	Pooley
Roger Cokayn	1471	1482	Pooley
Thomas Cokayn I	1459	1493	Pooley
Thomas Cokayn II	1493	*	Pooley
Hugh Cokesey	1407	1445	Hunningham
Thomas Cokesey	1473	1498	Milcote
Walter Cokesey	*	1404	Hunningham
Edmund Colshill	1421	1446	Binley
John Colyns	1422	1422	Warwickshire
Edmund Compton I	*	1408	Compton Wyniates
Edmund Compton II	1468	1493	Compton Wyniates
John Compton	1445	1456	Notts., Fenny Compton
Robert Compton	1452	1481/2	Compton Wyniates
William Compton I	1413	1429	Compton Wyniates
William Compton II	1493	*	Compton Wyniates
William Compton I	1428	1428	Notts., Fenny Compton
William Compton II	?	*	Notts., Fenny Compton
Edward Conway	1497	*	Arrow
Hugh Conway	1492	*	Arrow
Humphrey Conyngesby	1461	*c.* 1500	Morton Bagot
John Conyngesby	1480	1480	Morton Bagot
William Cope	1485	*	Wormleighton
Alexander Corbet	1492	*	Harbury
John Cotes I	*	1449	Hunningham
John Cotes II	1471	*	Hunningham
Richard Cotes	1486	*	Hunningham
Thomas Cotes	1452	1491	Hunningham
Thomas Cotton	1487	1497	Atherstone
William Couper I & II	1422	1453	Coleshill

[6] See above, p. 111 n. 57.

Name	1st	Last ref. or death	Residence
Thomas Crewe	*	1418	Moor Hall in Wixford
John de Crewenhale	early 15th c.		Crawenhall in Tanworth
John Croft	1451	1451	Coventry
John Croft	1487	*	Shotteswell
Thomas Croft	1472	1500	Shotteswell
Nicholas Croke	1453	1453	Charlecote
Alexander Culpepper	1485	*	Kent, Ansley
John Culpepper I	1400	1434	Kent, Ansley
John Culpepper II	1472	1482	Kent, Ansley
Walter Culpepper	1437	?	Kent, Ansley
John Curson	1478	*	Exhall nr. Coventry
Edmund Dalby	1435	1440	Over Pillerton
Edward Dalby	1428	1451	Over Pillerton
Hugh Dalby	*	1439	Brookhampton
Hugh Dalby I	1436	1453	Upton Tysoe, ? Over Pillerton
Hugh Dalby II	1453	1476	Over Pillerton
John Dalby	1402	1453	Over Pillerton
Richard Dalby	1434	1477	Brookhampton
Robert Dalby	1480	1489	Brookhampton
William Dalby I	1426	1452	Brookhampton
William Dalby II	1457	1487	Brookhampton
Gerard Danet	1488	*	Weston under Wetherley
Thomas Danyas	1473	1473	Coventry
John Daves	1470	1470	Balsall
Richard Delve	1420	1421	Kenilworth
John Denbawde	1457	1474	Coleshill
John Denton	1472	1497	Shelford
Thomas Denton	1496	*	Shelford
John Derset I	1416	1416	Thurlaston
John Derset II	1459	*	Thurlaston
Thomas Derset	1442	1485	Thurlaston
William Derset I	1416	1447	Thurlaston
William Derset II	?1477	*	Thurlaston
John Dey	1471	1475	Drakenage
Richard Dey	1485	1485	Coventry
Thomas Dey	1468	1489	Drakenage
Simon Digby	1495	*	Coleshill
Edward Dilcok	1436	1442	probably Coventry
William Dixwell	1436	1498	Coton on the Wold
Edward Doddingselles I	1403	1466	Long Itchington
Edward Doddingselles II	1481	*	Long Itchington
Gerard Doddingselles	1455	1493	Long Itchington
John Doddingselles	*	1404	Long Itchington

Name	1st	Last ref. or death	Residence
William Donyngton	1410	1449	Coventry
Roger Downe	1465	1465	Nuneaton
William Draycote	1439	1450	Maxstoke
Robert Dunton	1460s	?1483	Kenilworth
Edward Durant	1447	1474	Barcheston
Henry Durant	seised by 1507		Barcheston
John Durant	1409	1446	Barcheston
Nicholas Durant I	1409	1439	Barcheston
Nicholas Durant II	*c.* 1496	*	Barcheston
Richard Durant	1489	1490	Warwick
Thomas Durant	1442	1476	Barcheston
William Durant	1474	1498	Barcheston
John Duston ?I	1424	1455	Stretton on Dunsmore
John Duston ?II	1473	1488	Stretton on Dunsmore
Thomas Duston	1406	1439	Stretton on Dunsmore
Richard Empson	1490	*	Interests in estates of Straunge of Walton, Catesby of Ladbroke, and own property, Atherstone on Stour, from 1496/7
Thomas Erdington I	*	1433	Erdington
Thomas Erdington II	1431	1467	Erdington
Henry Est	1476	*	Yardley, Worcs., Witton
Thomas Est I	1420	1460	Yardley, Worcs., Witton
Thomas Est II	1476	1481	Yardley, Worcs., Witton
John Eton	*	?	?Warwick
Richard Eton I and II	1418	1463	Warwick
Henry Everingham	1450	1472	Withybrook
John Farndon	1497	1498	Woolscot
John Faukeswell	early 1460s		Coventry
Edward Ferrers	1493	*	Flecknoe, Baddesley Clinton
Henry Ferrers	1446	*	Flecknoe, Rutland and Kent
John Ferrers	1439	?1455	Chartley, Staffs., ? Nether Whitacre
John Ferrers I	1461	1485	Tamworth
John Ferrers II	1495	*	Tamworth
Richard Ferrers	1495	1495	Tamworth
Thomas Ferrers I	*c.* 1417	1459	Tamworth
Thomas Ferrers II	1448	1495	Tamworth
William Ferrers	1481	*	Tamworth
Everard Fielding	*c.* 1471	*	Leics., Newnham Paddox
John Fielding	1414	1436	Leics., Newnham Paddox
William Fielding	1439	1471	Leics., Newnham Paddox
Henry Fillongley I	*	1410	M'sex, Fillongley

Name	1st	Last ref. or death	Residence
Henry Fillongley II	1427	1460	M'sex, Fillongley
John Fillongley	1413	1436	Fillongley
John de Flandres	1405	c. 1434	Flanders in Kingsbury
John Folkesworth	1438	1438	Berkswell
John Fowne	1489	1489	Tamworth
Thomas Fowne	1489	1489	Tamworth
William Frank	1458	1458	Warwick
Henry Frebody	1454	1485	Berkswell
Thomas Frebody	1458	1484	Baddesley Clinton
Baldwin Freville I	*	1400	Tamworth
Baldwin Freville II	1400	1414	Tamworth
Francis Froxmere	1498	*	Fillongley
Henry Froxmere	1476	1476	Fillongley
Thomas Froxmere	1473	1498	Fillongley
John Fulbrook	1476	1476	Coventry
Thomas Fulthorp	1497	*	Yorks., Wishaw
John Fulwode	*	1449	Clay Hall in Tanworth
Richard Fulwode	1446	*	Clay Hall in Tanworth
Robert Fulwode	1448	*	Clay Hall in Tanworth
Edward Gamul	c. 1470s	1490	Wishaw
John Gamul	c. 1440	1482	Wishaw
William Gascoigne I	1482	1487	Oversley
William Gascoigne II	1487	*	Oversley
John Gerves	1471	1496	Kenilworth
Thomas Gerves	1483	1483	Coventry
Walter Goode	1434	1447	Harbury
Robert Goushill	*	1403	Notts., Warks.[7]
John Gower I	1454	1465	Cheswick, Worcs.
John Gower II	1475	1481	Cheswick, Worcs.
Robert Gower	1443	1456	Cheswick, Worcs.
Thomas Gower I	1401	1436	Cheswick, Worcs.
Thomas Gower II	1444	?*	Cheswick, Worcs.
William Grant	1498	1498	Warwickshire
Thomas Grene	?1401	1436	Solihull
John Greswold I	1426	1482	Solihull
John Greswold II	1472	*	Rowington/Solihull
Robert Greswold	1459	1486	Kenilworth
Roger Greswold	1452	*	Kenilworth/Solihull
Thomas Greswold	1415	1458	Solihull
Thomas Greswold I	1425	1452	Kenilworth
Thomas Greswold II	1492	1492	Kenilworth

7 Included as second husband of widow of Thomas duke of Norfolk (*c.* 1401) (*G.E.C.*, IX, p. 604).

Name	1st	Last ref. or death	Residence
William Greswold	1490	1490	Kenilworth
Edward Greville	1477	*	Milcote
Humphrey Greville	1499	*	Milcote
John Greville I	*	1444	Gloucs., Milcote[8]
John Greville II	1445	1480	Milcote
John Greville III	1474	*	Milcote
Robert Greville	1454	1466	?Milcote
Thomas Greville	1406	1418	?Milcote
William Greville	*	1401	Gloucs., Milcote
Edward Grey	1499	*	Staffs., Withybrook
Humphrey Grey	*c.* 1472	1499	Staffs., Withybrook
Robert Grey	1441	1460	Groby, Leics., Withybrook
Thomas Grey	?1471	?*	?Groby, Warwickshire[9]
Robert Grimshaw	1429	1430	Maxstoke
Robert Hadley	1461	1478	Coventry
Robert Hales	1480	*	Mollington
Robert Halford	1470	1487	Upton
John Hall	1449	1449	Marston ?nr. Wolston
Thomas Halle	1420	1426	Idlicote
William Haloughton	1450s	1466	Coventry
William Haltoft	1493	1494	Atherstone
John Halton/Hawton	1442	?1468	Castle Bromwich
John Hanham	1436	?1440s	Coventry, Bishops Tachbrook
Richard Hannys	1485	1485	Stratford on Avon
John Hardwick I	1409	1421	Leics., Flanders in Kingsbury
John Hardwick II	1459	*	Leics., Flanders
Richard Harecourt	1461	1486	Oxon., Shotteswell
William Harecourt	1450	1472	Maxstoke
John Harewell I	*	1428	Wootton Wawen
John Harewell	?1473	?*	Whitley
John Harewell II	1488	*	Wootton Wawen
Richard Harewell	1402	1435	Shottery
Roger Harewell	1415	1434	Wootton Wawen
Thomas Harewell	*	1443	Bidford
William Harewell	1452	1500	Wootton Wawen
Robert Harper	1471	1489	?Mancetter, ?Atherstone
William Harper	1432	1436	Mancetter
Leonard Hastings	1412	1455	Leics., Burton Hastings

8 See above, p. 111 n. 57.

9 Problems with identification: see app. 2 n. 16.

Name	1st	Last ref. or death	Residence
Richard Hastings	1410	1436	Yorks., Burton Hastings
Richard Hastings	1483	?	Drakenage
William Hastings	1455	1461[10]	Leics., Burton Hastings
John Hathewick	1442	1482	Harbury
Richard Haversham	1415	1430	Coleshill
Richard Hay	*c.* 1473	?1481	Warwick
John Hayton	1474	1474	Napton on the Hill
Thomas Hayton I	1412	1448	Napton on the Hill
Thomas Hayton II	1448	*	Napton on the Hill
Richard Hedley	1467	1497	Coventry
George Herthill	1432	1439	Woodloes
John Herthill	1438	1470	Woodloes
Richard Herthill	1452	1453	Warwick
Thomas Herthill	1435	1449	Woodloes
John Herward I, II and III	1427	*c.* 1480s	Notts., Frankton
Nicholas Herward	1486	1486	Notts., Frankton
Richard Herward	1503	*	Moreton Morrell
John Heryng	1503	*	Coventry
Baldwin Hethe	1489	*	Tanworth
John Hethe	1468	?1498	Brailes
Degory Heynes	1468	*	Warwick
Roger Holden	1472	1496	Erdington
Thomas Holden	1439	1481	Erdington
Bernard Holt	1458	1458	Warwick
John Holt	1422	1470s	Aston
Simon Holt	1402	1414	Birmingham
William Holt	?*	1414	Studley
William Holt	1415	1433	Alcester
William Holt I	*	1441	Aston
William Holt II	1474	*	Aston
Roger Holyes	*c.* 1464	?1478	Coventry
Henry Hopis	1483	1483	Nuneaton
Alan Hore	1452	1492	Elmdon
Edmund Hore	1464	?1481	Stoneythorpe
Gilbert Hore I	1427	1454	Cambs., Wishaw
Gilbert Hore II	1479	1497	Cambs., Wishaw
John Hore	1401	1434	Cambs., Wishaw
John Hore I	?1401	1439	Solihull
John Hore II	?1445	1482	Solihull
John Hore	?1456	*	Stoneythorpe

[10] Date of his ennoblement, at which point he ceases to be a member of the Warwickshire gentry (*G.E.C.*, VI, pp. 370–1).

Name	1st	Last ref. or death	Residence
Robert Hore	1410	1426	Solihull
Robert Hore	1464	*	Stoneythorpe
Robert Hore	1489	*	Little Kington
Thomas Hore I	1421	1427	Cambs., Wishaw
Thomas Hore II	1456	1479	Cambs., Wishaw
Thomas Hore	1410	1450	Elmdon
Thomas Hore I	*c.* 1410	1476	Solihull
Thomas Hore II	?1461	*	Solihull
William Hore I	*	1437	Stoneythorpe, Elmdon
William Hore II	1429	1456	Stoneythorpe
William Hore	1485	1485	Solihull
William Hore	1481	1488	Elmdon
Richard Hotoft	1421	1467	Leics., Marston nr. Wolston
Thomas Hotoft	1467	1473	Leics., Marston nr. Wolston
John Hoton	1491	1491	Coventry
William Hough	1478	1478	Warwick
Edward Hubaud	1455	1497	Ipsley
Humphrey Hubaud	1474	1488	Ipsley
John Hubaud	1430	1477	Ipsley
Richard Hubaud I	1410	1437	Ipsley
Richard Hubaud II	1481	*	Ipsley
Thomas Hubaud	1442/3	1480	Ipsley
William Hubaud	1471	1477	Ipsley
Robert Hubert	1488	1488	Sutton Coldfield
John Hugford I	1435	1478	Emscote, Shottery
John Hugford II	1446	1485	Emscote
John Hugford	1486	*	Princethorpe
Robert Hugford	*	1411	Emscote
Thomas Hugford	1416	1470	Emscote
William Hugford	1452	1492	Princethorpe
Edward Hungerford	1481	*	Charlecote
Richard Hungerford	1499	*	Charlecote
John Hyde	1453	1475	Coventry
Richard Hyde	1472	1490	Warwick
Thomas Hynkley	1417	1419	Coton
Richard Illingworth	1491	1491	Little Lawford
Thomas Ipstones	1411	1411	Warwickshire
John Ipwell	1461	1471	Exhall ?nr. Alcester
Thomas Ipwell	1480	1483	?Exhall
John Jakson	1446	1446	Castle Bromwich
Thomas Jenkins	1472	1492	Ansley
John Joce	1478	1487	Birmingham

Name	1st	Last ref. or death	Residence
John Kenwyk	1466	1480	Coventry
William Kilburn	1484	1484	Alcester
Bartholomew Knight	1455	1468	Alspath
John Knightley I	*	1426	Northants., Weston under Wetherley
John Knightley II	1478	1499	Northants., Weston under Wetherley
Richard Knightley I	1411	1442	Staffs., Weston under Wetherley
Richard Knightley II	1442	1475	Northants., Weston under Wetherley
Richard Knightley III	1474	*	Northants., Weston under Wetherley
John Ladbroke	1503	*	Kenilworth
Geoffrey Lambard	1449	1449	Atherstone
Reginald Langham	1442	1442	Coventry
John Langley I	1416	1459	Atherstone
John Langley II	1471	1474	Atherstone
John Langley III	1483	1496	Atherstone
Walter Langley	1466	1471	Atherstone
William Langley	1474	1483	Atherstone
William Laryngton	1446	1446	Coventry
Robert Lecroft	*temp.* Ric. II		Coleshill
William Lecroft I	1426	1449	Coleshill
William Lecroft II	1461	1490	Coleshill
Thomas Leder	1453	1453	Ryton ?on Dunsmore
Richard Lee	1476	1478	Warwick
Thomas Leek	1483	1483	?Coventry
John Leventhorpe	*	1433	Newnham Paddox
Hugh Lillburne	*	1417	Stockingford
Ralph Lingham	1496	1496	Morton Bagot
Henry Lisle	1466	*	Moxhull
John Lisle I	*	1418	Moxhull
John Lisle II	?1480	*	Moxhull
William Lisle	1417	1462	Moxhull
Richard Littleton	1476	*	Baxterley
Thomas Littleton	1440	1481	Baxterley/Grendon
George Longville	1423	1458	Bucks., share in Whitacre inheritance with Ferrers of Chartley
John Longville	1458	*	As for George[11]

[11] The family evinces no concern with its Warwickshire properties or its claim to them after George.

Name	1st	Last ref. or death	Residence
Richard Longville	1436	1458	As for George
Edmund Lucy	1487	1495	Charlecote
Edmund Lucy	1492	1497	Probably uncle of above
Edward Lucy	1468	1490	?Charlecote
Thomas Lucy I	*	1415	Charlecote
Thomas Lucy II	1495	*	Charlecote
William Lucy sr.	*	1401	Charlecote
William Lucy I	1415	1466	Charlecote
William Lucy II	1466	1492	Charlecote
John Ludford	1483	1483	Ansley
John Malory	1406	1434	Newbold Revel
John Malory I[12]	1412	1470	Leics., Bishops Tachbrook
John Malory II	?1480	1489	Leics., Bishops Tachbrook
John Malory III	1493	1494	Leics., Bishops Tachbrook
Nicholas Malory	1479	*	Newbold Revel
Robert Malory	?*c.* 1467	1479	Newbold Revel
Roger Malory	1453	1456	Ryton ?on Dunsmore
Simon Malory	1411	1480	Chilvers Coton
Thomas Malory	1407	?1422[13]	Bramcote
Thomas Malory	1421	1471	Newbold Revel
Henry Maners	1480	1480	Walton Deyville
Richard Marbroke	*	1438	Codbarrow in Tanworth
George Marlowe	1491	1491	Thelsford
John Marmeon	1489	*	Middleton
Thomas Marrowe	1491	*	M'sex., Kingswood
Ailred Marshall	1448	1475	Stretton
Nicholas Massy	1482	1482	Coventry
Robert Massy	1473	*	Erdington
Thomas de Merrington	*	1407	Lawford
Hugh Mervyn	1500	*	Lawford
Baldwin Metley	1427	1451	Coventry
Benedict Metley	1478	*	Whitnash
Edward Metley	*	1416	Wolston
Nicholas Metley	1425	1437	Wolston

12 There are the usual problems in disentangling Malory families, especially in this case from the family of Welton, Northamptonshire – as opposed to this one, of *Walton*, Leicestershire – which came to an end before 1430 (*Cat. Anc. Deeds,* IV, A8402, 9657). Hence, some of these dates may not be correct. Furthermore, Nichols (1795–1811: III, i, p. 501) has only two generations, both called John, covering the period 1429–1490, when the second died (1489 according to the I.P.M.: *I.P.M. Hen. VII,* II, 295), but the death is recorded of another John with land in Warwickshire and Leicestershire in 1470 (*Cal. Fine Rolls 1461–71*, p. 260) and there is no other family to which he could obviously belong.

13 There are serious problems in disentangling the Thomas of Bramcote and the more famous one of Newbold Revel (see Field 1979–80).

Name	1st	Last ref. or death	Residence
Thomas Metley	1438	1484	Rutland, Wolston
William Metley	1492	*	Whitnash
John de Middleham	1461	1461	Warwick
Edward Middlemore	1462	1460s	?Edgbaston
Henry Middlemore	1477	1477	?Edgbaston
John Middlemore I	1420	1447	Edgbaston
John Middlemore II	1492	*	Worcs., ?Edgbaston
Nicholas Middlemore	1437	1437	?Edgbaston
Richard Middlemore	1447	*	Edgbaston
Thomas Middlemore	1401	1428	Edgbaston
William Middlemore	1429	1429	Edgbaston
Leonard Middleton	1486	1486	Hunningham
Thomas Middleton	1439	1469	Walton Deyville
John Milward	1474	1485	Nuneaton
Roger Milward	1483	1483	Nuneaton
Thomas Milward	1475	1475	Nuneaton
Thomas Mollesley	1417	1449	Staffs., Moxhull
John Moreton	1432	1442	Hillmorton
Humphrey Morgan	1451	1495	Sambourn
Thomas Morgan	1475	*	Sambourn
William Morgan	1443	1455	?Sambourn
Baldwin Mountford	1434	1464	Hampton in Arden, Coleshill
Edmund Mountford	1431	1494	Berks., Coleshill
Henry Mountford	1492	1495	Coleshill
John Mountford	1479	1491/2	Coleshill, Monkspath
John Mountford	1491	*	Kington[14]
Richard Mountford	1488	*	Church Bickenhill
Robert Mountford	1458	?1494	Church Bickenhill
Robert Mountford	1437	1469	Coleshill, Monkspath
Simon Mountford	1453	1495	Hampton in Arden, Coleshill
Thomas Mountford I	1474	1491	Kington
Thomas Mountford II	1465	*	Coleshill, Sutton Coldfield
William Mountford I	*	1452	Coleshill
William Mountford II	1491	1491	Coleshill
John Mowton	1428	1428	Coventry
John Mudd	1461	1468	Warwick
George Muston	1462	1492	Hunscote
Thomas Muston	1431	1477	Hunscote

[14] This could be either Kineton Green in Bickenhill (now Solihull) or Kingsford, a Mountford property in Solihull.

Name	1st	Last ref. or death	Residence
William Muston	1417	?1455	Hunscote
John de Napton/Betons	1400	1401	Napton on the Hill
William de Napton/ Betons	1411	1411	Napton on the Hill
John Neville	1443	1482	Oversley
Ralph Neville	1411	1458	Oversley
Thomas Neville	1479	*	Leics., inherited minor interests in Warwickshire from Palmers of Holt, Leics.
William Neville	1476	1498	As for Thomas
Peter Newhall	1488	1488	Middleton
Edmund Newnham	1446	*	Northants., Stourton
John Newnham	1482	1498	Northants., Stourton
Thomas Newnham I	1413	1438	Northants., Stourton
Thomas Newnham II	1475	*	Northants., Stourton
William Newnham	1432	?1483	Northants., Stourton, Bishops Itchington
John Norbury	1473	*	No Warks. residence, although inherited substantial Warks. lands from Sudeley
John Norreys I	1438	1466	Berks., Codbarrow in Tanworth
John Norreys II	1473	1490	Codbarrow
William Norreys	1448	*	Berks., Codbarrow in Tanworth
John Norwood	1432	1466	Coventry
John Norwood	1468/9	1493	Snitterfield
Thomas Norwood	1465	1465	Coventry
Thomas Notyng	early 15th c.		Warwickshire
Thomas Odehill	1484	1484	Berkswell
John Onley I	*	1426	Bucks., Birdingbury
John Onley II	1420	1422	Bucks., Birdingbury
John Onley I	1402	1437/8	Bishops Tachbrook
John Onley II	1437/8	1450	Bishops Tachbrook
John Onley III	1483	1496	Bishops Tachbrook
Robert Onley	1435/6	1478	Bucks., Birdingbury
Robert Onley	1485	1494	Coventry
Thomas Onley I	1437/8	1473	Bishops Tachbrook
Thomas Onley II	1490s	1490s	Bishops Tachbrook
William Orchard	1502	*	Warwick
Richard Oresby	1498	1498	Coventry
John Otter	1455	1485	Warwick

Name	1st	Last ref. or death	Residence
Robert Otter	1470	1473	Alspath
Thomas Otter	1483	*	Berkswell
William Overton	1468	*	Brownsover
Richard Palmer	1477	1499	Ansley
Robert Palmer	before 1480		Ansley
Thomas Palmer	1408	1411	Frankton
Thomas Palmer	1426	1476	Northants., share in Bishopestone inheritance, but no Warks. residence
William Palmer	1490	1499	Ansley
John Parker	1473	1475	Coleshill
Thomas Parker I	1452	1474	Crawenhall in Tanworth
Thomas Parker II	1467	1474	Crawenhall
William Parker	1425	1452	Crawenhall
William Parys	*	1427	Warwick
John Peche	*	1401	Hampton in Arden
William Perkyns	1429	1429	Warwickshire
John Perot	1457	1457	'Alston' ? = Alveston
Adam Peshale	1401	1411	Staffs., Middleton
Edward Peyto	1487	1487	Chesterton
John Peyto I	1454	1487	Chesterton
John Peyto II	1487	*	Chesterton
Thomas Peyto	1467	1467	Chesterton
William Peyto sr.	*	1406/7	Chesterton
William Peyto	1406/7	1464	Chesterton
Thomas Plant	1483	1489	Coventry
John Pores	1457	1457	Warwick
Baldwin Porter	1448	1499	Eastcote and Longdon
Henry Porter	1430	1448	Solihull
John Porter	?1481	?*	Eastcote and Longdon
Robert Porter I	1435	1453	Upper Ettington
Robert Porter II	1482	*	Upper Ettington
Thomas Porter	?1411	1448	Eastcote and Longdon[15]
Thomas Porter	1435	1466	Upper Ettington
Thomas Porter	1451	1451	Kenilworth
William Porter	1444	1480	Upper Ettington
John Power	1478/9	1491	Stratford on Avon
Otwell Power	1412	1413	Stratford on Avon
Thomas Power	1437	1437	?Stratford on Avon
Walter Power	*	1402	?Stratford on Avon
John Prince	1497	1497	Barford
Richard Pudsey	1496	*	Hampton in Arden

[15] See discussion of origins, p. 124 n. 104.

Name	1st	Last ref. or death	Residence
Henry Purfrey	1488	1489	Saltley
John Purfrey I	1467	1472	Leics., Shelford in Burton Hastings
John Purfrey II	1482	1487	Leics., Shelford
Nicholas Purfrey I	?dead by 1482		Leics., Shelford
Nicholas Purfrey II	1491	*	Leics., Shelford
Philip Purfrey	1464	1468	Leics., Shelford
Thomas Purfrey[16]	*	1416	Leics., Shelford
Thomas Purfrey	1484/5	1484/5	Leics., Knightcote in Dassett
William Purfrey I	*	1414	Leics., Shelford
William Purfrey II	1426	1466	Leics., Shelford
William Purfrey III	1466	?1471	Leics., Shelford
William Purfrey	?end 15th cent.		Ansley
Edward Ralegh I	1460	*	Farnborough[17]
Edward Ralegh II	1488	*	Farnborough
Giles Ralegh	1481	*	Farnborough
Thomas Ralegh I	*	1404	Farnborough
Thomas Ralegh II	1454	1484	Farnborough
William Ralegh I	1404	1420/1	Farnborough
William Ralegh II	1436	1460	Farnborough
Thomas Rastell	1455/6	1479	Coventry
Thomas Raves	1471	1477	Worcs., Canley
William Raves I	1443	1465	Canley
William Raves II	1442	1493	Canley
William Repington I	1421	1468	Staffs., Amington
William Repington II	1472	*	Staffs., Amington
William Reynold	1409	1456	Attleborough
John Risley	1488	*	Granted various Catesby manors but no involvement in Warwickshire
Richard Rivell	1406	1438	Coventry
William Rodborn	1432	1448	Wilmcote
John Rody I	1408	1430	Warwick
John Rody II	1420	1437	Warwick
Nicholas Rody	1413	1458	Warwick
Thomas Rody	1411	1418	Warwick
William Rody	1423	1435	Warwick
Hugh Rogers	1431	1431	Birmingham

[16] The Purfrey genealogy is confused: I have followed *Dugdale*, p. 54 rather than Nichols 1795–1811: IV, ii, p. 599, because his version better fits the surviving evidence.

[17] See above, p. 111 n. 57.

Name	1st	Last ref. or death	Residence
John Rous sr.	*	1402/3	Ragley
John Rous I	1431	1470	Ragley
John Rous II	1463	1474	Ragley
Robert Rous I	between John sr. and William		Ragley[18]
Robert Rous II	1463	1464	Ragley
Thomas Rous	1464	1499	Ragley
William Rous	died 1420		Ragley
William Rudyng	*	1441	Warwick
Nicholas Ruggeley I	1400	1434[19]	Staffs., Dunton
Nicholas Ruggeley II	1437	1483	Staffs., Dunton
William Ruggeley	1487	*	Staffs., Dunton
Alexander Rushton	c. 1473	1486	Lancs., Studley
Henry Rushton	1445	1471	Lancs., Studley
Nicholas Rushton	1471	*	Lancs., Studley
Richard Rushton	1414	1472	Lancs., Studley
Richard Rushton	1498	*	Exhall nr. Coventry
William Rushton	1445	1445	?Studley
Geoffrey St. Germain	1472	1485	Ditchford Frary
Thomas Sampson	1439	1468	Coventry
Nicholas Sauser	*	1424	Stratford
Robert Scotte	1435	1435	Coventry
Thomas Scotte	1442	1442	Coventry
Thomas Seman	1471	1497	Temple Grafton
Thomas Seyville	*	1415	Bascote in Long Itchington
John Shaw	1491	1493	Alcester
James Sherard	c. 1479	1498	Napton on the Hill
Hugh Shirley I	*	1403	Derbys. etc., Lower Ettington, Newton Regis
Hugh Shirley II	1484	*	As for Hugh I
John Shirley	1466	1486	As for Hugh I
Ralph Shirley I	1410	1443	As for Hugh I[20]
Ralph Shirley II	1423	1466	As for Hugh I
Ralph Shirley III	1486	*	As for Hugh I
Robert Shirley	1493	1496	Little Bromwich
Thomas Shirley	1468	1480	As for Hugh I

[18] See above, p. 54 n. 78.

[19] Nicholas I was allegedly still alive in 1484 (Nott. Univ. Lib., Middleton MS 4509–10), but, circumstantial as this evidence is, there must be an error (PROB 11/3 fo. 193d.). The Ruggeleys are listed as a Warwickshire family as early as 1400, even though they did not acquire Dunton from the Stanhopes until 1422 (Bod. Lib. Dugdale MS 17, p. 38) because Nicholas I was serving the earls of Warwick within the county then (app. 3).

[20] Placed at Newton Regis in fig. 3.

Name	1st	Last ref. or death	Residence
Christopher Shirwode	1478	1478	Coventry
John Shirwode	1450	1488	Alspath
Thomas Shirwode	1465	*c.* 1493–1500	Alspath, Coventry
Balthasar Shukburgh	1484	*	Lower Shuckburgh
Giles Shukburgh	1408	1408	Upper Shuckburgh
Jasper Shukburgh	1480	1484	Lower Shuckburgh
John Shukburgh	*	1406	Upper Shuckburgh
Simon Shukburgh	1432	1433	Upper Shuckburgh
Thomas Shukburgh sr.	1404	t.Hen.V	Upper Shuckburgh
Thomas Shukburgh I	1436	1484	Upper Shuckburgh
Thomas Shukburgh II	1468	1499	Upper Shuckburgh
Thomas Shukburgh III	1484	*	Upper Shuckburgh
William Shukburgh I	1410	1432	Upper Shuckburgh
William Shukburgh II	1484	1492	Upper Shuckburgh
Robert Skerne	1405	1435	Surrey, Compton Murdack
Thomas Slade	1489	*	Maxstoke
William Sloley	1430	1430	Coventry
Robert Smalwode	1473	?1483	Alcott, Alcester
Henry Smyth	1493	*	Shelford
John Smyth	1459	*	Coventry
Thomas Smyth	*c.* 1467	*c.* 1467	Coventry ?error for John
Robert Solley	1489	1489	Barlichway Hundred
Henry Somerlane	1430	1466	Warwick
John Somerlane	?1474	1495	Warwick
Thomas Somerville	1489	*	Edstone
Giles Southam	1479	1479	Coventry
John Spenser	1459	1485	Wormleighton
John Spenser	1471	1496	Hodnell
John Spenser	1483	*	Hodnell, Wormleighton, Snitterfield
Thomas Spenser	1498	*	Wormleighton
William Spernore	*	1426	Spernall
Guy Spine	*	1412	Coughton
Humphrey Stafford sr.	*	?1401	Grafton, Worcs., Leamington Hastings
Humphrey Stafford jr.	1401	1419	As for Humphrey sr.
Humphrey Stafford I	1412	1450	As for Humphrey sr.
Humphrey Stafford II	1450	1486	As for Humphrey sr.
Humphrey Stafford III	1486	*	Eventually recovered part of inheritance
John Stafford	1415	1422	As for Humphrey sr.
Ralph Stafford	*	1410	As for Humphrey sr.
Richard Stafford	1422	1430	Wappenbury
Thomas Stafford	*	1425	Baginton

Name	1st	Last ref. or death	Residence
Thomas Stafford	1469	*	Grafton, Worcs., Northants.
William Stafford	1474	1494	Grafton, Worcs., Leamington (bastard)
Thomas Staffordshire	1481	1481	Ruin Clifford
Richard Stanhope	*	1422	Dunton
Edward Stanley	1499	1499	Milcote
Thomas Stanley	1475	1484	Alspath
Alexander Starkey	1480	1485	Stretton on Dunsmore
Edmund Starkey	?1414	1468	Stretton on Dunsmore
John Starkey	1499	*	Stretton on Dunsmore
Richard Starkey	1473	1493	Stretton on Dunsmore
Thomas Starkey	1429	1444	Stretton on Dunsmore
William Starkey	1458	1458	Stretton on Dunsmore
John Stokes	1463	1463	Brinklow
Robert Stokes	1415	1450	Staffs., Stoke nr. Coventry, Tamworth
Thomas Stokes I	*	1432	Staffs., Stoke nr. Coventry, Tamworth
Thomas Stokes II	1439	1469	Staffs., Polesworth
Alan Straunge	1417	1417	Walton Deyville
Baldwin Straunge	1408	1416	Walton Deyville
Thomas Straunge I	1417	1436	Walton Deyville
Thomas Straunge II	1458	1486	Walton Deyville
Thomas Stretton	1432	1472	Coventry
Henry Sutton	*	1408	Little Lawford
John Swayne	1468	1468	Coventry
John Swettenham	1428	1428	Coventry
Henry Sydenhale	1404	1404	Tanworth
John Sydenhale	1461	*	Tanworth
Thomas Sydenhale I	*	?1417	Tanworth
Thomas Sydenhale II	?1420	1460	Tanworth
William Tebottes	1448	?1483	Coventry, ?Offchurch
John Throgmorton I	1409	1445	Coughton
John Throgmorton II	1473	?1495	Coughton
Richard Throgmorton	1491	*	Coughton
Robert Throgmorton	1469	*	Coughton
Thomas Throgmorton I	*	1409	Worcs.
Thomas Throgmorton II	1443	1472	Coughton
William Tommes	1457	1457	Temple Grafton
George Tong	*c.* early 16th cent.		Warwickshire
Robert Topcliff	1487	1492	Warwickshire
Ailred Trussell	*	1424	Billesley Trussell
Edward Trussell	1481	*	Leics., Bilton

Name	1st	Last ref. or death	Residence
John Trussell	1432	1480	Billesley Trussell
Thomas Trussell	1441	1470	Leics., Bilton
Thomas Trussell	1477	*	Billesley Trussell
William Trussell I	1407	1464	Leics., Bilton
William Trussell II	1459	*	Leics., Bilton
William Trussell I	1425	1434	Billesley Trussell
William Trussell II	1470	*	Maxstoke, ?Billesley Trussell
Robert Twyford	1498	1498	Nuneaton
Richard Umfrey	1421	1421	Unknown
John Underhill	?1472	*	Lower Ettington
John Upton I	1408	1453	Warwick
John Upton II	1468	1482	Warwick
Giles Vale	1475	1475	Farnborough
William Vampage	1492/3	*	London, Hopsford
Peter Venables	1468	1468	Napton on the Hill
Edmund Verney	1457	1495	Compton Murdack
John Verney	1422	1435	Kingston, then Compton Murdack[21]
Leonard Verney	1494	*	Compton Murdack
Richard Verney I	1429	1490	Kingston, then Compton Murdack
Richard Verney II	1491	*	Compton Murdack
Robert Verney	1401	1417	Great Wolford
Thomas Verney	1479/80	1499	Great Wolford
Walter Verney	1424	1452	Great Wolford
William Verney	1441	1498	Great Wolford
Alan Waldeve	*	1406	Elmdon
John Waldeve	1407	1442	Alspath
John Waldeve I	1450	1470	?Plumpton
John Waldeve II	son and heir of Nich., seised by 1517		Plumpton
Nicholas Waldeve	1476	1484	Plumpton
Richard Waldeve	*	1403	Alspath
Thomas Waldeve	1432/3	1474	Plumpton
William Waldeve	1414	1448	Plumpton
Hugh Walford	1494	*	Wolverton

[21] Kingston acquired from Skerne in 1429 (S.B.T. D.R.98/460), but the family's earlier residence is not known. Possibly Great Wolford (above, p. 130 n. 127 for this and other problems in the Verney genealogy), especially as Richard Verney is described as 'of Wolverton', quite probably in error for Wolford, in the oath lists of 1434 (*Cal. Pat. Rolls 1429–36*, p. 384). The designation is in any case incorrect, as the Verneys had Kingston by then. They purchased Compton Murdack the following year (S.B.T. D.R.98/97).

Name	1st	Last ref. or death	Residence
John Walsh I	1426	1432	Alspath, Luddington
John Walsh II	?early 16th c.		Alspath, Luddington
Richard Walsh	between Alan Waldeve and John Walsh		Alspath, Luddington
William Warbelton	1478	1478	Tamworth
John Ward	1413	1436	Little Bromwich
Thomas Ward	1404	1417	Birmingham
Thomas Ward I	1467	1493	Little Bromwich
Thomas Ward II	1485	1494	Little Bromwich
William Ward	1479	1490	Little Bromwich
John Waryng I	1463	1478	Tanworth
John Warying II	1484	1495	Tanworth
Richard Warying	1478	1478	Tanworth
Thomas Warying I	1408	?1436	Tanworth
Thomas Warying II	?1441	?1472	Tanworth
Thomas Warying III	1470	*	Tanworth
William Warying	1473	1478	Tanworth
Henry Waver I	1451	1470	Cestersover
Henry Waver II	1472	1482	Cestersover
John Waver	*	1433	Marston Waver ?and Cestersover
Richard Waver		1490s	Mancetter
William Waver	1420	1433	Marston Waver
John Welay	1484	1484	Birmingham
John Welles	1485	1485	Coventry
John West	1445	1453	Solihull
John West	1465	1478	Little Bromwich
William West	?1474	*	Little Bromwich
George Westbury	1460	1460	Warwick
William Westley	1471	1471	Coventry
John Weston	1402	1433	Weston under Wetherley
Thomas Wexewode	1477	1477	Warwickshire
John Whalley	1434	1451	Coventry
Thomas Whalley	1480	1486	Southam
Richard Whitacre	dead by 1404		Nether Whitacre
Richard Whitacre	1423	1424	Warwickshire
Guy Willenhale	1421	1429	Canley
John Willenhale I	1421	1458	Grandborough
John Willenhale II	1467	*	Grandborough
Richard Willenhale	1421	1437	?Grandborough
Robert Willenhale ?I	1401	1411	Grandborough
Robert Willenhale ?II	1445	1458	Grandborough
Robert Willenhale ?III	1467	1467	Grandborough
Roger Willenhale	1422	1429	Grandborough

Name	1st	Last ref. or death	Residence
Humphrey Willingham	1454	*	Mollington
Thomas Willington	1475	1475	Coleshill
Henry Willoughby	1474	*	Notts., Middleton
Hugh Willoughby	*c.* 1417	1448	Notts., Middleton
John Willoughby	1486	*	Notts., Middleton, Grendon
Robert Willoughby	1462	1474	Notts. (Bingham had his Warks. land)
Richard Wilson	1499	1499	Coventry
Laurence Winstanley	1498	*	Exhall nr. Coventry
Edmund Wistowe	1464	*	Tamworth (Staffs. part)
William Wistowe	1453	1493	?Tamworth (Staffs. part)
Thomas atte Wode I	1415	1466	Woodhouse in Gt. Alne
Thomas atte Wode II	1471	*	Woodhouse
John Woodlow	*	1439	Woodloes
Thomas Woodlow	1408	1436	Woodloes
Thomas Woodshaw	1486	1488	Berkswell
John Wootton	1493	*	?Warwick
Roger Wootton	1442	1466	Warwick
Robert Worsley	1481	*	Cheping Kington
William Worsley	1457	1458	Warwick
John Wyard	*	1404	Alspath
John Wyldegrys	1444	1493	Coventry
Richard Wyldegrys	1459	1472	?Coventry
William Wymondeswold	1415	1436	Coventry
Christopher Wyncote	1491	*	prob. Binton
John Wyncote	between Rich. and Chris.		Binton
Richard Wyncote	1456	1493/4	Binton
Robert Wyncote	1430	1430	Binton
Thomas Wyncote	1401	1401	?Binton
Walter Wyncote	1415	1471	Binton
William Wyncote	1443	1467	Binton
Walter Yous	1441	1441	Knowle

Appendix 2

LISTS OF WARWICKSHIRE KNIGHTS, ESQUIRES AND GENTLEMEN

The following symbols are used: L – lawyer; + – a member of the family of appropriate status is known to hold lands but identity uncertain; & – heir is a minor; given status of father unless particular reasons not to do so; * – on income tax returns, 1436. References for lawyers appear after the lists.

1410

Knights

Ralph Brasebrugge I
Thomas Burdet I
John Cokayn I
& Baldwin Freville II
Thomas Lucy I
John Peche (wid.)
Adam Peshale (by marriage to Baldwin Freville's widow who had part of the estate)
Humphrey Stafford jr.
Baldwin Straunge
Ailred Trussell

Esquires

Thomas Archer
Ralph Ardern
Thomas Astley I
Roger Aylesbury
William Bermingham I[1]
William Bishopestone

[1] Although it is said that Elizabeth Clinton had Birmingham for life, William Bermingham presented to a chantry in the church and styled himself 'lord of Birmingham' (*Dugdale*, p. 901), and his activities in Warwickshire e.g. as M.P. 1413 (*Return: 1878*, I, p. 280) show that he must have been in possession of this, his only Warwickshire manor.

John Botreaux
Lewis Cardian
Robert Castell
L John Catesby I
John Chetwynd
Richard Chetwynd
Richard Clodesdale
\+ William or Edmund Compton of Compton Wyniates
L Thomas Crewe (by marriage to widow of Clopton of Moor Hall)[2]
John Culpepper I
Edward Doddingselles I
Thomas Erdington I
Henry Fillongley I
Thomas Grene
John Harewell I
L Thomas Harewell
Richard Hastings
William Holt of Aston I
Richard Hubaud I
L Robert Hugford
?L John Knightley I
Hugh Lillburne
John Lisle I (de Insula)
Thomas Malory of Bramcote
Richard Marbroke
William Mountford I
John Onley of Birdingbury I
William Peyto
William Purfrey I
Thomas Seyville
Ralph Shirley I
William Shukburgh I
Thomas Stafford of Baginton
Thomas Stokes I
William Trussell I of Bilton
John Waldeve of Alspath

Others

Henry Archer
Robert Ardern of Newbold
Giles Astley
L John Barbour I
William Barbour of Newbold

[2] Estate must have been shared by Crewe and William Clopton, the heir, since both were active in the county at the same time, so both are included.

	Thomas Baron
	James Bellers
	William Botener
	William Brett I
L	John Brewster
L	John Brome I
	John Clopton I
	William Clopton
&	Hugh Cokesey
	John Cotes I
	John de Crewenhale
L	Hugh Dalby of Brookhampton
+	–Derset
	Thomas Duston
+	John/Richard Eton
	John de Flandres
	John Fulwode
L	Thomas Gower I
L	Thomas Greswold of Solihull
	John Greville I
	Thomas Greville
	John Hardwick I
	Thomas Hayton I
	William Holt of Studley
	John Hore of Wishaw
	Thomas Hore of Elmdon
	Thomas Hore of Solihull I
	William Hore of Stoneythorpe I
+	William/Robert Lecroft
+	–Malory of Bishops Tachbrook
	John Malory of Newbold Revel
L	Edward Metley
	Thomas Middlemore
	William de Napton/Betons
	John Onley of Bishops Tachbrook I
	Thomas Palmer of Frankton
+	–Porter of Over Ettington
	Otwell Power
L	Thomas Purfrey
&	William Ralegh I
+	?Robert Rous I
	Nicholas Sauser
	Robert Skerne
	Guy Spine
	Henry Sutton
	Thomas Sydenhale I

Robert Verney
Richard Walsh
Thomas Ward of Birmingham
Thomas Waryng I
John Waver of Marston Waver ?and Cestersover
L John Weston
Richard Whitacre (wid.?)
Robert Willenhale ?I
+ –atte Wode
John Woodlow
+ Thomas/Walter Wyncote

Gentlemen

William de Alstre

1436

Knights

Roger Aston
* William Bishopestone
Nicholas Burdet
* Thomas Burdet I
Philip Chetwynd
* John Cokayn I
* Hugh Cokesey
John Culpepper I
* Edward Doddingselles I
Richard Hastings
* William Mountford
* Ralph Neville
* William Peyto
* Ralph Shirley I
* Humphrey Stafford I
Thomas Straunge I
* William Trussell I of Bilton
* Hugh Willoughby

Esquires

* Geoffrey Allesley
Richard Archer
* Robert Ardern of Castle Bromwich
John Aylesbury I
L* Thomas Beaufitz II
Ralph Bellers

	William Bermingham II
*	William Botener
&	Richard Brasebrugge
*	Edward Bromflete
	John Burgh
L	John Catesby II
	Robert Catesby
*	John Chetwynd
*	John Cotes I
*	Thomas Erdington II
*	Thomas Ferrers I
*	John Fielding[3]
*	Henry Fillongley II
	John Folkesworth (as husband of wid. of Robert Castell)
*	Thomas Grene
L*	Thomas Greswold of Solihull
L	John Greville I
	Richard Harewell (dau. and heiress)
*	Roger Harewell (wid.)
L*	Thomas Harewell
*	Thomas Herthill
*	William Holt of Aston I
*	Gilbert Hore I
*	Richard Hubaud I
	John Hugford I
*	Thomas Hugford
	Richard Knightley I
*	William Lisle
	George Longville[4]
*	William Lucy I
*	John Malory of Newbold Revel (wid.)
*	Simon Malory
	Richard Marbroke
L*	Nicholas Metley[5]
*	John Middlemore I
	Nicholas Middlemore
L	Thomas Mollesley
*	Baldwin Mountford
*	John Onley of Bishops Tachbrook I
*	Robert Onley

3 'Knight' according to Dugdale (p. 86), but nowhere else. Correspondence on the family connected with Dugdale's work suggests this came from a heralds' visitation of 1563, which is not likely to have been very reliable (W.C.R.O. C.R.2017/F105/30).

4 Entered on fig. 3, at Nether Whitacre, one of the estates of the Whitacre inheritance (see app. 1), as Richard, George's son, is once described as 'of Whitacre' (*Cal. Fine Rolls 1452–61*, p. 82).

5 His income and manors have been amalgamated with those of his mother, Margaret.

* Thomas Porter of Eastcote and Longdon
* William Purfrey II
L* William Repington I
* Nicholas Ruggeley I/II[6]
* Robert Stokes
* Thomas Sydenhale II
John Throgmorton I
& John Trussell
* Richard Verney
* John Waldeve of Alspath
William Waldeve
* Thomas Waryng ?II
* Thomas Woodlow

Gentlemen etc.

* Giles Astley (wid.)
L* William Betley I
Thomas Blankame
* ?John Botreaux[7]
* Thomas Boughton I[8]
L* John Bradwell
* William Brett I[9]
L* John Brome II
L Richard Broun
L* John Campion
* John Clopton I
L Edmund Colshill
Hugh Dalby of Brookhampton[10]
* Richard Dalby
* William Derset I

6 See app. 1, n. 19.

7 Although John Botreaux is listed in the tax return of 1436 (perhaps at too low an income level to be the main representative of this family), it has not proved possible to establish exactly which of the family held Alcester in 1436. There appear to have been two John Botreaux in successive generations; the first may well have been dead by 1436, as he is called 'esquire' as early as 1410 (*Cal. Close Rolls 1409–13*, p. 77); the latter, insofar as he has any title, is usually called 'gentleman'. There was also Thomas, the member of the family who sold Alcester to John Beauchamp of Powick in 1444 (*Cal. Pat. Rolls 1441–46*, p. 273), called 'esquire' in 1447 (K.B.27/746 Coram Rege rot.109d.).

8 Although he had yet to succeed to the lands of his father-in-law, Geoffrey Allesley (*V.C.H.*, VI, p. 189), he was assessed on lands in Warwickshire in 1436, presumably the jointure he had received on marrying the Allesley co-heiress.

9 First called 'gentleman' in 1443 (K.B.27/733 Coram Rege rot.95d.), but there is so little evidence for him that he has been given the benefit of the doubt.

10 No known title, but a lawyer, and the father of Richard, a 'gentleman' in 1433 and later an esquire, who was already independent by 1436.

*	William Dixwell
L*	William Donyngton
*	John Durant
*	John Duston ?I
	Thomas Est I[11]
+*	Richard Eton (probably I)
*	John Fulwode
L*	Thomas Gower I
	William Harper[12]
	Thomas Hayton I
	George Herthill
*	Thomas Hore of Elmdon
*	Thomas Hore of Solihull I
*	William Hore of Stoneythorpe I
*	William Lecroft I
*	John Malory of Bishops Tachbrook I[13]
?L	Baldwin Metley
	John Moreton
*	Thomas Muston[14]
*	John Norwood of Coventry
*	William Parker
*	Henry Porter
*	Robert Porter I
*	Richard Rivell
	William Rodborn
L	John Rody II
L*	Nicholas Rody
	John Rous I
*	Richard Rushton of Studley
*	Thomas Shukburgh I
	Henry Somerlane
*	Edmund Starkey
*	Thomas Stretton
*	Walter Verney[15]

[11] 'Valet' or 'yeoman of the crown' from the 1420s, 'esquire' just once, in 1446 (*Cal. Pat. Rolls 1422–29*, p. 35; B.R.L. 434594, 427016).

[12] Not included in calculations about social mobility (see table 4, ch. 4) because nothing at all is known about his origins.

[13] Although the family was still at Bishops Tachbrook in 1500, they have not been counted for that year, because they sold their second manor, Botley, in 1443 (S.B.T. D.R.37 Box 50 (deeds of 1443)) and were not sufficiently involved in the county to qualify for inclusion as a one-manor family.

[14] No title until 1450s, when 'esquire' (e.g. *Cal. Fine Rolls 1452–61*, p. 176), but already manorial lord in 1431/2 (*Dugdale*, p. 673) and features little in records at this time.

[15] No known title in 1436 but 'esquire' in 1446 (Nat. Lib. Wales Peniarth MS 280 fo. 71) and the owner of three Warwickshire manors.

+ ?John Walsh[16]
* John Whalley
* John Willenhale I
* Thomas atte Wode I
* William Wymondeswold
* Walter Wyncote

1500

Knights

Hugh Conway
Simon Digby
Henry Ferrers
John Ferrers II
William Gascoigne II
Richard Knightley III
Richard Pudsey
Edward Ralegh I
Ralph Shirley III
Henry Willoughby

Esquires

John Archer II
John Ardern
Walter Ardern
Thomas Astley of Hillmorton
William Astley of Wolvey II
John Aston II
& John Beaufo
Edward Belknap
William Bermingham III
John Boteller of Solihull II
Thomas Botreaux II
William Boughton
Baldwin Brasebrugge
John Brasebrugge
Richard Brasebrugge
Simon Brasebrugge
Thomas Brereton
Nicholas Brome
William Broun
John Burdet

[16] I have no definite identification of a member of this family between 1432 and 1510 (see app. 1), but it is clear that the family was at Luddington throughout the century (*V.C.H.*, III, p. 265; *Dugdale*, p. 704).

	George Catesby
	Nicholas Catesby
	Thomas Catesby
	William Chetwynd II
	John Cokayn III[17]
	Thomas Cokayn II
	William Cope
L	Gerard Danet
	Edward Doddingselles II
	Richard Empson
	Edward Ferrers
	Everard Fielding
&	Francis Froxmere
	Richard Fulwode
	Thomas Gower II
	John Greswold II
	John Greville III
	Edward Grey
	Thomas Grey[18]
	John Harewell II
L	William Harewell
	Richard Hubaud II
	Richard Hungerford
	Henry Lisle
	Richard Littleton
	Nicholas Malory
	Richard Middlemore
	John Mountford of Monkspath (wid.)
	John Mountford of Kington
	Thomas Mountford of Sutton Coldfield
	Thomas Neville[19]
	John Peyto II
	Nicholas Purfrey II
	William Repington II
&	?Thomas Rous
	Thomas Shukburgh III

[17] Counted separately because in receipt of a regular dole (see above, pp. 115-16).

[18] Some problems of identification, but probably the younger brother of Edward Lord Lisle; no Warwickshire manors if identification is correct, but almost certainly held private office in the county and may have been M.P. in 1491–2 (PROB 11/9 fo. 99, /14 fo. 135; Nott. Univ. Lib. Middleton MS Mi M 139–43; *Wedgwood: Biographies*, p. 399, where a different identification is made). Another possible candidate for the M.P. is Thomas, son of William Grey of Leics. and Lillington, Warks., who was 15 years old in 1495 and came of age in 1502 (*I.P.M. Hen. VII*, I, 1182–3, II, 543).

[19] Despite rather peripheral interests in Warwickshire, included in cross-section because sheriff of Warwickshire and Leicestershire in 1497 (*Lists and Indexes*, 9, p. 146), although this appointment clearly had more to do with his Leicestershire lands.

Thomas Somerville
& Thomas Spenser
Robert Throgmorton
& Edward Trussell
Thomas Trussell of Billesley
Richard Verney II
William Verney (d. *c.* 1497–8, co-heiresses minors in 1500)

Gentlemen

Thomas Andrewes
Ralph Aylesbury
John a Batre (d. 1497, heir a minor)
L John Boteller[20]
Thomas Boteller
Edward Bristowe
John Brome III
Henry Broun
Thomas Bury III
John Clinton
Thomas Clopton II
& William Clopton of Stratford on Avon
William Compton II of Compton Wyniates
L Humphrey Conyngesby
Alexander Corbet
Richard Cotes
Thomas Cotton
John Curson
\+ ?William Dalby II
John Derset II
William Dixwell
\+ William/Henry Durant[21]
Henry Est
John Farndon
L Robert Fulwode
William Grant
Roger Greswold
Robert Hales
L John Hardwick II
John Harewell of Whitley
Thomas Hayton II
Richard Herward

[20] There are serious difficulties in differentiating the various John Botellers of Coventry. This is probably the steward of Coventry (*Coventry Leet Book*, pp. 474, 602–3) and therefore a lawyer. See also above, p. 146 n. 180.

[21] Probably father and son.

John Heryng
Baldwin Hethe
Degory Heynes
+ Roger Holden[22]
William Holt of Aston II
John Hore of Stoneythorpe
Robert Hore of Little Kington
L Thomas Hore (probably II of Solihull)
John Ladbroke
John Lisle II
John Marmeon
L Thomas Marrowe
Robert Massy
Hugh Mervyn
Benedict Metley
Thomas Morgan
Richard Mountford of Church Bickenhill
Thomas Newnham II
Thomas Onley II
William Orchard
Richard Oresby
William Overton
Richard Palmer
John Porter
Robert Porter II
John Prince
Giles Ralegh
William Ruggeley
Nicholas Rushton
Thomas Seman
Thomas Shirwode
Balthasar Shukburgh
Henry Smyth
L John Smyth
John Spenser of Hodnell, Wormleighton etc.
John Starkey
George Tong
Robert Twyford
John Underhill
William Vampage
+ Nicholas/John Waldeve
Hugh Walford
Thomas Waryng III
William West
John Willenhale II

[22] Succeeded by son John some time after 1496 (*Dugdale*, p. 893; K.B.9/411/7.).

John Willoughby, son and heir of Henry
Richard Wilson
Laurence Winstanley
Thomas atte Wode II
Robert Worsley
Christopher Wyncote

References for lawyers (in order of appearance on lists) are given below. There are various indirect ways of identifying the 'legal proletariat', for which see Baker 1980: pp. 183–4, 1983: p. 56. Furthermore, by this time, lawyers were normally chosen for the post of estate steward and sometimes referred to, by virtue of one of their most important duties, as 'courtholders'; they not infrequently appear in *compoti* presiding over manorial courts (Ives 1983a: pp. 12, 29).

Br. Lib. Eg. Rolls 8769, 8772; *Register of Guild of Coventry*, p. 80; Br. Lib. Eg. Roll 8772; Bridges and Whalley 1791: I, p. 66; Br. Lib. Eg. Roll 8772; C.67/41 m. 21; Longleat MS Misc. IX m. 64; *Lists and Indexes*, 9, p. 145; *Marcher Lordships*, p. 49; Br. Lib. Eg. Roll 8772; K.B.27/646 Rex rot.3; S.B.T. D.R.37 Box 107/9; *Dugdale*, p. 54; *Cal. Pat. Rolls 1413–16*, p. 130; Br. Lib. Eg. Roll 8773; *Cal. Close Rolls 1435–41*, p. 147; Br. Lib. Eg. Roll 8772; S.C.R.O. D.641/1/2/162; Norris 1897, p. 17; Nat. Lib. of Wales Peniarth MS 280 fo. 25; Longleat MS 66; *Records of Lincoln's Inn*, I, p. 5 (Repington: no christian name given, but fits dates for William I); K.B.27/737 Coram Rege rot.95, /711 List of Fines; *Dugdale*, p. 970; K.B.27/738 Coram Rege rot.66d.; C.67/42 m.23; *Register of Gild of Stratford*, p. 40; S.C.6/1039/18; *Coventry Leet Book*, p. 99; *Coventry Leet Book*, pp. 157, 236; Br. Lib. Eg. Roll 8772; *Rot. Parl.*, IV, pp. 365–6; *Minister's Accounts of St. Mary's*, p. 7; S.B.T. D.R.10/2429; Cooper 1874: p. 227 ('Master Danet'); Cooper 1936: docs., pp. 6–7; *Coventry Leet Book*, pp. 474, 602–3; Baker 1980: p. 192; C.1/134/23; S.B.T. E.R.112/1/415; C.P.40/860 rot.557; S.B.T. D.R.10/2467; *Early Treatises*, p. 126; *Wedgwood: Biographies*, p. 777.

Appendix 3

NOBLE AND GENTRY MEMBERS OF NOBLE AFFINITIES IN WARWICKSHIRE

For nearly all those listed here there is evidence linking them with their lords' affinities well beyond the precise dates given here (for which, see the text of the book). Those with more tenuous connections, e.g. war service, wardship, have not been listed unless it is evident that their association went beyond this temporary form of association. Note that 'feed' covers fees and annuities.

BEAUCHAMP OF BERGAVENNY[1] AND BOTELLER OF ORMOND AND WILTSHIRE

Name	Date	Capacity	Refs.
John Basset I	1410	Servant	Br. Lib. Add. Ch. 8440
Thomas Blankame	1431–36	Co-def., legatee, servant	K.B.27/682 C.R. rot.69; *Test. Vetust.*, p. 229; S.C.6/767/8
Henry Fillongley	1431–55	Associate, legatee, officer, *de consilio*	K.B.27/682 C.R. rot.69; *Test. Vetust.*, p. 229; Br. Lib. Add. MS 74,169; B.R.L. 504041; S.C.6/1003/32
Thomas Gower I	1426	Officer	
John Harewell	1426	Officer	
Thomas Harewell	1426	Officer	
Thomas Littleton	1447–60	Feoffee, other evidence of assoc.	*H.M.C. Hastings*, I, pp. 1–2; C.P.40/802 rot.125; chs. 9–12, 16

[1] Unless otherwise specified, refs. are S.C.11/25; E.101/514/15.

Name	Date	Capacity	Refs.
John Onley of Birdingbury	*temp.* Ric. II–1416	Officer	B.R.L.168240; *Cal. Pat. Rolls 1401–05*, p. 152
Nicholas Sauser	*c.* 1418–21	Heavily involved in Joan's transactions	*Cal. Pat. Rolls 1416–22*, p. 305; *Cal. Close Rolls 1413–19*, p. 500, *1419–22*, pp. 86–90, 156, 167, 176, 183
Humphrey Stafford I	1448–9	Feed	Br. Lib. Add. Roll 74, 169
Humphrey Stafford II	1451–8	Feed	Br. Lib. Add. Roll 74, 171–8
	BEAUCHAMP OF POWICK[2]		
Thomas Burdet II	1440s	Evidence of association	See chs. 9 and 11
Thomas Littleton	1440s		
John Rous	1440s		
Humphrey Stafford I	*c.* 1446/7		
Humphrey Stafford II	1451–69	Feed, feoffee, bro.-in-law	Br. Lib. Add. Roll 74,171, Add.Ch. 73,926; *Wedgwood: Biographies*, p. 54
	BEAUCHAMP OF WARWICK[3]		
Henry Archer	1407–14	Servant	
Richard Archer	by *c.* 1433	Addresses earl as 'good lord'	S.B.T. D.R.37 Box 56
Thomas Archer	1396–1407	Agent, life ann.	Merevale MS

2 Because of the lack of records for the Beauchamp of Powick, Sudeley and Astley/Grey/Lisle/Bourchier families, much of the evidence for their affinities is cumulative and circumstantial. Only the more telling pieces of evidence have been included here, and for further details the reader is referred to part II of the text. Attention is drawn in particular to the account of the Astley/Grey of Ruthin following of the early fifteenth century in chs. 9 and 10 and to the intermingling of Grey and Sudeley associates from *c.* 1450, especially after Sudeley's death and the division of the estate, for which see ch. 16.

3 Unless otherwise specified, refs. are as follows: Br. Lib. Eg. Rolls 8477–8534, 8769–8775; E.368/220/107d.–9; S.C.12/18/45; Longleat MS 6414, Misc.IX; W.C.R.O. C.R.895/8/1–23; Worcs.R.O. 899:95/75–109 (for household and estate accounts) and Bod. Lib. Dugdale MS 2, p. 279; Br. Lib. Cotton Roll XIII.7, Add. MS 24,704/35–7; E.101/51/2 (for the war retinue: S.B.T. D.R.37 Box 48 (Alan Straunge's will) provides dating for those of 1417). Many of the affinity can be found in these documents as well as in the sources to which specific references are given, and the same point applies to other affinities for which blanket references are given, particularly Stafford.

Name	Date	Capacity	Refs.
Ralph Ardern	1396–1420	Officer, war ret., feed	
Robert Ardern	1420–36	Ward, uses earl as feoffee	C.139/153/21
John Barbour I	1408–18	Officer, ?war ret.	
John Barbour II	1408–09	*De consilio*	
John Basset ?II	1446	Officer	*Cal. Pat. Rolls 1452–61*, p. 587
John Beaufitz	1446–47	Feed by Beauchamp keepers	
William Bermingham I	1417	War ret.	
William Betley	1445	K.B. attorney to Warwick executors	K.B.27/737 C.R. rot.95
William Bishopestone	1414–15	War ret.	
Ralph Brasebrugge I	1415–20	War ret., preferential leases	*D.K.R.*, 44, p. 569; Bod. Lib. Dugdale MS 13, p. 434; Nott. Univ. Lib., Middleton MS Mi D 4743
Ralph Brasebrugge II	1420–1	Ward	
John Brewster	1410–25	Officer, war ret.	
John Brome I	1397–1431	War. M.P., officer	*Return: 1878*, 1
John Brome II	1429–47	War. M.P., officer, *de consilio*, under-sher. Worcs.	*Return: 1878*, 1; *Wedgwood: Register*, p. xliv; Bod. Lib. Dugdale MS 13, p. 434; *Lists and Indexes*, 9, p. 158
Robert Brome	1396– *temp.* earl Rich.	Officer	*Dugdale*, p. 970
Nicholas Burdet	1420–1	Wife in Warwick household	
Thomas Burdet I	1396–1411 and *temp.* Hen. VI	Officer, life ret.	S.B.T. D.R.37 Box 107/23, Strat. Corp. Recs. I/70
Robert Burguloyn	1396–7	?Agent	
John Catesby I	1396–7	Officer, feed	
John Catesby II	1417–31	Attorney, feed	
John Chetwynd	1425–34	Officer, feed	

Name	Date	Capacity	Refs.
William, Lord Clinton	1420–2	In household, has earl as feoffee	*Rot. Parl.*, IV, p. 152
Richard Clodesdale	1417–18	Officer	
William Clopton	1408–17	Life ret., war ret., under-sher. Worcs.	*Lists and Indexes*, 9, p. 157
Hugh Cokesey	1429–c. 31	Feed, under-sher. Worcs.	*Lists and Indexes*, 9, p. 158
John Cotes	1420–1	Officer	
Thomas Crewe	1400–16	Att. for mother, officer, councillor, under-sher. Worcs.	*Cal. Close Rolls 1399–1402*, p. 371; *Lists and Indexes*, 9, p. 157; Bod. Lib. Dugdale MS 13, p. 434; S.B.T. D.R.37 Box 107/13, 16, 20; B.R.L.434590
Thomas Erdington II	1432–3	Feed	B.R.L. 347934–6; S.B.T. Strat. Corp. Recs. XII/218
Thomas Est	1420–42	Officer	B.R.L. 434598–600
Richard Eton	1420–23	Officer, War. M.P.	*Return: 1878*, I
Edmund Lord Ferrers of Chartley	Hen. V and VI	Evidence of association	Chs. 9, 10; K.B.27/676 C.R. rot.49d. C.139/123/43
William Lord Ferrers of Chartley	Earl Rich. –1447	Life annuity	
John Fulwode	1396	Letters addressed to him (possibly merely as feudal tenant?)	
Thomas Gower I	1402–18	Officer, lawyer	
John Greville I	1420–21	In household of countess	
John Harewell	1417–21	Councillor, under-sher. Worcs.	*Lists and Indexes*, 9, p. 158
Thomas Harewell	1417	War ret.	
George Herthill	1437	'Dilecto fideli nostro'	S.B.T. E.R.1/65/448
Thomas Herthill	1417–47	War ret., feed by keepers	
Thomas Holden	1446–47	Feed by keepers	

Name	Date	Capacity	Refs.
William Holt I	1420–*c.* 31	In household, feed, under-sher. Worcs.	*Lists and Indexes*, 9, p. 158
John Hugford I	1433–37	Officer	S.B.T. D.R.37 Box 108; Oxon.L.R.O. Dillon MS I/b/1
John Hugford II	1446	Life annuity from keepers	D.L. 29/645/10464
Robert Hugford	1396–1409	Under-sher. Worcs., officer, life ret.	*Lists and Indexes*, 9, p. 157; *Dugdale*, p. 278; War. Castle MS 481–3; B.R.L.168234, 168024; S.B.T. D.R.37 Box 107/6, 10–12, 14, 16
Thomas Hugford	1417–47	Officer, councillor, executor, life annuitant, under-sher. Worcs.	*Dugdale*, p. 278; S.B.T. E.R.1/99 fo. 93, D.R.37 Box 108, D.R.10/2429; War. Corp. Muns. W.19/5; War. Castle MS 491; *Test. Vetust.*, p. 233; *Lists and Indexes*, 9, p. 158; Gloucs.R.O. D.184/M15/5–6, 16; B.R.L.434595
Richard Knightley	1417–21	Officer, councillor	
John Lisle	1414–15	War ret.	
Thomas Lucy	1408–09	Life ret.	
William Lucy I	1446–47	Feed by keepers	
Thomas Malory of Newbold Revel	?1414–1447	?War ret., feed by keepers	See app. 1 n. 13
Edward Metley	1397–1401	Officer	S.B.T. D.R.37 Box 107/8, 9; B.R.L.168234
Richard Middlemore	1428	Retinue	*Annales S. Albani*, 1, p. 68
Thomas Mollesley	1442–8	Agent, Henry to be prayed for in chantry	*Cal. Pat Rolls 1446–52*, p. 150
William Mountford	1415–41	War ret. officer, life ret., under-sher. Worcs., executor of Isabel, chief of	*D.K.R.*, 48, p. 569; B.R.L. 434594; *Lists*

Name	Date	Capacity	Refs.
		council	*and Indexes*, 9, p. 158; PROB 11/3 fo. 212d.; War. Castle MS 373,485; *Dugdale*, p. 1,009
William Muston	1439–46	Keeper of Isabel's lands, under-sher. Worcs.	*Cal. Pat. Rolls 1436–41*, p. 360; *Lists and Indexes*, 9, p. 158
Thomas Newnham I	1432	Officer	
John Norwood	1439	Executor of Isabel	PROB 11/3 fo. 212d.
John Onley of Tachbrook	1402–27	Officer, councillor	War. Castle MS 373; S.B.T. D.R.41/71 fo. 32, D.R.37 Box 107/13, 23
William Parys	1397–1421	Retainer	
William Peyto	1423–47	Life ret., feed by keepers	War. Corp. Muns. W.19/5; *Dugdale*, p. 476
Thomas Porter	1428–47	Retinue, officer, feed	*Annales S. Albani*, 1, p. 68; Bod. Lib. Dugdale MS 13, p. 434
Walter Power	1396–1402	Servant, life annuitant	B.R.L.168234; *Ministers' Accounts of St Mary's*, p. 69
Thomas Purfrey	1396– *temp.* earl Rich.	Councillor	*Dugdale* p. 54
William Ralegh	1436	Feed	C.139/123/43/28
William Repington I	1446	Remainders lands to Duke Henry's heirs	E.326/8627
John Rody II	1420–37	War. M.P.	*Return: 1878*, 1
Nicholas Rody	1413–47	War. M.P., under-sher. Worcs., executor, feed, officer	*Return: 1878*, 1; *Lists and Indexes*, 9, p. 158; *Test. Vetust.*, p. 233
William Rudyng	1399–1441	Warwick M.P.	*Return: 1878*, 1
Nicholas Ruggeley I	1400–32	Officer	Bod. Lib. Dugdale MS 13, p. 434
Robert Skerne	1425–29	Evidence of association, feudal tenant	S.B.T. D.R.98/85, 455, 460

Name	Date	Capacity	Refs.
William Spernore	1397–1401	Feoffee, ?officer	*Cal. Close Rolls 1396–99*, p. 157, *1399–1402*, pp. 113, 454
Guy Spine	1396–99[4]	Officer, feed	S.B.T. D.R.37 Box 107/7; War. Castle MS 481
Humphrey Stafford jr.	1412–14	War ret., under-sher. Worcs.	*Lists and Indexes*, 9, p. 157; above, p. 80 n. 156
Humphrey Stafford I	1431–49	Under-sher. Worcs., feed	*Lists and Indexes*, 9, p. 158; Br. Lib. Add. Roll 74,168; above, p. 80 n. 156
Thomas Stafford	1396–1427	Life ret.	S.B.T. D.R.10/2119a
Thomas Stokes I	1414–21	War ret., feed	
Alan Straunge	1417	War ret.	
Baldwin Straunge	1408–21	Officer, war ret., widow feed, dau. in earl's household, under-sher. Worcs.	*D.K.R.*, 44, p. 555; *Lists and Indexes*, 9, p. 158
Richard Lord Straunge	*c.* 1431	Feed	
Thomas Straunge	1420–36	Evidence of association and family tradition	W.C.R.O. C.R.133/12, 15; Alan and Baldwin, above
John Lord Talbot	1436	Annuitant	E.163/7/31 Part 1
John Throgmorton	1416–39	Feed, under-sher. Worcs., officer, councillor, life ret., executor, lawyer	Coughton Court Throgmorton MS Exhibition Box/18; *Lists and Indexes*, 9, p. 158; Roskell 1954: p. 224; Ross 1956: p. 12; War. Castle MS 373, 485, 490; Oxon.L.R.O. Dillon MS 1/b/1–2; *Dugdale*, p. 750; *Test. Vetust.*, p. 233

4 Served Surrey as holder of part of the estate 1398–99, which is no doubt why he had no further known employment on the Warwick estates.

Name	Date	Capacity	Refs.
Thomas Throgmorton I	1396–1404/5	Officer	Worcs. C.R.O. 705: 962 Boxes 5, 6; *Dugdale*, p. 750
Ailred Trussell	1396–1400	Retainer and feoffee	*Dugdale*, p. 716; *Cal. Close Rolls 1399–1402*, p. 113
William Trussell I of Bilton	1430	War ret.	*D.K.R.*, 48, p. 269
John Verney	1422–32	Officer	S.B.T. D.R.37 Box 108, D.R.98/722; War. Corp. Muns. W.19/5; War. Castle MS 373, 485–8; Gloucs.R.O. D.184/M15/1–4; Br. Lib. Add. Roll 26, 899–900; S.C.6/1303/13; B.R.L. 167998–9, 434595; above, p. 130 n. 127
Richard Verney	1428–46	Retinue, officer, Beauchamp arms in windows	*Annales S. Albani*, I, p. 68; S.B.T. D.R.98/722; *Dugdale*, p. 565
Alan Waldeve	1396	Letters addressed to him (possibly merely as feudal tenant?)	
John Waldeve	1408–28 (pos. 1432)	Life ret., war ret., officer	*Annales S. Albani*, I, p. 68
William Waldeve	1417–18	Officer	
William Waver	1420–21	Member of earl's household	
John Weston	1403–22	*De consilio*, under-sher., Worcs., War. M.P.	*Lists and Indexes*, 9, p. 158; *Return: 1878*, I
Thomas Woodlow	1408–23	Officer, life annuitant	War. Castle MS 373 B.R.L.434591
John Wyard	1396–1401	Feed	*V.C.H.*, III, p. 265

BOTELLER OF SUDELEY

Name	Date	Capacity	Refs.
John Aylesbury I	1451	Agent	W.C.R.O. L.1/78

Name	Date	Capacity	Refs.
John Aylesbury II	*c.* 1460s–71	Servant	S.B.T. D.R.41/20 fo. 47; C.67/49 m. 33
John Beaufitz	1439–73	Deputy at Kenilworth, feoffee, life annuitant, agent, remembers him in prayers, officer	D.L.29/463/7541; C.140/47/58; W.C.R.O. L.1/88; *C.A.D.*, II, B2510; PROB 11/8 fo. 161; C.P.40/856 rot.177d.
Thomas Beaufitz	1438	Acts as Sudeley's deputy	*Cal. Close Rolls 1435–41*, p. 147
Richard Bingham	1473	Executor	E.101/516/8
Henry Boteller	?–1473	Life annuitant, executor for Sudeley and Waldeve	C.140/47/58; S.B.T. D.R.41/20 fo. 47; W.C.R.O. C.R.136/C421; E.101/516/8
Richard Brasebrugge	1473	Executor	E101/516/8
William Bristowe	?–1473	Executor, feoffee for John Beaufitz	E.101/516/8; S.B.T. D.R.98/456
Thomas Clopton I	1460s	Servant	S.B.T. D.R.41/20 fo. 47
Richard Dalby	n.d.	Officer	Bod. Lib. Dugdale MS 15, pp. 225–6
Thomas Durant	*c.* 1464–5	Favoured/ protected by him	S.B.T. D.R.41/20 fo. 47; *Dugdale*, p. 602
Thomas Harewell	1441	Officer	S.B.T. D.R.3/815
William Lucy II	1473	Executor	E.101/516/8
Thomas Parker	1467–68	Servant	B.R.L. 168248
William Raves	1460s–1488	Servant, legatee of John Beaufitz	S.B.T. D.R.41/20 fo. 47; PROB 11/8 fo. 161
John Throgmorton	1439–45	Sudeley a witness and exec. for him	Coughton Court, Throckmorton MS Box 52 (deed of 1439); PROB 11/3 fo. 248d.
Thomas Throgmorton II	1450s–68	Evidence of assoc., feoffee, family tradition	W.C.R.O. L.1/79/81, 85; C.140/47/58
Thomas Waldeve	1468–73	Witness, executor	W.C.R.O. C.R.136/C420a; E.101/516/8
Thomas Waryng	1472	Officer	C.P.40/856 rot.177d.

Name	Date	Capacity	Refs.
Hugh Willoughby	1443	'My lord'	*Test. Ebor.*, II, p. 134
	FERRERS OF CHARTLEY		
Richard Archer	1448	Uses Ferrers as feoffee	S.B.T. D.R.37 Box 42/ 2503
John Bradwell	1431	Co-defendant	K.B.27/681 R. rot. 21
Robert Catesby	1422–24	Officer	Longleat MS 66
Edmund Colshill	1431	Co-defendant	K.B.27/681 R. rot.21
Thomas Erdington II	1431	Co-defendant	K.B.27/681 R. rot.21
Nicholas Metley	1436	Feed	E.163/7/31 Part I[5]
Thomas Mollesley	1422–25	*De consilio*	Longleat MS 66
William Parker	n.d.	Originally from Chartley	*Dugdale*, p. 783
William Repington I	1436	Feed	E.163/7/31 Part I
Thomas Stretton	1442	Feoffee	*Cal. Pat. Rolls 1441–46*, p. 52
John Throgmorton	1422–36	Dined and feed	Longleat MS 66; E.163/7/31 Part I
Thomas Waryng	1431	Co-defendant	K.B.27/681 R. rot.21
Richard Whitacre	1423	Co-defendant	K.B.9/203/18
	GEORGE DUKE OF CLARENCE[6]		
John Archer II	1475	War ret., 'good lord'	S.B.T. D.R.37 Box 83, E.R.3/667[7]
Richard Beauchamp of Powick	*c.* 1471–78	Officer	D.L.29/644/10458; *Cal. Pat. Rolls 1476–85*, p. 97
Thomas Burdet II	by 1477	'Servant'	*Rot. Parl.*, VI, p. 193; above, p. 521
William Catesby II	by 1478	Officer	D.L.29/640/10388; S.B.T. D.R.5/2870
Henry Ferrers	1461–72	Officer in Tutbury	Somerville 1953: p. 543
John Ferrers I	by 1478	Annuitant	D.L.29/645/10464;

5 List headed 'William Lord Ferrers': see Carpenter, M.C. 1976: app. 106 n. 1 for grounds for assigning it to Chartley rather than Groby.

6 The use of royal accounts for the Clarence affinity rests on the assumption (in some cases capable of confirmation) that the early appointment to offices etc. after Clarence's attainder represent reappointments to those granted by the duke.

7 Anonymous petition to Clarence but the contents make the identification of the petitioner almost certain.

Name	Date	Capacity	Refs.
William Harecourt	1472	Officer	S.B.T. D.R.5/2870 Bod. Lib. Dugdale MS 15, p. 278
Roger Harewell (of Worcs. branch)	by 1478	In household	*Rot. Parl.*, VI, p. 194
William Lord Hastings	1472	Officer	*H.M.C. Hastings*, I, p. 302
John Hethe	by 1478	Servant	D.L.29/642/10421
Roger Holden	by 1478	Officer	*Cal. Pat. Rolls 1476–85*, p. 163
John Hugford II	1472–78	Officer, life annuity	D.L.29/642/10421, 645/10464; S.B.T. D.R.5/2870; *Coventry Leet Book*, p. 381
William Hugford	by 1478	Annuitant	S.B.T. D.R.5/2870
Richard Hyde	1472–77	Servant, under-sher. Worcs.	*Cal. Pat. Rolls 1476–85*, p. 72; *Lists and Indexes*, 9, p. 158
Benedict Metley	by 1478	Servant	E.404/76/4/102
Humphrey Stafford II	by 1478	Feed	S.B.T. D.R.5/2870
Edmund and John Sutton of Dudley	1474	Officers, feed	E.159/258 adhuc Hil. between mm. 28 and 29
Edmund Verney	by 1478	Officer	D.L.29/643/10436
Richard Verney	1475	Duke arbitrates between him and collegiate church of Warwick	B.R.L.437204
GREY OF GROBY AND LISLE, ASTLEY AND BOURCHIER			
Thomas Astley I	early 15th *c.*	Family	*Colls. Hist. Staffs.*, n.s., I, p. 235
Thomas Bellers	1451–71	Evidence of assoc.	W.C.R.O. C.R.162/69, 227; *Dugdale*, p. 86; *I.P.M. Hen. VII*, II, 355; see also William Fielding, below.
Henry Boteller	1442–81	Assoc., attorney, feed	K.B.27/726 C.R. rot.60d., /754 C.R. rot.105d., /766 C.R. rot.64; *W.F.F.*, 2630: C.P.40/878 rot.466;

Name	Date	Capacity	Refs.
			Colls. Hist. Staffs., n.s., 6, i, p. 140; W.C.R.O. C.R.136/C422.
Thomas Boughton	1432–52	Officer, associate	W.C.R.O. C.R.136/156, 157; K.B.27/726 C.R. rot.60d., /738 C.R. rot.99, /766 C.R. rot.64
William Catesby II	1482	*De consilio*	*Cat. Anc. Deeds*, IV, A6600
Edward Durant	1450–53	Associate, attorney	K.B.27/766 C.R. rot.64, /769 C.R. Writs of Att.; C.P.40/756 rot.333
William Fielding	1452–70	Feoffee, other evidence of assoc.	C.1/27/268 (but NB /271c); *Cal. Close Rolls 1461–68*, p. 179; *H.M.C. Lothian*, p. 55; Nichols 1795–1811: IV, i, p. 287; see also Thomas Bellers, above.
Thomas Grey	by 1492	Officer	PROB 11/9 fo. 99
Richard Hotoft	1440–41	Feed	W.C.R.O. C.R.136/ C159
Edward Hungerford	1481–1500	In family deeds of Greys	*I.P.M. Hen. VII*, I, 249; Nott. Univ. Lib., Middleton MS Mi D 4798; *Cal. Close Rolls 1485–1500*, p. 365; E.326/9773
William Lucy II	1481	Relative, feoffee	*I.P.M. Hen. VII*, I, 249; *Dugdale*, p. 507; Nott. Univ. Lib., Middleton MS Mi D 4798
John Smyth	1474–96	Feoffee, attorney, legal adviser, associate, officer, agent	*Cal. Close Rolls 1485–1500*, pp. 150, 365; *I.P.M. Hen. VII*, I, 249, 764, II, 802; K.B.27/893 C.R. rot.45, /924 C.R. rot.59; C.P.40/852 rot.203, /890 rot.478 (*bis*); E.326/6810, 9773;

Name	Date	Capacity	Refs.
			W.C.R.O. C.R.136/ C312; Nott. Univ. Lib., Middleton MS 6/ 173/24; S.C.6/Hen. VII/1105
Henry Willoughby	1486–89	Lisle supervisor of his will, family tie	*H.M.C. Middleton*, p. 122; Nott. Univ. Lib., Middleton MS Mi D 4798
		WILLIAM LORD HASTINGS	
John Aston	21 Ed. IV	Life indenture	Dunham 1955: p. 120
Richard Boughton	19 Ed.IV	Life indenture	Dunham 1955: p. 120
John Burdet	22 Ed.IV	Life indenture	Dunham 1955: p. 120
William Catesby II	*c.* 1474–83	Officer of Ralph Hastings, evidence of assoc.	*Cat. Anc. Deeds,* IV, A9178; Ives 1983a: p. 94; Roskell 1981b: p. 315; above, pp. 00
John Cokayn III	15 Ed.IV	Life indenture	Dunham 1955: p. 119
Thomas Cokayn II	15 Ed.IV	Life indenture	Dunham 1955: p. 119
Ferrers of Tamworth	1448–83	Relatives, evidence of assoc., war ret.	*H.M.C. Hastings,* I, pp. 300, 2–3, 295–6; B.R.L.610247/47a; E.159/255 communia Hil. mm. 21–21d.; above p. 00
Simon Mountford	9 Ed.IV	Life indenture	Dunham 1955: p. 119
Nicholas Ruggeley II	21 Ed.IV	Life indenture	Dunham 1955: p. 120
John Shirley	14 Ed.IV	Life indenture	Dunham 1955: p. 119
Ralph Shirley III	21 Ed.IV	Life indenture	Dunham 1955: p. 120
Edward Trussell of Bilton	1481	Ward	PROB 11/7 fo. 76v.
William Trussell II of Bilton	15 Ed.IV	Life indenture	Dunham 1955: p. 119
Henry Willoughby	17 Ed.IV	Life indenture	Dunham 1955: p. 120
		MOWBRAY OF NORFOLK	
John Brome	?1422–45	?*De consilio*, agent, officer	Br. Lib. Add. Roll 17,209; E.101/514/17; Griffiths 1980b, p. 114
John Chetwynd	1428	Agent	E.101/514/17

Name	Date	Capacity	Refs.
Hugh Dalby	*temp*. Rich. II –1432	Feed, agent, officer, life ret.	*Dugdale*, p. 562; *Cal. Close Rolls 1422–29*, p. 221; *Marcher Lordships*, p. 49; E.101/514/17; C.139/60/43/14; Br. Lib. Add. Roll 17,209
Richard Dalby	1454–75	Officer, war ret.	*Dugdale*, p. 562; C.1/28/482
Richard Hastings	1429	General attorney	*North Country Wills*, p. 37
?Hugh Lillburne	?	Had served Nottingham before late 1399	*Cal. Pat. Rolls 1399–1401*, p. 207
Thomas Littleton	1449	Officer and farmer	N.R.A. 'College of Arms', 631–2
Nicholas Metley	1428	Legal agent	E.101/514/17
Edward Neville Lord Bergavenny	Life office	Br. Lib. Royal MS 17B XLVII fo. 113b	
		NEVILLE OF WARWICK	
John Archer I	1450–54	Uses earl as feoffee	S.B.T. D.R.37 Box 53
Thomas Bate	1451–56	Life annuitant	S.C.6/1038/2
Richard Beauchamp of Powick	1457–71	Officer	*Cal. Pat. Rolls 1476–85*, p. 97; D.L. 29/644/10458
John Beaufitz	1468	Witness for grant	Bod. Lib. Dugdale MS 15, p. 73
William Bermingham II	*c*. 1460–5	Feed	C.1/29/343
John Bourchier	1461–?68	Councillor	*Wedgwood: Biographies*, p. 616 n. 1; S.B.T. D.R.10/2000.
Thomas Burdet II	1451–60	Life annuitant	B.R.L.168023
William Catesby I	1460s	Uses earl as feoffee, said to be in favour	*Cat. Anc. Deeds*, III, A4251; P.R.O. Catesby Doc.
Richard Clapham	1455–70	Officer, fellow rebel	S.C.6/1038/2; Scofield 1923: I, pp. 51, 496, 521–2 (C.P.40/852 rot.339 probably

Name	Date	Capacity	Refs.
			confirms death in Readeption)
Edward Durant	1467–68	War. M.P.	*Return: 1878*, I
Thomas Erdington II	1453–70	Feed	Bod. Lib. Dugdale MS 13, p. 435; C.1/29/343; C.P.40/841 rot.130
Henry Everingham	1450–60	Life annuitant	S.C.6/1038/2; *Cal. Pat. Rolls 1452–61*, p. 587
Thomas Ferrers II	1455–?68	Feed; ?favour to earl's councillors as sheriff	B.R.L.434600; S.B.T. D.R.10/2000
John Greville II	1452–60	Life annuitant	B.R.L.168023
Robert Greville	1454–60	Life annuitant	B.R.L.168023
Edward Grey II of Groby	1461–70	Councillor, fellow rebel	*Wedgwood: Biographies*, p. 616 n. 1; Coughton Court, Throckmorton MS Exhibition Box; K.B.9/329/44
William Harecourt	1452–*c.* 65	Officer, feed	Bod. Lib. Dugdale MS 13, p. 434; C.1/29/343
William Harewell	1455–71	Feed, fellow rebel	S.B.T. D.R.37 Box 108; *Dugdale*, p. 810
William Hastings	1461–68	Councillor, officer	*Wedgwood: Biographies*, p. 616 n. 1; *H.M.C. Hastings*, I, p. 302
John Herthill	s.d.–1470	Officer, fellow rebel	*Dugdale*, p. 971; *Cal. Pat. Rolls 1467–77*, p. 218
John Hugford II	1449–71	Life annuitant, officer, fellow rebel	D.L.29/645/10464; Bod. Lib. Dugdale MS 13, p. 434; B.R.L.168023; K.B.27/836 Coram Rege rot.61d.
Thomas Hugford	1450–57	Life annuitant, officer	S.C.6/1038/2; War. Castle MS 491; Bod. Lib. Dugdale MS 13, p. 434; S.B.T. D.R.37 Box 108
William Hugford	by 1468–1471	Life annuitant, agent	C.81/1521/41; E.326/6461
Bartholomew Knight	1455–56	Agent (?officer)	Worcs.C.R.O. 899:95/112

Name	Date	Capacity	Refs.
Richard Knightley II	1468	Witness for earl in company with identifiable affinity	Bod. Lib. Dugdale MS 15, p. 73
John de Middleham	1450s	Brought to Warks.	Above, p. 126 n. 113
Thomas Middleton	1452–68	Life annuitant, witness, under-sher. Worcs.	B.R.L.168023; Bod. Lib. Dugdale MS 15, p. 73; *Lists and Indexes*, 9, p. 158
Baldwin Mountford	1451–56	Life annuitant	S.C.6/1038/2
Simon Mountford	1456/7	Retained as councillor	*Dugdale*, p. 1,011; Bod. Lib. Dugdale MS 13, p. 434
Thomas Muston	1468–9	Witness, has earl as feoffee	Bod. Lib. Dugdale MS 15, p. 73; K.B.9/324/25
William Muston	1455	Widow feed for life	Br. Lib. Eg. Roll 8540
John Otter	1458–70	Brought to Warks., servant, favoured by earl, fellow rebel	Above, p. 126 n. 113; *Cal. Fine Rolls 1452–61*, p. 199, *1467–77*, p. 218; *Paston Letters*, ed. Gairdner, III, p. 199; C.81/1378/16
Robert Otter	1450s–70	Brought to Warks., fellow rebel	Above, p. 126 n. 113; *Cal. Pat. Rolls 1467–77*, p. 218
Nicholas Rody	1449–58	Officer	K.B.27/765 Coram Rege rot.64; B.R.L.168023; W.C.R.O. C.R.26/1(1)/W.25, /xxx
John Rous I	1452–57	Life annuitant	S.B.T. D.R.37 Box 108
John Shirwode	1450s	Brought to Warks.	above. p. 126 n. 113
Thomas Shirwode	1462	?Servant of earl's bro., Geo.	*Cal. Close Rolls 1461–68*, p. 158
Henry Somerlane	1451–68	Officer, witness	War. Castle MS 491; Bod. Lib. Dugdale MS 15, p. 73
Humphrey Stafford II	1450–53	Feed, personal connections	Br. Lib. Add. MS 74,169, 74,171, 74,173
Thomas Stretton	1452–56	Life annuitant	S.C.6/1038/2

Name	Date	Capacity	Refs.
Thomas Throgmorton II	1451–69	Life annuitant, officer	Coughton Court, Throckmorton MS Box 59/8, Exhib. Box; S.B.T. D.R.37 Box 108; Worcs.C.R.O. 899:95/113

STAFFORD OF STAFFORD AND BUCKINGHAM[8]

Name	Date	Capacity	Refs.
Thomas Astley ?II	1450–51	Officer	
Roger Aston	1420–43	Custodian, executor, grantee	*Cal. Fine Rolls 1413–22*, p. 362; S.C.R.O. D 1721/11 fo. 22
John Aylesbury I	1449–50	Officer	
Thomas Bate	1444–53	Feed, *de consilio*	Longleat 6411; S.C.6/1040/15; B.R.L.168236
William Bermingham II	1456–57	Feed	
Richard Boteller ?I and II	1450–1501	Servant	Br. Lib. Add. MS 29,608
Thomas Burdet II	1442–45		
William Catesby II	1475–83	Receives regard, officer	*Cal. Pat. Rolls 1485–94*, p. 235; *Marcher Lordships*, p. 84; Rawcliffe 1978: p. 226
Philip Chetwynd	1431–44	Life ret., war ret.	*Colls. Hist. Staffs.*, o.s., 12, pp. 312–13, 318–20
William Chetwynd ?I	1485–88	Feed	
William Chetwynd II	1498–99	Feed	
Richard Clapham	1465–66	Feed	
John Cokayn I	1437	Held Duchy office with duke	Somerville 1953: p. 556
John Cokayn III	1438–54	Officer, life annuitant	
Richard Dalby	1434–68	Officer, war ret., lessee	*D.K.R.*, 48, pp. 361, 365; B.R.L.168236
William Draycote	1439–50	Officer	
Edmund Lord Ferrers of Chartley	1432	Justice	*Marcher Lordships*, p. 76
Henry Ferrers	1456–57	Feed	
John Ferrers [of Chartley]	1449–50	Servant	

[8] Unless otherwise specified, references are S.C.R.O. D.641/1/2/15–17, 21, 23, 26–8, 57, 59, 65, 76, 162, 174, 186, 254, 269–79; Nat. Lib. of Wales Peniarth MS 280; S.C.6/Hen.VII/450–3, 867–9.

Name	Date	Capacity	Refs.
John Greville ?I	1433–34	Officer	
John Greville II	1472–74	Officer	Br. Lib. Add. MS 29,608
William Greville	by 1504	Has given service, probably *de consilio*	
Edward Lord Grey of Groby	1440–*c.* 54	Life annuitant, associate	Above, chs. 11–12
Robert Grey of Groby	1444/5	Indentured annuitant	
William Harecourt	1460–66	Officer	
John Harewell II	1501	Officer	
William Lord Hastings	1461–67	Retained with annuity	S.C.6/1117/11
Richard Hotoft	1440–57	Annuitant, *de consilio*	Longleat 6411; B.R.L.168236
John Hugford II	1461–74	Officer	Br. Lib. Add. MS 29,608
Richard Littleton	1501	Officer	S.C.6/Hen.VII/1844
Thomas Littleton	1440s–63	Evidence of assoc., *de consilio*	Above, p. 412; S.C.6/1040/15
Thomas Mollesley	1440	Justice	
Edmund Mountford	1450s–77	Aided by duke, officer	Above, ch. 12
Robert Onley	1444–54	Officer, annuitant	Longleat 6411
Thomas Slade	1500–	Officer	
Humphrey Stafford I	1442–49	Officer, feed, war ret., justice	Br. Lib. Add. MS 74,168
John Trussell	1433–*c.* 46	In wardship	*Dugdale*, p. 761
Thomas Trussell	1440–51	Life ret., officer	
William Trussell [of Billesley]	1497–	Officer	
John Verney	1439–42	Feed	Wm. Salt Lib. Wm. Salt Orig. Coll. M.558
Richard Verney	?1440s	Stafford arms in his windows	*Dugdale*, p. 565
Walter Verney	1438–39	Wife feed	
Hugh Willoughby	1443	'My lord'	*Test. Ebor.*, II, p. 134

TALBOT OF SHREWSBURY AND LISLE

John Brome	1452	Executor	Pollard 1968: p. 420

Name	Date	Capacity	Refs.
William Catesby I	1452, 1453–	Executor, relative by marr.	Pollard 1968: pp. 225, 420
Hugh Cokesey	1419–24	Family connections	Pollard 1968: pp. 225–6; *Rot. Parl.*, IV, p. 254
Richard Dalby	1451	Officer	Pollard 1968: p. 310
Henry Everingham	1440s, 1460s	Close family links	Pollard 1968: pp. 222–4, 417–20; above, p. 461 n. 69
William Peyto	1434–43	Various capacities in war	Pollard 1968: pp. 422–3, 1983: p. 80
		OTHERS	
John Archer I	1453–60	M.P., officer to duke of Exeter	S.B.T. D.R.37 Box 91; *Wedgwood: Biographies*, p. 18; 'Worcestre', 'Annales', II, pp. 481–2
John Archer I	1459–60	Officer to Edward Neville Lord Bergavenny	S.B.T. E.R.1/65/456, D.R.37 Box 91
John Ardern	1488	Took Straunge livery	K.B.9/380/41(1)
John Lord Beauchamp of Powick	between 1422 and 1435	War ret., war councillor to Bedford	Bod. Lib. Dugdale MS 10 fo. 65
Richard Beauchamp of Powick	1470	Life annuity from Lord Berkeley	Br. Lib. Add. Ch. 72,687
Henry Boteller	1471	Steward to Lord Berkeley for Caludon	S.B.T. D.R.10/730
Henry Boteller	1461	Life ret. *de consilio* to Lord Zouche, officer	*I.P.M. Hen. VII*, III, 1144
James Boteller, Earl of Wiltshire	1450–53	Feed by duke of York	Br. Lib. Eg. Ch. 8773–4
Ralph Boteller Lord Sudeley	between 1422 and 1435	War ret., chamb. to Bedford	Bod. Lib. Dugdale MS 10 fo. 65
Edward Bromflete	1460	Will supervised by Henry Bromflete Lord	

Name	Date	Capacity	Refs.
		De Vesci	PROB 11/4 fo. 146
George Catesby	1477	Life annuitant of Lady Latimer	*Cat. Anc. Deeds,* IV, A7459
William Catesby II	1477	Life annuitant of Lady Latimer	*Test. Vetust.*, p. 360; *Cat. Anc. Deeds,* IV, A7459
William Catesby II	1481	Officer to John Lord Scrope	*Cat. Anc. Deeds,* IV, A8336
William Catesby II	1481	Officer to John Lord Zouche	*Cat. Anc. Deeds,* IV, A9650
William Catesby II	1483	Life annuity from Lord Stanley	*Cat. Anc. Deeds,* IV, A10182
Philip Chetwynd	1441	Allegedly friendly with Lord Bonville	*Procs. Priv. Counc.*, V, pp. 160–1
John Lord Clinton	1455–56	Fellow rebel, feed by York	*Paston Letters*, ed. Gairdner, III, p. 30; Rosenthal 1965: p. 191
Richard Clodesdale	1428	Bedford, '*dominum meum*', his executor	PROB 11/3 fo. 74
Richard Cotes	1488	Took Straunge livery	K.B.9/380/41(1)
Richard Dalby	1463	Officer to dowager duchess of York	*Sir Christopher Hatton*, p. 266
Henry Ferrers	1458	Dispute arbitrated by York	Rosenthal 1970
John Fielding	n.d.	War ret. of Bedford	*Dugdale*, p. 86
Leonard Hastings	1415–48	War ret. of, feed by March/ York family	Br. Lib. Harl. MS 782; *H.M.C. Hastings,* I, p. 158
William Hastings	1458–61	Agent, rebel for York	*Cat. Anc. Deeds,* IV, A6338; *G.E.C.*, VI, p. 370
William Lord Hastings	1477	Officer to Lord Bergavenny	*H.M.C. Hastings,* I, p. 271
William Lord Hastings	1461	Officer to John Lord Lovell	*Sir Christopher Hatton*, p. 21

Name	Date	Capacity	Refs.
William Lord Hastings	1480	Exec. and surveyor to Lady Latimer's will	*Test. Vetust.*, p. 360
William Lecroft II	by 1488	Feed by Lord Clinton	*I.P.M. Hen. VII*, I, 331
Thomas Littleton	1451–64	Life annuity *de consilio* from Lord Clinton	C.140/13/22/2
Edward Lucy	1468–80	Officer to Greys of Ruthin	Jack, ed., p. 54 n. 69
William Lucy II	1481–91	Connections with Greys of Ruthin and Dorset	*Cal. Close Rolls 1485–1500*, p. 181; *Cat. Anc. Deeds*, II, B3528; see above, p. 694, for his other Grey connections
Nicholas Metley	1436	Feed by John Lord Lescrope	E.163/7/31 Part I
Edmund Mountford	1485–94	Officer to duke of Bedford	PROB 11/10 fo. 82–82v.; Thomas 1971: p. 279; D.641/1/2/92
Simon Mountford	by 1488	Feed by Lord Clinton	*I.P.M. Hen. VII*, I, 331
Thomas Mountford II	1488	Took Straunge livery	K.B.9/380/41(1)
William Newnham	1467–8	Feed by earl of Kent	Jack, ed., p. 69
Robert Onley	[1438/9]–1456	Addressed as 'right wellbeloved friend' by Lord Zouche, life annuitant of same	Coughton Court, Throckmorton MS Box 53
William Peyto	1442–53	War ret., protected by Somerset	Br. Lib. Add. Ch. 12,167; E.101/54/11; *D.K.R.*, 48, pp. 390, 396; K.B.27/762 R. rot. 35; Pollard 1983, p. 80
William Repington I	1429	Officer to Bedford	*Coventry Leet Book*, p. 121
John Shirley	1485	Lord Mountjoy his 'good lord'	

Name	Date	Capacity	Refs.
		and supervisor to his will	Shirley 1873: p. 405
Thomas Shirwode	1475–82	Officer to Lord Ferrers [of Chartley], feoffee	C.244/120/129; Longleat MS Devereux Papers Box 1/27
Thomas Slade	*temp.* Hen. VII	Officer to duke of Bedford	Thomas 1971: p. 288
Thomas Slade	by 1505	Officer to Lord Clinton	Nott. Univ. Lib., Middleton MS Mi A 1/2, 5/167/103
Thomas Stokes II	1453	Feoffee to will of widow of Sir Thomas Clinton	*Cal. Close Rolls 1447–54*, p. 426
Thomas Throgmorton II	1452–1467	Officer to Edward Neville Lord Bergavenny	K.B.27/769 C. R. rot.53; W.C.R.O. C.R.623/1
Thomas Throgmorton II	1456	Life annuity from Lord Zouche	Coughton Court, Throckmorton MS Box 53
William Trussell [of Billesley]	1470	Feed by Lady Latimer	Bod. Lib. Dugdale MS 17, p. 35
William Trussell [of Billesley]	1486–97	Given office on Buckingham estate in minority for good service to Jasper of Bedford	*Cal. Pat. Rolls 1485–94*, p. 79; above, *sub* Stafford
Henry Willoughby	by 1488	Feed by Lord Clinton	*I.P.M. Hen. VII*, 1, 331
Henry Willoughby	1489	Shrewsbury supervisor of his will	*H.M.C. Middleton MS*, pp. 121–2
Henry Willoughby	*c.* 1487–89	Sutton of Dudley 'my lord' in will, invited to wedding	*H.M.C. Middleton MS*, pp. 122, 514
Henry Willoughby	*c.* 1488	Officer to duke of Bedford	Nott. Univ. Lib., Middleton MS 5/168/61; Thomas 1971: p. 288

Appendix 4

THE USE OF LEGAL RECORDS

Legal records are notoriously dangerous sources and their criticism is still at such an early stage that in principle it is foolhardy to place too much reliance on them.[1] However, the local historian of late-medieval England must use them, since they are far and away the best source for events in the localities. Reliance on legal records in itself is problematic, for one has to guard against assuming that conflict and violent or illegal behaviour were the norm and care must be taken to give equal weight to less obviously attractive and usable evidence indicating cooperation, such as deeds.

As is well known, these records give the authorities', or, alternatively, the lawyers', view of events.[2] In the latter case, a particular pitfall is the use of common form, for example the description of a killing in self-defence or the standard words used to describe a violent incident or a wounding.[3] At this period there is the added complication that the records may give the version of one faction trying to do down another. We cannot be sure that alleged offences really were committed or, if they were, that it was in exactly the form alleged. The more circumstantial the account, however, the more likely it is to contain some truth.

Two remarkable instances are the two different versions of the murder of William Chetwynd – one according to his widow, the other the coroner's verdict, probably 'massaged' by the Stanleys – and of the Coventry affray that initiated the Stafford–Harecourt feud. The second is particularly noteworthy. The King's Bench indictment not only minimises the role of the gentlefolk in the affair (presumably because having them hanged for felony was no use to anyone, since it was more desirable for both king and victims to have them fined) but it also makes it look like a premeditated assault by the Harecourts on the Staffords. Meanwhile the very graphic account in the Paston letters makes it quite clear that everybody in the two parties was involved in the melée, but that the fight itself was the outcome of an accidental loss of temper in an atmosphere between the two families that was probably already very highly charged.[4]

1 E.g. Hastings 1947; Blatcher 1936, 1978; Post 1976, 1987; Powell 1979; Baker ed., *Spelman*, II; Maddern 1985; Carpenter 1983: pp. 207–8. Also, on later periods, e.g. Cockburn ed. 1977; Sharpe 1984; Stone and Sharpe 1985; Beattie 1986; Gatrell, Lenman and Parker eds. 1980.

2 Post 1976: pp. 201–2; Powell 1979: ch. 5; Baker 1979: pp. 413–4; Sharpe 1984: chs. 6 and 7; Gatrell, Lenman and Parker eds. 1980: p. 3; Carpenter 1983: p. 208.

3 Above, p. 573.

4 Above, pp. 427–8; Powell 1979: pp. 115–16, 1988: pp. 101–4. Cf. Post 1976: p. 289.

While the official records may contain false or fabricated accusations, cases brought into King's Bench by writ, and indeed many others, were, as is well known, likely to end in acquittal. However, we cannot on those grounds assume that large numbers of people were being falsely accused.[5] Historians are coming to realise that the court case itself was only one aspect of an affair, not necessarily the most important, and that the verdict would normally have more to do with events behind the scenes than with absolute legal right or wrong.[6] Furthermore, the records are prone to error, discrepancies as to date, place and personnel being found between indictments recorded at different stages of the process.[7] In this context, when a large crowd is named as defendants in a case of riot or affray, it is worth asking how the names were reached. It is scarcely conceivable that anyone was able to note down the names of everyone present, and more probable that the ringleaders, usually members of the gentry, were noted and the presence of many of the others, as known friends or tenants, assumed.

Even if we could believe everything we read in the legal records, they would remain problematic to use for statistical purposes. As John Post has pointed out, to have a secure basis for statistical analysis of these records the historian has to read a prodigious number of documents.[8] And, even were this possible, we do not have complete series from the lower courts. Records of the sessions of the peace for the fifteenth century, in particular, tend to survive only in the King's Bench indictments or, occasionally, among private papers.[9] Neither are gaol delivery or assize records anything like complete for this century, and it cannot be assumed that there have been no losses from the legal records of chancery.[10] The hundred courts, some of them private, which have left few records or none at all, still handled a surprising amount of business,[11] although Warwickshire, fortunately, had few private liberties.[12] Then, special commissions, such as *oyer* and *terminers*, sent out in the wake of disorder, may grossly distort the statistics. Whether the injured party sought private redress through a plea of trespass, or a criminal prosecution for trespass or felony, or acted by appeal was likely to depend more on legal and political strategy than on the nature of the offence.[13] For example, there were clearly special privileges to be had in the pursuit of cases in chancery for those who were in any sense servants of the chancellor, although many may have been part of the chancery staff rather than people serving in a personal capacity.[14] Some cases were pursued in several different courts, again as a matter of strategy, and it is dangerous to count every one of such a case's multiple appearances as a criminal or legal statistic.

5 Blatcher 1978: pp. 56, 59; Powell 1979: pp. 282–4, 1988: pp. 100–1; Post 1976: p. 199, 1987, pp. 214–15; *Proceedings before the J.P.s*, p. cxxviii; Sharpe 1984: pp. 65–6.

6 Above, chs. 1, 9, 10–17.

7 Powell 1979: p. 202; Cockburn 1975: pp. 224–6, 228; Post 1973, 1976: pp. 182–91.

8 Post 1987: pp. 216–18.

9 *Proceedings before the J.P.s*, pp. lxiii–iv, lxix, 424; Post 1973, 1976: p. 159.

10 Powell 1988: pp. 80–1. However, it seems that cases were much less likely to be heard by assize in the fifteenth century (Baker 1979: pp. 203–4).

11 Post 1983.

12 Templeman 1948: p. 40; Post 1976: pp. 174–5.

13 Powell 1988: pp. 104–6; Post 1987: pp. 214–5, 1976: pp. 251–2; Powell 1979: ch. 5; Baker 1979: pp. 413–14; Whittick 1984.

14 C.244/3/31, 126, /4/144, /40/204; Barnes, '*Corpus Cum Causa* Files', p. 433; above, p. 499 n. 48.

Furthermore legislation, creating a new offence, like maintenance (or the non-wearing of seat-belts), can considerably increase the amount of crime.[15]

Here, there is an additional problem, for some lawyers and crown servants had privileged access to certain courts. If we know this to be true of men connected with the chancellor or his office, we can surmise it to be true in other instances. For example, Thomas Greswold, crown prosecutor and attorney in the King's Bench, was associated with numbers of west midland lawyers, most of them resident in the Arden, around Tanworth in Warwickshire and Yardley in Worcestershire. During Greswold's period of employment in the King's Bench, a substantial number of cases from this part of the world, several involving Greswold himself and sometimes also lawyers associated with Greswold, like his nephew John, reached this court.[16] It must be assumed that to some extent these cases reflect less the growth of local tension than ready access to this court. On the other hand, the very fact of there being numbers of locally-resident lawyers was likely to give rise to the sort of striving society that produced a lot of litigation, so to that extent the figures are not entirely unreal.[17]

If statistics are to be taken from legal records, it is best to avoid special commissions and to stick to courts for which the records are virtually complete. This means Common Pleas and King's Bench. The rolls of the Common Pleas are so bulky that to read them systematically for a hundred years was simply not feasible. They have been sampled, and, reassuringly, tend to confirm the view that they dealt mainly with minor business, a lot of it debt, much of it not of immediate interest to this study.[18] They could, however, almost certainly be made to yield extraordinarily interesting material on the credit system and on lords' relations with their tenants and those of others. The King's Bench rolls, which can and have been read for the full hundred years, are much richer in evidence for conflict among landowners, and it seems that a large proportion of significant cases involving landowners were by this time likely to turn up there, either *Coram Rege* or in the *Rex* section, sometimes in both.[19] Even so, in the first two decades, especially the first fifteen years, it is evident that there were important disputes that do not appear in the King's Bench, and the records of the court for this period are distinctly thin.[20] It should also be pointed out that these records do include some returned *oyer* and *terminer* commissions, but, as far as Warwickshire is concerned, these recorded mainly treasons, which have not been included in the graph, as they are not, strictly speaking, an index of local tension.

Of greater concern is what happened to King's Bench, both the *Coram Rege* and the *Rex* sides, between about 1471 and 1485. There is a decline in significant cases concerning landowners in this period (one masked to some extent in the graph by

[15] Harriss 1981: pp. xix–xx.

[16] Above, pp. 77, 297, 323, and app. 2. For John Greswold, see Blatcher 1936: p. 120. Other lawyers included John West I (*Cal. Pat. Rolls 1452–61*, p. 77) and Richard Broun (app. 2). Relevant cases include Greswold v. Hore (K.B.27/636 Coram Rege rot.9), Greswold v. Waldeve (K.B.27/660 Coram Rege rot.15), Greswold v. West and Benford (K.B.27/747 Coram Rege rot.33d.). Ives (1983a: p. 116) notes that most legal practices were in the midlands and the south-east, and this may well distort the King's Bench figures for the whole area.

[17] Above, chs. 2 and 4.

[18] Hastings 1947: ch. 2; Blatcher 1978: pp. 24–5.

[19] Baker 1979: pp. 56–9; Blatcher 1978: p. 51; Post 1976: chs. 5 and 6.

[20] Cf. K.B.27/554–604 and JUST 1/1514; above, p. 364.

numbers of smaller cases, by the fact that up to *c.* 1479 this was a fairly turbulent period anyway and by the disproportionate weight in the statistics of certain conflicts which gave rise to numbers of incidents, notably the Burdet inheritance dispute). Although it is known that King's Bench business began to decline from the 1470s, the Warwickshire evidence does not entirely support the hypothesis that this was a continuous downward spiral, to the benefit of the Common Pleas.[21] For one thing, King's Bench cases concerning Warwickshire landowners begin to increase in number from 1485. For another, although the Common Pleas, which were examined systematically for the period 1471–85, show some growth in significant business in which landowners were involved, there is not enough to compensate for the lack of King's Bench material unless we are to assume that Warwickshire landowners had suddenly become remarkably more law-abiding.[22]

An alternative explanation is that, in keeping with Edward IV's thoroughly interventionist rule in his second reign, the king's council was being used much more frequently to bypass the more formal courts and enforce summary and exemplary discipline. The *Corpus cum Causa* files suggest that Edward was already beginning to do this in the face of Warwick's evident failure in the west midlands in the 1460s. Indications that he was extending this policy both in Warwickshire and elsewhere in the period 1471–83 are the contents of the same files during this period, which reveal a lot of undertakings by major figures to keep the peace, and the proceedings of the King's Bench in the early years of Henry VII's reign. At this time indictments made under Edward IV, often with multiple defendants, which have never before appeared in this court and are not in the King's Bench indictment files, begin to be processed through the court. These include the indictment by the special commission of the ringleaders in the Alspath affray and murder of 1465; at the time only the minor participants were dealt with in this way. We may deduce that the indictment of the others was called into King's Bench, but that the king then administered a personal dressing-down followed possibly by demanding a bond that has since been lost. Henry VII then found these indictments, perhaps in the council records, and processed them through, usually ending with a pardon in return for a fine and a bond or mainprise, making some money and exerting some early control in his new kingdom.[23] The involvement of the council is evident in the Coventry–Bristowe affair, but without the Leet Book we should be ignorant both about much of what happened and of the king's concern (see above, pp. 540–2). Why under Richard III there should be a relative lack both of King's Bench records and of chancery recognisances concerning the aristocracy is unclear. The Burdet affair suggests that he

[21] Ives 1983a: p. 215; Blatcher 1978: ch. 2 and p. 45.

[22] C.P.40/841–83; above, pp. chs. 14–15. Legislation partly explains the increase in the amount of King's Bench business in the *Rex* side from 1487 (Hunnisett 1959: pp. 220–1).

[23] Barnes, '*Corpus cum Causa* Files', pp. 435–41; C.244/91–137; Bellamy 1985: pp. 149–50; K.B.27/907 Rex roti.9, 9d., 10, /908 Rex roti.4d., 16, 21, /916 Rex rot.6; K.B.9/311/10, /313/26; Williams 1928: p. 189 n.3; above, p. 502. It may be significant that there are indictments from Edward's second reign that reached the *Rex* proceedings only under Henry VII which survive in a series that is chronologically out of sequence with the rest of the K.B.9s (e.g. K.B.9/946/66 and K.B.27/907 Rex rot.9d.; K.B.9/992/76 and K.B.27/908 Rex rot.16). The last is especially noteworthy, as it is the Harecourt murder, in which Edward seems to have taken a particular interest (above, p. 512).

too was involving himself personally in such cases and he may have used other devices for securing the good behaviour of the participants.[24]

In conclusion, then, it is the King's Bench that has been used for figures on conflict and violence (figures 9 and 13). Virtually all midland counties have been combed for these. For the reasons given already, the figures cannot and are not intended to be absolute guides to conflict and violence, and it must not be forgotten that, especially under Henry IV and after about 1471, there is important additional evidence from other courts and judicial tribunals, but they do serve as a limited indicator of levels of local tension. Violent outbreaks obviously do this, but so does the very fact of a case reaching the courts, for it would not normally do so unless informal means of reconciliation had failed. The figures show conflicts between members of the gentry or nobility, or between gentry or nobility and religious institutions in which there was at least one participant with Warwickshire interests on each side, or, if only one of the parties was from Warwickshire, it was Warwickshire land that was at issue. These would seem to be the prime indicators of levels of tension. Each instance of alleged lawbreaking in a dispute has been counted, although a series of episodes taking place within a day or two has been counted as one. Disputes for which there are no details beyond the entry of the plea are included and are attributed to the year in which they appear in the Plea Rolls: cases known in greater detail usually reach the Plea Rolls not long after the offence has been committed. Cases reappearing in the rolls after a gap have been included, and these are normally accompanied anyway with dated details of new offences.[25]

It should be observed that individual cases can greatly distort the statistical profile: for example, the Burdet affair mentioned above, the main cause of the high levels of conflict in 1478–9 (although these clearly reflect a state of affairs evident from other sources (see above, p. 533)) and the relatively minor Ruggeley–Hardwick conflict of 1491. At the same time, the full extent of disorder early in the reign of Henry VII is not revealed in the graph because, being a regional conflict, it engulfed the north midlands and therefore, in most instances, does not qualify for inclusion in a list of Warwickshire incidents. Nor, of course, is the *quality* of violence revealed, a murder rating the same as a minor trespass. For qualitative judgements on local tension and violence, the reader is referred to the text. It is also worth noting that the real periods of crisis (notably 1459–60 and 1485) produce sudden falls in recorded conflict, followed by rapid rises, the reason being self-evidently that a climate of gross uncertainty led to abandonment of the courts, while the establishment of the new regime produced a rush to law on the part both of the injured parties of the crisis years and of those who felt able to exploit the new regime to deal with long-standing grievances.

[24] Above, p. 557.

[25] For a listing of most of these, and of other cases, up to 1472, see Carpenter, M.C. 1976: App. IX.

BIBLIOGRAPHY

(1) MANUSCRIPTS

London, Public Record Office
(all manuscript references are to P.R.O. unless otherwise indicated)

C.1 – Early Chancery Proceedings
C.47 – Chancery, Miscellanea (now reclassified: new classes used: C.88 and C.260)
C.54 – Chancery, Close Rolls
C.60 – Chancery, Fine Rolls
C.66 – Chancery, Patent Rolls
C.67 – Chancery, Patent Rolls, Supplementary (incl. Pardon Rolls).
C.81 – Chancery, Warrants for the Great Seal, series 1
C.138 – Chancery, Inquisitions *Post Mortem*, Henry V
C.139 – Chancery, Inquisitions *Post Mortem*, Henry VI
C.140 – Chancery, Inquisitions *Post Mortem*, Edward IV
C.141 – Chancery, Inquisitions *Post Mortem*, Richard III
C.142 – Chancery, Inquisitions *Post Mortem*, Henry VII to Charles II
C.143 – Chancery, Inquisitions *Ad Quod Damnum*
C.145 – Chancery, Miscellaneous Inquisitions
C.219 – Chancery, Election Indentures
C.244 – Chancery, *Corpus Cum Causa*
C.P.40 – Common Pleas, Plea Rolls
D.L.26 – Duchy of Lancaster, Deeds, series LL
D.L.29 – Duchy of Lancaster, Ministers' Accounts
D.L.41 – Duchy of Lancaster, Miscellanea
E.28 – Exchequer, T.R., Council and Privy Seal
E.40 – Exchequer, T.R., Deeds, series A
E.42 – Exchequer, T.R., Deeds, series AS
E.101 – Exchequer, K.R., Various Accounts
E.159 – Exchequer, K.R., Memoranda Rolls
E.163 – Exchequer, K.R., Miscellanea
E.179 – Exchequer, K.R., Subsidy Rolls etc.
E.198 – Exchequer, K.R., Serjeanties, Knights' Fees etc.

E.326 – Exchequer, L.T.R., Deeds, series B
E.368 – Exchequer, L.T.R. Memoranda Rolls
E.372 – Exchequer, L.T.R., Pipe Rolls
E.404 – Exchequer, T.R., Warrants for Issue
K.B.8 – King's Bench, *Baga de Secretis*
K.B.9 – King's Bench, Ancient Indictments
K.B.27 – King's Bench, Rolls *Coram Rege*
JUST 1 – Assize Rolls
JUST 3 – Gaol Delivery Rolls
PROB 2 – Prerogative Court of Canterbury, Inventories
PROB 11 – Prerogative Court of Canterbury, Wills
P.S.O.1 – Warrants for the Privy Seal, series 1
S.C.1 – Ancient Correspondence
S.C.6 – Ministers' and Receivers' Accounts
S.C.8 – Ancient Petitions
S.C.11, S.C.12 – Rentals and Surveys
STAC 1 – Star Chamber Proceedings, Henry VII
WARD 2 – Court of Wards, Deeds and Evidences

London, British Library

Additional Manuscripts, various
Additional Rolls and Charters, various – including Stafford of Grafton accounts, 74,129, 74,146–78
Egerton Charters and Rolls, various – including Beauchamp of Warwick Accounts, 8769–75
Harley Manuscripts, various
Cotton Manuscripts, various
Cotton Roll XIII.7 – Calais muster of the earl of Warwick, 1415
Royal Manuscripts, various
Stowe Manuscripts, various – including names of dukes etc. retained to serve king, 440

London, Westminster Abbey Muniments

Various manuscripts

Aberystwyth, National Library of Wales

Peniarth Manuscript 280

Cambridge, King's College Archives

WOW – Wootton Wawen Manuscripts

Gloucester, Gloucestershire Record Office

D.149 – Clifford of Frampton-on-Severn
D.184 – Craven

D.326 – Guise of Elmore
D.1086 – Hale of Alderley

Leicester, Leicestershire Record Office

44'28 – Documents relating to the manor and soke of Rothley
23 D 57 – Braye of Stanford
26 D 53 – Ferrers of Staunton Harold
D 611 – Conant
DE 170 – Fisher
DE 220, 221 – Peake (Nevill of Holt)
DE 1625 – Charters relating to Swithland etc.
DE 2242/3 – Additional Ferrers Manuscripts
DE 2242/6 – Medieval Leics. Deeds
DG 5 – Winstanley

Longleat, Manuscripts of the Marquess of Bath

66 – Ferrers of Chartley account 1422–5
6411 – Stafford valor 1444–5
6414 – Receiver-general account of earl of Warwick 1420–1
Devereux Papers
Misc.IX – Calendar of household of earl of Warwick 1420–1

Matlock, Derbyshire Record Office

D77 – Gresley
D156M – Burdet of Foremark
D185 – Taylor, Simpson and Moseley
D231M – Okeover
D410M – Vernon of Sudbury
D505M – Rodes
D518 – Harrington
D779 – Holden
D10052 – Leeke Cartulary

Northampton, Northamptonshire Record Office

Ashley (Ashby St. Ledgers)
Fitzwilliam Collection
Knightley Charters
Spencer Manuscripts
Temple (Stowe) Collection

Nottingham University Library

Middleton Manuscripts

Oxford, Bodleian Library

Manuscripts of Sir William Dugdale

Oxford, Magdalen College Muniments

Westcote and Willoughby deeds etc.

Oxford Local Record Office

Dillon Manuscripts
Parker Manuscripts

Stafford, Staffordshire Record Office

D.641 – Manuscripts of Lord Stafford
D.1721 – Bagot Collection
D.W.1744 – Documents deposited by Earl of Shrewsbury

Stafford, William Salt Library

William Salt Original Collection
William Salt Original Collection, Huntbach Manuscripts
H.M.Aston Coll.
H.M.Chetwynd Coll.
Vernon Coll.

Warwickshire

Birmingham Reference Library

Birmingham Collection
Moulton and Keen Collection
Wingfield Digby Manuscripts

Coughton Court, Alcester

Throckmorton Manuscripts (now in Warwick County Record Office (Class C.R. 1998))

Merevale Hall

Dugdale and other Manuscripts (consulted at Warwick County Record Office)

Stratford on Avon, Shakespeare Birthplace Trust, Archives Section

D.R.3 – Ferrers of Baddesley Clinton Collection
D.R.5 – Throckmorton Manuscripts, manorial records
D.R.10 – Gregory Hood Collection
D.R.18 – Leigh Family Papers

D.R.31 – Collection of Abstracts Relating to Warwickshire by J.H. Bloom
D.R.37 – Archer Collection
D.R.41 – Notes etc. from Warwickshire Documents by J.H. Bloom
D.R.98 – Willoughby de Broke Collection
D.R.503 – Archer Collection, genealogical material
E.R.1 – Saunders Collection
E.R.3/667 – Indenture of military service
E.R.112 – Aston Papers
Stratford Corporation Records – Div. I (deeds)
– Div. II (miscellaneous)
– Div. XII (accounts)

Warwick, Warwick Castle Manuscripts (now in County Record Office)

Warwick Corporation Records (consulted at Warwick County Record Office)

W.19/5 – accounts of earl of Warwick at Rouen, 1431

Warwick, Warwick County Record Office

C.R.26 – Walter of Woodcote
C.R.133 – Mordaunt of Walton
C.R.136 – Newdegate of Arbury
C.R.162 – Ward-Boughton-Leigh
C.R.229/18/4 – Shirley
C.R.299 – Greswold of Malvern Hall
C.R.456 – Philips of Weston Park
C.R.556/212 – Woodloes and Woodcote Account 1462–3
C.R.611 – Heath and Blenkinsop
C.R.623/1 – Allesley Account 1466–7
C.R.712 – Edstone Deeds
C.R.895 – Dormer of Grove Park
C.R.959 – Single deed
C.R.1248 – Shuckburgh of Upper Shuckburgh
C.R.1908 – Savage and Landor of Bishops Tachbrook
C.R.1911 – Ettington and Bishopton
C.R.2017 – Fielding
C.R.2026 – Documents Relating to Monks Kirby etc.
H.2 – Coleshill School
L.1 – Holbech of Farnborough
L.4 – Wolfhampcote
L.6 – Lucy
Z. – Photos and transcripts

Worcester, Hereford and Worcester Record Office

705:66 – Churchill Family Archives
705:139 – Holland and Martin (Upton-on-Severn)

705:962 – Robinson
899:95 – Holland and Martin (Elmley Castle Records)
Worcester Diocesan Wills

Bishops' Registers consulted on microfilm

Canterbury Diocese – Arundel (1399–1414)
– Stafford (1443–52)
– Kempe (1452–4)
Coventry and Lichfield Diocese – Burghill (1398–1414)
– Heyworth (1420–47)
– Booth (1447–52)
– Boulers (1453–9)
– Hales (1459–90)
– Arundel (1496–1502)
Worcester Diocese – Clifford (1401–7)
– Carpenter (1444–76)
– Alcock (1476–86)

California, Huntington Library

HM 19959 (consulted on microfilm)

(2) PRINTED SOURCES

The Account of the Great Household of Humphrey, First Duke of Buckingham; for the Year 1452–3, ed. M. Harris, intro. J. Thurgood, Camden Misc., 28, 4th ser., 29, 1984.

Actes de la Chancellerie d'Henri VI concernant la Normandie sous la domination anglaise (1425–35), ed. P. Le Cacheux, 2 vols., Société de l'histoire de Normandie, Rouen and Paris, 1907–8.

Annales Monasterii S. Albani a Johanne Amundesham, ed. H.T. Riley, Rolls Series, 2 vols., London, 1870–1.

Anstis, J., *The Register of the Most Noble Order of the Garter*, 2 vols., London, 1724.

Aquinas: Selected Political Writings, ed. A.P. D'Entrèves, trans. J.G. Dawson, Oxford, 1959.

Ashby, George, *Poems*, ed. M. Bateson, E.E.T.S., London, 1899.

Baker, J.H. (ed.), *The Reports of Sir John Spelman*, 2 vols., Selden Soc., 93–4, 1976–8.

Barnes, P.M. (ed.), 'The chancery *Corpus Cum Causa* file, 10–11 Edward IV', in Hunnisett and Post (eds.), *Medieval Legal Records Edited in Memory of C.A.F. Meekings*, pp. 430–76.

The Beauchamp Cartulary 1100–1268, ed. E. Mason, Pipe Roll Soc., n.s., 43, 1980.

Birrell, J. (ed.), 'The *Status Maneriorum* of John Catesby', in R. Bearman (ed.), *Miscellany I*, Dugdale Soc. Publications, 31, 1977.

The Boke of Noblesse, ed. J.G. Nichols, Roxburghe Club, London, 1860.

The Book of Bartholomew Bolney, ed. M. Clough, Sussex Rec. Soc., 63, 1964.

The Brut or the Chronicles of England, ed. F.W.D. Brie, E.E.T.S., 2 vols., o.s., 131, 136, 1906–8.

Calendar of the Close Rolls Preserved in the Public Record Office, 1399–1509, 18 vols., London, H.M.S.O., 1927–63.

Calendar of the Fine Rolls Preserved in the Public Record Office, 1399–1509, 11 vols., London, H.M.S.O., 1931–62.

Calendar of Inquisitions Miscellaneous, 7, 1399–1422, London, H.M.S.O., 1968.

Calendar of Inquisitions Post Mortem . . . Preserved in the P.R.O., 1–6 Henry IV, ed. J.L. Kirby, London, H.M.S.O., 1987.

Calendar of Inquisitions Post Mortem . . . Preserved in the Public Record Office, Hen. VII, 3 vols., London, H.M.S.O., 1898–1955.

Calendar of the Patent Rolls Preserved in the Public Record Office, 1399–1509, 17 vols., London, H.M.S.O., 1903–16.

Calendar of State Papers and Manuscripts Existing in the Archives and Collections of Milan, I, London, H.M.S.O., 1912.

Calendarium Inquisitionum Post Mortem Escaetarum, III, Ric. II–Hen. IV, Record Commissioners, London, 1821.

Calendarium Inquisitionum Post Mortem Escaetarum, IV, Hen. V–Ric. III, Record Commissioners, London, 1828.

Calendars of the Proceedings in Chancery in the Reign of Queen Elizabeth, to which are Prefixed Examples of Earlier Proceedings in that Court, 2 vols., Record Commissioners, London, 1827.

Caxton, William, (trans), *The Book of the Knight of the Tower*, ed. M.Y. Offord, E.E.T.S., suppl. ser., 2, 1971.

Chaucer, Geoffrey, *The Complete Works*, ed. F. Robinson, 2nd edn, Oxford, 1966.

Chronicles of London, ed. C.L. Kingsford, Oxford, 1905.

Civil Pleas of the Wiltshire Eyre, 1249, ed. M.T. Clanchy, Wiltshire Rec. Soc., 26, 1971.

Collections for a History of Staffordshire, ed. by the William Salt Archaeological Society, 1–, Kendal, 1880–.

Condon, M.M., (ed.), 'A Wiltshire sheriff's notebook, 1464–5', in Hunnisett and Post (eds.), *Medieval English Records Edited in Memory of C.A.F. Meekings*, pp. 410–28.

The Coronation of Richard III: the Extant Documents, ed. A.F. Sutton and P.W. Hammond, Gloucester, 1983.

Coss, P.R. (ed.), *The Early Records of Medieval Coventry*, Br. Acad. Records of Social and Economic Hist., n.s., 11, 1986.

The Court Rolls of the Manor of Bromsgrove and King's Norton 1494–1504, ed. A.F.C. Baber, Worcs. Hist. Soc., n.s., 3, 1963.

The Coventry Leet Book, ed. M.D. Harris, 4 vols. in one, E.E.T.S., o.s., 134, 135, 138, 146, 1907–13.

Derbyshire Feet of Fines, 1323–1546, ed. H.J.H. Garratt and C. Rawcliffe, Derbys. Rec. Soc., 11, 1985.

A Descriptive Catalogue of Ancient Deeds in the Public Record Office, 6 vols., London, H.M.S.O., 1890–1915.

Dobson, R.B. (ed.), *The Peasants' Revolt of 1381*, 2nd edn. London, 1983.

The Domesday of Enclosures 1517–1518, ed. I.S. Leadam, 2 vols., Roy. Hist. Soc., London, 1897.

The Duchy of Lancaster's Estates in Derbyshire 1485–1540, ed. I.S.W. Blanchard, Derbys. Rec. Soc., record ser., 3, 1971.

Early Records of Furnival's Inn, ed. D.S. Bland, Newcastle upon Tyne, 1957.

Early Treatises on the Practice of the Justices of the Peace in the Fifteenth and Sixteenth Centuries, ed. B.H. Putnam, Oxford, 1924.

An English Chronicle of the Reign of Richard II, Henry IV, Henry V, and Henry VI, ed. J.S. Davies, Camden, o.s., 64, 1855.

English Gilds, ed. T. Smith and L.T. Smith, E.E.T.S., o.s., 40, 1870.

English Historical Documents, III, 1189–1327, ed. H.A. Rothwell, London, 1975.

English Historical Documents, IV, 1327–1485, ed. A.R. Myers, London, 1969.

Excerpta Historica, ed. S. Bentley, London, 1831.

Fabyan, Robert, *The New Chronicles of England and France*, ed. H. Ellis, London, 1811.

Farnham, G.F., *Leicestershire Medieval Village Notes*, 6 vols., London, 1929–33.

Feodera, ed. T. Rymer, 10 vols., Hagae Comitis, 1745; rpt. Farnborough, 1967.

FitzHerbert, Anthony, *The New Natura Brevium*, London, 1652.

Fortescue, Sir John, *De Laudibus Legum Anglie*, ed. S.B. Chrimes, Cambridge, 1942.

The Governance of England, ed. C. Plummer, Oxford, 1885.

Génard, M., 'Marguerite d'Yorck, duchesse de Bourgogne, et la Rose Blanche (1495)', *Compte rendu des séances de la commission royale d'histoire ou receuil de ses bulletins*, 4th ser., 2, 1875, pp. 9–22.

Genet, J.P. (ed.), *Four English Political Tracts of the Later Middle Ages*, Camden, 4th ser., 18, 1977.

Gesta Henrici Quinti, ed. J.S. Roskell and F. Taylor, Oxford, 1975.

The Gild of St Mary, Lichfield, ed. F.J. Furnivall, E.E.T.S., extra series, 114, 1920 for 1914.

Gray, D. (ed.), *The Oxford Book of Late Medieval Verse and Prose*, Oxford, 1985.

The Great Chronicle of London, ed. A.H. Thomas and I.D. Thornley, London, 1938.

Green, R.F., 'Historical notes of a London citizen, 1483–1485', *Eng. Hist. Rev.*, 96, 1981, pp. 585–8.

Hale, M., *Pleas of the Crown*, London, 1682.

Halle, Edward, *The Union of the Twoo Noble and Illustre Famelies of Lancastre & York* . . ., London, 1550.

Harding, A. (ed.), 'Early trailbaston proceedings from the Lincoln roll of 1305', in Hunnisett and Post (eds), *Medieval Legal Records Edited in Memory of C.A.F. Meekings*, pp. 144–68.

Harrison, C.J., 'The Petition of Edmund Dudley', *Eng. Hist. Rev.*, 87, 1972, pp. 82–99.

Hilton, R.H. (ed.), *The Stoneleigh Leger Book*, Dugdale Soc. Publications, 24, 1960.

'Historia Croylandensis Continuatio', in *Rerum Anglicarum Scriptorum Veterum*, ed. W. Fulman, I, pp. 451–593, Oxford, 1684.

The Historical Collections of a Citizen of London in the Fifteenth Century, ed. J.G. Gairdner, Camden Soc., n.s., 17, 1876.

Historical Manuscripts Commission – Lechmere Manuscripts, Fifth Report, I, 1876.

– Eleventh Report, III, (Manuscripts of the Corporations of Southampton and Kings Lynn), 1887.

– Rutland Manuscripts, I (1888), IV (1905).

– Fifteenth Report, Appendix Part X, (Manuscripts of Shrewsbury and Coventry Corporations etc.), 1899.

– Various Collections, I, 1901.

– Various Collections, II, 1903.
– Lothian MS, 1905.
– Middleton MS, 1911.
– Various Collections, VII, 1914.
– Hastings Manuscripts, I, 1928.

Historie of the Arrivall of Edward IV . . ., ed. J. Bruce, Camden Series, London, 1838.

Hoccleve, Thomas, 'The Regiment of Princes', in *Hoccleve's Works*, III, ed. F.J. Furnivall, E.E.T.S., extra ser., 72, 1897.

Horrox, R.J. and Hammond, P. (eds.), *British Library Harleian Manuscript 433*, 4 vols., Gloucester, 1979–83.

Hunnisett, R.F. and Post, J.B. (eds.), *Medieval Legal Records Edited in Memory of C.A.F. Meekings*, London, 1978.

Ingulph's Chronicle of the Abbey of Croyland, ed. and trans. H.T. Riley, London, 1854.

Inquisitiones Post Mortem Relating to Nottinghamshire 1437–85, ed. M.A. Renshaw, Thoroton Soc., Rec. Series, 17, 1956.

Inquisitions and Assessments Relating to Feudal Aids . . . Preserved in the Public Record Office, 1284–1431, 6 vols., London, H.M.S.O., 1899–1920.

Jack, R.I. (ed.), *The Grey of Ruthin Valor*, Sydney, 1965.

Jeayes, I.H. (ed.), 'Descriptive Catalogue of the Charters and Muniments of the Spencer Family . . . at Althorp', MS, 1930, Northants.R.O..

Descriptive Catalogue of the Charters and Muniments . . . at Berkeley Castle, Bristol, 1892.

A Descriptive Catalogue of the Charters and Muniments of the Gresley Family . . ., London, 1895.

Descriptive Catalogue of the Charters and Muniments of the Lyttelton Family, London, 1893.

Descriptive Catalogue of Derbyshire Charters, London and Derby, 1906.

John Benet's Chronicle for the Years 1400 to 1462, ed. G.L. and M.A. Harriss, Camden Misc., 24, Camden, 4th ser., 9, 1972.

Kail, J. (ed.), *Twenty-Six Political and other Poems*, E.E.T.S., o.s., 124, 1904.

Landboc, Sive Registrum . . . de Winchelcumba, ed. D. Royce, 2 vols., Exeter, 1892–1903.

Langland, William, *The Vision of Piers Plowman*, B text, ed. A.V.C. Schmidt, London, 1978; rpt. 1982.

The Langley Cartulary, ed. P.R. Coss, Dugdale Soc. Publications, 32, 1980.

Leland, J., *De Rebus Britannicis Collectanea*, ed. T. Hearne, 2nd edn, 6 vols., London, 1774.

'A letter from the 'Kingmaker'', ed. J.H. Bloom, *Notes and Queries*, 12th ser., 5, 1919, p. 120.

Letters and Accounts of William Brereton of Malpas, ed. E.W. Ives, Lancs. and Chesh. Rec. Soc., 116, 1976.

Letters and Papers of the Reigns of Richard III and Henry VI, ed. J.G. Gairdner, 2 vols., Rolls Ser., 1861–3.

Letters of Queen Margaret of Anjou . . . and Others, ed. C. Monro, Camden Soc., o.s., 86, 1863.

The Libelle of Englyshe Polycye, ed. G. Warner, Oxford, 1926.

List of Inquisitions Ad Quod Damnum Preserved in the Public Record Office, II, P.R.O. Lists and Indexes, main ser., 22, London, H.M.S.O., 1906; rpt. New York, 1963.

Littleton's Tenures, ed. E. Wambaugh, Washington, D.C., 1903.

Madden, F., 'Documents relating to Perkin Warbeck, with remarks on his history', *Archaeologia*, 27, 1838, pp. 153–210.

Malory, Sir Thomas, *Works*, ed. E. Vinaver, 2nd edn, Oxford, 1971.

Manners and Meals in Olden Time, ed. F.J. Furnivall, E.E.T.S., o.s., 32, 1868.

The Marcher Lordships of South Wales 1415–1536: Select Documents, ed. T.B. Pugh, Cardiff, 1963.

Materials for a History of the Reign of Henry VII, ed. W. Campbell, 2 vols., Rolls Ser., 1873–7.

Ministers' Accounts of the Collegiate Church of St. Mary, Warwick 1432–85, ed. D. Styles, Dugdale Soc. Publications, 26, 1969.

Miscellanea Genealogica et Heraldica, 24 vols., London, 1866–1919.

'Modus Tenendi Parliamentum', in *Parliamentary Texts of the Later Middle Ages*, ed. N. Pronay and J. Taylor, Oxford, 1980.

Myers, A.R., *The Household of Edward IV: The Black Book and the Ordinance of 1478*, Manchester, 1959.

Myers, A.R. (ed.), 'The household of Queen Elizabeth Woodville, 1466–7', *Bulletin of the John Rylands Library*, 50, 1967–8, pp. 207–35, 443–81.

Nicolas, N.H. *History of the Battle of Agincourt*, 2nd edn, London, 1832; rpt. London, 1970.

National Register of Archives, MS lists
- 'Sutherland MS', Staffordshire Record Office.
- 'MS at Merevale Hall, Warwickshire'.
- 'Report on Miscellaneous Deeds in the Collection of the College of Arms', comp. L.M. Midgley
- 'Trusley Old Hall MS'

North Country Wills, ed. J.W. Clay, Surtees Soc., 116, 1908.

The Order of Chivalry, trans. William Caxton, ed. F.S. Ellis, Kelmscott, 1893.

Origines Juridiciales . . ., ed. W. Dugdale, London, 1666.

Oschinsky, D. (ed.), *Walter of Henley*, Oxford, 1971.

P.R.O. Lists and Indexes, Suppl. Ser., IX ii, Warrants for Issues, 1399–1485, New York, 1964.

Paris, M., *Chronica Majora*, ed. H.R. Luard, 7 vols., Rolls Ser., 1872–83.

Parliamentary Writs . . ., ed. F. Palgrave, 2 vols. in 4, Record Commissioners, London, 1827–34.

The Paston Letters, ed. J.G. Gairdner, 6 vols., London, 1904; rpt. in 1 vol., Gloucester, 1983.

Paston Letters and Papers of the Fifteenth Century, ed. N. Davis, 2 vols., Oxford, 1971–6.

Plumpton Correspondence, ed. T. Stapleton, Camden Ser., London, 1939.

'Political poems of the reigns of Henry VI and Edward IV', ed. F. Madden, *Archaeologia*, 29, 1842, pp. 318–47.

Post, J.B. (ed.), 'Courts, councils, and arbitrators in the Ladbroke manor dispute, 1382–1400', in Hunnisett and Post (eds), *Medieval Legal Records Edited in Memory of C.A.F. Meekings*, pp. 289–339.

Prerogativa Regis, by Robert Constable, ed. S.E. Thorne, New Haven, 1949.

Proceedings before the Justices of the Peace in the Fourteenth and Fifteenth Centuries, ed. B.H. Putnam, the Ames Foundation, London, 1938.

Proceedings and Ordinances of the Privy Council of England, ed. N.H. Nicolas, 7 vols., Record Commissioners, London, 1834–7.

Readings and Moots at the Inns of Court in the Fifteenth Century, 1, ed. S.E. Thorne, Selden Soc., 71, 1954.

Records of Early English Drama: Coventry, ed. R.W. Ingram, Manchester, 1981.

Records of the Honorable Society of Lincoln's Inn, 2 vols., London, 1896.

Records of King Edward VI's School Birmingham, 1, The 'Miscellany' Volume, ed. W.F. Carter, Dugdale Soc. Publications, 4, 1924.

Records of the Manor of Henley in Arden, Warwickshire, ed. W.F. Fieldhouse and F.C. Wellstood, Stratford-upon-Avon, 1919.

The Register of the Gild of the Holy Cross . . . of Stratford-upon-Avon, ed. J.H. Bloom, London, 1907.

The Register of the Guild . . . of Coventry, ed. M.D. Harris, Dugdale Soc. Publications, 13, 1935.

The Register of the Guild of Knowle in the County of Warwick, ed. W.B. Bickley *et al.*, Walsall, 1894.

The Register of Henry Chichele, Archbishop of Canterbury, 1414–43, ed. E.F. Jacob, 4 vols., Oxford, 1938–43.

The Reign of Henry VII from Contemporary Sources, ed. A.F. Pollard, 3 vols., London, 1913–14.

Les reports des cases . . . [Edward II–Henry VIII], 11 vols. in 7, London, 1678–80.

Reports of the Deputy Keeper of the Public Records –

No. 41, London, 1880, 'Calendar of Norman Rolls', Hen. V, pp. 671–810.

No. 44, London, 1883, 'Calendar of French Rolls', Hen. V., pp. 543–638.

No. 48, London, 1887, 'Calendar of French Rolls', Hen. VI, pp. 217–450.

'Roles Normands et Français . . . tirées des archives de Londres par Bréquigny (1764–6), ed. L. Puiseux, *Mémoires de la Société des Antiquaires de Normandie*, 3rd ser., 3, 1858.

Rolls of the Justices in Eyre for Gloucestershire, Warwickshire and Staffordshire, 1221, 1222, ed. D.M. Stenton, Selden Soc., 59, 1940.

Rolls of the Warwickshire and Coventry Sessions of the Peace, 1377–1397, ed. E.G. Kimball, Dugdale Soc. Publications, 16, 1939.

Rotuli Parliamentorum, 1377–1503, 4 vols., London, 1783.

Rous, John, *Historia Regum Angliae*, ed. T. Hearne, Oxford, 1745.

The Rous Roll, ed. C. Ross, Gloucester, 1980.

Russell, John, 'The Boke of Nurture', in *Manners and Meals in Olden Time*, ed. F.J. Furnivall, E.E.T.S., o.s., 32, 1868.

Rymes of Robyn Hood, ed. R.B. Dobson and J. Taylor, London, 1976.

St German's Doctor and Student, ed. T.F.T. Plucknett and J.L. Barton, Selden Soc., 91, 1974.

Secreta Secretorum: Nine English Versions, ed. M.A. Manzaloui, E.E.T.S., 276, 1977.

Selden, J., *Titles of Honour*, London, 1672.

Select Cases before the King's Council 1243–1482, ed. I.S. Leadam and J.F. Baldwin, Selden Soc., 35, 1918.

Select Cases in the Council of Henry VII, ed. C.G. Bayne and W.H. Dunham, Selden Soc., 75, 1956.

Select Cases in the Court of King's Bench under Edward II, ed. G.O. Sayles, Selden Soc., 74, 1955.

Select Pleas in the Manorial and other Seignorial Courts, I, Reigns of Henry III and Edward I, ed. F.W. Maitland, Selden Soc., 1889.

Sims, R., *Calendar of the Deeds and Documents belonging to the Corporation of Walsall*, Walsall, 1882.

Sir Christopher Hatton's Book of Seals, ed. L.C. Loyd and D.M. Stenton, Northants. Rec. Soc., 15, 1950.

Six Town Chronicles of England, ed. R. Flenley, Oxford, 1911.

The Statutes of the Realm, Hen. III–Hen. VII, 2 vols., London, 1810–16, rpt; London, 1963.

Stevenson, W.H., *Letters and Papers Illustrative of the Wars of the English in France during the Reign of Henry VI*, 2 vols. in 3, Rolls Ser., 1861–4.

The Stonor Letters and Papers 1290–1483, ed. C.L. Kingsford, 3 vols., Camden, 3rd ser., 29, 30, 34, 1919–24.

Stow, John, *Annales, or, a Generall Chronicle of England*, continued Edmund Howes, London, 1631.

Stratford-on-Avon Corporation Records, The Guild Accounts, in the archives of the Shakespeare Birthplace Trust, calendared by W.J. Hardy, Stratford, 1886.

The 1235 Surrey Eyre, I, ed. C.A.F. Meekings, Surrey Rec. Soc., 31, 1979.

Swanimote Rolls of Feckenham Forest, ed. R.H. Hilton, Worcs. Hist. Soc., Miscellany I, n.s., I, 1960.

Taylor, F. 'The chronicle of John Strecche for the reign of Henry V, 1414–22', *Bulletin of the John Rylands Library*, 16, 1932, pp. 137–87.

Testamenta Eboracensia, ed. J. Raine, II, III, IV, Surtees Soc., 30 (1855), 45 (1864), 53 (1869).

Testamenta Vetusta, ed. N.H. Nicolas, 2 vols. in one, London, 1826.

Three Prose Versions of the Secreta Secretorum, ed. R. Steele, E.E.T.S., extra ser., 74, 1898.

Upton, Nicholas, *The Essential Portions of Nicholas Upton's De Studio Militari* (before 1446, trans. John Blount *c.* 1500), ed. F.P. Barnard, Oxford, 1931.

Vergil, Polydore, *The Anglica Historia of Polydore Vergil* A.D. *1485–1537*, ed. D. Hay, Camden, 3rd ser., 74, 1950.

Virgoe, R. (ed.), 'Some Ancient Indictments in the King's Bench referring to Kent, 1450–1452', in F.R.H. Du Boulay (ed.), *Documents Illustrative of Medieval Kentish Society*, Kent Records, 18, 1964, pp. 214–65.

The Visitation of the County of Warwick in the Year 1619 by William Camden, ed. J. Fetherston, Harleian Soc. Publs., 12, London, 1877.

The Visitation of the County of Worcester in the year 1569, ed. W.P.W. Phillimore, Harleian Soc. Publs., 27, London, 1888.

Warkworth, John, *A Chronicle of the First Thirteen Years of King Edward the Fourth*, ed. J.O. Halliwell, Camden Ser., London, 1839.

Warwickshire Feet of Fines, III, ed. L. Drucker, Dugdale Soc. Publications, 18, 1943.

Wilson, T., *The State of England Anno Dom. 1600*, ed. F.J. Fisher, Camden Misc., 16, Camden, 3rd ser., 52, 1936.

A Worcestershire Miscellany compiled by John Northwood, c. *1400*, ed. N.S. Baugh, Philadelphia, 1956.

'William Worcestre', 'Annales', in *Liber Niger Scaccarii necnon Wilhelmi Worcestrii Annales . . .*, ed. T. Hearne, 2 vols., Oxford, 1774.

Worcestre, William, *Itineraries*, ed. J.H. Harvey, Oxford, 1969.

(3) SECONDARY WORKS

Agricola, 1762, 'Addenda' in Anon, 1762.

Ainsley, H., 1984, 'Keeping the peace in southern England in the thirteenth century', *South. Hist.*, 6, pp. 13–35.

Alcock, N.W., 1977, 'Enclosure and depopulation in Burton Dassett: a 16th-century view', *Warwickshire Hist.*, 3, pp. 180–4.

1978, 'Maxstoke Castle, Warwickshire', *The Archaeolog. Jnl.*, 135, pp. 195–233.

Alexander, J.J.G. and Binski, P., 1987 (eds.), *Age of Chivalry: Art in Plantaganet England 1200–1400*, Royal Academy of Arts, London.

Alexander, J.J.G. and Gibson, M.T., 1976, (eds.), *Medieval Learning and Literature*, Oxford, 1976.

Allmand, C., 1982, 'The civil lawyers', in Clough, C.H., 1982, (ed.), pp. 155–80.

1983, *Lancastrian Normandy 1415–1450*, Oxford.

1988, *The Hundred Years War: England and France at War* c. *1300* – c. 1450, Cambridge.

The Ancestor, 1902–05, London.

Anon, 1762, *The History of Sutton Coldfield*, London.

Archbold, W.A.J., 1899, 'Sir William Stanley and Perkin Warbeck', *Eng. Hist. Rev.*, 14, pp. 529–34.

Archer, R., 1984a, 'The Mowbrays, Earls of Nottingham and Dukes of Norfolk, to 1432', unpubl. D.Phil. thesis, Oxford University.

1984b, 'Rich old ladies: the problem of late medieval dowagers', in Pollard, A.J. (ed.), 1984, pp. 15–35.

Arlacchi, P., 1983, trans. J. Steinberg, *Mafia, Peasants and Great Estates: Society in Traditional Calabria*, Cambridge.

Armstrong, C.A.J., 1948, 'Some examples of the distribution and speed of news in England at the time of the Wars of the Roses', in Hunt, R.W., Pantin, W.A. and Southern, R.W. (eds.), 1948, pp. 429–54.

Arnold, C., 1984, 'The commission of the peace for the West Riding of Yorkshire, 1437–1509', in Pollard, A.J. (ed.) 1984, pp. 116–38.

Arnold, M.S., Green, T.A., Scully, S.A. and White, S.D. (eds.), 1981, *On the Laws and Customs of England*, Chapel Hill, N. Carolina.

Arthurson, I., 1981, '1497 and the Western Rising', unpubl. Ph.D. thesis, Keele University.

1987a, 'The king's voyage into Scotland: the war that never was', in Williams, D. (ed.) 1987, pp. 1–22.

1987b, 'The Rising of 1497: a revolt of the peasantry?', in Rosenthal, J.T. and Richmond, C. (eds.), 1987, pp. 1–18.

Astill, G.G., 1974, 'An early inventory of a Leicestershire Knight', *Midland Hist.*, 2, pp. 274–83.

1977, 'The medieval gentry: a study in Leicestershire society 1350–99', unpubl. Ph.D. thesis, Birmingham University.

Aston, M., 1984, 'Caim's castles: poverty, politics and disendowment', in Dobson, R.B. (ed.), 1984, pp. 45–81.

Aston, M. (ed.), 1988, *Medieval Fish, Fisheries and Fishponds in England*, British Archaeological Reports, British Ser., 182.

Aston, T.H. and Philpin, C.H.E. (eds.), 1985, *The Brenner Debate*, Cambridge.

Aston, T.H., Coss, P.R., Dyer, C. and Thirsk, J. (eds.), 1983, *Social Relations and Ideas*, Cambridge.

Atkyns, Sir Robert, 1712, *The Ancient and Present State of Gloucestershire*, 2 vols., London: rpt. East Ardsley, Wakefield, 1974.

Ault, W.O., 1970, 'The village church and the village community in medieval England', *Speculum*, 45, pp. 197–215.

Avrutick, J.B., 1967, 'Commissions of *oyer* and *terminer* in fifteenth century England', unpubl. M. Phil. thesis, University of London.

Aylmer, G.E., 1974, *The King's Servants: the Civil Service of Charles I 1625–42*, 2nd edn, London.

Aylmer, G.E. and Morrill, J.S. (eds.), 1983, *Land, Men and Beliefs* (collected essays of J.P. Cooper), London.

Bailey, M., 1988, 'The rabbit and the medieval East Anglian economy', *Agricultural Hist. Rev.*, 36, pp. 1–20.

Baker, A.R.H. and Butlin, R.A. (eds.), 1973, *Studies of Field Systems in the British Isles*, Cambridge.

Baker, D. (ed.), 1973, *Sanctity and Secularity: the Church and the World*, Studies in Church History, 10, Oxford.

1975, *Church, Society and Politics*, Studies in Church History, 12, Oxford.

Baker, G., 1822–41, *The History and Antiquities of the County of Northampton*, 2 vols., London.

Baker, J.H., 1979, *An Introduction to English Legal History*, 2nd edn, London.

1980, 'The attorneys and officers of the common law', *Jnl. Legal Hist.*, 1, pp. 182–203.

1981, 'The English legal profession, 1450–1550', in Prest, W. (ed.), 1981, pp. 16–41.

1983, 'Lawyers practising in chancery 1474–1486', *Jnl. of Legal Hist.*, 4, pp. 54–76.

Banton, M. (ed.), 1965, *Political Systems and the Distribution of Power*, London.

1966, *The Social Anthropology of Complex Societies*, London.

Barker, W.A., 1984–7, 'Warwickshire markets', *Warwickshire Hist.*, 6, pp. 161–75.

Barron, C., 1968, 'The tyranny of Richard II', *Bull. Inst. Hist. Res.*, 41, pp. 1–18.

1985, 'The parish fraternities of medieval London', in Barron, C.M. and Harper-Bill, C. (eds.), 1985, pp. 13–37.

Barron, C.M. and Harper-Bill, C. (eds.), 1985, *The Church in Pre-Reformation Society*, Woodbridge, Suffolk.

Bean, J.M.W., 1958, *The Estates of the Percy Family 1416–1537*, Oxford.

1959, 'Henry IV and the Percies', *History*, 44, pp. 212–27.

1968, *The Decline of English Feudalism 1215–1540*, Manchester.

1984, 'The financial position of Richard, duke of York', in Gillingham J. and Holt, J.C. (eds.), 1984, pp. 182–98.

Beauroy, J., 1986, 'Family patterns and relationships of Bishop's Lynn willmakers in the fourteenth century', in Bonfield, L., Smith, R.M. and Wrightson, K. (eds.), 1986, pp. 23–42.

Beattie, J., 1986, *Crime and the Courts in England, 1660–1800*, Oxford and Princeton.

Beckett, J.V., 1986, *The Aristocracy in England 1660–1914*, Oxford.

Beckinsale, R. and Beckinsale, M., 1980, *The English Heartland*, London.

Bellamy, J.G., 1964, 'The Coterel gang: an anatomy of a band of fourteenth-century criminals', *Eng. Hist. Rev.*, 79, pp. 698–717.

1965, 'Justice under the Yorkist kings', *American Jnl. of Legal Hist.*, 9, pp. 135–55.

1973, *Crime and Public Order in England in the Later Middle Ages*, London.

1984, *Criminal Law and Society in Late Medieval and Tudor England*, Gloucester.

Bennett, H.S., 1946–7, 'The production and dissemination of vernacular manuscripts in the fifteenth century', *The Library*, 5th ser., 1, pp. 167–78.

Bennett, M.J., 1973, 'A county community: social cohesion amongst the Cheshire gentry, 1400–1425', *North. Hist.*, 8, pp. 24–44.

1975, 'Late Medieval Society in North-West England: Cheshire and Lancashire, 1375–1425', unpubl. Ph.D. thesis, Lancaster University.

1978, 'Sources and problems in the study of social mobility: Cheshire in the later middle ages', *Trans. of the Historic Soc. of Lancs. and Chesh.*, 128, pp. 59–95.

1983, *Community, Class and Careerism: Cheshire and Lancashire Society in the Age of Sir Gawain and the Green Knight*, Cambridge.

1984, 'Provincial gentlefolk and legal education in the reign of Edward II', *Bull. Inst. Hist. Res.*, 57, pp. 203–8.

1985, *The Battle of Bosworth*, Gloucester.

1986, 'The status of the squire: the northern evidence', in Harper-Bill, C. and Harvey, R. (eds.), 1986, pp. 1–11.

1987a, 'Careerism in late medieval England', in Rosenthal, J. and Richmond, C. (eds.), 1987, pp. 19–39.

1987b, *Lambert Simnel and the Battle of Stoke*, Gloucester.

Beresford, M.W., 1945–6, 'The deserted villages of Warwickshire', *Trans. Birm. and Midland Inst.*, 66, pp. 49–106.

1971, 'A review of historical research', in Beresford, M.W. and Hurst, J.G. (eds.), 1971, pp. 3–75.

Beresford, M.W. and Hurst, J.G. (eds.), 1971, *Deserted Medieval Villages*, London.

Bernard, G., 1985, *The Power of the Early Tudor Nobility: a Study of the Fourth and Fifth Earls of Shrewsbury*, Brighton and Totowa, New Jersey.

Blanchard, I., 1970, 'Population, change, enclosure, and the early Tudor economy', *Ec. Hist. Rev.*, 2nd ser., 23, pp. 427–45.

Blatcher, M., 1935–6, 'Distress infinite and the contumacious sheriff', *Bull. Inst. Hist. Res.*, 13, pp. 146–50.

1936, 'The working of the court of King's Bench in the fifteenth century', unpubl. Ph.D. thesis, University of London.

1978, *The Court of King's Bench 1450–1550*, London.

Blomefield, F., 1805–10, *An Essay towards a Topographical History of the County of Norfolk* . . ., 11 vols., London.

Bois, G., 1985, 'Against the neo-Malthusian orthodoxy', in Aston, T.H. and Philpin, C.H.E. (eds.), 1985, pp. 107–18.

Boissevain, J., 1974, *Friends of Friends: Networks, Manipulators and Coalitions*, Oxford.

Boissevain, J. and Mitchell, J.C. (eds.), 1973, *Network Analysis: Studies in Human Interaction*, The Hague and Paris.

Bolton, J.L., 1980, *The Medieval English Economy 1150–1500*, London.

Bond, C.J., 1969, 'The deserted village of Billesley Trussell', *Warwickshire Hist.*, 1, pp. 16–24.

1973, 'The estates of Evesham Abbey: a preliminary survey of their medieval topography', *Vale of Evesham Hist. Soc. Research Papers*, 4, pp. 1–61.

1982, 'Deserted medieval villages in Warwickshire and Worcestershire', in Slater, T.R. and Jarvis, P.J. (eds.), 1982, pp. 141–71.

Bonfield, L., 1983, *Marriage Settlements 1601–1740: The Adoption of the Strict Settlement*, Cambridge.

1986, '"Affective Families", "Open Elites" and family settlements in early modern England', *Ec. Hist. Rev.*, 2nd ser., 39, pp. 341–54.

Bonfield, L., Smith, R.M. and Wrightson, K. (eds.), 1986, *The World we have Gained: Histories of Population and Social Structure*, Oxford.

Bonser, K.J., 1970, *The Drovers: Who They Were and How They Went*, London.

Born, L.K., 1928, 'The perfect prince: a study in thirteenth- and fourteenth-century ideals, *Speculum*, 3, pp. 470–504.

Bossy, J., 1973, 'Blood and baptism: kinship, community and Christianity in western Europe from the fourteenth to the seventeenth centuries', in Baker, D. (ed.), 1973, pp. 129–432.

1985, *Christianity in the West 1400–1700*, Oxford.

Bossy, J. (ed.), 1983, *Disputes and Settlements: Law and Human Relations in the West*, Cambridge.

Bourne, J.M., 1986, *Patronage and Society in Nineteenth-Century England*, London.

Brewer, J. and Styles, J. (eds.), 1980, *An Ungovernable People? The English and their Law in the Seventeenth and Eighteenth Centuries*, London.

Bridges, J. and Whalley, P., 1791, *The History and Antiquities of Northamptonshire*, 2 vols., Oxford.

British Association, 1950, *Birmingham and its Regional Setting, A Scientific Survey*, British Assoc. for the Advancement of Science.

Britnell, R.H., 1977, 'Agricultural technology and the margin of cultivation in the fourteenth century', *Ec. Hist. Rev.*, 2nd ser., 30, pp. 53–66.

1980, 'Minor landlords in England and medieval agrarian capitalism', *Past and Present*, 89, pp. 3–22.

1981, 'The proliferation of markets in England, 1200–1349', *Ec. Hist. Rev.*, 34, pp. 209–21.

Brooks, C.W., 1986, *Pettyfoggers and Vipers of the Commonwealth*, Cambridge.

Brown, A.L., 1969, 'The king's councillors in fifteenth-century England', *Trans. Roy. Hist. Soc.*, 5th ser., 19, pp. 95–118.

1972, 'The reign of Henry IV: the establishment of the Lancastrian regime', in Chrimes, S.B., Ross, C.D. and Griffiths, R.A. (eds.), 1972, pp. 1–28.

1981, 'Parliament, *c.* 1377–1422', in Davies, R.G. and Denton, J.H. (eds.), 1981, pp. 109–40.

Brown, J.M., 1977a, 'The exercise of power', in Brown, J.M. (ed.), 1977, pp. 33–65.

Brown, J.M. (ed.), 1977, *Scottish Society in the Fifteenth Century*, London.

Brown, R.A. (ed.), 1979, *Proceedings of the Battle Conference on Anglo-Norman Studies*, 2.

1980, *Proceedings of the Battle Conference on Anglo-Norman Studies*, 3.

1985, *Anglo-Norman Studies*, 8.

Buck, M.C., 1983, 'The reform of the exchequer, 1316–26, *Eng. Hist. Rev.*, 98, pp. 241–60.

Bullough, D.A. and Storey, R.L. (eds.), 1971, *The Study of Medieval Records*, Oxford.

Burgess, C., 1987, '"By quick and by dead": wills and pious bequests in late medieval Bristol', *Eng. Hist. Rev.*, 102, pp. 837–58.

Butterfield, H., 1957, *George III and the Historians*, London.

Butters, L., 1968, *Fairbairn's Crests of the Families of Great Britain and Ireland*, rev. edn, Rutland, Vermont.

Calnan, J., 1978, 'County society and local government in the county of Hertford *c.* 1580 – *c.* 1630, with special reference to the commission of the peace', unpubl. Ph.D. thesis, Cambridge University.

Cam, H.M., 1930, *The Hundred and the Hundred Rolls*, London; rpt. 1963.

1950, 'Shire officials, coroners, constables, and bailiffs', in Willard, J.F., Morris, W.A. and Dunham, W.H. (eds.) 1950, pp. 148–83.

1962, *Law-Finders and Law-Makers in Medieval England*, London.

1962a, 'The legislators of medieval England', in Cam, 1962, pp. 132–58.

1962b, 'The theory and practice of representation in medieval England', in Cam, 1962, pp. 159–75.

1963, *Liberties and Communities in Medieval England*, London.

1963a, 'The general eyres of 1329–30', in Cam, 1963, pp. 150–62.

1963b, 'The relation of English members of parliament to their constituencies in the fourteenth century', in Cam, 1963, pp. 223–35.

Camden, William, 1610, *Britain, or a Chrorographicall Description of . . . England, Scotland, and Ireland . . .*, trans. Philemon Holland, London.

Cameron, A., 1970, 'Sir Henry Willoughby of Wollaton', *Trans. of the Thoroton Soc.*, 74, pp. 10–21.

1972, 'A Nottinghamshire quarrel in the reign of Henry VII', *Bull. Inst. Hist. Res.*, 45, pp. 27–37.

1974, 'The giving of livery and retaining in Henry VII's reign', *Renaissance and Modern Studies*, 18, pp. 17–35.

1978, 'Complaint and reform in Henry VII's reign: the origins of the statute of 3 Henry VII, C.2?', *Bull. Inst. Hist. Res.*, 51, pp. 83–9.

Campbell, B.M.S., 1981, 'The population of early Tudor England', *Jnl. Hist. Geog.*, 7, pp. 145–54.

Campbell, J.K., 1964, *Honour, Family and Patronage: A Study of Institutions and Moral Values in a Greek Mountain Community*, Oxford.

Campbell, M., 1960, *The English Yeoman under Elizabeth and the Early Stuarts*, 2nd edn, London.

Cantor, L.M., 1970–1, 'The medieval parks of Leicestershire', *Trans. Leics. Archaeological Soc.*, 46, pp. 9–24.

Carpenter, D.A., 1976, 'The decline of the curial sheriff in England 1194–1258', *Eng. Hist. Rev.*, 91, pp. 1–32.

1981, 'Was there a crisis of the knightly class in the thirteenth century?: the Oxfordshire evidence', *Eng. Hist. Rev.*, 95, pp. 721–52.

Carpenter, M.C., 1976, 'Political Society in Warwickshire *c.* 1401–72', unpubl. Ph.D. thesis, Cambridge University.

1980a, 'The Beauchamp affinity: a study of bastard feudalism at work', *Eng. Hist. Rev.*, 95, pp. 514–32.

1980b, 'Sir Thomas Malory and 15th-century local politics', *Bull. Inst. Hist. Res.*, 53, pp. 31–43.

1982, 'Fifteenth-century biographies', *Hist. Jnl.*, 25, pp. 729–34.

1983, 'Law, justice and landowners in late-medieval England', *Law and Hist. Review*, 1, pp. 205–37.

1986a, 'The duke of Clarence and the midlands: a study in the interplay of local and national politics', *Midland Hist.*, 11, pp. 23–48.

1986b, 'The fifteenth-century English gentry and their estates', in Jones, M. (ed.), 1986, pp. 36–60.

1987, 'The religion of the gentry of fifteenth-century England', in Williams, D. (ed.), 1987, pp. 53–74.

1988, review of Bennett 1983 and Wright 1983, *Hist. Jnl.*, 31, pp. 753–7.

Carus-Wilson, E.M., 1959, 'Evidences of industrial growth on some fifteenth-century manors', *Ec. Hist. Rev.*, 2nd ser., 12, pp. 190–205.

Catto, J., 1985, 'The king's servants', in Harriss, G.L. (ed.), 1985, pp. 75–95.

Chatwin, P.B., 1947–8, 'Castles in Warwickshire', *Trans. Birm. and Midland Inst.*, 67, pp. 1–34.

1960–1, 'Long Itchington', *Trans. Birm. and Midland Inst.*, 79, pp. 1–10.

Cheney, C.R. (ed.), 1970, *Handbook of Dates for Students of English History*, Roy. Hist. Soc., London.

Cherry, M., 1979, 'The Courtenay earls of Devon: the formation and disintegration of a late medieval aristocratic affinity', *South. Hist.*, 1, pp. 71–97.

1981a, 'The crown and the political community in Devonshire 1377–1461', unpubl. Ph.D. thesis, University of Wales.

1981b, 'The struggle for power in mid-fifteenth-century Devonshire', in Griffiths, R.A. (ed.), 1981, pp. 123–44.

Chetwynd-Stapylton, H.E., 1892, *The Chetwynds of Ingestre*, London.

Chibnall, M., 1986, *Anglo-Norman England 1066–1166*, Oxford.

Chrimes, S.B., 1936, *English Constitutional Ideas in the Fifteenth Century*, Cambridge.

1966, *An Introduction to the Administrative History of Mediaeval England*, 3rd edn, Oxford.

1972a, *Henry VII*, London.

1972b, 'The reign of Henry VII', in Chrimes, S.B., Ross, C.D. and Griffiths, R.A. (eds.), 1972, pp. 67–85.

Chrimes, S.B., Ross, C.D. and Griffiths, R.A. (eds.), 1972, *Fifteenth-Century England 1399–1509*, Manchester.

Clanchy, M.T., 1974, 'Law, government, and society in medieval England', *History*, 59, pp. 73–8.

1979, *From Memory to Written Record: England 1066–1307*, London.

1983, 'Law and love in the middle ages', in Bossy, J. (ed.), 1983, pp. 47–67.

Clark, L. and Rawcliffe, C., 1983, 'The history of parliament, 1386–1422: a progress report', *Medieval Prosopography*, 4/2, pp. 9–41.

Clark, P., 1977, *English Provincial Society from the Reformation to the Revolution: Religion, Politics and Society in Kent 1500–1640*, Hassocks.

Clay, C.G.A., 1984, *Economic Expansion and Social Change: England 1500–1700*, 2 vols., Cambridge.

Clayton, D.J., 1985, 'Peace bonds and the maintenance of law and order in late medieval England: the example of Cheshire', *Bull. Inst. Hist. Res.*, 58, pp. 133–48.

Cliffe, J.T., 1969, *The Yorkshire Gentry from the Reformation to the Civil War*, London.

Clough, C.H. (ed.), 1982, *Profession, Vocation and Culture in Late Medieval England*, Liverpool.

Cockburn, J.S., 1975, 'Early modern assize records as historical evidence, *Jnl. Soc. Archivists*, 5, pp. 215–31.

Cockburn, J.S. (ed.), 1977, *Crime in England, 1550–1800*, London.

Cockburn, J.S. and Green, T.A. (eds.), 1988, *Twelve Good Men and True: the Criminal Jury in England, 1200–1800*, Princeton.

Coleman, C. and Starkey, D. (eds.), 1986, *Revolution Reassessed: Revisions in the History of the Tudor Government and Administration*, Oxford.

Coleman, D.C. and John, A.H. (eds.), 1976, *Trade, Government and Economy in Pre-Industrial England*, London.

Coleman, J., 1981, *Medieval Readers and Writers*, English Literature in History, 1350–1400, London.

Coles, G.M., 1961, 'The lordship of Middleham, especially in Yorkist and early Tudor times', unpubl. M.A. thesis, Liverpool University.

Condon, M.M., 1979, 'Ruling elites in the reign of Henry VII', in Ross, C. (ed.), 1979, pp. 109–42.

1986a, 'An anachronism with intent? Henry VII's council ordinance of 1491/2', in Griffiths, R.A. and Sherborne, J. (eds.), 1986, pp. 228–53.

1986b, 'The kaleidoscope of treason: fragments from the Bosworth story', *The Ricardian*, 7, pp. 208–12.

Cooper, C.H., 1874, *Memoir of Margaret, Countess of Richmond and Derby*, Cambridge.

Cooper, J.P., 1959, 'Henry VII's last years reconsidered', *Hist. Jnl.*, 2, pp. 103–29.

1967, 'The social distribution of land and men in England 1436–1700', *Ec. Hist. Rev.*, 2nd ser., 20, pp. 419–40.

1976, 'Patterns of inheritance and settlement by great landowners from the fifteenth to the eighteenth centuries', in Goody, J., Thirsk, J. and Thompson, E.P. (eds.), 1976, pp. 192–327.

1983a, 'Ideas of gentility in early modern England', in Aylmer, G.E. and Morrill, J.S. (eds.) 1983, pp. 43–77.

1983b, 'Retainers in Tudor England', in Aylmer and Morrill (eds.), 1983, pp. 78–96.

1985, 'In search of agrarian capitalism', in Aston, T.H. and Philpin, C.H.E. (eds.), 1985, pp. 138–91.

Cooper, W., 1936, *Wootton Wawen: Its History and Records*, Leeds.

1946, *Henley-in-Arden: An Ancient Market Town*, Birmingham.

Cornwall, J., 1964–5, 'The early Tudor gentry', *Ec. Hist. Rev.*, 2nd ser., 17, pp. 456–75.

Coss, P.R., 1974a, 'Coventry before incorporation', *Midland Hist.*, 2, pp. 137–51.

1974b, *The Langley Family and its Cartulary: A Study in Late Medieval 'Gentry'*, Dugdale Soc. Occasional Papers, 22.

1975, 'Sir Geoffrey Langley and the crisis of the knightly class in thirteenth-century England', *Past and Present*, 68, pp. 3–37.

1983, 'Literature and social terminology: the vavasour in England', in Aston, T.H., Coss, P.R., Dyer, C. and Thirsk, J. (eds.), 1983, pp. 109–50.

Coss, P.R. and Lloyd, S.D. (eds.), 1986, *Thirteenth-Century England*, Woodbridge, Suffolk, 1.

Coward, B., 1968, 'The Stanley family *c.* 1385–1461: a study of the origins, power and wealth of a landowning family', unpubl. Ph.D. thesis, Sheffield University.

1983, *The Stanleys Lords Stanley and Earls of Derby 1385–1672*, Chetham Soc., 3rd ser., 30, Manchester.

Craik, E.M. (ed.), 1984, *Marriage and Property*, Aberdeen.

Crawford, A., 1975, 'The career of John Howard, duke of Norfolk, 1420–1485', unpubl. M. Phil. thesis, University of London.

1985, 'The piety of late medieval English queens', in Barron, C.M. and Harper-Bill, C. (eds.), 1985, pp. 48–57.

1986, 'The private life of John Howard: a study of a Yorkist lord, his family and household', in Hammond, P.W. (ed.), 1986, pp. 6–24.

Cressy, D., 1986, 'Kinship and kin interaction in early modern England', *Past and Present*, 113, pp. 38–69.

Cronne, H.A., 1951, *The Borough of Warwick in the Middle Ages*, Dugdale Soc. Occasional Papers, 10.

Crouch, D., 1986, *The Beaumont Twins: The Roots and Branches of Power in the Twelfth Century*, Cambridge.

Crowley, D.A., 1975, 'The later history of frankpledge', *Bull. Inst. Hist. Res.*, 48, pp. 1–15.

Crump, C.G., 1924, 'A note on the criticism of records', *Bull. of the John Rylands Lib.*, 8, pp. 140–9.

Cuming, C.J. (ed.), 1967, *Studies in Church History*, 4, Leiden.

Darby, H.C. (ed.), 1951, *An Historical Geography of England before* A.D. *1800*, 2nd edn, Cambridge.

1976, *A New Historical Geography of England before 1600*, Cambridge, 1973; rpt. 1976.

Darby, H.C. and Terrett, I.B. (eds.), 1954, *The Domesday Geography of Midland England*, Cambridge.

Davenport, J., 1907, *The Washbourne Family*, London.

Davies, C.S.L., 1977, *Peace, Print and Protestantism*, Granada edn, London.

1987, 'Bishop John Morton, the Holy See and the accession of Henry VII', *Eng. Hist. Rev.*, 102, pp. 2–30.

Davies, J.C. (ed.), 1957, *Studies Presented to Sir Hilary Jenkinson*, London.

Davies, R.G., 1982, 'The episcopate', in Clough, C.H. (ed.), 1982, pp. 51–89.

Davies, R.G. and Denton, J.H. (eds.), 1981, *The English Parliament in the Middle Ages*, Manchester.

Davies, R.R., 1968, 'Baronial accounts, incomes, and arrears in the later middle ages', *Ec. Hist. Rev.*, 2nd ser., 21, pp. 211–29.

1971, 'Richard II and the principality of Chester 1397–9', in Du Boulay, F.R.H. and Barron, C.M. (eds.), 1971, pp. 256–79.

1972–3, Review of Maddicott 1970, *Welsh Hist. Rev.*, 6, pp. 201–10.

1978, *Lordship and Society in the March of Wales 1282–1400*, Oxford.

1987, *Conquest, Co-Existence, and Change: Wales 1063–1415*, Oxford.

Davies, W. and Fouracre, P. (eds.), 1986, *The Settlement of Disputes in Early Medieval Europe*, Cambridge.

Davis, R.H.C., 1967, *King Stephen 1135–1154*, London.

1976, *The Early History of Coventry*, Dugdale Soc. Occasional Papers, 24.

Davis, R.H.C. and Wallace-Hadrill, J.M. (eds.), 1981, *The Writing of History in the Middle Ages*, Oxford.

Denholm-Young, N., 1965, *History and Heraldry 1254–1310*, Oxford.

1969, *Collected Papers*, Cardiff.

1969a 'Feudal society in the thirteenth century: the knights', in Denholm-Young, N., 1969, pp. 83–94.

1969b, *The Country Gentry in the Fourteenth Century*, Oxford.

Dent, E., 1877, *Annals of Winchcombe and Sudeley*, London.

Derbyshire Archaeological Journal (formerly, *Jnl. of the Derbys. Archaeological and Natural Hist. Soc.*), 1879– , London, Derby, Kendal etc.

Deutsch, M., 1973, *The Resolution of Conflict; Constructive and Destructive Processes*, New Haven and London.

Dickens, Charles, 1950, *Nicholas Nickleby*, Oxford Illustrated Dickens.

Dobson, R.B., 1967, 'The foundation of perpetual chantries by the citizens of medieval York', in Cuming, G.J. (ed.), 1967, pp. 22–38.

1973, *Durham Priory 1400–1450*, Cambridge.

Dobson, R.B. (ed.), 1984, *The Church, Politics and Patronage in the Fifteenth Century*, Gloucester.

Dockray, K., 1986, 'Why did the fifteenth-century English gentry marry?', in Jones, M. (ed.), 1986, pp. 61–80.

Donkin, R.A., 1976, 'Changes in the early middle ages', in Darby, H.C. (ed.), 1976, pp. 75–135.

Driver, J.T., 1963, 'The knights of the shire for Worcestershire during the reigns of Richard II, Henry IV and Henry V', *Trans of the Worcs. Archaeological Soc.*, n.s., 40, 1963, pp. 42–64.

1986, 'Richard Quatremains: a 15th-century squire and knight of the shire for Oxfordshire', *Oxoniensa*, 51, 1986, pp. 87–103.

Du Boulay, F.R.H., 1965, 'Who were farming the English demesnes at the end of the middle ages?', *Ec. Hist. Rev.*, 2nd ser., 17, pp. 443–55.

1966, *The Lordship of Canterbury*, London.

1970, *An Age of Ambition: English Society in the late Middle Ages*, London.

1978, 'Law enforcement in medieval Germany', *History*, 63, pp. 345–55.

Du Boulay, F.R.H. and Barron, C.M. (eds.), 1971, *The Reign of Richard II*, London.

Duby, G., 1968, *Rural Economy and Country Life in the Medieval West*, trans. C. Postan, London.

1971, *La Société aux* XIe *et* XIIe *siècles dans la région Mâconnaise*, Paris.

1977, *The Chivalrous Society*, trans. C. Postan, London.

1977a, 'French genealogical literature', in Duby, G., 1977, pp. 149–57.

1977b, 'Lineage, nobility and knighthood', in Duby, G., 1977, pp. 59–80.

1977c, 'The structure of kinship and nobility', in Duby, G., 1977, pp. 134–48.

1977d, 'Youth in aristocratic society', in Duby, G., 1977, pp. 112–22.

1978, *Les Trois Ordres ou l'imaginaire du féodalisme*, Paris.

Dugdale, Sir William, 1675–6, *The Baronage of England*, 2 vols. in one, London.

1730, *The Antiquities of Warwickshire*, 2 vols. in one, London; rpt. Manchester, n.d.

1765, *The Antiquities of Warwickshire*, Coventry.

1817–30, *Monasticon Anglicanum*, 6 vols., London.

Dunham, W.H., 1955, *Lord Hastings' Indentured Retainers 1461–1483*, Transactions of the Connecticut Academy of Arts and Sciences, 39, Yale; rpt. Archon Books, 1970.

Dyer, C., 1965–7, 'The deserted medieval village of Woollashill, Worcestershire', *Trans. Worcs. Archaeological Soc.*, 3rd ser., 1, pp. 55–61.

1967–8, 'Population and agriculture on a Warwickshire manor in the later middle ages', *Univ. of Birm. Hist. Jnl.*, 11, pp. 113–27.

1968, 'A redistribution of incomes in fifteenth century England', *Past and Present*, 39, pp. 11–33.

1972, 'A small landowner in the fifteenth century', *Midland Hist.*, 1, pp. 1–14.

1980a, Addendum to Perry, J.G., 1980, *Trans. Birm. and Midland Inst.*, 90, pp. 63–4.

1980b, *Lords and Peasants in a Changing Society: The Estates of the Bishopric of Worcester, 680–1540*, Cambridge.

1981, *Warwickshire Farming 1349–c. 1520*, Dugdale Soc. Occasional Papers, 27.

1982 'Deserted medieval villages in the west midlands', *Ec. Hist. Rev.*, 2nd ser., 35, pp. 19–34.

1983, 'English diet in the later middle ages', in Aston, T.H., Coss, P.R., Dyer, C. and Thirsk, J. (eds.), 1983, pp. 191–216.

1984, 'Changes in the size of peasant holdings in some west midland villages 1400–1540', in Smith, R.M., (ed.), 1984, pp. 277–94.

1988a, 'Changes in diet in the late middle ages: the case of harvest workers', *Agricultural Hist. Rev.*, 36, pp. 21–37.

1988b, 'The consumption of fresh-water fish in medieval England', in Aston, M. (ed.) 1988, pp. 27–38.

Edwards, J.G., 1957, *The Commons in Medieval English Parliaments*, Creighton Lecture, University of London.

1964, 'The emergence of majority rule in English parliamentary elections', *Trans. Roy. Hist. Soc.*, 5th ser., 14, pp. 175–96.

1969, 'The Huntingdonshire parliamentary election of 1450', in Sandquist, T.A. and Powicke, M.R. (eds.), 1969, pp. 383–95.

1970, 'The *plena potestas* of English parliamentary representatives', in Fryde, E.B. and Miller, E. (eds.), 1970, pp. 136–49.

1979, *The Second Century of the English Parliament*, Oxford.
Ellis, S., 1985, *Tudor Ireland*, London.
Elton, G.R., 1958, 'Henry VII: rapacity and remorse', *Hist. Jnl.*, 1, pp. 21–39.
1961, 'Henry VII: a restatement', *Hist. Jnl.*, 4, pp. 1–29.
1969, *The Sources of History: England 1200–1640*, London.
1974, 'Tudor government: the points of contact: I. Parliament', *Trans. Roy. Hist. Soc.*, 5th ser., 24, pp. 183–200.
1976, 'Tudor government: the points of contact: III. The court', *Trans. Roy. Hist. Soc.*, 5th ser., 26, pp. 211–28.
Emden, A.B., 1957–9, *A Biographical Register of the University of Oxford to A.D.1500*, 3 vols., Oxford.
Emery, F.V., 1962, 'Moated settlements in England', *Geography*, 47, pp. 378–88.
Evans, H.T., 1915, *Wales and the Wars of the Roses*, Cambridge.
Everitt, A., 1966, 'Social mobility in early modern England', *Past and Present*, 33, pp. 56–73.
1968, 'The county community', in Ives, E.W. (ed.) 1968, pp. 48–63.
1985, *Landscape and Community in England*, London.
1985a, 'Country, county and town: patterns of regional evolution in England', in Everitt, 1985, pp. 11–40.
1985b, 'River and wold: reflections on the historical origin of regions and *pays*', in Everitt, 1985, pp. 41–59.
Faith, R., 1984, 'Berkshire: fourteenth and fifteenth centuries', in Harvey, P.D.A. (ed.), 1984, pp. 107–77.
Ferguson, A.B., 1960, *The Indian Summer of English Chivalry*, Durham, N. Carolina.
Field, P.J.C., 1979–80, 'Thomas Malory and the Warwick retinue roll', *Midland Hist.*, 5, pp. 20–30.
1981–2, 'The last years of Sir Thomas Malory', *Bulletin of the John Rylands Library*, 64, pp. 433–56.
Field, R.K., 1965, 'Worcestershire peasant buildings, household goods and farming equipment in the later middle ages', *Medieval Archaeology*, 9, 1965, pp. 105–45.
Finberg, H.P.R., 1975, *The Making of the Gloucestershire Landscape*, London.
1976, *The Formation of England 550–1042*, Paladin edn.
Finch, M.E., 1956, *The Wealth of Five Northamptonshire Families 1540–1640*, Northants. Rec. Soc. Publs., 19, Oxford.
Fleming, P.W., 1984, 'Charity, faith and the gentry of Kent 1422–1529', in Pollard, A.J. (ed.), 1984, pp. 36–58.
1987, 'The Hautes and their 'circle': culture and the English gentry', in Williams, D. (ed.) 1987, pp. 85–102.
Fletcher, A.J., 1975, *A County Community in Peace and War: Sussex 1600–1660*, London.
1983, 'National and local awareness in the county communities', in Tomlinson H. (ed.), 1983, pp. 151–74.
1985, 'Honour, reputation and local officeholding in Elizabethan and Stuart England', in Fletcher, A.J. and Stevenson, J. (eds.), 1985, pp. 92–115.
1986, *Reform in the Provinces: The Government of Stuart England*, Newhaven and London.

Fletcher, A.J. and Stevenson, J. (eds.), 1985, *Order and Disorder in Early Modern England*, Cambridge.

Ford, W.J., 1976, 'Some settlement patterns in the central region of the Warwickshire Avon', in Sawyer, P.H. (ed.), 1976, pp. 143–63.

Foss, E., 1848–64, *The Judges of England*, 9 vols., London.

1870, *A Biographical Dictionary of the Judges of England 1066–1870*, London.

Fowler, G.H., 1940, 'A household expense roll, 1328', *Eng. Hist. Rev.*, 55, pp. 630–4.

Fox, L., 1939, 'The honor and earldom of Leicester: origin and descent', *Eng. Hist. Rev.*, 54, pp. 385–402.

Fryde, E.B. and Miller, E. (eds.), 1970, *Historical Studies of the English Parliament*, I, Origins to 1399, Cambridge.

Fryde, N., 1979, *The Tyranny and Fall of Edward II 1321–26*, Cambridge.

Fuller, T., 1662, *The History of the Worthies of England*, 3 vols. in one, London.

Gatrell, P., 1982, 'Historians and peasants: studies of medieval English society in a Russian context', *Past and Present*, 96, pp. 22–50.

Gatrell, V.A.C., Lenman, B. and Parker, G. (eds.), 1980, *Crime and the Law: The Social History of Crime in Western Europe since 1500*, London.

Gellner, E., 1977, 'Patrons and clients', in Gellner, E. and Waterbury, J. (eds.), 1977, pp. 1–6.

Gellner, E. and Waterbury, J. (eds.), 1977, *Patrons and Clients in Mediterranean Societies*, London.

Genet, J.-P., 1981, 'Political theory and the relationship in England and France between the crown and the local communities', in Highfield, J.R. and Jeffs, R. (eds.), 1981, pp. 19–32.

1984, 'Ecclesiastics and political theory in late medieval England: the end of a monopoly', in Dobson, R.B. (ed.), 1984, pp. 23–44.

Gibbs, V., Doubleday, H.A. *et al.*, (eds.), 1910–40, *The Complete Peerage*, 13 vols., London.

Gill, C., 1930, *Studies in Midland History*, Oxford.

Gillespie, J.L., 1987, 'Cheshiremen at Blore Heath: a swan dive', in Rosenthal, J.T. and Richmond, C. (eds.), 1987, pp. 77–89.

Gillingham, J., 1981, *The Wars of the Roses: Peace and Conflict in Fifteenth-Century England*, London.

Gillingham, J. and Holt, J.C. (eds.), 1984, *War and Government in the Middle Ages*, Cambridge and Totowa, New Jersey.

Girouard, M., 1978, *Life in an English Country House: A Social and Architectural History*, New Haven and London.

Given, J.B., 1977, *Society and Homicide in Thirteenth-Century England*, Stanford.

Given-Wilson, C., 1978, 'Richard II and his grandfather's will', *Eng. Hist. Rev.*, 93, pp. 320–37.

1986, *The Royal Household and the King's Affinity*, Yale.

1987a, *The English Nobility in the Late Middle Ages: The Fourteenth-Century Political Community*, London and New York.

1987b, 'The king and the gentry in fourteenth-century England', *Trans. Roy. Hist. Soc.*, 5th ser., 37, pp. 87–102.

Glasscock, R.E., 1976, 'England *circa* 1334', in Darby, H.C. (ed.), 1976, pp. 136–85.

Glennie, P., 1988, 'In search of agrarian capitalism: manorial land markets and the acquisition of land in the Lea valley *c.* 1450 – *c.* 1560', *Continuity and Change*, 3, pp. 11–40.

Gluckman, M., 1955, 'The peace in the feud', *Past and Present*, 8, pp. 1–14.

1965, *Politics, Law and Ritual in Tribal Society*, Oxford.

Goodman, A.E., 1981a, 'Responses to requests in Yorkshire for military service under Henry V', *North. Hist.*, 17, pp. 240–52.

1981b, *The Wars of the Roses: Military Activity and English Society, 1452–97*, London.

1987, 'John of Gaunt: paradigm of the late fourteenth-century crisis', *Trans. Roy. Hist. Soc.*, 5th ser., 37, pp. 133–48.

Goody, J., Thirsk, J. and Thompson, E.P. (eds.), 1976, *Family and Inheritance: Rural Society in Western Europe, 1200–1800*, Cambridge.

Goring, J., 1975, 'Social change and military decline in mid-Tudor England', *History*, 60, pp. 185–97.

Gover, J.E.B., Mawer, A. and Stenton, F.M., 1936, *The Place-Names of Warwickshire*, English Place-Name Society, 13, Cambridge.

Gransden, A., 1982, *Historical Writing in England,* II, *c.* 1307 to the Early Sixteenth Century, London.

Grant, A., 1985, *Henry VII: The Importance of his Reign in English History*, London.

Gray, H.L., 1934, 'Incomes from land in England in 1436', *Eng. Hist. Rev.*, 49, pp. 607–39.

Green, J., 1986, *The Government of England under Henry I*, Cambridge.

Green, R.F., 1980, *Poets and Princepleasers: Literature and the English Court in the Late Middle Ages*, Toronto.

Green, T.A., 1972, 'Societal concepts of criminal liability for homicide in medieval England', *Speculum*, 47, pp. 669–94.

1985, *Verdict According to Conscience*, Chicago and London.

Greenway, D., Holdsworth, C. and Sayers, J. (eds.), 1985, *Tradition and Change*, Cambridge.

Griffith, M.C., 1940–1, 'The Talbot-Ormond struggle for control of the Anglo-Irish government, 1414–47', *Irish Hist. Studies*, 2, pp. 376–97.

Griffiths, R.A., 1968, 'Local rivalries and national politics – the Percies, the Nevilles, and the duke of Exeter, 1452–1455', *Speculum*, 43, pp. 589–632.

1972a, *The Principality of Wales in the Later Middle Ages: the Structure and Personnel of Government,* I, South Wales, 1277–1536, Cardiff.

1972b, 'Wales and the Marches', in Chrimes, S.B., Ross, C.D. and Griffiths, R.A. (eds.), 1972, pp. 145–72.

1974, 'Patronage, politics, and the principality of Wales, 1413–61', in Hearder, H. and Loyn, H.R. (eds.), 1974, pp. 69–86.

1975, 'Duke Richard of York's intentions in 1450 and the origins of the Wars of the Roses', *Jnl. Medieval Hist.*, 1, pp. 187–209.

1980a, 'The hazards of civil war: the Mountford family and the "Wars of the Roses"', *Midland Hist.* 5, pp. 1–19.

1980b, 'Public and private bureaucracies in England and Wales in the fifteenth century', *Trans. Roy. Hist. Soc.*, 5th ser., 30, pp. 109–30.

1981, *The Reign of King Henry VI*, London.

1984, 'The king's council and the first Protectorate of the duke of York, 1453–1454', *Eng. Hist. Rev.*, 99, pp. 67–82.

Griffiths, R.A. (ed.), 1981, *Patronage, the Crown and the Provinces in later Medieval England*, Gloucester.

Griffiths, R.A. and Sherborne, J. (eds.), 1986, *Kings and Nobles in the Later Middle Ages*, Gloucester.

Guenée, B., 1985, *States and Rulers in Later Medieval Europe*, trans. J. Vale, Oxford.

Gunn, S.J., 1988, *Charles Brandon, Duke of Suffolk* c. *1484–1545*, Oxford.

Guth, D.J., 1977, 'Fifteenth-century England: recent scholarship and future directions', *British Studies Monitor*, 7, pp. 3–50.

Guy, J.A. and Beale, H.G., 1984, (eds.), *Law and Social Change in British History*, Roy. Hist. Soc.

Haigh, C. (ed.), 1984, *The Reign of Elizabeth I*, London.

Haines, R.M., 1975, 'Church, society and politics in the early fifteenth century as viewed from an English pulpit', in Baker, D. (ed.), 1975, pp. 143–57.

Hammond, P.W. (ed.), 1986, *Richard III: Loyalty, Lordship and Law*, Richard III and Yorkist History Trust, London.

Hanawalt, B.A., 1975, 'Fur-collar crime: the pattern of crime among the fourteenth-century English nobility', *Jn. Social Hist.*, 8, pp. 1–17.

1979, *Crime and Conflict in English Communities 1300–1348*, Harvard.

Hanham, A., 1975, *Richard III and his Early Historians 1483–1535*, Oxford.

1985, *The Celys and their World*, Cambridge.

Hannett, J., 1894, *The Forest of Arden*, 2nd edn, Birmingham.

Harcourt, L.W.V., 1907, *His Grace the Steward and Trial of Peers*, London.

Harding, A., 1960, 'The origins and early history of the keeper of the peace', *Trans. Roy. Hist. Soc.*, 5th ser., 10, pp. 85–109.

1973, *The Law Courts of Medieval England*, London.

Hare, J.N., 1981, 'The demesne lessees of fifteenth-century Wiltshire', *Agricultural Hist. Rev.*, 29, pp. 1–15.

1982, 'The Wiltshire risings of 1450: political and economic discontent in mid-fifteenth century England', *South. Hist.*, 4, pp. 13–31.

1985, 'The monks as landlords: the leasing of the monastic demesnes in southern England', in Barron, C.M. and Harper-Bill, C. (eds.), 1985, pp. 82–94.

Harley, J.B., 1958–9, 'Population trends and agricultural developments from the Warwickshire Hundred rolls of 1279', *Ec. Hist. Rev.*, 2nd ser., 11, pp. 8–18.

1964, 'The settlement geography of early medieval Warwickshire', *Institute of British Geographers, Transactions and Papers*, 34, pp. 115–30.

Harper-Bill, C. and Harvey, R. (eds.), 1986, *The Ideals and Practice of Medieval Knighthood,* Woodbridge, Suffolk.

Harris, B.J., 1969, 'Landlords and tenants in England in the later middle ages: the Buckingham estates', *Past and Present*, 43, pp. 146–50.

1986, *Edward Stafford, Third Duke of Buckingham, 1478–1521*, Stanford.

Harris, M.D., 1894, 'Laurence Saunders, citizen of Coventry', *Eng. Hist. Rev.*, 9, pp. 633–51.

Harriss, G.L., 1957, 'Preference at the medieval exchequer', *Bull. Inst. Hist. Res.*, 30, pp. 17–40.

1960, 'The struggle for Calais: an aspect of the rivalry between Lancaster and York', *Eng. Hist. Rev.*, 75, pp. 30–53.

1975, *King, Parliament, and Public Finance in Medieval England to 1369*, Oxford.

1978, 'Medieval doctrines in the debates on supply, 1610–1629', in Sharpe, K. (ed.), 1978, pp. 73–103.

1981, 'Introduction' to McFarlane, K.B., 1981.

1985a, 'Introduction: the exemplar of kingship', in Harriss, G.L. (ed.), 1985, pp. 1–29.

1985b, 'Financial policy', in Harriss (ed.), 1985, pp. 159–79.

1985c, 'The king and his magnates', in Harriss (ed.), 1985, pp. 31–51.

1985d, 'The management of parliament', in Harriss (ed.), 1985, pp. 137–58.

1985e, 'Conclusion', in Harriss (ed.), 1985, pp. 201–10.

Harriss, G.L. (ed.), 1985, *Henry V: The Practice of Kingship*, Oxford.

Harte, N.B., 1976, 'State control of dress and social change in pre-industrial England', in Coleman, D.C. and John, A.H. (eds.), 1976. pp. 132–65.

Harte, N.B. and Ponting, K.G. (eds.), 1983, *Cloth and Clothing in Medieval Europe*, London.

Harvey, B., 1969, 'The leasing of the abbot of Westminster's demesnes in the later middle ages', *Ec. Hist. Rev.*, 2nd ser., 22, pp. 17–27.

1977, *Westminster Abbey and its Estates in the Middle Ages*, Oxford.

Harvey, J.H., 1944, 'Side-lights on Kenilworth castle', *Archaeological Jnl.*, 101, pp. 91–107.

Harvey, P.D.A. (ed.), 1984, *The Peasant Land Market in Medieval England*, Oxford.

Harvey, S.P.J., 1976, 'Evidence for settlement study: Domesday Book', in Sawyer, P. (ed.), 1976, pp. 105–09.

Hassell Smith, A., 1974, *County and Court: Government and Politics in Norfolk, 1558–1603*, Oxford.

Hastings, M., 1947, *The Court of Common Pleas in Fifteenth Century England*, Ithaca, New York.

Hatcher, J., 1970, *Rural Economy and Society in the Duchy of Cornwall, 1300–1500*, Cambridge.

1977, *Plague, Population and the English Economy 1348–1530*, London.

1986, 'Mortality in the fifteenth century: some new evidence', *Ec. Hist. Rev.*, 2nd ser., 39, pp. 19–38.

Hay, D., 1984, 'The criminal prosecution in England and its historians', *The Modern Law Review*, 47, pp. 1–29.

Heal, F., 1984, 'The idea of hospitality in early modern England', *Past and Present*, 102, pp. 66–93.

Heald, T., 1983, *Networks: Who We Know and How We Use Them*, London.

Hearder, H. and Loyn, H.R. (eds.), 1974, *British Government and Administration*, Cardiff.

Heath, P., 1974, 'The medieval church', in *V.C.H. Staffs.*, III, London, pp. 1–43.

1984, 'Urban piety in the later middle ages: the evidence of Hull wills', in Dobson, R.B. (ed.), 1984, pp. 209–29.

Heers, J., 1977, *Family Clans in the Middle Ages*, trans. B. Herbert, Amsterdam.

Helleiner, K.F., 1967, 'The population of Europe from the Black Death to the eve of the vital revolution', in Rich, E.E. and Wilson, C.H. (eds.), 1967, pp. 1–95.

Hess, H., 1973, *Mafia and Mafiosi: The Structure of Power*, trans. E. Osers, Farnborough, Hants.

Hexter, J.H., 1961, 'A new framework for social history', in Hexter, *Reappraisals in History*, London, pp. 14–25.

Hicks, M.A., 1974, 'The career of George Plantagenet, duke of Clarence 1449–78', unpubl. D.Phil. thesis, Oxford University.

1978, 'Dynastic change and northern society: the career of the fourth earl of Northumberland: 1476–89', *North. Hist.*, 14, pp. 78–107.

1979a, 'The changing role of the Wydevilles in Yorkist politics to 1483', in Ross, C. (ed.), 1979, pp. 60–86.

1979b, 'Descent, partition and extinction: the "Warwick inheritance"', *Bull. Inst. Hist. Res.*, 52, pp. 116–28.

1980, *False, Fleeting, Perjur'd Clarence*, Gloucester.

1981, 'The Beauchamp trust, 1439–87', *Bull. Inst. Hist. Res.*, 54, pp. 135–49.

1983, 'Restraint, mediation and private justice: George, duke of Clarence as "good lord"', *Jnl. Legal Hist.*, 4, pp. 56–71.

1984, 'Attainder, resumption and coercion 1461–1529', *Parliamentary Hist.*, 3, pp. 14–31.

1985a, 'Chantries, obits and almshouses: the Hungerford foundations, 1325–1478', in Barron, C.M. and Harper-Bill, C. (eds.), 1985, pp. 123–42.

1985b, Review of Wright, 1983, *Midland Hist.*, 10, pp. 112–13.

1986a, 'Counting the cost of war: the Moleyns ransom and the Hungerford land-sales 1453–87', *South. Hist.*, 8, pp. 11–35.

1986b, 'Piety and lineage in the Wars of the Roses: the Hungerford experience', in Griffiths and Sherborne (eds.), 1986, pp. 90–108.

1986c, *Richard III as Duke of Gloucester: A Study in Character*, Borthwick Papers, 70.

1986d, 'The Yorkshire rebellion of 1489 reconsidered', *North. Hist.*, 22, pp. 39–62.

1987, 'The piety of Margaret, Lady Hungerford (d. 1478)', *Jnl. Eccles. Hist.*, 38, pp. 19–38.

Highfield, J.R.L. and Jeffs, R. (eds.), 1981, *The Crown and Local Communities: England and France in the Fifteenth Century*, Gloucester.

Hilton, R.H., 1967, *A Medieval Society: The West Midlands at the End of the Thirteenth Century*, London.

1975, *The English Peasantry in the Later Middle Ages*, Oxford.

1975a, 'Lord and peasant in Staffordshire in the middle ages', in Hilton, 1975, pp. 215–43.

1975b, 'Rent and capital formation in feudal society' in Hilton, 1975, pp. 174–214.

1975c, 'Social structure of rural Warwickshire in the middle ages', in Hilton, 1975, pp. 113–38.

1975d, 'A study in the prehistory of English enclosure in the fifteenth century', in Hilton, 1975, pp. 161–73.

1985a, 'A crisis of feudalism', in Aston, T.H. and Philpin, C.H.E. (eds.), 1985, pp. 119–37.

1985b, 'Old enclosure in the west midlands', in Hilton, *Class Conflict and the Crisis of Feudalism*, London, 1985, pp. 36–47.

Hilton, R.H. and Aston, T.H. (eds.), 1984, *The English Rising of 1381*, Cambridge.

Hirst, D., 1978, 'Court, country and politics before 1629', in Sharpe, K. (ed.), 1978, pp. 105–37.

1981, 'Revisionism revised: the place of principle', *Past and Present*, 92, pp. 79–99.

Holdsworth, W.S., 1922, *A History of English Law*, 3rd edn, 17 vols., London.

Holmes, C., 1980, 'The county community in Stuart historiography', *Jnl. of Br. Studies*, 19, pp. 54–73.

Holmes, G., 1957, *The Estates of the Higher Nobility in Fourteenth-Century England*, Cambridge.

1962, *The Later Middle Ages 1272–1485*, London, Sphere edn, 1970.

Holmes, G.S., 1979, 'The professions and social change in England, 1680–1730, *Proc. Brit. Acad.*, 65, pp. 313–54.

1982, *Augustan England: Professions, Status and Society, 1680–1730*, London.

Holt, J.C., 1961a, *The Northerners*, Oxford.

1961b, 'Rights and liberties in Magna Carta', in *Album Helen Cam*, 2 vols., Paris and Louvain, 1, pp. 55–70.

1965, *Magna Carta*, Cambridge.

1972, 'Politics and property in early medieval England', *Past and Present*, 57, pp. 3–52.

1981, 'The prehistory of parliament', in Davies, R.G. and Denton, J.H. (eds.), 1981, pp. 1–28.

1982, *Robin Hood*, London.

1982–5, 'Feudal society and the family' four Presidential Addresses, *Trans. Roy. Hist. Soc.*, 5th ser.: 32, pp. 193–212; 33, pp. 193–220; 34, pp. 1–25; 35, pp. 1–28.

Holt, R., 1985, *The Early History of the Town of Birmingham 1166–1600*, Dugdale Soc. Occasional Papers, 30.

Hooke, D., 1982, 'The Anglo-Saxon Landscape', in Slater, T.R., and Jarvis, P.J. (eds.), 1982, pp. 79–103.

1985, *The Anglo-Saxon Landscape: The Kingdom of the Hwicce*, Manchester.

Horowitz, M.R., 1982, 'Richard Empson, minister of Henry VII', *Bull. Inst. Hist. Res.*, 55, pp. 35–49.

Horrox, R.J., 1981, 'Urban patronage and patrons in the fifteenth century', in Griffiths, R.A., (ed.), 1981, pp. 145–66.

1986a, 'Richard III and the East Riding', in Horrox, R.J. (ed.), 1986, pp. 82–107.

1988, 'The urban gentry in the fifteenth century', in Thomson, J.A.F. (ed.), 1988, pp. 22–44.

1989, *Richard III: A Study of Service*, Cambridge.

Horrox, R.J. (ed.), 1986, *Richard III and the North*, Hull.

Hoskins, W.G., 1950, *Essays in Leicestershire History*, Liverpool.

1950a, 'The deserted villages of Leicestershire', in Hoskins, 1950, pp. 67–107.

1957, *The Midland Peasant: The Economic and Social History of a Leicestershire Village*, London.

Houlbrooke, R.A., 1984, *The English Family 1450–1700*, London.

Howell, C., 1983, *Land, Family and Inheritance in Transition: Kibworth Harcourt 1280–1700*, Cambridge.

Hughes, A. (ed.), 1898, *A List of Sheriffs for England and Wales*, P.R.O. Lists and Indexes, main series, 9, London, H.M.S.O.; rpt. New York, 1963.

Hughes, A.F., 1981, 'Militancy and localism: Warwickshire politics and Westminster politics', *Trans. Roy. Hist. Soc.*, 5th ser., 31, pp. 51–68.

1982, 'Warwickshire on the eve of the civil war. A county community?', *Midland Hist.*, 7, pp. 42–72.

1987, *Politics, Society and Civil War in Warwickshire, 1620–60*, Cambridge.

Hunnisett, R.F., 1959, 'The medieval coroners' rolls', *Amer. Jnl. Legal Hist.*, 3, pp. 95–124, 205–21, 324–59, 383.

1961, *The Medieval Coroner*, Cambridge.

1971, 'The reliability of inquisitions as historical evidence', in Bullough, D. and Storey, R.L. (eds.), 1971, pp. 206–35.

Hunt, R.W., Pantin, W.A. and Southern, R.W. (eds.), 1948, *Studies in Medieval History presented to F.M. Powicke*, Oxford.

Hurstfield, J., 1967, 'Political corruption in modern England: the historian's problem', *History*, 52, pp. 16–34.

Hutchins, J., 1861–74, *The History and Antiquities of the County of Dorset*, 3rd edn, ed. W. Shipp and J.W. Hodson, 4 vols., Weston; rpt. East Ardsley, Wakefield, 1973.

Hyam, R., 1974, 'The expansion of Europe: imperial, African and Asian history', in R.F. Bennett (ed.), *First Class Answers in History*, London, pp. 135–65.

Illsley, J.S., 1976, 'Parliamentary elections in the reign of Edward I', *Bull. Inst. Hist. Res.*, 49, pp. 24–40.

Irvine, W.F., 1953, 'The early Stanleys', *Trans. of the Historic Soc. of Lancs. and Cheshire*, 105, pp. 45–68.

Ives, E.W., 1955, 'Some aspects of the legal profession in the late fifteenth and early sixteenth centuries', unpubl. Ph.D. thesis, University of London.

1968, 'The common lawyers in pre-Reformation England', *Trans. Roy. Hist. Soc.*, 5th ser., 18, pp. 145–73.

1969–70, 'Patronage at the court of Henry VIII: the case of Sir Ralph Egerton of Ridley', *Bulletin of the John Rylands Library*, 52, pp. 346–74.

1978, '"Agaynst taking awaye of women": the inception and operation of the abduction act of 1487', in Ives, E.W., Knecht, R.J., Scarisbrick, J.J. (eds.), 1978, pp. 21–44.

1979, *Faction in Tudor England*, Hist. Assoc.

1981a, 'Crime, sanctuary and royal authority under Henry VII: the exemplary sufferings of the Savage family', in Arnold, M.S., Green, T.A., Scully, S.A. and White, S.D. (eds.), 1981, pp. 296–320.

1981b, 'English law and English society', *History*, 66, pp. 50–60.

1982, 'The common lawyers', in Clough, C.H. (ed.), 1982, pp. 181–217.

1983a, *The Common Lawyers of Pre-Reformation England*, Cambridge.

1983b, 'Law, history and society: an eternal triangle', in Ives, E.W. and Manchester, A.H. (eds.), 1983, pp. 3–10.

Ives, E.W. (ed.), 1968, *The English Revolution 1600–1660*, London.

Ives, E.W., Knecht, R.J. and Scarisbrick, J.J. (eds.), 1978, *Wealth and Power in Tudor England*, London.

Ives, E.W. and Manchester, A.H. (eds.), 1983, *Law, Litigants and the Legal Profession*, Roy. Hist. Soc.

Jack, R.I., 1961, 'The Lords Grey of Ruthin, 1325–1490: a study in the lesser baronage', unpubl. Ph.D. thesis, University of London.

1965, 'Entail and descent: the Hastings inheritance, 1370–1436', *Bull. Inst. Hist. Res.*, 38, pp. 1–19.

Jalland, P., 1972, 'The influence of the aristocracy on shire elections in the north of England', *Speculum*, 47, pp. 483–507.

James, M.E., 1974, *Family, Lineage and Civil Society*, Oxford.

1986, *Society, Politics and Culture*, Cambridge.

1986a, 'Change and continuity in the Tudor north: Thomas first Lord Wharton', in James, 1986, pp. 91–147.

1986b, 'The concept of order and the Northern Rising, 1569', in James, 1986, pp. 270–307.

1986c, 'English politics and the concept of honour, 1485–1642', in James, 1986, pp. 308–415.

1986d, 'Obedience and dissent in Henrician England: the Lincolnshire rebellion, 1536', in James, 1986, pp. 188–269.

1986e, 'Ritual, drama and social body in the late medieval English town', in James, M.E., 1986, pp. 16–47.

Jefferies, P., 1979, 'The medieval use as family law and custom: the Berkshire gentry in the fourteenth and fifteenth centuries', *South. Hist.*, 1, pp. 45–69.

Jefferies, R., 1880, *Hodge and his Masters*, London.

Jeffs, R., 1961a, 'The later mediaeval sheriff and the royal household: a study in administrative change and political control', unpubl. D.Phil. thesis, Oxford University.

1961b, 'The Poynings–Percy dispute', *Bull. Inst. Hist. Res.*, 34, pp. 148–64.

Jewell, H.M., 1972, *English Local Administration in the Middle Ages*, Newton Abbot.

Jolliffe, J.E.A., 1963, *Angevin Kingship*, 2nd edn, London.

Johnson, P.A., 1988, *Duke Richard of York 1411–1460*, Oxford.

Jones, M. (ed.), 1986, *Gentry and Lesser Nobility in Late Medieval Europe*, Gloucester.

Jones, M.K., 1981, 'John Beaufort, duke of Somerset and the French expedition of 1443', in Griffiths, R.A. (ed.), 1981, pp. 79–102.

1982, 'The Beaufort family and the war in France 1421–1450', unpubl. Ph.D. thesis, Bristol University.

1986a, 'Richard III and Lady Margaret Beaufort', in Hammond, P.W. (ed.), 1986, pp. 25–37.

1986b, 'Richard III and the Stanleys', in Horrox, R. (ed.), 1986, pp. 27–50.

1987, 'Collyweston – an early Tudor palace', in Williams, D. (ed.), 1987, pp. 129–41.

1988, 'Sir William Stanley of Holt: politics and family allegiance in the late fifteenth century', *Welsh Hist. Rev.*, 14, pp. 1–22.

Jones, W.R., 1974, 'Keeping the peace: English society, local government, and the commissions of 1341–44', *American Jnl. of Legal Hist.*, 18, pp. 307–20.

Jordan, W.K., 1959, *Philanthropy in England 1480–1660*, London.

1961, 'Social institutions in Kent 1480–1660', *Archaeologia Cantiana*, 75.

Juriça, A.R.J. 1976, 'The Knights of Edward I', unpubl. Ph.D. thesis, Birmingham University.

Kantorowicz, E.H., 1957, *The King's Two Bodies*, Princeton.

Kaeuper, R.W., 1979, 'Law and order in fourteenth-century England: the evidence of special commissions of *oyer* and *terminer*', *Speculum*, 54, pp. 734–84.

1988, *War, Justice and Public Order: England and France in the Later Middle Ages*, Oxford.

Keefe, T.K., 1983, *Feudal Assessments and the Political Community under Henry II and his Sons*, Berkeley, Los Angeles and London.

Keen, M., 1973, *England in the Later Middle Ages*, London.

1983, 'Chaucer's knight, the English aristocracy and the crusade', in Scattergood, V.J. and Sherborne, J.W. (eds.), 1983, pp. 45–61.

1984, *Chivalry*, New Haven and London.

Kekewich, M., 1982, 'The attainder of the Yorkists in 1459: two contemporary accounts', *Bull. Inst. Hist. Res.*, 55, pp. 25–34.

Kendall, P.M., 1957, *Warwick the Kingmaker*, London.

Kent, G.H.R., 1973, 'The estates of the Herbert family in the mid fifteenth century', unpubl. Ph.D. thesis, Keele University.

Kent, J.R., 1986, *The English Village Constable 1580–1642: A Social and Administrative Study*, Oxford.

Kern, F., 1948, *Kingship and Law*, trans. S.B. Chrimes, Oxford.

Kerridge, E., 1955, 'The returns of the inquisition of depopulation', *Eng. Hist. Rev.*, 70, pp. 212–28.

Kershaw, I., 1973, *Bolton Priory: The Economy of a Northern Monastery 1286–1325*, Oxford.

Kettle, A.J., 1984, '"My wife shall have it": marriage and property in the wills and testaments of later mediaeval England', in Craik, E.M. (ed.), 1984, pp. 89–103.

1985, 'City and close: Lichfield in the century before the Reformation', in Barron, C.M. and Harper-Bill, C. (eds.), 1985, pp. 158–69.

King, E., 1970, 'Large and small landowners in thirteenth-century England', *Past and Present*, 47, pp. 26–50.

1973, *Peterborough Abbey 1086–1310*, Cambridge.

Kingsford, C.L., 1913, *English Historical Literature in the Fifteenth Century*, Oxford.

Kinvig, R.H., 1950, 'The Birmingham district in Domesday times', in British Association, 1950, pp. 113–34.

1954, 'Warwickshire', in Darby, H.C. and Terrett, I.B. (eds.), 1954, pp. 270–308.

1962, 'The west midlands', in Mitchell, J.B. (ed.), 1962, pp. 265–86.

Kishlansky, M.A., 1986, *Parliamentary Selection: Social and Political Choice in Early Modern England*, Cambridge.

Knafla, L.A., 1983, '"Sin of all sorts swarmeth": criminal litigation in an English county in the early seventeenth century', in Ives, E.W. and Manchester, A.H. (eds.), 1983, pp. 50–67.

Knowles, D.M., 1955, *The Religious Orders in England*, II, The End of the Middle Ages, Cambridge.

Kosminsky, E.A., 1956, *Studies in the Agrarian History of England in the Thirteenth Century*, trans. R. Kisch, ed. R.H. Hilton, Oxford.

Kratzmann, G. and Simpson, J. (eds.), 1986, *Medieval English Religious and Ethical Literature*, Cambridge.

Kreider, A., 1979, *English Chantries: The Road to Dissolution*, Harvard.

Lander, J.R., 1949, 'The administration of the Yorkist kings', unpubl. M.Litt. thesis, Cambridge University.

1969, *Conflict and Stability in Fifteenth-Century England*, London.

1976, *Crown and Nobility 1450–1509*, London.

1976a, 'Introduction: aspects of fifteenth-century studies', in Lander, 1976, pp. 1–56.

1976b, 'Attainder and forfeiture, 1453–1509', in Lander, 1976, pp. 127–58.

1976c, 'Bonds, coercion and fear: Henry VII and the peerage', in Lander, 1976, pp. 267–300.

1976d, 'Council, administration and councillors', in Lander, 1976, pp. 191–219.

1976e, 'Marriage and politics in the fifteenth century: the Nevilles and the Woodvilles', in Lander, 1976, pp. 94–126.

1980, *Government and Community: England 1450–1509*, London.

1986, 'Family, "friends" and politics in fifteenth-century England', in Griffiths, R.A. and Sherborne, J. (eds.), 1986, pp. 27–40.

Laslett, P., 1971, *The World We Have Lost*, 2nd edn, London.

Legge, M.D., 1979, 'Anglo-Norman as a spoken language', in Brown, R.A. (ed.), 1979, pp. 108–17.

Le Goff, J., 1984, *The Birth of Purgatory*, trans. A. Goldhammer, London.

Leland, J., 1907–10, *The Itinerary of John Leland in or about the years 1535–1543*, ed. L. Toulmin Smith, 5 vols., London.

Le Neve, J., 1964, *Fasti Ecclesiae Anglicanae 1300–1541*, x, Coventry and Lichfield, compiled B. Jones, London.

Levine, D., 1987, *Reproducing Families: The Political Economy of the English Population in History*, Cambridge.

Lewis, I.M. (ed.), 1968, *History and Social Anthropology*, London.

Lewis, P.S., 1958, 'Sir John Fastolf's lawsuit over Titchwell, 1448–1455', *Hist. Jnl.*, n.s., 1, pp. 1–20.

1964, 'Decayed and non-feudalism in later medieval France', *Bull. Inst. Hist. Res.*, 37, pp. 157–84.

1981, 'The centre, the periphery, and the problem of power distribution in later medieval France', in Highfield, J.R.L. and Jeffs, R. (eds.), 1981, pp. 33–50.

Loades, D., 1974, *Politics and the Nation 1450–1660*, London.

Lovatt, R., 1981, 'John Blacman: biographer of Henry VI', in Davis, R.H.C. and Wallace-Hadrill, J.M. (eds.), 1981, pp. 415–44.

1984, '"A collector of apocryphal anecdotes": John Blacman revisited', in Pollard, A.J. (ed.), 1984, pp. 172–97.

Lowe, D.E., 1980–2, 'Patronage and politics: Edward IV, the Wydevills, and the council of the Prince of Wales, 1471–83', *Bulletin Board of Celtic Studies*, 29, pp. 545–73.

Loyn, H.R., 1962, *Anglo-Saxon England and the Norman Conquest*, London.

MacCaffrey, W., 1965, 'England: the crown and the new aristocracy, 1540–1600', *Past and Present*, 30, pp. 52–64.

1975, *Exeter 1540–1640, the Growth of an English County Town*, 2nd edn, Harvard.

McClane, B., 1984, 'A case study of violence and litigation in the early fourteenth century: the disputes of Robert Godsfield of Sutton-le-Marsh', *Nottingham Mediaeval Studies*, 28, pp. 22–44.

MacCulloch, D., 1986, *Suffolk and the Tudors: Politics and Religion in an English County 1500–1600*, Oxford.

McFarlane, K.B., 1952, *Wycliffe and the Beginnings of English Nonconformity*, English University Press; rpt. Penguin, 1972.

1966, Review of *Calendar of Close Rolls 1500–1509, Eng. Hist. Rev.*, 81, pp. 153–4.

1972, *Lancastrian Kings and Lollard Knights*, Oxford.

1973, *The Nobility of Later Medieval England*, Oxford.

1973a, 'An early paper on crown and parliament in the later middle ages', in McFarlane, 1973, pp. 279–97.

1973b, 'Had Edward I a 'policy' towards the earls?', in McFarlane, 1973, pp. 248–67.

1981, *England in the Fifteenth Century: Collected Essays*, London.

1981a, 'Bastard feudalism', in McFarlane, 1981, pp. 23–43.

1981b, 'A business partnership in war and administration 1421–1445', in McFarlane, 1981, pp. 151–74.

1981c, 'The investment of Sir John Fastolf's profits of war', in McFarlane, 1981, pp. 175–97.

1981d, 'Parliament and "bastard feudalism"', in McFarlane, 1981, pp. 1–21.

1981e 'War, the economy and social change: England and the Hundred Years War', in McFarlane, 1981, pp. 139–49.

1981f, 'The Wars of the Roses', in McFarlane, 1981, pp. 231–61.

McIntosh, M.K., 1984, 'Social change and Tudor manorial leets', in Guy, J.A. and Beale, H.G. (eds.), 1984, pp. 73–85.

McKenna, J.W., 1979, 'The myth of parliamentary sovereignty in late-medieval England', *Eng. Hist. Rev.*, 94, pp. 481–506.

McKisack, M., 1932, *The Parliamentary Representation of the English Boroughs during the Middle Ages*, Oxford.

1959, *The Fourteenth Century*, Oxford.

McNiven, P., 1985, 'The problem of Henry IV's health', *Eng. Hist. Rev.*, 100, pp. 747–72.

1987, *Heresy and Politics in the Reign of Henry IV: The Burning of John Badby*, Woodbridge, Suffolk.

Maddern, P.C., 1985, 'Violence, crime and public disorder in East Anglia, 1422–42', unpubl. D.Phil. thesis, Oxford University.

Maddicott, J.R., 1970, *Thomas of Lancaster 1307–22*, Oxford.

1975, 'The English peasantry and the demands of the crown, 1294–1341', *Past and Present*, Suppl. 1.

1978a, 'The county community and the making of public opinion in fourteenth-century England', *Trans. Roy. Hist. Soc.*, 5th ser., 28, pp. 27–43.

1987b, 'Law and lordship: royal justices as retainers in thirteenth- and fourteenth-century England', *Past and Present* Suppl. 4.

1981, 'Parliament and the constituencies, 1272–1377', in Davies, R.G. and Denton, J.H. (eds.), 1981, pp. 61–87.

1984, 'Magna Carta and the local community 1215–1259', *Past and Present*, 102, pp. 25–65.

1986, 'Edward I and the lessons of baronial reform: local government, 1258–80', in Coss, P.R. and Lloyd, S.D. (eds.), 1986, pp. 1–30.

Mair, L., 1962, *Primitive Government: A Study of Traditional Political Systems in East Africa*, Penguin; rev. edn, London, 1977.

Maitland, F.W., 1911, 'The Shallows and Silences of real life', in *Collected Papers*, ed. H.A.L. Fisher, 3 vols., Cambridge, I, pp. 467–79.

Malinowski, B., 1926, *Crime and Custom in Savage Society*, London.

Mallory Smith, S.V., 1985, *A History of the Mallory Family*, Chichester.

Mann, J., 1973, *Chaucer and Medieval Estates Satire*, Cambridge.

Manning, B.L., 1919, *The People's Faith in the Time of Wyclif*, Cambridge; rpt. Hassocks, 1975.

Mason, E., 1976, 'The role of the English parishioner, 1100–1500', *Jnl. Eccles, Hist.*, 27, pp. 17–29.

1984, 'Legends of the Beauchamps' ancestors: the use of baronial propaganda in medieval England', *Jnl. Med. Hist.*, 10, pp. 25–40.

Massy, R., 1984, 'The land settlement in Lancastrian Normandy', in Pollard, A.J. (ed.), 1984, pp. 76–96.

Mate, M., 1987, 'Pastoral farming in south-east England in the fifteenth century', *Ec. Hist. Rev.*, 2nd ser., 40, pp. 523–36.

Mathew, G., 1948, 'Ideals of knighthood in late fourteenth-century England', in Hunt, R.W., Pantin, W.A. and Southern, R.W. (eds.), 1948, pp. 354–62.

Medcalf, S. (ed.), 1981, *The Context of English Literature: The Later Middle Ages*, London.

Meeson, R., 1983, 'The timber frame of the hall at Tamworth Castle, Staffordshire, and its contents', *Archaeological Jnl.*, 140, pp. 329–40.

Mertes, K., 1987, 'The household as a religious community', in Rosenthal, J. and Richmond, C. (eds.), 1987, pp. 123–39.

1988, *The English Noble Household 1250–1600*, Oxford.

Metcalfe, W.C., 1885, *A Book of Knights . . .*, London.

Miller, E., 1951, *The Abbey and Bishopric of Ely*, Cambridge; rpt. 1969.

Miller, E. and Hatcher, J., 1978, *Medieval England – Rural Society and Economic Change 1066–1348*, London.

Miller, H., 1986, *Henry VIII and the English Nobility*, Oxford.

Mills, M.H., 1957, 'The medieval shire house' in Davies, J.C. (ed.) 1957, pp. 254–71.

Millward, R., and Robinson, A., 1971, *The West Midlands*, London.

Milsom, S.F.C., 1969, *Historical Foundations of the Common Law*, 1st edn, London.

1981, *Historical Foundations of the Common Law*, 2nd edn, London.

Mingay, G.E., 1976, *The Gentry: The Rise and Fall of a Ruling Class*, London.

Mitchell, J.B. (ed.), 1962, *Great Britain: Geographical Essays*, Cambridge.

Mitchell, J.C., 1969, 'The concept and use of social networks', in Mitchell (ed.), *Social Networks in Urban Situations*, Manchester, pp. 1–50.

1973, 'Networks, norms and institutions', in Boissevain, J. and Mitchell, J.C. (eds.), 1973, pp. 15–35.

Morey, G.E., 1951, 'East Anglian Society in the Fifteenth Century', unpubl. Ph.D. thesis, University of London.

Morgan, D.A.L., 1973, 'The king's affinity in the polity of Yorkist England', *Trans. Roy. Hist. Soc.*, 5th ser., 23, pp. 1–25.
1986, 'The individual style of the English gentleman', in Jones, M. (ed.), 1986, pp. 15–35.
1987, 'The house of policy: the political role of the late Plantaganet household, 1422–1485' in Starkey, D. (ed.), 1987, pp. 25–70.
Morrill, J.S., 1976a, *The Cheshire Grand Jury 1625–1659: A Social and Administrative Study*, Leicester University Dept. of Eng. Local Hist., Occasional Papers, 3rd ser., 1.
1976b, *The Revolt of the Provinces*, London; rpt. 1980.
1984, 'The religious context of the English Civil War', *Trans. Roy. Hist. Soc.*, 5th ser., 34, pp. 155–78.
Morris, W.A., 1910, *The Frankpledge System*, New York.
1927, *The Mediaeval English Sheriff to 1300*, Manchester.
1947, 'The sheriff', in Morris, W.A. and Strayer, J.R. (eds.), 1947, pp. 41–108.
Morris, W.A. and Strayer, J.R. (eds.), 1947, *The English Government at Work, 1327–1336*, II, Fiscal Administration, Mediaeval Academy of America, Cambridge, Mass.
Morrison, J.H., 1932, *The Underhills of Warwickshire*, Cambridge.
Mortimer, R., 1985, 'Land and service: the tenants of the Honour of Clare', in Brown, R.A. (ed.), 1985, pp. 177–97.
Munro, J.H., 1983, 'The medieval scarlet and the economics of sartorial splendour', in Harte, N.B. and Ponting, K.G. (eds.), 1983, pp. 13–70.
Myers, A.R., 1981, 'Parliament, 1422–1509', in Davies, R.G. and Denton, J.H. (eds.), 1981, pp. 141–84.
Nash, T., 1781–82, *Collections for a History of Worcestershire*, 2 vols., London.
National Trust, 1987, *Baddesley Clinton*, National Trust.
Naughton, K.S., 1976, *The Gentry of Bedfordshire in the Thirteenth and Fourteenth Centuries*, Leicester University Dept. of Eng. Local Hist., Occasional Papers, 3rd ser., 2.
Nichols, F.M., 1863, 'On feudal and obligatory knighthood', *Archaeologia*, 39, pp. 189–244.
Nichols, J.G., 1795–1811, *The History and Antiquities of the County of Leicester*, 4 vols., London; rpt. Wakefield, 1971.
Nicklin, P.A., 1932, 'The early historical geography of the forest of Arden', *Trans. Birm. and Midland Inst.*, 56, pp. 71–6.
Nicholas, N.H., 1842, *History of the Orders of Knighthood of the British Empire*, 4th edn, 4 vols., London.
Noonan, J.T., 1984, *Bribes*, New York and London.
Norris, H., 1897, *Baddesley Clinton*, London and Leamington.
Orme, N., 1984, *From Childhood to Chivalry: The Education of the English Kings and Aristocracy 1066–1530*, London and New York.
Owen, D.M., 1971, *Church and Society in Medieval Lincolnshire*, Lincoln.
Owst, G.R., 1926, *Preaching in Medieval England*, Cambridge.
1961, *Literature and Pulpit in Medieval England*, Oxford.

Ozment, S., 1980, *The Age of Reform 1250–1550*, New Haven and London.

P.R.O. Lists and Indexes, 1892–1936, main ser., 55 vols., London, H.M.S.O.; rpt. New York, 1961–8.

1967– , suppl. ser., New York.

Painter, S., 1943, *Studies in the History of the English Feudal Barony*, Baltimore.

1961, 'The family and the feudal system in twelfth-century England', in Cazel, F.A., jr (ed.), *Feudalism and Liberty* (articles and addresses), Baltimore, pp. 195–219.

Palliser, D.M., 1976, *The Staffordshire Landscape*, London.

Palmer, C.F.R., 1845, *The History of the Town and Castle of Tamworth*, Tamworth.

Palmer, R.C., 1981, 'The feudal framework of English law', *Michigan Law Review*, 79, pp. 1,130–64.

1982, *The County Courts of Medieval England 1150–1350*, Princeton.

1984, *The Whilton Dispute, 1264–1380*, Princeton.

Pantin, W.A., 1955, *The English Church in the Fourteenth Century*, Cambridge.

1976, 'Instructions for a devout and literate layman', in Alexander, J.J.G. and Gibson, M.T. (eds.), 1976, pp. 398–422.

Payling, S.J., 1986, 'Inheritance and local politics in the later middle ages: the case of Ralph, Lord Cromwell, and the Heriz inheritance', *Nottingham Mediaeval Studies*, 30, pp. 67–96.

1987a, 'Law and arbitration in Nottinghamshire', in Rosenthal, J.T. and Richmond, C. (eds.), 1987, pp. 140–60.

1987b, 'Political society in Lancastrian Nottinghamshire', unpubl. D.Phil. thesis, Oxford University.

1987c, 'The widening franchise – parliamentary elections in Lancastrian Nottinghamshire', in Williams, D. (ed.) 1987, pp. 167–85.

Payne, A., 1987, 'The Salisbury roll of arms *c.* 1463', in Williams, D. (ed.), 1987, pp. 187–98.

Pearson, F.S., 1894, 'The manor of Northfield and Weoley in the reign of Henry VI', *Trans. Birm. and Midland Inst.*, 20, pp. 29–44.

1902, 'The manor and castle of Weoley', *Trans. Birm. and Midland Inst.*, 28, pp. 52–67.

Pelham, R.A., 1938, 'Trade relations of Birmingham during the middle ages', *Trans. Birm. and Midland Inst.*, 62, pp. 32–40.

1939–40, 'The early wool trade in Warwickshire and the rise of the merchant middle class', *Trans. Birm. and Midland Inst.*, 63, pp. 41–62.

1945–6, 'The cloth markets of Warwickshire during the later middle ages', *Trans. Birm. and Midland Inst.*, 66, pp. 131–41.

1950, 'The growth of settlement and industry *c.* 1100 – *c.* 1700', in British Association, 1950, pp. 135–48.

1951, 'Fourteenth-century England', in Darby, H.C. (ed.), 1951, pp. 230–65.

Perry, J.G., 1980, 'Interim report on the excavation at Sydenham's, Solihull', *Trans. Birm. and Midland Inst.*, 90, pp. 49–63.

Pevsner, N. and Wedgwood, A., 1966, *The Buildings of England: Warwickshire*, Harmondsworth.

Phillips, J.R.S., 1972, *Aymer De Valence Earl of Pembroke 1307–1324: Baronial Politics in the Reign of Edward II*, Oxford.

Phythian-Adams, C., 1979, *Desolation of a City: Coventry and the Urban Crisis of the late Middle Ages*, Cambridge.

Pierce, I., 1986, 'The knight, his arms and armour in the eleventh and twelfth centuries', in Harper-Bill, C. and Harvey, R. (eds.), 1986, pp. 152–64.

Pollard, A.J., 1968, 'The family of Talbot, Lords Talbot and earls of Shrewsbury in the fifteenth century', unpubl. Ph.D. thesis, Bristol University.

1972, 'Estate management in the later middle ages: the Talbots and Whitchurch, 1383–1525', *Ec. Hist. Rev.*, 2nd ser., 25, pp. 553–66.

1975–6, 'The northern retainers of Richard Nevill, earl of Salisbury', *North. Hist.*, 11, pp. 52–69.

1977, 'The tyranny of Richard III', *Jnl. Med. Hist.*, 3, pp. 147–65.

1979, 'The Richmondshire community of gentry during the Wars of the Roses', in Ross, C. (ed.), 1979, pp. 37–59.

1983, *John Talbot and the War in France 1427–1453*, Roy. Hist. Soc.

Pollard, A.J. (ed.), 1984, *Property and Politics*, Gloucester.

Pollock, F. and Maitland, F.W., 1968, *A History of English Law before the Time of Edward I*, 2 vols., 2nd edn, intro. S.F.C. Milsom, Cambridge.

Poos, L.R., 1985, 'The rural population of Essex in the later middle ages', *Ec. Hist. Rev.*, 2nd ser., 38, pp. 515–30.

Post, J.B., 1973, 'Some limitations of the medieval peace rolls', *Jnl. Soc. Archivists*, 4, pp. 633–9.

1976, 'Criminals and the law in the reign of Richard II', unpubl. D.Phil. thesis, Oxford University.

1983, 'Local jurisdictions and judgement of death in later medieval England', *Criminal Justice History*, 4, pp. 1–21.

1987, 'Crime in later medieval England: some historiographical limitations', *Continuity and Change*, 2, pp. 211–24.

Postan, M.M., 1967, 'Investment in medieval agriculture', *Jnl. Econ. Hist.*, 27, pp. 576–87.

1972, *The Medieval Economy and Society*, London.

1973, *Essays on Medieval Agriculture and General Problems of the Medieval Economy*, Cambridge.

1973a, 'The costs of the Hundred Years War', in Postan, 1973, pp. 63–80.

1973b, 'Some social consequences of the Hundred Years War', in Postan, 1973, pp. 49–62.

Postles, D., 1981, 'The *excessus* balance in manorial accounting', *Bull. Inst. Hist. Res.*, 54, pp. 105–10.

Powell, E., 1979, 'Public order and law enforcement in Shropshire and Staffordshire in the early fifteenth century', unpubl. D.Phil. thesis, Oxford University.

1983a, 'Arbitration and the law in England in the late middle ages', *Trans. Roy. Hist. Soc.*, 5th ser., 33, pp. 49–67.

1983b, 'The King's Bench in Shropshire and Staffordshire in 1414', in Ives, E.W. and Manchester, A.H. (eds.), 1983, pp. 94–103.

1984a, 'Proceedings before the justices of the peace at Shrewsbury in 1414: a supplement to the Shropshire peace roll', *Eng. Hist. Rev.*, 99, pp. 535–50.

1984b, 'Settlement of disputes by arbitration in fifteenth-century England', *Law and Hist. Rev.*, 2, pp. 21–43.

1985, 'The restoration of law and order', in Harriss, G.L. (ed.), 1985, pp. 53–74.
1988, 'Jury trial at gaol delivery in the late middle ages: the midland circuit, 1400–29', in Cockburn, J.S. and Green, T.A. (eds.), 1988, pp. 78–116.
1989, *Kingship, Law and Society: Criminal Justice in the Reign of Henry V*, Oxford.
Powell, J.E. and Wallis, K., 1968, *The House of Lords in the Middle Ages*, London.
Powicke, M.R., 1962, *Military Obligation in Medieval England*, Oxford.
1969, 'Lancastrian captains', in Sandquist, T.A. and Powicke, M.R. (eds.), 1969, pp. 371–82.
Prest, W. (ed.), 1981, *Lawyers in Early Modern Europe and America*, London.
Prestwich, M.C., 1972, *War, Politics and Finance under Edward I*, London.
1980, *The Three Edwards: War and State in England 1272–1377*, London.
1983, 'English armies in the early stages of the Hundred Years War: a scheme in 1341', *Bull. Inst. Hist. Res.*, 56, pp. 102–13.
1984, 'Cavalry service in early fourteenth century England', in Gillingham, J. and Holt, J.C. (eds.), 1984, pp. 147–58.
Pronay, N., 1974, 'The chancellor, the chancery, and the council at the end of the fifteenth century', in Hearder, H. and Loyn, H.R. (eds.), 1974, pp. 87–103.
Pugh, T.B., 1971, 'The Marcher lords of Glamorgan', in Pugh (ed.), *Glamorgan County History*, III, The Middle Ages, Cardiff, pp. 167–204.
1972, 'The magnates, knights and gentry', in Chrimes, S.B., Ross, C.D. and Griffiths, R.A. (eds.), 1972, pp. 86–128.
1986a, 'Richard Plantaganet (1411–60), duke of York as the king's lieutenant in England and Ireland', in Rowe, J.G. (eds.), 1986, pp. 107–41.
1986b, 'The Southampton Plot of 1415', in Griffiths, R.A. and Sherborne, J. (eds.), 1986, pp. 62–89.
Pugh, T.B. and Ross, C., 1953, 'The English baronage and the income tax of 1436', *Bull. Inst. Hist. Res.*, 26, pp. 1–28.
Putnam, B.H., 1908, *The Enforcement of the Statute of Labourers during the First Decade after the Black Death, 1349–1359*, Columbia.
1929, 'The transformation of the keepers of the peace into the justices of the peace, 1327–1380', *Trans. Roy. Hist. Soc.*, 4th ser., 12, pp. 19–48.
1950a, *The Place in Legal History of Sir William Shareshull, Chief Justice of the King's Bench, 1350–61*, Cambridge.
1950b, 'Shire officials: keepers of the peace and justices of the peace', in Willard, J.F., Morris, W.A. and Dunham, W.H. (eds.), 1950, pp. 185–217.
Raban, S., 1982, *Mortmain Legislation and the English Church 1279–1500*, Cambridge.
1985, 'The land market and the aristocracy in the thirteenth century', in Greenway, D., Holdsworth, C. and Sayers, J. (eds.), 1985, pp. 239–61.
Rahtz, P. and Hirst, S., 1976, *Bordesley Abbey*, British Archaeological Reports, 23.
Ramsay, N., 1985a, 'The English legal profession', unpubl. Ph.D. thesis, Cambridge University.
1985b, 'Retained legal counsel, *c.* 1275–*c.* 1475', *Trans. Roy. Hist. Soc.*, 5th ser., 35, pp. 95–112.
Rawcliffe, C., 1974, 'The Staffords, earls of Stafford and dukes of Buckingham 1394–1521', unpubl. Ph.D. thesis, Sheffield University.

1978, *The Staffords, Earls of Stafford and Dukes of Buckingham 1394–1521*, Cambridge.

1979, 'Baronial councils in the later middle ages', in Ross, C. (ed.), 1979, pp. 87–108.

1980, 'Henry VII and Edward, duke of Buckingham: the repression of an "over-mighty subject"', *Bull. Inst. Hist. Res.*, 53, pp. 114–18.

1984, 'The great lord as peacekeeper: arbitration by English noblemen and their councils in the later middle ages', in Guy, J.A. and Beale, H.G. (ed.), 1984, pp. 34–54.

Rawcliffe, C. and Flower, S., 1986, 'English noblemen and their advisers: consultation and collaboration in the later middle ages', *Jnl. British Studies*, 25, pp. 157–77.

Reader, W.J., 1966, *Professional Men: The Rise of the Professional Classes in Nineteenth-Century England*, London.

Return: Members of Parliament, 1878, 2 vols., London, House of Commons.

Reynolds, S., 1980, 'Decline and decay in late medieval towns', *Urban Hist. Yearbook*, pp. 76–8.

1984, *Kingdoms and Communities in Western Europe 900–1300*, Oxford.

Rich, E.E. and Wilson, C.H. (eds.), 1967, *The Cambridge Economic History of Europe*, IV, The Economy of Expanding Europe in the Sixteenth and Seventeenth Centuries, Cambridge.

Richardson, H.G., 1938, 'John of Gaunt and the parliamentary representation of Lancashire', *Bulletin of the John Rylands Library*, 22, pp. 175–222.

1946, 'The Commons and medieval politics', *Trans. Roy. Hist. Soc.*, 4th ser., 28, pp. 21–45.

Richardson, W.C., 1941, 'The surveyor of the king's prerogative', *Eng. Hist. Rev.*, 56, pp. 52–75.

Richmond, C., 1970, 'Fauconberg's Kentish rising of May 1471', *Eng. Hist. Rev.*, 85, pp. 673–92.

1977, 'The nobility and the Wars of the Roses 1459–61', *Nottingham Mediaeval Studies*, 21, pp. 71–85.

1981, *John Hopton: A Fifteenth Century Suffolk Gentleman*, Cambridge.

1983, 'After McFarlane', *History*, 68, pp. 46–60.

1984, 'Religion and the fifteenth-century English gentleman', in Dobson, R.B. (ed.), 1984, pp. 193–208.

1985a, 'The Battle of Bosworth', *History Today*, 35, 1985, pp. 17–22.

1985b, 'The Pastons revisited: marriage and the family in fifteenth-century England', *Bull. Inst. Hist. Res.*, 58, pp. 25–36.

1986, '1485 and all that, or what was going on at the Battle of Bosworth', in Hammond, P.W. (ed.), 1986, pp. 172–206.

1987, 'The Sulyard papers: the rewards of a small family archive', in Williams, D. (ed.), 1987, pp. 199–228.

Roberts, B.K., 1961–2, 'Moated sites in midland England', *Trans. Birm. and Mid. Inst.*, 80, pp. 26–37.

1962, 'Moated sites', *Amateur Historian*, 5, pp. 34–8.

1965, 'Settlement, land use and population in the western portion of the forest of Arden, Warwickshire between 1086 and 1350', unpubl. Ph.D. thesis, Birmingham University.

1968, 'A study of medieval colonization in the forest of Arden, Warwickshire', *Agric. Hist. Rev.*, 16, pp. 101–13.

1973, 'Field systems of the west midlands', in Baker, A.R.H. and Butlin, R.A. (eds.), 1973, pp. 188–231.

1976–7, 'The historical geography of moated homesteads: the forest of Arden, Warwickshire', *Trans. Birm. and Mid. Inst.*, 88, pp. 61–70.

1977, *Rural Settlement in Britain*, Folkestone.

Roberts, S., 1983, 'The study of dispute: anthropological perspectives', in Bossy, J. (ed.), 1983, pp. 1–24.

Rogers, A., 1966, 'The Lincolnshire county court in the fifteenth century', *Lincs. Hist. and Archaeology*, 1, pp. 64–78.

1969, 'Parliamentary elections in Grimsby in the fifteenth century', *Bull. Inst. Hist. Res.*, 42, pp. 212–20.

Rogers, J.E.T., 1866–1902, *A History of Agriculture and Prices in England, 1259–1703*, 7 vols., Oxford.

Roots, I., 1968, 'The central government and the local community', in Ives, E.W. (ed.), 1968, pp. 34–37.

Rosenthal, J.T., 1964, 'Fifteenth-century baronial incomes and Richard, duke of York', *Bull. Inst. Hist. Res.*, 37, pp. 233–9.

1965, 'The estates and finances of Richard, duke of York (1411–1460)', *Studies in Medieval and Renaissance History*, 2, pp. 115–204.

1970, 'Feuds and private peace-making: a fifteenth-century example', *Nottingham Mediaeval Studies*, 14, pp. 84–90.

1972, *The Purchase of Paradise; Gift Giving and the Aristocracy 1307–1485*, London.

1976, *Nobles and the Noble Life 1295–1500*, London.

1984, 'Heirs' ages and family succession in Yorkshire, 1399–1422', *Yorks. Archaeolog. Jnl.*, 56, pp. 87–94.

1987, 'Kings, continuity and ecclesiastical benefactors in 15th-century England', in Rosenthal, J. and Richmond, C. (eds.), 1987, pp. 161–75.

Rosenthal, J.T. and Richmond, C. (eds.), 1987, *People, Politics and Community in the Later Middle Ages*, Gloucester.

Roskell, J.S., 1937, *The Knights of the Shire for the County Palatine of Lancaster 1377–1460*, Chetham Soc., n.s., 96.

1954, *The Commons in the Parliament of 1422*, Manchester.

1965, *The Commons and their Speakers in English Parliaments 1376–1523*, Manchester.

1981, *Parliament and Politics in Late Medieval England*, II, London.

1981a, 'Sir William Oldhall, Speaker in the parliament of 1450–1' in Roskell, 1981, pp. 175–200.

1981b, 'William Catesby, counsellor to Richard III', in Roskell, 1981, pp. 307–36.

1983, *Parliament and Politics in Late Medieval England*, III, London.

1983a, 'William Burley of Broncroft, Speaker of the Commons in 1437 and 1445–6', in Roskell, 1983, pp. 343–52.

Ross, C., 1956, *The Estates and Finances of Richard Beauchamp, Earl of Warwick*, Dugdale Soc. Occasional Papers, 12.

1974, *Edward IV*, London.

1976, *The Wars of the Roses*, London.

1981, *Richard III*, London.

Ross, C. (ed.), 1979, *Patronage, Pedigree and Power in Later Medieval England*, Gloucester.

Ross, C.D. and Pugh, R.B., 1953–4, 'Materials for the study of baronies in fifteenth-century England', *Ec. Hist. Rev.*, 2nd ser., 6, pp. 185–94.

Rothwell, W., 1975–6, 'The role of French in thirteenth-century England', *Bulletin of the John Rylands Library*, 58, pp. 445–66.

Rowe, J.G. (ed.), 1986, *Aspects of Late Medieval Government and Society*, Toronto.

Rowlands, M.B., 1987, *The West Midlands from AD 1000*, Harlow.

Rowley, T. (ed.), 1981, *The Origins of Open-Field Agriculture*, London.

Rowney, I.D., 1981, 'The Staffordshire political community 1440–1500', unpubl. Ph.D. thesis, Keele University.

1982, 'Arbitration in gentry disputes of the later middle ages', *History*, 67, pp. 367–76.

1983, 'Government and patronage in the fifteenth century: Staffordshire, 1439–1459, *Midland Hist.*, 8, pp. 49–69.

1984a, 'The Hastings affinity in Staffordshire and the Honour of Tutbury', *Bull. Inst. Hist. Res.*, 57, pp. 35–45.

1984b, 'Resources and retaining in Yorkist England: William, Lord Hastings and the Honour of Tutbury', in Pollard, A.J. (ed.), 1984, pp. 139–55.

Rudder, S., 1779, *A New History of Gloucestershire*, Gloucester.

Russell, C., 1971, *The Crisis of Parliaments: English History 1509–1660*, Oxford; rpt. 1981.

Russell, J.C., 1948, *British Medieval Population*, Albuquerque.

Sabean, D., 1976, 'Aspects of kinship behaviour and property in rural western Europe before 1800', in Goody, J., Thirsk, J. and Thompson, E.P. (eds.), 1976, pp. 96–111.

Sanders, I.J., 1960, *English Baronies: A Study of their Origins and Descent 1086–1327*, Oxford.

Sandquist, T.A. and Powicke, M.R. (eds.), 1969, *Essays in Mediaeval History Presented to Bertie Wilkinson*, Toronto.

Saul, N., 1978, 'The Gloucestershire gentry in the fourteenth century', unpubl. D.Phil. thesis, Oxford University.

1980, 'The religious sympathies of the gentry in Gloucestershire, 1200–1500', *Bristol and Gloucs. Archaeological Soc. Trans.*, 98, pp. 99–112.

1981, *Knights and Esquires: the Gloucestershire Gentry in the Fourteenth Century*, Oxford.

1983, 'The social status of Chaucer's franklin: a reconsideration', *Medium Aevum*, 52, pp. 10–26.

1984, 'The Despensers and the downfall of Edward II', *Eng. Hist. Rev.*, 99, pp. 1–33.

1986, *Scenes from Provincial Life: Knightly Families in Sussex 1280–1400*, Oxford.

Sawyer, P.H. (ed.), 1976, *English Medieval Settlement*, London.

Sayer, M.J., 1979, *English Nobility: The Gentry, the Heralds and the Continental Context*, Norfolk Heraldry Soc.

Scammell, J., 1966, 'The origin and limitations of the Liberty of Durham', *Eng. Hist. Rev.*, 81, pp. 449–73.

Scarisbrick, J.J., 1968, *Henry VIII*, London.
1984, *The Reformation and the English People*, Oxford.

Scattergood, V.J., 1987, 'Fashion and morality in the late middle ages', in Williams, D. (ed.), 1987, pp. 255–72.

Scattergood, V.J. and Sherborne, J.W. (eds.), 1983, *English Court Culture in the Later Middle Ages*, London.

Scofield, C., 1923, *The Life and Reign of Edward the Fourth*, 2 vols., London.

Sellar, W.C. and Yeatman, R.J., 1975, *1066 and All That*, Methuen paperback edn, London.

Sharpe, J.A., 1982, 'The history of crime in late medieval and early modern England: a review of the field', *Social Hist.*, 7, pp. 187–203.
1983, '"Such disagreement betwyx neighbours": litigation and human relations in early modern England', in Bossy, J. (ed.), 1983, pp. 167–87.
1984, *Crime in Early Modern England 1550–1750*, London.

Sharpe, K., 1986, 'Crown, parliament and locality: government and communication in early Stuart England', *Eng. Hist. Rev.*, 101, pp. 321–50.
1987, 'The image of virtue: the court and household of Charles I 1625–1642', in Starkey, D. (ed.), 1987, pp. 226–60.

Sharpe, K. (ed.), 1978, *Faction and Parliament*, Oxford.

Shaw, S., 1798–1801, *The History and Antiquities of Staffordshire*, 2 vols., London.

Shaw, W.A., 1906, *The Knights of England*, 2 vols., London.

Shepherd, G., 1984, 'Poverty in *Piers Plowman*', in Aston, T.H., Coss, P.R., Dyer, C. and Thirsk, J. (eds.), 1983, pp. 169–89.

Sherborne, J.W., 1964, 'Indentured retinues and English expeditions to France, 1369–1380', *Eng. Hist. Rev.*, 79, pp. 718–46.

Shirley, E.P., 1873, *Stemmata Shirleiana*, 2nd edn, London.

Sinclair, A.F.J., 1987a, 'The Beauchamp earls of Warwick in the later middle ages', unpubl. Ph.D. thesis, University of London.
1987b, 'The great Berkeley law-suit revisited 1417–39', *South. Hist.*, 9, pp. 34–50.

Sitwell, G., 1902, 'The English gentleman', *The Ancestor*, 1, pp. 58–103.

Skipp, V.H., 1960, *Discovering Sheldon*, Dept. of Extra-Mural Studies, University of Birmingham.
1970a, 'Economic and social change in the forest of Arden, 1530–1649', *Agric. Hist. Rev.*, 18, pp. 84–111.
1970b, *Medieval Yardley: The Origin and Growth of a West Midland Community*, London and Chester.
1979, *The Centre of England*, London.
1981, 'The evolution of settlement and open-field topography in north Arden down to 1300', in Rowley, T. (ed.), 1981, pp. 162–83.

Skipp, V.H. and Hastings, R.P., 1963, *Discovering Bickenhill*, Dept. of Extra-Mural Studies, University of Birmingham.

Slater, T.R. and Jarvis, P.J. (eds.), 1982, *Field and Forest: An Historical Geography of Warwickshire and Worcestershire*, Norwich.

Smith, A., 1984, 'Litigation and politics: Sir John Fastolf's defence of his English property', in Pollard, A.J. (ed.), 1984, pp. 59–75.

Smith, L.W.D., 1980, 'A survey of building timber and other trees in the hedgerows of a Warwickshire estate, *c.* 1500', *Trans. Birm. and Midland Inst.*, 90, pp. 65–73.

Smith, R.B., 1970, *Land and Politics in the England of Henry VIII: The West Riding of Yorkshire: 1530–46*, Oxford.

Smith, R.M., 1979, 'Kin and neighbors in a thirteenth-century Suffolk community', *Jnl. of Family Hist.*, pp. 219–56.

Smith, R.M. (ed.), 1984, *Land, Kinship and Life Cycle*, Cambridge.

Smith, R.S., 1964, 'The Willoughbys of Wollaton 1500–1643, with special reference to early mining in Nottinghamshire', unpubl. Ph.D. thesis, Nottingham University.

Smythe-Palmer, A., n.d., *The Ideal of a Gentleman*, London.

Somerville, R., 1953, *History of the Duchy of Lancaster*, I, 1265–1603, London.

Southall, A., 1965, 'A critique of the typology of states and political systems', in Banton, M. (ed.), 1965, pp. 113–40.

Spufford, M., 1976, 'Peasant inheritance customs and land distribution in Cambridgeshire from the sixteenth to the eighteenth centuries', in Goody, J., Thirsk, J. and Thompson, E.P. (eds.), 1976, pp. 156–76.

Starkey, D., 1981, 'The age of the household: politics, society and the arts *c.* 1300–1550', in Medcalf, S. (ed.), 1981, pp. 225–90.

1986, 'Which age of reform?', in Coleman, C. and Starkey, D. (eds.), 1986, pp. 13–27.

Starkey, D., 1987, ed., *The English Court from the Wars of the Roses to the Civil War*, London.

1987a, 'Introduction: court history in perspective', in Starkey (ed.), 1987, pp. 1–24.

1987b, 'Intimacy and innovation: the rise of the privy chamber, 1485–1547', in Starkey (ed.), 1987, pp. 71–118.

Steane, J., 1974, *The Northamptonshire Landscape*, London.

Stenton, F.M., 1961, *The First Century of English Feudalism 1066–1166*, 2nd edn, Oxford.

Stephen, L. and Lee, S. (eds.), 1885–1900, ed., *Dictionary of National Biography*, 63 vols., London.

Stevenson, E.R., 1947 'The escheator', in Morris, W.A. and Strayer, J.R. (eds.), 1947, pp. 109–67.

Stone, L., 1966, 'Social mobility in England, 1500–1700', *Past and Present*, 33, pp. 16–55.

1967, *The Crisis of the Aristocracy 1558–1641*, abridged edn, Oxford.

1979, *The Family, Sex and Marriage in England 1500–1800*, abridged edn, Harmondsworth.

1983, 'Interpersonal violence in English society, 1300–1980', *Past and Present*, 101, pp. 22–33.

Stone, L. and Fawtier Stone, J.C., 1986, *An Open Elite? England 1540–1880*, abridged edn, Oxford.

Stone, L. and Sharpe, J.A., 1985, Debate on 'Interpersonal violence in English society', *Past and Present*, 108, pp. 206–24.

Stones, E.L.G., 1957, 'The Folvilles of Ashby-Folville, Leicestershire, and their associates in crime', *Trans. Roy. Hist. Soc.*, 5th ser., 7, pp. 117–36.

Storey, R.L., 1966, *The End of the House of Lancaster*, London.

1971, 'Liveries and commissions of the peace 1388–90', in Du Boulay, F.R.H. and Barron, C.M. (eds.), 1971, pp. 131–52.

1972, 'The north of England' in Chrimes, S.B., Ross, C.D. and Griffiths, R.A. (eds.), 1972, pp. 129–44.

1982, 'Gentleman-bureaucrats', in Clough, C.H. (eds.), 1982, pp. 90–129.

1987, 'The universities during the Wars of the Roses', in Williams, D. (ed.), 1987, pp. 315–27.

Sutherland, D.W., 1963, *Quo Warranto Proceedings in the Reign of Edward I, 1278–1294*, Oxford.

Sutton, A.F., 1986, '"A curious searcher for our weal public": Richard III, piety, chivalry and the concept of the good prince', in Hammond, P.W. (ed.), 1986, pp. 58–90.

Tanner, N., 1984, *The Church in late Medieval Norwich, 1370–1532*, Toronto.

Tate, W.E., 1943–4, 'Enclosure acts and awards relating to Warwickshire', *Trans. Birm. and Mid. Inst.*, 65, pp. 45–104.

Taylor, J., 1975, 'The Plumpton letters, 1416–1522', *Northern Hist.*, 10, pp. 72–87.

Taylor, M., 1982, *Community, Anarchy and Liberty*, Cambridge.

Templeman, G., 1948, *The Sheriffs of Warwickshire in the Thirteenth Century*, Dugdale Soc. Occasional Papers, 7.

Thirsk, J., 1964, 'The family', *Past and Present*, 27, pp. 116–22.

1967, 'Farming techniques: grassland and stock', in *The Agrarian History of England and Wales*, IV, 1500–1640, ed. J. Thirsk, Cambridge, pp. 179–95.

Thomas, R.S., 1971, 'The political career, estates and "connection" of Jasper Tudor, earl of Pembroke and duke of Bedford', unpubl. Ph.D. thesis, University of Wales.

Thompson, J.A.F., 1965, 'Piety and charity in late medieval London', *Jnl. Eccles. Hist.*, 16, pp. 178–95.

1972, 'The Courtenay family in the Yorkist period', *Bull. Inst. Hist. Res.*, 45, pp. 230–46.

1979, 'John de la Pole, duke of Suffolk', *Speculum*, 54, pp. 528–42.

1983, *The Transformation of Medieval England 1370–1529*, London.

1984, '"The well of grace": Englishmen and Rome in the fifteenth century', in Dobson, R.B. (ed.), 1984, pp. 99–114.

Thomson, J.A.F. (ed.), 1988, *Towns and Townspeople in the Fifteenth Century*, Gloucester.

Thoroton, R., 1790–96, *The Antiquities of Nottinghamshire*, ed. J. Throsby, Nottingham; rpt. East Ardsley, Wakefield, 1972.

Thorpe, H., 1962, 'The lord and the landscape', *Trans. Birm. and Mid. Inst.*, 8, pp. 38–77.

Thrupp, S.L., 1948, *The Merchant Class of Medieval London*, Chicago.

Tierney, B., 1963, 'Bracton on government', *Speculum*, 38, pp. 295–317.

Tomlinson, H. (ed.), 1983, *Before the English Civil War*, London.

Transactions of the Birmingham and Midland Institute Archaeological Society, 1870– , Birmingham.

Treharne, R.F., 1946–8, 'The knights in the period of baronial reform and rebellion, 1258–67', *Bull. Inst. Hist. Res.*, 21, pp. 1–12.

1969, 'The constitutional problem in thirteenth-century England', in Sandquist, T.A. and Powicke, M.R. (eds.), 1969, pp. 46–78.

Tuck, J.A., 1971, 'Richard II's system of patronage', in Du Boulay, F.R.H. and Barron, C.M. (eds.), 1971, pp. 1–20.

1973, *Richard II and the English Nobility*, London.

1984, 'Nobles, Commons and the great revolt of 1381', in Hilton, R.H. and Aston, T.H. (eds.), 1984, pp. 194–212.

1985a, *Crown and Nobility 1272–1461*, London.

1985b, 'War and society in the medieval north', *Northern Hist.*, 21, pp. 33–52.

Tudor-Craig, P., 1977, *Richard III*, 2nd edn, Ipswich and Toronto.

Tyldesley, C.J., 1978, 'The crown and the local communities in Devon and Cornwall from 1377 to 1422', unpubl. Ph.D. thesis, Exeter University.

Ussher, R., 1881, *An Historical Sketch of the Parish of Croxall*, London.

V.C.H. Bucks., 1905–28, *The Victoria History of the County of Buckingham*, 4 vols. with index, London.

V.C.H. Derbys., 1905–07, *The Victoria History of the County of Derby*, 2 vols., London.

V.C.H. Lancs., 1911, *The Victoria History of the County of Lancashire*, VI, London.

V.C.H. Leics., 1907– , *The Victoria History of the County of Leicester*, London.

V.C.H. Staffs., 1908– , *The Victoria History of the County of Stafford*, London.

V.C.H. Warwicks., 1904–69, *The Victoria History of the County of Warwick*, 8 vols. with index, London.

V.C.H. Worcs., 1901–26, *The Victoria History of the County of Worcester*, 4 vols. with index, London.

Vale, M.G.A., 1976, *Piety, Charity and Literacy among the Yorkshire Gentry, 1370–1480*, Borthwick Papers, 50.

Veale, E.M., 1966, *The English Fur Trade in the Later Middle Ages*, Oxford.

Virgoe, R., 1966, 'Three Suffolk parliamentary elections of the mid-fifteenth century', *Bull. Inst. Hist. Res.*, 39, pp. 185–96.

1971, 'The crown and local government: East Anglia under Richard II', in Du Boulay, F.R.H. and Barron, C.M. (eds.), 1971, pp. 218–41.

1972–3, 'William Tailboys and Lord Cromwell: crime and politics in Lancastrian England', *Bull. John Rylands Library*, 55, pp. 459–82.

1973, 'The Cambridgeshire election of 1439', *Bull. Inst. Hist. Res.*, 46, pp. 95–101.

1978, 'The recovery of the Howards in East Anglia, 1485–1529', in Ives, E.W., Knecht, R.J. and Scarisbrick, J.J. (eds.), 1978, pp. 1–20.

1980, 'The murder of James Andrew: Suffolk faction in the 1430s', *Procs. Suffolk Inst. of Archaeology and Hist.*, 34, pp. 263–8.

1981, 'The crown, magnates and local government in fifteenth-century East Anglia', in Highfield, J.R.L. and Jeffs, R. (eds.), 1981, pp. 72–87.

1987, 'An election dispute of 1483', *Historical Res.* (formerly *Bull. Inst. Hist. Res.*), 60, pp. 24–44.

Wagner, A., 1956, *Heralds and Heraldry in the Middle Ages*, 2nd edn, Oxford.

1967, *Heralds of England: A History of the Office and College of Arms*, Oxford.

1972, *English Genealogy*, 2nd edn, Oxford.

Walker, S.K., 1986, 'John of Gaunt and his retainers', unpubl. D.Phil. thesis, Oxford University.

Warren, W.L., 1987, *The Governance of Norman and Angevin England 1086–1272*, London.

Watkins, A., 1983–4, 'The development of Coleshill in the middle ages', *Warwickshire Hist.*, 5, pp. 167–84.

Watts, L., 1978–9, 'Birmingham Moat: its history, topography and destruction', *Trans. Birm. and Mid. Inst.*, 89, pp. 1–77.

Waugh, S.L., 1977, 'The profits of violence: the minor gentry in the rebellion of 1321–1322 in Gloucestershire and Herefordshire', *Speculum*, 52, pp. 843–69.

1983, 'Reluctant knights and jurors: respites, exemptions, and public obligations in the reign of Henry III', *Speculum*, 58, pp. 937–86.

Wedge, J., 1794, *A General View of the Agriculture of the County of Warwick*, London.

Wedgwood, J.C., 1936, *History of Parliament: Biographies of the Members of the Commons House 1439–1509*, London.

1938, *History of Parliament: Register of the Ministers and of the Members of both Houses 1439–1509*, London.

Weiss, M., 1976, 'A power in the north? the Percies in the fifteenth century', *Hist. Jnl.*, 19, pp. 501–9.

Weisser, M.R., 1979, *Crime and Punishment in Early Modern Europe 1350–1850*, Hassocks.

Westlake, H.F., 1919, *The Parish Gilds of Mediaeval England*, London.

Whittick, C., 1984, 'The role of the criminal appeal in the fifteenth century', in Guy, J.A. and Beale, H.G. (eds.), 1984, pp. 55–72.

Wilkinson, B., 1929, *The Chancery under Edward III*, Manchester.

1948–58, *Constitutional History of Medieval England 1216–1399*, 3 vols., London.

1964, *Constitutional History of England in the Fifteenth Century 1399–1485 with Illustrative Documents*, London.

Wilks, M., 1963, *The Problem of Sovereignty in the later Middle Ages*, Cambridge.

Willard, J.F., Morris, W.A. and Dunham, W.H. (eds.), 1950, *The English Government at Work 1327–1336*, III, Local Administration and Justice, Cambridge, Mass.

Williams, A., 1985, 'The knights of Shaftesbury Abbey', in Brown, R.A. (ed.), 1985, pp. 214–37.

Williams, C.H., 1925, 'A Norfolk parliamentary election, 1461', *Eng. Hist. Rev.*, 40, pp. 79–86.

1928, 'The rebellion of Humphrey Stafford in 1486', *Eng. Hist. Rev.*, 43, pp. 181–9.

Williams, D., 1975–6, 'The hastily drawn up will of William Catesby, esquire, 25 August 1485', *Trans. Leics. Archaeological and Hist. Soc.*, 51, pp. 43–51.

1984–5, 'From Towton to Bosworth: the Leicestershire community and the Wars of the Roses 1461–85', *Trans. Leics. Archaeological and Hist. Soc.*, 59, pp. 27–43.

Williams, D. (ed.), 1987, *England in the Fifteenth Century*, Woodbridge, Suffolk.

Williams, P., 1981, *The Tudor Regime*, corr. rpt., Oxford.

1984, 'The crown and the counties', in Haigh, C. (ed.), 1984, pp. 125–46.

Wilson, R.M., 1943, 'English and French in England 1100–1300', *History*, 28, pp. 37–60.

Winkler, F.H., 1943, 'The making of king's knights in England, 1399–1461', unpubl. Ph.D. thesis, Yale University.

Wolf, E.R., 1966, 'Kinship, friendship, and patron–client relations in complex societies', in Banton, M. (ed.), 1966, pp. 1–22.

Wolffe, B.P., 1970, *The Crown Lands 1461–1536*, London.

1972, 'The personal rule of Henry VI' in Chrimes, S.B., Ross, C.D. and Griffiths, R.A. (eds.), 1972, pp. 29–48.

1976, review of Ross, 1974, *Eng. Hist. Rev.*, 91, pp. 369–74.

1981, *Henry VI*, London.

Wood, A.C. 1971, *Typescript List of Escheators for England and Wales* in the P.R.O., issued as List and Index Society, 72, London, H.M.S.O., rpt. New York.

Wood, C.T., 1986, 'Richard III, William, Lord Hastings and Friday the thirteenth', in Griffiths, R.A. and Sherborne, J. (eds.), 1986, pp. 155–68.

Wood-Legh, K., 1931, 'Sheriffs, lawyers, and belted knights in the parliaments of Edward III', *Eng. Hist. Rev.*, 46, pp. 372–88.

1965, *Perpetual Chantries in Britain*, Cambridge.

Woodger, L.S., 1974, 'Henry Bourgchier, earl of Essex, and his family 1408–83', unpubl. D. Phil. thesis, Oxford University.

Wormald, J., 1980, 'Bloodfeud, kindred and government in early modern Scotland', *Past and Present*, 87, pp. 54–97.

1985, *Lords and Men in Scotland: the Bonds of Manrent 1442–1603*, Edinburgh.

1986a, 'An early modern postscript: the Sandlow dispute, 1546', in Davies, W. and Fouracre, P. (eds.), 1986, pp. 191–205.

1986b, 'Lords and lairds in fifteenth-century Scotland: nobles and gentry', in Jones, M. (ed.), 1986, pp. 181–200.

Wright, S.M., 1978, 'A gentry society of the fifteenth century: Derbyshire *c.* 1430–1509', unpubl. Ph.D. thesis, Birmingham University.

1983, *The Derbyshire Gentry in the Fifteenth Century*, Derbys. Rec. Soc., 8.

Wylie, J.H., 1884–98, *History of England under Henry the Fourth*, 4 vols., London.

Wylie, J.H. and Waugh, W.T., 1914–29, *The Reign of Henry the Fifth*, 3 vols., Cambridge.

Zell, M.L., 1977, 'Early Tudor J.P.s at work', *Archaeologia Cantiana*, 113, pp. 125–43.

INDEX